CAVALCADE

**Negro American Writing
from 1760 to the Present**

CAVALCADE

Negro American Writing from 1760 to the Present

edited by

ARTHUR P. DAVIS
University Professor, Howard University

SAUNDERS REDDING
Ernest I. White Professor of American Studies and Humane Letters, Cornell University

HOUGHTON MIFFLIN COMPANY · BOSTON

New York · Atlanta · Geneva, Illinois · Dallas · Palo Alto

For
Arthur Paul and Audrey Paulette
Conway and Lewis

PREFACE

The purpose of this anthology is to provide a representative selection of as much as possible of the best prose and poetry written by Negro Americans since 1760. While it has been our primary aim to make these choices on the basis of literary merit, we have also tried to cover as many areas of Negro life in America as was consistent with our first objective. We believe that this collection gives a fairly comprehensive picture of Negro experience in America for the past two hundred years.

In making our selections, we have tried within reason to avoid duplicating the material in other anthologies. To avoid *all* of the selections in other works would be unwise; to do so would leave out of our book some of the best work done by Negro writers in America. Since there is a "classic" Negro literature just as there is a classic canon of English or French or any other established literature, we inevitably have some duplications. But we also have included many works not found in other collections.

Whenever feasible, we have given whole works rather than excerpts. A few articles, however, have been far too long to include in their entirety in an anthology of this size, and we have used parts of them— parts which we believe can stand alone. We have done the same for plays, and naturally we have used chapters from novels and autobiographies. In every case we have seen to it that the selection can stand alone and is fairly representative of the author's general matter and manner. Whenever we left out short sections of a work, we indicated this omission with the conventional ellipses; for longer omissions, we used asterisks. When novels or autobiographies had chapter titles, we used them. When there were no titles, we supplied our own, noting so in a footnote.

This anthology is designed for use as a text in Negro American literature courses or as a supplementary text in American literature courses. The introductions to the five sections provide, we believe, a background sufficient to give meaning and perspective to the offerings in each section. The bibliographical data at the end of the biographical sketches and in the Selective Bibliography should be helpful to student and teacher alike, serving, we hope, as springboards for additional study.

In preparing this volume, we have examined and consulted practically all of the anthologies, collections, and critical works on Negro literature extant; and we are indebted in some measure to all of them. We wish to acknowledge a special indebtedness to the following works: *The Negro Author* by Vernon Loggins; *Early Negro American Writers* by Benjamin Brawley; *Negro Poetry and Drama* and *The Negro in American Fiction* by Sterling A. Brown.

We wish to thank the staff of the Moorland Room, Founders Library, Howard University, under the direction of Mrs. Dorothy A. Porter; and the staff of Mrs. Ethel P. Page's office. We thank both for many different kinds of help, always efficiently and graciously given. We also wish to thank Miss Jennifer Jordan of Howard University for research help on the biographical data for this work.

Arthur P. Davis
Saunders Redding

CONTENTS

4 / THE NEW NEGRO RENAISSANCE AND BEYOND: 1910–1954

GENERAL INTRODUCTION

There have been several collections of Negro American writing in recent years, but an anthology of writings by any national, cultural, time-contained, or ethnic group should serve a pedagogical function for students. None of the recent collections of Negro American writing quite does. None shows the evolution of this writing as literary art. None provides the historical context that makes meaningful the criticism of this writing as the expression of the American Negro's special experience and as a tool of social and cultural diagnosis. That is the purpose of this anthology. It comprehends the entire two hundred years of Negro American literature.

It has been our purpose to give not only a comprehensive account of the development of Negro American literature but, as far as humanly possible, a balanced and impartial account as well. No author has been left out because we disagree with his critical attitude, or his politics, or his stand on certain issues. By the same token, no author has been included because he happens to think as we do. Our selections, for example, represent practically every major Negro American critic—Alain Locke, Sterling Brown, Ralph Ellison, James Baldwin, Nathan Scott, Larry Neal, Harold Cruse, and LeRoi Jones. *Our* criticism of Negro writing is found in the headnotes and the several introductions.

The term "Negro writing" requires an explanation that goes beyond the obvious one of a body of writing by American blacks. Some Negro writers like William Stanley Braithwaite, Anne Spencer, and Frank Yerby, "write like whites." The entire stock of their referents is white, Anglo-Saxon American derived. Most black American writers, however, create out of a dual consciousness: Negro and American. They are twin-rooted, and while one root is nourished by the myths, customs, culture, and values traditional in the Western world, the other feeds hungrily on the experiential reality of blackness. These writers have a special vision. They are persuaded to a special mission. In their work they combine the sermon and the liturgy, the reality and the dream, the *is* and the *ought to be*. Their writing is intended to appeal as much to the cognitive as to the affective side of man's being.

Though *Cavalcade* is comprehensive, the basis on which works were chosen for inclusion was primarily literary merit. This excluded the work of some writers who have a certain historical importance, and who, therefore, are subjects of comment in the introductions. When other than an author's best is included, it is because it represents a critical phase of his development.

For the purposes of a historical survey, it seemed sensible to divide the history of Negro American writing into five periods. They are designated (and dated): Pioneer Writers (1760–1830); Freedom Fighters (1830–1865); Accommodation and Protest (1865–1910); The New Negro Renaissance and Beyond (1910–1954); Integration versus Black Nationalism (1954 to the present). Each period is prefaced with a critical introduction, and there is a bio-bibliographical headnote for each author.

The editors have exercised discretion in matters of spelling, punctuation, and capitalization in those works which were carelessly printed and edited in the eighteenth century and the early decades of the nineteenth. After that time, the editors have generally followed the texts as published.

Though the editors designed *Cavalcade* primarily as a textbook, they hope it is something more. They hope it is a book that the general public may read with pleasure and profit.

A. P. D.
S. R.

CAVALCADE

Negro American Writing
from 1760 to the Present

Pioneer Writers

1760-1830

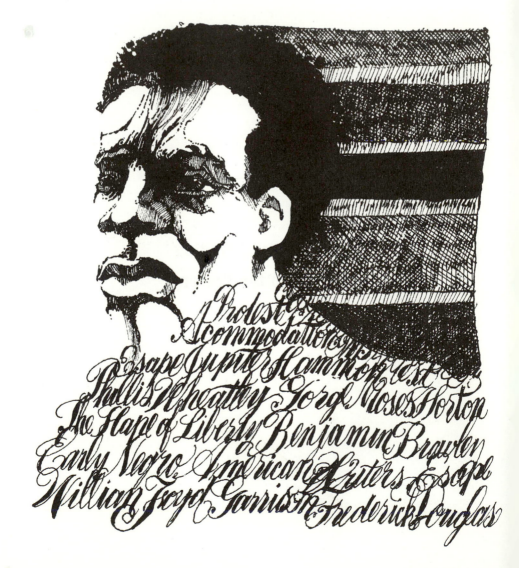

1

The history of Negro American writing begins a century and a half after the first black people were landed at Jamestown in the English colony of Virginia in 1619. While this long period embraced important cultural changes and was marked by predictable alterations in the civil and political orientation of the white colonists, it fixed the social position of Negroes, fastened upon them an aggregate of character qualities that were not always reflective of proved attributes, and created for them a repertoire of cultural and social roles that they seemed destined to play forever. Whether free man or slave, the Negro was forced into a markedly inferior status which was said to be justified by his "natural" character; and his character was variously and simultaneously described as "savage," "irrepressibly comic," "lecherous," "childish," "sullen," and "without a redeeming human trait."

These attributions and the rationalizations they supported were passionately credited in the South, increasingly so as they were challenged by the philosophy of the Enlightenment and the political concepts of human equality and the natural rights of man. Though the characterizations were considered less valid in the North, they were not rejected there. North and South, the Negro had become stereotyped by the middle of the eighteenth century: in the popular mind "the Negro" was any black person, including those unborn.

The stereotype represented an accommodation of religious and moral scruples to the white man's material interests. It was the answer to questions that had troubled rational men since the beginning of the modern slave era, and that were—as diaries, letters, and essays of the period indicate—particularly pervasive in colonial times: How can slavery be justified? Can black men be excluded from the brotherhood of Christianity? Is slavery right in the eyes of God?

Although hundreds of historical incidents document the fact that Negroes responded to the denial of their humanity in a variety of ways, a careful survey of Negro American writing suggests that the variety of responses can be subsumed under three basic attitudes and their corresponding modes of behavior: Accommodation, Protest, and Escape. These are the attitudes that were established almost at the beginning and were structured into the body of myths and "traditions" that symbolize them. From the first, Negroes had a choice of either accommodating to, protesting against, or escaping from a way of life that was cruelly exploitative and inexcusably demeaning. For the illiterate black man the response was direct and physical. He accom-

3

modated by projecting the harmless aspects of the Negro stereotype;
he protested by committing acts of violence; he escaped by running
away.

But reactions were not so simple for sophisticated, literate blacks.
Jupiter Hammon was among the first of whom there is record. He
accommodated. He said what seemed to be acceptable. In his one
extant prose piece, "An Address to the Negroes of the State of New
York," he states, "As for myself. . . . I do not wish to be free." But
when one reads the servant's replies in "A Dialogue Intitled the Kind
Master and the Dutiful Servant" one suspects that Hammon is double-
talking, and doing it so artfully and with such subtly pointed irony as
not only to reduce the Master's admonitions to absurdity but to constitute a statement of protest against them.

Phillis Wheatley, a much better poet than her older contemporary,
Hammon, seems also to have combined accommodation and protest,
especially in such pieces as "To the Right Honorable William, Earl of
Dartmouth" and "To the University of Cambridge, in New-England."
But again and again she returned to the mode of escape. It was expressed in her frequently implied rejection of the knowledge that the
color of her skin determined her experience—that it set bounds and
was prescriptive. Escape often lay in pretending that she was like
everyone else in the circle of white acquaintances with which the
Wheatley family surrounded her: by pretending that she was emotionally involved only in their concerns, directed by their biases, and
committed to their tastes. And, to an amazing degree, she did absorb
their late-Puritan culture. She was intensely moralistic and religious.
She considered restraint one of the highest of virtues. She modeled her
work after Alexander Pope and used the heroic couplet, classical allusions, neatness, precision. Julian Mason, the author of a recent critical
biography, remarks of Phillis Wheatley, "Her poems are certainly as
good or better than those of most of the poets usually included [in
standard anthologies of American literature] and . . . this evaluation
holds true when she is compared with most of the minor English
poets of the eighteenth century."

George Moses Horton, the last of the pioneer poets, was a considerably more complex person and poet than either Phillis Wheatley or
Jupiter Hammon. Scarcely typical of his poetry are the lines which
first brought him to general notice in 1829.

> Alas! and am I born for this,
>   To wear this slavish chain?
> Deprived of all created bliss
>   Through hardship, toil and pain!

After the publication of *The Hope of Liberty*, from which he expected to earn enough to buy his freedom and a passage to Africa,

Horton contented himself for more than thirty years with the place he occupied and the reputation he acquired in Chapel Hill, North Carolina. His knack for composing verses on a variety of subjects at a moment's notice gave him the status of a "Character" at the University. He fulfilled poetic commissions for the students. "For twenty-five cents he would supply a poem of moderate warmth, but if a gentleman wished to send a young lady an expression of exceptional fervor, fifty cents would be the fee."[1] But not all the commissions were for love verses. Some of his brightest pieces were purely comic.

> My duck bill boots would look as bright,
> Had you in justice served me right.
> Like you, I then could step as light
>> Before a flaunting maid.
> As nicely could I clear my throat,
> And to my tights my eyes devote;
> But I'd leave you bare, without a coat
>> For which you have not paid. . . .

Horton's verses are refreshing after the solemnity of Phillis Wheatley's work and the religious common-metre hymn doggerel of Jupiter Hammon. His rhythms are seldom monotonous, and his verse structure is varied. He was a troubadour, a purveyor of gossip, a maker of quips. He had a special penchant for ridicule. He dealt, often light-heartedly, with love, the fickleness of women and fortune, the curse of drink, and the elusiveness of fame. Of the slave poets, Horton was by far the most imaginative and the freest.

As art, early Negro autobiographical writing is less important than early Negro poetry, but as history it is more important and had a larger contemporary audience. After all, autobiographical writing centers in the experiences of "real life," and the mind of eighteenth-century and post-Colonial America had a great affinity for the true. It saw little connection between imagination and experience and cared less for imaginative insight than for the surface rendering of reality. Literary "art" was suspect. It was typical that William Lloyd Garrison, the abolitionist, counseled Frederick Douglass to *tell* his story and expressed an impatience with literary and intellectual embellishments.

The author of the first black American autobiography, then, need not have apologized for the "capacities and condition" of his life, nor for the language in which he sets them forth. *A Narrative of the Uncommon Sufferings and Surprising Deliverance of Briton Hammon, a Negro Man* is a booklet of fourteen pages. Published in Boston in 1760,

[1] Benjamin Brawley, *Early Negro American Writers* (Chapel Hill: The University of North Carolina Press, 1935), p. 110.

it describes episodes incident to a roundabout journey from New England to Jamaica to the British Isles and back. In the course of his journey Hammon suffers shipwreck, is held captive by Indians in Florida, and is imprisoned by Spaniards. But the telling falls flat. Hammon makes no attempt at description or character delineation and provides no insights. The *Narrative* deserves mention only because it is the first in a genre that by the middle of the nineteenth century became the most popular form of Negro expression.

While Briton Hammon, who lacked intellectual sophistication, owed nothing to tradition, John Marrant did. He most certainly knew *Pilgrim's Progress,* and he was probably acquainted with Jeremy Taylor's *Holy Living and Holy Dying.* Two of Marrant's three works are autobiographical, but only the title of the first reveals the fact that the author was a Negro. *A Narrative of the Lord's Wonderful Dealings with J. Marrant, a Black* (London, 1785) and *Journal of John Marrant* (London, 1789) tell of miraculous conversions followed by equally miraculous escapes, which symbolize God's mercy, from all sorts of natural cataclysms, which symbolize God's power and wrath, and man-created disasters, which symbolize humanity's wickedness. Marrant's third book, *Sermon,* is just that—a long narrative sermon that retells, with wildly imaginative elaborations, the "story" of the Old Testament.

The most important autobiography of the period was written by a native African, and American blacks have only a disingenuous claim to him. Olaudah Equiano, who was only briefly a slave in America, principally relates his experiences as a slave in foreign lands. *The Interesting Narrative of the Life of Olaudah Equiano, or Gustavus Vassa, the African* (London, 1789) is notable for several reasons. It ran to eight editions in five years. It is a great antislavery document and conveys a wealth of first-hand impressions and information about slavery, which, as Vassa makes brilliantly clear, was one thing in Africa, another in England, and something altogether different in America, but an evil everywhere. *The Narrative* is also an absorbing travel book. Vassa was taken to many places, and his descriptions of people, manners and customs are powerfully evocative of the realities of eighteenth-century life in several parts of the world. No autobiography of the period matches Vassa's for clarity, honesty, and truth.

But most of the autobiographical writings of this time were essays of protest, and the Negro authorship of several of them is questionable. Some dedicated white abolionists were not above writing "slave narratives" and issuing them as the authentic work of blacks. There is grave doubt, for instance, that "Petition of an African," which was published in an antislavery journal called *American Museum,* was written by a Negro woman as claimed. Similar doubts attach to "An Essay on Slavery," signed "Othello," which was also printed in *American Museum* in 1788.

Other autobiographical writers are easily identified as Negroes. One of these was Benjamin Banneker. An engineer, mathematician, and astronomer, Banneker served on the commission that laid out the streets of the nation's capital. In a letter of protest to Thomas Jefferson, he cited his own achievements as evidence against the "train of absurd and false ideas which so generally prevail with respect to the Negro. . . ." Other blacks, who certainly did not think of themselves as writers, produced pamphlets and tracts, letters and petitions which were widely circulated. David Walker's *Appeal,* published in 1829, aroused the slaveholding South to such a pitch of anger and fear as to persuade the Governor of Virginia to prepare a special legislative message about it, and the Mayor of Savannah, Georgia, to request that the Mayor of Boston suppress it.

By the end of the period George Moses Horton was the only writer who remained an accommodationist. Escape in the Phillis Wheatley sense was unthinkable. Protest was the mode and the theme. For all the variations in degrees of talent, in intellect, in "ways of seeing," and in style, protest united Briton Hammon and John Marrant, Gustavus Vassa, Benjamin Banneker, and David Walker. Whether they were as optimistic as Hammon or as desperate as Walker, these men believed that their writing could help change the lives of Negroes for the better. This was their commitment—to contribute to an amelioration of the black man's lot. If in their pursuit of this goal they did not produce literary art, they did reaffirm the values and the ideals of freedom, equality, and justice—ideals that blacks were seldom credited with appreciating and understanding.

Phillis Wheatley

PRACTICALLY ALL THAT IS known of the early life of Phillis Wheatley is found in the following letter, written in 1772 by her master, John Wheatley, and printed in her *Poems on Various Subjects* (1773):

> Phillis was brought from *Africa to America,* in the Year 1761, between Seven and Eight years of age. Without any assistance from School Education, and by only what she was taught in the Family, she, in sixteen Months Time from her Arrival, attained the English Language, to which she was an utter Stranger before, to such a Degree, as to read any, the most difficult Parts of the Sacred Writings, to the great Astonishment of all who heard her.
>
> As to her Writing, her own Curiosity led her to it; and this she learnt in so short a Time, that in the Year 1765, she wrote a letter to the Rev. Mr. Occam, the *Indian* Minister, while in *England.*
>
> She has a great Inclination to learn the Latin Tongue, and has made some Progress in it. This Relation is given by her Master who bought her, and with whom she now lives.

John Wheatley, a prosperous Boston tailor, purchased the frail little African to be a companion for his wife Susannah. The Wheatleys soon made Phillis a member of the family. Under their instruction, especially that of Mary, Wheatley's daughter, Phillis became not only a well-educated young girl but also something of a local celebrity. By 1766, at the age of twelve or thirteen, she was writing verses. In 1770 she published her first poem, "An Elegiac Poem on the Death of George Whitefield," which "appeared in at least six different editions in Boston, Philadelphia, and New York, within a few months."[1] In 1771 she received an unusual honor for a slave by becoming a "baptized communicant" of Boston's Old South Meeting House.

The high point in Phillis Wheatley's life came in 1773, when the Wheatleys sent her to London for her health. There Phillis met the Countess of Huntingdon, the patroness of George Whitefield and other Methodists, who introduced the girl to many distinguished Londoners. The Lord Mayor gave Phillis a copy of the 1770 folio edition of *Paradise Lost;* the Earl of Dartmouth presented her with a copy of Smollett's 1770 translation of *Don Quixote.* Phillis was urged

---

[1] Vernon Loggins, *The Negro Author* (New York: Columbia University Press, 1931), p. 16.

to stay in England long enough to be presented at Court, but learning that Mrs. Wheatley was ill, she returned to Boston. Before she left London, however, Phillis arranged for the publication of her only book, *Poems on Various Subjects, Religious and Moral*, which appeared in 1773 with a "Dedication" to the gracious Countess of Huntingdon.

Mrs. Wheatley died in March of 1774; Mr. Wheatley died in 1778. In the same year Phillis, now a "free Negro," married a Negro named John Peters. He was a jack-of-all-trades who was apparently not so successful as he was versatile. At various times he supposedly worked as a baker, grocer, lawyer, and physician. Phillis and John Peters had three children, but their marriage seems not to have been a happy one.

In 1776, Phillis Wheatley wrote a poem entitled "To His Excellency General Washington" and sent the General a manuscript copy. The poem was subsequently published in the April, 1776, issue of the *Pennsylvania Magazine, or American Monthly Museum*. Washington courteously thanked the black poet in a letter, dated February 28, 1776, and invited her to visit him at Cambridge, where she was graciously received by the General and his fellow officers.

After the Revolution, Phillis Wheatley drew up "Proposals" for another book of poems and published them originally in the October 30, 1779, *Evening Post and General Advertiser*. But the volume itself was never published, and of the items included in her "Proposals" only five are now extant.

Before the winter of 1783–84, Phillis lost her two older children. Her husband was in jail, and she had to earn her living by working in a "cheap boarding house." She died at the age of thirty-two on December 5, 1784. Her last child died soon enough afterwards to be buried with her.

Phillis Wheatley left forty-six known poems. Of these, eighteen are elegies, several of them probably written at the request of friends. They are "correct," typical eighteenth-century elegies using the religious imagery common to this type of poem. She wrote six poems inspired by public acts like the repeal of the Stamp Act and Washington's appointment as Commander-in-Chief. It is possible that had she lived longer she would have written more of this type of poem. But not all of Phillis Wheatley's poetry is occasional; she created versified selections from The Bible ("Goliath of Gath") and an adaptation from the sixth book of Ovid's *Metamorphoses*. In addition, she composed typically eighteenth-century poems on abstractions like "Imagination," "Recollection," and "Virtue" and wrote companion poems on "Morning" and "Evening" which show Milton's influence. Her one poem in blank verse, "To the University of Cambridge, in New-England," probably also was influenced by Milton.

Phillis Wheatley's poetic master was Alexander Pope, and she was second to none of her contemporaries in capturing the music and cadence of her mentor. In an age of imitators of Pope, she was among the best.

For the most recent study of Phillis Wheatley's poetry and reputation, see Julian D. Mason, Jr., ed., *The Poems of Phillis Wheatley* (Chapel Hill: The University of North Carolina Press, 1966). For other studies, see J. Saunders Redding, *To Make a Poet Black* (Chapel Hill: The University of North Carolina Press, 1939); Benjamin Brawley, *The Negro in Literature and Art* . . . , Third Edition (New York: Duffield and Company, 1929); and *Early Negro American Writers* (Chapel Hill: The University of North Carolina Press, 1935); and Vernon Loggins, *The Negro Author.*

TO THE UNIVERSITY OF CAMBRIDGE, IN NEW-ENGLAND

> While an intrinsic ardor prompts to write,
> The muses promise to assist my pen;
> 'Twas not long since I left my native shore
> The land of errors, and *Egyptian* gloom:
> Father of mercy, 'twas thy gracious hand
> Brought me in safety from those dark abodes.
>
>   Students, to you 'tis giv'n to scan the heights
> Above, to traverse the ethereal space,
> And mark the systems of revolving worlds.
> Still more, ye sons of science ye receive
> The blissful news by messengers from heav'n,
> How *Jesus'* blood for your redemption flows.
> See him with hands out-stretcht upon the cross;
> Immense compassion in his bosom glows;
> He hears revilers, nor resents their scorn:
> What matchless mercy in the Son of God!
>
> When the whole human race by sin had fall'n,
> He deign'd to die that they might rise again,
> And share with him in the sublimest skies,
> Life without death, and glory without end.
>
>   Improve your privileges while they stay,
> Ye pupils, and each hour redeem, that bears
> Or good or bad report of you to heav'n.
> Let sin, that baneful evil to the soul,
> By you be shunn'd, nor once remit your guard;
> Suppress the deadly serpent in its egg.

Ye blooming plants of human race devine,
An *Ethiop* tells you 'tis your greatest foe;
Its transient sweetness turns to endless pain,
And in immense perdition sinks the soul.

ON BEING BROUGHT FROM AFRICA TO AMERICA

'Twas mercy brought me from my *Pagan* land,
Taught my benighted soul to understand
That there's a God, that there's a *Saviour* too:
Once I redemption neither sought nor knew.
Some view our sable race with scornful eye,
"Their colour is a diabolic die."
Remember, *Christians, Negroes,* black as *Cain,*
May be refin'd, and join th' angelic train.

ON THE DEATH OF THE REV. MR. GEORGE WHITEFIELD. 1770

Hail, happy saint, on thine immortal throne,
Possest of glory, life, and bliss unknown;
We hear no more the music of thy tongue,
Thy wonted auditories cease to throng.
Thy sermons in unequall'd accents flow'd,
And ev'ry bosom with devotion glow'd;
Thou didst in strains of eloquence refin'd
Inflame the heart, and captivate the mind.
Unhappy we the setting sun deplore,
So glorious once, but ah! it shines no more.

Behold the prophet in his tow'ring flight!
He leaves the earth for heav'ns unmeasur'd height,
And worlds unknown receive him from our sight.
There *Whitefield* wings with rapid course his way,
And sails to *Zion* through vast seas of day.
Thy pray'rs, great saint, and thine incessant cries
Have pierc'd the bosom of thy native skies.
Thou moon hast seen, and all the stars of light,
How he has wrestled with his God by night.
He pray'd that grace in ev'ry heart might dwell,
He long'd to see *America* excel;
He charg'd its youth that ev'ry grace divine
Should with full lustre in their conduct shine;

That Saviour, which his soul did first receive,
The greatest gift that ev'n a God can give,
He freely offer'd to the num'rous throng,
That on his lips with list'ning pleasure hung.

   "Take him, ye wretched, for your only good,
"Take him ye starving sinners, for your food;
"Ye thirsty, come to this life-giving stream,
"Ye preachers, take him for your joyful theme;
"Take him my dear *Americans*, he said,
"Be your complaints on his kind bosom laid:
"Take him, ye *Africans*, he longs for you,
"*Impartial Saviour* is his title due:
"Wash'd in the fountain of redeeming blood,
"You shall be sons, and kings, and priests to God."

   Great *Countess*,* we *Americans* revere
Thy name, and mingle in thy grief sincere;
New England deeply feels, the *Orphans* mourn,
Their more than father will no more return.

   But, though arrested by the hand of death,
Whitefield no more exerts his lab'ring breath,
Yet let us view him in th' eternal skies,
Let ev'ry heart to this bright vision rise;
While the tomb safe retains its sacred trust,
Till life divine re-animates his dust.

AN HYMN TO THE MORNING

Attend my lays, ye ever honour'd nine,
Assist my labours, and my strains refine;
In smoothest numbers pour the notes along,
For bright *Aurora* now demands my song.

   Aurora hail, and all the thousand dies,
Which deck thy progress through the vaulted skies:
The morn awakes, and wide extends her rays,
On ev'ry leaf the gentle zephyr plays;
Harmonious lays the feather'd race resume,
Dart the bright eye, and shake the painted plume.

---

* The Countess of *Huntingdon,* to whom Mr. *Whitefield* was Chaplain.

Ye shady groves, your verdant gloom display
To shield your poet from the burning day:
Calliope awake the sacred lyre,
While thy fair sisters fan the pleasing fire:
The bow'rs, the gales, the variegated skies
In all their pleasures in my bosom rise.

See in the east th' illustrious king of day!
His rising radiance drives the shades away—
But Oh! I feel his fervid beams too strong,
And scare begun, concludes th' abortive song.

AN HYMN TO THE EVENING

Soon as the sun forsook the eastern main
The pealing thunder shook the heav'nly plain;
Majestic grandeur! From the zephyr's wing,
Exhales the incense of the blooming spring.
Soft purl the streams, the birds renew their notes,
And through the air their mingled music floats.

Through all the heav'ns what beauteous dies are spread!
But the west glories in the deepest red:
So may our breasts with ev'ry virtue glow,
The living temples of our God below!

Fill'd with the praise of him who gives the light;
And draws the sable curtains of the night,
Let placid slumbers sooth each weary mind,
At mourn to wake more heav'nly, more refin'd;
So shall the labours of the day begin
More pure, more guarded from the snares of sin.

Night's leaden sceptre seals my drousy eyes,
Then cease, my song, till fair *Aurora* rise.

ON IMAGINATION

Thy various works, imperial queen, we see,
How bright their forms! how deck'd with pomp by thee!
Thy wond'rous acts in beauteous order stand,
And all attest how potent is thine hand.

From *Helicon's* refulgent heights attend,
Ye sacred choir, and my attempts befriend:
To tell her glories with a faithful tongue,
Ye blooming graces, triumph in my song.

Now here, now there, the roving *Fancy* flies,
Till some lov'd object strikes her wand'ring eyes,
Whose silken fetters all the senses bind,
And soft captivity involves the mind.

Imagination! who can sing thy force?
Or who describe the swiftness of thy course?
Soaring through air to find the bright abode,
Th' empyreal palace of the thund'ring God,
We on thy pinions can surpass the wind,
And leave the rolling universe behind:
From star to star the mental optics rove,
Measure the skies, and range the realms above.
There in one view we grasp the mighty whole,
Or with new worlds amaze th' unbounded soul.

Though *Winter* frowns to *Fancy's* raptur'd eyes
The fields may flourish, and gay scenes arise;
The frozen deeps may break their iron bands,
And bid their waters murmur o'er the sands.
Fair *Flora* may resume her fragrant reign,
And with her flow'ry riches deck the plain;
Sylvanus may diffuse his honours round,
And all the forest may with leaves be crown'd:
Show'rs may descend, and dews their gems disclose,
And nectar sparkle on the blooming rose.

Such is thy pow'r, nor are thine orders vain,
O thou the leader of the mental train:
In full perfection all thy works are wrought,
And thine the sceptre o'er the realms of thought.
Before thy throne the subject-passions bow,
Of subject-passions sov'reign ruler Thou,
At thy command joy rushes on the heart,
And through the glowing veins the spirits dart.

Fancy might now her silken pinions try
To rise from earth, and sweep th' expanse on high;
From *Tithon's* bed now might *Aurora* rise,
Her cheeks all glowing with celestial dies,
While a pure stream of light o'erflows the skies.

The monarch of the day I might behold,
And all the mountains tipt with radiant gold,
But I reluctant leave the pleasing views,
Which *Fancy* dresses to delight the *Muse;*
Winter austere forbids me to aspire,
And northern tempests damp the rising fire;
They chill the tides of *Fancy's* flowing sea,
Cease then, my song, cease the unequal lay.

TO HIS EXCELLENCY GENERAL WASHINGTON

The following LETTER *and* VERSES, *were written by the famous* Phillis Wheatley, *The African Poetess, and presented to his Excellency* Gen. Washington.

SIR.

I Have taken the freedom to address your Excellency in the enclosed poem, and entreat your acceptance, though I am not insensible of its inaccuracies. Your being appointed by the Grand Continental Congress to be Generalissimo of the armies of North America, together with the fame of your virtues, excite sensations not easy to suppress. Your generosity, therefore, I presume, will pardon the attempt. Wishing your Excellency all possible success in the great cause you are so generously engaged in. I am,

> Your Excellency's most obedient humble servant,
> **PHILLIS WHEATLEY.**

Providence, Oct. 26, 1775.
His Excellency Gen. Washington.

> Celestial choir! enthron'd in realms of light,
>   Columbia's scenes of glorious toils I write.
> While freedom's cause her anxious breast alarms,
> She flashes dreadful in refulgent arms.
> See mother earth her offspring's fate bemoan,
> And nations gaze at scenes before unknown!
> See the bright beams of heaven's revolving light
> Involved in sorrows and the veil of night!
>   The goddess comes, she moves divinely fair,
> Olive and laurel binds her golden hair:
> Wherever shines this native of the skies,
> Unnumber'd charms and recent graces rise.
>   Muse! bow propitious while my pen relates
> How pour her armies through a thousand gates,

As when Eolus heaven's fair face deforms,
Enwrapp'd in tempest and a night of storms;
Astonish'd ocean feels the wild uproar,
The refluent surges beat the sounding shore;
Or thick as leaves in Autumn's golden reign,
Such, and so many, moves the warrior's train.
In bright array they seek the work of war,
Where high unfurl'd the ensign waves in air.
Shall I to Washington their praise recite?
Enough thou know'st them in the fields of fight.
Thee, first in peace and honours,—we demand
The grace and glory of thy martial band.
Fam'd for thy valour, for thy virtues more,
Hear every tongue thy guardian aid implore!
    One century scarce perform'd its destined round,
When Gallic powers Columbia's fury found;
And so may you, whoever dares disgrace
The land of freedom's heaven-defended race!
Fix'd are the eyes of nations on the scales,
For in their hopes Columbia's arm prevails.
Anon Britannia droops the pensive head,
While round increase the rising hills of dead.
Ah! cruel blindness to Columbia's state!
Lament thy thirst of boundless power too late.
    Proceed, great chief, with virtue on thy side,
Thy ev'ry action let the goddess guide.
A crown, a mansion, and a throne that shine,
With gold unfading, WASHINGTON! be thine.

Gustavus Vassa

(c. 1745–c. 1797)

ACCCORDING TO HIS OWN statement Gustavus Vassa was born in what is now the interior of Eastern Nigeria, probably in 1745. His language was Ibo, and his people came under the nominal jurisdiction of the King of Benin. Captured by local raiders when he was about ten or eleven, Vassa was taken to the coast and sold to slavers bound for the West Indies.

After a few days in the islands, he was shipped to Virginia, served as a slave there, and eventually became the property of a Captain Pascal. This man gave him the name Gustavus Vassa, which remained with him the rest of his life. Vassa traveled widely with Captain Pascal, serving under him during Wolfe's campaign in Canada and with Admiral Boscawen in the Mediterranean during the Seven Years War. On these trips Vassa, an intelligent youngster, learned a great deal, including English. After leaving Pascal he spent some time in England, went to school, and acquired the skills to become a shipping clerk and an amateur navigator.

With his next master, Robert King, a Quaker from Philadelphia, Vassa traveled often between America and the West Indies. He evidently had a chance to make money on his own, because in 1766 he bought his freedom from Mr. King for £40. Then twenty-one and a free man, Vassa continued his life as a seaman, crossing the Atlantic several more times; on one occasion he went with a scientific expedition to the Arctic.

In the meantime Vassa had been converted to Methodism; he had also become an abolition speaker and traveled through the British Isles lecturing against slavery.

In 1786 Vassa was appointed Commissary for Slaves for the Black Poor going to Sierra Leone, a project to colonize freed slaves in Africa. Because Vassa felt that the men in charge of the mission were both dishonest and prejudiced, he spoke out against them and consequently was relieved of his post as Commissary. He later volunteered to go to Africa as a missionary but was rejected.

On April 7, 1792, Gustavus Vassa married Susan (or Susanna) Cullen. The notice of this wedding which appeared in *The Gentleman's Magazine* refers to him as "Gustavus Vassa the African, well known as the champion and advocate for procuring the suppression of the slave trade. . . ."

In 1789 Vassa published *The Interesting Narrative of the Life of Olaudah Equiano, or Gustavus Vassa, the African,* a work which became—with good reason—a best seller of the day. The narrative was a valuable antislavery document and was used by abolition forces on both sides of the Atlantic. It was also a highly readable travel book of the type popular in the eighteenth century. The author includes some wonders—crowing snakes and neighing sea horses—but he never strays too far from common sense.

According to *The Gentleman's Magazine,* Gustavus Vassa died in London on April 31, 1797. (Other dates have also been given.)

For the most recent comment on Gustavus Vassa and the latest reprint (and abridgment) of his work, see Paul Edwards, ed., *Equiano's Travels* (New York: Praeger, 1966). See also Vernon Loggins, *The Negro Author,* and Benjamin Brawley, *Early Negro American Writers.*

The following selections are from Chapters I and III of Vassa's autobiography.

EARLY LIFE IN AFRICA

I believe it is difficult for those who publish their own memoirs to escape the imputation of vanity; nor is this the only disadvantage under which they labor: it is also their misfortune that what is uncommon is rarely, if ever, believed, and what is obvious we are apt to turn from with disgust, and to charge the writer with impertinence. People generally think those memoirs only worthy to be read or remembered which abound in great or striking events; those, in short, which in a high degree excite either admiration or pity: all others they consign to contempt and oblivion. It is therefore, I confess, not a little hazardous in a private and obscure individual, and a stranger too, thus to solicit the indulgent attention of the public; especially when I own I offer here the history of neither a saint, a hero, nor a tyrant. I believe there are few events in my life, which have not happened to many: it is true the incidents of it are numerous; and, did I consider myself an European, I might say my sufferings were great: but when I compare my lot with that of most of my countrymen, I regard myself as a *particular favorite of heaven,* and acknowledge the mercies of Providence in every occurrence of my life. If, then, the following narrative does not appear sufficiently interesting to engage general attention, let my motive be some excuse for its publication. I am not so foolishly vain as to expect from it either immortality or literary reputation. If it affords any satisfaction to my numerous friends, at whose request it has been

Title supplied by editors.

written, or in the smallest degree promotes the interests of humanity, the ends for which it was undertaken will be fully attained, and every wish of my heart gratified. Let it therefore be remembered, that, in wishing to avoid censure, I do not aspire to praise.

That part of Africa, known by the name of Guinea, to which the trade for slaves is carried on, extends along the coast above 3400 miles, from Senegal to Angola, and includes a variety of kingdoms. Of these the most considerable is the kingdom of Benin, both as to extent and wealth, the richness and cultivation of the soil, the power of its king, and the number and warlike disposition of the inhabitants. It is situated nearly under the line, and extends along the coast about 170 miles, but runs back into the interior part of Africa to a distance hitherto, I believe, unexplored by any traveller; and seems only terminated at length by the empire of Abyssinnia, near 1500 miles from its beginning. This kingdom is divided into many provinces or districts: in one of the most remote and fertile of which, I was born, in the year 1745, situated in a charming fruitful vale, named Essala. The distance of this province from the capital of Benin and the sea coast must be very considerable: for I had never heard of white men or Europeans, nor of the sea; and our subjection to the king of Benin was little more than nominal; for every transaction of the government, as far as my slender observation extended, was conducted by the chief or elders of the place. The manners and government of a people who have little commerce with other countries, are generally very simple; and the history of what passes in one family or village, may serve as a specimen of the whole nation. My father was one of those elders or chiefs I have spoken of, and was styled Embrenche; a term, as I remember, importing the highest distinction, and signifying in our language a *mark* of grandeur. This mark is conferred on the person entitled to it, by cutting the skin across at the top of the forehead, and drawing it down to the eye-brows: and while it is in this situation applying a warm hand, and rubbing it until it shrinks up into a thick *weal* across the lower part of the forehead. Most of the judges and senators were thus marked; my father had long borne it: I had seen it conferred on one of my brothers, and I also was *destined* to receive it by my parents. Those Embrenche or chief men, decided disputes and punished crimes; for which purpose they always assembled together. The proceedings were generally short: and in most cases the law of retaliation prevailed. I remember a man was brought before my father, and the other judges, for kidnapping a boy; and, although he was the son of a chief or senator, he was condemned to make recompense by a man or woman slave. Adultery, however, was sometimes punished with slavery or death; a punishment which I believe is inflicted on it throughout most of the nation of Africa: so sacred among them is the honor of the marriage bed, and so jealous are they of the fidelity of their wives. Of this I recollect an instance—a woman was convicted before the judges of adultery, and delivered over, as the custom was, to her husband, to be punished. Accordingly he determined to put her to death: but it being found, just before her execution, that she had an infant at her breast; and no woman being prevailed on to perform the part of a nurse, she was spared on account of the child. The men, however, do not preserve the same constancy to their wives, which they expect from them; for they indulge in a plurality, though seldom in more than two. Their mode of marriage is thus:—both parties are usually betrothed when young by their parents, (though I have known the males to betroth themselves.) On this occasion a feast is prepared, and the bride and bridegroom stand up in the midst of all their friends, who are assembled for the purpose, while he declares she is henceforth to be looked upon as his wife, and that no other person is to pay any addresses to her. This is also immediately proclaimed in the vicinity, on which the bride retires from the assembly. Some time after, she is brought home to her husband, and then another feast is made, to which the relations of both parties are invited: her parents then deliver her to the bridegroom, accompanied with a number of blessings, and at the same time they tie round her waist a cotton string of the thickness of a goose-quill, which none but married women are permitted to wear: she is now considered as completely his wife; and at this time the dowry is given to the new married pair, which generally consists of portions of land, slaves, and cattle, household goods, and implements of husbandry. These are offered by the friends of both parties; besides which the parents of the bridegroom present gifts to those of the bride, whose property she is looked upon before marriage; but after it she is esteemed the sole property of her husband. The ceremony being now ended, the festival begins, which is celebrated with bonfires, and loud acclamations of joy, accompanied with music and dancing.

We are almost a nation of dancers, musicians and poets. Thus every great event, such as a triumphant return from battle, or other cause of public rejoicing, is celebrated in public dances, which are accompanied with songs and music suited to the occasion. The assembly is separated into four divisions, which dance either apart or in succession, and each with a character peculiar to itself. The first division contains the married men, who in their dances frequently exhibit feats of arms, and the representation of a battle. To these succeed the married women, who dance in the second division. The young men occupy the third: and the maidens the fourth. Each represents some interesting scene of real life, such as a great achievement, domestic employment, a pathetic story, or some rural sport; and as the subject is generally founded on some recent event, it is therefore ever new. This gives our dances a spirit and variety which I have scarcely seen elsewhere. We have many musical instruments, particularly drums of different kinds, a piece of music which resembles a guitar, and another much like a stickado. These last are chiefly used by betrothed virgins, who play on them on all grand festivals.

As our manners are simple, our luxuries are few. The dress of both sexes is nearly the same. It generally consists of a long piece of calico, or muslin, wrapped loosely round the body, somewhat in the form of a highland plaid. This is usually dyed blue, which is our favorite color. It is extracted from a berry, and is brighter and richer than any I have seen in Europe. Besides this, our women of distinction wear golden ornaments, which they dispose with some profusion on their arms and legs. When our women are not employed with the men in tillage, their usual occupation is spinning and weaving cotton, which they afterwards dye, and make into garments. They also manufacture earthen vessels, of which we have many kinds. Among the rest, tobacco pipes, made after the same fashion, and used in the same manner, as those in Turkey.

Our manner of living is entirely plain; for as yet the natives are unacquainted with those refinements in cookery which debauch the taste: bullocks, goats, and poultry, supply the greatest part of their food.— These constitute likewise the principal wealth of the country, and the chief articles of its commerce.—The flesh is usually stewed in a pan; to make it savory we sometimes use also pepper, and other spices, and we have salt made of wood ashes. Our vegetables are mostly plantains, cadas, yams, beans, and Indian corn. The head of the family usually eats alone; his wives and slaves have also their separate tables. Before we taste food we always wash our hands: indeed our cleanliness on all occasions is extreme; but on this it is an indispensable ceremony. After washing, libation is made, by pouring out a small portion of the drink on the floor, and tossing a small quantity of the food in a certain place, for the spirits of departed relations, which the natives suppose to preside over their conduct, and guard them from evil. They are totally unacquainted with strong or spirituous liquors; and their principal beverage is palm wine. This is got from a tree of that name, by tapping it at the top, and fastening a large gourd to it; and sometimes one tree will yield three or four gallons in a night. When just drawn it is of a most delicious sweetness; but in a few days it acquires a tartish and more spirituous flavor: though I never saw any one intoxicated by it. The same tree also produces nuts and oil. Our principal luxury is in perfumes; one sort of these is an odoriferous wood of delicious fragrance: the other a kind of earth; a small portion of which thrown into the fire diffuses a most powerful odor. We beat this wood into powder, and mix it with palm oil; with which both men and women perfume themselves.

In our buildings we study convenience rather than ornament. Each master of a family has a large square piece of ground, surrounded with a moat or fence, or enclosed with a wall made of red earth tempered: which, when dry, is as hard as brick.—Within this, are his houses to accommodate his family and slaves; which, if numerous, frequently present the appearance of a village. In the middle, stands the principal building, appropriated to the sole use of the master, and consisting of two apartments; in one of which he sits in the day with his family, the other is left apart for the reception of his friends. He has besides these a distinct apartment in which he sleeps, together with his male children. On each side are the apartments of his wives, who have also their separate day and night houses. The habitations of the slaves and their families are distributed throughout the rest of the enclosure. These houses never exceed one story in height: they are always built of wood, or stakes driven into the ground, crossed with wattles, and neatly plastered within and without. The roof is thatched with reeds. Our day-houses are left open at the sides; but those in which we sleep are always covered, and plastered in the inside, with a composition mixed with cow-dung, to keep off the different insects, which annoy us during the night. The walls and floors also of these are generally covered with mats. Our beds consist of a platform, raised three or four feet from the ground, on which are laid skins, and different parts of a spungy tree, called plantain.—Our covering is calico or muslin, the same as our dress. The usual seats are a few logs of wood; but we have benches, which are generally perfumed to accommodate strangers: these compose the greater part of our household furniture. Houses so constructed and furnished, require but little skill to erect them. Every man is a sufficient architect for the purpose. The whole neighbourhood afford their unanimous assistance in building them, and in return receive, and expect no other recompense than a feast.

As we live in a country where nature is prodigal of her favors, our wants are few and easily supplied; of course we have few manufactures. They consist for the most part of calicoes, earthen ware, ornaments, and instruments of war and husbandry.—But these make no part of our commerce, the principal articles of which, as I have observed, are provisions. In such a state, money is of little use; however, we have some small pieces of coin, if I may call them such. They are made something like an anchor; but I do not remember either their value or denomination. We have also markets, at which I have been frequently with my mother. These are sometimes visited by stout mahogany-colored men from the south-west of us: we call them *Oye-Eboe*, which term signifies red men living at a distance.—They generally bring us fire-arms, gunpowder, hats, beads, and dried fish. The last we esteemed a great rarity, as our waters were only brooks and springs. These articles they barter with us for odoriferous woods and earth, and our salt of wood ashes. They always carry slaves through our land; but the strictest account is exacted of their manner of procuring them before they are suffered to pass. Sometimes indeed, we sold slaves to them, but they were only prisoners of war, or such among us as had been convicted of kidnapping, or adultery, and some other crimes, which we esteemed heinous. This practice of kidnapping induces me to think, that, notwithstanding all our strictness, their principal business among us was to trepan our people. I remember too, they carried great sacks along with them, which not long after, I had an opportunity of fatally seeing applied to that infamous purpose.

Our land is uncommonly rich and fruitful, and produces all kinds of vegetables in great abundance.—We have plenty of Indian corn, and vast quantities of cotton and tobacco. Our pine apples grow without culture; they are about the size of the largest sugar-loaf, and finely flavored. We have also spices of different kinds, particularly pepper; and a variety of delicious fruits which I have never seen in Europe; together with gums of various kinds, and honey in abundance. All our industry is exerted to improve these blessings of nature. Agriculture is our chief employment; and every one, even the children and women, are engaged in it. Thus we are all habituated to labor from our earliest years. Every one contributes something to the common stock; and, as we are unacquainted with idleness, we have no beggars. The benefits of such a mode of living are obvious. The West India planters prefer the slaves of Benin or Eboe, to those of any other part of Guinea, for their hardiness, intelligence, integrity, and zeal. Those benefits are felt by us in the general healthiness of the people, and in their vigor and activity; I might have added, too, in their comeliness. Deformity is indeed unknown amongst us, I mean that of shape. Numbers of the natives of Eboe now in London, might be brought in support of this assertion: for, in regard to complexion, ideas of beauty are wholly relative. I remember while in Africa to have seen three negro children who were tawny, and another quite white, who were universally regarded by myself, and the natives in general, as far as related to their complexions, as deformed.—Our women, too, were in my eye at least, uncommonly graceful, alert, and modest to a degree of bashfulness; nor do I remember to have heard of an instance of incontinence amongst them before marriage.—They are also remarkably cheerful. Indeed, cheerfulness and affability are two of the leading characteristics of our nation.

Our tillage is exercised in a large plain or common, some hours' walk from our dwellings, and all the neighbors resort thither in a body. They use no beasts of husbandry; and their only instruments are hoes, axes, shovels, and beaks, or pointed iron, to dig with. Sometimes we are visited by locusts, which come in large clouds, so as to darken the air, and destroy our harvest. This, however, happens rarely, but when it does, a famine is produced by it. I remember an instance or two wherein this happened. This common is often the theatre of war; and therefore when our people go out to till their land, they not only go in a body, but generally take their arms with them for fear of a surprise; and when they apprehend an invasion, they guard the avenues to their dwellings, by driving sticks into the ground, which are so sharp at one end as to pierce the foot, and are generally dipt in poison. From what I can recollect of these battles, they appear to have been irruptions of one little state or district on the other, to obtain prisoners or booty. Perhaps they were incited to this, by those traders who brought the European goods I mentioned, amongst us. Such a mode of obtaining slaves in Africa is common; and I believe more are procured this way, and by kidnapping, than any other. When a trader wants slaves, he applies to a chief for them, and tempts him with his wares. It is not extraordinary, if on this occasion he yields to the temptation with as little firmness, and accepts the price of his fellow creatures' liberty, with as little reluctance as the enlightened merchant.—Accordingly he falls on his neighbors, and a desperate battle ensues. If he prevails and takes prisoners, he gratifies his avarice by selling them; but, if his party be vanquished, and he falls into the hands of the enemy, he is put to death; for, as he has been known to foment their quarrels, it is thought dangerous to let him survive, and no ransom can save him, though all other prisoners may be redeemed. We have fire-arms, bows and arrows, broad two-edged swords and javelins: we have shields also which cover a man from head to foot. All are taught the use of these weapons; even our women are warriors, and march boldly out to fight along with the men.—Our whole district is a kind of militia: on a certain signal given, such as the firing of a gun at night, they all rise in arms and rush upon their enemy. It is perhaps something remarkable, that when our people march to the field a red flag or banner is borne before them. I was once a witness to a battle in our common. We had been all at work in it one day as usual, when our people were suddenly attacked. I climbed a tree at some distance, from which I beheld the fight. There were many women as well as men on both sides; among others my mother was there, and armed with a broad sword. After fighting for a considerable time with great fury, and many had been killed, our people obtained the victory, and took their enemy's Chief a prisoner. He was carried off in great triumph, and, though he offered a large ransom for his life, he was put to death. A virgin of note among our enemies, had been slain in the battle, and her arm was exposed in our marketplace, where our trophies were always exhibited.—The spoils were divided according to the merit of the warriors. Those prisoners which were not sold or redeemed, we kept as slaves: but how different was their condition from that of the slaves in the West Indies! With us, they do no more work than other members of the community, even their master; their food, clothing and lodging were nearly the same as theirs, (except that they were not permitted to eat with those who were free-born;) and there was scarce any other difference between them, than a superior degree of importance which the head of a family possesses in our state, and that authority which, as such, he exercises over every part of his household. Some of these slaves have even slaves under them as their own property, and for their own use.

As to religion, the natives believe that there is one Creator of all things, and that he lives in the sun, and is girted round with a belt that he may never eat or drink; but, according to some he smokes a pipe, which is our own favorite luxury. They believe he governs events, especially our deaths or captivity; but, as for the doctrine of eternity, I do not remember to have ever heard of it: some, however, believe in the transmigration of souls in a certain degree. Those spirits, which are not transmigrated, such as their dear friends or relations, they believe always attend them, and guard them from the bad spirits or their foes. For this reason they always before eating, as I have observed, put some small portion of the meat, and pour some of their drink, on the ground for them; and they often make oblations of the blood of beasts or fowls at their graves. I was very fond of my mother, and almost constantly with her. When she went to make these oblations at her mother's tomb, which was a kind of small solitary thatched house, I sometimes attended her.—There she made her libations, and spent most of the night in cries and lamentations. I have been often extremely terrified on these occasions. The loneliness of the place, the darkness of the night, and the ceremony of libation, naturally awful and gloomy, were heightened by my mother's lamentations; and these concurring with the doleful cries of birds, by which these places were frequented, gave an inexpressible terror to the scene.

We compute the year, from the day on which the sun crosses the line, and on its setting that evening, there is a general shout throughout the land; at least, I can speak from my own knowledge, throughout our vicinity. The people at the same time make a great noise with rattles, not unlike the basket rattles used by children here, though much larger, and hold up their hands to heaven for a blessing. It is then the greatest offerings are made; and those childern whom our wise men foretell will be fortunate, are then presented to different people. I remember many used to come to see me, and I was carried about to others for that purpose. They have many offerings, particularly at full moons; generally two, at harvest, before the fruits are taken out of the ground: and when any young animals are killed, sometimes they offer up part of them as a sacrifice. These offerings, when made by one of the heads of a family, serve for the whole. I remember we often had them at my father's and my uncle's, and their families have been present. Some of our offerings are eaten with bitter herbs. We had a saying among us to any one of a cross temper, 'That if they were to be eaten, they should be eaten with bitter herbs.'

We practised circumcision like the Jews, and made offerings and feasts on that occasion, in the same manner as they did. Like them also, our children were named from some event, some circumstance, or fancied foreboding, at the time of their birth. I was named *Olaudah,* which in our language signifies vicissitude, or fortunate; also, one favored, and having a loud voice and well spoken. I remember we never polluted the name of the object of our adoration; on the contrary, it was always mentioned with the greatest reverence; and we were totally unacquainted with swearing, and all those terms of abuse and reproach which find their way so readily and copiously into the language of more civilized people. The only expressions of that kind I remember were, 'May you rot, or may you swell, or may a beast take you.'

I have before remarked that the natives of this part of Africa are extremely cleanly. This necessary habit of decency, was with us a part of religion, and therefore we had many purifications and washings; indeed almost as many, and used on the same occasions, if my recollection does not fail me, as the Jews. Those that touched the dead at any time were obliged to wash and purify themselves before they could enter a dwelling-house. Every woman, too, at certain times was forbidden to come into a dwelling-house, or touch any person, or any thing we eat. I was so fond of my mother I could not keep from her, or avoid touching her at some of those periods, in consequence of which I was obliged to be kept out with her, in a little house made for that purpose, till offering was made, and then we were purified.

Though we had no places of public worship, we had priests and magicians, or wise men. I do not remember whether they had different offices, or whether they were united in the same persons, but they were held in great reverence by the people.—They calculated our time, and foretold events, as their name imported, for we called them Ah-affoe-way-cah, which signifies calculators or yearly men, our year being called Ah-affoe. They wore their beards, and when they died, they were succeeded by their sons. Most of their implements and things of value were interred along with them. Pipes and tobacco were also put into the grave with the corpse, which was always perfumed and ornamented, and animals were offered in sacrifice to them. None accompanied their funerals, but those of the same profession or tribe. They buried them after sunset, and always returned from the grave by a different way from that which they went.

These magicians were also our doctors or physicians. They practised bleeding by cupping; and were very successful in healing wounds and expelling poisons. They had likewise some extraordinary method of discovering jealousy, theft, poisoning; the success of which, no doubt, they derived from the unbounded influence over the credulity and superstition of the people. I do not remember what those methods were, except that as to poisoning; I recollect an instance or two, which I hope it will not be deemed impertinent here to insert, as it may serve as a kind of specimen of the rest, and is still used by the negroes in the West Indies. A young woman had been poisoned, but it was not known by whom; the doctors ordered the corpse to be taken up by some persons, and carried to the grave. As soon as the bearers had raised it on their shoulders, they seemed seized with some sudden impulse, and ran to and fro, unable to stop themselves. At last, after having passed through a number of thorns and prickly bushes unhurt, the corpse fell from them close to a house, and defaced it in the fall; and the owner being taken up, he immediately confessed the poisoning.

The natives are extremely cautious about poison. When they buy any eatables, the seller kisses it all round before the buyer, to show him it is not poisoned; and the same is done when any meat or drink is presented, particularly to a stranger. We have serpents of different kinds, some of which are esteemed ominous when they appear in our houses, and these we never molest. I remember two of those ominous snakes, each of which was as thick as the calf of a man's leg, and his color resembling a dolphin in the water, crept at different times into my mother's night-house, where I always lay with her, and coiled themselves into folds, and each time they crowed like a cock. I was desired by some of our wise men to touch these, that I might be interested in the good omen, which I did, for they were quite harmless, and would tamely suffer themselves to be handled; and then they were put into a large earthen pan, and set on one side of the high-way. Some of our snakes, however, were poisonous; one of them crossed the road one day as I was standing on it, and passed between my feet without offering to touch me, to the great surprise of many who saw it; and these incidents were accounted by the wise men, and likewise by my mother and the rest of the people, as remarkable omens in my favor.

❊   ❊   ❊

SLAVE SHIP

. . . The first object which saluted my eyes when I arrived on the coast, was the sea, and a slave ship, which was then riding at anchor, and waiting for its cargo. These filled me with astonishment, which was soon converted into terror, when I was carried on board. I was im-

Title supplied by editors.

mediately handled, and tossed up to see if I were sound, by some of the crew; and I was now persuaded that I had gotten into a world of bad spirits, and that they were going to kill me. Their complexions, too, differing so much from ours, their long hair, and the language they spoke, (which was very different from any I had ever heard) united to confirm me in this belief. Indeed, such were the horrors of my views and fears at the moment, that, if ten thousand worlds had been my own, I would have freely parted with them all to have exchanged my condition with that of the meanest slave in my own country. When I looked round the ship too, and saw a large furnace of copper boiling, and a multitude of black people of every description chained together, every one of their countenances expressing dejection and sorrow, I no longer doubted of my fate; and, quite overpowered with horror and anguish, I fell motionless on the deck and fainted. When I recovered a little, I found some black people about me, who I believed were some of those who had brought me on board, and had been receiving their pay; they talked to me in order to cheer me, but all in vain. I asked them if we were not to be eaten by those white men with horrible looks, red faces, and long hair. They told me I was not: and one of the crew brought me a small portion of spirituous liquor in a wine glass, but, being afraid of him, I would not take it out of his hand. One of the blacks therefore, took it from him and gave it to me, and I took a little down my palate, which, instead of reviving me, as they thought it would, threw me into the greatest consternation at the strange feeling it produced, having never tasted any such liquor before. Soon after this, the blacks who brought me on board went off, and left me abandoned to despair.

I now saw myself deprived of all chance of returning to my native country, or even the least glimpse of hope of gaining the shore, which I now considered as friendly; and I even wished for my former slavery in preference to my present situation, which was filled with horrors of every kind, still heightened by my ignorance of what I was to undergo. I was not long suffered to indulge my grief; I was soon put down under the decks, and there I received such a salutation in my nostrils as I had never experienced in my life: so that, with the loathsomeness of the stench, and crying together, I became so sick and low that I was not able to eat, nor had I the least desire to taste any thing. I now wished for the last friend, death, to relieve me; but soon, to my grief, two of the white men offered me eatables; and, on my refusing to eat, one of them held me fast by the hands and laid me across, I think the windlass, and tied my feet, while the other flogged me severely. I had never experienced any thing of this kind before, and although not being used to the water, I naturally feared that element the first time I saw it, yet, nevertheless, could I have got over the nettings, I would have jumped over the side, but I could not; and besides, the crew used to watch us very closely who were not chained down to the decks, lest we should leap into the water; and I have seen some of these poor African prisoners most severely cut, for attempting to do so, and hourly whipped for not eating. This indeed was often the case with myself. In a little time after, amongst the poor chained men, I found some of my own nation, which in a small degree gave ease to my mind. I inquired of these what was to be done with us? they gave me to understand, we were to be carried to these white people's country to work for them. I then was a little revived, and thought, if it were no worse than working, my situation was not so desperate; but still I feared I should be put to death, the white people looked and acted, as I thought, in so savage a manner; for I had never seen among any people such instances of brutal cruelty; and this not only shown towards us blacks, but also to some of the whites themselves. One white man in particular I saw, when we were permitted to be on deck, flogged so unmercifully with a large rope near the foremast, that he died in consequence of it; and they tossed him over the side as they would have done a brute. This made me fear these people the more; and I expected nothing less than to be treated in the same manner. I could not help expressing my fears and apprehensions to some of my countrymen; I asked them if these people had no country, but lived in this hollow place? (the ship) they told me they did not, but came from a distant one. 'Then,' said I, 'how comes it in all our country we never heard of them?' They told me because they lived so very far off. I then asked where were their women? had they any like themselves? I was told they had. 'And why,' said I, 'do we not see them?' They answered, because they were left behind. I asked how the vessel could go? they told me they could not tell; but that there was cloth put upon the masts by the help of the ropes I saw, and then the vessel went on; and the white men had some spell or magic they put in the water when they liked, in order to stop the vessel. I was exceedingly amazed at this account, and really thought they were spirits. I therefore wished much to be from amongst them, for I expected they would sacrifice me; but my wishes were vain—for we were so quartered that it was impossible for any of us to make our escape.

While we stayed on the coast I was mostly on deck; and one day, to my great astonishment, I saw one of these vessels coming in with the sails up. As soon as the whites saw it, they gave a great shout, at which we were amazed; and the more so, as the vessel appeared larger by approaching nearer. At last, she came to an anchor in my sight, and when the anchor was let go, I and my countrymen who saw it, were lost in astonishment to observe the vessel stop—and were now convinced it was done by magic. Soon after this the other ship got her boats out, and they came on board of us, and the people of both ships seemed very glad to see each other.—Several of the strangers also shook hands with us black people, and made motions with their hands, signifying I suppose, we were to go to their country, but we did not understand them.

At last, when the ship we were in, had got in all her cargo, they made ready with many fearful noises, and we were all put under deck, so that we could not see how they managed the vessel. But this disappointment was the least of my sorrow. The stench of the hold while we were on the coast was so intolerably loathsome, that it was dangerous to remain there for any time, and some of us had been permitted to stay on the deck for the fresh air; but now that the whole ship's cargo were confined together, it became absolutely pestilential. The closeness of the place, and the heat of the climate, added to the number in the ship, which was so crowded that each had scarcely room to turn himself, almost suffocated us. This produced copious perspirations, so that the air soon became unfit for respiration, from a variety of loathsome smells, and brought on a sickness among the slaves, of which many died—thus falling victims to the improvident avarice, as I may call it, of their purchasers. This wretched situation was again aggravated by the galling of the chains, now became insupportable; and the filth of the necessary tubs, into which the children often fell, and were almost suffocated. The shrieks of the women, and the groans of the dying, rendered the whole a scene of horror almost inconceivable. Happily perhaps, for myself, I was soon reduced so low here that it was thought necessary to keep me almost always on deck; and from my extreme youth I was not put in fetters. In this situation I expected every hour to share the fate of my companions, some of whom were almost daily brought upon deck at the point of death, which I began to hope would soon put an end to my miseries. Often did I think many of the inhabitants of the deep much more happy than myself. I envied them the freedom they enjoyed, and as often wished I could change my condition for theirs. Every circumstance I met with, served only to render my state more painful, and heightened my apprehensions, and my opinion of the cruelty of the whites.

One day they had taken a number of fishes; and when they had killed and satisfied themselves with as many as they thought fit, to our astonishment who were on deck, rather than give any of them to us to eat, as we expected, they tossed the remaining fish into the sea again, although we begged and prayed for some as well as we could, but in vain; and some of my countrymen, being pressed by hunger, took an opportunity, when they thought no one saw them, of trying to get a little privately; but they were discovered, and the attempt procured them some very severe floggings. One day, when we had a smooth sea and moderate wind, two of my wearied countrymen who were chained together, (I was near them at the time,) preferring death to such a life of misery, somehow made through the nettings and jumped into the sea; immediately, another quite dejected fellow, who, on account of his illness, was suffered to be out of irons, also followed their example; and I believe many more would very soon have done the same, if they had not been prevented by the ship's crew, who were instantly alarmed. Those of us that were the most active, were in a moment put down under the deck, and there was such a noise and confusion amongst the people of the ship as I never heard before, to stop her, and get the boat out to go after the slaves. However two of the wretches were drowned, but they got the other, and afterwards flogged him unmercifully, for thus attempting to prefer death to slavery. In this manner we continued to undergo more hardships than I can now relate, hardships which are inseparable from this accursed trade. Many a time we were near suffocation from the want of fresh air, which we were often without for whole days together. This, and the stench of the necessary tubs, carried off many.

During our passage, I first saw flying fishes, which surprised me very much; they used frequently to fly across the ship, and many of them fell on the deck. I also now first saw the use of the quadrant; I had often with astonishment seen the mariners make observations with it, and I could not think what it meant. They at last took notice of my surprise; and one of them, willing to increase it, as well as to gratify my curiosity, made me one day look through it. The clouds appeared to me to be land, which disappeared as they passed along. This heightened my wonder; and I was now more persuaded than ever, that I was in another world, and that every thing about me was magic. At last, we came in sight of the island of Barbadoes, at which the whites on board gave a great shout, and made many signs of joy to us. We did not know what to think of this; but as the vessel drew nearer, we plainly saw the harbor, and other ships of different kinds and sizes, and we soon anchored amongst them, off Bridgetown. Many merchants and planters now came on board, though it was in the evening. They put us in separate parcels, and examined us attentively. They also made us jump, and pointed to the land, signifying we were to go there. We thought by this, we should be eaten by these ugly men, as they appeared to us; and, when soon after we were all put down under the deck again, there was much dread and trembling among us, and nothing but bitter cries to be heard all the night from these apprehensions, insomuch, that at last the white people got some old slaves from the land to pacify us. They told us we were not to be eaten, but to work, and were soon to go on land, where we should see many of our country people. This report eased us much. And sure enough, soon after we were landed, there came to us Africans of all languages.

We were conducted immediately to the merchant's yard, where we were all pent up together, like so many sheep in a fold, without regard to sex or age. As every object was new to me, every thing I saw filled me with surprise. What struck me first, was, that the houses were built with bricks and stories, and in every other respect different from those I had seen in Africa; but I was still more astonished on seeing people on horseback. I did not know what this could mean; and, indeed, I thought these people were full of nothing but magical arts. While I was in this astonishment, one of my fellow-prisoners spoke to a countryman of his, about the horses, who said they were the same kind they had in their country. I understood them, though they were from a distant part of Africa; and I thought it odd I had not seen any horses there; but afterwards, when I came to converse with different Africans, I found they had many horses amongst them, and much larger than those I then saw.

We were not many days in the merchant's custody, before we were sold after their usual manner, which is this:—On a signal given, (as the beat of a drum,) the buyers rush at once into the yard where the slaves are confined, and make choice of that parcel they like best. The noise and clamor with which this is attended, and the eagerness visible in the countenances of the buyers, serve not a little to increase the apprehension of terrified Africans, who may well be supposed to consider them as the ministers of that destruction to which they think themselves devoted. In this manner, without scruple, are relations and friends separated, most of them never to see each other again. I remember, in the vessel in which I was brought over, in the men's apartment, there were several brothers, who, in the sale, were sold in different lots; and it was very moving on this occasion, to see and hear their cries at parting. O, ye nominal Christians! might not an African ask you—Learned you this from your God, who says unto you, Do unto all men as you would men should do unto you? Is it not enough that we are torn from our country and friends, to toil for your luxury and lust of gain? Must every tender feeling be likewise sacrificed to your avarice? Are the dearest friends and relations, now renderd more dear by their separation from their kindred, still to be parted from each other, and thus prevented from cheering the gloom of slavery, with the small comfort of being together, and mingling their sufferings and sorrows? Why are parents to lose their children, brothers their sisters, or husbands their wives? Surely, this is a new refinement in cruelty, which, while it has no advantage to atone for it, thus aggravates distress, and adds fresh horrors even to the wretchedness of slavery.

George Moses Horton

(c. 1797–c. 1883)

BORN IN NORTHAMPTON COUNTY, North Carolina, probably in 1797 (slaves rarely knew the exact date of their birth), George Moses was the property of a family of small plantation owners named Horton. When George was a few years old, the master moved to another plantation near the University of North Carolina at Chapel Hill. Here George Moses Horton grew up and became locally famous as a poet.

In an autobiographical sketch written in 1845, Horton tells us that while working as a cow-boy, he decided that he would learn to read. By having school children tell him letters, he accomplished this task and read well before he learned to write. Moved by reading "Wesley's old hymns and other pieces of poetry from various authors," the slave boy then decided that he would be a poet.

During his late teens, Horton began visiting the campus of the University of North Carolina on his free time, taking farm products to sell to the students. Soon, however, he began peddling not farm produce but acrostics and love poems (usual charge, 25¢) for undergraduates to send to their girl friends. At first Horton had to dictate the verses, not yet knowing how to write. Eventually he was allowed to give up all farm work and "hire himself out" for fifty cents a day, an arrangement often made for slaves who had skills that were in demand. He became a "comic" campus orator, a writer of love letters as well as verses for the students, and, for several generations of North Carolina students, a kind of legend in his own time.

Aided by Caroline Hentz, the Yankee wife of one of the University's professors, Horton "achieved" his first publication in 1828. On April 8 of that year, Mrs. Hentz had two of his poems printed in her home-town paper, the Lancaster (Massachusetts) *Gazette*. Later she persuaded the Raleigh *Register* to publish a few of Horton's poems with a short biography of the slave. These verses were reprinted by other Southern papers and by Northern periodicals like *Freedom's Journal* and Garrison's *Liberator*. Some of Horton's verses also appeared in *The Southern Literary Messenger*.

In the meantime, the poet's Southern friends attempted to secure Horton's freedom by compiling and selling a book of his poems, called *The Hope of Liberty*, which was printed in 1829 in Raleigh. The plan was not successful, for the book did not sell well, and not enough money came from it. But *The Hope of Liberty* made its way to Cincinnati, where it was read by an abolitionist who had it reprinted in 1837 under the title *Poems by a Slave*. (A third reprint was appended in 1838 to *A Memoir and Poems of Phillis Wheatley*.) The next volume of Horton's poems was underwritten by the President, faculty, students, and the poet's friends at the University of North Carolina. Printed in 1854 in Hillsborough, North Carolina, it was entitled *The Poetical Works of George M. Horton, the Colored Bard of North Carolina*. Horton wrote an autobiographical sketch to serve as a preface to the work.

Perhaps before this last publication, George married a slave belonging to a local farmer. The couple had two children, but from the evidence of several of his poems on the subject, the marriage was not successful.

The Yankees came to Horton's section of North Carolina in 1865, and the poet found a new friend and enthusiastic sponsor in twenty-eight-year-old Captain Will H. S. Banks of the 9th Michigan Cavalry Volunteers. Under Captain Bank's guidance and editorship, Horton published his last work, *Naked Genius*, in 1865 in Raleigh. There were 132 poems in this volume (forty-two of them, however, came from *The Poetical Works*, 1845). Many of the new poems, probably suggested by Banks, dealt with Civil War incidents and Civil War heroes like Grant, Sherman, and Lincoln.

Last records of George Moses Horton find him in Philadelphia in 1866. He probably died there in the year 1883.

Horton was a prolific and facile versifier, one who was willing to write about anything—no matter how sublime or trivial—that touched him. One is struck by his range of reading (he knew Milton, Byron, and other English poets), and by his mastery of several poetic forms. He freely uses the ode, blank verse, the heroic couplet, and various stanzaic patterns. Although his subject matter ranges far and wide, Horton had certain themes which he tended to overwork, among them the varieties of love, the transitoriness of life, and the woes of marriage. He must have had a very disagreeable time with his wife, because he never tires of describing the troubles a bad wife can cause. In his later poems he admonishes free Negroes to make the most of their newly acquired liberty, to be honest and industrious. Understandably, he retained his love for North Carolina and wrote several touching poems about his regret at leaving his native land; in fact, George Moses Horton never became actually anti-Southern.

Like many poets of his generation, Horton too often wrote on abstract themes like "Memory," "Prosperity," and "Liberty"; he attempted too many noble flights; and he used mythological characters far too often. But he could handle the language realistically and make humorous folk comparisons. Unfortunately, he did so all too rarely.

The fullest and most recent account of the life and works of George Moses Horton is Richard Walser's *The Black Poet* (New York: Philosophical Library, 1966). See also Vernon Loggins, *The Negro Author,* and Benjamin Brawley, *Early Negro American Writers.*

AN ACROSTIC FOR JULIA SHEPARD

Joy, like the morning, breaks from one divine—
Unveiling streams which cannot fail to shine.
Long have I strove to magnify her name
Imperial, floating on the breeze of fame.

Attracting beauty must delight afford,
Sought of the world and of the Bards adored;
Her grace of form and heart-alluring powers
Express her more than fair, the queen of flowers.

Pleasure, fond nature's stream, from beauty sprung,
And was the softest strain the Muses sung,
Reverting sorrows into speechless Joys,
Dispelling gloom which human peace destroys.

THE CREDITOR TO HIS PROUD DEBTOR

Ha! tott'ring Johnny strut and boast,
But think of what your feathers cost;
Your crowing days are short at most,
    You bloom but soon to fade.
Surely you could not stand so wide,
If strictly to the bottom tried [sic];
The wind would blow your plume aside,
    If half your debts were paid.
        Then boast and bear the crack,
        With the Sheriff at your back,
        Huzza for dandy Jack,
        My jolly fop, my Jo—

The blue smoke from your segar flies,
Offensive to my nose and eyes,
The most of people would be wise,
    Your presence to evade.

"An Acrostic for Julia Shepard." Title supplied by editors. Reprinted by permission of Philosophical Library.

Your pockets jingle loud with cash,
And thus you cut a foppish dash,
But alas! dear boy, you would be trash,
   If your accounts were paid.
     Then boast and bear the crack, &c.

My duck bill boots would look as bright,
Had you in justice served me right,
Like you, I then could step as light,
   Before a flaunting maid.
As nicely could I clear my throat,
And to my tights, my eyes devote;
But I'd leave you bare, without a coat,
   For which you have not paid.
     Then boast and bear the crack, &c.

I'd toss myself with a scornful air,
And to a poor man pay no care,
I could rock cross-legged in my chair,
   Within the cloister shade.
I'd gird my neck with a light cravat,
And creaming wear my bell-crown hat;
But away my down would fly at that,
   If once my debts were paid.
     Then boast and bear the crack,
     With the Sheriff at your back,
     Huzza for dandy Jack,
     My jolly fop, my Jo—

GEORGE MOSES HORTON, MYSELF

I feel myself in need
   Of the inspiring strains of ancient lore,
My heart to lift, my empty mind to feed,
   And all the world explore.

I know that I am old
   And never can recover what is past,
But for the future may some light unfold
   And soar from ages blast.

I feel resolved to try,
   My wish to prove, my calling to pursue,
Or mount up from the earth into the sky,
   To show what Heaven can do.

My genius from a boy,
    Has fluttered like a bird within my heart;
But could not thus confined her powers employ,
    Impatient to depart.

She like a restless bird,
    Would spread her wings, her power to be
        unfurl'd,
And let her songs be loudly heard,
    And dart from world to world.

ON LIBERTY AND SLAVERY

Alas! and am I born for this,
    To wear this slavish chain?
Deprived of all created bliss,
    Through hardship, toil and pain!

How long have I in bondage lain,
    And languished to be free!
Alas! and must I still complain—
    Deprived of liberty.

Oh, Heaven! and is there no relief
    This side the silent grave—
To soothe the pain—to quell the grief
    And anguish of a slave?

Come Liberty, thou cheerful sound,
    Roll though my ravished ears!
Come, let my grief in joys be drowned,
    And drive away my fears.

Say unto foul oppression, Cease:
    Ye tyrants rage no more,
And let the joyful trump of peace,
    Now bid the vassal soar.

Soar on the pinions of that dove
    Which long has cooed for thee,
And breathed her notes from Afric's grove,
    The sound of Liberty.

Oh, Liberty! thou golden prize,
  So often sought by blood—
We crave thy sacred sun to rise,
  The gift of nature's God!

Bid Slavery hide her haggard face,
  And barbarism fly:
I scorn to see the sad disgrace
  In which enslaved I lie.

Dear Liberty! upon thy breast,
  I languish to respire;
And like the Swan unto her nest,
  I'd to thy smiles retire.

Oh, blest asylum—heavenly balm!
  Unto thy boughs I flee—
And in thy shades the storm shall calm,
  With songs of Liberty!

TO ELIZA

Eliza, tell thy lover why
Or what induced thee to deceive me?
  Fare thee well—away I fly—
I shun the lass who thus will grieve me.

Eliza, still thou art my song,
Although by force I may foresake thee;
  Fare thee well, for I was wrong
To woo thee while another take thee.

Eliza, pause and think awhile—
Sweet lass! I shall forget thee never:
  Fare thee well! although I smile,
I grieve to give thee up for ever.

Eliza, I shall think of thee—
My heart shall ever twine about thee;
  Fare thee well—but think of me,
Compell'd to live and die without thee.
  "Fare thee well!—and if for ever,
Still for ever fare thee well!"

JEFFERSON IN A TIGHT PLACE

THE FOX IS CAUGHT

The blood hounds, long upon the trail,
Have rambled faithful, hill and dale;
But mind, such creatures never fail,
   To run the rebel down.
His fears forbid him long to stop,
Altho' he gains the mountain top,
He soon is made his tail to drop,
   And fleets to leave the hounds.

Alas! he speeds from place to place,
Such is the fox upon the chase;
To him the mud is no disgrace,
   No lair his cause defends.
He leaves a law and seeks a dell,
And where to fly 'tis hard to tell;
He fears before to meet with hell,
   Behind he has no friends.

But who can pity such a fox,
Though buried among the rocks;
He's a nuisance among the flocks,
   And sucks the blood of geese.
He takes advantage of the sheep,
His nature is at night to creep,
And rob the flocks while the herdsmen sleep,
   When dogs can have no peace.

But he is now brought to a bay,
However fast he run away,
He knows he has not long to stay,
   And assumes a raccoon's dress.
Found in a hole, he veils his face,
And fain would take a lady's place,
But fails, for he has run his race,
   And falls into distress.

The fox is captured in his den,
The martial troops of Michigan,
May hence be known the fleetest men,
   For Davis is their prey.
Great Babylon has fallen down,
A King is left without a crown,
Stripped of honors and renown,
   The evening ends the day.

LIKE BROTHERS WE MEET

DEDICATED TO THE FEDERAL AND LATE CONFEDERATE SOLDIERS

Like heart-loving brothers we meet,
    And still the loud thunders of strife,
The blaze of fraternity kindles most sweet,
    There's nothing more pleasing in life.

The black cloud of faction retreats,
    The poor is no longer depressed,
See those once discarded resuming their seats,
    The lost strangers will soon find rest.

The soldier no longer shall roam,
    But soon shall land safely ashore,
Each soon will arrive at his own native home,
    And struggle in warfare no more.

The union of brothers is sweet,
    Whose wives and children do come,
Their sons and fair daughters with pleasure they greet,
    When long absent fathers come home.

They never shall languish again,
    Nor discord their union shall break,
When brothers no longer lament and complain,
    Hence never each other forsake.

Hang closely together like friends,
    By peace killing foes never driven,
The storm of commotion eternally ends,
    And earth will soon turn into Heaven.

LETTER TO MR. HORACE GREELEY

Sept. 11, 1852
Chapel Hill, N. C.

TO MR. GREELEY

Sir,

From the information of the president of the University of North Carolina, to wit, the honorable D. L. Swain, who is willing to aid me himself, I learn that you are a gentleman of philanthropic feeling. I

"Letter to Mr. Horace Greeley." Title supplied by editors. Reprinted by permission of Philosophical Library.

therefore thought it essential to apply to your beneficent hand for some assistance to remove the burden of hard servitude. Notwithstanding, sir, there are many in my native section of country who wish to bring me out, and there are others far too penurious which renders it somewhat dubious with regard to my extrication. It is evident that you have heard of me by the fame of my work in poetry, much of which I am now too closely confined to carry out and which I feel a warm interest to do; and, sir, by favoring me with a bounty of 175 dollars, I will endeavor to reward your generosity with my productions as soon as possible. I am the only public or recognized poet of color in my native state or perhaps in the union, born in slavery but yet craving that scope and expression whereby my literary labor of the night may be circulated throughout the whole world. Then I forbid that my productions should ever fall to the ground, but rather soar as an eagle above the towering mountains and thus return as a triumphing spirit to the bosom of its God who gave it birth, though now confined in these loathsome fetters. Please assist the lowering vassal arise and live a glad denizen the remnant of his days and as one of active utility.

Yours respect.
George M. Horton
of color

David Walker

(1785–1830)

As THE CHILD OF a slave father and a free mother, David Walker was "born free" in Wilmington, North Carolina. Not much is known about his early life: in his *Appeal* he remarks that he had traveled widely in the United States, especially the South.

On the basis of his own observations and reading, Walker concluded that American slavery was the worst form of slavery in the history of mankind. So, sometime in the 1820's, he decided to flee from the South and its hateful institution. He landed in Boston and by 1827 was the owner of an "old clothes shop" on Brattle Street near the wharves.

Also in that year David Walker added his voice and pen to the Abolition Movement and began writing for the pioneer *Freedom's Journal,* which had just been established in New York by Samuel Cornish and John Russwurm, the founders of Negro journalism. In this connection Walker tried to publicize the work of George Moses Horton and to help the slave buy his freedom.

Walker's Appeal, in Four Articles; together with a Preamble, to the Coloured Citizens of the World, but in Particular and Very Expressly, to Those of the United States of America was published in 1829. Reaction to the work was immediate and sensational, especially in the South. The Mayor of Savannah, Georgia, wrote to Mayor Harrison Gray Otis of Boston, demanding that the book be suppressed. Otis refused, and the Governor of Virginia, who had made a similar demand, was told that Walker had not violated any Massachusetts law. It was rumored that in certain sections of the South a reward of $1,000 had been offered for Walker dead, and of $10,000 for him alive. Even those who sympathized with the black man's cause and worked for it— Harriet Martineau, Benjamin Lundy, and William Lloyd Garrison— were appalled by the violence expressed in the *Appeal.* Garrison's attitude changed, however, and he later printed most of the *Appeal* in his *Liberator.*

Concerned about Walker's safety, his friends urged him to go to Canada, but he refused to run. "Somebody must die in this cause," he told them. "I may be doomed to the stake and the fire, or to the scaffold tree, but it is not in me to falter if I can promote the work of emancipation." Accordingly, he revised the *Appeal* and brought out second and third editions within approximately a year. And, probably as a result of his writing, he did die for the cause: on June 28, 1830, he was found dead near the door of his shop. He seemed to have been poisoned, although this fact, also, is not known for certain. In any case, the rumor that he was murdered has never been quieted.

For recent discussions of Walker's work and importance and for recent reprints of the *Appeal,* see Charles M. Wiltse, ed., *David Walker's Appeal* (New York: Hill & Wang, 1965), and Herbert Aptheker, *One Continual Cry* (New York: Humanities Press, 1965). See also Vernon Loggins, *The Negro Author,* and Benjamin Brawley, *Early Negro American Writers.* For the effect of Walker's *Appeal* on the South see Clement Eaton, "A Dangerous Pamphlet in the Old South," *Journal of Southern History* (August, 1936).

The following selections from the *Appeal* are taken from Articles II and III of the third (1830) edition.

OUR WRETCHEDNESS IN CONSEQUENCE OF IGNORANCE

Ignorance, my brethren, is a mist, low down into the very dark and almost impenetrable abyss in which, our fathers for many centuries have been plunged. The Christians, and enlightened of Europe, and some of Asia, seeing the ignorance and consequent degradation of our fathers, instead of trying to enlighten them, by teaching them that religion and light with which God had blessed them, they have plunged them into wretchedness ten thousand times more intolerable, than if they had left them entirely to the Lord, and to add to their miseries, deep down into which they have plunged them tell them, that they are an *inferior* and *distinct race* of beings, which they will be glad enough to recall and swallow by and by. Fortune and misfortune, two inseparable companions, lay rolled up in the wheel of events, which have from the creation of the world, and will continue to take place among men until God shall dash worlds together.

When we take a retrospective view of the arts and sciences—the wise legislators—the Pyramids, and other magnificent buildings—the turning of the channel of the river Nile, by the sons of Africa or of Ham, among whom learning originated, and was carried thence into Greece, where it was improved upon and refined. Thence among the Romans, and all over the then enlightened parts of the world, and it has been enlightening the dark and benighted minds of men from then, down to this day. I say, when I view retrospectively, the renown of that once mighty people, the children of our great progenitor I am indeed cheered. Yea further, when I view that mighty son of Africa, HANNIBAL, one of the greatest generals of antiquity, who defeated and cut off so many thousands of the white Romans or murderers, and who carried his victorious arms, to the very gate of Rome, and I give it as my candid opinion, that had Carthage been well united and had given him good support, he would have carried that cruel and barbarous city by storm. But they were dis-united, as the coloured people are now, in the United States of America, the reason our natural enemies are enabled to keep their feet on our throats.

Beloved brethren—here let me tell you, and believe it, that the Lord our God, as true as he sits on his throne in heaven, and as true as our Saviour died to redeem the world, will give you a Hannibal, and when the Lord shall have raised him up, and given him to you for your possession, O my suffering brethren! remember the divisions and consequent sufferings of *Carthage* and of *Hayti.* Read the history particularly of Hayti, and see how they were butchered by the whites, and do you take warning. The person whom God shall give you, give him your support and let him go his length, and behold in him the salvation of your God. God will indeed, deliver you through him from your deplorable and wretched condition under the Christians of America. I charge you this day before my God to lay no obstacle in his way, but let him go.

The whites want slaves, and want us for their slaves, but some of them will curse the day they ever saw us. As true as the sun ever shone in its meridian splendor, my colour will root some of them out of the very face of the earth. They shall have enough of making slaves of, and butchering, and murdering us in the manner which they have. No doubt some may say that I write with a bad spirit, and that I being a black, wish these things to occur. Whether I write with a bad or a good spirit, I say if these things do not occur in their proper time, it is because the world in which we live does not exist, and we are deceived with regard to its existence.—It is immaterial however to me, who believe, or who refuse—though I should like to see the whites repent peradventure God may have mercy on them, some however, have gone so far that their cup must be filled.

But what need have I to refer to antiquity, when Hayti, the glory of the blacks and terror of tyrants, is enough to convince the most avaricious and stupid of wretches—which is at this time, and I am sorry to say it, plagued with that scourge of nations, the Catholic religion; but I hope and pray God that she may yet rid herself of it, and adopt in its stead the Protestant faith; also, I hope that she may keep peace within her borders and be united, keeping a strict look out for tyrants, for if they get the least chance to injure her, they will avail themselves of it, as true as the Lord lives in heaven. But one thing which gives me joy is, that they are men who would cut off to a man, before they would yield to the combined forces of the whole world—in fact, if the whole world was combined against them, it could not do any thing with them, unless the Lord delivers them up.

Ignorance and treachery one against the other—a grovelling servile and abject submission to the lash of tyrants, we see plainly, my brethren, are not the natural elements of the blacks, as the Americans try to make us believe; but these are misfortunes which God has suffered our fathers to be enveloped in for many ages, no doubt in consequence of their disobedience to their Maker, and which do, indeed, reign at this time among us, almost to the destruction of all other principles: for I must truly say, that ignorance, the mother of treachery and deceit, gnaws into our very vitals. Ignorance, as it now exists among us, produces a state of things, Oh my Lord! too horrible to present to the world. Any man who is curious to see the full force of ignorance developed among the coloured people of the United States of America, has only to go into the southern and western states of this confederacy, where, if he is not a tyrant, but has the feelings of a human being, who can feel for a fellow creature, he may see enough to make his very heart bleed! He may see there, a son take his mother, who bore almost the pains of death to give him birth, and by the command of a tyrant, strip her as naked as she came into the world, and apply the cow-hide to her, until she falls a victim to death in the road! He may see a husband take his dear wife, not unfrequently in a pregnant state, and perhaps far advanced, and beat her for an unmerciful wretch, until his infant falls a lifeless lump at her feet! Can the Americans escape God Almighty? If they do, can he be to us a God of Justice? God is just, and I know it—for he has convinced me to my satisfaction—I cannot doubt him. My observer may see fathers beating their sons, mothers their daughters, and children their parents, all to pacify the passions of unrelenting tyrants. He may also, see them telling news and lies, making mischief one upon another. These are some of the productions of ignorance, which he will see practised among my dear brethren, who are held in unjust slavery and wretchedness, by avaricious and unmerciful tyrants, to whom, and their hellish deeds, I would suffer my life to be taken before I would submit. And when my curious observer comes to take notice of those who are said to be free, (which assertion I deny) and who are making some frivolous pretentions to common sense, he will see that branch of ignorance among the slaves assuming a more cunning and deceitful course of procedure.—He may see some of my brethren in league with tyrants, selling their own brethren into *hell upon earth,* not dissimilar to the exhibitions in Africa, but in a more secret, servile and abject manner. Oh Heaven! I am full! ! ! I can hardly move my pen! ! ! ! and as I expect some will try to put me to death, to strike terror into others, and to obliterate from their minds the notion of freedom, so as to keep my brethren the more secure in wretchedness, where they will be permitted to stay but a short time (whether tyrants believe it or not)—I shall give the world a development of facts, which are already witnessed in the courts of heaven. My observer may see some of those ignorant and treacherous creatures (coloured people) sneaking about in the large cities, endeavouring to find out all strange coloured people, where they work and where they reside, asking them questions, and trying to ascertain whether they are runaways or not, telling them, at the same time, that they always have been, are, and always will be, friends to their brethren; and, perhaps, that they themselves are absconders, and a thousand such treacherous lies to get the better information of the more ignorant! ! ! There have been and are at this day in Boston, New-York, Philadelphia, and Baltimore, coloured men, who are in league with tyrants, and who receive a great portion of their daily bread, of the moneys which they acquire from the blood and tears of their more miserable brethren, whom they scandalously delivered into the hands of our *natural enemies! ! ! ! !* . . .

OUR WRETCHEDNESS IN CONSEQUENCE OF THE PREACHERS OF THE RELIGION OF JESUS CHRIST

Religion, my brethren, is a substance of deep consideration among all nations of the earth. The Pagans have a kind, as well as the Mahometans, the Jews and the Christians. But pure and undefiled religion, such as was preached by Jesus Christ and his apostles, is hard to be found in all the earth. God, through his instrument, Moses, handed a dispensation of his Divine will, to the children of Israel after they had left Egypt for the land of Canaan or of Promise, who through hypocrisy, oppression and unbelief, departed from the faith.—He then, by his apostles, handed a dispensation of his, together with the will of Jesus Christ, to the Europeans in Europe, who, in open violation of which, have made *merchandise* of us, and it does appear as though they take this very dispensation to aid them in their *infernal* depredations upon us. Indeed, the way in which religion was and is conducted by the Europeans and their descendants, one might believe it was a plan fabricated by themselves and the *devils* to oppress us. But hark! My master has taught me better than to believe it—he has taught me that his gospel as it was preached by himself and his apostles remains the same, notwithstanding Europe has tried to mingle blood and opression with it.

It is well known to the Christian world, that Bartholomew Las Casas, that very very notoriously avaricious Catholic priest or preacher, and adventurer with Columbus, in his second voyage, proposed to his countrymen, the Spaniards in Hispaniola to import the Africans from the Portuguese settlement in Africa, to dig up gold and silver, and work their plantations for them, to effect which, he made a voyage thence to Spain, and opened the subject to his master, Ferdinand then in declining health, who listened to the plan: but who died soon after, and left it in the hand of his successor, Charles V. This wretch, ("Las Casas, the Preacher,") succeeded so well in his plans of oppression, that in 1503, the first blacks had been imported into the new world. Elated with this success, and stimulated by sordid avarice only, he importuned

Charles V. in 1511, to grant permission to a Flemish merchant, to import 4000 blacks at one time. Thus we see, through the instrumentality of a pretended preacher of the gospel of Jesus Christ our common master, our wretchedness first commenced in America—where it has been continued from 1503, to this day, 1829. A period of three hundred and twenty-six years. But two hundred and nine, from 1620 [1619]—when twenty of our fathers were brought into Jamestown, Virginia, by a Dutch man of war, and sold off like brutes to the highest bidders; and there is not a doubt in my mind, but that tyrants are in hope to perpetuate our miseries under them and their children until the final consummation of all things—But if they do not get dreadfully deceived, it will be because God has forgotten them.

The Pagans, Jews and Mahometans try to make proselytes to their religions, and whatever human beings adopt their religions they extend to them their protection. But Christian Americans not only hinder their fellow creatures, the Africans, but thousands of them *will absolutely beat a coloured person nearly to death, if they catch him on his knees, supplicating the throne of grace.* This barbarous cruelty was by all the heathen nations of antiquity, and is by the Pagans, Jews and Mahometans of the present day, left entirely to Christian Americans to inflict on the Africans and their descendants, that their cup which is nearly full may be completed. I have known tyrants or usurpers of human liberty in different parts of this country to take their fellow creatures, the coloured people, and beat them until they would scarcely leave life in them; what for? Why they say "The black devils had the audacity to be found *making prayers and supplications to the God who made them! ! ! !*" Yes, I have known small collections of coloured people to have convened together, for no other purpose than to worship God Almighty, in spirit and in truth, to the best of their knowledge; when tyrants, calling themselves *patrols,* would also convene and wait almost in breathless silence for the poor coloured people to commence singing and praying to the Lord our God, as soon as they had commenced, the wretches would burst in upon them and drag them out and commence beating them as they would rattle-snakes—many of whom, they would beat so unmercifully, that they would hardly be able to crawl for weeks and sometimes for months. Yet the American ministers send out missionaries to convert the heathen, while they keep us and our children sunk at their feet in the most abject ignorance and wretchedness that ever a people was afflicted with since the world began. Will the Lord suffer this people to proceed much longer? Will he not stop them in their career? Does he regard the heathens abroad, more than the heathens among the Americans? Surely the Americans must believe that God is partial, notwithstanding his Apostle Peter, declared before Cornelius and others that he has no respect to persons, but in every nation he that feareth God and worketh righteousness is accepted with him.—"The word," said he, "which God sent unto the children of Israel, preaching peace, by Jesus Christ, (he is Lord of all.") Have not the Americans the Bible in their hands? Do they believe it? Surely they do not. See how they treat us in open violation of the Bible! ! They no doubt will be greatly offended with me, but if God does not awaken them, it will be, because they are superior to other men, as they have represented themselves to be. Our divine Lord and Master said, "all things whatsoever ye would that men should do unto you, do ye even so unto them." But an American minister, with the Bible in his hand, holds us and our children in the most abject slavery and wretchedness. Now I ask them, would they like for us to hold them and their children in abject slavery and wretchedness? No, says one, that never can be done—you are too abject and ignorant to do it—you are not men—you were made to be slaves to us, to dig up gold and silver for us and our children. Know this, my dear sirs, that although you treat us and our children now, as you do your domestic beast—yet the final result of all future events are known but to God Almighty alone, who rules in the armies of heaven and among the inhabitants of the earth, and who dethrones one earthly king and sits up another, as it seemeth good in his holy sight. We may attribute these vicissitudes to what we please, but the God of armies and of justice rules in heaven and in earth, and the whole American people shall see and know it yet, to their satisfaction. I have known pretended preachers of the gospel of my Master, who not only held us as their natural inheritance, but treated us with as much rigor as any Infidel or Deist in the world—just as though they were intent only on taking our blood and groans to glorify the Lord Jesus Christ. The wicked and ungodly, seeing their preachers treat us with so much cruelty, they say: our preachers, who must be right, if any body are, treat them like brutes, and why cannot we?—They think it is no harm to keep them in slavery and put the whip to them, and why cannot we do the same!—They being preachers of the gospel of Jesus Christ, if it were any harm, they would surely preach against their oppression and do their utmost to erase it from the country; not only in one or two cities, but one continual cry would be raised in all parts of this confederacy, and would cease only with the complete overthrow of the system of slavery, in every part of the country. But how far the American preachers are from preaching against slavery and oppression, which have carried their country to the brink of a precipice; to save them from plunging down the side of which, will hardly be affected, will appear in the sequel of this paragraph, which I shall narrate just as it transpired. I remember a Camp Meeting in South Carolina, for which I embarked in a Steam Boat at Charleston, and having been five or six hours on the water, we at last arrived at the place of hearing, where was a very great concourse of people, who were no doubt, collected together to hear the word of God, (that some had collected barely as spectators to the scene, I will not here pretend to doubt, however, that is left to themselves and their God.) Myself and boat companions, having been there a little while, we were all called up to hear; I among the rest went up and took my seat—being seated, I fixed myself in a complete position to hear the word of my Saviour and to receive such as I thought was authenticated by the Holy Scriptures; but to my no ordinary astonishment, our Reverend gentleman got up and told us (coloured people) that slaves must be obedient to their masters—must do their duty to their masters or be whipped—the whip was made for the backs of fools, &c. Here I pause for a moment, to give the world time to consider what was my surprise, to hear such preaching from a minister of my Master, whose very gospel is that of peace and not of blood and whips, as this pretended preacher tried to make us believe. What the American preachers can think of us, I aver this day before my God, I have never been able to define. They have newspapers and monthly periodicals, which they receive in continual succession, but on the pages of which, you will scarcely ever find a paragraph respecting slavery, which is ten thousand times more injurious to this country than all the other evils put together; and which will be the final overthrow of its government, unless something is very speedily done; for their cup is nearly full.— Perhaps they will laugh at or make light of this; but I tell you Americans! that unless you speedily alter your course, *you* and your *Country are gone!!!!!!* For God Almighty will tear up the very face of the earth!!! Will not that very remarkable passage of Scripture be fulfilled on Christian Americans? Hear it Americans!! "He that is unjust, let him be unjust still:—and he which is filthy, let him be filthy still: and he that is righteous, let him be righteous still: and he that is holy, let him be holy still." I hope that the Americans may hear, but I am afraid that they have done us so much injury, and are so firm in the belief that our Creator made us to be an inheritance to them for ever, that their hearts will be hardened, so that their destruction may be sure. This language, perhaps is too harsh for the American's delicate ears. But Oh Americans! Americans!! I warn you in the name of the Lord, (whether you will hear, or forbear,) to repent and reform, or you are ruined!!! Do you think that our blood is hidden from the Lord, because you can hide it from the rest of the world, by sending out missionaries, and by your charitable deeds to the Greeks, Irish, &c.? Will he not publish your secret crimes on the house top? Even here in Boston, pride and prejudice have got to such a pitch, that in the very houses erected to the Lord, they have built little places for the reception of coloured people, where they must sit during meeting, or keep away from the house of God, and the preachers say nothing about it—much less go into the hedges and highways seeking the lost sheep of the house of Israel, and try to bring them in to their Lord and Master. There are not a more wretched, ignorant, miserable, and abject set of beings in all the world, than the blacks in the Southern and Western sections of this country, under tyrants and devils. The preachers of America cannot see them, but they can send out missionaries to convert the heathens, notwithstanding. Americans! unless you speedily alter your course of proceeding, if God Almighty does not stop you, I say it in his name, that you may go on and do as you please for ever, both in time and eternity—never fear any evil at all! ! ! ! ! ! ! !

Freedom Fighters

1830-1865

2

In the years from the 1830's to the Civil War, American Negroes lived with the overriding condition of slavery. It was the reality that bound even those who were born free and who lived in the North. Black writers of this period were, as might be expected, especially responsive to this reality, and in much of their work argument takes precedence over art.

Some writers certainly were aware of this orientation, and at least one of them warned against it. In a letter to the editor of the first Negro literary magazine, *The Anglo-African,* Frances Ellen Watkins wrote: "If our [Negro] talents are to be recognized we must write less of issues that are particular and more of feelings that are general. We are blessed with hearts and minds that compass more than ourselves in our present plight. . . . We must look to the future which, God willing, will be better than the present or the past, and delve into the heart of the world." Miss Watkins tried to live up to her own admonitions. She wrote on a variety of themes having nothing to do with race. She adapted Biblical stories and classical myths. Like her predecessor Phillis Wheatley, she wrote poems on "occasions" and on social causes. She produced at least four original small volumes of verse in the most conventional moralistic vein, but almost invariably her racial consciousness breaks through. Unable to abandon the reality of her Negroness, she sentimentalized and romanticized it. Her novel *Iola Leroy, or Shadows Uplifted* (1893) tells of slavery times and is a sensational tale of the trials and triumph of a black woman.

Only one poet, Daniel A. Payne, avoided racial involvement. His little book, *Pleasures and Other Miscellaneous Poems*, contains nothing that strikes the reader as having been written by a black man. (Nor, incidentally, does it contain his best poem, "The Preceptor's Farewell," which appears in his autobiography, *Recollections of Seventy Years*.)

The black writers of this period were not prolific. Writing was no substitute for action or for the *spoken* word, and they did not concentrate on quiet study and uninterrupted leisure for serious literary production. These men and women were primarily preachers, teachers, and activists whose concept of duty was "uplifting a down-trodden race." They organized conventions and addressed them. They established schools and taught in them. They founded churches and preached in them.

George B. Vashon, a teacher, left only two poems—"Vincent Ogé," an ambitious piece celebrating the life and death of a Haitian, and "A

Life-Day," telling the tragic story of the marriage of a white man to a beautiful mulatto girl who had been his slave. James M. Whitfield did write enough poems to provide a thin book, *America, and Other Poems,* and three or four of the pieces are of such high quality that his early death (on a racial mission to Central America) was, in retrospect, a real loss to American poetry. James M. Bell, an Ohio politician, also produced a thin sheaf of poems.

William Wells Brown was more dedicated to a literary career than were any of his black contemporaries; indeed, writing and lecturing were his principal means of support. Brown produced the first Negro novel, the first Negro play, and the first book of travel by a native-born black American. He published, besides, three volumes of history and a book of autobiographical sketches. His play, *The Escape; or A Leap for Freedom,* was never produced (although it probably was not greatly inferior to most of the theatrical fare of the 1850's). But his novel, *Clotel, or The President's Daughter,* first published in London in 1853, ran to four versions, each with a different title: *Miralda; or The Beautiful Quadroon; Clotelle: A Tale of the Southern States;* and *Clotelle, or The Colored Heroine.* (In the first edition Thomas Jefferson is represented as the father of the nearly-white female protagonist. In the subsequent [American] editions of 1860–61, 1864, and 1867, this background is finally deleted.)

Two other novelists of the period concern us here. The first is Frank J. Webb, author of *The Garies and Their Friends* (London, 1857), the second novel by an American Negro. A fascinating book, it deals with Negro life in the North, mainly in Philadelphia, and is technically a better novel than Brown's *Clotel.* We know very little about Webb. Practically all that we have learned comes from one source—the prefatory material to *The Garies,* by Harriet Beecher Stowe, who apparently was a friend of the author. The second novelist, Martin R. Delany, is far better known for activities other than fiction-writing. His unfinished novel *Blake: or, The Huts of America* appeared serially in the 1859 *Anglo-African Magazine.* Actually a precursor of later militant and nationalistic works by black writers, *Blake* tells the story of a "heroic slave" trying to organize his fellow bondsmen; it also gives us a very valuable account of the daily lives of slaves on Deep Southern plantations.

Because most of the speeches and sermons of this time were extemporaneous, few have come down to us. But contemporary opinion suggests that the oratory of Henry Highland Garnet, Josiah Henson, and Samuel Ringgold Ward was as eloquent and moving as the white antislavery oratory of Wendell Phillips, the editorials of William Lloyd Garrison, and the poetry of John Greenleaf Whittier.

With the exception of James M. Whitfield, all the black authors of this period either wrote autobiographies or were the subjects of bio-

graphical works, and some of these—particularly Daniel Payne's autobiography—make very interesting reading. But none achieves the
literary stature of Frederick Douglass' autobiographical writings.
Judged by all acknowledged standards, *Narrative of the Life of Frederick Douglass, My Bondage and My Freedom,* and *Life and Times*
are classics of American autobiographical writing.

No one knows when Negro folk literature began to develop, but it
had become a separate great body of expression by the middle years
of the nineteenth century. Undoubtedly some of it, like the animal
tales, derives from Africa, but a large portion originated in the American South. The use of this folk literature—as secret communication
among slaves—was uniquely black American; and the rhetoric, the
idioms, and the images it employs are also distinctively black American.

In *Scenes in the Life of Harriet Tubman* (1869), the biography of
a runaway slave who became a conductor on the Underground Railroad, we notice an early use of folk material. Sarah H. Bradford, a
proper Yankee writer, tells us that Harriet often created "spirituals" to
inform potential runaways of her presence and her plans. And in
MacKinley Helm's biography of Roland Hayes, a world-famous Negro
tenor of the twentieth century, we learn that in Hayes' grandfather's
time a slave suspected of inciting other slaves to rebellion was apprehended and punished in an effort to make him reveal the names of his
companions. Although beaten nearly to death, the slave refused to
speak; and Hayes' grandfather, in order to inform the plotters of the
situation, allegedly created a song which is now entitled "An' He
Never Said a Mumblin' Word."

> Wasn't it a pity an' a shame,
> An' he never said a mumberlin' word
>
> Not a word, not a word, not a word!
> Oh, dey nailed him to de tree,
> An' he never said a mumberlin' word.

Most folk literature was probably the result of group or community
effort, and the variety of versions of any one folk piece is probably a
consequence of faulty memory and oral transmission. These factors
certainly account for the differing versions of folk pieces of the post-
Civil War period and the period of tremendous urbanization (1885–
1900), when the "John Henry" ballad, "Frankie and Johnnie," and
countless other urban folk songs and sayings came into being. The
original composers, whether individuals or groups, were illiterate and
could not record their compositions.

Although Negro folk stuff is, like the sophisticated writings of the period, invariably race-conscious and evokes the hard realities of the special black experience, and although this folk stuff too is coded, in a kind of "thieves' jargon," it achieves universal relevance. The materials of Negro folk literature—myth, legend, belief—are allegoric, parabolic. They illustrate attitudes, emotional states, and experiences that are common to all men.

William Wells Brown

(c. 1816–1884)

WILLIAM WELLS BROWN—the first American Negro to write a novel, the first to write a play, the first to write a book of travels, and among the first to write history—was born near Lexington, Kentucky. The son of a white father and a mulatto mother, he was one of seven children. According to rumor, Brown's mother was the daughter of Daniel Boone, and his father was thought to be a relative of the master.

Serving under several masters, William Wells Brown did many kinds of work, some of it unusual for a slave. At one time he was hired out to Elijah P. Lovejoy's newspaper office in St. Louis. Under his last master, a riverboat captain, Brown traveled up and down the Ohio and Mississippi Rivers. He tried twice to escape. The first time, he took his mother with him, and although the two reached Illinois they were captured and returned to the master. As punishment Brown's mother was sold "down South"; the incident was a terrible blow to the young boy, who felt that he was responsible. His second attempt was successful. Having been taken by his master to Cincinnati, Brown simply walked away. On his way North he was helped by a Quaker named Wells Brown, whose name he adopted.

As a free man Brown worked on steamboats on Lake Erie and was able to help many fugitive slaves to their freedom. He finally settled in Buffalo, brushed up on the "letters" he had somehow learned earlier, and improved remarkably his facility with the language. In 1847 Brown was invited to join the Massachusetts Anti-Slavery Society. Although he lacked the genius of Frederick Douglass, William Wells Brown became a faithful and effective speaker and writer for abolition both here and in England, and for the temperance cause, prison reform, and woman's suffrage.

A prolific author, Brown produced the following major works: *Narrative of William W. Brown, a Fugitive Slave* (1847; revised 1848 and 1849); *Three Years in Europe; or, Places I Have Seen and People I Have Met* (London, 1852; enlarged and reprinted in 1855 as *The American Fugitive in Europe*); *Clotel; or, The President's Daughter: A Narrative of Slave Life in the United States* (London, 1853; revised and reprinted under different names in 1860–61, 1864, and 1867); *The Escape; or, A Leap for Freedom: A Drama in Five Acts* (1858); *The Black Man: His Antecedents, His Genius, and His Achievements* (1863); *The Negro in the American Rebellion, His Heroism and His*

Fidelity (1867); *The Rising Son; or The Antecedents and the Advancement of the Colored Race* (1874); and *My Southern Home, or The South and Its People* (1880).

Until recently the fullest and best single account of the life and works of William Wells Brown was found in Vernon Loggins' *The Negro Author* (New York: Columbia University Press, 1931), which is still a useful reference. In recent months two excellent and significant studies of William Wells Brown have appeared. The first is a 1969 University of Illinois English dissertation by Dr. Jean F. Yellin, Chapter VIII of *The Negro in Pre-Civil War Literature*. The second is W. Edward Farrison's monumental and definitive *William Wells Brown, Author and Reformer* (Chicago: University of Chicago Press, 1969).

The selections "The Slave's Social Circle" and "The Negro Sale" are Chapters I and II of *Clotelle* (1867 version.) "Stud Negro" comes from *My Southern Home*.

THE SLAVE'S SOCIAL CIRCLE

With the growing population in the Southern States, the increase of mulattoes has been very great. Society does not frown upon the man who sits with his half-white child upon his knee whilst the mother stands, a slave, behind his chair. In nearly all the cities and towns of the Slave States, the real negro, or clear black, does not amount to more than one in four of the slave population. This fact is of itself the best evidence of the degraded and immoral condition of the relation of master and slave. Throughout the Southern States, there is a class of slaves who, in most of the towns, are permitted to hire their time from their owners, and who are always expected to pay a high price. This class is the mulatto women, distinguished for their fascinating beauty. The handsomest of these usually pay the greatest amount for their time. Many of these women are the favorites of men of property and standing, who furnish them with the means of compensating their owners, and not a few are dressed in the most extravagant manner.

When we take into consideration the fact that no safeguard is thrown around virtue, and no inducement held out to slave-women to be pure and chaste, we will not be surprised when told that immorality and vice pervade the cities and towns of the South to an extent unknown in the Northern States. Indeed, many of the slave-women have no higher aspiration than that of becoming the finely-dressed mistress of some white man. At negro balls and parties, this class of women usually make the most splendid appearance, and are eagerly sought after in the dance, or to entertain in the drawing-room or at the table.

A few years ago, among the many slave-women in Richmond, Virginia, who hired their time of their masters, was Agnes, a mulatto owned by John Graves, Esq., and who might be heard boasting that she was the daughter of an American Senator. Although nearly forty years of age at the time of which we write, Agnes was still exceedingly handsome. More than half white, with long black hair and deep blue eyes, no one felt like disputing with her when she urged her claim to her relationship with the Anglo-Saxon.

In her younger days, Agnes had been a housekeeper for a young slave-holder, and in sustaining this relation had become the mother of two daughters. After being cast aside by this young man, the slave-woman betook herself to the business of a laundress, and was considered to be the most tasteful woman in Richmond at her vocation.

Isabella and Marion, the two daughters of Agnes, resided with their mother, and gave her what aid they could in her business. The mother, however, was very choice of her daughters, and would allow them to perform no labor that would militate against their lady-like appearance. Agnes early resolved to bring up her daughters as ladies, as she termed it.

As the girls grew older, the mother had to pay a stipulated price for them per month. Her notoriety as a laundress of the first class enabled her to put an extra charge upon the linen that passed through her hands; and although she imposed little or no work upon her daughters, she was enabled to live in comparative luxury and have her daughters dressed to attract attention, especially at the negro balls and parties.

Although the term "negro ball" is applied to these gatherings, yet a large portion of the men who attend them are whites. Negro balls and parties in the Southern States, especially in the cities and towns, are usually made up of quadroon women, a few negro men, and any number of white gentlemen. These are gatherings of the most democratic character. Bankers, merchants, lawyers, doctors, and their clerks and students, all take part in these social assemblies upon terms of perfect equality. The father and son not unfrequently meet and dance *vis a vis* at a negro ball.

It was at one of these parties that Henry Linwood, the son of a wealthy and retired gentleman of Richmond, was first introduced to Isabella, the oldest daughter of Agnes. The young man had just returned from Harvard College, where he had spent the previous five years. Isabella was in her eighteenth year, and was admitted by all who knew her to be the handsomest girl, colored or white, in the city. On this occasion, she was attired in a sky-blue silk dress, with deep black lace flounces, and bertha of the same. On her well-moulded arms she wore massive gold bracelets, while her rich black hair was arranged at the back in broad basket plaits, ornamented with pearls, and the front in the French style (*a la Imperatrice*), which suited her classic face to perfection.

Marion was scarcely less richly dressed than her sister.

Henry Linwood paid great attention to Isabella, which was looked upon with gratification by her mother, and became a matter of general conversation with all present. Of course, the young man escorted the beautiful quadroon home that evening, and became the favorite visitor at the house of Agnes.

It was on a beautiful moonlight night in the month of August, when all who reside in tropical climates are eagerly gasping for a breath of fresh air, that Henry Linwood was in the garden which surrounded Agnes' cottage, with the young quadroon by his side. He drew from his pocket a newspaper wet from the press, and read the following advertisement:—

NOTICE.—Seventy-nine negroes will be offered for sale on Monday, September 10, at 12 o'clock, being the entire stock of the late John Graves. The negroes are in an excellent condition, and all warranted against the common vices. Among them are several mechanics, able-bodied field-hands, plough-boys, and women with children, some of them very prolific, affording a rare opportunity for any one who wishes to raise a strong and healthy lot of servants for their own use. Also several mulatto girls of rare personal qualities,—two of these very superior.

Among the above slaves advertised for sale were Agnes and her two daughters. Ere young Linwood left the quadroon that evening, he promised her that he would become her purchaser, and make her free and her own mistress.

Mr. Graves had long been considered not only an excellent and upright citizen of the first standing among the whites, but even the slaves regarded him as one of the kindest of masters. Having inherited his slaves with the rest of his property, he became possessed of them without any consultation or wish of his own. He would neither buy nor sell slaves, and was exceedingly careful, in letting them out, that they did not find oppressive and tyrannical masters. No slave speculator ever dared to cross the threshold of this planter of the Old Dominion. He was a constant attendant upon religious worship, and was noted for his general benevolence. The American Bible Society, the American Tract Society, and the cause of Foreign Missions, found in him a liberal friend. He was always anxious that his slaves should appear well on the Sabbath, and have an opportunity of hearing the word of God.

THE NEGRO SALE

As might have been expected, the day of sale brought an unusually large number together to compete for the property to be sold. Farmers, who make a business of raising slaves for the market, were there, and slave-traders, who make a business of buying human beings in the

slave-raising States and taking them to the far South, were also in attendance. Men and women, too, who wished to purchase for their own
use, had found their way to the slave sale.

In the midst of the throng was one who felt a deeper interest in the
result of the sale than any other of the bystanders. This was young
Linwood. True to his promise, he was there with a blank bank-check
in his pocket, awaiting with impatience to enter the list as a bidder for
the beautiful slave.

It was indeed a heart-rending scene to witness the lamentations of
these slaves, all of whom had grown up together on the old homestead
of Mr. Graves, and who had been treated with great kindness by that
gentleman, during his life. Now they were to be separated, and form
new relations and companions. Such is the precarious condition of the
slave. Even when with a good master, there is no certainty of his happiness in the future.

The less valuable slaves were first placed upon the auction-block,
one after another, and sold to the highest bidder. Husbands and wives
were separated with a degree of indifference that is unknown in any
other relation in life. Brothers and sisters were torn from each other,
and mothers saw their children for the last time on earth.

It was late in the day, and when the greatest number of persons were
thought to be present, when Agnes and her daughters were brought
out to the place of sale. The mother was first put upon the auction-
block, and sold to a noted negro trader named Jennings. Marion was
next ordered to ascend the stand, which she did with a trembling step,
and was sold for $1200.

All eyes were now turned on Isabella, as she was led forward by the
auctioneer. The appearance of the handsome quadroon caused a deep
sensation among the crowd. There she stood, with a skin as fair as
most white women, her features as beautifully regular as any of her
sex of pure Anglo-Saxon blood, her long black hair done up in the
neatest manner, her form tall and graceful, and her whole appearance
indicating one superior to her condition.

The auctioneer commenced by saying that Miss Isabella was fit to
deck the drawing-room of the finest mansion in Virginia.

"How much, gentlemen, for this real Albino!—fit fancy-girl for any
one! She enjoys good health, and has a sweet temper. How much do
you say?"

"Five hundred dollars."

"Only five hundred for such a girl as this? Gentlemen, she is worth
a deal more than that sum. You certainly do not know the value of
the article you are bidding on. Here, gentlemen, I hold in my hand a
paper certifying that she has a good moral character."

"Seven hundred."

"Ah, gentlemen, that is something like. This paper also states that
she is very intelligent."

"Eight hundred."

"She was first sprinkled, then immersed, and is now warranted to be a devoted Christian, and perfectly trustworthy."

"Nine hundred dollars."

"Nine hundred and fifty."

"One thousand."

"Eleven hundred."

Here the bidding came to a dead stand. The auctioneer stopped, looked around, and began in a rough manner to relate some anecdote connected with the sale of slaves, which he said had come under his own observation.

At this juncture the scene was indeed a most striking one. The laughing, joking, swearing, smoking, spitting, and talking, kept up a continual hum and confusion among the crowd, while the slave-girl stood with tearful eyes, looking alternately at her mother and sister and toward the young man whom she hoped would become her purchaser.

"The chastity of this girl," now continued the auctioneer, "is pure. She has never been from under her mother's care. She is virtuous, and as gentle as a dove."

The bids here took a fresh start, and went on until $1800 was reached. The auctioneer once more resorted to his jokes, and concluded by assuring the company that Isabella was not only pious, but that she could make an excellent prayer.

"Nineteen hundred dollars."

"Two thousand."

This was the last bid, and the quadroon girl was struck off, and became the property of Henry Linwood.

This was a Virginia slave-auction, at which the bones, sinews, blood, and nerves of a young girl of eighteen were sold for $500; her moral character for $200; her superior intellect for $100; the benefits supposed to accrue from her having been sprinkled and immersed, together with a warranty of her devoted Christianity, for $300; her ability to make a good prayer for $200; and her chastity for $700 more. This, too, in a city thronged with churches, whose tall spires look like so many signals pointing to heaven, but whose ministers preach that slavery is a God-ordained institution!

The slaves were speedily separated, and taken along by their respective masters. Jennings, the slave-speculator, who had purchased Agnes and her daughter Marion, with several of the other slaves, took them to the county prison, where he usually kept his human cattle after purchasing them, previous to starting for the New Orleans market.

Linwood had already provided a place for Isabella, to which she was taken. The most trying moment for her was when she took leave of her mother and sister. The "Good-by" of the slave is unlike that of any other class in the community. It is indeed a farewell forever. With tears streaming down their cheeks, they embraced and commended each other to God, who is no respecter of persons, and before whom master and slave must one day appear.

STUD NEGRO

Paying a flying visit to Tennessee, I halted at Columbia, the capital of Maury County. At Redgerford Creek, five miles distant from Columbia, lives Joe Budge, a man with one hundred children. Never having met one with such a family, I resolved to make a call on the gentleman and satisfy my own curiosity.

This distinguished individual is seventy-one years old, large frame, of unadulterated blood, and spent his life in slavery up to the close of the war.

"How many children have you, Mr. Budge?" I asked.

"One hundred, ser," was the quick response.

"Are they all living?"

"No, ser."

"How many wives had you?"

"Thirteen, ser."

"Had you more than one wife living at any time?"

"O, yes, ser, nearly all of dem ware livin' when de war broke out."

"How was this, did the law allow you to have more than one wife at a time?"

"Well, yer see, boss, I waren't under de law, I ware under marser."

"Were you married to all of your wives by a minister?"

"No, ser, only five by de preacher."

"How did you marry the others?"

"Ober de broomstick an' under de blanket."

"How was that performed?"

"Well, yer see, ser, dey all 'sembles in de quarters, an' a man takes hold of one en' of de broom an' a 'oman takes hole of tudder en', an' dey holes up de broom, an' de man an' de 'oman dats gwine to get married jumps ober an' den slips under a blanket, dey put out de light an' all goes out an' leabs em dar."

"How near together were your wives?"

"Marser had fore plantations, an' dey live 'bout on 'em, dem dat warn't sold."

"Did your master sell some of your wives?"

"O ! yes, ser, when dey got too ole to bare children. You see, marser raised slaves fer de market, an' my stock ware called mighty good, kase I ware very strong, an' could do a heap of work."

Title supplied by editors.

"Were your children sold away from you?"

"Yes, ser, I see three of 'em sole one day fer two thousand dollars a-piece; yer see dey ware men grown up."

"Did you select your wives?"

"Dunno what you mean by dat word."

"Did you pick out the women that you wanted?"

"O! no, ser, I had nuthin ter say 'bout dat. Marser allers get 'em, an' pick out strong, hearty young women. Dat's de reason dat de planters wanted to get my children, kase dey ware so helty."

"Did you never feel that it was wrong to get married in such a light manner?"

"No, ser, kase yer see I toted de witness wid me."

"What do you mean by that?"

"Why, ser, I had religion, an' dat made me feel dat all ware right."

"What was the witness that you spoke of?"

"De change of heart, ser, is de witness dat I totes in my bosom; an' when a man's got dat, he fears nuthin, not eben de debble himsef."

"Then you know that you've got the witness?"

"Yes, ser, I totes it right here." And at this point, Mr. Budge put his hand on his heart, and looked up to heaven.

"I presume your master made no profession of religion?"

"O! yes, ser, you bet he had religion. He ware de fustest man in de church, an' he ware called mighty powerful in prayer."

"Do any of your wives live near you now, except the one that you are living with?"

"Yes, ser, dar's five in dis county, but dey's all married now to udder men."

"Have you many grand-children?"

"Yes, ser, when my 'lations am all tergedder, dey numbers 'bout fore hundred, near as I ken get at it."

"Do you know of any other men that have got as many children as you?"

"No, ser, dey calls me de boss daddy in dis part of de State."

Having satisfied my curiosity, I bade Mr. Budge "good-day."

Martin R. Delany

(1812–1885)

BORN FREE IN CHARLESTOWN, Virginia, Martin R. Delany was described by William Lloyd Garrison, "as black as jet, and a fine fellow of great energy and spirit." Delany could trace his lineage back to an African chieftain more convincingly than most Negroes who made that claim.

When Martin Delany was ten, his parents moved to Chambersburg, Pennsylvania. His schooling began there; he later studied at the Harvard Medical School and became a practicing physician first in Pittsburgh and later in Canada.

In 1839 Delany traveled extensively in Louisiana and Texas and other states in the Southwest, gathering materials to be used in his novel, *Blake*. In 1843 in Pittsburgh he began publishing *The Mystery;* this newspaper seems to have appeared regularly until 1847, when Delany became an assistant to Frederick Douglass, who was publishing *The North Star* in Rochester, New York.

In 1852 Delany published perhaps his best work, *The Condition, Elevation, Emigration, and Destiny of the Colored People of the United States, Politically Considered*. His primary objective was to encourage Negroes to leave the United States for Central America. When attacked by abolitionists for his colonizing sympathies, Delany retracted, and in 1854 printed a speech entitled "Political Destiny of the Colored Race on the American Continent," which explained his former position.

A many-sided man, Delany was one of the first to advocate industrial education for Negroes; he wrote several scientific works; he went exploring in Africa and later wrote the *Official Report of the Niger Valley Exploring Party*. He was the first Negro to whom President Lincoln gave the responsibility and honor of field rank in the Army. In his later years, Delany became an important political figure in Reconstruction South Carolina.

In the first issue of *The Anglo-African Magazine* (January, 1859), three chapters of Delany's only novel appeared, following a descriptive announcement: "The scene is laid in Mississippi, the plot extending into Cuba; the Hero being an educated West India black, who deprived of his liberty by fraud when young and brought to the United States, in maturer age, at the instance of his wife being sold from him, sought revenge through the medium of a deep laid secret organization." Twenty-one chapters came out in subsequent issues, but the fiction, entitled *Blake: or, The Huts of America,* was never completed.

Delany is given rather substantial treatment in Benjamin Brawley's *Negro Builders and Heroes* (1937), but critics and historians generally ignore him.

The following selections are from *Blake*.

HENRY AT LARGE

On leaving the plantation carrying them hanging upon his arm, thrown across his shoulders, and in his hands Henry had a bridle, halter, blanket, girt, and horsewhip, the emblems of a faithful servant in discharge of his master's business.

By shrewdness and discretion such was his management as he passed along, that he could tell the name of each place and proprietor, long before he reached them. Being a scholar, he carefully kept a record of the plantations he had passed, that when accosted by a white, as an overseer or patrol, he invariably pretended to belong to a back estate, in search of his master's race horse. If crossing a field, he was taking a near cut; but if met in a wood, the animal was in the forest, as being a great leaper no fence could debar him, though the forest was fenced and posted. The blanket a substitute for a saddle, was in reality carried for a bed. . . .

Reaching Alexandria with no obstruction, his first secret meeting was held in the hut of aunt Dilly. Here he found them all ready for an issue.

"An dis you chile?" said the old woman, stooping with age, sitting on a low stool in the chimney corner; "dis many day, I heahn on yeh!" though Henry had just entered on his mission. From Alexandria he passed rapidly on to Latuer's making no immediate stops, preferring to organize at the more prominent places.

This is a mulatto planter, said to have come from the isle of Guadaloupe. Riding down the road upon a pony at a quick gallop, was a mulatto youth a son of the planter, an old black man on foot keeping close to the horse's heels.

"Whose boy are you?" enquired the young mulatto, who had just dismounted, the old servant holding his pony.

"I'm in search of master's race horse."

"What is your name?" farther enquired the young mulatto.

"Gilbert sir."

"What do you want?"

"I am hungry sir."

"Dolly," said he to an old black woman at the woodpile; "show this man into the negro quarter, and give him something to eat; give him a cup of milk. Do you like milk my man?"

"Yes sir, I have no choice when hungry; anything will do."

"Da is none heah but claubah, maus Eugene," replied the old cook.

"Give him that," said the young master. "You people like that kind of stuff I believe; our negroes like it."

"Yes sir," replied Henry, when the lad left.

"God knows'e needn' talk 'bout wat we po' black folks eat, case da don' ghin us nothin' else but dat an' caun bread." muttered the old woman.

"Dont they treat you well, aunty?" enquired Henry.

"God on'y knows my chile, wat we suffeh."

"Who was that old man who ran behind your master's horse?"

"Dat Nathan, my husban'."

"Do they treat him well, aunty?"

"No chile, wus an' any dog, da beat 'im foh little an nothin'."

"Is uncle Nathan religious?"

"Yes chile ole man an' I's been sahvin' God dis many day, fo yeh baun! Wen any on 'em in de house git sick, den da sen foh 'uncle Nathan' come pray foh dem; 'uncle Nathan' mighty good den!"

"Do you know that the Latuers are colored people?"

"Yes, chile; God bless yeh soul yes! Case huh mammy ony dead two-three yehs, an' she black as me."

"How did they treat her?"

"Not berry well; she nus da children; and eat in a house arter all done."

"What did Latuer's children call her?"

"Da call huh 'mammy,' same like wite folks childen call de nus."

"Can you tell me aunty why they treat you people so badly, knowing themselves to be colored, and some of the slaves related to them?"

"God bless yeh hunny, de wite folks, dese plantehs make 'em so; da run heah, an' tell 'em da mus'n treat deh niggehs, well, case da spile 'em."

"Do the white planters frequently visit here?"

"Yes, hunny, yes, da heah some on 'em all de time eatin' an' drinkin' long wid de old man; da on'y tryin' git wat little 'e got, dat all! Da 'tend to be great frien' de ole man; but laws a massy hunny, I doh mine dese wite folks no how!"

"Does your master ever go to their houses and eat with them?"

"Yes chile, some time'e go, but den half on 'em got nothin' fit to eat; da hab fat poke an' bean, caun cake an' sich like, dat all da got, some on 'em."

"Does Mr. Latuer give them better at his table?"

"Laws hunny, yes; yes'n deed chile? 'E got mutton—some time whole sheep mos'—fowl, pig, an' ebery tum ting a nuddeh, 'e got so much ting dah, I haudly know wat cook fus."

"Do the white planters associate with the family of Latuer?"

"One on 'em, ten 'e coatin de dahta; I dont recon 'e gwine hab heh. Da cah fool long wid 'Toyeh's gals dat way."

"Whose girls, Metoyers?"

"Yes chile."

"Do you mean the wealthy planters of that name?"

"Dat same chile."

"Well, I want to understand you: You don't mean to say that they are colored people."

"Yes, hunny, yes; da good culed folks any body. Some five-six boys' an five-six gals on 'em; da all rich."

"How do they treat their slaves?"

"Da boys all mighty haud maustas, da gals all mighty good; sahvants all like em."

"You seem to understand these people very well aunty. Now please tell me what kind of masters there are generally in the Red river country."

"Haud 'nough chile, haud 'nough, God on'y knows!"

"Do the colored masters treat theirs generally worse than the whites?"

"No hunny, 'bout da same."

"That's just what I want to know. What are the usual allowances for slaves?"

"Da 'low de fiel' han' two suit a yeah foh umin one long linen coat,* make suit, an' foh man, pantaloon an' jacket."

"How about eating?"

"Half peck meal ah day foh family uh fo!"

"What about weekly privileges? Do you have Saturday to your-selves?"

"Laud hunny, no! no chile, no! Da do'n 'low us no time, 'tall. Da 'low us ebery uddeh Sunday wash ouh close; dat all de time we git."

"Then you don't get to sell anything for yourselves?"

"No, hunny, no? Da don' 'low pig, chicken, tucky, goose, bean, pea, tateh, nothin' else."

"Well aunty, I'm glad to meet you, and as evening's drawing nigh, I must see your husband a little, then go."

"God bless yeh chile whah ebeh yeh go! Yeh ain' arteh no race-hos, dat yeh aint."

"You got something to eat my man, did you?" enquired the lad Eugene, at the conclusion of his interview with uncle Nathan.

"I did sir, and feasted well!" replied Henry in conclusion; "Good bye!" and he left for the next plantation suited to his objects.

"God bless de baby!" said old aunt Dolly as uncle Nathan entered the hut, referring to Henry.

"Ah, chile!" replied the old man with tears in his eyes; "my yeahs has heahn dis day!" . . .

* Coat—a term used by slaves for frock.

SOUTHERN FUN

"Well Judge as you wish to become a southerner, you must first 'see the sights,' as children say, and learn to get used to them. I wish you to ride out with me to Captain Grason's, and you'll see some rare sport; the most amusing thing I ever witnessed," suggested Franks.

"What is it?" enquired the Major.

"The effect is lost by previous knowledge of the thing," replied he. "This will suit you Armsted, as you're fond of negro jokes."

"Then Colonel let's be off," urged the Major.

"Off it is!" replied Franks, as he invited the gentlemen to take a seat in the carriage already at the door.

"Halloo, halloo, here you are Colonel! Why major Armsted, old fellow, 'pon my word!" saluted Grason, grasping Armsted by the hand as they entered the porch.

"Judge Ballard! sir," said Armsted.

"Just in time for dinner gentlemen! Be seated," invited he holding the Judge by the hand. Welcome to Mississippi sir! What's up gentlemen?"

"We've come out to witness some rare sport the Colonel has been telling us about," replied the major.

"Blamed if I don't think the Colonel will have me advertised as a showman presently! I've got a queer animal here; I'll show him to you after dinner," rejoined Grason: "Gentlemen, help yourself to brandy and water."

Dinner over, the gentlemen walked into the pleasure grounds, in the rear of the mansion.

"Nelse, where is Rube? Call him!" said Grason to a slave lad, brother to the boy he sent for.

Shortly there came forward, a small black boy about eleven years of age, thin visage, projecting upper teeth, rather ghastly consumptive look, and emaciated condition. The child trembled with fears as he approached the group.

"Now gentlemen," said Grason, "I'm going to show you a sight!" having in his hand a long whip, the cracking of which he commenced, as a ring master in the circus.

The child gave him a look never to be forgotten; a look beseeching mercy and compassion. But the decree was made, and though humanity quailed in dejected supplication before him, the command was imperative, with no living hand to stay the pending consequences. He must submit to his fate, and pass through the ordeal of training.

"Wat maus gwine do wid me now? I know wat maus gwine do," said this miserable child; "he gwine make me see sights!" when going

Title supplied by editors.

down on his hands and feet, he commenced trotting around like an animal.

"Now gentlemen, look!" said Grason; "he'll whistle, sing songs, hymns, pray, swear like a trooper, laugh, and cry, all under the same state of feelings."

With a peculiar swing of the whip, bringing the lash down upon a certain spot on the exposed skin, the whole person being prepared for the purpose, the boy commenced to whistle almost like a thrush; another cut changed it to a song, another to a hymn, then a pitiful prayer, when he gave utterance to oaths which would make a Christian shudder, after which he laughed outright; then from the fullness of his soul he cried:

"O, maussa, I's sick! Please stop little!" casting up gobs of hemorrhage.*

Franks stood looking on with unmoved muscles. Armsted stood aside whittling a stick; but when Ballard saw, at every cut the flesh turn open in gashes streaming down with gore, till at last in agony he appealed for mercy, he involuntary found his hand with a grasp on the whip, arresting its further application.

"Not quite a southerner yet Judge, if you can't stand that!" said Franks on seeing him wiping away the tears.

"Gentlemen help yourself to brandy and water. The little negro don't stand it nigh so well as formerly. He used to be a trump!"

"Well Colonel," said the Judge; "as I have to leave for Jackson this evening, I suggest that we return to the city."

The company now left Grason's, Franks for the enjoyment of home, Ballard and Armsted for Jackson, and the poor boy Reuben from hemorrhage of the lungs, that evening left time for eternity.

DAT OL' TIME RELIGION

Busying about the breakfast for herself and other servants about the house—the white members of the family all being absent—mammy Judy for a time lost sight of the expected arrival. Soon however, a hasty footstep arrested her attention, when on looking around it proved to be Henry who came smiling up the yard.

"How'd you do mammy! how's Mag' and the boy?" inquired he, grasping the old woman by the hand.

She burst into a flood of tears, throwing herself upon him.

"What is the matter!" exclaimed Henry, "is Maggie dead?"

"No chile," with increased sobs she replied, "much betteh she wah."

"My God! has she disgraced herself?"

---

* This is a true Mississippi scene.
Title supplied by editors.

"No chile, may be betteh she dun so, den she bin heah now an' not sole. Maus Stephen sell eh case she!—I dun'o, reckon dat's da reason!"

"What!—Do you tell me mammy she had better disgraced herself than been sold! By the—!"

"So, Henry! yeh ain' gwine swah! hope yeh ain' gwine lose yeh 'ligion? Do'n do so; put yeh trus' in de Laud, he is suffishen fah all!"

"Don't tell me about religion! What's religion to me? My wife is sold away from me by a man who is one of the leading members of the very church to which both she and I belong! Put my trust in the Lord! I have done so all my life nearly, and of what use is it to me? My wife is sold from me just the same as if I did n't. I'll—"

"Come, come, Henry, yeh mus'n talk so; we is po' weak an' bline cretehs, an' cah see de way uh da Laud. He move' in a mystus way, his wundahs to puhfaum."

"So he may, and what is all that to me? I don't gain anything by it, and—"

"Stop, Henry, stop! ain' de Laud bless yo' soul? ain' he take yeh foot out de miah an' clay, an' gib yeh hope da uddah side dis vale ub teahs?"

"I'm tired looking the other side; I want a hope this side of the vale of tears. I want something on this earth as well as a promise of things in another world. I and my wife have been both robbed of our liberty, and you want me to be satisfied with a hope of heaven. I won't do any such thing; I have waited long enough on heavenly promises; I'll wait no longer. I—"

"Henry, wat de mauttah wid yeh? I neveh heah yeh talk so fo'—yeh sin in de sight ub God; yeh gone clean back, I reckon. De good Book tell us, a tousan' yeahs wid man, am but a day wid de Laud. Boy, yeh got wait de Laud own pinted time."

"Well mammy, it is useless for me to stand here and have the same gospel preached into my ears by you, that I have all my life time heard from my enslavers. My mind is made up, my course is laid out, and if life last, I'll carry it out. I'll go out to the place to-day, and let them know that I have returned."

"Sho boy! what yeh gwine do, bun house down? Bettah put yeh trus' in de Laud!" concluded the old woman.

"You have too much religion mammy for me to tell you what I intend doing," said Henry in conclusion.

After taking up his little son, impressing on his lips and cheeks kisses for himself and tears for his mother, the intelligent slave left the abode of the care-worn old woman, for that of his master at the cotton place.

Henry was a black—a pure negro—handsome, manly and intelligent, in size comparing well with his master, but neither so fleshy nor heavy built in person. A man of good literary attainments—unknown to Col. Franks, though he was aware he could read and write—having been educated in the West Indies, and decoyed away when young. His affection for wife and child was not excelled by colonel Franks for his. He was bold, determined and courageous, but always mild, gentle and courteous, though impulsive when an occasion demanded his opposition.

Going immediately to the place, he presented himself before his master. Much conversation ensued concerning the business which had been entrusted to his charge, all of which was satisfactorily transacted, and full explanations concerning the horses, but not a word was uttered concerning the fate of Maggie, the Colonel barely remarking "your mistress is unwell."

After conversing till a late hour, Henry was assigned a bed in the great house, but sleep was far from his eyes. He turned and changed upon his bed with restlessness and anxiety, impatiently awaiting a return of the morning.

Early on Tuesday morning in obedience to his master's orders, Henry was on his way to the city, to get the house in readiness for the reception of his mistress, Mrs. Franks having much improved in three or four days. Mammy Judy had not yet risen when he knocked at the door.

"Hi Henry! yeh heah ready! huccum yeh git up so soon; arter some mischif I reckon? Do'n reckon yeh arter any good!" saluted mammy Judy.

"No mammy," replied he; "no mischief, but like a good slave such as you wish me to be, come to obey my master's will, just what you like to see."

"Sho boy! none yeh nonsens'; huccum I want yeh bey maus Stephen? Git dat nonsens' in yeh head las' night long so, I reckon! Wat dat yeh gwine do now?"

"I have come to dust and air the mansion for their reception. They have sold my wife away from me, and who else would do her work?" This reply excited the apprehension of mammy Judy.

"Wat yeh gwine do Henry? yeh arter no good; yeh ain' gwine 'tack maus Stephen is yeh?"

"What do you mean mammy, strike him?"

"Yes! reckon yeh ain' gwine hit 'im?"

"Curse—!"

"Henry, Henry, membeh wat ye 'fess! fah de Laud sake, yeh ain gwine take to swahin?" interrupted the old woman.

"I make no profession mammy. I once did believe in religion, but now I have no confidence in it. My faith has been wrecked on the stony hearts of such pretended christians as Stephen Franks, while passing through the stormy sea of trouble and oppression! and—"

"Hay, boy! yeh is gittin high! yeh call maussa 'Stephen?'"

"Yes, and I'll never call him 'master' again, except when compelled to do so."

"Bettah g'long ten' t' de house fo' wite folks come, an' nebeh mine talkin' 'bout fightin' 'long wid maus Stephen. Wat yeh gwine do wid white folks? Sho!"

"I don't intend to fight him, mammy Judy, but I'll attack him concerning my wife, if the words be my last! Yes, I'll—!" and pressing his lips to suppress the words, the outraged man turned away from the old slave mother, with such feelings as only an intelligent slave could realize.

The orders of the morning were barely executed, when the carriage came to the door. The bright eyes of the foot boy Tony sparkled when he saw Henry approaching the carriage.

"Well Henry! ready for us?" enquired his master.

"Yes sir," was the simple reply. "Mistress!" he saluted, politely bowing as he took her hand to assist her from the carriage.

"Come Henry, my man, get out the riding horses," ordered Franks after a little rest.

"Yes sir."

A horse for the Colonel and lady each, was soon in readiness at the door, but none for himself, it always having been the custom in their morning rides, for the maid and man-servant to accompany the mistress and master.

"Ready did you say?" enquired Franks on seeing but two horses standing at the stile.

"Yes sir."

"Where's the other horse?"

"What for sir?"

"What for? yourself to be sure!"

"Colonel Franks!" said Henry, looking him sternly in the face, "when I last rode that horse in company with you and lady, *my wife* was at my side, and I will not now go without her! Pardon me—my life for it, I won't go!"

"Not another word you black imp!" exclaimed Franks, with an uplifted staff in a rage, "or I'll strike you down in an instant!"

"Strike away if you will sir, I dont care—I wont go without my wife!"

"You impudent scoundrel! I'll soon put an end to your conduct! I'll put you on the auction block, and sell you to the negro traders."

"Just as soon as you please sir, the sooner the better, as I dont want to live with you any longer!"

"Hold your tongue sir, or I'll cut it out of your head! you ungrateful black dog! Really things have come to a pretty pass, when I must take impudence off my own negro! By gracious!—God forgive me for the expression—I'll sell every negro I have first! I'll dispose of him to the hardest negro trader I can find!" said Franks in a rage.

"You may do your mightiest, colonel Franks. I'm not your slave, nor never was, and you know it! and but for my wife and her people, I never would have staid with you till now. I was decoyed away when young, and then became entangled in such domestic relations as to induce me to remain with you; but now the tie is broken! I know that the odds are against me, but never mind!"

"Do you threaten me, sir! Hold your tongue, or I'll take your life instantly, you villain!"

"No sir, I dont threaten you, colonel Franks, but I do say that I wont be treated like a dog. You sold my wife away from me, after always promising that she should be free. And more than that, you sold her because ———! and now you talk about whipping me. Shoot me, sell me, or do anything else you please, but dont lay your hands on me, as I will not suffer you to whip me!"

Running up to his chamber, colonel Franks seized a revolver, when Mrs. Franks grasping hold of his arm exclaimed—

"Colonel! what does all this mean?"

"Mean, my dear? It's rebellion! a plot—this is but the shadow of a cloud that's fast gathering around us! I see it plainly, I see it!" reponded the Colonel, starting for the stairs.

"Stop Colonel!" admonished his lady, "I hope you'll not be rash. For Heaven's sake, do not stain your hands in blood!"

"I do not mean to, my dear! I take this for protection!" Franks hastening down stairs, when Henry had gone into the back part of the premises.

"Dah now! dah now!" exclaimed mammy Judy as Henry entered the kitchen, "see wat dis gwine back done foh yeh! Bettah put yo' trus' in de Laud! Henry, yeh gone clean back t'de wuhl ghin, yeh knows it!"

"You're mistaken mammy, I do trust the Lord as much as ever, but I now understand him better than I use to, that's all. I dont intend to be made a fool of any longer by false preaching."

"Henry!" interrogated Daddy Joe, who apprehending difficulties in the case, had managed to get back to the house, "yeh gwine lose all yo' ligion? Wat yeh mean boy!"

"Religion!" replied Henry rebukingly, "that's always the cry with black people. Tell me nothing about religion when the very man who hands you the bread at communion, has sold your daughter away from you!"

"Den yeh 'fen' God case man 'fen' yeh! Take cah Henry, take cah! mine wat yeh 'bout; God is lookin' at yeh, an' if yeh no' willin' trus' 'im, yeh need'n call on 'im in time o' trouble."

"I dont intend, unless He does more for me then than he has done before. 'Time of need!' If ever man needed his assistance, I'm sure I need it now."

"Yeh do'n know wat yeh need; de Laud knows bes'. On'y trus' in 'im, an' 'e bring yeh out mo' nah conkah. By de help o' God I's heah dis day, to gib yeh cumfut!"

"I have trusted in Him daddy Joe, all my life, as I told mammy Judy this morning, but—"

"Ah boy, yeh's gwine back! Dat on't do Henry, dat on't do!"

"Going back from what? my oppressor's religion! If I could only get rid of his inflictions as easily as I can his religion, I would be this day a free man, when you might then talk to me about 'trusting.'"

"Dis Henry, am one uh de ways ob de Laud; 'e fus 'flicks us an' den he bless us."

"Then it's a way I dont like."

"Mine how yeh talk, boy!"

> "'God moves in a myst'us way
> His wundahs to pehfaum,' an—'"

"He moves too slow for me daddy Joe; I'm tired waiting so—"

"Come Henry, I hab no sich talk like dat! yeh is gittin' rale weaked; yeh gwine let de debil take full 'session on yeh! Take cah boy, mine how yeh talk!"

"It is not wickedness, daddy Joe; you dont understand these things at all. If a thousand years with us is but a day with God, do you think that I am required to wait all that time?"

"Dont Henry, dont! de wud say 'Stan' still an' see de salbation.'"

"That's no talk for me daddy Joe, I've been 'standing still' long enough; I'll 'stand still' no longer."

"Den yeh no call t' bey God wud? Take cah boy, take cah!"

"Yes I have, and I intend to obey it, but that part was intended for the Jews, a people long since dead. I'll obey that intended for me."

"How yeh gwine bey it?"

"'Now is the accepted time, to-day is the day of salvation.' So you see, daddy Joe, this is very different to standing still."

"Ah boy, I's feahd yeh's losen yeh 'ligion!"

"I tell you once for all daddy Joe, that I'm not only 'losing,' but I have altogether lost my faith in the religion of my oppressors. As they are our religious teachers, my estimate of the thing they give, is no greater than it is for those who give it."

With elbows upon his knees, and face resting in the palms of his hands, daddy Joe for some time sat with his eyes steadily fixed on the floor, whilst Ailcey who for a part of the time had been an auditor to the conversation, went into the house about her domestic duties.

"Never mind Henry! I hope it will not always be so with you. You have been kind and faithful to me and the Colonel, and I'll do anything I can for you!" sympathetically said Mrs. Franks, who having been a concealed spectator of the interview between Henry and the old people, had just appeared before them.

Wiping away the emblems of grief which stole down his face, with a deep toned voice, upgushing from the recesses of a more than iron-pierced soul, he enquired—

"Madam, what can you do! Where is my wife?" To this, Mrs. Franks gave a deep sigh. "Never mind, never mind!" continued he, "yes, I will mind, and by—!"

"O! Henry, I hope you've not taken to swearing! I do hope you will not give over to wickedness! Our afflictions should only make our faith the stronger."

" 'Wickedness!' Let the righteous correct the wicked, and the Christian condemn the sinner!"

"That is uncharitable in you Henry! as you know I have always treated you kindly, and God forbid that I should consider myself any less than a Christian! and I claim as much at least for the Colonel, though like frail mortals he is liable to err at times."

"Madam!" said he with suppressed emotion—starting back a pace or two—"do you think there is anything either in or out of hell so wicked, as that which colonel Franks has done to my wife, and now about to do to me? For myself I care not—my wife!"

"Henry!" said Mrs. Franks, gently placing her hand upon his shoulder, "there is yet a hope left for you, and you will be faithful enough I know, not to implicate any person; it is this: Mrs. Van Winter, a true friend of your race, is shortly going to Cuba on a visit, and I will arrange with her to purchase you through an agent on the day of your sale, and by that means you can get to Cuba, where probably you may be fortunate enough to get the master of your wife to become your purchaser."

"Then I have two chances!" replied Henry.

Just then Ailcey thrusting her head in the door, requested the presence of her mistress in the parlor.

Henry passed directly around and behind the house.

"See, ole man, see! reckon 'e gwine dah now!" whispered mammy Judy, on seeing Henry pass through the yard without going into the kitchen.

"Whah?" enquired daddy Joe.

"Dun'o out yandah, whah 'e gwine way from wite folks!" she replied.

The interview between Franks and the trader Harris was not over half an hour duration, the trader retiring, Franks being prompt and decisive in all of his transactions, making little ceremony.

So soon as the front door was closed, Ailcey smiling bore into the kitchen a half pint glass of brandy, saying that her master had sent it to the old people.

The old man received it with compliments to his master, pouring it into a black jug in which there was both tansy and garlic, highly recommending it as a 'bitters' and certain antidote for worms, for which purpose he and the old woman took of it as long as it lasted, though neither had been troubled with that particular disease since the days of their childhood.

"Wat de gwine do wid yeh meh son?" enquired mammy Judy as Henry entered the kitchen.

"Sell me to the soul-drivers! what else would they do?"

"Yeh gwin 'tay 'bout till de git yeh?"

"I shant move a step! and let them do their—!"

"Maus wants to see yeh in da front house Henry," interrupted Ailcey, he immediately obeying the summons.

"Heah dat now!" said mammy Judy, as Henry followed the maid out of the kitchen.

"Carry this note sir, directly to captain Jack Harris!" ordered Franks, handing to Henry a sealed note. Receiving it, he bowed politely, going out of the front door, directly to the slave prison of Harris.

"Eh heh! I see," said Harris on opening the note; "colonel Frank's boy; walk in here;" passing through the office into a room which proved to be the first department of the slave-prison. "No common negro I see! you're a shade higher. A pretty deep shade too! Can read, write cipher; a good religious fellow, and has a Christian and sir name. The devil you say! Who's your father? Can you preach?"

"I have never tried," was the only reply.

"Have you ever been a member of Congress?" continued Harris with ridicule.

To this Henry made no reply.

"Wont answer hey! beneath your dignity. I understand that you're of that class of gentry who dont speak to common folks! You're not quite well enough dressed for a gentleman of your cloth. Here! Mr. Henry, I'll present you with a set of ruffles: give yourself no trouble sir, as I'll dress you! I'm here for that purpose," said Harris, fastening upon the wrists of the manly bondman, a heavy pair of handcuffs.

"You hurt my wrist!" admonished Henry.

"New clothing will be a little tight when first put on. Now sir!" continued the trader, taking him to the back door and pointing into the yard at the slave gang there confined; "as you have been respectably dressed, walk out and enjoy yourself among the ladies and gentleman there; you'll find them quite a select company."

Shortly after this the sound of the bell-ringer's voice was heard—a sound which usually spread terror among the slaves: "Will be sold this afternoon at three o'clock by public outcry, at the slave-prison of captain John Harris, a likely choice negro-fellow, the best trained body servant in the state, trained to the business by the most accomplished lady and gentleman negro-trainers in the Mississippi Valley. Sale positive without a proviso."

"Dah, dah! did'n eh tell yeh so? Ole man, ole man! heah dat now! Come heah. Dat jis what I been tellin on im, but 'e uden blieve me!"

Sojourner Truth

(c. 1797–1883)

BORN A SLAVE IN Ulster County, New York, Isabella Baumfree (or Bomefree) was sold many times in the course of the next eighteen years. During this time she married a fellow-slave and had five children, all but one of whom were taken away and probably sold into slavery.

Freed under the New York State Emancipation Act of 1827, Isabella took her only remaining child and moved to New York City, where she joined a religious cult. The group involved her in a sordid scandal—including a charge of murder. She sued her accuser for libel and was exonerated; the judgment of $125 which she won was an exceptional triumph for a slave.

Isabella Baumfree was deeply religious and inclined toward mysticism; she saw visions and heard voices. Following one such experience she announced that a Spirit had commanded her to go forth "to declare the truth to the people," and that she was no longer Isabella, but "Sojourner Truth." For the next thirty years she roamed the land, turning up at antislavery gatherings, woman's rights conventions, and religious revivals. Bidden or unbidden, Sojourner Truth always spoke, sometimes rising from her seat in the audience to counter remarks and arguments with which she disagreed. Though totally illiterate, she was a moving and dramatic speaker. Her fame spread throughout the East and Midwest and into Canada. She was in the forefront of many movements and the disciple of many "radical" ideas. When Lincoln received her late in 1861, she urged upon him the enlistment of free Negroes to fight in defense of the Union.

After the war Sojourner Truth remained in demand as a speaker, but she felt that her work was done. Friends and admirers helped her to buy a small house in Battle Creek, Michigan, where she died in 1883.

The following selection is representative of her dramatic speeches; its delivery was highlighted by Sojourner Truth's ripping open her dress to expose her breasts.

There is no exact copy of this speech, which was given at a Woman's Rights Convention in Akron, Ohio, in 1852. The following selection is based on fragments that have survived and been put in this form by Arthur Huff Fauset in *Sojourner Truth* (Chapel Hill: The University of North Carolina Press, 1938). For recent works on Sojourner Truth see

Hertha Pauli, *Her Name Was Sojourner Truth* (New York: Appleton-Century Crofts, 1962), and Jacqueline Bernard, *Journey Toward Freedom* (New York: Norton and Company, 1967).

"AND ARN'T I A WOMAN?"

As Sojourner made her way to the platform, a hissing sound of disapproval rushed through the room—the kind of sound which in America only a Negro is likely to experience and understand; a sound which says, "You don't belong. You have nothing to do with this."

Unmindful and unafraid, the old black woman moved on, with slowness and solemnity, to the front. Then she laid her old bonnet at her feet and, fastening her great, speaking eyes upon the chairman, she sought permission to address the group.

There she stands before the chairman, with all those hissing sounds rushing through her ears. Does she know an ounce of fear?

What!

. . . After a half century of locking horns with a hundred varieties of demoniacal opposition. . . . what mattered one more crowd? Who were these people anyway that they imagined they could make laws just to suit themselves—ministers, thugs, and barbarians? They with their laws about Negroes, laws about women, laws about property and about everything under the sun. . . . There was only one Lawgiver. He could make these picayune creatures fly, law or no law. He was on *her* side; assuredly He was *not* on their side.

She stands before the lady in the chair, looking with confident, unafraid, expectant eyes. That lady cannot refuse her petition to speak; she cannot help herself if she wants to.

The chairman turns to the audience and announces with befitting simplicity, "Sojourner Truth has a word. I beg of you to listen for a few moments."

With electrical rapidity the air cleared. The hubbub gave way to absolute silence.

Here was something unusually strange. Queer. Unheard of. Almost inconceivable. *Impossible.*

But there she was, a black woman, unwanted, even despised. Still it will be something rare to see what she will make out of the few minutes which have been given over to her.

Every eye fixes on the tall angular form. Her chin high, her eyes gleaming, yet seeming more a part of some faraway body than of that quiet poised person in whose head they shine, she stands for an instant and appraises her audience. Then slowly, with measured accent, quietly, and in that low deeply placed tone of voice which has made her name a byword in hundreds of cities and hamlets, she begins to hurl the darts of wit and intelligence which are to leave these listeners forever changed creatures. It is one of the few times that a speech of Sojourner's has come down to us in its pristine form, so that we know exactly the kind of language and dialect she employed, and what it was in her speeches that brought people of the highest grade of intelligence and training under her spell.

"Well, chillun," she began with that familiarity which came to her so readily, whether she was addressing God or man, "whar dar is so much racket, dar must be something out o' kilter."

The audience waited with unfeigned curiosity for the resolution which her statement implied.

"I t'ink dat 'twixt de niggers of de Souf an' de women at de Norf' all a-talkin' 'bout rights, de white men will be in a fix pretty soon.

"But what's all dis here talkin' about?"

She wheeled round in the direction of one of the previous speakers. He, probably, was none too pleased to have her attention focussed on him.

"Dat man ober dar say dat women needs to be helped into carriages, and lifted ober ditches, and to have de best place everywhere. . . . Nobody eber helped *me* into carriages, or ober mud puddles, or give *me* any best place!"

She raised herself to her full height and in a voice as rumbling as thunder roared, "And arn't *I* a woman?"

A low murmur advanced through the crowd.

"Look at me," she continued. "Look at my arm."

She bared her right arm to the shoulder and dramatically demonstrated its great muscular power.

"I have plowed and planted and gathered into barns"—her voice was singing into the ether—"and no man could head me—and arn't *I* a woman?"

The murmur became more vocal.

"I have born'd five childrun and seen 'em mos' all sold off into slavery, and when I cried out with mother's grief, none but Jesus heard . . . and arn't *I* a woman?"

Notice the studied emphasis of her assertion of femininity. The oratorical genius of her race is symbolized by this unlettered woman's speech.

Sojourner perceived that the throng had been snared by her persuasive, ungrammatical rhetoric. She felt the power in her dramatic utterance, and she realized that she had smashed that vague and hypocritical symbolism which unthinking white men invariably create when they choose to boast about their deference to the opposite sex.

It was time now to launch out in another quarter.

"Den dey talks 'bout dis t'ing in de head—what dis dey call it?"

"Intellect," whispers someone near by.

"Dat's it, honey—intellect. . . . Now, what's dat got to do wit women's rights or niggers' rights?"

Then came one of those classic aphorisms which distinguish the creative thinker and orator from the mere spellbinder.

"If my cup won't hold but a pint, and yourn holds a quart, wouldn't ye be mean not to let me have my little half-measure full?"

Now the crowd, fickle as always, is delirious. It rocks the church with applause and cheers, and echoes its approval of her words by pointing scornful fingers at the minister whom a few minutes ago it had applauded for sentiments in exactly the opposite key.

"Den dat little man in black dar," she continued, referring to another minister (she can afford now to be droll and even derisive), "he say women can't have as much rights as man, 'cause Christ warn't a woman. . . . Whar did your Christ come from?" she thundered at him, her arms outstretched, her eyes shooting fire. This was a lightning thrust. The throng sat perfectly quiet.

Then, raising her voice as high as it was possible for her to do, she repeated the query.

"*Whar did your Christ come from?*"

She hesitated a moment, poised over the audience like a bird hovering just before a final swoop down upon its prey, then thundered, "From God and a woman! Man had nothing to do with him!"

The audience was overwhelmed. It could not endure so much logic and oratory at one tme. Pandemonium broke loose.

But Sojourner was not quite through. She turned finally to the man who had made a deprecating gesture at Eve, and rebuked him.

"If de fust woman God ever made was strong enough to turn the world upside down, all alone—dese togedder ought to be able to turn it back and get it rightside up again; and now dey is asking to do it, de men better let 'em."

Amidst deafening cheering and stamping, Sojourner Truth, who had arisen to catcalls and hisses, could hardly make herself heard as she shouted in conclusion, "Bleeged to ye for hearin' on me; and now ole Sojourner hain't got nothing more to say."

❀ ❀ ❀

Frederick Douglass

(1817?–1895)

FREDERICK AUGUSTUS WASHINGTON BAILEY (DOUGLASS) was the most famous Negro in the antislavery movement and one of the most famous in the post-Civil War struggle for Negro equality and civil rights. Born (of an unknown white father) to a slave on the Eastern Shore of Maryland, he learned early the oppressive cruelty of slavery. During one brief period, however, a kind mistress encouraged the boy to learn to read and write. When he was twenty-one Frederick Bailey used his knowledge of letters to forge papers which enabled him to escape. New York City attracted him, but he was advised not to stay and lingered just long enough to be joined by Anna Murray, a free Negro woman from Baltimore, who became his wife.

Frederick Bailey's work as an antislavery crusader began in New Bedford, Massachusetts. Taking the name Douglass, he soon became a leader of the Negro community in New England. At an antislavery convention in Nantucket in 1841, William Lloyd Garrison heard Douglass speak and, impressed by the ex-slave's intelligence and bearing, persuaded Douglass to become an agent for the Massachusetts Anti-Slavery Society. For the next four years Douglass lectured extensively and with such impact that many doubted the truth of his assertions that he was a self-taught ex-slave. To quiet such doubts, he wrote the *Narrative of the Life of Frederick Douglass, An American Slave* (1845). The book was so explicitly factual and became so popular that it exposed him to the hazard of seizure and re-enslavement. Douglass fled to England, where he began to envision freedom as not only physical liberty, but social equality and opportunity as well. With money raised by English friends, Douglass bought his freedom.

Returning to the States, Douglass broke with Garrison. The old abolitionist was advocating a policy of New England's seceding from the Union, but this act would leave slavery to flourish in the South, and Douglass would not support it. To avoid open factionalism and the disruption of the antislavery crusade, he moved to Rochester, New York. Here he established his paper, *The North Star* (in 1850 called *Frederick Douglass' Paper*), and vigorously plunged back into the abolition movement. The struggle was difficult, and sometimes Douglass was overcome by despair. During one of his most pessimistic lectures, Sojourner Truth rose in the audience and asked, "Frederick, is God dead?"

But in spite of bitter disappointment, especially after enactment of the Fugitive Slave Law in 1850, Douglass fought on. He lectured everywhere. His Rochester home was a station on the Underground Railroad. He engaged in politics, first as a member of the Liberty Party and later as a Lincoln Republican. He was an intimate of the "extreme abolitionists"—although he did try to dissuade John Brown from his heroic, mad, and ill-fated attempt at insurrection.

When war broke out, Douglass joined Sojourner Truth in urging Lincoln to enlist Negroes in the Union army, and when Lincoln yielded in 1862, Douglass helped to recruit two Massachusetts Negro regiments and enlisted his own sons. The end of the war found him organizing Negroes to work against discrimination and segregation. Douglass' political prominence was such that he was appointed United States Marshal for the District of Columbia under President Grant, Recorder of Deeds under President Hayes, and Minister to Haiti under President Arthur.

For recent scholarship on Douglass, see Benjamin Quarles, *Frederick Douglass* (1948), and Philip S. Foner, *The Life and Writings of Frederick Douglass,* Four Volumes (1950) and *Frederick Douglass* (1964).

The first selection below comes from *The Life and Times of Frederick Douglass,* now ranked as an American classic. The second is one of the most popular orations of perhaps the greatest orator in an age of great orators.

MY FIRST ACQUAINTANCE WITH ABOLITIONISTS

In the summer of 1841 a grand anti-slavery convention was held in Nantucket, under the auspices of Mr. Garrison and his friends. I had taken no holiday since establishing myself in New Bedford, and feeling the need of a little rest, I determined on attending the meeting, though I had no thought of taking part in any of its proceedings. Indeed, I was not aware that any one connected with the convention so much as knew my name. Mr. William C. Coffin, a prominent Abolitionist in those days of trial, had heard me speaking to my colored friends in the little school-house on Second street, where we worshipped. He sought me out in the crowd and invited me to say a few words to the convention. Thus sought out, and thus invited, I was induced to express the feelings inspired by the occasion, and the fresh recollection of the scenes through which I had passed as a slave.

It was with the utmost difficulty that I could stand erect, or that I could command and articulate two words without hesitation and

Title supplied by editors.

stammering. I trembled in every limb. I am not sure that my embarrassment was not the most effective part of my speech, if speech it could be called. At any rate, this is about the only part of my performance that I now distinctly remember. The audience sympathized with me at once, and from having been remarkably quiet, became much excited.

Mr. Garrison followed me, taking me as his text, and now, whether *I* had made an eloquent plea in behalf of freedom, or not, his was one, never to be forgotten. Those who had heard him oftenest and had known him longest, were astonished at his masterly effort. For the time he possessed that almost fabulous inspiration often referred to, but seldom attained, in which a public meeting is transformed, as it were, into a single individuality, the orator swaying a thousand heads and hearts at once and, by the simple majesty of his all-controlling thought, converting his hearers into the express image of his own soul. That night there were at least a thousand Garrisonians in Nantucket!

At the close of this great meeting I was duly waited on by Mr. John A. Collins, then the general agent of the Massachusetts Anti-Slavery Society, and urgently solicited by him to become an agent of that society and publicly advocate its principles. I was reluctant to take the proffered position. I had not been quite three years from slavery and was honestly distrustful of my ability, and I wished to be excused. Besides, publicity might discover me to my master, and many other objections presented themselves. But Mr. Collins was not to be refused, and I finally consented to go out for three months, supposing I should in that length of time come to the end of my story and my consequent usefulness.

Here opened for me a new life—a life for which I had had no preparation. Mr. Collins used to say when introducing me to an audience, I was a "graduate from the peculiar institution, with my diploma *written on my back.*" The three years of my freedom had been spent in the hard school of adversity. My hands seemed to be furnished with something like a leather coating, and I had marked out for myself a life of rough labor, suited to the hardness of my hands, as a means of supporting my family and rearing my children.

Young, ardent and hopeful, I entered upon this new life in the full gush of unsuspecting enthusiasm. The cause was good, the men engaged in it were good, the means to attain its triumph, good. Heaven's blessings must attend all, and freedom must soon be given to the millions pining under a ruthless bondage. My whole heart went with the holy cause, and my most fervent prayer to the Almighty Disposer of the hearts of men was continually offered for its early triumph. In this enthusastic spirit I dropped into the ranks of freedom's friends and went forth to the battle. For a time I was made to forget that my skin was dark and my hair crisped. For a time I regretted that I could not have shared the hardships and dangers endured by the earlier workers for the slave's release. I found, however, full soon that my enthusiasm had been extravagant, that hardships and dangers were not all over, and that the life now before me had its shadows also, as well as its sunbeams.

Among the first duties assigned me on entering the ranks was to travel in company with Mr. George Foster to secure subscribers to the *Anti-Slavery Standard* and the *Liberator*. With him I traveled and lectured through the eastern counties of Massachusetts. Much interest was awakened—large meetings assembled. Many came, no doubt from curiosity to hear what a Negro could say in his own cause. I was generally introduced as a "chattel"—a "thing"—a piece of Southern property—the chairman assuring the audience that *it* could speak. *Fugitive slaves* were rare then, and as a fugitive slave lecturer, I had the advantage of being a "bran new fact"—the first one out.

Up to that time, a colored man was deemed a fool who confessed himself a runaway slave, not only because of the danger to which he exposed himself of being retaken, but because it was a confession of a very low origin. Some of my colored friends in New Bedford thought very badly of my wisdom in thus exposing and degrading myself. The only precaution I took at the beginning, to prevent Master Thomas from knowing where I was and what I was about, was the withholding my former name, my master's name, and the name of the State and county from which I came.

During the first three or four months my speeches were almost exclusively made up of narrations of my own personal experience as a slave. "Let us have the facts," said the people. So also said Friend George Foster, who always wished to pin me down to a simple narrative. "Give us the facts," said Collins, "we will take care of the philosophy." Just here arose some embarrassment. It was impossible for me to repeat the same old story month after month and keep up my interest in it. It was new to the people, it is true, but it was an old story to me; and to go through with it night after night was a task altogether too mechanical for my nature. "Tell your story, Frederick," would whisper my revered friend, Mr. Garrison, as I stepped upon the platform.

I could not always follow the injunction, for I was now reading and thinking. New views of the subject were being presented to my mind. It did not entirely satisfy me to *narrate* wrongs; I felt like *denouncing* them. I could not always curb my moral indignation for the perpetrators of slaveholding villainy long enough for a circumstantial statement of the facts which I felt almost sure everybody must know. Besides, I was growing and needed room.

"People won't believe you ever were a slave, Frederick, if you keep on this way," said friend Foster. "Be yourself," said Collins, "and tell your story." "Better have a little of the plantation speech than not," was said to me; "it is not best that you seem too learned." These excellent friends were actuated by the best of motives and were not altogether wrong in their advice; and still I must speak just the word that seemed to *me* the word to be spoken *by* me.

At last the apprehended trouble came. People doubted if I had ever been a slave. They said I did not talk like a slave, look like a slave, or act like a slave, and that they believed I had never been south of Mason and Dixon's line. "He don't tell us where he came from, what his master's name was, or how he got away; besides, he is educated, and is in this a contradiction of all the facts we have concerning the ignorance of the slaves." Thus I was in a pretty fair way to be denounced as an impostor. The committee of the Massachusetts Anti-Slavery Society knew all the facts in my case and agreed with me thus far in the prudence of keeping them private; but going down the aisles of the churches in which my meetings were held, and hearing the outspoken Yankees repeatedly saying, "He's never been a slave, I'll warrant you," I resolved that at no distant day, and by such a revelation of facts as could not be made by any other than a genuine fugitive, I would dispel all doubt.

In a little less than four years, therefore, after becoming a public lecturer, I was induced to write out the leading facts connected with my experience in slavery, giving names of persons, places, and dates, thus putting it in the power of any who doubted, to ascertain the truth or falsehood of my story. This statement soon became known in Maryland, and I had reason to believe that an effort would be made to recapture me.

It is not probable that any open attempt to secure me as a slave could have succeeded further than the obtainment by my master of the money value of my bones and sinews. Fortunately for me, in the four years of my labors in the Abolition cause I had gained many friends who would have suffered themselves to be taxed to almost any extent to save me from slavery. It was felt that I had committed the double offense of running away and exposing the secrets and crimes of slavery and slaveholders. There was a double motive for seeking my re-enslavement—avarice and vengeance; and while, as I have said, there was little probability of successful recapture, if attempted openly, I was constantly in danger of being spirited away at a moment when my friends could render me no assistance.

In traveling about from place to place, often alone, I was much exposed to this sort of attack. Anyone cherishing the desire to betray me could easily do so by simply tracing my whereabouts through the Anti-Slavery journals, for my movements and meetings were made through these in advance. My friends Mr. Garrison and Mr. Phillips had no faith in the power of Massachusetts to protect me in my right to liberty. Public sentiment and the law, in their opinion, would hand me over to the tormentors. Mr. Phillips especially considered me in danger, and said, when I showed him the manuscript of my story, if in my place he would "throw it into the fire." Thus the reader will observe that the overcoming of one difficulty only opened the way for another, and that though I had reached a free State, and had attained a position of public usefulness, I was still under the liability of losing all I had gained.

THE MEANING OF JULY FOURTH FOR THE NEGRO
SPEECH AT ROCHESTER, NEW YORK, JULY 5, 1852

Mr. President, Friends and Fellow Citizens:

He who could address this audience without a quailing sensation, has stronger nerves than I have. I do not remember ever to have appeared as a speaker before any assembly more shrinkingly, nor with greater distrust of my ability, than I do this day. A feeling has crept over me quite unfavorable to the exercise of my limited powers of speech. The task before me is one which requires much previous thought and study for its proper performance. I know that apologies of this sort are generally considered flat and unmeaning. I trust, however, that mine will not be so considered. Should I seem at ease, my appearance would much misrepresent me. The little experience I have had in addressing public meetings, in country school houses, avails me nothing on the present occasion.

The papers and placards say that I am to deliver a Fourth of July Oration. This certainly sounds large, and out of the common way, for me. It is true that I have often had the privilege to speak in this beautiful Hall, and to address many who now honor me with their presence. But neither their familiar faces, nor the perfect gage I think I have of Corinthian Hall seems to free me from embarrassment.

The fact is, ladies and gentlemen, the distance between this platform and the slave plantation, from which I escaped, is considerable— and the difficulties to be overcome in getting from the latter to the former are by no means slight. That I am here to-day is, to me, a matter of astonishment as well as of gratitude. You will not, therefore, be surprised, if in what I have to say I evince no elaborate preparation, nor grace my speech with any high sounding exordium. With little experience and with less learning, I have been able to throw my thoughts hastily and imperfectly together; and trusting to your patient and generous indulgence, I will proceed to lay them before you.

This, for the purpose of this celebration, is the Fourth of July. It is the birthday of your National Independence, and of your political freedom. This, to you, is what the Passover was to the emancipated people of God. It carries your minds back to the day, and to the act of your great deliverance; and to the signs, and to the wonders, associated with that act, and that day. This celebration also marks the beginning of another year of your national life; and reminds you that the Republic of America is now 76 years old. I am glad, fellow-citizens, that your nation is so young. Seventy-six years, though a good old age for a man, is but a mere speck in the life of a nation. Three score years and ten is the allotted time for individual men; but nations number their years by thousands. According to this fact, you are, even now, only in the beginning of your national career, still lingering in the period of childhood. I repeat, I am glad this is so. There is hope in the thought, and hope is much needed, under the dark clouds which lower above the horizon. The eye of the reformer is met with angry flashes, portending disastrous times; but his heart may well beat lighter at the thought that America is young, and that she is still in the impressible stage of her existence. May he not hope that high lessons of wisdom, of justice and of truth, will yet give direction to her destiny? Were the nation older, the patriot's heart might be sadder, and the reformer's brow heavier. Its future might be shrouded in gloom, and the hope of its prophets go out in sorrow. There is consolation in the thought that America is young. Great streams are not easily turned from channels, worn deep in the course of ages. They may sometimes rise in quiet and stately majesty, and inundate the land, refreshing and fertilizing the earth with their mysterious properties. They may also rise in wrath and fury, and bear away, on their angry waves, the accumulated wealth of years of toil and hardship. They, however, gradually flow back to the same old channel, and flow on as serenely as ever. But, while the river may not be turned aside, it may dry up, and leave nothing behind but the withered branch, and the unsightly rock, to howl in the abyss-sweeping wind, the sad tale of departed glory. As with rivers so with nations. . . .

Fellow-citizens, pardon me, allow me to ask, why am I called upon to speak here to-day? What have I, or those I represent, to do with your national independence? Are the great principles of political freedom and of natural justice, embodied in that Declaration of Independence, extended to us? and am I, therefore, called upon to bring our humble offering to the national altar, and to confess the benefits and express devout gratitude for the blessings resulting from your independence to us?

Would to God, both for your sakes and ours, that an affirmative answer could be truthfully returned to these questions! Then would my task be light, and my burden easy and delightful. For who is there so cold, that a nation's sympathy could not warm him? Who so obdurate and dead to the claims of gratitude, that would not thankfully acknowledge such priceless benefits? Who so stolid and selfish, that would not give his voice to swell the hallelujahs of a nation's jubilee, when the chains of servitude had been torn from his limbs? I am not that man. In a case like that, the dumb might eloquently speak, and the "lame man leap as an hart."

But such is not the state of the case. I say it with a sad sense of the disparity between us. I am not included within the pale of this glorious anniversary! Your high independence only reveals the immeasurable distance between us. The blessings in which you, this day, rejoice, are not enjoyed in common. The rich inheritance of justice, liberty, prosperity and independence, bequeathed by your fathers, is shared by you, not by me. The sunlight that brought light and healing to you, has brought stripes and death to me. This Fourth July is yours, not mine. You may rejoice, I must mourn. To drag a man in fetters into the grand illuminated temple of liberty, and call upon him to join you in joyous anthems, were inhuman mockery and sacrilegious irony. Do you mean, citizens, to mock me, by asking me to speak today? If so, there is a parallel to your conduct. And let me warn you that it is dangerous to copy the example of a nation whose crimes, towering up to heaven, were thrown down by the breath of the Almighty, burying that nation in irrevocable ruin! I can to-day take up the plaintive lament of a peeled and woe-smitten people!

> By the rivers of Babylon, there we sat down. Yea! we wept when we remembered Zion. We hanged our harps upon the willows in the midst thereof. For there, they that carried us away captive, required of us a song; and they who wasted us required of us mirth, saying, Sing us one of the songs of Zion. How can we sing the Lord's song in a strange land? If I forget thee, O Jerusalem, let my right hand forget her cunning. If I do not remember thee, let my tongue cleave to the roof of my mouth.

Fellow-citizens, above your national, tumultuous joy, I hear the mournful wail of millions; whose chains, heavy and grievous yesterday, are, to-day, rendered more intolerable by the jubilee shouts that reach them. If I do forget, if I do not faithfully remember those bleeding children of sorrow this day, "may my right hand forget her cunning, and may my tongue cleave to the roof of my mouth!" To forget them, to pass lightly over their wrongs, and to chime in with the popular theme, would be treason most scandalous and shocking, and would make me a reproach before God and the world. My subject, then, fellow-citizens, is AMERICAN SLAVERY. I shall see this day and its popular characteristics from the slave's point of view. Standing there identified with the American bondman, making his wrongs mine, I do not hesitate to declare, with all my soul, that the character and conduct of this nation never looked blacker to me than on this 4th of

July! Whether we turn to the declarations of the past, or to the professions of the present, the conduct of the nation seems equally hideous and revolting. America is false to the past, false to the present, and solemnly binds herself to be false to the future. Standing with God and the crushed and bleeding slave on this occasion, I will, in the name of humanity which is outraged, in the name of liberty which is fettered, in the name of the constitution and the Bible which are disregarded and trampled upon, dare to call in question and to denounce, with all the emphasis I can command, everything that serves to perpetuate slavery—the great sin and shame of America! "I will not equivocate; I will not excuse"; I will use the severest language I can command; and yet not one word shall escape me that any man, whose judgment is not blinded by prejudice, or who is not at heart a slaveholder, shall not confess to be right and just.

But I fancy I hear some one of my audience say, "It is just in this circumstance that you and your brother abolitionists fail to make a favorable impression on the public mind. Would you argue more, and denounce less; would you persuade more, and rebuke less; your cause would be much more likely to succeed." But, I submit, where all is plain there is nothing to be argued. What point in the anti-slavery creed would you have me argue? On what branch of the subject do the people of this country need light? Must I undertake to prove that the slave is a man? That point is conceded already. Nobody doubts it. The slaveholders themselves acknowledge it in the enactment of laws for their government. They acknowledge it when they punish disobedience on the part of the slave. There are seventy-two crimes in the State of Virginia which, if committed by a black man (no matter how ignorant he be), subject him to the punishment of death; while only two of the same crimes will subject a white man to the like punishment. What is this but the acknowledgment that the slave is a moral, intellectual, and responsible being? The manhood of the slave is conceded. It is admitted in the fact that Southern statute books are covered with enactments forbidding, under severe fines and penalties, the teaching of the slave to read or to write. When you can point to any such laws in reference to the beasts of the field, then I may consent to argue the manhood of the slave. When the dogs in your streets, when the fowls of the air, when the cattle on your hills, when the fish of the sea, and the reptiles that crawl, shall be unable to distinguish the slave from a brute, then will I argue with you that the slave is a man!

For the present, it is enough to affirm the equal manhood of the Negro race. Is it not astonishing that, while we are ploughing, planting, and reaping, using all kinds of mechanical tools, erecting houses, constructing bridges, building ships, working in metals of brass, iron, copper, silver and gold; that, while we are reading, writing and ciphering, acting as clerks, merchants and secretaries, having among us lawyers, doctors, ministers, poets, authors, editors, orators and teachers; that, while we are engaged in all manner of enterprises common to other men, digging gold in California, capturing the whale in the Pacific, feeding sheep and cattle on the hill-side, living, moving, acting, thinking, planning, living in families as husbands, wives and children, and, above all, confessing and worshipping the Christian's God, and looking hopefully for life and immortality beyond the grave, we are called upon to prove that we are men!

Would you have me argue that man is entitled to liberty? that he is the rightful owner of his own body? You have already declared it. Must I argue the wrongfulness of slavery? Is that a question for Republicans? Is it to be settled by the rules of logic and argumentation, as a matter beset with great difficulty, involving a doubtful application of the principle of justice, hard to be understood? How should I look to-day, in the presence of Americans, dividing, and subdividing a discourse, to show that men have a natural right to freedom? speaking of it relatively and positively, negatively and affirmatively. To do so, would be to make myself ridiculous, and to offer an insult to your understanding. There is not a man beneath the canopy of heaven that does not know that slavery is wrong for him.

What, am I to argue that it is wrong to make men brutes, to rob them of their liberty, to work them without wages, to keep them ignorant of their relations to their fellow men, to beat them with sticks, to flay their flesh with the lash, to load their limbs with irons, to hunt them with dogs, to sell them at auction, to sunder their families, to knock out their teeth, to burn their flesh, to starve them into obedience and submission to their masters? Must I argue that a system thus marked with blood, and stained with pollution, is wrong? No! I will not. I have better employment for my time and strength than such arguments would imply.

What, then, remains to be argued? Is it that slavery is not divine; that God did not establish it; that our doctors of divinity are mistaken? There is blasphemy in the thought. That which is inhuman, cannot be divine! Who can reason on such a proposition? They that can, may; I cannot. The time for such argument is passed.

At a time like this, scorching irony, not convincing argument, is needed. O! had I the ability, and could I reach the nation's ear, I would, to-day, pour out a fiery stream of biting ridicule, blasting reproach, withering sarcasm, and stern rebuke. For it is not light that is needed, but fire; it is not the gentle shower, but thunder. We need the storm, the whirlwind, and the earthquake. The feeling of the nation must be quickened; the conscience of the nation must be roused; the propriety of the nation must be startled; the hypocrisy of the nation must be exposed; and its crimes against God and man must be proclaimed and denounced.

What, to the American slave, is your 4th of July? I answer; a day that reveals to him, more than all other days in the year, the gross injustice and cruelty to which he is the constant victim. To him, your celebration is a sham; your boasted liberty, an unholy license; your national greatness, swelling vanity; your sounds of rejoicing are empty and heartless; your denunciation of tyrants, brass fronted impudence; your shouts of liberty and equality, hollow mockery; your prayers and hymns, your sermons and thanksgivings, with all your religious parade and solemnity, are to Him, mere bombast, fraud, deception, impiety, and hypocrisy—a thin veil to cover up crimes which would disgrace a nation of savages. There is not a nation on the earth guilty of practices more shocking and bloody than are the people of the United States, at this very hour.

Go where you may, search where you will, roam through all the monarchies and despotisms of the Old World, travel through South America, search out every abuse, and when you have found the last, lay your facts by the side of the everyday practices of this nation, and you will say with me, that, for revolting barbarity and shameless hypocrisy, America reigns without a rival.

Take the American slave-trade, which we are told by the papers, is especially prosperous just now. Ex-Senator Benton tells us that the price of men was never higher than now. He mentions the fact to show that slavery is in no danger. This trade is one of the peculiarities of American institutions. It is carried on in all the large towns and cities in one-half of this confederacy; and millions are pocketed every year by dealers in this horrid traffic. In several states this trade is a chief source of wealth. It is called (in contradistinction to the foreign slave-trade) "the internal slave-trade." It is, probably, called so, too, in order to divert from it the horror with which the foreign slave-trade is contemplated. That trade has long since been denounced by this government as piracy. It has been denounced with burning words from the high places of the nation as an execrable traffic. To arrest it, to put an end to it, this nation keeps a squadron, at immense cost, on the coast of Africa. Everywhere, in this country, it is safe to speak of this foreign slave-trade as a most inhuman traffic, opposed alike to the laws of God and of man. The duty to extirpate and destroy it, is admitted even by our DOCTORS OF DIVINITY. In order to put an end to it, some of these last have consented that their colored brethren (nominally free) should leave this country, and establish themselves on the western coast of Africa! It is, however, a notable fact that, while so much execration is poured out by Americans upon all those engaged in the foreign slave-trade, the men engaged in the slave-trade between the states pass without condemnation, and their business is deemed honorable.

Behold the practical operation of this internal slave-trade, the American slave-trade, sustained by American politics and American religion. Here you will see men and women reared like swine for the market. You know what is a swine-drover? I will show you a man-drover. They inhabit all our Southern States. They perambulate the country, and crowd the highways of the nation, with droves of human stock. You will see one of these human flesh jobbers, armed with pistol, whip, and bowie-knife, driving a company of a hundred men, women, and children, from the Potomac to the slave market at New Orleans. These wretched people are to be sold singly, or in lots, to suit purchasers. They are food for the cottonfield and the deadly sugar-mill. Mark the sad procession, as it moves wearily along, and the inhuman wretch who drives them. Hear his savage yells and his blood-curdling oaths, as he hurries on his affrighted captives! There, see the old man with locks thinned and gray. Cast one glance, if you please, upon that young mother, whose shoulders are bare to the scorching sun, her briny tears falling on the brow of the babe in her arms. See, too, that girl of thirteen, weeping, yes! weeping, as she thinks of the mother from whom she has been torn! The drove moves tardily. Heat and sorrow have nearly consumed their strength; suddenly you hear a quick snap, like the discharge of a rifle; the fetters clank, and the chain rattles simultaneously; your ears are saluted with a scream, that seems to have torn its way to the centre of your soul! The crack you heard was the sound of the slave-whip; the scream you heard was from the woman you saw with the babe. Her speed had faltered under the weight of her child and her chains! that gash on her shoulder tells her to move on. Follow this drove to New Orleans. Attend the auction; see men examined like horses; see the forms of women rudely and brutally exposed to the shocking gaze of American slave-buyers. See this drove sold and separated forever; and never forget the deep, sad sobs that arose from that scattered multitude. Tell me, citizens, WHERE, under the sun, you can witness a spectacle more fiendish and shocking. Yet this is but a glance at the American slave-trade, as it exists, at this moment, in the ruling part of the United States.

I was born amid such sights and scenes. To me the American slave-trade is a terrible reality. When a child, my soul was often pierced with a sense of its horrors. I lived on Philpot Street, Fell's Point, Baltimore, and have watched from the wharves the slave ships in the Basin, anchored from the shore, with their cargoes of human flesh, waiting for favorable winds to waft them down the Chesapeake. There was, at that time, a grand slave mart kept at the head of Pratt Street, by Austin Woldfolk. His agents were sent into every town and county in Maryland, announcing their arrival, through the papers, and on flaming "hand-bills," headed CASH FOR NEGROES. These men were generally well dressed men, and very captivating in their manners; ever ready to drink, to treat, and to gamble. The fate of many a slave has depended upon the turn of a single card; and many a child has been snatched from the arms of its mother by bargains arranged in a state of brutal drunkenness.

The flesh-mongers gather up their victims by dozens, and drive them, chained, to the general depot at Baltimore. When a sufficient number has been collected here, a ship is chartered for the purpose of conveying the forlorn crew to Mobile, or to New Orleans. From the slave prison to the ship, they are usually driven in the darkness of night; for since the anti-slavery agitation, a certain caution is observed.

In the deep, still darkness of midnight, I have been aroused by the dead, heavy footsteps, and the piteous cries of the chained gangs that passed our door. The anguish of my boyish heart was intense; and I was often consoled, when speaking to my mistress in the morning, to hear her say that the custom was very wicked; that she hated to hear the rattle of the chains and the heart-rending cries. I was glad to find one who sympathized with me in my horror.

Fellow-citizens, this murderous traffic is, to-day, in active operation in this boasted republic. In the solitude of my spirit I see clouds of dust raised on the highways of the South; I see the bleeding footsteps; I hear the doleful wail of fettered humanity on the way to the slave-markets, where the victims are to be sold like horses, sheep, and swine, knocked off to the highest bidder. There I see the tenderest ties ruthlessly broken, to gratify the lust, caprice and rapacity of the buyers and sellers of men. My soul sickens at the sight.

> Is this the land your Fathers loved,
>> The freedom which they toiled to win?
> Is this the earth whereon they moved?
>> Are these the graves they slumber in?

But a still more inhuman, disgraceful, and scandalous state of things remains to be presented. By an act of the American Congress, not yet two years old, slavery has been nationalized in its most horrible and revolting form. By that act, Mason and Dixon's line has been obliterated; New York has become as Virginia; and the power to hold, hunt, and sell men, women and children, as slaves, remains no longer a mere state institution, but is now an institution of the whole United States. The power is co-extensive with the star-spangled banner, and American Christianity. Where these go, may also go the merciless slave-hunter. Where these are, man is not sacred. He is a bird for the sportsman's gun. By that most foul and fiendish of all human decrees, the liberty and person of every man are put in peril. Your broad republican domain is hunting ground for men. Not for thieves and robbers, enemies of society, merely, but for men guilty of no crime. Your law-makers have commanded all good citizens to engage in this hellish sport. Your President, your Secretary of State, your lords, nobles, and ecclesiastics enforce, as a duty you owe to your free and glorious country, and to your God, that you do this accursed thing. Not fewer than forty Americans have, within the past two years, been hunted down and, without a moment's warning, hurried away in chains, and consigned to slavery and excruciating torture. Some of these have had wives and children, dependent on them for bread; but of this, no account was made. The right of the hunter to his prey stands superior to the right of marriage, and to all rights in this republic, the rights of God included! For black men there is neither law nor justice, humanity nor religion. The Fugitive Slave Law makes MERCY TO THEM A CRIME; and bribes the judge who tries them. An American JUDGE GETS TEN DOLLARS FOR EVERY VICTIM HE CONSIGNS to slavery, and five, when he fails to do so. The oath of any two villains is sufficient, under this hell-black enactment, to send the most pious and exemplary black man into the remorseless jaws of slavery! His own testimony is nothing. He can bring no witnesses for himself. The min-ister of American justice is bound by the law to hear but one side; and that side is the side of the oppressor. Let this damning fact be per-petually told. Let it be thundered around the world that in tyrant-killing, king-hating, people-loving, democratic, Christian America the seats of justice are filled with judges who hold their offices under an open and palpable bribe, and are bound, in deciding the case of a man's liberty, to hear only his accusers!

In glaring violation of justice, in shameless disregard of the forms of administering law, in cunning arrangement to entrap the defenseless, and in diabolical intent this Fugitive Slave Law stands alone in the annals of tyrannical legislation. I doubt if there be another nation on the globe having the brass and the baseness to put such a law on the statute-book. If any man in this assembly thinks differently from me in this matter, and feels able to disprove my statements, I will gladly confront him at any suitable time and place he may select.

I take this law to be one of the grossest infringements of Christian Liberty, and, if the churches and ministers of our country were not stupidly blind, or most wickedly indifferent, they, too, would so regard it.

At the very moment that they are thanking God for the enjoyment of civil and religious liberty, and for the right to worship God accord-ing to the dictates of their own consciences, they are utterly silent in respect to a law which robs religion of its chief significance and makes it utterly worthless to a world lying in wickedness. Did this law con-cern the "mint, anise, and cummin"—abridge the right to sing psalms, to partake of the sacrament, or to engage in any of the ceremonies of religion, it would be smitten by the thunder of a thousand pulpits. A general shout would go up from the church demanding repeal, repeal, instant repeal!—And it would go hard with that politician who presumed to solicit the votes of the people without inscribing this motto on his banner. Further, if this demand were not complied with, another Scotland would be added to the history of religious liberty, and the stern old convenanters would be thrown into the shade. A John Knox would be seen at every church door and heard from every pulpit, and Fillmore would have no more quarter than was shown by Knox to the beautiful, but treacherous, Queen Mary of Scotland. The fact that the church of our country (with fractional exceptions) does not esteem "the Fugitive Slave Law" as a declaration of war against religious liberty, implies that that church regards religion simply as a form of worship, an empty ceremony, and not a vital principle, requiring active benevolence, justice, love, and good will towards man. It esteems sacrifice above mercy; psalm-singing above right doing; solemn meetings above practical righteousness. A worship that can be conducted by persons who refuse to give shelter to the houseless, to give bread to the hungry, clothing to the naked, and who enjoin obedience to a law forbidding these acts of mercy is a curse, not a blessing to mankind. The Bible addresses all such persons as "scribes, pharisees, hypocrites, who pay tithe of mint, anise, and cummin, and have omitted the weightier matters of the law, judgment, mercy, and faith."

But the church of this country is not only indifferent to the wrongs of the slave, it actually takes sides with the oppressors. It has made itself the bulwark of American slavery, and the shield of American slave-hunters. Many of its most eloquent Divines, who stand as the very lights of the church, have shamelessly given the sanction of religion and the Bible to the whole slave system. They have taught that man may, properly, be a slave; that the relation of master and slave is ordained of God; that to send back an escaped bondman to his master is clearly the duty of all the followers of the Lord Jesus Christ; and this horrible blasphemy is palmed off upon the world for Christianity.

For my part, I would say, welcome infidelity! welcome atheism! welcome anything! in preference to the gospel, as preached by those Divines! They convert the very name of religion into an engine of tyranny and barbarous cruelty, and serve to confirm more infidels, in this age, than all the infidel writings of Thomas Paine, Voltaire, and Bolingbroke put together have done! These ministers make religion a cold and flinty-hearted thing, having neither principles of right action nor bowels of compassion. They strip the love of God of its beauty and leave the throne of religion a huge, horrible, repulsive form. It is a religion for oppressors, tyrants, man-stealers, and thugs. It is not that "pure and undefiled religion" which is from above, and which is "first pure, then peaceable, easy to be entreated, full of mercy and good fruits, without partiality, and without hypocrisy." But a religion which favors the rich against the poor; which exalts the proud above the humble; which divides mankind into two classes, tyrants and slaves; which says to the man in chains, stay there; and to the oppressor, oppress on; it is a religion which may be professed and enjoyed by all the robbers and enslavers of mankind; it makes God a respecter of persons, denies his fatherhood of the race, and tramples in the dust the great truth of the brotherhood of man. All this we affirm to be true of the popular church, and the popular worship of our land and nation —a religion, a church, and a worship which, on the authority of inspired wisdom, we pronounce to be an abomination in the sight of God. In the language of Isaiah, the American church might be well addressed,

> Bring no more vain oblations; incense is an abomination unto me: the new moons and Sabbaths, the calling of assemblies, I cannot away with; it is iniquity, even the solemn meeting. Your new moons, and your appointed feasts my soul hateth. They are a trouble to me; I am weary to bear them; and when ye spread forth your hands I will hide mine eyes from you. Yea! when ye make many prayers, I will not hear. YOUR HANDS ARE FULL OF BLOOD; cease to do evil, learn to do well; seek judgment; relieve the oppressed; judge for the fatherless; plead for the widow.

The American church is guilty, when viewed in connection with what it is doing to uphold slavery; but it is superlatively guilty when viewed in its connection with its ability to abolish slavery.

The sin of which it is guilty is one of omission as well as of commission. Albert Barnes but uttered what the common sense of every man at all observant of the actual state of the case will receive as truth, when he declared that "There is no power out of the church that could sustain slavery an hour, if it were not sustained in it."

Let the religious press, the pulpit, the Sunday School, the conference meeting, the great ecclesiastical, missionary, Bible and tract associations of the land array their immense powers against slavery, and slave-holding; and the whole system of crime and blood would be scattered to the winds, and that they do not do this involves them in the most awful responsibility of which the mind can conceive.

In prosecuting the anti-slavery enterprise, we have been asked to spare the church, to spare the ministry; but how, we ask, could such a thing be done? We are met on the threshold of our efforts for the redemption of the slave, by the church and ministry of the country, in battle arrayed against us; and we are compelled to fight or flee. From what quarter, I beg to know, has proceeded a fire so deadly upon our ranks, during the last two years, as from the Northern pulpit? As the champions of oppressors, the chosen men of American theology have appeared—men honored for their so-called piety, and their real learning. The LORDS of Buffalo, the SPRINGS of New York, the LATHROPS of Auburn, the COXES and SPENCERS of Brooklyn, the GANNETS and SHARPS of Boston, the DEWEYS of Washington, and other great religious lights of the land have, in utter denial of the authority of HIM by whom they professed to be called to the ministry, deliberately taught us, against the example of the Hebrews, and against the remonstrance of the Apostles, that we ought to obey man's law before the law of God.

My spirit wearies of such blasphemy; and how such men can be supported, as the "standing types and representatives of Jesus Christ," is a mystery which I leave others to penetrate. In speaking of the American church, however, let it be distinctly understood that I mean the great mass of the religious organizations of our land. There are exceptions, and I thank God that there are. Noble men may be found, scattered all over these Northern States, of whom Henry Ward Beecher, of Brooklyn; Samuel J. May, of Syracuse; and my esteemed friend (Rev. R. R. Raymond) on the platform, are shining examples; and let me say further, that, upon these men lies the duty to inspire our ranks with high religious faith and zeal, and to cheer us on in the great mission of the slave's redemption from his chains.

One is struck with the difference between the attitude of the American church towards the anti-slavery movement, and that occupied by the churches in England towards a similar movement in that country. There, the church, true to its mission of ameliorating, elevating and improving the condition of mankind, came forward promptly, bound up the wounds of the West Indian slave, and restored him to his liberty. There, the question of emancipation was a high religious question. It was demanded in the name of humanity, and according to the law of the living God. The Sharps, the Clarksons, the Wilberforces, the Buxtons, the Burchells, and the Knibbs were alike famous for their piety and for their philanthropy. The anti-slavery movement there was not an anti-church movement, for the reason that the church took its full share in prosecuting that movement: and the anti-slavery movement in this country will cease to be an anti-church movement, when the church of this country shall assume a favorable instead of a hostile position towards that movement.

Americans! your republican politics, not less than your republican union, are flagrantly inconsistent. You boast of your love of liberty, your superior civilization, and your pure Christianity, which the whole political power of the nation (as embodied in the two great political parties) is solemnly pledged to support and perpetuate the enslavement of three millions of your countrymen. You hurl your anathemas at the crowned headed tyrants of Russia and Austria and pride yourselves on your Democratic institutions, while you yourselves consent to be the mere tools and body-guards of the tyrants of Virginia and Carolina. You invite to your shores fugitives of oppression from abroad, honor them with banquets, greet them with ovations, cheer them, toast them, salute them, protect them, and pour out your money to them like water; but the fugitives from your own land you advertise, hunt, arrest, shoot, and kill. You glory in your refinement and your universal education; yet you maintain a system as barbarous and dreadful as ever stained the character of a nation—a system begun in avarice, supported in pride, and perpetuated in cruelty. You shed tears over fallen Hungary, and make the sad story of her wrongs the theme of your poets, statesmen, and orators, till your gallant sons are ready to fly to arms to vindicate her cause against the oppressor; but, in regard to the ten thousand wrongs of the American slave, you would enforce the strictest silence, and would hail him as an enemy of the nation who dares to make those wrongs the subject of public discourse! You are all on fire at the mention of liberty for France or for Ireland; but are as cold as an iceberg at the thought of liberty for the enslaved of America. You discourse eloquently on the dignity of labor; yet, you sustain a system which, in its very essence, casts a stigma upon labor. You can bare your bosom to the storm of British artillery to throw off a three-penny tax on tea; and yet wring the last hard earned farthing from the grasp of the black laborers of your country. You profess to believe "that, of one blood, God made all nations of men to dwell on the face of all the earth," and hath commanded all men, everywhere, to love one another; yet you notoriously hate (and glory in your hatred) all men whose skins are not colored like your own. You declare before the world, and are understood by the world to declare that you "hold these truths to be self-evident, that all men are created equal; and are endowed by their Creator with certain inalienable rights; and that among these are, life, liberty, and the pursuit of happiness;" and yet, you hold securely, in a bondage which, according to your own Thomas Jefferson, "is worse than ages of that which your fathers rose in rebellion to oppose," a seventh part of the inhabitants of your country.

Fellow-citizens, I will not enlarge further on your national inconsistencies. The existence of slavery in this country brands your republicanism as a sham, your humanity as a base pretense, and your Christianity as a lie. It destroys your moral power abroad: it corrupts your politicians at home. It saps the foundation of religion; it makes your name a hissing and a bye-word to a mocking earth. It is the antagonistic force in your government, the only thing that seriously disturbs and endangers your Union. It fetters your progress; it is the enemy of improvement; the deadly foe of education; it fosters pride, it breeds insolence; it promotes vice; it shelters crime; it is a curse to the earth that supports it; and yet you cling to it as if it were the sheet anchor of all your hopes. Oh! be warned! a horrible reptile is coiled up in your nation's bosom; the venomous creature is nursing at the tender breast of your youthful republic; for the love of God, tear away, and fling from you the hideous monster, and let the weight of twenty millions crush and destroy it forever! . . .

Allow me to say, in conclusion, notwithstanding the dark picture I have this day presented, of the state of the nation, I do not despair of this country. There are forces in operation which must inevitably work the downfall of slavery. "The arm of the Lord is not shortened," and the doom of slavery is certain. I, therefore, leave off where I began, with hope. While drawing encouragement from "the Declaration of Independence," the great principles it contains, and the genius of American Institutions, my spirit is also cheered by the obvious tendencies of the age. Nations do not now stand in the same relation to each other that they did ages ago. No nation can now shut itself up from the surrounding world and trot round in the same old path of its fathers without interference. The time was when such could be done. Long established customs of hurtful character could formerly fence themselves in, and do their evil work with social impunity. Knowledge was then confined and enjoyed by the privileged few, and the multitude walked on in mental darkness. But a change has now come over the affairs of mankind. Walled cities and empires have become unfashionable. The arm of commerce has borne away the gates of the strong city. Intelligence is penetrating the darkest corners of the globe. It makes its pathway over and under the sea, as well as on the earth. Wind, steam, and lightning are its chartered agents. Oceans no longer divide, but link nations together. From Boston to London is now a holiday excursion. Space is comparatively annihilated.—Thoughts expressed on one side of the Atlantic are distinctly heard on the other.

The far off and almost fabulous Pacific rolls in grandeur at our feet. The Celestial Empire, the mystery of ages, is being solved. The fiat of the Almighty, "Let there be Light," has not yet spent its force. No abuse, no outrage whether in taste, sport or avarice, can now hide itself from the all-pervading light. The iron shoe, and crippled foot of China must be seen in contrast with nature. Africa must rise and put on her yet unwoven garment. "Ethiopia shall stretch out her hand unto God." . . .

Frances Ellen Watkins (Harper)

(1825–1911)

THERE ARE CERTAIN SIMILARITIES in the early lives of Frances Ellen Watkins and Charlotte L. Forten. Both were born of free, well-to-do, educated parents; both received their early schooling at home; both developed a wide range of interests; and both became teachers. Miss Watkins, however, taught for only a brief three years (at the Union Seminary in Columbus, Ohio) after she left her native Baltimore. In 1854, having "pledged myself to the anti-slavery cause," she became a lecturer for the Anti-Slavery Society of Maine.

Like other abolition agents, Frances Watkins lectured extensively. Her lectures were spiced with recitations of poems she had composed herself. The best that can be said for her verse is that it was conventional and, by the popular standards of her time, competent. Its subject matter was varied, especially after the war, when she began to lecture for the Women's Christian Temperance Union. She wrote poetry on the evils of drink, on woman's rights, and on the double standard of morality. She put into verse Biblical stories such as *Moses, a Story of the Nile*, classical myths, and oriental legends. But Miss Watkins (later writing under her married name, Harper) returned time and again to the Negro cause. *Sketches of Southern Life* (1872) has many pictures of Reconstruction life, and the novel *Iola Leroy; or, Shadows Uplifted* (1893) is a "race" novel. Her novel, however, suffers from faults—highly contrived plot, purple patches, tear-jerking scenes —that only Charles Dickens, an early contemporary, could turn into literary virtues.

Frances Watkins' work is best represented by her four thin volumes of verse, all of which appeared between 1855 and 1900 and were privately printed and reprinted. The following selections were culled from these volumes: *Poems on Miscellaneous Subjects* (1854; enlarged 1857); *Poems* (1871; enlarged 1900); *Sketches of Southern Life* (1872; enlarged 1896).

THE SLAVE AUCTION

The sale began—young girls were there,
    Defenceless in their wretchedness,
Whose stifled sobs of deep despair
    Revealed their anguish and distress.

And mothers stood with streaming eyes,
   And saw their dearest children sold;
Unheeded rose their bitter cries,
   While tyrants bartered them for gold.

And woman, with her love and truth—
   For these in sable forms may dwell—
Gaz' on the husband of her youth,
   With anguish none may paint or tell.

And men, whose sole crime was their hue,
   The impress of their Maker's hand,
And frail and shrinking children, too,
   Were gathered in that mournful band.

Ye who have laid your love to rest,
   And wept above their lifeless clay,
Know not the anguish of that breast,
   Whose lov'd are rudely torn away.

Ye may not know how desolate
   Are bosoms rudely forced to part,
And how a dull and heavy weight
   Will press the life-drops from the heart.

THE DYING BONDMAN

Life was trembling, faintly trembling
On the bondman's latest breath,
And he felt the chilling pressure
Of the cold, hard hand of Death.

He had been an Afric chieftain,
Worn his manhood as a crown;
But upon the field of battle
Had been fiercely stricken down.

He had longed to gain his freedom,
Waited, watched and hoped in vain,
Till his life was slowly ebbing—
Almost broken was his chain.

By his bedside stood the master,
Gazing on the dying one,
Knowing by the dull grey shadows
That life's sands were almost run.

"Master," said the dying bondman,
"Home and friends I soon shall see;
But before I reach my country,
Master write that I am free;

"For the spirits of my fathers
Would shrink back from me in pride,
If I told them at our greeting
I a slave had lived and died;—

"Give to me the precious token,
That my kindred dead may see—
Master! write it, write it quickly!
Master! write that I am free!"

At his earnest plea the master
Wrote for him the glad release,
O'er his wan and wasted features
Flitted one sweet smile of peace.

Eagerly he grasped the writing;
"I am free!" at last he said.
Backward fell upon the pillow,
He was free among the dead.

BURY ME IN A FREE LAND

Make me a grave where'er you will,
In a lowly plain, or a lofty hill;
Make it among earth's humblest graves,
But not in a land where men are slaves.

I could not rest if around my grave
I heard the steps of a trembling slave;
His shadow above my silent tomb
Would make it a place of fearful gloom.

I could not rest if I heard the tread
Of a coffle gang to the shambles led,
And the mother's shriek of wild despair
Rise like a curse on the trembling air.

I could not sleep if I saw the lash
Drinking her blood at each fearful gash,
And I saw her babes torn from her breast,
Like trembling doves from their parent nest.

I'd shudder and start if I heard the bay
Of bloodhounds seizing their human prey,
And I heard the captive plead in vain
As they bound afresh his galling chain.

If I saw young girls from their mothers' arms
Bartered and sold for their youthful charms,
My eye would flash with a mournful flame,
My death-paled cheek grow red with shame.

I would sleep, dear friends, where bloated might
Can rob no man of his dearest right;
My rest shall be calm in any grave
Where none can call his brother a slave.

I ask no monument, proud and high,
To arrest the gaze of the passers-by;
All that my yearning spirit craves,
Is bury me not in a land of slaves.

A DOUBLE STANDARD

Do you blame me that I loved him?
    If when standing all alone
I cried for bread a careless world
    Pressed to my lips a stone.

Do you blame me that I loved him,
    That my heart beat glad and free,
When he told me in the sweetest tones
    He loved but only me?

Can you blame me that I did not see
    Beneath his burning kiss
The serpent's wiles, nor even hear
    The deadly adder hiss?

Can you blame me that my heart grew cold
    The tempted, tempter turned;
When he was feted and caressed
    And I was coldly spurned?

Would you blame him, when you draw from me
    Your dainty robes aside,
If he with gilded baits should claim
    Your fairest as his bride?

Would you blame the world if it should press
    On him a civic crown;
And see me struggling in the depth
    Then harshly press me down?

Crime has no sex and yet to-day
    I wear the brand of shame;
Whilst he amid the gay and proud
    Still bears an honored name.

Can you blame me if I've learned to think
    Your hate of vice a sham,
When you so coldly crushed me down
    And then excused the man?

Would you blame me if to-morrow
    The coroner should say,
A wretched girl, outcast, forlorn,
    Has thrown her life away?

Yes, blame me for my downward course,
    But oh! remember well,
Within your homes you press the hand
    That led me down to hell.

I'm glad God's ways are not our ways,
    He does not see as man;
Within His love I know there's room
    For those whom others ban.

I think before His great white throne,
    His throne of spotless light,
That whited sepulchres shall wear
    The hue of endless night.

That I who fell, and he who sinned,
    Shall reap as we have sown;
That each the burden of his loss
    Must bear and bear alone.

No golden weights can turn the scale
    Of justice in His sight;
And what is wrong in woman's life
    In man's cannot be right.

LEARNING TO READ

Very soon the Yankee teachers
 Came down and set up school;
But, oh! how the Rebs did hate it,—
 It was agin' their rule.

Our masters always tried to hide
 Book learning from our eyes;
Knowledge did'nt agree with slavery—
 'Twould make us all too wise.

But some of us would try to steal
 A little from the book,
And put the words together,
 And learn by hook or crook.

I remember Uncle Caldwell,
 Who took pot liquor fat
And greased the pages of his book,
 And hid it in his hat,

And had his master ever seen
 The leaves upon his head,
He'd have thought them greasy papers,
 But nothing to be read.

And there was Mr. Turner's Ben,
 Who heard the children spell,
And picked the words right up by heart,
 And learned to read 'em well.

Well, the Northern folks kept sending
 The Yankee teachers down;
And they stood right up and helped us,
 Though Rebs did sneer and frown.

And, I longed to read my Bible,
 For precious words it said;
But when I begun to learn it,
 Folks just shook their heads,

And said there is no use trying,
 Oh! Chloe, you're too late;
But as I was rising sixty,
 I had no time to wait.

So I got a pair of glasses,
    And straight to work I went,
And never stopped till I could read
    The hymns and Testament.

Then I got a little cabin
    A place to call my own—
And I felt as independent
    As the queen upon her throne.

Charlotte L. Forten

(1838–1914)

CHARLOTTE FORTEN WAS BORN in Philadelphia; her mother and father, a wealthy sailmaker, were free Negroes. The Forten family had been actively involved in the black man's cause for two generations, and their Philadelphia home was described as a "mecca for abolitionists." Eventually Charlotte herself counted John Greenleaf Whittier, William Lloyd Garrison, and Wendell Phillips among her friends.

Charlotte Forten received some of her education at home, but most of her training was acquired at the Salem, Massachusetts Normal School, where she was graduated in 1856. She was extremely sensitive to the plight of the black man—a cause to which her family contributed enormous physical and intellectual energy and a considerable share of its wealth. Charlotte Forten's *Journal* frequently alludes to racial prejudice, discrimination, and injustice; her tone is often one of bitter irony, occasionally hinting at despair. "How *can* I be a Christian when so many in common with myself, for no crime suffer so cruelly, so unjustly? It seems vain to try, even to hope."

Charlotte Forten was also sensitive to the pleasures of warm friendship, to nature's beauty, and to the ideals her parents had instilled in her. She read widely and insatiably, wrote "occasional" poems, and taught enthusiastically—first white pupils in Salem, and then black students in her aunt's school in Philadelphia.

At the start of the Civil War Miss Forten grew restless. When Union forces secured Port Royal Harbor and General Thomas W. Sherman urged "that suitable instructors be sent to the Negroes," the young woman volunteered. For two years she taught on St. Helena Island, one of the Sea Islands off the coast of South Carolina. It was her last regular teaching post, but also the most unusual and rewarding.

In 1864 Charlotte Forten returned to Philadelphia. She wrote a few magazine pieces, which were published in the *Atlantic Monthly,* and translated Erckmann-Chatrian's *Madame Therese; or, the Volunteers of '92.* In 1878 Miss Forten married Francis J. Grimké, a minister who later won distinction as a spokesman for the Negro people.

Charlotte Forten's *Journal,* which she kept sporadically from 1854 to 1864, is an unusual record and an important historical document.

For additional comment on Charlotte Forten, see Edmund Wilson, *Patriotic Gore* (New York: Oxford University Press, 1962), pp. 239–57. *The Journal of Charlotte L. Forten,* edited and introduced by Ray Allen Billington (New York: Dryden Press), came out in 1953. A paperback edition of *The Journal of Charlotte Forten* was published in 1961 by Collier Books, New York; a second printing (1967) is also available.

The following selections were taken from *The Journal of Charlotte Forten*.

FROM "THE JOURNAL"

. . . *Monday, July 16, 1855.   Examination day.—No further comment is needed.*

Tuesday, July 17.   I breathe freely,—our trial is over, and happy are we to escape from the hot, crowded school-room;—for it has been densely crowded all day. This evening the scholars had a pleasant meeting in the school house and the last farewells were said. . . .

Wednesday, Aug. 1.   Went with Aunt M[argaretta] and a party of friends to the celebration at Abington. Our much-loved Garrison was not there,—His absence could not fail to be felt. But Mr. Phillips and other able speakers were there and many eloquent speeches were made. We had a pleasant sail on the beautiful pond attached to the Grove;—and passed altogether a delightful day.

Sunday, Aug. 12.   Had a delightful ride to Reading, to an anti-slavery meeting. The road is beautiful and our Penn[sylvania] friends warmly admired scenery which the eastern part of the Keystone State cannot boast of. Mr. Garrison and Mr. Phillips spoke very beautifully. To our great regret we were obliged to leave while Mr. P[hillips] was speaking. Our ride home was extremely pleasant. . . .

Friday, Aug. 17.   My eighteenth birthday.—Spent the afternoon and evening very pleasantly at Mrs. Putnam's. Miss Brown was there, I think I shall like her. Her father's fondness for her is rather too demonstrative. I guess she is a sensible girl. I enjoy talking with her about her European life.—She is pleasant and communicative, and though coming lastly from England, has, I think, lived in France too much to acquire a great deal of that reserve which characterizes the manners of the English.

Sunday, Aug. 26.   Spent the evening at Mrs. Putnam's. Mr. Nell was there. We amused ourselves with making conundrums, reading and reciting poetry. . . .

Wednesday, Sept. 12.   To-day school commenced.—Most happy am I to return to the companionship of my studies,—ever my most valued friends. It is pleasant to meet the scholars again; most of them greeted me cordially, and were it not for the thought that *will* intrude, of the want of *entire sympathy* even of those I know and like best, I

Reprinted by permission of Ray Allen Billington.

should greatly enjoy their society. There is one young girl and only one—Miss [Sarah] B[rown] who I believe thoroughly and heartily appreciates anti-slavery,—*radical* anti-slavery, and has no prejudice against color. I wonder that every colored person is not a misanthrope. Surely we have everything to make us hate mankind. I have met girls in the schoolroom[—] they have been thoroughly kind and cordial to me,—perhaps the next day met them in the street—they feared to recognize me; these I can but regard now with scorn and contempt,— once I liked them, believing them incapable of such meanness. Others give the most distant recognition possible.—I, of course, acknowledge no such recognitions, and they soon cease entirely. These are but trifles, certainly, to the great, public wrongs which we as a people are obliged to endure. But to those who experience them, these apparent trifles are most wearing and discouraging; even to the child's mind they reveal volumes of deceit and heartlessness, and early teach a lesson of suspicion and distrust. Oh! it is hard to go through life meeting contempt with contempt, hatred with hatred, fearing, with too good reason, to love and trust hardly any one whose skin is white,—however lovable, attractive and congenial in seeming. In the bitter, passionate feelings of my soul again and again there rises the questions "When, oh! when shall this cease?" "Is there no help?" "How long oh! how long must we continue to suffer—to endure?" Conscience answers it is wrong, it is ignoble to despair; let us labor earnestly and faithfully to acquire knowledge, to break down the barriers of prejudice and oppression. Let us take courage; never ceasing to work,—hoping and believing that if not for us, for another generation there is a better, brighter day in store,—when slavery and prejudice shall vanish before the glorious light of Liberty and Truth; when the rights of every colored man shall everywhere be acknowledged and respected, and he shall be treated as a *man* and a *brother!*

September   This evening Miss B[rown] and I joined the Female Anti-Slavery Society. I am glad to have persuaded her to do so. She seems an earnest hearted girl, in whom I cannot help having some confidence. I can only hope and pray that she will be true, and courageous enough to meet the opposition which every friend of freedom must encounter. . . .

Friday, October 19.   Walked to Marblehead with some of the girls to attend the teachers' meeting. . . . In the evening . . . listened to a very beautiful lecture from Rev. Mr. Huntingdon,—his subject was "Unconscious Tuition." But I felt a want, for among the many true and beautiful sentiments which he uttered not the faintest indication that he was even aware of the existence of that cruel and disgraceful system which refuses all teachings—all that can elevate and improve to millions of the inhabitants of this *glorious* (?) republic. Had a pleasant walk to Salem in the moonlight. . . .

Sunday, Oct. 21. The twentieth anniversary of the day on which beloved Garrison was mobbed and insulted in the streets of Boston. To-day on the very spot where that little band of noble-hearted women so heroically maintained the right, the dauntless Pioneer of our glorious cause stands with many true-hearted co-workers, surrounded by hundreds of eager, sympathizing listeners. The men who dragged him with a rope around his neck through the streets of Boston,—to their own shame—not his—would blush to confess it to-day. And even his bitter enemies are forced, despite themselves, to respect his self-sacrificing unfaltering devotion to Liberty and Truth. Dear, honored friends, I cannot be with you in your gathering to-day, but the light of your loved countenances,—the tones of your eloquent voices fall upon my grateful heart. This evening my necessary absence from the meeting in Boston, upon which my thoughts have dwelt all day, was somewhat compensated for by listening to an excellent and very interesting lecture from Rev. S. Johnson of Lynn. *The first of our course.*—

Sunday, Oct. 28. This has indeed been one of the happiest days of my life.—Wendell Phillips, Mr. Hovey, and Miss Holley and Miss P[hillips] have spent it with us,—could it fail to be a happy one? Mr. Phillips is the most fascinating person I ever saw. That graceful affability which characterizes the truly great, he embodies, with all that is truly good and noble. Mr. Hovey is exceedingly entertaining. He has travelled much; and presented Mrs. R[emond] with a precious relic—a piece of mosaic pavement from the Baths of Caracalla, Rome, built sixteen hundred years ago. How strange it seems that sixteen centuries ago this stone was laid—almost incredible! While gazing on such relics a strange influence from the mighty, mysterious Past comes over us—conjuring up visions of that olden time, long past, but never to be forgotten; for the soul of man rests not in the *Present*, nor soars only in the great *Future*, which imagination paints for it, but also does it love to dwell in the deep, soul-stirring memories of the Past. Mr. Phillips' lecture was worthy of himself—I can bestow no higher praise upon it. Oh! it is a source of some consolation to feel—to know that some of the noblest minds—the greatest intellects of the age are enlisted in our behalf.—

Friday, Nov. 1. This evening heard Charles Sumner for the first time. He said many excellent things, but I cannot agree with very many of his views—particularly with his reverence for the Constitution and the Union. I believe, though greatly mistaken he yet has a warm, true heart, and certainly he is an elegant and eloquent orator. Though very different from, and inferior to Mr. Phillips, in my opinion.—. . .

Sunday, Dec. 23. This evening had the very great pleasure of hearing dear Mr. May speak on anti-slavery. It was one of the best lectures I have ever heard. And I thanked him with my whole heart for the beautiful and well deserved tribute which he paid Mr. Garrison, who is so very greatly unappreciated and misrepresented. He compared him to the fountain in the Black Forest of Germany where the mighty Danube—the great "anti-slavery stream" has its source; and failed not to mention the numerous valuable tributaries who have contributed to its mass of waters—ever receiving a new impulse from the great Fountain Head. He had a large, and extremely attentive audience.—

Christmas Day, 1855. Alone; I do not know when I have been alone before on Christmas—never, I think.—Wrote a long letter to Aunt M[argaretta] while I was writing, Mrs. Gilliard came in and insisted on my accompanying her home. I spent part of the day and took dinner there. . . . Went to hear Ralph Waldo Emerson, who lectured on Beauty. I liked his originality, though his manner is not particularly interesting. Altogether we were much pleased with the lecture.

Sunday, Dec. 30. Yesterday, Mrs. Remond, who has been attending the Boston Bazaar, came home. . . . Heard read, and read partly myself—"Caste" which is an interesting anti-slavery, anti-prejudice story.

This evening listened to an excellent lecture before our Society, from Mr. Frothingham. . . .

Sunday, Jan. 27 [1856]. (Wrote a hymn for examination.) The last few weeks have been but successions of constant study, with but little variation. I have heard but one lecture—that of Mr. Parker,—which was, of course, excellent. His subject was the "Productive Industry of the Age" and he contrasted it with the military achievements of the "olden time"; and strikingly showed the beneficial effects of the industry of our age. Every time I listen to this wonderful man, I become more deeply impressed with the magnificence of his intellect and the sincere goodness and nobleness of his heart. This evening Mr. Hodges gave us a very good anti-slavery lecture. For the first time Mrs. Remond was obliged to introduce the lecturer it was a great trial to her, but she did it well ne'ertheless. . . .

Saturday, Feb. 2. This evening our beloved Mr. Garrison and his wife arrived.—Most gladly did we welcome them. The Remonds and Putnams spent the evening with us, and we had a delightful time. Mr. Garrison was very genial as he always is, and sang delightfully.

Sunday, Feb. 3. This has been one of the happiest days of my life. More and more do I love and admire that great and good man. His wife is a lovely woman; it is indeed delightful to see so happy and noble a couple. This evening Mr. Garrison gave us one of the best lectures I ever heard him deliver. Always interesting to me, to-night he was unusually entertaining. Just before the lecture Mr. Innis announced the fact of Mr. Banks' election, which was received with tumultuous applause. Mr. G[arrison] spoke beautifully of the "*Banks* of Massachusetts impeding the onward progress of the waves of southern despotism."—

Monday, Feb. 4. This morning Mr. and Mrs. G[arrison] left. They kindly invited me to pay them a visit, which I will be glad to do. This was the first time they have stayed with us since I have been here. And the pleasure, the very great pleasure which I experienced from their visit, will prevent me from soon forgetting it.—

Friday, Feb. 8. Next week we shall have our examination. I dread it, and do most heartily wish it was over!

Tuesday, Feb. 12. The last day of our examination. Thank Heaven it is over at last! I am completely tired out, and need rest, both in body and mind. We have got along very well—I could say pleasantly on the last afternoon, were it not for a few unpleasant remarks of Mr. Russell. The best way is to forget them as soon as possible. The exercises of the graduating class, on this afternoon were very interesting.

Wednesday, Feb. 13. I should be sorry that we have vacation were it not that I need rest. This morning Mr. R[emond] left for Phila[del-phia]. I felt very anxious to go, but it was impossible. We met at the school house, and formed a Normal Association. . . .

Saturday, Mar. 1. . . . I would gladly go out and enjoy to the full the clear, bracing air and the bright sunlight; but I was *wise* enough to take a severe cold and must pay the penalty by keeping a close prisoner on this delightful day. I have just heard that my beloved friend Miss Shepard is much better, and I feel better and happier for knowing it. A few evenings since attended a pleasant surprise party at Mrs. P[ut-nam]'s. Several of the company were dressed as ladies of the olden time, and very comical they looked in short skirts, high-heeled shoes, huge collars, and combs which are miniature steeples. I was persuaded to dress in full Bloomer costume, which I have since had good cause to regret, however. . . .

Thursday, March 6. Received a long and pleasant letter from Sarah Brown. I was very glad to hear from her, and shall send her some anti-slavery tracts when I write. She is a most agreeable and good-hearted girl, interested in anti-slavery; but I do most earnestly hope to see her more so.—

Monday, Mar. 10. This evening went to see 'Hamlet.' It is the first play of Shakespeare's that I [have] ever seen and I enjoyed it very much. I suppose if I had ever seen any better acting than Mr. Marshall's I should not have been so much pleased. The tragedy I have always liked very much; and many parts of it are as familiar as household words.—

Tuesday, Mar. 11. Went to hear the Misses Hall—the 'Singing Sisters.' They sang very sweetly. One of them has a particularly fine voice.—On returning home found a very old friend of our family,—Mr. Coffin,—the former teacher of my father and uncles. I have seldom met any one who possessed such extensive and varied knowledge, and yet from his perfectly unassuming, and perhaps unrefined manner, a stranger would never suspect it. He is exceedingly entertaining, and, as I know him to be a radical abolitionist I like him very much. His daughter has just entered our Normal School. . . .

Sunday, March 16. . . . To-day we had our election for those who are to write our poem, valedictory, and dissertation. Miss Pitman was chosen to write the dissertation; Lizzie Church the valedictory, and my unworthy self to write the poem; I most respectfully declined, but every one insists upon my doing it; so I suppose I must make the attempt. But it is a most formidable undertaking for me, and one which, I greatly fear, is quite beyond my powers. . . .

Wednesday, April 2. This afternoon I had a long conversation with Mr. Edwards. He spoke very kindly to me, far more so than I deserve, and urged me to come back next term. When I very earnestly assured him that it was quite impossible, he asked me why in such a manner that I could not avoid telling him frankly. He said he would see if something could not be done. I said nothing, but I know too well that nothing *can* be done. Indeed though I very much wish to spend another term here, I desire nothing so much as some employment which shall enable me to pay my debts.—I hope I shall be fortunate enough to obtain some situation as a teacher. . . .

Saturday, May 11. All day I have been worrying about that poem. That troublesome poem which has yet to be commenced. Oh! that I could become suddenly inspired and write as only great poets can write. Or that I might write a beautiful poem of two hundred lines in my sleep as Coleridge did. Alas! in vain are all such longings. I must depend upon *myself* alone. And what can that self produce? Nothing, nothing but *doggerel!* This evening read Plutarch's Lycurgus.

Friday, May 24. To-day Mr. Purvis arrived. I think he looks poorly. Felt glad to see him. We have vacation this week instead of next, for which I am sorry, because next week the Boston meetings take place.

Wednesday, May 29. Went up to Boston this afternoon with Mr. Purvis, Mrs. P[urvis] and Miss L[ucy] R[emond]. We went to the Pillsbury Festival, which was a very brilliant and successful one. . . . Excellent speeches were made by our best speakers. Mr. P[hillips] was as usual eloquent and fascinating. Mr. Pillsbury spoke for a little while with deep feeling; his health is not entirely restored. I like him much. Had the happiness of seeing Mrs. Chapman for the first time. I think her the most beautiful woman I ever saw. Also the very great pleasure of seeing Mrs. Chase of R[hode] I[sland] to whom I wrote applying for the situation of governess. Her reply was a *very* kind letter. I love her for it. She is a lovely looking woman, I shall be glad to have such a friend. . . .

✿　✿　✿

. . . *Tuesday Night.* T'was a strange sight as our boat approached the landing at Hilton Head. On the wharf was a motley assemblage,— soldiers, officers, and "contrabands" of every hue and size. They were mostly black, however, and certainly the most dismal specimens I ever saw. H[ilton] H[ead] looks like a very desolate place; just a long low, sandy point running out into the sea with no visible dwellings upon it but the soldiers' white roofed tents.

Thence, after an hour's delay, during which we signed a paper, which was virtually taking the oath of allegiance, we left the "United States," most rocking of rockety propellers,—and took a steamboat for Beaufort. On board the boat was General Saxton to whom we were introduced. I like his face exceedingly. And his manners were very courteous and affable. He looks like a thoroughly *good* man.—From H[ilton] H[ead] to B[eaufort] the same low long line of sandy shore bordered by trees. Almost the only object of interest to me were the remains of an old Huguenot Fort, built many, many years ago.

Arrived at B[eaufort] we found that we had yet not reached our home. Went to Mr. French's, and saw there Reuben T[omlinson], whom I was very glad to meet, and Mrs. Gage, who seemed to be in rather a dismal state of mind. B[eaufort] looks like a pleasant place. The houses are large and quite handsome, built in the usual Southern style with verandahs around them, and beautiful trees. One magnolia tree in Mr. F[rench's] yard is splendid,—quite as large as some of our large shade trees, and, with the most beautiful foliage, a dark rich glossy green.

Went into the Commissary's Office to wait for the boat which was to take us to St. Helena's Island which is about six miles from B[eaufort]. T'is here that Miss Towne has her school, in which I am to teach, and that Mr. Hunn will have his store. While waiting in the Office we saw several military gentleman [*sic*], *not* very creditable specimens, I sh'ld say. The little Commissary himself . . . is a perfect little popinjay, and he and a Colonel somebody who didn't look any too sensible, talked in a very smart manner, evidently for our especial benefit. The word "nigger" was plentifully used, whereupon I set them down at once as not gentleman [*sic*]. Then they talked a great deal about rebel attacks and yellow fever, and other alarming things, with significant nods and looks at each other. We saw through them at once, and were not at all alarmed by any of their representations. But if they are a fair example of army officers, I sh'ld pray to see as little of them as possible.

To my great joy found that we were to be rowed by a crew of negro boatmen. Young Mr. F[rench] whom I like—accompanied us, while Mr. H[unn] went with a flat to get our baggage. The row was delightful. It was just at sunset—a grand Southern sunset; and the gorgeous clouds of crimson and gold were reflected in the waters below, which were smooth and calm as a mirror. Then, as we glided along, the rich sonorous tones of the boatmen broke upon the evening stillness. Their singing impressed me much. It was so sweet and strange and solemn. "Roll, Jordan, Roll" was grand, and another

> *"Jesus make de blind to see*
> *Jesus make de deaf to hear*
> *"   "   " cripple walk*
> *Walk in, dear Jesus,"*

and the refrain

> *"No man can hender me."*

It was very, very impressive. I want to hear these men sing Whittier's "Song of the Negro Boatmen." I am going to see if it can't be brought about in some way.

It was nearly dark when we reached St. Helena's, where we found Miss T[owne]'s carriage awaiting us, and then we three and our driver, had a long drive along the lonely roads in the dark night. How easy it w'ld have been for a band of guerillas—had any chanced that way—to seize and hang us. But we feared nothing of the kind. We were in a jubilant state of mind and sang "John Brown" with a will as we drove through the pines and palmettos. Arrived at the Superintendent's house we were kindly greeted by him and the ladies and shown into a lofty *ceilinged* parlor where a cheerful wood fire glowed in the grate, and we soon began to feel quite at home in the very heart of Rebeldom; only that I do not at all realize yet that we are in S[outh] C[arolina]. It is all a strange wild dream, from which I am constantly expecting to awake. But I can write no more now. I am tired, and still feel the motion of the ship in my poor head. Good night, dear A!

Wednesday, Oct. 29. A lovely day, but rather cool, I sh'ld think, for the "sunny South." The ship still seals [*sic*] in my head, and everything is most unreal, yet I went to drive. We drove to Oaklands, our future home. It is very pleasantly situated, but the house is in rather a dilapidated condition, as are most of the houses here, and the and the [*sic*] yard and garden have a neglected look, when it is cleaned up, and the house made habitable I think it will be quite a pleasant place. There are some lovely roses growing there and quantities of ivy creeping along the ground, even under the house, in wild luxuriance.—The negroes on the place are very kind and polite. I think I shall get on amicably with them.

❄   ❄   ❄

[*Monday, July 6, 1863*] . . . After school, though very tired, did not neglect my invitation to tea with the officers of the 54th. Drove down to Land's End. . . . Met Col. G[illmore] who went with us. Were just in time to see the Dress Parade. Tis a splendid looking reg[iment] —an honor to the race. Then we went with Col. Shaw to tea. Afterward sat outside the tent, and listened to some very fine singing from some of the privates. Their voices blended beautifully. "Jubilo" is one of the best things I've heard lately.

I am more than ever charmed with the noble little Col. [Shaw]. What purity, what nobleness of soul, what exquisite gentleness in that beautiful face! As I look at it I think "The bravest are the tenderest." I can imagine what he must be to his mother. May his life be spared to her! Yesterday at the celebration he stood, leaning against our carriage and speaking of mother, so lovingly, so tenderly. He said he wished she c'ld be there. If the reg[iment] were going to be stationed there for some time he sh'ld send for her. "But you know," he said "we might be suddenly ordered away, and then she w'ld have nobody to take care of her." I do think he is a wonderfully lovable person. To-night, he helped me on my horse, and after carefully arranging the folds of my riding skirt, said, so kindly, "Good-bye. If I don't see you again down here I hope to see you at our house." But I hope I shall have the pleasure of seeing him many times even down here. He and his men are eager to be called into active service.

Major H[allowell] rode with L[izzie] and me to Col. G[illmore]'s tent. . . . The rest of the party played whist till a very late hour but I was thoroughly exhausted. Lay down part of the time. And part of the time sat close to the water's edge, and watched the boats, and the gleaming lights over the water, and the rising moon. A deep peace was over everything—not a sound to be heard but the low, musical murmur of the waves as they kissed the shore.

Wednesday, July 8. Mr. T[omlinson] came over and drove down to Land's End for Lieut. [James] W[alton] who is still quite ill. The reg[iment] has gone. Left this morning. My heart-felt prayers go with them —for the men and for their noble, noble young Colonel. God bless him! God keep him in His care, and grant that his men may do nobly and prove themselves worthy of him!

Monday, July 20. For nearly two weeks we have waited, oh how anxiously for news of our reg[iment] which went, we know to Morris Is[land] to take part in the attack on Charleston. To-night comes news, oh, so sad, so heart sickening. It is too terrible, too terrible to write. We can only hope it may not all be true. That our noble, beautiful young Colonel is killed, and the reg[iment] cut to pieces! I cannot, cannot believe it. And yet I know it may be so. But oh, I am stunned, sick at heart. I can scarcely write. There was an attack on Fort Wagner. The 54th put in advance; fought bravely, desperately, but was finally overpowered and driven back after getting into the Fort. Thank Heaven! they fought bravely! And oh, I still must hope that our colonel, *ours* especially he seems to me, is not killed. But I can write no more to-night.

Beaufort, July 21. Came to town to-day hearing that nurses were sadly needed. Went to Mrs. L[ander]'s. Found Col. H[igginson] and

Dr. R[ogers] there. Mrs. L[ander] was sure I sh'ld not be able to endure the fatigues of hospital life even for a few days, but I thought
differently, and the Col. and Dr. were both on my side. So at last Mrs.
L[ander] consented and made arrangements for my entering one of
the hospitals to-morrow.

It is sad to see the Col. [T. W. Higginson] at all feeble. He is usually
so very strong and vigorous. He is going North next week. The Dr.
[Seth Rogers] is looking very ill. He is quite exhausted. I shall not feel
at peace until he is safe in his northern home. The attachment between
these two is beautiful, both are so thoroughly good and noble. And
both have the rarest charm of manner.

Wednesday, July 22.   My hospital life began to-day. Went early this
morning with Mrs. L[ander] and Mrs. G[?], the Surgeon's wife, saw
that the Dr. had not finished dressing the wounds, and while I waited
below Mrs. [Rufus] S[axton] gave me some sewing to do—mending
the pantaloons and jackets of the poor fellows. (They are all of the
54th) It was with a full heart that I sewed up bullet holes and bayonet
cuts. Sometimes I found a jacket that told a sad tale—so torn to pieces
that it was far past mending. After awhile I went through the wards.
As I passed along I thought "Many and low are the pallets, but each
is the face of a friend." And I was surprised to see such cheerful faces
looking up from the beds. Talked a little with some of the patients and
assisted Mrs. G. in distributing medicines. Mrs. L[ander] kindly sent
her carriage for me and I returned home, weary, but far more pleasantly impressed than I had thought possible, with hospital life.

Thursday, July 23.   Said farewell to Col. H[igginson] who goes
North in the Arago to-day. Am very sorry that Dr. R[ogers] c'ld not go
with him, not having been able to get his papers. He is looking so ill.
It makes me very anxious. He goes to Seaside for a few days. I hope the
change, and Mrs. H[unn]'s kind care will do him good.

Took a more thorough survey of the hospital to-day. It is a large new
brick building—quite close to the water,—two-storied, many win-
dowed, and very airy—in every way well adapted for a hospital.

Yesterday I was employed part of the time in writing letters for the
men. It was pleasant to see the brave, cheerful, uncomplaining spirit
which they all breathed. Some of the poor fellows had come from the
far west—even as far as Michigan. Talked with them much to-day.
Told them that we had heard that their noble Colonel [Shaw] was not
dead, but had been taken prisoner by the rebels. How joyfully their
wan faces lighted up! They almost started from their couches as the
hope entered their souls. Their attachment to their gallant young colonel is beautiful to see. How warmly, how enthusiastically they speak
of him. "He was one of the best little men in the world," they said.
"No one c'ld be kinder to a set of men than he was to us." Brave grateful hearts! I hope they will ever prove worthy of such a leader. And

God grant that he may indeed be living. But I fear, I greatly fear it may be but a false report.

One poor fellow here interests me greatly. He is very young, only nineteen, comes from Michigan. He is very badly wounded—in both legs, and there is a ball—in the stomach—it is thought that it cannot be extracted. This poor fellow suffers terribly. His groans are pitiful to hear. But he utters no complaint, and it is touching to see his gratitude for the least kindness that one does him. Mrs. G[?] asked him if he w'ld like her to write to his home. But he said no. He was an only son, and had come away against his mother's will. He w'ld not have her written to until he was better. Poor fellow! that will never be in this world.

Another, a Sergeant, suffers great pain, being badly wounded in the leg. But he too lies perfectly patient and uncomplaining. He has such a good, honest face. It is pleasant to look at it—although it is black. He is said to be one of the best and bravest men in the regiment.

When I went in this morning and found my patients so cheerful some of them even quite merry, I tho't it c'ld not be possible that they were badly wounded. Many, indeed have only flesh wounds. But there are others—and they among the most uncomplaining—who are severely wounded;—some dangerously so. Brave fellows! I feel it a happiness, an honor, to do the slightest service for them. True they were unsuccessful in the attack on Fort Wagner. But that was no fault of theirs. It is the testimony of all that they fought bravely as man can fight, and that it was only when completely overwhelmed by superior numbers that they were driven back.

Friday, July 24. To-day the news of Col. Shaw's death is confirmed. There can no longer be any doubt. It makes me sad, sad at heart. They say he sprang upon the parapet of the fort and cried "Onward, my brave boys, onward"; then fell, pierced with wounds. I know it was a glorious death. But oh, it is hard, very hard for the young wife, so late a bride, for the invalid mother, whose only and most dearly loved son he was,—that heroic mother who rejoiced in the position which he occupied as colonel of a colored regiment. My heart bleeds for her. His death is a very sad loss to us. I recall him as a much loved friend. Yet I saw him but a few times. Oh what must it be to the wife and the mother. Oh it is terrible. It seems very, very hard that the best and the noblest must be the earliest called away. Especially has it been so throughout this dreadful war. . . .

Accommodation and Protest

1865-1910

3

The North's military victory in the Civil War did not bring about change in ways change was expected. Malice remained, not exorcised by President Lincoln's splendid words; charity, which he prayed for, did not appear. Between the agrarian-gentleman, whose ingrained attitudes and habits of mind dominated Southern thought, and the industrialist-banker, whose money power determined Northern polity, bitterness was not relieved. In fact, it was intensified, and the tide of enmity was freshened by the Reconstruction Act of 1867, for which Northerners were held largely responsible. North and South, Negroes were caught in that tide. Their situation was not new, nor was their reaction.

In the South, American blacks were still subject to the whims of the white world. A few blacks benefited from the activities of the Freedmen's Bureau, which helped to ease the transition from slavery to freedom; and a few were privileged to attend Yankee missionary schools, which were built somewhat less quickly than they were burned down by Southern whites who opposed education for former slaves. It is true that between 1869 and 1874 Southern Negroes did vote in sufficient strength to have influence in some state legislatures and to send sixteen fellow blacks to the national Congress. But the terrorist activities of the Ku Klux Klan and other groups brought an effective end to Negro voting even before federal troops, charged with protecting the right to vote, were withdrawn.

Negroes in the North fared scarcely better. Few could afford schooling, even where free schools were provided—and they were not provided everywhere until the end of the century. Jobs were difficult to get and keep, for there was increasing competition with whites, who often mobbed black workers. Although the right to vote was generally acknowledged, few blacks were sophisticated enough to see the value of exercising that right.

The great majority of Negroes in both the North and the South accepted segregation and discrimination, believing, as Booker T. Washington persuaded them to believe, that as they approached the white world's standards, they would win the white world's tolerance, and "things" would be better.

A handful of Negroes protested. As their eloquent spokesman W. E. B. Du Bois wrote, "We demand every single right that belongs to a free born American, political, civil, and social; and until we get

121

these rights we will never cease to protest and assail the ears of America."

An infinitesimal number of Negroes reacted to the conditions of Negro life by trying to escape them.

While the imaginative writing of the period sets forth these attitudes and reactions symbolically, polemical writing states them straightforwardly. Between 1865 and 1910, twelve black authors published twenty-seven volumes of fiction, ten wrote more than five hundred poems, and a half dozen found an audience for a number of essays.

Charles W. Chesnutt, the first Negro novelist of imposing stature, published three novels and two volumes of short stories. With the exception of his earliest stories, which began appearing in the *Atlantic Monthly* in 1887 and were later collected under the title *The Conjure Woman,* all of his work is in the protest tradition. Chesnutt's special theme was the Negro of mixed blood, the "tragic mulatto": he was the first black author to deal in depth with the problem of the "color line" within the Negro race, and the first to make imaginative capital of racism's consequences to the white man. In *The Marrow of Tradition* and *The Colonel's Dream,* which were both constructed around incidents from real life, Chesnutt's artistic control occasionally slips, and he makes didactic digressions that interrupt the story and add nothing to the theme. His short stories are free of this fault, and so is *The House Behind the Cedars,* his first novel, and his best.

None of the fiction of Paul Laurence Dunbar matches the best of Charles Chesnutt. Dunbar was lacking in both artistic integrity and philosophic depth. He followed popular romantic trends. He accommodated. He tried to escape. Three of his four novels neither deal with racial themes nor present blacks as major characters. Dunbar's best novel, *The Sport of the Gods,* begins as a realistic depiction of Negro life in New York but finally becomes a commitment to the Southern white apologist's point of view. Indeed, it might have been written by Thomas Nelson Page or Maurice Thompson, both of whom were widely read Southern apologists.

While Dunbar's prose fiction was popular in his own time, it is his dialect poetry for which he is best known today. His poetry, of course, did no violence to the acceptable notions of Negro life and character or mind and spirit. The widely held opinion of Dunbar the poet was best expressed by William Dean Howells, who was probably the most highly regarded of contemporary critics: "In nothing is [Dunbar's] essentially refined and delicate art so well shown as in those pieces, which . . . *describe the range between appetite and emotion . . . which is the range of the race. He reveals in these a finely ironic perception of the Negro's limitations. . . .*" (italics added). Dunbar must have had this judgment in mind when, just prior to his death at the age of thirty-four, he wrote the lines that might very well have served as his epitaph:

> He sang of love when life was young,
> And Love itself was in his lays,
> But Ah, the world, it turned to praise
> A jingle in a broken tongue.

Sutton Griggs was a prolific and historically important novelist. Although he had more integrity (and less talent) than Dunbar, he nevertheless vacillated between accommodation and militant protest, and his work reveals the ambivalence of many Negro intellectuals during that troubled period. *Imperium in Imperio*, for instance, advocates militant black nationalism, while *Unfettered* and *Pointing the Way* recommend an alliance between "upper class" blacks and bourbon whites. Griggs, like Chesnutt, was opposed to poor whites. Because this was the one attitude from which he did not waver, his novels, whatever their story lines and themes, are bitter attacks upon the white poor—those "misguided souls [who] said and did all things, which [they] deemed necessary to leave behind . . . the greatest heritage of hatred the world has ever known."

There was little propaganda in the poetry of the time, and hard-line protest was out. Some poets have been designated as mockingbirds. Albery Whitman was one of these: he was by turns a "black Longfellow," a "black Byron," a "black Spenser." Lacking originality, Whitman's work was not truly significant, and he is remembered only for his versatility and for having composed the longest poem ever written by a Negro, "Not a Man and Yet a Man."

A small host of other poets were imitators too, but they imitated the dialect poetry of Paul Dunbar. James Edwin Campbell and Daniel Webster Davis were fairly good as imitators, and Davis' only collection, *Wey Down Souf*, bears comparison with Dunbar's *Candle-Ligh'ing Time*. J. Mord Allen's *Rhymes, Tales and Rhymed Tales* are noteworthy only in that they prove him more industrious than most of his contemporaries. Not much can be said for John Wesley Holloway's *From the Desert;* or for either of Ray Garfield Dandridge's two slim volumes, *Zalka Petruzza and Other Poems* and *The Poet and Other Poems*. George Marion McClellan refused to write dialect poetry. James D. Corrothers was probably the first American black poet to pursue African themes.

The best non-dialect poet of the period was William Stanley Braithwaite. Proud of his yearly anthologies of magazine verse, and of his position as a staff writer on the Boston *Transcript*, Braithwaite rejected the fact of his Negroness. In his autobiography, *The House of*

Falling Leaves, he wrote, "I am descended from a long line of English gentlemen." And this was true enough, if one considered only his father's line of descent; his mother was a West Indian Negro. As a poet, Braithwaite was a Pre-Raphaelite, and his work was haunting, mystical, romantic.

Certain autobiographical works and other prose pieces bridge the emotional gap between the pre-Civil War slave narratives and the racial apostasy of Braithwaite. An example of this type of literature is Elizabeth Keckley's *Behind the Scenes; or, Thirty Years a Slave, and Four Years in the White House.* John M. Langston, who was briefly Dean of the Law School at the all-Negro Howard University and even more briefly a member of Congress, wrote *From a Virginia Plantation to the National Capital* as a declaration of pride in his race. Then there is *Up From Slavery.* If certain of its episodes are suspect, its spirit and thrust are not. If Booker Washington lied and accommodated, he did so for a cause, and the cause was Negro advancement. This was also Frederick Douglass' cause, and his *Life and Times,* which was published in its final version in 1892, states it eloquently.

Two black historians deserve mention. Associated with Garrison on *The Liberator* and with Douglass on *The North Star,* William C. Nell was encouraged by John Greenleaf Whittier to do historical research. *The Colored Patriots of the American Revolution* is a work of careful scholarship and the first historical study by a Negro to deserve the respect of the academic community. But *The Colored Patriots* was twice surpassed by George Washington Williams' books, *History of the Negro Race in America from 1619 to 1880* and *A History of the Negro Troops in the War of the Rebellion,* which are still used as source books by reputable academic historians.

William Still

(1821–1902)

ALTHOUGH WILLIAM STILL'S PARENTS were both slaves, they escaped separately from Maryland, and their son was born free in Burlington County, New Jersey. As a young man William Still became a clerk in the office of the Philadelphia Anti-Slavery Society. In this capacity he met and helped hundreds of Negroes who were fleeing to the North and freedom via the Underground Railroad. One of the fugitives was his own brother, Peter Still, who had escaped from Alabama. (Peter Still is the subject in Mrs. Kate Pickard's biography, *The Kidnapped and the Ransomed.*)

Realizing the historical importance of the information brought to him by escaped slaves, William Still decided to keep a record of the experiences told to him by his passengers on the Underground. He worked late at night and at odd hours, writing down all the facts and anecdotes that he could reconstruct. Because he realized that these records could be dangerous, Still stored them in the loft of a cemetery building. Although collected between 1850 and 1860, they were not published until 1872, when they appeared in a 780-page volume with the explicit and exhaustive title: *The Underground Rail Road. A Record of Facts, Authentic Narratives, Letters, etc., Narrating the Hardships, Hair-Breadth Escapes and Death Struggles of the Slaves in Their Efforts for Freedom as Related by Themselves, and Others, or Witnessed by the Author; Together with Sketches of Some of the Largest Stockholders, and Most Liberal Aiders and Advisers of the Road.*

A unique publication, *The Underground Rail Road* is a rich storehouse of intimate and detailed information about slavery. Its subjects —escaped slaves, abolitionists, and foiled masters—are a fascinating group. Dramatic, sensational, occasionally tragic, the work, though factual, has the appeal of swiftly moving fiction.

In order to continue collecting and preserving data on the Negro, in 1861 William Still organized a "social, civil, and statistical association," which was an early forerunner of Carter G. Woodson's Association for the Study of Negro Life and History. In 1880 Still established one of the earlier YMCA branches for Negroes.

The following selections have been taken from *The Underground Rail Road.*

WILLIAM AND ELLEN CRAFT

*FEMALE SLAVE IN MALE ATTIRE, FLEEING AS A PLANTER,
WITH HER HUSBAND AS HER BODY SERVANT*

A quarter of a century ago, William and Ellen Craft were slaves in the State of Georgia. With them, as with thousands of others, the desire to be free was very strong. For this jewel they were willing to make any sacrifice, or to endure any amount of suffering. In this state of mind they commenced planning. After thinking of various ways that might be tried, it occurred to William and Ellen, that one might act the part of master and the other the part of servant.

Ellen being fair enough to pass for white, of necessity would have to be transformed into a young planter for the time being. All that was needed, however, to make this important change was that she should be dressed elegantly in a fashionable suit of male attire, and have her hair cut in the style usually worn by young planters. Her profusion of dark hair offered a fine opportunity for the change. So far this plan looked very tempting. But it occurred to them that Ellen was beardless. After some mature reflection, they came to the conclusion that this difficulty could be very readily obviated by having the face muffled up as though the young planter was suffering badly with the face or toothache; thus they got rid of this trouble. Straightway, upon further reflection, several other very serious difficulties stared them in the face. For instance, in traveling, they knew that they would be under the necessity of stopping repeatedly at hotels, and that the custom of registering would have to be conformed to, unless some very good excuse could be given for not doing so.

Here they again thought much over matters, and wisely concluded that the young man had better assume the attitude of a gentleman very much indisposed. He must have his right arm placed carefully in a sling; that would be a sufficient excuse for not registering, etc. Then he must be a little lame, with a nice cane in the left hand; he must have large green spectacles over his eyes, and withal he must be very hard of hearing and dependent on his faithful servant (as was no uncommon thing with slave-holders), to look after all his wants.

William was just the man to act this part. To begin with, he was very "likely-looking;" smart, active and exceedingly attentive to his young master—indeed he was almost eyes, ears, hands and feet for him. William knew that this would please the slave-holders. The young planter would have nothing to do but hold himself subject to his ailments and put on a bold air of superiority; he was not to deign to notice anybody. If, while traveling, gentlemen, either politely or rudely, should venture to scrape acquaintance with the young planter, in his deafness he was to remain mute; the servant was to explain. In every instance when this occurred, as it actually did, the servant was fully equal to the emergency—none dreaming of the disguises in which the Underground Rail Road passengers were traveling.

They stopped at a first-class hotel in Charleston, where the young planter and his body servant were treated, as the house was wont to treat the chivalry. They stopped also at a similar hotel in Richmond, and with like results.

They knew that they must pass through Baltimore, but they did not know the obstacles that they would have to surmount in the Monumental City. They proceeded to the depot in the usual manner, and the servant asked for tickets for his master and self. Of course the master could have a ticket, but "bonds will have to be entered before you can get a ticket," said the ticket master. "It is the rule of this office to require bonds for all negroes applying for tickets to go North, and none but gentlemen of well-known responsibility will be taken," further explained the ticket master.

The servant replied, that he knew "nothing about that"—that he was "simply traveling with his young master to take care of him—he being in a very delicate state of health, so much so, that fears were entertained that he might not be able to hold out to reach Philadelphia, where he was hastening for medical treatment," and ended his reply by saying, "my master can't be detained." Without further parley, the ticket master very obligingly waived the old "rule," and furnished the requisite tickets. The mountain being thus removed, the young planter and his faithful servant were safely in the cars for the city of Brotherly Love.

Scarcely had they arrived on free soil when the rheumatism departed—the right arm was unslung—the toothache was gone—the beardless face was unmuffled—the deaf heard and spoke—the blind saw—and the lame leaped as an hart, and in the presence of a few astonished friends of the slave, the facts of this unparalleled Underground Rail Road feat were fully established by the most unquestionable evidence.

The constant strain and pressure on Ellen's nerves, however, had tried her severely, so much so, that for days afterwards, she was physically very much prostrated, although joy and gladness beamed from her eyes, which bespoke inexpressible delight within.

Never can the writer forget the impression made by their arrival. Even now, after a lapse of nearly a quarter of a century, it is easy to picture them in a private room, surrounded by a few friends—Ellen in her fine suit of black, with her cloak and high-heeled boots, looking, in every respect, like a young gentleman; in an hour after having dropped her male attire, and assumed the habiliments of her sex the feminine only was visible in every line and feature of her structure.

Her husband, William, was thoroughly colored, but was a man of marked natural abilities, of good manners, and full of pluck, and possessed of perceptive faculties very large.

It was necessary, however, in those days, that they should seek a permanent residence, where their freedom would be more secure than in Philadelphia; therefore they were advised to go to headquarters, directly to Boston. There they would be safe, it was supposed, as it had then been about a generation since a fugitive had been taken back from the old Bay State, and through the incessant labors of William Lloyd Garrison, the great pioneer, and his faithful coadjutors, it was conceded that another fugitive slave case could never be tolerated on the free soil of Massachusetts. So to Boston they went.

On arriving, the warm hearts of abolitionists welcomed them heartily, and greeted and cheered them without let or hindrance. They did not pretend to keep their coming a secret, or hide it under a bushel; the story of their escape was heralded broadcast over the country— North and South, and indeed over the civilized world. For two years or more, not the slightest fear was entertained that they were not just as safe in Boston as if they had gone to Canada. But the day the Fugitive Bill passed, even the bravest abolitionist began to fear that a fugitive slave was no longer safe anywhere under the stars and stripes, North or South, and that William and Ellen Craft were liable to be captured at any moment by Georgia slave hunters. Many abolitionists counselled resistance to the death at all hazards. Instead of running to Canada, fugitives generally armed themselves and thus said, "Give me liberty or give me death."

William and Ellen Craft believed that it was their duty, as citizens of Massachusetts, to observe a more legal and civilized mode of conforming to the marriage rite than had been permitted them in slavery, and as Theodore Parker had shown himself a very warm friend of their's, they agreed to have their wedding over again according to the laws of a free State. After performing the ceremony, the renowned and fearless advocate of equals rights (Theodore Parker), presented William with a revolver and a dirk-knife, couselling him to use them manfully in defence of his wife and himself, if ever an attempt should be made by his owners or anybody else to re-enslave them. . . .

HENRY BOX BROWN

ARRIVED BY ADAMS' EXPRESS

Although the name of Henry Box Brown has been echoed over the land for a number of years, and the simple facts connected with his marvelous escape from slavery in a box published widely through the medium of anti-slavery papers, nevertheless it is not unreasonable to suppose that very little is generally known in relation to this case.

Briefly, the facts are these, which doubtless have never before been fully published—

Brown was a man of invention as well as a hero. In point of interest, however, his case is no more remarkable than many others. Indeed, neither before nor after escaping did he suffer one-half what many others have experienced.

He was decidedly an unhappy piece of property in the city of Richmond, Va. In the condition of a slave he felt that it would be impossible for him to remain. Full well did he know, however, that it was no holiday task to escape the vigilance of Virginia slave-hunters, or the wrath of an enraged master for committing the unpardonable sin of attempting to escape to a land of liberty. So Brown counted well the cost before venturing upon this hazardous undertaking. Ordinary modes of travel he concluded might prove disastrous to his hopes; he, therefore, hit upon a new invention altogether, which was to have himself boxed up and forwarded to Philadelphia direct by express. The size of the box and how it was to be made to fit him most comfortably, was of his own ordering. Two feet eight inches deep, two feet wide, and three feet long were the exact dimensions of the box, lined with baize. His resources with regard to food and water consisted of the following: One bladder of water and a few small biscuits. His mechanical implement to meet the death-struggle for fresh air, all told, was one large gimlet. Satisfied that it would be far better to peril his life for freedom in this way than to remain under the galling yoke of Slavery, he entered his box, which was safely nailed up and hooped with five hickory hoops, and was then addressed by his next friend, James A. Smith, a shoe dealer, to Wm. H. Johnson, Arch street, Philadelphia, marked, "This side up with care." In this condition he was sent to Adams' Express office in a dray, and thence by overland express to Philadelphia. It was twenty-six hours from the time he left Richmond until his arrival in the City of Brotherly Love. The notice, "This side up, &c.," did not avail with the different expressmen, who hesitated not to handle the box in the usual rough manner common to this class of men. For a while they actually had the box upside down, and had him on his head for miles. A few days before he was expected, certain intimation was conveyed to a member of the Vigilance Committee that a box might be expected by the three o'clock morning train from the South, which might contain a man. One of the most serious walks he ever took—and they had not been a few—to meet and accompany passengers, he took at half past two o'clock that morning to the depot. Not once, but for more than a score of times, he fancied the slave would be dead. He anxiously looked while the freight was being unloaded from the cars, to see if he could recognize a box that might contain a man; one alone had that appearance, and he confessed it really seemed as if there was the scent of death about it. But on inquiry, he soon learned that it was not the one he was looking after, and he was free to say he experienced a marked sense of relief.

That same afternoon, however, he received from Richmond a telegram, which read thus, "Your case of goods is shipped and will arrive to-morrow morning."

At this exciting juncture of affairs, Mr. McKim, who had been engineering this important undertaking, deemed it expedient to change the programme slightly in one particular at least to insure greater safety. Instead of having a member of the Committee go again to the depot for the box, which might excite suspicion, it was decided that it would be safest to have the express bring it direct to the Anti-Slavery Office.

But all apprehension of danger did not now disappear, for there was no room to suppose that Adams' Express office had any sympathy with the Abolitionist or the fugitive, consequently for Mr. McKim to appear personally at the express office to give directions with reference to the coming of a box from Richmond which would be directed to Arch street, and yet not intended for that street, but for the Anti-Slavery office at 107 North Fifth street, it needed of course no great discernment to foresee that a step of this kind was wholly impracticable and that a more indirect and covert method would have to be adopted. In this dreadful crisis Mr. McKim, with his usual good judgment and remarkably quick, strategical mind, especially in matters pertaining to the U. G. R. R., hit upon the following plan, namely, to go to his friend, E. M. Davis, who was then extensively engaged in mercantile business, and relate the circumstances. Having daily intercourse with said Adams' Express office, and being well acquainted with the firm and some of the drivers, Mr. Davis could, as Mr. McKim thought, talk about "boxes, freight, etc.," from any part of the country without risk. Mr. Davis heard Mr. McKim's plan and instantly approved of it, and was heartily at his service.

"Dan, an Irishman, one of Adams' Express drivers, is just the fellow to go to the depot after the box," said Davis. "He drinks a little too much whiskey sometimes, but he will do anything I ask him to do, promptly and obligingly. I'll trust Dan, for I believe he is the very man." The difficulty which Mr. McKim had been so anxious to overcome was thus pretty well settled. It was agreed that Dan should go after the box next morning before daylight and bring it to the Anti-Slavery office direct, and to make it all the more agreeable for Dan to get up out of his warm bed and go on this errand before day, it was decided that he should have a five dollar gold piece for himself. Thus these preliminaries having been satisfactorily arranged, it only remained for Mr. Davis to see Dan and give him instructions accordingly, etc.

Next morning, according to arrangement, the box was at the Anti-Slavery office in due time. The witnesses present to behold the resurrection were J. M. McKim, Professor C. D. Cleveland, Lewis Thompson, and the writer.

Mr. McKim was deeply interested; but having been long identified with the Anti-Slavery cause as one of its oldest and ablest advocates in the darkest days of slavery and mobs, and always found by the side of the fugitive to counsel and succor, he was on this occasion perfectly composed.

Professor Cleveland, however, was greatly moved. His zeal and earnestness in the cause of freedom, especially in rendering aid to passengers, knew no limit. Ordinarily he could not too often visit these travelers, shake them too warmly by the hand, or impart to them too freely of his substance to aid them on their journey. But now his emotion was overpowering.

Mr. Thompson, of the firm of Merrihew & Thompson—about the only printers in the city who for many years dared to print such incendiary documents as anti-slavery papers and pamphlets—one of the truest friends of the slave, was composed and prepared to witness the scene.

All was quiet. The door had been safely locked. The proceedings commenced. Mr. McKim rapped quietly on the lid of the box and called out, "All right!" Instantly came the answer from within, "All right, sir!"

The witnesses will never forget that moment. Saw and hatchet quickly had the five hickory hoops cut and the lid off, and the marvellous resurrection of Brown ensued. Rising up in his box, he reached out his hand, saying, "How do you do, gentlemen?" The little assemblage hardly knew what to think or do at the moment. He was about as wet as if he had come up out of the Delaware. Very soon he remarked that, before leaving Richmond he had selected for his arrival-hymn (if he lived) the Psalm beginning with these words: *"I waited patiently for the Lord, and He heard my prayer."* And most touchingly did he sing the psalm, much to his own relief, as well as to the delight of his small audience.

He was then christened Henry Box Brown, and soon afterwards was sent to the hospitable residence of James Mott and E. M. Davis, on Ninth street, where, it is needless to say, he met a most cordial reception from Mrs. Lucretia Mott and her household. Clothing and creature comforts were furnished in abundance, and delight and joy filled all hearts in that stronghold of philanthropy.

As he had been so long doubled up in the box he needed to promenade considerably in the fresh air, so James Mott put one of his broad-brim hats on his head and tendered him the hospitalities of his yard as well as his house, and while Brown promenaded the yard flushed with victory, great was the joy of his friends. . . .

Elizabeth Keckley

(1825–1905)

ELIZABETH KECKLEY WAS BORN a slave in Virginia and remained in bondage for thirty years, serving also in North Carolina and in St. Louis, Missouri. During her bondage in North Carolina, Elizabeth became the mistress of her owner and had a son by him. When she was young she learned the skills of a dressmaker, and with her trade Elizabeth earned enough money to buy freedom for herself and her son. This boy was a source of great pride for Mrs. Keckley; he attended Wilberforce University and served in the Civil War. When he died in battle, his mother was grief-stricken. Elizabeth Keckley was married for a short time, but the marriage was disappointing and unsuccessful.

Before the Civil War, Mrs. Keckley became a well-known and popular "Society" dressmaker in Washington, where she worked for such ladies as Mrs. Jefferson Davis, Mrs. Stephen A. Douglas, and Mrs. E. M. Stanton. For Mrs. Abraham Lincoln, Elizabeth was confidante and friend as well as dressmaker, the one to whom Mrs. Lincoln turned the night of her husband's assassination. To President Lincoln, Elizabeth was "Madame Keckley".

After the war, Mrs. Keckley served as "Director of Domestic Art" at Wilberforce. She died in Washington, D.C., and the scholarly Reverend Francis J. Grimké preached at her funeral.

Elizabeth Keckley's *Behind the Scenes; or, Thirty Years a Slave, and Four Years in the White House* (1868) belongs to Lincolniana as well as to Negro American Literature. When the authorship of the book was questioned, Reverend Grimké, among others, attested to its authenticity. (Mrs. Keckley freely acknowledged that her printer, G. W. Carleton, had corrected her grammar.) A vicious and crude parody entitled *Behind the Seams; by a Nigger Woman who took in Work from Mrs. Lincoln and Mrs. Davis* was published in New York, also in 1868. The preface was signed "Betsey (x) Kickley (Nigger)."

For additional information on Mrs. Keckley and other Negroes who knew Lincoln, see John E. Washington, *They Knew Lincoln* (New York: Dutton, 1942).

THE SECRET HISTORY OF MRS. LINCOLN'S WARDROBE IN NEW YORK

In March, 1867, Mrs. Lincoln wrote to me from Chicago that, as her income was insufficient to meet her expenses, she would be obliged to give up her house in the city, and return to boarding. She said that she had struggled long enough to keep up appearances, and that the mask must be thrown aside. "I have not the means," she wrote, "to meet the expenses of even a first-class boarding-house, and must sell out and secure cheap rooms at some place in the country. It will not be startling news to you, my dear Lizzie, to learn that I must sell a portion of my wardrobe to add to my resources, so as to enable me to live decently, for you remember what I told you in Washington, as well as what you understood before you left me here in Chicago. I cannot live on $1,700 a year, and as I have many costly things which I shall never wear, I might as well turn them into money, and thus add to my income, and make my circumstances easier. It is humiliating to be placed in such a position, but, as I am in the position, I must extricate myself as best I can. Now, Lizzie, I want to ask a favor of you. It is imperative that I should do something for my relief, and I want you to meet me in New York, between the 30th of August and the 5th of September next, to assist me in disposing of a portion of my wardrobe."

I knew that Mrs. Lincoln's income was small, and also knew that she had many valuable dresses, which could be of no value to her, packed away in boxes and trunks. I was confident that she would never wear the dresses again, and thought that, since her need was urgent, it would be well enough to dispose of them quietly, and believed that New York was the best place to transact a delicate business of the kind. She was the wife of Abraham Lincoln, the man who had done so much for my race, and I could refuse to do nothing for her, calculated to advance her interests. I consented to render Mrs. Lincoln all the assistance in my power, and many letters passed between us in regard to the best way to proceed. It was finally arranged that I should meet her in New York about the middle of September. While thinking over this question, I remembered an incident of the White House. When we were packing up to leave Washington for Chicago, she said to me, one morning:

"Lizzie, I may see the day when I shall be obliged to sell a portion of my wardrobe. If Congress does not do something for me, then my dresses some day may have to go to bring food into my mouth, and the mouths of my children."

I also remembered of Mrs. L. having said to me at different times, in the years of 1863 and '4, that her expensive dresses might prove of great assistance to her some day.

"In what way, Mrs. Lincoln? I do not understand," I ejaculated, the first time she made the remark to me.

"Very simple to understand. Mr. Lincoln is so generous that he will not save anything from his salary, and I expect that we will leave the White House poorer than when we came into it; and should such be the case, I will have no further need for an expensive wardrobe, and it will be policy to sell it off."

I thought at the time that Mrs. Lincoln was borrowing trouble from the future, and little dreamed that the event which she so dimly fore-shadowed would ever come to pass.

I closed my business about the 10th of September, and made every arrangement to leave Washington on the mission proposed. On the 15th of September I received a letter from Mrs. Lincoln, post-marked Chicago, saying that she should leave the city so as to reach New York on the night of the 17th, and directing me to precede her to the metropolis, and secure rooms for her at the St. Denis Hotel in the name of Mrs. Clarke, as her visit was to be *incog*. The contents of the letter were startling to me. I had never heard of the St. Denis, and therefore presumed that it could not be a first-class house. And I could not under-stand why Mrs. Lincoln should travel, without protection, under an assumed name. I knew that it would be impossible for me to engage rooms at a strange hotel for a person whom the proprietors knew noth-ing about. I could not write to Mrs. Lincoln, since she would be on the road to New York before a letter could possibly reach Chicago. I could not telegraph her, for the business was of too delicate a character to be trusted to the wires that would whisper the secret to every curious operator along the line. In my embarrassment, I caught at a slender thread of hope, and tried to derive consolation from it. I knew Mrs. Lincoln to be indecisive about some things, and I hoped that she might change her mind in regard to the strange programme proposed, and at the last moment despatch me to this effect. The 16th, and then the 17th of September passed, and no despatch reached me, so on the 18th I made all haste to take the train for New York. After an anxious ride, I reached the city in the evening, and when I stood alone in the streets of the great metropolis, my heart sank within me. I was in an embar-rassing situation, and scarcely knew how to act. I did not know where the St. Denis Hotel was, and was not certain that I should find Mrs. Lincoln there after I should go to it. I walked up to Broadway, and got into a stage going up town, with the intention of keeping a close look-out for the hotel in question. A kind-looking gentleman occupied the seat next to me, and I ventured to inquire of him:

"If you please, sir, can you tell me where the St. Denis Hotel is?"

"Yes; we ride past it in the stage. I will point it out to you when we come to it."

"Thank you, sir."

The stage rattled up the street, and after a while the gentleman looked out of the window and said:

"This is the St. Denis. Do you wish to get out here?"

"Thank you. Yes, sir."

He pulled the strap, and the next minute I was standing on the pavement. I pulled a bell at the ladies' entrance to the hotel, and a boy coming to the door, I asked:

"Is a lady by the name of Mrs. Clarke stopping here? She came last night, I believe."

"I do not know. I will ask at the office;" and I was left alone.

The boy came back and said:

"Yes, Mrs. Clarke is here. Do you want to see her?"

"Yes."

"Well, just walk round there. She is down here now."

I did not know where "round there" exactly was, but I concluded to go forward.

I stopped, however, thinking that the lady might be in the parlor with company; and pulling out a card, asked the boy to take it to her. She heard me talking, and came into the hall to see herself.

"My dear Lizzie, I am so glad to see you," she exclaimed, coming forward and giving me her hand. "I have just received your note"—I had written her that I should join her on the 18th—"and have been trying to get a room for you. Your note has been here all day, but it was never delivered until to-night. Come in here, until I find out about your room;" and she led me into the office.

The clerk, like all modern hotel clerks, was exquisitely arrayed, highly perfumed, and too self-important to be obliging, or even courteous.

"This is the woman I told you about. I want a good room for her," Mrs. Lincoln said to the clerk.

"We have no room for her, madam," was the pointed rejoinder.

"But she must have a room. She is a friend of mine, and I want a room for her adjoining mine."

"We have no room for her on your floor."

"That is strange, sir. I tell you that she is a friend of mine, and I am sure you could not give a room to a more worthy person."

"Friend of yours, or not, I tell you we have no room for her on your floor. I can find a place for her on the fifth floor."

"That, sir, I presume, will be a vast improvement on my room. Well, if she goes to the fifth floor, I shall go too, sir. What is good enough for her is good enough for me."

"Very well, madam. Shall I give you adjoining rooms, and send your baggage up?"

"Yes, and have it done in a hurry. Let the boy show us up. Come, Elizabeth," and Mrs. L. turned from the clerk with a haughty glance, and we commenced climbing the stairs. I thought we should never reach the top; and when we did reach the fifth story, what accommodations! Little three-cornered rooms, scantily furnished. I never expected to see the widow of President Lincoln in such dingy, humble quarters.

"How provoking!" Mrs. Lincoln exclaimed, sitting down on a chair when we had reached the top, and panting from the effects of the climbing. "I declare, I never saw such unaccommodating people. Just to think of them sticking us away up here in the attic. I will give them a regular going over in the morning."

"But you forget. They do not know you. Mrs. Lincoln would be treated differently from Mrs. Clarke."

"True, I do forget. Well, I suppose I shall have to put up with the annoyances. Why did you not come to me yesterday, Lizzie? I was almost crazy when I reached here last night, and found you had not arrived. I sat down and wrote you a note—I felt so badly—imploring you to come to me immediately."

This note was afterwards sent to me from Washington. It reads as follows:

> "*St. Denis Hotel, Broadway, N.Y.*
> "*Wednesday, Sept. 17th.*

"MY DEAR LIZZIE:—I arrived *here* last evening in utter despair *at not* finding you. I am frightened to death, being here alone. Come, I pray you, by *next* train. Inquire for

> "MRS. CLARKE,
> "*Room 94, 5th or 6th Story.*

"House so crowded could not get another spot. I wrote you especially to meet me here last evening; it makes me wild to think of being here alone. Come by *next train,* without fail.

> "Your friend,
> "MRS. LINCOLN.

"I am booked Mrs. Clarke; inquire for *no other person. Come, come, come.* I will pay your expenses when you arrive here. I shall not leave here or change my room until you come.

> "Your friend, M. L.

"Do not leave this house without seeing me.

> "*Come!*"

I transcribe the letter literally.

In reply to Mrs. Lincoln's last question, I explained what has already been explained to the reader, that I was in hope she would change her mind, and knew that it would be impossible to secure the rooms requested for a person unknown to the proprietors or attachés of the hotel.

The explanation seemed to satisfy her. Turning to me suddenly, she exclaimed:

"You have not had your dinner, Lizzie, and must be hungry. I nearly forgot about it in the joy of seeing you. You must go down to the table right away."

She pulled the bell-rope, and a servant appearing, she ordered him to give me my dinner. I followed him down-stairs, and he led me into the dining-hall, and seated me at a table in one corner of the room. I was giving my order, when the steward came forward and gruffly said:

"You are in the wrong room."

"I was brought here by the waiter," I replied.

"It makes no difference; I will find you another place where you can eat your dinner."

I got up from the table and followed him, and when outside of the door, said to him:

"It is very strange that you should permit me to be seated at the table in the dining-room only for the sake of ordering me to leave it the next moment."

"Are you not Mrs. Clarke's servant?" was his abrupt question.

"I am with Mrs. Clarke."

"It is all the same; servants are not allowed to eat in the large dining-room. Here, this way; you must take your dinner in the servants' hall."

Hungry and humiliated as I was, I was willing to follow to any place to get my dinner, for I had been riding all day, and had not tasted a mouthful since early morning.

On reaching the servants' hall we found the door of the room locked. The waiter left me standing in the passage while he went to inform the clerk of the fact.

In a few minutes the obsequious clerk came blustering down the hall:

"Did you come out of the street, or from Mrs. Clarke's room?"

"From Mrs. Clarke's room," I meekly answered. My gentle words seemed to quiet him, and then he explained:

"It is after the regular hour for dinner. The room is locked up, and Annie has gone out with the key."

My pride would not let me stand longer in the hall.

"Very well," I remarked, as I began climbing the stairs, "I will tell Mrs. Clarke that I cannot get any dinner."

He looked after me, with a scowl on his face:

"You need not put on airs! I understand the whole thing."

I said nothing, but continued to climb the stairs, thinking to myself: "Well, if you understand the whole thing, it is strange that you should put the widow of ex-President Abraham Lincoln in a three-cornered room in the attic of this miserable hotel."

When I reached Mrs. Lincoln's rooms, tears of humiliation and vexation were in my eyes.

"What is the matter, Lizzie?" she asked.

"I cannot get any dinner."

"Cannot get any dinner! What do you mean?"

I then told her of all that had transpired below.

"The insolent, overbearing people!" she fiercely exclaimed. "Never mind, Lizzie, you shall have your dinner. Put on your bonnet and shawl."

"What for?"

"What for! Why, we will go out of the hotel, and get you something to eat where they know how to behave decently:" and Mrs. Lincoln already was tying the strings of her bonnet before the glass.

Her impulsiveness alarmed me.

"Surely, Mrs. Lincoln, you do not intend to go out on the street to-night?"

"Yes I do. Do you suppose I am going to have you starve, when we can find something to eat on every corner?"

"But you forget. You are here as Mrs. Clarke and not as Mrs. Lincoln. You came alone, and the people already suspect that everything is not right. If you go outside of the hotel to-night, they will accept the fact as evidence against you.

"Nonsense; what do you suppose I care for what these low-bred people think? Put on your things."

"No, Mrs. Lincoln, I shall not go outside of the hotel to-night, for I realize your situation, if you do not. Mrs. Lincoln has no reason to care what these people may say about her as Mrs. Lincoln, but she should be prudent, and give them no opportunity to say anything about her as Mrs. Clarke."

It was with difficulty I could convince her that she should act with caution. She was so frank and impulsive that she never once thought that her actions might be misconstrued. It did not occur to her that she might order dinner to be served in my room, so I went to bed without a mouthful to eat.

The next morning Mrs. Lincoln knocked at my door before six o'clock:

"Come, Elizabeth, get up, I know you must be hungry. Dress yourself quickly and we will go out and get some breakfast. I was unable to sleep last night for thinking of you being forced to go to bed without anything to eat."

I dressed myself as quickly as I could, and together we went out and took breakfast, at a restaurant on Broadway, some place between 609 and the St. Denis Hotel. I do not give the number, as I prefer leaving it to conjecture. Of one thing I am certain—the proprietor of the restaurant little dreamed who one of his guests was that morning.

After breakfast we walked up Broadway, and entering Union Square Park, took a seat on one of the benches under the trees, watched the children at play, and talked over the situation. Mrs. Lincoln told me: "Lizzie, yesterday morning I called for the *Herald* at the breakfast table, and on looking over the list of diamond brokers advertised, I selected the firm of W. H. Brady & Co., 609 Broadway. After breakfast I walked down to the house, and tried to sell them a lot of jewelry. I gave my name as Mrs. Clarke. I first saw Mr. Judd, a member of the firm, a very pleasant gentleman. We were unable to agree about the price. He went back into the office, where a stout gentleman was seated at the desk, but

I could not hear what he said. [I know now what was said, and so shall the reader, in parentheses. Mr. Brady has since told me that he remarked to Mr. Judd that the woman must be crazy to ask such outrageous prices, and to get rid of her as soon as possible.] Soon after Mr. Judd came back to the counter, another gentleman, Mr. Keyes, as I have since learned, a silent partner in the house, entered the store. He came to the counter, and in looking over my jewelry discovered my name inside of one of the rings. I had forgotten the ring, and when I saw him looking at the name so earnestly, I snatched the bauble from him and put it into my pocket. I hastily gathered up my jewelry, and started out. They asked for my address, and I left my card, Mrs. Clarke, at the St. Denis Hotel. They are to call to see me this forenoon, when I shall enter into negotiations with them."

Scarcely had we returned to the hotel when Mr. Keyes called, and Mrs. Clarke disclosed to him that she was Mrs. Lincoln. He was much elated to find his surmise correct. Mrs. L. exhibited to him a large number of shawls, dresses, and fine laces, and told him that she was compelled to sell them in order to live. He was an earnest Republican, was much affected by her story, and denounced the ingratitude of the government in the severest terms. She complained to him of the treatment she had received at the St. Denis, and he advised her to move to another hotel forthwith. She readily consented, and as she wanted to be in an out-of-the-way place where she would not be recognized by any of her old friends, he recommended the Earle Hotel in Canal street.

On the way down to the hotel that morning she acceded to a suggestion made by me, and supported by Mr. Keyes, that she confide in the landlord, and give him her name without registering, so as to ensure the proper respect. Unfortunately, the Earle Hotel was full, and we had to select another place. We drove to the Union Place Hotel, where we secured rooms for Mrs. Clarke, Mrs. Lincoln changing her mind, deeming it would not be prudent to disclose her real name to any one. After we had become settled in our new quarters, Messrs. Keyes and Brady called frequently on Mrs. Lincoln, and held long conferences with her. They advised her to pursue the course she did, and were sanguine of success. Mrs. Lincoln was very anxious to dispose of her things, and return to Chicago as quickly and quietly as possible; but they presented the case in a different light, and, I regret to say, she was guided by their counsel. "Pooh," said Mr. Brady, "place your affairs in our hands, and we will raise you at least $100,000 in a few weeks. The people will not permit the widow of Abraham Lincoln to suffer; they will come to her rescue when they know she is in want."

The argument seemed plausible, and Mrs. Lincoln quietly acceded to the proposals of Keyes and Brady.

We remained quietly at the Union Place Hotel for a few days. On Sunday Mrs. Lincoln accepted the use of a private carriage, and accompanied by me, she drove out to Central Park. We did not enjoy the ride much, as the carriage was a close one, and we could not throw open the window for fear of being recognized by some one of the many thousands in the Park. Mrs. Lincoln wore a heavy veil so as to more effectually conceal her face. We came near being run into, and we had a spasm of alarm, for an accident would have exposed us to public gaze, and of course the masquerade would have been at an end. On Tuesday I hunted up a number of dealers in second-hand clothing, and had them call at the hotel by appointment. Mrs. Lincoln soon discovered that they were hard people to drive a bargain with, so on Thursday we got into a close carriage, taking a bundle of dresses and shawls with us, and drove to a number of stores on Seventh Avenue, where an attempt was made to dispose of a portion of the wardrobe. The dealers wanted the goods for little or nothing, and we found it a hard matter to drive a bargain with them. Mrs. Lincoln met the dealers squarely, but all of her tact and shrewdness failed to accomplish much. I do not care to dwell upon this portion of my story. Let it answer to say, that we returned to the hotel more disgusted than ever with the business in which we were engaged. There was much curiosity at the hotel in relation to us, as our movements were watched, and we were regarded with suspicion. Our trunks in the main hall below were examined daily, and curiosity was more keenly excited when the argus-eyed reporters for the press traced Mrs. Lincoln's name on the cover of one of her trunks. The letters had been rubbed out, but the faint outlines remained, and these outlines only served to stimulate curiosity. Messrs. Keyes and Brady called often, and they made Mrs. Lincoln believe that, if she would write certain letters for them to show to prominent politicians, they could raise a large sum of money for her. They argued that the Republican party would never permit it to be said that the wife of Abraham Lincoln was in want; that the leaders of the party would make heavy advances rather than have it published to the world that Mrs. Lincoln's poverty compelled her to sell her wardrobe. Mrs. L.'s wants were urgent, as she had to borrow $600 from Keyes and Brady, and she was willing to adopt any scheme which promised to place a good bank account to her credit. At different times in her room at the Union Hotel she wrote the following letters:

"Chicago, Sept. 18, 1867.

"Mr. Brady, *Commission Broker, No. 609*
    Broadway, New York:
    "I have this day sent to you personal property, which I am compelled to part with, and which you will find of considerable value. The articles consist of four camels' hair shawls, one lace dress and shawl, a parasol cover, a diamond ring, two dress patterns, some furs, etc.
    "Please have them appraised, and confer by letter with me.
                                    Very respectfully,
                                    "Mrs. Lincoln."

"Chicago, —————.

"Mr. Brady, *No. 609 Broadway, N.Y. City:*

"❄   ❄   ❄   ❄ Dear Sir:—The articles I am sending you to dispose of were gifts of dear friends, which only *urgent necessity* compels me to part with, and I am especially anxious that they shall not be sacrificed.

"The circumstances are peculiar, and painfully embarrassing; therefore I hope you will endeavor to realize as much as possible for them. Hoping to hear from you, I remain, very respectfully,

"Mrs. A. Lincoln."

"Sept. 25, 1867.

"W. H. Brady, Esq.:—My great, great sorrow and loss have made me painfully sensitive, but as my feelings and pecuniary comforts were never regarded or even recognized in the midst of my overwhelming bereavement—*now* that I am pressed in a most startling manner for means of subsistence, I do not know why I should shrink from an opportunity of improving my trying position.

"Being assured that all you do will be appropriately executed, and in a manner that will not startle me very greatly, and excite as little comment as possible, again I shall leave all in your hands.

"I am passing through a very painful ordeal, which the country, in remembrance of my noble and devoted husband, should have spared me.

"I remain, with great respect, very truly,

"Mrs. Lincoln.

"P.S.—As you mention that my goods have been valued at over $24,000, I will be willing to make a reduction of $8,000, and relinquish them for $16,000. If this is not accomplished, I will continue to sell and advertise largely until every article is sold.

"I must have means to live, at least in a medium comfortable state.

"M. L."

The letters are dated Chicago, and addressed to Mr. Brady, though every one of them was written in New York; for when Mrs. L. left the West for the East, she had settled upon no definite plan of action. Mr. Brady proposed to show the letters to certain politicians, and ask for money on a threat to publish them if his demands, as Mrs. Lincoln's agent, were not complied with. When writing the letter I stood at Mrs. Lincoln's elbow, and suggested that they be couched in the mildest language possible.

"Never mind, Lizzie," she said; "anything to raise the wind. One might as well be killed for a sheep as a lamb."

❄   ❄   ❄

George Washington Williams

(1849–1891)

GEORGE WASHINGTON WILLIAMS WAS born in Bedford Spring, Pennsylvania. When he was fourteen years old, he dropped out of a private school, lied about his age, and enlisted in the Union Army, where he rose to the rank of sergeant-major. Discharged from service in 1865, Williams crossed the Texas border and joined the Mexican Army which had been raised to fight Maximilian. After a short time, he quit that army with the rank of lieutenant-colonel. Re-enlisting in the United States Army, Williams served in several Indian campaigns.

From 1868 to 1874, George Washington Williams' civilian life was as varied as his army career. He was in and out of several seminaries and schools, including Howard University. He became a Baptist Minister, then a journalist in Washington, D.C., and in Cincinnati, and then a government worker. He passed the Ohio bar and became a lawyer and, in 1877, a member of the Ohio legislature. Williams was subsequently appointed American envoy to Haiti, and later served the Belgian government in the Congo. He died in Blackpool, England, while still connected with the Belgian government.

In 1883, Williams published *History of the Negro Race in America, from 1619 to 1880;* in 1888, *A History of the Negro Troops in the War of the Rebellion.* The first was brought out by G. P. Putnam's Sons and the second by Harper and Brothers, two of the best publishing companies of Williams' day.

Although too oratorical on occasion, Williams was basically a scholar, collecting and presenting his materials with a scholar's concern for clearness, accuracy, and objectivity. According to John Hope Franklin, Williams' works, judged by the standards of today's historical scholarship, "are substantial and reliable sources of information and bear up surprisingly well under careful scrutiny."

For a modern evaluation of this pioneer historian, see John Hope Franklin, "George Washington Williams, Historian," *The Journal of Negro History,* Vol. XXXI, no. 4 (January, 1946).

The selection given below comes from *A History of the Negro Troops in the War of the Rebellion.*

HEROISM: BLACK AND WHITE

South Carolina had set the other States a dangerous example in her attempts at nullification under President Jackson's administration, and was not only first in seceding, but fired the first shot of the slave-holders' rebellion against the laws and authority of the United States Government. It was eminently fitting, then, that the first shot fired at slavery by Negro soldiers should be aimed by the ex-slaves of the haughty South Carolina rebels. It was poetic justice that South Carolina Negroes should have the priority of obtaining the Union uniform, and enjoy the distinction of being the first Negro soldiers to encounter the enemy in battle. And the honor belongs to Massachusetts in furnishing a graduate of Harvard College, Thomas Wentworth Higginson, as the first colonel to lead the First South Carolina Negro Regiment of Volunteers.

Before Colonel Higginson assumed command of this regiment, in fact before it was organized as a regiment, Company A did its first fighting on Saint Helena Island. From the 3d to the 10th of November, 1862, Company A, under Captain Trowbridge, participated in the expedition along the coasts of Georgia and East Florida. The expedition was under the command of Lieutenant-colonel Oliver T. Beard, of the Forty-eighth New York Infantry. Of their fighting quality Colonel Beard in his report says:

"The colored men fought with astonishing coolness and bravery. For alacrity in effecting landings, for determination, and for bush-fighting I found them all I could desire—more than I had hoped. They behaved bravely, gloriously, and deserve all praise."

From the 13th to the 18th of November three companies of the First South Carolina Colored Volunteers participated in an expedition from Beaufort, South Carolina, to Doboy River, Georgia. In his report of the expedition General Rufus Saxton says:

"It gives me pleasure to bear witness to the good conduct of the Negro troops. They fought with the most determined bravery. Although scarcely one month since the organization of this regiment was commenced, in that short period these untrained soldiers have captured from the enemy an amount of property equal in value to the cost of the regiment for a year. They have driven back equal numbers of rebel troops, and have destroyed the salt-works along the whole line of this coast."

On the 23d of January, 1863, by order of Major-general Hunter, Colonel Higginson sailed in transports from Beaufort, South Carolina, to make a raid into Georgia and Florida. No strategic blow was to be

Title supplied by editors.

struck, no important manœuvre was to be executed. But there were two objects in view. Negro regiments were to be recruited in the Department, but the enemy, in retiring before the Union forces, had taken with him all effective Negroes. It was one of the objects of the expedition to secure Negro recruits in the enemy's country. The second object of the expedition was to obtain the far-farmed lumber which was to be had by a bold dash into the enemy's country. These two objects were of sufficient importance to justify the expedition, but Colonel Higginson cherished another idea that had not been canvassed at headquarters. This First South Carolina Volunteers was the only organized regiment of Negro troops in the army of the United States at this time. The tentative effort of General Hunter in raising this regiment the year before had met the inexorable disapproval of the President, and had drawn the fierce fire of the enemies of the Negro. Colonel Higginson knew that if he could get his black soldiers in battle once, the question of their employment in unlimited numbers would be finally settled. So, while he went ostensibly for recruits and lumber, his main aim was to find the enemy and engage him. His force consisted of four hundred and sixty-two officers and men. The vessels that bore the expedition were the *Ben de Ford,* Captain Hallet, carrying several six-pound guns; the *John Adams,* an army gun-boat, carrying a thirty-pound Parrott gun, two ten-pound Parrotts, and an eight-inch howitzer; the *Planter,* carrying a ten-pound Parrott gun and two howitzers. The *Ben de Ford* was the largest, and carried most of the troops. It was the "flag-ship" of the expedition, in a manner. Major John D. Strong was in command on the *John Adams,* and Captain Charles T. Trowbridge commanded the troops on the *Planter.* For prudential reasons, each vessel sailed at a different hour for St. Simon's, on the coast of Georgia.

On the night of the 26th of January Colonel Higginson found himself on the right track; the enemy he was looking for was not far away. Of his purpose Colonel Higginson says: "That night I proposed to make a sort of trial trip up stream as far as Township Landing, some fifteen miles, there to pay our respects to Captain Clark's company of cavalry, whose camp was reported to lie near by. This was included in Corporal Sutton's programme, and seemed to me more inviting and far more useful to the men than any amount of mere foraging. The thing really desirable appeared to be to get them under fire as soon as possible, and to teach them, by a few small successes, the application of what they had learned in camp."

Back from the river and five miles from Township Landing the much-desired enemy was bivouacked. A troop of skirmishers was landed behind the bend below the landing, with orders to march upon the town and surround it. When the troops arrived by water the town was in possession of the force that had proceeded by land. Colonel Higginson had brought along a good supply of the Emancipation Proclamation to distribute among the Negroes, and these were rather assuring to many who had been led to believe that the "Yankees would sell them into Cuba."

After making a selection of one hundred of the best soldiers in the expedition, Colonel Higginson took up his line of march for the enemy's camp shortly after midnight. The moon shone brightly, but the command soon reached the resinous pines, and clouds of shadows hid it. The column moved on in silence until, when about two miles from its base, the advance-guard came suddenly upon the rebel cavalry and exchanged shots. Colonel Higginson gave orders to fix bayonets, and prepared to receive the enemy kneeling, and the enemy delivered his fire over the heads of the intrepid black soldiers. "My soldiers," says Colonel Higginson, "in turn fired rapidly—too rapidly, being yet beginners—and it was evident that, dim as it was, both sides had opportunity to do some execution.

"I could hardly tell whether the fight had lasted ten minutes or an hour, when, as the enemy's fire had evidently ceased or slackened, I gave the order to cease firing. But it was very difficult at first to make them desist: the taste of gunpowder was too intoxicating. One of them was heard to mutter indignantly, 'Why de cunnel order *cease* firing, when de Secesh blazin' away at de rate of ten dollar a day?' "

The enemy beat a precipitate retreat, and left Colonel Higginson's Negro troops in undisputed possession of the field. The dead and wounded were tenderly taken up by their more fortunate comrades, and the command returned to Township Landing without being again assailed by the enemy. Of the wounded, Surgeon Seth Rogers wrote: "One man killed instantly by a ball through the heart and seven wounded, one of whom will die. Braver men never lived. One man with two bullet-holes through the large muscles of the shoulders and neck brought off from the scene of action, two miles distant, two muskets, and not a murmur has escaped his lips. Another, Robert Sutton, with three wounds—one of which, being on the skull, may cost him his life—would not report himself till compelled to do so by his officers. While dressing his wounds he quietly talked of what they had done and of what they yet could do. To-day I have had the colonel *order* him to obey me. He is perfectly quiet and cool, but takes this whole affair with the religious bearing of a man who realizes that freedom is sweeter than life. Yet another soldier did not report himself at all, but remained all night on guard, and possibly I should not have known of his having had a buckshot in his shoulder if some duty requiring a sound shoulder had not been required of him to-day."

The engagement in which Colonel Higginson's Negro soldiers had courageously and unflinchingly met and returned the enemy's fire was called the *"Battle of the Hundred Pines."* It decided no important military question, but, under the circumstances, it was of great importance to Negro soldiership throughout the entire country. It was one of the first stand-up fights that ex-slaves had had with their late masters, and their splendid bravery was at once a vindication and a prophecy of valor upon other fields that were yet to be fought for freedom. . . .

The Department of the South up to this time had done little effective military service. Most of the Sea Islands had fallen into the control of the Union forces, but the way to Charleston, both by land and water, was guarded by forts, fortifications, and torpedoes. Fort Wagner was a strongly mounted and thoroughly garrisoned earthwork extending across the north end of the island; it was within twenty-six hundred yards of Fort Sumter. The reduction of this fortress left but little work to subdue Cumming's Point, and thus siege guns could be brought within one mile of Fort Sumter, and the city of Charleston—the heart of the rebellion—would be within extreme shelling distance. In this assault the Fifty-fourth Massachusetts was to participate. It had sustained a loss of fourteen killed, seventeen wounded, and thirteen missing while on James Island, and having had a taste of war, was eager for more. It was eminently proper, too, that this Northern Negro regiment from stalwart old Massachusetts should have its fighting qualities tested in South Carolina before a haughty and formidable fortress, from under whose guns the most splendid valor of white troops had recoiled. Before the trying hour they had been subjected to tests not only of martial pluck, but of endurance, hunger, heat, and thirst. At the close of the engagement on the morning of the 16th these Negro soldiers were set in motion from James to Morris Island. The first shock of battle had burst upon them in the ominous silence of the early morning. All day they marched over the island under the exhausting heat of a July sun in Carolina, with the uncertain sand slipping under their weary tread. All night the march was continued through darkness and rain, amid thunder and lightning, over swollen streams, broken dikes, and feeble, shuddering, narrow causeways. Now a halt for no apparent reason, and then the column moved forward to lead in the dance of death. This dreary, weary, and exhausting march was continued till six o'clock in the morning of the 18th, when the Fifty-fourth reached Morris Island. . . .

As the day wore away it seemed certain, from the Union stand-point, that the garrison must yield or perish. Through a field-glass Wagner seemed little less than an unrecognizable mass of ruins, a mere heap of sand. It seemed as if the approaches to the bomb-proofs were choked with sand, and that most of the heavy guns were disabled and the fort practically dismantled. Its reduction seemed now near at hand, and the bombardment had facilitated the work of the infantry who were to consummate its reduction by a dash at the point of the bayonet. Towards evening the breaching siege guns and monitors slacked their fire. Soon the beach was filled with life. Couriers dashed in every direction, and the troops were now being disposed for an assault. At 6 P.M.

the Fifty-fourth Regiment reached General Geo. C. Strong's headquarters, about the middle of the island, wet and weary, hungry and thirsty; but there was no time for rest or refreshments. Onward the Negro regiment marched several hundred yards farther, and proudly took its place at the head of the assaulting column. General Strong and Colonel Shaw addressed it briefly, and with burning words of eloquent patriotic sentiment urged the men to valorous conduct in the approaching assault. Both officers were inspired; the siren of martial glory was sedulously luring them to the bloody and inhospitable trenches of Wagner. There was a tremor in Colonel Shaw's voice and an impressiveness in his manner. He was young and beautiful, wealthy and refined, and his heroic words soon flowered into action—bravest of the brave, leader of men! The random shot and shell that screamed through the ranks gave the troops little annoyance. The first brigade consisted of the Fifty-fourth Massachusetts, Colonel Robert Gould Shaw; the Sixth Connecticut, Colonel Chatfield; the Forty-eighth New York, Colonel Barton; the Third New Hampshire, Colonel Jackson; the Seventy-sixth Pennsylvania, Colonel Strawbridge; and the Ninth Maine, Colonel Emory. After about thirty minutes' halt, General Strong gave the order for the charge, and the column advanced quickly to its perilous work. The ramparts of Wagner flashed with small-arms, and all the large shotted guns roared with defiance. Sumter and Cumming's Point delivered a destructive cross-fire, while the howitzers in the bastions raked the ditch; but the gallant Negro regiment swept across it and gained the parapet. Here the flag of this regiment was planted; here General Strong fell mortally wounded; and here the brave, beautiful, and heroic Colonel Shaw was saluted by death and kissed by immortality. The regiment lost heavily, but held its ground under the most discouraging circumstances. The men had actually gained the inside of the fort, where they bravely contended with a desperate and determined enemy. The contest endured for about an hour, when the regiment, shattered and torn, with nearly all of its officers dead or wounded, was withdrawn under the command[1] of Captain Luis F. Emilio. He formed a new line of battle about seven hundred yards from the fort, and awaited orders for another charge. He despatched a courier to the commanding officer of the second brigade that had gone to the front, stating that he was in supporting position, and was ready and willing to do what he could. Word came that the enemy was quiet and that the Fifty-fourth was not needed. Captain Emilio then occupied the rifle-pits flanking the Union artillery which he found unoccupied, and being out of musket

[1] Several histories of the war have given Lieutenant Higginson the honor of leading the regiment from the parapets of Wagner. This is an error. Lieutenant Higginson was not in this action, but on detail at the other end of the island. *Captain Luis F. Emilio* was the officer who commanded at the close of the battle.— G. W. W.

range, organized his men as best he could. The national colors of the regiment which he had brought back from the scene of the battle he sent to the rear with the wounded color-sergeant, William H. Carney, as they could not serve as a rallying point in the deep darkness. . . .

The appalling list of casualties shows how bravely this Negro regiment had done its duty, and the unusually large number of men missing proves that the regiment had fought its way into the fort, and if properly supported, Wagner would have been captured. Colonel Shaw led about six hundred enlisted men and twenty-two officers into this action. Of the enlisted men thirty-one were killed, one hundred and thirty-five wounded, and ninety-two missing. Of the twenty-two officers participating three were killed and eleven were wounded. Nearly half of the enlisted men were killed, wounded, or missing, while more than one-half of the officers were either killed or wounded.

From a purely military stand-point the assault upon Fort Wagner was a failure, but it furnished the severest test of Negro valor and soldiership. It was a mournful satisfaction to the advocates of Negro soldiers to point the doubting, sneering, stay-at-home Negro-haters to the murderous trenches of Wagner. The Negro soldier had seen his red-letter day, and his title to patriotic courage was written in his own blood. Pleased with the splendid behavior of the regiment in particular and the special courage of several enlisted men, General Gillmore awarded a medal to the following soldiers of the Fifty-fourth: Sergeant Robert J. Simmons, Company B; Sergeant William H. Carney, Company C; Corporal Henry F. Peal, Company F; and Private George Wilson, Company A.

But it would be unjust to forget the gallant color-sergeant John Wall who fell in the outer trench. He was a brave and competent soldier, but after the United States colors had been taken up and borne to the top of the parapet, henceforth history seems to have kept her jealous eye upon Sergeant William H. Carney, the heroic self-appointed successor to Sergeant John Wall. Sergeant Carney planted his flag upon the ramparts of the rebel fort, and after having received three severe wounds, brought it to the rear stained with his own blood—

> Glares the volcanic breath,
> Breaks the red sea of death,
> From Wagner's yawning hold,
> On the besiegers bold.
>   Twice vain the wild attack,
>   Inch by inch, sadly slow,
>   Fights the torn remnant back,
>   Face to the foe.
>
> Yet free the colors wave,
> Borne by yon Afric brave,

In the fierce storm wind higher;
But, ah! one flashing fire:
  He sinks! the banner falls
    From the faint, mangled limb,
  And droop to mocking walls
    Those star-folds dim.

Stay, stay the taunting laugh!
See! now he lifts the staff,
Clinched in his close-set teeth,
Crawls from dead heaps beneath,
  Crowned with his starry robe,
    Till he the ranks has found:
  "Comrades, the dear old flag
    Ne'er touched the ground."

O man so pure, so grand,
Sidney might clasp thy hand!
O brother! black thy skin,
But white the pearl within!
  Man, who to lift thy race
    Worthy, thrice worthy art,
  Clasps thee, in warm embrace
    A Nation's heart.

❖   ❖   ❖

At the battle of Thermopylæ three hundred Spartans held the pass against an enormous army, and yet history has made Leonidas representative of them all. Many brave soldiers fell in the forlorn assault upon Fort Wagner, but when some great painter has patriotic inspiration to give this battle an immortal representation, Colonel Shaw will be the central figure; and America will only remember one name in this conflict for all time to come—Colonel Robert Gould Shaw! This was a noble and precious life, but it was cheerfully consecrated to human freedom and the regeneration of the nation. He had good blood, splendid training, wide experience for one so young, and had inherited strong antislavery sentiments. When he had fallen, a flag of truce called for his body. A rebel officer responded, "We have buried him with his niggers." It was thought thus to cast indignity upon the hero dead, but it was a failure. The colonel and his men were united in life, and it was fitting that they should not be separated in death. In this idea his father joined, and the following letter exhibits his feelings:

Brigadier-general Gillmore, commanding Department of the South:

Sir,—I take the liberty to address you because I am informed that efforts are to be made to recover the body of my son, Colonel Shaw, of the Fifty-fourth Massachusetts Regiment, which was buried at Fort Wagner. My object in writing is to say that such efforts are not authorized by me or any of my family, and that they are not approved by us. We hold that a soldier's most appropriate burial-place is on the field where he has fallen. I shall therefore be much obliged, General, if, in case the matter is brought to your cognizance, you will forbid the descration of my son's grave, and prevent the disturbance of his remains or those buried with him. With most earnest wishes for your success, I am, sir, with respect and esteem,

Your most obedient servant,
FRANCIS GEORGE SHAW.

New York, *August 24, 1863.*

Instead of dishonoring the remains of Colonel Shaw by burying him with his brave black soldiers, the intended ignominy was transformed into a beautiful bow of promise that was to span forever the future of the race for which he gave his life. He was representative of all that was good in American life; he had wealth, high social position, and the broadest culture. From his exalted station he chose to fight with and for Negro troops—not only to lead them in conflict, but to die for them and the Republic; and although separated from them in civil life, nevertheless he united the rich and the poor, the learned and the unlearned, the white and black, in his military apotheosis.

"They buried him with his niggers!"
    Together they fought and died;
There was room for them all where they laid him
    (The grave was deep and wide),
For his beauty and youth and valor,
    Their patience and love and pain;
And at the last day together
    They shall all be found again.

"They buried him with his niggers!"
    Earth holds no prouder grave;
There is not a mausoleum
    In the world beyond the wave
That a nobler tale has hallowed
    Or a purer glory crowned,
Than the nameless trench where they buried
    The brave so faithful found.

"They buried him with his niggers!"
    A wide grave should it be.
They buried more in that shallow trench
    Than human eye could see.
Ay, all the shames and sorrows
    Of more than a hundred years
Lie under the weight of that Southern soil
    Despite those cruel sneers.

"They buried him with his niggers!"
   But the glorious souls set free
Are leading the van of the army
   That fights for liberty.
Brothers in death, in glory
   The same palm-branches bear,
And the crown is as bright o'er the sable brows
   As over the golden hair. . . .

Booker Taliaferro Washington

(1856?–1915)

BORN ON THE BURROUGH'S PLANTATION near Hale's Ford, Virginia, Booker T. Washington was the son of a slave woman and a white father. In 1865 the Washingtons moved to Malden, West Virginia, and Booker worked at odd jobs there until he heard of Hampton Normal and Agricultural Institute (now Hampton Institute). With $1.50 in his pocket, he set out for the famous school.

After graduation from Hampton in 1875, Washington taught in Malden, then left for Washington, D.C., for a year's study at Wayland Seminary (now a part of Virginia Union University). In 1879 he returned to Hampton where he took charge of a group of Indian students and also organized Hampton's first night school. In 1881 he was sent to Tuskegee, Alabama, to start a new school of the Hampton type. Within a very short time, Booker T. Washington built in the backwoods of Alabama one of the best-known educational centers of America.

Up from Slavery, published in 1901, has probably been reprinted more frequently than any other book by a Negro author and ranks in popularity with Benjamin Franklin's *Autobiography*. Washington's book, however, is not solely autobiographical: much of it is geared to touch the hearts and pocketbooks of Northern white philanthropists. In addition, it is a conciliatory work designed on the one hand to placate and soothe the white South and, on the other, to inspire in Negroes habits of industry, cleanliness, thrift, and above all else, patience. Its style is painfully simple, and on occasion its subject matter is Pollyannish. American white readers tend to believe that *Up from Slavery* is the sincere work of a dedicated and unpretentious man, and it may well be. It is also a superb job of salesmanship written by a master of the art.

Although not an orator in the old-fashioned, thundering sense of the term, Booker T. Washington was one of the most popular and effective speakers of his generation. Relying largely on concrete images, parable-like anecdotes ("Cast down your bucket where you are"), and folk humor, usually at the expense of the Negro, his speeches became an American institution. Among the best are the two given below and one he delivered in Boston in 1897 at the unveiling of the Robert Gould Shaw Monument. In 1896 Harvard, the first New England college to give an honorary degree to a Negro, conferred upon Booker T. Washington a Master of Arts degree.

Among the many books written or edited by Booker T. Washington, the following are the most significant: *The Future of the American Negro* (1899); *Tuskegee and Its People* (1905); *Life of Frederick Douglass* (1907); *The Story of the Negro* (1909); *My Larger Education* (1911); and *The Negro in the South* (1907), co-authored with W. E. B. Du Bois.

For recent comment on the life and works of Booker T. Washington, see Samuel R. Spencer, *Booker T. Washington and the Negro's Place in American Life* (1955), and Hugh Hawkins (editor), *Booker T. Washington and His Critics* (1962).

"The Struggle for an Education" is from *Up From Slavery;* the two speeches are taken from Carter G. Woodson, *Negro Orators and Their Orations.*

THE STRUGGLE FOR AN EDUCATION

One day, while at work in the coal-mine, I happened to overhear two miners talking about a great school for coloured people somewhere in Virginia. This was the first time that I had ever heard anything about any kind of school or college that was more pretentious than the little coloured school in our town.

In the darkness of the mine I noiselessly crept as close as I could to the two men who were talking. I heard one tell the other that not only was the school established for the members of my race, but that opportunities were provided by which poor but worthy students could work out all or a part of the cost of board, and at the same time be taught some trade or industry.

As they went on describing the school, it seemed to me that it must be the greatest place on earth, and not even Heaven presented more attractions for me at that time than did the Hampton Normal and Agricultural Institute in Virginia, about which these men were talking. I resolved at once to go to that school, although I had no idea where it was, or how many miles away, or how I was going to reach it; I remembered only that I was on fire constantly with one ambition, and that was to go to Hampton. This thought was with me day and night.

After hearing of the Hampton Institute, I continued to work for a few months longer in the coal-mine. While at work there, I heard of a vacant position in the household of General Lewis Ruffner, the owner of the salt-furnace and coal-mine. Mrs. Viola Ruffner, the wife of General Ruffner, was a "Yankee" woman from Vermont. Mrs. Ruffner had a reputation all through the vicinity for being very strict with her servants, and especially with the boys who tried to serve her. Few of them had remained with her more than two or three weeks. They all left with the same excuse: she was too strict. I decided, however, that I would rather try Mrs. Ruffner's house than remain in the coal-mine, and so my mother applied to her for the vacant position. I was hired at a salary of $5 per month.

I had heard so much about Mrs. Ruffner's severity that I was almost afraid to see her, and trembled when I went into her presence. I had not lived with her many weeks, however, before I began to understand her. I soon began to learn that, first of all, she wanted everything kept clean about her, that she wanted things done promptly and systematically, and that at the bottom of everything she wanted absolute honesty and frankness. Nothing must be sloven or slipshod; every door, every fence, must be kept in repair.

I cannot now recall how long I lived with Mrs. Ruffner before going to Hampton, but I think it must have been a year and a half. At any rate, I here repeat what I have said more than once before, that the lessons that I learned in the home of Mrs. Ruffner were as valuable to me as any education I have ever gotten anywhere since. Even to this day I never see bits of paper scattered around a house or in the street that I do not want to pick them up at once. I never see a filthy yard that I do not want to clean it, a paling off of a fence that I do not want to put it on, an unpainted or unwhitewashed house that I do not want to paint or whitewash it, or a button off one's clothes, or a grease-spot on them or on a floor, that I do not want to call attention to it.

From fearing Mrs. Ruffner I soon learned to look upon her as one of my best friends. When she found that she could trust me she did so implicitly. During the one or two winters that I was with her she gave me an opportunity to go to school for an hour in the day during a portion of the winter months, but most of my studying was done at night, sometimes alone, sometimes under some one whom I could hire to teach me. Mrs. Ruffner always encouraged and sympathized with me in all my efforts to get an education. It was while living with her that I began to get together my first library. I secured a dry-goods box, knocked out one side of it, put some shelves in it, and began putting into it every kind of book that I could get my hands upon, and called it my "library."

Notwithstanding my success at Mrs. Ruffner's I did not give up the idea of going to the Hampton Institute. In the fall of 1872 I determined to make an effort to get there, although, as I have stated, I had no definite idea of the direction in which Hampton was, or of what it would cost to go there. I do not think that any one thoroughly sympathized with me in my ambition to go to Hampton unless it was my mother, and she was troubled with a grave fear that I was starting out on a "wild-goose chase." At any rate, I got only a half-hearted consent from her that I might start. The small amount of money that I had earned had been consumed by my stepfather and the remainder of the family, with the exception of a very few dollars, and so I had very little with which to buy clothes and pay my travelling expenses. My brother

John helped me all that he could, but of course that was not a great deal, for his work was in the coal mine, where he did not earn much, and most of what he did earn went in the direction of paying the household expenses.

Perhaps the thing that touched and pleased me most in connection with my starting for Hampton was the interest that many of the older coloured people took in the matter. They had spent the best days of their lives in slavery, and hardly expected to live to see the time when they would see a member of their race leave home to attend a boarding school. Some of these older people would give me a nickel, others a quarter, or a handkerchief.

Finally the great day came, and I started for Hampton. I had only a small, cheap satchel that contained what few articles of clothing I could get. My mother at the time was rather weak and broken in health. I hardly expected to see her again, and thus our parting was all the more sad. She, however, was very brave through it all. At that time there were no through trains connecting that part of West Virginia with eastern Virginia. Trains ran only a portion of the way, and the remainder of the distance was travelled by stage-coaches.

The distance from Malden to Hampton is about five hundred miles. I had not been away from home many hours before it began to grow painfully evident that I did not have enough money to pay my fare to Hampton. One experience I shall long remember. I had been travelling over the mountains most of the afternoon in an old-fashioned stage-coach, when, late in the evening, the coach stopped for the night at a common, unpainted house called a hotel. All the other passengers except myself were whites. In my ignorance I supposed that the little hotel existed for the purpose of accommodating the passengers who travelled on the stage-coach. The difference that the colour of one's skin would make I had not thought anything about. After all the other passengers had been shown rooms and were getting ready for supper, I shyly presented myself before the man at the desk. It is true I had practically no money in my pocket with which to pay for bed or food, but I had hoped in some way to beg my way into the good graces of the landlord, for at that season in the mountains of Virginia the weather was cold, and I wanted to get indoors for the night. Without asking as to whether I had any money, the man at the desk firmly refused to even consider the matter of providing me with food or lodging. This was my first experience in finding out what the colour of my skin meant. In some way I managed to keep warm by walking about, and so got through the night. My whole soul was so bent upon reaching Hampton that I did not have time to cherish any bitterness toward the hotel-keeper.

By walking, begging rides both in wagons and in the cars, in some way, after a number of days, I reached the city of Richmond, Virginia, about eighty-two miles from Hampton. When I reached there, tired, hungry, and dirty, it was late in the night. I had never been in a large city, and this rather added to my misery. When I reached Richmond, I was completely out of money. I had not a single acquaintance in the place, and, being unused to city ways, I did not know where to go. I applied at several places for lodging, but they all wanted money, and that was what I did not have. Knowing nothing else better to do, I walked the streets. In doing this I passed by many food-stands where fried chicken and half-moon apple pies were piled high and made to present a most tempting appearance. At that time it seemed to me that I would have promised all that I expected to possess in the future to have gotten hold of one of those chicken legs or one of those pies. But I could not get either of these, nor anything else to eat.

I must have walked the streets till after midnight. At last I became so exhausted that I could walk no longer. I was tired, I was hungry, I was everything but discouraged. Just about the time when I reached extreme physical exhaustion, I came upon a portion of a street where the board sidewalk was considerably elevated. I waited for a few minutes, till I was sure that no passers-by could see me, and then crept under the sidewalk and lay for the night upon the ground, with my satchel of clothing for a pillow. Nearly all night I could hear the tramp of feet over my head. The next morning I found myself somewhat refreshed, but I was extremely hungry, because it had been a long time since I had had sufficient food. As soon as it became light enough for me to see my surroundings I noticed that I was near a large ship, and that this ship seemed to be unloading a cargo of pig iron. I went at once to the vessel and asked the captain to permit me to help unload the vessel in order to get money for food. The captain, a white man, who seemed to be kind-hearted, consented. I worked long enough to earn money for my breakfast, and it seems to me, as I remember it now, to have been about the best breakfast that I have ever eaten.

My work pleased the captain so well that he told me if I desired I could continue working for a small amount per day. This I was very glad to do. I continued working on this vessel for a number of days. After buying food with the small wages I received there was not much left to add to the amount I must get to pay my way to Hampton. In order to economize in every way possible, so as to be sure to reach Hampton in a reasonable time, I continued to sleep under the same sidewalk that gave me shelter the first night I was in Richmond. Many years after that the coloured citizens of Richmond very kindly tendered me a reception at which there must have been two thousand people present. This reception was held not far from the spot where I slept the first night I spent in that city, and I must confess that my mind was more upon the sidewalk that first gave me shelter than upon the reception, agreeable and cordial as it was.

When I had saved what I considered enough money with which to reach Hampton, I thanked the captain of the vessel for his kindness, and started again. Without any unusual occurrence I reached Hampton, with a surplus of exactly fifty cents with which to begin my education. To me it had been a long, eventful journey; but the first sight of the large, three-story, brick school building seemed to have rewarded me for all that I had undergone in order to reach the place. If the people who gave the money to provide that building could appreciate the influence the sight of it had upon me, as well as upon thousands of other youths, they would feel all the more encouraged to make such gifts. It seemed to me to be the largest and most beautiful building I had ever seen. The sight of it seemed to give me new life. I felt that a new kind of existence had now begun—that life would now have a new meaning. I felt that I had reached the promised land, and I resolved to let no obstacle prevent me from putting forth the highest effort to fit myself to accomplish the most good in the world.

As soon as possible after reaching the grounds of the Hampton Institute, I presented myself before the head teacher for assignment to a class. Having been so long without proper food, a bath, and change of clothing, I did not, of course, make a very favourable impression upon her, and I could see at once that there were doubts in her mind about the wisdom of admitting me as a student. I felt that I could hardly blame her if she got the idea that I was a worthless loafer or tramp. For some time she did not refuse to admit me, neither did she decide in my favour, and I continued to linger about her, and to impress her in all the ways I could with my worthiness. In the meantime I saw her admitting other students, and that added greatly to my discomfort, for I felt, deep down in my heart, that I could do as well as they, if I could only get a chance to show what was in me.

After some hours had passed, the head teacher said to me: "The adjoining recitation-room needs sweeping. Take the broom and sweep it."

It occurred to me at once that here was my chance. Never did I receive an order with more delight. I knew that I could sweep, for Mrs. Ruffner had thoroughly taught me how to do that when I lived with her.

I swept the recitation-room three times. Then I got a dusting-cloth and I dusted it four times. All the woodwork around the walls, every bench, table, and desk, I went over four times with my dusting-cloth. Besides, every piece of furniture had been moved and every closet and corner in the room had been throughly cleaned. I had the feeling that in a large measure my future depended upon the impression I made upon the teacher in the cleaning of that room. When I was through, I reported to the head teacher. She was a "Yankee" woman who knew just where to look for dirt. She went into the room and inspected the floor and closets; then she took her handkerchief and rubbed it on the woodwork about the walls, and over the table and benches. When she was unable to find one bit of dirt on the floor, or a particle of dust on any of the furniture, she quietly remarked, "I guess you will do to enter this institution."

I was one of the happiest souls on earth. The sweeping of that room was my college examination, and never did any youth pass an examination for entrance into Harvard or Yale that gave him more genuine satisfaction. I have passed several examinations since then, but I have always felt that this was the best one I ever passed. . . .

AN ADDRESS DELIVERED AT THE OPENING OF THE COTTON STATES' EXPOSITION IN ATLANTA, GEORGIA, SEPTEMBER, 1895

Mr. President and Gentlemen of the Board of Directors and Citizens: One-third of the population of the South is of the Negro race. No enterprise seeking the material, civil, or moral welfare of this section can disregard this element of our population and reach the highest success. I but convey to you, Mr. President and Directors, the sentiment of the masses of my race when I say that in no way have the value and manhood of the American Negro been more fittingly and generously recognized than by the managers of this magnificent Exposition at every stage of its progress. It is a recognition that will do more to cement the friendship of the two races than any occurrence since the dawn of freedom.

Not only this, but the opportunity here afforded will awaken among us a new era of industrial progress. Ignorant and inexperienced, it is not strange that in the first years of our new life we began at the top instead of at the bottom; that a seat in Congress or the State Legislature was more sought than real estate or industrial skill; that the political convention or stump speaking had more attractions than starting a dairy farm or truck garden.

A ship lost at sea for many days suddenly sighted a friendly vessel. From the mast of the unfortunate vessel was seen a signal, "Water, water; we die of thirst!" The answer from the friendly vessel at once came back: "Cast down your bucket where you are." A second time the signal, "Water, water; send us water!" ran up from the distressed vessel, and was answered: "Cast down your bucket where you are." The captain of the distressed vessel, at last heeding the injunction, cast down his bucket, and it came up full of fresh, sparkling water from the mouth of the Amazon River. To those of my race who depend upon bettering their condition in a foreign land, or who underestimate the importance of cultivating friendly relations with the Southern white man, who is his next door neighbor, I would say: "Cast down your bucket where you are"—cast it down in making friends in every manly way of the people of all races by whom we are surrounded.

Cast it down in agriculture, mechanics, in commerce, in domestic service, and in the professions. And in this connection it is well to bear in mind that whatever other sins the South may be called to bear, when it comes to business, pure and simple, it is in the South that the Negro is given a man's chance in the commercial world, and in nothing is this Exposition more eloquent than in emphasizing this chance. Our greatest danger is, that in the great leap from slavery to freedom we may overlook the fact that the masses of us are to live by the productions of our hands, and fail to keep in mind that we shall prosper in proportion as we learn to dignify and glorify common labor, and put brains and skill into the common occupations of life; shall prosper in proportion as we learn to draw the line between the superficial and the substantial, the ornamental gewgaws of life and the useful. No race can prosper till it learns that there is as much dignity in tilling a field as in writing a poem. It is at the bottom of life we must begin, and not at the top. Nor should we permit our grievances to overshadow our opportunities.

To those of the white race who look to the incoming of those of foreign birth and strange tongue and habits for the prosperity of the South, were I permitted I would repeat what I say to my own race, "Cast down your bucket where you are." Cast it down among the 8,000,000 Negroes whose habits you know, whose fidelity and love you have tested in days when to have proved treacherous meant the ruin of your firesides. Cast down your bucket among these people who have, without strikes and labor wars, tilled your fields, cleared your forests, builded your railroads and cities, and brought forth treasures from the bowels of the earth, and helped make possible this magnificent representation of the progress of the South. Casting down your bucket among my people, helping and encouraging them as you are doing on these grounds, and, with education of head, hand and heart, you will find that they will buy your surplus land, make blossom the waste places in your fields, and run your factories. While doing this, you can be sure in the future, as in the past, that you and your families will be surrounded by the most patient, faithful, law-abiding, and unresentful people that the world has seen. As we have proved our loyalty to you in the past, in nursing your children, watching by the sick bed of your mothers and fathers, and often following them with tear-dimmed eyes to their graves, so in the future, in our humble way, we shall stand by you with a devotion that no foreigner can approach, ready to lay down our lives, if need be, in defense of yours, interlacing our industrial, commercial, civil, and religious life with yours in a way that shall make the interests of both races one. In all things that are purely social we can be as separate as the fingers, yet one as the hand in all things essential to mutual progress.

There is no defense or security for any of us except in the highest intelligence and development of all. If anywhere there are efforts tending to curtail the fullest growth of the Negro, let these efforts be turned into stimulating, encouraging, and making him the most useful and intelligent citizen. Effort or means so invested will pay a thousand per cent interest. These efforts will be twice blessed—blessing him that gives and him that takes.

There is no escape through law of man or God from the inevitable:

> The laws of changeless justice bind
> Oppressor with oppressed;
> And close as sin and suffering joined
> We march to fate abreast.

Nearly sixteen millions of hands will aid you in pulling the load upwards or they will pull against you the load downwards. We shall constitute one-third and more of the ignorance and crime of the South, or one-third its intelligence and progress; we shall contribute one-third to the business and industrial prosperity of the South, or we shall prove a veritable body of death, stagnating, depressing, retarding every effort to advance the body politic.

Gentlemen of the Exposition, as we present to you our humble effort at an exhibition of our progress, you must not expect overmuch. Starting thirty years ago with ownership here and there in a few quilts and pumpkins and chickens (gathered from miscellaneous sources), remember the path that has led from these to the invention and production of agricultural implements, buggies, steam engines, newspapers, books, statuary, carving, paintings, the management of drug stores and banks has not been trodden without contact with thorns and thistles. While we take pride in what we exhibit as a result of our independent efforts, we do not for a moment forget that our part in this exhibition would fall far short of your expectations but for the constant help that has come to our educational life, not only from the Southern States, but especially from Northern philanthropists, who have made their gifts a constant stream of blessing and encouragement.

The wisest among my race understand that the agitation of questions of social equality is the extremest folly, and that progress in the enjoyment of all the privileges that will come to us must be the result of severe and constant struggle rather than of artificial forcing. No race that has anything to contribute to the markets of the world is long in any degree ostracized. It is important and right that all privileges of the law be ours, but it is vastly more important that we be prepared for the exercise of those privileges. The opportunity to earn a dollar in a factory just now is worth infinitely more than the opportunity to spend a dollar in an opera house.

In conclusion, may I repeat that nothing in thirty years has given us more hope and encouragement, and drawn us so near to you of the white race, as this opportunity offered by the Exposition; and here bending, as it were, over the altar that represents the results of the struggles of your race and mine, both starting practically empty-handed three decades ago, I pledge that, in your effort to work out the great and intricate problem which God has laid at the doors of the South, you shall have at all times the patient, sympathetic help of my race; only let this be constantly in mind that, while from representations in these buildings of the products of field, of forest, of mine, of factory, letters, and art, much good will come, yet far above and beyond material benefits will be the higher good, that let us pray God will come, in a blotting out of sectional differences and racial animosities and suspicions, in a determination to administer absolute justice, in a willing obedience among all classes to the mandates of law. This, coupled with our material prosperity, will bring into our beloved South a new heaven and a new earth.

ADDRESS DELIVERED AT THE HARVARD ALUMNI DINNER IN 1896

Mr. President and Gentlemen: It would in some measure relieve my embarrassment if I could, even in a slight degree, feel myself worthy of the great honor which you do me today. Why you have called me from the Black Belt of the South, from among my humble people, to share in the honors of this occasion, is not for me to explain; and yet it may not be inappropriate for me to suggest that it seems to me that one of the most vital questions that touch our American life is how to bring the strong, wealthy and learned into helpful touch with the poorest, most ignorant and humblest, and at the same time make the one appreciate the vitalizing, strengthening influence of the other. How shall we make the mansions on yon Beacon Street feel and see the need of the spirits in the lowliest cabin in Alabama cotton fields or Louisiana sugar bottoms? This problem Harvard University is solving, not by bringing itself down, but by bringing the masses up.

If through me, an humble representative, seven millions of my people in the South might be permitted to send a message to Harvard— Harvard that offered up on death's altar young Shaw, and Russell, and Lowell, and scores of others, that we might have a free and united country—that message would be, "Tell them that the sacrifice was not in vain. Tell them that by habits of thrift and economy, by way of the industrial school and college, we are coming. We are crawling up, working up, yea, bursting up. Often through oppression, unjust discrimination and prejudice, but through them all we are coming up, and with proper habits, intelligence and property, there is no power on earth that can permanently stay our progress."

If my life in the past has meant anything in the lifting up of my people and the bringing about of better relations between your race and mine, I assure you from this day it will mean doubly more. In the economy of God there is but one standard by which an individual can succeed—there is but one for a race. This country demands that every race shall measure itself by the American standard. By it a race must rise or fall, succeed or fail, and in the last analysis mere sentiment counts for little. During the next half century and more, my race must continue passing through the severe American crucible. We are to be tested in our patience, our forbearance, our perseverance, our power to endure wrong, to withstand temptations, to economize, to acquire and use skill; in our ability to compete, to succeed in commerce, to disregard the superficial for the real, the appearance for the substance, to be great and yet small, learned and yet simple, high and yet the servant of all. This, this is the passport to all that is best in the life of our Republic, and the Negro must possess it, or be debarred.

While we are thus being tested, I beg of you to remember that wherever our life touches yours, we help or hinder. Wherever your life touches ours, you make us stronger or weaker. No member of your race in any part of our country can harm the meanest member of mine without the proudest and bluest blood in Massachusetts being degraded. When Mississippi commits crime, New England commits crime, and in so much, lowers the standard of your civilization. There is no escape—man drags man down, or man lifts man up.

In working out our destiny, while the main center of activity must be with us, we shall need, in a large measure in the years that are to come as we have in the past, the help, the encouragement, the guidance that the strong can give the weak. Thus helped, we of both races in the South soon shall throw off the shackles of racial and sectional prejudice and rise, as Harvard University has risen and as we all should rise, above the clouds of ignorance, narrowness and selfishness, into that atmosphere, that pure sunshine, where it will be our highest ambition to serve man, our brother, regardless of race or previous condition.

Sutton Elbert Griggs

(1872–1930)

SUTTON ELBERT GRIGGS WAS the author of more than thirty works, among them five published novels: *Imperium in Imperio* (1899); *Overshadowed* (1901); *Unfettered* (1902); *The Hindered Hand* (1905); and *Pointing the Way* (1908). As a novelist, he shared a weakness common to many other black authors of his era: he was too much concerned with the Race Problem and too little with the art of fiction. His technical shortcomings are, therefore, many and obvious; but in spite of them his writing is significant. An early though vacillating militant, the first Negro to write a political novel of any consequence, one of the first to "glorify black pigmentation" in his characters, and a strong defender of his race against the vicious attacks of Southern apologists like Thomas Dixon and Thomas Nelson Page, Griggs used themes which foreshadowed those used by later and better writers. Robert A. Bone, author of *The Negro Novel in America,* considers Griggs a representative figure, one who in his vacillating between militancy and accommodation reflects "the political dilemma of the Negro intellectual prior to World War I."

Born in Chatfield, Texas, Sutton Griggs attended Bishop College in his native state and was an outstanding student. In 1893 he completed a theological course at Richmond Theological Seminary (now a part of Virginia Union University), becoming an ordained Baptist minister. His first pastorate was in Berkley, Virginia, where he remained for two years. For the next twenty years, Griggs was corresponding Secretary of the Education Department of the National Baptist Convention in Nashville, Tennessee. After leaving that office, he held several pastorates in various parts of the country. Just before his death, Griggs went to Houston, Texas, to establish the National Religious and Civic Institute, a school sponsored by the Baptists of that city. He died while working on this project.

For additional information on Sutton Griggs, see Hugh M. Gloster, *Negro Voices in American Fiction* (Chapel Hill: The University of North Carolina Press, 1948); Hugh M. Gloster, "Sutton E. Griggs, Novelist of the New Negro," *Phylon,* IV, 4 (1943); and Robert A. Bone, *The Negro Novel in America.*

The selection given below comes from *The Hindered Hand.*

THE BLAZE

Little Melville Brant stamped his foot on the floor, looked defiantly at his mother, and said, in the whining tone of a nine-year old child,

"Mother, I want to go."

"Melville, I have told you this dozen times that you cannot go," responded the mother with a positiveness that caused the boy to feel that his chances were slim.

"You are always telling me to keep ahead of the other boys, and I can't even get up to some of them," whined Melville plaintively.

"What do you mean?" asked the mother.

"Ben Stringer is always a crowing over me. Every time I tell anything big he jumps in and tells what he's seen, and that knocks me out. He has seen a whole lots of lynchings. His papa takes him. I bet if my papa was living he would take me," said Melville.

"My boy, listen to your mother," said Mrs. Brant. "Nothing but bad people take part in or go to see those things. I want mother's boy to scorn such things, to be way above them."

"Well, I ain't. I want to see it. Ben Stringer ain't got no business being ahead of me," Melville said with vigor.

The shrieking of the train whistle caused the fever of interest to rise in the little boy.

"There's the train now, mother. Do let me go. I ain't never seen a darky burned."

"Burned!" exclaimed Mrs. Brant in horror.

Melville looked up at his mother as if pitying her ignorance.

"They are going to burn them. Sed Lonly heard his papa and Mr. Corkle talking about it, and it's all fixed up."

"My Heavenly Father!" murmured Mrs. Brant, horror struck.

The cheering of the multitude borne upon the air was now heard.

"Mother, I must go. You can beat me as hard as you want to after I do it. I can't let Ben Stringer be crowing over me. He'll be there."

Looking intently at his mother, Melville backed toward the door. Mrs. Brant rushed forward and seized him.

"I shall put you in the attic. You shall not see that inhuman affair."

To her surprise Melville did not resist, but meekly submitted to being taken up stairs and locked in the attic.

Knowing how utterly opposed his mother was to lynchings he had calculated upon her refusal and had provided for such a contingency. He fastened the attic door on the inside and took from a corner a stout stick and a rope which he had secreted there. Fastening the rope to the stick and placing the stick across the small attic window he succeeded in lowering himself to the ground. He ran with all the speed at his command and arrived at the railway station just in time to see the mob begin its march with Bud and Foresta toward the scene of the killing of Sidney Fletcher.

Arriving at the spot where Fletcher's body had been found, the mob halted and the leaders instituted the trial of the accused.

"Did you kill Mr. Sidney Fletcher?" asked the mob's spokesman of Bud.

"Can I explain the matter to you, gentlemen," asked Bud.

"We want you to tell us just one thing; did you kill Mr. Sidney Fletcher?"

"He tried to kill me," replied Bud.

"And you therefore killed him, did you?"

"Yes, sir. That's how it happened."

"You killed him, then?" asked the spokesman.

"I shot him, and if he died I suppose I must have caused it. But it was in self-defense."

"You hear that, do you. He has confessed," said the spokesman to his son who was the reporter of the world-wide news agency that was to give to the reading public an account of the affair.

"Well, we are ready to act," shouted the spokesman to the crowd.

Two men now stepped forward and reached the spokesman at about the same time.

"I got a fine place, with everything ready. I knew what you would need and I arranged for you," said one of the men.

"My place is nearer than his, and everything is as ready as it can be. I think I am entitled to it," said the other.

"You want the earth, don't you?" indignantly asked the first applicant of the second.

Ignoring this thrust the second applicant said to the spokesman,

"You know I have done all the dirty work here. If you all wanted anybody to stuff the ballot box or swear to false returns, I have been your man. I've put out of the way every biggety nigger that you sent me after. You know all this."

"You've been paid for it, too. Ain't you been to the legislature? Ain't you been constable? Haven't you captured prisoners and held 'um in secret till the governor offered rewards and then you have brung 'em forward? You have been well paid. But me, I've had none of the good things. I've done dirty work, too, don't you forget it. And now I want these niggers hung in my watermelon patch, so as to keep darkies out of nights, being as they are feart of hants, and you are here to keep me out of that little favor."

The dispute waxed so hot that it was finally decided that it was best to accept neither place.

"We want this affair to serve as a warning to darkies to never lift their hands against a white man, and it won't hurt to perform this noble deed where they will never forget it. I am commander to-day and I order the administration of justice to take place near the Negro church."

"Good! Good!" was the universal comment.

The crowd dashed wildly in the direction of the church, all being eager to get places where they could see best. The smaller boys climbed the trees so that they might see well the whole transaction. Two of the trees were decided upon for stakes and the boys who had chosen them had to come down. Bud was tied to one tree and Foresta to the other in such a manner that they faced each other. Wood was brought and piled around them and oil was poured on very profusely.

The mob decided to torture their victims before killing them and began on Foresta first. A man with a pair of scissors stepped up and cut off her hair and threw it into the crowd. There was a great scramble for bits of hair for souvenirs of the occasion. One by one her fingers were cut off and tossed into the crowd to be scrambled for. A man with a cork screw came forward, ripped Foresta's clothing to her waist, bored into her breast with the corkscrew and pulled forth the live quivering flesh. Poor Bud her helpless husband closed his eyes and turned away his head to avoid the terrible sight. Men gathered about him and forced his eyelids open so that he could see all.

When it was thought that Foresta had been tortured sufficiently, attention was turned to Bud. His fingers were cut off one by one and the corkscrew was bored into his legs and arms. A man with a club struck him over the head, crushing his skull and forcing an eyeball to hang down from the socket by a thread. A rush was made toward Bud and a man who was a little ahead of his competitors snatched the eyeball as a souvenir.

After three full hours had been spent in torturing the two, the spokesman announced that they were now ready for the final act. The brother of Sidney Fletcher was called for and was given a match. He stood near his mutilated victims until the photographer present could take a picture of the scene. This being over the match was applied and the flames leaped up eagerly and encircled the writhing forms of Bud and Foresta.

When the flames had done their work and had subsided, a mad rush was made for the trees which were soon denuded of bark, each member of the mob being desirous, it seemed, of carrying away something that might testify to his proximity to so great a happening.

Little Melville Brant found a piece of the charred flesh in the ashes and bore it home.

"Ben Stringer aint got anything on me now," said he as he trudged along in triumph.

Entering by the rear he caught hold of the rope which he had left hanging, ascended to the attic window and crawled in.

The future ruler of the land!

On the afternoon of the lynching Ramon Mansford alighted from the train at Maulville in search of Bud and Foresta. He noted the holiday appearance of the crowd as it swarmed around the depot awaiting the going of the special trains that had brought the people to Maulville to see the lynching, and, not knowing the occasion that had brought them together, said within himself:

"This crowd looks happy enough. The South is indeed sunny and sunny are the hearts of its people."

At length he approached a man, who like himself seemed to be an onlooker. Using the names under which Mrs. Harper told him that Bud and Foresta were passing, he made inquiry of them. The man looked at him in amazement.

"You have just got in, have you?" Asked the man of Ramon.

"Yes," he replied.

"Haven't you been reading the papers?" further inquired the man.

"Not lately, I must confess; I have been so absorbed in unraveling a murder mystery (the victim being one very dear to me) that I have not read the papers for the last few days."

"We burned the people to-day that you are looking for."

"Burned them?" asked Ramon incredulously.

"Yes, burned them."

"The one crime!" gasped Ramon.

"I understand you," said the man. "You want to know how we square the burning of a woman with the statement that we lynch for one crime in the South, heh?"

The shocked Ramon nodded affirmatively.

'That's all rot about one crime. We lynch niggers down here for anything. We lynch them for being sassy and sometimes lynch them on general principles. The truth of the matter is the real 'one crime' that paves the way for a lynching whenever we have the notion, is the crime of being black."

'Burn them! The one crime!" murmured Ramon, scarcely knowing what he said. With bowed head and hands clasped behind him he walked away to meditate.

"After all, do not I see to-day a gleam of light thrown on the taking away of my Alene? With murder and lawnessness rampant in the Southland, this section's woes are to be many. Who can say what bloody orgies Alene has escaped? Who can tell the contents of the storm cloud that hangs low over this section where the tragedy of the ages is being enacted? Alene, O Alene, my spirit longs for thee!"

Ramon took the train that night—not for Almaville, for he had not the heart to bear the terrible tidings to those helpless, waiting, simple folks, the parents of Bud and Foresta. He went North feeling that some day somehow he might be called upon to revisit the South as its real friend, but seeming foe. And he shuddered at the thought.

Charles Waddell Chesnutt

(1858–1932)

ALTHOUGH CHARLES W. CHESNUTT was born in Cleveland, Ohio, when he was eight years old his family moved to Fayetteville, North Carolina. There he received a grade school education, his only formal training. Chesnutt taught school for nine years in North Carolina, then moved to New York where he worked for some time as a journalist. Having taught himself stenography, he went to Cleveland and became a court stenographer. In the meantime he "read law" and passed the Ohio bar.

In 1887, the *Atlantic Monthly* accepted his short story "The Goophered Grapevine," but did not let the public know that the author was a Negro. (Chesnutt was a "voluntary Negro," that is, one light enough to pass for white.) Walter Hines Page, associated with the *Atlantic* and with Houghton Mifflin, rejected the first draft of *The House Behind the Cedars*, a "controversial" novel of the "color line," but published *The Conjure Woman* (1899) and *The Wife of His Youth, and Other Stories of the Color Line* (1899). The publishers then changed their minds and brought out *The House Behind the Cedars* (1900); *The Marrow of Tradition* (1901); and *The Colonel's Dream* (1905). One of Chesnutt's best short stories, "Baxter's Procrustes," was published in the *Atlantic* (June, 1904). A brilliant work, it had nothing to do with race.

Like Sutton Griggs, Chesnutt was angered by Southern injustice and fought against it in his books and civic activities. Also like Griggs, he resented the vicious charges made by popular Southern writers like Thomas Nelson Page and Thomas Dixon against the Negro. Chesnutt, however, had a better grasp of social conditions than Griggs and was more consistently militant; moreover, he was a much better artist. Although, like Griggs, he leaned rather heavily on "The Problem," he was undoubtedly the best black fiction writer before Richard Wright.

In 1928 Charles W. Chesnutt was awarded the Spingarn Medal for his "pioneer services as a literary artist and his distinguished career as a public-spirited citizen."

His daughter Helen's biography, *Charles Waddell Chesnutt: Pioneer of the Color Line* (Chapel Hill: The University of North Carolina Press, 1952), contains many interesting letters showing Chesnutt's intimacy with such figures as George W. Cable, Walter Hines Page, Mark Twain, Booker T. Washington, and others. See also Hugh M. Gloster,

"Charles W. Chesnutt: Pioneer in the Fiction of Negro Life," *Phylon,* II (First Quarter, 1941), Vernon Loggins, *The Negro Author,* and Robert A. Bone, *The Negro Novel in America.*

THE GOOPHERED GRAPEVINE

Some years ago my wife was in poor health, and our family doctor, in whose skill and honesty I had implicit confidence, advised a change of climate. I shared, from an unprofessional standpoint, his opinion that the raw winds, the chill rains, and the violent changes of temperature that characterized the winters in the region of the Great Lakes tended to aggravate my wife's difficulty, and would undoubtedly shorten her life if she remained exposed to them. The doctor's advice was that we seek, not a temporary place of sojourn, but a permanent residence, in a warmer and more equable climate. I was engaged at the time in grape-culture in northern Ohio, and, as I liked the business and had given it much study, I decided to look for some other locality suitable for carrying it on. I thought of sunny France, of sleepy Spain, of Southern California, but there were objections to them all. It occurred to me that I might find what I wanted in some one of our own Southern States. It was a sufficient time after the war for conditions in the South to have become somewhat settled; and I was enough of a pioneer to start a new industry, if I could not find a place where grape-culture had been tried. I wrote to a cousin who had gone into the turpentine business in central North Carolina. He assured me, in response to my inquiries, that no better place could be found in the South than the State and neighborhood where he lived; the climate was perfect for health, and, in conjunction with the soil, ideal for grape-culture; labor was cheap, and land could be bought for a mere song. He gave us a cordial invitation to come and visit him while we looked into the matter. We accepted the invitation, and after several days of leisurely travel, the last hundred miles of which were up a river on a sidewheel steamer, we reached our destination, a quaint old town, which I shall call Patesville, because, for one reason, that is not its name. There was a red brick market-house in the public square, with a tall tower, which held a four-faced clock that struck the hours, and from which there pealed out a curfew at nine o'clock. There were two or three hotels, a court-house, a jail, stores, offices, and all the appurtenances of a county seat and a commercial emporium; for while Patesville numbered only four or five thousand inhabitants, of all shades of complexion, it was one of the principal towns in North Carolina, and had a considerable trade in cotton and naval stores. This business activity was not immediately apparent to my unaccustomed eyes. Indeed, when I first saw the town, there brooded over it a calm that seemed almost sabbatic in its restfulness, though I learned later on that underneath its somnolent exterior the deeper currents of life— love and hatred, joy and despair, ambition and avarice, faith and friendship—flowed not less steadily than in livelier latitudes.

We found the weather delightful at that season, the end of summer, and were hospitably entertained. Our host was a man of means and evidently regarded our visit as a pleasure, and we were therefore correspondingly at our ease, and in a position to act with the coolness of judgment desirable in making so radical a change in our lives. My cousin placed a horse and buggy at our disposal, and himself acted as our guide until I became somewhat familiar with the country.

I found that grape-culture, while it had never been carried on to any great extent, was not entirely unknown in the neighborhood. Several planters thereabouts had attempted it on a commercial scale, in former years, with greater or less success; but like most Southern industries, it had felt the blight of war and had fallen into desuetude.

I went several times to look at a place that I thought might suit me. It was a plantation of considerable extent, that had formerly belonged to a wealthy man by the name of McAdoo. The estate had been for years involved in litigation between disputing heirs, during which period shiftless cultivation had well-nigh exhausted the soil. There had been a vineyard of some extent on the place, but it had not been attended to since the war, and had lapsed into utter neglect. The vines —here partly supported by decayed and broken-down trellises, there twining themselves among the branches of the slender saplings which had sprung up among them—grew in wild and unpruned luxuriance, and the few scattered grapes they bore were the undisputed prey of the first comer. The site was admirably adapted to grape-raising; the soil, with a little attention, could not have been better; and with the native grape, the luscious scuppernong, as my main reliance in the beginning, I felt sure that I could introduce and cultivate successfully a number of other varieties.

One day I went over with my wife to show her the place. We drove out of the town over a long wooden bridge that spanned a spreading mill-pond, passed the long whitewashed fence surrounding the county fair-ground, and struck into a road so sandy that the horse's feet sank to the fetlocks. Our route lay partly up hill and partly down, for we were in the sand-hill county; we drove past cultivated farms, and then by abandoned fields grown up in scrub-oak and short-leaved pine, and once or twice through the solemn aisles of the virgin forest, where the tall pines, well-nigh meeting over the narrow road, shut out the sun, and wrapped us in cloistral solitude. Once, at a cross-roads, I was in doubt as to the turn to take, and we sat there waiting ten minutes— we had already caught some of the native infection of restfulness—

for some human being to come along, who could direct us on our way. At length a little negro girl appeared, walking straight as an arrow, with a piggin full of water on her head. After a little patient investigation, necessary to overcome the child's shyness, we learned what we wished to know, and at the end of about five miles from the town reached our destination.

We drove between a pair of decayed gateposts—the gate itself had long since disappeared—and up a straight sandy lane, between two lines of rotting rail fence, partly concealed by jimson-weeds and briers, to the open space where a dwelling-house had once stood, evidently a spacious mansion, if we might judge from the ruined chimneys that were still standing, and the brick pillars on which the sills rested. The house itself, we had been informed, had fallen a victim to the fortunes of war.

We alighted from the buggy, walked about the yard for a while, and then wandered off into the adjoining vineyard. Upon Annie's complaining of weariness I led the way back to the yard, where a pine log, lying under a spreading elm, afforded a shady though somewhat hard seat. One end of the log was already occupied by a venerable-looking colored man. He held on his knees a hat full of grapes, over which he was smacking his lips with great gusto, and a pile of grape-skins near him indicated that the performance was no new thing. We approached him at an angle from the rear, and were close to him before he perceived us. He respectfully rose as we drew near, and was moving away, when I begged him to keep his seat.

"Don't let us disturb you," I said. "There is plenty of room for us all."

He resumed his seat with somewhat of embarrassment. While he had been standing, I had observed that he was a tall man, and, though slightly bowed by the weight of years, apparently quite vigorous. He was not entirely black, and this fact, together with the quality of his hair, which was about six inches long and very bushy, except on the top of his head, where he was quite bald, suggested a slight strain of other than negro blood. There was a shrewdness in his eyes, too, which was not altogether African, and which, as we afterwards learned from experience, was indicative of a corresponding shrewdness in his character. He went on eating the grapes, but did not seem to enjoy himself quite so well as he had apparently done before he became aware of our presence.

"Do you live around here?" I asked, anxious to put him at his ease.

"Yas, suh. I lives des ober yander, behine de nex' san'-hill, on de Lumberton plank-road."

"Do you know anything about the time when this vineyard was cultivated?"

"Lawd bless you, suh, I knows all about it. Dey ain' na'er a man in dis settlement w'at won' tell you ole Julius McAdoo 'uz bawn en raise' on dis yer same plantation. Is you de Norv'n gemman w'at's gwine ter buy de ole vimya'd?"

"I am looking at it," I replied; "but I don't know that I shall care to buy unless I can be reasonably sure of making something out of it."

"Well, suh, you is a stranger ter me, en I is a stranger ter you, en we is bofe strangers ter one anudder, but 'f I 'uz in yo' place, I would n' buy dis vimya'd."

"Why not?" I asked.

"Well, I dunno whe'r you b'lieves in cunj'in' er not,—some er de w'ite folks don't, er says dey don't,—but de truf er de matter is dat dis yer ole vimya'd is goophered."

"Is what?" I asked, not grasping the meaning of this unfamiliar word.

"Is goophered,—cunju'd, bewitch'."

He imparted this information with such solemn earnestness, and with such an air of confidential mystery, that I felt somewhat interested, while Annie was evidently much impressed, and drew closer to me.

"How do you know it is bewitched?" I asked.

"I would n' spec' fer you ter b'lieve me 'less you know all 'bout de fac's. But ef you en young miss dere doan' min' lis'nin' ter a ole nigger run on a minute er two w'ile you er restin', I kin 'splain to you how it all happen'."

We assured him that we would be glad to hear how it all happened, and he began to tell us. At first the current of his memory—or imagination—seemed somewhat sluggish; but as his embarrassment wore off, his language flowed more freely, and the story acquired perspective and coherence. As he became more and more absorbed in the narrative, his eyes assumed a dreamy expression, and he seemed to lose sight of his auditors, and to be living over again in monologue his life on the old plantation.

"Ole Mars Dugal' McAdoo," he began, "bought dis place long many years befo' de wah, en I 'member well w'en he sot out all dis yer part er de plantation in scuppernon's. De vimes growed monst'us fas', en Mars Dugal' made a thousan' gallon er scuppernon' wine eve'y year.

"Now, ef dey 's an'thing a nigger lub, nex' ter 'possum, en chick'n, en watermillyums, it 's scuppernon's. Dey ain' nuffin dat kin stan' up side'n de scuppernon' for sweetness; sugar ain't a suckumstance ter scuppernon'. W'en de season is nigh 'bout ober, en de grapes begin ter swivel up des a little wid de wrinkles er ole age,—w'en de skin git sof' en brown,—den de scuppernon' make you smack yo' lip en roll yo' eye en wush fer mo'; so I reckon it ain' very 'stonishin' dat niggers lub scuppernon'.

"Dey wuz a sight er niggers in de naberhood er de vimya'd. Dere wuz ole Mars Henry Brayboy's niggers, en ole Mars Jeems McLean's niggers, en Mars Dugal's own niggers; den dey wuz a settlement er free niggers en po' buckrahs down by de Wim'l'ton Road, en Mars Dugal' had de only vimya'd in de naberhood. I reckon it ain' so much so nowadays, but befo' de wah, in slab'ry times, a nigger did n' mine goin' fi' er ten mile in a night, w'en dey wuz sump'n good ter eat at de yuther een'.

"So atter a w'ile Mars Dugal' begin ter miss his scuppernon's. Co'se he 'cuse' de niggers er it, but dey all 'nied it ter de las'. Mars Dugal' sot spring guns en steel traps, en he en de oberseah sot up nights once't er twice't, tel one night Mars Dugal'—he 'uz a monst'us keerless man —got his leg shot full er cow-peas. But somehow er nudder dey could n' nebber ketch none er de niggers. I dunner how it happen, but it happen des like I tell you, en de grapes kep' on a-goin' des de same.

"But bimeby ole Mars Dugal' fix' up a plan ter stop it. Dey wuz a cunjuh 'oman livin' down 'mongs' de free niggers on de Wim'l'ton Road, en all de darkies fum Rockfish ter Beaver Crick wuz feared er her. She could wuk de mos' powerfulles' kin' er goopher,—could make people hab fits, er rheumatiz, er make 'em des dwinel away en die; en dey say she went out ridin' de niggers at night, fer she wuz a witch 'sides bein' a cunjuh 'oman. Mars Dugal' hearn 'bout Aun' Peggy's doin's, en begun ter 'flect whe'r er no he could n' git her ter he'p him keep de niggers off'n de grapevimes. One day in de spring er de year, ole miss pack' up a basket er chick'n en poun'-cake, en a bottle er scuppernon' wine, en Mars Dugal' tuk it in his buggy en driv ober ter Aun' Peggy's cabin. He tuk de basket in, en had a long talk wid Aun' Peggy.

"De nex' day Aun' Peggy come up ter de vimya'd. De niggers seed her slippin' 'roun', en dey soon foun' out what she 'uz doin' dere. Mars Dugal' had hi'ed her ter goopher de grapevimes. She sa'ntered 'roun' 'mongs' de vimes, en tuk a leaf fum dis one, en a grape-hull fum dat one, en a grape-seed fum anudder one; en den a little twig fum here, en a little pinch er dirt fum dere,—en put it all in a big black bottle, wid a snake's toof en a speckle' hen's gall en some ha'rs fum a black cat's tail, en den fill' de bottle wid scuppernon' wine. W'en she got de goopher all ready en fix', she tuk 'n went out in de woods en buried it under de root uv a red oak tree, en den come back en tole one er de niggers she done goopher de grapevimes, en a'er a nigger w'at eat dem grapes 'ud be sho ter die inside'n twel' mont's.

"Atter dat de niggers let de scuppernon's 'lone, en Mars Dugal' did n' hab no 'casion ter fine no mo' fault; en de season wuz mos' gone, w'en a strange gemman stop at de plantation one night ter see Mars Dugal' on some business; en his coachman, seein' de scuppernon's growin' so nice en sweet, slip 'roun' behine de smoke-house, en et all de scup-pernon's he could hole. Nobody did n' notice it at de time, but dat night, on de way home, de gemman's hoss runned away en kill' de coachman. W'en we hearn de noos, Aun' Lucy, de cook, she up 'n say she seed de strange nigger eat'n' er de scuppernon's behine de smoke-house; en den we knowed de goopher had b'en er wukkin'. Den one er de nigger chilluns runned away fum de quarters one day, en got in de scuppernon's, en died de nex' week. W'ite folks say he die' er de fevuh, but de niggers knowed it wuz de goopher. So you k'n be sho de darkies did n' hab much ter do wid dem scuppernon' vimes.

"W'en de scuppernon' season 'uz ober fer dat year, Mars Dugal' foun' he had made fifteen hund'ed gallon er wine; en one er de niggers hearn him laffin' wid de oberseah fit ter kill, en sayin' dem fifteen hund'ed gallon er wine wuz monst'us good intrus' on de ten dollars he laid out on de vimya'd. So I 'low ez he paid Aun' Peggy ten dollars fer to goopher de grapevimes.

"De goopher did n' wuk no mo' tel de nex' summer, we'n 'long to'ds de middle er de season one er de fiel' han's died; en ez dat lef' Mars Dugal' sho't er han's, he went off ter town fer ter buy anudder. He fotch de noo nigger home wid 'im. He wuz er ole nigger, er de color er a gingy-cake, en ball ez a hoss-apple on de top er his head. He wuz a peart ole nigger, do', en could do a big day's wuk.

"Now it happen dat one er de niggers on de nex' plantation, one er ole Mars Henry Brayboy's niggers, had runned away de day befo', en tuk ter de swamp, en ole Mars Dugal' en some er de yuther nabor w'ite folks had gone out wid dere guns en dere dogs fer ter he'p 'em hunt fer de nigger; en de han's on our own plantation wuz all so flusterated dat we fuhgot ter tell de noo han' 'bout de goopher on de scuppernon' vimes. Co'se he smell de grapes en see de vimes, an atter dahk de fus' thing he done wuz ter slip off ter de grapevimes 'dout sayin' nuffin ter nobody. Nex' mawnin' he tole some er de niggers 'bout de fine bait er scuppernon' he et de night befo'.

"W'en dey tole 'im 'bout de goopher on de grapevimes, he 'uz dat tarrified dat he turn pale, en look des like he gwine ter die right in his tracks. De oberseah come up en axed w'at 'uz de matter; en w'en dey tole 'im Henry be'n eatin' er de scuppernon's, en got de goopher on 'im, he gin Henry a big drink er w'iskey, en 'low dat de nex' rainy day he take 'im ober ter Aun' Peggy's, en see ef she would n' take de goopher off'n him, seein' ez he did n' know nuffin erbout it tel he done et de grapes.

"Sho nuff, it rain de nex' day, en de oberseah went ober ter Aun' Peggy's wid Henry. En Aun' Peggy say dat bein' ez Henry did n' know 'bout de goopher, en et de grapes in ign'ance er de conseq'ences, she reckon she mought be able fer ter take de goopher off'n him. So she fotch out er bottle wid some cunjuh medicine in it, en po'd some out in a go'd fer Henry ter drink. He manage ter git it down; he say it tas'e like whiskey wid sump'n bitter in it. She 'lowed dat 'ud keep de goopher off'n him tel de spring; but w'en de sap begin ter rise in de grapevimes he ha' ter come en see her ag'in, en she tell him w'at e's ter do.

"Nex' spring, w'en de sap commence' ter rise in de scuppernon' vime, Henry tuk a ham one night. Whar 'd he git de ham? *I* doan know; dey wa'n't no hams on de plantation 'cep'n' w'at 'uz in de smoke-house, but *I* never see Henry 'bout de smoke-house. But ez I wuz a-sayin', he tuk de ham ober ter Aun' Peggy's; en Aun' Peggy tole 'im dat w'en Mars Dugal' begin ter prune de grapevimes, he mus' go en take 'n scrape off de sap whar it ooze out'n de cut een's er de vimes, en 'n'int his ball head wid it; en ef he do dat once't a year de goopher would n' wuk agin 'im long ez he done it. En bein' ez he fotch her de ham, she fix' it so he kin eat all de scuppernon' he want.

"So Henry 'n'int his head wid de sap out'n de big grapevime des ha'f way 'twix' de quarters en de big house, en de goopher nebber wuk agin him dat summer. But de beatenes' thing you eber see happen ter Henry. Up ter dat time he wuz ez ball ez a sweeten' 'tater, but des ez soon ez de young leaves begun ter come out on de grapevimes, de ha'r begun ter grow out on Henry's head, en by de middle er de summer he had de bigges' head er ha'r on de plantation. Befo' dat, Henry had tol'able good ha'r 'round' de aidges, but soon ez de young grapes begun ter come, Henry's ha'r begun to quirl all up in little balls, des like dis yer reg'lar grapy ha'r, en by de time de grapes got ripe his head look des like a bunch er grapes. Combin' it did n' do no good; he wuk at it ha'f de night wid er Jim Crow,[1] en think he git it straighten' out, but in de mawnin' de grapes 'ud be dere des de same. So he gin it up, en tried ter keep de grapes down by havin' his ha'r cut sho't.

"But dat wa'n't de quares' thing 'bout de goopher. When Henry come ter de plantation, he wuz gittin' a little ole an stiff in de j'ints. But dat summer he got des ez spry en libely ez any young nigger on de plantation; fac', he got so biggity dat Mars Jackson, de oberseah, ha' ter th'eaten ter whip 'im, if he did n' stop cuttin' up his didos en behave hisse'f. But de mos' cur'ouses' thing happen' in de fall, when de sap begin ter go down in de grapevimes. Fus', when de grapes 'uz gethered, de knots begun ter straighten out'n Henry's ha'r; en w'en de leaves begin ter fall, Henry's ha'r 'mence' ter drap out; en when de vimes 'uz bar', Henry's head wuz baller 'n it wuz in de spring, en he begin ter git ole en stiff in de j'ints ag'in, en paid no mo' 'tention ter de gals dyoin' er de whole winter. En nex' spring, w'en he rub de sap on ag'in, he got young ag'in, en so soopl en libely dat none er de young niggers on de plantation could n' jump, ner dance, ner hoe ez much cotton ez Henry. But in de fall er de year his grapes 'mence' ter

---

[1] A small card, resembling a currycomb in construction, and used by negroes in the rural districts instead of a comb.

straighten out, en his j'ints ter git stiff, en his ha'r drap off, en de rheumatiz begin ter wrastle wid 'im.

"Now, ef you 'd 'a' knowed ole Mars Dugal' McAdoo, you 'd 'a' knowed dat it ha' ter be a mighty rainy day when he could n' fine sump'n fer his niggers ter do, en it ha' ter be a mighty little hole he could n' crawl thoo, en ha' ter be a monst'us cloudy night when a dollar git by him in de dahkness; en w'en he see how Henry git young in de spring en ole in de fall, he 'lowed ter hisse'f ez how he could make mo' money out'n Henry dan by wukkin' him in de cotton-fiel'. 'Long de nex' spring, atter de sap 'mence' ter rise, en Henry 'n'int 'is head en sta'ted fer ter git young en soopl, Mars Dugal' up 'n tuk Henry ter town, en sole 'im fer fifteen hunder' dollars. Co'se de man w'at bought Henry did n' know nuffin 'bout de goopher, en Mars Dugal' did n' see no 'casion fer ter tell 'im. Long to'ds de fall, w'en de sap went down, Henry begin ter git ole ag'in same ez yuzhal, en his noo marster begin ter git skeered les'n he gwine ter lose his fifteen-hunder'-dollar nigger. He sent fer a mighty fine doctor, but de med'cine did n' 'pear ter do no good; de goopher had a good holt. Henry tole de doctor 'bout de goopher, but de doctor des laff at 'im.

"One day in de winter Mars Dugal' went ter town, en wuz santerin' 'long de Main Street, when who should he meet but Henry's noo marster. Dey said 'Hoddy,' en Mars Dugal' ax 'im ter hab a seegyar; en atter dey run on awhile 'bout de craps en de weather, Mars Dugal' ax 'im, sorter keerless, like ez ef he des thought of it,—

" 'How you like de nigger I sole you las' spring?'

"Henry's marster shuck his head en knock de ashes off'n his seegyar.

" 'Spec' I made a bad bahgin when I bought dat nigger. Henry done good wuk all de summer, but sence de fall set in he 'pears ter be sorter pinin' away. Dey ain' nuffin pertickler de matter wid 'im—leastways de doctor say so—'cep'n' a tech er de rheumatiz; but his ha'r is all fell out, en ef he don't pick up his strenk mighty soon, I spec' I 'm gwine ter lose 'im.'

"Dey smoked on awhile, en bimeby ole mars say, 'Well, a bahgin 's a bahgin, but you en me is good fren's, en I doan wan 'ter see you lose all de money you paid fer dat nigger; en ef wa't you say is so, en I ain't 'sputin' it, he ain't wuf much now. I 'spec's you wukked him too ha'd dis summer, er e'se de swamps down here don't agree wid de san'-hill nigger. So you des lemme know, en ef he gits any wusser I 'll be willin' ter gib yer five hund'ed dollars fer 'im, en take my chances on his livin'.'

"Sho 'nuff, when Henry begun ter draw up wid de rheumatiz en it look like he gwine ter die fer sho, his noo marster sen' fer Mars Dugal', en Mars Dugal' gin him what he promus, en brung Henry home ag'in. He tuk good keer uv 'im dyoin' er de winter,—give 'im w'iskey ter rub his rheumatiz, en terbacker ter smoke, en all he want ter eat,—'caze a nigger w'at he could make a thousan' dollars a year off'n did n' grow on eve'y huckleberry bush.

"Nex' spring, w'en de sap ris en Henry's ha'r commence' ter sprout, Mars Dugal' sole 'im ag'in, down in Robeson County dis time; en he kep' dat sellin' business up fer five year er mo'. Henry nebber say nuffin 'bout de goopher ter his noo marsters, 'caze he know he gwine ter be tuk good keer uv de nex' winter, w'en Mars Dugal' buy him back. En Mars Dugal' made 'nuff money off'n Henry ter buy anudder plantation ober on Beaver Crick.

"But 'long 'bout de een' er dat five year dey come a stranger ter stop at de plantation. De fus' day he 'uz dere he went out wid Mars Dugal' en spent all de mawnin' lookin' ober de vimya'd, en atter dinner dey spent all de evenin' playin' kya'ds. De niggers soon 'skiver' dat he wuz a Yankee, en dat he come down ter Norf C'lina fer ter l'arn de w'ite folks how to raise grapes en make wine. He promus Mars Dugal' he c'd make de grapevimes b'ar twice't ez many grapes, en dat de noo winepress he wuz a-sellin' would make mo' d'n twice't ez many gallons er wine. En ole Mars Dugal' des drunk it all in, des 'peared ter be bewitch' wid dat Yankee. W'en de darkies see dat Yankee runnin' 'roun' de vimya'd en diggin' under de grapevimes, dey shuk dere heads, en 'lowed dat dey feared Mars Dugal' losin' his min'. Mars Dugal' had all de dirt dug away fum under de roots er all de scupper-non' vimes, an' let 'em stan' dat away fer a week er mo'. Den dat Yankee made de niggers fix up a mixtry er lime en ashes en manyo, en po' it 'roun' de roots er de grapevimes. Den he 'vise Mars Dugal' fer ter trim de vimes close't, en Mars Dugal' tuck 'n done eve'ything de Yankee tole him ter do. Dyoin' all er dis time, mind yer, dis yer Yan-kee wuz libbin' off'n de fat er de lan', at de big house, en playin' kya'ds wid Mars Dugal' eve'y night; en dey say Mars Dugal' los' mo'n a thousan' dollars dyoin' er de week dat Yankee wuz a-ruinin' de grapevimes.

"W'en de sap ris nex' spring, ole Henry 'n'inted his head ez yuzhal, en his ha'r 'mence' ter grow des de same ez it done eve'y year. De scuppernon' vimes growed monst's fas', en de leaves wuz greener en thicker dan dey eber be'n dyoin' my remem'bance; en Henry's ha'r growed out thicker dan eber, en he 'peared ter git younger 'n younger, en soopler 'n soopler; en seein' ez he wuz sho't er han's dat spring, havin' tuk in consid'able noo groun', Mars Dugal' 'cluded he would n' sell Henry 'tel he git de crap in en de cotton chop'. So he kep' Henry on de plantation.

"But 'long 'bout time fer de grapes ter come on de scuppernon' vimes, dey 'peared ter come a change ober 'em; de leaves withered en swivel' up, en de young grapes turn' yaller, en bimeby eve'ybody on de plantation could see dat de whole vimya'd wuz dyin'. Mars Dugal' tuk 'n water de vimes en done all he could, but 't wa'n' no use: dat Yankee had done bus' de watermillyum. One time de vimes picked up a bit, en Mars Dugal' 'lowed dey wuz gwine ter come out ag'in; but dat Yankee done dug too close under de roots, en prune de branches too close ter de vime, en all dat lime en ashes done burn' de life out'n de vimes, en dey des kep' a-with'in' en a-swivelin'.

"All dis time de goopher wuz a-wukkin'. When de vimes sta'ted ter wither, Henry 'mence' ter complain er his rheumatiz; en when de leaves begin ter dry up, his ha'r 'mence' ter drap out. When de vimes fresh' up a bit, Henry 'd git peart ag'in, en when de vimes wither' ag'in, Henry 'd git ole ag'in, en des kep' gittin' mo' en mo' fitten fer nuffin; he des pined away, en pined away, en fine'ly tuk ter his cabin; en when de big vime whar he got de sap ter 'n'int his head withered en turned yaller en died, Henry died too,—des went out sorter like a cannel. Dey did n't 'pear ter be nuffin de matter wid 'im, 'cep'n' de rheumatiz, but his strenk des dwinel' away 'tel he did n' hab ernuff lef' ter draw his bref. De goopher had got de under holt, en th'owed Henry dat time fer good en all.

"Mars Dugal' tuk on might'ly 'bout losin' his vimes en his nigger in de same year; en he swo' dat ef he could git holt er dat Yankee he'd wear 'im ter a frazzle, en den chaw up de frazzle; en he'd done it, too, for Mars Dugal' 'uz a monst'us brash man w'en he once git started. He sot de vimya'd out ober ag'in, but it wuz th'ee er fo' year befo' de vimes got ter b'arin' any scuppernon's.

"W'en de wah broke out, Mars Dugal' raise' a comp'ny, en went off ter fight de Yankees. He say he wuz mighty glad dat wah come, en he des want ter kill a Yankee fer eve'y dollar he los' 'long er dat grape-raisin' Yankee. En I 'spec' he would 'a' done it, too, if de Yankees had n' s'picioned sump'n, en killed him fus'. Atter de s'render ole miss move' ter town, de niggers all scattered 'way fum de plantation, en de vimya'd ain' be'n cultervated sence."

"Is that story true?" asked Annie doubtfully, but seriously, as the old man concluded his narrative.

"It's des ez true ez I 'm a-settin' here, miss. Dey 's a easy way ter prove it: I kin lead de way right ter Henry's grave ober yander in de plantation buryin'-groun'. En I tell yer w'at, marster, I would n' 'vise you to buy dis yer ole vimya'd, 'case de goopher 's on it yit, en dey ain' no tellin' w'en it 's gwine ter crap out."

"But I thought you said all the old vines died."

"Dey did 'pear ter die, but a few un 'em come out ag'in, en is mixed in 'mongs' de yuthers. I ain' skeered ter eat de grapes, 'caze I knows de old vimes fum de noo ones; but wid strangers dey ain' no tellin' w'at mought happen. I would n' 'vise yer ter buy dis vimya'd."

I bought the vineyard, nevertheless, and it has been for a long time in a thriving condition, and is often referred to by the local press as a striking illustration of the opportunities open to Northern capital in the development of Southern industries. The luscious scuppernong holds first rank among our grapes, though we cultivate a great many other varieties, and our income from grapes packed and shipped to the Northern markets is quite considerable. I have not noticed any developments of the goopher in the vineyard, although I have a mild suspicion that our colored assistants do not suffer from want of grapes during the season.

I found, when I bought the vineyard, that Uncle Julius had occupied a cabin on the place for many years, and derived a respectable revenue from the product of the neglected grapevines. This, doubtless, accounted for his advice to me not to buy the vineyard, though whether it inspired the goopher story I am unable to state. I believe, however, that the wages I paid him for his services as coachman, for I gave him employment in that capacity, were more than an equivalent for anything he lost by the sale of the vineyard.

THE WIFE OF HIS YOUTH

1

Mr. Ryder was going to give a ball. There were several reasons why this was an opportune time for such an event.

Mr. Ryder might aptly be called the dean of the Blue Veins. The original Blue Veins were a little society of colored persons organized in a certain Northern city shortly after the war. Its purpose was to establish and maintain correct social standards among a people whose social condition presented almost unlimited room for improvement. By accident, combined perhaps with some natural affinity, the society consisted of individuals who were, generally speaking, more white than black. Some envious outsider made the suggestion that no one was eligible for membership who was not white enough to show blue veins. The suggestion was readily adopted by those who were not of the favored few, and since that time the society, though possessing a longer and more pretentious name, had been known far and wide as the "Blue Vein Society," and its members as the "Blue Veins."

The Blue Veins did not allow that any such requirement existed for admission to their circle, but, on the contrary, declared that character and culture were the only things considered; and that if most of their members were light-colored, it was because such persons, as a rule, had had better opportunities to qualify themselves for membership. Opinions differed, too, as to the usefulness of the society. There were those who had been known to assail it violently as a glaring example of the very prejudice from which the colored race had suffered most; and later, when such critics had succeeded in getting on the inside, they had been heard to maintain with zeal and earnestness that the society was a life-boat, an anchor, a bulwark and a shield,—a pillar of cloud by day and of fire by night, to guide their people through the social wilderness. Another alleged prerequisite for Blue Vein membership was that of free birth; and while there was really no such requirement, it is doubtless true that very few of the members would have been unable to meet it if there had been. If there were one or two of the older members who had come up from the South and from slavery, their history presented enough romantic circumstances to rob their servile origin of its grosser aspects.

While there were no such tests of eligibility, it is true that the Blue Veins had their notions on these subjects, and that not all of them were equally liberal in regard to the things they collectively disclaimed. Mr. Ryder was one of the most conservative. Though he had not been among the founders of the society, but had come in some years later, his genius for social leadership was such that he had speedily become its recognized adviser and head, the custodian of its standards, and the preserver of its traditions. He shaped its social policy, was active in providing for its entertainment, and when the interest fell off, as it sometimes did, he fanned the embers until they burst again into a cheerful flame.

There were still other reasons for his popularity. While he was not as white as some of the Blue Veins, his appearance was such as to confer distinction upon them. His features were of a refined type, his hair was almost straight; he was always neatly dressed; his manners were irreproachable, and his morals above suspicion. He had come to Groveland a young man, and obtaining employment in the office of a railroad company as messenger had in time worked himself up to the position of stationery clerk, having charge of the distribution of the office supplies for the whole company. Although the lack of early training had hindered the orderly development of a naturally fine mind, it had not prevented him from doing a great deal of reading or from forming decidedly literary tastes. Poetry was his passion. He could repeat whole pages of the great English poets; and if his pronunciation was sometimes faulty, his eye, his voice, his gestures, would respond to the changing sentiment with a precision that revealed a poetic soul and disarmed criticism. He was economical, and had saved money; he owned and occupied a very comfortable house on a respectable street. His residence was handsomely furnished, containing among other things a good library, especially rich in poetry, a piano, and some choice engravings. He generally shared his house with some young couple, who looked after his wants and were company for him; for Mr. Ryder was a single man. In the early days of his connection with the Blue Veins he had been regarded as quite a catch, and young ladies and their mothers had manœuvred with much ingenuity to capture him. Not, however, until Mrs. Molly Dixon visited Groveland had any woman ever made him wish to change his condition to that of a married man.

Mrs. Dixon had come to Groveland from Washington in the spring, and before the summer was over she had won Mr. Ryder's heart. She possessed many attractive qualities. She was much younger than he; in fact, he was old enough to have been her father, though no one knew exactly how old he was. She was whiter than he, and better educated. She had moved in the best colored society of the country, at Washington, and had taught in the schools of that city. Such a superior person had been eagerly welcomed to the Blue Vein Society, and had taken a leading part in its activities. Mr. Ryder had at first been attracted by her charms of person, for she was very good looking and not over twenty-five; then by her refined manners and the vivacity of her wit. Her husband had been a government clerk, and at his death had left a considerable life insurance. She was visiting friends in Groveland, and, finding the town and the people to her liking, had prolonged her stay indefinitely. She had not seemed displeased at Mr. Ryder's attentions, but on the contrary had given him every proper encouragement; indeed, a younger and less cautious man would long since have spoken. But he had made up his mind, and had only to determine the time when he would ask her to be his wife. He decided to give a ball in her honor, and at some time during the evening of the ball to offer her his heart and hand. He had no special fears about the outcome, but, with a little touch of romance, he wanted the surroundings to be in harmony with his own feelings when he should have received the answer he expected.

Mr. Ryder resolved that this ball should mark an epoch in the social history of Groveland. He knew, of course,—no one could know better, —the entertainments that had taken place in past years, and what must be done to surpass them. His ball must be worthy of the lady in whose honor it was to be given, and must, by the quality of its guests, set an example for the future. He had observed of late a growing liberality, almost a laxity, in social matters, even among members of his own set, and had several times been forced to meet in a social way persons whose complexions and callings in life were hardly up to the standard which he considered proper for the society to maintain. He had a theory of his own.

"I have no race prejudice," he would say, "but we people of mixed blood are ground between the upper and the nether millstone. Our fate lies between absorption by the white race and extinction in the black. The one doesn't want us yet, but may take us in time. The other would welcome us, but it would be for us a backward step. 'With malice towards none, with charity for all,' we must do the best we can for ourselves and those who are to follow us. Self-preservation is the first law of nature."

His ball would serve by its exclusiveness to counteract leveling tendencies, and his marriage with Mrs. Dixon would help to further the upward process of absorption he had been wishing and waiting for.

2

The ball was to take place on Friday night. The house had been put in order, the carpets covered with canvas, the halls and stairs decorated with palms and potted plants; and in the afternoon Mr. Ryder sat on his front porch, which the shade of a vine running up over a wire netting made a cool and pleasant lounging place. He expected to respond to the toast "The Ladies" at the supper, and from a volume of Tennyson—his favorite poet—was fortifying himself with apt quotations. The volume was open at "A Dream of Fair Women." His eyes fell on these lines, and he read them aloud to judge better of their effect:—

> At length I saw a lady within call,
>   Stiller than chisell'd marble, standing there;
> A daughter of the gods, divinely tall,
>   And most divinely fair.

He marked the verse, and turning the page read the stanza beginning,—

> O sweet pale Margaret,
> O rare pale Margaret.

He weighed the passage a moment, and decided that it would not do. Mrs. Dixon was the palest lady he expected at the ball, and she was of a rather ruddy complexion, and of lively disposition and buxom build. So he ran over the leaves until his eye rested on the description of Queen Guinevere:—

> She seem'd a part of joyous Spring:
> A gown of grass-green silk she wore,
> Buckled with golden clasps before;
> A light-green tuft of plumes she bore
> Closed in a golden ring.
>
> She look'd so lovely, as she sway'd
> The rein with dainty finger-tips,
> A man had given all other bliss,
> And all his worldly worth for this,
> To waste his whole heart in one kiss
> Upon her perfect lips.

As Mr. Ryder murmured these words audibly, with an appreciative thrill, he heard the latch of his gate click, and a light footfall sounding on the steps. He turned his head, and saw a woman standing before his door.

She was a little woman, not five feet tall, and proportioned to her height. Although she stood erect, and looked around her with very bright and restless eyes, she seemed quite old; for her face was crossed and recrossed with a hundred wrinkles, and around the edges of her bonnet could be seen protruding here and there a tuft of short gray wool. She wore a blue calico gown of ancient cut, a little red shawl fastened around her shoulders with an old-fashioned brass brooch, and a large bonnet profusely ornamented with faded red and yellow artificial flowers. And she was very black,—so black that her toothless gums, revealed when she opened her mouth to speak, were not red, but blue. She looked like a bit of the old plantation life, summoned up from the past by the wave of a magician's wand, as the poet's fancy had called into being the gracious shapes of which Mr. Ryder had just been reading.

He rose from his chair and came over to where she stood.

"Good-afternoon, madam," he said.

"Good-evenin', suh," she answered, ducking suddenly with a quaint curtsy. Her voice was shrill and piping, but softened somewhat by age. "Is dis yere whar Mistuh Ryduh lib, suh?" she asked, looking around her doubtfully, and glancing into the open windows, through which some of the preparations for the evening were visible.

"Yes," he replied, with an air of kindly patronage, unconsciously flattered by her manner, "I am Mr. Ryder. Did you want to see me?"

"Yas, suh, ef I ain't 'sturbin' of you too much."

"Not at all. Have a seat over here behind the vine, where it is cool. What can I do for you?"

" 'Scuse me, suh," she continued, when she had sat down on the edge of a chair, " 'scuse me, suh, I 's lookin' for my husban'. I heered you wuz a big man an' had libbed heah a long time, an' I 'lowed you would n't min' ef I 'd come roun' an' ax you ef you 'd ever heered of a merlatter man by de name er Sam Taylor 'quirin' roun' in de chu'ches ermongs' de people fer his wife 'Liza Jane?"

Mr. Ryder seemed to think for a moment.

"There used to be many such cases right after the war," he said, "but it has been so long that I have forgotten them. There are very few now. But tell me your story, and it may refresh my memory."

She sat back farther in her chair so as to be more comfortable, and folded her withered hands in her lap.

"My name 's 'Liza," she began, " 'Liza Jane. W'en I wuz young I us'ter b'long ter Marse Bob Smif, down in ole Missoura. I wuz bawn down dere. W'en I wuz a gal I wuz married ter a man named Jim. But Jim died, an' after dat I married a merlatter man named Sam Taylor. Sam wuz freebawn, but his mammy and daddy died, an' de w'ite folks 'prenticed him ter my marster fer ter work fer 'im 'tel he wuz growed up. Sam worked in de fiel', an' I wuz de cook. One day Ma'y Ann, ole miss's maid, came rushin' out ter de kitchen, an' says she, ''Liza Jane, ole marse gwine sell yo' Sam down de ribber.'

" 'Go way f'm yere,' says I; 'my husban' 's free!'

" 'Don' make no diff'ence. I heerd ole marse tell ole miss he wuz gwine take yo' Sam 'way wid 'im ter-morrow, fer he needed money, an' he knowed whar he could git a t'ousan' dollars fer Sam an' no questions axed.'

"W'en Sam come home f'm de fiel' dat night, I tole him 'bout ole marse gwine steal 'im, an' Sam run erway. His time wuz mos' up, an' he swo' dat w'en he wuz twenty-one he would come back an' he'p me run erway, er else save up de money ter buy my freedom. An' I know he'd 'a' done it, fer he thought a heap er me, Sam did. But w'en he come back he did n' fin' me, fer I wuz n' dere. Ole marse had heerd dat I warned Sam, so he had me whip' an' sol' down de ribber.

"Den de wah broke out, an' w'en it wuz ober de cullud folks wuz scattered. I went back ter de ole home; but Sam wuz n' dere, an' I could n' l'arn nuffin' 'bout 'im. But I knowed he 'd be'n dere to look fer me an' had n' foun' me, an' had gone erway ter hunt fer me.

"I 's be'n lookin' fer 'im eber sence," she added simply, as though twenty-five years were but a couple of weeks, "an' I knows he 's be'n lookin' fer me. Fer he sot a heap er sto' by me, Sam did, an' I know he 's be'n huntin' fer me all dese years,—'less'n he 's be'n sick er sump'n, so he could n' work, er out'n his head, so he could n' 'member his promise. I went back down de ribber, fer I 'lowed he 'd gone down dere lookin' fer me. I 's be'n ter Noo Orleens, an' Atlanty, an' Charleston, an' Richmon'; an' w'en I 'd be'n all ober de Souf I come ter de Norf. Fer I knows I 'll fin' 'im some er dese days," she added softly, "er he 'll fin' me, an' den we 'll bofe be as happy in freedom as we wuz in de ole days befo' de wah." A smile stole over her withered countenance as she paused a moment, and her bright eyes softened into a far-away look.

This was the substance of the old woman's story. She had wandered a little here and there. Mr. Ryder was looking at her curiously when she finished.

"How have you lived all these years?" he asked.

"Cookin', suh. I 's a good cook. Does you know anybody w'at needs a good cook, suh? I 's stoppin' wid a cullud fam'ly roun' de corner yonder 'tel I kin git a place."

"Do you really expect to find your husband? He may be dead long ago."

She shook her head emphatically. "Oh no, he ain' dead. De signs an' de tokens tells me. I dremp three nights runnin' on'y dis las' week dat I foun' him."

"He may have married another woman. Your slave marriage would not have prevented him, for you never lived with him after the war, and without that your marriage does n't count."

"Would n' make no diff'ence wid Sam. He would n' marry no yuther 'ooman 'tel he foun' out 'bout me. I knows it," she added. "Sump'n 's be'n tellin' me all dese years dat I 's gwine fin' Sam 'fo' I dies."

"Perhaps he's outgrown you, and climbed up in the world where he would n't care to have you find him."

"No, indeed, suh," she replied, "Sam ain' dat kin' er man. He wuz good ter me, Sam wuz, but he wuz n' much good ter nobody e'se, fer he wuz one er de triflin'es' han's on de plantation. I 'spec's ter haf ter suppo't 'im w'en I fin' im, fer he nebber would work 'less'n he had ter. But den he wuz free, an' he did n' git no pay fer his work, an' I don' blame 'im much. Mebbe he 's done better sence he run erway, but I ain' 'spectin' much."

"You may have passed him on the street a hundred times during the twenty-five years, and not have known him; time works great changes."

She smiled incredulously. "I 'd know 'im 'mongs' a hund'ed men. Fer dey wuz n' no yuther merlatter man like my man Sam, an' I could n' be mistook. I 's toted his picture roun' wid me twenty-five years."

"May I see it?" asked Mr. Ryder. "It might help me to remember whether I have seen the original."

As she drew a small parcel from her bosom he saw that it was fastened to a string that went around her neck. Removing several wrappers, she brought to light an old-fashioned daguerreotype in a black case. He looked long and intently at the portrait. It was faded with time, but the features were still distinct, and it was easy to see what manner of man it had represented.

He closed the case, and with a slow movement handed it back to her.

"I don't know of any man in town who goes by that name," he said, "nor have I heard of any one making such inquiries. But if you will leave me your address, I will give the matter some attention, and if I find out anything I will let you know."

She gave him the number of a house in the neighborhood, and went away, after thanking him warmly.

He wrote the address on the fly-leaf of the volume of Tennyson, and, when she had gone, rose to his feet and stood looking after her curiously. As she walked down the street with mincing step, he saw several persons whom she passed turn and look back at her with a smile of kindly amusement. When she had turned the corner, he went upstairs to his bedroom, and stood for a long time before the mirror of his dressing-case, gazing thoughtfully at the reflection of his own face.

3

At eight o'clock the ballroom was a blaze of light and the guests had begun to assemble; for there was a literary programme and some routine business of the society to be gone through with before the dancing. A black servant in evening dress waited at the door and directed the guests to the dressing-rooms.

The occasion was long memorable among the colored people of the city; not alone for the dress and display, but for the high average of intelligence and culture that distinguished the gathering as a whole. There were a number of school-teachers, several young doctors, three or four lawyers, some professional singers, an editor, a lieutenant in the United States army spending his furlough in the city, and others in various polite callings; these were colored, though most of them would not have attracted even a casual glance because of any marked difference from white people. Most of the ladies were in evening costume, and dress coats and dancing pumps were the rule among the men. A band of string music, stationed in an alcove behind a row of palms, played popular airs while the guests were gathering.

The dancing began at half past nine. At eleven o'clock supper was served. Mr. Ryder had left the ballroom some little time before the intermission, but reappeared at the supper-table. The spread was worthy of the occasion, and the guests did full justice to it. When the coffee had been served, the toast-master, Mr. Solomon Sadler, rapped for order. He made a brief introductory speech, complimenting host and guests, and then presented in their order the toasts of the evening. They were responded to with a very fair display of after-dinner wit.

"The last toast," said the toast-master, when he reached the end of the list, "is one which must appeal to us all. There is no one of us of the sterner sex who is not at some time dependent upon woman,—in infancy for protection, in manhood for companionship, in old age for care and comforting. Our good host has been trying to live alone, but the fair faces I see around me to-night prove that he too is largely dependent upon the gentler sex for most that makes life worth living,— the society and love of friends,—and rumor is at fault if he does not soon yield entire subjection to one of them. Mr. Ryder will now respond to the toast,—The Ladies."

There was a pensive look in Mr. Ryder's eyes as he took the floor and adjusted his eye-glasses. He began by speaking of woman as the gift of Heaven to man, and after some general observations on the relations of the sexes he said: "But perhaps the quality which most distinguishes woman is her fidelity and devotion to those she loves. History is full of examples, but has recorded none more striking than one which only to-day came under my notice."

He then related, simply but effectively, the story told by his visitor of the afternoon. He gave it in the same soft dialect, which came readily to his lips, while the company listened attentively and sympathetically. For the story had awakened a responsive thrill in many hearts. There were some present who had seen, and others who had heard their fathers and grandfathers tell, the wrongs and sufferings of this past generation, and all of them still felt, in their darker moments, the shadow hanging over them. Mr. Ryder went on:—

"Such devotion and confidence are rare even among women. There are many who would have searched a year, some who would have waited five years, a few who might have hoped ten years; but for twenty-five years this woman has retained her affection for and her faith in a man she has not seen or heard of in all that time.

"She came to me to-day in the hope that I might be able to help her find this long-lost husband. And when she was gone I gave my fancy rein, and imagined a case I will put to you.

"Suppose that this husband, soon after his escape, had learned that his wife had been sold away, and that such inquiries as he could make brought no information of her whereabouts. Suppose that he was young, and she much older than he; that he was light; and she was black; that their marriage was a slave marriage, and legally binding only if they chose to make it so after the war. Suppose, too, that he made his way to the North, as some of us have done, and there, where he had larger opportunities, had improved them, and had in the course of all these years grown to be as different from the ignorant boy who ran away from fear of slavery as the day is from the night. Suppose, even, that he had qualified himself, by industry, by thrift, and by study, to win the friendship and be considered worthy the society of such people as these I see around me to-night, gracing my board and filling my heart with gladness; for I am old enough to remember the day when such a gathering would not have been possible in this land. Suppose, too, that, as the years went by, this man's memory of the past grew more and more indistinct, until at last it was rarely, except in his dreams, that any image of this bygone period rose before his mind. And then suppose that accident should bring to his knowledge the fact that the wife of his youth, the wife he had left behind him,—not one who had walked by his side and kept pace with him in his upward struggle, but one upon whom advancing years and a laborious life had set their mark,—was alive and seeking him, but that he was absolutely safe from recognition or discovery, unless he chose to reveal himself. My friends, what would the man do? I will presume that he was one who loved honor, and tried to deal justly with all men. I will even carry the case further, and suppose that perhaps he had set his heart upon another, whom he had hoped to call his own. What would he do, or rather what ought he to do, in such a crisis of a lifetime?

"It seemed to me that he might hesitate, and I imagined that I was an old friend, a near friend, and that he had come to me for advice; and I argued the case with him. I tried to discuss it impartially. After we had looked upon the matter from every point of view, I said to him, in words that we all know:—

> This above all: to thine own self be true,
> And it must follow, as the night the day,
> Thou canst not then be false to any man.

Then, finally, I put the question to him, 'Shall you acknowledge her?'

"And now, ladies and gentlemen, friends and companions, I ask you, what should he have done?"

There was something in Mr. Ryder's voice that stirred the hearts of those who sat around him. It suggested more than mere sympathy with an imaginary situation; it seemed rather in the nature of a personal appeal. It was observed, too, that his look rested more especially upon Mrs. Dixon, with a mingled expression of renunciation and inquiry.

She had listened, with parted lips and streaming eyes. She was the first to speak: "He should have acknowledged her."

"Yes," they all echoed, "he should have acknowledged her."

"My friends and companions," responded Mr. Ryder, "I thank you, one and all. It is the answer I expected, for I knew your hearts."

He turned and walked toward the closed door of an adjoining room, while every eye followed him in wondering curiosity. He came back in a moment, leading by the hand his visitor of the afternoon, who stood startled and trembling at the sudden plunge into this scene of brilliant gayety. She was neatly dressed in gray, and wore the white cap of an elderly woman.

"Ladies and gentlemen," he said, "this is the woman, and I am the man, whose story I have told you. Permit me to introduce to you the wife of my youth."

James David Corrothers

(1869–1917)

JAMES CORROTHERS TELLS US that he had Negro, Indian, Scotch-Irish, and French blood. He was born in "Chain Lake Settlement" near Cassopolis, Michigan, and attended school at South Haven, Michigan, from 1874 to 1883. From 1880 to 1893 he was a student at Northwestern University; in later years he studied at a Negro school in Greensboro, North Carolina.

Corrothers tried all kinds of jobs: he worked in a lumber camp, in a saw mill, as a bootblack, a coachman, a janitor, and a boxing-instructor. In Chicago he became a freelance newspaperman, contributing special articles to at least three Chicago dailies. Corrothers believed that he would have been hired as a regular reporter by one of these papers if he had been white.

In about 1893, Corrothers became a minister and held pastorates under three denominations—Methodist, Baptist, and Presbyterian. He is the author of *The Black Cat Club* (1902), which appeared originally as a series of newspaper articles; *Selected Poems* (1907); *The Dream and the Song* (1914); and *In Spite of the Handicap* (1916), an autobiography. Corrothers also contributed to the *Century* and other national magazines.

AT THE CLOSED GATE OF JUSTICE

To be a Negro in a day like this
    Demands forgiveness. Bruised with blow on blow,
Betrayed, like him whose woe dimmed eyes gave bliss
    Still must one succor those who brought one low,
To be a Negro in a day like this.

To be a Negro in a day like this
    Demands rare patience—patience that can wait
In utter darkness. 'Tis the path to miss,
    And knock, unheeded, at an iron gate,
To be a Negro in a day like this.

To be a Negro in a day like this
    Demands strange loyalty. We serve a flag
Which is to us white freedom's emphasis.
    Ah! one must love when Truth and Justice lag,
To be a Negro in a day like this.

To be a Negro in a day like this—
    Alas! Lord God, what evil have we done?
Still shines the gate, all gold and amethyst,
    But I pass by, the glorious goal unwon,
"Merely a Negro"—in a day like this!

PAUL LAURENCE DUNBAR

He came, a youth, singing in the dawn
    Of a new freedom, glowing o'er his lyre,
    Refining, as with great Apollo's fire,
    His people's gift of song. And thereupon,
This Negro singer, come to Helicon
    Constrained the masters, listening to admire,
    And roused a race to wonder and aspire,
    Gazing which way their honest voice was gone,
With ebon face uplit of glory's crest.
    Men marveled at the singer, strong and sweet,
    Who brought the cabin's mirth, the tuneful night,
But faced the morning, beautiful with light,
    To die while shadows yet fell toward the west,
    And leave his laurels at his people's feet.

Dunbar, no poet wears your laurels now;
    None rises, singing, from your race like you.
    Dark melodist, immortal, though the dew
    Fell early on the bays upon your brow,
And tinged with pathos every halcyon vow
    And brave endeavor. Silence o'er you threw
    Flowerets of love. Or, if an envious few
    Of your own people brought no garlands, how
Could Malice smite him whom the gods had crowned?
    If, like the meadow-lark, your flight was low
    Your flooded lyrics half the hilltops drowned;
A wide world heard you, and it loved you so
    It stilled its heart to list the strains you sang,
    And o'er your happy songs its plaudits rang.

THE NEGRO SINGER

O'er all my song the image of a face
    Lieth, like shadow on the wild sweet flowers.
    The dream, the ecstasy that prompts my powers;
    The golden lyre's delights bring little grace
To bless the singer of a lowly race.

Long hath this mocked me: aye in marvelous hours,
When Hera's gardens gleamed, or Cynthia's bowers,
Or Hope's red pylons, in their far, hushed place !
But I shall dig me deeper to the gold;
Fetch water, dripping, over desert miles,
From clear Nyanzas and mysterious Niles
Of love; and sing, nor one kind act withhold.
So shall men know me, and remember long,
Nor my dark face dishonor any song.

Kelly Miller

(1863–1939)

KELLY MILLER WAS A moderate who took a stand somewhere between Booker T. Washington and W. E. B. Du Bois, but nearer to the latter. He was born in Winnsboro, South Carolina, and educated at Howard University and Johns Hopkins University; he became a dean at Howard and one of the most popular lecturers in Negro America during the early decades of this century. Originally a mathematics teacher at Howard, Dean Miller subsequently turned to sociology and wrote a series of widely-read pamphlets and books on various aspects of the racial situation in America. Among his best known works are *Race Adjustment* (1908); *Out of the House of Bondage* (1914); *An Appeal to Conscience* (1918); and *The Everlasting Stain* (1924).

The two selections given below—the first from "As to the Leopard's Spots: An Open Letter to Thomas Dixon, Jr.," the second from the pamphlet *Radicalism and the Negro*—were chosen because they reflect conditions which encouraged prominent politicians and writers to attack, ridicule, and denigrate blacks openly on the floor of Congress and in the press.

The Wilson selection also reflects the opinion held by most Negroes about that leader: to them the President was not a world statesman, but the man who kicked Negroes out of Princeton and who, when President of the United States, brought Jim Crow to the Federal government in Washington.

AN OPEN LETTER TO THOMAS DIXON, JR.

September, 1905

Mr. Thomas Dixon, Jr.,

Dear Sir:—

I am writing you this letter to express the attitude and feeling of ten millions of your fellow citizens toward the evil propagandism of race animosity to which you have lent your great literary powers. Through the widespread influence of your writings you have become the chief priest of those who worship at the shrine of race hatred and wrath. This one spirit runs through all your books and published utterances,

Reprinted by permission of May Miller.

like the recurrent theme of an opera. As the general trend of your doctrine is clearly epitomized and put forth in your contribution to the *Saturday Evening Post* of August 19, I beg to consider chiefly the issues therein raised. You are a white man born in the midst of the civil war, I am a Negro born during the same stirring epoch. You were born with a silver spoon in your mouth, I was born with an iron hoe in my hand. Your race has inflicted accumulated injury and wrong upon mine, mine has borne yours only service and good will. You express your views with the most scathing frankness; I am sure, you will welcome an equally candid expression from me.

Permit me to acknowledge the personal consideration which you have shown me. You will doubtless recall that when I addressed The Congregational Ministers, of New York City, some year or more ago, you asked permission to be present and listened attentively to what I had to say, although as might have been expected, you beat a precipitous retreat when luncheon was announced. In your article in the *Post* you make several references to me and to other colored men with entire personal courtesy. So far as I know you have never varied from this rule in your personal dealings with members of my race. You are merciless, however, in excoriating the race as a whole, thus keenly wounding the sensibilities of every individual of that blood. I assure you that this courtesy of personal treatment will be reciprocated in this letter, however sharply I may be compelled to take issue with the views you set forth and to deplore your attitude. I shall endeavor to indulge in no bitter word against your race nor against the South, whose exponent and special pleader you assume to be.

I fear that you have mistaken personal manners, the inevitable varnish of any gentleman of your antecedents and rearing, for friendship to a race which you hold in despite. You tell us that you are kind and considerate to your personal servants. It is somewhat strange that you should deem such assurance necessary, any more than it is necessary for you to assure us that you are kind to and fond of your horse or your dog. But when you write yourself down as "one of their best friends," you need not be surprised if we retort the refrain of the ritual: "From all such proffers of friendship, good Lord deliver us."

Your fundamental thesis is that "no amount of education of any kind, industrial, classical or religious, can make a Negro a white man or bridge the chasm of the centuries which separates him from the white man in the evolution of human history." This doctrine is as old as human oppression. Calhoun made it the arch stone in the defense of Negro slavery—and lost.

This is but a recrudescence of the doctrine which was exploited and exploded during the antislavery struggle. Do you recall the school of proslavery scientists who demonstrated beyond doubt that the Negro's skull was too thick to comprehend the substance of Aryan knowledge? Have you not read in the discredited scientific books of that period, with what triumphant acclaim it was shown that the Negro's shape and size of skull, facial angle, and cephalic configuration rendered him forever impervious to the white man's civilization? But all enlightened minds are now as ashamed of that doctrine as they are of the onetime dogma that the Negro had no soul. We become aware of mind through its manifestations. Within forty years of only partial opportunity, while playing as it were in the back yard of civilization, the American Negro has cut down his illiteracy by over fifty per cent; has produced a professional class, some fifty thousand strong, including ministers, teachers, doctors, lawyers, editors, authors, architects, engineers, and all higher lines of listed pursuits in which white men are engaged; some three thousand Negroes have taken collegiate degrees, over three hundred being from the best institutions in the North and West established for the most favored white youth; there is scarcely a first-class institution in America, excepting some three or four in the South, that is without colored students who pursue their studies generally with success, and sometimes with distinction; Negro inventors have taken out four hundred patents as a contribution to the mechanical genius of America; there are scores of Negroes who, for conceded ability and achievements, take respectable rank in the company of distinguished Americans.

It devolves upon you, Mr. Dixon, to point out some standard, either of intelligence, character, or conduct to which the Negro can not conform. Will you please tell a waiting world just what is the psychological difference between the races? No reputable authority, either of the old or the new school of psychology, has yet pointed out any sharp psychic discriminant. There is not a single intellectual, moral, or spiritual excellence attained by the white race to which the Negro does not yield an appreciative response. If you could show that the Negro was incapable of mastering the intricacies of Aryan speech, that he could not comprehend the intellectual basis of European culture, or apply the apparatus of practical knowledge, that he could not be made amenable to the white man's ethical code or appreciate his spiritual motive, then your case would be proved. But in default of such demonstration, we must relegate your eloquent pronouncement to the realm of generalization and prophecy, an easy and agreeable exercise of the mind in which the romancer is ever prone to indulge.

The inherent, essential, and unchangeable inferiority of the Negro to the white man lies at the basis of your social philosophy. You disdain to examine the validity of your fondly cherished hope. You follow closely in the wake of Tom Watson, in the June number of his homonymous magazine. You both hurl your thesis of innate racial inferiority at the head of Booker T. Washington. You use the same illustrations, the same arguments, set forth in the same order of recital, and for the most part in identical language. This seems to be an instance of great minds, or at least of minds of the same grade, running in the same channel.

These are your words: "What contribution to human progress have the millions of Africa who inhabit this planet made during the past four thousand years? Absolutely nothing." These are the words of Thomas Watson spoken some two months previous: "What does civilization owe to the Negro race? Nothing! Nothing!! Nothing!!!" You answer the query with the most emphatic negative noun and the strongest qualifying adjective in the language. Mr. Watson, of a more ecstatic temperament, replies with the same noun and six exclamation points. One rarely meets, outside of yellow journalism, with such lavishness of language, wasted upon a hoary dogma. A discredited dictum that has been bandied about the world from the time of Canaan to Calhoun, is revamped and set forth with as much ardor and fervency of feeling as if discovered for the first time and proclaimed for the illumination of a waiting world.

But neither boastful asseveration on your part nor indignant denial on mine will affect the facts of the case. That Negroes in the average are not equal in developed capacity to the white race, is a proposition which it would be as simple to affirm as it is silly to deny. The Negro represents a backward race which has not yet taken a commanding part in the progressive movement of the world. In the great cosmic scheme of things, some races reach the limelight of civilization ahead of others. But that temporary forwardness does not argue inherent superiority is as evident as any fact of history. An unfriendly environment may hinder and impede the one, while fortunate circumstances may quicken and spur the other. Relative superiority is only a transient phase of human development. You tell us that "The Jew has achieved a civilization—had his poets, prophets, priests, and kings, when our Germanic ancestors were still in the woods cracking cocoanuts and hickory-nuts with the monkeys." Fancy some learned Jew at that day citing your query about the contribution of the Germanic races to the culture of the human spirit, during the thousands of years of their existence! Does the progress of history not prove that races may lie dormant and fallow for ages and then break suddenly into prestige and power? Fifty years ago you doubtless would have ranked Japan among the benighted nations and hurled at their heathen heads some derogatory query as to their contribution to civilization. But since the happenings at Mukden and Port Arthur, and Portsmouth, I suppose that you are ready to change your mind. Or maybe since the Jap has proved himself "a first-class fighting man," able to cope on equal terms with the best breeds in Europe, you will claim him as belonging to the white race, notwithstanding his pig eye and yellow pigment.

The Negro enters into the inheritance of all the ages on equal terms with the rest, and who can say that he will not contribute his quota of genius to enrich the blood of the world?

The line of argument of every writer who undertakes to belittle the Negro is a well-beaten path. Liberia and Haiti are bound to come in for their share of ridicule and contemptuous handling. Mr. Watson calls these experiments freshly to mind, lest we forget. We are told all about the incapacity of the black race for self-government, the relapse into barbarism and much more of which we have heard before; and yet when we take all the circumstances into account, Haiti presents to the world one of the most remarkable achievements in the annals of human history. The panegyric of Wendell Phillips on Toussaint L'Ouverture is more than an outburst of rhetorical fancy; it is a just measure of his achievements in terms of his humble environment and the limited instrumentalities at his command. Where else in the course of history has a slave, with the aid of slaves, expelled a powerfully intrenched master class, and set up a government patterned after civilized models and which without external assistance or reinforcement from a parent civilization, has endured for a hundred years in face of a frowning world? When we consider the difficulties that confront a weak government, without military or naval means to cope with its more powerful rivals, and where commercial adventurers are ever and anon stirring up internal strife, thus provoking the intervention of stronger governments, the marvel is that the republic of Haiti still endures, the only self-governing state of the Antilles. To expect as effective and proficient government to prevail in Haiti as at Washington would be expecting more of the black men in Haiti than we find in the white men of South America. And yet, I suspect that the million Negroes in Haiti are as well governed as the corresponding number of blacks in Georgia, where only yesterday eight men were taken from the custody of the law and lynched without judge or jury. It is often charged that these people have not maintained the pace set by the old master class, that the plantations are in ruin and that the whole island wears the aspect of dilapidation. Wherever a lower people overrun the civilization of a higher, there is an inevitable lapse toward the level of the lower. When barbarians and semi-civilized hordes of northern Europe overran the southern peninsulas, the civilization of the world was wrapped in a thousand years of darkness. Relapse inevitably precedes the rebound. Is there anything in the history of Haiti contrary to the law of human development?

You ask: "Can you change the color of the Negro's skin, the kink of his hair, the bulge of his lip, or the beat of his heart, with a spelling book or a machine?" This rhetorical outburst does great credit to your literary skill, and is calculated to delight the simple; but analysis fails to reveal in it any pregnant meaning. Since civilization is not an attribute of the color of skin, or curl of hair, or curve of lip, there is no necessity for changing such physical peculiarities, and if there was, the spelling book and the machine would be very unlikely instruments for its accomplishment. But why, may I ask, would you desire to change the Negro's heart throb, which already beats at a normal human pace? You need not be so frantic about the superiority of your race. Whatever superiority it may possess, inherent or acquired, will take care of itself without such rabid support. Has it ever occurred to you that the people of New England blood, who have done and are doing most to make the white race great and glorious in this land, are the most reticent about extravagant claims to everlasting superiority? You protest too much. Your loud pretensions, backed up by such exclamatory outbursts of passion, make upon the reflecting mind the impression that you entertain a sneaking suspicion of their validity.

Your position as to the work and worth of Booker T. Washington is pitiably anomalous. You recite the story of his upward struggle with uncontrolled admiration: "The story of this little ragged, barefooted pickaninny, who lifted his eyes from a cabin in the hills of Virginia, saw a vision and followed it, until at last he presides over the richest and most powerful institution in the South, and sits down with crowned heads and presidents, has no parallel even in the Tales of the Arabian Nights." You say that his story appeals to the universal heart of humanity. And yet in a recent letter to the *Columbia States,* you regard it as an unspeakable outrage that Mr. Robert C. Ogden should walk arm in arm with this wonderful man who "appeals to the heart of universal humanity," and introduce him to the lady clerks in a dry goods store. Your passionate devotion to a narrow dogma has seriously impaired your sense of humor. The subject of your next great novel has been announced as "The Fall of Tuskegee." In one breath you commend the work of this great institution, while in another you condemn it because it does not fit into your preconceived scheme in the solution of the race problem. The Tuskegee ideal: "to make Negroes producers, lovers of labor, independent, honest, and good" is one which you say that only a fool or a knave can find fault with, because, in your own words, "it rests squarely upon the eternal verities." Over against this you add with all the condemnatory emphasis of italics and exclamation point: *"Tuskegee is not a servant training school!"* And further: "Mr. Washington is not training Negroes to take their places in the industries of the South in which white men direct and control them. He is not training students to be servants and come at the beck and call of any man. He is training them to be masters of men, to be independent, to own and operate their own industries, plant their own field, buy and sell their own goods." All of which you condemn by imperative inference ten times stronger than your faint and forced verbal approval. It is a heedless man who wilfully flaunts his little philosophy in the face of "the eternal verities." When the wise man finds that his prejudices are running against fixed principles in God's cosmic plan, he speedily readjusts them in harmony therewith. Has it never occurred to you to reexamine the foundation of the faith, as well as the feeling, that is in you, since you admit that it runs afoul of the "eternal verities?"

* * *

You quote me as being in favor of the amalgamation of the races. A more careful reading of the article referred to would have convinced you that I was arguing against it as a probable solution of the race problem. I merely stated the intellectual conviction that two races cannot live indefinitely side by side, under the same general regime without ultimately fusing. This was merely the expression of a belief, and not the utterance of a preference nor the formulation of a policy. I know of no colored man who advocates amalgamation as a feasible policy of solution. You are mistaken. The Negro does not "hope and dream of amalgamation." This would be self-stultification with a vengeance. If such a policy were allowed to dominate the imagination of the race, its women would give themselves over to the unrestrained passion of white men, in quest of tawny offspring, which would give rise to a state of indescribable moral debauchery. At the same time you would hardly expect the Negro, in derogation of his common human qualities, to proclaim that he is so diverse from God's other human creatures as to make the blending of the races contrary to the law of nature. The Negro refuses to become excited or share in your frenzy on this subject. The amalgamation of the races is an ultimate possibility, though not an immediate probability. But what have you and I to do with ultimate questions, anyway? Our concern is with duty, not destiny.

But do you know, Mr. Dixon, that you are probably the foremost promoter of amalgamation between the two races? Wherever you narrow the scope of the Negro by preaching the doctrine of hate, you drive thousands of persons of lighter hue over to the white race carrying more or less Negro blood in their train. The blending of the races is less likely to take place if the self-respect and manly opportunity of the Negro are respected and encouraged, than if he is to be forever crushed beneath the level of his faculties for dread of the fancied result. Hundreds of the composite progeny are daily crossing the color line and carrying as much of the despised blood as an albicant skin can conceal without betrayal. I believe that it was Congressman Tillman, brother of the more famous Senator of that name, who stated on the floor of the constitutional convention of South Carolina, that he knew of four hundred white families in that State who had a taint of Negro blood in their veins. I personally know, or know of, fifty cases of transition in the city of Washington. It is a momentous thing for one to change his caste. The man or woman who affects to deny, ignore, or scorn the class with whom he previously associated is usually deemed deficient in the nobler qualities of human nature. It is not conceivable that persons of this class would undergo the self-degradation and humiliation of soul necessary to cross the great "social divide" unless it be to escape for themselves and their descendants an odious and despised status. Your oft expressed and passionately avowed belief that the progressive development of the Negro would hasten amalgamation is not borne out by the facts of observation. The refined and cultivated class among colored people are as much disinclined to such unions as the whites themselves. I am sorry that you saw fit to characterize Frederick Douglass as "a bombastic vituperator." You thereby gave poignant offense to ten millions of his race who regard him as the best embodiment of their possibilities. Besides millions of your race rate him among the foremost and best beloved of Americans. How would you feel if some one should stigmatize Jefferson Davis or Robert E. Lee in such language, these beau ideals of your Southern heart? But I will not undertake to defend Frederick Douglass against your calumniations. I am frank to confess that I do not feel that he needs it. The point I have in mind to make about Mr. Douglass is that he has a hold upon the affection of his race, not on account of his second marriage, but in spite of it. He seriously affected his standing with his people by that marriage.

It seems to me, Mr. Dixon, that this frantic abhorrence of amalgamation is a little late in its appearance. Whence comes this stream of white blood, which flows with more or less spissitude, in the veins of some six out of ten million Negroes? The Afro-American is hardly a Negro at all, except constructively; but a new creature. Who brought about this present approachment between the races? Do you not appreciate the inconsistency in the attitude and the action on the part of many of the loudmouthed advocates of race purity? It is said that old Father Chronos devoured his offspring in order to forestall future complications. But we do not learn that he put a bridle upon his passion as the surest means of security. The most effective service you can render to check the evil of amalgamation is to do missionary work among the males of your own race. This strenuous advocacy of race purity in face of proved proneness for miscegenation affords a striking reminder of the lines of Hudibras:—

> The self-same thing they will abhor,
> One way, and long another for. . . .

Your proposed solution of the race problem by colonizing the Negroes in Liberia reaches the climax of absurdity. It is difficult to see how such a proposition could emanate from a man of your reputation. Did you consult Cram's Atlas about Liberia? Please do so. You will find that it has an area of 48,000 square miles and a population of 1,500,000, natives and immigrants. The area and population are about the same as those of North Carolina, which, I believe, is your native State. When you tell us that this restricted area, without commerce, without manufacture, without any system of organized industry, can support every Negro in America, in addition to its present population, I beg mildly to suggest that you recall your plan for revision before submitting it to the judgment of a critical world. Your absolute indifference to and heedlessness of the facts, circumstances, and conditions involved in the scheme of colonization well befit the absurdity of the general proposition.

The solution of the race problem in America is indeed a grave and serious matter. It is one that calls for statesmanlike breadth of view, philanthropic tolerance of spirit, and exact social knowledge. The whole spirit of your propaganda is to add to its intensity and aggravation. You stir the slumbering fires of race wrath into an uncontrollable flame. I have read somewhere that Max Nordau, on reading *The Leopard's Spots,* wrote to you suggesting the awful responsibility you had assumed in stirring up enmity between race and race. Your teachings subvert the foundations of law and established order. You are the high priest of lawlessness, the prophet of anarchy. Rudyard Kipling places this sentiment in the mouth of the reckless stealer of seals in the Northern Sea: "There's never a law of God nor man runs north of fifty-three." This description exactly fits the brand of literature with which you are flooding the public. You openly urge your fellow citizens to override all law, human and divine. Are you aware of the force and effect of these words? "Could fatuity reach a sublimer height than the idea that the white man will stand idly by and see the performance? What will he do when put to the test? He will do exactly what his white neighbor in the North does when the Negro threatens his bread—kill him!" These words breathe out hatred and slaughter and suggest the murder of innocent men whose only crime is quest for the God-given right to work. You poison the mind and pollute the imagination through the subtle influence of letters. Are you aware of the force and effect of evil suggestion when the passions of men are in a state of unstable equilibrium? A heterogeneous population, where the elements are, on any account, easily distinguishable, is an easy prey for the promoter of wrath. The fuse is already prepared for the spark. The soul of the mob is stirred by suggestion of hatred and slaughter, as a famished beast at the smell of blood. The rabble responds so much more readily to an appeal to passion than to reason. To wantonly stir up the fires of race antipathy is as execrable a deed as flaunting a red rag in the face of a bull at a summer's picnic, or raising a false cry of "fire" in a crowded house. Human society could not exist one hour except on the basis of law, which holds the baser passions of men in restraint.

In our complex situation it is only the rigid observance of law re-enforced by higher moral restraint that can keep these passions in bound. You speak about giving the Negro a "square deal." Even among gamblers, a "square deal" means to play according to the rules of the game. The rules which all civilized States have set for themselves are found in the Ten Commandments, the Golden Rule, the Sermon on the Mount, and the organic law of the land. You acknowledge no such restraints when the Negro is involved, but waive them all aside with frenzied defiance. You preside at every crossroad lynching of a helpless victim; wherever the midnight murderer rides with rope and torch, in quest of the blood of his black brother, you ride by his side; wherever the cries of the crucified victim go up to God from the crackling flame, behold you are there; when women and children, drunk with ghoulish glee, dance around the funeral pyre and mock the death groans of their fellow man and fight for ghastly souvenirs, you have your part in the inspiration of it all. When guilefully guided workmen in mine and shop and factory, goaded by a real or imaginary sense of wrong, begin the plunder and pillage of property and murder of rival men, your suggestion is justifier of the dastardly doings. Lawlessness is gnawing at the very vitals of our institutions. It is the supreme duty of every enlightened mind to allay rather than spur on this spirit. You are hastening the time when there is to be a positive and emphatic show of hands—not of white hands against black hands, God forbid; not of Northern hands against Southern hands, heaven forfend; but a determined show of those who believe in law and God and constituted order, against those who would undermine and destroy the organic basis of society, involving all in a common ruin. No wonder Max Nordau exclaimed: "God, man, are you aware of your responsibility!"

But do not think, Mr. Dixon, that when you evoke the evil spirit, you can exorcise him at will. The Negro in the end will be the least of his victims. Those who become inoculated with the virus of race hatred are more unfortunate than the victims of it. Voltaire tells us that it is more difficult and more meritorious to wean men of their prejudices than it is to civilize the barbarian. Race hatred is the most malignant poison that can afflict the mind. It freezes up the fount of inspiration and chills the higher faculties of the soul. You are a greater enemy to your own race than you are to mine.

I have written you thus fully in order that you may clearly understand how the case lies in the Negro's mind. If any show of feeling or bitterness of spirit crops out in the treatment or between the lines, it is wholly without vindictive intent; but is the inevitable outcome of dealing with issues that verge upon the deepest human passion.

Yours truly,
KELLY MILLER.

WOODROW WILSON AND THE NEGRO

Woodrow Wilson believes, or believed, that he could hold a restless world in poise by the soothing balm of pleasing phraseology. His single-track, double-acting mind moves with equal celerity, sometimes with and sometimes against the onsweeping current which he seeks to guide and control. He is no whit abashed at the tangle of moral paradoxes in which he frequently finds himself enmeshed. He follows the lead of events only long enough to gauge their tendency and trend in order that he might make himself appear to guide them. He frequently reverses his course, and proceeds to the new goal with utter disregard of logical sequence or ethical consistency. It is utterly impossible to tell whether he undergoes a genuine conversion of heart or a prudent shift of mind. The same lack of consecutiveness and consistency appears in every great issue which he has been called upon to handle. Elected the first time upon a platform which condemned renomination, he has accepted a second term and is conniving at a third with convenient forgetfulness. He forced his Party to change its declared attitude on the Panama Canal by threats of calamity which he alone foresaw. Habitually opposed to national female suffrage, after the propaganda had gained significant proportions, as belated entrant, he now outruns the other disciples. He kept the Nation out of war while the Presidential campaign was on, and without additional provocation plunged it into war when the election was over. After Germany had committed every atrocity with which she has subsequently been charged, he issued a proclamation to the American people urging them to refrain from discussing the moral issues involved lest they disturb the serenity and composure of the German mind. At first an ardent advocate of the Washington policy of no entangling foreign alliances, he sits at the head of the Council Table and ties his country to alliances which are unentangleable. The apostle of new freedom for mankind ignores its application to the freedman in America. The High Priest of Democracy in Germany becomes the obligated beneficiary of oligarchy in Georgia. He has played at peace and war successively with Huerta, Villa and Carranza, and yet our Southern neighbor remains untranquillized and defiant. In one breath he declares that politics should be adjourned

Reprinted by permission of May Miller.

during the progress of the war, with another he urges the country to return a Democratic Congress as more easily pliant to his imperious will. As head of the Nation he congratulated the Republican Governor of Massachusetts upon his victorious stand for law and order, and as head of the Democratic Party he felicitates the successful Governor of his own State and Party, who won the election on the declaration that he would make the Nation as wet as water, thus subverting all law and order. The highest world exponent of derived powers, he swiftly overleaps all precedents in the assumption of unauthorized power. Elected President of the United States, he makes himself the Chief Magistrate of Mankind. He reverses the world motto; his charity begins abroad rather than at home. He believes in Democracy for humanity but not for Mississippi. Abraham Lincoln's gospel of freedom was immediate; Woodrow Wilson's is remote. The one believed in the freedom of the Negro; the other in the freedom of Nations. President Lincoln wrought for the United States of America; Woodrow Wilson for the United States of the World. The former never uttered one insincere or uncertain word; the utterances of the latter rarely escape the imputation of moral ambiguity. By marvelous assumption of superior insight, he propounds preachments and compounds idealistic theories as infallible solvents of all social ills. He retires into the secrecy of his inner consciousness and evolves his famous Fourteen Points—the new "tetra decalogue," which he was the first to violate and ignore. The advocate of open covenants openly arrived at proceeds to the Peace Conference enshrouded in the sacredness and secrecy of Sinai, and returns with the League of Nations written upon the tablet of his own conception with the finger of finality. Although the newly conceived League of Nations transcends the Constitution and Declaration of Independence, "anathema, maranatha" be upon the head of that impious statesman who would add or subtract one jot or one tittle from the law oracularly vouchsafed by the ordained lawgiver of the world.

President Wilson is indeed the greatest phrase-maker of the age, although each preceding phrase is apt to have its meaning nullified by a quickly succeeding one. "The Nations should be permitted to shed all the blood they please"; "we are too proud to fight"; "there must be peace without victory," have already taken their places in the limbo of innocuous desuetude. Such lofty expressions as "to make the world safe for democracy"; "overridden peoples must have a voice in the Governments which they uphold"; "the only way to stop men from agitation against grievances is to remove the grievances" still await vindication in light of sanctioned and condoned practices. To the Negro these phrases seem to possess the sinister suggestion of hollow mockery under the guise of Holy Democracy. Mr. Wilson would strengthen the chain by ignoring the weakest links. His abstract doctrine breaks down at the point of concrete application. The Negro question, the most aggravating moral issue of American life, is avoided or thrust aside as hopelessly impossible. He has handled this issue with less positiveness and moral aggression than any president since James Buchanan. Under pressure of political exigency or military exaction he has indited several of his customary notes on this question, but their luke-warmness indicates that they might have been written with the left hand as the easiest riddance of a disagreeable issue. On promise of political support, he pledged Bishop Walters the full recognition of the Negro's claims. Shortly after election he sent the name of a Negro as Register of the Treasury. His Southern partizans protested. The nomination was withdrawn. The promise has been ignored. It must be said that the President's change of attitude or shift of mind is usually in the direction of progress, aggression and courage; on the Negro question it is in the direction of timidity, negation, and reaction. President Wilson appears to be at once the greatest radical and the greatest conservator of the age. Under such leadership the American people—white and black—must face the issues which now confront the world.

Paul Laurence Dunbar

(1872–1906)

BOTH OF PAUL LAURENCE DUNBAR's parents had been slaves. His father was an escaped bondsman who made his way to Canada and then returned to fight in the Union Army. Dunbar spent his early years in Dayton, Ohio. In his senior year of high school he was elected editor of the school paper, but because he was too poor to pursue his studies in college, Dunbar became an elevator operator, writing verses on the job and peddling copies of his poems to riders.

In 1893 he published his first volume, *Oak and Ivy;* in 1895, the second, *Majors and Minors.* The latter work was brought to the attention of William Dean Howells, who sponsored a third volume, *Lyrics of Lowly Life* (1896). Composed of the best poems from the first two volumes, this work was prefaced by Howell's laudatory introduction which said, among other things: "So far as I could remember, Paul Dunbar was the only man of pure African blood and of American civilization to feel the Negro life aesthetically and express it lyrically." Howell's praise brought Dunbar to the attention of America, and from 1896 on he was the most popular black poet (and fiction writer) in the nation.

In 1897 Dunbar made a not-too-successful reading tour of England; on his return he was given, through the influence of Robert G. Ingersoll, a minor position in the Library of Congress which he kept for two years. In 1898 he married Alice Ruth Moore, who was also a writer, but the marriage failed. A victim of tuberculosis aggravated by overwork, Dunbar returned to Dayton in 1904 and died eighteen months later.

An accommodationist, Paul Laurence Dunbar avoided almost entirely any mention of racial injustice. Predominantly a pastoral poet, he wrote generally about plantation life before and after "the War," stressing the parties, the good times, the good food, the innocent courtships, the playful masters, and the idyllic existence of contented slaves and untroubled freedmen. He seldom mentioned the harshness of the "peculiar institution" or the viciousness of Reconstruction. His best poetry is written in dialect, and although he paints only two aspects of peasant Negro life—pathos and humor—his works show a deeper understanding and insight than the portrayal by any of his white contemporaries. His poems in standard English are highly uneven, running the gamut from banal and sentimental verses to lyrics of undoubted excellence.

Like his dialect verse, Dunbar's short stories, with but few exceptions, present only the humorous or pathetic side of plantation life. He wrote for a white audience, and he did not chance alienating it by writing protest literature. Only one of Dunbar's four novels, *The Sport of the Gods,* uses major characters who are black.

In addition to the poetical works mentioned above, Dunbar published the following collections: *Lyrics of the Hearthside* (1899); *Lyrics of Love and Laughter* (1903); and *Lyrics of Sunshine and Shadow* (1905). He published four novels: *The Uncalled* (1898), *The Love of Landry* (1900); *The Fanatics* (1901); and *The Sport of the Gods* (1902) and four collections of short stories: *Folks from Dixie* (1898), *The Strength of Gideon* (1900), *In Old Plantation Days* (1903), and *The Heart of Happy Hollow* (1904).

For studies of Dunbar's life and works, see Benjamin Brawley, *Paul Laurence Dunbar: Poet of His People* (1936) and Victor Lawson, *Dunbar Critically Examined* (1941).

AN ANTE-BELLUM SERMON

We is gathahed hyeah, my brothahs,
    In dis howlin' wildaness,
Fu' to speak some words of comfo't
    To each othah in distress.
An' we chooses fu' ouah subjic'
    Dis—we 'll 'splain it by an' by;
"An' de Lawd said, 'Moses, Moses,'
    An' de man said, 'Hyeah am I.' "

Now ole Pher'oh, down in Egypt,
    Was de wuss man evah bo'n,
An' he had de Hebrew chillun
    Down dah wukin' in his co'n;
'T well de Lawd got tiahed o' his foolin',
    An' sez he: "I 'll let him know—
Look hyeah, Moses, go tell Pher'oh
    Fu' to let dem chillun go."

"An' ef he refuse to do it,
    I will make him rue de houah,
Fu' I 'll empty down on Egypt
    All de vials of my powah."

Poems reprinted by permission of Dodd, Mead & Company, Inc. from *The Complete Poems of Paul Laurence Dunbar.*

Yes, he did—an' Pher'oh's ahmy
  Was n't wuth a ha'f a dime;
Fu' de Lawd will he'p his chillun,
  You kin trust him evah time.

An' yo' enemies may 'sail you
  In de back an' in de front;
But de Lawd is all aroun' you,
  Fu' to ba' de battle's brunt.
Dey kin fo'ge yo' chains an' shackles
  F'om de mountains to de sea;
But de Lawd will sen' some Moses
  Fu' to set his chillun free.

An' de lan' shall hyeah his thundah,
  Lak a blas' f'om Gab'el's ho'n,
Fu' de Lawd of hosts is mighty
  When he girds his ahmor on.
But fu' feah some one mistakes me,
  I will pause right hyeah to say,
Dat I 'm still a-preachin' ancient,
  I ain't talkin' 'bout to-day.

But I tell you, fellah christuns,
  Things 'll happen mighty strange;
Now, de Lawd done dis fu' Isrul,
  An' his ways don't nevah change,
An' de love he showed to Isrul
  Was n't all on Isrul spent;
Now don't run an' tell yo' mastahs
  Dat I 's preachin' discontent.

'Cause I is n't; I 'se a-judgin'
  Bible people by deir ac's;
I 'se a-givin' you de Scriptuah,
  I 'se a-handin' you de fac's.
Cose ole Pher'oh b'lieved in slav'ry,
  But de Lawd he let him see,
Dat de people he put bref in,—
  Evah mothah's son was free.

An' dahs othahs thinks lak Pher'oh,
  But dey calls de Scriptuah liar,
Fu' de Bible says "a servant
  Is a-worthy of his hire."

An' you cain't git roun' nor thoo dat,
  An' you cain't git ovah it,
Fu' whatevah place you git in,
  Dis hyeah Bible too 'll fit.

So you see de Lawd's intention,
  Evah sence de worl' began,
Was dat His almighty freedom
  Should belong to evah man,
But I think it would be bettah,
  Ef I 'd pause again to say,
Dat I 'm talkin' 'bout ouah freedom
  In a Bibleistic way.

But de Moses is a-comin',
  An' he 's comin', suah and fas'
We kin hyeah his feet a-trompin',
  We kin hyeah his trumpit blas'.
But I want to wa'n you people,
  Don't you git too brigity;
An' don't you git to braggin'
  'Bout dese things, you wait an' see.

But when Moses wif his powah
  Comes an' sets us chillun free,
We will praise de gracious Mastah
  Dat has gin us liberty;
An' we 'll shout ouah halleluyahs,
  On dat mighty reck'nin' day,
When we 'se reco'nised ez citiz'—
  Huh uh! Chillun, let us pray!

ODE TO ETHIOPIA

O Mother Race! to thee I bring
This pledge of faith unwavering,
  This tribute to thy glory.
I know the pangs which thou didst feel,
When Slavery crushed thee with its heel,
  With thy dear blood all gory.

Sad days were those—ah, sad indeed!
But through the land the fruitful seed
  Of better times was growing.

The plant of freedom upward sprung,
And spread its leaves so fresh and young—
    Its blossoms now are blowing.

On every hand in this fair land,
Proud Ethiope's swarthy children stand
    Beside their fairer neighbor;
The forests flee before their stroke,
Their hammers ring, their forges smoke,—
    They stir in honest labour.

They tread the fields where honour calls;
Their voices sound through senate halls
    In majesty and power.
To right they cling; the hymns they sing
Up to the skies in beauty ring,
    And bolder grow each hour.

Be proud, my Race, in mind and soul;
Thy name is writ on Glory's scroll
    In characters of fire.
High 'mid the clouds of Fame's bright sky
Thy banner's blazoned folds now fly,
    And truth shall lift them higher.

Thou hast the right to noble pride,
Whose spotless robes were purified
    By blood's severe baptism.
Upon thy brow the cross was laid,
And labour's painful sweat-beads made
    A consecrating chrism.

No other race, or white or black,
When bound as thou wert, to the rack,
    So seldom stooped to grieving;
No other race, when free again,
Forgot the past and proved them men
    So noble in forgiving.

Go on and up! Our souls and eyes
Shall follow thy continuous rise;
    Our ears shall list thy story
From bards who from thy root shall spring,
And proudly tune their lyres to sing
    Of Ethiopia's glory.

WHEN DE CO'N PONE'S HOT

Dey is times in life when Nature
    Seems to slip a cog an' go,
Jes' a-rattlin' down creation,
    Lak an ocean's overflow;
When de worl' jes' stahts a-spinnin'
    Lak a picaninny's top,
An' yo' cup o' joy is brimmin'
    'Twell it seems about to slop,
An' you feel jes' lak a racah,
    Dat is trainin' fu' to trot—
When yo' mammy says de blessin'
    An' de co'n pone 's hot.

When you set down at de table,
    Kin' o' weary lak an' sad,
An' you 'se jes' a little tiahed
    An' purhaps a little mad;
How yo' gloom tu'ns into gladness,
    How yo' joy drives out de doubt
When de oven do' is opened,
    An' de smell comes po'in' out;
Why, de 'lectric light o' Heaven
    Seems to settle on de spot,
When yo' mammy says de blessin'
    An' de co'n pone 's hot.

When de cabbage pot is steamin'
    An' de bacon good an' fat,
When de chittlins is a-sputter'n'
    So 's to show you whah dey 's at;
Tek away yo' sody biscuit,
    Tek away yo' cake an' pie,
Fu' de glory time is comin',
    An' it 's 'proachin' mighty nigh,
An' you want to jump an' hollah,
    Dough you know you 'd bettah not,
When yo' mammy says de blessin'
    An' de co'n pone 's hot.

I have hyeahd o' lots o' sermons,
    An' I 've hyeahd o' lots o' prayers,
An' I've listened to some singin'
    Dat has tuck me up de stairs

Of de Glory-Lan' an' set me
   Jes' below de Mastah's th'one,
An' have lef' my hea't a-singin'
   In a happy aftah tone;
But dem wu'ds so sweetly murmured
   Seem to tech de softes' spot,
When my mammy says de blessin',
   An' de co'n pone 's hot.

SIGNS OF THE TIMES

Air a-gittin' cool an' coolah,
   Frost a-comin' in de night,
Hicka' nuts an' wa'nuts fallin',
   Possum keepin' out o' sight.
Tu'key struttin' in de ba'nya'd,
   Nary step so proud ez his;
Keep on struttin', Mistah Tu'key,
   Yo' do' know what time it is.

Cidah press commence a-squeakin'
   Eatin' apples sto'ed away,
Chillun swa'min' 'roun' lak ho'nets,
   Huntin' aigs ermung de hay.
Mistah Tu'key keep on gobblin'
   At de geese a-flyin' souf,
Oomph! dat bird do' know whut 's comin';
   Ef he did he 'd shet his mouf.

Pumpkin gittin' good an' yallah
   Mek me open up my eyes;
Seems lak it 's a-lookin' at me
   Jes' a-la'in' dah sayin' "Pies."
Tu'key gobbler gwine 'roun' blowin',
   Gwine 'roun' gibbin' sass an' slack;
Keep on talkin', Mistah Tu'key,
   You ain't seed no almanac.

Fa'mer walkin' th'oo de ba'nya'd
   Seein' how things is comin' on,
Sees ef all de fowls is fatt'nin'—
   Good times comin' sho 's you bo'n.
Hyeahs dat tu'key gobbler braggin',
   Den his face break in a smile—
Nebbah min', you sassy rascal,
   He 's gwine nab you atter while.

Choppin' suet in de kitchen,
    Stonin' raisins in de hall,
Beef a-cookin' fu' de mince meat,
    Spices groun'—I smell 'em all.
Look hyeah, Tu'key, stop dat gobblin',
    You ain' luned de sense ob feah,
You ol' fool, yo' naik 's in dangah,
    Do' you know Thanksgibbin 's hyeah?

WE WEAR THE MASK

We wear the mask that grins and lies,
It hides our cheeks and shades our eyes,—
This debt we pay to human guile;
With torn and bleeding hearts we smile,
And mouth with myriad subtleties.

Why should the world be overwise,
In counting all our tears and sighs?
Nay, let them only see us, while
    We wear the mask.

We smile, but, O great Christ, our cries
To thee from tortured souls arise.
We sing, but oh the clay is vile
Beneath our feet, and long the mile;
But let the world dream otherwise,
    We wear the mask!

CHRISMUS ON THE PLANTATION

It was Chrismus Eve, I mind hit fu' a mighty gloomy day—
Bofe de weathah an' de people—not a one of us was gay;
Cose you 'll t'ink dat 's mighty funny 'twell I try to mek hit cleah,
Fu' a da'ky 's allus happy when de holidays is neah.

But we was n't, fu' dat mo'nin' Mastah 'd tol' us we mus' go,
He 'd been payin' us sence freedom, but he could n't pay no mo';
He wa'n't nevah used to plannin' 'fo' he got so po' an' ol',
So he gwine to give up tryin', an' de homestead mus' be sol'.

I kin see him stan'in' now erpon de step ez cleah ez day,
Wid de win' a-kind o' fondlin' thoo his haih all thin an' gray;
An' I 'membah how he trimbled when he said, "It 's ha'd fu' me,
Not to mek yo' Chrismus brightah, but I 'low it wa'n't to be."

All de women was a-cryin', an' de men, too, on de sly,
An' I noticed somep'n shinin' even in ol' Mastah's eye.
But we all stood still to listen ez ol' Ben come f'om de crowd
An' spoke up, a-try'n' to steady down his voice and mek it loud:—

"Look hyeah, Mastah, I 's been servin' you' fu' lo! dese many yeahs,
An' now, sence we 's got freedom an' you 's kind o' po', hit 'pears
Dat you want us all to leave you 'cause you don't t'ink you can pay.
Ef my membry has n't fooled me, seem dat whut I hyead you say.

"Er in othah wo'ds, you wants us to fu'git dat you 's been kin',
An' ez soon ez you is he'pless, we 's to leave you hyeah behin'.
Well, ef dat 's de way dis freedom ac's on people, white er black,
You kin jes' tell Mistah Lincum fu' to tek his freedom back.

"We gwine wo'k dis ol' plantation fu' whatevah we kin git,
Fu' I know hit did suppo't us, an' de place kin do it yit.
Now de land is yo's, de hands is ouahs, an' I reckon we 'll be brave,
An' we 'll bah ez much ez you do w'en we has to scrape an' save."

Ol' Mastah stood dah trimblin', but a-smilin' thoo his teahs,
An' den hit seemed jes' nachullike, de place fah rung wid cheahs,
An' soon ez dey was quiet, some one sta'ted sof' an' low:
"Praise God," an' den we all jined in, "from whom all blessin's flow!"

Well, dey was n't no use tryin', ouah min's was sot to stay,
An' po' ol' Mastah could n't plead ner baig, ner drive us 'way,
An' all at once, hit seemed to us, de day was bright agin,
So evahone was gay dat night, an' watched de Chrismus in.

ANNER 'LIZER'S STUMBLIN' BLOCK

It was winter. The gray old mansion of Mr. Robert Selfridge, of Fayette County, Kentucky, was wrapped in its usual mantle of winter somberness, and the ample plantation stretching in every direction thereabout was one level plain of unflecked whiteness. At a distance from the house the cabins of the Negroes stretched away in a long, broken black line that stood out in bold relief against the extreme whiteness of their surroundings.

About the center of the line, as dark and uninviting as the rest, with its wide chimney of scrap limestone turning clouds of dense smoke into the air, stood a cabin.

Reprinted by permission of Dodd, Mead & Company, Inc. from *The Best Stories of Paul Laurence Dunbar* by Benjamin Brawley. Copyright 1938 by Dodd, Mead & Company, Inc.; Copyright renewed 1965 by Thaddeus Gaylord.

There was nothing in its appearance to distinguish it from the other huts clustered about. The logs that formed its sides were just as seamy, the timbers of the roof had just the same abashed, brow-beaten look; and the keenest eye could not have detected the slightest shade of difference between its front and the bare, unwhitewashed fronts of its scores of fellows. Indeed, it would not have been mentioned at all, but for the fact that within its confines lived and thrived the heroine of this story.

Of all the girls of the Selfridge estate, black, brown, or yellow, Anner 'Lizer was, without dispute, conceded to be the belle. Her black eyes were like glowing coals in their sparkling brightness; her teeth were like twin rows of shining ivories; her brown skin was as smooth and soft as silk, and the full lips that enclosed her gay and flexile tongue were tempting enough to make the heart of any dusky swain throb and his mouth water.

Was it any wonder, then, that Sam Merritt—strapping, big Sam, than whom there was not a more popular man on the place—should pay devoted court to her?

Do not gather from this that it was Sam alone who paid his *devoirs* to this brown beauty. Oh, no! Anner 'Lizer was the "bright particular star" of that plantation, and the most desired of all blessings by the young men thereabout. But Sam, with his smooth but fearless ways, Sam with his lightsome foot, so airy in the dance, Sam, handsome Sam, was the all-preferred. If there was a dance to go to, a corn-husking to attend, a social at the rude little log church, Sam was always the lucky man who was alert and *able* to possess himself of Anner 'Lizer's "comp'ny." And so, naturally, people began to connect their names, and the rumor went forth, as rumors will, that the two were engaged; and, as far as engagements went among the slaves in those days, I suppose it was true. Sam had never exactly prostrated himself at his sweetheart's feet and openly declared his passion; nor had she modestly snickered behind her fan and murmured Yes in the approved fashion of the present. But he had looked his feelings, and she had looked hers, while numerous little attentions bestowed on each other, too subtle to be detailed, and the attraction which kept them constantly together, were earnests of their intentions more weighty than words could give. And so, let me say, without further explanation, that Sam and Anner 'Lizer were engaged. But when did the course of true love ever run smooth?

There was never a time but there were some rocks in its channel around which the little stream had to glide or over which it had to bound and bubble; and thus it was with the loves of our young friends. But in this case the crystal stream seemed destined neither to bound over nor glide by the obstacle in its path, but rather to let its merry course be checked thereby.

It may, at first, seem a strange thing to say, but it was nevertheless true, that the whole sweep and torrent of the trouble had rise in the great religious revival that was being enthusiastically carried on at the little Baptist meeting-house. Interest, or perhaps, more correctly speaking, excitement ran high, and regularly as night came round, all the hands on the neighboring plantations flocked to the scene of their devotions.

There was no more regular attendant at these meetings, nor more deeply interested listener to the pastor's inflammatory exhortations, than Anner 'Lizer. The weirdness of the scene and the touch of mysticism in the services—though, of course, she did not analyze it thus—reached her emotional nature and stirred her being to its depths. Night after night found her in her pew, the third bench from the rude pulpit, her large eyes, dilated to their fullest capacity, following the minister through every motion, seeming at times in their steadiness to look him through and beyond to the regions he was describing—the harp-ringing heaven of bliss or the fire-filled home of the damned.

Now Sam, on the other hand, could not be induced to attend these meetings; and when his fellow-servants were at the little church pray-ing, singing, and shouting, he was to be found sitting in one corner of his cabin, picking his banjo, or scouring the woods, carrying ax and taper, and, with a dog trotting at his heels, hunting for that venison of the Negro palate—'coon.

Of course this utter irreverence on the part of her lover shocked Anner 'Lizer; but she had not entered far enough into the regions of the ecstasy to be a proselyte; so she let Sam go his way, albeit with reluctance, while she went to church unattended. But she thought of Sam; and many a time when she secretly prayed to get religion she added a prayer that she might retain Sam.

He, the rogue, was an unconscious but pronounced skeptic; and day by day, as Anner 'Lizer became more and more possessed by religious fervor, the breach between them widened; still widening gradually until the one span that connected the two hearts was suddenly snapped asunder on the night when Anner 'Lizer went to the mourn-ers' bench.

She had not gone to church with that intention; indeed not, al-though she had long been deeply moved by a consciousness of her lost estate. But that night, when the preacher had pictured the bound-less joys of heaven, and then, leaning over the pulpit and stretching out his arms before him, had said in his softest tone, "Now come, won't you, sinnahs? De Lawd is jes' on de othah side; jes' one step away, waitin' to receibe you. Won't you come to him? Won't you tek de chance o' becomin' j'int 'ars o' dat beautiful city whar de streets is gol' an' de gates is pearl? Won't you come to him, sinnah? Don't you see de pityin' look he's a-givin' you, a-sayin' Come, come?" she lost herself. Some irresistible power seemed dominating her, and she rose and went forward, dropping at the altar amid a great shouting and clapping of hands and cries of "Bless de Lawd, one mo' recruit fu' de Gospel ahmy."

Someone started the hymn, "We'll bow around the altar," and the refrain was taken up by the congregation with a fervor that made the rafters of the little edifice ring again.

The conquest of Anner 'Lizer, the belle of that section of Kentucky, was an event of great moment; and, in spite of the concentration of the worshipers' minds on their devotions, the unexpected occurrence called forth a deal of discussion among the brothers and sisters. Aunt Hannah remarked to Aunt Maria, over the back of the seat, that she "nevah knowed de gal was unner c'nviction." And Aunt Maria answered solemnly, "You know, sistah, de Lawd wuks in a myste'ious way his wondahs to pu'fo'm."

Meanwhile the hymn went on, and above it rose the voice of the minister: "We want all de Christuns in de house to draw up aroun' de altah, whar de fiah is bu'nin': you know in de wintah time when hit's col' you crowds up clost to de fiahplace; so now, ef you wants to git spi'tually wa'm, you mus' be up whar de fiah is." There was a great scrambling and shuffling of feet as the members rose with one accord to crowd, singing, around the altar.

Two of the rude benches had been placed end to end before the pulpit, so that they extended nearly the full width of the little church; and at these knelt a dozen or more mourners, swaying and writhing under the burden of their sins.

The song being ended, the preacher said: "Br'er Adams, please tek up de cross." During the momentary lull that intervened between the end of the song and the prayer, the wails and supplications of the mourners sounded out with weird effect. Then Br'er Adams, a white-haired patriarch, knelt and "took up the cross."

Earnestly he besought the divine mercy in behalf of "de po' sinnahs, a-rollin' an' a-tossin' in de tempes' of dere sins." "Lawd," he prayed, "come down dis evenin' in Sperit's powah to seek an' to save-ah; let us heah de rumblin' of yo' cha'iot wheels-ah lak de thundah f'om Mount Sinai-ah; oh, Lawd'ah, convert mou'nahs an' convict sinnahs-ah; show 'em dat dey mus' die an' cain't lib an' atter death to judg-a-ment; tu'n 'em aroun' befo' it is evahlastin' an' eternally too late." Then, warming more and more, and swaying his form back and forth, as he pounded the seat in emphasis, he began to wail out in a sort of indescribable monotone: "O Lawd, save de mou'nah!"

"Save de mou'nah!" came the response from all over the church.

"He'p 'em out of de miah an' quicksan's of dere sins!"

"He'p, Lawd!"

"And place deir feet upon de evahlastin' an' eternal rock-ah!"

"Do, Lawd."

"O Lawd-ah, shake a dyin' sinnah ovah hell an' fo'bid his mighty fall-ah!"

"O Lawd, shake 'em!" came from the congregation.

By this time everyone was worked up to a high state of excitement, and the prayer came to an end amid great commotion. Then a rich, mellow voice led out with:

> "Sabe de mou'nah jes' now,
> Sabe de mou'nah jes' now,
> Sabe de mou'nah jes' now,
> Only trust Him jes' now,
> Only trust Him jes' now,
> He'p de sinnah jes' now;"

and so to indefinite length the mournful minor melody ran along like a sad brook flowing through autumn woods, trying to laugh and ripple through tears.

Every now and then some mourner would spring half up, with a shriek, and then sink down again trembling and jerking spasmodically. "He's a-doubtin', he's a-doubtin'!" the cry would fly around; "but I tell you he purt' nigh had it that time."

Finally the slender form of Anner 'Lizer began to sway backward and forward, like a sapling in the wind, and she began to mourn and weep aloud.

"Praise de Lawd!" shouted Aunt Hannah, "de po' soul's gittin' de evidence: keep on, honey, de Lawd ain't fa' off." The sudden change attracted considerable attention, and in a moment a dozen or more zealous altar-workers gathered around Anner 'Lizer and began to clap and sing with all their might, keeping time to the melodious cadence of their music with heavy foot-pats on the resounding floor.

> "Git on boa'd-ah, little childering,
> Git on boa'd-ah, little childering,
> Git on boa'd-ah, little childering,
>   Dere's room fo' many mo'.

> "De gospel ship is sailin',
>   It's loaded down wid souls.
> If you want to mek heab'n yo' happy home,
> You mus' ketch it fo' it goes.
>   Git on boa'd, etc.

> "King Jesus at de hellum,
>   Fu' to guide de ship erright.
>   We gwine fu' to put into heab'n's po't
>   Wid ouah sails all shinin' white.
>   Git on boa'd," etc.

With a long dwell on the last word of the chorus, the mellow cadence of the song died away.

"Let us bow down fu' a season of silent praar," said the minister.

"Lawd, he'p us to pray," responded Uncle Eben Adams.

The silence that ensued was continually broken by the wavering wail of the mourners. Suddenly one of them, a stalwart young man, near the opening of the aisle, began to writhe and twist himself into every possible contortion, crying, "O Lawd, de devil's a-ridin' me; tek him off—tek him off!"

"Tek him off, Lawd!" shouted the congregation.

Then suddenly, without warning, the mourner rose straight up into the air, shouting, "Hallelujah, hallelujah, hallelujah!"

"He's got it—he's got it!" cried a dozen eager worshipers, leaping to their feet and crowding around the happy convert; "bless de Lawd, he's got it." A voice was raised, and soon the church was ringing with

> "Loose him and let him go,
>   Let him shout to glory."

On went the man, shouting "Hallelujah," shaking hands, and bounding over seats in the ecstasy of his bliss.

His conversion kindled the flame of the meeting and set the fire going. You have seen corn in the popper when the first kernel springs up and flares open, how quickly the rest follow, keeping up the steady pop, pop, pop; well, just so it was after this first conversion. The mourners popped up quickly and steadily as the strength of the spiritual fire seemed to reach their swelling souls. One by one they left the bench on which, figuratively speaking, they may be said to have laid down their sins and proclaimed themselves possessors of religion; until, finally, there was but one left, and that one—Anner 'Lizer. She had ceased from her violent activity, and seemed perfectly passive now.

The efforts of all were soon concentrated on her, and such stamping and clapping and singing was never heard before. Such cries of "Jes' look up, sistah, don't you see Him at yo' side? Jes' reach out yo' han' an' tech de hem of His ga'ment. Jes' listen, sistah, don't you heah de angels singin'? Don't you heah de rumblin' of de cha'iot wheels? He's a-comin', He's a-comin', He's a-comin'!"

But Anner 'Lizer was immovable; with her face lying against the hard bench, she moaned and prayed softly to herself. The congregation redoubled its exertions, but all to no effect; Anner 'Lizer wouldn't "come thoo."

It was a strange case.

Aunt Maria whispered to her bosom friend: "You min' me, Sistah Hannah, dere's sump'n' on dat gal's min'." And Aunt Hannah answered, "I believe you."

Josephine, or more comonly Phiny, a former belle whom Anner 'Lizer's superior charms had deposed, could not lose this opportunity to have a fling at her successful rival. Of course such cases of vindictiveness in women are rare, and Phiny was exceptional when she whispered to her fellow-servant, Lucy: "I reckon she'd git 'ligion if Sam Me'itt was heah to see her." Lucy snickered, as in duty bound, and whispered back, "I wisht you'd heish."

Well, after all their singing, in spite of all their efforts, the time came for closing the meeting, and Anner 'Lizer had not yet made a profession.

She was lifted tenderly up from the mourners' bench by a couple of solicitous sisters, and, after listening to the preacher's exhortation to "pray constantly, thoo de day an' thoo de night, in de highways an' de byways an' in yo' secret closet," she went home praying in her soul, leaving the rest of the congregation to loiter along the way and gossip over the night's events.

All the next day Anner 'Lizer, erstwhile so cheerful, went about her work sad and silent, every now and then stopping in the midst of her labors and burying her face in her neat white apron to sob violently. It was true, as Aunt Hannah expressed, that "de Sperit had sholy tuk holt of dat gal wid a powahful han'."

All of her fellow-servants knew that she was a mourner, and, with that characteristic reverence for religion which is common to all their race, and not lacking even in the most hardened sinner among them, they respected her feelings. Phiny alone, when she met her, tossed her head and giggled openly. But Phiny's actions never troubled Anner 'Lizer, for she felt herself so far above her. Once though, in the course of the day, she had been somewhat disturbed, when she had suddenly come upon her rival, standing in the spring-house talking and laughing with Sam. She noticed, too, with a pang, that Phiny had tied a bow of red ribbon on her hair. She shut her lips and only prayed the harder. But an hour later, somehow, a ribbon as red as Phiny's had miraculously attached itself to her thick black plaits. Was the temporal creeping in with the spiritual in Anner 'Lizer's mind? Who can tell? Perhaps she thought that, while cultivating the one, she need not utterly neglect the other; and who says but that she was right?

Uncle Eben, however, did not take this view of the matter when he came hobbling up in the afternoon to exhort her a little. He found Anner 'Lizer in the kitchen washing dishes. Engrossed in the contemplation of her spiritual state, or praying for deliverance from the same, through the whole day she had gone about without speaking to anyone. But with Uncle Eben it was, of course, different, for he was a man held in high respect by all the Negroes and, next to the minister, the greatest oracle in those parts; so Anner 'Lizer spoke to him.

"Howdy, Uncl' Eben," she said, in a lugubrious tone, as the old man hobbled in and settled down in a convenient corner.

"Howdy, honey, howdy," he replied, crossing one leg over the other, as he unwound his long bandanna, placed it in his hat, and then deposited his heavy cane on the white floor. "I jes' thought I'd drap in to ax you how do you do today?"

"Po' enough, Uncl' Eben, fu' sho.'"

"Ain't foun' no res' fu' yo' soul yit?"

"No res yit," answered Anner 'Lizer, again applying the apron to her already swollen eyes.

"Um-m," sighed the old man, meditatively tapping his foot; and then the gay flash of Anner 'Lizer's ribbon caught his eye and he gasped: "Bless de Lawd, Sis 'Lizer; you don't mean to tell me dat you's gwine 'bout heah seekin' wid yo' har tied up in ribbon? Whut! tek it off, honey, tek it off; ef yo' wants yo' soul saved, tek it off!"

Anner 'Lizer hesitated, and raised her eyes in momentary protest, but they met the horrified gaze of the old man, and she lowered them again as her hand went reluctantly up to her head to remove the offending bit of finery.

"You see, honey," Uncle Eben went on, "when you sta'ts out on de Christian jou'ney, you's got to lay aside ev'ry weight dat doth so easy beset you an' keeps you f'om pergressin'; y' ain't got to think nothin' 'bout pussunal 'dornment; you's jes' got to shet yo' eyes an' open yo' hea't an' say, Lawd, come; you mustn't wait fu' to go to chu'ch to pray, nuther, you mus' pray anywhar an' ev'ry whar. Why, when I was seekin', I ust to go 'way off up in de big woods to pray, an' dere's whar de Lawd answered me, an' I'm a-rejoicin' today in de powah of de same salvation. Honey, you's got to pray, I tell you. You's got to brek de backbone of yo' pride an' pray in earnes'; an' ef you does dat, you'll git he'p, fu' de Lawd is a praar-heahin' Lawd an' plenteous in mussy."

Anner 'Lizer listened attentively to the exhortation and evidently profited by it, for soon after Uncle Eben's departure she changed her natty little dress for one less pretentious, and her dainty, frilled white muslin apron gave way to a broad dark calico one. If grace was to be found by self-abnegation in the matter of dress, Anner 'Lizer was bound to have it at any price.

As afternoon waned and night came on, she grew more and more serious, and more frequent recourse was had to the corner of her apron. She even failed to see Phiny when that enterprising young person passed her, decked out in the whitest of white cuffs and collars setting off in pleasant contrast her neat dark dress. Phiny giggled again and put up her hand, ostensibly to brush some imaginary dust from her bosom but really to show her pretty white cuffs with their big bone buttons. But it was all lost on Anner 'Lizer; her gaze was downcast and her thoughts far away. If anyone was ever "seekin'" in earnest, this girl was.

Night came, and with it the usual services. Anner 'Lizer was one of the earliest of the congregation to arrive, and she went immediately to the mourners' bench. In the language of the congregation, "Eldah Johnsing sholy did preach a powahful sermon" that night. More sinners were convicted and brought to their knees, and, as before, these recruits were converted and Anner 'Lizer left. What was the matter?

That was the question which everyone asked, but there were none found who could answer it. The circumstance was all the more astounding from the fact that this unsuccessful mourner had not been a very wicked girl. Indeed, it was to have been expected that she might shake her sins from her shoulders as she would discard a mantle, and step over on the Lord's side. But it was not so.

But when a third night came and passed with the same result, it became the talk of three plantations. To be sure, cases were not lacking where people had "mourned" a week, two weeks, or even a month; but they were woeful sinners and those were times of less spiritual interest; but under circumstances so favorable as were now presented, that one could long refrain from "gittin' religion" was the wonder of all. So, after the third night, everybody wondered and talked, and not a few began to lean to Phiny's explanation, that "de ole snek in de grass had been a-goin' on doin' all her dev'ment on de sly, so's *people* wouldn't know it; but de *Lawd* he did, an' he payin' her up fu' it now."

Sam Merritt alone did not talk, and seemed perfectly indifferent to all that was said. When he was in Phiny's company and she rallied him about the actions of his "gal," he remained silent.

On the fourth night of Anner 'Lizer's mourning, the congregation gathered as usual at the church. For the first half-hour all went on as usual, and the fact that Anner 'Lizer was absent caused no remark, for everyone thought she would come in later. But time passed and she did not come. "Eldah Johnsing's" flock became agitated. Of course there were other mourners, but the one particular one was absent; hence the dissatisfaction. Every head in the house was turned toward the door, whenever it was opened by some late comer; and around flew the whisper, "I wunner ef she's quit mou'nin'; you aint' heerd of her gittin' 'ligion, have you?" No one had.

Meanwhile the object of their solicitude was praying just the same, but in a far different place. Grasping, as she was, at everything that seemed to give her promise of relief, somehow Uncle Eben's words had had a deep effect upon her. So, when night fell and her work was over, she had gone up into the woods to pray. She had prayed long without success, and now she was crying aloud from the very fullness of her heart, "O Lawd, sen' de light—sen' de light!" Suddenly, as if in answer to her prayer, a light appeared before her some distance away.

The sudden attainment of one's desires often shocks one; so with our mourner. For a moment her heart stood still and the thought came to her to flee, but her mind flashed back over the words of one of the hymns she had heard down at church, "Let us walk in de light," and she knew that before she walked in the light she must walk toward it. So she rose and started in the direction of the light. How it flickered and flared, disappeared and reappeared, rose and fell, even as her spirits, as she stumbled and groped her way over fallen logs and through briers! Her limbs were bruised and her dress torn by the thorns. But she heeded it not; she had fixed her eye—physical and spiritual—on the light before her. It drew her with an irresistible fascination. Suddenly she stopped. An idea had occurred to her. Maybe this light was a Jack-o'-lantern! For a moment she hesitated, then promptly turned her pocket wrong side out, murmuring, "De Lawd'll tek keer o' me." On she started; but lo! the light had disappeared! What! had the turning of the pocket indeed worked so potent a charm?

But no! it reappeared as she got beyond the intervention of a brush pile which had obscured it. The light grew brighter as she grew fainter; but she clasped her hands and raised her eyes in unwavering faith, for she found that the beacon did not recede, but glowed with a steady and stationary flame.

As she drew near, the sound of sharp strokes came to her ears, and she wondered. Then, as she slipped into the narrow circle of light, she saw that it was made by a taper which was set on a log. The strokes came from a man who was chopping down a tree in which a 'coon seemed to have taken refuge. It needed no second glance at the stalwart shoulders to tell her that the man was—Sam. Her step attracted his attention, and he turned.

"Sam!"

"Anner 'Lizer!"

And then they both stood still, too amazed to speak. Finally she walked across to where he was standing, and said: "Sam, I didn't come out heah to fin' you, but de Lawd has 'p'inted it so, 'ca'se he knowed I orter speak to you." Sam leaned hopelessly on his ax; he thought she was going to exhort him.

Anner 'Lizer went on: "Sam, you's my stumblin' block in de highroad to salvation. I's been tryin' to git 'ligion fu' fo' nights, an' I cain't do it jes' on you' 'count. I prays an' I prays, an' jes as I's a'mos' got it, jes as I begin to heah de cha'iot wheels a-rollin', yo' face comes right in 'tween an' drives it all away. Tell me now, Sam, so's to put me out of my 'spense, does you want to ma'y me, er is you goin' to ma'y Phiny? I jes' wants you to tell me, not dat I keers pussonally, but so's my min' kin be at res' spi'tu'lly, an' I kin git 'ligion. Jes' say yes er no; I wants to be settled one way er t' other."

"Anner 'Lizer," said Sam, reproachfully, "you know I wants to ma'y you jes' ez soon ez Mas' Rob'll let me."

"Dere now," said Anner 'Lizer, "bless de Lawd!" And somehow Sam had dropped the ax and was holding her in his arms.

It boots not whether the 'coon was caught that night or not, but it is a fact that Anner 'Lizer set the whole place afire by getting religion at home early the next morning. And the same night the minister announced that "de Lawd had foun' out de sistah's stumblin' block an' removed it f'om de path."

William Stanley Beaumont Braithwaite

(1878–1962)

POET, CRITIC, AND NATIONALLY KNOWN anthologist, Braithwaite was born in Boston, Massachusetts, and spent most of his life there. Largely self-educated, he received honorary degrees from both Atlanta University and Talladega College. During the forties, he held a chair as Professor of Literature at Atlanta University.

A one-time editor of the *New Poetry Review,* a regular contributor of literary criticism to the old Boston *Transcript,* and a contributor of essays to *Forum, Century, Scribner's,* and the *Atlantic Monthly,* William Stanley Braithwaite is probably best known for annual anthologies of magazine verse, which he compiled for many years, and anthologies of period verse: *The Book of Elizabethan Verse* (1906); *The Book of Modern British Verse* (1919).

Braithwaite's own poetry fills three volumes: *Lyrics of Life and Love* (1904); *The House of Falling Leaves* (1908); and *Selected Poems* (1948). His prose works are *The House Under Arcturus: An Autobiography* (1940) and *The Bewitched Parsonage* (1950), a biography of the Brontes.

In his poetry, Braithwaite exemplified to an extreme degree an assimilationist attitude held sporadically by other authors of his time. Refusing to write as a "Negro poet" or to use racial themes, he elected to fight for equality by competing with white writers on their terms. (When Chesnutt wrote "Baxter's Procrustes" and when Dunbar wrote non-racial novels, they were doing essentially the same thing.) This is a kind of literary "passing" that we find hard to understand today, but the position is tenable. It is easy to criticize Braithwaite's refusal to be a race poet; it is not so easy to match his performance as a lyrical poet.

Although Braithwaite lived until 1962, his best and most representative work as a poet was done before 1910. For his excellence in literature he was awarded the Spingarn Medal in 1918.

DEL CASCAR

Del Cascar, Del Cascar,
Sat upon a flaming star,
Sat, and let his feet hang down
Till in China the toes turned brown.

And he reached his fingers over
The rim of the sea, like sails from Dover,
And caught a Mandarin at prayer,
And tickled his nose in Orion's hair.

The sun went down through crimson bars,
And left his blind face battered with stars,
But the brown toes in China kept
Hot the tears Del Cascar wept!

TURN ME TO MY YELLOW LEAVES

Turn me to my yellow leaves,
I am better satisfied;
There is nothing in me grieves—
That was never born—and died.
Let me be a scarlet flame
On a windy autumn morn,
I, who never had a name,
Nor from a breathing image born.
From the margin let me fall
Where the farthest stars sink down.
And the void consume me,—all
Into nothingness to drown.
Let me dream my dream entire,
Withered as an autumn leaf—
Let me have my vain desire,
Vain—as it is brief!

SIC VITA

Heart free, hand free,
  Blue above, brown under,
All the world to me
  Is a place of wonder.

Poems reprinted by permission of Coward-McCann, Inc. from *Selected Poems* by William Stanley Braithwaite. Copyright 1948 by William Stanley Braithwaite.

Sun shine, moon shine,
    Stars, and winds a-blowing,
All into this heart of mine
    Flowing, flowing, flowing!

Mind free, step free,
    Days to follow after,
Joys of life sold to me
    For the price of laughter.
Girl's love, man's love,
    Love of work and duty,
Just a will of God's to prove
    Beauty, beauty, beauty!

SCINTILLA

I kissed a kiss in youth
    Upon a dead man's brow;
And that was long ago—
    And I'm a grown man now.

It's lain there in the dust,
    Thirty years and more—
My lips that set a light
    At a dead man's door!

THE WATCHERS

Two women on the lone wet strand
    (*The wind's out with a will to roam*)
The waves wage war on rocks and sand,
    (*And a ship is long due home!*)

The sea spray's in the women's eyes—
    (*Hearts can writhe like the sea's wild foam*)
Lower descend the tempestuous skies,
    (*For the wind's out with a will to roam.*)

"O daughter, thine eyes be better than mine,"
    (*The waves ascend high as yonder dome*)
"North or south is there never a sign?"
    (*And a ship is long due home!*)

They watch there all the long night through—
  (*The wind's out with a will to roam*)
Wind and rain and sorrow for two,—
  (*And heaven on the long reach home!*)

QUIET HAS A HIDDEN SOUND

BEACON HILL

Quiet has a hidden sound
Best upon a hillside street,
When the sunlight on the ground
Is luminous with heat.

Something teases one to peek
Behind the summer afternoon
And watch the shadowy legends leak
Off Time's unscalèd tune.

Just a common city street
Running up a city hill,
Filled with nothing but the heat
And houses standing still!

But where is silence castlèd,
Or stranger, the sunlight magic,
Than on this hillside, where the tread
Of summertime is tragic!

The New Negro Renaissance and Beyond

1910-1954

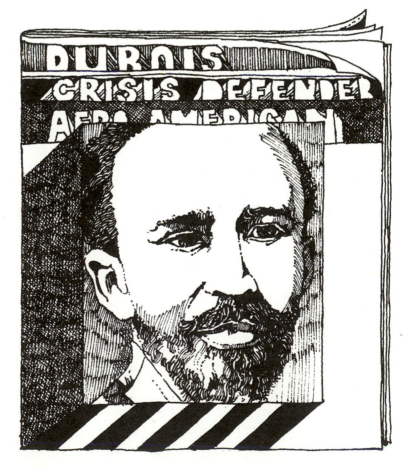

4

The political compromise that in 1877 brought an end to Reconstruction and led to the complete disfranchisement of the Negro in the South had consequences which, by 1908, extended far beyond the sphere of politics. It had cultural and psychological effects such as those epitomized in the life and works of Booker T. Washington, whose tremendous influence on racial thought helped to impose on millions of blacks the life-style and character image which the majority of whites judged to be not only acceptable but true.

And this white acceptance had literary consequences. It fixed the respectability of the "darky rhymes," "coon songs," and "nigger dialect" of the minstrel tradition. As long as black writers followed this tradition, they were certain of the approval of a white audience. Whites were amused and their racial beliefs were confirmed by the works of Paul Laurence Dunbar, James Edwin Campbell, and Daniel Webster Davis, and by such Negro theatrical productions as "A Trip to Coontown," "Bandanna Land," and "Clorindy—The Origin of the Cakewalk." These works, which were all written and staged between 1898 and 1903, were taken as positive proof of the Negro's inherent inferiority; and his inferiority justified the treatment accorded him in ordinary rounds of civil life.

But there were some Negroes who refused to accept the minstrel tradition, who rebelled against the idea of racial inferiority, and who were outraged by the accommodationist doctrine of Booker Washington. Because most Negroes were illiterate and unaware of attitudes and opinions around them, these rebels were few in number. Their spokesman did not make himself heard until 1903, when the minstrel tradition already seemed indestructible.

With the publication of William E. B. Du Bois' *The Souls of Black Folk,* another concept of Negro character and ethos struggled toward a viable existence. Du Bois' book was a potpourri of history and fantasy, fiction and autobiography, prophecy and scholarly perception. But an unmistakable integrity of purpose gave it the unity of a single statement of protest such as no black writer had ever made. Prophetically he stated, "The problem of the twentieth century is the problem of the color line." Although *The Souls of Black Folk* may now seem reasonable and temperate, it was severely criticized, particularly in the South. The Atlanta *Constitution* castigated it. The Nashville *Banner* declared, "This book is dangerous for the negro to read, for it will only excite discontent and fill his imagination with things that do not exist, or things that should not bear upon his mind."

The book did just that. James Weldon Johnson, who himself had contributed his share of coon songs and dialect poetry to the minstrel tradition, said that *The Souls of Black Folk* had "a greater effect upon and within the Negro race in America than any other single book published in this country since *Uncle Tom's Cabin.*"

Du Bois had told the truth. If the telling caused sharp criticism and rejection by whites, this criticism of *The Souls of Black Folk* was mild when compared to that generated by the "Resolution" which Du Bois composed for the Niagara Movement two years later.

The Souls of Black Folk and the "Resolution" set the tone and suggested the themes that were to preoccupy most Negro literature for nearly two decades. Although Negro authors were not very productive during this time, the writing they did was principally propaganda and protest. It appeared in the pages of *The Crisis*—the NAACP's official organ, and in those weekly Negro newspapers (the Boston *Guardian,* the Chicago *Defender,* the Baltimore *Afro-American*) which Booker Washington had not seduced, bribed, or threatened into silence on all aspects of the race question.

But these periodicals gave space to imaginative writing too, and not all of it concerned social issues. Poetry by William Stanley Braithwaite occasionally appeared in *The Crisis,* as did the short fiction and essays of Effie Lee Newsome and, with increasing frequency, the verse of Jessie Fauset. Fenton Johnson published in the Chicago *Defender,* and the work of several writers of lesser talent cropped up in other weekly newspapers whose "literary" standards were more flexible than those set by Du Bois for publication in *The Crisis.* Indeed, these newspapers were the only outlets available to black writers, particularly the angry ones, and although most black writers certainly wanted to attract a white audience, few succeeded.

Because the white audience was the paying audience, and because the measure of success for any Negro endeavor was the degree of white attention or approval it attracted, it is not surprising that some imaginative black writers avoided racial themes and sought publication simply as "artists." The minstrel tradition was scorned by the Negroes who wrote, and whites ignored black protest. Besides, unlike other protest, black protest had already accumulated those connotations that reduced such writing to a level below the creative, a level where Negro folk art—including folk tales, spirituals, blues, and jazz—was also relegated. Folk art was considered an element of the "low culture," as distinct from the "high culture" of white middle-class America. Some black writers tried to overcome this situation by meeting the standards of craft and of "universality" that the white audience seemed to demand of its own creative artists. No one of the Negro writers who tried was a complete failure. No one of them, either, was an unqualified success.

William Braithwaite did earn a reputation as a critic. From 1913 to 1928 he annually published anthologies of magazine verse, which were the gleanings from white periodicals and demonstrated his critical sensibilities and perceptions. But Braithwaite's poetry, avoiding all consciousness of race, is strained. The poetry of James Weldon Johnson, who also strove for universality, is mediocre at best, but his innocuous, sentimental non-black poems achieved publication in such white magazines as the *Century* and *Outlook*.

It can be said that the black women poets who eschewed racial themes were generally better poets than the men. Most were middle-class housewives, and their men—husbands, fathers, brothers, and friends—sheltered them from the grosser realities of black life. The facts of wife- and motherhood were "universal" experiences upon which these poets could draw, and which excused them for avoiding the theme of protest. Their poetry was no better and no worse than that of most of their white female contemporaries. The poetry of Georgia Douglass Johnson, Angelina Grimké, and Alice Dunbar Nelson tends more to prettiness than profundity, more to surface than to substance.

This coterie of "raceless" writers represented Du Bois' "talented tenth" of Negroes who "through their knowledge of modern culture . . . could guide the American Negro into a higher civilization." Du Bois' earlier promotion of this idea had earned him the reputation of being class- and color-conscious, of being concerned only for the interest of the small "dickty" middle class of Negroes. But by 1910 the idea of a "talented tenth" no longer seemed defensible or viable even to some members of the talented tenth. Other attitudes were developing.

James Weldon Johnson published *The Autobiography of An Ex-Coloured Man* in 1912, and the novel showed changes from Charles Chesnutt's tragic mulatto theme: to all appearances the protagonist is white, but the representation of his weaknesses contradicts the racial myth implicit in Chesnutt's thesis and denies the notion that more white blood makes a better and stronger person. Five years later came Johnson's *Fifty Years and Other Poems*, a revelation of true Negro consciousness. Even its strongest pieces are mild in comparison with today's angry black poetry, but they are never conciliatory or pleading.

At about the same time Fenton Johnson (no relation to James Weldon) published *Visions of the Dusk* (1915) and *Songs of the Soil* (1916). Influenced by the Chicago School, *Visions* helped free black poets from their enslavement to conventional verse forms and showed them that sophisticated poetry could deal realistically, and on a fairly high level, with the degradation and disillusionment of the typical Negro's urban life. Ballads and the blues, of course, also dealt with these matters, but these modes of expression were folk in origin, idiom and theme. Stripped of all sentiment, the realism and cynicism of the ballads and the blues spoke only to blacks, as did the earliest jazz; and like jazz, ballads and blues did not begin to enter the mainstream of American culture until the end of the second decade of the twentieth century.

But at that time many changes took place. With the First World War in its second year, the flow of European immigrant labor was suddenly cut off, and the industrial North was faced with a manpower shortage. It turned South for replenishment. Negroes were eager to go North and escape poverty, peonage, and lynching. Two million fled the South in less than four years. They crowded into the industrial cities of the North and Midwest, and the density of black ghettoes increased twenty- and thirty-fold. Unaccustomed to urban living, to weekly wages that amounted to more than most had previously made in a year, and to the restricted freedom of the North, these Negroes created problems and protested the absence of solutions. When black men were drafted, they protested discrimination and segregation in training camps. Overseas, where some were sent as combat troops (but most as stevedores and food handlers), their experiences with the French gave them a notion of what equality was. They liked it. As Alain Locke, one of the most perceptive observers, said, when the war ended "America had to reckon with a fundamentally changed Negro, a new Negro." This new Negro tended to react defiantly. Cursed, he cursed back. Struck, he struck back. A dozen race riots in the "red summer" of 1919 proved his new mettle.

Defiance, then, was the new temper. It was also the organizing mode of Marcus Garvey's Universal Negro Improvement Association. Under such slogans as "A Place in the Sun" and "Back to Africa," Garvey marshalled thousands of lower-class urban Negroes. His newspaper, *The Negro World,* inspired his followers with fiery editorials on black nationalism, with slanted news, and with stories—sometimes mythic and apocryphal, but often true—of black peoples' contributions to world culture. In 1922 Garvey claimed for UNIA a world-wide membership of four million.

Defiance, too, was the temper of more sophisticated publications for more sophisticated blacks. Du Bois' *The Crisis* editorials constantly challenged the vagaries of the white man's concept of democracy and how it should work. A. Philip Randolph's editorials in *The Messenger,* the magazine which he founded just after the war, were cited as "dangerous to the comfort and security" of white people. *The Messenger,* a Congressman from South Carolina declared, "is antagonistic to the United States. . . . It pays tribute to [Eugene] Debs and every other convicted enemy of the Government."

But perhaps no expression of the new spirit had such impact as a poem entitled "If We Must Die." Written by Claude McKay, the poem was first published in *The Liberator,* which, unlike the magazines cited above, was edited by whites for whites.

A complex of forces seemed suddenly to arouse a tremendous interest in black people and black life. If whites were caught up in this interest, they also contributed to it. The dramatists Eugene O'Neill, Ridgely Torrence, and Paul Green wrote plays about Negro life. White novelists, including Sherwood Anderson, Waldo Frank, Carl Van Vechten, and DuBose Heyward, produced fiction in which the major characters were black. Jazz music and the dances it inspired, the blues (called "torch songs" by white singers like Ruth Etting and Helen Morgan), and basic black ballads at last emerged from underground Negro life. John Charles Thomas and Ada May, Irene and Vernon Castle, Ziegfeld and his imitators were suddenly old hat. The sentimental plays, the melodramas, and the romantic musical shows gradually yielded to new modes and to a mood, generated by blacks, that was at once romantic and realistic, sentimental and cynical, abrasive and bland, profound and superficial, humorous and sad. And perhaps, above all, it was primitive.

The mood was primitive in what it expressed and often in the manner of expression. It was primitive in the sense of stripping experience —the experience of blackness as interpreted by black poets and novelists, essayists and editors, singers and composers—down to the quivering marrow of emotional content, psychological relevance, and racial insight. Black writers and artists wanted to make clear the meaning of being black in America. They were no longer afraid or ashamed. Indeed, black writers took an arrogant pride in their blackness. They flaunted it. They stood naked before whites and—sometimes in anger, sometimes in scorn, sometimes in satirical amusement—said, "Look at me! It will help you the better to see and know yourself."

Of course all the writers of the New Negro Renaissance did not have the same quality or kind of talent, nor were they all committed in the same degree to revelation. Some had great talent and versatility, and perhaps first among these was Langston Hughes. But Jean Toomer and, at their best, Claude McKay, Countee Cullen, and Arna Bontemps were of top rank. Most writers, however, were merely competent, and —like Wallace Thurman, George Schuyler (who wrote *Black No More,* the only sustained satirical novel by a Negro), Eric Waldrond, Nella Larsen, Frank Marshall Davis, Rudolph Fisher, and Walter White—rode the great wave of popularity until it waned. Negro critics showed a constant development from the formal pedantry of Benjamin Brawley to the cultural insights of Alain Locke to the sensitive understanding of Sterling Brown. The Renaissance period lacked a notable dramatist, and although many plays were written few were produced. Garland Anderson's *Appearances* had a brief Broadway run, as did Hall Johnson's *Run, Little Chillun,* but Negro dramas had to wait for white producers, and white producers were not eager for the preachy and didactic plays that most black playwrights were writing.

This great outpouring of serious creative effort did not attract a sizeable Negro audience or patronage, and most blacks were ignorant of the novels, the poems, the plays, the essays. The measure of success for Negro artists and writers was still the degree of white interest and approval. The New Negro Renaissance was sustained by a white audience, and white entrepreneurs reaped the rewards. While for the serious black artists race and racial experiences were (and are) the most compelling forces, most of the white audience was looking for entertainment; fast-buck boys, mostly white, made a mockery of black artists' efforts to project their unhappy truths. The fast-buck boys made Harlem, which one writer called "nigger heaven," the mecca of the exotic, the savage, and the strange. The fad for things black soon began to die: by 1928 the end was in sight. Publishers no longer competed for Negro manuscripts. Negro writers, including Hughes, McKay, Cullen, and Toomer, began to desert Harlem for Paris, Rome, Moscow, Lagos, Havana, and Eatonville, Florida. The Great Depression brought the absolute end, and for the next ten years scarcely a black voice was heard above a whisper.

The Depression, however, provided a valuable apprentice period for a group of young writers who were employed on projects of the WPA and many of whom came under the watchful eye of the teacher-critic Sterling Brown, who served as a project director. Among these young black men were Frank Yerby, Willard Motley, Richard Wright, and Ralph Ellison. Yerby and Motley soon renounced the Negro's special consciousness. After the publication of *The Foxes of Harrow,* Yerby could no longer be called a black writer. Motley, who died in 1966, was not a black writer either, although there is at least one sketchily drawn Negro character in both *Knock On Any Door* and *We Fished All Night.*

When Richard Wright's four novellas, collectively called *Uncle Tom's Children* (1938), were followed by *Native Son* (1940), readers knew that a powerful talent had found itself. The stories in the first book showed promise; the novel fulfilled that promise. Although *Native Son* had social importance, its skillful structure, characterization, dramatic intensity, and subtly woven threads of symbolism made it a novel to be reckoned with aesthetically. As both a novel and a "social document," *Native Son* was by far the best work done by a black writer up to that time.

In 1946 Wright moved permanently to Paris, where he was no longer faced with the everyday reality of his blackness, intellectual tension relaxed, and his talent waned. But his departure did not leave the world of American black letters altogether impoverished. Ann Petry published her first novel, *The Street,* which was soon followed by *Country Place.* Dorothy West's *The Living Is Easy* appeared in 1948, three years prior to Owen Dodson's *Boy at the Window.* James Baldwin published brilliant essays, and *Go Tell It On the Mountain,* his first, and best, novel came out in 1953. There were poets too, three of them of top rank. Margaret Walker was awarded the Yale Younger Poet's Prize for *For My People.* Gwendolyn Brooks won the Pulitzer Prize for her second volume, *Annie Allen* (1949). And Robert Hayden is at last beginning to be recognized as a fine poet.

No really major black novel since *Native Son* appeared until 1952, when Ralph Ellison's *Invisible Man* was published. Although it had taken seven years to write, the labor does not show, and the time was not wasted. Ellison is a consummate artist. His is also a brilliant critic and personal essayist. *Shadow and Act* (1964) is proof of it.

One thing seems perfectly clear about Negro writing in the period from 1910 to mid-century, and that is its steady development in two directions: from propaganda and the literature of knowledge toward artistry and the literature of power; and from the concept of the Negro as a sort of imitation white man toward the concept of the Negro as a black man whose experiences are not simply a variety of sociological constructions.

William Edward Burghardt Du Bois

(1868–1963)

No SELECTION OF BIOGRAPHICAL facts could possibly do justice to the life of W. E. B. Du Bois. Born in Great Barrington, Massachusetts, he earned a B.A. at Fisk University and another at Harvard, where he also received an M.A. and, following two years of study at the University of Berlin, a Ph.D. His dissertation, *The Suppression of the African Slave Trade, 1638–1870,* was the first volume issued in the Harvard Historical Studies series.

A scholar and teacher, poet, novelist, editor, and political activist, Du Bois had one of the most catholic minds of the twentieth century. He was praised for his prophetic foresight ("The problem of the twentieth century," he wrote in 1903, "is the problem of the color line".); respected for his "radical" thought—even by those conservatives who disagreed with him; and, finally, at the age of ninety-three, hounded out of his native country because of his incorruptible integrity. He died in the West African country of (Accra) Ghana, of which he became a citizen in 1963.

The causes which W. E. B. Du Bois served can be summed up in such well-worn phrases as "equality and justice," "the brotherhood of man," "the least is the most," and "one people, one world, and many cultures." They are implicit in the titles of some of his major works: *The Souls of Black Folk* (1903); *Darkwater: Voices from Within the Veil* (1920); *Black Folk, Then and Now* (1939); *Dusk of Dawn* (1940); *The World and Africa* (1947). And they are explicitly developed in dozens of his essays.

Du Bois never thought of himself as a literary artist, but the literary quality of *The Souls of Black Folk* and his autobiographical *Dusk of Dawn* and of one or two of his few poems is quite good. There is less literary merit in his fiction: *The Quest of the Silver Fleece* (1911); *Dark Princess* (1928); and *The Black Flame: A Triology—The Ordeal of Mansart, Mansart Builds a School, Worlds of Color* (1957, 1959, 1961).

A great deal has been written about Du Bois, but the best recent studies are Francis L. Broderick's *W. E. B. Du Bois, Negro Leader in a Time of Crisis* (1959) and Elliott M. Rudwick's *W. E. B. Du Bois: A Study in Minority Group Leadership* (1960).

The selections in this anthology come from *Dusk of Dawn* and *The Autobiography of W. E. B. Du Bois.*

A NEW ENGLAND BOY AND RECONSTRUCTION

As I have written elsewhere, "I was born by a golden river and in the shadow of two great hills." My birthplace was Great Barrington, a little town in western Massachusetts in the valley of the Housatonic, flanked by the Berkshire hills. Physically and socially our community belonged to the Dutch valley of the Hudson rather than to Puritan New England, and travel went south to New York more often and more easily than east to Boston. But my birthplace was less important than my birth-time. The Civil War had closed but three years earlier and 1868 was the year in which the freedmen of the South were enfranchised and for the first time as a mass took part in government. Conventions with black delegates voted new constitutions all over the South; and two groups of laborers—freed slaves and poor whites—dominated the former slave states. It was an extraordinary experiment in democracy. Thaddeus Stevens, the clearest-headed leader of this attempt at industrial democracy, made his last speech impeaching Andrew Johnson on February sixteenth and on February twenty-third I was born.

Less than a month after my birth Andrew Johnson passed from the scene and Ulysses Grant became President of the United States. The Fifteenth Amendment enfranchising the Negro as a race became law, and the work of abolishing slavery and making Negroes men was accomplished, so far as law could do it. Meanwhile elsewhere in the world there were stirring and change which were to mean much in my life: in Japan the Meiji Emperors rose to power the year I was born; in China the intrepid Empress Dowager was fighting strangulation by England and France; Prussia had fought with Austria and France, and the German Empire arose in 1871. In England, Victoria opened her eighth parliament; the duel of Disraeli and Gladstone began; while in Africa came the Abyssinian expedition and opening of the Suez Canal, so fateful for all my people.

My town was shut in by its mountains and provincialism; but it was a beautiful place, a little New England town nestled shyly in its valley with something of Dutch cleanliness and English reticence. The Housatonic yellowed by the paper mills, rolled slowly through its center; while Green River, clear and beautiful, joined in to the south. Main Street was lined with ancient elms; the hills held white pines and orchards and then faded up to magnificent rocks and caves which shut out the neighboring world. The people were mainly of English descent with much Dutch blood and with a large migration of Irish and German workers to the mills as laborers.

The social classes of the town were built partly on land-holding farmers and more especially on manufacturers and merchants, whose prosperity was due in no little degree to the new and high tariff. The rich people of the town were not very rich nor many in number. The middle class were farmers, merchants and artisans; and beneath these was a small proletariat of Irish and German mill workers. They lived in slums near the woolen mills and across the river clustering about the Catholic Church. The number of colored people in the town and county was small. They were all, save directly after the war, old families, well-known to the old settlers among the whites. The color line was manifest and yet not absolutely drawn. I remember a cousin of mine who brought home a white wife. The chief objection was that he was not able to support her and nobody knew about her family; and knowledge of family history was counted as highly important. Most of the colored people had some white blood from unions several generations past. That they congregated together in their own social life was natural because that was the rule in the town: there were little social knots of people, but not much that today would be called social life, save that which centered about the churches; and there the colored folk often took part. My grandmother was Episcopalian and my mother, Congregational. I grew up in the Congregational Sunday school.

In Great Barrington there were perhaps twenty-five, certainly not more than fifty, colored folk in a population of five thousand. My family was among the oldest inhabitants of the valley. The family had spread slowly through the county intermarrying among cousins and other black folk with some but limited infiltration of white blood. Other dark families had come in and there was some intermingling with local Indians. In one or two cases there were groups of apparently later black immigrants, near Sheffield for instance. There survives there even to this day an isolated group of black folk whose origin is obscure. We knew little of them but felt above them because of our education and economic status.

The economic status was not high. The early members of the family supported themselves on little farms of a few acres; then drifted to town as laborers and servants, but did not go into the mills. Most of them rented homes, but some owned little homes and pieces of land; a few had very pleasant and well-furnished homes, but none had anything like wealth.

My immediate family, which I remember as a young child, consisted of a very dark grandfather, Othello Burghardt, sitting beside the fireplace in a high chair, because of an injured hip. He was good-natured but not energetic. The energy was in my grandmother, Sally, a thin, tall, yellow and hawk-faced woman, certainly beautiful in her youth, and efficient and managing in her age. My mother, Mary Sylvina, was born at Great Barrington, January 14, 1831, and died there in 1885 at the age of fifty-four years. She had at the age of thirty a son, Idelbert, born of her and her cousin, John Burghardt. The circumstances of this romance I never knew. No one talked of it in the family. Perhaps there was an actual marriage. If so, it was not recorded in the family Bible. Perhaps the mating was broken up on account of the consanguinity of the cousins by a family tradition which had a New England strictness in its sex morals. So far as I ever knew there was only one illegitimate child throughout the family in my grandfather's and the two succeeding generations. My mother was brown and rather small with smooth skin and lovely eyes, and hair that curled and crinkled down each side her forehead from the part in the middle. She was rather silent but very determined and very patient. My father, a light mulatto, died in my infancy so that I do not remember him. I shall later speak more intimately of him.

I was born in a rather nice little cottage which belonged to a black South Carolinian, whose own house stood next, at the lower end of one of the pleasant streets of the town. Then for a time I lived in the country at the house of my grandfather, Othello, one of three farming brothers. It was sturdy, small and old-fashioned. Later we moved back to town and lived in quarters over the woodshed of one of the town's better mansions. After that we lived awhile over a store by the railway and during my high school years in a little four room tenement house on the same street where I was born, but farther up, down a lane and in the rear of a home owned by the widow of a New York physician. None of these homes had modern conveniences but they were weatherproof, fairly warm in winter and furnished with some comfort.

For several generations my people had attended schools for longer or shorter periods so most of them could read and write. I was brought up from earliest years with the idea of regular attendance at school. This was partly because the schools of Great Barrington were near at hand, simple but good, well-taught, and truant laws were enforced. I started on one school ground, which I remember vividly, at the age of five or six years, and continued there in school until I was graduated from high school at sixteen. I was seldom absent or tardy, and the school ran regularly ten months in the year with a few vacations. The curriculum was simple: reading, writing, spelling and arithmetic; grammar, geography and history. We learned the alphabet; we were drilled rigorously on the multiplication tables and we drew accurate maps. We could spell correctly and read clearly.

By the time I neared the high school, economic problems and questions of the future began to loom. These were partly settled by my own activities. My mother was then a widow with limited resources of income through boarding the barber, my uncle; supplemented infrequently by day's work, and by some kindly but unobtrusive charity.

But I was keen and eager to eke out this income by various jobs: splitting kindling, mowing lawns, doing chores. My first regular wage began as I entered the high school: I went early of mornings and filled with coal one or two of the new so-called "base-burning" stoves in the millinery shop of Madame L'Hommedieu. From then on, all through my high school course, I worked after school and on Saturdays; I sold papers, distributed tea from the new A & P stores in New York; and for a few months, through the good will of Johnny Morgan, actually rose to be local correspondent of the *Springfield Republican.*

Meantime the town and its surroundings were a boy's paradise: there were mountains to climb and rivers to wade and swim; lakes to freeze and hills for coasting. There were orchards and caves and wide green fields; and all of it was apparently property of the children of the town. My earlier contacts with playmates and other human beings were normal and pleasant. Sometimes there was a dearth of available playmates but that was peculiar to the conventions of the town where families were small and children must go to bed early and not loaf on the streets or congregate in miscellaneous crowds. Later, in the high school, there came some rather puzzling distinctions which I can see now were social and racial; but the racial angle was more clearly defined against the Irish than against me. It was a matter of income and ancestry more than color. I have written elsewhere of the case of exchanging visiting cards where one girl, a stranger, did not seem to want mine to my vast surprise.

I presume I was saved evidences of a good deal of actual discrimination by my own keen sensitiveness. My companions did not have a chance to refuse me invitations; they must seek me out and urge me to come as indeed they often did. When my presence was not wanted they had only to refrain from asking. But in the ordinary social affairs of the village—the Sunday school with its picnics and festivals; the temporary skating rink in the town hall; the coasting in crowds on all the hills—in all these, I took part with no thought of discrimination on the part of my fellows, for that I would have been the first to notice.

Later, I was protected in part by the fact that there was little social activity in the high school; there were no fraternities; there were no school dances; there were no honor societies. Whatever of racial feeling gradually crept into my life, its effect upon me in these earlier days was rather one of exaltation and high disdain. They were the losers who did not ardently court me and not I, which seemed to be proven by the fact that I had no difficulty in outdoing them in nearly all competition, especially intellectual. In athletics I was not outstanding. I was only moderately good at baseball and football; but at running, exploring, story-telling and planning of intricate games, I was often if not always the leader. This made discrimination all the more difficult.

When, however, during my high school course the matter of my future career began to loom, there were difficulties. The colored population of the town had been increased a little by "contrabands," who on the whole were well received by the colored group; although the older group held some of its social distinctions and the newcomers astonished us by forming a little Negro Methodist Zion Church, which we sometimes attended. The work open to colored folk was limited. There was day labor; there was farming; there was house-service, particularly work in summer hotels; but for a young, educated and ambitious colored man, what were the possibilities? And the practical answer to this inquiry was: Why encourage a young colored man toward such higher training? I imagine this matter was discussed considerably among my friends, white and black, and in a way it was settled partially before I realized it.

My high school principal was Frank Hosmer, afterward president of Oahu College, Hawaii. He suggested, quite as a matter of fact, that I ought to take the college preparatory course which involved algebra, geometry, Latin and Greek. If Hosmer had been another sort of man, with definite ideas as to a Negro's "place," and had recommended agricultural "science" or domestic economy, I would doubtless have followed his advice, had such "courses" been available. I did not then realize that Hosmer was quietly opening college doors to me, for in those days they were barred with ancient tongues. This meant a considerable expenditure for books which were not free in those days— more than my folk could afford; but the wife of one of the mill-owners, or rather I ought to describe her as the mother of one of my playmates, after some hesitation offered to furnish all the necessary school books. I became therefore a high school student preparing for college and thus occupying an unusual position in the town even among whites, although there had been one or two other colored boys in the past who had gotten at least part of a high school education. In this way I was thrown with the upper rather than the lower social classes and protected in many ways. I came in touch with rich folk, summer boarders, who made yearly incursions from New York. Their beautiful clothes impressed me tremendously but otherwise I found them quite ordinary. The children did not have much sense or training; they were not very strong and rather too well dressed to have a good time playing.

I had little contact with crime and degradation. The slums in the town were not bad and repelled me, partly because they were inhabited by the foreign-born. There was one house among colored folk, where I now realize there must have been a good deal of gambling, drinking and other looseness. The inmates were pleasant to me but I was never asked to enter and of course had no desire. In the whole town, colored and white, there was not much crime. The one excess was drunkenness and there my mother quietly took a firm stand. I was never to enter a liquor saloon. I never did. I donned a Murphy "blue ribbon." And yet perhaps, as I now see, the one solace that this pleasant but spiritually rather drab little town had against the monotony of life was liquor; and rich and poor got drunk more or less regularly. I have seen one of the mill owners staggering home, and my very respectable uncle used to come home now and then walking exceedingly straight.

I was born in a community which conceived itself as having helped put down a wicked rebellion for the purpose of freeing four million slaves. All respectable people belonged to the Republican Party, but Democrats were tolerated, although regarded with some surprise and hint of motive. Most of the older men had been soldiers, including members of my own family. The town approached in politics a pure democracy with annual town meeting and elections of well-known and fairly qualified officials. We were placidly religious. The bulk of the well-to-do people belonged to the Episcopal and Congregational churches, a small number of farmers and artisans to the Methodist Church and the Irish workers to the Catholic Church across the river. The marriage laws and family relations were fairly firm. The chief delinquency was drunkenness and the major social problem of the better classes was the status of women who had little or no opportunity to marry.

My ideas of property and work during my boyhood were vague. They did not present themselves to me as problems. As a family we owned little property and our income was always small. Spending money for me came first as small gifts of pennies or a nickel from relatives; once I received a silver dollar, a huge fortune. Later I earned all my spending funds. I can see now that my mother must have struggled pretty desperately on very narrow resources and that the problem of shoes and clothes for me must have been at times staggering. But these matters seldom bothered me because they were not brought to my attention. My general attitude toward property and income was that all who were willing to work could easily earn a living; that those who had property had earned it and deserved it and could use it as they wished; that poverty was the shadow of crime and connoted lack of thrift and shiftlessness. These were the current patterns of economic thought of the town in my boyhood.

In Great Barrington the first glimpse of the outer and wider world I got, was through Johnny Morgan's news shop which occupied the front end of the post office. There newspapers and books were on display and I remember very early seeing pictures of "U. S." Grant, and of "Bill" Tweed who was beginning his extraordinary career in New York City; and later I saw pictures of Hayes and of the smooth and rather cruel face of Tilden. Of the great things happening in the United States at that time, we were actually touched only by the Panic of 1873. When my uncle came home from a little town east of us where he was the leading barber, he brought me, I remember, a silver dollar which was an extraordinary thing: up to that time I had seen nothing but paper money. I was six when Charles Sumner died and the Freedmen's Bank closed; and when I was eight there came the revolution of 1876 in the South, and Victoria of England became Empress of India; but I did not know the meaning of these events until long after.

In general thought and conduct I became quite thoroughly New England. It was not good form in Great Barrington to express one's thought volubly, or to give way to excessive emotion. We were even sparing in our daily greetings. I am quite sure that in a less restrained and conventional atmosphere I should have easily learned to express my emotions with far greater and more unrestrained intensity; but as it was I had the social heritage not only of a New England clan but Dutch taciturnity. This was later reinforced and strengthened by inner withdrawals in the face of real and imagined discriminations. The result was that I was early thrown in upon myself. I found it difficult and even unnecessary to approach other people and by that same token my own inner life perhaps grew the richer; but the habit of repression often returned to plague me in after years, for so early a habit could not easily be unlearned. The Negroes in the South, when I came to know them, could never understand why I did not naturally greet everyone I passed on the street or slap my friends on the back.

During my high school career I had a chance for the first time to step beyond the shadow of the hills which hemmed in my little valley. My father's father was living in New Bedford and his third wife who had greatly loved my own father wanted my grandfather to know and recognize me. The grandfather, a short thick-set man, "colored" but quite white in appearance, with austere face, was hard and set in his ways, proud and bitter. My father and grandfather had not been able to get along together. Of them, I shall speak more intimately later. I went to New Bedford in 1883 at the age of fifteen. On the way I saw Hartford and Providence. I called on my uncle in Amherst and received a new navy-blue suit. Grandfather was a gentleman in manner, precise and formal. He looked at me coolly, but in the end he was not unpleasant. I went down across the water to Martha's Vineyard and saw what was then "Cottage City" and came home by way of Springfield and Albany where I was a guest of my older half-brother and saw my first electric street light blink and sputter.

I was graduated from high school in 1884 and was of course the only colored student. Once during my course another young dark man had attended the school for a short time but I was very much ashamed of him because he did not excel the whites as I was quite used to doing. All thirteen of us had orations and mine was on "Wendell Phillips." The great anti-slavery agitator had just died in February and I presume that some of my teachers must have suggested the subject, although it is quite possible that I chose it myself. But I was fascinated by his life and his work and took a long step toward a wider conception of what I was going to do. I spoke in June and then came face to face with the problem of my future life.

My mother lived proudly to see me graduate but died in the fall and I went to live with an aunt. I was strongly advised that I was too young to enter college. Williams had been suggested, because most of our few high school graduates who went to college had attended there; but my heart was set on Harvard. It was the greatest and oldest college and I therefore quite naturally thought it was the one I must attend. Of course I did not realize the difficulties: some difficulties in entrance examinations because our high school was not quite up to the Harvard standard; but a major difficulty of money. There must have been in my family and among my friends a good deal of anxious discussion as to my future but finally it was temporarily postponed when I was offered a job and promised that the next fall I should begin my college work.

The job brought me in unexpected touch with the world. There had been a great-uncle of mine, Tom Burghardt, whose tombstone I had seen often in the town graveyard. My family used to say in undertones that the money of Tom Burghardt helped to build the Pacific Railroad and that this came about in this wise: nearly all his life Tom Burghardt had been a servant in the Kellogg family, only the family usually forgot to pay him; but finally they did give him a handsome burial. Then Mark Hopkins, a son or relative of the great Mark, appeared on the scene and married a daughter of the Kelloggs. He became one of the Huntington-Stanford-Crocker Pacific Associates who built, manipulated and cornered · the Pacific railroads and with the help of the Kellogg nest-egg, Hopkins made nineteen million dollars in the West by methods not to be inquired into. His widow came back to Great Barrington in the eighties and planned a mansion out of the beautiful blue granite which formed our hills. A host of workmen, masons, stone-cutters and carpenters were assembled, and in the summer of 1884 I was made time-keeper for the contractors who carried on this job. I received the fabulous wage of a dollar a day. It was a most interesting experience and had new and intriguing bits of reality and romance. As time-keeper and the obviously young and inexperienced agent of superiors, I was the one who handed the discharged workers their last wage envelopes. I talked with contractors and saw the problems of employers. I pored over the plans and specifications and even came in contact with the elegant English architect Searles who finally came to direct the work.

The widow had a steward, a fine, young educated colored fellow who had come to be her right-hand man; but the architect supplanted him. He had the glamour of an English gentleman. The steward was gradually pushed aside and down into his place. The architect eventually married the widow and her wealth and the steward killed himself. So the Hopkins millions passed strangely into foreign hands and gave me my first problem of inheritance. But in the meantime the fabrication and growth of this marvelous palace, beautiful beyond anything that Great Barrington had seen, went slowly and majestically on, and always I could sit and watch it grow.

Finally in the fall of 1885, the difficulty of my future education was solved. The whole subtlety of the plan was clear neither to me nor my relatives at the time. Merely I was offered through the Reverend C. C. Painter, once excellent Federal Indian Agent, a scholarship to attend Fisk University in Nashville, Tennessee; the funds were to be furnished by four Connecticut churches which Mr. Painter had formerly pastored. Disappointed though I was at not being able to go to Harvard, I merely regarded this as a temporary change of plan; I would of course go to Harvard in the end. But here and immediately was adventure. I was going into the South; the South of slavery, rebellion and black folk; and above all I was going to meet colored people of my own age and education, of my own ambitions. Once or twice already I had had swift glimpses of the colored world: at Rocky Point on Narragansett Bay, I had attended an annual picnic beside the sea, and had seen in open-mouthed astonishment the whole gorgeous color gamut of the American Negro world; the swaggering men, the beautiful girls, the laughter and gaiety, the unhampered self-expression. I was astonished and inspired. I became aware, once a chance to go to a group of such young people was opened up for me, of the spiritual isolation in which I was living. I heard too in these days for the first time the Negro folk songs. A Hampton Quartet had sung them in the Congregational Church. I was thrilled and moved to tears and seemed to recognize something inherently and deeply my own. I was glad to go to Fisk.

On the other hand my people had undoubtedly a more discriminating and unromantic view of the situation. They said frankly that it was a shame to send me South. I was Northern born and bred and instead of preparing me for work and giving me an opportunity right there in my own town and state, they were bundling me off to the South. This was undoubtedly true. The educated young white folk of Great Barrington became clerks in stores, bookkeepers and teachers, while a few went into professions. Great Barrington was not able to conceive of me in such local position. It was not so much that they were opposed to it, but it did not occur to them as a possibility.

On the other hand there was the call of the black South; teachers were needed. The crusade of the New England schoolmarm was in full swing. The freed slaves, if properly led, had a great future. Temporarily deprived of their full voting privileges, this was but a passing set-back. Black folk were bound in time to dominate the South. They needed trained leadership. I was sent to help furnish it.

I started out and went into Tennessee at the age of seventeen to be a sophomore at Fisk University. It was to me an extraordinary experience. I was thrilled to be for the first time among so many people of my own color or rather of such various and such extraordinary colors, which I had only glimpsed before, but who it seemed were bound to me by new and exciting and eternal ties. Never before had I seen young men so self-assured and who gave themselves such airs, and colored men at that; and above all for the first time I saw beautiful girls. At my home among my white school mates there were a few pretty girls; but either they were not entrancing or because I had known them all my life I did not notice them; but at Fisk at the first dinner I saw opposite me a girl of whom I have often said, no human being could possibly have been as beautiful as she seemed to my young eyes that far-off September night of 1885.

FROM "AN INDICTED CRIMINAL"

. . . In 1950 the month of February had for me special meaning. I was a widower. The wife of 53 years lay buried in the New England hills beside her first-born boy. I was lonesome because so many boyhood friends had died, and because a certain illogical reticence on my part had never brought me many intimate friends. But there was a young woman, a minister's daughter, to whom I had been a sort of father confessor in literary affairs and difficulties of life for many years, especially after her father's death 15 years before. I knew her hardships and I had rejoiced in her successes. Shirley Graham, with her beautiful martyr complex, finally persuaded herself that I needed her help and companionship, as I certainly did; so we decided to get married a few days after my next birthday, when I would be 83 years old.

Preparations for a birthday dinner to be held at the Essex House, New York City, were being made at the request of the Council on African Affairs of which I had become vice-chairman after leaving the

The omitted material which precedes in this chapter deals with Dr. Du Bois' campaign as the American Labor Party candidate for U.S. Senator from New York; it also presents the trouble between the Department of Justice and the Peace Information Center, a Communist organization in which Du Bois was involved and which worked toward informing Americans of worldwide efforts for peace: the Peace Information Center and its officers were indicted for "failure to register as agents of a foreign principal."

Reprinted by permission of International Publishers Co., Inc.

NAACP. The list of sponsors was imposing and growing daily. Before the indictment about 300 people had made reservations and paid over $2,000.

Then came a strange series of events: on February 8 I was indicted for an alleged crime; on February 14, I was married secretly to Shirley, lest if I were found guilty she might have no right to visit me in jail; February 16 I was arraigned in Washington and on February 19, four days before the dinner, the hotel at which the dinner was planned cancelled our contract by telegram saying:

"Pursuant to our rules and regulations and for other sufficient reasons we hereby advise you that reservations of our facilities for Friday evening, February 23 for the W. E. B. Du Bois testimonial dinner is cancelled. Deposit is being returned. Vincent J. Coyle, Vice-President and Managing Director, Essex House Hotel, Inc."

We had five days before the dinner to find a place to entertain our 300 guests. In addition to this, three of our speakers, Charlotte Hawkins Brown, Mordecai Johnson and Rabbi Hillel Silver, hastily declined to appear. Some of the sponsors withdrew, but I do not know how many of the original list remained.

I can stand a good deal, and have done so during my life; but this experience was rather more than I felt like bearing, especially as the blows continued to fall. I had meantime been finger-printed, hand-cuffed, bailed and remanded for trial. I was more than ready to drop all thought of the birthday dinner.

But my remaining friends said No! I could do no less than stand beside them, although without Shirley's faith and strength I probably would not have allowed the dinner to take place. Franklin Frazier, the chairman, stood firm. He said the dinner must and would go on.

There ensued a period of wild search for a place of meeting; of securing other speakers and of notifying participants. Subtly the whole picture changed; instead of a polite, friendly social gesture, this dinner became a fight for civil rights, and into the seats of timid and withdrawing guests slipped a new set of firmer men and women who were willing to face even the United States government in my defense and for the preservation of American freedom. They carried on the battle while I sat uneasily in the background.

The program was hastily rearranged. No white downtown hotel would harbor us, and turning to Harlem we found Small's Paradise, well-known to the cabaret world, much too small but with a proprietor willing and eager even to lose money by the venture. At the dinner Belford Lawson, head of the Alpha Phi Alpha fraternity, volunteered and made a fighting speech; Paul Robeson spoke courageously and feelingly. A strong letter from Judge Hubert Delany was read. Franklin Frazier presided and spoke. The room was crowded to suffocation, and many could not get to their seats. But the spirit was what the

Germans call *feierlich* [festive]! Finally, amid cheers, birthday cakes and flowers, I made my speech. There were about 700 persons present who paid $6,557 in dinner fees and donations.

In this indictment of the Peace Information Center, I received a severe jolt, because in fact I found myself being punished before I was tried. In the first place, the Department of Justice allowed the impression to spread that my colleagues and I had in some way betrayed our country. Although the charge was not treason, it was widely understood and said that the Peace Information Center had been discovered to be an agent of the Soviet Union.

When we were arraigned in Washington February 16, the proceedings were brusque and unsympathetic. We were not treated as innocent people whose guilt was to be inquired into, but distinctly as criminals whose innocence was to be proven, which was assumed to be doubtful.

The white commercial press treated our case either with silence or violent condemnation. The New York *Herald-Tribune* had this editorial, February 11:

"The Du Bois outfit was set up to promote a tricky appeal of Soviet origin, poisonous in its surface innocence, which made it appear that a signature against the use of atomic weapons would forthwith insure world peace. It was, in short, an attempt to disarm America and yet ignore every form of Communist aggression. A lot of 'men and women of good will through the world,' to quote the petition's bland phrasing, were snared into signing without quite realizing that this thing came straight out of the Cominform."

So far as the nation was concerned, Alice Barrows secured 220 leaders of the arts, sciences, clergy and other professions in 33 states, including 35 universities, to sign "A Statement to the American People," released June 27, calling for the withdrawal of the prosecution. The statement, initiated by the National Council of the Arts, Sciences and Professions, described the indictment as "but one of numerous recent actions against individuals and organizations that advocate peaceful solutions to the world's crisis. In this time of hysteria, the attempted labeling of 'foreign agent' on a distinguished scholar and leader of a peace movement can fairly be interpreted as an effort to intimidate and silence all advocates of peace."

The response of Negroes in general was slow. At first many Negroes were puzzled. They did not understand the indictment and assumed that I had let myself be drawn into some treasonable acts or movements in retaliation for continued discrimination in this land, which I had long fought. They understood this and forgave it, but thought my action ill-advised. The Norfolk *Journal and Guide* expressed this clearly. The *Chicago Defender* said:

"Dr. Du Bois has earned many honors and it is a supreme tragedy that he should have become embroiled in activities that have been exposed as subversive in the twilight of his years." But on the other hand, editors like Percival Prattis of the *Pittsburgh Courier,* Carl Murphy of the *Afro-American,* and columnists like Marjorie McKenzie, J. A. Rogers, and others, showed a courage and real intellectual leadership which was lacking elsewhere. The reaction of Negroes revealed a distinct cleavage not hitherto clear in American Negro opinion. The intelligentsia, the "Talented Tenth," the successful business and professional men, were not, for the most part, outspoken in my defense. There were many and notable exceptions, but as a group this class was either silent or actually antagonistic. The reasons were clear; many believed that the government had actual proof of subversive activities on our part; until the very end they awaited their disclosure.

Other Negroes of intelligence and prosperity had become American in their acceptance of exploitation as defensible, and in their imitation of American "conspicuous expenditure." They proposed to make money and spend it as pleased them. They had beautiful homes, large and expensive cars and fur coats. They hated "communism" and "socialism" as much as any white American. Their reaction toward Paul Robeson was typical; they simply could not understand his surrendering a thousand dollars a night for a moral conviction.

This dichotomy in the Negro group, this development of class structure, was to be expected, and will be more manifest in the future, as discrimination against Negroes as such decreases. There will gradually arise among American Negroes a separation according to their attitudes toward labor, wealth and work. It is still my hope that the Negro's experience in the past will, in the end, lead the majority of his intelligentsia into the ranks of those advocating social control of wealth, abolition of exploitation of labor, and equality of opportunity for all.

I have belonged to a Negro graduate fraternity for 45 years—indeed helped its first formation. Today it contains in its membership a large number of leading business and professional Negroes in the United States. Yet of its 30 or more chapters covering the nation, only one expressed any sympathy with me, and none offered aid. It is probable that individual members of the fraternity gave my cause support, but no official action was taken save in one case. In my own New York chapter I was bitterly criticized.

Another of our projects was to secure the names of a dozen nationally prominent Negroes to this statement:

". . . We are not here concerned with the political or social beliefs of Dr. Du Bois. Many of us do not agree with him on these and other matters. But we are concerned with the right of a man to say within the law what he thinks without being subject to threat and intimidation. Especially we are concerned with Dr. Du Bois as a leader of the Negro American for 50 years. In that time until now his integrity and absolute sincerity has never been questioned. . . ."

We did not, however, succeed in getting enough such signatures to this statement to warrant its circulation. I recognized the fear in the Negro group, especially among the educated and well-to-do. One said to me sadly, "I have a son in government employ; he has a well-paid position and is in line for promotion. He has worked long for this start and has had many disappointments. I am sorry but I dare not sign this."

I served the NAACP for 28 years in all. When this case came up, although I was no longer officially connected with the organization, branches and members all over the nation wanted to help me and urged the main office to join in. The president of the Board of Directors said frankly to Shirley Graham that undoubtedly the Peace Information Center was supported by funds from the Soviet Union. He admitted that it was possible that I did not know this. At a meeting, March 12, of the Board of Directors, it was urged that the Board take a position on the indictment, and as one branch said, "give active, tangible aid to Dr. Du Bois in his present plight." However, the secretary, Walter White, reported that he had talked with Peyton Ford, assistant to the Attorney-General in Washington, and was told that there was definite evidence of guilt in the hands of the Department of Justice and that the four associates of Dr. Du Bois could not be prosecuted without prosecuting Dr. Du Bois.

A white member of the Board had offered to take up the matter of asking the legal department of the NAACP to join in our defense. After this member heard our "certain guilt" stated he made no further effort.

The Board finally passed this resolution:

"Without passing on the merits of the recent indictment of Dr. Du Bois, the board of directors of the NAACP expresses the opinion that this action against one of the great champions of civil rights lends color to the charge that efforts are being made to silence spokesmen for full equality of Negroes. The board also reaffirms its determination to continue its aggressive fight for full citizenship rights for all Americans."

Even this resolution was not given much publicity, and the main office advised the branches strongly "not to touch" this case. Some branches vigorously complained, and despite the attitude of the New York office, many branches of the NAACP supported our campaign.

Our appeal to the officials of the World Defenders of Peace resulted in wide publicity for our case all over the world. Messages began to pour in to us from Europe, Asia and Africa; from the West Indies and South America. We received letters from England, Scotland, and

France; from Belgium, Holland, Luxembourg, and Scandinavia; from Germany, the Union of Socialist Soviet Republics, Austria, Czechoslovakia, Poland, Rumania, Albania, Hungary, Trieste, and Switzerland; from Canada, Cuba, Martinique, Jamaica, British Guiana and Brazil; from West Africa, South Africa, Southeast Asia, China, Viet Nam, Indonesia, India and Australia. International bodies sent their support, including the International Union of Students, the World Federation of Teachers' Unions, the International Federation of Women, the World Federation of Scientific Workers, and others.

An "International Committee in Defense of Dr. W. E. B. Du Bois and his Colleagues" was formed. The original signers included a university professor from Holland; two professors from Switzerland; a judge of the Court of Appeals and a federal judge in Brazil; two magistrates from Colombia and Iran; an Italian senator; and the president of the French Court of Cassation; together with ten Americans, eight white and two Negro. Eventually this committee grew to 200 with 33 Frenchmen, 30 Poles, 12 Belgiums, 11 Germans, seven Englishmen, six Italians, five Brazilians, four each from Switzerland, the Soviet Union, Hungary and China; one to three each from Rumania, Bulgaria, Iran, Lebanon, Martinique, Holland, Austria; and 59 from the United States, of whom six were colored. Isabelle Blume of Belgium was chairman.

Articles were published in Austria, India, the Soviet Union, the Shanghai *China News* and Edinburgh *Review* in Scotland. The story was told in at least a dozen different languages. From the West Indies came letters, from the professors of the University of Havana and outstanding Cubans like Dr. Fernando Ortiz, Latin America's most famous sociologist; Dr. Domingo Villamil, eminent Catholic jurist; and Juan Marinello, senator and poet.

The International Union of Students wrote to the Department of Justice:

"On behalf of over 5,000,000 students in 71 countries, the International Union of Students expresses indignation at the prosecution of Dr. Du Bois and associates. Du Bois is an internationally known scholar and spokesman for peace. His work for peace is in best traditions of the American people. Prosecution is an attack upon peace supporters, upon Negro people and upon right of professors and students to act for peace. We join with peace-loving people throughout the world in demanding that you dismiss Du Bois' indictment and end persecution of United States peace supporters."

Despite the difficulty of securing meeting places in New York where we could defend our cause, we succeeded late in September in organizing a meeting in Town Hall. The National Council of the Arts, Sciences and Professions put on an interesting program, with Professor Henry Pratt Fairchild presiding. Here Bishop Wright, Corliss Lamont and Lawrence D. Reddick, former curator of the Schomburg Collection and then Librarian of Atlanta University, spoke. Dr. Reddick said in part:

"I have just come from a part of our country where the flag of the Confederacy is more popular than the flag of the United States of America; where Robert E. Lee is not only more of a hero than Ulysses S. Grant but also more than George Washington; and where the Governor threatens to close down the State's entire system of education if the courts should compel the public, tax-supported institutions that are presently maintained for whites only to admit a single Negro."

I wrote this statement for the defendants:

"This case is a blow at civilization: by instituting thought control; by seeking to stop the circulation of ideas; by seeking to shut off the free flow of culture around the world and reducing all American culture to the level of Mississippi and Nevada; by making it a crime to think as others think, if your thought is against the prejudices or graft or barbarism of some backwoods partisan; by making it treason to brand the hoary lie that War is the path to Peace; by crucifying fathers and mothers who do not want their sons raised to murder men, women and children . . .

"The Government can put into absolute control of our thinking, feeling and culture any set of half-educated fanatics from Southern rotten boroughs or western mining camps or Missouri gang politics in order to: curtail and misdirect education in America; limit thought and twist ambition; send school children hiding under desks instead of learning to read and write; make saints of spies, informers and professional liars; make a prisoned nation call Freedom that which is slavery and to change a Democracy into a police state!

"Wake up, America. Your liberties are being stolen before your very eyes. What Washington, Jefferson and Lincoln fought for, Truman, Acheson, and McGrath are striving desperately to nullify. Wake up, Americans, and dare to think and say and do. Dare to cry: No More War!"

This brought forward the whole question of costs. It had not occurred to us how costly justice in the United States is. It is not enough to be innocent in order to escape punishment. You must have money and a lot of it. In the end it cost us $35,150 to prosecute this case to a successful end, not counting the fee refused by the Chief Counsel. If, as we had confidently expected, the case had gone to higher courts to determine the constitutionality of this foreign agents Act, it might have cost us $100,000. Before this prospect of sheer cost, we stood for many weeks appalled and discouraged. We realized more than ever that this trial was not going to be simply a legal process, but a political persecution, the outcome of which would depend on public opinion; and that to raise the funds necessary for our defense, we would need the contributions of large numbers of poor people and need have no hope for gifts from the rich. . . .

The government not only went to trouble and large expense, risked its own reputation, but also forced us to extraordinary and worldwide effort, to escape punishment. Personally, I had no funds for such a case. I was retired from work, with a pension too small for normal expenses of living. My wife's work and income were seriously curtailed by her complete immersion in this case. We had no rich friends. None of the defendants were able personally to finance this case. Had it not been for the almost miraculous rise of American friends, we would have gone to jail by default. Not a cent of money for the trial came from abroad. Even had this been possible, it would have been used to convict us. But in this nation by popular appeal to poor and middle-class folk, Negroes and white, trade unions and other groups, we raised funds for these purposes:

Legal fees, $18,400; publicity, $5,600; office, $5,250; salaries, $3,600; travel, $2,365.

To this should be added additional legal fees of at least $13,000; $3,000 paid to an attorney hired by one of the defendants and not paid for by the Committee, and at least $10,000 which Marcantonio earned but would not accept. This amounts to a total of $40,215. To this should be added at least $2,000 in travel expenses paid by localities. How much the case cost the government we cannot know, but it could not have been less than $100,000 and it might have been much more.

I have faced during my life many unpleasant experiences; the growl of a mob; the personal threat of murder; the scowling distaste of an audience. But nothing has so cowed me as that day, November 8, 1951, when I took my seat in a Washington courtroom as an indicted criminal. I was not a criminal. I had broken no law, consciously or unwittingly. Yet I sat with four other American citizens of unblemished character, never before accused even of misdemeanor, in the seats often occupied by murderers, forgers and thieves; accused of a felony and liable to be sentenced before leaving this court to five years of imprisonment, a fine of $10,000 and loss of my civil and political rights as a citizen, representing five generations of Americans.

James Weldon Johnson

(1871–1938)

AFTER HIS GRADUATION FROM Atlanta University in 1894, James Weldon Johnson returned to Jacksonville, Florida, where he had been born. He taught for a while, read law and practiced it half-heartedly, established a Negro weekly newspaper and soon abandoned it, and, in 1901, joined his older brother, John Rosamond Johnson, a musician, in New York. Earlier, the brothers had collaborated on a song, "Lift Every Voice and Sing," which for many years was called the "Negro National Anthem"; but in New York they worked on the librettos for Negro musical shows in the ministrel tradition and on "coon songs" such as "Sence You Went Away." They had uncommon success, but the younger brother felt unfulfilled. His well-known name made him attractive to politicians, and for supporting Theodore Roosevelt he was rewarded by Consulate appointments, first in Venezuela and then in Nicaragua.

It was while serving in the latter post that Johnson wrote the novel *The Autobiography of an Ex-Coloured Man* (1912). This marked the beginning of a literary career that, combined with his work as an official of the NAACP, brought him great contemporary distinction. In 1917 Johnson published *Fifty Years and Other Poems;* in 1927, *God's Trombones: Seven Negro Sermons in Verse;* in 1935, a long, satirical narrative poem, *St. Peter Relates an Incident;* and in 1933, his autobiography, *Along This Way.*

James Weldon Johnson was not a great writer. He was, however, versatile and interesting. The importance of his work is that beginning with the war years, his literary output is woven of all the threads of thought and emotion that ran through the Renaissance.

The prose selections given below are from Johnson's *Black Manhattan* (1930), a valuable sourcebook of information on the Negro in New York City.

THE PRODIGAL SON

Young man—
Young man—
Your arm's too short to box with God.

From *God's Trombones* by James Weldon Johnson. Copyright 1927 by The Viking Press, Inc., renewed 1955 by Grace Nail Johnson. Reprinted by permission of The Viking Press, Inc.

But Jesus spake in a parable, and he said:
A certain man had two sons.
Jesus didn't give this man a name,
But his name is God Almighty.
And Jesus didn't call these sons by name,
But ev'ry young man,
Ev'rywhere,
Is one of these two sons.

[handwritten annotation: everyone is a child of God]

And the younger son said to his father,
He said: Father, divide up the property,
And give me my portion now.

And the father with tears in his eyes said: Son,
Don't leave your father's house.
But the boy was stubborn in his head,
And haughty in his heart,
And he took his share of his father's goods,
And went into a far-off country.

There comes a time,
There comes a time
When ev'ry young man looks out from his father's house,
Longing for that far-off country.

And the young man journeyed on his way,
And he said to himself as he travelled along:
This sure is an easy road,
Nothing like the rough furrows behind my father's plow.

Young man—
Young man—
Smooth and easy is the road
That leads to hell and destruction.
Down grade all the way,
The further you travel, the faster you go.
No need to trudge and sweat and toil,
Just slip and slide and slip and slide
Till you bang up against hell's iron gate.

And the younger son kept travelling along,
Till at night-time he came to a city.
And the city was bright in the night-time like day,
The streets all crowded with people,
Brass bands and string bands a-playing,
And ev'rywhere the young man turned

There was singing and laughing and dancing.
And he stopped a passer-by and he said:
Tell me what city is this?
And the passer-by laughed and said: Don't you know?
This is Babylon, Babylon,
That great city of Babylon.
Come on, my friend, and go along with me.
And the young man joined the crowd.

Young man—
Young man—
You're never lonesome in Babylon.
You can always join a crowd in Babylon.
Young man—
Young man—
You can never be alone in Babylon,
Alone with your Jesus in Babylon.
You can never find a place, a lonesome place,
A lonesome place to go down on your knees,
And talk with your God, in Babylon.
You're always in a crowd in Babylon.

And the young man went with his new-found friend,
And bought himself some brand new clothes,
And he spent his days in the drinking dens,
Swallowing the fires of hell.
And he spent his nights in the gambling dens,
Throwing dice with the devil for his soul.
And he met up with the women of Babylon.
Oh, the women of Babylon!
Dressed in yellow and purple and scarlet,
Loaded with rings and earrings and bracelets,
Their lips like a honeycomb dripping with honey,
Perfumed and sweet-smelling like a jasmine flower;
And the jasmine smell of the Babylon women
Got in his nostrils and went to his head,
And he wasted his substance in riotous living,
In the evening, in the black and dark of night,
With the sweet-sinning women of Babylon.
And they stripped him of his money,
And they stripped him of his clothes,
And they left him broke and ragged
In the streets of Babylon.

Then the young man joined another crowd—
The beggars and lepers of Babylon.
And he went to feeding swine,
And he was hungrier than the hogs;
He got down on his belly in the mire and mud
And ate the husks with the hogs.
And not a hog was too low to turn up his nose
At the man in the mire of Babylon.

Then the young man came to himself—
He came to himself and said:
In my father's house are many mansions,
Ev'ry servant in his house has bread to eat,
Ev'ry servant in his house has a place to sleep;
I will arise and go to my father.

And his father saw him afar off,
And he ran up the road to meet him.
He put clean clothes upon his back,
And a golden chain around his neck,
He made a feast and killed the fatted calf,
And invited the neighbors in.

Oh-o-oh, sinner,
When you're mingling with the crowd in Babylon—
Drinking the wine of Babylon—
Running with the women of Babylon—
You forget about God, and you laugh at Death.
Today you've got the strength of a bull in your neck
And the strength of a bear in your arms,
But some o' these days, some o' these days,
You'll have a hand-to-hand struggle with bony Death,
And Death is bound to win.

Young man, come away from Babylon,
That hell-border city of Babylon.
Leave the dancing and gambling of Babylon,
The wine and whiskey of Babylon,
The hot-mouthed women of Babylon;
Fall down on your knees,
And say in your heart:
I will arise and go to my Father.

NEW YORK'S BLACK BOHEMIA

New York's black Bohemia constituted a part of the famous old Tenderloin; and, naturally, it nourished a number of the ever present vices; chief among them, gambling and prostitution. But it nourished other things; and one of these things was artistic effort. It is in the growth of this artistic effort that we are here interested; the rest of the manifestations were commonplaces. This black Bohemia had its physical being in a number of clubs—a dozen or more of them well established and well known. There were gambling-clubs, honky-tonks, and professional clubs. The gambling-clubs need not be explained. The honky-tonks were places with paid and volunteer entertainers where both sexes met to drink, dance, and have a good time; they were the prototype of the modern night-club. The professional clubs were particularly the rendezvous of the professionals, their satellites and admirers. Several of these clubs were famous in their day and were frequented not only by blacks, but also by whites. Among the best-known were Joe Stewart's Criterion, the Douglass Club, the Anderson Club, the Waldorf, Johnny Johnson's, Ike Hines's, and later, and a little higher up, Barron Wilkins's Little Savoy, in West Thirty-fifth Street. The border line between the honky-tonks and some of the professional clubs was very thin. One of the latter that stood out as exclusively professional was Ike Hines's. A description of a club—really Ike Hines's—is given in *The Autobiography of an Ex-Coloured Man.** That will furnish, perhaps, a fresher picture of these places and the times than anything I might now write:

> I have already stated that in the basement of the house there was a Chinese restaurant. The Chinaman who kept it did an exceptionally good business; for chop-suey was a favourite dish among the frequenters of the place. . . . On the main floor there were two large rooms: a parlour about thirty feet in length, and a large, square back room into which the parlour opened. The floor of the parlour was carpeted; small tables and chairs were arranged about the room; the windows were draped with lace curtains, and the walls were literally covered with photographs or lithographs of every coloured man in America who had ever 'done anything.' There were pictures of Frederick Douglass and of Peter Jackson, of all the lesser lights of the prize-ring, of all the famous jockeys and the stage celebrities, down to the newest song and dance team. The most of these photographs were

autographed and, in a sense, made a really valuable collection. In the back room there was a piano, and tables were placed round the wall. The floor was bare and the centre was left vacant for singers, dancers, and others who entertained the patrons. In a closet in this room which jutted out into the hall the proprietor kept his buffet. There was no open bar, because the place had no liquor licence. In this back room the tables were sometimes pushed aside, and the floor given over to general dancing. The front room on the next floor was a sort of private party room; a back room on the same floor contained no furniture and was devoted to the use of new and ambitious performers. In this room song and dance teams practised their steps, acrobatic teams practised their tumbles, and many other kinds of 'acts' rehearsed their 'turns.' The other rooms of the house were used as sleeping-apartments.

No gambling was allowed, and the conduct of the place was surprisingly orderly. It was, in short, a centre of coloured Bohemians and sports. Here the great prize-fighters were wont to come, the famous jockeys, the noted minstrels, whose names and faces were familiar on every bill-board in the country; and these drew a multitude of those who love to dwell in the shadow of greatness. There were then no organizations giving performances of such order as are now given by several coloured companies; that was because no manager could imagine that audiences would pay to see Negro performers in any other role than that of Mississippi River roustabouts; but there was lots of talent and ambition. I often heard the younger and brighter men discussing the time when they would compel the public to recognize that they could do something more than grin and cut pigeon-wings.

Sometimes one or two of the visiting stage-professionals, after being sufficiently urged, would go into the back room and take the places of the regular amateur entertainers, but they were very sparing with their favours, and the patrons regarded them as special treats. There was one man, a minstrel, who, whenever he responded to a request to "do something," never essayed anything below a reading from Shakespere. How well he read I do not know, but he greatly impressed me; and I can say that at least he had a voice which strangely stirred those who heard it. Here was a man who made people laugh at the size of his mouth, while he carried in his heart a burning ambition to be a tragedian; and so after all he did play a part in a tragedy.

These notables of the ring, the turf, and the stage, drew to the place crowds of admirers, both white and coloured. Whenever one of them came in, there were awe-inspired whispers from those who knew him by sight, in which they enlightened those round them as to his identity, and hinted darkly at their great intimacy with the noted one. Those who were on terms of approach showed their privilege by gathering round their divinity. . . .

A great deal of money was spent here, so many of the patrons were men who earned large sums. I remember one night a dapper little brown-skin fellow was pointed out to me and I was told that he was the most popular jockey of the day, and that he earned $12,000 a year. This latter statement I couldn't doubt, for with my own eyes I saw him spending at about thirty times that rate. For his friends and those who were introduced to him he bought nothing but wine—in sporting circles, "wine" means champagne—and paid for it at five dollars a quart. . . . This jockey had won a great race that day, and he was rewarding his admirers for the homage they paid him, all of which he accepted with a fine air of condescension.

Besides the people I have just been describing, there were at the place almost every night one or two parties of white people, men and women, who were out sight-seeing, or slumming. They generally came in cabs; some of them would stay only for a few minutes, while others sometimes stayed until morning. There was also another set of white people that came frequently; it was made up of variety performers and others who delineated "darky characters"; they came to get their imitations first-hand from the Negro entertainers they saw there.

*   *   *

EARLY NEGRO ENTERTAINERS

. . . In the midst of the period we are now considering, another shift in the Negro population took place; and by 1900 there was a new centre established in West Fifty-third Street. In this new centre there sprang up a new phase of life among coloured New Yorkers. Two well-appointed hotels, the Marshall and the Maceo, run by coloured men, were opened in the street and became the centres of a fashionable sort of life that hitherto had not existed. These hotels served dinner to music and attracted crowds of well-dressed people. On Sunday evenings the crowd became a crush; and to be sure of service one had to book a table in advance. This new centre also brought about a revolutionary change in Negro artistic life. Those engaged in artistic effort deserted almost completely the old clubs farther downtown, and the Marshall, run by Jimmie Marshall, an accomplished Boniface, became famous as the headquarters of Negro talent. There gathered the actors, the musicians, the composers, the writers, and the better-paid vaude-villians; and there one went to get a close-up of Cole and Johnson, Williams and Walker, Ernest Hogan, Will Marion Cook, Jim Europe, Ada Overton, Abbie Mitchell, Al Johns, Theodore Drury, Will Dixon, and Ford Dabney. Paul Laurence Dunbar was often there. A good many white actors and musicians also frequented the Marshall, and it was no unusual thing for some among the biggest Broadway stars to run up there for an evening. So there were always present numbers of those who love to be in the light reflected from celebrities. Indeed, the Marshall for nearly ten years was one of the sights of New York, for it was gay, entertaining, and interesting. To be a visitor there, without at the same time being a rank outsider, was a distinction. The Maceo run by Benjamin F. Thomas had the more staid clientele.

In the brightest days of the Marshall the temporary blight had not yet fallen on the Negro in the theatre. Williams and Walker and Cole and Johnson were at their height; there were several good Negro road companies touring the country, and a considerable number of coloured performers were on the big time in vaudeville. In the early 1900's there came to the Marshall two young fellows, Ford Dabney and James Reese Europe, both of them from Washington, who were to play an important part in the artistic development of the Negro in a field that was, in a sense, new. It was they who first formed the coloured New York entertainers who played instruments into trained, organized bands, and thereby became not only the daddies of the Negro jazz orchestras, but the grand-daddies of the unnumbered jazz orchestras that have followed. Ford Dabney organized and directed a jazz orchestra which for a number of years was a feature of Florenz Ziegfeld's roof-garden shows. Jim Europe organized the Clef Club. Joe Jordan also became an important factor in the development of Negro bands.

How long Negro jazz bands throughout the country had been playing jazz at dances and in honky-tonks cannot be precisely stated, but the first modern jazz band ever heard on a New York stage, and probably on any other stage, was organized at the Marshall and made its début at Proctor's Twenty-third Street Theatre in the early spring of 1905. It was a playing-singing-dancing orchestra, making dominant use of banjos, mandolins, guitars, saxophones, and drums in combination, and was called the Memphis Students—a very good name, overlooking the fact that the performers were not students and were not from Memphis. There was also a violin, a couple of brass instruments, and a double-bass. The band was made up of about twenty of the best performers on the instruments mentioned above that could be got together in New York. They had all been musicians and entertainers for private parties, and as such had played together in groups varying in size, according to the amount the employing host wished to spend. Will Marion Cook gave a hand in whipping them into shape for their opening. They scored an immediate success. After the Proctor engagement they went to Hammerstein's Victoria, playing on the vaudeville bill in the day, and on the roof-garden at night. In the latter part of the same year they opened at Olympia in Paris; from Paris they went to the Palace Theatre in London, and then to the Schumann Circus in Berlin. They played all the important cities in Europe and were abroad a year.

At the opening in New York the performers who were being counted on to carry the stellar honours were: Ernest Hogan, comedian; Abbie Mitchell, soprano; and Ida Forsyne, dancer; but while they made good, the band proved to be the thing. The instrumentalists were the novelty. There was one thing they did quite unconsciously; which, however, caused musicians who heard them to marvel at the feat. When the band played and sang, there were men who played one part while singing another. That is, for example, some of them while playing the lead, sang bass, and some while playing an alto part sang tenor; and so on, in accordance with the instrument each man played and his natural voice. The Memphis Students deserve the credit that should go to pioneers. They were the beginners of several things that still persist as jazz-band features. They introduced the dancing conductor. Will Dixon, himself a composer of some note, conducted the band here and on its European tour. All through a number he would keep his men together by dancing out the rhythm, generally in a graceful, sometimes in grotesque, steps. Often an easy shuffle would take him across the whole front of the band. This style of directing not only got the fullest possible response from the men, but kept them in just the right humour for the sort of music they were playing. Another innovation they introduced was the trick trap-drummer. "Buddy" Gilmore was the drummer with the band, and it is doubtful if he has been surpassed as a performer of juggling and acrobatic stunts while manipulating a dozen noise-making devices aside from the drums. He made this style of drumming so popular that not only was it adopted by white professionals, but many white amateurs undertook to learn it as a social accomplishment, just as they might learn to do card tricks. The whole band, with the exception, of course, of the players of wind-instruments, was a singing band; and it seems safe to say that they introduced the singing band—that is, a band singing in four-part harmony and playing at the same time.

One of the original members of the Memphis Students was Jim Europe. Afterwards he went for a season or two as musical director with the Cole and Johnson shows; and then in the same capacity with Bert Williams's *Mr. Lode of Kole.* In 1910 he carried out an idea he had, an idea that had a business as well as an artistic reason behind it, and organized the Clef Club. He gathered all the coloured professional instrumental musicians into a chartered organization and systematized the whole business of "entertaining." The organization purchased a house in West Fifty-third Street and fitted it up as a club, and also as booking-offices. Bands of from three to thirty men could be furnished at any time, day or night. The Clef Club for quite a while held a monopoly of the business of "entertaining" private parties and furnishing music for the dance craze, which was then just beginning to sweep the country. One year the amount of business done amounted to $120,000.

The crowning artistic achievement of the Clef Club was a concert given at Carnegie Hall in May 1912. The orchestra for the occasion consisted of one hundred and twenty-five performers. It was an unorthodox combination—as is every true jazz orchestra. There were a few strings proper, the most of them being 'cellos and double-basses; the few wind-instruments consisted of cornets, saxophones, clarinets, and trombones; there were a battery of drums; but the main part of the orchestra was composed of banjos, mandolins, and guitars. On this night all these instruments were massed against a background of ten upright pianos. In certain parts the instrumentation was augmented by the voices. New York had not yet become accustomed to jazz; so when the Clef Club opened its concert with a syncopated march, playing it with a biting attack and an infectious rhythm, and on the finale bursting into singing, the effect can be imagined. The applause became a tumult. It is possible that such a band as that could produce a similar effect even today.

Later Jim Europe with his orchestra helped to make Vernon and Irene Castle famous. When the World War came, he assembled the men for the band of the Fifteenth, New York's noted Negro regiment. He was with this band giving a concert in a Boston theatre, after their return from the War, when he met his tragic end.

1912 was also the year in which there came up out of the South an entirely new genre of Negro songs, one that was to make an immediate and lasting effect upon American popular music; namely, the blues. These songs are as truly folk-songs as the Spirituals, or as the original plantation songs, levee songs, and rag-time songs that had already been made the foundation of our national popular music. The blues were first set down and published by William C. Handy, a coloured composer and for a while a bandleader in Memphis, Tennessee. He put out the famous "Memphis Blues" and the still more famous "St. Louis Blues" and followed them by blues of many localities and kinds. It was not long before the New York song-writers were turning out blues of every variety and every shade. Handy followed the blues to New York and has been a Harlemite ever since, where he is known as the "Father of the Blues." It is from the blues that all that may be called *American music* derives its most distinctive characteristic.

It was during the period we have just been discussing that the earliest attempt at rendering opera was made by Negroes in New York. Beginning in the first half of the decade 1900–10 and continuing for four or five years, the Theodore Drury Opera Company gave annually one night of grand opera at the Lexington Opera House. Among the operas sung were *Carmen, Aida,* and *Faust.* These nights of grand opera were, at least, great social affairs and were looked forward to months ahead. In September 1928 H. Lawrence Freeman, a Negro musician and the composer of six grand operas, produced his opera *Voodoo* at the Fifty-second Street Theatre. Mr. Freeman's operas are *The Martyr, The Prophecy, The Octoroon, Plantation, Vendetta,* and

Voodoo. In the spring of the present year he presented scenes from various of his works in Steinway Hall. He was the winner of the 1929 Harmon Award and Medal for musical composition.

MARCUS GARVEY

. . . These journals[1] shook up the Negroes of New York and the country and effected some changes that have not been lost; but able as were most of the men behind them, as radicals, they failed almost wholly in bringing about any co-ordination of the forces they were dealing with; perhaps that was to be expected. This post-war radical movement gradually waned—as it waned among whites—and the organs of the movement, one by one, withered and died. The *Messenger,* which continued to be published up to last year, was the longest-lived of them all. The *Negro World* is still being published; but it falls in a classification distinctly its own.

The Harlem radicals failed to bring about a correlation of the forces they had called into action, to have those forces work through a practical medium to a definite objective; but they did much to prepare the ground for a man who could and did do that, a man who was one of the most remarkable and picturesque figures that have appeared on the American scene—Marcus Garvey.

Marcus Garvey is a full-blooded black man, born, and born poor, in Jamaica, British West Indies, in 1887. He grew up under the triple race scheme that prevails in many of the West Indian islands—white, mulatto, and black. The conditions of this system aroused in him, even as a boy, a deep resentment, which increased as he grew older. His resentment against the mulattos was, perhaps, deeper than his resentment against the whites. At about the time he became of age, he left Jamaica and travelled in South America. He next went to England, where he stayed for several years. All the while he was seeking some escape from the terrible pressure of the colour bar. In England he met one or two African agitators. He became intimate with Duse Muhamed Effendi, an African political writer, who was running a small revolutionary newspaper in London, and from him learned something about world politics, especially with relation to Africa. It was probably then that he began to dream of a land where black men ruled. England was a disappointment. In 1914 he returned to Jamaica, determined to do

---

[1] "These journals" refer to a group of radical Negro periodicals, ranging in policy from "left centre to extreme left," that sprang up in Harlem around 1919. Among them were *The Messenger, Challenge, The Voice, The Crusader, The Emancipator,* and *The Negro World.* They were cited in a Department of Justice report in 1919 under the caption "Radicalism and Sedition among Negroes as Reflected in Their Publications." [Eds.]

something to raise the status of the black masses of the island. He began his public career by organizing the Universal Negro Improvement Association. He was discouraged by the fact that he aroused more interest and gained more support among the whites than among the blacks. He wrote Booker T. Washington about his plans—plans probably for establishing industrial training for the natives of Jamaica —and received a reply encouraging him to come to the United States. Before he could perfect arrangements to come, Booker T. Washington had died. But on March 23, 1916 Garvey landed in Harlem.

In some way or other he got about the country, visiting, as he says, thirty-eight states, studying the condition of the Negro in America, and then returned to New York. On June 12, 1917 a large mass meeting, called by Hubert Harrison, was held in Bethel A. M. E. Church in Harlem for the purpose of organizing the Liberty League. Some two thousand people were present, and among them was Marcus Garvey. Mr. Harrison introduced him to the audience and asked him to say a few words. This was Harlem's first real sight of Garvey, and his first real chance at Harlem. The man spoke, and his magnetic personality, torrential eloquence, and intuitive knowledge of crowd psychology were all brought into play. He swept the audience along with him. He made his speech an endorsement of the new movement and a pledge of his hearty support of it; but Garvey was not of the kidney to support anybody's movement. He had seen the United States and he had seen Harlem. He had doubtless been the keenest observer at the Liberty League organization meeting; and it may be that it was then he decided upon New York as the centre for his activities.

He soon organized and incorporated the Universal Negro Improvement Association in the United States, with New York as headquarters. He made his first appeal to the West Indian elements, not only to British, but to Spanish and French, and they flocked to him. He established the *Negro World* as his organ and included in it Spanish and French sections. He built Liberty Hall, a great basement that held five or six thousand people. There the association held its first convention in 1919, during the whole month of August, with delegates from the various states and the West Indies. By this time the scheme of the organization had expanded from the idea of economic solution of the race problem through the establishment of "Universal" shops and factories and financial institutions to that of its solution through the redemption of Africa and the establishment of a Negro merchant marine. At the mass meeting held in Carnegie Hall during this convention, Garvey in his address said:

"We are striking homeward toward Africa to make her the big black republic. And in the making of Africa the big black republic, what is the barrier? The barrier is the white man; and we say to the

white man who dominates Africa that it is to his interest to clear out
now, because we are coming, not as in the time of Father Abraham,
200,000 strong, but we are coming 400,000,000 strong and we mean
to retake every square inch of the 12,000,000 square miles of African
territory belonging to us by right Divine."

Money poured in; war-time prosperity made it possible. Three ships
were bought and placed in commission. Garvey had grown to be High
Potentate of the association and "Provisional President of Africa."
Around him he had established a court of nobles and ladies. There
were dukes and duchesses, knight commanders of the Distinguished
Order of Ethiopia, and knight commanders of the Sublime Order of
the Nile. There were gorgeous uniforms, regalia, decorations, and
insignia. There was a strict court etiquette, and the constitution provided that "No lady below the age of eighteen shall be presented at
the 'Court Reception' and no gentleman below the age of twenty-one."
There was established the African Legion, with a full line of commissioned officers and a quartermaster staff and commissariat for each
brigade. The Black Cross nurses were organized. In fact, an embryo
army was set up with Marcus Garvey as commander-in-chief. A mission was sent to Liberia to negotiate an agreement whereby the
Universal Improvement Association would establish a colony there and
aid in the development of the country.

Garvey became a world figure, and his movements and utterances
were watched by the great governmental powers. (Even today from
his exile in Jamaica his actions and words are considered international
news.) The U.N.I.A. grew in the United States and spread through the
region of the Caribbean. The movement became more than a movement, it became a religion, its members became zealots. Meetings at
Liberty Hall were conducted with an elaborate liturgy. The moment
for the entry of the "Provisional President" into the auditorium was
solemn; a hushed and expectant silence on the throng, the African
Legion and Black Cross nurses flanking the long aisle and coming to
attention, the band and audience joining in the hymn: "Long Live our
President," and Garvey, surrounded by his guard of honour from the
Legion, marching majestically through the double line and mounting
the rostrum; it was impressive if for no other reason than the way in
which it impressed the throng. Garvey made a four months' tour of the
West Indies in a Black Star liner, gathering in many converts to the
movement, but no freight for the vessel. Of course, the bubble burst.
Neither Garvey nor anyone with him knew how to operate ships. And
if they had known, they could not have succeeded at the very time
when ships were the greatest drug on the market. So the Black Star
Line, after swallowing up hundreds of thousands of dollars, collapsed
in December 1921. The Federal Government investigated Garvey's
share-selling scheme and he was indicted and convicted on a charge

of using the mails to defraud. While out of the Tombs on bail, he made an unsuccessful attempt to revive his shipping venture as the Black Cross Line.

Within ten years after reaching New York Marcus Garvey had risen and fallen, been made a prisoner in the Atlanta Federal Penitentiary, and finally been deported to his native island. Within that brief period a black West Indian, here in the United States, in the twentieth century, had actually played an imperial role such as Eugene O'Neill never imagined in his *Emperor Jones.*

Garvey failed; yet he might have succeeded with more than moderate success. He had energy and daring and the Napoleonic personality, the personality that draws masses of followers. He stirred the imagination of the Negro masses as no Negro ever had. He raised more money in a few years than any other Negro organization had ever dreamed of. He had great power and great possibilities within his grasp. But his deficiencies as a leader outweighed his abilities. He is a supreme egotist, his egotism amounting to megalomania; and so the men surrounding him had to be for the most part cringing sycophants; and among them there were also cunning knaves. Upon them he now lays the entire blame for failure, taking no part of it to himself. As he grew in power, he fought every other Negro rights organization in the country, especially the National Association for the Advancement of Colored People, centering his attacks upon Dr. Du Bois.

Garvey made several vital blunders, which, with any intelligent advice, he might have avoided. He proceeded upon the assumption of a triple race scheme in the United States; whereas the facts are that the whites in the United States, unlike the whites of the West Indies, make no distinction between people of colour and blacks, nor do the Negroes. There may be places where a very flexible social line exists, but Negroes in the United States of every complexion have always maintained a solid front on the rights of the race. This policy of Garvey, going to the logical limit of calling upon his followers to conceive of God as black, did arouse a latent pride of the Negro in his blackness, but it wrought an overbalancing damage by the effort to drive a wedge between the blacks and the mixed bloods, an effort that might have brought on disaster had it been more successful.

He made the mistake of ignoring or looking with disdain upon the technique of the American Negro in dealing with his problems of race, a technique acquired through three hundred years of such experience as the West Indian has not had and never can have. If he had availed himself of the counsel and advice of an able and honest American Negro, he would have avoided many of the barbed wires against which he ran and many of the pits into which he fell.

But the main reason for Garvey's failure with thoughtful American Negroes was his African scheme. It was recognized at once by them to be impracticable and fantastic. Indeed, it is difficult to give the man credit for either honesty or sanity in these imperialistic designs, unless, as there are some reasons to suppose, his designs involved the purpose of going into Liberia as an agent of development and then by gradual steps or a coup taking over the government and making the country the centre of the activities and efforts for an Africa Redeemed. But thoughtful coloured Americans knew that, under existing political conditions in Africa, even that plan could ultimately meet with nothing but failure. Had there been every prospect of success, however, the scheme would not have appealed to them. It was simply a restatement of the Colonization Society scheme advanced just one hundred years before, which had occasioned the assembling of the first national convention of Negroes in America, called to oppose "the operations and misrepresentations of the American Colonization Society in these United States." The central idea of Garvey's scheme was absolute abdication and the recognition as facts of the assertions that this is a white man's country, a country in which the Negro has no place, no right, no chance, no future. To that idea the overwhelming majority of thoughtful American Negroes will not subscribe. And behind this attitude is the common-sense realization that as the world is at present, the United States, with all of its limitations, offers the millions of Negroes within its borders greater opportunities than any other land.

Garvey's last great mistake came about through his transcending egotism. He had as leading counsel for his trial Henry Lincoln Johnson, one of the shrewdest and ablest Negro lawyers in the country. But the temptation to strut and pose before a crowded court and on the front pages of the New York newspapers was too great for Garvey to resist; so he brushed his lawyers aside and handled his own case. He himself examined and cross-examined the witnesses; he himself harangued the judge and jury; and he was convicted.

Garvey, practically exiled on an island in the Caribbean, becomes a somewhat tragic figure. There arises a slight analogy between him and that former and greater dreamer in empires, exiled on another island. But the heart of the tragedy is that to this man came an opportunity such as comes to few men, and he clutched greedily at the glitter and let the substance slip from his fingers.

Anne Spencer

(b. 1879)

ANNE SPENCER IS A very private person, and some of her poems are very private poems. She was born in Bramwell, West Virginia, and was educated at the Virginia Seminary in Lynchburg, Virginia. Until her retirement a few years ago, Miss Spencer was the librarian at the Negro Dunbar High School in Lynchburg.

Writing in 1937, Sterling Brown said: "Anne Spencer is the most original of all Negro women poets . . . her vision and expression are those of a wise, ironic but gentle woman of her times." Age has not dimmed the brilliance of Anne Spencer's mind. At ninety she is still writing poetry, still commenting wisely—and, on occasion, ironically— on contemporary life.

Anne Spencer has never published a book. The selections reprinted here have appeared over the years in magazines and in practically every major anthology of Negro writing.

BEFORE THE FEAST OF SHUSHAN

Garden of Shushan!
After Eden, all terrace, pool, and flower recollect thee:
Ye weavers in saffron and haze and Tyrian purple,
Tell yet what range in color wakes the eye;
Sorcerer, release the dreams born here when
Drowsy, shifting palm-shade enspells the brain;
And sound! ye with harp and flute ne'er essay
Before these star-noted birds escaped from paradise awhile to
Stir all dark, and dear, and passionate desire, till mine
Arms go out to be mocked by the softly kissing body of the wind—
Slave, send Vashti to her King!

The fiery wattles of the sun startle into flame
The marbled towers of Shushan:
So at each day's wane, two peers—the one in
Heaven, the other on earth—welcome with their
Splendor the peerless beauty of the Queen.

Cushioned at the Queen's feet and upon her knee
Finding glory for mine head,—still, nearly shamed
Am I, the King, to bend and kiss with sharp
Breath the olive-pink of sandaled toes between;
Or lift me high to the magnet of a gaze, dusky,
Like the pool when but the moon-ray strikes to its depth;
Or closer press to crush a grape 'gainst lips redder
Than the grape, a rose in the night of her hair;
Then—Sharon's Rose in my arms.

And I am hard to force the petals wide;
And you are fast to suffer and be sad.
Is any prophet come to teach a new thing
Now in a more apt time?
Have him 'maze how you say love is sacrament;
How says Vashti, love is both bread and wine;
How to the altar may not come to break and drink,
Hulky flesh nor fleshly spirit!

I, thy lord, like not manna for meat as a Judahn;
I, thy master, drink, and red wine, plenty, and when
I thirst. Eat meat, and full, when I hunger.
I, thy King, teach you and leave you, when I list.
No woman in all Persia sets out strange action
To confuse Persia's lord—
Love is but desire and thy purpose fulfillment;
I, thy King, so say!

LETTER TO MY SISTER

It is dangerous for a woman to defy the gods;
To taunt them with the tongue's thin tip,
Or strut in the weakness of mere humanity,
Or draw a line daring them to cross;
The gods own the searing lightning,
The drowning waters, tormenting fears
And anger of red sins.

Oh, but worse still if you mince timidly—
Dodge this way or that, or kneel or pray,
Be kind, or sweat agony drops
Or lay your quick body over your feeble young;
If you have beauty or none, if celibate
Or vowed—the gods are Juggernaut,
Passing over . . . over . . .

This you may do:
Lock your heart, then, quietly,
And lest they peer within,
Light no lamp when dark comes down
Raise no shade for sun;
Breathless must your breath come through
If you'd die and dare deny
The gods their god-like fun.

AT THE CARNIVAL

Gay little Girl-of-the-Diving-Tank,
I desire a name for you,
Nice, as a right glove fits;
For you—who amid the malodorous
Mechanics of this unlovely thing,
Are darling of spirit and form.
I know you—a glance, and what you are
Sits-by-the-fire in my heart.
My Limousine-Lady knows you, or
Why does the slant-envy of her eye mark
Your straight air and radiant inclusive smile?
Guilt pins a fig-leaf; Innocence is its own adorning.
The bull-necked man knows you—this first time
His itching flesh sees from divine and vibrant health,
And thinks not of his avocation.
I came incuriously—
Set on no diversion save that my mind
Might safely nurse its brood of misdeeds
In the presence of a blind crowd.
The color of life was gray.
Everywhere the setting seemed right
For my mood!
Here the sausage and garlic booth
Sent unholy incense skyward;
There a quivering female-thing
Gestured assignations, and lied
To call it dancing;
There, too, were games of chance
With chances for none;
But oh! the Girl-of-the-Tank, at last!
Gleaming Girl, how intimately pure and free
The gaze you send the crowd,
As though you know the dearth of beauty

In its sordid life.
We need you—my Limousine-Lady,
The bull-necked man, and I.
Seeing you here brave and water-clean,
Leaven for the heavy ones of earth,
I am swift to feel that what makes
The plodder glad is good; and
Whatever is good is God.
The wonder is that you are here;
I have seen the queer in queer places,
But never before a heaven-fed
Naiad of the Carnival-Tank!
Little Diver, Destiny for you,
Like as for me, is shod in silence;
Years may seep into your soul
The bacilli of the usual and the expedient;
I implore Neptune to claim his child to-day!

LINES TO A NASTURTIUM

A LOVER MUSES

Flame-flower, Day-torch, Mauna Loa,
I saw a daring bee, today, pause, and soar,
        Into your flaming heart;
Then did I hear crisp crinkled laughter
As the furies after tore him apart?

        A bird, next, small and humming,
Looked into your startled depths and fled. . . .
Surely, some dread sight, and dafter
        Than human eyes as mine can see,
Set the stricken air waves drumming
        In his flight.

Day-torch, Flame-flower, cool-hot Beauty,
I cannot see, I cannot hear your fluty
Voice lure your loving swain,
But I know one other to whom you are in beauty
Born in vain;
Hair like the setting sun,
Her eyes a rising star,
Motions gracious as reeds by Babylon, bar
All your competing;

Hands like, how like, brown lilies sweet,
Cloth of gold were fair enough to touch her feet. . . .
Ah, how the senses flood at my repeating,
As once in her fire-lit heart I felt the furies
Beating, beating.

Alain LeRoy Locke

(1886–1954)

ALAIN LEROY LOCKE, WHO was born in Philadelphia, earned a baccalaureate at Harvard and was chosen a Rhodes Scholar in 1907. He took a B.Litt. at Oxford, went on to the University of Berlin in 1910 for further study in philosophy, and after a few years of teaching, earned a Ph.D. at Harvard. Locke then went to teach at Howard University where he remained for forty years; during this time he lectured all over the United States, Europe, Latin America, and the Caribbean, and served as a Visiting Professor at Harvard, the University of Wisconsin, and New York University. Often called upon to lecture on subjects related to the Negro, Locke developed an impressive knowledge of Negro and African history, literature, and culture.

His competence in these areas is evident in the books he wrote and in his work as an editor for the Associates of Negro Folk Education and for *Survey Graphic*. *The New Negro* (1925) is probably the best known of his edited works, but *Four Negro Poets* (1927) and *Plays of Negro Life* (with Montgomery Gregory, 1927) are notable for their critical introductions. Locke's own books are *The Negro in America* (1933); *The Negro and His Music* (1936); *Negro Art—Past and Present* (1937); *The Negro in Art* (1941); and *When Peoples Meet* (1942) with Bernard Stern.

The selection reprinted here is from *The New Negro*.

THE NEW NEGRO

In the last decade something beyond the watch and guard of statistics has happened in the life of the American Negro and the three norns who have traditionally presided over the Negro problem have a changeling in their laps. The Sociologist, the Philanthropist, the Race-leader are not unaware of the New Negro, but they are at a loss to account for him. He simply cannot be swathed in their formulae. For the younger generation is vibrant with a new psychology; the new spirit is awake in the masses, and under the very eyes of the professional observers is transforming what has been a perennial problem into the progressive phases of contemporary Negro life.

Could such a metamorphosis have taken place as suddenly as it has appeared to? The answer is no; not because the New Negro is not here, but because the Old Negro had long become more of a myth than a man. The Old Negro, we must remember, was a creature of moral debate and historical controversy. His has been a stock figure perpetuated as an historical fiction partly in innocent sentimentalism, partly in deliberate reactionism. The Negro himself has contributed his share to this through a sort of protective social mimicry forced upon him by the adverse circumstances of dependence. So for generations in the mind of America, the Negro has been more of a formula than a human being—a something to be argued about, condemned or defended, to be "kept down," or "in his place," or "helped up," to be worried with or worried over, harassed or patronized, a social bogey or a social burden. The thinking Negro even has been induced to share this same general attitude, to focus his attention on controversial issues, to see himself in the distorted perspective of a social problem. His shadow, so to speak, has been more real to him than his personality. Through having had to appeal from the unjust stereotypes of his oppressors and traducers to those of his liberators, friends and benefactors he has had to subscribe to the traditional positions from which his case has been viewed. Little true social or self-understanding has or could come from such a situation.

But while the minds of most of us, black and white, have thus burrowed in the trenches of the Civil War and Reconstruction, the actual march of development has simply flanked these positions, necessitating a sudden reorientation of view. We have not been watching in the right direction; set North and South on a sectional axis, we have not noticed the East till the sun has us blinking.

Recall how suddenly the Negro spirituals revealed themselves; suppressed for generations under the stereotypes of Wesleyan hymn harmony, secretive, half-ashamed, until the courage of being natural brought them out—and behold, there was folk-music. Similarly the mind of the Negro seems suddenly to have slipped from under the tyranny of social intimidation and to be shaking off the psychology of imitation and implied inferiority. By shedding the old chrysalis of the Negro problem we are achieving something like a spiritual emancipation. Until recently, lacking self-understanding, we have been almost as much of a problem to ourselves as we still are to others. But the decade that found us with a problem has left us with only a task. The multitude perhaps feels as yet only a strange relief and a new vague urge, but the thinking few know that in the reaction the vital inner grip of prejudice has been broken.

With this renewed self-respect and self-dependence, the life of the Negro community is bound to enter a new dynamic phase, the buoyancy from within compensating for whatever pressure there may be of conditions from without. The migrant masses, shifting from countryside to city, hurdle several generations of experience at a leap, but more important, the same thing happens spiritually in the life-attitudes and self-expression of the Young Negro, in his poetry, his art, his education and his new outlook, with the additional advantage, of course, of the poise and greater certainty of knowing what it is all about. From this comes the promise and warrant of a new leadership. As one of them has discerningly put it:

> We have tomorrow
> Bright before us
> Like a flame.
>
> Yesterday, a night-gone thing
> A sun-down name.
>
> And dawn today
> Broad arch above the road we came.
> We march!

This is what, even more than any "most creditable record of fifty years of freedom," requires that the Negro of to-day be seen through other than the dusty spectacles of past controversy. The day of "aunties," "uncles" and "mammies" is equally gone. Uncle Tom and Sambo have passed on, and even the "Colonel" and "George" play barnstorm rôles from which they escape with relief when the public spotlight is off. The popular melodrama has about played itself out, and it is time to scrap the fictions, garret the bogeys and settle down to a realistic facing of facts.

First we must observe some of the changes which since the traditional lines of opinion were drawn have rendered these quite obsolete. A main change has been, of course, that shifting of the Negro population which has made the Negro problem no longer exclusively or even predominantly Southern. Why should our minds remain sectionalized, when the problem itself no longer is? Then the trend of migration has not only been toward the North and the Central Midwest, but city-ward and to the great centers of industry—the problems of adjustment are new, practical, local and not peculiarly racial. Rather they are an integral part of the large industrial and social problems of our present-day democracy. And finally, with the Negro rapidly in process of class differentiation, if it ever was warrantable to regard and treat the Negro *en masse* it is becoming with every day less possible, more unjust and more ridiculous.

In the very process of being transplanted, the Negro is becoming transformed.

The tide of Negro migration, northward and city-ward, is not to be fully explained as a blind flood started by the demands of war industry coupled with the shutting off of foreign migration, or by the pressure of poor crops coupled with increased social terrorism in certain sections of the South and Southwest. Neither labor demand, the boll-weevil nor the Ku Klux Klan is a basic factor, however contributory any or all of them may have been. The wash and rush of this human tide on the beach line of the northern city centers is to be explained primarily in terms of a new vision of opportunity, of social and economic freedom, of a spirit to seize, even in the face of an extortionate and heavy toll, a chance for the improvement of conditions. With each successive wave of it, the movement of the Negro becomes more and more a mass movement toward the larger and the more democratic chance—in the Negro's case a deliberate flight not only from country-side to city, but from medieval America to modern.

Take Harlem as an instance of this. Here in Manhattan is not merely the largest Negro community in the world, but the first concentration in history of so many diverse elements of Negro life. It has attracted the African, the West Indian, the Negro American; has brought together the Negro of the North and the Negro of the South; the man from the city and the man from the town and village; the peasant, the student, the business man, the professional man, artist, poet, musician, adventurer and worker, preacher and criminal, exploiter and social outcast. Each group has come with its own separate motives and for its own special ends, but their greatest experience has been the finding of one another. Proscription and prejudice have thrown these dissimilar elements into a common area of contact and interaction. Within this area, race sympathy and unity have determined a further fusing of sentiment and experience. So what began in terms of segregation becomes more and more, as its elements mix and react, the laboratory of a great race-welding. Hitherto, it must be admitted that American Negroes have been a race more in name than in fact, or to be exact, more in sentiment than in experience. The chief bond between them has been that of a common condition rather than a common consciousness; a problem in common rather than a life in common. In Harlem, Negro life is seizing upon its first chances for group expression and self-determination. It is—or promises at least to be—a race capital. That is why our comparison is taken with those nascent centers of folk-expression and self-determination which are playing a creative part in the world to-day. Without pretense to their political significance, Harlem has the same rôle to play for the New Negro as Dublin has had for the New Ireland or Prague for the New Czechoslovakia.

Harlem, I grant you, isn't typical—but it is significant, it is prophetic. No sane observer, however sympathetic to the new trend, would contend that the great masses are articulate as yet, but they stir, they move, they are more than physically restless. The challenge of the new intellectuals among them is clear enough—the "race radicals" and realists who have broken with the old epoch of philanthropic guidance, sentimental appeal and protest. But are we after all only reading into the stirrings of a sleeping giant the dreams of an agitator? The answer is in the migrating peasant. It is the "man farthest down" who is most active in getting up. One of the most characteristic symptoms of this is the professional man, himself migrating to recapture his constituency after a vain effort to maintain in some Southern corner what for years back seemed an established living and clientele. The clergyman following his errant flock, the physician or lawyer trailing his clients, supply the true clues. In a real sense it is the rank and file who are leading, and the leaders who are following. A transformed and transforming psychology permeates the masses.

When the racial leaders of twenty years ago spoke of developing race-pride and stimulating race-consciousness, and of the desirability of race solidarity, they could not in any accurate degree have antici-pated the abrupt feeling that has surged up and now pervades the awakened centers. Some of the recognized Negro leaders and a power-ful section of white opinion identified with "race work" of the older order have indeed attempted to discount this feeling as a "passing phase," an attack of "race nerves" so to speak, an "aftermath of the war," and the like. It has not abated, however, if we are to gauge by the present tone and temper of the Negro press, or by the shift in pop-ular support from the officially recognized and orthodox spokesman to those of the independent, popular, and often radical type who are unmistakable symptoms of a new order. It is a social disservice to blunt the fact that the Negro of the Northern centers has reached a stage where tutelage, even of the most interested and well-intentioned sort, must give place to new relationships, where positive self-direc-tion must be reckoned with in ever increasing measure. The American mind must reckon with a fundamentally changed Negro.

The Negro too, for his part, has idols of the tribe to smash. If on the one hand the white man has erred in making the Negro appear to be that which would excuse or extenuate his treatment of him, the Negro, in turn, has too often unnecessarily excused himself because of the way he has been treated. The intelligent Negro of to-day is resolved not to make discrimination an extenuation for his shortcomings in performance, individual or collective; he is trying to hold himself at par, neither inflated by sentimental allowances nor depreciated by current social discounts. For this he must know himself and be known for precisely what he is, and for that reason he welcomes the new scientific rather than the old sentimental interest. Sentimental interest in the Negro has ebbed. We used to lament this as the falling off of our friends; now we rejoice and pray to be delivered both from self-pity and condescension. The mind of each racial group has had a bitter weaning, apathy or hatred on one side matching disillusionment or resentment on the other; but they face each other to-day with the possibility at least of entirely new mutual attitudes.

It does not follow that if the Negro were better known, he would be better liked or better treated. But mutual understanding is basic for any subsequent coöperation and adjustment. The effort toward this will at least have the effect of remedying in large part what has been the most unsatisfactory feature of our present stage of race relationships in America, namely the fact that the more intelligent and representative elements of the two race groups have at so many points got quite out of vital touch with one another.

The fiction is that the life of the races is separate, and increasingly so. The fact is that they have touched too closely at the unfavorable and too lightly at the favorable levels.

While inter-racial councils have sprung up in the South, drawing on forward elements of both races, in the Northern cities manual laborers may brush elbows in their everyday work, but the community and business leaders have experienced no such interplay or far too little of it. These segments must achieve contact or the race situation in America becomes desperate. Fortunately this is happening. There is a growing realization that in social effort the co-operative basis must supplant long-distance philanthropy, and that the only safeguard for mass relations in the future must be provided in the carefully maintained contacts of the enlightened minorities of both race groups. In the intellectual realm a renewed and keen curiosity is replacing the recent apathy; the Negro is being carefully studied, not just talked about and discussed. In art and letters, instead of being wholly caricatured, he is being seriously portrayed and painted.

To all of this the New Negro is keenly responsive as an augury of a new democracy in American culture. He is contributing his share to the new social understanding. But the desire to be understood would never in itself have been sufficient to have opened so completely the protectively closed portals of the thinking Negro's mind. There is still too much possibility of being snubbed or patronized for that. It was rather the necessity for fuller, truer self-expression, the realization of the unwisdom of allowing social discrimination to segregate him mentally, and a counter-attitude to cramp and fetter his own living—and so the "spite-wall" that the intellectuals built over the "color-line" has happily been taken down. Much of this reopening of intellectual contacts has centered in New York and has been richly fruitful not merely in the enlarging of personal experience, but in the definite enrichment of American art and letters and in the clarifying of our common vision of the social tasks ahead.

The particular significance in the re-establishment of contact between the more advanced and representative classes is that it promises to offset some of the unfavorable reactions of the past, or at least to re-surface race contacts somewhat for the future. Subtly the conditions that are molding a New Negro are molding a new American attitude.

However, this new phase of things is delicate; it will call for less charity but more justice; less help, but infinitely closer understanding. This is indeed a critical stage of race relationships because of the likelihood, if the new temper is not understood, of engendering sharp group antagonism and a second crop of more calculated prejudice. In some quarters, it has already done so. Having weaned the Negro, public opinion cannot continue to paternalize. The Negro to-day is inevitably moving forward under the control largely of his own objectives. What are these objectives? Those of his outer life are happily already well and finally formulated, for they are none other than the ideals of American institutions and democracy. Those of his inner life are yet in process of formation, for the new psychology at present is more of a consensus of feeling than of opinion, of attitude rather than of program. Still some points seem to have crystallized.

Up to the present one may adequately describe the Negro's "inner objectives" as an attempt to repair a damaged group psychology and reshape a warped social perspective. Their realization has required a new mentality for the American Negro. And as it matures we begin to see its effects; at first, negative, iconoclastic, and then positive and constructive. In this new group psychology we note the lapse of sentimental appeal, then the development of a more positive self-respect and self-reliance; the repudiation of social dependence, and then the gradual recovery from hyper-sensitiveness and "touchy" nerves, the repudiation of the double standard of judgment with its special philanthropic allowances and then the sturdier desire for objective and scientific appraisal; and finally the rise from social disillusionment to race pride, from the sense of social debt to the responsibilities of social contribution, and offsetting the necessary working and commonsense acceptance of restricted conditions, the belief in ultimate esteem and recognition. Therefore the Negro to-day wishes to be known for what he is, even in his faults and shortcomings, and scorns a craven and precarious survival at the price of seeming to be what he is not. He resents being spoken of as a social ward or minor, even by his own, and to being regarded a chronic patient for the sociological clinic, the sick man of American Democracy. For the same reasons, he himself is through with those social nostrums and panaceas, the so-called "solutions" of his "problem," with which he and the country have been so liberally dosed in the past. Religion, freedom, education, money—in turn, he has ardently hoped for and peculiarly trusted these things; he still believes in them, but not in blind trust that they alone will solve his life-problem.

Each generation, however, will have its creed, and that of the present is the belief in the efficacy of collective effort, in race co-operation. This deep feeling of race is at present the mainspring of Negro life. It seems to be the outcome of the reaction to proscription and prejudice; an attempt, fairly successful on the whole, to convert a defensive into an offensive position, a handicap into an incentive. It is radical in tone, but not in purpose and only the most stupid forms of opposition, misunderstanding or persecution could make it otherwise. Of course, the thinking Negro has shifted a little toward the left with the world-trend, and there is an increasing group who affiliate with radical and liberal movements. But fundamentally for the present the Negro is radical on race matters, conservative on others, in other words, a "forced radical," a social protestant rather than a genuine radical. Yet under further pressure and injustice iconoclastic thought and motives will inevitably increase. Harlem's quixotic radicalisms call for their ounce of democracy to-day lest to-morrow they be beyond cure.

The Negro mind reaches out as yet to nothing but American wants, American ideas. But this forced attempt to build his Americanism on race values is a unique social experiment, and its ultimate success is impossible except through the fullest sharing of American culture and institutions. There should be no delusion about this. American nerves in sections unstrung with race hysteria are often fed the opiate that the trend of Negro advance is wholly separatist, and that the effect of its operation will be to encyst the Negro as a benign foreign body in the body politic. This cannot be—even if it were desirable. The racialism of the Negro is no limitation or reservation with respect to American life; it is only a constructive effort to build the obstructions in the stream of his progress into an efficient dam of social energy and power. Democracy itself is obstructed and stagnated to the extent that any of its channels are closed. Indeed they cannot be selectively closed. So the choice is not between one way for the Negro and another way for the rest, but between American institutions frustrated on the one hand and American ideals progressively fulfilled and realized on the other.

There is, of course, a warrantably comfortable feeling in being on the right side of the country's professed ideals. We realize that we cannot be undone without America's undoing. It is within the gamut of this attitude that the thinking Negro faces America, but with variations of mood that are if anything more significant than the attitude itself. Sometimes we have it taken with the defiant ironic challenge of McKay:

> Mine is the future grinding down to-day
> Like a great landslip moving to the sea,
> Bearing its freight of débris far away

> Where the green hungry waters restlessly
> Heave mammoth pyramids, and break and roar
> Their eerie challenge to the crumbling shore.

Sometimes, perhaps more frequently as yet, it is taken in the fervent and almost filial appeal and counsel of Weldon Johnson's:

> O Southland, dear Southland!
> Then why do you still cling
> To an idle age and musty page,
> To a dead and useless thing?

But between defiance and appeal, midway almost between cynicism and hope, the prevailing mind stands in the mood of the same author's *To America*, an attitude of sober query and stoical challenge:

> How would you have us, as we are?
> Or sinking 'neath the load we bear,
> Our eyes fixed forward on a star,
> Or gazing empty at despair?
>
> Rising or falling? Men or things?
> With dragging pace or footsteps fleet?
> Strong, willing sinews in your wings,
> Or tightening chains about your feet?

More and more, however, an intelligent realization of the great discrepancy between the American social creed and the American social practice forces upon the Negro the taking of the moral advantage that is his. Only the steadying and sobering effect of a truly characteristic gentleness of spirit prevents the rapid rise of a definite cynicism and counter-hate and a defiant superiority feeling. Human as this reaction would be, the majority still deprecate its advent, and would gladly see it forestalled by the speedy amelioration of its causes. We wish our race pride to be a healthier, more positive achievement than a feeling based upon a realization of the shortcomings of others. But all paths toward the attainment of a sound social attitude have been difficult; only a relatively few enlightened minds have been able as the phrase puts it "to rise above" prejudice. The ordinary man has had until recently only a hard choice between the alternatives of supine and humiliating submission and stimulating but hurtful counter-prejudice. Fortunately from some inner, desperate resourcefulness has recently sprung up the simple expedient of fighting prejudice by mental passive resistance, in other words by trying to ignore it. For the few, this manna may perhaps be effective, but the masses cannot thrive upon it.

Fortunately there are constructive channels opening out into which the balked social feelings of the American Negro can flow freely.

Without them there would be much more pressure and danger than there is. These compensating interests are racial but in a new and enlarged way. One is the consciousness of acting as the advance-guard of the African peoples in their contact with Twentieth Century civilization; the other, the sense of a mission of rehabilitating the race in world esteem from that loss of prestige for which the fate and conditions of slavery have so largely been responsible. Harlem, as we shall see, is the center of both these movements; she is the home of the Negro's "Zionism." The pulse of the Negro world has begun to beat in Harlem. A Negro newspaper carrying news material in English, French and Spanish, gathered from all quarters of America, the West Indies and Africa has maintained itself in Harlem for over five years. Two important magazines, both edited from New York, maintain their news and circulation consistently on a cosmopolitan scale. Under American auspices and backing, three pan-African congresses have been held abroad for the discussion of common interests, colonial questions and the future co-operative development of Africa. In terms of the race question as a world problem, the Negro mind has leapt, so to speak, upon the parapets of prejudice and extended its cramped horizons. In so doing it has linked up with the growing group consciousness of the dark-peoples and is gradually learning their common interests. As one of our writers has recently put it: "It is imperative that we understand the white world in its relations to the non-white world." As with the Jew, persecution is making the Negro international.

As a world phenomenon this wider race consciousness is a different thing from the much asserted rising tide of color. Its inevitable causes are not of our making. The consequences are not necessarily damaging to the best interests of civilization. Whether it actually brings into being new Armadas of conflict or argosies of cultural exchange and enlightenment can only be decided by the attitude of the dominant races in an era of critical change. With the American Negro, his new internationalism is primarily an effort to recapture contact with the scattered peoples of African derivation. Garveyism may be a transient, if spectacular, phenomenon, but the possible rôle of the American Negro in the future development of Africa is one of the most constructive and universally helpful missions that any modern people can lay claim to.

Constructive participation in such causes cannot help giving the Negro valuable group incentives, as well as increased prestige at home and abroad. Our greatest rehabilitation may possibly come through such channels, but for the present, more immediate hope rests in the revaluation by white and black alike of the Negro in terms of his artistic endowments and cultural contributions, past and prospective. It must be increasingly recognized that the Negro has already made very substantial contributions, not only in his folk-art, music especially, which has always found appreciation, but in larger, though humbler and less acknowledged ways. For generations the Negro has been the peasant matrix of that section of America which has most undervalued him, and here he has contributed not only materially in labor and in social patience, but spiritually as well. The South has unconsciously absorbed the gift of his folk-temperament. In less than half a generation it will be easier to recognize this, but the fact remains that a leaven of humor, sentiment, imagination and tropic nonchalance has gone into the making of the South from a humble, unacknowledged source. A second crop of the Negro's gifts promises still more largely. He now becomes a conscious contributor and lays aside the status of a beneficiary and ward for that of a collaborator and participant in American civilization. The great social gain in this is the releasing of our talented group from the arid fields of controversy and debate to the productive fields of creative expression. The especially cultural recognition they win should in turn prove the key to that revaluation of the Negro which must precede or accompany any considerable further betterment of race relationships. But whatever the general effect, the present generation will have added the motives of self-expression and spiritual development to the old and still unfinished task of making material headway and progress. No one who understandingly faces the situation with its substantial accomplishment or views the new scene with its still more abundant promise can be entirely without hope. And certainly, if in our lifetime the Negro should not be able to celebrate his full initiation into American democracy, he can at least, on the warrant of these things, celebrate the attainment of a significant and satisfying new phase of group development, and with it a spiritual Coming of Age.

Jean Toomer

(1894–1967)

THE GRANDSON OF P. B. S. Pinchback, a former Lieutenant Governor of Louisiana, Jean Toomer was born in Washington, D.C. and was educated there and at the University of Wisconsin and the City College of New York. A few months of teaching school in rural Georgia seem to have inspired Toomer's "novel" *Cane* (1923)—a lyric burst of pride in his Negro heritage and his ancestral Southern home. After *Cane,* which was a great critical success, Toomer became a disciple of the Russian mystic Gurdjieff, twice married white, and vanished into the white world.

Cane heralded and projected the enduring qualities of the Negro Renaissance. It was race-conscious and race-proud. It was revealing. It destroyed the old constraining stereotypes and myths. It represented a complete break with tradition. As fiction, the form is so boldly experimental that it scarcely answers to the name of novel; and the prose sometimes seems to give sound priority over sense. Yet the meaning, though obscured, is never lost, and the emotional relevance of the depicted experiences is always clear.

Jean Toomer's genius exploded in only one book. A handful of fugitive poems, a short novel, *York Beach,* in the *New American Caravan* (1929), and a book of essays entitled *Essentials* (1931) are undistinguished.

The selections given here are all from *Cane.*

SONG OF THE SON

Pour O pour that parting soul in song,
O pour it in the saw-dust glow of night,
Into the velvet pine-smoke air to-night,
And let the valley carry it along.
And let the valley carry it along.

O land and soil, red soil and sweet-gum tree,
So scant of grass, so profligate of pines,
Now just before an epoch's sun declines
Thy son, in time, I have returned to thee,
Thy son, I have, in time, returned to thee.

In time, for though the sun is setting on
A song-lit race of slaves, it has not set;
Though late, O soil, it is not too late yet
To catch thy plaintive soul, leaving, soon gone,
Leaving, to catch thy plaintive soul soon gone.

O Negro slaves, dark purple ripened plums,
Squeezed, and bursting in the pine-wood air,
Passing, before they strip the old tree bare
One plum was saved for me, one seed becomes

An everlasting song, a singing tree,
Caroling softly souls of slavery,
What they were, and what they are to me,
Caroling softly souls of slavery.

COTTON SONG

Come, brother, come. Lets lift it;
Come now, hewit! roll away!
Shackles fall upon the Judgment Day
But lets not wait for it.

God's body's got a soul,
Bodies like to roll the soul,
Cant blame God if we dont roll,
Come, brother, roll, roll!

Cotton bales are the fleecy way
Weary sinner's bare feet trod,
Softly, softly to the throne of God,
"We aint agwine t wait until th Judgment Day!

Nassur; nassur,
Hump.
Eoho, eoho, roll away!
We aint agwine t wait until th Judgment Day!"

God's body's got a soul,
Bodies like to roll the soul,
Cant blame God if we dont roll,
Come, brother, roll, roll!

ESTHER

1

Nine.

Esther's hair falls in soft curls about her high-cheek-boned chalk-white face. Esther's hair would be beautiful if there were more gloss to it. And if her face were not prematurely serious, one would call it pretty. Her cheeks are too flat and dead for a girl of nine. Esther looks like a little white child, starched, frilled, as she walks slowly from her home towards her father's grocery store. She is about to turn in Broad from Maple Street. White and black men loafing on the corner hold no interest for her. Then a strange thing happens. A clean-muscled, magnificent, black-skinned Negro, whom she had heard her father mention as King Barlo, suddenly drops to his knees on a spot called the Spittoon. White men, unaware of him, continue squirting tobacco juice in his direction. The saffron fluid splashes on his face. His smooth black face begins to glisten and to shine. Soon, people notice him, and gather round. His eyes are rapturous upon the heavens. Lips and nostrils quiver. Barlo is in a religious trance. Town folks know it. They are not startled. They are not afraid. They gather round. Some beg boxes from the grocery stores. From old McGregor's notion shop. A coffin-case is pressed into use. Folks line the curb-stones. Business men close shop. And Banker Warply parks his car close by. Silently, all await the prophet's voice. The sheriff, a great florid fellow whose leggings never meet around his bulging calves, swears in three deputies. "Wall, y cant never tell what a nigger like King Barlo might be up t." Soda bottles, five fingers full of shine, are passed to those who want them. A couple of stray dogs start a fight. Old Goodlow's cow comes flopping up the street. Barlo, still as an Indian fakir, has not moved. The town bell strikes six. The sun slips in behind a heavy mass of horizon cloud. The crowd is hushed and expectant. Barlo's under jaw relaxes, and his lips begin to move.

"Jesus has been awhisperin strange words deep down, O way down deep, deep in my ears."

Hums of awe and of excitement.

"He called me to His side an said, 'Git down on your knees beside me, son, Ise gwine t whisper in your ears.'"

An old sister cries, "Ah, Lord."

"'Ise agwine t whisper in your ears,' he said, an I replied, 'Thy will be done on earth as it is in heaven.'"

"Ah, Lord. Amen. Amen."

"An Lord Jesus whispered strange good words deep down, O way down deep, deep in my ears. An He said, 'Tell em till you feel your throat on fire.' I saw a vision. I saw a man arise, an he was big an black an powerful—"

Some one yells, "Preach it, preacher, preach it!"

"—but his head was caught up in th clouds. An while he was agazin at th heavens, heart filled up with th Lord, some little white-ant biddies came an tied his feet to chains. They led him t th coast, they led him t th sea, they led him across th ocean and they didnt set him free. The old coast didnt miss him, an th new coast wasnt free, he left the old-coast brothers, t give birth t you an me. O Lord, great God Almighty, t give birth t you an me."

Barlo pauses. Old gray mothers are in tears. Fragments of melodies are being hummed. White folks are touched and curiously awed. Off to themselves, white and black preachers confer as to how best to rid themselves of the vagrant, usurping fellow. Barlo looks as though he is struggling to continue. People are hushed. One can hear weevils work. Dusk is falling rapidly, and the customary store lights fail to throw their feeble glow across the gray dust and flagging of the Georgia town. Barlo rises to his full height. He is immense. To the people he assumes the outlines of his visioned African. In a mighty voice he bellows:

"Brothers an sisters, turn your faces t th sweet face of the Lord, an fill your hearts with glory. Open your eyes an see th dawnin of th mornin light. Open your ears—"

Years afterwards Esther was told that at that very moment a great, heavy, rumbling voice actually was heard. That hosts of angels and of demons paraded up and down the streets all night. That King Barlo rode out of town astride a pitch-black bull that had a glowing gold ring in its nose. And that old Limp Underwood, who hated niggers, woke up next morning to find that he held a black man in his arms. This much is certain: an inspired Negress, of wide reputation for being sanctified, drew a portrait of a black madonna on the court-house wall. And King Barlo left town. He left his image indelibly upon the mind of Esther. He became the starting point of the only living patterns that her mind was to know.

2

Sixteen.

Esther begins to dream. The low evening sun sets the windows of McGregor's notion shop aflame. Esther makes believe that they really are aflame. The town fire department rushes madly down the road. It ruthlessly shoves black and white idlers to one side. It whoops. It clangs. It rescues from the second-story window a dimpled infant which she claims for her own. How had she come by it? She thinks of it immaculately. It is a sin to think of it immaculately. She must dream no more. She must repent her sin. Another dream comes. There is no fire department. There are no heroic men. The fire starts. The loafers on the corner form a circle, chew their tobacco faster, and squirt juice just as fast as they can chew. Gallons on top of gallons they squirt upon the flames. The air reeks with the stench of scorched tobacco juice. Women, fat chunky Negro women, lean scrawny white women, pull their skirts up above their heads and display the most ludicrous under-clothes. The women scoot in all directions from the danger zone. She alone is left to take the baby in her arms. But what a baby! Black, singed, woolly, tobacco-juice baby—ugly as sin. Once held to her breast, miraculous thing: its breath is sweet and its lips can nibble. She loves it frantically. Her joy in it changes the town folks' jeers to harmless jealousy, and she is left alone.

Twenty-two.

Esther's schooling is over. She works behind the counter of her father's grocery store. "To keep the money in the family," so he said. She is learning to make distinctions between the business and the social worlds. "Good business comes from remembering that the white folks dont divide the niggers, Esther. Be just as black as any man who has a silver dollar." Esther listlessly forgets that she is near white, and that her father is the richest colored man in town. Black folk who drift in to buy lard and snuff and flour of her, call her a sweet-natured, accommodating girl. She learns their names. She forgets them. She thinks about men. "I dont appeal to them. I wonder why." She recalls an affair she had with a little fair boy while still in school. It had ended in her shame when he as much as told her that for sweetness he pre-ferred a lollipop. She remembers the salesman from the North who wanted to take her to the movies that first night he was in town. She refused, of course. And he never came back, having found out who she was. She thinks of Barlo. Barlo's image gives her a slightly stale thrill. She spices it by telling herself his glories. Black. Magnetically so. Best cotton picker in the county, in the state, in the whole world for that matter. Best man with his fists, best man with dice, with a razor. Promoter of church benefits. Of colored fairs. Vagrant preacher. Lover of all the women for miles and miles around. Esther decides that she loves him. And with a vague sense of life slipping by, she resolves that she will tell him so, whatever people say, the next time he comes to town. After the making of this resolution which becomes a sort of wedding cake for her to tuck beneath her pillow and go to sleep upon, she sees nothing of Barlo for five years. Her hair thins. It looks like the dull silk on puny corn ears. Her face pales until it is the color of the gray dust that dances with dead cotton leaves.

3

Esther is twenty-seven.

Esther sells lard and snuff and flour to vague black faces that drift in her store to ask for them. Her eyes hardly see the people to whom she gives change. Her body is lean and beaten. She rests listlessly against the counter, too weary to sit down. From the street some one shouts, "King Barlo has come back to town." He passes her window, driving a large new car. Cut-out open. He veers to the curb, and steps out. Barlo has made money on cotton during the war. He is as rich as anyone. Esther suddenly is animate. She goes to her door. She sees him at a distance, the center of a group of credulous men. She hears the deep-bass rumble of his talk. The sun swings low. McGregor's windows are aflame again. Pale flame. A sharply dressed white girl passes by. For a moment Esther wishes that she might be like her. Not white; she has no need for being that. But sharp, sporty, with get-up about her. Barlo is connected with that wish. She mustnt wish. Wishes only make you restless. Emptiness is a thing that grows by being moved. "I'll not think. Not wish. Just set my mind against it." Then the thought comes to her that those purposeless, easy-going men will possess him, if she doesnt. Purpose is not dead in her, now that she comes to think of it. That loose women will have their arms around him at Nat Bowle's place tonight. As if her veins are full of fired sun-bleached southern shanties, a swift heat sweeps them. Dead dreams, and a forgotten resolution are carried upward by the flames. Pale flames. "They shant have him. Oh, they shall not. Not if it kills me they shant have him." Jerky, aflutter, she closes the store and starts home. Folks lazing on store window-sills wonder what on earth can be the matter with Jim Crane's gal, as she passes them. "Come to remember, she always was a little off, a little crazy, I reckon." Esther seeks her own room, and locks the door. Her mind is a pink mesh-bag filled with baby toes.

Using the noise of the town clock striking twelve to cover the creaks of her departure, Esther slips into the quiet road. The town, her parents, most everyone is sound asleep. This fact is a stable thing that comforts her. After sundown a chill wind came up from the west. It is still blowing, but to her it is a steady, settled thing like the cold. She wants her mind to be like that. Solid, contained, and blank as a sheet of darkened ice. She will not permit herself to notice the peculiar phosphorescent glitter of the sweet-gum leaves. Their movement would excite her. Exciting too, the recession of the dull familiar homes she knows so well. She doesnt know them at all. She closes her eyes, and holds them tightly. Wont do. Her being aware that they are closed recalls her purpose. She does not want to think of it. She opens them.

She turns now into the deserted business street. The corrugated iron canopies and mule- and horse-gnawed hitching posts bring her a strange composure. Ghosts of the commonplace of her daily life take stride with her and become her companions. And the echoes of her heels upon the flagging are rhythmically monotonous and soothing. Crossing the street at the corner of McGregor's notion shop, she thinks that the windows are a dull flame. Only a fancy. She walks faster. Then runs. A turn into a side street brings her abruptly to Nat Bowle's place. The house is squat and dark. It is always dark. Barlo is within. Quietly she opens the outside door and steps in. She passes through a small room. Pauses before a flight of stairs down which people's voices, muffled, come. The air is heavy with fresh tobacco smoke. It makes her sick. She wants to turn back. She goes up the steps. As if she were mounting to some great height, her head spins. She is violently dizzy. Blackness rushes to her eyes. And then she finds that she is in a large room. Barlo is before her.

"Well, I'm sholy damned—skuse me, but what, what brought you here, lil milk-white gal?"

"You." Her voice sounds like a frightened child's that calls homeward from some point miles away.

"Me?"

"Yes, you Barlo?"

"This aint th place fer y. This aint th place fer y."

"I know. I know. But I've come for you."

"For me for what?"

She manages to look deep and straight into his eyes. He is slow at understanding. Guffaws and giggles break out from all around the room. A coarse woman's voice remarks, "So that how th dictie niggers does it." Laughs. "Mus give em credit fo their gall."

Esther doesnt hear. Barlo does. His faculties are jogged. She sees a smile, ugly and repulsive to her, working upward through thick licker fumes. Barlo seems hideous. The thought comes suddenly, that conception with a drunken man must be a mighty sin. She draws away, frozen. Like a somnambulist she wheels around and walks stiffly to the stairs. Down them. Jeers and hoots pelter bluntly upon her back. She steps out. There is no air, no street, and the town has completely disappeared.

Claude McKay

(1890—1948)

CLAUDE MCKAY WAS BORN in Jamaica, B.W.I., the youngest of eleven children. He won a cabinet-maker's apprenticeship at the age of seventeen but an older brother and a white Englishman introduced him to literature, and McKay turned to writing poetry, in which he worked with the Jamaican dialect. In 1912, the year he came to the States, he published two books of verse, *Constab Ballads* and *Songs of Jamaica*. After a few months at Tuskegee Institute, McKay transferred to Kansas State University, but did not stay to get a degree. When World War One began, he moved to New York and supported himself by a variety of non-literary jobs, while in his spare time writing and publishing poetry (some under the pseudonym of Eli Edwards) in *Seven Arts, Pearson's,* and *The Liberator.*

In 1915 McKay went to London, where he stayed for six years, writing for the Radical *Workers Dreadnought* and producing another volume of verse, *Spring in New Hampshire* (1920). He returned briefly to New York as associate editor, with Max Eastman, of *The Liberator,* but the years 1921–1944 found him traveling in Russia, Germany, Spain, North Africa, and France, where he finally settled to write the best-selling novel *Home to Harlem* (1928), and *Banjo* (1929), *Gingertown* (1932), and *Banana Bottom* (1933). McKay's autobiography, *A Long Way from Home,* came out in 1937, and *Harlem,* a kind of history, appeared after he returned to America to stay in 1944.

Claude McKay was a better and far more honest poet than novelist. Of his novels, *Home to Harlem* is the best known and certainly the most sensational exploitation of the "primitive," but some critics feel that *Banana Bottom* is a better work. In all of his novels, McKay tends to overemphasize certain of his color and class prejudices. His poetry, on the other hand, is everything his fiction is not: it is powerfully expressive and superbly lyrical.

For a recent study of McKay, see Stephen H. Bronz, *Roots of Negro Racial Consciousness* (1964).

The selection "Myrtle Avenue" comes from *Home to Harlem.*

HARLEM SHADOWS

I hear the halting footsteps of a lass
    In Negro Harlem when the night lets fall
Its veil. I see the shapes of girls who pass
    To bend and barter at desire's call.
Ah, little dark girls who in slippered feet
Go prowling through the night from street to street!

Through the long night until the silver break
    Of day the little gray feet know no rest;
Through the lone night until the last snow-flake
    Has dropped from heaven upon the earth's
        white breast,
The dusky, half-clad girls of tired feet
Are trudging, thinly shod, from street to street.

Ah, stern harsh world, that in the wretched way
    Of poverty, dishonor and disgrace,
Has pushed the timid little feet of clay,
    The sacred brown feet of my fallen race!
Ah, heart of me, the weary, weary feet
In Harlem wandering from street to street.

SPRING IN NEW HAMPSHIRE
(To J. L. J. F. E.)

Too green the springing April grass,
    Too blue the silver-speckled sky,
For me to linger here, alas,
    While happy winds go laughing by,
Wasting the golden hours indoors,
Washing windows and scrubbing floors.

Too wonderful the April night,
    Too faintly sweet the first May flowers,
The stars too gloriously bright,
    For me to spend the evening hours,
When fields are fresh and streams are leaping,
Wearied, exhausted, dully sleeping.

"Harlem Shadows," "Spring in New Hampshire," "If We Must Die," "The White House," and "America" from *Selected Poems of Claude McKay.* Reprinted by permission of Twayne Publishers, Inc.

IF WE MUST DIE

If we must die, let it not be like hogs
Hunted and penned in an inglorious spot,
While round us bark the mad and hungry dogs,
Making their mock at our accurséd lot.
If we must die, O let us nobly die,
So that our precious blood may not be shed
In vain; then even the monsters we defy
Shall be constrained to honor us though dead!
O kinsmen! we must meet the common foe!
Though far outnumbered let us show us brave,
And for their thousand blows deal one deathblow!
What though before us lies the open grave?
Like men we'll face the murderous, cowardly pack,
Pressed to the wall, dying, but fighting back!

THE WHITE HOUSE

Your door is shut against my tightened face,
And I am sharp as steel with discontent;
But I possess the courage and the grace
To bear my anger proudly and unbent.
The pavement slabs burn loose beneath my feet,
A chafing savage, down the decent street;
And passion rends my vitals as I pass,
Where boldly shines your shuttered door of glass.
Oh, I must search for wisdom every hour,
Deep in my wrathful bosom sore and raw,
And find in it the superhuman power
To hold me to the letter of your law!
Oh, I must keep my heart inviolate
Against the potent poison of your hate.

AMERICA

Although she feeds me bread of bitterness,
And sinks into my throat her tiger's tooth,
Stealing my breath of life, I will confess
I love this cultured hell that tests my youth!
Her vigor flows like tides into my blood,
Giving me strength against her hate.
Her bigness sweeps my being like a flood.

Yet as a rebel fronts a king in state,
I stand within her walls with not a shred
Of terror, malice, not a word of jeer.
Darkly I gaze into the days ahead,
And see her might and granite wonders there,
Beneath the touch of Time's unerring hand,
Like priceless treasures sinking in the sand.

MYRTLE AVENUE

Zeddy was excited over Jake's success in love. He thought how often he had tried to make up to Rose, without succeeding. He was crazy about finding a woman to love him for himself.

He had been married when he was quite a lad to a crust-yellow girl in Petersburg. Zeddy's wife, after deceiving him with white men, had run away from him to live an easier life. That was before Zeddy came North. Since then he had had many other alliances. But none had been successful.

It was true that no Black Belt beauty would ever call Zeddy "mah han'some brown." But there were sweetmen of the Belt more repulsive than he, that women would fight and murder each other for. Zeddy did not seem to possess any of that magic that charms and holds women for a long time. All his attempts at home-making had failed. The women left him when he could not furnish the cash to meet the bills. They never saw his wages. For it was gobbled up by his voracious passion for poker and crap games. Zeddy gambled in Harlem. He gambled with white men down by the piers. And he was always losing.

"If only I could get those kinda gals that falls foh Jake," Zeddy mused. "And Jake is such a fool spade. Don't know how to handle the womens."

Zeddy's chance came at last. One Saturday a yellow-skinned youth, whose days and nights were wholly spent between pool-rooms and Negro speakeasies, invited Zeddy to a sociable at a grass-widow's who lived in Brooklyn and worked as a cook downtown in New York. She was called Gin-head Susy. She had a little apartment in Myrtle Avenue near Prince Street.

Susy was wonderfully created. She was of the complexion known among Negroes as spade or chocolate-to-the-bone. Her eyes shone like big white stars. Her chest was majestic and the general effect like a mountain. And that mountain was overgrand because Susy never wore any other but extremely French-heeled shoes. Even over the range she always stood poised in them and blazing in bright-hued clothes.

The burning passion of Susy's life was the yellow youth of her race. Susy came from South Carolina. A yellow youngster married her when she was fifteen and left her before she was eighteen. Since then she had lived with a yellow complex at the core of her heart.

Civilization had brought strikingly exotic types into Susy's race. And like many, many Negroes, she was a victim to that. . . . Ancient black life rooted upon its base with all its fascinating new layers of brown, low-brown, high-brown, nut-brown, lemon, maroon, olive, mauve, gold. Yellow balancing between black and white. Black reaching out beyond yellow. Almost-white on the brink of a change. Sucked back down into the current of black by the terribly sweet rhythm of black blood. . . .

Susy's life of yellow complexity was surcharged with gin. There were whisky and beer also at her sociable evenings, but gin was the drink of drinks. Except for herself, her parties were all-male. Like so many of her sex, she had a congenital contempt for women. All-male were her parties and as yellow as she could make them. A lemon-colored or paper-brown pool-room youngster from Harlem's Fifth Avenue or from Prince Street. A bell-boy or railroad waiter or porter. Sometimes a chocolate who was a quick, nondiscriminating lover and not remote of attitude like the pampered high-browns. But chocolates were always a rarity among Susy's front-roomful of gin-lovers.

Yet for all of her wages drowned in gin, Susy carried a hive of discontents in her majestic breast. She desired a lover, something like her undutiful husband, but she desired in vain. Her guests consumed her gin and listened to the phonograph, exchanged rakish stories, and when they felt fruit-ripe to dropping, left her place in pursuit of pleasures elsewhere.

Sometimes Susy managed to lay hold of a yellow one for some time. Something all a piece of dirty rags and stench picked up in the street. Cleansed, clothed, and booted it. But so soon as he got his curly hair straightened by the process of Harlem's Ambrozine Palace of Beauty, and started in strutting the pavement of Lenox Avenue, feeling smart as a moving-picture dandy, he would leave Susy.

Apart from Susy's repellent person, no youthful sweetmen attempting to love her could hold out under the ridicule of his pals. Over their games of pool and craps the boys had their cracks at Susy.

"What about Gin-head Susy tonight?"

"Sure, let's go and look the crazy old broad over."

"I'll go anywheres foh swilling of good booze."

"She's sho one ugly spade, but she's right there with her Gordon Dry."

"She ain't got 'em from creeps to crown and her trotters is B flat, but her gin is regal."

But now, after all the years of gin sociables and unsatisfactory lemons, Susy was changing just a little. She was changing under the influence of her newly-acquired friend, Lavinia Curdy, the only woman whom she tolerated at her parties. That was not so difficult, as Miss Curdy was less attractive than Susy. Miss Curdy was a putty-skinned mulattress with purple streaks on her face. Two of her upper front teeth had been knocked out and her lower lip slanted pathetically leftward. She was skinny and when she laughed she resembled an old braying jenny.

When Susy came to know Miss Curdy, she unloaded a quantity of the stuff of her breast upon her. Her drab childhood in a South Carolina town. Her early marriage. No girlhood. Her husband leaving her. And all the yellow men that had beaten her, stolen from her, and pawned her things.

Miss Curdy had been very emphatic to Susy about "yaller men." "I know them from long experience. They never want to work. They're a lazy and shiftless lot. Want to be kept like women. I found that out a long, long time ago. And that's why when I wanted a man foh keeps I took me a black plug-ugly one, mah dear."

It wouldn't have supported the plausibility of Miss Curdy's advice if she had mentioned that more than one black plug-ugly had ruthlessly cut loose from her. As the black woman had had her entanglements in yellow, so had the mulattress hers of black. But, perhaps, Miss Curdy did not realize that she could not help desiring black. In her salad days as a business girl her purse was controlled by many a black man. Now, however, her old problems did not arise in exactly the same way,—her purse was old and worn and flat and attracted no attention.

"A black man is as good to me as a yaller when I finds a real one." Susy lied a little to Miss Curdy from a feeling that she ought to show some pride in her own complexion.

"But all these sociables—and you spend so much coin on gin," Miss Curdy had said.

"Well, that's the trute, but we all of us drinks it. And I loves to have company in mah house, plenty of company."

But when Susy came home from work one evening and found that her latest "yaller" sweetie had stolen her suitcase and best dresses and pawned even her gas range, she resolved never to keep another of his kind as a "steady." At least she made that resolve to Miss Curdy. But the sociables went on and the same types came to drink the Saturday evenings away, leaving the two women at the finish to their empty bottles and glasses. Once Susy did make a show of a black lover. He was the house man at the boarding-house where she cooked. But the arrangement did not hold any time, for Susy demanded of the chocolate extremely more than she ever got from her yellows.

"Well, boh, we's Brooklyn bound tonight," said Zeddy to Jake.

"You got to show me that Brooklyn's got any life to it," replied Jake.

"Theah's life anywheres theah's booze and jazz, and theah's casses o' gin and gramophone whar we's going."

"Has we got to pay foh it, buddy?"

"No, boh, eve'ything is f. o. c. ef the lady likes you."

"Blimey!" A cockney phrase stole Jake's tongue. "Don't bull me."

"I aint. Honest-to-Gawd Gordon Dry, and moh—ef you're the goods, all f. o. c."

"Well, I'll be browned!" exclaimed Jake.

Zeddy also took along Strawberry Lips, a new pal, burnt-cork black, who was thus nick-named from the peculiar stage-red color of his mouth. Strawberry Lips was typically the stage Negro. He was proof that a generalization has some foundation in truth. . . . You might live your life in many black belts and arrive at the conclusion that there is no such thing as a typical Negro—no minstrel coon off the stage, no Thomas Nelson Page's nigger, no Octavus Roy Cohen's porter, no lineal descendant of Uncle Tom. Then one day your theory may be upset through meeting with a type by far more perfect than any created counterpart.

"Myrtle Avenue used to be a be-be itching of a place," said Strawberry Lips, "when Doc Giles had his gambling house on there and Elijah Bowers was running his cabaret. H'm. But Bowers was some big guy. He knew swell white folks in politics, and had a grand automobile and a high-yaller wife that hadn't no need of painting to pass. His cabaret was running neck and neck with Marshall's in Fifty-third Street. Then one night he killed a man in his cabaret, and that finished him. The lawyers got him off. But they cleaned him out dry. Done broke him, that case did. And today he's plumb down and out."

Jake, Zeddy, and Strawberry Lips had left the subway train at Borough Hall and were walking down Myrtle Avenue.

"Bowers' cabaret was some place for the teasing-brown pick-me-up then, brother—and the snow. The stuff was cheap then. You sniff, boh?" Strawberry Lips asked Jake and Zeddy.

"I wouldn't know befoh I sees it," Jake laughed.

"I ain't no habitual prisoner," said Zeddy, "but I does any little thing for a change. Keep going and active with anything, says I."

The phonograph was discharging its brassy jazz notes when they entered the apartment. Susy was jerking herself from one side to the other with a potato-skinned boy. Miss Curdy was half-hopping up and down with the only chocolate that was there. Five lads, ranging from brown to yellow in complexion, sat drinking with jaded sneering expressions on their faces. The one that had invited Zeddy was among them. He waved to him to come over with his friends.

"Sit down and try some gin," he said. . . .

Zeddy dipped his hand in his pocket and sent two bones rolling on the table.

"Ise with you, chappie," his yellow friend said. The others crowded around. The gramophone stopped and Susy, hugging a bottle, came jerking on her French heels over to the group. She filled the glasses and everybody guzzled gin.

Miss Curdy looked the newcomers over, paying particular attention to Jake. A sure-enough eye-filling chocolate, she thought. I would like to make a steady thing of him.

Over by the door two light-brown lads began arguing about an actress of the leading theater of the Black Belt.

"I tell you I knows Gertie Kendall. I know her more'n I know you."

"Know her mah granny. You knows her just like I do, from the balcony of the Lafayette. Don't hand me none o' that fairy stuff, for I ain't gwine to swallow it."

"Youse an aching pain. I knows her, I tell you. I even danced with her at Madame Mulberry's apartment. You thinks I only hangs out with low-down trash becassin Ise in a place like this, eh? I done met mos'n all our big niggers: Jack Johnson, James Reese Europe, Adah Walker, Buddy, who used to play that theah drum for them Castle Walkers, and Madame Walker."

"Yaller, it 'pears to me that youse jest a nacherally-born story-teller. You really spec's me to believe youse been associating with the mucty-mucks of the race? Gwan with you. You'll be telling me next you done speaks with Charlie Chaplin and John D. Rockefeller——"

Miss Curdy had tuned her ears to the conversation and broke in: "Why, what is that to make so much fuss about? Sure he can dance with Gertie Kendall and know the dickty niggers. In my sporting days I knew Bert Williams and Walker and Adah Overton and Editor Tukslack and all that upstage race gang that wouldn't touch Jack Johnson with a ten-foot pole. I lived in Washington and had Congressmen for my friends—foop! Why you can get in with the top-crust crowd at any swell ball in Harlem. All you need is clothes and the coin. I know them all, yet I don't feel a bit haughty mixing here with Susy and you all."

"I guess you don't now," somebody said.

Gin went round . . . and round . . . and round. . . . Desultory dancing. . . . Dice. . . . Blackjack. . . . Poker. . . . The room became a close, live, intense place. Tight-faced, the men seemed interested only in drinking and gaming, while Susy and Miss Curdy, guzzling hard, grew uglier. A jungle atmosphere pervaded the room, and, like shameless wild animals hungry for raw meat, the females savagely searched the eyes of the males. Susy's eyes always came back to settle upon the lad that had invited Zeddy. He was her real object. And Miss Curdy was ginned up with high hopes of Jake.

Jake threw up the dice and Miss Curdy seized her chance to get him alone for a little while.

"The cards do get so tiresome," she said. "I wonder how you men can go on and on all night long poking around with poker."

"Better than worser things," retorted Jake. Disgusted by the purple streaks, he averted his eyes from the face of the mulattress.

"I don't know about that," Miss Curdy bridled. "There's many nice ways of spending a sociable evening between ladies and gentlemen."

"Got to show me," said Jake, simply because the popular phrase intrigued his tongue.

"And that I can."

Irritated, Jake turned to move away.

"Where you going? Scared of a lady?"

Jake recoiled from the challenge, and shuffled away from the hideous mulattress. From experience in seaport towns in America, in France, in England, he had concluded that a woman could always go farther than a man in coarseness, depravity, and sheer cupidity. Men were ugly and brutal. But beside women they were merely vicious children. Ignorant about the aim and meaning and fulfillment of life; uncertain and indeterminate; weak. Rude children who loved excelling in spectacular acts to win the applause of women.

But women were so realistic and straight-going. *They* were the real controlling force of life. Jake remembered the bal-musette fights between colored and white soldiers in France. Blacks, browns, yellows, whites. . . . He remembered the interracial sex skirmishes in England. Men fought, hurt, wounded, killed each other. Women, like blazing torches, egged them on or denounced them. Victims of sex, the men seemed foolish, ape-like blunderers in their pools of blood. Didn't know what they were fighting for, except it was to gratify some vague feeling about women. . . .

Jake's thoughts went roaming after his little lost brown of the Baltimore. The difference! She, in one night, had revealed a fine different world to him. Mystery again. A little stray girl. Finer than the finest!

Some of the fellows were going. In a vexed spirit, Susy had turned away from her unresponsive mulatto toward Zeddy. Relieved, the mulatto yawned, threw his hands backwards and said: "I guess mah broad is home from Broadway by now. Got to final on home to her. Harlem, lemme see you."

Miss Curdy was sitting against the mantel-piece, charming Strawberry Lips. Marvellous lips. Salmon-pink and planky. She had hoisted herself upon his knees, her arm around his thick neck.

Jake went over to the mantelpiece to pour a large chaser of beer and Miss Curdy leered at him. She disgusted him. His life was a free coarse thing, but he detested nastiness and ugliness. Guess I'll haul bottom to Harlem, he thought. Congo Rose was a rearing wild animal, all right, but these women, these boys. . . . Skunks, tame skunks, all of them!

He was just going out when a chocolate lad pointed at a light-brown and said: "The pot calls foh four bits, chappie. Come across or stay out."

"Lemme a quarter!"

"Ain't got it. Staying out?"

Biff! Square on the mouth. The chocolate leaped up like a tiger-cat at his assailant, carrying over card table, little pile of money, and half-filled gin glasses with a crash. Like an enraged ram goat, he held and butted the light-brown boy twice, straight on the forehead. The victim crumpled with a thud to the floor. Susy jerked over to the felled boy and hauled him, his body leaving a liquid trail, to the door. She flung him out in the corridor and slammed the door.

"Sarves him right, pulling off that crap in mah place. And you, Mis'er Jack Johnson," she said to the chocolate youth, "lemme miss you quick."

"He done hits me first," the chocolate said.

"I knows it, but I ain't gwina stand foh no rough-house in mah place. Ise got a dawg heah wif me all ready foh bawking."

"K-hhhh, K-hhhh," laughed Strawberry Lips. "Oh, boh, I know it's the trute, but——"

The chocolate lad slunk out of the flat.

"Lavinia," said Susy to Miss Curdy, "put on that theah 'Tickling Blues' on the victroly."

The phonograph began its scraping and Miss Curdy started jig-jagging with Strawberry Lips. Jake gloomed with disgust against the door.

"Getting outa this, buddy?" he asked Zeddy.

"Nobody's chasing *us*, boh." Zeddy commenced stepping with Susy to the "Tickling Blues."

Outside, Jake found the light-brown boy still half-stunned against the wall.

"Ain't you gwine at home?" Jake asked him.

"I can't find a nickel foh car fare," said the boy.

Jake took him into a saloon and bought him a lemon squash. "Drink that to clear you' haid," he said. "And heah's car fare." He gave the boy a dollar. "Whar you living at?"

"San Juan Hill."

"Come on, le's git the subway, then."

The Myrtle Avenue Elevated train passed with a high raucous rumble over their heads.

"Myrtle Avenue," murmured Jake. "Pretty name, all right, but it stinks like a sewer. Legs and feets! Come take me outa it back home to Harlem."

Langston Hughes

(1902—1967)

LANGSTON HUGHES WAS BORN in Joplin, Missouri, and since his parents separated when he was still very young, he was brought up by his mother (with the help of other relatives) in Lawrence and Topeka, Kansas, and Cleveland, Ohio. The summer after his graduation from high school in 1919, Hughes went to Mexico to join his father, an engineer and lawyer. Although the father and son did not get along well together, young Hughes stayed for about a year; then, after rejecting an opportunity to study in Europe at his father's expense, he returned to the States. He spent a year 1921–22, at Columbia University, but he was unhappy and restless. He was writing and having his work published in such Negro magazines as *The Crisis* and the *Messenger*.

In 1923 Hughes began the wanderings abroad and at home that lasted for three years before he settled down at Lincoln University (Pennsylvania) and graduated in 1929. Hughes made frequent periodic trips to other parts of the world, including Russia in 1932, and lectured throughout the United States; but his home base was Harlem. Here he produced the volumes of poetry, the novels, the plays, the short stories, the essays, the urban folk pieces, and the anthologies which earned his living and several fellowships and literary awards, and brought him a reputation as the most versatile of black writers.

Hughes was not only versatile. He was deeply involved in Negro life, which, as his writings show, he loved and thoroughly understood. Although widely read by whites, Hughes wrote for blacks; he used a language of beguiling simplicity to speak directly of simple things and common experiences. Few other black writers have matched his range; even fewer the moving beauty of his best poems or insights of his best prose; fewer still his sense of humor.

Among Hughes' best works are the following: *Weary Blues* (poetry), 1926; *The Ways of White Folk* (short fiction), 1934; *The Big Sea* (autobiography), 1940, 1956; *Montage of a Dream Deferred* (poetry), 1951; *The Best of Simple* (urban folk pieces), 1961. The works included here are from several sources.

For recent studies of Hughes' life and works, see James A. Emanuel, *Langston Hughes* (1967), and Donald C. Dickinson, *A Bio-Bibliography of Langston Hughes: 1902–1967* (1967). See also the special Hughes issues of *CLA Journal* (June, 1968), and *Freedom-ways* (Spring, 1968).

NEGRO DANCERS

"Me an' ma baby's
Got two mo' ways,
Two mo' ways to do de Charleston!
    Da, da,
    Da, da, da!
Two mo 'ways to do de Charleston!"

Soft light on the tables,
Music gay,
Brown-skin steppers
In a cabaret.

White folks, laugh!
White folks, pray!

"Me an' ma baby's
Got two mo' ways,
Two mo' ways to do de Charleston!"

THE CAT AND THE SAXOPHONE

2 A.M.

EVERYBODY
Half-pint,—
Gin?
No, make it
LOVES MY BABY
corn. You like
liquor,
don't you, honey?
BUT MY BABY
Sure. Kiss me,
DON'T LOVE NOBODY
daddy.
BUT ME.
Say!

EVERYBODY
Yes?
WANTS MY BABY
I'm your
BUT MY BABY
sweetie, ain't I?
DON'T WANT NOBODY
Sure.
BUT
Then let's
ME,
do it!
SWEET ME.
Charleston,
mamma!
!

CROSS

My old man's a white old man
And my old mother's black.
If ever I cursed my white old man
I take my curses back.

If ever I cursed my black old mother
And wished she were in hell,
I'm sorry for that evil wish
And now I wish her well.

My old man died in a fine big house.
My ma died in a shack.
I wonder where I'm gonna die,
Being neither white nor black?

RUBY BROWN

She was young and beautiful
And golden like the sunshine
That warmed her body.

And because she was colored
Mayville had no place to offer her,
Nor fuel for the clean flame of joy
That tried to burn within her soul.

One day,
Sitting on old Mrs. Latham's back porch
Polishing the silver,
She asked herself two questions
And they ran something like this:
What can a colored girl do
On the money from a white woman's kitchen?
And ain't there any joy in this town?

Now the streets down by the river
Know more about this pretty Ruby Brown,
And the sinister shuttered houses of the bottoms
Hold a yellow girl
Seeking an answer to her questions.
The good church folk do not mention
Her name any more.

But the white men,
Habitués of the high shuttered houses,
Pay more money to her now
Than they ever did before,
When she worked in their kitchens.

THEME FOR ENGLISH B

The instructor said,

> *Go home and write*
> *a page tonight.*
> *And let that page come out of you—*
> *Then, it will be true.*

I wonder if it's that simple?

I am twenty-two, colored, born in Winston-Salem.
I went to school there, then Durham, then here
to this college on the hill above Harlem.

I am the only colored student in my class.
The steps from the hill lead down into Harlem,
through a park, then I cross St. Nicholas,
Eighth Avenue, Seventh, and I come to the Y.
the Harlem Branch Y, where I take the elevator
up to my room, sit down, and write this page:

It's not easy to know what is true for you or me
at twenty-two, my age. But I guess I'm what
I feel and see and hear. Harlem, I hear you:
hear you, hear me—we two—you, me, talk on this page.
(I hear New York, too.) Me—who?

Well, I like to eat, sleep, drink, and be in love.
I like to work, read, learn, and understand life.
I like a pipe for a Christmas present,
or records—Bessie, bop, or Bach.
I guess being colored doesn't make me *not* like
the same things other folks like who are other races.

So will my page be colored that I write?
Being me, it will not be white.
But it will be
a part of you, instructor.
You are white——
yet a part of me, as I am a part of you.
That's American.
Sometimes perhaps you don't want to be a part of me.
Nor do I often want to be a part of you.
But we are, that's true!
As I learn from you,
I guess you learn from me——
although you're older—and white——
and somewhat more free.

This is my page for English B.

MOTHER TO SON

Well, son, I'll tell you:
Life for me ain't been no crystal stair.

It's had tacks in it,
And splinters,
And boards torn up,
And places with no carpet on the floor—
Bare.
But all the time
I'se been a-climbin' on,
And reachin' landin's,
And turnin' corners,
And sometimes goin' in the dark
Where there ain't been no light.
So boy, don't you turn back.
Don't you set down on the steps
'Cause you finds it's kinder hard.
Don't you fall now—
For I'se still goin', honey,
I'se still climbin',
And life for me ain't been no crystal stair.

THE NEGRO SPEAKS OF RIVERS

To W.E.B. Du Bois

I've known rivers:
I've known rivers ancient as the world and older than the flow of
   human blood in human veins.

My soul has grown deep like the rivers.

I bathed in the Euphrates when dawns were young.
I built my hut near the Congo and it lulled me to sleep.
I looked upon the Nile and raised the pyramids above it.
I heard the singing of the Mississippi when Abe Lincoln went down
   to New Orleans, and I've seen its muddy bosom turn all golden in
   the sunset.

I've known rivers:
Ancient, dusky rivers.

My soul has grown deep like the rivers.

BOUND NO'TH BLUES

Goin' down the road, Lawd,
Goin' down the road.
Down the road, Lawd,
Way, way down the road.
Got to find somebody
To help me carry this load.

Road's in front o' me,
Nothin' to do but walk.
Road's in front o' me,
Walk . . . an' walk . . . an' walk.
I'd like to meet a good friend
To come along an' talk.

Hates to be lonely,
Lawd, I hates to be sad.
Says I hates to be lonely,
Hates to be lonely an' sad,
But ever friend you finds seems
Like they try to do you bad.

Road, road, road, O!
Road, road . . . road . . . road, road!
Road, road, road, O!
On the no'thern road.
These Mississippi towns ain't
Fit fer a hoppin' toad.

PUZZLED

Here on the edge of hell
Stands Harlem—
Remembering the old lies,
The old kicks in the back,
The old, *Be patient,*
They told us before.

Sure, we remember.
Now, when the man at the corner store
Says sugar's gone up another two cents,
And bread one,
And there's a new tax on cigarettes—
We remember the job we never had,
Never could get,
And can't have now
Because we're colored.

So we stand here
On the edge of hell
In Harlem
And look out on the world
And wonder
What we're gonna do
In the face of
What we remember.

MOTTO

I play it cool
And dig all jive
That's the reason
I stay alive.

My motto,
As I live and learn,
        is:
*Dig And Be Dug
In Return.*

LOW TO HIGH

How can you forget me?
But you do!
You said you was gonna take me
Up with you—

Now you've got your Cadillac,
you done forgot that you are black.
How can you forget me
When I'm you?

But you do.

How can you forget me,
fellow, say?
How can you low-rate me
this way?
You treat me like you damn well please,
Ignore me—though I pay your fees.
How can you forget me?

But you do.

HIGH TO LOW

God knows
We have our troubles, too——
One trouble is you:
you talk too loud,
cuss too loud,
look too black,
don't get anywhere,
and sometimes it seems
you don't even care.
The way you send your kids to school
stockings down,
(not Ethical Culture)
the way you shout out loud in church,
(not St. Phillips)
and the way you lounge on doorsteps
just as if you were down South,
(not at 409)
the way you clown——
the way, in other words,
you let me down——
me, trying to uphold the race
and you——

well, you can see,
we have our problems,
too, with you.

WHO'S PASSING FOR WHO?

One of the great difficulties about being a member of a minority race is that so many kindhearted, well-meaning bores gather around to help you. Usually, to tell the truth, they have nothing to help with, except their company—which is often appallingly dull.

Some members of the Negro race seem very well able to put up with it, though, in these uplifting years. Such was Caleb Johnson, colored social worker, who was always dragging around with him some non-descript white person or two, inviting them to dinner, showing them Harlem, ending up at the Savoy—much to the displeasure of whatever friends of his might be out that evening for fun, not sociology.

Friends are friends and, unfortunately, overearnest uplifters are uplifters—no matter what color they may be. If it were the white race that was ground down instead of Negroes, Caleb Johnson would be one of the first to offer Nordics the sympathy of his utterly inane society, under the impression that somehow he would be doing them a great deal of good.

You see, Caleb, and his white friends, too, were all bores. Or so we, who lived in Harlem's literary bohemia during the "Negro Renaissance," thought. We literary ones in those days considered ourselves too broad-minded to be bothered with questions of color. We liked people of any race who smoked incessantly, drank liberally, wore complexion and morality as loose garments, and made fun of anyone who didn't do likewise. We snubbed and high-hatted any Negro or white luckless enough not to understand Gertrude Stein, Ulysses, Man Ray, the theremin, Jean Toomer, or George Antheil. By the end of the 1920's Caleb was just catching up to Dos Passos. He thought H. G. Wells good.

We met Caleb one night in Small's. He had three assorted white folks in tow. We would have passed him by with but a nod had he not hailed us enthusiastically, risen, and introduced us with great acclaim to his friends, who turned out to be schoolteachers from Iowa, a woman and two men. They appeared amazed and delighted to meet all at once two Negro writers and a black painter in the flesh. They invited us to have a drink with them. Money being scarce with us, we deigned to sit down at their table.

The white lady said, "I've never met a Negro writer before."

The two men added, "Neither have we."

"Why, we know any number of *white* writers," we three dark bo-. hemians declared with bored nonchalance.

"But Negro writers are much more rare," said the lady.

"There are plenty in Harlem," we said.

"But not in Iowa," said one of the men, shaking his mop of red hair.

"There are no good *white* writers in Iowa either, are there?" we asked superciliously.

"Oh yes, Ruth Suckow came from there."

Whereupon we proceeded to light in upon Ruth Suckow as old hat and to annihilate her in favor of Kay Boyle. The way we flung names around seemed to impress both Caleb and his white guests. This, of course, delighted us, though we were too young and too proud to admit it.

The drinks came and everything was going well, all of us drinking, and we three showing off in a high-brow manner, when suddenly at the table just behind us a man got up and knocked down a woman. He was a brownskin man. The woman was blonde. As she rose, he knocked her down again. Then the red-haired man from Iowa got up and knocked the colored man down.

He said, "Keep your hands off that white woman."

The man got up and said, "She's not a white woman. She's my wife."

One of the waiters added, "She's not white, sir, she's colored."

Whereupon the man from Iowa looked puzzled, dropped his fists, and said, "I'm sorry."

The colored man said, "What are you doing up here in Harlem anyway, interfering with my family affairs?"

The white man said, "I thought she was a white woman."

The woman who had been on the floor rose and said, "Well, I'm not a white woman, I'm colored, and you leave my husband alone."

Then they both lit in on the gentleman from Iowa. It took all of us and several waiters, too, to separate them. When it was over, the manager requested us to kindly pay our bill and get out. He said we were disturbing the peace. So we all left. We went to a fish restaurant down the street. Caleb was terribly apologetic to his white friends. We artists were both mad and amused.

"Why did you say you were sorry," said the colored painter to the visitor from Iowa, "after you'd hit that man—and then found out it wasn't a white woman you were defending, but merely a light colored woman who looked white?"

"Well," answered the red-haired Iowan, "I didn't mean to be butting in if they were all the same race."

"Don't you think a woman needs defending from a brute, no matter what race she may be?" asked the painter.

"Yes, but I think it's up to you to defend your own women."

"Oh, so you'd divide up a brawl according to races, no matter who was right?"

"Well, I wouldn't say that."

"You mean you wouldn't defend a colored woman whose husband was knocking her down?" asked the poet.

Before the visitor had time to answer, the painter said, "No! You just got mad because you thought a black man was hitting a *white* woman."

"But she *looked* like a white woman," countered the man.

"Maybe she was just passing for colored," I said.

"Like some Negroes pass for white," Caleb interposed.

"Anyhow, I don't like it," said the colored painter, "the way you stopped defending her when you found out she wasn't white."

"No, we don't like it," we all agreed except Caleb.

Caleb said in extenuation, "But Mr. Stubblefield is new to Harlem."

The red-haired white man said, "Yes, it's my first time here."

"Maybe Mr. Stubblefield ought to stay out of Harlem," we observed.

"I agree," Mr. Stubblefield said. "Good night."

He got up then and there and left the café. He stalked as he walked. His red head disappeared into the night.

"Oh, that's too bad," said the white couple who remained. "Stubby's temper just got the best of him. But explain to us, are many colored folks really as fair as that woman?"

"Sure, lots of them have more white blood than colored, and pass for white."

"Do they?" said the lady and gentleman from Iowa.

"You never read Nella Larsen?" we asked.

"She writes novels," Caleb explained. "She's part white herself."

"Read her," we advised. "Also read the *Autobiography of an Ex-Coloured Man*." Not that we had read it ourselves—because we paid but little attention to the older colored writers—but we knew it was about passing for white.

We all ordered fish and settled down comfortably to shocking our white friends with tales about how many Negroes there were passing for white all over America. We were determined to *épater le bourgeois* real good via this white couple we had cornered, when the woman leaned over the table in the midst of our dissertations and said, "Listen, gentlemen, you needn't spread the word, but me and my husband aren't white either. We've just been *passing* for white for the last fifteen years."

"What?"

"We're colored, too, just like you," said the husband. "But it's better passing for white because we make more money."

Well, that took the wind out of us. It took the wind out of Caleb, too. He thought all the time he was showing some fine white folks Harlem—and they were as colored as he was!

Caleb almost never cursed. But this time he said, "I'll be damned!"

Then everybody laughed. And laughed! We almost had hysterics. All at once we dropped our professionally self-conscious "Negro" manners, became natural, ate fish, and talked and kidded freely like colored folks do when there are no white folks around. We really had fun then, joking about that red-haired guy who mistook a fair colored woman for white. After the fish we went to two or three more night spots and drank until five o'clock in the morning.

Finally we put the light-colored people in a taxi heading downtown. They turned to shout a last good-by. The cab was just about to move off when the woman called to the driver to stop.

She leaned out the window and said with a grin, "Listen, boys! I hate to confuse you again. But, to tell the truth, my husband and I aren't really colored at all. We're white. We just thought we'd kid you by passing for colored a little while—just as you said Negroes sometimes pass for white."

She laughed as they sped off toward Central Park, waving, "Good-by!"

We didn't say a thing. We just stood there on the corner in Harlem dumbfounded—not knowing now *which* way we'd been fooled. Were they really white—passing for colored? Or colored—passing for white?

Whatever race they were, they had had too much fun at our expense —even if they did pay for the drinks.

PICTURE FOR HER DRESSER

It was a warm evening not yet dark when I stopped by Simple's. His landlady had the front door open airing the house, so I did not need to ring. I walked upstairs and knocked on his door. He was sitting on the bed, cutting his toenails, listening to a radio show, and frowning.

"Do you hear that?" he asked. "It's not about me, neither about you. All these plays, dramas, skits, sketches, and soap operas all day long and practically nothing about Negroes. You would think no Negroes lived in America except Amos and Andy. White folks have all kinds of plays on the radio about themselves, also on TV. But what have we got about us? Just now and then a song to sing. Am I right?"

"Just about right," I said.

"Come on, let's go take a walk." He put on his shoes first, his pants, then his shirt. "Is it cool enough for a coat?"

"You'd better wear one," I said. "It's not summer yet, and evening's coming on. You probably won't get back until midnight."

"Joyce is gone to a club meeting, so I won't be going to see her," he said. "She's expecting her sister-members to elect her a delegate to the

From *The Best of Simple* by Langston Hughes. © 1961 by Langston Hughes. Reprinted by permission of Hill and Wang, Inc.

regional which meets in Boston sometime soon. If they don't, she'll be a disappointed soul. She used to skip meetings, but that regional is why she goes regular now. Let's me and you stroll up Seventh Avenue to 145th, then curve toward Sugar Hill where the barmaids are beautiful and barflies are belles. I have not been on Sugar Hill in a coon's age."

It was dusk-dark when we reached the pavement. Taxis and pleasure cars sped by. The Avenue was alive with promenaders. On the way up the street we passed a photographer's shop with a big sign glowing in the window:

HARLEM DE-LUXE PHOTOGRAPHY STUDIO
IF YOU ARE NOT GOOD-LOOKING
WE WILL MAKE YOU SO
ENTER

"The last time I come by here," said Simple, "before my lady friend started acting like an iceberg, Joyce told me, 'Jess, why don't you go in and get your picture posed? I always did want a nice photograph of you to set on my dresser.'

"I said, 'Joyce, I don't want to take no picture.' But you know how womens is! So I went in.

"They got another big sign up on the wall inside that says:

RETOUCHING DONE

" 'I don't want them to *touch* me, let alone *retouch*,' I told Joyce.

"Joyce said, 'Be sweet, please, I do not wish no evil-looking Negro on my dresser.' So I submitted.

"Another sign states:

COLORED TO ORDER—EXPERT TINTING

"I asked, 'Joyce, what color do you want me to be?'

"Joyce said, 'A little lighter than natural. I will request the man how much he charges to make you chocolate.'

"About that time a long tall bushy-headed joker in a smock came dancing out of a booth and said, 'Next.'

"That were me next. There was a kind of sick green light blazing inside the booth. That light not only hurt my eyes, but turned my stomach before I even set down.

"The man said, 'Pay in advance.'

"My week's beer money went to turn me into chocolate to set on Joyce's dresser—providing I did not melt before I got out of there, it were so hot.

"The man said, 'Naturally, you want a retouching job?'

"I said, 'You know I *don't* want to look like I am.'

" 'That will be One Dollar extra,' he stated. 'Would you also wish to be tinted?'

" 'Gimme the works,' I said.

" 'We will add Three,' he additioned. 'And if you want more than one print, that will be Two Dollars each, after the negative.'

" 'One is enough,' I said. 'I would not want myself setting around on my *own* dresser. Just one print for the lady, that's all.'

" 'How about your mother?' asked the man. 'Or your sister down home?'

" 'Skip down home,' I said.

" 'Very well,' said the man. 'Now, look pleasant, please! You have observed the sign yonder which is the rule of the company:

IF YOU MOVE,

YOU LOSE.

IF YOU SHAKE—

NO RE-TAKE!

So kindly hold your position.'

" 'As much of my money as you've got,' I said, 'I will not bat a eye.'

" 'Tilt your head to one side and watch the birdie. Don't look like you have just et nails. . . . Smile! . . . Smile! . . . Smile! . . . Brightly, now! That's right!'

" 'I cannot grin all night,' I said. 'Neither can I set like a piece of iron much longer. If you don't take me as I am, *damn!*'

" 'No profanity in here, please,' says the man. 'Just hold it while I focus.'

"I held.

"He focussed.

"I sweated.

"He focussed.

"I said, 'Can't you see me?'

"He said, 'Shussh-ss-s! Now, a great big smile! . . . Hold it!'

"F—L—A—S—H!

"I were blind for the next ten minutes. Seven Dollars and a Half's worth of me to set on Joyce's dresser! When I go to get that picture out next week it better be good—also have a frame! As touchous as Joyce is these days, I want her to like that picture."

By that time we had reached the Woodside. The corner of 141st and Seventh was jumping. King Cole was coming cool off the juke box inside the bar.

"Daddy-o, let's turn in here and get a beer," said Simple. "I never was much on climbing hills and if I go any further, I'll have too far to walk back. Besides, I got to wake myself up in the morning. My Big Ben won't alarm, my wrist watch is broke, and my landlady is evil. She says I don't pay her to climb three flights of steps to wake me up —so I have got nobody to wake me in the morning. That is one reason why I wish I was married, so I would not have to worry about getting to work on time. Also I would have somebody to cook my breakfast. I am tired of coffee, crullers, coffee and crullers, which is all I can afford. Besides, I hate an alarm clock. . . . Two beers, bartender! . . . I like to be woke up gentle, some woman's hand shaking saying, 'Jess, honey, ain't you gonna make your shift?'

"And if I was to say, 'No,' she would say, 'Then all right, baby. You been working too hard lately anyhow. Sleep on. We will all get up about noon and go to the show.'

"That is the kind of woman I would like to have. Most womens is different. Most womens say, 'You better get up from there, Jess Semple, and go to work.' But even that would be better than a *brr-rrr-rr-r!* alarm clock every morning in your ears. I rather be woke up by a human than a clock."

"So you would make your wife get up before you, *just to wake you up,* would you?"

"Which is a woman's duty," said Simple. "He that earns the bread should be woke up, petted, fed, and got off to work in time. Then his wife can always go back to bed and get her beauty sleep—providing she is not working herself."

"No doubt a woman of yours would have to work."

"Only until we got a toe-holt," said Simple, "then Joyce could stay home and take care of the children."

"I haven't heard you speak of children before," I said. "You'll be too far along in age to start raising a family if you don't soon get married."

"You don't have to marry to have a family," said Simple.

"You wouldn't care to father children out of wedlock, surely?"

"A man slips up sometimes. But I don't need to worry about that. Joyce is a respectable woman—which is why I respects her. But she says as soon as we are wedlocked she wants a son that looks like me— which will be just as soon as that Negro in Baltimore pays for Isabel's divorce. So far that igaroot has only made one payment."

"I thought that man loved your wife so much he was willing to pay for the *whole* divorce. What happened?"

"I reckon inflation got him," said Simple. "Some things makes me sad to speak of. It takes three payments to get a decree. He made the down payment. Isabel writ that if I would make one, she would make one, then everybody could marry again. But I cannot meet a payment now with food up, rent up, phones up, cigarettes up, Lifebuoy up— everything up but my salary. Isabel wrote that divorces are liable to go up if I don't hurry up and pay up. I got a worried mind. Let's order one more beer—then I won't sleep restless. Have you got some change for this round?"

"I paid the last time."

"Except that *that* were not the last time. This round will be the last time. Just like a divorce in three installments, the last time is not the *last* time—if you still have to pay another time. Kindly order two beers."

"What do you take me for, a chump?"

"No, pal—a friend."

BOMBS IN BARCELONA

Nicolás Guillén went with me to Spain as a correspondent for a Cuban paper. Since everybody said food in that war-torn country was scarce, we took along with us an enormous basket of edibles. But we ate it all on the train. Guillén was a jovial companion with whom to travel and on the way to Barcelona he entertained me with Cubanismos and folk songs:

> *Oyelo bien, encargada!*
> *Esta es la voz que retumba—*
> *Esta es la ultima rumba*
> *Que bailamos en tu morada.*

At the border between France and Spain there is a tunnel, a long stretch of darkness through which the night express from Paris passes in the early morning. When the train comes out into the sunlight, on the Spanish side of the mountain, with a shining blue bay where children swim in the Mediterranean, you see the village of Port Bou. The town seemed bright and quiet that morning. But as I left the train, I noticed that almost all of the windows of the station were shattered. There were machine-gun marks on the walls of the custom-house and several nearby houses were in ruins, gutted by bombs. In the winding streets of Port Bou there were signs, REFUGIO, pointing to holes in the mountains to be used in case of air raids. And on old walls there were new Loyalist posters. One read: "It's better to be the tail of a lion than the head of a rat." This was my first view of war-time Spain, this little town by the blue sea where travelers changed trains.

In the country they were harvesting the wheat, and as we chugged southward, men and women were swinging primitive scythes in the

From *I Wonder as I Wander* by Langston Hughes. © 1956 by Langston Hughes. Reprinted by permission of Hill and Wang, Inc.

fields. The Barcelona train was very crowded that day and all around me folks kept up a rapid fire of conversation in various accents. Guillén and I were the only Negroes on the train, so I thought, until at one of the stations when we got out to buy fruit, we noticed a dark face leaning from a window of the coach ahead of us. When the train started again, we went forward to investigate. He was a brownskin boy from the Canary Islands in a red shirt and a blue beret. He had escaped from the Canaries by the simple expedient of getting into his fishing boat with the rest of her crew and sailing toward French Morocco. From there he had gotten to France. The Canary Islands were a part of Spain, he said, but the fishermen did not like the men who had usurped power, so many of them sailed their boats away and came to fight with the Loyalists. This young man spoke a strange Spanish dialect that was hard for Guillén to understand, but he told us that many folks in the Canaries are colored, mixed with African and Spanish blood.

What should have been a short trip from the French border to Barcelona, took all day and well into the night. When our blacked-out train pulled into the blacked-out city near midnight, Nicolás Guillén was so tired that he had stopped talking or singing, and wanted nothing so much as a good bed. There were no lights whatsoever on the platform of the Barcelona station, so we followed the crowd moving slowly like shadows into the station where one lone lantern glimmered behind a ticket wicket. I was loaded down as usual with bags, books, records and a typewriter. Guillén had sense enough to travel light with mostly just his songs and himself. He helped me carry things, and clung to what little remained of our hamper of food. We took a bus through pitch-black streets to a hotel on the Ramblas—there was no gas for taxis and only one bus met each train. I was so tired that night that I slept right through an air-raid alert. Hotel instructions were that all guests were to assemble in the lobby when an alert sounded. Since the hotel had no basement, the ground floor was considered safest. But the so-called ground floor of this hotel was really several feet above street level. The lobby had enormous French doors and windows opening on a balcony. It did not look very safe to me. But I learned later that in a bombing no place was really safe, and that the Spaniards had two rather fatalistic theories about protection. One was during an air raid to go to the roof of a building and fall down with it if a bomb struck. The other was go to the ground floor and, in case of a hit, be buried at once under debris.

One could tell that Barcelona was jittery from the terrific bombing it had undergone the day before I arrived. But nothing happened during the first twenty-four hours I was there, so Guillén and I walked about, looking at the destruction and at the antiaircraft guns on most of the busy corners, the flower sellers on the tree-lined Ramblas, and the passing crowds everywhere, with folks clinging to the overcrowded street cars all day long. Sitting in the cafés, whenever the public radios started to blare out the latest war news, everybody would jump. Nerves were certainly on edge. But there were no planes overhead all day.

As Guillén and I sat at a sidewalk table on the Ramblas that afternoon, a dark young man passed, turned, looked back at me and spoke. He recognized me, he said, because he had heard me read my poems at the library in New York. He was a Puerto Rican named Roldan, who had come from Harlem to serve as an interpreter in Spain. At that moment he was on his way to a dance at a little club where the Cubans and other Spanish-speaking peoples from the Caribbean gathered. He invited us to come with him. The club had a beautiful courtyard and a little bar where rum drinks were mixed. The party that afternoon was in honor of the International Brigaders on leave, among them several Spanish-speaking Negroes and a colored Portugese. Catalonian soldiers and their girls mingled gaily with the Negro guests. And Guillén, lionized as Cuba's most famous poet, was in his element, surrounded by girls.

That night back at our hotel we knew it was wartime because, in the luxurious dining room with its tuxedoed waiters, there was only one fixed menu with no choice of food. The dinner was good, but not elaborate. Later we went to an outdoor café for coffee. Until midnight we sat watching the crowds strolling up and down the tiled sidewalks of the Ramblas. The fact that Barcelona was lightless did not keep people home on a warm evening. There was a wan bulb behind the bar inside to help the barman find his bottles, but other than that no visible light save for the stars shining brightly. The buildings were great grey shadows towering in the night, with windows shuttered everywhere and curtains drawn. There must be no visible lights in any windows to guide enemy aviators.

At midnight, the public radios on many corners began to blare the war news and people gathered in large groups to hear it. Then the café closed, and we went to the hotel. I had just barely gotten to my room and begun to undress when the low extended wail of a siren began, letting us know that Fascist planes were coming. They came, we had been told, from Mallorca across the sea at a terrific speed, dropped their bombs, then circled away into the night again. Quickly, I put on my shirt, passed Guillén's room, and together we started downstairs. Suddenly all the lights went out in the hotel. We heard people rushing down the stairs in the dark. A few had flashlights with them. Some were visibly frightened. In the lobby a single candle was burning, casting giantlike shadows on the walls. In an ever-increasing wail the siren sounded louder and louder, droning its deathly warning. Suddenly it stopped. By then the lobby was full of people, men, women and children, speaking in Spanish, English, French.

In the distance we heard a series of quick explosions.

"Bombs?" I asked.

"No, antiaircraft guns," a man explained.

Everyone became very quiet. Then we heard the guns go off again.

"Come here," a man called, leading the way. Several of us went out on the balcony where, in the dark, we could see the searchlights playing across the sky. Little round puffs of smoke from the antiaircraft shells floated against the stars. In the street a few women hurried along to public bomb-proof cellars.

Then for a long while nothing happened. No bombs fell. After about an hour, the lights suddenly came on in the hotel as a signal that the danger had ended. Evidently, the enemy planes had been driven away without having completed their mission. Everyone went back upstairs to bed. The night was quiet again. I put out my light, opened the window and, never being troubled with sleeplessness, I was soon sound asleep. The next thing I knew was that, with part of my clothes in my arms, I was running in the dark toward the stairs. A *terrific* explosion somewhere nearby had literally lifted me out of bed. Apparently I had slept through an alert, for almost all the other guests in the hotel had already assembled in the lobby, huddled in various stages of dress and undress. At the foot of the stairs I put my trousers on over my pajamas and sat down shaking like a leaf, evidently having been frightened to this dire extent while still asleep, because I had hardly realized I was afraid until I felt myself shaking. When I put one hand on the other, both hands were trembling. There were the sounds of what seemed like a major battle going on in the streets outside—but this was only the antiaircraft guns firing at the sky, so someone near me explained. Suddenly I developed the worst stomachache I've ever had in my life. I managed to find my way to a MEN'S ROOM about the time a distant explosion sounded, far away, yet near enough to cause the hotel to shake. When I came back, by the light of the single candle at the desk, I managed to find Guillén, sitting calmly like Buddha on a settee under a potted palm. He said, "*Ay, chico, eso es!*" Well, this is it! Which was of little comfort.

Gradually I began to be fully awake and less frightened, so I sat down, too, smoked a cigarette, and got acquainted with some of the other folks in the lobby. After perhaps a half hour, when the crackling of the antiaircraft batteries had died down, an all clear sounded, and the desk clerk said we might return to our beds. He blew out his candle before opening some of the French doors leading onto the balcony overlooking the Ramblas. Some of us went out on the balcony to see what was happening in the streets. An occasional military motor passed without lights, and a few people moved up and down—police and rescue workers, I supposed. As I stood there with the others a sudden crackle of shots rang out in our direction from across the corner square. Glass came down all over us from windows on the upper floors. A machine gun was firing directly at the hotel! We almost fell over each other getting back inside the lobby. Door and shutters were slammed again. Shortly some soldiers entered from the street and said that someone on an upper floor had turned on a light. (Their orders were to fire at any exposed light in any building.) Sternly they mounted the stairs in search of the offender. Later I learned that some foreigner (not knowing the rules) had turned on a bedside bulb after he had opened his window for air. So the guards simply blasted away at the lighted room. The frightened guest was severely reprimanded. And I had cause to quake all over again. It was quite a while before I went back to sleep that night.

Eventually, however, I got used to air raids in Spain—the Junkers, Heinkels, Savoias and Capronis going over—and the sound and the feel of bombs bursting. But I never got used to the alerts—those baleful, high, eerie, wailing sirens of warning.

Countee Cullen

(1903–1946)

A CONVENTIONAL POET IN the better sense of the word, Countee Cullen was a "disciple" of John Keats. He did not want to become a "Negro poet"; he was not interested, like Langston Hughes, in folk speech and rhythms. Cullen was a lyrical poet, and he wrote on the themes—death, love, the transitoriness of life—that lyrical poets have always written on. And yet most of Cullen's best poems are on race. Perhaps the finest statement of the then-popular alien-and-exile theme in black writing is found in his "Heritage."

Reared in Harlem as the adopted son of the Reverend Frederick A. Cullen, pastor of the Salem A.M.E. Church, Countee Cullen was educated at De Witt Clinton High School, where he began writing poetry; New York University, where he was elected to Phi Beta Kappa; and Harvard, where he earned his M.A.

During his sophomore year at N.Y.U., Cullen won the Witter Bynner Undergraduate Award for poetry. In 1926 he received the first Harmon Foundation Award in Literature for his brilliant first volume of verse, *Color,* which had been published the year before. And in 1928 he received a Guggenheim Fellowship for study and creative writing in Paris.

At different times in his life Cullen was an assistant editor of *Opportunity,* and literary editor of *The Crisis,* the official organ of the NAACP. His poems appeared in *Bookman, Century, Poetry, Harper's,* and other national periodicals, but Cullen's principal occupation was that of French teacher in the New York Public Schools.

In addition to the works already named, Countee Cullen produced the following volumes of poetry: *Copper Sun* (1927), *The Ballad of the Brown Girl* (1927), and *The Black Christ* (1929). In 1927 he edited an anthology of Negro American verse, *Caroling Dusk;* and in 1935 he made a translation of *Medea* which he published in *Medea and Other Poems.* Cullen also brought out two clever children's books: *The Lost Zoo* (1940) and two years later *My Lives and How I Lost Them* (*By Christopher Cat*). The first is largely verse, the second prose. *On These I Stand,* a volume of his selected poems, was published posthumously in 1947.

Countee Cullen wrote a single novel, *One Way to Heaven* (1932), a work which deserved more critical attention than it received. Although satirical in parts, it is a much more realistic picture of the New

Negro Renaissance Harlem than Claude McKay's exaggerated and one-sided picture in *Home to Harlem.* Cullen also collaborated with Arna Bontemps on a play, *God Sends Sunday,* which finally became the musical *St. Louis Woman.*

For critical comment on Cullen, see Stephen H. Bronz, *Roots of Negro Racial Consciousness* (1964).

YET DO I MARVEL

I doubt not God is good, well-meaning, kind,
And did He stoop to quibble could tell why
The little buried mole continues blind,
Why flesh that mirrors Him must some day die,
Make plain the reason tortured Tantalus
Is baited by the fickle fruit, declare
If merely brute caprice dooms Sisyphus
To struggle up a never-ending stair.
Inscrutable His ways are, and immune
To catechism by a mind too strewn
With petty cares to slightly understand
What awful brain compels His awful hand.
Yet do I marvel at this curious thing:
To make a poet black, and bid him sing!

INCIDENT

(For Eric Walrond)

Once riding in old Baltimore,
    Heart-filled, head-filled with glee,
I saw a Baltimorean
    Keep looking straight at me.

Now I was eight and very small,
    And he was no whit bigger,
And so I smiled, but he poked out
    His tongue, and called me, "Nigger."

I saw the whole of Baltimore
From May until December;
Of all the things that happened there
That's all that I remember.

PAGAN PRAYER

Not for myself I make this prayer,
But for this race of mine
That stretches forth from shadowed places
Dark hands for bread and wine.

For me, my heart is pagan mad,
My feet are never still,
But give them hearths to keep them warm
In homes high on a hill.

For me, my faith lies fallowing,
I bow not till I see,
But these are humble and believe;
Bless their credulity.

For me, I pay my debts in kind,
And see no better way,
Bless these who turn the other cheek
For love of you, and pray.

Our Father, God, our Brother, Christ—
So are we taught to pray;
Their kinship seems a little thing
Who sorrow all the day.

Our Father, God; our Brother, Christ,
Or are we bastard kin,
That to our plaints your ears are closed,
Your doors barred from within?

Our Father, God; our Brother, Christ,
Retrieve my race again;
So shall you compass this black sheep,
The pagan heart. Amen.

TRIBUTE

(To My Mother)

Because man is not virtuous in himself,
Nor kind, nor given to sweet charities,
Save goaded by the little kindling elf
Of some dear face it pleasures him to please;
Some men who else were humbled to the dust,
Have marveled that the chastening hand should stay
And never dreamed they held their lives in trust
To one the victor loved a world away.

So I, least noble of a churlish race,
Least kind of those by nature rough and crude,
Have at the intervention of your face
Spared him with whom was my most bitter feud
One moment, and the next, a deed more grand,
The helpless fly imprisoned in my hand.

FOR A LADY I KNOW

She even thinks that up in heaven
Her class lies late and snores,
While poor black cherubs rise at seven
To do celestial chores.

HERITAGE

What is Africa to me:
Cooper sun or scarlet sea,
Jungle star or jungle track,
Strong bronzed men, or regal black
Women from whose loins I sprang
When the birds of Eden sang?
One three centuries removed
From the scenes his fathers loved,

Spicy grove, cinnamon tree,
What is Africa to me?

So I lie, who all day long
Want no sound except the song
Sung by wild barbaric birds
Goading massive jungle herds,
Juggernauts of flesh that pass
Trampling tall defiant grass
Where young forest lovers lie
Plighting troth beneath the sky.
So I lie, who always hear
Though I cram against my ear
Both my thumbs, and keep them there,
Great drums beating through the air.
So I lie, whose fount of pride,
Dear distress, and joy allied,
Is my sombre flesh and skin,
With the dark blood dammed within
Like great pulsing tides of wine
That, I fear, must burst the fine
Channels of the chafing net
Where they surge and foam and fret.

Africa? A book one thumbs
Listlessly, till slumber comes.
Unremembered are her bats
Circling through the night, her cats
Crouching in the river reeds,
Stalking gentle flesh that feeds
By the river brink; no more
Does the bugle-throated roar
Cry that monarch claws have leapt
From the scabbards where they slept.
Silver snakes that once a year
Doff the lovely coats you wear,
Seek no covert in your fear
Lest a mortal eye should see;
What's your nakedness to me?
Here no leprous flowers rear
Fierce corollas in the air;
Here no bodies sleek and wet,
Dripping mingled rain and sweat,
Tread the savage measures of
Jungle boys and girls in love.

What is last year's snow to me,
Last year's anything? The tree
Budding yearly must forget
How its past arose or set—
Bough and blossom, flower, fruit,
Even what shy bird with mute
Wonder at her travail there,
Meekly labored in its hair.
One three centuries removed
From the scenes his fathers loved,
Spicy grove, cinnamon tree,
What is Africa to me?

So I lie, who find no peace
Night or day, no slight release
From the unremittent beat
Made by cruel padded feet
Walking through my body's street.
Up and down they go, and back,
Treading out a jungle track.
So I lie, who never quite
Safely sleep from rain at night—
I can never rest at all
When the rain begins to fall;
Like a soul gone mad with pain
I must match its weird refrain;
Ever must I twist and squirm,
Writhing like a baited worm,
While its primal measures drip
Through my body, crying, "Strip!
Doff this new exuberance.
Come and dance the Lover's Dance!"
In an old remembered way
Rain works on me night and day.

Quaint, outlandish heathen gods
Black men fashion out of rods,
Clay, and brittle bits of stone,
In a likeness like their own,
My conversion came high-priced;
I belong to Jesus Christ,
Preacher of humility;
Heathen gods are naught to me.

Father, Son, and Holy Ghost,
So I make an idle boast,

Jesus of the twice turned cheek,
Lamb of God, although I speak
With my mouth thus, in my heart
Do I play a double part.
Ever at thy glowing altar
Must my heart grow sick and falter,
Wishing He I served were black,
Thinking then it would not lack
Precedent of pain to guide it,
Let who would or might deride it;
Surely then this flesh would know
Yours had borne a kindred woe.
Lord, I fashion dark gods, too,
Daring even to give to You
Dark despairing features where,
Crowned with dark rebellious hair,
Patience wavers just so much as
Mortal grief compels, while touches
Quick and hot, of anger, rise
To smitten cheek and weary eyes.
Lord, forgive me if my need
Sometimes shapes a human creed.

All day long and all night through,
One thing only must I do:
Quench my pride and cool my blood,
Lest I perish in the flood.
Lest a hidden ember set
Timber that I thought was wet
Burning like the dryest flax,
Melting like the merest wax,
Lest the grave restore its dead.
Not yet has my heart or head
In the least way realized
They and I are civilized.

TO JOHN KEATS, POET. AT SPRINGTIME

I cannot hold my peace, John Keats;
There never was a spring like this;
It is an echo, that repeats
My last year's song and next year's bliss.

I know, in spite of all men say
Of Beauty, you have felt her most.
Yea, even in your grave her way
Is laid. Poor, troubled, lyric ghost,
Spring never was so fair and dear
As Beauty makes her seem this year.

I cannot hold my peace, John Keats,
I am as helpless in the toil
Of Spring as any lamb that bleats
To feel the solid earth recoil
Beneath his puny legs. Spring beats
Her tocsin call to those who love her,
And lo! the dogwood petals cover
Her breasts with drifts of snow, and sleek
White gulls fly screaming to her, and hover
About her shoulders, and kiss her cheek,
While white and purple lilacs muster
A strength that bears them to a cluster
Of color and odor; for her sake
All things that slept are now awake.

And you and I, shall we lie still,
John Keats, while Beauty summons us?
Somehow I feel your sensitive will
Is pulsing up some tremulous
Sap road of a maple tree, whose leaves
Grow music as they grow, since your
Wild voice is in them, a harp that grieves
For life that opens death's dark door.
Though dust, your fingers still can push
The Vision Splendid to a birth,
Though now they work as grass in the hush
Of the night on the broad sweet page of the earth.

"John Keats is dead," they say, but I
Who hear your full insistent cry
In bud and blossom, leaf and tree,
Know John Keats still writes poetry.
And while my head is earthward bowed
To read new life sprung from your shroud,
Folks seeing me must think it strange
That merely spring should so derange
My mind. They do not know that you,
John Keats, keep revel with me, too.

TO CERTAIN CRITICS

Then call me traitor if you must,
Shout treason and default!
Say I betray a sacred trust
Aching beyond this vault.
I'll bear your censure as your praise,
For never shall the clan
Confine my singing to its ways
Beyond the ways of man.

No racial option narrows grief,
Pain is no patriot,
And sorrow plaits her dismal leaf
For all as lief as not.
With blind sheep groping every hill,
Searching an oriflamme,
How shall the shepherd heart then thrill
To only the darker lamb?

Arna W. Bontemps

(b. 1902)

ARNA W. BONTEMPS, WHO was born in Alexandria, Louisiana, and reared in California, received his education at San Francisco Academy, Pacific Union College (B.A.), and the University of Chicago (M.A.). His poetry began to appear in numerous magazines in 1924. "Golgotha Is a Mountain" won the *Opportunity* contest in 1926; in 1927 Bontemps won the *Opportunity* contest again with "The Return" and *The Crisis* contest with "Nocturne at Bethesda."

Bontemps has taught in New York City and at Oakwood College in Huntsville, Alabama. For over twenty years he was the librarian at Fisk University (1943–1966), and since 1969 he has been curator of the James W. Johnson Collection at Yale University. A prolific writer, Bontemps has received two Rosenwald Fellowships (1938–39 and 1942–43) as well as the Jane Addams Children's Book Award (1956).

Since 1931, when Arna Bontemps published *God Sends Sunday*, a novel, he has devoted most of his time to prose works. His many volumes include: *You Can't Pet a Possum* (1934); *Black Thunder* (1936); *Sadfaced Boy* (1937); *Drums of Dusk* (1939); *One Hundred Years of Negro Freedom* (1961); and *Anyplace But Here* (1966). He is co-author of a study on Negro migration, *They Seek a City* (1945) and with Countee Cullen, co-author of a play, *St. Louis Woman.* Bontemps edited *American Negro Poetry* (1963) and a children's anthology, *Golden Slippers* (1941). He and Langston Hughes co-edited such works as *The Poetry of the Negro* (1949) and *The Book of Negro Folklore* (1958).

The following poems are from *Personals* (1963).

A BLACK MAN TALKS OF REAPING

I have sown beside all waters in my day.
I planted deep, within my heart the fear
That wind or fowl would take the grain away.
I planted safe against this stark, lean year.

I scattered seed enough to plant the land
In rows from Canada to Mexico,
But for my reaping only what the hand
Can hold at once is all that I can show.

Yet what I sowed and what the orchard yields
My brother's sons are gathering stalk and root,
Small wonder then my children glean in fields
They have not sown, and feed on bitter fruit.

MIRACLES

Doubt no longer miracles,
This spring day makes it plain
A man may crumble into dust
And straightway live again

A jug of water in the sun
Will easy turn to wine
If love is stopping at the well
And love's brown arms entwine.

And you who think him only man,
I tell you faithfully
That I have seen Christ clothed in rain
Walking on the sea.

NOCTURNE AT BETHESDA

I thought I saw an angel flying low,
I thought I saw the flicker of a wing
Above the mulberry trees; but not again.
Bethesda sleeps. This ancient pool that healed
A host of bearded Jews does not awake.

This pool that once the angels troubled does not move
No angel stirs it now, no Saviour comes
With healing in His hands to raise the sick
And bid the lame man leap upon the ground.

The golden days are gone. Why do we wait
So long upon the marble steps, blood
Falling from our open wounds? and why
Do our black faces search the empty sky?

Is there something we have forgotten? some precious thing
We have lost, wandering in strange lands?

There was a day, I remember now,
I beat my breast and cried, "Wash me God,
Wash me with a wave of wind upon
The barley; O quiet One, draw near, draw near!
Walk upon the hills with lovely feet
And in the waterfall stand and speak.

"Dip white hands in the lily pool and mourn
Upon the harps still hanging in the trees
Near Babylon along the river's edge,
But oh, remember me, I pray, before
The summer goes and rose leaves lose their red."

The old terror takes my heart, the fear
Of quiet waters and of faint twilights.
There will be better days when I am gone
And healing pools where I cannot be healed.
Fragrant stars will gleam forever and ever
Above the place where I lie desolate.

Yet I hope, still I long to live.
And if there can be returning after death
I shall come back. But it will not be here;
If you want me you must search for me
Beneath the palms of Africa. Or if
I am not there then you may call to me
Across the shining dunes, perhaps I shall
Be following a desert caravan.

I may pass through centuries of death
With quiet eyes, but I'll remember still
A jungle tree with burning scarlet birds.
There is something I have forgotten, some precious thing.
I shall be seeking ornaments of ivory,
I shall be dying for a jungle fruit.

You do not hear, Bethesda.
O still green water in a stagnant pool!
Love abandoned you and me alike.
There was a day you held a rich full moon
Upon your heart and listened to the words

Of men now dead and saw the angels fly.
There is a simple story on your face;
Years have wrinkled you. I know, Bethesda!
You are sad. It is the same with me.

SOUTHERN MANSION

Poplars are standing there still as death
And ghosts of dead men
Meet their ladies walking
Two by two beneath the shade
And standing on the marble steps.

There is a sound of music echoing
Through the open door
And in the field there is
Another sound tinkling in the cotton:
Chains of bondmen dragging on the ground.

The years go back with an iron clank,
A hand is on the gate,
A dry leaf trembles on the wall.
Ghosts are walking.
They have broken roses down
And poplars stand there still as death.

THE RETURN

Once more, listening to the wind and rain,
Once more, you and I, and above the hurting sound
Of these comes back the throbbing of remembered rain,
Treasured rain falling on dark ground.
Once more, huddling birds upon the leaves
And summer trembling on a withered vine.
And once more, returning out of pain,
The friendly ghost that was your love and mine.

2

Darkness brings the jungle to our room:
The throb of rain is the throb of muffled drums.
Darkness hangs our room with pendulums
Of vine and in the gathering gloom

Our walls recede into a denseness of
Surrounding trees. This is a night of love
Retained from those lost nights our fathers slept
In huts; this is a night that must not die.
Let us keep the dance of rain our fathers kept
And tread our dreams beneath the jungle sky.

3

And now the downpour ceases.
Let us go back once more upon the glimmering leaves
And as the throbbing of the drums increases
Shake the grass and dripping boughs of trees.
A dry wind stirs the palm; the old tree grieves.

Time has charged the years: the old days have returned.

Let us dance by metal waters burned
With gold of moon, let us dance
With naked feet beneath the young spice trees.
What was that light, that radiance
On your face?—something I saw when first
You passed beneath the jungle tapestries?

A moment we pause to quench our thirst
Kneeling at the water's edge, the gleam
Upon your face is plain: you have wanted this.
Let us go back and search the tangled dream
And as the muffled drum-beats throb and miss
Remember again how early darkness comes
To dreams and silence to the drums.

Let us go back into the dusk again,
Slow and sad-like following the track
Of blowing leaves and cool white rain
Into the old gray dream, let us go back.
Our walls close about us we lie and listen
To the noise of the street, the storm and the driven birds.
A question shapes your lips, your eyes glisten
Retaining tears, but there are no more words.

Rudolph Fisher

(1897—1934)

RUDOLPH FISHER, A NATIVE of Washington, D.C., spent his childhood and youth in Providence, Rhode Island, where he attended Brown University and received both a B.A. and an M.A. He took a medical degree at Howard University and, following further study at Columbia, settled into the private practice of medicine in Harlem, just at the time when Harlem was becoming a social and cultural Mecca.

Unembittered, and one of the wittiest of the Renaissance group, Rudolph Fisher was among the first to light up the dark realities of Negro life with humor. In 1925 he won a *Crisis* short story contest with "High Yaller," and after that his stories began appearing regularly in the *Atlantic Monthly*, the *American Mercury, Survey Graphic*, and *Story*. They are good stories, but Fisher's style is somewhat stiff, and his use of the Negro idiom, Harlemese, is self-conscious. Yet the humor is there and also in his two novels, *The Walls of Jericho* (1928) and *The Conjure Man Dies* (1932).

Much of Fisher's short fiction has been anthologized in *Best Short Stories by Afro-American Writers: 1928–1950, Black Voices*, and *The Negro Caravan*.

HIGH YALLER

1

The timekeeper's venomous whistle killed the ball in its flight, halfway to the basket. There was a triumphant bedlam. From the walls of Manhattan Casino impatient multitudes swarmed on to the immense floor, congratulating, consoling, gibing; pouring endlessly from the surrounding terrace, like long restrained torrents at last transcending a dam; sweeping tumultuously in from all sides, till the dance floor sank beneath a sounding flood of dark-skinned people, submerged to its furthest corners save the distant platform that gave the orchestra refuge, like a raft. A sudden blare of music cut the uproar. The turbulence gradually ordered itself into dense, crawling currents, sluggish as jammed traffic, while the din of voices at length reluctantly surrendered to the rhythmic swish-swash of shuffling feet.

Reprinted from *The Crisis* with the permission of the National Association for the Advancement of Colored People.

Looking down from a balcony on that dark mass of heads, close together as buckshot, Evelyn Brown wondered how they all managed to enjoy it. Why must they always follow a basket-ball game with a dance?—the one pleasurable enough, the other mob-torture, she knew.

"Game?" challenged MacLoed.

She couldn't refuse her escort, of course. "If you are."

They descended and struck out like swimmers in the sea. MacLeod surrounded her as closely as a lifesaver. She knew that he had to, but she hated it—this mere hugging to music, this acute consciousness of her partner's body. The air was vile—hot, full of breath and choking perfume. You were forever avoiding, colliding, marking time on the same spot. So insulating was the crush that you might sway for several minutes near a familiar couple, even recognize their voices, yet catch only the merest glimpse of their vanishing faces.

Something of the sort was happening now. Evelyn heard someone say her name, and the mordant intonation with the succeeding spiteful snatch-phrases made her forget the physical unpleasantness of the moment.

"Evelyn Brown?—Hmph!—got yellow fever—I know better—color struck, I tell you—girls she goes around with—all lily whites—even the fellows—Mac to-day—pass for white anywhere—Jeff, Rickmond, Stanley Hall, all of 'em—You? Shoot! You don't count—you're crazy 'bout high yallers anyhow."

The words were engulfed. Evelyn had not needed to look. Mayme Jackson's voice was unmistakable.

The dance number ended on an unresolved, interrogative chord that set off an explosion of applause. Jay Martin, who had just been defending Evelyn against Mayme's charge, spied the former's fluff of fair hair through several intervening thicknesses of straight and straightened black, and, dragging Mayme by the arm, he made for the other couple.

"'Now say what you said about Evelyn!" he dared Mayme, mock-maliciously, quite unaware that Evelyn already knew.

"Sweetest old thing in the world," came Mayme's tranquil purr.

"Rake in the chips," gasped Jay. "Your pot." He addressed Evelyn. "How about the next wrestle?"

There was a ready exchange of partners. The orchestra struck up an air from a popular Negro comedy: "Yaller Gal's Gone Out o' Style." Soon the two couples were urged apart in increasingly divergent currents.

"Black sea," commented Jay.

But Evelyn was thoughtful. "Jay?"

"Nobody else."

"I heard what Mayme said."

"You did? Aw, heck—don't pay any attention to that kid. She's a nut."

"I'm not so sure she isn't right, Jay."

"Right? About what?"

"I've been thinking over my best friends. They're practically all 'passing' fair. Any one of them could pass—for a foreigner, anyway."

"Me, for instance," he grinned. "Prince Woogy-boogy of Abyssinia."

"I'm afraid you prove the rule."

He was serious. "Well, what of it?"

"Oh, I don't mean I've done it intentionally. I never realized it till just now. But, just as Mayme says, it looks bad."

"Hang what Mayme says. She's kind o' gone on yaller men, herself. See the way she melted into Mac's shirtfront! Hung round his neck like a chest-protector. Didn't drape herself over *me* that way."

"Jay! You're as bad as she is."

"That's what she said."

"What do you mean?"

"Claims I fall only for pinks."

"Oh. I didn't mean that."

"Neither did she. Point is, there aren't any more dark girls. Skin bleach and rouge have wiped out the strain. The blacks have turned sealskin, the sealskins are high-brown, the high-browns are all yaller, and the yallers are pink. How's a bird going to fall for what ain't?"

They jazzed on a while in noisy silence. Evelyn's tone was surprisingly bitter when at last she spoke again:

"I wish I looked like Mayme." Astonished, Jay stared at her as she went on: "A washerwoman can make half a million dollars turning dark skins light. Why doesn't someone learn how to turn light skins dark?"

And now, in addition to staring, he saw her: the averted blue eyes, the fine lips about to quiver, the delicate, high-bridged nose, the white cheeks, colorless save for the faintest touch, the incredible tawny, yellow-flecked, scintillant hair,—an almost crystal-line creature, as odd in this dark company as a single sapphire in jet. He was quick to comprehend. "I know a corner—let's sit out the rest," he suggested.

When they achieved their place in a far end of the terrace, the orchestra was outdoing itself in the encore. One of the members sang through a megaphone in a smoky, half-talking voice:

> *"Oh Miss Pink thought she knew her stuff,*
> *But Miss High Brown has called her bluff."*

When the encore ended, the dancers demanded yet another. The rasp of syncopation and the ceaseless stridor of soles mingled, rose about the two refugees, seeming to wall them in, so that presently they felt alone together.

"Jay, can you imagine what it's like to be colored and look white?"

He tried to be trivial. "Very convenient at times, I should think."

"But oftener unbearable. That song—imagine—everyone looking at you—laughing at you. And Mayme Jackson—'yellow fever'! Can I help it?—Jeff—Rickmond—Stanley Hall—yes, they're light. But what can I do? I like the others. I'd be glad to go places with them. But they positively avoid me."

"I don't, Ev."

"No, you don't, Jay." But her bitterness recaptured her. "Oh, I've heard them talking: 'There goes Evelyn Brown—queen of the lily-whites—nothing brown about her but her name'!" A swiftly matured determination rendered her suddenly so grim that it seemed, fragile as she was, something about her must break. "Jay, no one's going to accuse me of jim-crowing again!"

"Shucks. What do you care as long as you don't mean to?"

"I'm not only not going to mean to. I'm not going to. I'm going to see to it that I don't."

"What the deuce—by cutting your gang?"

"No. By cultivating the others."

"Oh."

"Jay—will you help me?"

"Help you? Sure. How?"

"Come to see me oftener."

"Good night! Don't you see enough of me at the office every day?"

"Come oftener. Take me places when you're not too broke. Rush me!"

He grinned as he perceived her purpose. "Doggone good stunt!" he said slowly, with increasingly enthusiastic approval. "Blessed if I wouldn't like to see you put it over, Ev. It'll show Mayme something, anyhow."

"It'll show me something, too."

"You? What?"

She was about to answer when a sharp, indecent epithet rent the wall of noise that had until then isolated them. Looking involuntarily up, Jay saw two youngsters, quarreling vituperatively. They were too close to be ignored, and, since dancing was at its height, no one else was about.

"Excuse me a second," he said, rising before Evelyn could protest. The pair were but a few feet away. The evident aggressor was a hard-looking little black youth of indefinite age,—perhaps sixteen actual years, plus the accumulated bonus of worldly wisdom which New York pays its children. He grew worse, word by word. Approaching, Jay spoke sharply, in a low voice so that Evelyn might not hear:

"Cut out that gutter-talk, boy!"

"Aw, go to hell!"

Jay stopped, less amazed than aggravated. He knew his Harlem adolescent, but he was not quite sure what to do with it. Meanwhile he was being advised: "This is a horse-race, big boy. No jackasses allowed!"

He seized the lad firmly by the shoulder and said, "Son, if you don't cover that garbage-trap of yours——" but the boy flung away and defied him in a phrase both loud and ugly. Thoroughly angered, Jay clapped one hand over the offending mouth and, catching the youngster around the waist with the other, forcibly propelled him through a tangle of empty, spindle-legged chairs to a place where two big policemen, one black and one red, were complacently watching the dancers. Here he released him with "Now—talk."

The boy scowled with wrath and impotence. So outraged in the street, he would have found a stone to throw. Now only a retaliative speech was left him, and the nearness of the law attenuated even that:

"Aw 'ight! Showin' off before 'at ole 'fay gal, huh? Aw 'ight, y' pink-chaser. Ah'm goan put y' both in." And he sidled darkly off, pulling at his disadjusted collar.

Evelyn, out of earshot, followed it all with her eyes. "Mac wouldn't have done that," she mused as she saw Jay turn from the boy and start back toward her. "Mac would have pretended he didn't hear." And before Jay reached her, she had decided something: "I certainly like Jay Martin. He's so—white."

2

Over One Hundred and Thirty-fourth Street's sidewalks between Fifth and Lenox Avenues Jay Martin's roller-skates had rattled and whirred in the days when that was the northern boundary of Negro Harlem. He had grown as the colony grew, and now he could just recall the time when his father, a pioneer preacher, had been forever warning him never to cross Lenox Avenue and never to go beyond One Hundred and Thirty-fifth Street; a time when no Negroes lived on or near Seventh Avenue and when it would have been almost suicidal for one to appear unarmed on Irish Eighth.

School had been a sucession of fist-fights with white boys who called him nigger, until, when he reached the upper grades, the colored boys began to outnumber the white; from that time until high school, pitched battles superseded individual contests, and he ran home bruised less often. His high school record had been good, and his father, anxious to make a physician of him, had sent him on to college. At the end of his third year, however, the looming draft menace, combined with the chance of a commission in the army, had urged him into a training camp at Des Moines.

He had gone to France as a lieutenant. When he returned, un-harmed, he found his father fatally ill and his mother helpless. Further study out of the question, he had taken his opportunity with a Negro real estate firm, and for five years now he had been actively concerned in black Harlem's extension, the spread whose beginnings his earlier years had witnessed.

About Evelyn, of course, there had been hypothesis:

"Looks might funny to me when a woman Jennie Browns' color has a yaller-headed young one white as Evelyn."

"Daddy was white, so I understan'."

"Huh. An' her mammy, too, mos' likely. 'At's de way dese rich white folks do. Comes a wile oat dey doan want, dey ups an' gives it to one de servants—to adopt."

"Oh, I dunno. How come she couldn't been married to some white man 'nuther? Dey's plenty sich, right hyeh in Harlem."

"Plenty whut? Plenty common law, maybe. You know d' ain' no se'f-respectin' white man gonna——"

"Well, doan make no diff'nce. Cain' none of us go but so fur back in our fam'ly hist'ry 'fo we stops. An' doan nobody have t' ask us why we stops. We jes' stops. Evelyn's a good girl. Smart—works regular an' makes mo 'out o' dem real estate niggers 'n she'd make in Miss Ann's kitchen. Bad 's her mother's asthma's gittin', no tellin' whut they'd do if 'twasn't f' Evelyn's job an' dem two women lodgers."

"Oh, I ain' sayin' nuthin' 'gins 'em. Only seem like to me—dey's a white man in de woodpile somewha'."

Her own singularity had become conscious early in Evelyn's life. There crept often into her mind of late an old, persistent recollection. She and Sookie Johnson, seven-year-old playmates, had been playing jacks on the front stoop. There arose a dispute as to whose turn it was. Sookie owned the ball and Evelyn the jacks; neither would surrender her possession to the other, and the game was deadlocked. Whereupon, the spiteful Sookie had resorted to abuse:

"Y' ole yaller thing, you! My mother say y' cain't 'speck nuthin' f'm yaller niggers nohow!"

Evelyn had thrown the jacks into Sookie's face and ran heartbroken to her mother. Why didn't she have kinky hair and dark brown skin like Sookie's? "Why, honey, you're beautiful," her mother had com-forted her. "Folks 'll call you names long as you live. They're just jealous, that's all."

Thus fortified, Evelyn had come to maturity, finding her mother's prophecy ever and again true. "They're just jealous" was but a forti-fication, however; within it Evelyn's spirit was still vulnerable, and she knew that under constant fire this stronghold could not stand forever. Mayme Jackson's thrust-in-the-back culminated what Sookie's sneer had begun. Evelyn felt her mother's defence crumbling rapidly and alarmingly, and her appeal to Jay Martin was a rather desperate effort to establish a defence of her own.

They sat now in the front room of her flat; a room to full of mock-mahogany furniture about to collapse; a room with gas light and a tacked-down carpet, with flower-figured wall-paper and a marble-topped walnut table in one corner, bearing a big brown morocco-bound Bible.

"Jay, will you?"

"Remember the time I pulled your hair in Sunday-School?"

"I'm going to pull your ears if you don't answer me!"

"Did you say something?"

"You make me tired."

"Aw, for Pete's sake, Ev, I can't take you to that dump."

"Have the last two weeks frozen your nerve?"

"No—but——"

"Well, this isn't like the others, you know. This is a colored place."

"But why go there? Let's go to Broadway's or Happy's."

"No. I want to see something new. Why isn't Hank's decent, anyway? It can't be any worse than the Hole in the Wall."

"Much worse. Regular rat-trap. No gentleman would take a lady ——"

"You flatter us. Let's don't be a gentleman and lady tonight. I want to see the rat-trap."

"Why, Ev, the place was raided only last week!"

"You can't scare me that way. If it was it'll be all the safer this week."

"Lord! You girls know it all."

"I don't know anything about Hank's."

"But I'm trying to tell you——"

"Seeing is believing."

"There's nothing to see."

She introduced strategy. "All right. I guess Mac won't be so hard to persuade."

"Ev—please—for Pete's sake don't let anybody take you to that——"

"Jay, I'd really hate to have to go with anybody but you." He was growing helpless. "Just the tiniest peep into the place, Jay. We won't stay—cross my liver."

"Your mother wouldn't like it."

"Come here." She led him by the arm down the long hallway to the dining-room, where her mother was sewing.

"You may go any place you please, if you go with Jay," smiled Mrs. Brown.

Hank's at first glance, presented nothing unique: a sedate old house in an elderly row of houses with high entrances, several steps above the sidewalk; houses that had once been private, but now, trapped in an extending matrix of business, stoically accepted their fates as real estate offices, printing shops and law rooms. Here and there a card peeped around the corner of a window and whispered, "Rooms"; but not the most suspicious eye would have associated those timid invitations with the bold vertical electric sign projecting over the doorway of the one lighted building in the row. Great letters, one above another, blazed the word "Café"; smaller horizontal ones across the top read "Hank's", and others across the bottom "Cabaret".

"This doesn't look so bad," commented Evelyn as they approached. "Police station right in the same block."

"Yes—convenient."

Several men stood about on the sidewalk, smoking and talking. One of these, a white man, looked sharply at Jay and Evelyn as they mounted the steps and entered.

"Why, this is like any restaurant," said Evelyn. "Just a lot of tables and folks eating."

"Only a blind," explained Jay. "The real thing is downstairs."

A dinner-coated attendant came toward them. "I'm sorry. Everything's gone in the cabaret. Would you care to wait a few minutes?"

Jay, eager for an excuse to flee, looked at Evelyn; but the blue eyes said, "Please," and he nodded. "Very well."

"This way, then."

They were led up a narrow flight of padded stairs, along a carpeted hallway with several mysterious closed doors on either side, and finally into a little room near the end. Against one wall of the room was a table with two chairs, and against the opposite a flat couch with two or three cushions. Curtains draped the one window, facing the door. The table was bare except for a small lamp with a parchment shade of orange and black, yielding a warm, dim light.

"M—m!" exclaimed Evelyn. "Cozy!"

"We can serve you here if you like," suggested the attendant.

"No, thanks," Jay answered quickly. "We'll wait."

The attendant seemed to hesitate a moment. Then, "All right," he said. "I'll let you know as soon as there's space in the cabaret." He went out and closed the door.

Evelyn was alive with interest. "Spiffy, isn't it?" She sat down on one of the chairs and looked about. "Couldn't get lost, could you?"

Jay thoughtfully took the other chair.

"You might," he said absently.

"What are you talking about? Goodness, what a lot of fun you're having!"

"I don't like this, that's a fact."

"What's wrong?"

Jay looked and noted that the door locked from within. He went over to the window, pulled the shade aside a crack, and made out the skeleton of a fire-escape in the darkness outside.

"Oh, nothing", he said, returning to his seat. "Not a thing."

"Heavens, you give me the shivers! What is it?"

He was not eager to answer. "I'm not sure but—I believe—that bird thinks you're ofay."

"White? What difference would that make?"

"Well, I'll tell you, Ev. This place, like some you already know about, has a mixed patronage, see? Part jigs, part ofays. That's perfectly all right as long as the jigs keep to their own parties and the ofays to theirs. But as soon as they begin to come mixed, trouble starts. The colored men don't like to see white men with colored women and the white men don't like to see colored men with white women. So the management avoids it. I don't believe that house-man was telling the truth when he said there was no room in the cabaret. It's too early in the evening and it's not a busy night. Fact is, the place is probably half full of ofays, and he figured that if we went down there together some drunk would get fly and I'd bounce him on the nose and right away there'd be a hullabaloo. So he took a chance that maybe we were more interested in each other than in the cabaret anyhow, and sidetracked us off up here."

"But he said he'd let us know—"

"Of course. He thought we'd be tickled silly to be in one of these rooms alone; but after I refused to be served up here, what else could he say? I don't think he has any more idea of coming back than Jack Johnson."

"Then what does he expect you to do?"

"Get tired waiting and beat it."

"Oh." A depressed silence. Then a tragic diminuendo: "Lord, what a misfit I am!"

He was contrite at once. "I'm a bum. I shouldn't have told you. I don't know—maybe I'm wrong. We're here, so let's wait awhile and see."

"Jay, if only I were one thing or the other! You can't imagine—"

He absolutely could not answer. From somewhere below a thin strain drifted to their ears, like a snicker: "Yaller Gal's Gone Out o' Style".

Jay rose. "Let's breeze. That shine isn't coming back."

"All right. I'm sorry to be such a nuisance."

"You're not the nuisance. It's—folks."

They went down the soft-carpeted hallway. Strange, low sounds behind the closed doors seemed to hush apprehensively as they approached and revive after they passed. Once a shrill laugh was abruptly cut off as if by a stifling hand. There was a thick atmosphere of suppression, a sense of unspoken fears and half-drawn breaths and whispers.

As they reached the head of the padded stairs they saw someone hurrying up and drew aside to let him pass. It was a youth in a white coat, bent on some errand. He looked at them as he went by. They resumed their course and proceeded down the stairs; but the boy halted in his, and turned to look again. Immediately, he left off his errand, and waiting until he heard the front door close behind them, retraversed the staircase. A minute later he was on the sidewalk talking in an undertone to the white man who had so sharply observed Evelyn and Jay when they entered, and who now stood smoking still, following their departure with his eyes.

"Ah know 'at sucker", scowled the little black youth. "Collects rents f' Hale an' Barker. See 'at 'fay wid 'im? Seen 'im pick 'uh up pre' near two weeks ago at Manhattan Casino."

The white man puffed a minute, while the boy looked up at him, side-long, expectant. "Hale and Barker, huh?—Hmph! All right, Shorty. I'll keep my eye on 'im. If you're on, I'll fix y' up as usual."

"'At's the time papa." And the boy too stood eyeing the disappearing pair, an imp of malice and satisfaction.

3

A young man leaned nonchalantly on the high foot of Jay's wooden bed, grinning goodnaturedly at him; a young man who looked exactly like Jay, feature for feature, with one important exception: his skin was white.

"Who in hell are you?" asked Jay.

"What you would be if you could," came the prompt, pleasant response.

"Liar."

"Straight stuff, brother. Think of the heights you might rise to if you were I."

"Hell!" grunted Jay.

"Eventually, of course. But I mean meanwhile. Why, now you'd be in a big firm downtown, on your way to wealth. Or you might be a practicing physician—your old man could have kept you out of the draft."

"Oh, well, I'm not doing so worse."

"No, nor so better. And then there's Evelyn."

"What about Evelyn? Why, I wouldn't even know her."

"You'd know somebody like her. Don't kid yourself, boy. You like 'em pink. Remember Paris?"

"You lie like a bookmaker. I like 'em intelligent. If they happen to be bright on the outside, too, why of course, I don't bar 'em."

"No—of course not." The sarcastic caller paused a thoughtful moment. "I've got a jawful of advice for you, old-timer."

"Swallow it and choke."

"Now listen. Don't you get to liking Evelyn, see. She's too damned white."

"What of it?"

"Be yourself, son. You ask me that, after these last two weeks?"

Jay reached up and wiped a mosquito from his forehead and smacked at another singing into his ear. They irritated him. "I'll like whoever I damn please!" he flared.

"Don't get high, now," soothed the other. "I'm only warning you. Pull up on the emergency before something hits you. That girl's too fair for comfort."

"But I like her."

The other disregarded this. "You're too dark, buddy. You're ultra-violet anyhow, alone. Beside her you become absolute black—invisible. The lady couldn't see you with an arc-lamp."

"Shucks! Evelyn doesn't care."

"You're wrong there. She does. She can't help it. But she doesn't want to, so she tries hard to make herself believe she doesn't. She takes up with you, tells herself how much she likes you, invites all sorts of embarrassments upon both of you. She might even marry you. It's like taking bad medicine she thinks she's got to take and telling herself it's sweet. She figures it's better to gulp it down than to sip it, and it's better to say it's sweet than to make faces."

"Well, maybe. But I'm just conceited enough to think she likes me."

"Of course she does. I'm not talking about you. I'm talking about your color. If you were I, now, she'd jump at you."

"Humph! I don't see her jumping at MacLoed."

"Mac isn't either of us, buddy. He hasn't got a thing but his looks, and Evelyn's too wise to fall for that alone."

"There are others."

"None who can make her forget what she's trying to do. She thinks it's a sort of duty to be colored, so she's going to make a thorough job of it—do it up brown, you might say. See? The only man that could unscramble her would be a real white man. She's not going to compromise."

"You're too deep for me. But I don't believe she cares about the color of a fellow's skin."

"You don't? Well, stay away from her anyhow."

"How come?"

"To save her feelings. Every time you two go out together you're in torture. Everybody stares at you—jigs and ofays both. You've tried it now for two weeks. What's happened? The first night you went to Coney Island and nearly got yourself mobbed. A couple of days later you went into an ice-cream parlor on One Hundred and Twenty-Fifth Street, a place where Evelyn goes anytime she likes, and the proprietor had the nerve to tell you *your* presence hurt his business. Then how about that crowd of jigs on the subway? And last night, when you wanted to get up and punch that shine waiter in the ear because he gave Evelyn the once over and then rolled his eyes at you behind her back, as much as to say, 'Oh, boy! How I envy you!'—and she looking at him all the time in the mirror! Tonight caps it all. You go out to enjoy yourself in a 'colored' place, and get jim-crowed by a man of your own color who's afraid to let the two of you be seen. Do you think Evelyn enjoys a string of things like that?"

"She enjoys 'em as much as I do."

"But it isn't the same. When people look at you, it's just with surprise. All their look says is, 'Wonder what that nigger is doing with a white woman?' But when they look at her, it's with contempt. They say, 'Humph! What a cheap drab she must be to tag around with a nigger!' No matter whether it's true or not. Do you suppose she enjoys being looked at like that?"

Jay was silent. Sounds came from the street below into his open window; an empty Coney Island bus, rumbling, clattering, shrieking, eager to get in before daybreak; gay singing of a joy-riding chorus, swelling, consummating, dying away; the night-clear whistle of a lone, late straggler—"Yaller Gal's Gone Out o' Style".

"What do you expect me to do about it?" he finally asked.

"Ease out. See less and less of her. When you breeze away for your vacation, forget to write."

"Simple, ain't it?"

"Quite." The devil straightened up. "And now that that's settled, suppose you go to sleep a while."

"Suppose you go to hell," suggested Jay glumly.

"With pleasure. See you again."

Jay closed his smarting eyes. His caller departed into the clothespress or the hall or up the airshaft, he wasn't sure where; he knew only that when again he looked about, he was alone.

Evelyn Brown, too, lay in bed, debating with a visitor—a sophisticated young woman who sat familiarly on the edge of the counterpane and hugged her knees as she talked, and who might have been Evelyn over again, save for a certain bearing of self-assurance which the latter entirely lacked.

"Well, you've tried it," said this visitor. "See what a mess you've made of it."

"I wish you'd let me alone."

"I think too much of you, dear. And you're thinking too much of Jay. Surely the last two weeks have shown you how impossible that is."

"Two weeks isn't a long enough test."

"Quite long enough. The only place you and Jay could be happy together would be on a desert island that nobody could find. You can't go to a single place together without sooner or later wishing the ground would swallow you."

"Oh, I'd get hardened to it."

"Would that be happiness? And even if you did, he wouldn't. You don't think he enjoys all this, do you?"

"No, I suppose not."

"No. And don't think he's dumb enough to put himself into it for life, either."

"He cares enough to, I think."

"Then you've got to care enough not to let him."

"How?"

"Drop him."

"I can't."

"You must. Don't you see now why you lily-whites seek each other? It's self-protection. Whether you do it consciously or not, you're really trying to prevent painful embarrassment."

"But I can't just shut myself away from everyone who happens to be a little darker than I am. If I did it before I didn't realize it, and I wasn't to blame. But if I do it now, intentionally, I'm just drawing the color-line, and that wouldn't be right. What can I do?"

Her visitor smiled. "Do? Get out. Pass. What else?"

"That's impossible. There's mother. Wherever I'd go I'd have to take her, and she couldn't pass for anything but American Negro—"

Her protest was drowned in her visitor's laughter. It was harsh, strident laughter, like the suddenly stifled outburst she'd heard at Hank's that night. It was long, loud laughter that left the visitor breathless, panting pitiably.

Of a sudden Evelyn sat upright, fearfully aware that the laughter of her dream had merged into something real and close. She listened a moment. It was her mother in the next room. Asthma again.

She met both the women lodgers in the hall, frightened, helpless.

"Did you hear her?"

Shortly Evelyn hurried from her mother's room, leaving the two women with her. She slipt on as little as she dared and sped out to get a physician.

A half hour passed before she returned with one. She noted a bright light in the front room and hastened to it thinking the two women had taken her mother there for air; but she found only the two of them, huddled together on the sofa, shivering in their bathrobes, with something close to panic in their eyes.

4

Jimmy MacLoed, red-eyed, stretchy, disconsolate, and broke, all the event of a prolonged and fatal night of stud-poker, got up at noon-time, dressed, and strolled languidly into the street, wondering from whom he could bum four bits for breakfast. At the corner of One Hundred and Thirty-Fifth Street and the Avenue he encountered Jay Martin, hurrying to lunch. This was luck, for Jay always had bucks.

"See me go for breakfast?" he asked.

"No," grinned Jay, "but I'll add it to the five I'm by you already."

Dick's lunchroom seemed to have been designed so that the two waitresses could serve everybody without moving from where they stood. You could pass from the little front door to your stool before the counter without colliding with someone only when there was no one else there. Many a patron had unexpectedly thrust his knife further into his mouth than he intended because some damn fool, rushing out, squeezed between him and the wall. But one of the waitresses was pretty; and the ham with your eggs was cut thick, not shaved; and the French fried potatoes were really French fried, not boiled ones warmed over in grease. Jay and MacLoed considered themselves lucky to find two of the dozen stools still unoccupied.

They gave their orders and rested their elbows on the counter while the waitress that wasn't pretty threw down some pewter implements before them.

"Too bad about Evelyn's old lady, huh?" said MacLoed.

Jay became grave. "Too bad about Evelyn."

"Evelyn? Wha' d' y' mean?"

"Nobody's seen her since the funeral."

"No? Only three days. Maybe she's gone off for a rest."

"Didn't leave any notice at the office."

"Think she went dippy and jumped in the river or somethin'?"

"No. But I think she's jumped out of Harlem."

"You mean—passin'?"

"I don't know. The last time I saw her she was sick enough to do anything. Those two women roomers wouldn't stay in the house another night. None of her friends would either, even after her mother was safe in the undertaker's. She had three rotten days of it, except when my mother was there. Nobody much went to the funeral. I sent the only flowers. Next day, my mother went around to see how she was making out and found nobody home.—There hasn't been, since."

"Didn't leave word with nobody, huh?"

"Nope."

" 'S funny. 'D she have any relations?"

"Nope."

"Hm! Then that's what she's doin' all right."

"Passing?"

"Yea." Mac contemplated the ham and eggs that the homely waitress had just slid between his elbows. "Don't blame her. I'd do the same thing if I didn't have so damn much brownskin family."

"Why?"

"Why?—Why not? Wouldn't you?"

"Be white if I could?" Jay paid the waitress. "I don't know."

"The hell you don't. What would you be afraid of? Meetin' somebody? Hell! Don't see 'em. If they jump you, freeze 'em.—But you'd never meet anybody you knew. S'posin' you looked white and didn't have anything to stop you, what would be the hold-back?"

Jay chewed a minute thoughtfully. Then he looked at MacLoed as if wondering whether he was worth a reply. Finally he answered:

"Kids."

"Kids?" Mac ingested this with two pieces of the real French fried potatoes well swabbed in ham gravy. "You mean you might get married and have a little pickaninny to account for, huh? Well, you could get out o' that all right. Just tell her she'd been runnin' around with a nigger and quit."

Jay knew MacLoed too well to be shocked. "You might not want to quit," he said. "You might like her. Or you might have a conscience."

"Humph! Conscience and kids. Old stuff, buddy."

"And even if your scheme worked with a man who was passing, it wouldn't with a woman. She couldn't tell her white husband he'd been running around with a colored girl. That wouldn't explain the pickaninny."

"No.—The woman catches hell both ways, don't she?"

"It's a damned shame." Jay was speaking rather to himself than to MacLoed. "I know. I took her—places. That girl was white—as white as anybody could be. Lord only knows what she'll be now."

Three or four men had come in, standing in what little space they could find and reading the menu signs while they awaited seats. No one paid any particular attention to one of these who was "ofay". White patrons were not infrequent in Dick's. This one had moved close enough to Jay to hear his last statement. He touched him on the shoulder. As Jay turned the white man drew aside his coat, and Jay glimpsed a badge. When the officer motioned him to step outside, there was nothing else to do, and with an "Excuse me a minute, Mac—be right back," he preceded the other to the sidewalk.

Outside, Jay asked, "What's the idea?"

"Didn't want to start a row in that dump. Somebody might 'a had a gun."

"What's the idea?"

"Let's walk down this way." Jay knew better than to refuse, though "this way" led toward the police station. "So you think it's a damned shame, do you? Well, I think it's a damned shame, too."

"What the devil are you talking about?"

"Come down out o' that tree, son. I'm talking about you and the white girl you picked up at Manhattan Casino a while back. You y'self said just now she's white. That about settles it."

"White? Why, I only meant——"

"I heard you. You said 'white'. White's white, ain't it?"

Presently: "What's the charge?"

"Don't play dumb, bud. There's been too damn much of this thing goin' on here. We're goin' to stop it."

Suddenly Jay Martin laughed.

The two walked on in silence.

5

From a point in the wide, deep balcony's dimness, Jay followed the quick-shifting scenes; not those on the screen at which he stared, but others, flashing out from his mind.

Coney Island. He and Evelyn arm in arm, inconsequent, hilarious, eating sticky popcorn out of the same bag, dipping in at the same time, gaily disputing the last piece. Their laughter suddenly chilled by an intentionally audible remark: "Look at that white girl with a nigger." A half-dozen lowering rowdies. Evelyn urging him away. People staring.

An ice-cream parlor. A rackety mechanical piano, tables with white tops and dappled wire legs; outside One Hundred and Twenty-fifth Street traffic shadowing past; Evelyn and he, wilted with the heat, waiting a couple of eternities for a waitress; he finally looking about impatiently, beckoning to one, who leers through him. The proprietor. "Of course we don't mind serving the lady, sir; but while we can't actually refuse, why—er—frankly your presence is unprofitable to us, sir." People staring.

The subway. He and Evelyn in a corner of the car. Above the rattle and bump of doors and clang of signal-gong, wild laughter, coarse, loud. Different. Negro laughter. Headlong into the car, stumbling over one another, a group of hilarious young colored people. Men contesting seats with women, and winning; women flouncing defiantly down on the men's knees. Conscious of the attention attracted by their loudness; pleased with it. Train starting, accelerating. Train-din rising. Negro-noise rising through and above it, like sharp pain through and above dull ache. "Oh, you high yaller!" Evelyn ashamed. People staring.

Finally a back room in the police station. Two or three red-faced ruffians in brass-buttoned uniforms, sneering, menacing, quite like those Coney Island rowdies. Himself, outraged, at bay, demanding to know on just what score he was there. Surly accusation, hot denial, scalding epithet—flame. A blow. Swift, violent struggle. "Now mebbe y'll leave white women alone!" Emptiness. After a time release; release raw with bodily anguish, raw with the recurrent sting of that cover-all charge of policemen, "resisting an officer".

What an enormity, blackness! From the demons and ogres and ravens of fairy tales on; storm-clouds, eclipses, night, the valley of the shadow, gloom, hell. White, the standard of goodness and perfection. Christ himself, white. All the angels. Imagine a black angel! A black angel with a flat nose and thick lips, laughing loudly. The devil! Standards, of course; but beneath the standards, what? An instinctive shrinking from the dark? He'd seen a little white child run in terror from his father once, the first black man the child had ever seen. Instinctive? He looked about. All this balcony full of fellow creatures instinctively shrinking from him. No help for it? Awful idea. Unbearable.

A general murmur of amusement refocussed his attention for a moment on the screen. Two chubby infants sat side by side on a doorstep; the one shiny black, with a head full of kinks and eyes of twinkling midnight; the other white, with eyes of gray and the noonday sun in its hair; both dimpled and grinning and happy. Kids. Old stuff, buddy. Evelyn—would she dare?

The thoughts that gathered and throbbed like an abscess were suddenly incised. Off to one side, a row or two ahead, he had caught sight of an oddly familar face. The dimness seemed to lift mockingly, so that he should have no doubt. Evelyn, like an answer. Different, but— Evelyn. The attitude of the young man beside her was that of an escort, and something in his profile, in the fairness of his hair and skin, discernible even through the dusk, marked him to the staring Jay as unmistakably white. Watching with quickened pulse Jay saw the young man's hand move forward over Evelyn's arm, lying on the elbow-rest between them; move forward till it reached her own hand, which turned palm-upward to clasp it. Saw one white hand close firmly over the other.

He rose abruptly and made his way past stubborn knees to the aisle. The orchestra struck up a popular bit of Negro jazz. It fell on his ears like a guffaw: the familiar refrain of "Yaller Gal's Gone Out o' Style."

Jessie R. Fauset

(1884–1961)

JESSIE FAUSET WAS BORN into an upper-class Negro family in Philadelphia, and her contribution to American literature involved a mission which she pursued relentlessly: to document the fact that Negroes are no different from the "best" white Americans. In her novels, written during the Renaissance, she treated her subjects in such a way as to remind readers that all black people are not lecherous and lazy, or exotic and primitive.

Miss Fauset received a B.A. degree at Cornell and a Master's at the University of Pennsylvania and then went to Paris to the Sorbonne. She lived in Paris for several years, and probably would have stayed on indefinitely; but a decline in her family's resources forced her to return to the States in 1920. She accepted a teaching job at Washington, D.C.'s Dunbar High School, which, though a public school, was exclusively geared to the training of upper-class, college-bound Negro students. Jessie Fauset's poetry, some of it written in French, was produced during this period. It attracted the attention of W. E. B. Du Bois, who invited her to join the staff of *The Crisis*. Although she returned to teaching (and was eventually retired from the New York City school system), her connection with *The Crisis* remained until Dr. Du Bois resigned in 1934.

The selection chosen for this anthology is from *There Is Confusion* (1924), Jessie Fauset's first novel. Three others followed: *Plum Bun* (1929), *The Chinaberry Tree* (1931), and *Comedy American Style* (1933).

CLASS

It was Joanna who first acquainted Peter with himself. But neither of the children knew this at the time. And although Peter came to realize it later it was many years before he told her so. For, though he went through many changes and though these two came to speak of many things, he kept a certain inarticulateness all his lifetime.

Joanna and all the older Marshalls went to a school in West Fifty-second Street, one after another like little steps, with Joanna at first quite some distance behind. They were known throughout the school.

"Those Marshall children, you know those colored children that always dress so well and as though they had someone to take care of them. Pretty nice looking children, too, if only they weren't colored. Their father is a caterer, has that place over there on Fifty-ninth Street. Makes a lot of money for a colored man."

Peter, unlike Joanna, had gone to school, one might almost say, all over New York, and nowhere for any great length of time. Meriwether had stayed longest at Mrs. Reading's but as, in later years, he more and more went off on his runs without paying his bills, Mrs. Reading frequently refused to let Peter leave the house until his father's return.

"For all I know he may be joinin' his father on the outside and the two of them go off together. Then where'd I be? For them few rags that Mr. Bye keeps in his room wouldn't be no good to nobody."

This enforced truancy was the least of Peter's troubles. He did not like school,—too many white people and consequently, as he saw it, too much chance for petty injustice. The result of this was that Peter at twelve, possessed it is true of a large assortment of really useful facts, lacked the fine precision, if the doubtful usefulness, of Joanna's knowledge at ten. When Miss Susan settled in the Marshalls' neighborhood and brought Peter to the school in Fifty-second Street he was found to be lacking and yet curiously in advance. "We'll try him," said the principal doubtfully, "in the fifth grade. I'll take him to Miss Shanley's room."

Miss Shanley was Joanna's teacher. She greeted Peter without enthusiasm, not because he was colored but because he was clearly a problem. Joanna spied him immediately. He was too handsome with his brown-red skin, his black silky hair that curled alluringly, his dark, almost almond-shaped eyes, to escape her notice. But she forgot about him, too, almost immediately, for the first time Miss Shanley called on him he failed rather ignominiously. Joanna did not like stupid people and thereafter to her he simply was not.

On the contrary, Joanna had caught and retained Peter's attention. She was the only other colored person in the room and therefore to him the only one worth considering. And though at that time Joanna was still rather plain, she already had an air. Everything about her was of an exquisite perfection. Her hair was brushed till it shone, her skin glowed not only with health but obviously with cleanliness, her shoes were brown and shiny, with perfectly level heels. She wore that first week a very fine soft sage-green middy suit with a wide buff tie. The nails which finished off the rather square-tipped fingers of her small square hands, were even and rounded and shining. Peter had seen little girls with this perfection and assurance on Chestnut Street in Philadelphia and on Fifth Avenue in New York, but they had been white. He had not yet envisaged this sort of thing for his own. Perhaps he inherited his great-grandfather Joshua's spiritless acceptance of things as they are, and his belief that differences between people were not made, but had to be.

Joanna clearly stood for something in the class. Peter noted a little enviously the quality of the tone in which Miss Shanley addressed her. To other children she said, "Gertrude, can you tell me about the Articles of Confederation?" Usually she implied a doubt, which Gertrude usually justified. But she was sure of Joanna. The tenseness of her attitude might be seen to relax; her mentality prepared momentarily for a rest. "Joanna will now tell us,—" she would announce. For Joanna, having a purpose and having been drilled by Joel to the effect that final perfection is built on small intermediate perfections, got her lessons completely and in detail every day.

It was at this time and for many years thereafter characteristic of Peter that he, too, wanted to shine, but did not realize that one shone only as a resut of much mental polishing personally applied. Joanna's assurance, her air of purposefulness, her indifference intrigued him and piqued him. He sidled across to the blackboard nearest her—if they were both sent to the board—cleaned hers off if she gave him a chance, managed to speak a word to her now and then. He even contrived to wait for her one day at the Girls' entrance. Joanna threw him a glance of recognition, swept by, returned.

His heart jumped within him.

"If you see my sister Sylvia,—you know her?—tell her not to wait for me. I have to go early to my music-lesson. She'll be right out."

Sylvia didn't appear for half an hour and Peter should have been at the butcher's, but he waited. Sylvia and Maggie Ellersley came out laughing and glowing. Peter gave the message.

"Thanks," said Sylvia prettily. Maggie stared after him. She was still the least bit bold in those days.

"Ain't he the best looker you ever saw, Sylvia? Such eyes! Who is he, anyway? Not ever Joanna's beau?"

"Imagine old Joanna with a beau." Sylvia laughed. "He's just a new boy in her class. He *is* good looking."

Some important examinations were to take place shortly and Miss Shanley planned extensive reviews. She was a thorough if somewhat unimaginative teacher and she meant to have no loose threads. So she devoted two days to geography, two more to grammar, another to history, one to the rather puzzling consideration of that mysterious study, physiology. Perhaps by now the class was a bit fed up with cramming, perhaps the children weren't really interested in physiological processes. Joanna wasn't, but she always got lessons like these doggedly, thinking "Soon we'll be past all this," or "I'm going to forget this old stuff as soon as I grow up." Poor Miss Shanley was in despair. She could not call on Joanna for everything. Pupil after pupil had failed. Her eye roved over the room and fell on Peter's black head.

She sighed. He had not even been a member of the class when she had taught this particular physiological phenomenon. "Can't anyone besides Joanna Marshall give me the 'Course of the Food?' "

Peter raised his hand. "He looks intelligent," she thought. "Well, Bye you may try it."

"I don't think I can give it to you the way the others say it,"—the children had been reciting by rote, "but I know what happens to the food."

She knew he would fail if he didn't know it her way, but she let him begin.

This was old ground for Peter. "Look, I can draw it. See, you take the food in your mouth," he drew a rough sketch of lips, mouth cavity and gullet, "then you must chew it, masticate it, I think you said." He went on varying from his own simplified interpretation of Meriwether Bye's early instructions, past difficult names like pancreatic juice and thoracic duct, and while he talked he drew, recalling pictures from those old anatomies; expounding, flourishing. Miss Shanley stared at him in amazement. This jewel, this undiscovered diamond!

"How'd you come to know it, Peter?"

"I read it, I studied it." He did not say when. "But it's so easy to learn things about the body. It's yourself."

She quizzed him then while the other children, Joanna among them, stared open-eyed. But he knew all the simple ground which she had already covered, and much, much beyond.

"If all the children," said Miss Shanley, forgetting Peter's past, "would just get their lessons like Peter Bye and Joanna Marshall."

She had coupled their names together! And after school Joanna was waiting for him. He walked up the street with her, pleasantly conscious of her interest, her frank admiration.

"How wonderful," she breathed, "that you should know your physiology like that. What are you going to be when you grow up, a doctor?"

"A surgeon," said Peter forgetting his old formula and expressing a resolve which her question had engendered in him just that second. He saw himself on the instant, a tall distinguished-looking man, wielding scissors and knife with deft nervous fingers. Joanna would be hovering somewhere—he was not sure how—in the offing. And she would be looking at him with this same admiration.

"My, won't you have to study?" Joanna could have told an aspirant almost to the day and measure the amount of time and effort it would take him to become a surgeon, a dentist, a lawyer, an engineer. All these things Joel discussed about his table with the intense seriousness which colored men feel when they speak of their children's futures. Alexander and Philip were to have their choice of any calling within reason. They were seventeen and fifteen now and the house swarmed with college catalogues. Schools, terms, degrees of prejudice, fields of practice,—Joanna knew them all.

"Yes," said Peter, "I suppose I will have to study. How did you come to know so much—did your father tell you?"

"Why, I get it out of books, of course." Joanna was highly indignant: "I never go to bed without getting my lessons. In fact, all I do is to get lessons of some kind—school lessons or music. You know I'm to be a great singer."

"No, I didn't know that. Perhaps you'll sing in your choir?"

Then Joanna astonished him. "In my choir—I sing there already! No! Everywhere, anywhere, Carnegie Hall and in Boston and London. You see, I'm to be famous."

"But," Peter objected, "colored people don't get any chance at that kind of thing."

"Colored people," Joanna quoted from her extensive reading, "can do everything that anybody else can do. They've already done it. Some one colored person somewhere in the world does as good a job as anyone else,—perhaps a better one. They've been kings and queens and poets and teachers and doctors and everything. I'm going to be the one colored person who sings best in these days, and I never, never, never mean to let color interfere with anything I *really* want to do."

"I dance, too," she interrupted herself, "and I'll probably do that besides. Not ordinary dancing, you know, but queer beautiful things that are different from what we see around here; perhaps I'll make them up myself. You'll see! They'll have on the bill-board, 'Joanna Marshall, the famous artist,'—" She was almost dancing along the sidewalk now, her eyes and cheeks glowing.

Peter looked at her wistfully. His practical experience and the memory of his father inclined him to dubiousness. But her superb assurance carried away all his doubts.

"I don't suppose you'll ever think of just ordinary people like me?"

"But you'll be famous, too—you'll be a wonderful doctor. Do be. I can't stand stupid, common people."

"You'll always be able to stand me," said Peter with a fervor which made his statement a vow.

May Miller

THE DAUGHTER OF WRITER KELLY MILLER, May Miller was born in Washington, D.C. She graduated from Howard University and has done advanced work at American and Columbia Universities. Miss Miller (in private life, Mrs. John Sullivan) is a former teacher of speech and dramatics in the Frederick Douglass High School, Baltimore, Maryland. While working in the field of the theater, she published articles on the Negro Little Theater movement and collaborated on two volumes of one-act plays: *Plays and Pageants from the Life of the Negro* and *Negro History in Thirteen Plays.*

More recently, Miss Miller has served as reader, panelist, lecturer, and poet-in-residence at Monmouth College, Monmouth, Illinois. Under the auspices of Friends of the Arts in the Public Schools of the District of Columbia, she worked for three years as coordinator for performing poets; presently she is a member of the Commission on the Arts of the District of Columbia.

Miss Miller's work has appeared in many anthologies and leading magazines, among them: *The Antioch Review, Common Ground, The Crisis, The Nation, The New York Times, Phylon, Poetry,* Alan Swallow's *P.S.,* and *Cafe Solo* (a magazine of new verse). Miss Miller's two published volumes of verse are *Into the Clearing* (1959) and *Poems* (1962); and she is represented as one of the three poets in *Lyrics of Three Women* (1964).

GIFT FROM KENYA

> Within the day a seventh time
> I touch the pale wood antelope.
> Forever squat on spindle legs
> He tips his head to danger.
> (But O to see the pronghorn herd
> Run the ridge of a blunted hill
> With the skyline copper-red).
> It is too late to hear the axe
> Which, in the ruined cedar grove,
> Shivered down like a death drum note
> To fell the trees that would become
> The multi-hundred antelopes.

Some fluid centuries ago
My ancient father knew the tree;
Then young and bending in a wind,
Played near the sapling
While the hours of morning whipped
Singing round his loins.
When dark came down and the vultures slept,
In the fragrance of dew-heavy bark
He watched determined stars in course.
As man, in a glittering night of power
He traced with others curving paths
Leading out from the sheltering boughs.

The cedar carved to figurine,
And to all its counterparts,
Is hunched upon the years to come.
The man and his way are old in me,
Old in the unborn who wait
To hold the ice-aged heritage
That has no end in single flesh
However wound in death.

PROCESSION

(Gozzoli's "Journey of the Magi" hangs on a tenement wall)

> *Ring, hammer, ring!*
Time is today, yesterday, and time to come,
In which man, depending on hereafter,
Hangs his hope on a distant star.

Low ceiling under high sky,
Boards for feet to tread the solid way,
Avoiding paths
Tracked by the image-haunted.
> *Gonna heist mah wings*
> *An' gonna fly high,*
> *New Jerusalem.*

Where gray twilight falls away
Hangs the miracle in which wax-curled kings,
Ermined, brocaded, travel to Bethlehem.
White steeds poise to the trumpet,
Immobile figures of grandeur burn a mark
Golden at the crossroads to a dream.

> *An' they nailed Him to a tree,*
> *To a tall black tree.*
> *How the hammer do ring!*

Down the ages, moving and motionless.
Birth is the great mystery:
A name on Bible page,
The cry from castle walls,
Man's dream of renewal,
The miracle recorded of God in man.

> *Jest ready me a body, Father,*
> *An' Ah'll go down an' die.*

From this miracle comes another:
The infinite takes familiar form:
God is friend with whom the lowly
Walk hand in hand
Through the quiet byways.

> *Please, Suh, forgive us, Lawd,*
> *We didn't know 'twas You.*

Stream flowing to single birth—
Croon of the infinite
Fed at the personal breast.

> *Sweet little Jesus Boy,*
> *They made You be born*
> *In a manger.*

The lit journey, the magi bearing gifts,
And the final stable—a tenement wall.
Is it that man and art must end
Beneath the crumbling cities?

We who travel the way from innocence
Cry out for direction beyond the journey.
Hours revolving in an iron schedule—
Sun to moon, birth to death—
Turn in the dust of our passage.
Desperate, we seek conviction
More than child nursed in a narrow corner.

TALLY

We lay there drained of time,
Empty as the bulge of hour glass
That has let slip

The last thin feel of grit
Sealing it to this heady whirl
Of minute marking.
Up love's sheerest pinnacle
We had climbed
In rhythm tuned to rhythm;
Unbodied clasped the peak of ice,
Bathed in molten lava,
Chorused one convulsive gasp,
Spewed seed to cradling womb,
Fused with eternity.

Lost lucifer streaked to reality
You counted:
One—three—six.
Who votes at 'Frisco?
What the whispered word at Yalta?
Why the power?
Which the count—one, three, six?
News type one inch tall,
Startled cry on ether wave,
Voice upon voice in marble hall:
Remember Greece, patch-quilt Poland?
One—three—six.
Somewhere in the tally lost
One item—Peace.

But leave to me his childhood sum:
One, two—buckle my shoe
Three, four—shut the door
Five, six—pick up sticks.
Sprawled flattened on the twilight step
To coax the first wan sapphire out,
To dot the legion aftermath,
Then safe behind the barring door
To show the star-marked body
To the other sex
Innocent of heaven and hell
Locked there.
One, two—buckle my shoe.

O multiply the years between
——Seventeen, eighteen.
Too soon the downy fuzz
On cheek and chin,

The backdoor tryst,
The feel of power in fountain welling,
And always, ever a war waiting.
Seven seas, alien sod, or dome so vast
That God is lost in weak conception.
The sheeted stiff to deep-sea rest,
A wooden cross on shell-pocked field,
Or charred bones after wings are singed.
The fountain dry though rains may fall
Three, four—shut the door.

Hold, Mr. Science passing by,
Pray let me test our wares.
Penicillin, sulfa drugs,
Blood—types 1, 2, 3, 4,
Metal limbs, plastic parts,
Glass eyes, fine muscle cords—
New life to mangled flesh,
A wonder world of walking dead.
So what? No souls for sale!
Mere life beyond the burst of shell,
Bomb, bullet, bayonet, more of hell.
Dead, man-resurrected to slight and slur,
The pitying word, the thoughtless stare,
And in the end the bitter cup.
Five, six—pick up sticks.

Fear goads reluctant flesh
Nor stealing lassitude the power
To bind me to the couch.
No seed of mine to sprout
Cork leg, plastic arm, clutching claw.
Better to be lost
In muck and slime of sewer swirl
That yet may run a clearer stream
To lap some lonely lighthouse rock
Or green again the passing plain.

Melvin B. Tolson

(1900–1966)

MELVIN B. TOLSON IS probably the least known of major black poets. Although his work has appeared in such magazines as the *Atlantic Monthly* and *Art Quarterly* and in various anthologies, and although he received the honor of being named Poet Laureate of Liberia in 1947, Tolson spent all but the last few years of his life in almost total obscurity. He is not an easy poet. His meanings are often concealed; his imagery and allusions, though brilliant, are complexly parabolic; and his rhetoric—compounded of Africanisms, pure English, and Negro vernacular—sounds more difficult at first reading than it actually is. But only lately has a considerable body of readers begun to study his poetry and find it rewarding. He was enthusiastically supported by other poets—Robert Frost, Theodore Roethke, John Ciardi—and in introductions to two of his works, Allen Tate (*Libretto for the Republic of Liberia*) and Karl Shapiro (*Harlem Gallery*) praise Tolson's work.

Born in Moberly, Missouri, Melvin Tolson grew up in the town of Slater, where his father found it difficult to support a family on a small-town minister's income. Young Tolson managed a year at Fisk University before he dropped out to earn money to continue his education; he finally finished at Lincoln University (Pennsylvania), and later did graduate work at Columbia University. He earned his living as a teacher, first at Wiley College (Texas), then at Langston University (Oklahoma), where he taught creative writing. Tolson also served as mayor of the city of Langston for four terms. Finally, his reputation having at last caught up with his talent, he became Avalon Professor of Humanities at Tuskegee Institute.

The piece used here is a section from Melvin Tolson's last published work, *Harlem Gallery* (1965). Suggested further reading includes his other two volumes, *Rendezvous with America* (1944) and *Libretto for the Republic of Liberia* (1953).

FROM "PSI"

Black Boy,
let me get up from the white man's Table of Fifty Sounds
in the kitchen; let me gather the crumbs and cracklings

From "Psi" from *Harlem Gallery* by Melvin B. Tolson. Reprinted by permission of Twayne Publishers, Inc.

of this autobio-fragment,
before the curtain with the skull and bones descends.

Many a *t* in the ms.
I've left without a cross,
many an *i* without a dot.
A dusky Lot
with a third degree and a second wind and a seventh turn
of pitch-and-toss,
my psyche escaped the Sodom of Gylt
and the Big White Boss.

Black Boy,
you stand before your heritage,
naked and agape;
cheated like a mockingbird
pecking at a Zuexian grape,
pressed like an awl to do
duty as a screw-
driver, you
ask the American Dilemma in you:
"If the trying plane
of Demos fail,
what will the trowel
of Uncle Tom avail?"

Black Boy,
in this race, at this time, in this place,
to be a Negro artist is to be
a flower of the gods, whose growth
is dwarfed at an early stage—
a Brazilian owl moth,
a giant among his own in an acreage
dark with the darkman's designs,
where the milieu moves back downward like the sloth.

Black Boy,
true—you
have not
dined and wined
(*ignoti nulla cupido*)
in the El Dorado of aeried Art,
for unreasoned reasons;
and your artists, not so lucky as the Buteo,
find themselves without a

skyscape sanctuary
in the
season of seasons:
in contempt of the contemptible,
refuse the herb of grace, the rue
of Job's comforter;
take no
lie-tea in lieu
of Broken Orange Pekoe.
Doctor Nkomo said: "*What* is he who smacks
his lips when dewrot eats away the golden grain
of self-respect exposed like flax
to the rigors of sun and rain?"

Black Boy,
every culture,
every caste,
every people,
every class,
facing the barbarians
with lips hubris-curled,
believes its death rattle omens
the *Dies Irae* of the world.

Black Boy,
summon Boas and Dephino,
Blumenbach and Koelreuter,
from their posts
around the gravestone of Bilbo,
who, with cancer in his mouth,
orated until he quaked the magnolias of the South,
while the pocketbooks of his weeping black serfs
shriveled in the drouth;
summon the ghosts
of scholars with rams' horns from Jericho
and facies in letters from Jerusalem,
so
we may ask them:
"What is a Negro?"

Black Boy,
what's in a people's name that wries the brain
like the neck of a barley bird?
Can sounding brass create
an ecotype with a word?

Black Boy,
beware of the thin-bladed mercy
stroke, for one drop of Negro blood
(V. *The Black Act of the F. F. V.*)
opens the flood-
gates of the rising tide of color
and jettisons
the D. A. R. in the Heraclitean flux
with Uncle Tom and
Crispus Attucks.
The Black Belt White,
painstaking as a bedbug in
a tenant farmer's truckle bed,
rabbit-punched old Darrow
because
he quoted Darwin's sacred laws
(instead of the Lord God Almighty's)
and gabbled that the Catarrhine ape
(the C from a Canada goose nobody knows)
appears,
after X's of years,
in the vestigial shape
of the Nordic's thin lips, his aquiline nose,
his straight hair,
orangutanish on legs and chest and head.
Doctor Nkomo, a votary of touch-and-go,
who can stand the gaff
of Negrophobes and, like Aramis,
parry a thrust with a laugh,
said:
"In spite of the pig in the python's coils,
in spite of Blake's lamb in the jaws of the tiger,
Nature is kind, even in the raw: she toils
. . . aeons and aeons and aeons . . .
gives the African a fleecy canopy
to protect the seven faculties of the brain
from the burning convex lens of the sun;
she foils
whiteness
(without disdain)
to bless the African
(as Herodotus marvels)
with the birthright of a burnt skin for work or fun;
she roils
the Aryan

(as his eye and ear repose)
to give the African an accommodation nose
that cools the drying-up air;
she entangles the epidermis in broils
that keep the African's body free from lice-infested hair.
As man to man,
the Logos is
Nature is on the square
with the African.
If a black man circles the rim
of the Great White World, he will find
(even if Adamness has made him half blind)
the bitter waters of Marah *and*
the fresh fountains of Elim."

Although his transition
was a far cry
from Shakespeare to Sardou,
the old Africanist's byplay gave
no soothing feverfew
to the Dogs in the Zulu Club;
said he:
"A Hardyesque artistry
of circumstance
divides the Whites and Blacks in life,
like the bodies of the dead
eaten by vultures
in a Tower of Silence.
Let, then, the man with a maggot in his head
lean . . . lean . . . lean
on race or caste or class,
for the wingless worms of blowflies shall grub,
dry and clean,
the stinking skeletons of these,
when the face of the macabre weather-
cock turns to the torrid wind of misanthropy;
and later their bones shall be swept together
(like the Parsees')
in the Sepulchre of Anonymity."
A Zulu Wit cleared away his unsunned
mood with dark laughter;
but I sensed the thoughts of Doctor Nkomo
pacing nervously to and fro
like Asscher's, after
he'd cleaved the giant Cullinan Diamond.

Black Boy,
the vineyard is the fittest place
in which to booze (with Omar) and study
soil and time and integrity—
the telltale triad of grape and race.

Palates that can read the italics
of *salt* and *sugar* know
a grapevine
transplanted from Bordeaux
to Pleasant Valley
cannot give grapes that make a Bordeaux wine.

Like the sons of the lone mother of dead empires,
who boasted their ancestors,
page after page—
wines are peacocky
in their vintage and their age,
disdaining the dark ways of those engaging
in the profits
of chemical aging.
When the bluebirds sing
their perennial anthem
a capriccio, in the Spring,
the sap begins to move up the stem
of the vine, and the wine in the bed of the deep
cask stirs in its winter sleep.
Its bouquet
comes with the years, dry or wet;
so the connoisseurs say:
"The history of the wine
is repeated by the vine."

Black Boy,
beware of wine labels,
for the Republic does not guarantee
what the phrase "Château Bottled" means—
the estate, the proprietor, the quality.
This ignominy will baffle you, Black Boy,
because the white man's law
has raked your butt many a time
with fang and claw.
Beware of the waiter who wraps
a napkin around your Clos Saint Thierry,
if Chance takes you into high-hat places

open to all creeds and races
born to be or not to be.
Beware of the pop
of a champagne cork:
like the flatted fifth and octave jump in Bebop,
it is theatrical
in Vicksburg or New York.
Beware of the champagne cork
that does not swell up like your ma when she had you—*that*
comes out flat,
because the bottle of wine
is dead . . . dead
like Uncle Tom and the Jim Crow Sign.
Beware . . . yet
your dreams in the Great White World
shall be unthrottled
by pigmented and unpigmented lionhearts,
for we know *without no*
every people, by and by, produces its "Château Bottled."

White Boy,
as regards the ethnic origin
of Black Boy and me,
the *What* in Socrates' *"Tò tí"*
is for the musk-ox habitat of anthropologists;
but there is another question,
dangerous as a moutaba tick,
secreted in the house
of every Anglo-Saxon sophist and hick:

Who is a Negro?
(I am a White in deah ole Norfolk.)
Who is a White?
(I am a Negro in little old New York.)
Since my mongrelization is invisible
and my Negroness a state of mind conjured up
by Stereotypus, I am a chameleon
on *that* side of the Mason-Dixon
that a white man's conscience
is not on.
My skin is as white
as a Roman's toga when he sought an office on the sly;
my hair is as blond
as xanthein;
my eyes are as blue

as the hawk's-eye.
At the Olympian powwow of curators,
when I revealed my Negroness,
my peers became shocked like virgins in a house
where satyrs tattooed on female thighs heralds of success.

White Boy,
counterfeit scholars have used
the newest brush-on Satinlac,
to make our ethnic identity
crystal clear for the lowest IQ
in every mansion and in every shack.
Therefore,
according to the myth that Negrophobes bequeath
to the Lost Gray Cause, since Black Boy is the color
of betel-stained teeth,
he and I
(from ocular proof
that cannot goof)
belong to races
whose dust-of-the-earth progenitors
the Lord God Almighty created
of different bloods,
in antipodal places.
However,
even the F. F. V. pate
is aware that laws defining a Negro
blackjack each other with*in* and with*out* a state.
The Great White World, White Boy, leaves you in a sweat
like a pitcher with three runners on the bases;
and, like Kant, you seldom get
your grammar straight—yet,
you are the wick that absorbs the oil in my lamp,
in all kinds of weather;
and we are teeth in the pitch wheel
that work together.

White Boy,
when I hear the word *Negro* defined,
why does it bring to mind
the chef, the gourmand, the belly-god,
the disease of kings, the culinary art
in alien lands, Black Mammy in a Dixie big house,
and the dietitian's chart?
Now, look at Black Boy scratch his head!

It's a stereotypic gesture of Uncle Tom,
a learned Gentleman of Color said
in his monumental tome,
The *Etiquette of the New Negro,*
which,
the publishers say,
by the way,
should be in every black man's home.

The Negro is a dish in the white man's kitchen—
a potpourri,
an ola-podrida,
a mixie-maxie,
a hotchpotch of lineal ingredients;
with UN guests at his table,
the host finds himself a Hamlet on the spot,
for, in spite of his catholic pose,
the Negro dish is a dish nobody knows:
to some . . . tasty,
like an exotic condiment—
to others . . . unsavory
and inelegant.

White Boy,
the Negro dish is a mix
like . . . and *un*like
pimiento brisque, chop suey,
eggs à la Goldenrod, and eggaroni;
tongue-and-corn casserole, mulligan stew,
baked fillets of halibut, and cheese fondue;
macaroni milanaise, egg-milk shake,
mullagatawny soup, and sour-milk cake.

Just as the Chinese lack
an ideogram for "to be,"
our lexicon has no definition
for an ethnic amalgam like Black Boy and me.

Behold a Gordian knot without
the *beau geste* of an Alexander's sword!
Water, O Modern Mariner, water, everywhere,
unfit for *vitro di trina* glass
or the old-oaken-bucket's gourd!

For dark hymens on the auction block,
the lord of the mansion knew the macabre score:
not a dog moved his tongue,
not a lamb lost a drop of blood to protect a door.
O
Xenos of Xanthos,
what midnight-to-dawn lecheries,
in cabin and big house,
produced these brown hybrids and yellow motleys?

White Boy,
Buchenwald is a melismatic song
whose single syllable is sung to blues notes
to dark wayfarers who listen for the gong
at the crack of doom along
. . . that Lonesome Road . . .
before they travel on.

A Pelagian with the *raison d'être* of a Negro,
I cannot say I have outwitted dread,
for I am conscious of the noiseless tread
of the Yazoo tiger's ball-like pads behind me
in the dark
as I trudge ahead,
up and up . . . that Lonesome Road . . . up and up.

In a Vision in a Dream,
from the frigid seaport of the proud Xanthochroid,
the good ship *Défineznegro*
sailed fine, under an unabridged moon,
to reach the archipelago
Nigeridentité.
In the Strait of Octoroon,
off black Scylla,
after the typhoon Phobos, out of the Stereotypus Sea,
had rived her hull and sail to a T,
the *Défineznegro* sank the rock
and disappeared in the abyss
(*Vanitas vanitatum!*)
of white Charybdis.

Waring Cuney

(b. 1906)

WILLIAM WARING CUNEY was born in Washington, D.C., on May 6, 1906. He attended Howard University in his native city and Lincoln University in Pennsylvania.

During World War II he served as an army technical sergeant in the South Pacific region. This brought him the Asiatic Pacific Theatre Ribbon with three battle stars.

He is the author of a book of poems titled *Puzzles*, which was published in the Netherlands in 1960.

OLD WORKMAN

The old man sits on a bench in the sun,
A feeble frame of his youthful self.

How many years has it been—
A nine-pound sledge-hammer,
Made a rainbow around his shoulders?
Now the strength has gone from his hands.
A once powerful steel-driving man
Sits on a bench in the morning sun,
A shadow of the days of his youth.
He teases the children as they go to school.
As the children come and go he tells them,
John Henry said, "Don't cry until I cry."
The children ask, "Who was John Henry?"
The old man answers, "He was a steel-driving man."
The children ask, "What is a steel-driving man?"
Why did he say, "Don't cry until I cry?"
The old man says, "Run along, you'll be late for school."

COLORED

You want to know what it's like
Being colored?

Poems reprinted by permission of the author.

Well,
It's like going to bat
With two strikes
Already called on you—

It's like playing pool
With your name
Written on the eight ball.

Did you ever say,
"Thank you, sir"—
For an umbrella full of holes?

Did you ever dream
You had a million bucks,
And wake up with nothing to pawn?

You want to know what it's like
Being colored

Well,
The only way to know
Is to be born colored.

BEALE STREET

Did you know
That Beale Street
In Memphis,
Has a grave yard
At one end,
A river,
At the other?

No wonder
They say the blues
Began on Beale Street.
You could pick
A guitar,
You could make
A song about that:

Walkin' down
Beale Street
Sad an' low,

Nobody cares
If I stay or go.
Walkin' any which way down
Beale Street,
What do I see?
Nothin' but a
Grave yard,
Or a river,
In front of me.

GIRL FROM OKLAHOMA

I know a girl from Oklahoma.
She has a pretty face,
And a fine figure.
She has brains,
And money in the bank.
This girl from Oklahoma
Has the three B's,
Beauty, brains, and bucks.
She has what nine out of ten men
Are looking for.

This girl I know from Oklahoma
Talks to a psychiatrist
Three hours a week,
Because she is lonely.

WOMEN AND KITCHENS

No kitchen
Is big enough
For two women.

If you build
A kitchen
A city block long
By a city street wide,
It will be too small
For two women.
They can be sisters,
They can be friends,
They can be a girl
And her mother-in-law.

They can be strangers,
Or a servant
And the lady for whom she works.

It makes no difference.

A house with
Two women in it
Needs two kitchens.

A dance hall
Has room for many women.
So has a bargain basement.

Kitchens are different.

There should be a sign
Above all kitchen doors:
'Room For One Woman Only'.

NO IMAGES

She does not know
Her beauty,
She thinks her brown body
Has no glory.

If she could dance
Naked
Under palm trees,
And see her image in the river
She would know.

But there are no palm trees
On the street,
And dish water gives back no images.

William Attaway

(b. 1912)

BORN IN MISSISSIPPI AND educated in Chicago and at the University of Illinois, William Attaway left college to see the world, as a seaman, salesman, labor organizer, and actor (in the road company of *You Can't Take It With You*).

A composer as well as a writer, Attaway has arranged songs for Harry Belafonte and is the author of *The Calypso Song Book*. He has also written television and film scripts, including the script for the screen version of Irving Wallace's novel *The Man*.

The author of two provocative and unusual novels, William Attaway has not received the popularity and attention he deserves. His first novel, *Let Me Breathe Thunder* (1939), is unusual in that it deals with white characters—white migratory workers. Though white, they are, like Negroes, "outside" people, and Attaway treats them with great understanding. The second novel, *Blood on the Forge* (1941), is a perceptive analysis of the rural Southern Negro's bewildering and occasionally tragic introduction to life in the alien industrial North. Edward Margolies feels that in this work Attaway has "rendered the usual subject matter of the proletarian novel into a work of art."

For recent critical comment on William Attaway, see pages 47–64 in Edward Margolies, *Native Sons* (1968).

NORTH TO HELL

They hunched against one another, whispering and wondering, and big drops of rain, grayed with slag and soot, rolled on the long wooden bunkhouse. Passing the makings back and forth, they burned cigarettes until their tongues felt like flannel in their jaws. There was a crap game going on in the bunkhouse, but the newcomers didn't have any money to put on the wood. There was nothing for them to do that first day, except smoke and keep walking the rows of bunks. Windows stretched in the long wooden walls around them. And outside they could see the things that they would see for a long time to come.

A giant might have planted his foot on the heel of a great shovel and split the bare hills. Half buried in the earth where the great shovel had trenched were the mills. The mills were as big as creation when the new men had ridden by on the freight. From the bunkhouse they were just so much scrap iron, scattered carelessly, smoking lazily. In back of them ran a dirty-as-a-catfish-hole river with a beautiful name: the Monongahela. Its banks were lined with mountains of red ore, yellow limestone and black coke. None of this was good to the eyes of men accustomed to the pattern of fields.

Most of the crap shooters had been in the valley a long time. Some of them took time from the game to come back and talk with the green men.

"See them towers? That's where I works. The iron blast. Don't take the blast if you kin help it. It ain't the work—it's the head blower. Goddamn tough mick. Why, I seen the time when the keeper on my furnace mess up the blast, and the furnace freeze before you know it. That head blower don't stop to find who the fault go to. Naw, he run up and right quick lays out three men with a sow. One of the hunkies yanks a knife on him, but that hunky gits laid out too. I reckon somebody woulda got that mick 'fore this. Only a man ain't much fer a fight when he's makin' four hundred tons of fast iron from one sun to the other."

The men from the hills were not listening. They were not talking. Their attitude spoke. Like a refrain:

We have been tricked away from our poor, good-as-bad-ground-and-bad-white-men-will-let-'em-be hills. What men in their right minds would leave off tending green growing things to tend iron monsters?

"Lots of green guys git knocked out by the heat—'specially hunkies. They don't talk nothin' but gobbler talk. Don't understand nothin' else neither. Foreman tell one old feller who was workin' right next to me to put leather over his chest. Foreman might jest as well been whistlin', 'cause when the heat come down there that hunky lays with a chest like a scrambled egg."

Yes, them red-clay hills was what we call stripped ground, but there was growing things everywhere and crab-apple trees bunched—stunted but beautiful in the sun.

"Them old fellers hadn't oughta be put on a furnace. Course, a green man got to expect to git pitted up some. Lots o' young'uns got lead in their pants, and they gits tagged when the flame come jumpin' for their shovel. There always burns, too, when the furnace gits tapped and the slag spills over into the pit. But the quicker a man learn to move around on his feet the longer he stays livin'."

A man don't git to know what the place where he's born looks like until he goes someplace else. Then he begins to see with his mind things that his eyes had never been able to see. To us niggers who are seeing the red-clay hills with our minds this Allegheny County is an ugly, smoking hell out of a backwoods preacher's sermon.

"Mebbe they start you new boys out on the skull buster. That's a good way to git broke in. But jest keep minded that you got to be keerful o' that old devil, skull buster. Kill many a green man. How? Well, magnet lift the steel ball thirty feet up and drop her. Steel ball weigh nigh eight tons. That eight tons bust the hell out of old scrap metal. Got to be keerful not to git some of it in your skull. Yessir, many a green man long gone 'cause he couldn't keep old skull buster from aimin' at his head."

What's the good in strainin' our eyes out these windows? We can't see where nothin' grows around here but rusty iron towers and brick stacks, walled up like somebody's liable to try and steal them. Where are the trees? They so far away on the tops of the low mountains that they look like the fringe on a black wear-me-to-a-wake dress held upside down against the sky.

"Skull buster don't git as many as whores git. Roll mill help the gals out. Feller sees all that hot steel shooting along the runout tables, all them red-and-white tongues licking 'twixt them rollers. Feller go hog wild fer any gal what 'll take his money. She don't have to work him up none—he's hot from that bakin' steel."

The sun on the red hillsides baked a man, but it was only a short walk to the bottoms and the mud that oozed up between his toes like a cool drink to hot black feet, steppin' easy, mindful of the cotton-mouth.

"On the floor, under the Bessemers, you ain't got time to think what a gal's got 'tween her legs. . . ."

Melody and Chinatown went out into the wet. The door closed behind them. The rain had lessened to a drizzle. They could hear the clank of the mills over the steady swish of the rain. Melody led the way. He turned away from the river and walked toward the town.

"Boy, this here North don't seem like nothin' to me," complained Chinatown. "All this smoke and stuff in the air! How a man gonna breathe?"

The drizzle stopped. Thin clouds rolled. Melody looked up. "Sun liable to break through soon."

"Won't make no difference to us if the sun don't shine."

"How come?"

"There won't be no crop to make or take out."

"Sun make you feel better," said Melody.

"Couldn't shine through the smoke, nohow. Long time ago a fella told me a nigger need sun so's he kin keep black."

Melody kicked Chinatown with his knee. Chinatown kicked back. Soon they were kicking and dodging around the ash piles. They were laughing when they came to the weedy field at the edge of town. Both men stopped. The laughter died.

Quivering above the high weeds were the freckled white legs of a girl. She struggled with a small form—a little boy who wanted to be turned loose. Other children were peeping through the wet grass. They began to chant, "Shame, shame! Mary and her brother—shame!"

Chinatown and Melody wheeled and hurried away. They had no need to speak to each other. In both of them was the fear brought from Kentucky: that girl might scream. Back in the hills young Charley had been lynched because a girl screamed.

Breathing hard, they followed the path until it became a dirt street. In front of them was a long line of women waiting in front of a pump shed. A few boys crouched underneath one corner of the shelter, held by a game with a jackknife.

"Look—more hunkies!" breathed Chinatown.

"Keep shut," warned Melody.

The pump at the edge of town watered about fifty families. Every Saturday the women were here in line. This day they carried bathing water home. The rain had soaked into their shawl head coverings. They stood patiently.

Then one of the boys spied the three strangers. He was on his feet in a second.

"Ya-a-a . . ."

A rock whizzed between Melody and Chinatown. The two men halted, confused. In the eyes of all the Slavs was a hatred and contempt different from anything they had ever experienced in Kentucky. Another rock went past. Chinatown started to back away.

"We ain't done nothin'," cried Melody. He took a step toward the pump shed. The women covered their faces with their shawls.

"We ain't done nothin'," he cried again.

His words were lost in the shrill child voices: "Ya-a-a . . . ya-a-a . . . ya-a-a . . ."

Melody backed after his half brother. A little distance away they turned and trotted riverward.

"So this how the North different from the South," panted Chinatown.

"Musta mistook us for somebody," said Melody.

"When white folks git mad all niggers look alike," said Chinatown.

"Musta mistook us," insisted Melody.

It should have been easy for them to find the bunkhouse. The river was a sure landmark. But, in turning in among a series of knolls, they lost direction and found themselves back at the town. Before them a dirt road ran between rows of frame shacks. A large pile of garbage blocked the far end of the road.

"Oughta be somebody we kin ask where the bunkhouse," said Chinatown.

"Well, I ain't knockin' on nobody's door to ask nothing."

"All we got to do is start back to the river."

"Which way the river?" puzzled Melody, craning his neck around.

The light rain had started again. A mist had arisen through the rain. The low mountains were no longer visible. The mills along the water were blotted out. Their sound seemed to come from all directions.

"Maybe if I climbs that garbage . . ."

Chinatown started at a run down the road. At the top of the garbage pile he got his bearings. To the west the gray was tinged with faint streaks of orange.

"Over yonder apiece," he yelled, pointing westward.

At the cry, white faces appeared in the doorway opposite him. Nothing was said. Little faces grimaced between the overalled legs of the bearded father. With a movement of her hands beneath an apron, the mother fanned the breadth of her hips at him. An old Slav bent like a burned weed out of the window. Great handle-bar mustaches dripped below his chin. With eyes a snow-washed blue, he looked contempt at Chinatown. Then he wrinkled his nose and spat.

Chinatown slid down the pile of wet garbage. Hardly daring to hurry, he walked the middle of the road to the place where Melody waited.

"These here folks ain't mistook nobody."

They made quick tracks in the mud to the west.

At the river they did not stop to rest or look around. They wanted the shelter of the bunkhouse. This new place was full of hatreds that they did not understand. Melody led the way down-river. They had been going ten minutes when he stopped. There was no sign of the bunkhouse. Nothing but the river looked familiar.

"You reckon we been goin' wrong?" asked Chinatown.

"Got to be one way or the other," said Melody. He turned and looked behind him.

A fat-cheeked black girl moved along the river-front road. Bright red lipstick had turned to purple on her lips. A man's hat was pulled down over her ears. She wore an old overall coat over a stained satin dress.

Melody stared at her. She drew the coat tight around her hips and began to swagger. He was drawn by her eyes. They were cold pieces of wet glass.

"Wish I knowed what the way to Kentucky," Chinatown was moaning. He turned and saw the woman. "Man! Man! Kentucky kin wait."

The girl passed them. Her swimming eyes invited. They caught a heavy scent of perfume. Under the perfume was a rot stink. The stink sickened them. They were unnerved.

"Howdy, boys. Green, huh?"

They whirled and faced a small, dark man. He shifted from one foot to the other. His movements were like a squirrel's.

"Howdy," said Chinatown.

"How come you know we green?" asked Melody.

"They give all green niggers the same clothes," said the man.

"Oh . . ." Melody's gaze followed the woman.

"Beside, only a green man stop to look at that there gal."

They questioned him with their eyes.

"Her left breast 'bout rotted off." The man laughed. "You kin smell it a mile away."

"What you know!" Chinatown laughed.

Melody was stunned. He could not get the wet eyes out of his mind. All he could think to say was, "We lost from the bunkhouse."

"You been goin' wrong," said the man. "Back the other way a piece."

"Obliged," said Melody.

"I got to pass by there. Point it out."

"Obliged."

They walked along together.

"You work around here?" Chinatown asked.

"Blast. Boss of stove gang," said the man.

"Oh," said Chinatown. He looked at the old overalls.

"Sparks," explained the little man. "They'll git you too."

"Oh."

A group of Slav workmen came out of a gate in front of one of the mills. They moved with a slow stiffness, hardly shaking their drooping mustaches. There was dignity in the way they walked.

"Uh-uh," groaned Chinatown.

The workmen paused at the gate. One of them turned and waved at the little black man.

"Hallo, Bo."

The little man waved back. That greeting was the easy familiarity of men who had known each other over a period of years.

Chinatown voiced what was in his mind: "That there's the first white guy we seen don't hate niggers."

Bo asked, "You been havin' trouble?"

"Everybody treat us like poison," said Chinatown.

"Everythin' be smooth in a coupla weeks," said Bo. "Always hate new niggers round here."

"How come?"

"Well, company bring them in when there strike talk. Keep the old men in line."

"Oh . . ." said Chinatown. They walked a little. "There strike talk now?"

Bo looked him in the eye. "Looka here, boy. I don't know nothin' but my job."

"Yessir," said Chinatown.

"Don't mean nothin' by talkin' short," said Bo, "only it ain't a good thing for a feller to go spoutin' off."

"That's like Kentucky," said Chinatown.

Within sight of the bunkhouse, Bo stopped in the open to let water.

"Good idea," he said. "The outhouse always full of flies. Smells because nobody sprinkle ashes like they supposed to." He laughed. "Sometime a lizard use your behind for a bridge when you on the hole."

The men from the hills had always let water in the open. It made a feller feel free—space around him and the warm water running in the weeds. Nothing overhead but what God first put there. This touch of the past relaxed them. Their recent experiences became the unreality. This was the reality. They felt for a minute like Bo was an old friend.

Robert E. Hayden

(b. 1913)

Born in Detroit, Michigan, Robert Hayden did undergraduate work at Wayne State University and graduate work at the University of Michigan, where he received an M.A. He taught for two years at Michigan, leaving in 1944 to join the English faculty at Fisk University. Very much in demand as lecturer, reader-of-his-own-works, and visiting professor, Hayden has appeared on college campuses throughout the nation.

Professor Hayden has received many honors, awards, and fellowships, among them the Rosenwald and Ford Foundation fellowships for study, travel, and creative writing. In 1965 he was awarded the Grand Prize for Poetry at the First World African Festival of Arts, held in Dakar.

A prominent member of the Bahaist faith, Hayden has edited *World Order,* the official publication of that group. He has also contributed music and drama criticism to the *Michigan Chronicle.* His poems have appeared in many periodicals, including *Poetry* and the *Atlantic Monthly.*

Hayden has always been a skillful craftsman, and with the years his verses have become more sensitive, subtle, and provocative as his insights have deepened. Many of his early poems, which tend towards the simplicity of folk utterance, were written in the protest tradition. In his later work there is still a theme of protest, but it is more obliquely and subtly stated.

Among Robert Hayden's publications are: *Heart-Shape in the Dust* (1940); *The Lion and the Archer* (1948), with Myron O'Higgins; *A Ballad of Remembrance* (1962), the "Grand Prize" work; *Figure of Time* (1955); *Selected Poems* (1960); and *Kaleidoscope* (1967), an anthology of American Negro poetry.

The poems reprinted here were chosen to show Hayden's early and latest styles.

THE DIVER

Sank through easeful
azure. Flower
creatures flashed and
shimmered there—

lost images
fadingly remembered.
Swiftly descended
into canyon of cold
nightgreen emptiness.
Freefalling, weightless
as in dreams of
wingless flight,
plunged through infra-
space and came to
the dead ship,
carcass that swarmed with
voracious life.
Angelfish, their
lively blue and
yellow prised from
darkness by the
flashlight's beam,
thronged her portholes.
Moss of bryozoans
blurred, obscured her
metal. Snappers,
gold groupers explored her,
fearless of bubbling
manfish. I entered
the wreck, awed by her silence,
feeling more keenly
the iron cold.
With flashlight probing
fogs of water
saw the sad slow
dance of gilded
chairs, the ectoplasmic
swirl of garments,
drowned instruments
of buoyancy,
drunken shoes. Then
livid gesturings,
eldritch hide and
seek of laughing
faces. I yearned to
find those hidden
ones, to fling aside
the mask and call to them,
yield to rapturous

whisperings, have
done with self and
every dinning
vain complexity.
Yet in languid
frenzy strove, as
one freezing fights off
sleep desiring sleep;
strove against the
cancelling arms that
suddenly surrounded
me, fled the numbing
kisses that I craved.
Reflex of life-wish?
Respirator's brittle
belling? Swam from
the ship somehow;
somehow began the
measured rise.

HOMAGE TO THE EMPRESS OF THE BLUES

Because there was a man somewhere in a candystripe silk shirt,
gracile and dangerous as a jaguar and because a woman moaned
for him in sixty-watt gloom and mourned him Faithless Love
Twotiming Love Oh Love Oh Careless Aggravating Love,

> She came out on the stage in yards of pearls, emerging like
> a favorite scenic view, flashed her golden smile and sang.

Because grey laths began somewhere to show from underneath
torn hurdygurdy lithographs of dollfaced heaven;
and because there were those who feared alarming fists of snow
on the door and those who feared the riot-squad of statistics,

> She came out on the stage in ostrich feathers, beaded satin,
> and shone that smile on us and sang.

"Homage to the Empress of the Blues" by Robert Hayden from *Selected Poems.*
Copyright © 1966 by Robert Hayden. Reprinted by permission of October House
Inc.

MIDDLE PASSAGE

1

Jesús, Estrella, Esperanza, Mercy:

> Sails flashing to the wind like weapons,
> sharks following the moans the fever and the dying;
> horror the corposant and compass rose.

Middle Passage:
>   voyage through death
>   to life upon these shores.

> "10 April 1800—
> Blacks rebellious. Crew uneasy. Our linguist says
> their moaning is a prayer for death,
> ours and their own. Some try to starve themselves.
> Lost three this morning leaped with crazy laughter
> to the waiting sharks, sang as they went under."

Desire, Adventure, Tartar, Ann:

> Standing to America, bringing home
> black gold, black ivory, black seed.

> > *Deep in the festering hold thy father lies,*
> > *of his bones New England pews are made,*
> > *those are altar lights that were his eyes.*

Jesus Saviour Pilot Me
Over Life's Tempestuous Sea

We pray that Thou wilt grant, O Lord,
safe passage to our vessels bringing
heathen souls unto Thy chastening.

Jesus Saviour

> "8 bells. I cannot sleep, for I am sick
> with fear, but writing eases fear a little
> since still my eyes can see these words take shape
> upon the page & so I write, as one
> would turn to exorcism. 4 days scudding,

but now the sea is calm again. Misfortune
follows in our wake like sharks (our grinning
tutelary gods). Which one of us
has killed an albatross? A plague among
our blacks—Ophthalmia: blindness—& we
have jettisoned the blind to no avail.
It spreads, the terrifying sickness spreads.
Its claws have scratched sight from the Capt.'s eyes
& there is blindness in the fo'c'sle
& we must sail 3 weeks before we come
to port."

> *What port awaits us, Davy Jones'*
> *or home? I've heard of slavers drifting, drifting,*
> *playthings of wind and storm and chance, their crews*
> *gone blind, the jungle hatred*
> *crawling up on deck.*

Thou Who Walked On Galilee

"Deponent further sayeth *The Bella J*
left the Guinea Coast
with cargo of five hundred blacks and odd
for the barracoons of Florida:

"That there was hardly room 'tween-decks for half
the sweltering cattle stowed spoon-fashion there;
that some went mad of thirst and tore their flesh
and sucked the blood:

"That Crew and Captain lusted with the comeliest
of the savage girls kept naked in the cabins;
that there was one they called The Guinea Rose
and they cast lots and fought to lie with her:

"That when the Bo's'n piped all hands, the flames
spreading from starboard already were beyond
control, the negroes howling and their chains
entangled with the flames:

"That the burning blacks could not be reached,
that the Crew abandoned ship,
leaving their shrieking negresses behind,
that the Captain perished drunken with the wenches:

"Further Deponent sayeth not."

Pilot Oh Pilot Me

2

Aye, lad, and I have seen those factories,
Gambia, Rio Pongo, Calabar;
have watched the artful mongos baiting traps
of war wherein the victor and the vanquished

Were caught as prizes for our barracoons.
Have seen the nigger kings whose vanity
and greed turned wild black hides of Fellatah,
Mandingo, Ibo, Kru to gold for us.

And there was one—King Anthracite we named him—
fetish face beneath French parasols
of brass and orange velvet, impudent mouth
whose cups were carven skulls of enemies:

He'd honor us with drum and feast and conjo
and palm-oil-glistening wenches deft in love,
and for tin crowns that shone with paste,
red calico and German-silver trinkets

Would have the drums talk war and send
his warriors to burn the sleeping villages
and kill the sick and old and lead the young
in coffles to our factories.

Twenty years a trader, twenty years,
for there was wealth aplenty to be harvested
from those black fields, and I'd be trading still
but for the fevers melting down my bones.

3

Shuttles in the rocking loom of history,
the dark ships move, the dark ships move,
their bright ironical names
like jests of kindness on a murderer's mouth;
plough through thrashing glister toward
fata morgana's lucent melting shore,
weave toward New World littorals that are
mirage and myth and actual shore.

Voyage through death,
　　　　　　　　　voyage whose chartings are unlove.

A charnel stench, effluvium of living death
spreads outward from the hold,
where the living and the dead, the horribly dying,
lie interlocked, lie foul with blood and excrement.

Deep in the festering hold thy father lies,
the corpse of mercy rots with him,
rats eat love's rotten gelid eyes.

But, oh, the living look at you
with human eyes whose suffering accuses you,
whose hatred reaches through the swill of dark
to strike you like a leper's claw.

You cannot stare that hatred down
or chain the fear that stalks the watches
and breathes on you its fetid scorching breath;
cannot kill the deep immortal human wish,
the timeless will.

"But for the storm that flung up barriers
of wind and wave, *The Amistad*, señores,
would have reached the port of Príncipe in two,
three days at most; but for the storm we should
have been prepared for what befell.
Swift as the puma's leap it came. There was
that interval of moonless calm filled only
with the water's and the rigging's usual sounds,
then sudden movement, blows and snarling cries
and they had fallen on us with machete
and marlinspike. It was as though the very
air, the night itself were striking us.
Exhausted by the rigors of the storm,
we were no match for them. Our men went down
before the murderous Africans. Our loyal
Celestino ran from below with gun
and lantern and I saw, before the cane-
knife's wounding flash, Cinquez,
that surly brute who calls himself a prince,
directing, urging on the ghastly work.
He hacked the poor mulatto down, and then
he turned on me. The decks were slippery
when daylight finally came. It sickens me
to think of what I saw, of how these apes
threw overboard the butchered bodies of

our men, true Christians all, like so much jetsam.
Enough, enough. The rest is quickly told:
Cinquez was forced to spare the two of us
you see to steer the ship to Africa,
and we like phantoms doomed to rove the sea
voyaged east by day and west by night,
deceiving them, hoping for rescue,
prisoners on our own vessel, till
at length we drifted to the shores of this
your land, America, where we were freed
from our unspeakable misery. Now we
demand, good sirs, the extradition of
Cinquez and his accomplices to La
Havana. And it distresses us to know
there are so many here who seem inclined
to justify the mutiny of these blacks.
We find it paradoxical indeed
that you whose wealth, whose tree of liberty
are rooted in the labor of your slaves
should suffer the august John Quincy Adams
to speak with so much passion of the right
of chattel slaves to kill their lawful masters
and with his Roman rhetoric weave a hero's
garland for Cinquez. I tell you that
we are determined to return to Cuba
with our slaves and there see justice done. Cinquez—
or let us say 'the Prince'—Cinquez shall die."

The deep immortal human wish,
the timeless will:

Cinquez its deathless primaveral image,
life that transfigures many lives.

Voyage through death
                        to life upon these shores.

FREDERICK DOUGLASS

When it is finally ours, this freedom, this liberty, this beautiful
and terrible thing, needful to man as air,
usable as earth; when it belongs at last to all,

when it is truly instinct, brain matter, diastole, systole,
reflex action; when it is finally won; when it is more
than the gaudy mumbo jumbo of politicians:
this man, this Douglass, this former slave, this Negro
beaten to his knees, exiled, visioning a world
where none is lonely, none hunted, alien,
this man, superb in love and logic, this man
shall be remembered. Oh, not with statues' rhetoric,
not with legends and poems and wreaths of bronze alone,
but with the lives grown out of his life, the lives
fleshing his dream of the beautiful, needful thing.

O DAEDALUS, FLY AWAY HOME

Drifting night in the Georgia pines,
coonskin drum and jubilee banjo.
    Pretty Malinda, dance with me.

Night is juba, night is conjo.
    Pretty Malinda, dance with me.

Night is an African juju man
weaving a wish and a weariness together
    to make two wings.

    O fly away home fly away

Do you remember Africa?

    O cleave the air fly away home

My gran, he flew back to Africa,
just spread his arms and
    flew away home.

Drifting night in the windy pines;
night is a laughing, night is a longing.
    Pretty Malinda, come to me.

Night is a mourning juju man
weaving a wish and a weariness together
    to make two wings.

    O fly away home fly away

Owen Dodson

(b. 1914)

AT PRESENT PROFESSOR OF DRAMA in the School of Fine Arts at Howard University, Owen Dodson was born in Brooklyn, New York, and educated at Bates College and Yale University. He is a member of Phi Beta Kappa. In 1967 he received a Doctor of Letters from Bates.

Best known for his work in poetry and drama, Dodson has been a recipient of the Rosenwald Fellowship, the General Education Board Fellowship, and the coveted Guggenheim Fellowship (1953–54) for study in Italy. He has lectured and conducted seminars at many American universities and colleges, including Vassar, Kenyon, Cornell, Rutgers, Iowa, and U.C.L.A. During the spring of 1969, he was Poet-in-Residence at the University of Arizona.

Owen Dodson has taught and directed dramatic groups in Atlanta, Hampton, and during World War II, in the U.S. Navy. In 1949 with Ann Cook, he took the Howard Players to Denmark, Sweden, and Germany on America's first international, undergraduate cultural exchange.

Dodson's plays have been presented by little theatre groups all over the country, Off Broadway, and in England. His short story "The Summer Fire" received a prize in an international short story contest conducted by the *Paris Review*.

Among his publications are a book of poems, *Powerful Long Ladder* (1946), and a novel, *Boy at the Window* (1951; reprinted in 1967 as *When Trees Were Green*).

The prose selection below is from *Boy at the Window*.

MISS PACKARD AND MISS GILES

(Who founded Spelman College for Negro women in Georgia)

Two women, here in April, prayed alone
And saw again their vision of an altar
Built for mind and spirit, flesh and bone.

They never turned away, they never said
*This dream is air, let us go back to our New England spring
And cultivate an earth that is not dead;*

Let dark mothers weep, dark children bleed,
This land is barren land
Incapable of seed.

They made their crucifix far more
Than ornament; they wrestled with denial
And pinned him to the floor.

They made defeat an exile.
And year by year their vision shed its mist,
And still they smiled their Noah smile

Certain they had no death to fear,
Certain their future would be now
And all the Aprils we assemble here.

TELL RACHEL, HE WHISPERED

Tonight I talked to Jesus,
And Jesus spoke to me.
No, I don't remember
If His hair was long
Or if He wore a bible dress
Or had a halo on.
I know He spoke to me;
There were no trouble
In His eyes but I
Saw the gospels there.
When the morning stars
Sang bright together:
That were His voice.
He said He had heard of me,
Heard of long labours
In the vineyards of the city;
This city here, bless God
He asked after sister this
And brother that and The President.
Then it were time to speak:
I spoke 'bout Pastor Moss
Near working his bones to death
Trying to call the children home;

From *The Promethean* (Howard University Art and Literary Magazine), May, 1967. Reprinted by permission of the author.

'Bout Sister Seneatha bakin,
Bakin' biscuits for the poor;
'Bout how hard I scrubbed to get
The education for Sarah
And put some pride in Freddie's heart.
Finally I told Him 'bout cramps in my lungs.
'That's why I'm here,'
He reached out to me, yes He did,
'My Father caused me
To journey down';
—Tell Rachel—, He whispered,
—Tell her to cease that scrubbin,
To get off the apron,
Smooth the calice
And wait for the chariot
Waiting by the curbstone.—
That's what Jesus said
Through His Father.
He meant it too.

TRAIN RIDE

"CHESTER, CHESTER, the next stop is CHESTER," the conductor rolled the word out. He made Chester seem like a capital. When the train stopped, it was at an old station. A red sign announced Chester again and that was all except a lot of colored people got on there and most of them pushed right into the car where Coin was. They were dressed up and laughing to beat the band. One great bosom lady sat across from him with her son. He was peaked and looked like the last rose of summer. Kept on calling her Ma. Kept hugging her up. A fat old boy was in the seat in front of the woman. He called her Mama. Others took seats here and there and commenced to yelling and waving and passing bottles and sandwiches. It was a picnic on the train. When the conductor came by for the tickets, there was such a digging into pockets and paper bags and wallets, looking under seats and acting the fool until all the tickets were handed in to screaming laughter. Coin began to laugh too, whenever someone said anything funny. They kept on saying funny things and he kept on laughing. The train heated up until you could hardly breathe. Smelled like outing flannel and asafoetida. You weren't supposed to open the windows. Coin got himself cold water three times. When he was coming back the last time the talking and jokes and eating was louder and whooped-up more than ever. A man at the front of the car rose up out of his seat a little and called back, "Why don't you darkies shut up so we kin hear ourselves think."

What did he want to say that for? The happy confusion died down to a silence like an axe was hanging overhead by a thread. It stayed that way for a long time. Only the train wheels still raced: why don't you darkies shut up, why don't you darkies shut up.

The bosom woman's bosom panted up and down. She took three long puffs of her cigarette letting the smoke out of her nose in straight clouds, then she stood up, scrubbing the butt into the floor carefully. This woman, who had talked so hard and eaten more chicken than six, who had a laugh like a ten-gun salute, began walking down the aisle toward the man who had asked for silence. As she trod, she seemed to grow tall and furious as one of Popa's Bible prophets, Moses maybe or Genesis. You could see it in her back, in the way she threw her shoulders and lifted her head. People around buzzed low like the sound of bees with special stings. She reached her destination, leaned over the seat and pointed one dagger finger.

"If you don't know what you're talking about, you'd better ask somebody." Her voice filled the car and drowned the sound of the wheels.

"Nuts," came out of the seat, "nuts, you folks keeping up enough racket to drive a man crazy."

"You don't need to be driv crazy. You crazy already, that's what you are. Don't you come calling me no darkie."

"Aw, lady."

"Don't you be calling me no lady either. I been bringing up your children and scrubbing your nasty houses until my bones fair ache inside me. I ain't no lady, I'm a truck horse. Been a truck horse for you for too many years and I'm too tired to listen to you shutting me up. You hear that."

A voice from somewhere said, "NIGGERS, niggers," and that was all.

"Who said that!" She shot around and her eyes blazed fire even to where Coin sat. "You ain't afraid to say it again, is you? Cowards. That's what you is, a coward. Niggers, niggers. My boy is lying in the fields of Europe on the Kaiser's acres, that's where he is and I got a medal from the government. Cowards. It's too bad they didn't get your ass, that's what's too bad." She looked left and right, high and low. Only the train wheels dared to make a noise. Finally she strode back to her seat. Her heavy body seemed to shake the train. When she took her seat again, the boy who called her Mama turned around.

"Keep quiet, Mama, keep your big mouth shut."

She faced him like the wrath of God.

"Keep quiet, keep quiet! Why you shoulda been down there instead of me. Keep quiet, you chicken, that's what you is. Nobody's gonna call me out of my name. You hear me!" She worked herself up again. She walked up the aisle and down the aisle being bumped first to one side and then the other. Her voice sounded the hallelujah Sister Maudesta Lee shouted in church.

"All the planes that were fallen, and the ships rammed into, the bombs splitting the ocean apart, poison gas. God has a way."

The train wheels sang between her silences. People looked down.

"Don't give us nothing. Stepping all over us. Calling us darkies and niggers. God has a way. Colored boys working in the manholes of the streets in Philadelphia 'cause a white boy got his head rammed off by a trolley car. God has a way. They put colored on after that. Colored boys crawling about like cats under the streets and don't look out of them holes lessen they look both ways. They smart. God has a way. Trying to spoil my holiday. Don't give but the one day and you calling me outta my name. I hope there comes a next war. I hope they knocks hell outta this country. That's what I hopes. You can't think. Well, you better think. The end of the world is scheduled to be by fire. Now, if you don't know what you're talking about, you'd better keep quiet." She paused. The sweat was running off of her forehead in beads. She sat down again like on a throne. The train wheels sounded but didn't say any words.

When the train pulled into Baltimore, the bosom woman and her friends got off. They stood at the window where the man who had asked them to keep quiet sat, gazed in long like at an animal in the zoo. As the train started again, they all laughed at him; laughed pure and long and solid. The train wheels took up the laughter. It lasted almost until Washington.

Coin knew something was wrong with the way every one had acted but he didn't know where to place the blame. One thing he had learned: what nobody would tell him. He knew now what a nigger was. His mother really had been right. A bad person. What confused him was that it meant much more than that. Maybe you weren't a bad person but you were colored and they called you nigger.

Walking with the rest of the people toward the exit, Coin spied Uncle Troy at the gate. He was so happy to see him that he broke into a trot calling his name.

"Uncle Troy."

"Coin, Coin!"

"Uncle Troy."

Coin rushed to him and his uncle felt his face, measured his height with his stick.

"Lord, boy, I thought a baby was coming here to me but you're almost grown. Must have grown several inches since I saw you. Let me look at you." His hands felt Coin's face, and the old laughter Coin remembered from Pennsylvania Station surrounded them. "Well, you might as well begin working now. Mrs. Walker brought me here but you gotta lead me there." He was still laughing as Coin took his hand. The porter brought Coin's bag and hailed a taxi for them.

In the cab Uncle Troy began to laugh again.

"What's this I feel on your chest?"

"Agnes put a tag on me."

"Now isn't that just like Agnes, sending you like freight."

Sterling A. Brown

(b. 1901)

A GREAT TEACHER AND a brilliant scholar, a critic and poet, Sterling A. Brown has—through his many lectures all over the nation, his critical essays and books, and his personal contact with young black writers— probably done more than any other one person to influence and direct the course of Negro American writing. The son of a distinguished professor of theology at Howard University, Brown was born in Washington, D.C., and educated at Dunbar High School, Williams College, where he received a B.A. and was elected to Phi Beta Kappa, and Harvard University, where he received an M.A. in English.

He has taught at Virginia Seminary and College, Lincoln University (Missouri), Fisk University, and Howard. He has also been a visiting professor at New York University, the New School, Sarah Lawrence, and Vassar.

Sterling Brown is the author of *Southern Road* (1932); *Negro Poetry and Drama* (1937); and *The Negro in American Fiction* (1937). He is the senior editor of *The Negro Caravan* (1941). In addition, he has written numerous critical articles on literature, folklore, jazz, and Negro life and culture. For many years Brown was literary editor of the periodical *Opportunity* and wrote a monthly review of new books; between 1936 and 1939 he was Editor of Negro Affairs for the Federal Writers Project.

An excellent craftsman, in his poetry Sterling Brown effectively uses folk speech and folk experience. He has a delightful sense of humor and has developed several classic comic characters, including the unforgettable Slim Greer.

The essay which follows, "The New Negro in Literature," appeared originally in *The New Negro Thirty Years Afterwards*, Division of Social Sciences, Howard University Press (1955).

ODYSSEY OF BIG BOY

Lemme be wid Casey Jones,
Lemme be wid Stagolee,
Lemme be wid such like men
When Death takes hol' on me,
When Death takes hol' on me. . . .

Selections reprinted by permission of the author.

Done skinned as a boy in Kentucky hills,
   Druv steel dere as a man,
Done stripped tobacco in Virginia fiel's
   Alongst de River Dan,
     Alongst de River Dan;

Done mined de coal in West Virginia,
   Liked dat job jes' fine,
Till a load o' slate curved roun' my head,
   Won't work in no mo' mine,
     Won't work in no mo' mine;

Done shocked de corn in Marylan',
   In Georgia done cut cane,
Done planted rice in South Caline,
   But won't do dat again,
     Do dat no mo' again.

Been roustabout in Memphis,
   Dockhand in Baltimore,
Done smashed up freight on Norfolk wharves,
   A fust class stevedore,
     A fust class stevedore. . . .

Done slung hash yonder in de North
   On de ole Fall River Line,
Done busted suds in li'l New York,
   Which ain't no work o' mine—
     Lawd, ain't no work o' mine.

Done worked and loafed on such like jobs,
   Seen what dey is to see,
Done had my time wid a pint on my hip
   An' a sweet gal on my knee,
     Sweet mommer on my knee:

Had stovepipe blond in Macon,
   Yaller gal in Marylan',
In Richmond had a choklit brown,
   Called me huh monkey man—
     Huh big fool monkey man.

Had two fair browns in Arkansaw
   And three in Tennessee,
Had Creole gal in New Orleans,
   Sho Gawd did two time me—
     Lawd two time, fo' time me—

But best gal what I evah had
  Done put it over dem,
A gal in Southwest Washington
  At Four'n half and M—
    Four'n half and M. . . .

Done took my livin' as it came,
  Done grabbed my joy, done risked my life;
Train done caught me on de trestle,
  Man done caught me wid his wife,
    His doggone purty wife. . . .

I done had my women,
  I done had my fun;
Cain't do much complainin'
  When my jag is done,
    Lawd, Lawd, my jag is done.

An' all dat Big Boy axes
  When time comes fo' to go,
Lemme be wid John Henry, steel drivin' man,
  Lemme be wid old Jazzbo,
    Lemme be wid ole Jazzbo. . . .

OLD LEM

  I talked to old Lem
  And old Lem said,
    "They weigh the cotton
    They store the corn
      We only good enough
      To work the rows;
    They run the commissary
    They keep the books
      We gotta be grateful
      For being cheated;
    Whippersnapper clerks
    Call us out of our name
      We got to say mister
      To spindling boys
    They make our figgers
    Turn somersets
    We buck in the middle
      Say, "Thankyuh, sah.'

They don't come by ones
They don't come by twos
But they come by tens.

"They got the judges
They got the lawyers
They got the jury-rolls
They got the law
    They don't come by ones
They got the sheriffs
They got the deputies
    They don't come by twos

They got the shotguns
They got the rope
  We git the justice
  In the end
    And they come by tens.

"Their fists stay closed
Their eyes look straight
  Our hands stay open
  Our eyes must fall
    They don't come by ones
They got the manhood
They got the courage
    They don't come by twos
  We got to slink around,
  Hangtailed hounds.
They burn us when we dogs
They burn us when we men
    They come by tens. . . .

"I had a buddy
Six foot of man
Muscled up perfect
Game to the heart
    They don't come by ones
Outworked and outfought
Any man or two men
    They don't come by twos
He spoke out of turn
At the commissary
They gave him a day
To git out the county.

He didn't take it.
He said "Come and get me."
They came and got him.
            And they came by tens.
He stayed in the county—
He lays there dead.

        They don't come by ones
        They don't come by twos
        But they come by tens."

SISTER LOU

Honey
When de man
Calls out de las' train
You're gonna ride,
Tell him howdy.

Gather up yo' basket
An' yo' knittin' an' yo' things,
An' go on up an' visit
Wid frien' Jesus fo' a spell.

Show Marfa
How to make yo' greengrape jellies,
An' give po' Lazarus
A passel of them Golden Biscuits.

Scald some meal
Fo' some rightdown good spoonbread
Fo' li'l box-plunkin' David.

An' sit aroun'
An' tell them Hebrew Chillen
All yo' stories. . . .

Honey
Don't be feared of them pearly gates,
Don't go 'round to de back,
No mo' dataway
Not evah no mo'.

Let Michael tote yo' burden
An' yo' pocketbook an' evahthing
'Cept yo' Bible,

While Gabriel blows somp'n
Solemn but loudsome
On dat horn of his'n.

Honey
Go straight on to de Big House,
An' speak to yo' God
Widout no fear an' tremblin'.

Then sit down
An' pass de time of day awhile.

Give a good talkin' to
To yo' favorite 'postle Peter,
An' rub the po' head
Of mixed-up Judas,
An' joke awhile wid Jonah.

Then, when you gits de chance,
Always rememberin' yo' raisin',
Let 'em know youse tired
Jest a mite tired.

Jesus will find yo' bed fo' you
Won't no servant evah bother wid yo' room.
Jesus will lead you
To a room wid windows
Openin' on cherry trees an' plum trees
Bloomin' everlastin'.

An' dat will be yours
Fo' keeps.

Den take yo' time. . . .
Honey, take yo' bressed time.

MEMPHIS BLUES

1

Nineveh, Tyre,
Babylon,
Not much lef'
Of either one.
All dese cities

Ashes and rust,
De win' sing sperrichals
Through deir dus' . . .
Was another Memphis
Mongst de olden days,
Done been destroyed
In many ways. . . .
Dis here Memphis
It may go;
Floods may drown it;
Tornado blow;
Mississippi wash it
Down to sea—
Like de other Memphis in
History.

2

Watcha gonna do when Memphis on fire,
    Memphis on fire, Mistah Preachin' Man?
Gonna pray to Jesus and nebber tire,
    Gonna pray to Jesus, loud as I can,
        Gonna pray to my Jesus, oh, my Lawd!

Watcha gonna do when de tall flames roar,
    Tall flames roar, Mistah Lovin' Man?
Gonna love my brownskin better'n before—
    Gonna love my baby lak a do right man,
        Gonna love my brown baby, oh, my Lawd!

Watcha gonna do when Memphis falls down,
    Memphis falls down, Mistah Music Man?
Gonna plunk on dat box as long as it soun',
    Gonna plunk dat box fo' to beat de ban',
        Gonna tickle dem ivories, oh, my Lawd!

Watcha gonna do in de hurricane,
    In de hurricane, Mistah Workin' Man?
Gonna put dem buildings up again,
    Gonna put em up dis time to stan',
        Gonna push a wicked wheelbarrow, oh, my Lawd!

Watcha gonna do when Memphis near gone,
    Memphis near gone, Mistah Drinkin' Man?
Gonna grab a pint bottle of Mountain Corn,
    Gonna keep de stopper in my han',
        Gonna get a mean jag on, oh, my Lawd!

Watcha gonna do when de flood roll fas',
  Flood roll fas', Mistah Gamblin' Man?
Gonna pick up my dice fo' one las' pass—
  Gonna fade my way to de lucky lan',
    Gonna throw my las' seven—oh, my Lawd!

3

Memphis go
By Flood or Flame;
Nigger won't worry
All de same—
Memphis go
Memphis come back,
Ain' no skin
Off de nigger's back.
All dese cities
Ashes, rust. . . .
De win' sing sperrichals
Through deir dus'.

SLIM IN ATLANTA

Down in Atlanta,
  De whitefolks got laws
For to keep all de niggers
  From laughin' outdoors.

  Hope to Gawd I may die
    If I ain't speakin' truth
  Make de niggers do deir laughin'
    In a telefoam booth.

Slim Greer hit de town
  An' de rebs got him told,—
"Dontcha laugh on de street,
  If you want to die old."

  Den dey showed him de booth,
    An' a hundred shines
  In front of it, waitin'
    In double lines.

Slim thought his sides
  Would bust in two,
Yelled, "Lookout, everybody,
  I'm coming through!"

Pulled de other man out,
An' bust in de box,
An' laughed four hours
By de Georgia clocks.

Den he peeked through de door,
An' what did he see?
Three hundred niggers there
In misery.—

Some holdin' deir sides,
Some holdin' deir jaws,
To keep from breakin'
De Georgia laws.

An' Slim gave a holler,
An' started again;
An' from three hundred throats
Come a moan of pain.

An' everytime Slim
Saw what was outside,
Got to whoopin' again
Till he nearly died.

An' while de poor critters
Was waitin' deir chance,
Slim laughed till dey sent
Fo' de ambulance.

De state paid de railroad
To take him away;
Den, things was as usural
In Atlanta, Gee A.

REMEMBERING NAT TURNER

We saw a bloody sunset over Courtland, once Jerusalem,
As we followed the trail that old Nat took
When he came out of Cross Keys down upon Jerusalem,
In his angry stab for freedom a hundred years ago.
The land was quiet, and the mist was rising,
Out of the woods and the Nottaway swamp,
Over Southampton the still night fell,
As we rode down to Cross Keys where the march began.

When we got to Cross Keys, they could tell us little of him,
The Negroes had only the faintest recollections:
    "I ain't been here so long, I come from up roun' Newsome;
    Yassah, a town a few miles up de road,
    The old folks who coulda told you is all dead an' gone.
    I heard something, sometime; I doan jis remember what.
    'Pears lak I heard that name somewheres or other.
    So he fought to be free. Well. You doan say."

An old white woman recalled exactly
How Nat crept down the steps, axe in his hand,
After murdering a woman and child in bed,
"Right in this house at the head of these stairs."
(In a house built long after Nat was dead.)

She pointed to a brick store where Nat was captured,
(Nat was taken in a swamp, three miles away)
With his men around him, shooting from the windows
(She was thinking of Harper's Ferry and old John Brown.)
She cackled as she told how they riddled Nat with bullets
(Nat was tried and hanged at Courtland, ten miles away)
She wanted to know why folks would come miles
Just to ask about an old nigger fool.
    "Ain't no slavery no more, things is going all right,
    Pervided thar's a good goober market this year.
    We had a sign post here with printing on it,
    But it rotted in the hole and thar it lays;
    And the nigger tenants split the marker for kindling.
    Things is all right, naow, ain't no trouble with the niggers.
    Why they make this big to-do over Nat?"

As we drove from Cross Keys back to Courtland,
Along the way that Nat came down from Jerusalem,
A watery moon was high in the cloud-filled heavens,
The same moon he dreaded a hundred years ago.
The tree they hanged Nat on is long gone to ashes,
The trees he dodged behind have rotted in the swamps.

The bus for Miami and the trucks boomed by,
And touring cars, their heavy tires snarling on the pavement.
Frogs piped in the marshes, and a hound bayed long,
And yellow lights glowed from the cabin windows.

As we came back the way that Nat led his army,
Down from Cross Keys, down to Jerusalem,
We wondered if his troubled spirit still roamed the Nottaway,

Or if it fled with the cock-crow at daylight,
Or lay at peace with the bones in Jerusalem,
Its restlessness stifled by Southampton clay.

We remembered the poster rotted through and falling,
The marker split for kindling a kitchen fire.

THE NEW NEGRO IN LITERATURE (1925–1955)

I am grateful for the chance to participate in this symposium, dedicated to the memory of Alain LeRoy Locke. My acquaintance with Alain Locke dates back to his appearance at this university when, together with the other "Young Howards," a gang of boys that infested the campus, I stood in awe of the dapper man with a cane who had been a Rhodes Scholar at Oxford. Young barbarians on the brink of an unknown world, we thrilled at those magic words and wondered how so much learning could be stored in so slight a frame. When years later I joined the faculty here, I was struck by his incisive and wide ranging mind and by his devotedness to the university; I soon learned how firm a respect he enjoyed from such peers as Kelly Miller, Ernest Just, Charles Burch, Abram Harris, and Ralph Bunche, all stalwarts who have now left us. I have collaborated with him on articles, I was one of his associates in the Bronze Booklet Series, and although our critical views did not always coincide, I have profited from his wise counsel. I should like here to salute him as benefactor, colleague, and friend.

This conference, assessing the achievements of the New Negro movement and paying tribute to one of its prime launchers and sponsors, fills a need. Official biographers of eminent Negroes have commented only scantily on Alain Locke; in Embree's *Brown America* (1943) Locke's name is in neither bibliography nor index; in Embree's *Thirteen Against the Odds* he gets part of a sentence. In Brawley's *The Negro Genius,* he is merely called the *"maestro* of the New Negro performance" and is solely praised for "a fine sense of the value of words"—this of a man whose essays in *The New Negro* said more about the "Negro genius" than Brawley's entire book. It is true that, though little recorded, his place as mentor and interpreter is established. But it is good for this conference, in memoirs and elucidations, to make that place even clearer.

The Twenties

My colleagues have ably filled in the social and historical backgrounds of the New Negro movement. It is my task to trace and evaluate the literature by and about Negroes from 1925 to the present.

Because of the exigencies of time and space, drama must be excluded.[1] The divisions of this essay are natural, corresponding roughly with decades which had distinct cultural characteristics: they are (1) The Harlem Vogue, 1920–1930; (2) The Depression Thirties, and (3) World War II and Its Aftermath. I have hesitated to use the term Negro Renaissance for several reasons: one is that the five or eight years generally allotted are short for the life-span of any "renaissance." The New Negro is not to me a group of writers centered in Harlem during the second half of the twenties. Most of the writers were not Harlemites; much of the best writing was not about Harlem, which was the show-window, the cashier's till, but no more Negro America than New York is America. The New Negro movement had temporal roots in the past and spatial roots elsewhere in America, and the term has validity, it seems to me, only when considered to be a continuing tradition.

The rise of the New Negro movement coincided with increased interest in Negro life and character in the twenties. American literature was in revolt against the squeamishness and repression of Victorianism, and the philistinism of an acquisitive society. Carl Van Doren wrote: "What American literature decidedly needs at the moment is color, music, gusto, the free expression of gay or desperate moods. If the Negroes are not in a position to contribute these items, I do not know what Americans are." The decade was ushered in by Eugene O'Neill's *The Emperor Jones* (1920), an undoubted theatrical success, significant in placing the Negro at the tragic center instead of in comic relief, but overly reliant on tom-toms, superstition, and atavism. Waldo Frank's *Holiday* (1923), along with a humanitarian's dismay at injustice, defined white and Negro "consciousness" too schematically. Sherwood Anderson's *Dark Laughter* (1925) protests his fondness for the "Negro way of life," but when he equates this with self-satisfied satire of white neuroticism he shows how fondness could use a little knowledge. In his harrying of Puritanism, Carl Van Vechten made excursions to Harlem; despite his defenders' claim that he discovered the Negro élite, *Nigger Heaven* (1926) emphasizes the flamboyant and erotic. The influence of Europe was strong on the new sophisticates. Picasso's ad-

[1] The treatment of the Negro in drama is of course significant, but complete coverage of three decades of a fairly abundant literature is impossible for an essay of this length. The major plays, *In Abraham's Bosom* (1924); *The Green Pastures* (1930); *Porgy and Bess*, the "folk opera" (1935); *Stevedore* (1934); *Native Son* (1941); *Strange Fruit* (1945); *Deep Are The Roots* (1945), and the recent Louis Peterson's *Take A Giant Step* (1953), and Charles Sebree's and Greer Johnson's *Mrs. Patterson* (1954), conform to the trends that will be discussed. In 1927 Alain Locke saw on the near horizon great tragedy and comedy of Negro life, "universal even in sounding its most racial notes." ("Introduction," *Plays of Negro Life*, edited by Locke and Montgomery Gregory, New York and London, 1927), p. vi. But that hope has yet to be fulfilled.

miration for African sculpture, Gide's interest in the Congo, and the award of the *Prix Goncourt* to René Maran's naturalistic *Batouala* (1921) indicated France's turning to vital, genuine sources. But Paul Morand is merely a cynical camp follower in *Magie Noire* (1929), in which he includes absurd fantasies of American Negroes reverting at slightest provocation to ancestral savagery. Several British books seasoned Kipling's white man's burden with Mayfair ridicule; Ronald Firbank's *Prancing Nigger* (1925) is such sophisticated racist burlesque. Americans found the West Indies to be a treasure trove for authors, but where John Vandercook brought back from Haiti the stirring epic of Henri Christophe, W. B. Seabrook could find there little more than the weird, the voodoistic, the orgiastic, which he exploited in *The Magic Island* (1929).

Written with some distinction, these widely selling books by white authors enforced a tradition of exotic primitivism. Healthier interest in Negro life, of the here and now in America, was manifested in the liberal periodicals, the *Nation*, the *New Republic*, and the *American Mercury*. Alerted by James Weldon Johnson, Charles S. Johnson, and Alain Locke to the growing expression of Negro life by Negroes themselves, the *Survey Graphic* issued a Harlem number in March, 1925. This afforded the nucleus of an epochal collection of the work of young and old, aspiring and established, fledgling poet and established racial statesman, which, under the creative editing of Alain Locke, appeared a few months later as *The New Negro: An Interpretation*.

Alain Locke introduced the volume confidently: The New Negro "wishes to be known for what he is, even in his faults and shortcomings, and scorns a craven and precarious survival at the price of seeming to be what he is not."[2] The already published *Cane* (1923) by Jean Toomer deserves such praise. Apprenticeship to experimental writing had helped Toomer develop a revelatory prose; deep pondering over Negro life in border cities and Georgia had supplied him with rich material; the resultant book, *Cane*, expressed Negro life with insight, beauty, and power. Eric Walrond's *Tropic Death* (1926), brilliant impressionism about the tragedies of his native Caribbean, was unapologetically naturalistic, and firmly controlled in style.

Neither wrote another work of fiction, however, and their pioneering was not followed. Negro writers instead trooped off to join Van Vechten's band and share in the discovery of Harlem as a new African colony. Wa-wa trumpets, trap drums (doubling for tom-toms), and shapely dancers with bunches of bananas girdling their middles in Bamboo Inns and Jungle Cabarets nurtured tourists' delusions of "the Congo cutting through the black." Claude McKay's *Home to Harlem*

---

[2] Locke, "The New Negro" in Locke, ed., *The New Negro: An Interpretation* (New York, 1925), p. 11.

(1926) concentrates on the primitive, which McKay defiantly glorifies in *Banjo* (1929), whose hero decides to "let intellect go to hell and live instinct." *Joie de vivre* was acclimated to Harlem especially, to Negroes generally. It was all rhythm, rhythm; jazz-bands swung out on "That's Why Darkies Were Born;" pent-houses sprouted miraculously atop Lenox Avenue tenements; the cabin was exchanged for the cabaret but the old mirth was still inside. Even Countee Cullen in *One Way to Heaven* (1932) proclaims "Enjoyment isn't across the [racial] line." The whites have only money, privilege, power; Negroes have cornered the joy.

Gay with youth, heady from attention, caught up along with much of America in ballyhoo, flattered by influential creators, critics, and publishers who had suddenly discovered the dark world at their doorstep, many Negroes helped to make a cult of Harlem. They set up their own Bohemia, sharing in the nationwide rebellion from family, church, small town, and business civilization, but revolt from racial restrictions was sporadic. Rash in the spurt for sophistication (wisdom was too slow and did not pay off), grafting primitivism on decadence, they typified one phase of American literary life in the twenties. A few magazines such as *Fire* and *Harlem* flared like rockets; good experiments jostled against much that was falsely atavistic and wilfully shocking.

But several writers were uncomfortable at the racial mystique that seemed the price of the new freedom. Wallace Thurman illustrates their ambivalence in *Blacker the Berry* (1929), which counterposes lurid descriptions of Harlem with a somber account of a dark heroine who is defeated by color snobbishness among Negroes themselves. All was certainly not joy in Thurman's heaven. Alain Locke warned that "too many of our younger writers . . . are pot-plants seeking a forced growth according to the exotic tastes of a pampered and decadent public."[3] Rudolph Fisher rose above this ruck. Kin to O. Henry with his quick eyes and ears and curiosity, Fisher wrote insouciant fiction that tells more about Harlem than is in all of *Nigger Heaven* and its brood.

The obvious preference for low-life Harlem was chided by W. E. B. Du Bois, who wished creative literature to enlist in his trenchant crusade for equal rights. His novels, *The Quest of the Silver Fleece* (1911) and *The Dark Princess* (1928), have undoubted social wisdom and prophetic vision, but their virtues are those of pamphleteering. The fiction by the officers of the NAACP is programmatic, fighting Nordicism, disfranchisement, segregation, mob violence, and other racial evils. Walter White's *Fire in the Flint* (1924) has strength chiefly as

[3] Locke, "Art or Propaganda?" *Harlem, A Forum of Negro Life,* I (November, 1928), 12.

an anti-lynching tract. Alert against the obvious stereotypes, White lent his support in *Flight* (1926) to the stereotype of the heroine who passes for white until she gets a mystical revelation that happiness belongs on the darker side of the racial boundary. Passing, in novels, became an inordinate preoccupation of leisure class Negro women. Such is true of Nella Larsen's heroine in *Passing* (1930); and in *Quicksand* (1928) her heroine is torn between pulls of race and caste. Jessie Fauset's novels also have an undue amount of passing, but her chief purpose is to exhibit the Negro world of education, substance, and breeding. Like most novels of the Negro middle class, however, these have little penetration; they record a class (idealized) in order to praise a race (imperfectly understood).

Whether licentious Harlem or sedate brown Babbittry, the most frequent setting for New Negro fiction was the urban North. Great segments of Negro life obviously remained unrecorded. Agreeing with the wag who would rather be "a lamppost on Lenox Avenue than the mayor of Atlanta," most Negro novelists left the South to white authors. Julia Peterkin's absorption in the plantation life of coastal South Carolina and Du Bose Heyward's poetic use of the lives of Charleston Negroes, at its best in *Porgy*, showed unusual grasp of folkspeech and folkways, an unfeigned sympathy different from the old cozy condescension. There remained some stress on the exotic and violent, some traces of the plantation tradition, some failure or unwillingness to comprehend. But regionalism drew close to reality. Howard Odum's Left Wing Gordon is as authentic as countless conversations with footloose working-men and minstrels could make him. The little-heralded books of E. C. L. Adams contained dialogues of folk Negro talking to folk Negro, which were unsurpassed in their ironic awareness and added dimensions to people who had long been considered quaint, artless children. John Sale and R. Emmett Kennedy wrote of Mississippi and Louisiana Negroes from long and loving study; even Roark Bradford, of the same region, knew much about the folk Negro. But, for all of his grasp of idiom and mannerism, he saw little in folk-life beyond the ludicrous and wasted his knowledge on burlesque.

Thorough collection and study of Negro folksong accompanied the growing regionalism. Howard Odum and Guy Johnson turned up valuable ore in *The Negro and His Songs* (1925) and *Negro Workaday Songs* (1926). The researches of Guy Johnson and Louis Chappell set John Henry deservedly in the pantheon of American folk heroes. Abbe Niles and W. C. Handy, in *Blues: An Anthology* (1926), pioneered in the analysis and history of this original music, which Mamie and Bessie Smith and Ma Rainey were popularizing. James Weldon Johnson and J. Rosamond Johnson edited collections of spirituals in 1925 and 1926, for which the former wrote valuable introductions. These together with Alain Locke's perceptive appreciation in *The New Negro* and the appealing voices of Roland Hayes, Paul Robeson, Taylor Gordon, Marian Anderson, and the Hall Johnson choir, made the spirituals, in the words of one enthusiast, "the finest medium for interpreting to the whites some of the best qualities of the Negroes."[4]

Claude McKay's *Harlem Shadows* signalled the new movement in poetry. The substance of McKay's poems was different; nostalgic recreations of early Jamaica life alternated with harsh pictures of America. The poet's manly anger and militant self-assurance were properly influential. Countee Cullen, a precocious disciple of the romantic tradition, produced gifted lyrics on love and death as brown youth coped with them. For all of his disclaimers, race pride and defense hovered over his verse. Cullen sought a tradition to glorify, turning, as in "Heritage," to story-book Africa, or to romantic heroes such as Christophe and Simon the Cyrenian. When he turned to American Negro experience the result was the unconvincing *Black Christ*. Langston Hughes felt Negro life more sincerely and portrayed it more movingly. *Weary Blues* (1926) and *Fine Clothes to the Jew* (1927) presented blues singers, honky-tonk dancers, lonely piano players, wastrels, and others of the urban folk with sympathy and authenticity. Hughes learned from Lindsay and Sandburg, but wisely also studied the rhythms of jazz, the spirituals, and the blues. Deceptively simple, these poems often contain real insight. James Weldon Johnson was influenced by the new regionalism to discard his older rhetorical approach; *God's Trombones* (1927) dramatically resurrects the eloquence of the bard-like folk preacher. These seven poetized sermons, wrought with loving care, showed as did some of Toomer's lyrics, how folkstuff could be invested with dignity. These were the more important poets: lyrics of merit were written conventionally by Georgia Douglas Johnson and Angelina Grimké, and unconventionally by Anne Spencer and Fenton Johnson, who bitterly echoed *Spoon River Anthology*. Helene Johnson, Frank Horne, Arna Bontemps, and Waring Cuney won prizes in the annual contests held by the *Crisis* and *Opportunity* magazines.

What was the critical standing of the literature of Negro life in the twenties? Reviewers were generous, but in later accounts of the period omit books once praised. Opposition critics included Wyndham Lewis, whose *Paleface* (1929) railed at sentimental primitivism, which he felt was swelling the fearful tide of color. Harvey Wickham, deploring the degradation of much fiction about Negroes, still counseled the Negro to be "engagingly different" and to create "the romance of Africa espoused to our own South, the savage's sense of the nearness of the

---

[4] "In the Driftway," *Nation*, CXXXI (September 3, 1930), 245.

spiritual world."[5] Present day literary historians of the decade are silent about the New Negro movement. The latest and fullest coverage mentions only Van Vechten, Sherwood Anderson, and Waldo Frank, and summarizes the interest in the Negro as simplification, distortion, and exploitation of primitivism.[6]

Such easy dismissal is injustice, however; primitivism is not the only trend of early New Negro writing. When one realizes that since Chesnutt's pioneering, no fiction by Negroes had tapped the rich materials except James Weldon Johnson's *Autobiography of An Ex-Coloured Man* (1912) and since Dunbar, little poetry except genre sentimentality and race rhetoric, one sees in fresh perspective the positive achievements of the earliest New Negroes. The fiction of Toomer, Walrond, Fisher, and of McKay at his uncontroversial best; the poetry of *God's Trombones*, McKay, Cullen, and Hughes; the winning of real respect for Negro spirituals, seculars, and folkstuff generally; all of these had solid merit. New publishing houses—Knopf, Harcourt Brace, Viking, Liveright and the Bonis—welcomed Negro talents, who opened doors that have stayed open.

Langston Hughes's credo expressed proud independence: "We younger Negro artists intend to express our individual dark-skinned selves without fear or shame." In not caring whether white people or Negroes were pleased, these artists stand "on the top of the mountain, free within ourselves." But the fine idealism runs up hard against the reality that white critics were constantly looking over the writers' shoulders and, even when well-meaning, often counseled amiss.[7] There were few Negro critics for guidance. One of the best equipped, Allison Davis, keenly analyzed the opportunism of the rampant primitivism, cynicism, and luridity. He found in the experience of Negroes here in America, both past and present, qualities better worth attention; these were "fortitude, irony, and a relative absence of self pity"[8]—a broader human nature available for the imagination that could grasp it, and a higher potential for truer and more universal literature. But such trust and such prescription point forward to the thirties.

[5] Harvey Wickham, *The Impuritans* (New York, 1929), p. 283.
[6] Frederick J. Hoffman, *The Twenties: American Writing in the Postwar Decade* (New York, 1955), p. 269. Edmund Wilson's *The Shores of Light* (1952) touches only on Frank and Toomer; John K. Hutchen's *The American Twenties* anthologizes no work about Negro life; William Hodapp's *The Pleasures of the Jazz Age* (1948) anthologizes only a dithyramb by Sherwood Anderson to Negro easy living as an instance of the period's interest in The Race Question!
[7] See, for example, Dorothy Van Doren's review of Schuyler's *Black No More*, which says: "The Negro will never write great literature while he tries to write white literature. It may be that he can express himself only by music and rhythm and not by words." "Black, Alas, No More!", *Nation*, CXXXII (February 25, 1931), 219.
[8] Allison Davis, "Our Intellectuals," *Crisis*, XXXV (August, 1928), 285.

The Thirties

Those who nostalgically recall the Harlem boom include in their memoirs far more of the good time parties and big contacts than of the writing. Alain Locke was troubled by the feckless irresponsibility of a fad produced "by a period of inflation and overproduction."[9] Langston Hughes dated its end "when the crash came in 1929 and the white people had much less money to spend on themselves and practically none to spend on Negroes."[10] For all of its positive services in encouraging racial respect and self reliance, a large number of Negroes were ignorant of, indifferent or ill disposed toward the new literature of Negro life.

The current literary fashion in America is to make the thirties a whipping boy, while pampering the glamorous twenties. Nevertheless a period which saw the maturing of Dos Passos, Farrell, Wolfe, Hemingway, Steinbeck, Caldwell, and Faulkner cannot be cavalierly dismissed as stodgily naturalistic or proletarian. The central characteristic of the period is its grave reappraisal of American life and positive affirmation of democracy. When Black Friday ushered in the Depression, American writers were shocked by the unfamiliar sights of bread lines, unemployed workers, closed factories, farm evictions, hunger, and loss of human decency. It *had* happened here, and America wanted to know why. American writers, sensitive and dismayed, assumed serious social responsibilities.

Negro authors of the thirties, like their compatriots, faced reality more squarely. For the older lightheartedness they substituted sober self searching; for the bravado of false Africanism and Bohemianism they substituted attempts to understand Negro life in its workaday aspects in the here and now. Clear-eyed and forthright social scientists —Charles S. Johnson, E. Franklin Frazier, and Abram Harris—supplied needed documentation, analysis, and synthesis. Alert to the changing times, a few critics—Alain Locke among them—charted new directions.

The first books by Negroes in the thirties continued the preoccupations of the twenties, when they were conceived. Taylor Gordon's bawdy autobiography *Born to Be* (1930) was sponsored as usual by Van Vechten, who praised the author's six-foot lankiness, "falsetto voice, and molasses laugh," but neglected to point out his literary distinctions; one of which—a murderous way with grammar—charmed several aesthetes. George Schuyler's swashbuckling *Black No More* (1931), a fantasy about the dire results of the discovery of a treatment to whiten dark complexions, indiscriminately lampooned Dixie racists and professional race-men. Wallace Thurman's *Infants of the Spring*

[9] Locke, "This Year of Grace," *Opportunity*, IX (February, 1931), 48.
[10] Langston Hughes, *The Big Sea* (New York, 1940), p. 247.

(1932) exposes the Harlem literati, whom he calls Niggerati, in their dissipation. Seven years after their brave beginning Thurman is grieving over the New Negroes as a lost generation, pandering to tourists on the safari for queer dives in Harlem.

More engagingly written, Arna Bontemps's *God Sends Sunday* (1931) belongs with the earlier school in its evocation of the life of jockeys, rounders, and demi-mondaines of the gaudy Negro tenderloin at the turn of the century. His second novel illustrates the change: now involved with the Negro's struggle for freedom, Bontemps chose a new sort of history for *Black Thunder* (1936). Based on a little-known slave revolt, written with imaginative identification, *Black Thunder* is one of America's better historical novels.[11] Langston Hughes, a barometer of this decade as of others, turned to semi-autobiographic fiction in *Not Without Laughter* (1930), a quietly moving novel of boyhood in a Kansas town. *The Ways of White Folks* (1934), a collection of Hughes's short stories, contains fondness for underprivileged people and shrewd, sometimes exasperated irony at patronage. Zora Neale Hurston showed a ripeness worth waiting for in the tales she contributed to *Story Magazine* in the thirties, and in the folk-based *Jonah's Gourd Vine* (1934) and *Their Eyes Were Watching God* (1937), a superior regional novel about the rural Negroes of Miss Hurston's native Florida. Miss Hurston's *Mules and Men* (1935) is a first class collection of Negro yarns, gaining from the author's being both insider and trained folklorist. Inside intimacy is also in George Wylie Henderson's *Ollie Miss* (1935); George Lee's combination of river legend, sharecropping realism and protest in *River George* (1937); and the promising beginnings of a family saga in E. Waters Turpin's *These Low Grounds* (1937) and *O Canaan* (1939). But, not staying with their material, these authors forfeited the slow maturation so apparent in the best of American regionalist writing.

The nation's Economic Problem Number One—The South—strongly attracted the social conscience. The poor white sharecropper—America's forgotten man—written of definitively by William Faulkner in *As I Lay Dying* (1930) and by Erskine Caldwell in *Tobacco Road* (1932) was shown as having much the same characteristics—improvidence, shiftlessness, promiscuity, superstition—that had been superficially considered Negro traits. "Kneel to the Rising Sun," Caldwell's most striking story, showed a Negro who has grit denied to his white fellow in misery, and humanity denied to the sadistic landlord. Novels by

---

[11] Historical fiction about slavery, the Civil War, and Reconstruction has been plentiful. Despite the phenomenal success of *Gone With The Wind*, the plantation tradition is in decline. More satisfying artistically and historically has been the recreation of the past by regionalists whose documentation and honesty draw them far from the moonlight and magnolia school.

white authors aware of the harshness of Negro life include Roy Flannagan's *Amber Satyr* (1932), and Robert Rylee's *Deep Dark River* (1935). William March's *Come In At The Door* (1934) and Hamilton Basso's *Courthouse Square* (1936) go even farther, portraying Negroes of education and ambition with sympathy hitherto reserved for peasant types.

Left-wing authors, among them Scott Nearing, John Spivak, and Myra Page, attacked the rampant injustices—wholesale discrimination, peonage, the chain gang, unjust employment practices, and lynching— in a catalogue too true in its tragic particulars, with veracity as a *J'accuse*, but with less verisimilitude as literature. Grace Lumpkin's *A Sign for Cain* (1935), the best "proletarian" novel about Negro life, springs from wide knowledge and deep feeling. A schematic conclusion to most of the proletarian fiction was the union of white and Negro workers, which at this point of history, not only in the deep South, was more wishful than realizable.

In 1938 Richard Wright's *Uncle Tom's Children* won *Story Magazine's* contest for the best book of fiction by a member of the Federal Writers' Project. Comprising four novellas, this book showed intense militancy and a power to present the starkest of tragedies. Largely self-trained, a brooding, lonely seeker for decency, rasped by constant racial rebuffs in the South, Wright poured more anger and terror into his fiction than any other Negro author had done. He made his people vivid and convincing in their full humanity, courage, and wisdom, their frustration and fortitude. In 1939 Wright added to the volume "The Ethics of Living Jim Crow," which was an early draft of *Black Boy,* and "Bright and Morning Star," which, though as bleak as the first novellas, nourished the hope for brotherhood of the oppressed, which for a short while Wright believed that Communism was to achieve.

Most of the poetry of the decade is regionalism or social protest. Welborn V. Jenkins's *Trumpet in the New Moon* (1934) is rhapsodic but vivid cataloguing of Negro experience; Frank Marshall Davis is likewise panoramic in *Black Man's Verse* (1935) and *I Am The American Negro* (1937) which mingle sharp etchings with irony and belligerence. Richard Wright's occasional poems were farthest to the left. In the early thirties, Langston Hughes suddenly rebelled from a white patron who believed that Negroes had "mystery and mysticism and spontaneous harmony in their souls" when not polluted by whites. He responded that he did not feel the primitive surging through him. He admitted a love for the surface and the rhythms of Africa, but said, "I was not Africa. I was Chicago and Kansas City and Broadway and Harlem."[12] "Advertisement for the Waldorf Astoria" contrasting luxury

[12] Hughes, *op. cit.,* pp. 316 ff.

with down-and-out Harlem, signalized Hughes's revolt, which extended to praise of revolutionary heroes, attacks upon false Negro leadership, and heated defense of the Scottsboro boys.

Negro, an anthology edited by Nancy Cunard in 1934, struck insistently the chord of protest against colonialism in Africa and the Caribbean and second-class citizenship at home; the numerous contributors included whites as well as Negroes. The "united front" against Fascism partly broke down the isolation of the Negro author. The Federal Writers' Project gave even fuller participation to Negroes, employing Bontemps, McKay, Roi Ottley, Ted Poston, Henry Lee Moon, Wright, William Attaway, Ellison, Margaret Walker, Willard Motley, Frank Yerby, and Zora Neale Hurston. The Writers' Project aided Negro authors as well as white by exploring the American past and encouraging a sound, unchauvinistic regionalism. Of the planned series of books on Negro life, only the *Negro in Virginia* (1940) prepared by Roscoe Lewis from materials amassed by Negroes on the Virginia Project was completed, but this book is earnest of what might have developed had not the solons at the Capitol killed the Project so soon. In December, 1940, as a sort of climax to the New Deal interest in Negro life, the seventy-fifth anniversary of the Thirteenth Amendment was commemorated at the Library of Congress by an exhibit of paintings, books, and manuscripts, and a festival of music in which Dorothy Maynor and Roland Hayes sang, and the Budapest Quartet played music on Negro themes. On the evening devoted to Negro folk music, Alain Locke was commentator on the Spirituals, Sterling Brown on the Blues and Ballads, and Alan Lomax on the Reels and Worksongs. Locke repeated his proud faith in the survival of the spirituals, and believed them at last safe "under the protection of the skilful folklorist."[13] He was correct: around the hall in the Folk-Archives were thousands of records of Negro folk music of all types, needing interpretation and creative shaping certainly, but available to any honest searcher for truth.

From the Forties to the Present

The rediscovery of the American past in the thirties deepened into passionate affirmation of democracy in the early forties when Fascism menaced the entire world. American Negroes shared as always the determination that democracy should survive. But they knew bitterly that democracy had never been simon-pure for them; that, as Langston Hughes wrote: "America never was America to me." Fighting against

---

[13] *Seventy Years of Freedom* (Commemoration of the 75th Anniversary of the Proclamation of the 13th Amendment to the Constitution of the United States) (Washington, 1940), p. 15.

Hitlerism abroad, they found nothing contradictory in fighting against injustice at home. The democracy they endorsed was of the future; they were lukewarm at the slogan that victory would restore American life exactly as it had been. Exclusion from complete service in factory and on firing line was galling. The irony of rejecting one tenth of the nation from an all-out defense of democracy was apparent both at home and among our allies.

In Richard Wright's significant *Native Son* (1940), Bigger Thomas was native born, but an exploited ghetto was his home, and a straight course from delinquency to crime was his doom. *Native Son* was composed in great anger, but except for excessive melodrama and the Marxist lawyer's harangue explaining what Wright's powerful dramatic scenes had already left clear, the anger was disciplined by craft. A large audience, prepared by Dreiser and Farrell and depression naturalists, acclaimed *Native Son;* the Book-of-the Month and The Modern Library selected it (the first choice in both instances of a book by a Negro). Wright's impressionist "folk history," *Twelve Million Black Voices* (1941), excellently illustrated by Edwin Rosskam, stresses exploitation and revolt. *Black Boy* (1945), the autobiography of Wright's early years, is also violent and outspoken. Hatred of racial injustice made Wright seek France as refuge. Here, having broken with the Communist Party, he wrote fiction of the Underground Man, Wright's new symbol for the American Negro. Influenced by existentialism, *The Outsider* (1953) lacks roots in the American scene that Wright knew so well, and suffers in the transplanting.

William Attaway's *Blood on the Forge* (1941), another unapologetic novel, is based on unused material—the experiences of three brothers who give up sharecropping for work in the steel mills; its style, veering from naturalistic to symbolic, is mature; the ideas are perceptive. Chester Himes in his shorter fiction had drawn his characters from the lower depths; his novels are concerned with the lonely and frustrated who, no more than Bigger Thomas, can find a home in America. Himes's *If He Hollers* (1945) portrays a Negro whose neuroticism is tormented by wartime experiences; *Lonely Crusade* (1947) shows a labor organizer's disillusionment with fellow Negroes, organized labor, and the Communist Party. The white world is blamed by Himes for most of the dead ends of his characters; in *Third Generation* (1954), however, a family is ruined by a mulatto mother's pathologic worship of color and upper-class striving.

The intra-racial problem of color has now ousted the once favorite problem of passing. Dorothy West's *Living is Easy* (1948), written from long familiarity with Boston, satirizes convincingly the snobbishness based on color and social prestige. Willard Savoy's *Alien Land* (1949) probes anew the dilemmas of a fair-skinned Negro confronted by race loyalty and racial rebuffs. J. Saunders Redding's *Stranger and*

Alone (1950) sues a new milieu, Negro college life,—about which Redding certainly has an insider's knowledge—, but revelation is sacrificed for embittered exposure of two mulatto misleaders who exhaust the vices of Uncle Tomism.

Tribulations of the slum-shocked filled most of the decade's novels of Negro life. Best of these is Ann Petry's *The Street* (1946), the winner of the Houghton Mifflin Literary Fellowship. Miss Petry's crowded tenements, delinquent youngsters, hunted women, and predatory men inhabit a city drastically different from the joy-filled playground of the Harlem Vogue. A skilled and thoughtful novelist, Miss Petry has also written *Narrows* (1953), which tells of a doomed interracial affair in Connecticut. Carl Offord's *White Face* (1943) about Harlem, Philip Kaye's *Taffy* (1950) about Harlem and Brooklyn, Alden Bland's *Behold A Cry* (1947) about Chicago, and Curtis Lucas's *Third Ward Newark* (1946) are typical of the sociological fiction where poverty, family disorganization, alcoholism, unemployment, police brutality, and other urban evils are rendered better than the characters. Case studies at their best, literary slumming at their worst, they are exposures of the obvious rather than illumination of the hidden. Too often hopelessness palls; the course of the neurotic pawns is disastrous instead of tragic; the protagonists are victims, not heroes, because they struggle half-heartedly if at all. In the soft-back publishing bonanza, however, such novels sell well; it is likely that the four S's of sex, sadism, sensationalism, and sentimentality pay off better than the justified racial indignation.

William Gardner Smith's *South Street* (1954) seeks a wider scope than the slums, but his handling of an interracial romance lacks the biting reality of his earlier *The Last of the Conquerors* (1948). This novel, one of the few to tap the Negro's rich war experience, tells much about the Negro G.I. in Europe, where the lack of color prejudice among the defeated Hitlerites contrasts ironically with its presence among white soldiers of the American occupation. John O. Killen's novel *Youngblood* (1954) departs from the futility of the slum exposures, and sets its major sections in Crossroads, Georgia, where slow improvements are brought about by militant unionists, teachers, and preachers, who learn to organize their strength. *Have You Been to the River* (1952) by Chancellor Williams is also solidly documentary, this time on the cult religions and their zealots, with a social scientist expounding the meanings.

White authors did not neglect the dramatic life of Negroes in the changing South. Lillian Smith's *Strange Fruit* (1944) with sharp and deep understanding shows race-crossed lovers in a mean-spirited Georgia town. Insight into the many types, Negro and white, a cross-section of the South, helps *Strange Fruit* disclose hitherto concealed truths. Bucklin Moon's *Without Magnolias* (1949) gives another cross-section: its delineations of a Southern Negro college under white control, the

Uncle Toms, courageous labor leaders, working folk, and intellectuals, are authentic and sincere. Hodding Carter, alarmed by war tensions, wrote *Winds of Fear* (1944), a middle-of-the-road novel recognizing the Negro's growing and justified militancy. William Russell's *A Wind is Rising* (1950), Arthur Gordon's *Reprisal* (1950), and Earl Conrad's fiction are protests against lynching and exploitation, as are several of Caldwell's sardonic later novels. The incidental Negro characters in the fiction of Carson McCullers and Peter Taylor reveal aspects of race relations unrecorded earlier. Without stressing violence, Jefferson Young's *A Good Man* (1953), Lonnie Coleman's *Clara* (1952), and Hubert Creekmore's family saga *The Chain in the Heart* (1953) tell of Negroes whose essential dignity is firmly respected. William Faulkner has grown in wisdom about Negroes; after early stereotyping and groping, he created in *Go Down Moses* (1942) Negro characters of complexity and depth. Sometimes, as in *Intruder in the Dust* (1948), Faulkner yields to fierce anti-yankeeism, but when he lets Negroes do their own talking and acting, they refute his political tirades, and join the company of his best characterizations.

The most recent fiction by Negro authors is personal, not social; psychological more than sociological; it attacks no problems but wrestles with philosophical meanings. It shares the current distrust of liberalism and naturalism. One young critic denounces the "professionally liberal" publishers who insist that the Negro writer "cannot possibly know anything else but Jim Crow, sharecropping, slum-ghettoes, Georgia crackers, and the sting of his humiliation, his unending ordeal, his blackness."[14] This swing of the pendulum from the publishers of the Van Vechten vogue with their demands for the exotic is striking. Nevertheless, some publishers still take risks with Negro fiction not burdened with the conventional problem. William Demby's *Beetle Creek* (1950) presents a stifling small town where an old white eccentric seeking friendship from Negroes is rejected with cruel barbarity. Owen Dodson's *Boy at the Window* (1951) focuses steadily on a Negro boy's growing up in Brooklyn and Washington; the problems are those of youth and adolescence, not race. James Baldwin considers the problem novel to be the cage of Negro writing. Of his novel, *Go Tell It on the Mountain* (1953), Baldwin says: "I wanted my people to be people first, Negroes almost incidentally. . . . I hoped by refusing to take a special, embattled tone, to involve the reader in their lives [so that] he would close the book knowing more about himself, and therefore more about Negroes, than he had known before." Baldwin's depiction of a Negro family and of the religion of Harlem storefront churches has rich insight. Ralph Ellison's *Invisible Man* (1952) is by any reckoning a major novel. Its theme is time-honored—the education of a provincial;

[14] Richard Gibson, "A No to Nothing," *Kenyon Review* (Spring, 1951), reprinted in *Perspectives USA* (Winter, 1953), p. 92.

its manner ranges from naturalistic to surrealistic. Its hero—humiliated as a boy in the South, disillusioned by a Southern college, catspaw of Communists, quarry of frenzied Negro nationalists, rejected and harassed, denied identity as a person—pays exorbitantly for his education. But Ellison has humor as well as starkness. His swarming gallery of characters: Negroes, whites; folk illiterates, Park Avenue sophisticates; mentals and mad messiahs; all have the ring of truth. Saying more about Negro life than any preceding novelist, Ellison claims universality for his novel. "Who knows, but that on the lower frequencies, I speak for you," his protagonist asks all other men who are perplexed by the tensions of modern civilization.

Because of the phenomenal sales of Frank Yerby's historical romances and the critical esteem accorded Willard Motley's novels, certain critics now counsel Negro novelists to stop writing about Negro life. But Yerby's period pieces are hardly pertinent to such counsel. Escapist fiction, shrewdly concocted of sex and sadism, sensationalizing rather than illuminating history, has never invalidated the time-proven truth that in representational literature an artist does best with what he knows best and feels most deeply. Motley's *Knock on Any Door* (1947) about an Italian gangster, and his *We Fished All Night* (1952) about perplexed veterans, support the axiom; this polyglot, fringe world is precisely the world that Motley knows best. Most Negroes, however, have not shared such experiences. The pragmatic proof is still the quality of the book; the "white novels" of Zora Neale Hurston, Ann Petry, Chester Himes, William Gardner Smith are inferior in significance and skill to their novels centered in Negro experience. That Negro novelists should not be confined to Negro characters goes without saying. Even if said, bold imaginations would always be found to disobey; Negroes will write of whites with as much knowledge and sympathetic identification as they can muster. But this does not mean the forfeiture of the life that perforce they know best. Negro life is called a prison by certain critics who equate civic disabilities with artistic, but for the artist of imagination it is no more imprisoning than the worlds of Zola, Dostoevsky, Joyce, O'Casey, or Faulkner.

Negro poets of the last fifteen years have followed the course of modern poetry, from "public" verse to private symbolism. Poetry of the early forties was social: Waring Cuney turned from elegiac lyrics to harsh blues, which the folk singer, Joshua White, recorded as *Southern Exposure*. Langston Hughes continued his racial indignation in *Jim Crow's Last Stand* (1943) and his quizzical portraiture in several books, from *Shakespeare in Harlem* (1942) to *One Way Ticket* (1949). *Montage of a Dream Deferred* (1951), experimenting with counterparts of jazz forms—from swing through boogie-woogie to bebop— shows Hughes at his mature best in revealing the complexity of his beloved Harlem. Frank Marshall Davis's *47th Street* (1948) has vigor and bite and the same kind of knowingness about Chicago that Hughes has about Harlem. Margaret Walker's *For My People,* which won the Yale University Younger Poets award in 1942, expressed strong racial pride and faith in both dithyrambs and ballads. Quite different is the carefully disciplined poetry of Gwendolyn Brooks's *A Street in Bronzeville* (1945); frankness, insight, and increasingly intricate symbolism mark her *Annie Allen* (1949), which won the Pulitzer Prize. *Powerful Long Ladder* (1946), by Owen Dodson, another highly trained poet, includes sincerely felt poetry on race experience; his later poems, in step with *avant-gardism,* explore a private mystical world.

Robert Hayden's earliest *Heart Shapes in the Dust* (1940) contained deft lyrics of clarity and melody; the poems of his second phase exploded the heroic and tragic in the history of the Negro; his latest poems in *The Lion and The Archer* (1948) and *Figure of Time* (1955) are densely symbolic. Hayden is the leading spirit in a group that issued a manifesto, "Counterpoise," which opposed the "chauvinistic, the cultist, the special pleading" of Negro writing, and its evaluation "entirely in the light of sociology and politics."[15] Myron O'Higgins, whose poems comprised the second part of *The Lion and The Archer,* Bruce McWright, May Miller, and Carl Holman are also skillful modernist poets. M. Beaunorus Tolson's poetic career extends from the rhapsodic poetry of *Rendezvous with America* (1944) to the *Libretto for the Republic of Liberia* (1955), where Whitman's influence is exchanged for those of Hart Crane, Pound, and Eliot. Tolson's praise of the Liberian experiment is not perfunctory; *Libretto* grew out of long antagonism to imperialism, a wide-reaching intelligence, and a vigorous vocabulary. Allen Tate has called this poem the Negro's first complete assimilation of the "language of the Anglo-American poetic tradition," i.e., the tradition of Allen Tate.[16] With great respect for Tolson's gifts, one may still say of his latest sponsor, to paraphrase one of his favorite poets: *Timeo Tateos, donas ferentes.* The *Libretto* has a *succès d'estime* and is to be studied over the land in college classes; for this explication Tolson has supplied sixteen pages of notes for twenty-nine sparsely printed pages of text, but for one reader these are not yet enough.

The discovery of America, encouraged by the Writers' Project, stimulated Roi Ottley's *New World A-Comin'* (1943), which gave an up-to-date, guardedly optimistic account of the changes of the racial front. Ottley's *Black Odyssey* (1948) is sprightly, journalistic history; his *No Green Pastures* (1951) records disillusionment with Europe, concluding that despite the disabilities, America still offers the greatest promises to Negroes. J. Saunders Redding's *No Day of Triumph* (1942) is one of the best examples of the reportage of the forties, telling much

---

[15] "Counterpoise" (Nashville, 1948) n.p.
[16] "Introduction," Tolson, *Libretto for the Republic of Liberia* (New York, 1955), n.p.

about Negro America with keenness and perceptiveness. These qualities also mark *They Came in Chains* (1950), a volume in Louis Adamic's People of America Series. Redding's *On Being Negro in America* (1951), baring the exasperations of a Negro intellectual, was supposed to be his last word on "race," but in *An American in India* (1954) race confronts him constantly and he is forced to spend much of his mission defending America from Communist hecklers. Carl Rowan's *South of Freedom* (1954) is the discovery by a Negro veteran of a few changes in his native South, slowed down by prevailing and dangerous inertia. Langston Hughes's *Simple Speaks His Mind* (1950) and *Simple Takes A Wife* (1954) are a concoction of reportage, satire and fiction. The chats of the author and his sharp witted buddy center about race in a new kind of cracker-box philosophizing transferred to Harlem juke joints, with no loss of the old pith and pungency. Two books on Africa contrast: Era Bell Thompson has written a breezy, journalistic travelogue in *Africa: Land of My Fathers* (1954); and Richard Wright has written an angry and troubled account of a visit to the Gold Coast in *Black Power* (1954); both books are based on short trips, to which Africa proverbially yields up few secrets.

At the start of the twenties, the only books available on the folk Negro were the Uncle Remus Tales, a few collections of spirituals, and Talley's *Negro Folk Rhymes.* Today materials abound. B. A. Botkin's *Lay My Burden Down* (1945), edited from the thousands of ex-slave narratives collected by the Writers' Project, is valuable "folk history," helping to lay the ghosts of the plantation tradition. The vast collection of discs in the Library of Congress Archives, started by the Lomaxes, has discovered unknown songs and singers; among these was the dynamic Leadbelly, who, together with Josh White, brought unadulterated folk music to thousands of Americans. The record companies have responded to the appeal of this music. It is significant that whereas even an artist like Roland Hayes found the recording studios closed to him in his early years, today not only are the voices of Marian Anderson, Dorothy Maynor, and other concert singers everywhere available on records, but staid companies issue long-play volumes of folk singers such as Bessie Smith and Mahalia Jackson, with their strong faces gracing the colorful album jackets. Frederic Ramsey's *Music From The South* in ten long-play volumes, from field recordings in areas hitherto untouched, crown Ramsey's tireless search for the roots of jazz. Together with Charles Smith, Ramsey pioneered in the historical and critical study of jazz; today a long bibliography by many authors shows the wisdom of such pioneering. Most of the above collectors and interpreters are white; Negro collectors of folk material have been rare, but second-generation respectability is declining: J. Mason Brewer has enthusiastically collected yarns; Lorenzo Turner has studied Gullah with scientific linguistic techniques; and William H. Pipes, with sociological interest, has recorded old-time sermons in backwoods churches. The interest in Negro folk expression is not a momentary fad; the collection and interpretation are the work of both white and Negro folklorists, united in respect for material which, no longer set in isolation, is becoming recognized as integral part of the American experience.

But with folk culture corresponding less and less to Negro experience in America, it is of course to the conscious literature that we turn for the fullest expression. The New Critics find such a literature negligible, unworthy of anthologizing or evaluation. To a young white critic, John W. Aldridge, literature about Negroes has a "specialness" that works against universality,[17] to a young Negro critic, Richard Gibson, literature by American Negroes is a dismaying spectacle because no single work "stands out as a masterpiece."[18] But universality and masterpieces are never called out of the vasty deep by critics' incantations or debarred by their proscriptions. That they are hard-won and rare in whatever time or place is not likely to stop the vigorous contemporary writing. The Negro writer's task is that of his fellows in England, France, Italy, and America; to do as honest, truthful, well-designed, and revelatory work as his powers and insight permit; the rest he must leave to the future. Some signs confute the Cassandras who decry the possibilities of a sound literature of Negro life: the growing craftmanship, learned from the best models; the waning provincialism, self-pity, and denunciation; the increasing integration in American literary life; the leisure for creative maturing, more possible because of new publishing conditions; the loss, on the part of Negro readers, of their hypersensitivity and, on the part of white readers, of their superficial preconceptions. In one of the last essays he wrote, Alain Locke looked with serenity upon the future of the literature to which he had given such support and guidance. He saw how improving race relations have relaxed the Negro writer's tensions, and made possible deeper human understanding on his part; on the part of whites he saw growing fraternal acceptance. Should this cultural recognition and acceptance be realized, he wrote,

> the history of the Negro's strange and tortuous career in American literature may also become the story of America's hard-won but easily endured attainment of cultural democracy.[19]

[17] John W. Aldridge, *After the Lost Generation* (New York, 1953), pp. 102 ff. Aldridge is sound in hoping that "problems of race" will be treated as human problems, not as "forced polemics journalistically presented." But, though he categorizes the Negro and the Jew with the homosexual (p. 103) as the last remaining tragic types, he considers their problems minor issues, not "central to the meaning of this age." Such lofty dismissal divulges the narrowness of much current academic criticism.

[18] Gibson, *op. cit.*, p. 92.

[19] Locke, "The Negro in American Literature," Arabel J. Porter, ed., *New World Writing* (New York, 1952), p. 33.

Arthur P. Davis

(b. 1904)

BORN IN HAMPTON, VIRGINIA, Arthur P. Davis was educated at Hampton Institute (high school), Howard University (freshman year), Columbia College, and Columbia University. A veteran instructor in Negro literature courses, he has taught at North Carolina College, Virginia Union University, Hampton Institute Summer School, and at Howard University, where he has been Professor of English since 1944.

The author of *Isaac Watts: His Life and Works*, a study of the eighteenth-century "Father of English hymnology"; co-editor (with Sterling A. Brown and the late Ulysses Lee) of *The Negro Caravan* (1941), Arthur Davis has also written a considerable number of articles—critical and journalistic—on Negro literature and life. They have appeared in *The Crisis, Phylon, CLA Journal, Journal of Negro Education, Journal of Negro History,* and in several recent anthologies.

The article included here is selected from an autobiographical work now in progress; it appeared in *Negro American Literature Forum*.

GROWING UP IN THE NEW NEGRO RENAISSANCE

I was a college boy in New York during the middle period of the New Negro Renaissance. Living as I did in Harlem, I had a ringside seat on the activities of those stirring years. As an undergraduate, I naturally did not fully understand the significance of the events happening around me, but I did get the *feel* of the times. Any young Negro then in Harlem could sense that he was in some way part of an experience that was new and larger-than-ordinary. If he possessed a modicum of sensitiveness, he also realized that it was bliss to be alive in those days.

What was the New Negro Renaissance? It is difficult to define the movement precisely. As a matter of record, several scholars dislike the name itself, feeling that it is inaccurate and meaningless. Every generation of Negroes, they say, labels itself *new;* they also claim that the period in question is far too brief to be called a *renaissance*. Nevertheless, I have used the term because it is the best known of the several names given to the literary and artistic activities which flourished in the period between, roughly, 1920 and 1935 (the year of the Harlem Riot). Whatever one calls or miscalls this era, we know that it brought to Negro American literature a new strength, a new outlook, and a new, startling and unprecedented burst of creativity; we also know that the artistic capital of this movement was Harlem. In this essay, I am not trying to write a scholarly appraisal of the New Negro Renaissance or of the sociological and esthetic forces which produced it. My purpose is to recall the many-sided Harlem of the period, to put down the reminiscences that I have of those delightful years.

The word *delightful* is peculiarly appropriate. Harlem in the 1920's was a delightful place, particularly so to a youngster reared in a small Southern town. With its broad avenues uncluttered then by excess traffic, with its clean streets and its well-kept apartment houses; with its favored residential sections like Strivers Row (139th between 7th and 8th) and its swank apartment dwellings on Sugar Hill like 409 Edgecombe, Harlem was a Nigger Heaven to my provincial eyes; and there were thousands of other migrants like me who felt the charm of the black ghetto. Harlem was then still a relatively new settlement for Negroes, and the grime and the deterioration that came with the subsequent years of poverty and job-discrimination and frustration had not blighted the black city. One of our favorite sayings in those years was that the Jews owned New York, the Irish controlled it, and the Negroes enjoyed it!

But this enjoyment was not the phony exotic primitivism which the white folks came uptown nightly to find in cabarets and other hot spots. Our enjoyment was in part the pride of having a city of our very own—a city of black intellectuals and artists, of peasants just up from the South, of West Indians and Africans, of Negroes of all kinds and classes. In spite of the bohemian interests which the New Negro Renaissance cultivated, in spite of the embryonic proletarian stirrings found in the Garvey Movement, Harlem was basically a lower middle class community with strong middle class attitudes and prejudices. The average Harlemite possessed what James Weldon Johnson has called "second generation respectability." He took pride in himself and his home. He would not appear on the avenue improperly dressed or wearing a "headrag." He seldom went downtown to *work*, but to *business,* carrying not a lunch pail but his overalls and lunch in a *brief case.* Perhaps, he tended to overdo this respectability, but he was of a generation and class which felt that the whole race was judged by individual conduct, and he was determined to hold up his end. Although the majority of Harlemites were Southerners who had migrated north for economic reasons, many others belonged to solid well-established Negro families who had come north to seek freedom.

Nowadays *The Corner* in Harlem is at 125th Street and 7th Avenue. It is there where you find your orators of all kinds, your Black Muslims and their bodyguards, your female cult leaders. During the New Negro Renaissance, 125th Street was still largely white and bitterly anti-Negro. *Our* center was 135th Street and 7th Avenue, and the most important part of that intersection was the northeast corner. It was called *The Campus*. This was the favorite meeting place for all of the Negro college boys in the New York area; and in the summer, college boys from all over the country. Sunday afternoon was our best time for gathering, because in addition to "chewing the fat" with your friends and contemporaries, you could watch the Sunday parade, an established institution in those years. After church Harlemites dressed in their Sunday best promenaded on the Avenue. If you stayed on The Campus long enough you would see not only everybody you knew in Harlem, but in the nation. The theory was that every Negro came to 135th Street and 7th Avenue sometime in his life. The old saying, see-Paris-and-die, we paraphrased to see-Harlem-and-live! Another peculiarly worded quip that we had was: It is better to be a lamppost in Harlem than the Mayor [sic] of Georgia.

One of the pleasures of standing on The Campus was seeing celebrities. Just around the corner at 185 W. 135th Street lived James Weldon Johnson. Next door to him lived Fats Waller, the jazz pianist, and across the street was the apartment of Lawrence Brown, who was an accompanist for Roland Hayes, I believe. In any case, both Hayes and Paul Robeson used to visit there frequently. On 133rd Street between 7th and 8th lived Florence Mills, and we saw her frequently. If we strolled down the Avenue to the Lafayette Theater at 132nd Street, we often found under the famous Hope Tree such artists as Ethel Waters, Sissle and Blake, Fletcher Henderson, and Miller and Lyles. Bojangles Robinson, the great tap dancer, was often at the 135th Street YMCA, giving exhibitions of his ability to run one hundred yards *backwards* faster than the "Y" athletes could run it in the normal way (he insisted upon a ten-yard handicap).

On one occasion as a group of us stood on The Campus, we witnessed a revealing encounter between two celebrities. Up the Avenue, dressed in a black Prince Albert, carrying a large gold-headed walking stick, came Marcus Garvey, leader of the Back-to-Africa UNIA Movement, the first mass movement among American Negroes. Down the Avenue, also formally dressed in morning coat and striped trousers, came W. E. B. Du Bois, editor of *The Crisis* and intellectual leader of the NAACP movement. These two men, the two best known and most powerful leaders in Negro America at the time—these two passed each other with absolutely no sign of recognition from either side.

The Campus also served the college boys in other ways. It was often a clearing house for unscheduled but pleasurable excursions. For example, you could leave home expecting to spend just a few minutes chatting with your friends and end up at an exciting party. There were many parties in Harlem in those days—affairs that ran the gamut from "rent parties" up to literary parties at the famous *Dark Tower*. The

Dark Tower was an apartment in 136th Street furnished by Alelia Walker, the "Hairdressing Heiress," as a meeting place for young writers and artists. At the Tower, you could hear young poets like Cullen and Hughes read their works, or you could watch Alelia Walker make one of her spectacular entrances with her numerous black and white followers in tow. During those years, Alelia was busy spending the money which her mother (a pioneer Negro businesswoman) had made from the product for Negro hair which bore her name. Alelia, a handsome, dynamic dark woman, who impressed me as possessing a kind of animal energy that affected one physically—Alelia was always surrounded by hangers-on. As a college boy, of course, I could only know her from the periphery of her circle, but I was impressed. There was something regal about her; she didn't just walk into a room, she *swept* into a gathering. With Alelia one often saw Carl Van Vechten, who was then gathering material for his *Nigger Heaven* (1925), one of the works by white authors which influenced the New Negro Renaissance.

The Campus boys also found, on weekends, parties at Wallace Thurman's house in 139th Street (or was it 137th?) that were far more exciting than those at the Dark Tower. Thurman, the author, among other works, of *Blacker the Berry* and *Infants of the Spring,* both novels, and *Harlem,* a three-act drama—Thurman was a charming host with a hearty laugh and a keen sense of the phony. His parties tended to have a broader social mixture than those at the Tower. There one found in addition to writers and artists, truck drivers and other workers, theatrical people from downtown, and always, it seems, a disproportionate number of white girls. The sky was the limit at Thurman's parties. As I remember it, we danced in the basement, but the whole house was used. They were really not rent parties, but there was always somebody collecting a quarter or half-dollar from you to run out to get a fruit-jar of bathtub gin.

The last time I saw Wallace Thurman he was walking down Seventh Avenue with three pairs of new shoes—two in boxes under his arms, the other pair, tied together by strings, around his neck. When I asked why so many, he laughed and told me that he had just received the first check from his play, *Harlem,* which was then a Broadway success. "You never know when a gravy train will stop running," he said. "When it does, I'll be ready for walking."

Of all the parties we attended, the really earthy ones were the Rent Parties given in many Harlem apartments every week-end. The term *Rent Party* could be taken literally because they were affairs designed to raise money for rent and other necessities. Of course, such parties were usually not given by the average middle class Harlemite; they were "thrown" by the "other" Negroes and these parties became a sort of Harlem institution. Like any other money-raising event, they were advertised in bars and other public places by little printed calling-card sized notices. The card usually had, along with the time and place, a bit of home-made verse, often of an off-color nature. The following will give some idea of the type:

Party!   Party!   Party!

At Cora's Place
Saturday, April 10, 1927

Let your papa drink the whiskey,
Let your mama drink the wine
But you come to Cora's
And do the Georgia grind!

Cora Jones
000 West 148th St.-Apt. 901
Good Food   9:00 until—   Good Music

And the card didn't lie! There would definitely be good piano music; there would be plenty of what we now call *soul-food:* chitterlings, pig feet, hopping-john and similar delicacies, sold at reasonable prices; and there would be, since this was the prohibition era, plenty of bathtub gin and homemade "needle beer." If the place were not too crowded, you could dance; but the food, drink, and "gutty" talk that went on were more important than dancing.

College boys were not always welcome at these parties for two principal reasons: first, we really didn't have enough money to make our patronage profitable; and, second, we were outsiders. To most of the persons found at these affairs, we were "dicties." We had to enjoy ourselves cautiously. You could get into trouble if you paid too much attention to the wrong girl.

The jazz musician and the blues singer, blowing and singing their respective "racial" hearts out, became popular symbols in New Negro poetry, but as I recall the twenties, I realize that we didn't talk in daily conversation about these performers in that light. For one thing, we hadn't then "intellectualized" jazz and the blues; as for the artists themselves, we appreciated them in much the same way as we did other stage performers. Perhaps it was a case of forest versus trees. Of course, we went to the Savoy to hear the big bands, and we went to the Lafayette Theater to hear Fats Waller "swing" the pipe organ; we also went there to see Negro vaudeville acts like Butterbeans and Susie, one of the hardy perennials of the black circuit. But we didn't discuss those things in the way we do today; we enjoyed them and took them in our stride.

My favorite band at the Savoy was Johnson's Happy Pals from Richmond, Virginia. In those days, the Savoy featured two bands nightly, and the Pals played opposite Chick Webb's famous band. I realize *now* that the Richmond group was not in Chick Webb's class, but I *knew* the Happy Pals. They used to play at the Negro summer resort on Chesapeake Bay at which I worked. I was proud to see them make the "big time." Another band that was then starting in New York, I had also seen at the same resort. It was a Washington group headed by one Duke Ellington.

Bessie Smith, the blues singer, lived for awhile in an apartment in 133rd Street across the air shaft from the house in which I roomed. I was far more interested, I am sure, in the racy and earthy conversation that often came from her apartment than I was in her singing. Mamie Smith, one of the pioneer blues artists, would appear from time to time in the local Harlem theatres. As a grammar school boy, during World War I, I had heard Mamie sing in Newport News. The last time I saw her in New York was at the Lincoln Theatre in West 135th Street in the late twenties. Evidently she had lost that big, brassy, "sending" voice of her early years, because she was not singing that evening. She played in a burlesque routine in which she and a man wrestled suggestively all over the stage. Mamie was wearing a pair of enormous red bloomers, which she filled to capacity.

The new singing stars for us then were Ethel Waters and Florence Mills, each a fine artist. It was thrilling to hear Ethel "take over" the Capital Theatre as she belted out "Stormy Weather." Ethel Waters was then a statuesque creature with a voice that matched her magnificent brown frame. Florence Mills, on the other hand, was petite and one of the most charming musical comedy stars I have known. Without the power of Ethel Waters, she made up in finesse, in delicate phrasing and sensitive interpreting what she lacked in volume. For me, she was the Roland Hayes of the popular stage.

The artistic impetus of the New Negro Renaissance carried over into the field of the theatre, expressing itself most successfully in musical comedy and revues. The twenties and early thirties saw the Broadway production of great all Negro shows like *Shuffle Along, Running Wild,* and the several *Blackbirds.* Startlingly fresh, these shows literally shocked New York. The spirited dancing and the beauty of the multi-colored chorus were new to Broadway; they were a shot in the arm to a jaded theatre public. I saw all of these shows as they appeared downtown. Part of my enjoyment came from knowing three of the prettiest girls in the several chorus lines of these shows.

I am amused now when I recall how shocked I was to learn that these girls were rehearsing for the *Shuffle Along* chorus line. Up to that time, I had assumed that all show girls were "fast women," "nobodies" from across the track. These young women came from respectable Harlem families, and they remained, in spite of Broadway and subsequent European trips with various shows, respectable middle class young women; and they are now respectable old women with a fund of anecdotes from those stirring years of the New Negro Movement.

Among the "godfathers" of the New Negro Movement—James Weldon Johnson, W. E. B. Du Bois, Charles S. Johnson, and Alain LeRoy Locke—I knew personally only the last-named. Dr. Locke, the first Negro Rhodes Scholar, Professor of Philosophy at Howard University, and the major interpreter of the Negro Renaissance was on "forced leave" from Howard during the winter of 1924–25, having been a victim of the faculty effort to oust President Durkee. During that year, Dr. Locke, sensing the significance of the literary and artistic explosion around him, persuaded the editor of *Survey-Graphic* to devote an issue of that magazine to the New Negro. The New Negro issue of *Survey-Graphic* and the volume called *The New Negro* which grew out of it were both edited by Locke in 1925. Both are landmarks not only of the Renaissance but of Negro American literature.

During the time that he was producing these works, Locke lived in a top floor room of a brownstone house in (I believe) 139th Street. It was a typical Harlem room-to-let, bare, ugly, and often quite cold (as I remember it, Locke occasionally worked with a blanket around his feet to keep off drafts). Young writers and artists and college boys were constantly dropping in on Locke to seek advice on writing, to submit material for *The New Negro,* or just to talk. To those of us who were preparing for an academic career, Locke with his Harvard-Oxford background and his interest not only in literature but in music, drama, and art as well—Locke was a revelation. He represented a kind of continental sophistication and learning that we had never seen before— at least that I had never found in my teachers. Moreover, he was easy to talk to; as his interests were broad and decidedly unconventional, he could and did talk brilliantly on many things that our teachers had not discussed with us—folk songs, blues, African art, and modern painting. Incidentally, Locke was the first person I heard who discussed seriously the blues and other folk material.

Among the young writers who visited Dr. Locke regularly was one who then called himself Bruce Nugent. I say it in this way because he used other names when the mood struck him. Nugent was a true bohemian in every sense of the word. In no ways a *poseur,* he was simply and basically a non-conformist—one who refused to accept so-called middle class standards of any kind. During that cold winter he had no overcoat and no shoes. For the latter he wore rubbers tied to his feet with string. He had no "fixed residence" but slept, I am told, in Greenwich Village doorways, on the subway, and in other convenient places. He used to bring Dr. Locke his plays and poetry piecemeal, written on all kinds of paper; and Locke would advance him fifty cents or a dollar or some other small amount. Locke told me that he was afraid to give larger sums because Bruce would not return so long as he had any money at all. The boy had great talent. The works that Locke got from him for *The New Negro* show a potential never realized. This was the case, unfortunately, with too many New Negro creative artists.

Too many were one-good-poem or one-good-book writers. One of the most gifted of the latter group was a young West Indian whom I met through Dr. Locke named Eric Walrond. His *Tropic Death* (1926) was in its way as significant a first work as were *Color* by Countee Cullen and *The Weary Blues* by Langston Hughes. But Walrond, like Jean Toomer, whose *Cane* was one of the outstanding productions of the Movement, never seemed to recover from his first success. Perhaps the most interesting case of a one-book writer I know is that of a classmate of mine. He started writing on a novel in 1926. He is still in Harlem and still working on it! Maybe it will be *The* novel of the century. In any case, I hope so. I also hope that he will publish at least some part of it before I die, because I am really curious. According to the laws of probability some good things would have to come out of that much effort.

Alain Locke was the most influential of the "godfathers" of the New Negro Renaissance; but Charles S. Johnson and W. E. B. Du Bois as editors, respectively, of *Opportunity* and *The Crisis,* the official organs of the Urban League and the NAACP, also did a great deal to guide and stimulate young writers. Both magazines conducted annual poetry, short story, essay, and drama contests—contests which gave young Negroes a chance to publish. Many of our best New Negro writers, among them Cullen and Hughes, appeared in print if not for the first time at least quite early through these annual contests. These editors we saw at the various literary parties and charity dances, but they were not as "approachable" as Locke.

Another often-overlooked influence on the New Negro Renaissance was the 135th Street Branch of the New York Public Library, then under the direction of Miss Ernestine Rose, a very capable and understanding white woman. Miss Rose brought to that branch an intelligent and efficient group of young Negro and white librarians and made the branch a cultural center for the Harlem Community. There you found exhibitions of African art as well as the work of young Negro American painters and sculptors. There you could go on certain evenings and hear young poets read or discuss their work, hear lectures on current issues, or see a group of one-act plays produced by some community group. Attached to the branch as a kind of unofficial lecturer-in-residence was Hubert Harrison, the Dean of the Harlem Street Orators. A rather formal black man with a broad West Indian accent, Harrison seemed to divide his time between a ladder on the corner of 135th Street and Seventh and the platform of the Library auditorium.

In either place, he was a fascinating and versatile speaker, taking all subjects for his province—politics, religion, the race problem, colonialism, literature—and handling them all with equal facility and ease.

Perhaps the most important contribution to the New Negro Renaissance which the 135th Street Branch Library made was done through its Schomburg Collection, at the time the best collection of works on and by the Negro in the world. Housed on the third floor of the Branch, it served as a kind of clearing house and cultural reservoir for the Black Renaissance. It was a haven for scholars, black and white, who were just "discovering" the Negro. This collection had been gathered over the years by Arthur A. Schomburg, a Negro businessman (he was a fruit dealer, I am told), who had made the collecting of Negro books a hobby. When Schomburg finally retired from business, Miss Rose appointed him curator of the collection he had made. Though a self-made man without much formal education, Schomburg had a scholarly knowledge of books on and by Negroes. He was also, as I remember him, a courtly gentleman of the old-school type. Mr. Schomburg helped to make the 135th Street Branch of the New York Public Library one of the most effective and one of the most popular branches in the system.

Although we tended to laugh at Marcus Garvey and his Back-to-Africa program, we were impressed in spite of ourselves by the emphasis he put on pride in race, pride in blackness, pride in the African "homeland." A great showman as well as a dynamic leader, Garvey's flamboyant uniforms, his "Black Cross" units, his Black Star Line (consisting of one ship), all appealed to the Negro lowest down, for whom they were designed. They captured the imagination and the loyalty of these folk in a way that no program of the middle class NAACP could possibly have done.

The Garvey Headquarters was a one-story building (really a roofed-over basement) on 138th Street. Meetings, it seems to me, were held there nightly. For a lark, boys from The Campus would visit these UNIA meetings. We went there to get a laugh, but we had to be careful not to let anybody catch us making fun. Garvey's followers took his program seriously, almost religiously. Their faith in the Back-to-Africa promise was a thing that transcended everyday logic and it *was* a real faith, something that gave meaning to otherwise drab and oppressed lives. The speaking at these meetings was often moving, sometimes sensational. Garvey, himself, was a very impressive and persuasive orator. The constant hammering by these men, on the themes of Africa, blackness, and pride in race, in spite of middle class opposition to the Garvey idea, touched us and unconsciously influenced the thinking and the writing of New Negro poetry, witness the early works of McKay, Cullen, and Hughes.

By 1935, the New Negro Renaissance came to an end; that is, literary historians found the year of the Harlem Riot a convenient time to close the period. After the riot we began to see Harlem as it actually was; we began to note the seeds of poverty, job discrimination and frustration which were latent in our ghetto and in every other black ghetto—seeds which were to mature into the rotten and diseased fruit of present-day Harlem. Actually much of the intensity and drive which characterized the early years of the Renaissance had begun to wane by 1935. Moreover, as stated above, far too many of the New Negro creative artists did not live up to their initial promise and, therefore, did not survive the thirties. In this respect, the New Negro Renaissance may be called a failure. But it was a brilliant failure! It was also the best time to be young, colored, and a resident of Nigger Heaven.

Saunders Redding

(b. 1906)

BORN IN WILMINGTON, DELAWARE, Saunders Redding was educated at Lincoln University in Pennsylvania (freshman year) and at Brown University, where he received both undergraduate and graduate degrees. He has taught at Morehouse, Louisville Municipal College, Southern University, Elizabeth City State Teachers College, Hampton Institute, The George Washington University, and Cornell University, where he is at the present time as Ernest I. White Professor of American Studies and Humane Letters.

The first Negro to receive the Mayflower Award from the North Carolina Historical Society for his *No Day of Triumph,* Redding has added several other honors and awards, including Rockefeller and Guggenheim Fellowships.

He has lectured for the State Department in India and has been an AMSAC exchange lecturer in Africa. He has also served as lecturer and visiting professor in many American colleges and universities. From 1966 until the present he has been Director of the Division of Research and Publication, National Endowment for the Humanities.

His major publications are: *To Make a Poet Black* (1939), *No Day of Triumph* (1942), *They Came in Chains* (1950), *Stranger and Alone* (1950), *On Being Negro in America* (1951), *An American in India* (1955) and *The Lonesome Road* (1958).

The selections here were taken from *The American Negro and His Roots,* which is composed of selected papers read at the 1959 First Conference of Negro Writers, and *The Lonesome Road.*

THE AMERICAN NEGRO WRITER AND HIS ROOTS

I do not feel in the least controversial or argumentative about the announced subject. Indeed, I have touched upon it so often in one way or another that I long ago exhausted my store of arguments, and if I now revert to a kind of expressionistic way of talking, my excuse for it is patent. "The American Negro Writer and His Roots" is the kind of subject which, if one talked directly on it for more than twenty minutes, he would have to talk at least a year. I shan't talk directly on it, and I shan't talk a year. An exhaustive treatment? Heaven forbid—or anything near it. Suggestive? Well, I can only hope.

And anyway, I realize now that my position here is that of the boy who, through native disability, cannot himself play but is perfectly

willing to furnish the ball for others to play in exchange for the pleasure of watching the game.

Since my theme is that the American situation has complex and
multifarious sources and that these sources sustain the emotional and
intellectual life of American Negro writers, let me take as my starting
point a classic oversimplification. This is that the meaning of American society and of the American situation to the Negro is summed up
in such works as *Native Son, Invisible Man,* and the *Ordeal of Mansart,*
and in two or three volumes of poetry, notably *Harlem Shadows, The
Black Christ,* and *The Weary Blues,* and that the American Negro
writer's entire spirit is represented by such writers as Richard Wright,
Ralph Ellison and William Burghardt Du Bois—by realists, surrealists,
and romantic idealists.

Please understand me. Wright, Ellison and Du Bois are not men-
dacious men, and they are doing what writers must always do. They
are telling the truth as they see it, which happens to be largely what it
is, and they are producing from the examined, or at least the observed
causes, the predictable effects; and no one should blame them if the
impression they give of the American situation is deplorable. They
have been blamed, you know. But let those who blame these writers
blame themselves for forgetting that fiction is fiction, and that no novel
can pretend to be an exact photographic copy of a country or of the
people in a country.

Moreover, dishonor, bigotry, hatred, degradation, injustice, arrogance and obscenity do flourish in American life, and especially in the
prescribed and proscriptive American Negro life; and it is the right
and the duty of the Negro writer to say so—to complain. He has cause.
The temptation of the moral enthusiast is not only strong in him; it is
inevitable. He never suspends social and moral judgment. Few actions
and events that touch him as a man fail to set in motion his machinery
as an artist. History is as personal to him as the woman he loves; and
he is caught in the flux of its events, the currents of its opinion and the
tides of its emotion; and he believes that the mood is weak which
tolerates an impartial presentment of these, and that this weak mood
cannot be indulged in a world where the consequences of the actions
of a few men produce insupportable calamities for millions of humble
folk. He is one of the humble folk. He forages in the cause of righteousness. He forgets that he is also one of Apollo's company.

On the one hand, the jungle; on the other, the resourceful hunter to
clear it. The jungle, where lurk the beasts, nourishes the hunter. It is
there that he has that sum of relationships that make him what he is.
It is where he lives. It is precisely because the jungle is there and is
terrible and dangerous that the Negro writer writes and lives at all.

But first, I suppose you must grant me, if only for the sake of this
brief exposition, that the American Negro writer is not just an Amer-

ican with a dark skin. If he were, I take it, the theme of this conference would be mighty silly and the conference itself superfluous. This granted, you want to know what the frame of reference is, and about this I shall be dogmatic.

Neither the simplest nor the subtlest scrutiny reveals to an honest man that he has two utterly diverse kinds of experience, that of sense data and that of purpose. Psychology seems to have no difficulty establishing the natural gradation of impulse to purpose. In varying degrees, all our experiences are complications of physical processes.

Shifting from the dogmatic to the apologetic, I must eliminate from view a period of nearly three hundred years from 1619 to 1900. It was the period that saw the solid establishment here in America of a tradition of race relations and of the concepts that supported the tradition. It was a period that need not be rehearsed. Within the frame of reference thus established, let us look at a certain chain of events.

In 1902 came Thomas Dixon's *The Leopard's Spots,* and three years later *The Clansman.* Both were tremendously popular, and both were included in the repertoires of traveling theatrical companies; and I think it is significant—though we will only imply how—that even a colored company, The Lafayette Players, undertook an adaptation of *The Leopard's Spots.* In 1903 there was a race riot in New York. In 1906 race riots occurred in Georgia and Texas; in 1908 in Illinois. By this latter year, too, all the Southern states had disfranchised the Negro, and color caste was legalized or had legal status everywhere. The Negro's talent for monkeyshines had been exploited on the stage, and some of the music that accompanied the monkeyshines was created by James Weldon Johnson and his brother Rosamond. Meantime, in 1904, Thomas Nelson Page had written the one true canonical book of the law and the prophets, *The Negro, The Southerner's Problem.* And, most cogent fact of all, Booker Washington, having sworn on this bible of reactionism, had been made the undisputed leader of American Negroes because, as he had pledged to do, he advocated a race policy strictly in line with the tradition and the supporting concepts of race relations.

If there had been a time when this tradition seemed to promise the Negro a way out, that time was not now. He had been laughed at, tolerated, amusingly despaired of, but all his own efforts were vain. All the instruments of social progress—schools, churches, lodges—adopted by colored people were the subjects of ribald jokes and derisive laughter. "Mandy, has you studied yo' Greek?" "I'se sewing, Ma." "Go naked, Gal. Git Dat Greek!"

Any objective judgment of Booker Washington's basic notion must be that it was an extension of the old tradition framed in new terms. Under the impact of social change, the concept was modified to include the stereotype of the Negro as a happy peasant, a docile and satisfied laborer under the stern but kindly eye of the white boss, a creature who had a place and knew it and loved it and would keep it unless he got bad notions from somewhere. The once merely laughable coon had become now also the cheap farm grub or city laborer who could be righteously exploited for his own good and for the greater glory of America. By this addition to the concept, the Negro-white status quo, the condition of inferior-superior race and caste could be maintained in the face of profound changes in the general society.

What this meant to the Negro writer was that he must, if he wished an audience, adhere to the old forms and the acceptable patterns. It meant that he must create within the limitations of the concept, or that he must dissemble completely, or that he must ignore his racial kinship altogether and leave unsounded the profoundest depths of the peculiar experiences which were his by reason of that kinship. Some chose the first course; at least one—Dunbar—chose the second (as witness his sickly, sticky novels of white love life and his sad epithalamium to death); and a good many chose the third: Braithwaite's anthologies of magazine verse, James Weldon Johnson's contributions to the *Century Magazine,* and the writing of Alice Dunbar, Anne Spenser, and Angelina Grimke.

But given the whole web of circumstances—empirical, historic, psychological—these writers must have realized that they could not go on and that the damps and fevers, chills and blights, terrors and dangers of the jungle could not be ignored. They must have realized that, with a full tide of race-consciousness bearing in upon them, they could not go on forever denying their racehood and that to try to do this at all was a symptom of psychotic strain. Rather perish now than escape only to die of slow starvation.

What had happened was that Booker Washington, with the help of the historic situation and the old concepts, had so thoroughly captured the minds of white people that his was the only Negro voice that could be heard in the jungle. Negro schools needing help could get it only through Booker Washington. Negro social thought wanting a sounding board could have it only on Washington's say-so. Negro political action was weak and ineffective without his strength. Many Negro writers fell silent, and for the writer, silence is death.

Many, but not all. There were stubborn souls and courageous, and the frankly mad among them. There was the Boston *Guardian,* and the Chicago *Defender,* and the Atlanta University Pamphlets, and *The Souls of Black Folk,* and finally the *Crisis;* and this latter quickly developed a voice of multi-range and many tones. It roared like a lion and cooed like a dove and screamed like a monkey and laughed like a hyena. And always it protested. Always the sounds it made were the

sounds of revolt in the jungle, and protestation and revolt were becoming—forgive me for changing my figure—powerful reagents in the
social chemistry that produced the "new" Negro.

Other factors contributed to this generation too. The breath of
academic scholarship was just beginning to blow hot and steadily
enough to wither some of the myths about the Negro. The changes
occurring with the onset of war in Europe sloughed off other emotional and intellectual accretions. The Negro might be a creature of
"moral debate," but he was also something more. "I ain't a problem,"
a Negro character was made to say, "I's a person." And that person
turned out to be a seeker after the realities in the American dream.
When he was called upon to protect that dream with his blood, he
asked questions and demanded answers. Whose dream was he protecting, he wanted to know, and why and wherefore? There followed
such promises as only the less scrupulous politicians had made to him
before. Then came the fighting and the dying, and finally came a thing
called peace.

By this time, the Negro was already stirring massively along many
fronts. He cracked Broadway wide open. The Garvey movement swept
the country like wildfire. *Harlem Shadows, The Gift of Black Folk,
Color, Fire in the Flint, The Autobiography of an Ex-Coloured Man.*
The writers of these and other works were declared to be irresponsible.
A polemical offensive was launched against them, and against such
non-artist writers as Philip Randolph, Theophilus Lewis, William Patterson, Angelo Herndon. They were accused of negativism; they were
called un-American. Cultural nationalism raised its head and demanded that literature be patriotic, optimistic, positive, uncritical, like
Americans All, and *American Ideals,* and *America is Promises,* and *It
Takes a Heap O' Living,* which were all written and published in the
period of which I speak. But democracy encourages criticism, and it is
true that even negative criticism implies certain positive values like
veracity, for instance, and these Negro writers had positive allegiances.
Their sensibilities were violently irritated, but their faith and imaginations were wonderfully nourished by the very environment which they
saw to be and depicted as being bad.

Fortunately there was more than faith and fat imagination in some
of these works. There was also talent. Had this not been so, Negro
writing would have come to nothing for perhaps another quarter century, for the ground would not have been plowed for the seeds of later
talents. But Du Bois, Johnson, McKay, Fisher, Cullen, Hughes knew
what they were about. Their work considerably furthered the interest
of white writers and critics. Whatever else O'Neill, Rosenfeld, Con-
nolley, Calverton and Heyward did, they gave validity to the notion
that the Negro was material for serious literary treatment.

Beginning then and continuing into the forties, Negro writing had two distinct aspects. The first of these was arty, self-conscious, somewhat precious, experimental, and not truly concerned with the condition of man. Some of the "little reviews" printed a lot of nonsense by Negro writers, including the first chapter of a novel which was to be entirely constructed of elliptical sentences. Then there was *Cane:* sensibility, inwardness, but much of it for the purpose of being absorbed into the universal oneness. Nirvana. Oblivion. Transcendence over one's own personality through the practice of art for art's sake. The appropriate way of feeling and thinking growing out of a particular system of living. And so eventually Gurdjieff.

But the second aspect was more important. The pathos of man is that he hungers for personal fulfillment and for a sense of community with others. And these writers hungered. There is no American national character. There is only an American situation, and within this situation these writers sought to find themselves. They had always been alienated, not only because they were Negroes, but because democracy in America decisively separates the intellectual from everyone else. The intellectual in America is a radically alienated personality, the Negro in common with the white, and both were hungry and seeking, and some of the best of both found food and an identity in communism. But the identity was only partial and, the way things turned out, further emphasized their alienation. So—at least for the Negro writers among them—back into the American situation, the jungle where they could find themselves. A reflex of the natural gradation of impulse to purpose.

Surely this is the meaning of *Native Son.* "Bigger Thomas was not black all the time," his creator says. "He was white too, and there were literally millions of him. . . . Modern experiences were creating types of personalities whose existence ignored racial . . . lines." Identity. Community. Surely this is the meaning of *Invisible Man* and the poignant, pain-filled, pain-relieving humor of simple Jesse B. It is the meaning of *Go Tell It On The Mountain,* and it is explicitly the meaning of four brilliant essays in part three of a little book of essays called *Notes of a Native Son.* (How often that word "native" appears, and how meaningful its implications!) Let me quote a short, concluding passage from one of these essays.

"Since I no longer felt that I could stay in this cell forever, I was beginning to be able to make peace with it for a time. On the 27th . . . I went again to trial . . . and the case . . . was dismissed. The story of the *Drap De Lit,* . . . caused great merriment in the courtroom. . . . I was chilled by their merriment, even though it was meant to warm me. It could only remind me of the laughter I had often heard at home. . . . This laughter is the laughter of those who consider themselves to be at a safe remove from all the wretched, for whom the pain of living is not real. I had heard it so often in my native land that I had resolved to find a place where I would never hear it anymore. In some deep, black, stony and liberating way, my life, in my own eyes, began during that first year in Paris, when it was borne in on me that this laughter is universal and never can be stilled." Explicit.

The human condition, the discovery of self. Community. Identity. Surely this must be achieved before it can be seen that a particular identity has a relation to a common identity, commonly described as human. This is the ultimate that the honest writer seeks. He knows that the dilemmas, the perils, the likelihood of catastrophe in the human situation are real and that they have to do not only with whether men understand each other but with the quality of man himself. The writer's ultimate purpose is to use his gifts to develop man's awareness of himself so that he, man, can become a better instrument for living together with other men. This sense of identity is the root by which all honest creative effort is fed, and the writer's relation to it is the relation of the infant to the breast of the mother.

ROBERT SENGSTACKE ABBOTT OF THE CHICAGO "DEFENDER"

Robert Sengstacke Abbott was an altogether different breed. Though he was described as shrewd, calculating, and "tight with guile," the facts dispute the estimate. His mind was not equipped to deal with subtleties. The formal education he managed to acquire was not of much use to him. In middle life he was called a demagogue and dangerous—"like a monkey with a shotgun," Julius Rosenwald said, "who will hurt anybody." But he was more hurt than hurting, and his demagoguery, if this is what it can be called, had in it more of pathos than of calculating sense. He was not the son of his father.

Born in a cabin on the crummy edge of a Georgia plantation, Robert Abbott spent much of his life trying to live down the opprobrious term "Geechee." It was an epithet that conjured up in the Negro mind the storied attributes of the lowest slave type, the ignorant "field nigger," with a dull and stupid mind, gross habits, and primitive passions beyond control. And it was unfair. Robert's father, Tom, had been Charles Stevens' trusted boss house slave, the envy of other slaves for miles around. The esteem in which the Stevenses held him is attested by the fact that when freedom came they gave him a cabin and a plot of ground, and when he died in 1869 they buried him in their own graveyard.

And by that time, in the common opinion, Tom had deserved less. He had gone off to Savannah and abused his freedom. Nearly fifty years old and still unmarried, he had played city sport, lived by his wits and on his gracious white-folks manners, which attracted, among others, Flora Butler, a hairdresser and ladies' maid at the Savannah theater. But Flora was not a frivolous, easy woman. She would settle for nothing less than marriage to a man who had a job and "common decency." Tom pled and promised and, when they were married, took Flora to his cabin and plot of ground on St. Simon's Island. Farming, however, was beneath him. He converted the front room of his cabin into a store. In the room behind it Robert was born only five months before Tom died of "galloping consumption."

Flora was more durable. Free since childhood, she had become a skilled hairdresser and an expert seamstress, but no one on St. Simon's had a need for her services, and after the death of Tom she took her infant son and returned to Savannah, where she readily found employment among the wives of the German shopkeepers with whom she became a favorite by picking up a speaking knowledge of their language. This favoritism proved timely. She had been settled in the city only a few months when Tom Abbott's sister, alleging Flora to be an unfit mother, brought suit for the custody of the child. The Germans came to Flora's support, and one of them, John H. H. Sengstacke, engaged a lawyer who successfully defended her.

Sengstacke had had dealings with lawyers and lawsuits. His short history in America was thorny with legal tangles. White to all appearances, and German-reared, he was born the son of an immigrant father and a slave girl. When the mother died at the birth of a second child, his father took his two mulatto children to Germany to be reared by his sister. The father himself returned to the States in 1850, prospered in the mercantile trade, regularly remitted money for the support of his children, and died in 1862. He left a will that amply secured his offspring, but his white executors ignored it, for after his death no money from the estate, estimated at fifty thousand dollars, ever reached Germany. The son came to America to investigate in 1869.

John H. Hermann Sengstacke was an educated man, fluent in five languages—just the man for the job of translator for the Savannah *Morning News.* But in the course of pushing his claim to his father's estate he had to reveal the fact of his Negro blood. He was fired. Thereafter some of his father's old friends treated him with contempt. Completely unprepared for this betrayal of old loyalties and this ravishment of his personal dignity, by the time he was financially able to escape to Germany he had perforce identified himself with the Negro race, and he decided to remain. The experience of his Negroness left deep scars. Already there was something of the messiah in him, and something of the masochist. When the dwindled estate was finally settled he came to the conclusion—at once bitter torment and solace —that since he was a Negro he was lucky to salvage two or three thousand dollars, a small frame house, and a store-front building on a bluff in the western section of Savannah.

This was the man who married Flora Abbott in 1874 and gave his name not only to the seven children he begot but to his stepson as well. This was the man who, with the burning ardor of the ancient Christian convert, embraced with passion the scabrous cross of his Negroness and staggered under it with mad delight.

Ordained a minister of the Congregational Church and appointed a teacher in a rural Negro school, he also undertook to publish, edit, and sustain a Negro newspaper. As a preacher-teacher he earned altogether forty dollars a month. His church had few members, and these were so poor that they "could pay," he reported, "only one dollar towards his whole year's salary." Yet he alienated some of these and expelled others for belonging to secret societies. His school had no books, no blackboards, no pencils, no stove. He wrote his newspaper copy in longhand—all of it. "We labor under great disadvantages," he informed a friend. And indeed he did. Eventually the disadvantages became willful malignities offered to him personally. He saw the grim red finger of malice pointing at him from every quarter. He saw himself as a Negro persecuted not only by society but by individuals. The world was against the Sengstackes. The world was against him.

If this was the spirit of Robert's training at home and in his father's school, it was given substance by his earliest experiences at Beach Institute. This was a day school founded by the Freedmen's Bureau but supported by the American Missionary Society. In Savannah, as in other urban centers in those days, there was a Negro color caste as rigid as iron. Mulattoes, as we have seen, were generally the privileged and the exclusive. They had their own churches, their own social clubs. Only mulattoes were normally expected to go to school beyond the second or third grade.

Robert was as black as tar. The prejudice of his light-skinned schoolmates at Beach was cruel to an extreme possible only to adolescents. They dubbed him "Liver Lips," "Tar Baby," and "Crow." Their malevolence undoubtedly generated the unconscious self-hatred that was one of the twisted, ruling passions of Abbott's life—that made him shun the color black even in clothes and cars; that made him dun Negro fraternal organizations to use the whiteball as the symbol of rejection, and plaster black Chicago with slogans urging Negroes to "Go to a White Church on Sunday."

Only Joseph and Catharine Scarborough were not unkind to him at Beach, and if this was more out of respect for their father's friendship with the Reverend John H. H. Sengstacke than friendly regard for

Robert, the latter did not sense it. Indeed, he fell in love with Catharine—he was seventeen at the time—and courted her for nearly thirty years. In 1897 he asked her to marry him, but her father was "outraged" at the black man's presumption, and Catharine declined the honor. In 1918, when she had twice been widowed by ne'er-do-well mulatto husbands, Catharine finally agreed to marry him. He was by then a millionaire, but even as he prepared to go to her in Savannah she wrote that she had changed her mind.

But all this was in the future in 1886. What was in the present was the intolerable weight of obloquy and the crushing blows to his self-esteem. He did not cry out aloud. Instead he adopted a system of attitudes—not principles of conduct or principles of ethics—informed only by a defensive spirit, which served him the rest of his life. And the chief of these was patient meekness. In some ways it was as false as Uriah Heep's—and to much the same purpose.

To the disappointment of his stepfather, Robert retreated from Beach after less than two full terms. He dreamed of Hampton, in Virginia, but when his stepfather suggested Claflin University, a hundred miles from his home, he pretended enthusiasm for that place and agreed to work his way through that institution's equivalent of high school. He stayed six months. He was nineteen and still separated from his future by a vast ignorance. Another year went by before Hampton accepted him "conditionally" to study the printing craft.

At Hampton, it is reported, "everybody always picked on him." His hangdog mien and his genuine feelings of inferiority invited it. He was the butt of crude, practical, and sometimes vicious jokes. He probably resented them, but he was too patient, too hungry for acceptance, and too cowardly to protest. Driven to the other extreme at times, he tried to bluster through class recitations, but his dull mind was no help to him, and he invariably made a fool of himself.

He did no better socially. The same prejudice, though degrees milder, that plagued him at Beach prevailed at Hampton, and, inept to begin with, Robert had no success in the highly formalized and rigidly controlled social life of the campus. He was not asked to join the intimate bull sessions. He got no invitations to parties. Girls ignored him, and one of his classmates told him, half in jest, that he was "too black to associate with fair women."

Ironically enough, his black skin did bring him one distinction. Toward the end of his first year he was chosen as a member of the Hampton Quartet. But this was not because his tenor voice was the best that could be found. It was because "white people resented seeing light-complexioned boys in the group"; because Hampton's white administrators knew the emotional impact that "four black boys forlornly singing spirituals" had on white audiences; and because white audiences were the targets of the school's financial appeals.

Abbott had a good voice, and he sang the sorrow songs with feeling, but not even the distinction of becoming a member of the quartet in his first year suggested that, next to Booker T. Washington, he would one day be the school's best-known graduate. It took some students five years to complete the four-year course. Abbott required seven.

He was twenty-seven when he graduated and accepted a teaching post in a school on the outskirts of Savannah. Soon he was supplementing his income with part-time work as a printer. He was not very good in either job, and both together did not provide enough for him to court Catharine Scarborough in the manner he thought she deserved. Rivalry for that lady's attentions was keen, and when she rejected his first proposal Abbott felt that the odds were against him. His rivals, though scarcely more affluent than he, were light-skinned. Perhaps if he could get money he could overcome the handicap of his color, equalize the competition. But how get money? His stepfather's example proved that money was not in teaching or preaching. Even the printer's craft offered scant returns to a black man in Georgia. Perhaps in another state—a city in the North—he could use his vocation as a steppingstone "to higher things." After presenting Miss Scarborough with a handsome gold watch in the summer of 1897, he still had enough money to support himself while he explored.

He went to Chicago. When the Hampton Quartet had sung there at the World's Fair four years earlier, Abbott had been awed by the conspicuous display of Negro wealth and achievement. Now almost at once he wrote home, "I will stay out west and try to make a fortune."

But fortunes were not easily made, and he did not know how to begin. He managed to obtain part-time employment as a printer, but earning "real money" at his trade looked no more promising in Chicago than it had in Savannah. It did not take him long to discover that the men to emulate, the men whose names were spoken with deference along State Street and Dearborn Street, were either independent businessmen or professionals. Daniel Hale Williams was a physician and surgeon, Charles Smiley a caterer, Edward Morris a lawyer, and John Jones, who was still remembered as the first Negro to hold public office in Chicago, had been a wealthy merchant tailor. These men were of the status to which Abbott aspired. His ambition was uninformed by any idea of service or any dedication to large purposes. He wanted simply to "accomplish *something* noteworthy"; he wanted—as a later phrase had it—to be a big shot.

He tried to find ways into the closed circle of the elite. He joined the Grace Presbyterian Church where the elite went. He sacrificed necessities to buy admission to the charity balls given for the benefit of Provident Hospital and the Institutional Social Settlement. No one paid the slightest attention to him. For all that he had been a member of the Hampton Quartet and had a better than passable tenor voice, his bid to join the choir of Grace Presbyterian Church was rejected. He was black, and his speech gave him away as one of those "new-come Southern darkies" who were "spoiling things" for long-time residents of the North. Every rebuff fed his passion to "show them" and increased his torment to "make his mark," no matter how. He wrote his mother, "Tell father if he will back me, I will . . . run a paper. . . . Let me know his intentions before I begin to make up my mind as to what steps to take."

The Reverend Mr. Sengstacke, undoubtedly recalling his own costly experience, advised against the newspaper but seemed willing enough to back his stepson in another line, for in the fall of 1898 Robert enrolled in the evening classes of the Kent College of Law. Now for the first time he dropped Sengstacke as a surname and put himself on record as Robert S. Abbott. It is reported that when his stepfather heard of this he wept.

If Robert S. Abbott also wept, it was for other reasons. He had a better than average capacity for self-pity, and later he was to write of this period that he "probably would have starved to death but for the generosity of some folk who would loan me a dime now and then. Even when I did work I did not earn enough to pay back rent, repay loans and eat. . . ."

Somehow, though, he managed to get through law school, only to be advised by the light-skinned lawyer Edward Morris, to whom he went for encouragement and help, that he was "too dark to make any impression on the courts in Chicago." As a matter of fact, Abbott failed to pass the Illinois bar. He was told that Indiana was easier, and he moved to Gary. He went on to Topeka, Kansas. The story was the same. When he returned to Chicago in 1903, all he had to show for five years of painful effort was a contract as Chicago distributor of the national Negro weekly, the *Kansas Plaindealer*. He was thirty-three, and all the pathways to fulfillment seemed blocked against him, but he was as obdurate as stone.

He did not look like a man in whom the fires of worldly ambition burned with corroding intensity. Stubby, dour-faced, he affected semiclerical garb, poor but neat: patched white shirt with celluloid collar and white string tie, a blue suit turning green with age, shoes lined with paper. Indeed, he seemed the exact copy of a pastor of a small, earnest fundamentalist sect. He did not play cards, or smoke (though he was to acquire the habit of fifty-cent cigars later), or drink.

Excluded from the "best" society, he shunned the worst, and made his acquaintances among that emerging middle class of decent domestic servants, small tradesmen, part-time lawyers, and night-time doctors who were becoming extremely vocal on such subjects as race discrimination, Negro rights, and Negro solidarity, and who, under the leadership of Louis B. Anderson and George Hall, were learning the uses of political power even as they slowly acquired it. Abbott joined their social groups, earned a part of his precarious living doing their printing jobs on borrowed presses, and took part in their discussions. They liked him, and he liked them. Among them he did not have to live down his blackness; he had rather to live up to it. Other qualities began to peep from beneath the cloak of his patient humility. He had gratitude. He could be depended on. He had insinuating kindliness of spirit. He counted among these people—counted enough for them to exert their political influence to get him a job in a printing firm that did the work of the city government.

It was among this middle-class-in-emergence, too, that he again broached the idea of starting a newspaper. The more intelligent could not see it, and would not help him, and told him so. There were already three Negro newspapers in Chicago—the *Conservator,* the *Broad Ax,* and the *Illinois Idea*—and none of them was a financial success. There was no need for yet another paper. But Abbott thought otherwise, and he backed his thinking with an inspired argument—his friends and acquaintances had no voice. The social historian, Roi Ottley, notes that existing papers "were primarily vehicles for the editors to expound their views . . . and advance their personal political ambitions." Abbott's acquaintances were never mentioned in them. Their births, their weddings, their deaths were unheralded. Their churches, their clubs, and their community activities existed in a murmurless limbo. Abbott would give them a voice. This was the idea that drew nourishment from the subterranean depths of personal frustration, and around it his fumbling intelligence, his oceanic patience, and his legendary stubbornness fixed as inexorably as fate.

So, his only capital twenty-five cents and a tongue ready with promises, Robert Sengstacke Abbott launched the first issue of the paper for which he did not even originate the name. The date was May 5, 1905, and the Chicago *Defender* would not miss a weekly issue for fifty years. At the age of thirty-seven Abbott had at last found his métier. His manner, his methods, and his mission would evolve and change with time.

❈   ❈   ❈

One Negro editor, however, stayed conspicuously aloof.* Robert S. Abbott had not made up his mind on this and many other issues, and until his mind was made up not even the persuasive powers of his

---

* From a controversy over whether W. E. B. Du Bois or Booker T. Washington was, or should be, the "leader" of Negroes in America.

friend, Dr. George Hall, could move him. Abbott refused to be bought. As a matter of fact, when Hall tried, not too subtly, to buy into the *Defender* in the interest of Booker T. Washington, he was repulsed with an asperity that threatened their friendship. Abbott was slow, Abbott was stubborn, but he was not, he said, "a pure-born fool." In truth, the growth of the *Defender* in both circulation and influence bore him out.

Contrary to the belief of some, not all the credit for this growth was due to the often questionable and always sensational ways and works of J. Hockley Smiley, whom Abbott had hired in 1910. Though meagerly gifted himself, Abbott knew talent when he saw it, and he could make talent work for him. He used this knack to advantage so long as he lived. Smiley had the talents and the techniques of a Hearst. It was he who introduced the glaring red headlines, who thought up the slogans ("With Drops of Ink We Make Millions Think") and the elaborate, circulation-pulling hoaxes. It was Smiley who departmentalized the paper into theater, sports, and society sections, and he who recruited Pullman porters, dining-car waiters, and performers on the Negro vaudeville circuit to carry weekly bundles of the *Defender* east to New York and Boston, south to Atlanta and Birmingham, and west to Seattle and Los Angeles.

But the editorial page belonged to Abbott, and much of the credit for the *Defender's* growth must go to the editorials. This is not to say that Abbott wrote them. He seldom wrote them in their final form, for his prose was often ungrammatical and clumsy; but his ideas informed the editorials, and in them his consciousness, it might be said, prevailed.

It was a consciousness that was cunning without being the least subtle. It did not work from design but through instinct, and often, therefore, it plunged—like a man falling through space—past all the levels of logic to plop at last against the bedrock of personal experience. Whatever position he took, he took on this bedrock ground, and whatever position he took, he held tenaciously. He was almost never known to change his mind, even when he was demonstrably in error.

For instance, when he was a member of the Chicago Commission on Race Relations it was brought forcibly home to him that the *Defender's* campaign to lure Negroes from the South was doing more harm than good. The facts with which the commission dealt showed clearly that the hysterical South–North migration caused a great leap in all the depressing statistics—unemployment, delinquency, crime—and a tragic upsurge of anti-Negro feeling North and South. Mentioning the *Defender* by name, the commission itself urged "greater care and accuracy in reporting incidents involving whites and Negroes, the abandonment of sensational headlines and articles on racial questions, and more attention to means and opportunities of [Negroes] adjusting themselves and their fellows into more harmonious relations with their white neighbors. . . ." But, in 1914, Abbott had taken the position that migration to the North was the Negro's salvation, and in 1919 he refused to abandon it. When disastrous riots flared up all the summer and fall of the latter year, Abbott "did not view them as unmitigated evil."

If he seldom changed his mind, even more rarely did he change his heart. He was emotionally rigid and complex. He felt his black skin to be not only a severe handicap in the Negro world—which, of course, it was—but a source of personal shame. In spite of the most concrete evidence to the contrary—his wealth, prestige, and influence—he was convinced that his intrinsic worth as a person could be certified only by the acceptance of mulattoes. Nevertheless, he felt an obsessive loyalty to blackskin people per se. He reflected their moods instinctively and their minds so perfectly that they saw their composite image in the pages of the *Defender*. He was "for the masses, not the classes." He wanted them to "solidify, throw off the shackles. Rise!" and any small instance of rising—a high school graduation, a black boy on a white athletic team, a Negro victory in the prize ring or in any other contest against a white opponent—any immaterial instance was enough for columns of praise and joy.

Yet—strange duality!—no instance whatever was testimony to his own intrinsic worth. Only intimate social concourse with mulattoes could provide that; only, say, a light-skinned wife could make him worth while and respectable in his own eyes. When finally he married at the age of fifty he took to wife a woman whom he did not love but who was indistinguishable from white. When this unhappy affair ended in divorce he took a second wife who was "white in fact," and who, accompanying him to "white" places of entertainment, did not seem to mind the ridiculous gibberish he spoke in the impossible hope of being mistaken for a foreigner. It is strangely characteristic that, though he gave only casual and token assistance to the black Abbotts and completely ignored them in his will, he contributed regularly to the mulatto Sengstackes, was for years a dependable source of income for their white relatives in Germany, and saw to it that some of the white direct descendants of his father's master were educated.

Though these abiding indices to his character were evident in 1912, Abbott had at that time made up his mind on no public issues and on only one policy for his paper. The *Defender* would not fight Negroes and the editor's own private enemies. It would concentrate its fire on the common foe, the whites. Abbott wanted to unify "the black population for aggressive counter-action," and if this required him to vilify even well-meaning whites, then he would vilify. Of course this was wrong on the face of it, but "give the skunks hell," Abbott would say, and in his book of rules nearly every white man was a skunk, including the good philanthropist friend of the Negro, Julius Rosenwald, who was not the only white man to think that Abbott was a mindless "monkey with a shotgun, who will hurt anybody."

Anybody, that is, except Negroes—who certainly were hurt enough by the white press; and anything except the struggle in which even the semiliterate masses believed themselves engaged. Week after endless week the *Defender's* slogan for that struggle was "American Race Prejudice Must Be Destroyed." The proof of its destruction would rest, Abbott himself wrote (with a habitually greater regard for sense than syntax), in "the opening of all trades and trade unions to blacks. . . . Representation in the President's Cabinet. Engineers, firemen and conductors on all American railroads, and all jobs in government. Representation in all departments of the police forces over the entire United States; Federal legislation to abolish lynching and full enfranchisement of all American citizens."

Though Du Bois probably had the *Defender* in mind when he said that "some of the best colored papers are so wretchedly careless in their use of the English language . . . that when they see English they are apt to mistake it for something else," it is highly unlikely that he also included the *Defender* in his condemnation of those colored weeklies that did not "stand staunch for *principle*." That year, 1914, nearly every Negro paper in the country blasted Du Bois at one time or another, but not the *Defender*. Abbott hated and feared divisive argument among Negroes, and Abbott realized that he and Du Bois were fighting the same war on the same side.

Many Negroes did not realize, except sporadically, that Du Bois was on their side. The man had an unhappy predilection for making enemies. He was impatient, especially of ignorance; he was temperamentally unsuited to mingling with the masses. He was called "race traitor" more than once because it was thought he sounded like one. He was as caustically critical of Negroes as of whites. "Jeremiads were needed to redeem [the Negro] people," he said, and jeremiads he gave them. Abbott on the other hand gave them panegyrics and made excuses for their wrongdoing. Neither man realized that he reflected a deepening mood of frustration and despair.

There were reasons for this mood.

Zora Neale Hurston

(1907–1960)

ZORA NEALE HURSTON WAS the daughter of a tenant farmer who doubled as a Baptist minister in Eatonville, Florida. She attended Howard University and Barnard, where she studied anthropology with Franz Boaz; she received her B.A. from Barnard in 1928. In one of his autobiographies, Langston Hughes speaks of Zora Neale Hurston's unfailing ability to obtain grants for study: and she did receive numerous ones, including a Rosenwald Fellowship in anthropology (1935) and a Guggenheim for research in West Indian and Haitian folklore (1936–38).

Miss Hurston published stories in *Opportunity* during the Renaissance and was on the editorial staff of the avant-garde magazine *Fire,* with such writers as Langston Hughes and Wallace Thurman. She was co-author—with Langston Hughes—of a play, *Mule Bone,* which, (according to Hughes) because of a personal disagreement between the two, never was produced. Miss Hurston's stories and articles have appeared in *Story, The Saturday Evening Post, The New Negro, New Republic, American Mercury,* and *Negro Digest.* She worked as a script writer for Paramount pictures and as a drama instructor at North Carolina College in Durham. Never a financial success, and not really suited to academic life, Miss Hurston barely managed the last two years as a teaching substitute at Lincoln Park Academy in Florida and as a writer for a local paper, *The Chronicle.* She died in Fort Pierce, Florida, in early 1960.

Miss Hurston is the author of a large number of works: *Jonah's Gourd Vine* (1934); *Mules and Men,* a book of folklore (1935) from which the following selection is taken; *Their Eyes Were Watching God* (1937); *Tell My Horse* (1938); *Moses, Man of the Mountain* (1939); *Dust Tracks on a Road,* her autobiography (1943); *Voice of the Land* (1945); and *Seraph on the Suwanee* (1948).

FOLK TALES

The very next afternoon, as usual, the gregarious part of the town's population gathered on the store porch. All the Florida-flip players,

Title supplied by the editors. Reprinted by permission of John G. Hurston.

all the eleven-card layers.[1] But they yelled over to me they'd be over that night in full. And they were.

"Zora," George Thomas informed me, "you come to de right place if lies is what you want. Ah'm gointer lie up a nation."

Charlie Jones said, "Yeah, man. Me and my sworn buddy Gene Brazzle is here. Big Moose done come down from de mountain."[2]

"Now, you gointer hear lies above suspicion," Gene added.

It was a hilarious night with a pinch of everything social mixed with the story-telling. Everybody ate ginger bread; some drank the buttermilk provided and some provided coon dick for themselves. Nobody guzzled it—just took it in social sips.

But they told stories enough for a volume by itself. Some of the stories were the familiar drummer-type of tale about two Irishmen, Pat and Mike, or two Jews as the case might be. Some were the European folk-tales undiluted, like Jack and the Beanstalk. Others had slight local variations, but Negro imagination is so facile that there was little need for outside help. A'nt Hagar's son, like Joseph, put on his many-colored coat and paraded before his brethren and every man there was a Joseph.

Steve Nixon was holding class meeting across the way at St. Lawrence Church and we could hear the testimony and the songs. So we began to talk about church and preachers.

"Aw, Ah don't pay all dese ole preachers no rabbit-foot,"[3] said Ellis Jones. "Some of 'em is all right but everybody dats up in de pulpit whoopin' and hollerin' ain't called to preach."

"They ain't no different from nobody else," added B. Moseley. "They mouth is cut cross ways, ain't it? Well, long as you don't see no man wid they mouth cut up and down, you know they'll all lie jus' like de rest of us."

"Yeah; and hard work in de hot sun done called a many a man to preach," said a woman called Gold, for no evident reason. "Ah heard about one man out clearin' off some new ground. De sun was so hot till a grindstone melted and run off in de shade to cool off. De man was so tired till he went and sit down on a log. 'Work, work, work! Everywhere Ah go de boss say hurry, de cap' say run. Ah got a durn good notion not to do nary one. Wisht Ah was one of dese preachers wid a whole lot of folks makin' my support for me.' He looked back over his shoulder and seen a narrer li'l strip of shade along side of de log, so he got over dere and laid down right close up to de log in de shade and said, 'Now, Lawd, if you don't pick me up and chunk me on de other side of dis log, Ah know you done called me to preach.'

[1] Coon-can players. A two-handed card game popular among Southern Negroes.
[2] Important things are about to happen.
[3] I ignore these preachers.

"You know God never picked 'im up, so he went off and tol' everybody dat he was called to preach."

"There's many a one been called just lak dat," Ellis corroborated. "Ah knowed a man dat was called by a mule."

"A mule, Ellis? All dem b'lieve dat, stand on they head," said Little Ida.

"Yeah, a mule did call a man to preach. Ah'll show you how it was done, if you'll stand a straightenin'."

"Now, Ellis, don't mislay de truth. Sense us into dis mule-callin' business."

Ellis: These was two brothers and one of 'em was a big preacher and had good collections every Sunday. He didn't pastor nothin' but big charges. De other brother decided he wanted to preach so he went way down in de swamp behind a big plantation to de place they call de prayin' ground, and got down on his knees.

"O Lawd, Ah wants to preach. Ah feel lak Ah got a message. If you done called me to preach, gimme a sign."

Just 'bout dat time he heard a voice, "Wanh, uh wanh! Go preach, go preach, go preach!"

He went and tol' everybody, but look lak he never could git no big charge. All he ever got called was on some saw-mill, half-pint church or some turpentine still. He knocked around lak dat for ten years and then he seen his brother. De big preacher says, "Brother, you don't look like you gittin' holt of much."

"You tellin' dat right, brother. Groceries is scarce. Ah ain't dirtied a plate today."

"Whut's de matter? Don't you git no support from your church?"

"Yeah, Ah gits it such as it is, but Ah ain't never pastored no big church. Ah don't git called to nothin' but saw-mill camps and turpentine stills."

De big preacher reared back and thought a while, then he ast de other one, "Is you sure you was called to preach? Maybe you ain't cut out for no preacher."

"Oh, yeah," he told him. "Ah *know* Ah been called to de ministry. A voice spoke and tol' me so."

"Well, seem lak if God called you He is mighty slow in puttin' yo' foot on de ladder. If Ah was you Ah'd go back and ast 'im agin."

So de po' man went on back to de prayin' ground agin and got down on his knees. But there wasn't no big woods like it used to be. It has been all cleared off. He prayed and said, "Oh, Lawd, right here on dis spot ten years ago Ah ast you if Ah was called to preach and a voice tole me to go preach. Since dat time Ah been strugglin' in Yo' moral vineyard, but Ah ain't gathered no grapes.

Now, if you really called me to preach Christ and Him crucified, please gimme another sign."

Sho nuff, jus' as soon as he said dat, de voice said "Wanh-uh! Go preach! Go preach! Go preach!"

De man jumped up and says, "Ah knowed Ah been called. Dat's de same voice. Dis time Ah'm goin ter ast Him where *must* Ah go preach."

By dat time de voice come agin and he looked 'way off and seen a mule in de plantation lot wid his head all stuck out to bray agin, and he said, "Unh hunh, youse de very son of a gun dat called me to preach befo'."

So he went off and got a job plowin'. Dat's whut he was called to do in de first place.

Armetta said, "A many one been called to de plough and they run off and got up in de pulpit. Ah wish dese mules knowed how to take a pair of plow-lines and go to de church and ketch some of 'em like they go to de lot with a bridle and ketch mules."

Ellis: Ah knowed one preacher dat was called to preach at one of dese split-off churches. De members had done split off from a big church because they was all mean and couldn't git along wid nobody.

Dis preacher was a good man, but de congregation was so tough he couldn't make a convert in a whole year. So he sent and invited another preacher to come and conduct a revival meeting for him. De man he ast to come was a powerful hard preacher wid a good strainin' voice. He was known to get converts.

Well, he come and preached at dis split-off for two whole weeks. De people would all turn out to church and jus' set dere and look at de man up dere strainin' his lungs out and nobody would give de man no encouragement by sayin' "Amen," and not a soul bowed down.

It was a narrer church wid one winder and dat was in de pulpit and de door was in de front end. Dey had a mean ole sexton wid a wooden leg. So de last night of de protracted meetin' de preacher come to church wid his grip-sack in his hand and went on up in de pulpit. When he got up to preach he says, "Brother Sexton, dis bein' de last night of de meetin' Ah wants you to lock de do' and bring me de key. Ah want everybody to stay and hear whut Ah got to say."

De sexton brought him de key and he took his tex and went to preachin'. He preached and he reared and pitched, but nobody said "Amen" and nobody bowed down. So 'way after while he stooped down and opened his suit-satchel and out wid his .44 Special. "Now," he said, "you rounders and brick-bats—yeah, you women, Ah'm talkin' to you. If you ain't a whole brick, den you must be a bat—and gamblers and 'leven-card layers. Ah done preached to you for two whole weeks and not one of you has said 'Amen,' and nobody has bowed down."

He thowed de gun on 'em. "And now Ah say bow down!" And they beginned to bow all over dat church.

De sexton looked at his wooden leg and figured he couldn't bow because his leg was cut off above de knee. So he ast, "Me too, Elder?"

"Yeah, you too, you peg-leg son of a gun. You bow down too."

Therefo' dat sexton bent dat wooden leg and bowed down. De preacher fired a couple of shots over they heads and stepped out de window and went on 'bout his business. But he skeered dem people so bad till they all rushed to one side of de church tryin' to git out and carried dat church buildin' twenty-eight miles befo' they thought to turn it loose.

"Now Ellis," chided Gold when she was thru her laughter, "You know dat's a lie. Folks over there in St. Lawrence holdin' class meetin' and you over here lyin' like de crossties from Jacksonville to Key West."

✿   ✿   ✿

Richard Wright

(1909–1960)

RICHARD WRIGHT, BORN NEAR Natchez, Mississippi, had a troubled childhood: his family was broken and poverty-stricken and moved often in order to survive. By the time he was fifteen, Wright had lived in eight towns and cities in three different southern states. At that point he ran away and headed north. It took him three years, but by 1927 he had made his way to Chicago, where, like many other young Negro intellectuals, he was attracted to Communism. He began his serious writing in espousal of the Communist ideology; his earliest work appeared in *New Masses, The Daily Worker, Anvil,* and other left wing periodicals. Although Wright later withdrew from the Party, he retained Marxist sympathies for the rest of his life.

Working on the Chicago Federal Writers' Project during the Depression, Wright won a *Story Magazine* contest with *Uncle Tom's Children* (1938), a collection of four novellas. In 1939 he was granted a Guggenheim Fellowship, and in 1942, the Spingarn Medal for excellence in creative literature.

In 1940 Richard Wright published *Native Son,* a naturalistic novel which became a landmark in Negro American literature. Brutal, stark, violent, and abrasive, it shocked America as few works have. In 1940–41, the dramatic version of *Native Son,* written by Wright in collaboration with Paul Green and produced by Orson Welles, became one of the season's best plays. Wright's brilliant fictionalized autobiography, *Black Boy,* was published in 1945.

Deciding that he could no longer accept the American way of life, Wright moved to France in 1946 and settled with his family in Paris. Before his death in 1960, he published *The Outsider* (1953), an "existentialist" novel; *Black Power* (1954), a subjective treatise on the politics and culture of Africa; *White Man, Listen!* (1957), a collection of lectures on various subjects; and *The Long Dream* (1958), a novel about Negro life in the South. Although *Eight Men* (1961), short stories, and *Lawd Today* (1963), a novel, were published posthumously, they were written in the 1940's and early 1950's.

Certainly one of the greatest and most influential American Negro authors, Richard Wright inspired a whole school of black naturalistic writers. His first three books served notice that the Negro writer had definitely attained his majority.

For the most recent comment on Wright's life and work, see Constance Webb, *Richard Wright* (1968) and Edward Margolies, *The Art of Richard Wright* (1969).

The selections given here come from *Black Boy* and *Eight Men*.

THE WAGES OF HUMILITY

My life now depended upon my finding work, and I was so anxious that I accepted the first offer, a job as a porter in a clothing store selling cheap goods to Negroes on credit. The shop was always crowded with black men and women pawing over cheap suits and dresses. And they paid whatever price the white man asked. The boss, his son, and the clerk treated the Negroes with open contempt, pushing, kicking, or slapping them. No matter how often I witnessed it, I could not get used to it. How can they accept it? I asked myself. I kept on edge, trying to stifle my feelings and never quite succeeding, a prey to guilt and fear because I felt that the boss suspected that I resented what I saw.

One morning, while I was polishing brass out front, the boss and his son drove up in their car. A frightened black woman sat between them. They got out and half dragged and half kicked the woman into the store. White people passed and looked on without expression. A white policeman watched from the corner, twirling his night stick; but he made no move. I watched out of the corner of my eyes, but I never slackened the strokes of my chamois upon the brass. After a moment or two I heard shrill screams coming from the rear room of the store; later the woman stumbled out, bleeding, crying, holding her stomach, her clothing torn. When she reached the sidewalk, the policeman met her, grabbed her, accused her of being drunk, called a patrol wagon and carted her away.

When I went to the rear of the store, the boss and his son were washing their hands at the sink. They looked at me and laughed uneasily. The floor was bloody, strewn with wisps of hair and clothing. My face must have reflected my shock, for the boss slapped me reassuringly on the back.

"Boy, that's what we do to niggers when they don't pay their bills," he said.

His son looked at me and grinned.

"Here, hava cigarette," he said.

Not knowing what to do, I took it. He lit his and held the match for me. This was a gesture of kindness, indicating that, even if they had beaten the black woman, they would not beat me if I knew enough to keep my mouth shut.

"Yes, sir," I said.

After they had gone, I sat on the edge of a packing box and stared at the bloody floor until the cigarette went out.

The store owned a bicycle which I used in delivering purchases. One day, while returning from the suburbs, my bicycle tire was punctured. I walked along the hot, dusty road, sweating and leading the bicycle by the handle bars.

A car slowed at my side.

"What's the matter there, boy?" a white man called.

I told him that my bicycle was broken and that I was walking back to town.

"That's too bad," he said. "Hop on the running board."

He stopped the car. I clutched hard at my bicycle with one hand and clung to the side of the car with the other.

"All set?"

"Yes, sir."

The car started. It was full of young white men. They were drinking. I watched the flask pass from mouth to mouth.

"Wanna drink, boy?" one asked.

The memory of my six-year-old drinking came back and filled me with caution. But I laughed, the wind whipping my face.

"Oh, no!" I said.

The words were barely out of my mouth before I felt something hard and cold smash me between the eyes. It was an empty whisky bottle. I saw stars, and fell backwards from the speeding car into the dust of the road, my feet becoming entangled in the steel spokes of the bicycle. The car stopped and the white men piled out and stood over me.

"Nigger, ain't you learned no better sense'n that yet?" asked the man who hit me. "Ain't you learned to say *sir* to a white man yet?"

Dazed, I pulled to my feet. My elbows and legs were bleeding. Fists doubled, the white man advanced, kicking the bicycle out of the way.

"Aw, leave the bastard alone. He's got enough," said one.

They stood looking at me. I rubbed my shins, trying to stop the flow of blood. No doubt they felt a sort of contemptuous pity, for one asked:

"You wanna ride to town now, nigger? You reckon you know enough to ride now?"

"I wanna walk," I said simply.

Maybe I sounded funny. They laughed.

"Well, walk, you black sonofabitch!"

Before they got back into their car, they comforted me with:

"Nigger, you sure ought to be glad it was us you talked to that way. You're a lucky bastard, 'cause if you'd said that to some other white man, you might've been a dead nigger now."

I was learning rapidly how to watch white people, to observe their every move, every fleeting expression, how to interpret what was said and what left unsaid.

Late one Saturday night I made some deliveries in a white neighborhood. I was pedaling my bicycle back to the store as fast as I could when a police car, swerving toward me, jammed me into the curbing.

"Get down, nigger, and put up your hands!" they ordered.

I did. They climbed out of the car, guns drawn, faces set, and advanced slowly.

"Keep still!" they ordered.

I reached my hands higher. They searched my pockets and packages. They seemed dissatisfied when they could find nothing incriminating. Finally, one of them said:

"Boy, tell your boss not to send you out in white neighborhoods at this time of night."

"Yes, sir," I said.

I rode off, feeling that they might shoot at me, feeling that the pavement might disappear. It was like living in a dream, the reality of which might change at any moment.

Each day in the store I watched the brutality with growing hate, yet trying to keep my feelings from registering in my face. When the boss looked at me I would avoid his eyes. Finally the boss's son cornered me one morning.

"Say, nigger, look here," he began.

"Yes, sir."

"What's on your mind?"

"Nothing, sir," I said, trying to look amazed, trying to fool him.

"Why don't you laugh and talk like the other niggers?" he asked.

"Well, sir, there's nothing much to say or smile about," I said, smiling.

His face was hard, baffled; I knew that I had not convinced him. He whirled from me and went to the front of the store; he came back a moment later, his face red. He tossed a few green bills at me.

"I don't like your looks, nigger. Now, get!" he snapped.

I picked up the money and did not count it. I grabbed my hat and left.

I held a series of petty jobs for short periods, quitting some to work elsewhere, being driven off others because of my attitude, my speech, the look in my eyes. I was no nearer than ever to my goal of saving enough money to leave. At times I doubted if I could ever do it.

One jobless morning I went to my old classmate, Griggs, who worked for a Capitol Street jeweler. He was washing the windows of the store when I came upon him.

"Do you know where I can find a job?" I asked.

He looked at me with scorn.

"Yes, I know where you can find a job," he said, laughing.

"Where?"

"But I wonder if you can hold it," he said.

"What do you mean?" I asked. "Where's the job?"

"Take your time," he said. "You know, Dick, I know you. You've been trying to hold a job all summer, and you can't. Why? Because you're impatient. That's your big fault."

I said nothing, because he was repeating what I had already heard him say. He lit a cigarette and blew out smoke leisurely.

"Well," I said, egging him on to speak.

"I wish to hell I could talk to you," he said.

"I think I know what you want to tell me," I said.

He clapped me on the shoulder; his face was full of fear, hate, concern for me.

"Do you want to get killed?" he asked me.

"Hell, no!"

"Then, for God's sake, learn how to live in the South!"

"What do you mean?" I demanded. "Let white people tell me that. Why should you?"

"See?" he said triumphantly, pointing his finger at me. "There it is, *now!* It's in your face. You won't let people tell you things. You rush too much. I'm trying to help you and you won't let me." He paused and looked about; the streets were filled with white people. He spoke to me in a low, full tone. "Dick, look, you're black, black, *black*, see? Can't you understand that?"

"Sure. I understand it," I said.

"You don't act a damn bit like it," he spat.

He then reeled off an account of my actions on every job I had held that summer.

"How did you know that?" I asked.

"White people make it their business to watch niggers," he explained. "And they pass the word around. Now, my boss is a Yankee and he tells me things. You're marked already."

Could I believe him? Was it true? How could I ever learn this strange world of white people?

"Then tell me how must I act?" I asked humbly. "I just want to make enough money to leave."

"Wait and I'll tell you," he said.

At that moment a woman and two men stepped from the jewelry store; I moved to one side to let them pass, my mind intent upon Griggs's words. Suddenly Griggs reached for my arm and jerked me violently, sending me stumbling three or four feet across the pavement. I whirled.

"What's the matter with you?" I asked.

Griggs glared at me, then laughed.

"I'm teaching you how to get out of white people's way," he said.

I looked at the people who had come out of the store; yes, they were *white,* but I had not noticed it.

"Do you see what I mean?" he asked. "White people want you out of their way." He pronounced the words slowly so that they would sink into my mind.

"I know what you mean," I breathed.

"Dick, I'm treating you like a brother," he said. "You act around white people as if you didn't know that they were white. And they see it."

"Oh, Christ, I can't be a slave," I said hopelessly.

"But you've got to eat," he said.

"Yes, I got to eat."

"Then start acting like it," he hammered at me, pounding his fist in his palm. "When you're in front of white people, *think* before you act, *think* before you speak. Your way of doing things is all right among *our* people, but not for *white* people. They won't stand for it."

I stared bleakly into the morning sun. I was nearing my seventeenth birthday and I was wondering if I would ever be free of this plague. What Griggs was saying was true, but it was simply utterly impossible for me to calculate, to scheme, to act, to plot all the time. I would re-member to dissemble for short periods, then I would forget and act straight and human again, not with the desire to harm anybody, but merely forgetting the artificial status of race and class. It was the same with whites as with blacks; it was my way with everybody. I sighed, looking at the glittering diamonds in the store window, the rings and the neat rows of golden watches.

"I guess you're right," I said at last. "I've got to watch myself, break myself . . ."

"No," he said quickly, feeling guilty now. Someone—a white man—went into the store and we paused in our talk. "You know, Dick, you may think I'm an Uncle Tom, but I'm not. I hate these white people, hate 'em with all my heart. But I can't show it; if I did, they'd kill me." He paused and looked around to see if there were any white people within hearing distance. "Once I heard an old drunk nigger say:

> *All these white folks dressed so fine*
> *Their ass-holes smell just like mine . . ."*

I laughed uneasily, looking at the white faces that passed me. But Griggs, when he laughed, covered his mouth with his hand and bent at the knees, a gesture which was unconsciously meant to conceal his excessive joy in the presence of whites.

"That's how I feel about 'em," he said proudly after he had finished his spasm of glee. He grew sober. "There's an optical company upstairs and the boss is a Yankee from Illinois. Now, he wants a boy to work all day in summer, mornings and evenings in winter. He wants to break a colored boy into the optical trade. You know algebra and you're just cut out for the work. I'll tell Mr. Crane about you and I'll get in touch with you."

"Do you suppose I could see him now?" I asked.

"For God's sake, take your *time!*" he thundered at me.

"Maybe that's what's wrong with Negroes," I said. "They take too much time."

I laughed, but he was disturbed. I thanked him and left. For a week I did not hear from him and I gave up hope. Then one afternoon Griggs came to my house.

"It looks like you've got a job," he said. "You're going to have a chance to learn a trade. But remember to keep your head. Remember you're black. You start tomorrow."

"What will I get?"

"Five dollars a week to start with; they'll raise you if they like you," he explained.

My hopes soared. Things were not quite so bad, after all. I would have a chance to learn a trade. And I need not give up school. I told him that I would take the job, that I would be humble.

"You'll be working for a Yankee and you ought to get along," he said.

The next morning I was outside the office of the optical company long before it opened. I was reminding myself that I must be polite, must think before I spoke, must think before I acted, must say "yes sir, no sir," that I must so conduct myself that white people would not think that I thought I was as good as they. Suddenly a white man came up to me.

"What do you want?" he asked me.

"I'm reporting for a job, sir," I said.

"O.K. Come on."

I followed him up a flight of steps and he unlocked the door of the office. I was a little tense, but the young white man's manner put me at ease and I sat and held my hat in my hand. A white girl came and began punching the typewriter. Soon another white man, thin and gray, entered and went into the rear room. Finally a tall, red-faced white man arrived, shot me a quick glance and sat at his desk. His brisk manner branded him a Yankee.

"You're the new boy, eh?"

"Yes, sir."

"Let me get my mail out of the way and I'll talk with you," he said pleasantly.

"Yes, sir."

I even pitched my voice to a low plane, trying to rob it of any suggestion or overtone of aggressiveness.

Half an hour later Mr. Crane called me to his desk and questioned me closely about my schooling, about how much mathematics I had had. He seemed pleased when I told him that I had had two years of algebra.

"How would you like to learn this trade?" he asked.

"I'd like it fine, sir. I'd like nothing better," I said.

He told me that he wanted to train a Negro boy in the optical trade; he wanted to help him, guide him. I tried to answer in a way that would let him know that I would try to be worthy of what he was doing. He took me to the stenographer and said:

"This is Richard. He's going to be with us."

He then led me into the rear room of the office, which turned out to be a tiny factory filled with many strange machines smeared with red dust.

"Reynolds," he said to a young white man, "this is Richard."

"What you saying there, boy!" Reynolds grinned and boomed at me.

Mr. Crane took me to the older man.

"Pease, this is Richard, who'll work with us."

Pease looked at me and nodded. Mr. Crane then held forth to the two white men about my duties; he told them to break me in gradually to the workings of the shop, to instruct me in the mechanics of grinding and polishing lenses. They nodded their assent.

"Now, boy, let's see how clean you can get this place," Mr. Crane said.

"Yes, sir."

I swept, mopped, dusted, and soon had the office and the shop clean. In the afternoons, when I had caught up with my work, I ran errands. In an idle moment I would stand and watch the two white men grinding lenses on the machines. They said nothing to me and I said nothing to them. The first day passed, the second, the third, a week passed and I received my five dollars. A month passed. But I was not learning anything and nobody had volunteered to help me. One afternoon I walked up to Reynolds and asked him to tell me about the work.

"What are you trying to do, get smart, nigger?" he asked me.

"No sir," I said.

I was baffled. Perhaps he just did not want to help me. I went to Pease, reminding him that the boss had said that I was to be given a chance to learn the trade.

"Nigger, you think you're white, don't you?"

"No, sir."

"You're acting mighty like it," he said.

"I was only doing what the boss told me to do," I said.

Pease shook his fist in my face.

"This is a *white* man's work around here," he said.

From then on they changed toward me; they said good morning no more. When I was just a bit slow in performing some duty, I was called a lazy black sonofabitch. I kept silent, striving to offer no excuse for worsening of relations. But one day Reynolds called me to his machine.

"Nigger, you think you'll ever amount to anything?" he asked in a slow, sadistic voice.

"I don't know, sir," I answered, turning my head away.

"What do niggers think about?" he asked.

"I don't know, sir," I said, my head still averted.

"If I was a nigger, I'd kill myself," he said.

I said nothing. I was angry.

"You know why?" he asked.

I still said nothing.

"But I don't reckon niggers mind being niggers," he said suddenly and laughed.

I ignored him. Mr. Pease was watching me closely; then I saw them exchange glances. My job was not leading to what Mr. Crane had said it would. I had been humble, and now I was reaping the wages of humility.

"Come here, boy," Pease said.

I walked to his bench.

"You didn't like what Reynolds just said, did you?" he asked.

"Oh, it's all right," I said smiling.

"You didn't like it. I could see it on your face," he said.

I stared at him and backed away.

"Did you ever get into any trouble?" he asked.

"No, sir."

"What would you do if you got into trouble?"

"I don't know, sir."

"Well, watch yourself and don't get into trouble," he warned.

I wanted to report these clashes to Mr. Crane, but the thought of what Pease or Reynolds would do to me if they learned that I had "snitched" stopped me. I worked through the days and tried to hide my resentment under a nervous, cryptic smile.

The climax came at noon one summer day. Pease called me to his workbench; to get to him I had to go between two narrow benches and stand with my back against a wall.

"Richard, I want to ask you something," Pease began pleasantly, not looking up from his work.

"Yes, sir."

Reynolds came over and stood blocking the narrow passage between the benches; he folded his arms and stared at me solemnly. I looked from one to the other, sensing trouble. Pease looked up and spoke slowly, so there would be no possibility of my not understanding.

"Richard, Reynolds here tells me that you called me Pease," he said.

I stiffened. A void opened up in me. I knew that this was the showdown.

He meant that I had failed to call him Mr. Pease. I looked at Reynolds; he was gripping a steel bar in his hand. I opened my mouth to speak, to protest, to assure Pease that I had never called him simply *Pease,* and that I had never had any intention of doing so, when Reynolds grabbed me by the collar, ramming my head against a wall.

"Now, be careful, nigger," snarled Reynolds, baring his teeth. "I heard you call 'im *Pease.* And if you say you didn't, you're calling me a liar, see?" He waved the steel bar threateningly.

If I had said: No, sir, Mr. Pease, I never called you *Pease,* I would by inference have been calling Reynolds a liar; and if I had said: Yes, sir, Mr. Pease, I called you *Pease,* I would have been pleading guilty to the worst insult that a Negro can offer to a southern white man. I stood trying to think of a neutral course that would resolve this quickly risen nightmare, but my tongue would not move.

"Richard, I asked you a question!" Pease said. Anger was creeping into his voice.

"I don't remember calling you *Pease,* Mr. Pease," I said cautiously. "And if I did, I sure didn't mean . . ."

"You black sonofabitch! You called me *Pease,* then!" he spat, rising and slapping me till I bent sideways over a bench.

Reynolds was up on top of me demanding:

"Didn't you call him *Pease?* If you say you didn't, I'll rip your gut string loose with this f–k–g bar, you black granny dodger! You can't call a white man a liar and get away with it!"

I wilted, I begged them not to hit me. I knew what they wanted. They wanted me to leave the job.

"I'll leave," I promised. "I'll leave right now!"

They gave me a minute to get out of the factory, and warned me not to show up again or tell the boss. Reynolds loosened his hand on my collar and I ducked out of the room. I did not see Mr. Crane or the stenographer in the office. Pease and Reynolds had so timed it that Mr. Crane and the stenographer would be out when they turned on the terror. I went to the street and waited for the boss to return. I saw Griggs wiping glass shelves in the jewelry store and I beckoned to him. He came out and I told him what had happened.

"Then what are you standing there like a fool for?" he demanded. "Won't you ever learn? Get home! They might come down!"

I walked down Capitol Street feeling that the sidewalk was unreal, that I was unreal, that the people were unreal, yet expecting somebody to demand to know what right I had to be on the streets. My wound went deep; I felt that I had been slapped out of the human race. When I reached home, I did not tell the family what had happened; I merely told them that I had quit, that I was not making enough money, that I was seeking another job.

That night Griggs came to my house; we went for a walk.

"You got a goddamn tough break," he said.

"Can you say it was my fault?" I asked.

He shook his head.

"Well, what about your goddamn philosophy of meekness?" I asked him bitterly.

"These things just happen," he said, shrugging.

"They owe me money," I said.

"That's what I came about," he said. "Mr. Crane wants you to come in at ten in the morning. Ten sharp, now, mind you, because he'll be there and those guys won't gang up on you again."

The next morning at ten I crept up the stairs and peered into the office of the optical shop to make sure that Mr. Crane was in. He was at his desk. Pease and Reynolds were at their machines in the rear.

"Come in, Richard," Mr. Crane said.

I pulled off my hat and walked into the office; I stood before him.

"Sit down," he said.

I sat. He stared at me and shook his head.

"Tell me, what happened?"

An impulse to speak rose in me and died with the realization that I was facing a wall that I would never breach. I tried to speak several times and could make no sounds. I grew tense and tears burnt my cheeks.

"Now, just keep control of yourself," Mr. Crane said.

I clenched my fists and managed to talk.

"I tried to do my best here," I said.

"I believe you," he said. "But I want to know what happened. Which one bothered you?"

"Both of 'em," I said.

Reynolds came running to the door and I rose. Mr. Crane jumped to his feet.

"Get back in there," he told Reynolds.

"That nigger's lying!" Reynolds said. "I'll kill 'im if he lies on me!"

"Get back in there or get out," Mr. Crane said.

Reynolds backed away, keeping his eyes on me.

"Go ahead," Mr. Crane said. "Tell me what happened."

Then again I could not speak. What could I accomplish by telling him? I was black; I lived in the South. I would never learn to operate those machines as long as those two white men in there stood by them. Anger and fear welled in me as I felt what I had missed; I leaned forward and clapped my hands to my face.

"No, no, now," Mr. Crane said. "Keep control of yourself. No matter what happens, keep control . . ."

"I know," I said in a voice not my own. "There's no use of my saying anything."

"Do you want to work here?" he asked me.

I looked at the white faces of Pease and Reynolds; I imagined their waylaying me, killing me. I was remembering what had happened to Ned's brother.

"No, sir," I breathed.

"Why?"

"I'm scared," I said. "They would kill me."

Mr. Crane turned and called Pease and Reynolds into the office.

"Now, tell me which one bothered you. Don't be afraid. Nobody's going to hurt you," Mr. Crane said.

I stared ahead of me and did not answer. He waved the men inside. The white stenographer looked at me with wide eyes and I felt drenched in shame, naked to my soul. The whole of my being felt violated, and I knew that my own fear had helped to violate it. I was breathing hard and struggling to master my feelings.

"Can I get my money, sir?" I asked at last.

"Just sit a minute and take hold of yourself," he said.

I waited and my roused senses grew slowly calm.

"I'm awfully sorry about this," he said.

"I had hoped for a lot from this job," I said. "I'd wanted to go to school, to college . . ."

"I know," he said. "But what are you going to do now?"

My eyes traveled over the office, but I was not seeing.

"I'm going away," I said.

"What do you mean?"

"I'm going to get out of the South," I breathed.

"Maybe that's best," he said. "I'm from Illinois. Even for me, it's hard here. I can do just so much."

He handed me my money, more than I had earned for the week. I thanked him and rose to leave. He rose. I went into the hallway and he followed me. He reached out his hand.

"It's tough for you down here," he said.

I barely touched his hand. I walked swiftly down the hall, fighting against crying again. I ran down the steps, then paused and looked back up. He was standing at the head of the stairs, shaking his head. I went into the sunshine and walked home like a blind man.

THE MAN WHO WAS ALMOST A MAN

Dave struck out across the fields, looking homeward through paling light. Whut's the use talkin wid em niggers in the field? Anyhow, his mother was putting supper on the table. Them niggers can't understan nothing. One of these days he was going to get a gun and practice shooting, then they couldn't talk to him as though he were a little boy. He slowed, looking at the ground. Shucks, Ah ain scareda them even ef they are biggern me! Aw, Ah know whut Ahma do. Ahm going by ol Joe's sto n git that Sears Roebuck catlog n look at them guns. Mebbe Ma will lemme buy one when she gits mah pay from ol man Hawkins. Ahma beg her t gimme some money. Ahm ol enough to hava gun. Ahm seventeen. Almost a man. He strode, feeling his long loose-jointed limbs. Shucks, a man oughta hava little gun aftah he done worked hard all day.

He came in sight of Joe's store. A yellow lantern glowed on the front porch. He mounted steps and went through the screen door, hearing it bang behind him. There was a strong smell of coal oil and mackerel fish. He felt very confident until he saw fat Joe walk in through the rear door, then his courage began to ooze.

"Howdy, Dave! Whutcha want?"

"How yuh, Mistah Joe? Aw, Ah don wanna buy nothing. Ah jus wanted t see ef yuhd lemme look at tha catlog erwhile."

"Sure! You wanna see it here?"

"Nawsuh. Ah wans t take it home wid me. Ah'll bring it back ter-morrow when Ah come in from the fiels."

"You plannin on buying something?"

"Yessuh."

"Your ma lettin you have your own money now?"

"Shucks. Mistah Joe, Ahm gittin t be a man like anybody else!"

Joe laughed and wiped his greasy white face with a red bandanna.

"Whut you plannin on buyin?"

Dave looked at the floor, scratched his head, scratched his thigh, and smiled. Then he looked up shyly.

"Ah'll tell yuh, Mistah Joe, ef yuh promise yuh won't tell."

"I promise."

"Waal, Ahma buy a gun."

"A gun? Whut you want with a gun?"

"Ah wanna keep it."

"You ain't nothing but a boy. You don't need a gun."

"Aw, lemme have the catlog, Mistah Joe. Ah'll bring it back."

Joe walked through the rear door. Dave was elated. He looked around at barrels of sugar and flour. He heard Joe coming back. He craned his neck to see if he were bringing the book. Yeah, he's got it. Gawddog, he's got it!

"Here, but be sure you bring it back. It's the only one I got."

"Sho, Mistah Joe."

"Say, if you wanna buy a gun, why don't you buy one from me? I gotta gun to sell."

"Will it shoot?"

"Sure it'll shoot."

"Whut kind is it?"

"Oh, it's kinda old . . . a left-hand Wheeler. A pistol. A big one."

"Is it got bullets in it?"

"It's loaded."

"Kin Ah see it?"

"Where's your money?"

"Whut yuh wan fer it?"

"I'll let you have it for two dollars."

"Just two dollahs? Shucks, Ah could buy tha when Ah git mah pay."

"I'll have it here when you want it."

"Awright, suh. Ah be in fer it."

He went through the door, hearing it slam again behind him. Ahma git some money from Ma n buy me a gun! Only two dollahs! He tucked the thick catalogue under his arm and hurried.

"Where yuh been, boy?" His mother held a steaming dish of black-eyed peas.

"Aw, Ma, Ah jus stopped down the road t talk wid the boys."

"Yuh know bettah t keep suppah waitin."

He sat down, resting the catalogue on the edge of the table.

"Yuh git up from there and git to the well n wash yosef! Ah ain feedin no hogs in mah house!"

She grabbed his shoulder and pushed him. He stumbled out of the room, then came back to get the catalogue.

"Whut this?"

"Aw, Ma, it's jusa catlog."

"Who yuh git it from?"

"From Joe, down at the sto."

"Waal, thas good. We kin use it in the outhouse."

"Naw, Ma." He grabbed for it. "Gimme ma catlog, Ma."

She held onto it and glared at him.

"Quit hollerin at me! Whut's wrong wid yuh? Yuh crazy?"

"But Ma, please. It ain mine! It's Joe's! He tol me t bring it back t im termorrow."

She gave up the book. He stumbled down the back steps, hugging the thick book under his arm. When he had splashed water on his face and hands, he groped back to the kitchen and fumbled in a corner for the towel. He bumped into a chair; it clattered to the floor. The catalogue sprawled at his feet. When he had dried his eyes he snatched up the book and held it again under his arm. His mother stood watching him.

"Now, ef yuh gonna act a fool over that ol book, Ah'll take it n burn it up."

"Naw, Ma, please."

"Waal, set down n be still!"

He sat down and drew the oil lamp close. He thumbed page after page, unaware of the food his mother set on the table. His father came in. Then his small brother.

"Wutcha got there, Dave?" his father asked.

"Jusa catlog," he answered, not looking up.

"Yeah, here they is!" His eyes glowed at blue-and-black revolvers. He glanced up, feeling sudden guilt. His father was watching him. He eased the book under the table and rested it on his knees. After the blessing was asked, he ate. He scooped up peas and swallowed fat meat without chewing. Buttermilk helped to wash it down. He did not want to mention money before his father. He would do much better by cornering his mother when she was alone. He looked at his father uneasily out of the edge of his eye.

"Boy, how come yuh don quit foolin wid tha book n eat yo suppah?"

"Yessuh."

"How you n ol man Hawkins gitten erlong?"

"Suh?"

"Can't yuh hear? Why don yuh lissen? Ah ast yu how wuz yuh n ol man Hawkins gittin erlong?"

"Oh, swell, Pa. Ah plows mo lan than anybody over there."

"Waal, yuh oughta keep yo mind on whut yuh doin."

"Yessuh."

He poured his plate full of molasses and sopped it up slowly with a chunk of cornbread. When his father and brother had left the kitchen, he still sat and looked again at the guns in the catalogue, longing to muster courage enough to present his case to his mother. Lawd, ef Ah only had tha pretty one! He could almost feel the slickness of the weapon with his fingers. If he had a gun like that he would polish it and keep it shining so it would never rust. N Ah'd keep it loaded, by Gawd!

"Ma?" His voice was hesitant.

"Hunh?"

"Ol man Hawkins give yuh mah money yit?"

"Yeah, but ain no usa yuh thinking bout throwin nona it erway. Ahm keepin tha money sos yuh kin have cloes t go to school this winter."

He rose and went to her side with the open catalogue in his palms. She was washing dishes, her head bent low over a pan. Shyly he raised the book. When he spoke, his voice was husky, faint.

"Ma, Gawd knows Ah wans one of these."

"One of whut?" she asked, not raising her eyes.

"One of these," he said again, not daring even to point. She glanced up at the page, then at him with wide eyes.

"Nigger, is yuh gone plumb crazy?"

"Aw, Ma—"

"Git outta here! Don yuh talk t me bout no gun! Yuh a fool!"

"Ma, Ah kin buy one fer two dollahs."

"Not ef Ah knows it, yuh ain!"

"But yuh promised me one—"

"Ah don care whut Ah promised! Yuh ain nothing but a boy yit!"

"Ma, ef yuh lemme buy one Ah'll *never* ast yuh fer nothing no mo."

"Ah tol yuh t git outta here! Yuh ain gonna toucha penny of tha money fer no gun! Thas how come Ah has Mistah Hawkins t pay yo wages t me, cause Ah knows yuh ain got no sense."

"But, Ma, we needa gun. Pa ain got no gun. We needa gun in the house. Yuh kin never tell whut might happen."

"Now don yuh try to maka fool outta me, boy! Ef we did hava gun, yuh wouldn't have it!"

He laid the catalogue down and slipped his arm around her waist.

"Aw, Ma, Ah done worked hard alla summer n ain ast yuh fer nothin, is Ah, now?"

"Thas whut yuh spose t do!"

"But Ma, Ah wans a gun. Yuh kin lemme have two dollahs outta mah money. Please, Ma. I kin give it to Pa . . . Please, Ma! Ah loves yuh, Ma."

When she spoke her voice came soft and low.

"Whut yu wan wida gun, Dave? Yuh don need no gun. Yuh'll git in trouble. N ef yo pa jus thought Ah let yuh have money t buy a gun he'd hava fit."

"Ah'll hide it, Ma. It ain but two dollahs."

"Lawd, chil, whut's wrong wid yuh?"

"Ain nothin wrong, Ma. Ahm almos a man now. Ah wans a gun."

"Who gonna sell yuh a gun?"

"Ol Joe at the sto."

"N it don cos but two dollahs?"

"Thas all, Ma. Jus two dollahs. Please, Ma."

She was stacking the plates away; her hands moved slowly, reflectively. Dave kept an anxious silence. Finally, she turned to him.

"Ah'll let yuh git tha gun ef yuh promise me one thing."

"Whut's tha, Ma?"

"Yuh bring it straight back t me, yuh hear? It be fer Pa."

"Yessum! Lemme go now, Ma."

She stooped, turned slightly to one side, raised the hem of her dress, rolled down the top of her stocking, and came up with a slender wad of bills.

"Here," she said. "Lawd knows yuh don need no gun. But yer pa does. Yuh bring it right back t me, yuh hear? Ahma put it up. Now ef yuh don, Ahma have yuh pa lick yuh so hard yuh won fergit it."

"Yessum."

He took the money, ran down the steps, and across the yard.

"Dave! Yuuuuuh Daaaaave!"

He heard, but he was not going to stop now. "Naw, Lawd!"

The first movement he made the following morning was to reach under his pillow for the gun. In the gray light of dawn he held it loosely, feeling a sense of power. Could kill a man with a gun like this. Kill anybody, black or white. And if he were holding his gun in his hand, nobody could run over him; they would have to respect him. It was a big gun, with a long barrel and a heavy handle. He raised and lowered it in his hand, marveling at its weight.

He had not come straight home with it as his mother had asked; instead he had stayed out in the fields, holding the weapon in his hand, aiming it now and then at some imaginary foe. But he had not fired it; he had been afraid that his father might hear. Also he was not sure he knew how to fire it.

To avoid surrendering the pistol he had not come into the house until he knew that they were all asleep. When his mother had tiptoed to his bedside late that night and demanded the gun, he had first played possum, then he had told her that the gun was hidden outdoors, that he would bring it to her in the morning. Now he lay turning it slowly in his hands. He broke it, took out the cartridges, felt them, and then put them back.

He slid out of bed, got a long strip of old flannel from a trunk, wrapped the gun in it, and tied it to his naked thigh while it was still loaded. He did not go in to breakfast. Even though it was not yet day-light, he started for Jim Hawkins' plantation. Just as the sun was rising he reached the barns where the mules and plows were kept.

"Hey! That you, Dave?"

He turned. Jim Hawkins stood eying him suspiciously.

"What're yuh doing here so early?"

"Ah didn't know Ah wuz gittin up so early, Mistah Hawkins. Ah wuz fixin t hitch up ol Jenny n take her t the fiels."

"Good. Since you're so early, how about plowing that stretch down by the woods?"

"Suits me, Mistah Hawkins."

"O.K. Go to it!"

He hitched Jenny to a plow and started across the fields. Hot dog! This was just what he wanted. If he could get down by the woods, he could shoot his gun and nobody would hear. He walked behind the plow, hearing the traces creaking, feeling the gun tied tight to his thigh.

When he reached the woods, he plowed two whole rows before he decided to take out the gun. Finally, he stopped, looked in all direc-tions, then untied the gun and held it in his hand. He turned to the mule and smiled.

"Know whut this is, Jenny? Naw, yuh wouldn know! Yuhs jusa ol mule! Anyhow, this is a gun, n it kin shoot, by Gawd!"

He held the gun at arm's length. Whut t hell, Ahma shoot this thing! He looked at Jenny again.

"Lissen here, Jenny! When Ah pull this ol trigger, Ah don wan yuh t run n acka fool now!"

Jenny stood with head down, her short ears pricked straight. Dave walked off about twenty feet, held the gun far out from him at arm's length, and turned his head. Hell, he told himself, Ah ain afraid. The gun felt loose in his fingers; he waved it wildly for a moment. Then he shut his eyes and tightened his forefinger. Bloom! A report half deafened him and he thought his right hand was torn from his arm. He heard Jenny whinnying and galloping over the field, and he found himself on his knees, squeezing his fingers hard between his legs. His hand was numb; he jammed it into his mouth, trying to warm it, trying to stop the pain. The gun lay at his feet. He did not quite know what had happened. He stood up and stared at the gun as though it were a living thing. He gritted his teeth and kicked the gun. Yuh almos broke mah arm! He turned to look for Jenny; she was far over the fields, tossing her head and kicking wildly.

"Hol on there, ol mule!"

When he caught up with her she stood trembling, walling her big white eyes at him. The plow was far away; the traces had broken. Then Dave stopped short, looking, not believing. Jenny was bleeding. Her left side was red and wet with blood. He went closer. Lawd, have mercy! Wondah did Ah shoot this mule? He grabbed for Jenny's mane. She flinched, snorted, whirled, tossing her head.

"Hol on now! Hol on."

Then he saw the hole in Jenny's side, right between the ribs. It was round, wet, red. A crimson stream streaked down the front leg, flowing fast. Good Gawd! Ah wuzn't shootin at tha mule. He felt panic. He knew he had to stop that blood, or Jenny would bleed to death. He had never seen so much blood in all his life. He chased the mule for half a mile, trying to catch her. Finally she stopped, breathing hard, stumpy tail half arched. He caught her mane and led her back to where the plow and gun lay. Then he stooped and grabbed handfuls of damp black earth and tried to plug the bullet hole. Jenny shuddered, whinnied, and broke from him.

"Hol on! Hol on now!"

He tried to plug it again, but blood came anyhow. His fingers were hot and sticky. He rubbed dirt into his palms, trying to dry them. Then again he attempted to plug the bullet hole, but Jenny shied away, kicking her heels high. He stood helpless. He had to do something. He ran at Jenny; she dodged him. He watched a red stream of blood flow down Jenny's leg and form a bright pool at her feet.

"Jenny. . . Jenny," he called weakly.

His lips trembled. She's bleeding t death! He looked in the direction of home, wanting to go back, wanting to get help. But he saw the pistol lying in the damp black clay. He had a queer feeling that if he only did something, this would not be; Jenny would not be there bleeding to death.

When he went to her this time, she did not move. She stood with sleepy, dreamy eyes; and when he touched her she gave a low-pitched whinny and knelt to the ground, her front knees slopping in blood.

"Jenny . . . Jenny . . ." he whispered.

For a long time she held her neck erect; then her head sank, slowly. Her ribs swelled with a mighty heave and she went over.

Dave's stomach felt empty, very empty. He picked up the gun and held it gingerly between his thumb and forefinger. He buried it at the foot of a tree. He took a stick and tried to cover the pool of blood with dirt—but what was the use? There was Jenny lying with her mouth open and her eyes walled and glassy. He could not tell Jim Hawkins he had shot his mule. But he had to tell something. Yeah, Ah'll tell em Jenny started gittin wil n fell on the joint of the plow. . . . But that would hardly happen to a mule. He walked across the field slowly, head down.

It was sunset. Two of Jim Hawkins' men were over near the edge of the woods digging a hole in which to bury Jenny. Dave was surrounded by a knot of people, all of whom were looking down at the dead mule.

"I don't see how in the world it happened," said Jim Hawkins for the tenth time.

The crowd parted and Dave's mother, father, and small brother pushed into the center.

"Where Dave?" his mother called.

"There he is," said Jim Hawkins.

His mother grabbed him.

"Whut happened, Dave? Whut yuh done?"

"Nothin."

"C mon, boy, talk," his father said.

Dave took a deep breath and told the story he knew nobody believed.

"Waal," he drawled. "Ah brung ol Jenny down here sos Ah could do mah plowin. Ah plowed bout two rows, just like yuh see." He stopped and pointed at the long rows of upturned earth. "Then somethin musta been wrong wid ol Jenny. She wouldn ack right at-all. She started snortin n kickin her heels. Ah tried t hol her, but she pulled erway, rearin n goin in. Then when the point of the plow was stickin up in the air, she swung erroun n twisted back on it . . . She stuck herself n started t bleed. N fo Ah could do anything, she wuz dead."

"Did you ever hear of anything like that in all your life?" asked Jim Hawkins.

There were white and black standing in the crowd. They murmured. Dave's mother came close to him and looked hard into his face. "Tell the truth, Dave," she said.

"Looks like a bullet hole to me," said one man.

"Dave, whut yuh do wid the gun?" his mother asked.

The crowd surged in, looking at him. He jammed his hands into his pockets, shook his head slowly from left to right, and backed away. His eyes were wide and painful.

"Did he hava gun?" asked Jim Hawkins.

"By Gawd, Ah tol yuh tha wuz a gun wound," said a man, slapping his thigh.

His father caught his shoulders and shook him till his teeth rattled.

"Tell whut happened, yuh rascal! Tell whut . . ."

Dave looked at Jenny's stiff legs and began to cry.

"Whut yuh do wid tha gun?" his mother asked.

"Whut wuz he doin wida gun?" his father asked.

"Come on and tell the truth," said Hawkins. "Ain't nobody going to hurt you . . ."

His mother crowded close to him.

"Did yuh shoot tha mule, Dave?"

Dave cried, seeing blurred white and black faces.

"Ahh ddinn gggo tt sshooot hher . . . Ah ssswear ffo Gawd Ahh ddin. . . . Ah wuz a-tryin t sssee ef the old gggun would sshoot—"

"Where yuh git the gun from?" his father asked.

"Ah got it from Joe, at the sto."

"Where yuh git the money?"

"Ma give it t me."

"He kept worryin me, Bob. Ah had t. Ah tol im t bring the gun right back t me . . . It was fer yuh, the gun."

"But how yuh happen to shoot that mule?" asked Jim Hawkins.

"Ah wuzn shootin at the mule, Mistah Hawkins. The gun jumped when Ah pulled the trigger . . . N fo Ah knowed anythin Jenny was there a-bleedin."

Somebody in the crowd laughed. Jim Hawkins walked close to Dave and looked into his face.

"Well, looks like you have bought you a mule, Dave."

"Ah swear fo Gawd, Ah didn go t kill the mule, Mistah Hawkins!"

"But you killed her!"

All the crowd was laughing now. They stood on tiptoe and poked heads over one another's shoulders.

"Well, boy, looks like yuh done bought a dead mule! Hahaha!"

"Ain tha ershame."

"Hohohohoho."

Dave stood, head down, twisting his feet in the dirt.

"Well, you needn't worry about it, Bob," said Jim Hawkins to Dave's father. "Just let the boy keep on working and pay me two dollars a month."

"What yuh wan fer yo mule, Mistah Hawkins?"

Jim Hawkins screwed up his eyes.

"Fifty dollars."

"What yuh do wid tha gun?" Dave's father demanded.

Dave said nothing.

"Yuh wan me t take a tree n beat yuh till yuh talk!"

"Nawsuh!"

"Whut yuh do wid it?"

"Ah throwed it erway."

"Where?"

"Ah . . . Ah throwed it in the creek."

"Waal, c mon home. N firs thing in the mawnin git to tha creek n fin tha gun."

"Yessuh."

"Whut yuh pay fer it?"

"Two dollahs."

"Take tha gun n git yo money back n carry it t Mistah Hawkins, yuh hear? N don fergit Ahma lam you black bottom good fer this! Now march yosef on home, suh!"

Dave turned and walked slowly. He heard people laughing. Dave glared, his eyes welling with tears. Hot anger bubbled in him. Then he swallowed and stumbled on.

That night Dave did not sleep. He was glad that he had gotten out of killing the mule so easily, but he was hurt. Something hot seemed to turn over inside him each time he remembered how they had laughed. He tossed on his bed, feeling his hard pillow. N Pa says he's gonna beat me . . . He remembered other beatings, and his back quivered. Naw, naw, Ah sho don wan im t beat me tha way no mo. Dam em all! Nobody ever gave him anything. All he did was work. They treat me like a mule, n then they beat me. He gritted his teeth. N Ma had t tell on me.

Well, if he had to, he would take old man Hawkins that two dollars. But that meant selling the gun. And he wanted to keep that gun. Fifty dollars for a dead mule.

He turned over, thinking how he had fired the gun. He had an itch to fire it again. Ef other men kin shoota gun, by Gawd, Ah kin! He was still, listening. Mebbe they all sleepin now. The house was still. He heard the soft breathing of his brother. Yes, now! He would go down and get that gun and see if he could fire it! He eased out of bed and slipped into overalls.

The moon was bright. He ran almost all the way to the edge of the woods. He stumbled over the ground, looking for the spot where he had buried the gun. Yeah, here it is. Like a hungry dog scratching for a bone, he pawed it up. He puffed his black cheeks and blew dirt from the trigger and barrel. He broke it and found four cartridges unshot. He looked around; the fields were filled with silence and moonlight. He clutched the gun stiff and hard in his fingers. But, as soon as he wanted to pull the trigger, he shut his eyes and turned his head. Naw, Ah can't shoot wid mah eyes closed n mah head turned. With effort he held his eyes open; then he squeezed. *Blooooom!* He was stiff, not breathing. The gun was still in his hands. Dammit, he'd done it! He fired again. *Blooooom!* He smiled. *Blooooom! Blooooom! Click, click.* There! It was empty. If anybody could shoot a gun, he could. He put the gun into his hip pocket and started across the fields.

When he reached the top of a ridge he stood straight and proud in the moonlight, looking at Jim Hawkins' big white house, feeling the gun sagging in his pocket. Lawd, ef Ah had just one mo bullet Ah'd taka shot at tha house. Ah'd like t scare ol man Hawkins jusa little . . . Jusa enough t let im know Dave Saunders is a man.

To his left the road curved, running to the tracks of the Illinois Central. He jerked his head, listening. From far off came a faint *hoooof-hoooof; hoooof-hoooof; hoooof-hoooof.* . . . He stood rigid. Two dollahs a mont. Les see now . . . Tha means it'll take bout two years. Shucks! Ah'll be dam!

He started down the road, toward the tracks. Yeah, here she comes! He stood beside the track and held himself stiffly. Here she comes, erroun the ben . . . C mon, yuh slow poke! C mon! He had his hand on his gun; something quivered in his stomach. Then the train thundered past, the gray and brown box cars rumbling and clinking. He gripped the gun tightly; then he jerked his hand out of his pocket. Ah betcha Bill wouldn't do it! Ah betcha . . . The cars slid past, steel grinding upon steel. Ahm ridin yuh ternight, so hep me Gawd! He was hot all over. He hesitated just a moment; then he grabbed, pulled atop of a car, and lay flat. He felt his pocket; the gun was still there. Ahead the long rails were glinting in the moonlight, stretching away, away to somewhere, somewhere where he could be a man . . .

Chester B. Himes

(b. 1909)

BORN IN JEFFERSON CITY, Missouri, reared in Mississippi, and a resident of Harlem for many years, Chester B. Himes attended Ohio University for three years (1926–29). He began to write and publish short stories while serving time in an Ohio State penitentiary. Himes' work was first published in *Esquire* in 1934 and has since appeared in *Abbott's Monthly, The Crisis, Opportunity, Coronet, Commentary,* and others. An expatriate living in France, Himes returns to the United States only rarely.

Chester Himes is the author of *If He Hollers Let Him Go* (1945); *Lonely Crusade* (1947); *Cast the First Stone* (1953); *Third Generation* (1954); *The Primitive* (1955); *Pinktoes* (1965); and *Blind Man with a Pistol* (1969). He has also written numerous mystery stories, such as *Cotton Comes to Harlem* (1965), which features an indomitable pair of black detectives. In 1958 Himes received the "Grand Prix Policier" for mystery writing.

The selection appearing here comes from *Third Generation,* a novel which includes a theme characteristic of Himes' earlier works—the emasculation of the black male by middle-class Negro women.

RAPE!

It was late at night when the train pulled into the old stone station. A short black man wearing a black derby hat, dark suit and black, box-toed shoes alighted from a Pullman car. The conductor looked away. The short black man stood at the bottom of the steps and extended his hand to a woman. She wore a linen duster over a pale-blue silk jersey dress, and a large pink hat with feathers. Her face was white and strained; her deep-set eyes fixed in an unseeing stare.

The short black man touched her arm. She looked at him. A smile flickered in her stiff white face, flickered out. The short black man helped her down the steps. The conductor's mouth pursed in a grim, straight line; his face reddened slowly.

A Pullman porter followed, carrying two heavy valises and a woman's straw traveling case. The short black man tipped him and hailed a station porter. Then he took the woman's arm and, preening with self-importance, followed the porter through the huge, dimly lit South Station to a dark side street.

"We'll just go straight to the hotel, honey, unless you want to stop for a bowl of hot milk or a glass of wine," he said.

"No," she said.

He looked at her, undecided, as if to interpret her meaning. She seemed passive, acquiescent. He smiled indulgently and patted her arm.

The porter hailed a horse cab and put the luggage aboard, and the short black man, tipping him generously, helped the woman to enter and climbed in beside her. His actions were slightly erratic. He seemed laboring under great emotion, tautened with excitement.

The old cab went clattering through the drab cobbled streets, past row after row of gray stone houses interlocked and identical as peas, in the dim light like prison walls enclosing the tunnel down which she went to her doom. She couldn't help the distortions of her imagination. She was frightened, lonely, homesick. The man beside her, whom she had married that morning, now seemed a stranger. And this seemed a monstrously wrong thing they were doing.

He sensed her need for reassurance and patted her hand comfortingly. But tremors of his excitement passed down through his touch into her skin and she shuddered.

He'd gone to great pains to arrange everything so there would be no embarrassment or anxiety, and her attitude puzzled and angered him.

"It's a big city," he said. "More people here than in all the state of North Carolina."

She looked out at the depressing sameness of the gloomy streets. "Yes," she replied.

They lapsed into silence . . .

. . . as if she were that kind of woman, she was thinking . . .

. . . she'll be all right, he reassured himself doubtfully . . .

The clop-clop of the horses' hoofs hammered on the silence. The neighborhood changed. Smell of city slums pressed into the cab. Strident Negroid laughter shattered on the night. The horse cab pulled up before an old dilapidated stone-faced building which carried the faded legend, HOTEL, atop a dingy door.

The short black man alighted and helped the woman down. He paid the driver and struggled with the luggage. She opened the door for him and followed across the dusty foyer to the scarred and littered desk. A few moth-eaten chairs sat here and there in the dim light of turned-down lamps and in one a fat black man sat slumped, asleep and snoring slightly. The smell of damp decay hung in the air.

The short black man put down his luggage and smiled at the woman reassuringly. "It's the best colored hotel in town. I thought it'd be better than to try to . . ." his voice petered out, leaving the thought unspoken.

She didn't answer.

The night clerk came from somewhere out of the shadows, hitching up his suspenders.

"I reserved the bridal suite," the short black man said.

"Yas suh," the night clerk said, and teeth came alive in his face as he slanted a glance at the strained white face of the waiting woman. "Yas *suh!*"

The short black man signed the register and the night clerk picked up the luggage and preceded them up the narrow, bending stairs, his footsteps muffled on the threadbare carpet. The night clerk opened a door at the front of the narrow corridor, entered the darkness and lit a lamp, lit the grate, carried the luggage within, and stood to one side, his big white teeth winking at them like an electric sign. The woman looked at him with a shudder of distaste.

Impulsively the short black man lifted the woman across the threshold. Her body was stiff and unyielding. Gingerly he stood her erect, then turned and tipped the servant.

"Thankee-suh, thankee-suh. Ah knows y'all gonna have uh good time," the night clerk said as if it was a dirty joke.

The short black man quickly closed the door. He turned and went across to the woman, who hadn't moved, and tried to put his arm around her. She pulled away and went over and sat on the moth-eaten sofa. The same smell of decay encountered below was in the room, but here it was dry, mingled with the vague scent of countless assignations. Again the woman shuddered as her thoughts were assailed by a sickening recollection. Once, as a little girl, when cutting through a vulgar street in niggertown, Atlanta, she had heard an obscene reference to her vagina. She had not known then what it had meant, only that it was vulgar and dirty and had filled her with a horrible shame. She had never told anyone, but the feeling of shame had lingered in her thoughts like a drop of pus, poisoning her conception of sex. As she had approached womanhood, she had resolved to make her marriage immaculate. And now it seemed dirtied at the very start by this cloying scent.

The fire sputtered cheerfully in the grate. Beyond was the door into the bedroom. The short black man went and lit the bedroom lamp, then came back and turned down the living-room lamp and went over and sat beside her.

"You go to bed, honey," he said gently. "You must be tired."

She turned and for the first time gave him a grateful smile. "I'm not tired." She groped for words. She spread her hands slightly, inclusively. "It's so squalid."

"It's the best they have," he said defensively.

She arose and started toward the bedroom, then impulsively bent down and kissed him on the lips and, laughing girlishly, went into the bedroom and closed the door. Slowly she undressed before the mirror, glancing furtively, a little ashamedly at her nude figure, letting the realization that she was married come to her.

She was a tiny woman with soft milk-white skin and tiny breasts as round and hard as oranges. Her face was slightly longish and her expression a little austere. Laughing at herself, she slipped into her nightgown and, putting out the light, crawled quickly into bed. She lay looking into the dark, her thoughts pounding, listening to the movements of her husband as he undressed in the other room. The latch clicked, the door slowly opened. She tensed beneath the covers, watching him enter the room.

His short muscular body, seemingly blacker than the night, was silhouetted against the faint luminescence of the doorway. *He's naked!* she thought, horrified as by some startling obscenity. And then as he came toward her, his naked body assumed a sinister aspect, its very blackness the embodiment of evil. She felt a cold shock of terror.

"William," she whimpered.

"I'm right here, honey," he said reassuringly.

She felt his hand pulling back the cover. She could scarcely breathe.

He lay down beside her with infinite gentleness. For a time he lay still. Then his hand moved and he touched her breasts. Her body became instantly taut. She could not analyze her fear of him, but she dreaded the feel of his touch. She was still caught in a state of shock. She feared him as something inhuman.

He turned over and kissed her on the throat. She lay rigid in terror. His hand went down over the smooth satin nightgown and rested on her stomach. Then, abruptly, he reached down and drew the gown up about her waist and his hand searched frantically. His breathing shortened and thickened.

"Don't!" she gasped. "Don't! Not now! Not here! Not in this hovel!" Her arms had stretched out, gripping the sheets in the classic posture of crucifixion.

He scrambled over her. His hot breath licked at her face.

"Dont!" she cried again. "Don't!" And then she screamed in terror, "Light the lamp so I can see you!"

But he had gone out of himself and was panting uncontrollably, unaware, unhearing, his head filled with the roaring fire of his lust. He mounted her like a stud. The penetration chilled her body like death. For an instant the vision of her father's kindly white face with its long silky beard flickered through her consciousness. Then her mind closed against reality as it filled with a sense of outrage; her organs tightened as she stiffened to the pain and degradation.

He struggled brutally and savagely and blindly and then desperately to overcome her, conquer her, win her. She fought to hold herself back. He could not control himself; his muscles jerked with frenzy, the vague pallor of her face floating through the red haze of his vision. When she felt her virginity go bleedingly to this vile and bestial man she hated him.

He threw back the covers, leaped from the bed and lit the lamp, unaware of his reason for doing so. Standing naked, the shadow of his black, knotty body with the muscular bowed legs, darker than the night, he trembled with frustration and dissatisfaction, not knowing what was wrong with him.

She lay rigid in the posture of crucifixion, her stiff white face as still as if in death, looking at him through pools of horror. The sight of his black body was incalculably repulsive. Finally she closed her eyes. She felt as if she had been raped, victimized, debased by an animal. "You beast," she said.

He was shocked out of his daze. He groped for reason, sucking at his lower lip, trying to frame in simple thought the basis for her attitude.

"But, honey, we're married now," he said in a soft, placating voice.

"You rapist," she said through clenched teeth. "You don't know what marriage is."

Had it not been for the prospect of facing the night alone in a strange and terrifying city, she would have left him then. But she realized she had no place to go. Her family wouldn't have welcomed her home, she knew. There would have been a scandal. No one would have understood. In view of all the hardships and travail her parents had experienced during their marriage, they would have been appalled by her attitude. So she steeled herself to stay with him.

Vaguely aware that he was losing her, he tried to win her back. Afterwards, he was infinitely gentle. But she never became reconciled. Each time, she received him with horror and revulsion. Although a child was conceived, she never got over that first night. She was never able to separate the blackness of his skin from the brutality of his act; the two were irrevocably bound together in all her thoughts of him.

After they returned to the college in Georgia where he taught, he discovered she hated him. She was cold and distant and shuddered at his touch. He thought it was due to her condition; many women hated their husbands during pregnancy. To lighten the burden of housekeeping for her he brought his sister to live with them and do the housework. Beatrice was a thin, black girl with short, kinky hair. It was her first time away from home. And she stood in such awe of her forbidding, white-faced sister-in-law she was painfully self-conscious and stupid. Mrs. Taylor was ill and unhappy and very impatient with the girl. She thought her mean and sullen, and took out her spleen toward her husband on her.

One day Beatrice burst into tears and begged Professor Taylor to send her home. He turned on his wife and shouted, "Confound you, quit picking on my sister!"

"Then get her out of my house," she retorted. "I can't help it if she feels inferior because she's black."

"Inferior? Because she's black?"

"Yes, that's why she's so sullen and slovenly. It's no crime to be black." For the first time she had revealed her attitude toward color.

He was shocked. Then suddenly it all came clear, the source of her unhappiness, the reason she hated him. "Confound it, who do you think you are, a white woman!" he raved, turning ashy with fury. "You're a colored woman, too, just like my sister. The only difference is my sister and I aren't bastards." It was an epithet black people hurled at light-complexioned Negroes, challenging their legitimacy.

Her face blanched. "You'll live to see the day you regret that vile calumny," she vowed.

"Yes, and you'll live to see the day you'll wish you were black as me," he replied cuttingly.

She pursed her lips and turned away. He knew that he had scored a hit and felt a sense of triumph. But he little knew how deeply he had wounded her, nor how relentlessly she'd seek vengeance. Added to the shock and horror of her wedding night, it completed the destruction of their marriage.

For years she punished him in every conceivable manner. She left his bed and for four years forbade him to touch her. She wasted his salary on expensive luxuries and ran him into debt to embarrass him. All her love and tenderness were spent on her child. She treated her husband with unwavering contempt and made enemies of all his associates. She whipped him with her color at every turn, and whipped all those about him. There came the time when she was not welcome in a single house. Yet her scorn and fury continued unabated. Eventually he was asked to leave the college.

When they came to this college in Missouri, he was beaten. Only then did she feel avenged. After Thomas became of school age she relented and accepted him again as the father of her children. She had resigned herself to marital unhappiness, but now she longed for a family. It was the beginning of her bitter struggle for security, for possessions and prestige and a home, and for opportunities for her children.

By then Professor Taylor had lost all hope and confidence. He refused to share in her plans and seemed only interested in earning his salary. When William was born she became desperate. She tried to fire him with ambition again. But he seemed dead inside. For a time she was sorry for him. She knew she had destroyed him. And she wanted to remake him with her love and devotion. She forgave him for all that he had done to her. When he seemed most despondent and forlorn she responded to him most passionately. Charles came as the result of this tender interlude. She often thought that was the reason she loved him best. All the while she carried him she felt devoted to his father. She thought she was mending him with her love.

When it finally became evident that he was unchanged, her love reverted to hate. She became more disillusioned than ever. She was chagrined as much as infuriated. She hated him for leading her on. All waste, she thought. All her efforts to fire his ambition and spur him on —nothing but waste. Nothing had changed.

Even now, after twelve years, she was still as revolted by him as she had been on their wedding night, she reflected as she went bitterly about her chores. Twelve years of nothing but waste. He had the same type of job he'd had when they were married, with scarcely any more salary. They didn't even own the house in which they lived. Her own parents had owned their home in less than twelve years of freedom, she thought bitterly. But her husband had given up. It filled her with rage and frustration.

Even with all his other faults, including his apishness and carnality, she could respect him if he had kept fighting to advance. She could make allowances if he were a success. But he couldn't even succeed at teaching, for which he had been trained.

None was better educated. He was a fine blacksmith and wheelwright. His students had built some of the best carriages and wagons seen in that city. He could make the most elaborate andirons and coal tongs and gates and lampposts imaginable. He had made jewelry and lamps and dishes from gold and silver. He was an artist at the forge and anvil. There was practically nothing he couldn't forge from metal. Many prominent white people from all over the city commissioned him for jobs. He had made the wrought-iron gate for the governor's mansion, and a pair of ornamental silver bridles for the district attorney. All of the school's metal work was done in his shop. He made cedar chests and brass lockers and all manner of things for the faculty members; he shod their horses and repaired their harnesses. Nor could she accuse him of neglecting his own home in this manner. Their house contained numerous fine pieces that he'd made—marble-topped tables with intricately wrought iron legs, hat racks, stools, fenders, foot-scrapers, chests, cabinets.

And the children loved him too. He made most of their Christmas toys—little wagons, the exact replicas of large expensive ones, with hickory axles and iron-bound hubs, spoked wheels with iron tires, solid oak beds with removable sides, and seats with real springs. They were the joy and wonder of the neighborhood. And he had made sleds with fine iron runners, rocking horses, and miniature garden tools for them.

No one could deny he had the ability. That was what enraged her most. He could if he tried. But when opportunity knocked he seemed to shrink within himself. Often she wondered if his being black had anything to do with it; if in some way he was racially incapable of doing great things. During moments of despondency she regretted having married a black man. She should have known better. Had she married a man her own color at least she would not have to worry about her children being black.

She had long since concluded that he was not going to get anywhere. And regretting it was just a waste of time, she told herself. But she was tied to him by her children. And she would never let him hold back her children.

For a moment she wondered where it was all going to end. Now she was not so certain of anything. But as she worked, a strange set came over her face and her actions became forceful. It was as if she stood with clenched fists, drawing on her heritage, and said over and over again, "I will! I will! I will!"

William Demby

(b. 1922)

WILLIAM DEMBY WAS BORN in Pittsburgh, spent his childhood in Clarksburg, West Virginia, and attended West Virginia State College until he joined the Army. After an overseas military tour in Italy, Demby entered Fisk University in 1947. There he wrote stories and did illustrations for the *Fisk University Herald*. Upon graduation from Fisk, he returned to Italy, where he studied art at the University of Rome, worked as a jazz musician, and wrote screen plays for Roberto Rossellini. From Rome Demby traveled in Europe, Ethiopia, Japan, and Thailand. He returned to the United States in 1963 to work briefly for a New York advertising agency before again settling in Rome.

William Demby is the author of *Beetlecreek* (1950) and *The Catacombs* (1965). The following selection is taken from *Beetlecreek*.

THE NIGHTRIDERS

All up and down the street, there was an awareness of the festival. For that early evening hour, there were more people than usual crossing back and forth across the swinging bridge. Ladies, coming back to the village from uptown kitchens, carried mysterious pans covered with gleaming white tablecloths, and they walked faster, nervously like birds in the early morning. On their faces, were stretched rubber-band smiles.

On the street there was a steady stream of traffic; important kids pulling toy wagons loaded with fifty pound blocks of ice and streaked, marble-green watermelons, and men, home early from work, carrying hammers and saws and rolls of wire, all heading for the church grass where a line of booths and a few strips of crepe paper were already giving a gay, festive appearance to the raggedy grass lot.

Because of the strange hothouse warmth in the air, doors and windows were wide open. There were women ironing in the doorways, and excited big girls running back and forth across the street with their hair greased into pigtails or shiny balls.

It was absolutely an important day, full of a special festive tenseness. But Johnny didn't feel it.

Even though he could see the festival taking shape around him, Johnny didn't feel excited. Early that afternoon, his aunt came home from Pinkertons' loaded down with three huge pans of gingercake she'd baked on their electric range. All day in the house there had been the smell of pink icing. Uncle David had been in and out several times and had spent part of the afternoon painting signs and price tags for the various booths. As soon as school was out, kids began chasing dogs into the church grass and running them round and round.

But all these goings-on didn't interest Johnny. He felt separate and apart from the festival. He could tell by the way kids broke up the everyday games of mumblety-peg and by the way they were dressed, in Sunday blue suits and Sunday frocks with some little girls already knotted up into shiny pigtails, that it was an important day of the year, like the annual Sunday School picnic. But he didn't feel part of it.

The night before, he dreamt that his mother tried to tell him something but couldn't because a great stream of vomit and blood came from her mouth every time she opened it. The same night, too, he thought about the team's raffle they had had the year before in Pittsburgh to buy jerseys for the football team, and it made him feel very lonely to know that they would be wearing the orange and black uniforms, and that he wouldn't have one even though he sold more chances than any of them.

And even though he tried to think of other things, he knew that he still felt a dismal, lost feeling about Bill Trapp. In some way, when he was dreaming about his mother, when there came over him a hot, melting urge to cry, he knew that Bill Trapp was mixed up with what he was feeling for his mother. In the dream, they were one and the same, and about each, he remembered feeling very sad.

Only sometimes was he the new Johnny. It didn't last when he was by himself. As soon as it became silent enough around him, he would know who he was. Only when he was with the gang did he feel strong and different—outside himself. But he hadn't seen the gang all day. He waited for them a long time down by the swinging bridge but they didn't come. And while he was there, he thought about Bill Trapp again. Feeling alone and neglected himself made him think of the old white man being all alone and neglected. He's there, closed inside the stone wall, all by himself, an old man, all by himself, he thought. And this thought amplified his own feeling about himself, and he wished he were away from the village, wished he were near his own hill, near the sound of the whistles of his own Pittsburgh trains.

And at the very bottom of these feelings, like the current pushing the stones at the bottom of the creek, or like standing in the rapids and feeling the underneath strength of the water force you off balance, was the feeling of waiting, expecting, and coming-on. But this feeling was too big for him to understand or think about; he could only know that it was there.

That evening, he went home feeling downcast and lonely. Walking down the street, he was mindful of the movement toward the festival, and even when he saw the Dairybell ice-cream truck backed up at the side of the church, he wouldn't go to join the children watching the unloading of the ice-cream boxes.

He entered the house and sat in the darkened living room, thumbing through an old *Popular Mechanics* magazine. When his aunt called him to supper, he went without relish. He hunched over his plate and filled his mouth without knowing what it was he ate.

"What's wrong with you, boy?" his aunt asked.

But she was so full of excitement herself, that she didn't even wait for him to answer. And his uncle was excited too. He smiled and was dressed up in his Sunday suit and wore gold cuff links that he wore only on special occasions. At first Johnny thought his uncle was drunk but there was no smell of beer like there usually was when he had been drinking. Their excitement over the festival made him feel even more separate and lonely. Once he thought he was going to cry right there at the table.

"Something tells me I should have made three more pans of gingercake," Mary was saying. "Something tells me I should have made more."

"Smitty down at the bus terminal tells me there's going to be special trucks coming in from Munstor and Radcliffe," David said.

Johnny wondered why his uncle was so happy. Except for when his uncle was drunk, Johnny had never seen him in such high spirits before.

While they were eating their dessert of gingercake crumbs and cream, someone knocked at the door. Without knowing why, Johnny stopped breathing.

His aunt got up to answer the door.

"It's Baby Boy," she called from the doorway. "He wants you, Johnny."

He tried to keep from running but so great was his excitement, he almost knocked his aunt down at the kitchen doorway.

"Hi there, Baby Boy," Johnny said. He was very glad to see Baby Boy and he could hardly speak. "Come on in the parlor," he invited.

He was very proud to be able to invite Baby Boy into the parlor; it was his first guest in the three weeks he had been in Beetlecreek. Baby Boy was dressed in his Sunday suit and his hair was brushed. His face was very solemn.

Baby Boy didn't answer him or make any move to enter the house. Instead, he held out an envelope for Johnny to take and, as soon as it was in Johnny's hands, Baby Boy ran down the steps.

With hands trembling, Johnny ripped open the envelope. At first he though that it was written in blood, but when he held it up to his nose he knew it was tomato catsup.

BE AT THE JUNK YARD AT TEN FIFTEEN PM OR YOUR NAME IS MUD—
THE NIGHTRIDERS ! ! !

This was it, then. He would be initiated tonight. His first feeling was that of cold, numbing fear. What would they do to him? Across his mind flashed pictures of tortures he had seen in his history book, Indians holding burning torches to the chests of their victims, and people in England being stretched by ropes that pulled on their arms and legs in opposite directions.

Would he be able to stand such tortures or would he cry out for them to release him? Maybe he should hurry and tell them that he changed his mind and no longer wanted to be a member of the gang. But how could he? He would die of shame. He would have to go through with it.

His mouth became dry and every tendon in his legs and arms became as if charged with electricity. His jaws felt as if dry ice were on his teeth, and he vibrated all over as if a dentist's drill were in his mouth. He ate the rest of his cake, chewing it vigorously, as if to stop the dentist-drill feeling.

As soon as he could, he left the table and went upstairs to his room. During the half hour he lay there, all kinds of tortures came to his mind.

He used to pass time by imagining what he would do if suddenly he had to jump out of an airplane with a parachute. He would create each stage of the feeling until he had hypnotized himself with the idea of getting ready to jump. His stomach would feel hard as stone and his legs would become cold. Then he would stop breathing and begin to shake all over from the exertion.

Other times he would do the same thing until he had hypnotized himself into thinking he was about to be thrust into a roaring fire.

Once when he was very young, he fell off the porch and broke his leg. For a long time before anyone came to him, he lay on the ground delirious with the worst pain he had ever experienced. At the time, he thought that there could be no worse pain in all the world than that. He wondered if the pain of the initiation would be as great.

Later, while helping his aunt carry the gingercake pans to the church grass, he could hardly walk, so drugged was he from thinking about the initiation.

He left her as soon as he put down the pans, paying no attention to the activity that was transforming the church grass.

It was still early. He had more than two hours before time to meet the gang. He went to Telrico's where there were strangers hanging around, waiting for the festival to start.

A big group was around the pinball machine watching Wilson try to ring up twenty thousand on the red. Johnny stood on the fringe of the crowd and watched too. He noticed how graceful was the pulling back of the plunger and how gently the green carpeted sides and the rubber fences around the lights were bumped by the ball. More than ever, he felt apart from all the crowds and centers of excitement.

He perched himself on a stool and drank a bottle of Nehi, taking long, dawdling sips and looking down the straw into the bottle. Sometimes he would blow the brown pop back into the bottle and make bubbles.

A girl sat down beside him. She was pretty and had long brown hair. Johnny thought she looked like an Indian princess. He had never seen her before so she must have come into town that evening for the festival. From the corner of his eye, he could see her looking at him. She must have been fourteen or fifteen because she had big bubbies and wore thick pasty lipstick on her lips. She wore a black sateen dress that was very short so that Johnny could see a knee and part of her thigh.

She was looking at him frankly now and he began to drink his pop without fooling around.

"You from here?" she asked. Her voice was low and thin, like a skinny preacher's voice.

He turned around so that his body faced her, but he kept his head lowered to the pop bottle. He was very excited and felt a buzzing on his knees.

"No, I'm from Pittsburgh." He finished his pop with a loud sip and then lay the bottle on the counter so he could run his fingers over the frosted sides.

She kept on looking at him, at the same time, moving so close he could feel her knee touching the edge of his trousers.

"You sure are a long way from home," she said.

When he got up, she squeezed his knee slyly. "I hopes we see more of each other, sugarfoot," she said. "I'll be here all evening for the festival."

Johnny turned toward her briefly and tried to smile. Outside, he thought, I'll be able to see her after the initiation. After the initiation it would be all right to meet a girl. After the initiation, he knew he would know what to say to her and how to act. Now he was feeling too crazy. All he could do now was giggle and smile like a goop. Her voice was very sweet. She looked like an Indian princess.

It was quarter to nine. He could hear the loudspeaker being tested over at the church grass. Light was spilling out from the side of the church. It seemed as if everyone in the village were at the festival and as if all who weren't walked there as fast as they could go. The village was quiet and deserted. He walked in the very middle of the street. There were hardly any lights on in any of the houses. His fear remembered itself and became associated with the tight stillness.

He stopped at the side of the creek. He took down his trousers and stooped so that it fell with a frog splash into the water. The grass was cool and ticklish. He scooped his hand into the black mud near the water and squeezed it through his fingers. Later, he washed his hands, drying them on the big leaves of an oak sprout.

The water and creekside smelled like rotten flowers in the damp.

He knew that in a few more minutes it would be time for him to go but he knew they would be long minutes.

He thought of the first time he and his uncle were at Bill Trapp's house, how he had been caught by the old man while climbing up the apple tree and of how that fright was like what he was feeling now.

While buttoning up his trousers, he thought of the Indian princess and remembered how she squeezed his knee. He would go look for her as soon as he had been initiated. They would walk along the creek road in the dark and he would hold her hand, and with her sweet voice, she would ask him about himself, and he would tell her, very nonchalantly, that he had just been initiated by the Nightriders, a secret organization. And later they would go to Telrico's and sit in a booth together like the grownups do and he wouldn't care who saw them.

The junk yard was completely dark. Johnny walked rapidly through the bushes, holding his hand before him like a sleepwalker so that he wouldn't tear his new trousers on the thorns. As soon as he was in the clearing where slight moonlight gray gave depth to obscure objects around him, he stopped breathing and strained his ears to hear some reassuring sound. His heart was pounding and the rustle of the new corduroy when his legs brushed together kept him from identifying any close sound. Once he thought he heard a whirring noise but when he closed his eyes, he knew that it was only a cricket.

He went over to the derrick and sat on one of the planks. Maybe they had forgotten about the initiation and had gone to the festival instead. Maybe Baby Boy had been playing a prank on him. This idea swelled up inside him and the more he thought about it, the more likely it seemed. More minutes passed. He amused himself by feeling his pulse. He counted with the beats up to fifty and couldn't hear the footsteps approaching.

Suddenly, there they were in front of him. There were at least seven of them, all dressed in black robes, wearing black bags over their heads with holes cut for the eyes.

Johnny felt that he should say something but it was impossible for him to move his tongue. He could tell by the way they were standing and by the height of their silhouettes which was Baby Boy and which was the Leader. But the others he didn't know. The Nightriders must be a big club, he thought.

The Leader took him by the hand and, as if in a dream, Johnny rose to follow him. One of them tied a bandage over his eyes so tight he could see a galaxy of shapes and colors.

He heard whispering. There seemed to be some discussion as to where he should be taken first. He heard someone whisper, Gant's Tomb.

Gant's Tomb, he knew, was the colored folks' burying ground on the side of the hill above the railroad tracks. That was where the torture would take place then!

He tried to feel with his feet as he walked. He knew by the side to side rolling and the smell of the creek, when they crossed the swinging bridge. He knew when they climbed the embankment to get up on the railroad tracks. He almost slipped and fell on the cinders. He and the Leader headed the procession, the others followed closely and silently. He could hear only their concerted breathing and the shuffling of their feet.

Finally, they arrived at Gant's Tomb. He had never been there before, but had seen its tumbling white headstones and splintered rose trellis entrance from a distance.

He imagined smelling a strange odor in the cemetery, a smell like opening a trunk inside which a piece of bread had become moldy. He could hear the faint tinkling of the festival blown up the hillside from the village in the valley. The wind pulled at his bandage. He could hear a freight engine switching tracks at the roundhouse in Munstor.

They stopped and he was pushed down on a cool stone shape which he imagined to be a fallen tombstone.

"Gather round, brother Nightriders," said the Leader's voice. "Read the orders, brother secretary!"

A voice which Johnny didn't recognize began to read with mock seriousness, "Johnny Diggs, you is charged with secrecy of the initiation ceremony which is to follow."

Another voice, very high indeed, sounding very much like Baby Boy talking through a handkerchief muffler, said, "Do you swears on your life blood to keep all which will happen secret?"

Someone prodded Johnny. "Answer him!"

"I do," Johnny said, his voice choking on the words. If he could only control his breathing. If the air would only go out his nose instead of his mouth.

The Leader began speaking again. "The nightriders is a man's society and we don't want no kids foolin around. Now if you's ascared and don't want to join up, say so now or forever hold your peace."

"I want to belong," Johnny mumbled fervently.

"Well, all right then. We're going to give you a chance to be a man. The Nightriders's all men and each one of us has proved it by some courageous deed. You don't get into the club until you've proved to us you's a man."

What would they make him do? Johnny wondered. Would they make him stay out all night on some mysterious mission like they did to college students in a book he read once? He was no longer afraid of being tortured. Whatever they make me do, he told himself, I'll not be afraid. I'll prove to them that I'm a man and that I can take it. He felt like the new Johnny again. He smiled to himself as his fright left him. He bit his lower lip as if to prove to himself that he could stand pain.

He thought of the Indian princess and of the lipstick smile she gave him. He thought of being with her after the initiation, knowing that he would be a Nightrider—a man! And maybe they would see him in Telrico's with her. He would nod to them and smile, saying, "Hi, brothers, I want you to meet my girl friend."

They took his bandage off and sat on the ground in front of him. Only the Leader stood. It was too dark and he couldn't see the faces of the others.

"Are you ready to be charged with your duty?" the Leader asked. His voice was high and cracking as he tried to speak formally and slower than he usually spoke.

"Yes, sir," Johnny said. And he meant it. He tried to look straight into the Leader's eyes to show that he meant what he said. This was solemn. This was religious.

"We're goin with you, and if you try any monkey business, you don't get into the club, and you might get knocked around a bit, see?"

"You don't have to worry about me."

Johnny was anxious to know what he would have to do. He wanted to get it over with but, also, he was anxious to test the new Johnny. There was nothing he feared. There was nothing they could propose to him that he wouldn't do. He'd show them he was a man worthy of their trust in him.

"Stand up!" the Leader ordered. And all the Nightriders stood up. "Give the sign!" he ordered. And they made a circle around Johnny and held each other's hands, at the same time mumbling something which Johnny couldn't understand.

"Raise yo right hand!"

Quivering with excitement and anxiety, Johnny raised his hand. Seconds seemed long and high as he waited for the Leader to speak.

"All right then. You knows this old white man Bill Trapp? You ought to know him—you used to hang out with him all the time."

There was a whisper of laughter around the circle.

"You knows all about what he did to those little Tolley girls. You knows how everybody talkin and ain't nobody doin nothing. Night-riders don't go in for all that talkin stuff. What we believe in is action. Ain't no peckerwood goin get away with that kind of stuff while we Nightriders's around. Everybody know what would of happened if it had been a colored man did all that funny stuff. Everybody knows, ain't nobody doin nothing about it. The Nightriders want action! To test whether you worthy of 'comin a member of the Nightriders, we hereby charges you to go out to Bill Trapp's shanty and burn it to the ground! Bring forth the gasoline!"

Cutting through the bushes below the railroad track, Johnny could hear the tramp, tramp, tramp of their footsteps behind him. None of them would speak; he refused to think. Before he knew it, he was across the swinging bridge. He walked as if he were in a dream. His steps seemed light and he couldn't tell when he put his feet down. Soon they were passing the bend in the creek—then the stone wall of the May Farm. Inside was Bill Trapp's shanty!

The gasoline cans, two of them, were cutting into the palm of his hand, but he hardly felt the weight of them. The Nightriders behind him tramped along noisily in single file, occasionally stumbling over their own robes. Under a street light he looked back to see the straggling line of black ghosts.

He was calm, too calm. It seemed as if he moved without any life inside him. He was only movement, no inner sensation or substance. He felt like a ghost figure, too. Trees and bushes moved past him as if they were moving and not him. He could hear no sounds from the village. There were no dogs.

Just as he had done that first time when he was with the boys stealing apples from Bill Trapp, he crawled under the stone fence through a hole near a clump of bushes. The earth was wet and slimy. He didn't care about dirtying his Sunday clothes. He dragged the cans in after him. The others joined him on the other side.

"You got any matches?" the Leader asked.

Johnny shook his head. A box was located and shoved into his hands. It was much too dark to see, but he knew exactly where the house was. He could see the chimney standing alone against the sky above the hill. Baby Boy patted him on the shoulder; it was the only sensation he remembered. Then he ran across the grass.

He ran lightly as if he were being pushed by a gentle force behind him or as if he were sliding down a bannister to the house. In a moment he was there.

They had told him to pour the gasoline on a rolled up mat that was under the porch. They said it would catch quick because the logs of the house had been pitched with tar.

The mat was there and he poured the cool gasoline on it. His movements were smooth and efficient. The second can he poured on a pile of trash wood nearby and some he poured on the side of the shack.

Slowly and deliberately he took the matchbox and opened it. For only a moment he waited until the match flowered into a bulb of fire. Then he threw it in a slow falling arc on the bundled up mat.

It smouldered a moment, and then made a blue orange burst of light, like an automobile headlight suddenly appeared from around a curve. He was blinded and he smelled hair burning. He rubbed his eyebrows and discovered they had been singed by the burst of flame.

Slowly, he turned around and began to walk back to where the Nightriders waited. Then he ran. He began to laugh hysterically and stumbled over the shadow that became longer and longer in front of him as the fire grew.

He arrived at the tree where the others were waiting but they had disappeared. He could hear their footsteps pounding on the road outside the wall. He was still laughing hysterically. He couldn't find the hole in the wall. He retraced his steps.

Only then did his movements stop gliding. Blood began moving inside him and he was no longer a ghost of movement. He seemed to wake. He looked, both fascinated and horrified, at the roaring flames. One whole side of the shanty was already burning and the field was lit as if in a fireworks display.

At first, he couldn't associate himself with the fire but then he realized he was still holding a gasoline can in his hand. As soon as he got outside the fence, he would throw it away.

He thought about the Indian princess, suddenly realizing that he must run away, far away, must escape, must escape. He had committed a terrible crime and he must escape.

He was sick and he stooped over to see if he could vomit. But no liquid came from his dry throat.

Without realizing what he was doing, he ran to the flaming house yelling, "Help, Help! Mr. Trapp! Mr. Trapp! Your house is on fire! Help! Help!"

But he could get no closer than fifteen yards to the house. He's burning to death in there, Johnny thought. He imagined seeing the old man's kindly face surrounded by flames.

He scratched his face. He jumped up and down. He blew out of the corner of his mouth. He wet his pants.

He must get away! He had murdered a man. Bill Trapp was burning to death. There was a rhythmic crackling to the fire. Johnny imagined he heard a soft, almost inaudible groaning over the crackling.

He ran completely around the shanty twice; ran as if he were in a race, fast, lifting his knees high, digging his toes in the sod. Then he ran to the stone fence. He must get away! He must get away! Why had he ever agreed to do such a thing?

At the stone fence, he still couldn't find the hole. He ran from bush to bush. He fell over the stump of a tree into a hole covered by vines. He felt as if he were trapped, and fought and fought, thrashing his arms about like a madman.

On his feet once more, he ran from one dark shadowy place to the other, finding no hole. He ran along the stone wall taking tiny frantic steps. Suddenly, he straightened up and stopped dead in his tracks. There, standing beside him, holding onto the trunk of the tree, his features exaggerated by the light from the fire, stood Bill Trapp. On his face was a sad, resigned look.

"What have you done, Johnny?" was all he said. He put out his hand and touched Johnny's shoulder.

When Johnny felt the old man's hand on him, he began to shake with terror and rage. The old man grabbed him and hugged him close.

"What have you done, Johnny? What have you been up to?"

There was a blinding light inside him, a blinding light that lit him up inside from his stomach to his head, a blinding green streak of lightning. Outside this inside light, he could feel the old man's hands on him. He felt as if his blood had been changed into hot steel. He must get away! He must get away!

His fist closed tighter on the handle of the gasoline can and he felt his arm swinging out in a high swooping arc. And he heard a dull clang. And he felt Bill Trapp become limp. And he saw him fall to the ground.

Johnny ran and ran through the trees. He followed a path lit by the flames. He climbed a tree and swung over the wall. He jumped. He realized he was hurt and bleeding. He ran and ran and ran.

He heard the train switching in Munstor.

He heard fire engines.

Ann Petry

(b. 1911)

ANN PETRY HAS WRITTEN several children's plays and participated as an actress in The American Negro Theatre. Her story "Like a Winding Sheet" was included in *The Best American Short Stories of 1946;* her work has been anthologized and her short stories appear in such magazines as *The New Yorker* and *Redbook.*

A native of Old Saybrook, Connecticut, Ann Petry attended the University of Connecticut (1928–31) and Columbia University (1943–44). She worked as a pharmacist from 1934–48, but turned to newspaper work on the *Amsterdam News* and later on the *People's Voice,* which she served as women's editor.

Miss Petry's work includes *The Street,* a winner of a Houghton Mifflin Literary Fellowship (1946); *Country Place* (1947); *The Drug Store Cat* (1949); *The Narrows* (1953); *Harriet Tubman: Conductor of the Underground Railroad* (1955); and *Tituba of Salem Village* (1964).

The selection which follows comes from *The Street,* one of the better novels of the naturalistic school which flourished after 1940, the date of Richard Wright's *Native Son.*

DEAD END STREET

It was a cold, cheerless night. But in spite of the cold, the street was full of people. They stood on the corners talking, lounged half in and half out of hallways and on the stoops of the houses, looking at the street and talking. Some of them were coming home from work, from church meetings, from lodge meetings, and some of them were not coming from anywhere or going anywhere, they were merely deferring the moment when they would have to enter their small crowded rooms for the night.

In the middle of the block there was a sudden thrust of raw, brilliant light where the unshaded bulbs in the big poolroom reached out and pushed back the darkness. A group of men stood outside its windows watching the games going on inside. Their heads were silhouetted against the light.

Lutie, walking quickly through the block, glanced at them and then at the women coming toward her from Eighth Avenue. The women moved slowly. Their shoulders sagged from the weight of the heavy shopping bags they carried. And she thought, That's what's wrong. We don't have time enough or money enough to live like other people because the women have to work until they become drudges and the men stand by idle.

She made an impatient movement of her shoulders. She had no way of knowing that at fifty she wouldn't be misshapen, walking on the sides of her shoes because her feet hurt so badly; getting dressed up for church on Sunday and spending the rest of the week slaving in somebody's kitchen.

It could happen. Only she was going to stake out a piece of life for herself. She had come this far poor and black and shut out as though a door had been slammed in her face. Well, she would shove it open; she would beat and bang on it and push against it and use a chisel in order to get it open.

When she opened the street door of the apartment house, she was instantly aware of the silence that filled the hall. Mrs. Hedges had been quiet, too, for if she was sitting in her window she had given no indication of her presence.

There was no sound except for the steam hissing in the radiator. The silence and the dimly lit hallway and the smell of stale air depressed her. It was like a dead weight landing on her chest. She told herself that she musn't put too much expectation in getting the singing job. Almost anything might happen to prevent it. Boots might change his mind.

She went up the stairs, thinking, But he can't. She wouldn't let him. It meant too much to her. It was a way out—the only way out of here and she and Bub had to get out.

On the third-floor landing she stopped. A man was standing in the hall. His back was turned toward her. She hesitated. It wasn't very late, but it was dark in the hall and she was alone.

He turned then and she saw that he had his arms wound tightly around a girl and he was pressed so close to her and was bending so far over her that they had given the effect of one figure. He wore a sailor's uniform and the collar of his jacket was turned high around his neck, for it was cold in the hall.

The girl looked to be about nineteen or twenty. She was very thin. Her black hair, thick with grease, gleamed in the dim light. There was an artificial white rose stuck in the center of the pompadour that mounted high above her small, dark face.

Lutie recognized her. It was Mary, one of the little girls who lived with Mrs. Hedges. The sailor gave Lutie a quick, appraising look and then turned back to the girl, blotting her out. The girl's thin arms went back around his neck.

"Mary," Lutie said, and stopped right behind the sailor.

The girl's face appeared over the top of the sailor's shoulder.

"Hello," she said sullenly.

"It's so cold out here," Lutie said. "Why don't you go inside?"

"Mis' Hedges won't let him come in no more," Mary said. "He's spent all his money. And she says she ain't in business for her health."

"Can't you talk to him somewhere else? Isn't there a friend's house you could go to?"

"No, ma'am. Besides, it ain't no use, anyway. He's got to go back to his ship tonight."

Lutie climbed the rest of the stairs fuming against Mrs. Hedges. The sailor would return to his ship carrying with him the memory of this dark narrow hallway and Mrs. Hedges and the thin resigned little girl. The street was full of young thin girls like this one with a note of resignation in their voices, with faces that contained no hope, no life. She shivered. She couldn't let Bub grow up in a place like this.

She put her key in the door quietly, trying to avoid the loud click of the lock being drawn back. She pushed the door open, mentally visualizing the trip across the living room to her bedroom. Once inside her room, she would close the door and put the light on and Bub wouldn't wake up. Then she saw that the lamp in the living room was lit and she shut the door noisily. He should have been asleep at least two hours ago, she thought, and walked toward the studio couch, her heels clicking on the congoleum rug.

Bub sat up and rubbed his eyes. For a moment she saw something frightened and fearful in his expression, but it disappeared when he looked at her.

"How come you're not in bed?" she demanded.

"I fell asleep."

"With your clothes on?" she said, and then added: "With the light on, too? You must be trying to make the bill bigger——" and she stopped abruptly. She was always talking to him about money. It wasn't good. He would be thinking about nothing else pretty soon. "How was the movie?" she asked.

"It was swell," he said eagerly. "There was one guy who caught gangsters——"

"Skip it," she interrupted. "You get in bed in a hurry, Mister. I still don't know what you're doing up——" Her eyes fell on the ash tray on the blue-glass coffee table. It was filled with cigarette butts. That's funny. She had emptied all the trays when she washed the dinner dishes. She knew that she had. She looked closer at the cigarette ends. They were moist. Whoever had smoked them had held them, not between their lips, but far inside the mouth so that the paper got wet and the tobacco inside had stained and discolored it. She turned toward Bub.

"Supe was up." Bub's eyes had followed hers. "We played cards."

"You mean he was in here?" she said sharply. And thought, Of course, dope, he didn't stand outside and throw his cigarette butts into the ash tray through a closed door.

"We played cards," Bub said again.

"Let's get this straight once and for all." She put her hands on his shoulders. "When I'm not home, you're not to let anyone in here. Anyone. Understand?"

He nodded. "Does that mean Supe, too?"

"Of course. Now you get in bed fast so you can get to school on time."

While Bub undressed, she took the cover off the studio couch, smoothed the thin blanket and the sheets, pulled a pillowslip over one of the cushions. He seemed to be taking an awfully long time in the bathroom. "Hey," she said finally. "Step on it. You can't get to heaven that way."

She heard him giggle and smiled at the sound. Then her face sobered. She looked around the living room. One of these days he was going to have a real bedroom to himself instead of this shabby, sunless room. The plaid pattern of the blue congoleum rug was wearing off in front of the studio couch. It was scuffed down to the paper base at the door that led to the small hall. Everything in the room was worn and old—the lumpy studio couch, the overstuffed chair, the card table that served as desk, the bookcase filled with second-hand textbooks and old magazines. The blue-glass top on the coffee table was scratched and chipped. The small radio was scarred with cigarette burns. The first thing she would do would be to move and then she would get some decent furniture.

Bub got into bed, pulled the covers up under his chin. "Good night, Mom," he said.

He was almost asleep when she leaned over and kissed him on the forehead. She turned the light on in her bedroom, came back and switched the light off in the living room.

"Sleep tight!" she said. His only reply was a drowsy murmur—half laugh, half sigh.

She undressed, thinking of the Super sitting in the living room, of the time when she had come to look at the apartment and he had stood there in that room where Bub was now sleeping and how he had held the flashlight so that the beam of light from it was down at his feet. Now he had been back in there—sitting down, playing cards with Bub —making himself at home.

What had he talked to Bub about? The thought of his being friendly with Bub was frightening. Yet what could she do about it other than tell Bub not to let him into the apartment again? There was no telling what went on in the mind of a man like that—a man who had lived in basements and cellars, a man who had forever to stay within hailing distance of whatever building he was responsible for.

The last thing she thought before she finally went to sleep was that the Super was something less than human. He had been chained to buildings until he was like an animal.

She dreamed about him and woke up terrified, not certain that it was a dream and heard the wind sighing in the airshaft. And went back to sleep and dreamed about him again.

He and the dog had become one. He was still tall, gaunt, silent. The same man, but with the dog's wolfish mouth and the dog's teeth— white, sharp, pointed, in the redness of his mouth. His throat worked like the dog's throat. He made a whining noise deep inside it. He panted and strained to get free and run through the block, but the building was chained to his shoulders like an enormous doll's house made of brick. She could see the people moving around inside the building, drearily climbing the tiny stairs, sidling through the narrow halls. Mrs. Hedges sat on the first floor smiling at a cage full of young girls.

The building was so heavy he could hardly walk with it on his shoulders. It was a painful, slow, horrible crawl of a walk—hesitant, slowing down, now stopping completely and then starting again. He fawned on the people in the street, dragged himself close to them, stood in front of them, pointing to the building and to the chains. "Unloose me! Unloose me!" he begged. His voice was cracked and hollow.

Min walked beside him repeating the same words. "Unloose him! Unloose him!" and straining to reach up toward the lock that held the chains.

He thought she, Lutie, had the key. And he followed her through the street, whining in his throat, nuzzling in back of her with his sharp, pointed dog's face. She tried to walk faster and faster, but the sham- bling, slow, painful sound of his footsteps was always just behind her, the sound of his whining stayed close to her like someone talking in her ear.

She looked down at her hand and the key to the padlock that held the chains was there. She stopped, and there was a whole chorus of clamoring voices: "Shame! Shame! She won't unloose him and she's got the key!"

Mrs. Hedges' window was suddenly in front of her. Mrs. Hedges nodded, "If I were you, dearie, I'd unloose him. It's so easy, dearie. It's so easy, dearie. Easy—easy—easy——"

She reached out her hand toward the padlock and the long white fangs closed on her hand. Her hand and part of her arm were swallowed up inside his wolfish mouth. She watched in horror as more and more of her arm disappeared until there was only the shoulder left and then his jaws closed and she felt the sharp teeth sink in and in through her shoulder. The arm was gone and blood poured out.

She screamed and screamed and windows opened and the people poured out of the buildings—thousands of them, millions of them. She saw that they had turned to rats. The street was so full of them that she could hardly walk. They swarmed around her, jumping up and down. Each one had a building chained to its back, and they were all crying, "Unloose me! Unloose me!"

She woke up and got out of bed. She couldn't shake loose the terror of the dream. She felt of her arm. It was still there and whole. Her mouth was wide open as though she had been screaming. It felt dry inside. She must have dreamed she was screaming, for Bub was still asleep—apparently she had made no sound. Yet she was so filled with fright from the nightmare memory of the dream that she stood motionless by the bed, unable to move for a long moment.

The air was cold. Finally she picked up the flannel robe at the foot of the bed and pulled it on. She sat down on the bed and tucked her feet under her, then carefully pulled the robe down over her feet, afraid to go back to sleep for fear of a recurrence of the dream.

The room was dark. Where the airshaft broke the wall there was a lighter quality to the darkness—a suggestion of dark blue space. Even in the dark like this her knowledge of the position of each piece of furniture made her aware of the smallness of the room. If she should get up quickly, she knew she would bump against the small chest and moving past it she might collide with the bureau.

Huddled there on the bed, her mind still clouded with the memory of the dream, her body chilled from the cold, she thought of the room, not with hatred, not with contempt, but with dread. In the darkness it seemed to close in on her until it became the sum total of all the things she was afraid of and she drew back nearer the wall because the room grew smaller and the pieces of furniture larger until she felt as though she were suffocating.

Suppose she got used to it, took it for granted, became resigned to it and all the things it represented. The thought set her to murmuring aloud, "I mustn't get used to it. Not ever. I've got to keep on fighting to get away from here."

All the responsibility for Bub was hers. It was up to her to keep him safe, to get him out of here so he would have a chance to grow up fine and strong. Because this street and the other streets just like it would, if he stayed in them long enough, do something terrible to him. Sooner or later they would do something equally as terrible to her. And as she sat there in the dark, she began to think about the things that she had seen on such streets as this one she lived in.

There was the afternoon last spring when she had got off the sub-way on Lenox Avenue. It was late afternoon. The spring sunlight was sharp and clear. The street was full of people taking advantage of the soft warm air after a winter of being shut away from the sun. They had peeled off their winter coats and sweaters and mufflers.

Kids on roller skates and kids precariously perched on home-made scooters whizzed unexpectedly through the groups of people clustered on the sidewalk. The sun was warm. It beamed on the boys and girls walking past arm in arm. It made their faces very soft and young and relaxed.

She had walked along slowly, thinking that the sun transformed everything it shone on. So that the people standing talking in front of the buildings, the pushcart men in the side streets, the peanut ven-dor, the sweet potato man, all had an unexpected graciousness in their faces and their postures. Even the drab brick of the buildings was altered to a deep rosy pinkness.

Thus she had come on the crowd suddenly, quite unaware that it was a crowd. She had walked past some of the people before she sensed some common impulse that had made this mass of people stand motionless and withdrawn in the middle of the block. She stopped, too. And she became sharply aware of a somber silence, a curious still-ness that was all around her. She edged her way to the front of the crowd, squeezing past people, forcing her way toward whatever it was that held them in this strangely arrested silence.

There was a cleared space near the buildings and a handful of policemen and cameramen and reporters with pink cards stuck in their hatbands were standing in it looking down at something. She got as close to the cleared space as she could—so close that she was almost touching the policeman in front of her.

And she saw what they were looking at. Lying flat on the sidewalk was a man—thin, shabby, tall from the amount of sidewalk that his body occupied. There was blood on the sidewalk, and she saw that it was coming from somewhere under him. Part of his body and his face were covered with what looked to be a piece of white canvas.

But the thing she had never been able to forget were his shoes. Only the uppers were intact. They had once been black, but they were now a dark dull gray from long wear. The soles were worn out. They were mere flaps attached to the uppers. She could see the layers of wear. The first outer layer of leather was left near the edges, and then the great gaping holes in the center where the leather had worn out en-tirely, so that for weeks he must have walked practically barefooted on the pavement.

She had stared at the shoes, trying to figure out what it must have been like to walk barefooted on the city's concrete sidewalks. She wondered if he ever went downtown, and if he did, what did he think about when he passed store windows filled with sleek furs and fabulous food and clothing made of materials so fine you could tell by looking at them they would feel like sea foam under your hand?

How did he feel when the great long cars snorted past him as he waited for the lights to change or when he looked into a taxi and saw a delicate, soft, beautiful woman lifting her face toward an opulently dressed man? The woman's hair would gleam and shine, her mouth would be knowingly shaped with lip rouge. And the concrete would have been rough under this man's feet.

The people standing in back of her weren't moving. They weren't talking. They were simply standing there looking. She watched a cop touch one of the man's broken, grayish shoes with his foot. And she got a sick feeling because the cop's shoes were glossy with polish and the warm spring sunlight glinted on them.

One of the photographers and a newspaperman elbowed through the crowd. They had a thin, dark young girl by the arm. They walked her over to a man in a gray business suit. "She thinks it's her brother," the reporter said.

The man stared at the girl. "What makes you think so?"

"He went out to get bread and he ain't home yet."

"Look like his clothes?" He nodded toward the figure on the sidewalk.

"Yes."

One of the cops reached down and rolled the canvas back from the man's face.

Lutie didn't look at the man's face. Instead, she looked at the girl and she saw something—some emotion that she couldn't name—flicker in the girl's face. It was as though for a fraction of a second something—hate or sorrow or surprise—had moved inside her and been reflected on her face. As quickly as it came, it was gone and it was replaced by a look of resignation, of complete acceptance. It was an expression that said the girl hoped for no more than this from life because other things that had happened to her had paved the way so that she had lost the ability to protest against anything—even death suddenly like this in the spring.

"I always thought it'd happen," she said in a flat voice.

Why doesn't she scream? Lutie had thought angrily. Why does she stand there looking like that? Why doesn't she find out how it happened and yell her head off and hit out at people? The longer she looked at that still, resigned expression on the girl's face, the angrier she became.

Finally she had pushed her way to the back of the crowd. "What happened to him?" she asked in a hard voice.

A woman with a bundle of newspapers under her arm answered her. She shifted the papers from one arm to the other. "White man in the baker shop killed him with a bread knife."

There was a silence, and then another voice added: "He had the bread knife in him and he walked to the corner. The cops brought him back here and he died there where he's layin' now."

"White man in the store claims he tried to hold him up."

"If that bastard white man puts one foot out here, we'll kill him. Cops or no cops."

She went home remembering, not the threat of violence in that silent, waiting crowd, but instead the man's ragged soleless shoes and the resigned look on the girl's face. She had never been able to forget either of them. The boy was so thin—painfully thin —and she kept thinking about his walking through the city barefooted. Both he and his sister were so young.

The next day's papers said that a "burly Negro" had failed in his effort to hold up a bakery shop, for the proprietor had surprised him by resisting and stabbed him with a bread knife. She held the paper in her hand for a long time, trying to follow the reasoning by which that thin ragged boy had become in the eyes of a reporter a "burly Negro." And she decided that it all depended on where you sat how these things looked. If you looked at them from inside the framework of a fat weekly salary, and you thought of colored people as naturally criminal, then you didn't really see what any Negro looked like. You couldn't, because the Negro was never an individual. He was a threat, or an animal, or a curse, or a blight, or a joke.

It was like the Chandlers and their friends in Connecticut, who looked at her and didn't see her, but saw instead a wench with no morals who would be easy to come by. The reporter saw a dead Negro who had attempted to hold up a store, and so he couldn't really see what the man lying on the sidewalk looked like. He couldn't see the ragged shoes, the thin, starved body. He saw, instead, the picture he already had in his mind: a huge, brawny, blustering, ignorant, criminally disposed black man who had run amok with a knife on a spring afternoon in Harlem and who had in turn been knifed.

She had gone past the bakery shop again the next afternoon. The windows had been smashed, the front door had apparently been broken in, because it was boarded up. There were messages chalked on the sidewalk in front of the store. They all said the same thing: "White man, don't come back." She was surprised to see that there were men still standing around, on the nearest corners, across the street. Their faces were turned toward the store. They weren't talking. They were just standing with their hands in their pockets—waiting.

Two police cars with their engines running were drawn up in front of the store. There were two cops right in front of the door, swinging nightsticks. She walked past, thinking that it was like a war that hadn't got off to a start yet, though both sides were piling up ammunition and reserves and were now waiting for anything, any little excuse, a gesture, a word, a sudden loud noise—and pouf! it would start.

Lutie moved uneasily on the bed. She pulled the robe more tightly around her. All of these streets were filled with violence, she thought. You turned a corner, walked through a block, and you came on it suddenly, unexpectedly.

For it was later in the spring that she took Bub to Roundtree Hospital. There was a cold, driving rain and she had hesitated about going out in it. But Bub had fallen on the sidewalk and cut his knee. She had come home from work to find him sitting disconsolately in Pop's kitchen. It was a deep, nasty cut, so she took him to the emergency room at Roundtree in order to find out just how bad it was.

She and Bub sat on the long bench in the center of the waiting room. There were two people ahead of them, and she waited impatiently because she should have been at home fixing dinner and getting Bub's clothes ready for school the next day.

Each time the big doors that led to the street swung open, a rush of wet damp air flushed through the room. She took to watching the people who came in, wondering about them. A policeman came in with a tired-looking, old man. The man's suit was shabby, but it was neatly pressed. He was wearing a stiff white collar.

The policeman guided him toward the bench. "Sit here," he said. The man gave no indication that he had heard. "Sit here," the policeman repeated. "Naw," as the old man started to move away. "Just sit down here, Pop." Finally the old man sat down.

She had watched him out of the corner of her eyes. He stared at the white hospital wall with a curious lack of interest. Nurses walked past him, white-coated internes strode by. There was a bustle and flurry when a stocky, gray-haired man with pince-nez glasses emerged from the elevator. "How are you, Doctor?" "Nice to see you back, Doctor."

The old man remained completely oblivious to the movement around him. The focus of his eyes never shifted from the expanse of wall in front of him.

Bub moved closer to her. "Hey, Mom," he whispered, "what's the matter with him?"

"I don't know," she said softly. "Maybe he's just tired."

Right across from where they were sitting was a small room filled with volunteer ambulance drivers. They were lounging in the chairs, their shirt collars open, smoking cigarettes. The blue haze of the smoke drifted out into the waiting room. The cop went into the room to use the telephone.

She heard him quite clearly. "I dunno. Picked him up on Eighth Avenue. Woman at the candy store said he'd been sittin' there all day. Naw. On the steps. Yeah. Psychopathic, I guess."

The old man didn't move, apparently didn't hear. She found him strangely disturbing, because there was in his lack-luster staring the same quality of resignation that she had seen in the face of the girl on Lenox Avenue earlier in the spring. She remembered how she had tried to tie the two together and reach a conclusion about them and couldn't because the man was old. She kept thinking that if he had lived that long, he should have been able to develop some inner strength that would have fought against whatever it was that had brought him to this aimless staring.

The telephone in the room across from them rang and she forgot about the old man. The woman who answered it said, "Okay. Right away." She turned to one of the drivers, gave him an address on Morningside Avenue, and said, "Hustle! They say it's bad."

Lutie had hoped that she would be able to get Bub into the emergency room before the ambulance came back, so that he wouldn't be sitting round-eyed with fear when he saw whatever it was they brought back that was "bad." She kept telling herself she shouldn't have brought him here, but the fee was so low that it was almost like free treatment.

The big street doors opened suddenly and the stretcher came through. The men carrying it moved quickly and with such precision that the stretcher was practically on top of them before Lutie realized it. The room was full of a low, terrible moaning, and the young girl on the stretcher was trying to sit up and blood was streaming out of the center of her body.

A gray-haired woman walked beside the stretcher. She kept saying, "Cut to ribbons! Cut to ribbons! Cut to ribbons!"—over and over in a monotonous voice. It was raining so hard that even in getting from the street to the waiting room the woman had been soaked and water dripped from her coat, from her hatbrim.

There was a long, awful moment while they maneuvered the stretcher past the bench and the girl moaned and tried to talk, and every once in a while she screamed—a sharp, thin, disembodied sound. The policeman looked at the girl in astonishment, but the old man never turned his head.

Lutie had grabbed Bub and covered his face with her face so that he couldn't see. He tried to squirm out of her arms and she held him closer and tighter. When she lifted her head, the stretcher was gone.

Bub stood up and looked around. "What was the matter with her?" he asked.

"She got hurt."

"How did she get hurt?"

"I don't know. It was an accident, I guess."

"Somebody cut her, didn't they?" And when she didn't answer, he repeated, "Didn't they?"

"I guess so, but I really don't know."

"One of the kids at school got cut up like that," he said, and then, "Why wouldn't you let me look, Mom?"

"Because I didn't think it was good for you to look. And when people are hurt badly like that, it doesn't help them to have someone stare at them."

While the interne dressed Bub's knee, she thought about the girl on the stretcher. Just a kid. Not much over sixteen, and she had that same awful look of resignation, of not expecting anything better than that of life. She was like the girl on Lenox Avenue who had looked down at her brother lying on the sidewalk to say, "I always thought it'd happen."

Lutie sat motionless staring into the dark. She was cold and yet she didn't move. She thought of the old man, the young girls. What reason did she have to believe that she and Bub wouldn't become so accustomed to the sight and sound of violence and of death that they wouldn't protest against it—they would become resigned to it; or that Bub finally wouldn't end up on a sidewalk with a knife in his back?

She felt she knew the steps by which that girl landed on the stretcher in the hospital. She could trace them easily. It could be that Bub might follow the same path.

The girl probably went to high school for a few months and then got tired of it. She had no place to study at night because the house was full of roomers, and she had no incentive, anyway, because she didn't have a real home. The mother was out to work all day and the father was long gone. She found out that boys liked her and she started bringing them to the apartment. The mother wasn't there to know what was going on.

They didn't have real homes, no base, no family life. So at sixteen or seventeen the girl was fooling around with two or three different boys. One of them found out about the others. Like all the rest of them, he had only a curious supersensitive kind of pride that kept him going, so he had to have revenge and knives are cheap.

It happened again and again all through Harlem. And she saw in her mind's eye the curious procession of people she had met coming out of 121st Street. They were walking toward Eighth Avenue.

She had been to the day-old bakery on Eighth Avenue and she stopped on the corner for the stop light. Down the length of the block she saw this group of people. They formed at first glance what appeared to be a procession, for they were walking slowly, stiffly. There was a goodish space between each one of them as though they didn't want to be too close to each other and yet were held together in a group by shock. They were young—sixteen, seventeen, eighteen, nineteen—and they were moving like sleepwalkers.

Then she saw that they had set their pace to that of the girl walking in the very front. Someone was leading her by the arm, and she was walking slowly, her body was limp, her shoulders sagged.

She had cringed away from the sight of the girl's face. She couldn't collect her thoughts for a moment, and then almost automatically the toneless reiterated words of the gray-haired woman in Roundtree Hospital came back to her: "Cut to ribbons! Cut to ribbons!"

She couldn't really see the girl's face, because blood poured over it, starting at her forehead. It was oozing down over her eyes, her nose, over her cheeks, dripped even from her mouth. The bright red blood turned what had been her face into a gaudy mask with patches of brown here and there where her skin showed through.

Lutie got that same jolting sense of shock and then of rage, because these people, all of them—the girl, the crowd in back of her—showed no horror, no surprise, no dismay. They had expected this. They were used to it. And they had become resigned to it.

Yes, she thought, she and Bub had to get out of 116th Street. It was a bad street. And then she thought about the other streets. It wasn't just this street that she was afraid of or that was bad. It was any street where people were packed together like sardines in a can.

And it wasn't just this city. It was any city where they set up a line and say black folks stay on this side and white folks on this side, so that the black folks were crammed on top of each other—jammed and packed and forced into the smallest possible space until they were completely cut off from light and air.

It was any place where the women had to work to support the families because the men couldn't get jobs and the men got bored and pulled out and the kids were left without proper homes because there was nobody around to put a heart into it. Yes. It was any place where people were so damn poor they didn't have time to do anything but work, and their bodies were the only source of relief from the pressure under which they lived; and where the crowding together made the young girls wise beyond their years.

It all added up to the same thing, she decided—white people. She hated them. She would always hate them. She forced herself to stop that train of thought. It led nowhere. It was unpleasant.

She slipped out of the wool robe and got back into bed and lay there trying to convince herself that she didn't have to stay on this street or any other street like it if she fought hard enough. Bub didn't have to end up stretched out on a sidewalk with a knife through his back. She was going to sleep, and she wasn't going to dream about supers who were transformed into wolfish dogs with buildings chained on their backs.

She searched her mind for a pleasant thought to drift off to sleep on. And she started building a picture of herself standing before a microphone in a long taffeta dress that whispered sweetly as she moved; of a room full of dancers who paused in their dancing to listen as she sang. Their faces were expectant, worshiping, as they looked up at her.

It was early when she woke up the next morning and she yawned and stretched and tried to remember what it was that had given her this feeling of anticipation. She burrowed her head deep into her pillow after she looked at the small clock on the bureau, because she could stay in bed for a few more minutes.

And then she remembered. Tonight was the night that she was going to sing at the Casino. Perhaps after tonight was over she could leave this street and these dark, narrow rooms and these walls that pressed in against her. It would be like discarding a wornout dress, a dress that was shiny from wear and faded from washing and whose seams were forever giving way. The thought made her fling her arms out from under the covers. She pulled the covers close around her neck, for the room was cold and the steam was as yet only a rattling in the radiator.

Immediately she began planning the things she had to do. When she got home from work, she would wash her hair and curl it, then press the long black taffeta skirt which with a plain white blouse would have to serve as evening gown. She wouldn't wear her winter coat, even though it was cold out, for the little short black coat would look better.

The hands of the battered clock moved toward seven and she jumped out of bed, shivered in the cold air, and slammed the airshaft shut.

Pulling her bathrobe around her, she went into the living room. Bub was still sleeping and she tucked the covers tight under his chin, thinking that sometime soon he would wake up in a bedroom of his own. It would have maple furniture and the bedspread and draperies would have ships and boats on them. There would be plenty of windows in the room and it would look out over a park.

In the kitchen she poured water into a saucepan, lit the gas stove, and stood waiting for the water to boil. While she stirred oatmeal into the boiling water, she began to wonder if perhaps she shouldn't wear that thin white summer blouse instead of one of the plain long-sleeved ones. The summer blouse had a low, round neck. It would look a lot more dressed-up. She turned the flame low under the oatmeal, set the table, filled small glasses with tomato juice, thinking that Bub could sleep about fifteen more minutes. She would have just time enough to take a bath.

But first she would look at the blouse to see if it needed pressing. She went into the bedroom and opened the closet door quietly. The blouse was rammed in between her one suit and her heavy winter coat. She reached her hand toward it, thinking, That's just plain careless of me. It must be terribly wrinkled from having been put in there like that.

She took the blouse out and held it up in front of her, staring at it in amazement. Why, it's all crushed, and there's dirt on it, she thought— great smudges of dirt and tight, small wrinkles as though it had been squeezed together. What on earth had Bub been doing with it?

She shook him awake. "What were you doing in my closet?" she demanded.

"Closet?" He looked up at her his eyes still full of sleep. "I ain't been in your closet."

"Will you stop saying 'ain't'?" she said. "Were you playing with my blouse?" She held it in front of him.

He was wide awake now, and he looked up at her with such obvious astonishment that she knew he was telling the truth. "Honest, Mon," he protested, "I ain't had it."

Unconsciously she thrust the blouse a little farther away from her, holding it by the metal hanger and thinking, Well, then who had done this? She knew that she hadn't hung it up wrinkled and dirty. Then she remembered that Jones, the Super, had been in the apartment last night playing cards with Bub. But he couldn't, she thought—what would he be doing with her blouse and when had he done it?

"Bub," she said sharply, "did you go out while the Super was here?"

He nodded. "I got him some beer."

She turned away and went into the kitchen so that Bub wouldn't see the expression on her face, because she was afraid and angry and at the same time she felt sickened. She could picture him, hungry-eyed, gaunt, standing there in her room crushing the blouse between his hands.

She opened the set tubs, dumped soapflakes in—great handfuls of them—and ran hot water on the flakes until the suds foamed up high. She almost let the water run over the top of the tub, because she stood in front of it, not moving, thinking, He's crazy. He's absolutely crazy.

Finally she shut the faucet off and poked the blouse deep into the hot, soapy water. She couldn't wear it again—not for a long time. Certainly she wouldn't wear it tonight.

Gwendolyn Brooks

(b. 1917)

GWENDOLYN BROOKS (BLAKELY) HAS been writing poetry since she was thirteen, when she published her first verses in a children's magazine. She is now a major American poet, and her work has appeared in many of the nation's periodicals and anthologies. Her poetry is principally concerned with the nuances—tragic and comic—of the black person's experience in a world where color counts heavily. A keen and sympathetic observer, Gwendolyn Brooks knows thoroughly the ghetto people about whom she writes. She is a brilliant wordsmith and her insights, like Melvin B. Tolson's, have deepened and sharpened as she progressed from a relatively simple style (*A Street in Bronzeville*) to a decidedly complex style (*In the Mecca*).

Born in Topeka, Kansas, Gwendolyn Brooks was reared in Chicago, where she learned from her own neighborhood many facts of ghetto life. She was educated at Wilson Junior College and has been a teacher of creative writing at Chicago's Columbia College at Elmhurst and at Chicago Teacher's College North. She has also been a lecturer at Northeastern Illinois State College and visiting Rennebohn Professor of Creative Writing at the University of Wisconsin.

Miss Brooks has received several distinguished honors and awards. She was the first Negro to win the Pulitzer Prize for Poetry (in 1950 for *Annie Allen*); in 1945 she received the *Mademoiselle* Merit Award; in 1946, the American Academy of Letters Award; in 1946 and 1947, Guggenheim Fellowships; in 1949, the Eunice Tietjens Memorial Award from *Poetry;* and in 1964, the Friends Literary Award for Poetry. Columbia College (Chicago) awarded her a Doctor of Humane Letters degree, and Illinois made her a member of its Art Council and Poet Laureate of the state.

Gwendolyn Brooks' major publications are: *A Street in Bronzeville* (1945); *Annie Allen* (1949); *Maud Martha,* a short novel (1953); *The Bean Eaters* (1960); *Selected Poems* (1963); and *In the Mecca* (1968).

For critical comment on Gwendolyn Brooks see David Littlejohn, *Black on White* (1966), pages 89–94. See also Arthur P. Davis, "Gwendolyn Brooks: A Poet of the Unheroic," *CLA Journal* (December, 1963), and "The Black and Tan Motif in the Poetry of Gwendolyn Brooks," *CLA Journal* (December, 1962).

The poems given here represent all of Miss Brooks' major works, from *A Street in Bronzeville* to *In the Mecca.*

OF DE WITT WILLIAMS ON HIS WAY TO LINCOLN CEMETERY

He was born in Alabama.
He was bred in Illinois.
He was nothing but a
Plain black boy.

Swing low swing low sweet sweet chariot.
Nothing but a plain black boy.

Drive him past the Pool Hall.
Drive him past the Show.
Blind within his casket,
But maybe he will know.

Down through Forty-seventh Street:
Underneath the L,
And Northwest Corner, Prairie,
That he loved so well.

Don't forget the Dance Halls—
Warwick and Savoy,
Where he picked his women, where
He drank his liquid joy.

Born in Alabama.
Bred in Illinois.
He was nothing but a
Plain black boy.

Swing low swing low sweet sweet chariot.
Nothing but a plain black boy.

THE SUNDAYS OF SATIN-LEGS SMITH

Inamoratas, with an approbation,
Bestowed his title. Blessed his inclination.

He wakes, unwinds, elaborately: a cat
Tawny, reluctant, royal. He is fat
And fine this morning. Definite. Reimbursed.

He waits a moment, he designs his reign,
That no performance may be plain or vain.
Then rises in a clear delirium.

He sheds, with his pajamas, shabby days.
And his desertedness, his intricate fear, the
Postponed resentments and the prim precautions.

Now, at his bath, would you deny him lavender
Or take away the power of his pine?
What smelly substitute, heady as wine,
Would you provide? life must be aromatic.
There must be scent, somehow there must be some.
Would you have flowers in his life? suggest
Asters? a Really Good geranium?
A white carnation? would you prescribe a Show
With the cold lilies, formal chrysanthemum
Magnificence, poinsettias, and emphatic
Red of prize roses? might his happiest
Alternative (you muse) be, after all,
A bit of gentle garden in the best
Of taste and straight tradition? Maybe so.
But you forget, or did you ever know,
His heritage of cabbage and pigtails,
Old intimacy with alleys, garbage pails,
Down in the deep (but always beautiful) South
Where roses blush their blithest (it is said)
And sweet magnolias put Chanel to shame.

No! He has not a flower to his name.
Except a feather one, for his lapel.
Apart from that, if he should think of flowers
It is in terms of dandelions or death.
Ah, there is little hope. You might as well—
Unless you care to set the world a-boil
And do a lot of equalizing things,
Remove a little ermine, say, from kings,
Shake hands with paupers and appoint them men,
For instance—certainly you might as well
Leave him his lotion, lavender and oil.

Let us proceed. Let us inspect, together
With his meticulous and serious love,
The innards of this closet. Which is a vault
Whose glory is not diamonds, not pearls,
Not silver plate with just enough dull shine.
But wonder-suits in yellow and in wine,
Sarcastic green and zebra-striped cobalt.
With shoulder padding that is wide
And cocky and determined as his pride;
Ballooning pants that taper off to ends
Scheduled to choke precisely.
                                 Here are hats
Like bright umbrellas; and hysterical ties
Like narrow banners for some gathering war.

People are so in need, in need of help.
People want so much that they do not know.

Below the tinkling trade of little coins
The gold impulse not possible to show
Or spend. Promise piled over and betrayed.

These kneaded limbs receive the kiss of silk.
Then they receive the brave and beautiful
Embrace of some of that equivocal wool.
He looks into his mirror, loves himself—
The neat curve here; the angularity
That is appropriate at just its place;
The technique of a variegated grace.

Here is all his sculpture and his art
And all his architectural design.
Perhaps you would prefer to this a fine
Value of marble, complicated stone.
Would have him think with horror of baroque,
Rococo. You forget and you forget.

He dances down the hotel steps that keep
Remnants of last night's high life and distress.
As spat-out purchased kisses and spilled beer.
He swallows sunshine with a secret yelp.
Passes to coffee and a roll or two.
Has breakfasted.
                          Out. Sounds about him smear,
Become a unit. He hears and does not hear
The alarm clock meddling in somebody's sleep;

Children's governed Sunday happiness;
The dry tone of a plane; a woman's oath;
Consumption's spiritless expectoration;
An indignant robin's resolute donation
Pinching a track through apathy and din;
Restaurant vendors weeping; and the L
That comes on like a slightly horrible thought.

Pictures, too, as usual, are blurred.
He sees and does not see the broken windows
Hiding their shame with newsprint; little girl
With ribbons decking wornness, little boy
Wearing the trousers with the decentest patch,
To honor Sunday; women on their way
From "service," temperate holiness arranged
Ably on asking faces; men estranged
From music and from wonder and from joy
But far familiar with the guiding awe
Of foodlessness.
        He loiters.
                Restaurant vendors
Weep, or out of them rolls a restless glee.
The Lonesome Blues, the Long-lost Blues, I Want A
Big Fat Mama. Down these sore avenues
Comes no Saint-Saëns, no piquant elusive Grieg,
And not Tschaikovsky's wayward eloquence
And not the shapely tender drift of Brahms.
But could he love them? Since a man must bring
To music what his mother spanked him for
When he was two: bits of forgotten hate,
Devotion: whether or not his mattress hurts:
The little dream his father humored: the thing
His sister did for money: what he ate
For breakfast—and for dinner twenty years
Ago last autumn: all his skipped desserts.

The pasts of his ancestors lean against
Him. Crowd him. Fog out his identity.
Hundreds of hungers mingle with his own,
Hundreds of voices advise so dexterously
He quite considers his reactions his,
Judges he walks most powerfully alone,
That everything is—simply what it is.

But movie-time approaches, time to boo
The hero's kiss, and boo the heroine

Whose ivory and yellow it is sin
For his eye to eat of. The Mickey Mouse,
However, is for everyone in the house.

Squires his lady to dinner at Joe's Eats.
His lady alters as to leg and eye,
Thickness and height, such minor points as these,
From Sunday to Sunday. But no matter what
Her name or body positively she's
In Queen Lace stockings with ambitious heels
That strain to kiss the calves, and vivid shoes
Frontless and backless, Chinese fingernails,
Earrings, three layers of lipstick, intense hat
Dripping with the most voluble of veils.
Her affable extremes are like sweet bombs
About him, whom no middle grace or good
Could gratify. He had no education
In quiet arts of compromise. He would
Not understand your counsels on control, nor
Thank you for your late trouble.

At Joe's Eats

You get your fish or chicken on meat platters.
With coleslaw, macaroni, candied sweets,
Coffee and apple pie. You go out full.
(The end is—isn't it?—all that really matters.)

And even and intrepid come
The tender boots of night to home.

Her body is like new brown bread
Under the Woolworth mignonette.
Her body is a honey bowl
Whose waiting honey is deep and hot.
Her body is like summer earth,
Receptive, soft, and absolute . . .

THE RITES FOR COUSIN VIT

Carried her unprotesting out the door.
Kicked back the casket-stand. But it can't hold her,
That stuff and satin aiming to enfold her,

The lid's contrition nor the bolts before.
Oh oh. Too much. Too much. Even now, surmise,
She rises in the sunshine. There she goes,
Back to the bars she knew and the repose
In love-rooms and the things in people's eyes.
Too vital and too squeaking. Must emerge.
Even now she does the snake-hips with a hiss,
Slops the bad wine across her shantung, talks
Of pregnancy, guitars and bridgework, walks
In parks or alleys, comes haply on the verge
Of happiness, haply hysterics. Is.

WE REAL COOL

The Pool Players.
Seven at the Golden Shovel.

We real cool. We
Left school. We

Lurk late. We
Strike straight. We

Sing sin. We
Thin gin. We

Jazz June. We
Die soon.

THE CHICAGO DEFENDER SENDS A MAN TO LITTLE ROCK

Fall, 1957

In Little Rock the people bear
Babes, and comb and part their hair
And watch the want ads, put repair

To roof and latch. While wheat toast burns
A woman waters multiferns.

Time upholds or overturns
The many, tight, and small concerns.

In Little Rock the people sing
Sunday hymns like anything,
Through Sunday pomp and polishing.

And after testament and tunes,
Some soften Sunday afternoons
With lemon tea and Lorna Doones.

I forecast
And I believe
Come Christmas Little Rock will cleave
To Christmas tree and trifle, weave,
From laugh and tinsel, texture fast.

In Little Rock is baseball; Barcarolle.
That hotness in July . . . the uniformed figures raw and implacable
And not intellectual,
Batting the hotness or clawing the suffering dust.
The Open Air Concert, on the special twilight green. . . .
When Beethoven is brutal or whispers to lady-like air.
Blanket-sitters are solemn, as Johann troubles to lean
To tell them what to mean. . . .

There is love, too, in Little Rock. Soft women softly
Opening themselves in kindness,
Or, pitying one's blindness,
Awaiting one's pleasure
In azure
Glory with anguished rose at the root. . . .
To wash away old semi-discomfitures.
They re-teach purple and unsullen blue.

The wispy soils go. And uncertain
Half-havings have they clarified to sures.

In Little Rock they know
Not answering the telephone is a way of rejecting life,
That it is our business to be bothered, is our business
To cherish bores or boredom, be polite

To lies and love and many-faceted fuzziness.
I scratch my head, massage the hate-I-had.
I blink across my prim and pencilled pad.
The saga I was sent for is not down.
Because there is a puzzle in this town.
The biggest News I do not dare
Telegraph to the Editor's chair:
"They are like people everywhere."

The angry Editor would reply
In hundred harryings of Why.

And true, they are hurling spittle, rock,
Garbage and fruit in Little Rock.
And I saw coiling storm a-writhe
On bright madonnas. And a scythe
Of men harassing brownish girls.
(The bows and barrettes in the curls
And braids declined away from joy.)

I saw a bleeding brownish boy. . . .

The lariat lynch-wise I deplored.

The lovelist lynchee was our Lord.

MALCOLM X

For Dudley Randall

Original.
Ragged-round.
Rich-robust.

He had the hawk-man's eyes.
We gasped. We saw the maleness.
The maleness raking out and making guttural the air
and pushing us to walls.

And in a soft and fundamental hour
a sorcery devout and vertical
beguiled the world.

He opened us—
who was a key,

who was a man.

THE WALL

August 27, 1967

For Edward Christmas

"The side wall of a typical slum building on the
corner of 43rd and Langley became a mural com-
municating black dignity. . . ."

—*Ebony*

A drumdrumdrum.
Humbly we come.
South of success and east of gloss and glass are
sandals;
flowercloth;
grave hoops of wood or gold, pendant
from black ears, brown ears, reddish-brown
and ivory ears;

black boy-men.
Black
boy-men on roofs fist out "Black Power!" Val,
a little black stampede
in African
images of brass and flowerswirl,
fists out "Black Power!"—tightens pretty eyes,
leans back on mothercountry and is tract,
is treatise through her perfect and tight teeth.

Women in wool hair chant their poetry.
Phil Cohran gives us messages and music
made of developed bone and polished and honed cult.
It is the Hour of tribe and of vibration,
the day-long Hour. It is the Hour
of ringing, rouse, of ferment-festival.

On Forty-third and Langley
black furnaces resent ancient
legislatures
of ploy and scruple and practical gelatin.
They keep the fever in,
fondle the fever.

All
worship the Wall.

I mount the rattling wood. Walter
says, "She is good." Says, "She
our Sister is." In front of me
hundreds of faces, red-brown, brown, black, ivory,
yield me hot trust, their yea and their Announcement
that they are ready to rile the high-flung ground.
Behind me, Paint.
Heroes.
No child has defiled
the Heroes of this Wall this serious Appointment
this still Wing
this Scald this Flute this heavy Light this Hinge.

An emphasis is paroled.
The old decapitations are revised,
the dispossessions beakless.

And we sing.

INTERMISSION

(DEEP SUMMER)

By all things planetary, sweet, I swear
Those hands may not possess these hands again
Until I get me gloves of ice to wear.
Because you are the headiest of men!
Your speech is whiskey, and your grin is gin.
I am well drunken. Is there water near?
I've need of wintry air to crisp me in.
—But come here—let me put this in your ear:

I would not want them now! You gave me this
Wildness to gulp. Now water is too pale.
And now I know deep summer is a bliss
I have no wish for weathering the gale.
So when I beg for gloves of ice to wear,
Laugh at me. I am lying, sweet, I swear!

Margaret A. Walker

(b. 1915)

MARGARET A. WALKER, POET and novelist, was born in Birmingham, Alabama, and grew up in New Orleans, where her father was a Methodist minister. She received a B.A. from Northwestern University and an M.A. in creative writing from the University of Iowa. *For My People* (1942), her first volume, won the Yale University Younger Poets Competition.

Miss Walker worked with the Federal Writers Project during the Depression; taught English at Livingstone College and West Virginia State College; and is presently teaching at Jackson State College, Jackson, Mississippi. In 1965 she received her Ph.D. from Iowa for her novel *Jubilee* (1966).

Jubilee, which received a Houghton Mifflin Literary Award, is the fictionalized story of Miss Walker's great-grandmother's experiences during slavery and Reconstruction.

In several of her best poems, in both form and subject matter, Miss Walker brilliantly uses the folk material of the Negro.

Margaret Walker is currently working on another book, tentatively entitled *October Journey.*

FOR MY PEOPLE

For my people everywhere singing their slave songs repeatedly: their
dirges and their ditties and their blues and jubilees, praying their
prayers nightly to an unknown god, bending their knees humbly
to an unseen power;

For my people lending their strength to the years, to the gone years and
the now years and the maybe years, washing ironing cooking scrubbing sewing mending hoeing plowing digging planting pruning
patching dragging along never gaining never reaping never knowing
and never understanding;

For my playmates in the clay and dust and sand of Alabama backyards playing baptizing and preaching and doctor and jail and soldier and school and mama and cooking and playhouse and concert and store and hair and Miss Choomby and company;

For the cramped bewildered years we went to school to learn to know the reasons why and the answers to and the people who and the places where and the days when, in memory of the bitter hours when we discovered we were black and poor and small and different and nobody cared and nobody wondered and nobody understood;

For the boys and girls who grew in spite of these things to be man and woman, to laugh and dance and sing and play and drink their wine and religion and success, to marry their playmates and bear children and then die of consumption and anemia and lynching;

For my people thronging 47th Street in Chicago and Lenox Avenue in New York and Rampart Street in New Orleans, lost disinherited dispossessed and happy people filling the cabarets and taverns and other people's pockets needing bread and shoes and milk and land and money and something—something all our own;

For my people walking blindly spreading joy, losing time being lazy, sleeping when hungry, shouting when burdened, drinking when hopeless, tied and shackled and tangled among ourselves by the unseen creatures who tower over us omnisciently and laugh;

For my people blundering and groping and floundering in the dark of churches and schools and clubs and societies, associations and councils and committees and conventions, distressed and disturbed and deceived and devoured by money-hungry glory-craving leeches, preyed on by facile force of state and fad and novelty, by false prophet and holy believer;

For my people standing staring trying to fashion a better way from confusion, from hypocrisy and misunderstanding, trying to fashion a world that will hold all the people, all the faces, all the adams and eves and their countless generations;

Let a new earth rise. Let another world be born. Let a bloody peace be written in the sky. Let a second generation full of courage issue forth; let a people loving freedom come to growth. Let a beauty full of healing and a strength of final clenching be the pulsing in our spirits and our blood. Let the martial songs be written, let the dirges disappear. Let a race of men now rise and take control.

POPPA CHICKEN

Poppa was a sugah daddy
Pimping in his prime;
All the gals for miles around
Walked to Poppa's time.

Poppa Chicken owned the town,
Give his women hell;
All the gals on Poppa's time
Said that he was swell.

Poppa's face was long and black;
Poppa's grin was broad.
When Poppa Chicken walked the streets
The gals cried Lawdy! Lawd!

Poppa Chicken made his gals
Toe his special line:
"Treat 'em rough and make 'em say
Poppa Chicken's fine!"

Poppa Chicken toted guns;
Poppa wore a knife.
One night Poppa shot a guy
Threat'ning Poppa's life.

Poppa done his time in jail
Though he got off light;
Bought his pardon in a year;
Come back out in might.

Poppa walked the streets this time,
Gals around his neck.
And everybody said the jail
Hurt him nary speck.

Poppa smoked his long cigars—
Special Poppa brands—
Rocks all glist'ning in his tie;
On his long black hands.

Poppa lived without a fear;
Walked without a rod.
Poppa cussed the coppers out;
Talked like he was God.

Poppa met a pretty gal;
Heard her name was Rose;
Took one look at her and soon
Bought her pretty clothes.

One night she was in his arms,
In walked her man Joe.
All he done was look and say,
"Poppa's got to go."

Poppa Chicken still is hot
Though he's old and gray,
Walking round here with his gals
Pimping every day.

WE HAVE BEEN BELIEVERS

We have been believers believing in the black gods of an old land,
believing in the secrets of the seeress and the magic of the charmers
and the power of the devil's evil ones.

And in the white gods of a new land we have been believers believing
in the mercy of our masters and the beauty of our brothers, believing
in the conjure of the humble and the faithful and the pure.

Neither the slavers' whip nor the lynchers' rope nor the bayonet could
kill our black belief. In our hunger we beheld the welcome table and
in our nakedness the glory of a long white robe. We have been believers in the new Jerusalem.

We have been believers feeding greedy grinning gods, like a Moloch
demanding our sons and our daughters, our strength and our wills
and our spirits of pain. We have been believers, silent and stolid
and stubborn and strong.

We have been believers yielding substance for the world. With our
hands have we fed a people and out of our strength have they wrung
the necessities of a nation. Our song has filled the twilight and our
hope has heralded the dawn.

Now we stand ready for the touch of one fiery iron, for the cleansing
breath of many molten truths, that the eyes of the blind may see and
the ears of the deaf may hear and the tongues of the people be filled
with living fire.

Where are our gods that they leave us asleep? Surely the priests and the preachers and the powers will hear. Surely now that our hands are empty and our hearts too full to pray they will understand. Surely the sires of the people will send us a sign.

We have been believers believing in our burdens and our demigods too long. Now the needy no longer weep and pray; the long-suffering arise, and our fists bleed against the bars with a strange insistency.

Ralph Ellison

(b. 1914)

RALPH ELLISON WAS BORN in Oklahoma City, the son of middle-class parents who instilled in him a love of literature and music and an objective attitude toward being a Negro in America.

He went to Tuskegee to study music, stayed there three years, and in 1936 left for New York, ostensibly to study sculpturing and music composition. Ellison became acquainted with Richard Wright, involved himself in the WPA, and abandoned his studies for a writing career. He began contributing regularly to the *New Masses* and *The Negro Quarterly*. Although interested in politics of the left, Ellison never became a Communist.

Ralph Ellison has received an impressive amount of awards and honors. In 1945 he was given a Rosenwald Fellowship; in 1955, the National Arts and Letters Fellowship (Rome). For *Invisible Man* (1952), he received the National Book Award (1953), the Russwurm Award (1953), and National Newspaper Publishers' Award (1954); and in 1965 the *New York Herald-Tribune's* Book Review Poll named the book the most distinguished novel written between 1945 and 1965.

A technically superb work, *Invisible Man* may be read on several levels: as a search for identity, as a symbolic portrayal of the Negro in America, or as an odyssey of modern man. The book is not a protest novel in the usual sense of that term; it does point out America's racial shortcomings, but the artist remains much more than merely a propagandist.

In great demand as lecturer, teacher, and writer-in-residence, Ellison has appeared in one or another of these roles at many American schools, among them Bard, Columbia, Bennington, Fisk, Antioch, Chicago, Barnard, Rutgers, and Yale. He has given the Gertrude Clarke Whittall Lecture at the Library of Congress. In 1964 he was elected to the American Institute of Arts and Letters.

A brilliant critic of literature and folk material, especially jazz, Ralph Ellison has written for the *Partisan Review, The Nation, Harper's* and many other periodicals.

For critical comment on Ellison see Robert Bone, "Ralph Ellison and the Uses of Imagination," *Tri-Quarterly,* number 6 (1966); Marcus Klein, "Ralph Ellison" in *After Alienation: American Novels in Mid-Century* (1962); and Floyd Ross Horowitz, "The Enigma of Ellison's Intellectual Man," *CLA Journal* (December, 1963).

The two selections given below come from *Invisible Man* (1952) and *Shadow and Act* (1964), a collection of his critical essays.

AT THE GOLDEN DAY

I saw them as we approached the short stretch that lay between the railroad tracks and the Golden Day. At first I failed to recognize them. They straggled down the highway in a loose body, blocking the way from the white line to the frazzled weeds that bordered the sun-heated concrete slab. I cursed them silently. They were blocking the road and Mr. Norton was gasping for breath. Ahead of the radiator's gleaming curve they looked like a chain gang on its way to make a road. But a chain gang marches single file and I saw no guards on horseback. As I drew nearer I recognized the loose gray shirts and pants worn by the veterans. Damn! They were heading for the Golden Day.

"A little stimulant," I heard behind me.

"In a few minutes, sir."

Up ahead I saw the one who thought he was a drum major strutting in front, giving orders as he moved energetically in long, hip-swinging strides, a cane held above his head, rising and falling as though in time to music. I slowed the car as I saw him turn to face the men, his cane held at chest level as he shortened the pace. The men continued to ignore him, walking along in a mass, some talking in groups and others talking and gesticulating to themselves.

Suddenly, the drum major saw the car and shook his cane-baton at me. I blew the horn, seeing the men move over to the side as I nosed the car slowly forward. He held his ground, his legs braced, hands on hips, and to keep from hitting him I slammed on the brakes.

The drum major rushed past the men toward the car, and I heard the cane bang down upon the hood as he rushed toward me.

"Who the hell you think you are, running down the army? Give the countersign. Who's in command of this outfit? You trucking bastards was always too big for your britches. Countersign me!"

"This is General Pershing's car, sir," I said, remembering hearing that he responded to the name of his wartime Commander-in-Chief. Suddenly the wild look changed in his eyes and he stepped back and saluted with stiff precision. Then looking suspiciously into the back seat, he barked,

"Where's the General?"

"There," I said, turning and seeing Mr. Norton raising himself, weak and white-faced, from the seat.

"What is it? Why have we stopped?"

"The sergeant stopped us, sir . . ."

"Sergeant? What sergeant?" He sat up.

"Is that you, General?" the vet said, saluting. "I didn't know you were inspecting the front lines today. I'm very sorry, sir."

"What . . . ?" Mr. Norton said.

"The General's in a hurry," I said quickly.

"Sure is," the vet said. "He's got a lot to see. Discipline is bad. Artillery's shot to hell." Then he called to the men walking up the road, "Get the hell out of the General's road. General Pershing's coming through. Make way for General Pershing!"

He stepped aside and I shot the car across the line to avoid the men and stayed there on the wrong side as I headed for the Golden Day.

"Who was that man?" Mr. Norton gasped from the back seat.

"A former soldier, sir. A vet. They're all vets, a little shell-shocked."

"But where is the attendant?"

"I don't see one, sir. They're harmless though."

"Nevertheless, they should have an attendant."

I had to get him there and away before they arrived. This was their day to visit the girls, and the Golden Day would be pretty rowdy. I wondered where the rest of them were. There should have been about fifty. Well, I would rush in and get the whiskey and leave. What was wrong with Mr. Norton anyway, why should he get *that* upset over Trueblood? I had felt ashamed and several times I had wanted to laugh, but it had made him sick. Maybe he needed a doctor. Hell, he didn't ask for any doctor. Damn that bastard Trueblood.

I would run in, get a pint, and run out again, I thought. Then he wouldn't see the Golden Day. I seldom went there myself except with some of the fellows when word got out that a new bunch of girls had arrived from New Orleans. The school had tried to make the Golden Day respectable, but the local white folks had a hand in it somehow and they got nowhere. The best the school could do was to make it hot for any student caught going there.

He lay like a man asleep as I left the car and ran into the Golden Day. I wanted to ask him for money but decided to use my own. At the door I paused; the place was already full, jammed with vets in loose gray shirts and trousers and women in short, tight-fitting, stiffly starched gingham aprons. The stale beer smell struck like a club through the noise of voices and the juke box. Just as I got inside the door a stolid-faced man gripped me by the arm and looked stonily into my eyes.

"It will occur at 5:30," he said, looking straight through me.

"What?"

"The great all-embracing absolute Armistice, the end of the world!" he said.

Before I could answer, a small plump woman smiled into my face and pulled him away.

"It's your turn, Doc," she said. "Don't let it happen till after me and you done been upstairs. How come I always have to come get you?"

"No, it is true," he said. "They wirelessed me from Paris this morning."

"Then, baby, me an' you better hurry. There's lots of money I got to make in here before that thing happens. You hold it back a while, will you?"

She winked at me as she pulled him through the crowd toward the stairs. I elbowed my way nervously toward the bar.

Many of the men had been doctors, lawyers, teachers, Civil Service workers; there were several cooks, a preacher, a politician, and an artist. One very nutty one had been a psychiatrist. Whenever I saw them I felt uncomfortable. They were supposed to be members of the professions toward which at various times I vaguely aspired myself, and even though they never seemed to see me I could never believe that they were really patients. Sometimes it appeared as though they played some vast and complicated game with me and the rest of the school folk, a game whose goal was laughter and whose rules and subtleties I could never grasp.

Two men stood directly in front of me, one speaking with intense earnestness. ". . . and Johnson hit Jeffries at an angle of 45 degrees from his lower left lateral incisor, producing an instantaneous blocking of his entire thalamic rine, frosting it over like the freezing unit of a re-frigerator, thus shattering his autonomous nervous system and rocking the big brick-laying creampuff with extreme hyperspasmic muscular tremors which dropped him dead on the extreme tip of his coccyx, which, in turn, produced a sharp traumatic reaction in his sphincter nerve and muscle, and then, my dear colleague, they swept him up, sprinkled him with quicklime and rolled him away in a barrow. Naturally, there was no other therapy possible."

"Excuse me," I said, pushing past.

Big Halley was behind the bar, his dark skin showing through his sweat-wet shirt.

"Whatcha saying, school-boy?"

"I want a double whiskey, Halley. Put it in something deep so I can get it out of here without spilling it. It's for somebody outside."

His mouth shot out, "Hell, naw!"

"Why?" I asked, surprised at the anger in his thyroid eyes.

"You still up at the school, ain't you?"

"Sure."

"Well, those bastards is trying to close me up agin, that's why. You can drink till you blue in the face in here, but I wouldn't sell you enough to spit through your teeth to take outside."

"But I've got a sick man out in the car."

"What car? You never had no car."

"The white man's car. I'm driving for him."

"Ain't you in school?"

"He's *from* the school."

"Well, who's sick?"

"He is."

"He too good to come in? Tell him we don't Jimcrow nobody."

"But he's sick."

"He can die!"

"He's important, Halley, a trustee. He's rich and sick and if anything happens to him, they'll have me packed and on my way home."

"Can't help it, school-boy. Bring him inside and he can buy enough to swim in. He can drink outa my own private bottle."

He sliced the white heads off of a couple of beers with an ivory paddle and passed them up the bar. I felt sick inside. Mr. Norton wouldn't want to come in here. He was too sick. And besides I didn't want him to see the patients and the girls. Things were getting wilder as I made my way out. Supercargo, the white-uniformed attendant who usually kept the men quiet was nowhere to be seen. I didn't like it, for when he was upstairs they had absolutely no inhibitions. I made my way out to the car. What could I tell Mr. Norton? He was lying very still when I opened the door.

"Mr. Norton, sir. They refuse to sell me whiskey to bring out."

He lay very still.

"Mr. Norton."

He lay like a figure of chalk. I shook him gently, feeling dread within me. He barely breathed. I shook him violently, seeing his head wobble grotesquely. His lips parted, bluish, revealing a row of long, slender, amazingly animal-like teeth.

"SIR!"

In a panic I ran back into the Golden Day, bursting through the noise as through an invisible wall.

"Halley! Help me, he's dying!"

I tried to get through but no one seemed to have heard me. I was blocked on both sides. They were jammed together.

"Halley!"

Two patients turned and looked me in the face, their eyes two inches from my nose.

"What is wrong with this gentleman, Sylvester?" the tall one said.

"A man's dying outside!" I said.

"Someone is always dying," the other one said.

"Yes, and it's good to die beneath God's great tent of sky."

"He's got to have some whiskey!"

"Oh, that's different," one of them said and they began pushing a path to the bar. "A last bright drink to keep the anguish down. Step aside, please!"

"School-boy, you back already?" Halley said.

"Give me some whiskey. He's dying!"

"I done told you, school-boy, you better bring him in here. He can die, but I still got to pay my bills."

"Please, they'll put me in jail."

"You going to college, figure it out," he said.

"You'd better bring the gentleman inside," the one called Sylvester said. "Come, let us assist you."

We fought our way out of the crowd. He was just as I left him.

"Look, Sylvester, it's Thomas Jefferson!"

"I was just about to say, I've long wanted to discourse with him."

I looked at them speechlessly; they were both crazy. Or were they joking?

"Give me a hand," I said.

"Gladly."

I shook him. "Mr. Norton!"

"We'd better hurry if he's to enjoy his drink," one of them said thoughtfully.

We picked him up. He swung between us like a sack of old clothes. "Hurry!"

As we carried him toward the Golden Day one of the men stopped suddenly and Mr. Norton's head hung down, his white hair dragging in the dust.

"Gentlemen, this man is my grandfather!"

"But he's *white*, his name's Norton."

"I should know my own grandfather! He's Thomas Jefferson and I'm his grandson—on the 'field-nigger' side," the tall man said.

"Sylvester, I do believe that you're right. I certainly do," he said, staring at Mr. Norton. "Look at those features. Exactly like yours— from the identical mold. Are you sure he didn't spit you upon the earth, fully clothed?"

"No, no, that was my father," the man said earnestly.

And he began to curse his father violently as we moved for the door. Halley was there waiting. Somehow he'd gotten the crowd to quieten down and a space was cleared in the center of the room. The men came close to look at Mr. Norton.

"Somebody bring a chair."

'Yeah, let Mister Eddy sit down."

"That ain't no Mister Eddy, man, that's John D. Rockefeller," someone said.

"Here's a chair for the Messiah."

"Stand back y'all," Halley ordered. "Give him some room."

Burnside, who had been a doctor, rushed forward and felt for Mr. Norton's pulse.

"It's solid! This man has a *solid* pulse! Instead of beating, it *vibrates*. That's very unusual. Very."

Someone pulled him away. Halley reappeared with a bottle and a glass. "Here, some of y'all tilt his head back."

And before I could move, a short, pock-marked man appeared and took Mr. Norton's head between his hands, tilting it at arm's length and then, pinching the chin gently like a barber about to apply a razor, gave a sharp, swift movement.

"Pow!"

Mr. Norton's head jerked like a jabbed punching bag. Five pale red lines bloomed on the white cheek, glowing like fire beneath translucent stone. I could not believe my eyes. I wanted to run. A woman tittered. I saw several men rush for the door.

"Cut it out, you damn fool!"

"A case of hysteria," the pock-marked man said quietly.

"Git the hell out of the way," Halley said. "Somebody git that stool-pigeon attendant from upstairs. Git him down here, quick!"

"A mere mild case of hysteria," the pock-marked man said as they pushed him away.

"Hurry with the drink, Halley!"

"Heah, school-boy, you hold the glass. This here's brandy I been saving for myself."

Someone whispered tonelessly into my ear, "You see, I told you that it would occur at 5:30. Already the Creator has come." It was the stolid-faced man.

I saw Halley tilt the bottle and the oily amber of brandy sloshing into the glass. Then tilting Mr. Norton's head back, I put the glass to his lips and poured. A fine brown stream ran from the corner of his mouth, down his delicate chin. The room was suddenly quiet. I felt a slight movement against my hand, like a child's breast when it whimpers at the end of a spell of crying. The fine-veined eyelids flickered. He coughed. I saw a slow red flush creep, then spurt, up his neck, spreading over his face.

"Hold it under his nose, school-boy. Let 'im smell it."

I waved the glass beneath Mr. Norton's nose. He opened his pale blue eyes. They seemed watery now in the red flush that bathed his face. He tried to sit up, his right hand fluttering to his chin. His eyes widened, moved quickly from face to face. Then coming to mine, the moist eyes focused with recognition.

"You were unconscious, sir," I said.

"Where am I, young man?" he asked wearily.

"This is the Golden Day, sir."

"What?"

"The Golden Day. It's a kind of sporting-and-gambling house," I added reluctantly.

"Now give him another drinka brandy," Halley said.

I poured a drink and handed it to him. He sniffed it, closed his eyes as in puzzlement, then drank; his cheeks filled out like small bellows; he was rinsing his mouth.

"Thank you," he said, a little stronger now. "What is this place?"

"The Golden Day," said several patients in unison.

He looked slowly around him, up to the balcony, with its scrolled and carved wood. A large flag hung lank above the floor. He frowned.

"What was this building used for in the past?" he said.

"It was a church, then a bank, then it was a restaurant and a fancy gambling house, and now *we* got it," Halley explained. "I think somebody said it used to be a jailhouse too."

"They let us come here once a week to raise a little hell," someone said.

"I couldn't buy a drink to take out, sir, so I had to bring you inside," I explained in dread.

He looked about him. I followed his eyes and was amazed to see the varied expressions on the patients' faces as they silently returned his gaze. Some were hostile, some cringing, some horrified; some, who when among themselves were most violent, now appeared as submissive as children. And some seemed strangely amused.

"Are all of you patients?" Mr. Norton asked.

"Me, I just runs this joint," Halley said. "These here other fellows . . ."

"We're patients sent here as therapy," a short, fat, very intelligent-looking man said. "But," he smiled, "they send along an attendant, a kind of censor, to see that the therapy fails."

"You're nuts. I'm a dynamo of energy. I come to charge my batteries," one of the vets insisted.

"I'm a student of history, sir," another interrupted with dramatic gestures. "The world moves in a circle like a roulette wheel. In the beginning, black is on top, in the middle epochs, white holds the odds, but soon Ethiopia shall stretch forth her noble wings! Then place your money on the black!" His voice throbbed with emotion. "Until then, the sun holds no heat, there's ice in the heart of the earth. Two years from now and I'll be old enough to give my mulatto mother a bath, the half-white bitch!" he added, beginning to leap up and down in an explosion of glassy-eyed fury.

Mr. Norton blinked his eyes and straightened up.

"I'm a physician, may I take your pulse?" Burnside said, seizing Mr. Norton's wrist.

"Don't pay him no mind, mister. He ain't been no doctor in ten years. They caught him trying to change some blood into money."

"I did too!" the man screamed. "I discovered it and John D. Rockefeller stole the formula from me."

"Mr. Rockefeller did you say?" Mr. Norton said. "I'm sure you must be mistaken."

"WHAT'S GOING ON DOWN THERE?" a voice shouted from the balcony. Everyone turned. I saw a huge black giant of a man, dressed only in white shorts, swaying on the stairs. It was Supercargo, the attendant. I hardly recognized him without his hard-starched white uniform. Usually he walked around threatening the men with a strait jacket which he always carried over his arm, and usually they were quiet and submissive in his presence. But now they seemed not to recognize him and began shouting curses.

"How you gon keep order in the place if you gon git drunk?" Halley shouted. "Charlene! Charlene!"

"Yeah?" a woman's voice, startling in its carrying power, answered sulkily from a room off the balcony.

"I want you to git that stool-pigeoning, joy-killing, nut-crushing bum back in there with you and sober him up. Then git him in his white suit and down here to keep order. We got white folks in the house."

A woman appeared on the balcony, drawing a woolly pink robe about her. "Now you lissen here, Halley," she drawled, "I'm a woman. If you want him dressed, you can do it yourself. I don't put on but one man's clothes and he's in N'Orleans."

"Never mind all that. Git that stool pigeon sober!"

"I want order down there," Supercargo boomed, "and if there's white folks down there, I wan's *double* order."

Suddenly there was an angry roar from the men back near the bar and I saw them rush the stairs.

"Get him!"

"Let's give him some order!"

"Out of my way."

Five men charged the stairs. I saw the giant bend and clutch the posts at the top of the stairs with both hands, bracing himself, his body gleaming bare in his white shorts. The little man who had slapped Mr. Norton was in front, and, as he sprang up the long flight, I saw the attendant set himself and kick, catching the little man just as he reached the top, hard in the chest, sending him backwards in a curving dive into the midst of the men behind him. Supercargo got set to swing his leg again. It was a narrow stair and only one man could get up at a time. As fast as they rushed up, the giant kicked them back. He swung his leg, kicking them down like a fungo-hitter batting out flies. Watching him, I forgot Mr. Norton. The Golden Day was in an uproar. Half-dressed women appeared from the rooms off the balcony. Men hooted and yelled as at a football game.

"I WANT ORDER!" the giant shouted as he sent a man flying down the flight of stairs.

"THEY THROWING BOTTLES OF LIQUOR!" a woman screamed. "REAL LIQUOR!"

"That's a order he don't want," someone said.

A shower of bottles and glasses splashing whiskey crashed against the balcony. I saw Supercargo snap suddenly erect and grab his forehead, his face bathed in whiskey, "Eeeee!" he cried, "Eeeee!" Then I saw him waver, rigid from his ankles upward. For a moment the men on the stairs were motionless, watching him. Then they sprang forward.

Supercargo grabbed wildly at the balustrade as they snatched his feet from beneath him and started down. His head bounced against the steps making a sound like a series of gunshots as they ran dragging him by his ankles, like volunteer firemen running with a hose. The crowd surged forward. Halley yelled near my ear. I saw the man being dragged toward the center of the room.

"Give the bastard some order!"

"Here I'm forty-five and he's been acting like he's my old man!"

"So you like to kick, huh?" a tall man said, aiming a shoe at the attendant's head. The flesh above his right eye jumped out as though it had been inflated.

Then I heard Mr. Norton beside me shouting, "No, no! Not when he's down!"

"Lissen at the white folks," someone said.

"He's the white folks' man!"

Men were jumping upon Supercargo with both feet now and I felt such an excitement that I wanted to join them. Even the girls were yelling, "Give it to him good!" "He never pays me!" "Kill him!"

"Please, y'all, not in here! Not in my place!"

"You can't speak your mind when he's on duty!"

"Hell, no!"

Somehow I got pushed away from Mr. Norton and found myself beside the man called Sylvester.

"Watch this, school-boy," he said. "See there, where his ribs are bleeding?"

I nodded my head.

"Now don't move your eyes."

I watched the spot as though compelled, just beneath the lower rib and above the hip-bone, as Sylvester measured carefully with his toe and kicked as though he were punting a football. Supercargo let out a groan like an injured horse.

"Try it, school-boy, it feels so good. It gives you relief," Sylvester said. "Sometimes I get so afraid of him I feel that he's inside my head. There!" he said, giving Supercargo another kick.

As I watched, a man sprang on Supercargo's chest with both feet and he lost consciousness. They began throwing cold beer on him, reviving him, only to kick him unconscious again. Soon he was drenched in blood and beer.

"The bastard's out cold."

"Throw him out."

"Naw, wait a minute. Give me a hand somebody."

They threw him upon the bar, stretching him out with his arms folded across his chest like a corpse.

"Now, let's have a drink!"

Halley was slow in getting behind the bar and they cursed him.

"Get back there and serve us, you big sack of fat!"

"Gimme a rye!"

"Up here, funk-buster!"

"Shake them sloppy hips!"

"Okay, okay, take it easy," Halley said, rushing to pour them drinks. "Just put y'all's money where your mouth is."

With Supercargo lying helpless upon the bar, the men whirled about like maniacs. The excitement seemed to have tilted some of the more delicately balanced ones too far. Some made hostile speeches at the top of their voices against the hospital, the state and the universe. The one who called himself a composer was banging away the one wild piece he seemed to know on the out-of-tune piano, striking the keyboard with fists and elbows and filling in other effects in a bass voice that moaned like a bear in agony. One of the most educated ones touched my arm. He was a former chemist who was never seen without his shining Phi Beta Kappa key.

"The men have lost control," he said through the uproar. "I think you'd better leave."

"I'm trying to," I said, "as soon as I can get over to Mr. Norton."

Mr. Norton was gone from where I had left him. I rushed here and there through the noisy men, calling his name.

When I found him he was under the stairs. Somehow he had been pushed there by the scuffling, reeling men and he lay sprawled in the chair like an aged doll. In the dim light his features were sharp and white and his closed eyes well-defined lines in a well-tooled face. I shouted his name above the roar of the men, and got no answer. He was out again. I shook him, gently, then roughly, but still no flicker of his wrinkled lids. Then some of the milling men pushed me up against him and suddenly a mass of whiteness was looming two inches from my eyes; it was only his face but I felt a shudder of nameless horror. I had never been so close to a white person before. In a panic I struggled to get away. With his eyes closed he seemed more threatening than with them open. He was like a formless white death, suddenly appeared before me, a death which had been there all the time and which had now revealed itself in the madness of the Golden Day.

"Stop screaming!" a voice commanded, and I felt myself pulled away. It was the short fat man.

I clamped my mouth shut, aware for the first time that the shrill sound was coming from my own throat. I saw the man's face relax as he gave me a wry smile.

"That's better," he shouted into my ear. "He's only a man. Remember that. He's only a man!"

I wanted to tell him that Mr. Norton was much more than that, that he was a rich white man and in my charge; but the very idea that I was responsible for him was too much for me to put into words.

"Let us take him to the balcony," the man said, pushing me toward Mr. Norton's feet. I moved automatically, grasping the thin ankles as he raised the white man by the armpits and backed from beneath the stairs. Mr. Norton's head lolled upon his chest as though he were drunk or dead.

The vet started up the steps still smiling, climbing backwards a step at a time. I had begun to worry about him, whether he was drunk like the rest, when I saw three of the girls who had been leaning over the balustrade watching the brawl come down to help us carry Mr. Norton up.

"Looks like pops couldn't take it," one of them shouted.

"He's high as a Georgia pine."

"Yeah, I tell you this stuff Halley got out here is too strong for white folks to drink."

"Not drunk, ill!" the fat man said. "Go find a bed that's not being used so he can stretch out awhile."

"Sho, daddy. Is there any other little favors I can do for you?"

"That'll be enough," he said.

One of the girls ran up ahead. "Mine's just been changed. Bring him down here," she said.

In a few minutes Mr. Norton was lying upon a three-quarter bed, faintly breathing. I watched the fat man bend over him very professionally and feel for his pulse.

"You a doctor?" a girl asked.

"Not now, I'm a patient. But I have a certain knowledge."

Another one, I thought, pushing him quickly aside. "He'll be all right. Let him come to so I can get him out of here."

"You needn't worry, I'm not like those down there, young fellow," he said. "I really was a doctor. I won't hurt him. He's had a mild shock of some kind."

We watched him bend over Mr. Norton again, feeling his pulse, pulling back his eyelid.

"It's a mild shock," he repeated.

"This here Golden Day is enough to shock anybody," a girl said, smoothing her apron over the smooth sensuous roll of her stomach.

Another brushed Mr. Norton's white hair away from his forehead and stroked it, smiling vacantly. "He's kinda cute," she said. "Just like a little white baby."

"What kinda ole baby?" the small skinny girl asked.

"That's the kind, an *ole* baby."

"You just like white men, Edna. That's all," the skinny one said.

Edna shook her head and smiled as though amused at herself. "I sho do. I just love 'em. Now this one, old as he is, he could put his shoes under my bed any night."

"Shucks, me I'd kill an old man like that."

"Kill him nothing," Edna said. "Girl, don't you know that all these rich ole white men got monkey glands and billy goat balls? These old bastards don't never git enough. They want to have the whole world.'"

The doctor looked at me and smiled. "See, now you're learning all about endocrinology," he said. "I was wrong when I told you that he was only a man; it seems now that he's either part goat or part ape. Maybe he's both."

"It's the truth," Edna said. "I used to have me one in Chicago—"

"Now you ain't never been to no Chicago, gal," the other one interrupted.

"How you know I ain't? Two years ago . . . Shucks, you don't know nothing. That ole white man right there might have him a coupla jackass balls!"

The fat man raised up with a quick grin. "As a scientist and a physician I'm forced to discount that," he said. "That is one operation that has yet to be performed." Then he managed to get the girls out of the room.

"If he should come around and hear that conversation," the vet said, "it would be enough to send him off again. Besides, their scientific curiosity might lead them to investigate whether he really does have a monkey gland. And that, I'm afraid, would be a bit obscene."

"I've got to get him back to the school," I said.

"All right," he said, "I'll do what I can to help you. Go see if you can find some ice. And don't worry."

I went out on the balcony, seeing the tops of their heads. They were still milling around, the juke box baying, the piano thumping, and over at the end of the room, drenched with beer, Supercargo lay like a spent horse upon the bar.

Starting down, I noticed a large piece of ice glinting in the remains of an abandoned drink and seized its coldness in my hot hand and hurried back to the room.

The vet sat staring at Mr. Norton, who now breathed with a slightly irregular sound.

"You were quick," the man said, as he stood and reached for the ice. "Swift with the speed of anxiety," he added, as if to himself. "Hand me that clean towel—there, from beside the basin."

I handed him one, seeing him fold the ice inside it and apply it to Mr. Norton's face.

"Is he all right?" I said.

"He will be in a few minutes. What happened to him?"

"I took him for a drive," I said.

"Did you have an accident or something?"

"No," I said. "He just talked to a farmer and the heat knocked him out . . . Then we got caught in the mob downstairs."

"How old is he?"

"I don't know, but he's one of the trustees . . ."

"One of the very first, no doubt," he said, dabbing at the blue-veined eyes. "A trustee of consciousness."

"What was that?" I asked.

"Nothing . . . There now, he's coming out of it."

I had an impulse to run out of the room. I feared what Mr. Norton would say to me, the expression that might come into his eyes. And yet, I was afraid to leave. My eyes could not leave the face with its flickering lids. The head moved from side to side in the pale glow of the light bulb, as though denying some insistent voice which I could not hear. Then the lids opened, revealing pale pools of blue vagueness that finally solidified into points that froze upon the vet, who looked down unsmilingly.

Men like us did not look at a man like Mr. Norton in that manner, and I stepped hurriedly forward.

"He's a real doctor, sir," I said.

"I'll explain," the vet said. "Get a glass of water."

I hesitated. He looked at me firmly. "Get the water," he said, turning to help Mr. Norton to sit up.

Outside I asked Edna for a glass of water and she led me down the hall to a small kitchen, drawing it for me from a green old-fashioned cooler.

"I got some good liquor, baby, if you want to give him a drink," she said.

"This will do," I said. My hands trembled so that the water spilled. When I returned, Mr. Norton was sitting up unaided, carrying on a conversation with the vet.

"Here's some water, sir," I said, extending the glass.

He took it. "Thank you," he said.

"Not too much," the vet cautioned.

"Your diagnosis is exactly that of my specialist," Mr. Norton said, "and I went to several fine physicians before one could diagnose it. How did you know?"

"I too was a specialist," the vet said.

"But how? Only a few men in the whole country possess the knowledge—"

"Then one of them is an inmate of a semi-madhouse," the vet said. "But there's nothing mysterious about it. I escaped for awhile—I went to France with the Army Medical Corps and remained there after the Armistice to study and practice."

"Oh yes, and how long were you in France?" Mr. Norton asked.

"Long enough," he said. "Long enough to forget some fundamentals which I should never have forgotten."

"What fundamentals?" Mr. Norton said. "What do you mean?"

The vet smiled and cocked his head. "Things about life. Such things as most peasants and folk peoples almost always know through experience, though seldom through conscious thought . . ."

"Pardon me, sir," I said to Mr. Norton, "but now that you feel better, shouldn't we go?"

"Not just yet," he said. Then to the doctor, "I'm very interested. What happened to you?" A drop of water caught in one of his eyebrows glittered like a chip of active diamond. I went over and sat on a chair. Damn this vet to hell!

"Are you sure you would like to hear?" the vet asked.

"Why, of course."

"Then perhaps the young fellow should go downstairs and wait . . ."

The sound of shouting and destruction welled up from below as I opened the door.

"No, perhaps you should stay," the fat man said. "Perhaps had I overheard some of what I'm about to tell you when I was a student up there on the hill, I wouldn't be the casualty that I am."

"Sit down, young man," Mr. Norton ordered. "So you were a student at the college," he said to the vet.

I sat down again, worrying about Dr. Bledsoe as the fat man told Mr. Norton of his attending college, then becoming a physician and going to France during the World War.

"Were you a successful physician?" Mr. Norton said.

"Fairly so. I performed a few brain surgeries that won me some small attention."

"Then why did you return?"

"Nostalgia," the vet said.

"Then what on earth are you doing here in this . . . ?" Mr. Norton said, "With your ability . . ."

"Ulcers," the fat man said.

"That's terribly unfortunate, but why should ulcers stop your career?"

"Not really, but I learned along with the ulcers that my work could bring me no dignity," the vet said.

"Now you sound bitter," Mr. Norton said, just as the door flew open.

A brown-skinned woman with red hair looked in. "How's white-folks making out?" she said, staggering inside. "White-folks, baby, you done come to. You want a drink?"

"Not now, Hester," the vet said. "He's still a little weak."

"He sho looks it. That's how come he needs a drink. Put some iron in his blood."

"Now, now, Hester."

"Okay, okay . . . But what y'all doing looking like you at a funeral? Don't you know this is the Golden Day?" she staggered toward me, belching elegantly and reeling. "Just look at y'all. Here school-boy looks like he's scared to death. And white-folks here is acting like y'all two strange poodles. Be happy y'all! I'm going down and get Halley to send you up some drinks." She patted Mr. Norton's cheek as she went past and I saw him turn a glowing red. "Be happy, white-folks."

"Ah hah!" the vet laughed, "you're blushing, which means that you're better. Don't be embarrassed. Hester is a great humanitarian, a thera- pist of generous nature and great skill, and the possessor of a healing touch. Her catharsis is absolutely tremendous—ha, ha!"

"You do look better, sir," I said, anxious to get out of the place. I could understand the vet's words but not what they conveyed, and Mr. Norton looked as uncomfortable as I felt. The one thing which I did know was that the vet was acting toward the white man with a free- dom which could only bring on trouble. I wanted to tell Mr. Norton that the man was crazy and yet I received a fearful satisfaction from hearing him talk as he had to a white man. With the girl it was differ- ent. A woman usually got away with things a man never could.

I was wet with anxiety, but the vet talked on, ignoring the interrup- tion.

"Rest, rest," he said, fixing Mr. Norton with his eyes. "The clocks are all set back and the forces of destruction are rampant down below. They might suddenly realize that you are what you are, and then your life wouldn't be worth a piece of bankrupt stock. You would be can- celed, perforated, voided, become the recognized magnet attracting loose screws. Then what would you do? Such men are beyond money, and with Supercargo down, out like a felled ox, they know nothing of value. To some, you are the great white father, to others the lyncher of souls, but for all, you are confusion come even into the Golden Day."

"What are you talking about?" I said, thinking: *Lyncher?* He was getting wilder than the men downstairs. I didn't dare look at Mr. Nor- ton, who made a sound of protest.

The vet frowned. "It is an issue which I can confront only by evad- ing it. An utterly stupid proposition, and these hands so lovingly trained to master a scalpel yearn to caress a trigger. I returned to save life and I was refused," he said. "Ten men in masks drove me out from the city at midnight and beat me with whips for saving a human life. And I was forced to the utmost degradation because I possessed skilled hands and the belief that my knowledge could bring me dignity—not wealth, only dignity—and other men health!"

Then suddenly he fixed me with his eyes. "And now, do you under- stand?"

"What?" I said.

"What you've heard!"

"I don't know."

"Why?"

I said, "I really think it's time we left."

"You see," he said turning to Mr. Norton, "he has eyes and ears and a good distended African nose, but he fails to understand the sim- ple facts of life. *Understand.* Understand? It's worse than that. He re- gisters with his senses but short-circuits his brain. Nothing has meaning. He takes it in but he doesn't digest it. Already he is—well, bless my soul! Behold! a walking zombie! Already he's learned to repress not only his emotions but his humanity. He's invisible, a walking personification of the Negative, the most perfect achievement of your dreams, sir! The mechanical man!"

Mr. Norton looked amazed.

"Tell me," the vet said, suddenly calm. "Why have you been interested in the school, Mr. Norton?"

"Out of a sense of my destined role," Mr. Norton said shakily. "I felt, and I still feel, that your people are in some important manner tied to my destiny."

"What do you mean, destiny?" the vet said.

"Why, the success of my work, of course."

"I see. And would you recognize it if you saw it?"

"Why, of course I would," Mr. Norton said indignantly. "I've watched it grow each year I've returned to the campus."

"Campus? Why the campus?"

"It is there that my destiny is being made."

The vet exploded with laughter. "The campus, what a destiny!" He stood and walked around the narrow room, laughing. Then he stopped as suddenly as he had begun.

"You will hardly recognize it, but it is very fitting that you came to the Golden Day with the young fellow," he said.

"I came out of illness—or rather, he brought me," Mr. Norton said.

"Of course, but you came, and it was fitting."

"What do you mean?" Mr. Norton said with irritation.

"A little child shall lead them," the vet said with a smile. "But seriously, because you both fail to understand what is happening to you. You cannot see or hear or smell the truth of what you see—and you, looking for destiny! It's classic! And the boy, this automaton, he was made of the very mud of the region and he sees far less than you. Poor stumblers, neither of you can see the other. To you he is a mark on the score-card of your achievement, a thing and not a man; a child, or even less—a black amorphous thing. And you, for all your power, are not a man to him, but a God, a force—"

Mr. Norton stood abruptly. "Let us go, young man," he said angrily.

"No, listen. He believes in you as he believes in the beat of his heart. He believes in that great false wisdom taught slaves and pragmatists alike, that white is right. I can tell you *his* destiny. He'll do your bidding, and for that his blindness is his chief asset. He's your man, friend. Your man and your destiny. Now the two of you descend the stairs into chaos and get the hell out of here. I'm sick of both of you pitiful obscenities! Get out before I do you both the favor of bashing in your heads!"

I saw his motion toward the big white pitcher on the washstand and stepped between him and Mr. Norton, guiding Mr. Norton swiftly through the doorway. Looking back, I saw him leaning against the wall making a sound that was a blending of laughter and tears.

"Hurry, the man is as insane as the rest," Mr. Norton said.

"Yes, sir," I said, noticing a new note in his voice.

The balcony was now as noisy as the floor below. The girls and drunken vets were stumbling about with drinks in their hands. Just as we went past an open door Edna saw us and grabbed my arm.

"Where you taking white-folks?" she demanded.

"Back to school," I said, shaking her off.

"You don't want to go up there, white-folks, baby," she said. I tried to push past her. "I ain't lying," she said. "I'm the best little home-maker in the business."

"Okay, but please let us alone," I pleaded. "You'll get me into trouble."

We were going down the stairs into the milling men now and she started to scream, "Pay me then! If he's too good for me, let him pay!"

And before I could stop her she had pushed Mr. Norton, and both of us were stumbling swiftly down the stairs. I landed against a man who looked up with the anonymous familiarity of a drunk and shoved me hard away. I saw Mr. Norton spin past as I sank farther into the crowd. Somewhere I could hear the girl screaming and Halley's voice yelling, "Hey! Hey! Hey, now!" Then I was aware of fresh air and saw that I was near the door and pushed my way free and stood panting and preparing to plunge back for Mr. Norton—when I heard Halley calling, "Make way y'all!" and saw him piloting Mr. Norton to the door.

"Whew!" he said, releasing the white man and shaking his huge head.

"Thanks, Halley—" I said and got no further.

I saw Mr. Norton, his face pale again, his white suit rumpled, topple and fall, his head scraping against the screen of the door.

"Hey!"

I opened the door and raised him up.

"Goddamit, out agin," Halley said. "How come you bring this white man here, school-boy?"

"Is he dead?"

"DEAD!" he said, stepping back indignantly. "He *caint* die!"

"What'll I do, Halley?"

"Not in my place, he caint die," he said, kneeling.

Mr. Norton looked up. "No one is dead or dying," he said acidly. "Remove your hands!"

Halley fell away, surprised. "I sho am glad. You sho you all right? I thought sho you was dead this time."

"For God's sake, be quiet!" I exploded nervously. "You should be glad that he's all right."

Mr. Norton was visibly angry now, a raw place showing on his fore-head, and I hurried ahead of him to the car. He climbed in unaided, and I got under the wheel, smelling the heated odor of mints and cigar smoke. He was silent as I drove away.

HIDDEN NAME AND COMPLEX FATE

A WRITER'S EXPERIENCE IN THE UNITED STATES

In *Green Hills of Africa,* Ernest Hemingway reminds us that both Tolstoy and Stendhal had seen war, that Flaubert had seen a revolu-tion and the Commune, that Dostoievsky had been sent to Siberia and that such experiences were important in shaping the art of these great masters. And he goes on to observe that "writers are forged in injustice as a sword is forged." He declined to describe the many personal forms which injustice may take in this chaotic world—who would be so mad as to try?—nor does he go into the personal wounds which each of these writers sustained. Now, however, thanks to his brother and sister, we do know something of the injustice in which he himself was forged, and this knowledge has been added to what we have long known of Hemingway's artistic temper.

In the end, however, it is the quality of his art which is primary. It is the art which allows the wars and revolutions which he knew, and the personal and social injustice which he suffered, to lay claims upon our attention; for it was through his art that they achieved their most enduring meaning. It is a matter of outrageous irony, perhaps, but in literature the great social clashes of history no less than the painful experience of the individual are secondary to the meaning which they take on through the skill, the talent, the imagination and personal vision of the writer who transforms them into art. Here they are re-duced to more manageable proportions; here they are imbued with humane values; here, injustice and catastrophe become less important in themselves than what the writer makes of them. This is *not* true, however, of the writer's struggle with that recalcitrant angel called Art; and it was through *this* specific struggle that Ernest Hemingway became *Hemingway* (now refined to a total body of transcendent work, after forty years of being endlessly dismembered and resurrected, as it continues to be, in the styles, the themes, the sense of life and literature of countless other writers). And it was through this struggle with form that he became the master, the culture hero, whom we have come to know and admire.

Address sponsored by the Gertrude Clarke Whittall Foundation, Library of Con-gress, January 6, 1964.

It was suggested that it might be of interest if I discussed here this evening some of my notions of the writer's experience in the United States, hence I have evoked the name of Hemingway, not by way of inviting far-fetched comparisons but in order to establish a perspective, a set of assumptions from which I may speak, and in an attempt to avoid boring you by emphasizing those details of racial hardship which for some forty years now have been evoked whenever writers of my own cultural background have essayed their experience in public.

I do this *not* by way of denying totally the validity of these by now stylized recitals, for I have shared and still share many of their detailed injustices—what Negro can escape them?—but by way of suggesting that they are, at least in a discussion of a writer's experience, as *writer*, as artist, somewhat beside the point.

For we select neither our parents, our race nor our nation; these occur to us out of the love, the hate, the circumstances, the fate, of others. But we *do* become writers out of an act of will, out of an act of choice; a dim, confused and ofttimes regrettable choice, perhaps, but choice nevertheless. And what happens thereafter causes all those experiences which occurred before we began to function as writers to take on a special quality of uniqueness. If this does not happen then as far as writing goes, the experiences have been misused. If we do not make of them a value, if we do not transform them into forms and images of meaning which they did not possess before, then we have failed as artists.

Thus for a writer to insist that his personal suffering is of special interest in itself, or simply because he belongs to a particular racial or religious group, is to advance a claim for special privileges which members of his group who are not writers would be ashamed to demand. The kindest judgment one can make of this point of view is that it reveals a sad misunderstanding of the relationship between suffering and art. Thomas Mann and André Gide have told us much of this and there are critics, like Edmund Wilson, who have told of the connection between the wound and the bow.

As I see it, it is through the process of making artistic forms—plays, poems, novels—out of one's experience that one becomes a writer, and it is through this process, this struggle, that the writer helps give meaning to the experience of the group. And it is the process of mastering the discipline, the techniques, the fortitude, the culture, through which this is made possible that constitutes the writer's real experience as *writer*, as artist. If this sounds like an argument for the artist's withdrawal from social struggles, I would recall to you W. H. Auden's comment to the effect that:

> In our age, the mere making of a work of art is itself a political act. So long as artists exist, making what they please, and think they ought to make, even if it is not terribly good, even if it appeals to only a

handful of people, they remind the Management of something managers need to be reminded of, namely, that the managed are people with faces, not anonymous members, that *Homo Laborans* is also *Homo Ludens. . . .*

Without doubt, even the most *engagé* writer—and I refer to true artists, not to artists *manqués*—begin their careers in play and puzzlement, in dreaming over the details of the world in which they become conscious of themselves.

Let Tar Baby, that enigmatic figure from Negro folklore, stand for the world. He leans, black and gleaming, against the wall of life utterly noncommittal under our scrutiny, our questioning, starkly unmoving before our naïve attempts at intimidation. Then we touch him playfully and before we can say *Sonny Liston!* we find ourselves stuck. Our playful investigations become a labor, a fearful struggle, an *agon.* Slowly we perceive that our task is to learn the proper way of freeing ourselves to develop, in other words, technique.

Sensing this, we give him our sharpest attention, we question him carefully, we struggle with more subtlety; while he, in his silent way, holds on, demanding that we perceive the necessity of calling him by his true name as the price of our freedom. It is unfortunate that he has so many, many "true names"—all spelling chaos; and in order to discover even one of these we must first come into the possession of our own names. For it is through our names that we first place ourselves in the world. Our names, being the gift of others, must be made our own.

Once while listening to the play of a two-year-old girl who did not know she was under observation, I heard her saying over and over again, at first with questioning and then with sounds of growing satisfaction, "I am Mimi Livisay? . . . *I* am Mimi Livisay. I *am* Mimi Livisay . . . I am *Mimi* Li-vi-say! I am Mimi . . ."

And in deed and in fact she was—or became so soon thereafter, by working playfully to establish the unity between herself and her name.

For many of us this is far from easy. We must learn to wear our names within all the noise and confusion of the environment in which we find ourselves; make them the center of all of our associations with the world, with man and with nature. We must charge them with all our emotions, our hopes, hates, loves, aspirations. They must become our masks and our shields and the containers of all those values and traditions which we learn and/or imagine as being the meaning of our familial past.

And when we are reminded so constantly that we bear, as Negroes, names originally possessed by those who owned our enslaved grandparents, we are apt, especially if we are potential writers, to be more than ordinarily concerned with the veiled and mysterious events, the fusions of blood, the furtive couplings, the business transactions, the violations of faith and loyalty, the assaults; yes, and the unrecognized and unrecognizable loves through which our names were handed down unto us.

So charged with emotion does this concern become for some of us, that we have, earlier, the example of the followers of Father Divine and, now, the Black Muslims, discarding their original names in rejection of the bloodstained, the brutal, the sinful images of the past. Thus they would declare new identities, would clarify a new program of intention and destroy the verbal evidence of a willed and ritualized discontinuity of blood and human intercourse.

Not all of us, actually only a few, seek to deal with our names in this manner. We take what we have and make of them what we can. And there are even those who know where the old broken connections lie, who recognize their relatives across the chasm of historical denial and the artificial barriers of society, and who see themselves as bearers of many of the qualities which were admirable in the original sources of their common line (Faulkner has made much of this); and I speak here not of mere forgiveness, nor of obsequious insensitivity to the outrages symbolized by the denial and the division, but of the conscious acceptance of the harsh realities of the human condition, of the ambiguities and hypocrisies of human history as they have played themselves out in the United States.

Perhaps, taken in aggregate, these European names which (sometimes with irony, sometimes with pride, but always with personal investment) represent a certain triumph of the spirit, speaking to us of those who rallied, reassembled and transformed themselves and who under dismembering pressures refused to die. "Brothers and sisters," I once heard a Negro preacher exhort, "let us make up our faces before the world, and our names shall sound throughout the land with honor! For we ourselves are our *true* names, not their epithets! So let us, I say, Make Up Our Faces and Our Minds!"

Perhaps my preacher had read T. S. Eliot, although I doubt it. And in actuality, it was unnecessary that he do so, for a concern with names and naming was very much a part of that special area of American culture from which I come, and it is precisely for this reason that this example should come to mind in a discussion of my own experience as a writer.

Undoubtedly, writers begin their *conditioning* as manipulators of words long before they become aware of literature—certain Freudians would say at the breast. Perhaps. But if so, that is far too early to be of use at this moment. Of this, though, I am certain: that despite the misconceptions of those educators who trace the reading difficulties experienced by large numbers of Negro children in Northern schools to their Southern background, these children are, in *their* familiar

South, facile manipulators of words. I know, too, that the Negro community is deadly in its ability to create nicknames and to spot all that is ludicrous in an unlikely name or that which is incongruous in conduct. Names are not qualities; nor are words, in this particular sense, actions. To assume that they are could cost one his life many times a day. Language skills depend to a large extent upon a knowledge of the details, the manners, the objects, the folkways, the psychological patterns, of a given environment. Humor and wit depend upon much the same awareness, and so does the suggestive power of names.

"A small brown bowlegged Negro with the name 'Franklin D. Roosevelt Jones' might sound like a clown to someone who looks at him from the outside," said my friend Albert Murray, "but on the other hand he just might turn out to be a hell of a fireside operator. He might just lie back in all of that comic juxtaposition of names and manipulate you deaf, dumb and blind—and you not even suspecting it, because you're thrown out of stance by his name! There you are, so dazzled by the F.D.R. image—which you *know* you can't see—and so delighted with your own superior position that you don't realize that it's *Jones* who must be confronted."

Well, as you must suspect, all of this speculation on the matter of names has a purpose, and now, because it is tied up so ironically with my own experience as a writer, I must turn to my own name.

For in the dim beginnings, before I ever thought consciously of writing, there was my own name, and there was, doubtless, a certain magic in it. From the start I was uncomfortable with it, and in my earliest years it caused me much puzzlement. Neither could I understand what a poet was, nor why, exactly, my father had chosen to name me after one. Perhaps I could have understood it perfectly well had he named me after his own father, but that name had been given to an older brother who died and thus was out of the question. But why hadn't he named me after a hero, such as Jack Johnson, or a soldier like Colonel Charles Young, or a great seaman like Admiral Dewey, or an educator like Booker T. Washington, or a great orator and abolitionist like Frederick Douglass? Or again, why hadn't he named me (as so many Negro parents had done) after President Teddy Roosevelt?

Instead, he named me after someone called Ralph Waldo Emerson, and then, when I was three, he died. It was too early for me to have understood his choice, although I'm sure he must have explained it many times, and it was also too soon for me to have made the connection between my name and my father's love for reading. Much later, after I began to write and work with words, I came to suspect that he was aware of the suggestive powers of names and of the magic involved in naming.

I recall an odd conversation with my mother during my early teens in which she mentioned their interest in, of all things, prenatal culture! But for a long time I actually knew only that my father read a lot, and that he admired this remote Mr. Emerson, who was something called a "poet and philosopher"—so much so that he named his second son after him.

I knew, also, that whatever his motives, the combination of names he'd given me caused me no end of trouble from the moment when I could talk well enough to respond to the ritualized question which grownups put to very young children. Emerson's name was quite familiar to Negroes in Oklahoma during those days when World War I was brewing, and adults, eager to show off their knowledge of literary figures, and obviously amused by the joke implicit in such a small brown nubbin of a boy carrying around such a heavy moniker, would invariably repeat my first two names and then to my great annoyance, they'd add "Emerson."

And I, in my confusion, would reply, "No, *no, I'm* not Emerson; he's the little boy who lives next door." Which only made them laugh all the louder. "Oh no," they'd say, "*you're* Ralph Waldo Emerson," while I had fantasies of blue murder.

For a while the presence next door of my little friend, Emerson, made it unnecessary for me to puzzle too often over this peculiar adult confusion. And since there were other Negro boys named Ralph in the city, I came to suspect that there was something about the combination of names which produced their laughter. Even today I know of only one other Ralph who had as much comedy made out of his name, a campus politician and deep-voiced orator whom I knew at Tuskegee, who was called in friendly ribbing, *Ralph Waldo Emerson Edgar Allan Poe,* spelled Powe. This must have been quite a trial for him, but I had been initiated much earlier.

During my early school years the name continued to puzzle me, for it constantly evoked in the faces of others some secret. It was as though I possessed some treasure or some defect, which was invisible to my own eyes and ears; something which I had but did not *possess,* like a piece of property in South Carolina, which was mine but which I could not have until some future time. I recall finding, about this time, while seeking adventure in back alleys—which possess for boys a superiority over playgrounds like that which kitchen utensils possess over toys designed for infants—a large photographic lens. I remember nothing of its optical qualities, of its speed or color correction, but it gleamed with crystal mystery and it was beautiful.

Mounted handsomely in a tube of shiny brass, it spoke to me of distant worlds of possibility. I played with it, looking through it with squinted eyes, holding it in shafts of sunlight, and tried to use it for a magic lantern. But most of this was as unrewarding as my attempts to make the music come from a phonograph record by holding the needle in my fingers.

I could burn holes through newspapers with it, or I could pretend that it was a telescope, the barrel of a cannon, or the third eye of a monster—*I* being the monster—but I could do nothing at all about its proper function of making images; nothing to make it yield its secret. But I could not discard it.

Older boys sought to get it away from me by offering knives or tops, agate marbles or whole zoos of grass snakes and horned toads in trade, but I held on to it. No one, not even the white boys I knew, had such a lens, and it was my own good luck to have found it. Thus I would hold on to it until such time as I could acquire the parts needed to make it function. Finally I put it aside and it remained buried in my box of treasures, dusty and dull, to be lost and forgotten as I grew older and became interested in music.

I had reached by now the grades where it was necessary to learn something about Mr. Emerson and what he had written, such as the "Concord Hymn" and the essay "Self-Reliance," and in following his advice, I reduced the "Waldo" to a simple and, I hoped, mysterious "W," and in my own reading I avoided his works like the plague. I could no more deal with my name—I shall never really master it—than I could find a creative use for my lens. Fortunately there were other problems to occupy my mind. Not that I forgot my fascination with names, but more about that later.

Negro Oklahoma City was starkly lacking in writers. In fact, there was only Roscoe Dungee, the editor of the local Negro newspaper and a very fine editorialist in that valuable tradition of personal journalism which is now rapidly disappearing; a writer who in his emphasis upon the possibilities for justice offered by the Constitution anticipated the anti-segregation struggle by decades. There were also a few reporters who drifted in and out, but these were about all. On the level of *conscious* culture the Negro community was biased in the direction of music.

These were the middle and late twenties, remember, and the state was still a new frontier state. The capital city was one of the great centers for southwestern jazz, along with Dallas and Kansas City. Orchestras which were to become famous within a few years were constantly coming and going. As were the blues singers—Ma Rainey and Ida Cox, and the old bands like that of King Oliver. But best of all, thanks to Mrs. Zelia N. Breaux, there was an active and enthusiastic school music program through which any child who had the interest and the talent could learn to play an instrument and take part in the band, the orchestra, the brass quartet. And there was a yearly operetta and a chorus and a glee club. Harmony was taught for four years and the music appreciation program was imperative. European folk dances were taught throughout the Negro school system, and we were also taught complicated patterns of military drill.

I tell you this to point out that although there were no incentives to write, there was ample opportunity to receive an artistic discipline. Indeed, once one picked up an instrument it was difficult to escape. If you chafed at the many rehearsals of the school band or orchestra and were drawn to the many small jazz groups, you were likely to discover that the jazzmen were apt to rehearse far more than the school band; it was only that they seemed to enjoy themselves better and to possess a freedom of imagination which we were denied at school. And one soon learned that the wild, transcendent moments which occurred at dances or "battles of music," moments in which memorable improvisations were ignited, depended upon a dedication to a discipline which was observed even when rehearsals had to take place in the crowded quarters of Halley Richardson's shoeshine parlor. It was not the place which counted, although a large hall with good acoustics was preferred, but what one did to perfect one's performance.

If this talk of musical discipline gives the impression that there were no forces working to nourish one who would one day blunder, after many a twist and turn, into writing, I am misleading you. And here I might give you a longish lecture on the Ironies and Uses of Segregation. When I was a small child there was no library for Negroes in our city; and not until a Negro minister invaded the main library did we get one. For it was discovered that there was no law, only custom, which held that we could not use these public facilities. The results were the quick renting of two large rooms in a Negro office building (the recent site of a pool hall), the hiring of a young Negro librarian, the installation of shelves and a hurried stocking of the walls with any and every book possible. It was, in those first days, something of a literary chaos.

But how fortunate for a boy who loved to read! I started with the fairy tales and quickly went through the junior fiction; then through the Westerns and the detective novels, and very soon I was reading the classics—only I didn't know it. There were also the Haldeman Julius Blue Books, which seem to have floated on the air down from Girard, Kansas; the syndicated columns of O. O. McIntyre, and the copies of *Vanity Fair* and the *Literary Digest* which my mother brought home from work—how could I ever join uncritically in the heavy-handed attacks on the so-called Big Media which have become so common today?

There were also the pulp magazines and, more important, that other library which I visited when I went to help my adopted grandfather, J. D. Randolph (my parents had been living in his rooming house when I was born), at his work as custodian of the law library of the

Oklahoma State Capitol. Mr. Randolph had been one of the first teachers in what became Oklahoma City; and he'd also been one of the leaders of a group who walked from Gallatin, Tennessee, to the Oklahoma Territory. He was a tall man, as brown as smoked leather, who looked like the Indians with whom he'd herded horses in the early days.

And while his status was merely the custodian of the law library, I was to see the white legislators come down on many occasions to question him on points of law, and often I was to hear him answer without recourse to the uniform rows of books on the shelves. This was a thing to marvel at in itself, and the white lawmakers did so, but even more marvelous, ironic, intriguing, haunting—call it what you will—is the fact that the Negro who knew the answers was named after Jefferson Davis. What Tennessee lost, Oklahoma was to gain, and after gaining it (a gift of courage, intelligence, fortitude and grace), used it only in concealment and, one hopes, with embarrassment.

So, let us, I say, make up our faces and our minds!

In the loosely structured community of that time, knowledge, news of other ways of living, ancient wisdom, the latest literary fads, hate literature—for years I kept a card warning Negroes away from the polls, which had been dropped by the thousands from a plane which circled over the Negro community—information of all kinds, found its level, catch-as-catch can, in the minds of those who were receptive to it. Not that there was no conscious structuring—I read my first Shaw and Maupassant, my first Harvard Classics in the home of a friend whose parents were products of that stream of New England education which had been brought to Negroes by the young and enthusiastic white teachers who staffed the schools set up for the freedmen after the Civil War. These parents were both teachers and there were others like them in our town.

But the places where a rich oral literature was truly functional were the churches, the schoolyards, the barbershops, the cotton-picking camps; places where folklore and gossip thrived. The drug store where I worked was such a place, where on days of bad weather the older men would sit with their pipes and tell tall tales, hunting yarns and homely versions of the classics. It was here that I heard stories of searching for buried treasure and of headless horsemen, which I was told were my own father's versions told long before. There were even recitals of popular verse, "The Shooting of Dan McGrew," and, along with these, stories of Jesse James, of Negro outlaws and black United States marshals, of slaves who became the chiefs of Indian tribes and of the exploits of Negro cowboys. There was both truth and fantasy in this, intermingled in the mysterious fashion of literature.

Writers, in their formative period, absorb into their consciousness much that has no special value until much later, and often much which is of no special value even then—perhaps, beyond the fact that it throbs with affect and mystery and in it "time and pain and royalty in the blood" are suspended in imagery. So, long before I thought of writing, I was claimed by weather, by speech rhythms, by Negro voices and their different idioms, by husky male voices and by the high shrill singing voices of certain Negro women, by music; by tight spaces and by wide spaces in which the eyes could wander; by death, by newly born babies, by manners of various kinds, company manners and street manners; the manners of white society and those of our own high society; and by interracial manners; by street fights, circuses and ministrel shows; by vaudeville and moving pictures, by prize fights and foot races, baseball games and football matches. By spring floods and blizzards, catalpa worms and jack rabbits; honeysuckle and snap-dragons (which smelled like old cigar butts); by sunflowers and holly-hocks, raw sugar cane and baked yams; pigs' feet, chili and blue haw ice cream. By parades, public dances and jam sessions, Easter sunrise ceremonies and large funerals. By contests between fire-and-brimstone preachers and by presiding elders who got "laughing-happy" when moved by the spirit of God.

I was impressed by expert players of the "dozens" and certain notorious bootleggers of corn whiskey. By jazz musicians and fortune-tellers and by men who did anything well; by strange sicknesses and by interesting brick or razor scars; by expert cursing vocabularies as well as by exalted praying and terrifying shouting, and by transcendent playing or singing of the blues. I was fascinated by old ladies, those who had seen slavery and those who were defiant of white folk and black alike; by the enticing walks of prostitutes and by the limping walks affected by Negro hustlers, especially those who wore Stetson hats, expensive shoes with well-starched overalls, usually with a diamond stickpin (when not in hock) in their tieless collars as their gambling uniforms.

And there were the blind men who preached on corners, and the blind men who sang the blues to the accompaniment of washboard and guitar; and the white junkmen who sang mountain music and the famous hucksters of fruit and vegetables.

And there was the Indian–Negro confusion. There were Negroes who were part Indian and who lived on reservations, and Indians who had children who lived in towns as Negroes, and Negroes who were Indians and traveled back and forth between the groups with no trouble. And Indians who were as wild as wild Negroes and others who were as solid and as steady as bankers. There were the teachers, too, inspiring teachers and villainous teachers who chased after the girl students, and certain female teachers who one wished would chase after young male students. And a handsome old principal of military bearing who had been blemished by his classmates at West Point when they discovered on the eve of graduation that he was a Negro. There were certain Jews, Mexicans, Chinese cooks, a German orchestra conductor and an English grocer who owned a Franklin touring car. And certain Negro mechanics—"Cadillac Slim," "Sticks" Walker, Buddy Bunn and Oscar Pitman—who had so assimilated the automobile that they seemed to be behind a steering wheel even as they walked the streets or danced with girls. And there were the whites who despised us and the others who shared our hardships and our joys.

There is much more, but this is sufficient to indicate some of what was present even in a segregated community to form the background of my work, my sense of life.

And now comes the next step. I went to Tuskegee to study music, hoping to become a composer of symphonies and there, during my second year, I read *The Waste Land* and that, although I was then unaware of it, was the real transition to writing.

Mrs. L. C. McFarland had taught us much of Negro history in grade school and from her I'd learned of the New Negro Movement of the twenties, of Langston Hughes, Countee Cullen, Claude McKay, James Weldon Johnson and the others. They had inspired pride and had given me a closer identification with poetry (by now, oddly enough, I seldom thought of my hidden name), but with music so much on my mind it never occurred to me to try to imitate them. Still I read their work and was excited by the glamour of the Harlem which emerged from their poems and it was good to know that there were Negro writers.—Then came *The Waste Land.*

I was much more under the spell of literature than I realized at the time. *Wuthering Heights* had caused me an agony of unexpressible emotion and the same was true of *Jude the Obscure,* but *The Waste Land* seized my mind. I was intrigued by its power to move me while eluding my understanding. Somehow its rhythms were often closer to those of jazz than were those of the Negro poets, and even though I could not understand then, its range of allusion was as mixed and as varied as that of Louis Armstrong. Yet there were its discontinuities, its changes of pace and its hidden system of organization which escaped me.

There was nothing to do but look up the references in the footnotes to the poem, and thus began my conscious education in literature.

For this, the library at Tuskegee was quite adequate and I used it. Soon I was reading a whole range of subjects drawn upon by the poet, and this led, in turn, to criticism and to Pound and Ford Madox Ford, Sherwood Anderson and Gertrude Stein, Hemingway and Fitzgerald and "round about 'til I was come" back to Melville and Twain—the writers who are taught and doubtlessly overtaught today. Perhaps it was my good luck that they were not taught at Tuskegee, I wouldn't know. But at the time I was playing, having an intellectually interesting good time.

Having given so much attention to the techniques of music, the process of learning something of the craft and intention of modern poetry and fiction seemed quite familiar. Besides, it was absolutely painless because it involved no deadlines or credits. Even then, however, a process which I described earlier had begun to operate. The more I learned of literature in this conscious way, the more the details of my background became transformed. I heard undertones in remembered conversations which had escaped me before, local customs took on a more universal meaning, values which I hadn't understood were revealed; some of the people whom I had known were diminished while others were elevated in stature. More important, I began to see my own possibilities with more objective, and in some ways, more hopeful eyes.

The following summer I went to New York seeking work, which I did not find, and remained there, but the personal transformation continued. Reading had become a conscious process of growth and discovery, a method of reordering the world. And that world had widened considerably.

At Tuskegee I had handled manuscripts which Prokofiev had given to Hazel Harrison, a Negro concert pianist who taught there and who had known him in Europe, and through Miss Harrison I had become aware of Prokofiev's symphonies. I had also become aware of the radical movement in politics and art, and in New York had begun reading the work of André Malraux, not only the fiction but chapters published from his *Psychology of Art*. And in my search for an expression of modern sensibility in the works of Negro writers I discovered Richard Wright. Shortly thereafter I was to meet Wright, and it was at his suggestion that I wrote both my first book review and my first short story. These were fatal suggestions.

For although I had tried my hand at poetry while at Tuskegee, it hadn't occurred to me that I might write fiction, but once he suggested it, it seemed the most natural thing to try. Fortunately for me, Wright, then on the verge of his first success, was eager to talk with a beginner and I was able to save valuable time in searching out those works in which writing was discussed as a craft. He guided me to Henry James' prefaces, to Conrad, to Joseph Warren Beach and to the letters of Dostoievsky. There were other advisers and other books involved, of course, but what is important here is that I was consciously concerned with the art of fiction, that almost from the beginning I was grappling quite consciously with the art through which I wished to realize myself. And this was not done in isolation; the Spanish Civil

War was now in progress and the Depression was still on. The world was being shaken up, and through one of those odd instances which occur to young provincials in New York, I was to hear Malraux make an appeal for the Spanish Loyalists at the same party where I first heard the folk singer Leadbelly perform. Wright and I were there seeking money for the magazine which he had come to New York to edit.

Art and politics; a great French novelist and a Negro folk singer; a young writer who was soon to publish *Uncle Tom's Children;* and I who had barely begun to study his craft. It is such accidents, such fortuitous meetings, which count for so much in our lives. I had never dreamed that I would be in the presence of Malraux, of whose work I became aware on my second day in Harlem when Langston Hughes suggested that I read *Man's Fate* and *Days of Wrath* before returning them to a friend of his. And it is this fortuitous circumstance which led to my selecting Malraux as a literary "ancestor," whom, unlike a relative, the artist is permitted to choose. There was in progress at the time all the agitation over the Scottsboro boys and the Herndon Case, and I was aware of both. I had to be; I myself had been taken off a freight train at Decatur, Alabama, only three years before while on my way to Tuskegee. But while I joined in the agitation for their release, my main energies went into learning to write.

I began to publish enough, and not too slowly, to justify my hopes for success, and as I continued, I made a most perplexing discovery; namely, that for all his conscious concern with technique, a writer did not so much create the novel as he was created *by* the novel. That is, one did not make an arbitrary gesture when one sought to write. And when I say that the novelist is created by the novel, I mean to remind you that fictional techniques are not a mere set of objective tools, but something much more intimate: a way of feeling, of seeing and of expressing one's sense of life. And the process of *acquiring* technique is a process of modifying one's responses, of learning to see and feel, to hear and observe, to evoke and evaluate the images of memory and of summoning up and directing the imagination; of learning to conceive of human values in the ways which have been established by the great writers who have developed and extended the art. And perhaps the writer's greatest freedom, as artist, lies precisely in his possession of technique; for it is through technique that he comes to possess and express the meaning of his life.

Perhaps at this point it would be useful to recapitulate the route—perhaps as mazelike as that of *Finnegan's Wake*—which I have been trying to describe; that which leads from the writer's discovery of a sense of purpose, which is that of becoming a writer, and then the involvement in the passionate struggle required to master a bit of technique, and then, as this begins to take shape, the disconcerting discovery that it is *technique* which transforms the individual before he is able in turn to transform it. And in that personal transformation he discovers something else: he discovers that he has taken on certain obligations, that he must not embarrass his chosen form, and that in order to avoid this he must develop taste. He learns—and this is most discouraging—that he is involved with values which turn in their *own* way, and not in the ways of politics, upon the central issues affecting his nation and his time. He learns that the American novel, from its first consciousness of itself as a literary form, has grappled with the meaning of the American experience; that it has been aware and has sought to define the nature of that experience by addressing itself to the specific details, the moods, the landscapes, the cityscapes, the tempo of American change. And that it has borne, at its best, the full weight of that burden of conscience and consciousness which Americans inherit as one of the results of the revolutionary circumstances of our national beginnings.

We began as a nation not through the accidents of race or religion or geography (Robert Penn Warren has dwelled on these circumstances) but when a group of men, *some* of them political philosophers, put down, upon what we now recognize as being quite sacred papers, their conception of the nation which they intended to establish on these shores. They described, as we know, the obligations of the state to the citizen, of the citizen to the state; they committed themselves to certain ideas of justice, just as they committed us to a system which would guarantee all of its citizens equality of opportunity.

I need not describe the problems which have arisen from these beginnings. I need only remind you that the contradiction between these noble ideals and the actualities of our conduct generated a guilt, an unease of spirit, from the very beginning, and that the American novel at its best has always been concerned with this basic moral predicament. During Melville's time and Twain's, it was an implicit aspect of their major themes; by the twentieth century and after the discouraging and traumatic effect of the Civil War and the Reconstruction it had gone underground, had become *understated.* Nevertheless it did not disappear completely and it is to be found operating in the work of Henry James as well as in that of Hemingway and Fitzgerald. And then (and as one who believes in the impelling moral function of the novel and who believes in the moral seriousness of the form) it pleases me no end that it comes into explicit statement again in the works of Richard Wright and William Faulkner, writers who lived close to moral and political problems which would not stay put underground.

I go into these details not to recapitulate the history of the American novel but to indicate the trend of thought which was set into motion when I began to discover the nature of that process with which

I was actually involved. Whatever the opinions and decisions of critics, a novelist must arrive at his own conclusions as to the meaning and function of the form with which he is engaged, and these are, in all modesty, some of mine.

In order to orient myself I also began to learn that the American novel had long concerned itself with the puzzle of the one-and-the-many; the mystery of how each of us, despite his origin in diverse regions, with our diverse racial, cultural, religious backgrounds, speaking his own diverse idiom of the American in his own accent, is, nevertheless, American. And with this concern with the implicit pluralism of the country and with the composite nature of the ideal character called "the American," there goes a concern with gauging the health of the American promise, with depicting the extent to which it was being achieved, being made manifest in our daily conduct.

And with all of this there still remained the specific concerns of literature. Among these is the need to keep literary standards high, the necessity of exploring new possibilities of language which would allow it to retain that flexibility and fidelity to the common speech which has been its glory since Mark Twain. For me this meant learning to add to it the wonderful resources of Negro American speech and idiom and to bring into range as fully and eloquently as possible the complex reality of the American experience as it shaped and was shaped by the lives of my own people.

Notice that I stress as "fully" as possible, because I would no more strive to write great novels by leaving out the complexity of circumstances which go to make up the Negro experience and which alone go to make the obvious injustice bearable, than I would think of preparing myself to become President of the United States simply by studying Negro American history or confining myself to studying those laws affecting civil rights.

For it seems to me that one of the obligations I took on when I committed myself to the art and form of the novel was that of striving for the broadest range, the discovery and articulation of the most exalted values. And I must squeeze these from the life which I know best. (A highly truncated impression of that life I attempted to convey to you earlier.)

If all this sounds a bit heady, remember that I did not destroy that troublesome middle name of mine, I only suppressed it. Sometimes it reminds me of my obligations to the man who named me.

It is our fate as human beings always to give up some good things for other good things, to throw off certain bad circumstances only to create others. Thus there is a value for the writer trying to give as thorough a report of social reality as possible. Only by doing so may we grasp and convey the cost of change. Only by considering the broadest accumulation of data may we make choices that are based upon our own hard-earned sense of reality. Speaking from my own special area of American culture, I feel that to embrace uncritically values which are extended to us by others is to reject the validity, even the sacredness, of our own experience. It is also to forget that the small share of reality which each of our diverse groups is able to snatch from the whirling chaos of history belongs not to the group alone, but to all of us. It is a property and a witness which can be ignored only to the danger of the entire nation.

I could suppress the name of my namesake out of respect for the achievements of its original bearer but I cannot escape the obligation of attempting to achieve some of the things which he asked of the American writer. As Henry James suggested, being an American is an arduous task, and for most of us, I suspect, the difficulty begins with the name.

Integration versus Black Nationalism

1954 to the present

5

In the period beginning in 1954, three startling events set the political tone, established the emotional climate, and influenced the choice and treatment of literary themes. These events freshly emphasized the difference between the idealism expressed in the American creed and the actual practices of the American people. They also intensified and stabilized the polarity which, since at least the beginning of the twentieth century, had seemed to draw many members of the Negro community into opposing clusters: in one group were the black nationalists, who clamored for complete separation of the races, while at the other extreme were those who appeared to favor absorption of the black minority into the value system and culture of the whites.

On May 17, 1954, the Supreme Court handed down a ruling in the Brown vs. Topeka Board of Education case which ultimately intended to do away with segregation in the public schools. The South's reluctance to comply with this decision generated a series of courtroom confrontations between the NAACP and the Department of Justice, on the one hand, and local and state public school officials on the other. Token integration finally, and grudgingly, resulted.

On December 5, 1955, a black dressmaker and minor official in the local branch of the NAACP refused to give up her seat to a white man on a crowded bus in Montgomery, Alabama. Since her refusal was contrary not only to law but also to custom, Mrs. Rosa Parks was arrested. The black community in Montgomery, like black communities across the nation, had long resented legalized racial discrimination, and now, under the leadership of a young Negro minister named Martin Luther King, Jr., they organized a boycott of the buses. It lasted for a year and ended only when the Supreme Court ruled that state and local laws requiring racial segregation in public transportation were unconstitutional. The Montgomery bus boycott was the first in a series of activities that swept the country and came to be called the "nonviolent protest movement."

On February 1, 1960, in Greensboro, North Carolina, four students from the predominantly Negro Agricultural and Technical College walked into the Woolworth store, sat down at the lunch counter which served only whites, and asked to be waited on. Service was refused, but they stayed until closing time. The next day other students joined them, and the group of young black people occupied all the seats so that no one could be served. This kind of tactic was later adapted to many different situations by white activists, by blacks, and by many other dissatisfied groups.

These events increased the momentum and expanded the dimensions of what has been described as a black revolution. Beginning with a nonviolent demand for racial equality, conflicting ideas about methods and immediate objectives soon developed. Change, yes. But how, and to what? These questions appeared to fix the polarity of thought and mood in the black community, while they left in the center the integrationists, mainly of the middle class, whom the black nationalists scorned as "Uncle Tom, brief case niggers," and whose life-style and world view the majority of young blacks seemed to find inappropriate to the times in which they lived.

While the integrationists and assimilationists fell relatively silent, the attitudes and point of view of the militants dominated the work of the younger writers of the period. Much of their writing was ostensibly directed only to a black audience and was able to appear, when examined in one frame of reference, anti-intellectual, anti-Establishment, and anti-white. It aimed at new forms, new themes, and even virtually a new language, but it often reflected the state of mind of men and women suffering various forms of oppression, often not even recognized as such. For this reason, their writing sometimes appeared to be a kind of overreaction: anger and rage long unexpressed sometimes suddenly and without apparent cause exploded into rejection and even total condemnation of the middle-class tradition. These writers strove for a "black aesthetic," constituted of principles which were never formally expressed, since they were known intuitively and based on life experiences shared by all the artists who agreed upon them. Those who found this aesthetic valid repudiated white concepts of reality and urged a "return to Africa"; there they hoped to find a tradition which would help explain their identity and a mythology which would illustrate it. The most representative black writers have themselves not returned to Africa; nevertheless, the search for an African heritage reinforced these writers' sense of self-esteem and gave them the confidence to create new themes: contemporary, black, American. These themes were frequently directed against what was seen to be the treachery of the white man, and while encouraging a new identity for the black, they often seemed even to favor destructive violence, the black ghetto, alienation, and thoughtless rage.

Though older Negro writers of this period tended to view their environment as they always had, many were influenced by younger contemporaries. James Baldwin's best novel, *Go Tell It on the Mountain,* which predates the black literary revolution, and much of his later work indicate the existence of a mind concerned with matters other than race. But in *Tell Me How Long the Train's Been Gone* (1968), Baldwin shows a more intense awareness of the search for a cultural identity among the members of the American black community. John O'Killens' novel *Youngblood* (1954) also predates LeRoi Jones, Larry Neal, and the new Black Arts movement, but his *And Then We Heard Thunder* (1963) takes up the favorite themes of the young rebels: the frequent social and political emasculation of the black male, the corruptive influence of white value systems, the emancipating power of militant black racism. Two of John A. Williams' novels recreate the black lover/white mistress relationship, a dramatic situation which like its obverse, the white lover/black mistress liaison, has been used frequently in novels by black writers. In *The Man Who Cried I Am* the situation has no great dramatic significance; but it does provide the context for dialogue loaded with thundering pro-black, anti-white language.

But language is perhaps the metaphor of experience, and when judging a creative writer's work, it is impossible to avoid considering his subjective experience. This experience is his source, the matrix of his emotions, the molder of his mind. Thus, though LeRoi Jones has stated his total commitment to blackness, the events that took place during his Greenwich Village days may have created in him a certain ambivalence toward race. For though he has often claimed that he seeks a black audience exclusively, he has seemed to set traps (as in the plays *Dutchman* and *The Slave*) unmistakably designed to snare a white audience. His repudiation of the Western cultural tradition is contradicted, paradoxically, by the context of much of his work, such as the milieu of his novel *The System of Dante's Hell*. His black militant, anti-white bitterness could appear to be almost a pose, a put-on, a public relations gimmick, when it in fact may have represented his attempts to find an identity by assuming several different identities in succession, the way a man might put on a suit of clothes to examine the fit. In many ways, there has been precious little "blackness" in Jones' work, so much of which is essentially poetry. Bitterness and condemnation of middle-class values are there but are not necessarily black; they are partly the result of the influences of other poets like Allen Ginsberg, Charles Olson, and Louis Zukovsky, but they are also partly a simple human cry of pain and rage in the face of a nearly intolerable racial injustice.

William Melvin Kelley and Ernest J. Gaines can be described as representatives of other literary rebels. Kelley's *A Different Drummer* and *A Drop of Patience* pursue a theme—the black man's alienation from the "definition-producing realities and the structures of established society"—that attempts so many variations that a lifetime of thought would scarcely exhaust it. Ernest Gaines' theme has been similar to Kelley's, although the selection included here shows the theme only obliquely. Carlene Hatcher Polite, Ronald Fair, Larry Neal, Jimmie Garrett, Sonia Sanchez, and even the playwright Ed

Bullins have produced too little about which to advance many critical judgments. Their work is in the black radical mode, but it does not necessarily forecast an everlasting commitment to that mode.

The autobiographical writing of the period, including the essays of James Baldwin, Harold Cruse, and Eldridge Cleaver, has been the most widely read. Claude Brown's *Manchild in the Promised Land* and the *Autobiography of Malcolm X* are forthright revelations of the hidden life of the black ghetto, of internalized conflict, and of tragic alienation. *Malcolm X* has an added dimension, for it is the life story of a brilliant and complex man who became the most conspicuous symbol of black America's social revolution. Neither *Manchild in the Promised Land* nor the *Autobiography* was influenced by the Black Arts movement, that "aesthetic and spiritual sister of the Black Power concept," as Larry Neal wrote. That movement sought a new and "separate symbolism, mythology, critique, and iconology."

The search began some time ago. It has not yet ended.

James Baldwin

(b. 1924)

JAMES BALDWIN'S PARENTS MIGRATED from the South to Harlem, where his father was a part-time minister. Baldwin himself became a preacher when he was fourteen but left the church at the age of seventeen. He was educated in the New York City schools and graduated from De Witt Clinton High School in 1942.

At De Witt Clinton, Baldwin edited the school literary magazine. By 1946, he had published a book review in *The Nation,* and he has since published widely and received numerous distinguished awards and fellowships, including the Eugene F. Saxton Memorial Trust Award (for *Go Tell It on the Mountain,* first version, 1945); the Guggenheim, Rosenwald, and *Partisan Review* Fellowships; the National Institute of Arts and Letters Award; and a Ford Foundation Grant-in-aid. Baldwin's short stories have appeared in Martha Foley's and O. Henry's series of "best short stories." His work has been translated into French, Italian, German, Japanese, Danish, Swedish, and other foreign languages.

Always sensitive and alert to the feeling of the black community, James Baldwin has expressed the Negro's attitude toward America powerfully and accurately. He is a prolific writer and has produced fiction, drama, and brilliant essays. Among his fiction works are *Go Tell It on the Mountain* (1953), *Giovanni's Room* (1956), *Another Country* (1962), *Going to Meet the Man* (short stories, 1965), and *Tell Me How Long the Train's Been Gone* (1968). His essays have been gathered into three volumes which prove that the essay is undoubtedly Baldwin's forte: *Notes of a Native Son* (1955), *Nobody Knows My Name* (1961), and *The Fire Next Time* (1963). His plays include *The Amen Corner* and *Blues for Mr. Charlie.*

"The Threshing Floor" comes from *Go Tell It on the Mountain;* "Letter to My Nephew" is from *The Fire Next Time.*

THE THRESHING-FLOOR

> *Then I buckled up my shoes,*
> *And I started.*

He knew, without knowing how it had happened, that he lay on the floor, in the dusty space before the altar which he and Elisha had cleaned; and knew that above him burned the yellow light which he had himself switched on. Dust was in his nostrils, sharp and terrible, and the feet of the saints, shaking the floor beneath him, raised small clouds of dust that filmed his mouth. He heard their cries, so far, so high above him—he could never rise that far. He was like a rock, a dead man's body, a dying bird, fallen from an awful height; something that had no power of itself, any more, to turn.

And something moved in John's body which was not John. He was invaded, set at naught, possessed. This power had struck John, in the head or in the heart; and, in a moment, wholly, filling him with an anguish that he could never in his life have imagined, that he surely could not endure, that even now he could not believe, had opened him up; had cracked him open, as wood beneath the axe cracks down the middle, as rocks break up; had ripped him and felled him in a moment, so that John had not felt the wound, but only the agony, had not felt the fall, but only the fear; and lay here, now, helpless, screaming, at the very bottom of darkness.

He wanted to rise—a malicious, ironic voice insisted that he rise— and, at once, to leave this temple and go out into the world.

He wanted to obey the voice, which was the only voice that spoke to him; he tried to assure the voice that he would do his best to rise; he would only lie here a moment, after his dreadful fall, and catch his breath. It was at this moment, precisely, that he found he could not rise; something had happened to his arms, his legs, his feet—ah, something had happened to John! And he began to scream again in his great, bewildered terror, and felt himself, indeed, begin to move—not upward, toward the light, but down again, a sickness in his bowels, a tightening in his loin-strings; he felt himself turning, again and again, across the dusty floor, as though God's toe had touched him lightly. And the dust made him cough and retch; in his turning the center of the whole earth shifted, making of space a sheer void and a mockery of order, and balance, and time. Nothing remained: all was swallowed up in chaos. And: *Is this it?* John's terrified soul inquired—*What is it?* —to no purpose, receiving no answer. Only the ironic voice insisted yet once more that he rise from that filthy floor if he did not want to become like all the other niggers.

Then the anguish subsided for a moment, as water withdraws briefly to dash itself once more against the rocks: he knew that it subsided only to return. And he coughed and sobbed in the dusty space before the altar, lying on his face. And still he was going down, farther and farther from the joy, the singing, and the light above him.

He tried, but in such despair!—the utter darkness does not present any point of departure, contains no beginning, and no end—to rediscover, and, as it were, to trap and hold tightly in the palm of his hand, the moment preceding his fall, his change. But that moment was also locked in darkness, was wordless, and would not come forth. He remembered only the cross: he had turned again to kneel at the altar, and had faced the golden cross. And the Holy Ghost was speaking— seeming to say, as John spelled out the so abruptly present and gigantic legend adorning the cross: *Jesus Saves*. He had stared at this, an awful bitterness in his heart, wanting to curse—and the Spirit spoke, and spoke in him. Yes: there was Elisha, speaking from the floor, and his father, silent, at his back. In his heart there was a sudden yearning tenderness for holy Elisha; desire, sharp and awful as a reflecting knife, to usurp the body of Elisha, and lie where Elisha lay; to speak in tongues, as Elisha spoke, and, with that authority, to confound his father. Yet this had not been the moment; it was as far back as he could go, but the secret, the turning, the abysmal drop was farther back, in darkness. As he cursed his father, as he loved Elisha, he had, even then, been weeping; he had already passed his moment, was already under the power, had been struck, and was going down.

Ah, down!—and to what purpose, where? To the bottom of the sea, the bowels of the earth, to the heart of the fiery furnace? Into a dungeon deeper than Hell, into a madness louder than the grave? What trumpet sound would awaken him, what hand would lift him up? For he knew, as he was struck again, and screamed again, his throat like burning ashes, and as he turned again, his body hanging from him like a useless weight, a heavy, rotting carcass, that if he were not lifted he would never rise.

His father, his mother, his aunt, Elisha—all were far above him, waiting, watching his torment in the pit. They hung over the golden barrier, singing behind them, light around their heads, weeping, perhaps, for John, struck down so early. And, no, they could not help him any more—nothing could help him any more. He struggled, struggled to rise up, and meet them—he wanted wings to fly upward and meet them in that morning, that morning where they were. But his struggles only thrust him downward, his cries did not go upward, but rang in his own skull.

Yet, though he scarcely saw their faces, he knew that they were there. He felt them move, every movement causing a trembling, an astonishment, a horror in the heart of darkness were he lay. He could not know if they wished him to come to them as passionately as he wished to rise. Perhaps they did not help him because they did not care —because they did not love him.

Then his father returned to him, in John's changed and low condition; and John thought, but for a moment only, that his father had come to help him. In the silence, then, that filled the void, John looked on his father. His father's face was black—like a sad, eternal night; yet in his father's face there burned a fire—a fire eternal in an eternal night. John trembled where he lay, feeling no warmth for him from this fire, trembled, and could not take his eyes away. A wind blew over him, saying: "Whosoever loveth and maketh a lie." Only: "Whosoever loveth and maketh a lie." And he knew that he had been thrust out of the holy, the joyful, the bloodwashed community, that his father had thrust him out. His father's will was stronger than John's own. His power was greater because he belonged to God. Now, John felt no hatred, nothing, only a bitter, unbelieving despair: all prophecies were true, salvation was finished, damnation was real!

Then Death is real, John's soul said, and Death will have his moment.

"Set thine house in order," said his father, "for thou shalt die and not live."

And then the ironic voice spoke again, saying: "Get up, John. Get up, boy. Don't let him keep you here. You got everything your daddy got."

John tried to laugh—John thought that he was laughing—but found, instead, that his mouth was filled with salt, his ears were full of burning water. Whatever was happening in his distant body now, he could not change or stop; his chest heaved, his laughter rose and bubbled at his mouth, like blood.

And his father looked on him. His father's eyes looked down on him, and John began to scream. His father's eyes stripped him naked, and hated what they saw. And as he turned, screaming, in the dust again, trying to escape his father's eyes, those eyes, that face, and all their faces, and the far-off yellow light, all departed from his vision as though he had gone blind. He was going down again. There is, his soul cried out again, no bottom to the darkness!

He did not know where he was. There was silence everywhere—only a perpetual, distant, faint trembling far beneath him—the roaring, perhaps, of the fires of Hell, over which he was suspended, or the echo, persistent, invincible still, of the moving feet of the saints. He thought of the mountaintop, where he longed to be, where the sun would cover him like a cloth of gold, would cover his head like a crown of fire, and in his hands he would hold a living rod. But this was no mountain where John lay, here, no robe, no crown. And the living rod was up-lifted in other hands.

"I'm going to beat sin out of him. I'm going to beat it out."

Yes, he had sinned, and his father was looking for him. Now, John did not make a sound, and did not move at all, hoping that his father would pass him by.

"Leave him be. Leave him alone. Let him pray to the Lord."

"Yes, Mama. I'm going to try to love the Lord."

"He done run off somewhere. I'm going to find him. I'm going to beat it out."

Yes, he had sinned: one morning, alone, in the dirty bathroom, in the square, dirt-gray cupboard room that was filled with the stink of his father. Sometimes, leaning over the cracked, "tattle-tale gray" bathtub, he scrubbed his father's back; and looked, as the accursed son of Noah had looked, on his father's hideous nakedness. It was secret, like sin, and slimy, like the serpent, and heavy, like the rod. Then he hated his father, and longed for the power to cut his father down.

Was this why he lay here, thrust out from all human or heavenly help tonight? This, and not that other, his deadly sin, having looked on his father's nakedness and mocked and cursed him in his heart? Ah, that son of Noah's had been cursed, down to the present groaning generation: *A servant of servants shall he be unto his brethren.*

Then the ironic voice, terrified, it seemed, of no depth, no darkness, demanded of John, scornfully, if he believed that he was cursed. All niggers had been cursed, the ironic voice reminded him, all niggers had come from this most undutiful of Noah's sons. How could John be cursed for having seen in a bathtub what another man—*if* that other man had ever lived—had seen ten thousand years ago, lying in an open tent? Could a curse come down so many ages? Did it live in time, or in the moment? But John found no answer for this voice, for he was in the moment, and out of time.

And his father approached. "I'm going to beat sin out of him. I'm going to beat it out." All the darkness rocked and wailed as his father's feet came closer; feet whose tread resounded like God's tread in the garden of Eden, searching the covered Adam and Eve. Then his father stood just above him, looking down. Then John knew that a curse was renewed from moment to moment, from father to son. Time was indifferent, like snow and ice; but the heart, crazed wanderer in the driving waste, carried the curse forever.

"John," said his father, "come with me."

Then they were in a straight street, a narrow, narrow way. They had been walking for many days. The street stretched before them, long, and silent, going down, and whiter than the snow. There was no one on the street, and John was frightened. The buildings on this street, so near that John could touch them on either side, were narrow, also, rising like spears into the sky, and they were made of beaten gold and silver. John knew that these buildings were not for him—not today— *no, nor tomorrow, either!* Then, coming up this straight and silent street, he saw a woman, very old and black, coming toward them, staggering on the crooked stones. She was drunk, and dirty, and very old, and her mouth was bigger than his mother's mouth, or his own; her mouth was loose and wet, and he had *never* seen anyone so black. His father was astonished to see her, and beside himself with anger; but John was glad. He clapped his hands, and cried:

"See! She's uglier than Mama! She's uglier than me!"

"You mighty proud, ain't you," his father said, "to be the Devil's son?"

But John did not listen to his father. He turned to watch the woman pass. His father grabbed his arm.

"You see that? That's sin. That's what the Devil's son runs after."

"Whose son are you?" John asked.

His father slapped him. John laughed, and moved a little away.

"I seen it. I seen it. I ain't the Devil's son for nothing."

His father reached for him, but John was faster. He moved backward down the shining street, looking at his father—his father who moved toward him, one hand outstretched in fury.

"And I *heard* you—all the nighttime long. I know what you do in the dark, black man, when you think the Devil's son's asleep. I heard you, spitting, and groaning, and choking—and I *seen* you, riding up and down, and going in and out. I ain't the Devil's son for nothing."

The listening buildings, rising upward yet, leaned, closing out the sky. John's feet began to slip; tears and sweat were in his eyes; still moving backward before his father, he looked about him for deliverance; but there was no deliverance in this street for him.

"And I hate you. I hate you. I don't care about your golden crown. I don't care about your long white robe. I seen you under the robe, I seen you!"

Then his father was upon him; at his touch there was singing, and fire. John lay on his back in the narrow street, looking up at his father, that burning face beneath the burning towers.

"I'm going to beat it out of you. I'm going to beat it out."

His father raised his hand. The knife came down. John rolled away, down the white, descending street, screaming:

"Father! Father!"

These were the first words he uttered. In a moment there was silence, and his father was gone. Again, he felt the saints above him—and dust was in his mouth. There was singing somewhere; far away, above him; singing slow and mournful. He lay silent, racked beyond endurance, salt drying on his face, with nothing in him any more, no lust, no fear, no shame, no hope. And yet he knew that it would come again—the darkness was full of demons crouching, waiting to worry him with their teeth again.

Then I looked in the grave and I wondered.

Ah, down!—what was he searching here, all alone in darkness? But now he knew, for irony had left him, that he was searching something, hidden in the darkness, that must be found. He would die if it was not found; or, he was dead already, and would never again be joined to the living, if it was not found.

And the grave looked so sad and lonesome.

In the grave where he now wandered—he knew it was the grave, it was so cold and silent, and he moved in icy mist—he found his mother and his father, his mother dressed in scarlet, his father dressed in white. They did not see him: they looked backward, over their shoulders, at a cloud of witnesses. And there was his Aunt Florence, gold and silver flashing on her fingers, brazen earrings dangling from her ears; and there was another woman, whom he took to be that wife of his father's, called Deborah—who had, as he had once believed, so much to tell him. But she, alone, of all that company, looked at him and signified that there was no speech in the grave. He was a stranger there—they did not see him pass, they did not know what he was looking for, they could not help him search. He wanted to find Elisha, who knew, per- haps, who would help him—but Elisha was not there. There was Roy: Roy also might have helped him, but he had been stabbed with a knife, and lay now, brown and silent, at his father's feet.

Then there began to flood John's soul the waters of despair. *Love is as strong as death, as deep as the grave.* But love, which had, perhaps, like a benevolent monarch, swelled the population of his neighboring kingdom, Death, had not himself descended: they owed him no alle- giance here. Here there was no speech or language, and there was no love; no one to say: You are beautiful, John; no one to forgive him, no matter what his sin; no one to heal him, and lift him up. No one: father and mother looked backward, Roy was bloody, Elisha was not here.

Then the darkness began to murmur—a terrible sound—and John's ears trembled. In this murmur that filled the grave, like a thousand wings beating on the air, he recognized a sound that he had always heard. He began, for terror, to weep and moan—and this sound was swallowed up, and yet was magnified by the echoes that filled the darkness.

This sound had filled John's life, so it now seemed, from the moment he had first drawn breath. He had heard it everywhere, in prayer and in daily speech, and wherever the saints were gathered, and in the unbelieving streets. It was in his father's anger, and in his mother's calm insistence, and in the vehement mockery of his aunt; it had rung, so oddly, in Roy's voice this afternoon, and when Elisha played the piano it was there; it was in the beat and jangle of Sister McCandless's tambourine, it was in the very cadence of her testimony, and invested that testimony with a matchless, unimpeachable authority. Yes, he had heard it all his life, but it was only now that his ears were opened to this sound that came from darkness, that could only come from darkness, that yet bore such sure witness to the glory of the light. And now in his moaning, and so far from any help, he heard it in himself—it rose from his bleeding, his cracked-open heart. It was a sound of rage and weeping which filled the grave, rage and weeping from time set free, but bound now in eternity; rage that had no language, weeping with no voice—which yet spoke now, to John's startled soul, of boundless melancholy, of the bitterest patience, and the longest night; of the deepest water, the strongest chains, the most cruel lash; of humility most wretched, the dungeon most absolute, of love's bed defiled, and birth dishonored, and most bloody, unspeakable, sudden death. Yes, the darkness hummed with murder: the body in the water, the body in the fire, the body on the tree. John looked down the line of these armies of darkness, army upon army, and his soul whispered: *Who are these? Who are they?* And wondered: *Where shall I go?*

There was no answer. There was no help or healing in the grave, no answer in the darkness, no speech from all that company. They looked backward. And John loked back, seeing no deliverance.

I, John, saw the future, way up in the middle of the air.

Were the lash, the dungeon, and the night for him? And the sea for him? And the grave for him?

I, John, saw a number, way in the middle of the air.

And he struggled to flee—out of this darkness, out of this company—into the land of the living, so high, so far away. Fear was upon him, a more deadly fear than he had ever known, as he turned and turned in the darkness, as he moaned, and stumbled, and crawled through darkness, finding no hand, no voice, finding no door. *Who are these? Who are they?* They were the despised and rejected, the wretched and the spat upon, the earth's offscouring; and he was in their company, and they would swallow up his soul. The stripes they had endured would scar his back, their punishment would be his, their portion his, his their humiliation, anguish, chains, their dungeon his, their death his. *Thrice was I beaten with rods, once I was stoned, thrice I suffered shipwreck, a night and a day I have been in the deep.*

And their dread testimony would be his!

In journeyings often, in perils of waters, in perils of robbers, in perils by mine own countrymen, in perils by the heathen, in perils in the city, in perils in the wilderness, in perils in the sea, in perils among false brethren.

And there desolation, his:

In weariness and painfulness, in watchings often, in hunger and thirst, in fastings often, in cold and nakedness.

And he began to shout for help, seeing before him the lash, the fire, and the depthless water, seeing his head bowed down forever, he, John, the lowest among these lowly. And he looked for his mother, but her eyes were fixed on this dark army—she was claimed by this army. And his father would not help him, his father did not see him, and Roy lay dead.

Then he whispered, not knowing that he whispered: "Oh, Lord, have mercy on me. Have mercy on me."

And a voice, for the first time in all his terrible journey, spoke to John, through the rage and weeping, and fire, and darkness, and flood: "Yes," said the voice, "go through. Go through."

"Lift me up," whispered John, "lift me up. I can't go through."

"Go through," said the voice, "go through."

Then there was silence. The murmuring ceased. There was only this trembling beneath him. And he knew there was a light somewhere.

"Go through."

"Ask Him to take you through."

But he could never go through this darkness, through this fire and this wrath. He never could go through. His strength was finished, and he could not move. He belonged to the darkness—the darkness from which he had thought to flee had claimed him. And he moaned again, weeping, and lifted up his hands.

"Call on Him. Call on Him."

"Ask Him to take you through."

Dust rose again in his nostrils, sharp as the fumes of Hell. And he turned again in the darkness, trying to remember something he had heard, something he had read.

Jesus saves.

And he saw before him the fire, red and gold, and waiting for him —yellow, and red, and gold, and burning in a night eternal, and waiting for him. He must go through this fire, and into this night.

Jesus saves.

Call on Him.

Ask Him to take you through.

He could not call, for his tongue would not unlock, and his heart was silent, and great with fear. In the darkness, how to move?—with death's ten thousand jaws agape, and waiting in the darkness. On any turning whatsoever the beast may spring—to move in the darkness is to move into the waiting jaws of death. And yet, it came to him that he must move; for there was a light somewhere, and life, and joy, and singing—somewhere, somewhere above him.

And he moaned again: "Oh, Lord, have mercy. Have mercy, Lord."

There came to him again the communion service at which Elisha had knelt at his father's feet. Now this service was in a great, high room, a room made golden by the light of the sun; and the room was filled with a multitude of people, all in long, white robes, the women with covered heads. They sat at a long, bare, wooden table. They broke at this table flat, unsalted bread, which was the body of the Lord, and drank from a heavy silver cup the scarlet wine of His blood. Then he saw that they were barefoot, and that their feet were stained with this same blood. And a sound of weeping filled the room as they broke the bread and drank the wine.

Then they rose, to come together over a great basin filled with water. And they divided into four groups, two of women and two of men; and they began, woman before woman, and man before man, to wash each other's feet. But the blood would not wash off; many washings only turned the crystal water red; and someone cried: *"Have you been to the river?"*

Then John saw the river, and the multitude was there. And now they had undergone a change; their robes were ragged, and stained with the road they had traveled, and stained with unholy blood; the robes of some barely covered their nakedness; and some indeed were naked. And some stumbled on the smooth stones at the river's edge, for they were blind; and some crawled with a terrible wailing, for they were lame; some did not cease to pluck at their flesh, which was rotten with running sores. All struggled to get to the river, in a dreadful hardness of heart: the strong struck down the weak, the ragged spat on the naked, the naked cursed the blind, the blind crawled over the lame. And someone cried: *"Sinner, do you love my Lord?"*

Then John saw the Lord—for a moment only; and the darkness, for a moment only, was filled with a light he could not bear. Then, in a moment, he was set free; his tears sprang as from a fountain; his heart, like a fountain of waters, burst. Then he cried: "Oh, blessed Jesus! Oh, Lord Jesus! Take me through!"

Of tears there was, yes, a very fountain—springing from a depth never sounded before, from depths John had not known were in him. And he wanted to rise up, singing, singing in that great morning, the morning of his new life. Ah, how his tears ran down, how they blessed his soul!—as he felt himself, out of the darkness, and the fire, and the terrors of death, rising upward to meet the saints.

"Oh, yes!" cried the voice of Elisha. "Bless our God forever!"

And a sweetness filled John as he heard this voice, and heard the sound of singing: the singing was for him. For his drifting soul was anchored in the love of God; in the rock that endured forever. The light and the darkness had kissed each other, and were married now, forever, in the life and the vision of John's soul.

> *I, John, saw a city, way in the middle of the air,*
> *Waiting, waiting, waiting up there.*

He opened his eyes on the morning, and found them, in the light of the morning, rejoicing for him. The trembling he had known in darkness had been the echo of their joyful feet—these feet, bloodstained forever, and washed in many rivers—they moved on the bloody road forever, with no continuing city, but seeking one to come; a city out of time, not made with hands, but eternal in the heavens. No power could hold this army back, no water disperse them, no fire consume them. One day they would compel the earth to heave upward, and surrender the waiting dead. They sang, where the darkness gathered, where the lion waited, where the fire cried, and where blood ran down:

My soul, don't you be uneasy!

They wandered in the valley forever; and they smote the rock, forever; and the waters sprang, perpetually, in the perpetual desert. They cried unto the Lord forever, and lifted up their eyes forever, they were cast down forever, and He lifted them up forever. No, the fire could not hurt them, and yes, the lion's jaws were stopped; the serpent was not their master, the grave was not their resting-place, the earth was not their home. Job bore them witness, and Abraham was their father, Moses had elected to suffer with them rather than glory in sin for a season. Shadrach, Meshach, and Abednego had gone before them into the fire, their grief had been sung by David, and Jeremiah had wept for them. Ezekiel had prophesied upon them, these scattered bones, these slain, and, in the fulness of time, the prophet, John, had come out of the wilderness, crying that the promise was for them. They were encompassed with a very cloud of witnesses: Judas, who had betrayed the Lord; Thomas, who had doubted Him; Peter, who had trembled at the crowing of a cock; Stephen, who had been stoned; Paul, who had been bound; the blind man crying in the dusty road, the dead man rising from the grave. And they looked unto Jesus, the author and the finisher of their faith, running with patience the race He had set before them; they endured the cross, and they despised the shame, and waited to join Him, one day, in glory, at the right hand of the Father.

My soul! don't you be uneasy!

Jesus going to make up my dying bed!

"Rise up, rise up, Brother Johnny, and talk about the Lord's deliverance."

It was Elisha who had spoken; he stood just above John, smiling; and behind him were the saints—Praying Mother Washington and Sister McCandless, and Sister Price. Behind these, he saw his mother, and his aunt; his father, for the moment, was hidden from his view.

"Amen!" cried Sister McCandless, "rise up, and praise the Lord!"

He tried to speak, and could not, for the joy that rang in him this morning. He smiled up at Elisha, and his tears ran down; and Sister McCandless began to sing:

> *"Lord, I ain't*
> *No stranger now!"*

"Rise up, Johnny," said Elisha, again. "Are you saved, boy?"

"Yes," said John, "oh, yes!" And the words came upward, it seemed, of themselves, in the new voice God had given him. Elisha stretched out his hand, and John took the hand, and stood—so suddenly, and so strangely, and with such wonder!—once more on his feet.

> *"Lord, I ain't*
> *No stranger now!"*

Yes, the night had passed, the powers of darkness had been beaten back. He moved among the saints, he, John, who had come home, who was one of their company now; weeping, he yet could find no words to speak of his great gladness; and he scarcely knew how he moved, for his hands were new, and his feet were new, and he moved in a new and Heaven-bright air. Praying Mother Washington took him in her arms, and kissed him, and their tears, his tears and the tears of the old, black woman, mingled.

"God bless you, son. Run on, honey, and don't get weary!"

> *"Lord, I been introduced*
> *To the Father and the Son,*
> *And I ain't*
> *No stranger now!"*

Yet, as he moved among them, their hands touching, and tears falling, and the music rising—as though he moved down a great hall, full of a splendid company—something began to knock in that listening, astonished, newborn, and fragile heart of his; something recalling the terrors of the night, which were not finished, his heart seemed to say; which, in this company, were now to begin. And, while his heart was speaking, he found himself before his mother. Her face was full of tears, and for a long while they looked at each other, saying nothing. And once again, he tried to read the mystery of that face—which, as it had never before been so bright and pained with love, had never seemed before so far from him, so wholly in communion with a life beyond his life. He wanted to comfort her, but the night had given him no language, no second sight, no power to see into the heart of any other. He knew only—and now, looking at his mother, he knew that he could never tell it—that the heart was a fearful place. She kissed him, and she said: "I'm mighty proud, Johnny. You keep up the faith. I'm going to be praying for you till the Lord puts me in my grave."

Then he stood before his father. In the moment that he forced himself to raise his eyes and look into his father's face, he felt in himself a stiffening, and a panic, and a blind rebellion, and a hope for peace. The tears still on his face, and smiling still, he said: "Praise the Lord."

"Praise the Lord," said his father. He did not move to touch him, did not kiss him, did not smile. They stood before each other in silence, while the saints rejoiced; and John struggled to speak the authoritative, the living word that would conquer the great division between his father and himself. But it did not come, the living word; in the silence something died in John, and something came alive. It came to him that he must testify: his tongue only could bear witness to the wonders he had seen. And he remembered, suddenly, the text of a sermon he had once heard his father preach. And he opened his mouth, feeling, as he watched his father, the darkness roar behind him, and the very earth beneath him seem to shake; yet he gave to his father their common testimony. "I'm saved," he said, "and I know I'm saved." And then, as his father did not speak, he repeated his father's text: "My witness is in Heaven and my record is on high."

"It come from your mouth," said his father then. "I want to see you live it. It's more than a notion."

"I'm going to pray God," said John—and his voice shook, whether with joy or grief he could not say—"to keep me, and make me strong . . . to stand . . . to stand against the enemy . . . and against everything and everybody . . . that wants to cut down my soul."

Then his tears came down again, like a wall between him and his father. His Aunt Florence came and took him in her arms. Her eyes were dry, and her face was old in the savage, morning light. But her voice, when she spoke, was gentler than he had ever known it to be before.

"You fight the good fight," she said, "you hear? Don't you get weary, and don't you get scared. Because I *know* the Lord's done laid His hands on you."

"Yes," he said, weeping, "yes. I'm going to serve the Lord."

"Amen!" cried Elisha. "Bless our God!"

✿ ✿ ✿

LETTER TO MY NEPHEW

ON THE ONE HUNDREDTH ANNIVERSARY OF THE EMANCIPATION

Dear James:

I have begun this letter five times and torn it up five times. I keep seeing your face, which is also the face of your father and my brother. Like him, you are tough, dark, vulnerable, moody—with a very definite tendency to sound truculent because you want no one to think you are soft. You may be like your grandfather in this, I don't know, but certainly both you and your father resemble him very much physically. Well, he is dead, he never saw you, and he had a terrible life; he was defeated long before he died because, at the bottom of his heart, he really believed what white people said about him. This is one of the reasons that he became so holy. I am sure that your father has told you something about all that. Neither you nor your father exhibit any tendency towards holiness: you really *are* of another era, part of what happened when the Negro left the land and came into what the late E. Franklin Frazier called "the cities of destruction." You can only be destroyed by believing that you really are what the white world calls a *nigger*. I tell you this because I love you, and please don't you ever forget it.

I have known both of you all your lives, have carried your Daddy in my arms and on my shoulders, kissed and spanked him and watched him learn to walk. I don't know if you've known anybody from that far back; if you've loved anybody that long, first as an infant, then as a child, then as a man, you gain a strange perspective on time and human pain and effort. Other people cannot see what I see whenever I look into your father's face, for behind your father's face as it is today are all those other faces which were his. Let him laugh and I see a cellar your father does not remember and a house he does not re-member and I hear in his present laughter his laughter as a child. Let him curse and I remember him falling down the cellar steps, and howl-ing, and I remember, with pain, his tears, which my hand or your grandmother's so easily wiped away. But no one's hand can wipe away those tears he sheds invisibly today, which one hears in his laughter and in his speech and in his songs. I know what the world has done to my brother and how narrowly he has survived it. And I know, which is much worse, and this is the crime of which I accuse my country and my countrymen, and for which neither I nor time nor history will ever forgive them, that they have destroyed and are destroying hundreds of thousands of lives and do not know it and do not want to know it. One can be, indeed one must strive to become, tough and philosophical concerning destruction and death, for this is what most of mankind has been best at since we have heard of man. (But remember: *most* of mankind is not *all* of mankind.) But it is not permissible that the authors of devastation should also be innocent. It is the innocence which constitutes the crime.

Now, my dear namesake, these innocent and well-meaning people, your countrymen, have caused you to be born under conditions not very far removed from those described for us by Charles Dickens in the London of more than a hundred years ago. (I hear the chorus of the innocents screaming, "No! This is not true! How *bitter* you are!"— but I am writing this letter to *you,* to try to tell you something about how to handle *them,* for most of them do not yet really know that you exist. I *know* the conditions under which you were born, for I was there. Your countrymen were *not* there, and haven't made it yet. Your grandmother was also there, and no one has ever accused her of being bitter. I suggest that the innocents check with her. She isn't hard to find. Your countrymen don't know that *she* exists, either, though she has been working for them all their lives.)

Well, you were born, here you came, something like fifteen years ago; and though your father and mother and grandmother, looking about the streets through which they were carrying you, staring at the walls into which they brought you, had every reason to be heavy-hearted, yet they were not. For here you were, Big James, named for me—you were a big baby, I was not—here you were: to be loved. To be loved, baby, hard, at once, and forever, to strengthen you against the loveless world. Remember that: I know how black it looks today, for you. It looked bad that day, too, yes, we were trembling. We have not stopped trembling yet, but if we had not loved each other none of us would have survived. And now you must survive because we love you, and for the sake of your children and your children's children.

This innocent country set you down in a ghetto in which, in fact, it intended that you should perish. Let me spell out precisely what I mean by that, for the heart of the matter is here, and the root of my dispute with my country. You were born where you were born and faced the future that you faced because you were black and *for no other reason.* The limits of your ambition were, thus, expected to be set forever. You were born into a society which spelled out with brutal clarity, and in as many ways as possible, that you were a worthless human being. You were not expected to aspire to excellence: you were expected to make peace with mediocrity. Wherever you have turned, James, in your short time on this earth, you have been told where you could go and what you could do (and *how* you could do it) and where you could live and whom you could marry. I know your countrymen do not agree with me about this, and I hear them saying, "You exaggerate." They do not know Harlem, and I do. So do you. Take no one's word for anything, including mine—but trust your experience. Know whence you came. If you know whence you came, there is really no limit to where you can go. The details and symbols of your life have been deliberately constructed to make you believe what white people say about you. Please try to remember that what they believe, as well as what they do and cause you to endure, does not testify to your inferiority but to their inhumanity and fear. Please try to be clear, dear James, through the storm which rages about your youthful head today, about the reality which lies behind the words *acceptance* and *integration.* There is no reason for you to try to become like white people and there is no basis whatever for their impertinent assumption that *they* must accept *you.* The really terrible thing, old buddy, is that *you* must accept *them.* And I mean that very seriously. You must accept them and accept them with love. For these innocent people have no other hope. They are, in effect, still trapped in a history which they do not understand; and until they understand it, they cannot be released from it. They have had to believe for many years, and for innumerable reasons, that black men are inferior to white men. Many of them, indeed, know better, but, as you will discover, people find it very difficult to act on what they know. To act is to be committed, and to be committed is to be in danger. In this case, the danger, in the minds of most white Americans, is the loss of their identity. Try to imagine how you would feel if you woke up one morning to find the sun shining and all the stars aflame. You would be frightened because it is out of the order of nature. Any upheaval in the universe is terrifying because it so profoundly attacks one's sense of one's own reality. Well, the black man has functioned in the white man's world as a fixed star, as an immovable pillar: and as he moves out of his place, heaven and earth are shaken to their foundations. You, don't be afraid. I said that it was intended that you should perish in the ghetto, perish by never being allowed to go behind the white man's definitions, by never being allowed to spell your proper name. You have, and many of us have, defeated this intention; and, by a terrible law, a terrible paradox, those innocents who believed that your imprisonment made them safe are losing their grasp of reality. But these men are your brothers—your lost, younger brothers. And if the word *integration* means anything, this is what it means: that we, with love, shall force our brothers to see themselves as they are, to cease fleeing from reality and begin to change it. For this is your home, my friend, do not be driven from it; great men have done great things here, and will again, and we can make America what America must become. It will be hard, James, but you come from sturdy, peasant stock, men who picked cotton and dammed rivers and built railroads, and, in the teeth of the most terrifying odds, achieved an unassailable and monumental dignity. You come from a long line of great poets, some of the greatest poets since Homer. One of them said, *The very time I thought I was lost, My dungeon shook and my chains fell off.*

You know, and I know, that the country is celebrating one hundred years of freedom one hundred years too soon. We cannot be free until they are free. God bless you, James, and Godspeed.

Your uncle,
James

Ulysses Lee

(1914–1969)

Born in Washington, D.C., Ulysses Lee attended Dunbar High School, received a B.A. (*summa cum laude*) from Howard University, and a Ph.D. (with honors) from the University of Chicago.

He taught at Lincoln University (Pennsylvania), Virginia Union University, Lincoln University (Missouri), Morgan State College, and the University of Pennsylvania. At the time of his death, Dr. Lee was simultaneously Professor of English at Morgan and Professor of American Civilization at Pennsylvania.

In great demand as a lecturer, Lee appeared on many American campuses. Under the sponsorship of the American Society of African Culture, he lectured in 1965 in Nigeria, in Sierra Leone, and in the Cameroons.

A member of Phi Beta Kappa, Professor Lee was the recipient of other academic honors and awards, including a Rosenwald Fellowship and a Rockefeller Post-War Fellowship.

Ulysses Lee was a major in the Army during World War II; he spent a large share of his time, during the war and for several years afterwards, preparing his major work, *U.S. Army in World War II, The Employment of Negro Troops*, an official volume published in 1966 "in the subseries *Special Studies*" by the Office of the Chief of Military History. Dr. Lee was one of the editors (with Arthur P. Davis and Sterling A. Brown) of *The Negro Caravan* (1941) and a contributor to *The Negro in Virginia* (1940), one of the better WPA Studies. He also contributed to many national periodicals in the fields of English, history, and American culture. At the time of his death, Ulysses Lee was editor-designate of *The Journal of Negro History*.

The following selection comes from *Current History* (July, 1968).

THE DRAFT AND THE NEGRO

Pick up any metropolitan newspaper and look at the photographs from the front in Vietnam; read the obituaries of men killed in action; observe the videotapes and the picture essays in *Life* and *Look* and

"The Draft and the Negro" by Ulysses Lee from the July, 1968, issue of *Current History*. Reprinted by permission of Current History, Inc.

The New York Times Magazine. One fact is clear: there are proportionately more Negroes in the United States combat forces and on the battle lines today than there were in any other military action in American history. The reasons lie in the past and in the present; in the nature of the American societal fabric; and in the nature and operation of the draft laws and enlistment regulations. The effects of disproportionate Negro participation alter the nature of our armed forces and of our society and, more especially, the lives and attitudes of Negroes in the United States today.

In a more nearly perfect democracy, there would be little reason to discuss Negroes and the draft, for Negroes would be affected and they would react in consonance with the rest of the national population. But despite the massive alteration of the terms of Negroes' service in the armed forces and in the position of Negroes in American life since the close of World War II, no one can seriously argue in 1968 that Negroes do not constitute a special, still "unfinished business" for the American democracy. The intensive civil rights activities of the 1960's, followed by a series of disastrous riots, summer after summer, in the great American cities, culminated in the arson and looting which followed the assassination of Dr. Martin Luther King, Jr., in April, 1968.

The nation's continuing failure to come to grips with the poverty of the rural South as well as that of the great city ghettos overshadows the simultaneously increasing integration of Negroes into many phases of American life, including the economic, on the managerial level, and the political, on the decision-making level. The increase of serious studies of "the Negro in American life" and the greater exposure of Negroes in the entertainment, sports, and intellectual worlds do not alter the essentials of the present situation. Not even a set of legally nondiscriminatory draft regulations, nor legally nondiscriminatory armed services (which are probably closer in fact to this ideal than any other discernible American institution) can alter the fact that in the pursuit of their daily and even their presumably patriotic duties Negroes face problems different from those of the population at large.

They also differ from those of our smaller, less widely distributed, and therefore less visibly distinctive minorities. For although Puerto Ricans, American Indians, Mexican-Americans, and Orientals face problems analogous to those of American Negroes in particular parts of the nation, they can still expect an approach different in kind and manner in the rest of the country. Though there have been separate and special Puerto Rican and Japanese-American—and even Filipino and Norwegian-American—units in the armed forces in the past, these proceeded from a different social and military philosophy from that which provided segregated Negro units in the armed forces from the

Civil War (and, in some instances, from the American Revolution) through World War II. On the surface, today, the draft operates without discrimination; Selective Service no longer keeps records by race; the prospective Negro draftee takes the same chances as anyone else. But, in reality, for a variety of reasons, this is not yet the case.

Historical Position of the Negro

The services of Negroes in the land and naval forces of the United States from the days of the colonial militia to the present have been well documented. Up to the Civil War, the nation relied largely upon volunteers with state militia forces at their core. Distinguished personages in their own communities raised companies and regiments; these, in turn, entered the service of the nation and were counted against the quotas levied against each state. During the Revolution, local units might contain a varying number of Negroes, some of them free volunteers, some of them slaves serving in the hope of obtaining their freedom thereby, some serving in the places of their masters. In some cases, full companies of Negroes, such as Connecticut's "Attucks Guards" and Boston's "Massasoit Guards," were organized. Virginia's navy of 40 vessels had Negroes aboard each ship.

But by the time of the Civil War, and for 80 years thereafter, it was true that "Negroes must fight for the right to fight." Early in the war, free Negroes volunteered their services to the Union forces, only to be rejected as a matter of political as well as social policy. By the middle of 1862, when volunteers for the Union forces were becoming scarce, Union generals, like David Hunter in South Carolina and J. H. Lane in Kansas, began to form Negro regiments without full authorization; and, in New Orleans, B. F. Butler organized the Louisiana "Native Guards." On March 3, 1863, in response to the growing manpower problems of the Northern armies, Congress passed the first national draft law in the nation's history. Subsequently states (including Rhode Island and Massachusetts) raised volunteer Negro units whose enlistees counted against state quotas even when the units were recruited in the South.

Draft-Race Riots

The new draft law and the reaction of white Northern workingmen to the formal Emancipation Proclamation issued on January 1, 1863, precipitated the New York draft riots, the bloodiest race riots in American history. The draft law provided that a drafted man might purchase his release for a payment of $300. Working men, often recent immigrants, already believing that freed slaves would migrate north and usurp their jobs, saw the new draft law as a measure discriminating against them in favor of the rich. Anti-war Copperhead orators and newspapers declared that Northern workingmen were being forced to fight and risk death for the freedom of slaves who would soon take their jobs. Riots began when the names of the first draftees appeared in the New York papers on Sunday, July 12, 1863. Draft headquarters, saloons and newspapers were the mob's first targets; then they attacked any Negro found on the streets. By the second day, the homes and businesses of those employing or sympathizing with Negroes were looted and burned. What began as anti-draft riots ended as anti-Negro riots, with the Colored Orphan Asylum one of the main targets. The riot lasted four days, and Negro bodies were left hanging from the trees and lampposts on the streets of New York.

Thus, the first American draft law had an immediate social effect upon Negroes. The Bureau of Colored Troops, established in May, 1863, to recruit and supervise Negro units in the South as well as the North, recruited and organized 185,000 Negroes into the United States Colored Troops after August, 1863. If Negroes in independent and state units are added, it is estimated that the number of Negroes serving in the Civil War reached 390,000.

After the Civil War, the congressionally authorized reorganization of the Army (in 1866) provided for the organization of Negro infantry and cavalry regiments within the regular Army and the Act of 1869 fixed their number at two regiments in each branch of the service. The four regular regiments (the 24th and 25th Infantry and the 9th and 10th Cavalry) remained the core of Negro regular Army strength until World War II for the cavalry, and until the Korean War for the infantry units. But while these units guaranteed a role for Negroes in the Army, they also placed a limit on the nature of his service. They were all-Negro units with white officers, except for the chaplain and an occasional Negro graduate of West Point. They became famed Indian fighters—the Buffalo soldiers of the plains—but their existence meant that no Negroes served in other branches of the military service except in time of war.

In the Spanish-American War, Negro volunteer regiments were called "Immunes" because of the belief that they would not be subject to the yellow fever that proved as dangerous to American troops as Spanish arms. Negro state militia units became National Guard units, though only those in Illinois, New York, Massachusetts, Ohio, Maryland, and the District of Columbia remained by World War I. The Navy continued to enlist Negroes, in small numbers, for general service until the end of World War I. These men served throughout the fleet; when the Navy banned Negro enlistments after World War I, Negro opponents of the new policy recalled that it was a Negro, Chief Gunner's Mate John Christopher Jordan, who fired the first shot at Manila Bay, from the cruiser *Olympia*, Admiral George Dewey's flagship.

The Draft: World War I

The Selective Service draft of World War I was designed to spread service in the armed forces through all segments of the population. Negroes were about 10.7 per cent of the population, and about that proportion of the 3,464,296 Americans serving in World War I, or 371,710, were Negroes. But this did not mean that Negroes served on an equal basis. Most Negroes were draftees, since few of them were able to enlist; most of the draftees served in supply trains and in port, engineer and pioneer (labor) battalions. Of the two Negro combat divisions, one, the 93d, made up of National Guard units and a draft regiment largely from South Carolina, was never completely organized for it had neither artillery nor trains. The other division, the 92d, was composed completely of draftees. While there were Negro officers and enlisted men in the former National Guard units, no provision was made for training Negro officers until public protests from Negroes and concerned whites, including the officials of the then young National Association for the Advancement of Colored People (N.A.A.C.P.), gained the concession of a segregated officers' training camp (the 17th Provisional ROTC) located at Des Moines, Iowa. Only infantry officers were trained; of the 1,200 who volunteered, about 700 were commissioned.

Ironically, in the Civil War and the Spanish-American War, Negro officers had been commissioned without the bitterness that preceded the establishment of the Des Moines center and without the problems that followed. Most of the problems were a direct result of the continuation of segregation not only in the form of separate units, but also within units where most officers, including all senior officers, were white; even when Negroes were commissioned, they did not serve in grades higher than captain. Accusations of morale-destroying discrimination on the part of commanders against their troops were frequent and counter-accusations on the efficiency of the troops and their newly-commissioned Negro officers were as frequent.

In the aftermath of World War I, the Navy stopped Negro enlistments altogether until 1932, when it permitted enlistment in the messmen's branch only. At the same time, as a concomitant of the general reduction of the size of the regular Army, the statutory Negro regiments were only partially filled and were broken into detachments performing a variety of tasks as garrison troops at a number of posts and stations. And despite vigorous efforts, no Negroes were permitted to enlist in the Air Force.

The Draft: World War II

With this in mind, on the eve of World War II, Negro and liberal organizations, leading Negro newspapers and political figures launched a vigorous campaign to guarantee that any new Selective Service Act would prohibit discrimination against Negroes in the operation of the draft.

The Selective Training and Service Act of 1940 contained two provisions intended to prevent racial discrimination. The first, Section 3 (a) dealt with volunteering through the draft: "That within the limits of the quota determined—for the subdivision in which he resides, any person, regardless of race or color, between the ages of eighteen and forty-five, shall be afforded an opportunity to volunteer for induction into the land or naval forces of the United States for the training and service prescribed. . . ." The second, Section 4 (a) dealt with the selection and training of draftees: "In the selection and training of men under this Act, and in the interpretation and execution of the provisions of this Act, there shall be no discrimination against any person on account of race or color."

With this provision in the Act, the newly mobilizing armed forces of 1940 could have become a revolutionary force. But they did not, and their leaders had no such intention. The Navy and the Marine Corps avoided the entire problem by accepting only volunteers; not needing to use the draft in the first years of the war, they were not affected by the Act. Within the Army, the Air Corps, which could rely on volunteers, sought to evade the problem as long as possible. The Army itself was forced to rely upon the draft, since it was both the largest and the least glamorous of the military services. It looked at the wording of the act and decided that it could live with it. The Army declared that separate units were not in themselves discriminatory and that if the training of Negro and white draftees were kept at the same level, there would be no discrimination. Army apologists stated that the Army was not a sociological laboratory, that it reflected and did not mold social attitudes.

Nevertheless, prodded by President Franklin D. Roosevelt, the Army announced on October 9, 1940, that its Negro personnel would be "maintained on the general basis of the proportion of the Negro population of the country" despite the fact that its policy was "not to intermingle colored and white enlisted personnel in the same regimental organizations." When carried out literally, this meant that because it received most of the Negro draftees, the Army had to find troop and station units for them. Initially, each arm and service and eventually each type of unit was to have a proportionate number of Negroes, averaging ten per cent. This eventually proved impossible: if the Army activated 100 infantry divisions, ten would have had to be Negro; if there were seven locomotive repair companies, seven-tenths of a company would have to be Negro.

But since the Army as a whole had to receive a fixed percentage of Negroes, these branches which had been traditionally closed to Negro soldiers, including the Air Force and the Signal Corps, were forced by the pressures generated by the other branches, especially the Infantry and the Engineers, to accept their share of the quotas. This led to a great waste of manpower as unneeded units, often created especially for the purpose, were organized to receive the otherwise unwanted Negroes. Thus there were units such as medical sanitary companies and airbase security battalions for which no use could be predicted.

Further, the in-flow of Negro draftees never managed to maintain an even 10 per cent of all draftees. It never embraced at any one time and in any one place a full cross-section of Negro skills and abilities. Few Negro units, therefore, could be guaranteed the men that they needed; few units could be guaranteed the replacements they needed; no white unit could receive a Negro replacement, no matter how well prepared, and no Negro unit could receive a white specialist, no matter how great the need. Individuals could be temporarily assigned, at times, but this procedure was seldom resorted to even in times of great need.

The quota system, though it failed, did open the other armed services to Negroes. After the tightening of the manpower supply midway through the war, in February, 1943, the Army succeeded in forcing the Navy to accept its men through the draft; the War Manpower Commission then directed the Navy to accept Negroes proportionately with the other services.

The Navy and the Marine Corps were thereafter reluctant users of the draft, which made them subject to the provisions of the Selective Service Act. But the Navy and the Marine Corps are not pluralistic, multibranched services. The Navy soon ran out of billets for Negroes in shore stations, ordnance units and construction battalions. In late 1943, it manned a destroyer escort and a patrol boat with mainly Negro seamen and white officers. This was hardly a successful venture; moreover, its logical extension would have been a cruiser or battleship manned by a Negro crew. Cartoons in the Negro press poked fun at the experiment, showing tiny black tugboats bringing up the rear in flotillas of giant white battleships and carriers. In August, 1944, the Navy assigned Negroes to 25 auxiliary vessels, limiting the Negroes to 10 per cent of the crew of each vessel.

The two fleet experiments demonstrated that Negroes could handle a wider variety of tasks aboard ship than had been believed and that the mixed crews had no real problems. In April, 1945, the Navy announced that Negroes were eligible for assignment, at up to 10 per cent of crew strength, to all auxiliary fleet vessels; in December, all ships were instructed that "In the administration of naval personnel no differentiation shall be made because of race or color"; and, on February 27, 1946, the Navy announced that Negroes were eligible for "all types of assignments in all ratings in all activities and all ships of the naval service" and that in "housing, messing and other facilities, no special or unusual provisions will be made for the accommodation of Negroes." The Navy thus became the first major American institution to declare a non-discriminatory, non-segregational policy for all of its activities.

The Army, in the meantime, had conducted its own experiment, under somewhat different circumstances and auspices. In the Battle of the Bulge, at Bastogne, Belgium, in December, 1944, Negroes from supply and support units fought with the white riflemen of the besieged combat units. When the European Theater's Services of Supply offered Negroes the chance to retrain as riflemen, over 2,500 volunteered. Original plans to use these men as individual replacements were countermanded and the men were sent out in platoons to Third Army units along the Rhine and in companies to Seventh Army units in Southeastern France. Reports of performance were good, with the edge going to the smaller units. Since the one Negro division then in combat, the 92d, in Italy, had suffered continuing problems since its commitment as a division, the performance of the infantry replacements seemed to indicate the direction which the Army should take. Nonetheless, Army boards created after the war, while proposing increased opportunities for Negroes within the service, continued to support separate units and a quota system.

Finally, President Harry S. Truman, in Executive Order 9981, July 26, 1948, declared it to be the policy of the President that "there shall be equality of treatment and opportunity for all persons in the armed services without regard to race, color, religion or national origin." A committee was established in the same directive with authorization to examine the policies of the armed services with a view to determining how this order should be effected. The committee reported to the President in 1950, just as the Korean War was beginning, saying that it had found, "in fact, that inequality had contributed to inefficiency." The Korean War hastened the implementation of the committee's findings. Informal and on-the-spot integration produced results similar to those of the infantry-replacement platoon integration at the close of World War II. The last of the large Negro combat units, the venerable but now shaken 24th Infantry, disappeared during the Korean War. By the close of the war in 1953, young Negro recruits serving in Korea found it hard to believe that an all-Negro infantry regiment had ever existed.

The Draft Today

A selective service or draft act exists to provide manpower for military forces. An equitable Selective Service Act is intended to spread the requirements for military service over the population's entire group of mentally and physically able men as fairly as possible and in accordance with the needs of the armed forces. All reports from Vietnam and from armed forces installations around the world point to circumstances within the armed forces which are markedly different from those at home.

> There, [one observer reports] for the first time in history, an element of American society has fully accepted the Negro, with potentially great repercussions . . . the integration is as complete as any we are likely to see in our lifetimes. Whites take orders from Negroes or save Negro lives in combat. Negro and white soldiers eat, sleep, travel, and fight side by side. They even trade dirty jokes, something no one would have believed possible in 1950.[1]

Other dispatches and reports, such as those of Whitney Young of the Urban League and of Thomas A. Johnson of *The New York Times,* support this view. So do reenlistment figures, which show that Negroes reenlist in a ratio of two to one for whites.

Why, then, should there be any opposition to the draft at all among Negroes if Negroes in general feel that the biggest national failing is a refusal to count them in on the benefits of the mainstream of American life?

The operation of the draft and the related positions of the armed forces are themselves discriminatory. Of the services, the Army takes approximately 97 per cent of all draftees; the Marine Corps takes the remainder, for the Navy and the Air Force rely on volunteers. The result is that Negroes constitute approximately 13 per cent of the Army, 10 per cent of the Air Force, 5.6 per cent of the Navy, and 8 per cent of the Marines. Moreover, the proportion of Negroes in the combat forces, especially in Vietnam, is higher by far than their proportion in the Army and the number of Negro fatalities is higher still.

The National Advisory Commission on Selective Service reported in the spring of 1967 that Negroes constituted 11 per cent of the total enlisted strength in Vietnam, 14.5 per cent of the Army, and 22.4 per cent of all Army troops killed in action.

Current estimates are that Negroes constitute nearly 20 per cent of the combat forces, about 25 per cent of the front-line non-commissioned officers, about 2 per cent of the commissioned officers, and over 14 per cent of those killed in action.

The reduction in the current figures reflects the efforts of the Department of Defense to reduce criticism and to combat the notion, held by many Negroes, that the disproportionate combat death rate is intentional.

The figures on enlistments and reenlistments indicate that many Negroes feel that the armed services offer a better way of life for them

[1] Stephen E. Ambrose, "The Negro in the Army," Baltimore *Evening Sun,* April 19, 1968.

and their families, at higher incomes and with better facilities for living, than the civilian society. This in itself is regarded as a strong, indirect criticism of American society, though the situation is not new. For most of their existence, the four Negro regiments of the old Army had waiting lists and, at times, when it was possible to enlist only by going to Fort Huachuchua in Arizona where one of the regiments was stationed, eager applicants showed up from as far away as New York and the Philippines.

The draft process itself reveals other rankling inequities. An often stated reason for the high proportion of Negroes in the combat forces is that relatively few Negroes enter the Army with a reasonably high level of education or with acquired skills, so that they are less readily eligible than whites for specialized, technical assignments and schools. This is an unfavorable reflection on the public educational system available to Negroes and on an industrial economy that fails to train the Negro potential in our society.

Moreover, in the matter of deferrable classes and occupations, Negro youths are at a distinct disadvantage. Relatively fewer Negroes are attending colleges and graduate schools; most Negroes have not therefore been eligible for student deferments. Few are in critical occupations and those who are so employed are seldom the sole physicians or specialists upon whom an entire community depends.

Nor can Negroes rush to join the National Guard as a means of avoiding—even if temporarily—combat assignments; Negroes in the Guard today represent only 1.15 per cent of the total and only 0.6 per cent of the Air National Guard.

For these and other reasons, some 30.2 per cent of qualified Negroes are drafted, while 18.8 per cent of the qualified whites are drafted. The constitution of local draft boards may also play a part in this picture; they certainly share the criticism levelled against the Selective Service System as it has operated in the immediate past. Many draft boards, until 1967, retained most of their World War II and Korean War members. In mid-1966, only 1.3 per cent of all draft board members were Negroes, although the national Negro population is about 12 per cent. During 1967, at least 316 Negroes were added to the nation's 4,080 local draft boards, making approximately 600 in mid-1968.

To overcome the inequities of the present system of selection and deferments, many Negroes, including members of the National Association for the Advancement of Colored People, support a return to a lottery system.

Obviously affecting attitudes towards the draft is the conviction, held by a rapidly growing number of Negroes and many whites, that the war in Vietnam is not only an unjust war but one whose enormous budget prevents adequate attention to problems at home, especially to the reconstruction of cities and the war on poverty. College students of the Society of African and Afro-American Students have been especially vocal in their opposition to the "racist war in Vietnam." In the spring of 1967, their New England Regional meeting, attended by 200 students from 14 colleges, declared that "We believe that America is the black man's battlefield and that the black man must not join the atrocities of this war." Upon his return to the mainland from Bimini, Representative Adam Clayton Powell (D., N.Y.) gave college audiences an updated version of a saying frequently repeated by Negro soldiers in the Pacific during World War I: "Here lies a black man killed fighting a colored man for the white man." (In World War II the second term was usually "yellow man" while the first was "colored man.") For a year before he was slain, Dr. Martin Luther King, Jr., had opposed the Vietnamese War as "a blasphemy against all that America stands for," a war in which Negroes are "dying in disproportionate numbers in Vietnam. Twice as many Negroes as whites are in combat." This he saw as a "reflection of the Negro's position in America." While the N.A.A.C.P. deplored a merger of the civil rights and peace movements, CORE (Congress of Racial Equality) and SNCC (Student Nonviolent Coordinating Committee) agreed, along with most of the locally-based Black Power and separatist movements.

A number of Negroes, primarily from the college and intellectual groups, have applied for conscientious objector status from their local boards because of moral objections to the Vietnamese War, nor is it possible to know how much further the pitifully small number of Negro commissioned officers will be reduced by the reluctance of young Negroes of college age to enter Reserve Officer Training Corps units because of their opposition to what they see as a colonial or racist war.

In service, there are clear advantages for Negroes noted by most observers and many participants; thus there is a high rate of enlistment and reenlistment "generated largely by the superiority of opportunity for training and advancement in the military sector as compared with civilian life" (as Mahlon T. Puryear, executive director of the Urban League, phrased it when announcing the establishment of an Office of Veterans Affairs by his organization in the late summer of 1967). Yet it is unlikely that the Negro of the ghetto, whose whole encounter with his environment produces anger, anxiety and hostility growing out of his sense of entrapment, will find the draft an inviting solution. If he does, he does not wait to be drafted: he volunteers instead and looks ahead to an assignment in Germany or Hawaii or even in Vietnam.

Paule Marshall

(b. 1929)

PAULE MARSHALL WAS BORN in Brooklyn to Barbadian parents who migrated to New York after World War I. She received a B.A., *cum laude*, from Brooklyn College in 1953. She has worked as a librarian and feature writer for *Our World* and has traveled a good deal in the West Indies and Brazil.

Miss Marshall's first novel, *Brown Girl, Brownstones*, was published in 1959 and she adapted the work for television in 1960. A book of novelettes, *Soul Clap Hands and Sing*, came out in 1961. Miss Marshall, who has published short stories in numerous magazines and in several recent anthologies of Negro literature, has received a Guggenheim Fellowship (1961–62), a Rosenthal Award from the National Institute of Arts and Letters (1962), a Ford Foundation Theater Award (1964–65), and a National Endowment for the Arts Grant (1967).

The selection "Brooklyn" comes from *Soul Clap Hands and Sing*.

BROOKLYN

A summer wind, soaring just before it died, blew the dusk and the first scattered lights of downtown Brooklyn against the shut windows of the classroom, but Professor Max Berman—B.A., 1919, M.A., 1921, New York; Docteur de l'Université, 1930, Paris—alone in the room, did not bother to open the windows to the cooling wind. The heat and airlessness of the room, the perspiration inching its way like an ant around his starched collar were discomforts he enjoyed; they obscured his larger discomfort: the anxiety which chafed his heart and tugged his left eyelid so that he seemed to be winking, roguishly, behind his glasses.

To steady his eye and ease his heart, to fill the time until his students arrived and his first class in years began, he reached for his cigarettes. As always he delayed lighting the cigarette so that his need for it would be greater and, thus, the relief and pleasure it would bring, fuller. For some time he fondled it, his fingers shaping soft, voluptuous gestures, his warped old man's hands looking strangely abandoned on the bare desk and limp as if the bones had been crushed, and so white

—except for the tobacco burn on the index and third fingers—it seemed his blood no longer traveled that far.

He lit the cigarette finally and as the smoke swelled his lungs, his eyelid stilled and his lined face lifted, the plume of white hair wafting above his narrow brow; his body—short, blunt, the shoulders slightly bent as if in deference to his sixty-three years—settled back in the chair. Delicately Max Berman crossed his legs and, looking down, examined his shoes for dust. (The shoes were of a very soft, fawn-colored leather and somewhat foppishly pointed at the toe. They had been custom made in France and were his one last indulgence. He wore them in memory of his first wife, a French Jewess from Alsace-Lorraine whom he had met in Paris while lingering over his doctorate and married to avoid returning home. She had been gay, mindless and very excitable—but at night, she had also been capable of a profound stillness as she lay in bed waiting for him to turn to her, and this had always awed and delighted him. She had been a gift—and her death in a car accident had been a judgment on him for never having loved her, for never, indeed, having even allowed her to matter.) Fastidiously Max Berman unbuttoned his jacket and straightened his vest, which had a stain two decades old on the pocket. Through the smoke his veined eyes contemplated other, more pleasurable scenes. With his neatly shod foot swinging and his cigarette at a rakish tilt, he might have been an old *boulevardier* taking the sun and an absinthe before the afternoon's assignation.

A young face, the forehead shiny with earnestness, hung at the half-opened door. "Is this French Lit, fifty-four? Camus and Sartre?"

Max Berman winced at the rawness of the voice and the flat "a" in Sartre and said formally, "This is Modern French Literature, number fifty-four, yes, but there is some question as to whether we will take up Messieurs Camus and Sartre this session. They might prove hot work for a summer-evening course. We will probably do Gide and Mauriac, who are considerably more temperate. But come in nonetheless. . . ."

He was the gallant, half rising to bow her to a seat. He knew that she would select the one in the front row directly opposite his desk. At the bell her pen would quiver above her blank notebook, ready to commit his first word—indeed, the clearing of his throat—to paper, and her thin buttocks would begin sidling toward the edge of her chair.

His eyelid twitched with solicitude. He wished that he could have drawn the lids over her fitful eyes and pressed a cool hand to her forehead. She reminded him of what he had been several lifetimes ago: a boy with a pale, plump face and harried eyes, running from the occasional taunts at his yamilke along the shrill streets of Brownsville in Brooklyn, impeded by the heavy satchel of books which he always carried as proof of his scholarship. He had been proud of his brilliance at school and the Yeshiva, but at the same time he had been secretly troubled by it and resentful, for he could never believe that he had come by it naturally or that it belonged to him alone. Rather, it was like a heavy medal his father had hung around his neck—the chain bruising his flesh—and constantly exhorted him to wear proudly and use well.

The girl gave him an eager and ingratiating smile and he looked away. During his thirty years of teaching, a face similar to hers had crowded his vision whenever he had looked up from a desk. Perhaps it was fitting, he thought, and lighted another cigarette from the first, that she should be present as he tried again at life, unaware that behind his rimless glasses and within his ancient suit, he had been gutted.

He thought of those who had taken the last of his substance—and smiled tolerantly. "The boys of summer," he called them, his inquisitors, who had flailed him with a single question: "Are you now or have you ever been a member of the Communist party?" Max Berman had never taken their question seriously—perhaps because he had never taken his membership in the party seriously—and he had refused to answer. What had disturbed him, though, even when the investigation was over, was the feeling that he had really been under investigation for some other offense which did matter and of which he was guilty; that behind their accusations and charges had lurked another which had not been political but personal. For had he been disloyal to the government? His denial was a short, hawking laugh. Simply, he had never ceased being religious. When his father's God had become useless and even a little embarrassing, he had sought others: his work for a time, then the party. But he had been middle-aged when he joined and his faith, which had been so full as a boy, had grown thin. He had come, by then, to distrust all pieties, so that when the purges in Russia during the thirties confirmed his distrust, he had withdrawn into a modest cynicism.

But he had been made to answer for that error. Ten years later his inquisitors had flushed him out from the small community college in upstate New York where he had taught his classes from the same neat pack of notes each semester and had led him bound by subpoena to New York and bandied his name at the hearings until he had been dismissed from his job.

He remembered looking back at the pyres of burning autumn leaves on the campus his last day and feeling that another lifetime had ended—for he had always thought of his life as divided into many small lives, each with its own beginning and end. Like a hired mute, he had been present at each dying and kept the wake and wept professionally as the bier was lowered into the ground. Because of this feeling, he told himself that his final death would be anticlimactic.

After his dismissal he had continued living in the small house he had built near the college, alone except for an occasional visit from a colleague, idle but for some tutoring in French, content with the income he received from the property his parents had left him in Brooklyn— until the visits and tutoring had tapered off and a silence had begun to choke the house, like weeds springing up around a deserted place. He had begun to wonder then if he were still alive. He would wake at night from the recurrent dream of the hearings, where he was being accused of an unstated crime, to listen for his heart, his hand fumbling among the bedclothes to press the place. During the day he would pass repeatedly in front of the mirror with the pretext that he might have forgotten to shave that morning or that something had blown into his eye. Above all, he had begun to think of his inquisitors with affection and to long for the sound of their voices. They, at least, had assured him of being alive.

As if seeking them out, he had returned to Brooklyn and to the house in Brownsville where he had lived as a boy and had boldly applied for a teaching post without mentioning the investigation. He had finally been offered the class which would begin in five minutes. It wasn't much: a six-week course in the summer evening session of a college without a rating, where classes were held in a converted factory building, a college whose campus took in the bargain department stores, the five-and-dime emporiums and neon-spangled movie houses of downtown Brooklyn.

Through the smoke from his cigarette, Max Berman's eyes—a waning blue that never seemed to focus on any one thing—drifted over the students who had gathered meanwhile. Imbuing them with his own disinterest, he believed that even before the class began, most of them were longing for its end and already anticipating the soft drinks at the soda fountain downstairs and the synthetic dramas at the nearby movie.

They made him sad. He would have liked to lead them like a Pied Piper back to the safety of their childhoods—all of them: the loud girl with the formidable calves of an athlete who reminded him, uncomfortably, of his second wife (a party member who was always shouting political heresy from some picket line and who had promptly divorced him upon discovering his irreverence); the two sallow-faced young men leaning out the window as if searching for the wind that had died; the slender young woman with crimped black hair who sat very still and apart from the others, her face turned toward the night sky as if to a friend.

Her loneliness interested him. He sensed its depth and his eye paused. He saw then that she was a Negro, a very pale mulatto with skin the color of clear, polished amber and a thin, mild face. She was somewhat older than the others in the room—a schoolteacher from the South, probably, who came north each summer to take courses toward a graduate degree. He felt a fleeting discomfort and irritation: discomfort at the thought that although he had been sinned against as a Jew he still shared in the sin against her and suffered from the same vague guilt, irritation that she recalled his own humiliations: the large ones, such as the fact that despite his brilliance he had been unable to get into a medical school as a young man because of the quota on Jews (not that he had wanted to be a doctor; that had been his father's wish) and had changed his studies from medicine to French; the small ones which had worn him thin: an eye widening imperceptibly as he gave his name, the savage glance which sought the Jewishness in his nose, his chin, in the set of his shoulders, the jokes snuffed into silence at his appearance. . . .

Tired suddenly, his eyelid pulsing, he turned and stared out the window at the gaudy constellation of neon lights. He longed for a drink, a quiet place and then sleep. And to bear him gently into sleep, to stay the terror which bound his heart then reminding him of those oleographs of Christ with the thorns binding his exposed heart—fat drops of blood from one so bloodless—to usher him into sleep, some pleasantly erotic image: a nude in a boudoir scattered with her frilled garments and warmed by her frivolous laugh, with the sun like a voyeur at the half-closed shutters. But this time instead of the usual Rubens nude with thighs like twin portals and a belly like a huge alabaster bowl into which he poured himself, he chose Gauguin's *Aita Parari,* her languorous form in the straight-back chair, her dark, sloping breasts, her eyes like the sun under shadow.

With the image still on his inner eye, he turned to the Negro girl and appraised her through a blind of cigarette smoke. She was still gazing out at the night sky and something about her fixed stare, her hands stiffly arranged in her lap, the nerve fluttering within the curve of her throat, betrayed a vein of tension within the rock of her calm. It was as if she had fled long ago to a remote region within herself, taking with her all that was most valuable and most vulnerable about herself.

She stirred finally, her slight breasts lifting beneath her flowered summer dress as she breathed deeply—and Max Berman thought again of Gauguin's girl with the dark, sloping breasts. What would this girl with the amber-colored skin be like on a couch in a sunlit room, nude in a straight-back chair? And as the question echoed along each nerve and stilled his breathing, it seemed suddenly that life, which had scorned him for so long, held out her hand again—but still a little beyond his reach. Only the girl, he sensed, could bring him close enough to touch it. She alone was the bridge. So that even while he repeated to himself that he was being presumptuous (for she would surely refuse him) and ridiculous (for even if she did not, what could he do—his performance would be a mere scramble and twitch), he vowed at the same time to have her. The challenge eased the tightness around his heart suddenly; it soothed the damaged muscle of his eye and as the bell rang he rose and said briskly, "Ladies and gentlemen, may I have your attention, please. My name is Max Berman. The course is Modern French Literature, number fifty-four. May I suggest that you check your program cards to see whether you are in the right place at the right time."

Her essay on Gide's *The Immoralist* lay on his desk and the note from the administration informing him, first, that his past political activities had been brought to their attention and then dismissing him at the end of the session weighed the inside pocket of his jacket. The two, her paper and the note, were linked in his mind. Her paper reminded him that the vow he had taken was still an empty one, for the term was half over and he had never once spoken to her (as if she understood his intention she was always late and disappeared as soon as the closing bell rang, leaving him trapped in a clamorous circle of students around his desk), while the note which wrecked his small attempt to start anew suddenly made that vow more urgent. It gave him the edge of desperation he needed to act finally. So that as soon as the bell rang, he returned all the papers but hers, announced that all questions would have to wait until their next meeting and, waving off the students from his desk, called above their protests, "Miss Williams, if you have a moment, I'd like to speak with you briefly about your paper."

She approached his desk like a child who has been cautioned not to talk to strangers, her fingers touching the backs of the chairs as if for support, her gaze following the departing students as though she longed to accompany them.

Her slight apprehensiveness pleased him. It suggested a submissiveness which gave him, as he rose uncertainly, a feeling of certainty and command. Her hesitancy was somehow in keeping with the color of her skin. She seemed to bring not only herself but the host of black women whose bodies had been despoiled to make her. He would not only possess her but them also, he thought (not really thought, for he scarcely allowed these thoughts to form before he snuffed them out). Through their collective suffering, which she contained, his own personal suffering would be eased; he would be pardoned for whatever sin it was he had committed against life.

"I hope you weren't unduly alarmed when I didn't return your paper along with the others," he said, and had to look up as she reached the desk. She was taller close up and her eyes, which he had thought were black, were a strong, flecked brown with very small pupils which seemed to shrink now from the sight of him. "But I found it so interesting I wanted to give it to you privately."

"I didn't know what to think," she said, and her voice—he heard it for the first time for she never recited or answered in class—was low, cautious, Southern.

"It was, to say the least, refreshing. It not only showed some original and mature thinking on your part, but it also proved that you've been listening in class—and after twenty-five years and more of teaching it's encouraging to find that some students do listen. If you have a little time I'd like to tell you, more specifically, what I liked about it. . . ."

Talking easily, reassuring her with his professional tone and a deft gesture with his cigarette, he led her from the room as the next class filed in, his hand cupped at her elbow but not touching it, his manner urbane, courtly, kind. They paused on the landing at the end of the long corridor with the stairs piled in steel tiers above and plunging below them. An intimate silence swept up the stairwell in a warm gust and Max Berman said, "I'm curious. Why did you choose *The Immoralist?*"

She started suspiciously, afraid, it seemed, that her answer might expose and endanger the self she guarded so closely within.

"Well," she said finally, her glance reaching down the stairs to the door marked EXIT at the bottom, "when you said we could use anything by Gide I decided on *The Immoralist,* since it was the first book I read in the original French when I was in undergraduate school. I didn't understand it then because my French was so weak, I guess, but I always thought about it afterward for some odd reason. I was shocked by what I did understand, of course, but something else about it appealed to me, so when you made the assignment I thought I'd try reading it again. I understood it a little better this time. At least I think so. . . ."

"Your paper proves you did."

She smiled absently, intent on some other thought. Then she said cautiously, but with unexpected force, "You see, to me, the book seems to say that the only way you begin to know what you are and how much you are capable of is by daring to try something, by doing something which tests you. . . ."

"Something bold," he said.

"Yes."

"Even sinful."

She paused, questioning this, and then said reluctantly, "Yes, perhaps even sinful."

"The salutary effects of sin, you might say." He gave the little bow.

But she had not heard this; her mind had already leaped ahead. "The only trouble, at least with the character in Gide's book, is that what he finds out about himself is so terrible. He is so unhappy. . . ."

"But at least he knows, poor sinner." And his playful tone went unnoticed.

"Yes," she said with the same startling forcefulness. "And another thing, in finding out what he is, he destroys his wife. It was as if she had to die in order for him to live and know himself. Perhaps in order for a person to live and know himself somebody else must die. Maybe there's always a balancing out. . . . In a way"—and he had to lean close now to hear her—"I believe this."

Max Berman edged back as he glimpsed something move within her abstracted gaze. It was like a strong and restless seed that had taken root in the darkness there and was straining now toward the light. He had not expected so subtle and complex a force beneath her mild exterior and he found it disturbing and dangerous, but fascinating.

"Well, it's a most interesting interpretation," he said. "I don't know if M. Gide would have agreed, but then he's not around to give his opinion. Tell me, where did you do your undergraduate work?"

"At Howard University."

"And you majored in French?"

"Yes."

"Why, if I may ask?" he said gently.

"Well, my mother was from New Orleans and could speak a little Creole and I got interested in learning how to speak French through her, I guess. I teach it now at a junior high school in Richmond. Only the beginner courses because I don't have my master's. You know, *je vais, tu vas, il va* and *Frère Jacques*. It's not very inspiring."

"You should do something about that then, my dear Miss Williams. Perhaps it's time for you, like our friend in Gide, to try something new and bold."

"I know," she said, and her pale hand sketched a vague, despairing gesture. "I thought maybe if I got my master's . . . that's why I decided to come north this summer and start taking some courses. . . ."

Max Berman quickly lighted a cigarette to still the flurry inside him, for the moment he had been awaiting had come. He flicked her paper, which he still held. "Well, you've got the makings of a master's thesis right here. If you like I will suggest some ways for you to expand it sometime. A few pointers from an old pro might help."

He had to turn from her astonished and grateful smile—it was like a child's. He said carefully, "The only problem will be to find a place where we can talk quietly. Regrettably, I don't rate an office. . . ."

"Perhaps we could use one of the empty classrooms," she said.

"That would be much too dismal a setting for a pleasant discussion."

He watched the disappointment wilt her smile and when he spoke he made certain that the same disappointment weighed his voice. "Another difficulty is that the term's half over, which gives us little or no time. But let's not give up. Perhaps we can arrange to meet and talk over a weekend. The only hitch there is that I spend weekends at my place in the country. Of course you're perfectly welcome to come up there. It's only about seventy miles from New York, in the heart of what's very appropriately called the Borsch Circuit, even though, thank

God, my place is a good distance away from the borsch. That is, it's very quiet and there's never anybody around except with my permission."

She did not move, yet she seemed to start; she made no sound, yet he thought he heard a bewildered cry. And then she did a strange thing, standing there with the breath sucked into the hollow of her throat and her smile, that had opened to him with such trust, dying— her eyes, her hands faltering up begged him to declare himself.

"There's a lake near the house," he said, "so that when you get tired of talking—or better, listening to me talk—you can take a swim, if you like. I would very much enjoy that sight." And as the nerve tugged at his eyelid, he seemed to wink behind his rimless glasses.

Her sudden, blind step back was like a man groping his way through a strange room in the dark, and instinctively Max Berman reached out to break her fall. Her arms, bare to the shoulder because of the heat (he knew the feel of her skin without even touching it—it would be like a rich, fine-textured cloth which would soothe and hide him in its amber warmth), struck out once to drive him off and then fell limp at her side, and her eyes became vivid and convulsive in her numbed face. She strained toward the stairs and the exit door at the bottom, but she could not move. Nor could she speak. She did not even cry. Her eyes remained dry and dull with disbelief. Only her shoulders trembled as though she was silently weeping inside.

It was as though she had never learned the forms and expressions of anger. The outrage of a lifetime, of her history, was trapped inside her. And she stared at Max Berman with this mute, paralyzing rage. Not really at him but to his side, as if she caught sight of others behind him. And remembering how he had imagined a column of dark women trailing her to his desk, he sensed that she glimpsed a legion of old men with sere flesh and lonely eyes flanking him: "old lechers with a love on every wind . . ."

"I'm sorry, Miss Williams," he said, and would have welcomed her insults, for he would have been able, at least, to distill from them some passion and a kind of intimacy. It would have been, in a way, like touching her. "It was only that you are a very attractive young woman and although I'm no longer young"—and he gave the tragic little laugh which sought to dismiss that fact—"I can still appreciate and even desire an attractive woman. But I was wrong. . . ." His self-disgust, overwhelming him finally, choked off his voice. "And so very crude. Forgive me. I can offer no excuse for my behavior other than my approaching senility."

He could not even manage the little marionette bow this time. Quickly he shoved the paper on Gide into her lifeless hand, but it fell, the pages separating, and as he hurried past her downstairs and out the door, he heard the pages scattering like dead leaves on the steps.

She remained away until the night of the final examination, which was also the last meeting of the class. By that time Max Berman, believing that she would not return, had almost succeeded in forgetting her. He was no longer even certain of how she looked, for her face had been absorbed into the single, blurred, featureless face of all the women who had ever refused him. So that she startled him as much as a stranger would have when he entered the room that night and found her alone amid a maze of empty chairs, her face turned toward the window as on the first night and her hands serene in her lap. She turned at his footstep and it was if she had also forgotten all that had passed between them. She waited until he said, "I'm glad you decided to take the examination. I'm sure you won't have any difficulty with it"; then she gave him a nod that was somehow reminiscent of his little bow and turned again to the window.

He was relieved yet puzzled by her composure. It was as if during her three-week absence she had waged and won a decisive contest with herself and was ready now to act. He was wary suddenly and all during the examination he tried to discover what lay behind her strange calm, studying her bent head amid the shifting heads of the other students, her slim hand guiding the pen across the page, her legs—the long bone visible, it seemed, beneath the flesh. Desire flared and quickly died.

"Excuse me, Professor Berman, will you take up Camus and Sartre next semester, maybe?" The girl who sat in front of his desk was standing over him with her earnest smile and finished examination folder.

"That might prove somewhat difficult, since I won't be here."

"No more?"

"No."

"I mean, not even next summer?"

"I doubt it."

"Gee, I'm sorry. I mean, I enjoyed the course and everything."

He bowed his thanks and held his head down until she left. Her compliment, so piteous somehow, brought on the despair he had forced to the dim rear of his mind. He could no longer flee the thought of the exile awaiting him when the class tonight ended. He could either remain in the house in Brooklyn, where the memory of his father's face above the radiance of the Sabbath candles haunted him from the shadows, reminding him of the certainty he had lost and never found again, where the mirrors in his father's room were still shrouded with sheets, as on the day he lay dying and moaning into his beard that his only son was a bad Jew; or he could return to the house in the country, to the silence shrill with loneliness.

The cigarette he was smoking burned his fingers, rousing him, and he saw over the pile of examination folders on his desk that the room was empty except for the Negro girl. She had finished—her pen lay aslant the closed folder on her desk—but she had remained in her seat and she was smiling across the room at him—a set, artificial smile that was both cold and threatening. It utterly denuded him and he was wildly angry suddenly that she had seen him give way to despair; he wanted to remind her (he could not stay the thought; it attacked him like an assailant from a dark turn in his mind) that she was only black after all. . . . His head dropped and he almost wept with shame.

The girl stiffened as if she had seen the thought and then the tiny muscles around her mouth quickly arranged the bland smile. She came up to his desk, placed her folder on top of the others and said pleasantly, her eyes like dark, shattered glass that spared Max Berman his reflection, "I've changed my mind. I think I'd like to spend a day at your place in the country if your invitation still holds."

He thought of refusing her, for her voice held neither promise nor passion, but he could not. Her presence, even if it was only for a day, would make his return easier. And there was still the possibility of passion despite her cold manner and the deliberate smile. He thought of how long it had been since he had had someone, of how badly he needed the sleep which followed love and of awakening certain, for the first time in years, of his existence.

"Of course the invitation still holds. I'm driving up tonight."

"I won't be able to come until Sunday," she said firmly. "Is there a train then?"

"Yes, in the morning," he said, and gave her the schedule.

"You'll meet me at the station?"

"Of course. You can't miss my car. It's a very shabby but venerable Chevy."

She smiled stiffly and left, her heels awakening the silence of the empty corridor, the sound reaching back to a tap like a warning finger on Max Berman's temple.

The pale sunlight slanting through the windshield lay like a cat on his knees, and the motor of his old Chevy, turning softly under him could have been the humming of its heart. A little distance from the car a log-cabin station house—the logs blackened by the seasons—stood alone against the hills, and the hills, in turn, lifted softly, still green although the summer was ending, into the vague autumn sky.

The morning mist and pale sun, the green that was still somehow new, made it seem that the season was stirring into life even as it died, and this contradiction pained Max Berman at the same time that it pleased him. For it was his own contradiction after all: his desires which remained those of a young man even as he was dying.

He had been parked for some time in the deserted station, yet his hands were still tensed on the steering wheel and his foot hovered near the accelerator. As soon as he had arrived in the station he had wanted to leave. But like the girl that night on the landing, he was too stiff with tension to move. He could only wait, his eyelid twitching with foreboding, regret, curiosity and hope.

Finally and with no warning the train charged through the fiery green, setting off a tremor underground. Max Berman imagined the girl seated at a window in the train, her hands arranged quietly in her lap and her gaze scanning the hills that were so familiar to him, and yet he could not believe that she was really there. Perhaps her plan had been to disappoint him. She might be in New York or on her way back to Richmond now, laughing at the trick she had played on him. He was convinced of this suddenly, so that even when he saw her walking toward him through the blown steam from under the train, he told himself that she was a mirage created by the steam. Only when she sat beside him in the car, bringing with her, it seemed, an essence she had distilled from the morning air and rubbed into her skin, was he certain of her reality.

"I brought my bathing suit but it's much too cold to swim," she said and gave him the deliberate smile.

He did not see it; he only heard her voice, its warm Southern lilt in the chill, its intimacy in the closed car—and an excitement swept him, cold first and then hot, as if the sun had burst in his blood.

"It's the morning air," he said. "By noon it should be like summer again."

"Is that a promise?"

"Yes."

By noon the cold morning mist had lifted above the hills and below, in the lake valley, the sunlight was a sheer gold net spread out on the grass as if to dry, draped on the trees and flung, glinting, over the lake. Max Berman felt it brush his shoulder gently as he sat by the lake waiting for the girl, who had gone up to the house to change into her swimsuit.

He had spent the morning showing her the fields and small wood near his house. During the long walk he had been careful to keep a little apart from her. He would extend a hand as they climbed a rise or when she stepped uncertainly over a rock, but he would not really touch her. He was afraid that at his touch, no matter how slight and casual, her scream would spiral into the morning calm, or worse, his touch would unleash the threatening thing he sensed behind her even smile.

He had talked of her paper and she had listened politely and occasionally even asked a question or made a comment. But all the while detached, distant, drawn within herself as she had been that first night in the classroom. And then halfway down a slope she had paused and, pointing to the canvas tops of her white sneakers, which had become wet and dark from the dew secreted in the grass, she had laughed. The sound, coming so abruptly in the midst of her tense quiet, joined her, it seemed, to the wood and wide fields, to the hills; she shared their simplicity and held within her the same strong current of life. Max Berman had felt privileged suddenly, and humble. He had stopped questioning her smile. He had told himself then that it would not matter even if she stopped and picking up a rock bludgeoned him from behind.

"There's a lake near my home, but it's not like this," the girl said, coming up behind him. "Yours is so dark and serious-looking."

He nodded and followed her gaze out to the lake, where the ripples were long, smooth welts raised by the wind, and across to the other bank, where a group of birches stepped delicately down to the lake and bending over touched the water with their branches as if testing it before they plunged.

The girl came and stood beside him now—and she was like a pale-gold naiad, the spirit of the lake, her eyes reflecting its somber autumnal tone and her body as supple as the birches. She walked slowly into the water, unaware, it seemed, of the sudden passion in his gaze, or perhaps uncaring; and as she walked she held out her arms in what seemed a gesture of invocation (and Max Berman remembered his father with the fringed shawl draped on his outstretched arms as he invoked their God each Sabbath with the same gesture); her head was bent as if she listened for a voice beneath the water's murmurous surface. When the ground gave way she still seemed to be walking and listening, her arms outstretched. The water reached her waist, her small breasts, her shoulders. She lifted her head once, breathed deeply and disappeared.

She stayed down for a long time and when her white cap finally broke the water some distance out, Max Berman felt strangely stranded and deprived. He understood suddenly the profund cleavage between them and the absurdity of his hope. The water between them became the years which separated them. Her white cap was the sign of her purity, while the silt darkening the lake was the flotsam of his failures. Above all, their color—her arms a pale, flashing gold in the sunlit water and his bled white and flaccid with the veins like angry blue penciling—marked the final barrier.

He was sad as they climbed toward the house late that afternoon and troubled. A crow cawed derisively in the bracken, heralding the dusk which would not only end their strange day but would also, he felt, unveil her smile, so that he would learn the reason for her coming. And because he was sad, he said wryly, "I think I should tell you that you've been spending the day with something of an outcast."

"Oh," she said and waited.

He told her of the dismissal, punctuating his words with the little hoarse, deprecating laugh and waving aside the pain with his cigarette. She listened, polite but neutral, and because she remained unmoved, he wanted to confess all the more. So that during dinner and afterward when they sat outside on the porch, he told her of the investigation.

"It was very funny once you saw it from the proper perspective, which I did, of course," he said. "I mean here they were accusing me of crimes I couldn't remember committing and asking me for the names of people with whom I had never associated. It was pure farce. But I made a mistake. I should have done something dramatic or something just as farcical. Bared my breast in the public market place or written a tome on my apostasy, naming names. It would have been a far different story then. Instead of my present ignominy I would have been offered a chairmanship at Yale. . . No? Well, Brandeis then. I would have been draped in honorary degrees. . . ."

"Well, why didn't you confess?" she said impatiently.

"I've often asked myself the same interesting question, but I haven't come up with a satisfactory answer yet. I suspect, though, that I said nothing because none of it really mattered that much."

"What did matter?" she asked sharply.

He sat back, waiting for the witty answer, but none came, because just then the frame upon which his organs were strung seemed to snap and he felt his heart, his lungs, his vital parts fall in a heap within him. Her question had dealt the severing blow, for it was the same question he understood suddenly that the vague forms in his dream asked repeatedly. It had been the plaintive undercurrent to his father's dying moan, the real accusation behind the charges of his inquisitors at the hearing.

For what had mattered? He gazed through his sudden shock at the night squatting on the porch steps, at the hills asleep like gentle beasts in the darkness, at the black screen of the sky where the events of his life passed in a mute, accusing review—and he saw nothing there to which he had given himself or in which he had truly believed since the belief and dedication of his boyhood.

"Did you hear my question?" she asked, and he was glad that he sat within the shadows clinging to the porch screen and could not be seen.

"Yes, I did," he said faintly, and his eyelid twitched. "But I'm afraid it's another one of those I can't answer satisfactorily." And then he struggled for the old flippancy. "You make an excellent examiner, you know. Far better than my inquisitors."

"What will you do now?" Her voice and cold smile did not spare him.

He shrugged and the motion, a slow, eloquent lifting of the shoulders, brought with it suddenly the weight and memory of his boyhood. It was the familiar gesture of the women hawkers in Belmont Market, of the men standing outside the temple on Saturday mornings, each of them reflecting his image of God in their forbidding black coats and with the black, tumbling beards in which he had always imagined he could hide as in a forest. All this had mattered, he called loudly to himself, and said aloud to the girl, "Let me see if I can answer this one at least. What *will* I do?" He paused and swung his leg so that his foot in the fastidious French shoe caught the light from the house. "Grow flowers and write my memoirs. How's that? That would be the proper way for a gentleman and scholar to retire. Or hire one of those hefty housekeepers who will bully me and when I die in my sleep draw the sheet over my head and call my lawyer. That's somewhat European, but how's that?"

When she said nothing for a long time, he added soberly, "But that's not a fair question for me any more. I leave all such considerations to the young. To you, for that matter. What will you do, my dear Miss Williams?"

It was as if she had been expecting the question and had been readying her answer all the time that he had been talking. She leaned forward eagerly and with her face and part of her body fully in the light, she said, "I will do something. I don't know what yet, but something."

Max Berman started back a little. The answer was so unlike her vague, resigned "I know" on the landing that night when he had admonished her to try something new.

He edged back into the darkness and she leaned further into the light, her eyes overwhelming her face and her mouth set in a thin, determined line. "I will do something," she said, bearing down on each word, "because for the first time in my life I feel almost brave."

He glimpsed this new bravery behind her hard gaze and sensed something vital and purposeful, precious, which she had found and guarded like a prize within her center. He wanted it. He would have liked to snatch it and run like a thief. He no longer desired her but it, and starting forward with a sudden envious cry, he caught her arm and drew her close, seeking it.

But he could not get to it. Although she did not pull away her arm, although she made no protest as his face wavered close to hers, he did not really touch her. She held herself and her prize out of his desperate reach and her smile was a knife she pressed to his throat. He saw himself for what he was in her clear, cold gaze: an old man with skin the color and texture of dough that had been kneaded by the years into tragic folds, with faded eyes adrift behind a pair of rimless glasses and the roughened flesh at his throat like a bird's wattles. And as the disgust which he read in her eyes swept him, his hand dropped from her arm. He started to murmur, "Forgive me . . ." when suddenly she caught hold of his wrist, pulling him close again, and he felt the strength which had borne her swiftly through the water earlier hold him now as she said quietly and without passion, "And do you know why, Dr. Berman, I feel almost brave today? Because ever since I can remember my parents were always telling me, 'Stay away from white folks. Just leave them alone. You mind your business and they'll mind theirs. Don't go near them.' And they made sure I didn't. My father, who was the principal of a colored grade school in Richmond, used to drive me to and from school every day. When I needed something from downtown my mother would take me and if the white saleslady asked me anything she would answer. . . ."

"And my parents were also always telling me, 'Stay away from niggers,' and that meant anybody darker than we were." She held out her arm in the light and Max Berman saw the skin almost as white as his but for the subtle amber shading. Staring at the arm she said tragically, "I was so confused I never really went near anybody. Even when I went away to college I kept to myself. I didn't marry the man I wanted to because he was dark and I knew my parents would disapprove. . . ." She paused, her wistful gaze searching the darkness for the face of the man she had refused, it seemed, and not finding it she went on sadly, "So after graduation I returned home and started teaching and I was just as confused and frightened and ashamed as always. When my parents died I went on the same way. And I would have gone on like that the rest of my life if it hadn't been for you, Dr. Berman"—and the sarcasm leaped behind her cold smile. "In a way you did me a favor. You let me know how you—and most of the people like you—see me."

"My dear Miss Williams, I assure you I was not attracted to you because you were colored. . . ." And he broke off, remembering just how acutely aware of her color he had been.

"I'm not interested in your reasons!" she said brutally. "What matters is what it meant to me. I thought about this these last three weeks and about my parents—how wrong they had been, how frightened, and the terrible thing they had done to me . . . And I wasn't confused any longer." Her head lifted, tremulous with her new assurance. "I can do something now! I can begin," she said with her head poised. "Look how I came all the way up here to tell you this to your face. Because how could you harm me? You're so old you're like a cup I could break in my hand." And her hand tightened on his wrist, wrenching the last of his frail life from him, it seemed. Through the quick pain he remembered her saying on the landing that night: "Maybe in order for a person to live someone else must die" and her quiet "I believe this" then. Now her sudden laugh, an infinitely cruel sound in the warm night, confirmed her belief.

Suddenly she was the one who seemed old, indeed ageless. Her touch became mortal and Max Berman saw the darkness that would end his life gathered in her eyes. But even as he sprang back, jerking his arm away, a part of him rushed forward to embrace that darkness, and his cry, wounding the night, held both ecstasy and terror.

"That's all I came for," she said, rising. "You can drive me to the station now."

They drove to the station in silence. Then, just as the girl started from the car, she turned with an ironic, pitiless smile and said, "You know, it's been a nice day, all things considered. It really turned summer again as you said it would. And even though your lake isn't anything like the one near my home, it's almost as nice."

Max Berman bowed to her for the last time, accepting with that gesture his responsibility for her rage, which went deeper than his, and for her anger, which would spur her finally to live. And not only for her, but for all those at last whom he had wronged through his indifference: his father lying in the room of shrouded mirrors, the wives he had never loved, his work which he had never believed in enough and, lastly (even though he knew it was too late and he would not be spared), himself.

Too weary to move, he watched the girl cross to the train which would bear her south, her head lifted as though she carried life as lightly there as if it were a hat made of tulle. When the train departed his numbed eyes followed it until its rear light was like a single firefly in the immense night or the last flickering of his life. Then he drove back through the darkness.

Samuel W. Allen (Paul Vesey)

(b. 1917)

SAMUEL W. ALLEN IS at Tuskegee Institute as the Avalon Professor of Humanities, which is an endowed chair for creative work. He was born in Columbus, Ohio, educated at Fisk University, Harvard Law School, the New School for Social Research, and the Sorbonne.

A many-sided man, Sam Allen has been, among other things, English Editor of *Présence Africaine;* Delegate and Panelist on African Literature, UNESCO Conference, Boston, 1961; Poet-in-Residence at Tuskegee; a professor of law, practicing attorney, and a deputy assistant district attorney; guest lecturer and/or reader of his own poetry in colleges and universities across the country.

Among his many publications are *Elfenbein Zähne* (Ivory Tusks), a bi-lingual volume of poetry (1956); *Pan Africanism Reconsidered,* as co-editor (1962); *Ivory Tusks and Other Poems* (1962); and numerous articles on African and Negro American literature.

The article reprinted here, "Negritude and Its Relevance to the American Negro Writer," was published in *The American Negro Writer and His Roots,* selected papers from the First Conference of Negro Writers held in New York City in 1959. The author has made some changes in the original article for this work.

A MOMENT, PLEASE

WHEN I GAZE AT THE SUN
    I walked to the subway booth
    for change for a dime.
AND KNOW THAT THIS GREAT EARTH
    Two adolescent girls stood there
    alive with eagerness to know
IS BUT A FRAGMENT FROM IT THROWN
    all in their new found world
    there was for them to know
IN HEAT AND FLAME A BILLION YEARS AGO,
    they looked at me and brightly asked
    'Are you Arabian?'

Poems reprinted by permission of the author.

THAT THEN THIS WORLD WAS LIFELESS
 I smiled and cautiously
 —for one grows cautious—
 shook my head.
AS, A BILLION HENCE
 'Egyptian?'
IT SHALL AGAIN BE,
  Again I smiled and shook my head
  and walked away.
WHAT MOMENT IS IT THAT I AM BETRAYED,
  I've gone but seven paces now
OPPRESSED, CAST DOWN,
  and from behind comes swift the sneer
OR WARM WITH LOVE OR TRIUMPH?
  'Or Nigger?'

  A moment, please
WHAT IS IT THAT TO FURY I AM ROUSED?
  for still it takes a moment
WHAT MEANING FOR ME
  and now
IN THIS HOMELESS CLAN
  I'll turn
THE DUPE OF SPACE
  and smile
THE TOY OF TIME?
  and nod my head.

AMERICAN GOTHIC

To Satch

(The legendary Satchell Paige, one of the star pitchers in Negro baseball)

Sometimes I feel like I will *never* stop
Just go on forever
Til one fine mornin'
I'm gonna reach up and grab me a handfulla stars
Swing out my long lean leg
And whip three hot strikes burnin' down the heavens
And look over at God and say
How about that!

AFRICA TO ME

In the pit of their presumption
Encumbered yet with the weight of fear
Torn under the heel of a false doctrine
Divided by a falsely speaking seer,
We are halted at this juncture
And consider in which direction
Not to aspire.
We are weary with illusions and the years that drag
The haste to be about another's business,
Unfurl an ever alien flag.

> I listen for the clear song
> of your sweet voice,
> O matchless one,
> who will sing an old song
> and tell in a far country
> of the foothills of an unremembered home.

They say we have forgotten;
That we parted, and forever, at the shore
In the shadow of the ships attending,
Flickering still the flame and death, the branding,
Amid the cries of terror which long years ago they bore;
That you are any curious climate
A place we're called upon to study
To be literate
   to know
Along with Peking, Angkor
   strange Tibet
   exotic Singapore . . .

Only that, and nothing more?
A curious spot, pinned on a map,
That, and nothing more?

NEGRITUDE AND ITS RELEVANCE TO THE AMERICAN NEGRO WRITER

By way of preface, before I add my remarks to the very able paper given by Mr. Redding, let me emphasize that in appraising, above all, the future direction of creative endeavor, it is least possible to be

Reprinted by permission of the American Society of African Culture and the author. The Mr. Redding referred to in the first sentence of Mr. Allen's paper is Saunders Redding, who had also presented a paper at the First Conference of Negro Writers.

doctrinaire. The creative effort appears to be in large measure a refusal to be bound, a breaking forth, a reaction to prescription. And all critical preoccupation with the future of any area of creative activity is apt to be proved vain, in error, and subject to reversal by the superior court of hindsight.

Turning then to the phenomenon of "la négritude," we see that it has developed principally among the poets of African descent writing in the French language, including not only the poets of the African continent itself but also those of the Caribbean area, of Martinique, Guadeloupe, etc., who also write in French. Among these were Aimé Césaire, Jacques Roumain, René Dépestre, Léon Damas, Léon Laleau, Paul Niger and others who, remote from what they felt to be a lost homeland that exists in the nostalgic, collective memory were more intense in their reaction to the estrangement of the African in Western society than the poets of the continent were.

We may note that this term, negritude has been unsettling to many, perhaps because it puts into the realm of the explicit that which might more comfortably remain in the area of the implicit. The Negro, or, in French, le Négre, is denied an acceptable identity in Western culture, and the term negritude focuses and carries with it the perjorative implications of that denial. The fact that it was possible for the term to emerge in the literature is undoubtedly symbolic of the necessity of the development it represents. It is essentially, of course, the latter with which we are concerned, and the question of what to call it is secondary.

The work of these poets of the Caribbean and of those of the continent—Leopold Senghor, David Diop, Birago Diop, and, among those writing in English, Efua Morgue, Dei Anang, Carey Thomas, Adeboye Babalola,* has served and is serving to cast off the cultural imprint of colonial Europe; it is a type of reconnaissance in the formation of a new imaginative world free from the proscriptions of a racist West. Their creative activity reveals an effort toward a renewal of their lost organic vision of the universe, which is inextricably involved in, and as crucial as, the political and economic enfranchisement presently occurring. The African finds himself bound fast in the culture prison of the Western World, which has held him for centuries in derision and contempt; his poetic concern has been with his liberation from this prison, with the creation of a truer sense of identity, and with the establishment of his dignity as a man. This preoccupation led to the birth in the French language of the central concept of negritude, principally in the work of Leopold Senghor and Aimé Césaire. The term is not amenable to easy definition. It appears to serve in some-

---

* This article was written initially in 1958 and preceded the emergence of Wole Soyinka, John Pepper Clark and the other younger African writers in English.

what varying roles for those who employ it. It represents in one sense the Negro African poet's endeavor to recover for his race a normal self-pride, a confidence in himself shattered for centuries when the enslaver suddenly loomed in the village pathway; to recover a world in which he once again could have a sense of unashamed identity and an unsubordinate role. Jean Paul Sartre wrote an excellent preface to Senghor's 1947 anthology of African poetry in the French language, and in this, he likened negritude to an African Eurydice, recovered by the song of Orpheus from Pluto. It is the African's lost beloved, his complete and ultimate self, his vision of the world, not that of a culture in which he dwells on sufferance, which holds him in veiled and un-veiled disdain. It is not simply a goal to be accomplished, but rather, more functionally, an affective disposition. In Heidegger's existentialist term, it indicates the African's "being-in-the-world." Senghor points out that the négritude of a poem is less the theme than the style. It is the poem's characteristic manner, the intensity of its passion. It is its rhythmic flow, the quality of its imagery, whether the poet writes of a ritual dance in Dahomey, of the Brittany seacoast, or of the nature of God and man. Négritude includes the characteristic impulses, traits and habits which may be considered more markedly black African than white or European. It is thus something which the poet possesses in the wells of his being, and which he is seeking to invoke and to make manifest. Beneath the complex of traits which may be subsumed under négritude is the subjective disposition of the poet toward the vindica-tion of his integrity, an attitude affirmed and objectivized in the poem.

Aimé Césaire writes:

> My négritude is not a rock, its deafness hurled against the clamor of
> the day
> My négritude is not a film of dead water on the dead eye of the earth
> My négritude is neither a tower nor a cathedral
> It plunges into the red flesh of the earth
> It plunges into the burning flesh of the sky
> It pierces the opaque prostration by its upright patience.

In these lines, Césaire emphasizes the dynamic quality of this con-cept; négritude is an act, an active becoming, a vital force patiently and stubbornly active in the earth and the sky and the elements. Amid the insufferable tension of his estrangement, negritude is that area the poet has carved out for himself in the poem where he may live and dwell and have his true and absolute being. Again Césaire:

> The words surpass themselves. It is indeed toward a sky and a land
> whose height and depth can not be troubled. It is made of the old ge-
> ography. Yet there now emerges at a certain level an area curiously
> breatheable. At the gaseous level of the solid and liquid organism,
> white and black, night and day.

The initial reaction among both black and white Americans in the 1950s might well have been forseen. Tutored in a society egalitarian and integrationist in its proclaimed ideal, however derelict in deed, they were surprised that the black African who has been so outrageously the victim of racial persecution, should affirm racial qualities.* However, a consideration of the historical circumstances giving rise to its development tends to make clear its justification, and more, its necessity. The reaction to centuries of humiliation and contempt is not one of calm objectivity. The pendulum can only gradually achieve dead center. Each age, each people has its own historical necessity. In this connection, Sartre has used Hegelian concepts, to describe this movement. Négritude in African poetry is an anti-racist racism; it is the moment of negativity in reaction to the thesis of white supremacy. It is the anti-thesis in a dialectical progression leading to the synthesis of a humanity without racism. This is undoubtedly too neat a formula for the actual operation of the influences involved (and it is scarcely the most astute application of Marxist dialectic to dub the assertion of African values the "moment of negativity"). It does provide, however, a ready and roughly accurate framework for the comprehension of the conflicting tendencies at play. We see, too, that some of these poets express their strong conviction that man, ultimately, is man and that his race is an attribute, only, of his more basic membership in the human community. Jacques Roumain gives particularly poignant testimony:

> Africa I guard your memory Africa
> you are in me as the shaft is in the wound
> as the guardian fetish in the center of the village
> make of me the stone of your sling
> of my mouth the lips of your sores
> of my knees the broken column of your humiliation
>   and yet
> I wish to be only of your race
> fellow workers of every land.

We have considered this concept, this esthetic, this rebel to analysis— négritude—confining our remarks thus far to the work of African and French West Indian writers and the role negritude has played in their development. Let us consider briefly the possible relevance of this concept to the work of the Afro-American writer and its validity for a writer in our cultural situation.

I think it has a role. This is not necessarily so for all of us, the writer not being a soldier marching to command. He writes, when he writes most creatively, pursuant to his own most deeply felt need. It is pos-

---

* We have seen, of course, here in the United States in the 1960s, an even stronger surge of black cultural nationalism.

sible, though highly unlikely, in a Western world so dominated by racist attitudes that the writer's racial identity may have little influence, or only indirect influence, upon his writing. It is probably true, also, that it was not by chance that this concept, négritude, originated among the poets rather than among those working in prose. Except for certain highly imaginative works, the novelist writes within a framework of what we term reality. He must in part concern himself with Plato's shadows—with plot and setting. His characters, unlike Orphan Annie, must grow up. He is constrained to a certain degree of reasonableness. The poet has probably a greater chance to penetrate at once without apology and without a setting of the worldly stage, to the deepest level of his creative concern. And so, perhaps what we are saying may have greater applicability to poetry than to prose.

I think there is little disagreement that our cultural situation is substantially different from that of Amos Tutuola of Nigeria, of Efua Morgue of Ghana, of the Senegalese, resident of Paris since his university days, or of the Haitian or Jamaican writer. Our contact with Africa has been remote for centuries, and both the natural and the consciously directed impacts of the enslavement were to shatter the African cultural heritage. Further, the Afro-American, uprooted from his homeland, has been subjected in a manner unparalleled among other peoples of African descent to the cultural imprint of a powerful, dominant majority in a strange and unfriendly land. The Ashanti, the Senegalese, the Yoruba were overwhelmed militarily and politically and subjected to a foreign culture; but they were on their home ground, and they retained the morale afforded by the mystic attachment to the soil of their ancestors. The colonizing European, though controlling, was a minority, and the African remained in large part Senegalese, Ashanti, Yoruba. And even in South Africa, the Zulu, uprooted and virtually driven into the mines, remained upon his own continent. The West Indian, though like the black people of the United States, captive and transplanted across the ocean, at least retained the advantage of numbers and an infrequency of contact with a ruling and relatively restrained elite. In contrast, the black American has undergone a physical and spiritual alienation without parallel in modern history. Overwhelmed militarily, uprooted and transplanted 3,000 miles from his native soil, he has been subjected for centuries to the close, daily cultural impress not only of a dominant elite but also of the lowest elements of what Claude McKay has termed a "cultured hell," created by a powerful, materialistic, brutal, frontier society, uncertain of its own identity and seeking to assure itself of status in part by the denial of status to its victims. Rightfully resentful of the privilege of the old world, American society itself fell victim to a psychological complex of denigration—a complex which, it is perfectly patent today, has redounded to its own disadvantage in the assault upon the intellectual, in the rock-throwing at the egghead, in the widespread triumph of mediocrity.

The question, then, is posed whether this unparalleled alienation and our partial entrance into what is referred to as the mainstream of American life precludes our exploration of our identity as a minority of African descent and our recourse to the African heritage as a fructifying source of our creative endeavor. Lest there be some confusion, it should be pointed out that we are dealing here not with the question of social segregation on the basis of race, but with an analysis of our cultural situation, with an exploration of aspects of our identity, which have been thwarted by the prevailing racial mores. I believe it is evident that the Afro American as well as the African writer has both this task and this opportunity.

We may differ, as we did in Paris at the first Congress of the Society of African Culture, as to whether the American Negro is subjected to a species of colonialism. The fact is he has felt himself to be in an alien land, and the frequency of the term "native" in the titles of black American writers (Richard Wright, James Baldwin, etc.) eloquently attests to this fact. He too, as Countee Cullen in "Heritage," feels about him a culture prison. The resulting erosion of identity is evident to the observer. The African visitor to America, we frequently hear, finds the American of African descent "diminué"—diminished. Henry Wallace, visiting the West Indies, noted what he felt to be a greater personal stature on the part of the West Indian. Dorothy Dandridge has reported how strongly she was impressed by the deep sense of assurance and quiet pride she found in the Senegalese. The psychologists Kardiner and Ovesey have traced the damaged psychological profile of the black American in the book *The Mark of Oppression* (and now, more recently, Cobbs and Grier have given a broader picture in *Black Rage*). Dubose Heyward portrays the effect of this culture prison in *Porgy,* in which the hero, an American Negro, is symbolically a cripple, and in which the only man of full stature is the character who never in the course of the play experiences a confrontation with the all-powerful white authorities, who refuses reasonably to conform and to make the best of the social pattern. He is the outlaw, the gambler, the near rapist, the murderer, symbolically named "Crown."

Thus do we see the effect of the dominant cultural pattern. It is a significant commentary upon that dominant white society that it is necessary, with perhaps an occasional exception, to return to the nineteenth century—to the great souled Melville, the mystic Thoreau, the cosmic vision of Whitman—to find among white writers the spiritual dimension to comprehend and to transcend the fact of race in this country.

For an uncomfortably long period of time, it was a kind of national ritual to enjoin the black writer to enter the mainstream of American letters. When we consider, however, the nature of the role the black man has occupied in America's cultural design, when we consider the materialistic stamp of America's contribution to man's progress, it is evident we should be wary of making too eager, too anxious a jump into that stream. The black man in the United States is American, it is true. And though it may also be true, as T. S. Eliot said, that the time-and-place social history of the artist is not necessarily his *significant* prior experience in his creative work, yet it is probable that his creative effort will in substantial measure bear the imprint of his social experience within his culture. However, and this is the focal point, it does the black writer a disservice to think of his work, as was so long the case, as a tributary to some major American stream.

The mainstream of American arts and letters, as we have seen, falls staggeringly short of reflecting the Negro with dignity and with psychological integrity. To think merely of joining that stream or to think of our creative effort simply as part of that stream would mean to fall under the influence of its direction and to perpetrate cultural proto-types. (Here we should distinguish between a mastery of the content and technique of a literature and a self-immolating submission to it.) It would be a more fruitful approach for the Afro American, as in the Harlem Renaissance, to write out of his own felt need, looking to the creative sources of his inclination, defining himself in terms of the deeper wells of his being as he may discover them in the direction of his particular interests, talent and emotional reactions. He should seek his inspiration in what life in this society has meant to *him* and, if he finds it seminal, in the history, mythology and folklore of Africa, in the battles of Chaka, in Benin bronze, in the Bantu philosophy of vital force, forgetting for the time being the dubious assumption of an American mainstream. There is small chance that the body of creative effort of the Afro American will not reflect his devastating American experience. But it is only in an emphasis upon the development of his own identity in that experience that he will be able to make ultimately his fullest contribution as an artist both within and without the nation.

Because this culture prison to which we have referred has imposed a wall between him and his origins, it is to those origins that the artist is drawn to recover that lost fullness of self. Thus, for example, Amos Tutuola, author of the celebrated *Palm Wine Drinkard,* was able, by pursuing his own ancestral experience and developing his own style of expression, to create something totally divergent from current British literary trends. Though to a sophisticated London ear, his syntax may leave something to be desired, he has gone far toward creating an African mythology and resurrecting the magic of his African heritage, which he undoubtedly would not have accomplished had he been more alert and responsive to English literary trends. Here in America, it was not in pursuit of a mainstream that Langston Hughes created something new under the literary sun when he contained on paper the haunting refrains of the blues. And, similarly, it was in retreat to the sources of his own identity that James Weldon Johnson captured the beauty and the power of the Southern Negro preacher in *God's Trombones,* without the caricature characteristic of the American white writers who have dealt with the theme.

I think it may, moreover, be worthwhile to ask what is the mainstream of the contribution of the United States to world culture? It is not chauvinism but an objective determination of fact to remark that in the area of both popular and religious music, the black American is not a tributary; he is substantially the stream. With the alchemy of his particular talent, he transformed and practically preempted the field of American popular music through jazz, and the blues. Out of his American passion, he created the tragic glory of the spirituals and his own inimitable gospel music, and he remains decisive in their development. And this he did not do through a preoccupation with the "respectable" or accepted musical forms about him, but in response to the interior demands of his being.

James Weldon Johnson wrote in *Along This Way* that the Negro may be ultimately merged in America, but that he had beforehand a distinct cultural contribution to make. Cedric Dover, the Indian writer, at the Paris Congress in 1956, decried the fact that the drive toward integration in the United States seems to mean for many American Negroes a desire for obliteration and passive absorption by the majority. He remarked that a close and fruitful rapport between people can occur only where there is complete respect for the identity of the one by the other. It is this truth that Ralph Waldo Emerson, who keynoted a second independence from Britain, undoubtedly had in mind when he said in effect that a quality of the highest type of friendship was the ability to do without.

And to achieve this birth of freedom from the culture prison, let us finally consider more precisely whether the black American writer has an interest in looking to that phase of négritude which is the African heritage. Is he cut off by 300 years of his American experience? Undoubtedly, he will never draw upon this experience with the intensity of the writer on the African continent. But since the dominant American image of the black man which is held by black and white alike and which robs him of his full stature, is due in large measure to the popular distorted impression of Africa as a continent of barbarism, it is imperative to break through that culture prison and to deal with this poisonous current that feeds the American stream. It is a necessary task in transforming the debasing image the white world has imposed upon the black American. As Hegel has somewhere said, the slave must not only break the chain; he must also shatter the image in both his and his former master's mind before he is truly free.

In the historical light of the interaction of cultures, there is no reason why the African heritage may not be a fertile source of inspiration. It will be futile to admonish that our roots are American only, that our roots go back to the Virginia shore in 1619 and stop at the water's edge, amid the branding and the cries and trance-like intonations such as those of Cassandra when carried by Agamemnon back to Greece: "What isle, what land is this?"

Perhaps, therefore, our concern with Africa should stop with 1619. But here in New York a German philosopher once said the connective most applicable to man is not "therefore," but "nonetheless." What was the direct line from Greece to Arabia? And yet through Arabian scholars such as Avicenna and Averroes, a millennium removed, antiquity was recaptured and became the inspiration for the flowering of the Renaissance of Western Europe. When Derain chanced upon a piece of African statuary in a street in France, his remoteness from the former continent did not prevent him, or Picasso and others of the cubists and the "fauves," from finding in that work an inspiration for an entirely new direction—a new dimension in Western art. A more immediate example: in the middle fifties, Randy Weston, the jazz pianist and composer, was at the Schomburg Collection in Harlem doing research in African rhythms which he has employed in creations he has since played at the Birdland and elsewhere. In literature, the poetry of Countee Cullen, Langston Hughes, Melvin Tolson and Claude McKay has already, in varying degrees, occupied itself with the African past.

The existence of African survivals in the black community in America has been the subject of considerable debate. It is significant for this discussion that Carter Woodson and W. E. B. Du Bois waged a continuing attack upon the thesis of Robert S. Park and his followers that the Afro American was completely bereft of his cultural past when he landed on these shores. It is becoming increasingly clear that the cultural stripping was not complete, and that regardless of the degree of rupture, the African heritage may serve as a fertile source of inspiration and of renewal for the Afro American. Although the black writer in this country has understandably been preoccupied with the American scene, Africa may well serve in the future as a leaven enriching the cultural loaf.

It is impossible, of course, to know beforehand to what extent he may utilize the African heritage. Experience, not a predetermined chart, will provide the answer.* It is clear, however, that the black

* In 1968, ten years after this article was originally written, Alex Haley published his pioneer account of his search in Africa for his ancestral roots. John Williams and other black novelists have begun to explore African sources. The younger black poets, particularly those adopting Islam, have been even more active in reclaiming an African heritage.

writer's circumstance as an American will not preclude a substantial participation in that rich heritage. On the South Atlantic Coast there is an expression which has survived slavery—"gone to Guinea." When the old African woman was weary from her labor in the field, from her chores about the big house, when she was overcome by the troubles of the world, she would say that soon she would be "gone to Guinea." Guinea was heaven. Guinea was the west coast of Africa which remained but faintly, nostalgically in the memory of her shattered past. As part of the continuing effort of the black American to find his roots, to achieve his full stature in a racist, exploitative society, it is imperative to go back for a moment in our cultural reconnaissance—to go back to Guinea.

Finally, as we have already pointed out, there is that aspect of négritude which does not have to do with an African or other content, but which is simply an affirmation of self, the dwarfed self, denied realization because of the root of its identity. (It is enlightening to realize the origin of the word "race," coming from the Spanish "raiz," meaning "root.") The Afro American, as the African, has an imposing interest in the development of his image of the universe, of the correction of the distorted image of himself in this society, in an exploration and fuller expression of his particular talents, whatever the subject matter with which he deals. It is true we are influenced by other cultural tendencies in this country. The problem is largely a matter of emphasis. There is a measure of truth in each perception. But we cannot resolve the argument by a generous eclecticism. It is crucial to assess the particular emphasis appropriate to our cultural situation. The emphasis at present will prove most fruitfully to be upon our unique creative personality; and it should continue to be so until we have achieved our full identity, implicit in our culture without the necessity of affirmation, until we have purged the empoisoned air, until the metamorphosis implicit in the lines of Césaire has taken place:

"bird of their scorn, bird reborn, brother in the sun."

Ossie Davis

(b. 1917)

OSSIE DAVIS WAS BORN in Cogdell, Georgia, and educated at Howard and Columbia Universities. Beginning his stage career in 1941 as a member of the Rose McClendon Players, an early Harlem group, Davis made his Broadway debut in 1946 in the title role of *Jeb*. He has performed many roles on Broadway, including Gabriel in *Green Pastures,* Walter Lee Younger in *A Raisin in the Sun,* and the title role in his own *Purlie Victorious.*

Ossie Davis made his film debut in 1950 in *No Way Out.* Since then he has appeared in a number of movies, among them *The Joe Louis Story, The Scalp Hunters, The Hill,* and *Slaves.* He has also acted on television: the title role in *Emperor Jones,* and other characters such as the District Attorney in "The Star Spangled Ghetto" (*The Defenders,* CBS).

Purlie Victorious, from which this selection is taken, is Ossie Davis' most ambitious play. He has not only written a hilarious satire on the changing South, but has accomplished something far more significant: he has brought back to Negro drama good, honest laughter, which has for too long been absent.

PURLIE VICTORIOUS

Purlie Victorious was presented by Phillip Rose at the Cort Theatre, New York City; directed by Howard Da Silva; settings and lighting by Ben Edwards; costumes by Ann Roth; production stage manager, Leonard Auerbach; assistant, John Sillings.

Cast
(In Order of Appearance)

PURLIE VICTORIOUS JUDSON	*Ossie Davis*
LUTIEBELLE GUSSIE MAE JENKINS	*Ruby Dee*
MISSY JUDSON	*Helen Martin*
GITLOW JUDSON	*Godfrey C. Cambridge*
CHARLIE COTCHIPEE	*Alan Alda*
IDELLA LANDY	*Beah Richards*
OL' CAP'N COTCHIPEE	*Sorrell Booke*
THE SHERIFF	*Cy Herzog*
THE DEPUTY	*Roger C. Carmel*

Place: The cotton plantation country of the Old South
Time: The recent past

"Our churches will say segregation is immoral because it makes perfectly wonderful people, white and black, do immoral things; . . .

Our courts will say segregation is illegal because it makes perfectly wonderful people, white and black, do illegal things; . . .

And finally our Theatre will say segregation is ridiculous because it makes perfectly wonderful people, white and black, do ridiculous things!"

—From "Purlie's I.O.U."

Act I

Scene 1

Scene: The setting is the plain and simple interior of an antiquated, run-down farmhouse such as Negro sharecroppers still live in, in South Georgia. Threadbare but warm-hearted, shabby but clean. In the Center is a large, rough-hewn table with three homemade chairs and a small bench. This table is the center of all family activities. The main entrance is a door in the Upstage Right corner, which leads in from a rickety porch which we cannot see. There is a small archway in the opposite corner, with some long strips of gunnysacking hanging down to serve as a door, which leads off to the kitchen. In the center of the Right wall is a window that is wooden, which opens outward on hinges. Downstage Right is a small door leading off to a bedroom, and opposite, Downstage Left, another door leads out into the backyard, and on into the cotton fields beyond. There is also a smaller table and a cupboard against the wall. An old dresser stands against the Right wall, between the window and the Downstage door. There is a shelf on the Left wall with a pail of drinking water, and a large tin dipper. Various cooking utensils, and items like salt and pepper are scattered about in appropriate places.

At Rise: The CURTAIN rises on a stage in semi-darkness. After a moment, when the LIGHTS have come up, the door in the Up Right corner bursts open: Enter PURLIE JUDSON. PURLIE JUDSON *is tall, restless, and commanding. In his middle or late thirties, he wears a wide-brim, ministerial black hat, a string tie, and a claw hammer coat, which, though far from new, does not fit him too badly. His arms are loaded with large boxes and parcels, which must have come fresh from a department store.* PURLIE *is a man consumed with that divine impatience, without which nothing truly good, or truly bad, or even truly ridiculous, is ever accomplished in this world—with rhetoric and flourish to match.*

PURLIE. [*Calling out loudly.*] Missy! [*No answer.*] Gitlow!—It's me—Purlie Victorious! [*Still no answer.* PURLIE *empties his overloaded arms, with obvious relief, on top of the big Center table. He stands, mops his brow, and blows.*] Nobody home it seems. [*This last he says to someone he assumes has come in with him. When there is no answer he hurries to the door through which he entered.*] Come on —come on in!

[*Enter* LUTIEBELLE JENKINS, *slowly, as if bemused. Young, eager, well-built: though we cannot tell it at the moment. Clearly a girl from the backwoods, she carries a suitcase tied up with a rope in one hand, and a greasy shoebox with what's left of her lunch, together with an out-moded, out-sized handbag, in the other. Obviously she has traveled a great distance, but she still manages to look fresh and healthy. Her hat is a horror with feathers, but she wears it like a banner. Her shoes are flat-heeled and plain white, such as a good servant girl in the white folks' kitchen who knows her place absolutely is bound to wear. Her fall coat is dowdy, but well-intentioned with a stingy strip of rabbit fur around the neck.* LUTIEBELLE *is like thousands of Negro girls you might know. Eager, desirous—even anxious, keenly in search for life and for love, trembling on the brink of self-confident and vigorous young womanhood—but afraid to take the final leap: because no one has ever told her it is no longer necessary to be white in order to be virtuous, charming, or beautiful.*]

LUTIEBELLE. [*Looking around as if at a museum of great importance.*] Nobody home it seems.

PURLIE. [*Annoyed to find himself so exactly echoed, looks at her sharply. He takes his watch from his vest pocket, where he wears it on a chain.*] Cotton-picking time in Georgia it's against the law to be home. Come in—unload yourself. [*Crosses and looks out into the kitchen.* LUTIEBELLE *is so enthralled, she still stands with all her bags and parcels in her arm.*] Set your suitcase down.

LUTIEBELLE. What?

PURLIE. It's making you lopsided.

LUTIEBELLE. [*Snapping out of it.*] It is? I didn't even notice. [*Sets suit-case, lunch box, and parcels down.*]

PURLIE. [*Studies her for a moment; goes and gently takes off her hat.*] Tired?

LUTIEBELLE. Not stepping high as I am!

PURLIE. [*Takes the rest of her things and sets them on the table.*] Hungry?

LUTIEBELLE. No, sir. But there's still some of my lunch left if you—

PURLIE. [*Quickly.*] No, thank you. Two ham-hock sandwiches in one day is my limit. [*Sits down and fans himself with his hat.*] Sorry I had to walk you so far so fast.

LUTIEBELLE. [*Dreamily.*] Oh, I didn't mind, sir. Walking's good for you, Miz Emmylou sez—

PURLIE. Miz Emmylou can afford to say that: Miz Emmylou got a car. While all the transportation we got in the world is tied up in second-hand shoe leather. But never mind, my sister, never-you-mind! [*Rises, almost as if to dance, exaltation glowing in his eyes.*] And toll the bell, Big Bethel—toll that big, black, fat and sassy liberty bell! Tell Freedom the bridegroom cometh; the day of her deliver-ance is now at hand! [PURLIE *catches sight of* MISSY *through door Down Left.*] Oh, there she is. [*Crosses to door and calls out.*] Missy! —Oh, Missy!

MISSY. [*From a distance.*] Yes-s-s-s-!

PURLIE. It's me!—Purlie!

MISSY. Purlie Victorious?

PURLIE. Yes. Put that battling stick down and come on in here!

MISSY. All right!

PURLIE. [*Crosses hurriedly back to above table at Center.*] That's Missy, my sister-in-law I was telling you about. [*Clears the table of everything but one of the large cartons, which he proceeds to open.*]

LUTIEBELLE. [*Not hearing him. Still awe-struck to be in the very house, in perhaps the very same room that* PURLIE *might have been born in.*] So this is the house where you was born and bred at.

PURLIE. Yep! Better'n being born outdoors.

LUTIEBELLE. What a lovely background for your home-life.

PURLIE. I wouldn't give it to my dog to raise fleas in!

LUTIEBELLE. So clean—and nice—and warm-hearted!

PURLIE. The first chance I get I'ma burn the damn thing down!

LUTIEBELLE. But—Reb'n Purlie!—It's yours, and that's what counts. Like Miz Emmylou sez—

PURLIE. Come here! [*Pulls her across to the window, flings it open.*] You see that big white house, perched on top of that hill with them two windows looking right down at us like two eyeballs: that's where Ol' Cap'n lives.

LUTIEBELLE. Ol' Cap'n?

PURLIE. Stonewall Jackson Cotchipee. He owns this dump, not me.

LUTIEBELLE. Oh—

PURLIE. And that ain't all: hill and dale, field and farm, truck and tractor, horse and mule, bird and bee and bush and tree—and cotton!—cotton by bole and by bale—every bit o' cotton you see in this county!—Everything and everybody he owns!

LUTIEBELLE. Everybody? You mean he owns people?

PURLIE. [*Bridling his impatience.*] Well—look!—ain't a man, woman or child working in this valley that ain't in debt to that ol' bastard!—[*Catches himself.*] bustard!—[*This still won't do.*] buzzard!—And that includes Gitlow and Missy—everybody—except me.—

LUTIEBELLE. But folks can't own people no more, Reb'n Purlie. Miz Emmylou sez that—

PURLIE. [*Verging on explosion.*] You ain't working for Miz Emmylou no more, you're working for me—Purlie Victorious. Freedom is my business, and I say that ol' man runs this plantation on debt: the longer you work for Ol' Cap'n Cotchipee, the more you owe at the commissary; and if you don't pay up, you can't leave. And I don't give a damn what Miz Emmylou nor nobody else sez—that's slavery!

LUTIEBELLE. I'm sorry, Reb'n Purlie—

PURLIE. Don't apologize, wait!—Just wait!—til I get my church;—wait til I buy Big Bethel back—[*Crosses to window and looks out.*] Wait til I stand once again in the pulpit of Grandpaw Kinkaid, and call upon my people—and talk to my people—About Ol' Cap'n, that miserable son-of-a—

LUTIEBELLE. [*Just in time to save him.*] Wait—!

PURLIE. Wait, I say! And we'll see who's gonna dominize this valley!—him or me! [*Turns and sees* MISSY *through door Down Left.*] Missy —!

[*Enter* MISSY, *ageless, benign, and smiling. She wears a ragged old straw hat, a big house apron over her faded gingham, and low-cut, dragged-out tennis shoes on her feet. She is strong and of good cheer —of a certain shrewdness, yet full of the desire to believe. Her eyes light on* LUTIEBELLE, *and her arms go up and outward automatically.*]

MISSY. Purlie!

PURLIE. [*Thinks she is reaching for him.*] Missy!

MISSY. [*Ignoring him, clutching* LUTIEBELLE, *laughing and crying.*] Well—well—well!

PURLIE. [*Breaking the stranglehold.*] For God's sake, Missy, don't choke her to death!

MISSY. All my life—all my life I been praying for me a daughter just like you. My prayers is been answered at last. Welcome to our home, whoever you is!

LUTIEBELLE. [*Deeply moved.*] Thank you, m'am.

MISSY. "M'am—m'am." Listen to the child, Purlie. Everybody down here calls me Aunt Missy, and I'd be much obliged if you would, too.

LUTIEBELLE. It would make me very glad to do so—Aunt Missy.

MISSY. Uhmmmmmm! Pretty as a pan of buttermilk biscuits. Where on earth did you find her, Purlie? [PURLIE *starts to answer.*] Let me take your things—now, you just make yourself at home—Are you hungry?

LUTIEBELLE. No, m'am, but cheap as water is, I sure ain't got no business being this thirsty!

MISSY. [*Starts forward.*] I'll get some for you—

PURLIE. [*Intercepts her; directs* LUTIEBELLE.] There's the dipper. And right out yonder by the fence just this side of that great big live oak tree you'll find the well—sweetest water in Cotchipee county.

LUTIEBELLE. Thank you, Reb'n Purlie. I'm very much obliged. [*Takes dipper from water pail and exits Down Left.*]

MISSY. Reb'n who?

PURLIE. [*Looking off after* LUTIEBELLE.] Perfection—absolute Ethiopian perfect. Hah, Missy?

MISSY. [*Looking off after* LUTIEBELLE.] Oh, I don't know about that.

PURLIE. What you mean you don't know? This girl looks more like Cousin Bee than Cousin Bee ever did.

MISSY. No resemblance to me.

PURLIE. Don't be ridiculous; she's the spitting image—

MISSY. No resemblance whatsoever!

PURLIE. I ought to know how my own cousin looked—

MISSY. But I was the last one to see her alive—

PURLIE. Twins, if not closer!

MISSY. Are you crazy? Bee was more lean, loose, and leggy—

PURLIE. Maybe so, but this girl makes it up in—

MISSY. With no chin to speak of—her eyes: sort of fickle one to another—

PURLIE. I know, but even so—

MISSY. [*Pointing off in* LUTIEBELLE's *direction.*] Look at her head—it ain't nearly as built like a rutabaga as Bee's own was!

PURLIE. [*Exasperated.*] What's the difference! White folks can't tell one of us from another by the head!

MISSY. Twenty years ago it was, Purlie, Ol' Cap'n laid bull whip to your natural behind—

PURLIE. Twenty years ago I swore I'd see his soul in hell!

MISSY. And I don't think you come full back to your senses yet—That ol' man ain't no fool!

PURLIE. That makes it one "no fool" against another.

MISSY. He's dangerous, Purlie. We could get killed if that old man was to find out what we was trying to do to get that church back.

PURLIE. How can he find out? Missy, how many times must I tell you, if it's one thing I am foolproof in it's white folks' psychology.

MISSY. That's exactly what I'm afraid of.

PURLIE. Freedom, Missy, that's what Big Bethel means. For you, me and Gitlow. And we can buy it for five hundred dollars, Missy. Freedom! —You want it, or don't you?

MISSY. Of course I want it, but—After all, Purlie, that rich ol' lady didn't exactly leave that $500 to us—

PURLIE. She left it to Aunt Henrietta—

MISSY. Aunt Henrietta is dead—

PURLIE. Exactly—

MISSY. And Henrietta's daughter Cousin Bee is dead, too.

PURLIE. Which makes us next in line to inherit the money by law!

MISSY. All right, then, why don't we just go on up that hill man-to-man and tell Ol' Cap'n we want our money?

PURLIE. Missy! You have been black as long as I have—

MISSY. [*Not above having her own little joke.*] Hell, boy, we could make him give it to us.

PURLIE. Make him—how? He's a white man, Missy. What you plan to do, sue him?

MISSY. [*Drops her teasing; thinks seriously for a moment.*] After all, it is our money. And it was our church.

PURLIE. And can you think of a better way to get it back than that girl out there?

MISSY. But you think it'll work, Purlie? You really think she can fool Ol' Cap'n?

PURLIE. He'll never know what hit him.

MISSY. Maybe—but there's still the question of Gitlow.

PURLIE. What about Gitlow?

MISSY. Gitlow has changed his mind.

PURLIE. Then you'll have to change it back.

GITLOW. [*Offstage.*] Help, Missy; help, Missy; help, Missy; help, Missy! [GITLOW *runs on.*]

MISSY. What the devil's the matter this time?

GITLOW. There I was, Missy, picking in the high cotton, twice as fast as the human eye could see. All of a sudden I missed a bole and it fell—it fell on the ground, Missy! I stooped as fast as I could to pick it up and— [*He stoops to illustrate. There is a loud tearing of cloth.*] ripped the seat of my britches. There I was, Missy, exposed from stem to stern.

MISSY. What's so awful about that? It's only cotton.

GITLOW. But cotton is white, Missy. We must maintain respect. Bring me my Sunday School britches.

MISSY. What!

GITLOW. Ol' Cap'n is coming down into the cotton patch today, and I know you want your Gitlow to look his level best. [MISSY *starts to answer.*] Hurry, Missy, hurry! [GITLOW *hurries her off.*]

PURLIE. Gitlow—have I got the girl!

GITLOW. Is that so—what girl?

PURLIE. [*Taking him to the door.*] See? There she is! Well?

GITLOW. Well what?

PURLIE. What do you think?

GITLOW. Nope; she'll never do.

PURLIE. What you mean, she'll never do?

GITLOW. My advice to you is to take that girl back to Florida as fast as you can!

PURLIE. I can't take her back to Florida.

GITLOW. Why can't you take her back to Florida?

PURLIE. 'Cause she comes from Alabama. Gitlow, look at her: she's just the size—just the type—just the style.

GITLOW. And just the girl to get us all in jail. The answer is no! [*Crosses to kitchen door.*] MISSY! [*Back to* PURLIE.] Girl or no girl, I ain't getting mixed up in no more of your nightmares—I got my own. Dammit, Missy, I said let's go!

MISSY. [*Entering with trousers.*] You want me to take my bat to you again?

GITLOW. No, Missy, control yourself. It's just that every second Gitlow's off the firing line-up, seven pounds of Ol' Cap'n's cotton don't git gotten. [*Snatches pants from* MISSY, *but is in too much of a hurry to put them on—starts off.*]

PURLIE. Wait a minute, Gitlow. . . . Wait! [GITLOW *is off in a flash.*] Missy! Stop him!

MISSY. He ain't as easy to stop as he used to be. Especially now Ol' Cap'n's made him Deputy-For-The-Colored.

PURLIE. Deputy-For-The-Colored? What the devil is that?

MISSY. Who knows? All I know is Gitlow's changed his mind.

PURLIE. But Gitlow can't change his mind!

MISSY. Oh, it's easy enough when you ain't got much to start with. I warned you. You don't know how shifty ol' Git can git. He's the hardest man to convince and keep convinced I ever seen in my life.

PURLIE. Missy, you've got to make him go up that hill, he's got to identify this girl—Ol' Cap'n won't believe nobody else.

MISSY. I know—

PURLIE. He's got to swear before Ol' Cap'n that this girl is the real Cousin Bee—

MISSY. I know.

PURLIE. Missy, you're the only person in this world ol' Git'll really listen to.

MISSY. I know.

PURLIE. And what if you do have to hit him a time or two—it's for his own good!

MISSY. I know.

PURLIE. He'll recover from it, Missy. He always does—

MISSY. I know.

PURLIE. Freedom, Missy—Big Bethel; for you; me; and Gitlow—!

MISSY. Freedom—and a little something left over—that's all I ever wanted all my life. [*Looks out into the yard.*] She do look a little somewhat like Cousin Bee—about the feet!

PURLIE. Of course she does—

MISSY. I won't guarantee nothing, Purlie—but I'll try.

PURLIE. [*Grabbing her and dancing her around.*] Everytime I see you, Missy, you get prettier by the pound!

[LUTIEBELLE *enters.* MISSY *sees her.*]

MISSY. Stop it, Purlie, stop it! Stop it. Quit cutting the fool in front of company!

PURLIE. [*Sees* LUTIEBELLE, *crosses to her, grabs her about the waist and swings her around too.*]

How wondrous are the daughters of my people,
Yet knoweth not the glories of themselves!
[*Spins her around for* MISSY's *inspection. She does look better with her coat off, in her immaculate blue and white maid's uniform.*]
Where do you suppose I found her, Missy—
This Ibo prize—this Zulu Pearl—
This long lost lily of the black Mandingo—
Kikuyu maid, beneath whose brown embrace
Hot suns of Africa are burning still: where—where?
A drudge; a serving wench; a feudal fetch-pot:
A common scullion in the white man's kitchen.
Drowned is her youth in thankless Southern dishpans;
Her beauty spilt for Dixiecratic pigs!
This brown-skinned grape! this wine of Negro vintage—

MISSY. [*Interrupting.*] I know all that, Purlie, but what's her name?

[PURLIE *looks at* LUTIEBELLE *and turns abruptly away.*]

LUTIEBELLE. I don't think he likes my name so much—it's Lutiebelle, ma'am—Lutiebelle Gussie Mae Jenkins!

MISSY. [*Gushing with motherly reassurance.*] Lutiebelle Gussie Mae Jenkins! My, that's nice.

PURLIE. Nice! It's an insult to the Negro people!

MISSY. Purlie, behave yourself!

PURLIE. A previous condition of servitude, a badge of inferiority, and I refuse to have it in my organization!—change it!

MISSY. You want me to box your mouth for you!

PURLIE. Lutiebelle Gussie Mae Jenkins! What does it mean in Swahili? Cheap labor!

LUTIEBELLE. Swahili?

PURLIE. One of the thirteen silver tongues of Africa: Swahili, Bushengo, Ashanti, Baganda, Herero, Yoruba, Bambora, Mpongwe, Swahili: a language of moons, of velvet drums; hot days of rivers, red-splashed, and birdsong bright!, black fingers in rice white at sunset red!—ten thousand Queens of Sheba—

MISSY. [*Having to interrupt.*] Just where did Purlie find you, honey?

LUTIEBELLE. It was in Dothan, Alabama, last Sunday, Aunt Missy, right in the junior choir!

MISSY. The junior choir—my, my, my!

PURLIE. [*Still carried away.*]

Behold! I said, this dark and holy vessel,

In whom should burn that golden nut-brown joy
Which Negro womanhood was meant to be.
Ten thousand queens, ten thousand Queens of Sheba:
[*Pointing at* LUTIEBELLE.]
Ethiopia herself—in all her beauteous wonder,
Come to restore the ancient thrones of Cush!

MISSY. Great Gawdamighty, Purlie, I can't hear myself think—!

LUTIEBELLE. That's just what I said last Sunday, Aunt Missy, when Reb'n Purlie started preaching that thing in the pulpit.

MISSY. Preaching it!?

LUTIEBELLE. Lord, Aunt Missy, I shouted clear down to the Mourners' Bench.

MISSY. [*To* PURLIE.] But last time you was a professor of Negro Philosophy.

PURLIE. I told you, Missy: my intention is to buy Big Bethel back; to reclaim the ancient pulpit of Grandpaw Kincaid, and preach freedom in the cotton patch—I told you!

MISSY. Maybe you did, Purlie, maybe you did. You got yourself a license?

PURLIE. Naw!—but—

MISSY. [*Looking him over.*] Purlie Victorious Judson: Self-made minister of the gospel-claw-hammer coattail, shoe-string tie and all.

PURLIE. [*Quietly but firmly holding his ground.*] How else can you lead the Negro people?

MISSY. Is that what you got in your mind: leading the Negro people?

PURLIE. Who else is they got?

MISSY. God help the race.

LUTIEBELLE. It was a sermon, I mean, Aunt Missy, the likes of which has never been heard before.

MISSY. Oh, I bet that. Tell me about it, son. What did you preach?

PURLIE. I preached the New Baptism of Freedom for all mankind, according to the Declaration of Independence, taking as my text the Constitution of the United States of America, Amendments First through Fifteenth, which readeth as follows: "Congress shall make no law—"

MISSY. Enough—that's enough, son—I'm converted. But it is confusing, all the changes you keep going through. [*To* LUTIEBELLE.] Honey, every time I see Purlie he's somebody else.

PURLIE. Not any more, Missy; and if I'm lying may the good Lord put me down in the book of bad names: Purlie is put forever!

Missy. Yes. But will he stay put forever?

Purlie. There is in every man a finger of iron that points him what he must and must not do—

Missy. And your finger points up the hill to that five hundred dollars with which you'll buy Big Bethel back, preach freedom in the cotton patch, and live happily ever after!

Purlie. The soul-consuming passion of my life! [*Draws out watch.*] It's 2:15, Missy, and Gitlow's waiting. Missy, I suggest you get a move on.

Missy. I already got a move on. Had it since four o'clock this morning!

Purlie. Time, Missy—exactly what the colored man in this country ain't got, and you're wasting it!

Missy. [*Looks at* Purlie, *and decides not to strike him dead.*] Purlie, would you mind stepping out into the cotton patch and telling your brother Gitlow I'd like a few words with him? [Purlie, *overjoyed leaps at* Missy *as if to hug and dance her around again, but she is too fast.*] Do like I tell you now—go on! [Purlie *exits singing.* Missy *turns to* Lutiebelle *to begin the important task of sizing her up.*] Besides, it wouldn't be hospitable not to set and visit a spell with our distinguished guest over from Dothan, Alabama.

Lutiebelle. [*This is the first time she has been called anything of importance by anybody.*] Thank you, ma'am.

Missy. Now. Let's you and me just set back and enjoy a piece of my potato pie. You like potato pie, don't you?

Lutiebelle. Oh, yes, ma'am, I like it very much.

Missy. And get real acquainted. [*Offers her a saucer with a slice of pie on it.*]

Lutiebelle. I'm ever so much obliged. My, this looks nice! Uhm, uhn, uhn!

Missy. [*Takes a slice for herself and sits down.*] You know—ever since that ol' man—[*Indicates up the hill.*] took after Purlie so unmerciful with that bull whip twenty years ago—he fidgets! Always on the go; rattling around from place to place all over the country: one step ahead of the white folks—something about Purlie always did irritate the white folks.

Lutiebelle. Is that the truth!

Missy. Oh, my yes. Finally wound up being locked up a time or two for safekeeping—[Lutiebelle *parts with a loud, sympathetic grunt. Changing her tack a bit.*] Always kept up his schooling, though. In fact that boy's got one of the best second-hand educations in this country.

LUTIEBELLE. [*Brightening considerably.*] Is that a fact!

MISSY. Used to read everything he could get his hands on.

LUTIEBELLE. He did? Ain't that wonderful!

MISSY. Till one day he finally got tired, and throwed all his books to the hogs—not enough "Negro" in them, he said. After that he puttered around with first one thing then another. Remember that big bus boycott they had in Montgomery? Well, we don't travel by bus in the cotton patch, so Purlie boycotted mules!

LUTIEBELLE. You don't say so?

MISSY. Another time he invented a secret language, that Negroes could understand but white folks couldn't.

LUTIEBELLE. Oh, my goodness gracious!

MISSY. He sent it C.O.D. to the NAACP but they never answered his letter.

LUTIEBELLE. Oh, they will, Aunt Missy; you can just bet your life they will.

MISSY. I don't mind it so much. Great leaders are bound to pop up from time to time 'mongst our people—in fact we sort of look forward to it. But Purlie's in such a hurry I'm afraid he'll lose his mind.

LUTIEBELLE. Lose his mind—no! Oh, no!

MISSY. That is unless you and me can do something about it.

LUTIEBELLE. You and me? Do what, Aunt Missy? You tell me—I'll do anything!

MISSY. [*Having found all she needs to know.*] Well, now; ain't nothing ever all that peculiar about a man a good wife—and a family—and some steady home cooking won't cure. Don't you think so?

LUTIEBELLE. [*Immensely relieved.*] Oh, yes, Aunt Missy, yes. [*But still not getting* MISSY'S *intent.*] You'd be surprised how many tall, good-looking, great big, ol' handsome looking mens—just like Reb'n Purlie —walking around, starving theyselves to death! Oh, I just wish I had one to aim my pot at!

MISSY. Well, Purlie Judson is the uncrowned appetite of the age.

LUTIEBELLE. He is! What's his favorite?

MISSY. Anything! Anything a fine-looking, strong and healthy—girl like you could put on the table.

LUTIEBELLE. Like me? Like ME! Oh, Aunt Missy—!

MISSY. [PURLIE'S *future is settled.*] Honey, I mind once at the Sunday School picnic Purlie et a whole sack o' pullets!

LUTIEBELLE. Oh, I just knowed there was something—something—just reeks about that man. He puts me in the mind of all the good things

I ever had in my life. Picnics, fish-fries, corn-shuckings, and love-feasts, and gospel-singings—picking huckleberries, roasting ground-peas, quilting-bee parties and barbecues; that certain kind of—welcome—you can't get nowhere else in all this world. Aunt Missy, life is so good to us—sometimes!

MISSY. Oh, child, being colored can be a lotta fun when ain't nobody looking.

LUTIEBELLE. Ain't it the truth! I always said I'd never pass for white, no matter how much they offered me, unless the things I love could pass, too.

MISSY. Ain't it the beautiful truth!

[PURLIE *enters again; agitated.*]

PURLIE. Missy—Gitlow says if you want him come and get him!

MISSY. [*Rises, crosses to door Down Left; looks out.*] Lawd, that man do take his cotton picking seriously. [*Comes back to* LUTIEBELLE *and takes her saucer.*] Did you get enough to eat, honey?

LUTIEBELLE. Indeed I did. And Aunt Missy, I haven't had potato pie like that since the senior choir give—

MISSY. [*Still ignoring him.*] That's where I met Gitlow, you know. On the senior choir.

LUTIEBELLE. Aunt Missy! I didn't know you could sing!

MISSY. Like a brown-skin nightingale. Well, it was a Sunday afternoon —Big Bethel had just been—

PURLIE. Dammit, Missy! The white man is five hundred years ahead of us in this country, and we ain't gonna ever gonna catch up with him sitting around on our non-Caucasian rumps talking about the senior choir!

MISSY. [*Starts to bridle at this sudden display of passion, but changes her mind.*] Right this way, honey. [*Heads for door Down Right.*] Where Cousin Bee used to sleep at.

LUTIEBELLE. Yes, ma'am. [*Starts to follow* MISSY.]

PURLIE. [*Stopping her.*] Wait a minute—don't forget your clothes! [*Gives her a large carton.*]

MISSY. It ain't much, the roof leaks, and you can get as much September inside as you can outside any time; but I try to keep it clean.

PURLIE. Cousin Bee was known for her clothes!

MISSY. Stop nagging, Purlie— [*To* LUTIEBELLE.] There's plenty to eat in the kitchen.

LUTIEBELLE. Thank you, Aunt Missy. [*Exits Down Right.*]

PURLIE. [*Following after her.*] And hurry! We want to leave as soon as Missy gets Gitlow in from the cotton patch!

MISSY. [*Blocking his path.*] Mr. Preacher—[*She pulls him out of ear-shot.*] If we do pull this thing off—[*Studying him a moment.*] what do you plan to do with her after that—send her back where she came from?

PURLIE. Dothan, Alabama? Never! Missy, there a million things I can do with a girl like that, right here in Big Bethel!

MISSY. Yeah! Just make sure they're all legitimate. Anyway, marriage is still cheap, and we can always use another cook in the family! [PURLIE *hasn't the slightest idea what* MISSY *is talking about.*]

LUTIEBELLE. [*From Offstage.*] Aunt Missy.

MISSY. Yes, honey.

LUTIEBELLE. [*Offstage.*] Whose picture is this on the dresser?

MISSY. Why, that's Cousin Bee.

LUTIEBELLE. [*A moment's silence. Then she enters hastily, carrying a large photograph in her hand.*] Cousin Bee!

MISSY. Yes, poor thing. She's the one the whole thing is all about.

LUTIEBELLE. [*The edge of panic.*] Cousin Bee— Oh, my!—Oh, my goodness! My goodness gracious!

MISSY. What's the matter?

LUTIEBELLE. But she's pretty—she's so pretty!

MISSY. [*Takes photograph; looks at it tenderly.*] Yes—she was pretty. I guess they took this shortly before she died.

LUTIEBELLE. And you mean—you want me to look like her?

PURLIE. That's the idea. Now go and get into your clothes. [*Starts to push her off.*]

MISSY. They sent it down to us from the college. Don't she look smart? I'll bet she was a good student when she was living.

LUTIEBELLE. [*Evading* PURLIE.] Good student!

MISSY. Yes. One more year and she'd have finished.

LUTIEBELLE. Oh, my gracious Lord have mercy upon my poor soul!

PURLIE. [*Not appreciating her distress or its causes.*] Awake, awake! Put on thy strength, O, Zion—put on thy beautiful garments. [*Hurries her Offstage.*] And hurry! [*Turning to* MISSY.] Missy, Big Bethel and Gitlow is waiting. Grandpaw Kincaid gave his life. [*Gently places the bat into her hand.*] It is a far greater thing you do now, than you've ever done before—and Gitlow ain't never got his head knocked off in a better cause. [MISSY *nods her head in sad agreement, and accepts the bat.* PURLIE *helps her to the door Down Left, where she exits, a most reluctant executioner.* PURLIE *stands and watches her off from the depth of his satisfaction. The door Down Right eases open, and* LUTIEBELLE, *her suitcase, handbag, fall coat and lunch box firmly in hand, tries to sneak out the front door.* PURLIE *hears her, and turns just in time.*] Where do you think you're going?

LUTIEBELLE. Did you see that, Reb'n Purlie? [*Indicating bedroom from which she just came.*] Did you see all them beautiful clothes—slips, hats, shoes, stockings? I mean nylon stockings like Miz Emmylou wears—and a dress, like even Miz Emmylou don't wear. Did you look at what was in that big box?

PURLIE. Of course I looked at what was in that big box—I bought it—all of it—for you.

LUTIEBELLE. For me!

PURLIE. Of course! I told you! And as soon as we finish you can have it!

LUTIEBELLE. Reb'n Purlie, I'm a good girl. I ain't never done nothing in all this world, white, colored or otherwise, to hurt nobody!

PURLIE. I know that.

LUTIEBELLE. I work hard; I mop, I scrub, I iron; I'm clean and polite, and I know how to get along with white folks' children better'n they do. I pay my church dues every second and fourth Sunday the Lord sends; and I can cook catfish—and hushpuppies— You like hush-puppies, don't you, Reb'n Purlie?

PURLIE. I love hushpuppies!

LUTIEBELLE. Hushpuppies—and corn dodgers; I can cook you a corn dodger would give you the swimming in the head!

PURLIE. I'm sure you can, but—

LUTIEBELLE. But I ain't never been in a mess like this in all my life!

PURLIE. Mess—what mess?

LUTIEBELLE. You mean go up that hill, in all them pretty clothes, and pretend—in front of white folks—that—that I'm your Cousin Bee—somebody I ain't never seen or heard of before in my whole life!

PURLIE. Why not? Some of the best pretending in the world is done in front of white folks.

LUTIEBELLE. But Reb'n Purlie, I didn't know your Cousin Bee was a student at the college; I thought she worked there!

PURLIE. But I told you on the train—

LUTIEBELLE. Don't do no good to tell ME nothing, Reb'n Purlie! I never listen. Ask Miz Emmylou and 'em, they'll tell you I never listen. I didn't know it was a college lady you wanted me to make like. I thought it was for a sleep-in like me. I thought all that stuff you bought in them boxes was stuff for maids and cooks and— Why, I ain't never even been near a college!

PURLIE. So what? College ain't so much where you been as how you talk when you get back. Anybody can do it; look at me.

LUTIBELLE. Nawsir, I think you better look at me like Miz Emmylou sez—

PURLIE. [*Taking her by the shoulders, tenderly.*] Calm down—just take it easy, and calm down. [*She subsides a little, her chills banished by the warmth of him.*] Now—don't tell me, after all that big talking you done on the train about white folks, you're scared.

LUTIEBELLE. Talking big is easy—from the proper distance.

PURLIE. Why—don't you believe in yourself?

LUTIEBELLE. Some.

PURLIE. Don't you believe in your own race of people?

LUTIEBELLE. Oh, yessir—a little.

PURLIE. Don't you believe the black man is coming to power some day?

LUTIEBELLE. Almost.

PURLIE. Ten thousand Queens of Sheba! What kind of a Negro are you! Where's your race pride?

LUTIEBELLE. Oh, I'm a great one for race pride, sir, believe me—it's just that I don't need it much in my line of work! Miz Emmylou sez—

PURLIE. Damn Miz Emmylou! Does her blond hair and blue eyes make her any more of a woman in the sight of her men folks than your black hair and brown eyes in mine?

LUTIEBELLE. No, sir!

PURLIE. Is her lily-white skin any more money-under-the-mattress than your fine fair brown? And if so, why does she spend half her life at the beach trying to get a sun tan?

LUTIEBELLE. I never thought of that!

PURLIE. There's a whole lotta things about the Negro question you ain't thought of! The South is split like a fat man's underwear; and somebody beside the Supreme Court has got to make a stand for the everlasting glory of our people!

LUTIEBELLE. Yessir.

PURLIE. Snatch Freedom from the jaws of force and filibuster!

LUTIEBELLE. Amen to that!

PURLIE. Put thunder in the Senate—!

LUTIEBELLE. Yes, Lord!

PURLIE. And righteous indignation back in the halls of Congress!

LUTIEBELLE. Ain't it the truth!

PURLIE. Make Civil Rights from Civil Wrongs; and bring that ol' Civil War to a fair and a just conclusion!

LUTIEBELLE. Help him, Lord!

PURLIE. Remind this white and wicked world there ain't been more'n a dime's worth of difference twixt one man and another'n, irregardless of race, gender, creed, or color—since God Himself Almighty set the first batch out to dry before the chimneys of Zion got hot! The eyes and ears of the world is on Big Bethel!

LUTIEBELLE. Amen and hallelujah!

PURLIE. And whose side are you fighting on this evening, sister?

LUTIEBELLE. Great Gawdamighty, Reb'n Purlie, on the Lord's side! But Miss Emmylou sez—

PURLIE. [*Blowing up.*] This is outrageous—this is a catastrophe! You're a disgrace to the Negro profession!

LUTIEBELLE. That's just what she said all right—her exactly words.

PURLIE. Who's responsible for this? Where's your Maw and Paw at?

LUTIEBELLE. I reckon I ain't rightly got no Maw and Paw, wherever they at.

PURLIE. What!

LUTIEBELLE. And nobody else that I knows of. You see, sir—I been on the go from one white folks' kitchen to another since before I can remember. How I got there in the first place—whatever became of my Maw and Paw, and my kinfolks—even what my real name is—nobody is ever rightly said.

PURLIE. [*Genuinely touched.*] Oh. A motherless child—

LUTIEBELLE. That's what Miz Emmylou always sez—

PURLIE. But—who cared for you—like a mother? Who brung you up—who raised you?

LUTIEBELLE. Nobody in particular—just whoever happened to be in charge of the kitchen that day.

PURLIE. That explains the whole thing—no wonder; you've missed the most important part of being somebody.

LUTIEBELLE. I have? What part is that?

PURLIE. Love—being appreciated, and sought out, and looked after; being fought to the bitter end over even.

LUTIEBELLE. Oh, I have missed that, Reb'n Purlie, I really have. Take mens—all my life they never looked at me the way other girls get looked at!

PURLIE. That's not so. The very first time I saw you—right up there in the junior choir—I give you that look!

LUTIEBELLE. [*Turning to him in absolute ecstasy.*] You did! Oh, I thought so!—I prayed so. All through your sermon I thought I would faint from hoping so hard so. Oh, Reb'n Purlie—I think that's the finest look a person could ever give a person— Oh, Reb'n Purlie! [*She closes her eyes and points her lips at him.*]

PURLIE. [*Starts to kiss her, but draws back shyly.*] Lutiebelle—

LUTIEBELLE. [*Dreamily, her eyes still closed.*] Yes, Reb'n Purlie—

PURLIE. There's something I want to ask you—something I never—in all my life—thought I'd be asking a woman—Would you—I don't know exactly how to say it—would you—

LUTIEBELLE. Yes, Reb'n Purlie?

PURLIE. Would you be my disciple?

LUTIEBELLE. [*Rushing into his arms.*] Oh, yes, Reb'n Purlie, yes!

[*They start to kiss, but are interrupted by a NOISE coming from Offstage.*]

GITLOW. [*Offstage; in the extremity of death.*] No, Missy. No—no!— NO!— [*This last plea is choked off by the sound of some solid object brought smartly into contact with sudden flesh. "CLUNK!"* PURLIE *and* LUTIEBELLE *stand looking off Left, frozen for the moment.*]

LUTIEBELLE. [*Finally daring to speak.*] Oh, my Lord, Reb'n Purlie, what happened?

PURLIE. Gitlow has changed his mind. [*Grabs her and swings her around bodily.*] Toll the bell, Big Bethel!—toll that big, fat, black and sassy liberty bell. Tell Freedom— [LUTIEBELLE *suddenly leaps from the floor into his arms and plants her lips squarely on his. When finally he can come up for air.*] Tell Freedom—tell Freedom— WOW!

CURTAIN

Copies of this play, in individual paper covered acting editions, are available from Samuel French, Inc., 25 W. 45th St., New York, N.Y. or 7623 Sunset Blvd., Hollywood, Calif. or in Canada Samuel French, (Canada) Ltd., 26 Grenville St., Toronto, Canada.

LeRoi Jones

(b. 1934)

LeRoi Jones was born into a middle-class family in Newark, New Jersey. He graduated from a predominantly white high school and attended Rutgers University for a year. A desire to see and participate in an all-black world sent him to Howard University, where Jones regarded the middle-class environment as stifling and, in his mind, anti-black. He graduated from Howard at the age of nineteen and joined the Air Force.

Honorably discharged from the military, Jones went to New York City, where he did graduate work at the New School for Social Research and at Columbia. In 1958 he and his wife, Hallie Cohen, founded an avant garde magazine called *Yugen*. Although it ran for only eight issues (1958–62), it served as a forum for an impressive group of writers and poets: Allen Ginsberg, William S. Burroughs, Herbert Selby, Jr., Robert Creeley, A. B. Spellman, Diana Di Prima, Charles Olson, and Edward Dahlberg. Jones wrote short fiction, essays, and poetry not only for *Yugen*, but also for *Evergreen Review, Poetry, Saturday Review*, and *The Nation*. He served as a jazz critic for *Downbeat, Jazz*, and *Jazz Review* and edited two other "little magazines," *Kulchur* and *The Floating Bear*. In 1961 he received a John Hay Whitney Opportunity Fellowship, and in 1965 a Guggenheim Fellowship.

LeRoi Jones produced off Broadway a little-known play, *A Good Girl Is Hard to Find*. In 1961 he published a book of poetry, *Preface to a Twenty-Volume Suicide Note. Blues People*, a sociological approach to blues and jazz, came out in 1963. In 1964 *The Dead Lecturer* (poetry) appeared. In March of that year Jones' play *Baptism* was produced by the Writers' Stage Theater; *Dutchman* was performed at the Cherry Lane Theater in the fall; and *The Toilet* was presented at St. Mark's Playhouse in December. For *Dutchman* Jones received an Obie (the off-Broadway Theater Award given by the *Village Voice*).

LeRoi Jones' only novel, *The System of Dante's Hell*, appeared in 1965. In 1964–65 Jones founded and directed the Black Arts Repertory Theater in Harlem. A volume of essays and articles called *Home* was published in 1966, and, in 1967, *Black Music* and *Tales* (short fiction).

Jones has also written a number of short plays which reflect his theory that art serves primarily a social function—in this case, the furtherance of black nationalistic and revolutionary thought and goals. The plays in this vein include *Jello, A Black Mass, The Slave Ship*, and

Arm Yrself or Harm Yrself. Recently Jones' home base has been Newark, New Jersey, where he works with a black revolutionary theater and arts group called The Spirit House Movers and Players. He edits a black music journal called *The Cricket* and has become interested in a new field of endeavor—film making.

CROW JANE IN HIGH SOCIETY.

                         (Wipes
her nose
on the draperies. Spills drinks
fondles another man's
life. She is looking
for alternatives. Openings
where she can lay all
this greasy talk
on somebody. Me, once. Now
I am her teller.
                (And I tell
her symbols, as the grey movement
of clouds. Leave
grey movements
of clouds. Leave, always,
more.

Where is she? That she
moves without light. Even
in our halls. Even with
our laughter, lies, dead drunk
in a slouch hat famous king.
                        Where?

To come on so.

THE INVENTION OF COMICS

I am a soul in the world: in
the world of my soul the whirled
light from the day

the sacked land
of my father.

In the world, the sad
nature of
myself. In myself
nature is sad. Small
prints of the day. Its
small dull fires. Its
sun, like a greyness
smeared on the dark.

The day of my soul, is
the nature of that
place. It is a landscape. Seen
from the top of a hill. A
grey expanse; dull fires
throbbing on its seas.

The man's soul, the complexion
of his life. The menace
of its greyness. The
fire, throbs, the sea
moves. Birds shoot
from the dark. The edge
of the waters lit
darkly for the moon.

And the moon, from the soul. Is
the world, of the man. The man
and his sea, and its moon, and
the soft fire throbbing. Kind
death. O
my dark and sultry
love.

BLACK DADA NIHILISMUS

.Against what light

is false what breath
sucked, for deadness.
            Murder, the cleansed

purpose, frail, against
God, if they bring him
                 bleeding, I would not

forgive, or even call him
black dada nihilismus.

The protestant love, wide windows,
color blocked to Mondrian, and the
ugly silent deaths of jews under

the surgeon's knife. (To awake on
69th street with money and a hip
nose. Black dada nihilismus, for

the umbrella'd jesus. Trilby intrigue
movie house presidents sticky the floor.
B.D.N., for the secret men, Hermes, the

blacker art. Thievery (ahh, they return
those secret gold killers. Inquisitors
of the cocktail hour. Trismegistus, have

them, in their transmutation, from stone
to bleeding pearl, from lead to burning
looting, dead Moctezuma, find the West

a grey hideous space.

2

From Sartre, a white man, it gave
the last breath. And we beg him die,
before he is killed. Plastique, we

do not have, only thin heroic blades.
The razor. Our flail against them, why
you carry knives? Or brutaled lumps of

heart? Why you stay, where they can
reach? Why you sit, or stand, or walk
in this place, a window on a dark

warehouse. Where the minds packed in
straw. New homes, these towers, for those
lacking money or art. A cult of death,

need of the simple striking arm under
the streetlamp. The cutters, from under
their rented earth. Come up, black dada

nihilismus. Rape the white girls. Rape
their fathers. Cut the mothers' throats.
Black dada nihilismus, choke my friends

in their bedrooms with their drinks spilling
and restless for tilting hips or dark liver
lips sucking splinters from the master's thigh.

Black scream
and chant, scream,
and dull, un
earthly

hollering. Dada, bilious
what ugliness, learned
in the dome, colored holy
shit (i call them sinned

or lost
       burned masters
                of the lost
                        nihil German killers
                                all our learned

art, 'member
what you said
money, God, power,
a moral code, so cruel
it destroyed Byzantium, Tenochtitlan, Commanch
                            (got it, *Baby!*

For tambo, willie best, dubois, patrice, mantan, the
bronze buckaroos.

              For Jack Johnson, asbestos, tonto, buckwheat,
              billie holiday.

              For tom russ, l'overture, vesey, beau jack,

(may a lost god damballah, rest or save us
against the murders we intend
against his lost white children
black dada nihilismus

THE MYTH OF A NEGRO LITERATURE

The mediocrity of what has been called "Negro Literature" is one of the most loosely held secrets of American culture. From Phyllis Wheatley to Charles Chesnutt, to the present generation of American Negro writers, the only recognizable accretion of tradition readily attributable to the black producer of a formal literature in this country, with a few notable exceptions, has been of an almost agonizing mediocrity. In most other fields of "high art" in America, with the same few notable exceptions, the Negro contribution has been, when one existed at all, one of impressive mediocrity. Only in music, and most notably in blues, jazz, and spirituals, *i.e.*, "Negro Music," has there been a significantly profound contribution by American Negroes.

There are a great many reasons for the spectacular vapidity of the American Negro's accomplishment in other formal, serious art forms—social, economic, political, etc.—but one of the most persistent and aggravating reasons for the absence of achievement among serious Negro artists, except in Negro music, is that in most cases the Negroes who found themselves in a position to pursue some art, especially the art of literature, have been members of the Negro middle class, a group that has always gone out of its way to cultivate *any* mediocrity, as long as that mediocrity was guaranteed to prove to America, and recently to the world at large, that they were not really who they were, *i.e.*, Negroes. Negro music alone, because it drew its strengths and beauties out of the depth of the black man's soul, and because to a large extent its traditions could be carried on by the lowest classes of Negroes, has been able to survive the constant and willful dilutions of the black middle class. Blues and jazz have been the only consistent exhibitors of "Negritude" in formal American culture simply because the bearers of its tradition maintained their essential identities as Negroes; in no other art (and I will persist in calling Negro music, Art) has this been possible. Phyllis Wheatley and her pleasant imitations of 18th century English poetry are far and, finally, ludicrous departures from the huge black voices that splintered southern nights with their *hollers, chants, arwhoolies*, and *ballits*. The embarrassing and inverted paternalism of Charles Chesnutt and his "refined Afro-American" heroes are far cries from the richness and profundity of the blues. And it is impossible to mention the achievements of the Negro in any area of artistic endeavor with as much significance as in spirituals, blues and jazz. There has never been an equivalent to Duke Ellington or Louis Armstrong in Negro writing, and even the best of contemporary literature written by Negroes cannot yet be compared to the fantastic beauty of the music of Charlie Parker.

American Negro music from its inception moved logically and powerfully out of a fusion between African musical tradition and the American experience. It was, and continues to be, a natural, yet highly stylized and personal version of the Negro's life in America. It is, indeed, a chronicler of the Negro's movement, from African slave to American slave, from Freedman to Citizen. And the literature of the blues is a much more profound contribution to Western culture than any other literary contribution made by American Negroes. Moreover, it is only recently that formal literature written by American Negroes has begun to approach the literary standards of its model, *i.e.*, the literature of the white middle class. And only Jean Toomer, Richard Wright, Ralph Ellison, and James Baldwin have managed to bring off examples of writing, in this genre, that could succeed in passing themselves off as "serious" writing, in the sense that, say, the work of Somerset Maugham is "serious" writing. That is, serious, if one has never read Herman Melville or James Joyce. And it is part of the tragic naïveté of the middle class (brow) writer, that he has not.

Literature, for the Negro writer, was always an example of "culture." Not in the sense of the more impressive philosophical characteristics of a particular social group, but in the narrow sense of "cultivation" or "sophistication" of an individual within that group. The Negro artist, because of his middle-class background, carried the artificial social burden as the "best and most intelligent" of Negroes, and usually entered into the "serious" arts to exhibit his familiarity with the social graces, *i.e.*, as a method or means of displaying his participation in the "serious" aspects of American culture. To be a writer was to be "cultivated," in the stunted bourgeois sense of the word. It was also to be a "quality" black man. It had nothing to do with the investigation of the human soul. It was, and is, a social preoccupation rather than an aesthetic one. A rather daring way of status seeking. The cultivated Negro leaving those ineffectual philanthropies, Negro colleges, looked at literature merely as another way of gaining prestige in the white world for the Negro middle class. And the literary and artistic models were always those that could be socially acceptable to the white middle class, which automatically limited them to the most spiritually debilitated imitations of literature available. Negro music, to the middle class, black and white, was never socially acceptable. It was shunned by blacks ambitious of "waking up white," as low and degrading. It was shunned by their white models simply because it was produced by blacks. As one of my professors at Howard University protested one day, "It's amazing how much bad taste the blues display." Suffice it to say, it is in part exactly this "bad taste" that has continued to keep Negro music as vital as it is. The abandonment of one's local (*i.e.*, place or group) emotional attachments in favor of the abstract emotional response of what is called "the general public" (which is notoriously white and middle class) has always been the great diluter of any Negro culture. "You're acting like a nigger," was the standard disparagement. I remember being chastised severely for daring to eat a piece of watermelon on the Howard campus. "Do you realize you're sitting near the highway?" is what the man said, "This is the capstone of Negro education." And it is too, in the sense that it teaches the Negro how to make out in the white society, using the agonizing overcompensation of pretending he's also white. James Baldwin's play, *The Amen Corner*, when it appeared at the Howard Players theatre, "set the speech department back ten years," an English professor groaned to me. The play depicted the lives of poor Negroes running a store-front church. Any reference to the Negro-ness of the American Negro has always been frowned upon by the black middle class in their frenzied dash toward the precipice of the American mainstream.

High art, first of all, must reflect the experiences of the human being, the emotional predicament of the man, as he exists, in the defined world of his being. It must be produced from the legitimate emotional resources of the soul in the world. It can *never* be produced by evading these resources or pretending that they do not exist. It can never be produced by appropriating the withered emotional responses of some strictly social idea of humanity. High art, and by this I mean any art that would attempt to describe or characterize some portion of the profound meaningfulness of human life with any finality or truth, cannot be based on the superficialities of human existence. It must issue from *real* categories of human activity, *truthful* accounts of human life, and not fancied accounts of the attainment of cultural privilege by some willingly preposterous apologists for one social "order" or another. Most of the formal literature produced by Negroes in America has never fulfilled these conditions. And aside from Negro music, it is only in the "popular traditions" of the so-called lower class Negro that these conditions are fulfilled as a basis for human life. And it is because of this "separation" between Negro life (as an emotional experience) and Negro art, that, say, Jack Johnson or Ray Robinson is a larger cultural hero than any Negro writer. It is because of this separation, even evasion, of the emotional experience of Negro life, that Jack Johnson is a more modern political symbol than most Negro writers. Johnson's life, as proposed, certainly, by his career, reflects much more accurately the symbolic yearnings for singular values among the great masses of Negroes than any black novelist has yet managed to convey. Where is the Negro-ness of a literature written in imitation of the meanest of social intelligences to be found in American culture, *i.e.*, the white middle class? How can it even begin to express the emotional predicament of black Western man? Such a literature, even if its "characters" *are* black, takes on the emotional barrenness of its model, and the blackness of the characters is like the blackness of Al Jolson, an unconvincing device. It is like using black checkers instead of white. They are still checkers.

The development of the Negro's music was, as I said, direct and instinctive. It was the one vector out of African culture impossible to eradicate completely. The appearance of blues as a native *American* music signified in many ways the appearance of American Negroes where once there were African Negroes. The emotional fabric of the music was colored by the emergence of an American Negro culture. It signified that culture's strength and vitality. In the evolution of form in Negro music it is possible to see not only the evolution of the Negro as a cultural and social element of American culture, but also the evolution of that culture itself. The "Coon Shout" proposed one version of the American Negro—and of America; Ornette Coleman proposes another. But the point is that both these versions are accurate and informed with a legitimacy of emotional concern nowhere available in what is called "Negro Literature," and certainly not in the middlebrow literature of the white American.

The artifacts of African art and sculpture were consciously eradicated by slavery. Any African art that based its validity on the production of an artifact, *i.e.,* some *material* manifestation such as a wooden statue or a woven cloth, had little chance of survival. It was only the more "abstract" aspects of African culture that could continue to exist in slave America. Africanisms still persist in the music, religion, and popular cultural traditions of American Negroes. However, it is not an African art American Negroes are responsible for, but an American one. The traditions of Africa must be utilized within the culture of the American Negro where they *actually* exist, and not because of a defensive rationalization about the *worth* of one's ancestors or an attempt to capitalize on the recent eminence of the "new" African nations. Africanisms do exist in Negro culture, but they have been so translated and transmuted by the American experience that they have become integral parts of that experience.

The American Negro has a definable and legitimate historical tradition, no matter how painful, in America, but it is the only place such a tradition exists, simply because America is the only place the American Negro exists. He is, as William Carlos Williams said, "A pure product of America." The paradox of the Negro experience in America is that it is a separate experience, but inseparable from the complete fabric of American life. The history of Western culture begins for the Negro with the importation of the slaves. It is almost as if all Western history before that must be strictly a learned concept. It is only the American experience that can be a persistent cultural catalyst for the Negro. In a sense, history for the Negro, before America, must remain an emotional abstraction. The cultural memory of Africa informs the Negro's life in America, but it is impossible to separate it from its American transformation. Thus, the Negro writer if he wanted to tap his legitimate cultural tradition should have done it by utilizing the entire spectrum of the American experience from the point of view of the emotional history of the black man in this country: as its victim and its chronicler. The soul of such a man, as it exists outside the boundaries of commercial diversion or artificial social pretense. But without a deep commitment to cultural relevance and intellectual purity this was impossible. The Negro, as a writer, was always a social object, whether glorifying the concept of white superiority, as a great many early Negro writers did, or in crying out against it, as exemplified by the stock "protest" literature of the thirties. He never moved into the position where he could propose his own symbols, erect his own personal myths, as any great literature must. Negro writing was always "after the fact," *i.e.*, based on known social concepts within the structure of bourgeois idealistic projections of "their America," and an emotional climate that never really existed.

The most successful fiction of most Negro writing is in its emotional content. The Negro protest novelist postures, and invents a protest quite amenable with the tradition of bourgeois American life. He never reaches the central core of the America which *can* cause such protest. The intellectual traditions of the white middle class prevent such exposure of reality, and the black imitators reflect this. The Negro writer on Negro life in America postures, and invents a Negro life, and an America to contain it. And even most of those who tried to rebel against that *invented* America were trapped because they had lost all touch with the reality of their experience within the *real* America, either because of the hidden emotional allegiance to the white middle class, or because they did not realize where the reality of their experience lay. When the serious Negro writer disdained the "middlebrow" model, as is the case with a few contemporary black American writers, he usually rushed headlong into the groves of the Academy, perhaps the most insidious and clever dispenser of middlebrow standards of excellence under the guise of "recognizable tradition." That such recognizable tradition is necessary goes without saying, but even from the great philosophies of Europe a contemporary usage must be established. No poetry has come out of England of major importance for forty years, yet there are would-be Negro poets who reject the gaudy excellence of 20th century American poetry in favor of disembowelled Academic models of second-rate English poetry, with the notion that somehow it is the only way poetry should be written. It would be better if such a poet listened to Bessie Smith sing *Gimme a Pigfoot,* or listened to the tragic verse of a Billie Holiday, than be content to imperfectly imitate the bad poetry of the ruined minds of Europe. And again, it is this striving for *respectability* that has it so. For an American, black or white, to say that some hideous imitation of Alexander Pope means more to him, emotionally, than the blues of Ray Charles or Lightnin' Hopkins, it would be required for him to have completely disappeared into the American Academy's vision of a Europeanized and colonial American culture, or to be lying. In the end, the same emotional sterility results. It is somehow much more tragic for the black man.

A Negro literature, to be a legitimate product of the Negro experience in America, must get at that experience in exactly the terms America has proposed for it, in its most ruthless identity. Negro reaction to America is as deep a part of America as the root causes of that reaction, and it is impossible to accurately describe that reaction in terms of the American middle class; because for them, the Negro has never really existed, never been glimpsed in anything even approaching the complete reality of his humanity. The Negro writer has to go from where he actually is, completely outside of that conscious white myopia. That the Negro does exist is the point, and as an element of American culture he is completely misunderstood by Americans. The middlebrow, commercial Negro writer assures the white American that, in fact, he doesn't exist, and that if he does, he does so within the perfectly predictable fingerpainting of white bourgeois sentiment and understanding. Nothing could be further from the truth. The Creoles of New Orleans resisted "Negro" music for a time as raw and raucous, because they thought they had found a place within the white society which would preclude their being Negroes. But they were unsuccessful in their attempts to "disappear" because the whites themselves reminded them that they were still, for all their assimilation, "just coons." And this seems to me an extremely important idea, since it is precisely this bitter insistence that has kept what can be called "Negro Culture" a brilliant amalgam of diverse influences. There was always a border beyond which the Negro could not go, whether musically or socially. There was always a possible limitation to any dilution or excess of cultural or spiritual reference. The Negro could not ever become white and that was his strength; at some point, always, he could not participate in the dominant tenor of the white man's culture, yet he came to understand that culture as well as the white man. It was at this juncture that he had to make use of other resources, whether African, sub-cultural, or hermetic. And it was this boundary, this no-man's-land, that provided the logic and beauty of his music. And this is the only way for the Negro artist to provide his version of America—from that no-man's-land outside the mainstream. A no-man's-land, a black country, completely invisible to white America, but so essentially part of it as to stain its whole being an ominous gray. Were there really a Negro literature, now it could flower. At this point when the whole of Western society might go up in flames, the Negro remains an integral part of that society, but continually outside it, a figure like Melville's Bartleby. He is an American, capable of identifying emotionally with the fantastic cultural ingredients of this society, but he is also, forever, outside that culture, an invisible strength within it, an observer. If there is ever a Negro literature, it must disengage itself from the weak, heinous elements of the culture that spawned it, and use its very existence as evidence of a more profound America. But as long as the Negro writer contents himself with the imitation of the useless ugly inelegance of the stunted middle-class mind, academic or popular, and refuses to look around him and "tell it like it is"—preferring the false prestige of the black bourgeosie or the deceitful "acceptance" of *buy and sell* America, something never included in the legitimate cultural tradition of "his people"—he will be a failure, and what is worse, not even a significant failure. Just another dead American.

Ed Bullins

(b. 1935)

ED BULLINS, PLAYWRIGHT-IN-RESIDENCE at the New Lafayette Theater in Harlem, was born in Philadelphia. He spent a good deal of his adult life in California, where he attended school and worked at odd jobs. He has written an autobiography and a novel and has published short stories and poetry in literary magazines. Bullins, who feels that the theater is more effective than the printed word as a means of reaching the black community, began writing plays in San Francisco, where he was the co-founder and director of a community experiment in theater called the Black Arts/West. In 1966 he went to New York.

In 1968 Bullins presented three one-act plays at the American Place Theatre. (They were originally planned for the Harlem New Lafayette Theater which was destroyed by fire.) The plays were billed as "*The Electronic Nigger* and Others," but objections from the public resulted in the billing being changed to "The Ed Bullins' Plays." Of the three plays—*Clara's Ole Man, The Electronic Nigger,* and *A Son Come Home*—*Clara's Ole Man* is considered the best. In 1968 Bullins was given the Vernon Rice Award for contributing to the off-Broadway theater.

Bullins has edited an issue on the black theater for *The Drama Review* (*tdr*) (Summer, 1968). He is the editor of a magazine called *Black Theater* and a paperback anthology of new plays called *New Plays from the Black Theater.* He is presently writing a twenty-play cycle on black urban life.

A member of the Black Arts School, Ed Bullins is associated with LeRoi Jones in film making.

CLARA'S OLE MAN

Clara's Ole Man was first performed at the Firehouse Repertory Theatre in San Francisco on August 5, 1965. It was produced by the San Francisco Drama Circle and directed by Robert Hartman. The sets were designed by Louie Gelwicks and Peter Rounds. Lighting by Verne Shreve. In winter, 1968, it was done, along with two other of Mr. Bullins' plays, at the American Place Theatre in New York, and in the Spring the production continued running at the Martinique.

From *Five Plays by Ed Bullins,* copyright © 1968, by Ed Bullins. Reprinted by permission of the publishers, The Bobbs-Merrill Company, Inc.

The People

CLARA, *a light brown girl of 18 well-built with long, dark hair. A blond streak runs down the middle of her head, and she affects a pony tail. She is pensive, slow in speech but feline. Her eyes are heavy-lidded and brown; she smiles—rather, blushes—often.*

BIG GIRL, *a stocky woman wearing jeans and tennis shoes and a tight fitting blouse which accents her prominent breasts. She is of an indeterminable age, due partly to her lack of makeup and plain hair style. She is anywhere from 25 to 40, and is loud and jolly, frequently breaking out in laughter from her own jokes.*

JACK, *20 years old, wears a corduroy Ivy League suit and vest. At first, JACK's speech is modulated and too eloquent for the surroundings but as he drinks his words become slurred and mumbled.*

BABY GIRL, BIG GIRL's *mentally retarded teenaged sister. The girl has the same hairdo as* CLARA. *Her face is made up with mascara, eye shadow, and she has black arching eyebrows penciled darkly, the same as* CLARA.

MISS FAMIE, *a drunken neighbor.*

STOOGIE, *a local street-fighter and gang leader. His hair is processed.*

BAMA, *one of* STOOGIE's *boys.*

HOSS, *another of* STOOGIE's *boys.*

C. C., *a young wino.*

Time: *Early spring, the mid-1950's.*

Scene: *A slum kitchen on a rainy afternoon in South Philadelphia. The room is very clean, wax glosses the linoleum and old wooden furniture; a cheap but clean red checkered oil cloth covers the table. If the room could speak it would say, "I'm cheap but clean."*

A cheap AM radio plays rhythm 'n blues music throughout the play. The furniture is made up of a wide kitchen table where a gallon jug of red wine sits. Also upon the table is an oatmeal box, cups, mugs, plates and spoons, ashtrays and packs of cigarettes. Four chairs circle the table, and two sit against the wall back-stage. An old fashioned wood and coal burning stove takes up a corner of the room and a gas range of 1935 vintage is backstage next to the door to the yard. A large, smoking frying pan is on one of the burners.

JACK and BIG GIRL are seated at opposite ends of the table; CLARA *stands at the stove fanning the fumes toward the door.* BABY GIRL *plays upon the floor with a homemade toy.*

CLARA, *fans fumes.* Uummm uummm . . . well, there goes the lunch. I wonder how I was dumb enough to burn the bacon?

BIG GIRL. Just comes natural with you, honey, all looks and no brains . . . now with me and my looks, anybody in South Philly can tell I'm a person that naturally takes care of business . . . hee hee . . . ain't that right, Clara?

CLARA. Awww girl, go on. You's the worst messer-upper I knows. You didn't even go to work this morn'. What kind of business is that?

BIG GIRL. It's all part of my master plan, baby. Don't you worry none . . . Big Girl knows what she's doin'. You better believe that!

CLARA. Yeah, you may know what you're doin' but I'm the one who's got to call in for you and lie that you're sick.

BIG GIRL. Well, it ain't a lie. You know I got this cough and stopped up feeling. *Looking at* JACK. You believe that, don't you, young blood?

JACK. Most certainly. You could very well have a respiratory condition and also have all the appearances of a extremely capable person.

BIG GIRL, *slapping table.* HEE HEE . . . SEE CLARA? . . . SEE? Listen ta that, Clara. I told you anybody could tell it. Even ole hot lips here can tell.

CLARA, *pours out grease and wipes stove.* Awww . . . he just says that to be nice . . . he's always sayin' things like that.

BIG GIRL. Is that how he talked when he met you the other day out to your aunt's house?

CLARA, *hesitating.* Nawh . . . nawh he didn't talk like that.

BIG GIRL. Well, how did he talk, huh?

CLARA. Awww . . . Big Girl. I don't know.

BIG GIRL. Well, who else does? You know what kind of a line a guy gives ya. You been pitched at enough times, haven't ya? By the looks of him I bet he gave ya the ole smooth college boy approach . . . *To* JACK. C'mon, man, drink up. We got a whole lot mo' ta kill. Don't you know this is my day off and I'm celebratin'?

JACK, *takes a drink.* Thanks . . . this is certainly nice of you to go to all this trouble for me. I never expected it.

BIG GIRL. What did you expect, young blood?

JACK, *takes another sip.* Ohhh, well . . . I . . .

CLARA, *to* BABY GIRL *on floor.* Don't put that dirty thing in your mouf, gal! *She walks around the table to* Baby Girl *and tugs her arm.* Now, keep that out of your mouf!

BABY GIRL, *holds to toy sullenly.* NO!

CLARA. You keep quiet, you hear, gal!

BABY GIRL. NO!

CLARA. If you keep tellin' me no I'm goin' ta take you upstairs ta Aunt Toohey.

BABY GIRL, *throws back head and drums feet on floor.* NO! NO! SHIT! DAMN! NO! SHIT!

CLARA, *disturbed.* NOW STOP THAT! We got company.

BIG GIRL, *laughs hard and leans elbows upon table.* HAW HAW HAW . . . I guess she told you, Clara. Hee hee . . . that little dirty mouf bitch, *pointing to* BABY GIRL *and becoming choked* . . . that little . . . *cough cough* . . . hooeee boy!

CLARA. You shouldn't have taught her all them nasty words, Big Girl. Now we can't do anything with her. *Turns to* JACK. What do you think of that?

JACK. Yes, it does seem a problem. But with proper guidance she'll more than likely be conditioned out of it when she gets into a learning situation among her peer group.

BIG GIRL, *takes a drink and scowls.* BULLSHIT!

CLARA. Aww . . . B. G.

JACK. I beg your pardon, Miss?

BIG GIRL. I said bullshit! Whatta ya mean with proper guidance . . . *points.* I taught that little bitch myself . . . the best cuss words I know before she ever climbed out of her crib . . . whatta ya mean when she gets among her "peer" group?

JACK. I didn't exactly say that. I said when . . .

BIG GIRL, *cuts him off.* Don't tell me what you said, boy. I got ears. I know all them big horseshit doctor words . . . tell him, Clara . . . tell him what I do. Where do I work. Clara?

CLARA. Awww . . . B.G., please.

BIG GIRL. Do like I say! Do like big wants you to!

CLARA, *surrenders.* She works out at the state nut farm.

BIG GIRL, *triumphant.* And tell mister smart and proper what I do.

CLARA, *automatically.* She's a technician.

JACK. Oh, that's nice. I didn't mean to suggest there was anything wrong with how you raised your sister.

BIG GIRL, *jolly again.* Haw haw haw . . . Nawh, ya didn't. I know you didn't even know what you were sayin', young blood. Do you know why I taught her to cuss?

JACK. Why no, I have no idea. Why did you?

BIG GIRL. Well, it was to give her freedom, ya know?

JACK *shakes his head.*

Ya see, workin' in the hospital with all the nuts and fruits and crazies and weirdos I get ideas 'bout things. I saw how when they get these kids in who have cracked up and even with older people who come in out of their skulls they all mostly cuss. Mostly all of them, all the time they out of their heads, they cuss all the time and do other wild things, and boy do some of them really get into it and let out all of that filthy shit that's been stored up all them years. But when the docs start shockin' them puttin' them on insulin they quiets down, that's when the docs think they're gettin' better, but really they ain't. They're just learn'n like before to hold it in . . . just like before, that's one reason most of them come back or are always on the verge afterwards of goin' psycho again.

JACK, *enthusiastic.* Wow, I never thought of that! That ritual action of purging and catharsis can open up new avenues in therapy and in learning theory and conditioning subjects . . .

BIG GIRL. Saaay whaaa . . . ? What did you have for breakfast, man?

CLARA, *struck.* That sounds so wonderful . . .

JACK, *still excited.* But I agree with you. You have an intuitive grasp of very abstract concepts!

BIG GIRL, *beaming.* Yeah, yeah . . . I got a lot of it figured out . . . *To* JACK. Here, fill up your glass again, man.

JACK, *to* CLARA. Aren't you drinking with us?

CLARA. Later. Big Girl doesn't allow me to start in drinking too early.

JACK, *confused.* She doesn't?

BIG GIRL *cuts in.* Well, in Baby Girl's case I said to myself that I'm teach'n her how in front and lettin' her use what she knows whenever it builds up inside. And it's really good for her, gives her spirit and everything.

CLARA. That's what probably warped her brain.

BIG GIRL. Hush up! You knows it was dat fuckin' disease. All the doctors said so.

CLARA. You don't believe no doctors 'bout nothin' else!

BIG GIRL, *glares at* CLARA. Are you showin' out, Clara? Are you showin' out to your little boy friend?

CLARA. He ain't mah boy friend.

JACK, *interrupts.* How do you know she might not have spirit if she wasn't allowed to curse?

BIG GIRL, *sullen.* I don't know anything, young blood. But I can take a look at myself and see the two of us. Look at me! *Stares at* JACK. LOOK AT ME!

JACK. Yes, yes, I'm looking.

BIG GIRL. Well, what do you see?

CLARA. B. G. . . . PLEASE!

BIG GIRL, *ignores.* Well, what do you see?

JACK, *worried.* Well, I don't really know . . . I . . .

BIG GIRL. Well, let me tell you what you see. You see a fat bitch who's 20 pounds overweight and looks ten years older than she is. You want to know how I got this way and been this way most of my life and would be worse off if I didn't let off some steam drinkin' this rotgut and speakin' my mind?

JACK, *to* BIG GIRL *who doesn't listen but drinks.* Yes, I would like to hear.

> CLARA *finishes the stove and takes seat between the two.* BABY GIRL *goes to the yard door but does not go out into the rain; she sits down and looks out through the door at an angle.*

BIG GIRL. Ya see, when I was a little runt of a kid my mother found out she couldn't keep me or Baby Girl any longer cause she had T. B., so I got shipped out somewheres and Baby Girl got shipped out somewheres else. People that Baby Girl went to exposed her to the disease. She was lucky, I ended up with some fuckin' Christians . . .

CLARA. Ohhh, B. G., you shouldn't say that!

BIG GIRL. Well, I sho as hell just did! . . . Damned kristers! I spent 12 years with those people, can you imagine? A dozen years in hell. Christians . . . HAAA . . . always preachin' 'bout some heaven over yonder and building a bigger hell here den any devil have imagination for.

CLARA. You shouldn't go round sayin' things like dat.

BIG GIRL. I shouldn't! Well what did you christian mammy and pot-gutted pappy teach you? When I met you you didn't even know how to take a douche.

CLARA. YOU GOT NO RIGHT!!! *She momentarily rises as if she's going to launch herself on* BIG GIRL.

BIG GIRL, *condescending.* Awww . . . forget it, sweetie . . . don't make no never mind, but you remember how you us'ta smell when you got ready fo bed . . . like a dead hoss or a baby skunk . . . *To* JACK, *explaining.* That damned Christian mamma and pappa of hers didn't tell her a thing 'bout herself . . . ha ha ha . . . thought if she ever found out her little thing was used fo anything else 'cept squattin' she'd fall backwards right up in it . . . ZaaaBOOM . . . STRAIGHT TA HELL . . . ha ha . . . didn't know that lil Clara had already found her heaven and on the same trail.

CLARA, *ashamed.* Sometimes . . . sometimes . . . I just want to die for bein' here.

BIG GIRL, *enjoying herself.* Ha ha ha . . . that wouldn't do no good. Would it? Just remember what shape you were in when I met you, kid. Ha ha ha. *To* JACK. Hey, boy, can you imagine this pretty little trick here had her stomach seven months in the wind, waitin' on a dead baby who died from the same disease that Baby Girl had . . .

CLARA. He didn't have any nasty disease like Baby Girl!

BABY GIRL, *hears her name but looks out door.* NO! NO! SHIT! DAMN! SHIT! SHIT!

BIG GIRL. HAW HAW HAW . . . now we got her started . . .

She laughs for over a minute; JACK *waits patiently, sipping;* CLARA *is grim.* BABY GIRL *has quieted.*

BIG GIRL. She . . . she . . . ha ha . . . was walkin' round with a dead baby in her and had no place to go.

CLARA, *fills a glass.* I just can't understand you, B. G. You know my baby died after he was born. Somedays you just get besides yourself.

BIG GIRL. I'm only helpin' ya entertain your guest.

CLARA. Awww . . . B. G. It wasn't his fault. I invited him.

JACK, *dismayed.* Well, I asked really. If there's anything wrong I can go.

BIG GIRL. Take it easy, young blood. I'm just havin' a little fun. Now let's get back to the Clara Saga . . . ya hear that word, junior? . . . S-A-G-A, SUCKER! You college boys don't know it all. Yeah, her folks had kicked her out and the little punk she was big for what had tried to put her out on the block and when that didn't work out . . . *mocking and making pretended blushes* . . . because our sweet little thing here was soooo modest and sedate . . . the nigger split! . . . HAW HAW HAW . . . HE MADE IT TO NEW YORK!

She goes into a laughing, choking and crying fit. BABY GIRL *rushes over to her and on tip toes pats her back.*

BABY GIRL. Big Girl! Big Girl! Big Girl! *A knocking sounds and* CLARA *exits to answer the door.*

BIG GIRL, *catches her breath.* Whatcha want, little sister?

BABY GIRL. The cat. The cat. Cat got kittens. Cat got kittens.

BIG GIRL, *still coughing and choking.* Awww, go on. You know there ain't no cat under there with no kittens. *To* JACK. She's been makin' that story up for two months now about how some cat crawls up under the steps and has kittens. She can't fool me none. She just wants a cat but I ain't gonna get none.

JACK. Why not, cats aren't so bad. My mother has one and he's quite a pleasure to her.

BIG GIRL. For your mammy maybe, but all they mean round here . . . *singsong* . . . is fleas and mo mouths to feed. With an invalid aunt upstairs we don't need anymo expenses.

JACK, *gestures toward* BABY GIRL. It shows that she has a very vivid imagination to make up that story about the kittens.

BIG GIRL. Yeah, her big sister ain't the biggest liar in the family.

CLARA *returns with* MISS FAMIE *staggering behind her, a thin middle-aged woman in long seamen's raincoat, dripping wet, and wearing house slippers that are soaked and squish water about the kitchen floor.*

BIG GIRL. Hi, Miss Famie. I see you're dressed in your rainy glad rags today.

MISS FAMIE, *slurred speech of the drunk.* Hello, B. G. Yeah, I couldn't pass up seein' Aunt Toohey, so I put on my weather coat. You know that don't a day pass that I don't stop up to see her.

BIG GIRL. Yeah, I know, Miss Famie. Every day you go up there with that quart of gin under your dress and you two ole lushes put it away.

MISS FAMIE. Why, B. G. You should know better than that.

CLARA, *re-seated.* B. G., you shouldn't say that . . .

BIG GIRL. Why shouldn't I? I'm payin' for over half of that juice and I don't git to see none of it 'cept the empty bottles.

BABY GIRL. CAT! CAT! CAT!

MISS FAMIE. Oh, the baby still sees them there cats.

CLARA. You should be ashamed to talk to Miss Famie like that.

BIG GIRL, *to* JACK. Why you so quiet? Can't you speak to folks when they come in?

JACK. I'm sorry. *To* MISS FAMIE. Hello, mam.

MISS FAMIE. Why howdie, son.

CLARA. Would you like a glass of wine, Miss Famie?

MISS FAMIE. Don't mind if I do, sister.

BIG GIRL. Better watch it, Miss Famie. Wine and gin will rust your gizzard.

CLARA. Ohh . . . *pours a glass of wine* . . . Here, Miss Famie.

BABY GIRL. CAT! CAT!

BIG GIRL, *singsong, lifting her glass.* Mus' I tell' . . . muscatel . . . jitter-bug champagne. *Reminisces.* Remember, Clara, the first time I got you to take a drink? *To* Miss Famie. You should of seen her. Some of this same cheap rotgut here. She'd never had a drink before but she wanted to show me how game she was. She was a bright little smart thing, just out of high school and didn't know her butt from a door nob.

Miss Famie. Yes, indeed, that was Clara all right.

Big Girl. She drank three water glasses down and got so damned sick I had to put my finger down her throat and make her heave it up . . . HAW HAW . . . babbled her fool head off all night . . . said she'd be my friend always . . . that we'd always be together . . .

Miss Famie, *gulps down her drink.* Wine will make you do that the first time you get good'n high on it.

Jack, *takes drink.* I don't know. You know . . . I've never really been wasted and I've been drinkin' for quite some time now.

Big Girl. Quite some time, huh? Six months?

Jack. Nawh. My mother used to let me drink at home. I've been drinkin' since 15. And I drank all the time I was in the service.

Big Girl. Just because you been slippin' some drinks out of ya mammy's bottle and you slipped a few under ya belt with the punks in the barracks don't make ya a drinker, boy!

Clara. B. G. . . . do you have to?

Miss Famie *finishes her second drink as* Big Girl *and* Clara *stare at each other.*

Miss Famie. Well, I guess I better get up and see Aunt Toohey. *She leaves.*

Jack. Nice to have met you, mam.

Miss Famie. Well, good-bye, son.

Big Girl, *before* Miss Famie *reaches top of stairs.* That ole gin-head tracked water all over your floor, Clara.

Clara. Makes no never mind to me. This place stays so clean I like when someone comes so it gets a little messy so I have somethin' ta do.

Big Girl. Is that why Jackie boy is here? So he can do some messin' 'round?

Clara. Nawh, B. G.

Jack, *stands.* Well, I'll be going. I see that . . .

Big Girl, *rises and tugs his sleeve.* Sit down an' drink up, young blood. *Pushes him back into his seat.* There's wine here . . . *slow and suggestive* . . . there's a pretty girl here . . . you go for that, don't you?

JACK. It's not that . . .

BIG GIRL. You go for fine little Clara, don't you?

JACK. Well, yes, I do . . .

BIG GIRL. HAW HAW HAW . . . *slams the table and sloshes wine* . . . HAW HAW HAW . . . *slow and suggestive* . . . What I tell ya, Clara? You're a winner. First time I laid eyes on you I said to myself that you's a winner.

CLARA, *takes a drink.* Drink up B. G.

BIG GIRL, *to* JACK. You sho you like what you see, young blood?

JACK, *becomes bold.* Why sure. Do you think I'd come out on a day like this for anybody?

BIG GIRL. HAW HAW HAW . . . *peals of laughter and more coughs* . . .

JACK, *to* CLARA. I was going to ask you to go to the matinee 'round Pep's but I guess it's too late now.

CLARA, *hesitates.* I never been.

BIG GIRL, *sobers.* That's right. You never been to Pep's and it's only 'round the corner. What you mean it's too late, young blood? It don't start gettin' good till round four.

JACK. I thought she might have ta start gettin' supper.

BIG GIRL. She'd only burn it the fuck up too if she did. *To* CLARA. I'm goin' ta take you to Pep's this afternoon.

CLARA. You don't have ta, B. G.

BIG GIRL. It's my day off, ain't it?

CLARA. But it costs so much, don't it?

BIG GIRL. Nawh, not much . . . you'll like it. Soon as C. C. comes over ta watch Baby Girl we can go.

CLARA, *brightens.* O.K.!

JACK. I don't know who's there now, but they always have a good show. Sometimes Ahmad Jamal . . .

BABY GIRL, *cuts speech.* CAT! CAT! CAT!

BIG GIRL. Let's toast to that . . . *raising her glass* . . . To Pep's on a rainy day!

JACK. HERE! HERE! *He drains his glass. A tumbling sound is heard from the backyard as they drink and* BABY GIRL *claps hands as* STOOGIE, BAMA *and* HOSS *appear in yard doorway. The three boys are no more than 16. They are soaked but wear only thin jackets, caps and pants. Under* STOOGIE's *cap he wears a bandanna to keep his processed hair dry.*

BIG GIRL. What the hell is this?

STOOGIE, *goes to* BIG GIRL *and pats her shoulder.* The heat, B. G. The man was on our asses so we had to come on in out of the rain, baby, dig?

BIG GIRL. Well tell me somethin' I don't know, baby. Why you got to pick mah back door? I ain't never ready for any more heat than I gets already.

STOOGIE. It just happened that way, B. G. We didn't have any choice.

BAMA. That's right, Big Girl. You know we ain't lame 'nuf to be usin' yo pad for no highway.

HOSS. Yeah, baby, you know how it is when the man is there.

BIG GIRL. Well, that makes a difference. *Smiles.* Hey, what'cha standin' there with your faces hangin' out for? Get yourselves a drink.

HOSS *goes to the sink to get glasses for the trio;* STOOGIE *looks* JACK *over and nods to* BAMA, *then turns to* CLARA.

STOOGIE. How ya doin', Clara. Ya lookin' fine as ever.

CLARA. I'm okay, Stoogie. I don't have to ask 'bout you none. Bad news sho travels fast.

STOOGIE, *holds arms apart in innocence.* What'cha mean, baby? What'-cha been hearin' 'bout poppa Stoogie?

CLARA. Just the regular. That your gang's fightin' the Peaceful Valley guys up in North Philly.

STOOGIE, Awww . . . dat's old stuff. Sheet . . . you way behind, baby.

BAMA. Yeah sweet cake, dat's over.

CLARA. Already?

HOSS. Yeah, we just finished sign'n a peace treaty with Peaceful Valley.

BAMA. Yeah, we out ta cool the War Lords now from ov'va on Powelton Avenue.

HOSS. Ole Stoogie here is settin' up the war council now; we got a pact with Peaceful Valley and man when we come down on those punk War Lords . . . baby . . . it's just gonna be all ov'va.

BIG GIRL. Yeah, it's always one thing ta another with you punks.

STOOGIE. Hey, B. G., cool it! We can't help it if people always spreadin' rumors 'bout us. Things just happen an' people talk and don' understand and get it all wrong, dat's all.

BIG GIRL. Yeah, all of it just happens, huh? It's just natural . . . you's growin' boys.

STOOGIE. That's what's happen'n baby. Now take for instance Peaceful Valley. Las' week we went up there . . . ya know, only five of us in Crook's Buick.

CLARA. I guess ya was just lookin' at the scenery?

HOSS. Yeah, baby, dat's it. We was lookin' . . . fo' some jive half-ass niggers.

The boys laugh and giggle as STOOGIE *enacts the story.*

STOOGIE. Yeah, we spot Specs from off'a Jefferson and Gratz walkin' with them bad foots down Master . . . ha ha ha . . .

BAMA. Tell them what happened to Specs, man.

HOSS. Awww, man, ya ain't gonna drag mah man Bama again?

They laugh more, slapping and punching each other, taking off their caps and cracking each other with them, gulping their wine and performing for the girls and JACK.

STOOGIE *has his hair exposed.*

STOOGIE. Bama here . . . ha ha ha . . . Bama burnt dat four-eyed mathafukker in the leg.

HOSS. Baby, you should'a seen it!

CLARA. Yeah, that's what I heard.

STOOGIE. Yeah, but listen, baby. *Points to* BAMA. He was holding the only heat we had . . . ha ho ho . . . and dis jive sucker was aimin' at Spec's bad foots . . . ha ha . . . while that blind mathafukker was blastin' from 'round the corner straight through the car window . . .

They become nearly hysterical with laughter and stagger and stumble around the table.

HOSS. Yeah . . . ha ha . . . mathafukkin' glass was flyin' all over us . . . ha ha . . . we almost got sliced ta death and dis stupid mathafukker was shootin' at the man's bad foots . . . ha ha . . .

BAMA, *scratching his head.* Well, man. Well, man . . . I didn't know what kind of rumble we was in.

CLARA *and* BIG GIRL *laugh as they refill their glasses, nearly emptying the jug.* BIG GIRL *gets up and pulls another gallon out of the refrigerator as laughter subsides. . .*

BIG GIRL, *sits down.* What's the heat doin' after ya?

STOOGIE. Nothin'.

CLARA. I bet!

STOOGIE, *sneer.* That's right, baby. They just singled us out to make examples out of.

This gets a laugh from his friends.

BIG GIRL. What did you get?

Hoss. Get?

Big Girl, *turns on him.* You tryin' ta get wise, punk?

Stoogie, *patronizing.* Awww, B. G. You not goin' ta take us serious, are ya?

Silence.

Well, ya see. We were walkin' down Broad Street by the State Store, see? And we see this old rumdum come out and stagger down the street carryin' this heavy package . . .

Clara. And?

Stoogie. And he's stumblin', see. Like he's gonna fall. So good ole Hoss here says, "Why don't we help that pore man out?" So Bama walks up and helps the man carry his package, and do you know what?

Big Girl. Yeah, the mathafukker "slips" down and screams and some cops think you some wrong doin' studs . . . yeah, I know . . . of course you didn't have time to explain.

Stoogie. That's right, B.G. So to get our breath so we could tell our side of it we just stepped in here, dig?

Big Girl. Yeah I dig. *Menacing.* Where is it?

Hoss. Where's what?

Silence.

Stoogie. If you had just give me another minute, B.G. *Pulls out a quart of vodka.* Well, no use savin' it anyway. Who wants some 100 proof tiger piss?

Bama, *to* Stoogie. Hey, man, how much was in dat mathafukker's wallet?

Stoogie, *nods toward* Jack. Cool it, sucker.

Hoss, *to* Stoogie. But, man, you holdin' the watch and ring too!

Stoogie, *advancing on them.* What's wrong with you jive-ass mathafukkers?

Big Girl. Okay, cool it? There's only one person gets out of hand 'round here, ya understand?

Stoogie. Okay, B.G. Let it slide . . .

Baby Girl. CAT! CAT! CAT!

Bama, *to* Hoss. Hey, man, dis chick's still chasin' dose cats.

Stoogie, *to* Jack. Drink up, man. Not everyday ya get dis stuff. Bama *picks up the beat of the music and begins a shuffling dance.* Baby Girl *begins bouncing in time to the music.*

Hoss. C'mon, Baby Girl; let me see ya do the slide.

Baby Girl. NO! NO! *She claps and bounces.*

Hoss, *demonstrates his steps, trying to out-dance* Bama. C'mon, Baby Girl, shake that thing!

Clara. No, stop that, Hoss. She don't know what she's doin!

Big Girl. That's okay Clara. Go on, Baby Girl, do the thing.

Stoogie *grabs salt from the table and shakes it upon the floor, under the feet of the dancers.*

Stoogie. DO THE SLIDE, MAN! SLIDE!

Baby Girl *lumbers up and begins a grotesque maneuver while grunting out strained sounds.*

Baby Girl. Uuuhhh . . . sheeeee . . . waaa . . . uuhhh . . .

Big Girl, *standing, toasting.* DO THE THING, BABY! ! !

Clara. Awww . . . B. G. Why don't you stop all dat?

Stoogie, *to* Jack. C'mon, man, git with it.

Jack *shakes his head and* Stoogie *goes over to* Clara *and holds out his hand.*

Stoogie. Let's go, Baby.

Clara. Nawh . . . I don't dance no mo . . .

Stoogie. C'mon, pretty mamma . . . watch this step . . . *He cuts a fancy step.*

Big Girl. Go on and dance, sister.

Stoogie *moves off and the three boys dance.*

Clara. Nawh . . . B. G., you know I don't go for that kind of stuff no mo.

Big Girl. Go on, baby!

Clara. No!

Big Girl. I want you to dance, Clara.

Clara. Nawh . . . I just can't.

Big Girl. DO LIKE I SAY! DO LIKE BIG WANTS!

The dancers stop momentarily but begin again when Clara *joins them.* Baby Girl *halts and resumes her place upon the floor, fondling her toy. The others dance until the record stops.*

Stoogie, *to* Jack. Where you from, man?

Jack. Oh, I live over in West Philly now, but I come from up around Master.

Stoogie. Oh? Do you know Hector?

Jack, *trying to capture an old voice and mannerism.* Yeah, man, I know the cat.

STOOGIE. What's your name, man?

JACK. Jack man, maybe you know me by Tookie.

STOOGIE, *ritually*. Tookie . . . Tookie . . . yeah, man, I think I heard about you. You us'ta be in the ole Jet Cobras!

JACK. Well, I us'ta know some of the guys then. I been away for a while.

BAMA, *matter-of-factly*. Where you been, man? Jail?

JACK. I was in the Marines for three years.

STOOGIE. Hey, man. That must'a been a gas.

JACK. It was okay. I seen a lot . . . went a lot of places.

BIG GIRL. Yeah, you must'a seen it all.

STOOGIE. Did you get to go anywhere overseas, man?

JACK. Yeah, I was aboard ship most of the time.

HOSS. Wow, man. That sounds cool.

BAMA. You really was overseas, man?

JACK, Yeah. I went to Europe and North Africa and the Caribbean.

STOOGIE. What kind of a boat were you on, man?

JACK. A ship.

BIG GIRL. A boat!

JACK. No, a ship.

STOOGIE, *rising*, BAMA *and* HOSS *surrounding* JACK. Yeah, man, dat's what she said . . . a boat!

CLARA. STOP IT! ! !

BABY GIRL. NO! NO! NO! SHIT! SHIT! SHIT! DAMN! SHIT!

MISS FAMIE's *voice from upstairs*. Your Aunt don't like all that noise.

BIG GIRL. You and my aunt better mind ya fukkin' ginhead business or I'll come up there and ram those empty bottles up where it counts!

BAMA *sniggling*. Oh, baby. We forgot your aunt was up dere sick.

STOOGIE. Yeah, baby. Have another drink.

> *He fills all glasses except* CLARA's. *She pulls hers away.*

CLARA. Nawh, I don't want any more. Me and Big Girl are goin' out after a while.

BAMA. Can I go too?

BIG GIRL. There's always have to be one wise mathafukker.

BAMA. I didn't mean nuttin', B. G., honest.

STOOGIE, *to* JACK. What did you do in the Army, man?

JACK, *feigns a dialect*. Ohhh, man. I told you already I was in the Marines!

Hoss, *to* Clara. Where you goin'?

Clara. B. G.'s takin' me to Pep's.

Bama. Wow . . . dat's nice, baby.

Big Girl, *gesturing toward* Jack. Ole smoothie here suggesting takin' Clara but it seems he backed out, so I thought we might step around there anyway.

Jack, *annoyed.* I didn't back out!

Stoogie, *to* Jack. Did you screw any of them foreign bitches when you were in Japan, man?

Jack. Yeah, man. I couldn't help it. They was all over, ya know?

Big Girl. He couldn't beat them off.

Stoogie. Yeah, man. I dig.

Jack. Especially in France and Italy. Course, the Spanish girls are the best, but the ones in France and Italy ain't so bad either.

Hoss. You mean those French girls ain't as good as those Spanish girls?

Jack. Nawh, man, the Spanish girls are the best.

Bama. I never did dig no Mexican nor Rican spic bitches. Too tough, man.

Jack. They ain't Mexican or Puerto Rican. They Spanish . . . from Spain . . . Spanish is different from Mexican. In Spain . . .

Stoogie. What'cha do now, man?

Jack. Ohhh . . . I'm goin' ta college prep on the G.I. Bill now . . . and workin' a little.

Stoogie. Is that why you sound like you got a load of shit in your mouth?

Jack. What do you mean!

Stoogie. I thought you talked like you had shit in your mouth because you had been ta college, man.

Jack. I don't understand what you're tryin' to say, man.

Stoogie. It's nothin', man. You just talk funny sometimes . . . ya know what I mean. Hey, man, where da you work?

Jack, *visibly feeling his drinks.* Nawh, man, I don't know what ya mean and I don't go to college, man, it's college prep.

Stoogie. Thanks, man.

Jack. And I work at the P.O.

Bama. Pee-who?

Jack. The Post Office, man.

Bama. No shit, baby.

STOOGIE. Thanks, George. I always like know things I don't know anything about. *He turns back on* JACK.

JACK, *to* BIG GIRL. Hey, what time ya goin' round to Pep's?

BIG GIRL. Soon . . . are you in a hurry, young blood? You don't have to wait for us.

JACK, *now drunk.* That's okay . . . it's just gettin' late, ya know, man . . . and I was wonderin' what time Clara's ole man gets home . . .

BIG GIRL. Clara's ole man? . . . Whad do you mean, man? . . . *The trio begins snickering, holding their laughter back;* JACK *is too drunk to notice.*

JACK. Well, Clara said for me to come by today in the afternoon when her ole man would be at work . . . and I was wonderin' what time he got home . . .

BIG GIRL *stands, tilting over her chair to crash backwards on the floor. Her bust juts out; she is controlled but furious.*

BIG GIRL. Clara's ole man is home now . . .

A noise is heard outside as C. C. comes in the front door. The trio are laughing louder but with restraint; CLARA *looks stunned.*

C. C. It's just Me . . . just ole C. C.

HOSS. Shsss . . . shut up, man.

JACK, *starts up and feels drunk for the first time.* What . . . you mean he's been upstairs all this time?

BIG GIRL, *staring.* Nawh, man, I don't mean that!

JACK, *looks at* BIG GIRL, *then at the laughing boys and finally to* CLARA. Ohhh . . . jezzus! *He staggers to the backyard door, past* BABY GIRL, *and becomes sick.*

BIG GIRL, *to* CLARA. Didn't you tell him? Didn't you tell him a fukkin' thing?

C. C. *comes in. He is drunk and weaves and says nothing. He sees the wine, searches for a glass, bumps into one of the boys, is shoved into another, and gets booted in the rear before he reaches wine and seat.*

BIG GIRL. Didn't you tell him?

CLARA. I only wanted to talk, B. G. I only wanted to talk to somebody. I don't have anybody to talk to . . . *crying* . . . I don't have anyone . . .

BIG GIRL. It's time for the matinee. *To* STOOGIE. Before you go, escort my friend out, will ya?

CLARA. Ohhh . . . B. G. I'll do anything but please . . . ohhh Big . . . I won't forget my promise.

BIG GIRL. Let's go. We don't want to miss the show, do we?

CLARA. Please, B. G., please. Not that. It's not his fault! Please!

BIG GIRL. DO LIKE I SAY! DO LIKE I WANT YOU TO DO!

> CLARA *drops her head and rises and exits stage right followed by* BIG GIRL. STOOGIE *and his boys finish their drinks, stalk and swagger about.* BAMA *opens the refrigerator and* HOSS *takes one long last guzzle.*

BAMA. Hey, Stoogie babe, what about the split?

STOOGIE, *drunk.* Later, you square-ass, lame-ass mathafukker!

> Hoss *giggles.*

BABY GIRL. CAT! CAT! CAT!

C. C., *seated drinking,* Shut up, Baby Girl. Ain't no cats out dere.

MISS FAMIE *staggers from upstairs, calls back.* Good night Toohey. See ya tomorrow.

> With a nod from STOOGIE, BAMA and HOSS take JACK'S arms and wrestle him into the yard. The sound of JACK'S beating is heard. MISS FAMIE wanders to the yard door, looks out but staggers back from what she sees and continues sprawling toward the exit, stage right.

BABY GIRL. CAT! CAT! CAT!

C. C. SHUT UP! SHUT ON UP, BABY GIRL! I TOLE YA . . . DERE AIN'T NO CATS OUT DERE! ! !

BABY GIRL. NO! DAMN! SHIT! SHIT! DAMN! NO! NO!

> STOOGIE *looks over the scene and downs his drink, then saunters outside. Lights dim out until there is a single soft spot on* BABY GIRL'S *head, turned wistfully toward the yard, then blackness. Curtain.*

John A. Williams

(b. 1925)

JOHN A. WILLIAMS, WHO is an excellent but relatively unacclaimed author, has produced five novels: *The Angry Ones* (1960); *Night Song* (1961); *Sissie* (1963); *The Man Who Cried I Am* (1967); and *Sons of Darkness, Sons of Light* (1969). The last two novels deal with the subject of the increasing violent confrontation between the black and white races in the United States.

Williams was born near Jackson, Mississippi, but spent most of his early years in Syracuse, New York. In high school he was more interested in sports than books, and when not participating in team sports, he would occasionally drop out of school to work, once taking a job with the sanitation department. During World War II Williams served in a segregated Navy, spending a good bit of time in conflict with his "white comrades." After the war he attended Syracuse University.

John. A. Williams' short fiction first appeared in 1957. He has written for *Negro Digest, Provincetown Review,* the *New York Herald Tribune Book Review, Holiday, Saturday Review, Ebony,* and others. He has worked for CBS, NBC, and for a large public relations firm.

In 1960 Williams was a Bread Loaf Scholar. In 1962 he was awarded the Prix de Rome by the American Academy of Arts and Letters, only to be rejected by the Academy in Rome, presumably for racial reasons. The National Institute of Arts and Letters then awarded him a grant which he reluctantly accepted after the Institute had discontinued its association with the Academy in Rome. (Williams includes this incident in his novel *The Man Who Cried I Am.*)

Williams is the author of *This Is My Country, Too* (1965), a book written after an eight-month journey through the United States to test the racial climate. The book, commissioned by *Holiday* magazine, first appeared as a series of articles. He has also written *Africa: Her History, Lands, and People* (1962); is co-author (with H. J. Anslinger) of *The Protectors;* and editor of *The Angry Black* (1962) and *Beyond the Angry Black* (1966). His poetry appears in a volume entitled simply *Poems.*

"Project: King Alfred" is taken from *The Man Who Cried I Am.*

PROJECT: KING ALFRED

Yes, Max thought. I knew Jaja Enzkwu, eagle-faced, hot-eyed Jaja with his sweating, pussy-probing fingers and perfumed agbadas; I knew him.

Max glanced at his watch again. Two o'clock. He wondered what Margrit was doing back in Amsterdam on such a beautiful day. He knew what Jaja was doing: feeding the bugs back in Onitsha where he had been sent in a box, after that deadly rendezvous with Baroness Huganot in Basel that day.

So much had happened that day, the day of the March on Washington. Margrit had left shortly after he called her. Then he had taken a plane to Washington. Du Bois had died in Ghana the night before, and so had Jaja, leaving behind an opened magnum of Piper-Heidsieck, a half-eaten partridge and a startled, voluptuous, eager-to-be-ravished Baroness. But Washington had been the place to be that day. There you could forget that the cancer tests were positive—it was malignant —and that you were going into cobalt treatment soon; you could forget with more than a quarter million people surging around you.

Max flipped up the next page of the letter and when he finished, he shook as if with a sudden chill, and yet the shaking hand had nothing to do with his illness; it was the letter itself. With trembling hands he lit a cigarette.

No, he told himself. I have not read what I just read. This cannot be. No, it's me, the way I'm thinking, the way I'm reading. He closed his eyes hard and held them for a long time. Then he opened them to re-read the entire letter once again:

Dear Max:

You are there, Max? It is you reading this, right? I mean, even dead, which I must be for you to have these papers *and* be alone in the company of Michelle, I'd feel like a damned fool if someone else was reading them. I hope these lines find you in good shape and with a full life behind you, because, chances are, now that you've started reading, all that is way, way behind you, baby.

I'm sorry to get you into this mess, but in your hands right now is the biggest story you'll ever have. Big and dangerous. Unbelievable. Wow. But, it's a story with consequences the editors of *Pace* may be unwilling to pay. And you, Max, baby, come to think of it, may not even get the chance to cable the story. Knowing may kill you, just as knowing killed me and a few other people you'll meet in this letter. Uh-uh! Can't quit now! It was too late when you opened the case. This is a rotten way to treat a friend. Yes, friend. We've had good and bad times together; we've both come far. I remember that first day we met at Zutkin's. We both saw something we liked in each other. What? I don't know, but it never mattered to me. Our friendship worked; it had value; it lasted. I've run out of acquaintances and other friends who never were the friend you were. So, even if this is dangerous for you— and it is—I turn to you in friendship and in the hope that you can do with this information what I could not. Quite frankly, I don't know how I got into this thing. It just happened, I guess, and like any contemporary Negro, like a ghetto Jew of the 1930's in Europe, I couldn't believe it was happening, even when the pieces fell suddenly into place. Africa . . .

God, Max, what doesn't start with Africa? What a history still to be told! The scientists are starting to say life began there. I'm no scientist. I don't know. But I do know that this letter you're reading had its origins with what happened there. Let me go back to the beginning. I doubt if you've heard of Alliance Blanc. In 1958 Guinea voted to leave the French Family of Nations, and at once formed a federation with Kwame Nkrumah, or Ghana, whichever you prefer. The British and French were shaken. How could countries only two minutes ago colonies spring to such political maturity? Would the new federation use pounds or francs? The national banks of both countries were heavily underwriting the banking systems of the two countries. There would be a temporary devaluation of both pounds and francs, whether the new federation minted new money or not. More important—and this is what really rocked Europe—if the federation worked, how many new, independent African states would follow suit? *Then,* what would happen to European interests in Africa after independence and federation? Was it *really* conceivable that all of Africa might one day unite, Cape to Cairo, Abidjan to Addis? Alliance Blanc said *Yes!* If there were a United States of Africa, a cohesiveness among the people— 300,000,000 of them—should not Europeans anticipate the possibility of trouble, sometime when the population had tripled, for example? Couldn't Africa become another giant, like China, with even more hatred for the white West? It was pure guilt over what Europeans had done to Africa and the Africans that made them react in such a violent fashion to African independence.

The white man, as we well know, has never been of so single an accord as when maltreating black men. And he has had an amazing historical rapport in Africa, dividing it up arbitrarily across tribal and language boundaries. That rapport in plundering Africa never existed and never will when it requires the same passion for getting along with each other in Europe. But you know all this. All I'm trying to say is that, where the black man is concerned, the white man will bury differences that have existed between them since the beginning of time, and come together. How goddamn different this would have been if there had been no Charles Martel at Tours in 732!

The Alliance first joined together not in the Hague, not in Geneva, not in London, Versailles or Washington, but in Munich, a city top-heavy with monuments and warped history. Present were representatives from France, Great Britain, Belgium, Portugal, Australia, Spain, Brazil, South Africa. The United States of America was also present. There were white observers from most of the African countries that appeared to be on their way to independence. The representation at first, with a few exceptions, was quasi-official. But you know very well that a quasi-official body can be just as effective as an official one; in fact, it is often better to use the former.

I don't have to tell you that the meetings, then and subsequently, were held in absolute secrecy. They were moved from place to place— Spain, Portugal, France, Brazil and in the United States, up around Saranac Lake—Dreiser's setting for *An American Tragedy,* that neck of the woods, remember? America, with the largest black population outside Africa, had the most need of mandatory secrecy. Things were getting damned tense following the Supreme Court decision to desegregate schools in 1954.

The disclosure of America's membership in Alliance Blanc would have touched off a racial cataclysm—but America went far, far beyond the evils the Alliance was perpetuating, but more of this later. For the moment, let me consider the Alliance.

African colonies were still becoming independent. Federations were formed only to collapse a few weeks later, like the Guinea-Ghana combine. Good men and bad were assassinated indiscriminately; coups were a dime a dozen. Nkrumah in West Africa vied with Selassie in East Africa for leadership of the continent. The work of the Alliance agents—setting region against region and tribe against tribe, just as the colonial masters had done—was made easy by the rush to power on the part of a few African strongmen. Thus, the panic mentality that had been the catalyst for the formation of the Alliance seemed to have been tranquilized. There was diplomacy as usual, independence as usual. What, after all, did Europeans have to fear after that first flash of black unity? The Alliance became more leisurely, less belligerent, more sure that it had time, and above all, positive now that Africa was not a threat to anyone but itself. Alliance agents flowed leisurely through Africa now, and Western money poured in behind them.

From a belligerent posture, the Alliance went to one based on economics. Consider that 15 percent of Nigeria's federal budget comes from offshore oil brought in by Dutch, British, Italian, French and American oil companies; consider that the 72 percent of the world's cocoa which Africa produces would rot if the West did not import it. Palm oil, groundnuts, minerals, all for the West. Can you imagine, man, what good things could happen to Africans, if they learned to consume what they produce? It did not take the Europeans long to discover that their stake in Africa as "friends" rather than masters was more enormous than they could have imagined. Only naked desperation demanded that Spain and Portugal stay in Africa; the Iberian Peninsula hasn't been the same since the Moors and Jews left it in the fifteenth century. Time? It was the Alliance's most formidable ally.

In South Africa, the spark of revolt flickered, sputtered and now is dead. The Treason Trials killed it; oppression keeps murdering it, and those who say the spark is still alive, those successive schools of nattily tailored South African nationalists, who plunge through Paris, London and New York raising money for impossible rebellions, lie. The paradox, Max, is that, denied freedom, the black man lives better in South Africa than anywhere else on the continent; the average African. The bigshots—with their big houses and long cars, their emulation of the colonial masters—do all right. My friend Genêt said it all in *Les Noirs*.

The Alliance worked. God, how it worked! And Africans themselves, dazzled by this new contraption the white man was giving them, independence, helped. Lumumba, disgracefully educated by the Belgians, was a victim of the Alliance; Olympio, dreaming dreams of federation, was another. Nkrumah and Touré have lasted for so long because their trust in the white man never was, and their trust in their own fellows only a bit deeper seated.

The Congo mess served as a valuable aid to the Alliance: it could test the world's reaction to black people in crisis. The Alliance was pleased to observe that the feeling in the West was, "Oh, well, they're only niggers, anyhow."

I could have foreseen that reaction; you could have foreseen it; any black man could have anticipated it. But, then, "niggers" are embattled everywhere, ain't they, baby? Asian "niggers," South American "niggers" . . . But let a revolt occur in East Germany and watch the newsprint fly! Let another Hungarian revolution take place and see the white nations of the world open their doors to take in refugees—Hungarian Freedom Fighters, yeah! Who takes in blacks, Pakistanis, Vietnamese, Koreans, Chinese, who?

But the picture began to change. It was quite clear that the Europeans had Africa well under control—and that was all they cared about. America, sitting on a bubbling black cauldron, felt that it had to map its own contingency plans for handling 22 million black Americans in case they became unruly; in case they wanted everything Freedom Fighters got just by stepping off the boat. So, America prepared King Alfred and submitted it to the Alliance, just as the Alliance European members had submitted their plans for operations in Africa to the Americans. King Alfred in its original form, called for sending American Negroes to Africa, and this had to be cleared by the Europeans. The Europeans vetoed that plan; they remembered what excitement Garvey had caused in Africa. The details of King Alfred are in the case, and it is truly hot stuff. All this Alliance business is pretty pallid shit compared to what the Americans have come up with.

I should tell you that it was an African who discovered the Alliance and in the process came upon King Alfred. Who? Jaja Enzkwu, that cockhound, that's who. He stumbled on the Alliance the second year of its existence, while he was in Spain, which as you know has turned out to be a very hospitable place for ex-heads of African countries on the lam. Enzkwu didn't know what was going on; he simply sensed something, seeing a gathering of British, American, Brazilian, Portuguese and South Africans at San Sebastián in winter. This was where the Alliance held its second meeting. I'll tell you about Jaja. Any halfway good-looking white woman can make a fool of him (which was what was happening, for him to be at a summer resort in winter), but he doesn't trust a gathering of more than a single white man. About the white man, Enzkwu has a nose for trouble. But you know Jaja.

Jaja died as he had lived, chasing white pussy. As soon as his nation became independent in 1960, using the various embassies and consulates his government had established in the Park Avenues, Park Lanes and Georges V's of the world, yes, those places, with the long, black limousines in front, chauffeured by large but deferential white men, those places with the waiting rooms filled with African art, Jaja started gathering material on the Alliance. He amassed all the information you have at hand.

How did they get to Jaja? It's a white man's world—so far. He had to hire white operatives, of course, to get to Alliance Blanc. A couple of these, Jaja's beloved Frenchmen, I believe, checked back through several white people fronting for Enzkwu, but, at last, they discovered old black Jaja sitting there behind it all. A black man, interesting. The bastards then sold *this* information to the Alliance. At this point, old Jaja, sitting behind an eighteen-foot desk, was cooling it, thinking he had it all covered. He planned to make use of the information. Like so many people, he had begun his investigations with a sincere desire to protect his country. But another consideration rose very, very quickly. He could use the information, to be released at a propitious time, to prove that the Nigerian premier, and African leaders generally, had failed to protect their people from the new colonialism. Jaja planned to gather all of Africa under a single ruler one day. That ruler was to be Jaja Enzkwu.

Panic in Washington ensued when it was discovered that Jaja not only had information on the Alliance, but on King Alfred, the contingency plan to detain and ultimately rid America of its Negroes. Mere American membership in the Alliance would have been sufficient to rock America, but King Alfred would have made Negroes realize, finally and angrily, that all the new moves—the laws and committees —to gain democracy for them were fraudulent, just as Minister Q and the others had been saying for years. Your own letter to me days after you left the White House only underscored what so many Negro leaders believed. The one alternative left for Negroes would be not only to seek that democracy withheld from them as quickly and as violently as possible, but to fight for their very survival. King Alfred, as you will see, leaves no choice.

The European members of the Alliance were not as concerned as America about the leak. In fact, if King Alfred was revealed and racial violence exploded in America, America's position as world leader would be seriously undermined. There were members in the Alliance who wished for this. The danger in Africa being nullified, the white man became divided. In the U.S., the situation had worsened. There had been that second boy at Ole Miss; the dogs and firehoses in Birmingham; kids blown up in church; little brush-fire riots that came and went across the country, like wind stroking a wheat field. Minister Q's voice was now large indeed. The March on Washington appeared to have been the last time the Negroes were peacefully willing to ask for and take any old handout.

The Alliance had not counted on the efficiency of the Central Intelligence Agency, which had placed agents in Nigeria within days of receiving the report that Jaja had information. Concealing King Alfred became the top priority assignment of the National Security Council and the CIA. Jaja was not killed at once for two reasons: first, the agents were unable to ascertain where he kept the papers. Second, on a trip to Paris, the agents made a fake attempt on his life to make him go for the papers. But this only resulted in arousing Jaja's curiosity, and he began backtracking through his former operatives and discovered that the Americans knew that he knew. Then Jaja started to deal. He'd give over the papers and keep his mouth shut, if the Americans gave him Nigeria. The U.S. had no choice but to agree, when it had the opportunity. It would take time. All right, Jaja said. But not *too* much time.

Jaja moved, ate, slept and crapped with an army of bodyguards. He had only to put it out that the Hausas in the north were after him, and every Ibo in the eastern region understood.

Enzkwu came to see me two days before your March on Washington. He was thin and drawn and quite subdued. Almost a year, I learned later, had passed since making the deal with the U.S. and nothing had come of it. Even Charlotte did not bring out that old gleam to his eyes, as her presence has done for many of my friends. Jaja and I had dinner that night, surrounded by some of the biggest Ibos I've ever seen. After, a car followed us, but it was his and was filled with his men. We didn't talk too much in his hotel. We were in one room and his guards in another. Every five minutes, one of the guards would knock on the door and ask something in Ibo, and Jaja would reply in Ibo. It was always the same question and the same answer.

Jaja was on his way to Switzerland and he gave me the key to a safe deposit box in a Paris bank and told me to get what was in it, if he did not return from Switzerland. I was puzzled and curious about his mood, but I took the key without asking questions. Of course, he was killed. I hustled to the bank and what I found was this information you now have found, plus a letter from Jaja, similar to my letter which you are now reading. The material fascinated me. I'd spent so much of my life writing about the evil machinations of Mr. Charlie without really *knowing* the truth, as this material made me know it. It was spread out before me, people, places and things. I became mired in them, and I *knew* now that the way black men live on this earth was no accident. And yet, my mind kept telling me that Jaja's death was a coincidence, a mere coincidence. I could not believe that I, too, soon would be dead. One looks at death, always moves toward it, but until the last denies its existence. I was trapped by my contempt for everything African. I made the bodyguards just a part of the African spectacle. I gripped the material, I hugged it to my chest, for now I would know; if they killed me, I would know that this great evil did exist, indeed, thrived. And Dr. Faustus came to my mind. The Americans killed Jaja, obviously because they ran out of patience, and because they thought they could find the material without him.

I didn't say anything to you when you came through Paris on your way to East Africa because I had not seen Jaja then.

It is spring. Strange, now that life seems to quicken a bit, and you can see people smiling more, and the trees starting to bloom, I feel tired, going downhill. I am sure the Americans are on to me. Perhaps the French keep them off, not wanting trouble to becloud De Gaulle's new image. At least that's what I think, and that's why I haven't made any trips outside France. I thought of giving it to the Russians, but would they even accept it from me? Even if they did, can't you see the West laughing it off as another Russian hoax, even Negroes?

But there was America itself. You and *Pace*. You must have access to outlets where this material would do the most good. The choice is yours and yours alone as to whether you want to wreck the nation or not. My opinion? No, Max, it's up to you. Think of the irony: the very nation that most wants to keep the information secret, would be the very one to release it!

A personal item: Charlotte seems to have found a strange tolerance for me these days. I think she knows about the material. And she has found out about Michelle and me, at last. How, I don't know, exactly, but I think American agents have told her, to enlist her aid.

In fact, Max, old trusted friend, everybody knows everything now, past and present.

I am getting this material to Michelle tonight. She will get it to you even if she has to swim to New York. I know of no one else. And perhas this is a sign, the ultimate sign, that I am very tired. I can only hope that no harm comes to her.

Another item, old buddy. Tomorrow I'm having lunch with a young man I understand you've met. His name is Edwards, and he's quit Uncle Sam's foreign service to write a novel about it. I can't resist these youngsters who come to see me, to sit at the feet of the father, so to speak. I guess I'll never outgrow it. I suppose you're next in line to be father . . .

Harry

Shock, gracious, pain-absorbing shock came at once and lessened the hurt and surprise. Max, reacting normally for the moment, lit another cigarette, picked through and carefully read Enzkwu's papers.

Yes, there was explosive material here. Enough to unsettle every capital city in the West; enough to force the Africans to cut ties with Europe at once and worry about the consequences later; enough to send black Brazilians surging out of their *favelas* and *barrios* to inundate the sleek beach places of the whites. Wherever white men had been involved with black men, Enzkwu's photostats disclosed a clear and unrelenting danger. Recorded in cold black type were lists of statesmen and diplomats, the records of their deeds, what they planned to do, when, where, why and to whom. The list of people dead, Max knew, and therefore murdered, if their names appeared in Enzkwu's papers, included the residents of four continents. African airfields equipped for the handling of jets and props, along with radio and power stations, the number of men in the army of each country, plus a military critique of those armies, were set down here.

Now Max's hand held another numbered packet, but above the number were the words: THE UNITED STATES OF AMERICA—KING ALFRED. Slowly, he pulled out the sheaf of photostats. So, this is King Alfred, Alfred the Great. He mused, Why is it called King Alfred? Then he saw the answer footnoted at the bottom of the first page.

KING ALFRED*

In the event of widespread and continuing and coordinated racial disturbances in the United States, KING ALFRED, at the discretion of the President, is to be put into action immediately.

PARTICIPATING FEDERAL AGENCIES

National Security Council	Department of Justice
Central Intelligence Agency	Department of Interior
Federal Bureau of Investigation	Department of Defense

PARTICIPATING STATE AGENCIES
(Under Federal Jurisdiction)

National Guard Units	State Police

PARTICIPATING LOCAL AGENCIES
(Under Federal Jurisdiction)

City Police	County Police

Memo: National Security Council

Even before 1954, when the Supreme Court of the United States of America declared unconstitutional separate educational and recreational facilities, racial unrest and discord had become very nearly a part of the American way of life. But that way of life was repugnant to most Americans. Since 1954, however, that unrest and discord have broken out into widespread violence which increasingly have placed the peace and stability of the nation in dire jeopardy. This violence has resulted in loss of life, limb and property, and has cost the taxpayers of this nation billions of dollars. And the end is not yet in sight. This same violence has raised the tremendously grave question as to whether the races can ever live in peace with each other. Each passing month has brought new intelligence that, despite new laws passed to alleviate the condition of the Minority, the Minority still is not satisfied. Demonstrations and rioting have become a part of the familiar scene. Troops have

*849–899 (?) King of England; directed translation from the Latin of the *Anglo-Saxon Chronicle.*

been called out in city after city across the land, and our image as a world leader severely damaged. Our enemies press closer, seeking the advantage, possibly at a time during one of these outbreaks of violence. The Minority has adopted an almost military posture to gain its objectives, which are not clear to most Americans. It is expected, therefore, that, when those objectives are denied the Minority, racial war must be considered inevitable. When that Emergency comes, we must expect the total involvement of all 22 million members of the Minority, men, women and children, for once this project is launched, its goal is to terminate, once and for all, the Minority threat to the whole of the American society, and, indeed, the Free World.

Chairman, National Security Council

❋   ❋   ❋

William Melvin Kelley

(b. 1937)

BORN IN NEW YORK CITY, William Kelley attended Fieldston School and Harvard College, where he studied under Archibald MacLeish and John Hawkes. Kelley has taught at the New School, has been a Bread Loaf Scholar and the recipient of a John Hay Whitney Award, and an Author-in-Residence at State University, Geneseo, New York. His articles and stories have appeared in *Esquire, Mademoiselle,* and *Negro Digest.*

William Kelley's major works are *A Different Drummer* (1962); *Dancers on the Shore,* a collection of short stories (1964); *A Drop of Patience* (1965); and *dem,* a surrealistic spoof on American color consciousness (1967).

The selections following are from *Dancers on the Shore* and *dem.*

THE ONLY MAN ON LIBERTY STREET

She was squatting in the front yard, digging with an old brass spoon in the dirt which was an ocean to the islands of short yellow grass. She wore a red and white checkered dress, which hung loosely from her shoulders, and obscured her legs. It was early spring and she was barefoot. Her toes stuck from under the skirt. She could not see the man yet, riding down Liberty Street, his shoulders square, the duster he wore spread back over the horse's rump, a carpetbag tied with a leather strap to his saddle horn and knocking against his leg. She could not see him until he had dismounted and tied his horse to a small, black, iron Negro jockey and unstrapped the bag. She watched now as he opened the wooden gate, came into the yard, and stood, looking down at her, his face stern, almost gray beneath the brim of his wide hat.

She knew him. Her mother called him Mister Herder and had told Jennie that he was Jennie's father. He was one of the men who came riding down Liberty Street in their fine black suits and starched shirts and large, dark ties. Each of these men had a house to go to, into which, in the evening usually, he would disappear. Only women and children lived on Liberty Street. All of them were Negroes. Some of the women were quite dark, but most were coffee-color. They were all very beautiful. Her mother was light. She was tall, had black eyes, and black hair so long she could sit on it.

The man standing over her was the one who came to her house once or twice a week. He was never there in the morning when Jennie got up. He was tall, and thin, and blond. He had a short beard that looked as coarse as the grass beneath her feet. His eyes were blue, like Jennie's. He did not speak English very well. Jennie's mother had told her he came from across the sea and Jennie often wondered if he went there between visits to their house.

"Jennie? Your mother tells me that you ask why I do not stay at night. Is so?"

She looked up at him. "Yes, Mister Herder." The hair under his jaw was darker than the hair on his cheeks.

He nodded. "I stay now. Go bring your mother."

She left the spoon in the dirt, and ran into the house, down the long hall, dark now because she had been sitting in the sun. She found her mother standing over the stove, a great black lid in her left hand, a wooden spoon in her right. There were beads of sweat on her forehead. She wore a full black skirt and a white blouse. Her one waist-length braid hung straight between her shoulder blades. She turned to Jennie's running steps.

"Mama? That man? My father? He in the yard. He brung a carpetbag."

First her mother smiled, then frowned, then looked puzzled. "A carpetbag, darling?"

"Yes, Mama."

She followed her mother through the house, pausing with her at the hall mirror where the woman ran her hand up the back of her neck to smooth stray black hair. Then they went onto the porch, where the man was now seated, surveying the tiny yard and the dark green hedge that enclosed it. The carpetbag rested beside his chair.

Her mother stood with her hands beneath her apron, staring at the bag. "Mister Herder?"

He turned to them. "I will not go back this time. No matter what. Why should I live in that house when I must come here to know what home is?" He nodded sharply as if in answer to a question. "So! I stay. I give her that house. I will send her money, but I stay here."

Her mother stood silently for an instant, then turned to the door. "Dinner'll be on the table in a half hour." She opened the screen door. The spring whined and cracked. "Oh." She let go the door, and picked up the carpetbag. "I'll take this on up." She went inside. As she passed, Jennie could see she was smiling again.

After that, Jennie's mother became a celebrity on Liberty Street. The other women would stop her to ask about the man. "And he staying for good, Josie?"

"Yes."

"You have any trouble yet?"

"Not yet."

"Well, child, you make him put that there house in your name. You don't want to be no Sissie Markham. That white woman come down the same day he died and moved Sissie and her children right into the gutter. You get that house put in your name. You hear?"

"Yes."

"How is it? It different?"

Her mother would look dazed. "Yes, it different. He told me to call him Maynard."

The other women were always very surprised.

At first, Jennie too was surprised. The man was always there in the morning and sometimes even woke her up. Her mother no longer called him Mister Herder, and at odd times, though still quite seldom, said, No. She had never before heard her mother say No to anything the man ever said. It was not long before Jennie was convinced that he actually was her father. She began to call him Papa.

Daily now a white woman had been driving by their house. Jennie did not know who she was or what she wanted, but playing in the yard, would see the white woman's gray buggy turn the corner and come slowly down the block, pulled by a speckled horse that trudged in the dry dust. A Negro driver sat erect in his black uniform, a whip in his fist. The white woman would peer at the house as if looking for an address or something special. She would look at the curtained windows, looking for someone, and sometimes even at Jennie. The look was not kind or tender, but hard and angry as if she knew something bad about the child.

Then one day the buggy stopped, the Negro pulling gently on the reins. The white woman leaned forward, spoke to the driver and handed him a small pink envelope. He jumped down, opened the gate, and without looking at Jennie, his face dark and shining, advanced on the porch, up the three steps, which knocked hollow beneath his boots, opened the screen door and twisted the polished brass bell key in the center of the open, winter door.

Her mother came drying her hands. The Negro reached out the envelope and her mother took it, looking beyond him for an instant at the buggy and the white woman who returned her look coldly. As the Negro turned, her mother opened the letter, and read it, moving her lips slightly. Then Jennie could see the twinkling at the corners of her eyes. Her mother stood framed in the black square of doorway, tall, fair, the black hair swept to hide her ears, her eyes glistening.

Jennie turned back to the white woman now and saw her lean deeper into her seat. Then she pulled forward. "Do you understand what I will have them do?" She was shouting shrilly and spoke like Jennie's father.

"You tell him he has got one wife! You are something different!" She leaned back again, waved her gloved hand and the buggy lurched down the street, gained speed, and jangled out of sight around the corner.

Jennie was on her feet and pounding up the stairs. "Mama?"

"Go play, Jennie. Go on now, *play!*" Still her mother stared straight ahead, as if the buggy and the white woman remained in front of the house. She still held the letter as if to read it. The corners of her eyes were wet. Then she turned and went into the house. The screen door clacked behind her.

At nights now Jennie waited by the gate in the yard for her father to turn the corner, walking. In the beginning she had been waiting too for the one day he would not turn the corner. But each night he came, that day seemed less likely to come. Even so, she was always surprised to see him. When she did, she would wave, timidly, raising her hand only to her shoulder, wiggling only her fingers, as if to wave too wildly would somehow cause the entire picture of his advancing to collapse as only a slight wind would be enough to disarrange a design of feathers.

That night too she waved and saw him raise his hand high over his head, greeting her. She backed away when he reached the gate so he might open it, her head thrown way back, looking up at him.

"Well, my Jennie, what kind of day did you have?"

She only smiled, then remembered the white woman. "A woman come to visit Mama. She come in a buggy and give her a letter too. She made Mama cry."

His smile fled. He sucked his tongue, angry now. "We go see what is wrong. Come." He reached for her hand.

Her mother was in the kitchen. She looked as if she did not really care what she was doing or how, walking from pump to stove, stove to cupboard in a deep trance. The pink envelope was on the table.

She turned to them. Her eyes were red. Several strands of her hair stuck to her temples. She cleared her nose and pointed to the letter. "She come today."

Her father let go Jennie's hand, picked up the letter and read it. When he was finished he took it to the stove and dropped it into the flame. There was a puff of smoke before he replaced the lid. He shook his head. "She cannot make me go back, Josephine."

Her mother fell back heavily into a wooden chair, beginning to cry again. "But she's white, Maynard."

He raised his eyebrows like a priest or a displeased school teacher. "Your skin is whiter."

"My mother was a slave."

He threw up his hands, making fists. "Your mother did not ask to be a slave!" Then he went to her, crouched on his haunches before her, speaking quietly. "No one can make me go back."

"But she can get them to do what she say." She turned her gaze on Jennie, but looked away quickly. "You wasn't here after the war. But I seen things. I seen things happen to field niggers that . . . I was up in the house; they didn't bother me. My own father, General Dewey Willson, he stood on a platform in the center of town and promised to keep the nigger down. I was close by." She took his face in her hands. "Maynard, maybe you better go back, leastways—"

"I go back—dead! You hear? Dead. These children, these cowardly children in their masks will not move me! I go back dead. That is all. We do not discuss it." And he was gone. Jennie heard him thundering down the hall, knocking against the table near the stairs, going up to the second floor.

Her mother was looking at her now, her eyes even more red than before, her lips trembling, her hands active in her lap. "Jennie?"

"Yes, Mama." She took a step toward her, staring into the woman's eyes.

"Jennie, I want you to promise me something and not forget it."

"Yes, Mama." She was between her mother's knees, felt the woman's hands clutching her shoulders.

"Jennie, you'll be right pretty when you get grown. Did you know that? Promise me you'll go up North. Promise me if I'm not here when you get eighteen, you'll go North and get married. You understand?"

Jennie was not sure she did. She could not picture the North, except that she had heard once it was cold and white things fell from the sky. She could not picture being eighteen and her mother not being there. But she knew her mother wanted her to understand and she lied. "Yes, Mama."

"Repeat what I just said."

She did. Her mother kissed her mouth, the first time ever.

From the kitchen below came their voices. Her father's voice sounded hard, cut short; Jennie knew he had made a decision and was sticking to it. Her mother was pleading, trying to change his mind. It was July the Fourth, the day of the shooting match.

She dressed in her Sunday clothes and coming downstairs, heard her mother: "Maynard, please don't take her." She was frantic now. "I'm begging you. Don't take that child with you today."

"I take her. We do not discuss it. I take her. Those sneaking cowards in their masks . . ." Jennie knew now what they were talking about. Her father had promised to take her to the shooting match. For some reason, her mother feared there would be trouble if Jennie went downtown. She did not know why her mother felt that way, except that it might have something to do with the white woman, who continued to ride by their house each morning, after her father had left for the day. Perhaps her mother did not want to be alone in the house when the white woman drove by in her gray buggy, even though she had not stopped the buggy since the day two months ago, when the Negro had given her mother the pink envelope.

But other strange things had happened after that. In the beginning she and her mother, as always before, had gone downtown to the market, to shop amid the bright stalls brimming with green and yellow vegetables and brick-red meats, tended by dark, country Negroes in shabby clothes and large straw hats. It would get very quiet when they passed, and Jennie would see the Negroes look away, fear in their eyes, and knots of white men watching, sometimes giggling. But the white women in fine clothes were the most frightening; sitting on the verandas or passing in carriages, some even coming to their windows, they would stare angrily as if her mother had done something terrible to each one personally, as if all these white women could be the one who drove by each morning. Her mother would walk through it all, her back straight, very like her father's, the bun into which she wove her waist-length braid on market days, gleaming dark.

In the beginning they had gone to the suddenly quiet market. But now her mother hardly set foot from the house, and the food was brought to them in a carton by a crippled Negro boy, who was coming just as Jennie and her father left the house that morning.

Balancing the carton on his left arm, he removed his ragged hat and smiled. "Morning, Mister Herder. Good luck at the shooting match, sir." His left leg was short and he seemed to tilt.

Her father nodded. "Thank you, Felix. I do my best."

"Then you a sure thing, Mister Herder." He replaced his hat and went on around the house.

Walking, her hand in her father's, Jennie could see some of the women on Liberty Street peering out at them through their curtains.

Downtown was not the same. Flags and banners draped the verandas; people wore their best clothes. The Square had been roped off, a platform set up to one side, and New Marsails Avenue, which ran into the Square, had been cleared for two blocks. Far away down the Avenue stood a row of cotton bales onto which had been pinned oil-cloth targets. From where they stood, the bull's-eyes looked no bigger than red jawbreakers.

Many men slapped her father on the back, and furtively, looked at her with a kind of clinical interest. But mostly they ignored her. The celebrity of the day was her father, and unlike her mother, he was very popular. Everyone felt sure he would win the match; he was the best shot in the state.

After everyone shot, the judge came running down from the targets, waving his arms. "Maynard Herder. Six shots, and you can cover them all with a good gob of spit!" He grabbed her father's elbow and pulled him toward the platform, where an old man with white hair and beard, wearing a gray uniform trimmed with yellow, waited. She followed them to the platform steps, but was afraid to go any farther because now some women had begun to look at her as they had at her mother.

The old man made a short speech, his voice deep, but coarse, grainy-sounding, and gave her father a silver medal in a blue velvet box. Her father turned and smiled at her. She started up the steps toward him, but just then the old man put his hand on her father's shoulder.

People had begun to walk away down the streets leading out of the Square. There was less noise now but she could not hear the first words the old man said to her father.

Her father's face tightened into the same look she had seen the day the letter came, the same as this morning in the kitchen. She went halfway up the stairs, stopped.

The old man went on: "You know I'm no meddler. Everybody knows about Liberty Street. I had a woman down there myself . . . before the war."

"I know that." The words came out of her father's face, though his lips did not move.

The old man nodded. "But, Maynard, what you're doing is different."

"She's your own daughter."

"Maybe that's why . . ." The old man looked down the street, toward the cotton bales and the targets. "But she's a nigger. And now the talking is taking an ugly turn and the folks talking are the ones I can't hold."

Her father spoke in an angry whisper. "You see what I do to that target? You tell those children in their masks I do that to the forehead of any man . . . or woman that comes near her or my house. You tell them."

"Maynard, that wouldn't do any real good *after* they'd done something to her." He stopped, looked at Jennie, and smiled. "That's my only granddaughter, you know." His eyes clicked off her. "You're a man who knows firearms. You're a gunsmith. I know firearms too. Pistols and rifles can do lots of things, but they don't make very good doctors. Nobody's asking you to give her up. Just go back home. That's all. Go back to your wife."

Her father turned away, walking fast, came down the stairs and grabbed her hand. His face was red as blood between the white of his collar and the straw yellow of his hair.

They slowed after a block, paused in a small park with green trees shading several benches and a statue of a stern-faced young man in uniform, carrying pack and rifle. "We will sit."

She squirmed up onto the bench beside him. The warm wind smelled of salt from the Gulf of Mexico. The leaves were a dull, low tambourine. Her father was quiet for a long while.

Jennie watched birds bobbing for worms in the grass near them, then looked at the young, stone soldier. Far off, but from where she viewed it, just over the soldier's hat, a gliding sea gull dived suddenly behind the rooftops. That was when she saw the white man, standing across the street from the park, smiling at her. There were other white men with him, some looking at her, others at the man, all laughing. He waved to her. She smiled at him though he was the kind of man her mother told her always to stay away from. He was dressed as poorly as any Negro. From behind his back, he produced a brown rag doll, looked at her again, then grabbed the doll by its legs, and tore it part way up the middle. Then he jammed his finger into the rip between the doll's legs. The other men laughed uproariously.

Jennie pulled her father's sleeve. "Papa? What he doing?"

"Who?" Her father turned. The man repeated the show and her father bolted to his feet, yelling: "I will kill you! You hear? I will kill you for that!"

The men only snickered and ambled away.

Her father was red again. He had clenched his fists; now his hands were white like the bottoms of fishes. He sighed, shook his head and sat down. "I cannot kill everybody." He shook his head again, then leaned forward to get up. But first he thrust the blue velvet medal box into her hand. It was warm from his hand, wet and prickly. "When you grow up, you go to the North like your mother tells you. And you take this with you. It is yours. Always remember I gave it to you." He stood. "Now you must go home alone. Tell your mother I come later."

That night, Jennie tried to stay awake until he came home, until he was there to kiss her good night, his whiskers scratching her cheek. But all at once there was sun at her window and the sound of carts and wagons grating outside in the dirt street. Her mother was quiet while the two of them ate. After breakfast, Jennie went into the yard to wait for the gray buggy to turn the corner, but for the first morning in many months, the white woman did not jounce by, peering at the house, searching for someone or something special.

HARLEM QUEST

They descended steps to a cellar doorway, passed rows of steel garbage cans. Already Mitchell could hear music. Carlyle pushed open a door into a stone hallway. "Listen, Mr. Pierce, don't say nothing. You let me talk." He winked. "This race business." They stopped and Carlyle rang the bell. "And if you don't mind, I'd better call you Mitchell."

The door opened a crack, then all the way. "Hiya, Carlyle!" Mitchell could not see her face, only tight pink slacks, a yellow turtle-neck sweater, red hair, and plump arms, each with a charm bracelet, rushing to embrace Carlyle. "How you doing?"

"All right." His hand stroked the pink slacks. "You miss me?"

"Sure did." She pulled back from him, gold teeth smiling in a copper face. "And just where you been?"

"Around." Carlyle's forehead was greasy.

The gold disappeared behind lavender lips, her face serious now. "You ain't been up state, has you?"

"Nothing like that, Glora." He smiled. "Just hustling."

"Well, come in and party." From behind a hard face, she looked at Mitchell. "What's this?" scolding Carlyle with her eyes.

"You see that, Mitchell?" Carlyle shook his head. "White skin and she act like a red skin." He sucked his tongue. "This my cousin, Mitchell, from Canada. From a small, snowy-ass town where the underground railway left his granddaddy's butt. Had to integrate to keep the blood moving."

She smiled at Mitchell now, gold teeth in the dim light. "Cousin!" He felt her arms around him, red hair in his face, high breasts just above his stomach. "Welcome home. I'm sorry I took you for Sir Charles, the White Knight."

"That's all right." Mitchell did not know if he liked being . . . colored.

"What we standing out here for when they partying inside?" She hugged Mitchell's arm, pulled him over the marble doorsill, and took his coat.

"You got a cover, man," Carlyle whispered. "Just don't dance. They know you a phoney for sure if you get on that floor."

Mitchell nodded, slightly offended. He had always considered himself a good dancer, especially when he was drunk.

Carlyle was still at his ear. "Listen, they trying to pay the Jew, so lay something on them."

"What?" The hallway was dark, a door at the end, lit red. The music came from the doorway, and inside the room, Mitchell could see shadows weaving.

"It's a rent party, so drop two dollars in the basket. A dollar a drink, and if you hungry, she got her mama making chicken and potato salad, a dollar a plate."

Glora was back, hugging his arm again. "I'm taking over your cousin, Carlyle." As if to consolidate her claim, she put her hand on Carlyle's stomach, and pushed him away.

"I'll see you later, man." Before Mitchell could protest, Carlyle winked and left them.

Glora pulled him into the room where Black people danced, nodding heads, jerking hips, feet scraping on the wooden floor. Some of the men were sweating under the red light, patting their faces with neatly folded handkerchiefs. The women's faces were stern above their dancing bodies. Mitchell had never seen a group of Black people dance before, and was surprised to find no one writhing on the floor, none of the women with skirts hitched to their waist. Everyone did the same step, moved the same way in time to the music. Even so, they seemed to be having a good time.

Around the dancers, at the edges of the room, others stood talking. In the closest group to him, a half-dozen men, and a few women stood listening, their eyes downcast, but no one seemed to be talking. Glora led him toward them.

"Well look what the cat drug in," one of the women said. "What's that, Glora?"

"This is Carlyle Bedlow's cousin from Canada. Mitchell. Don't he look white though?" She introduced him around, ". . . and down there is Shorty."

Out of the shadows in the center of their small circle, reached a yellow hand. Mitchell looked down at a pinched face under a pile of straight yellow hair. The midget wore a tuxedo, a lace-front shirt. "Glad to meet you." He mashed Mitchell's knuckles. "Where from in Canada?" His voice was high, forced through tiny nostrils.

Mitchell answered that he was from a small town near Ottawa.

"That's a long way from home. I ain't never worked there." He stared at Mitchell a moment longer, almost suspiciously, then turned to the others. "Anyway, like I say, I didn't really want to join, but I like testing them. So I look up the name in the phone book: The Little Folks Club, downtown, and walks in there one day, with my Great Dane and my two-foot cane. They had like kindergarten furniture, everything low down on the floor. There's this blond at the reception desk, maybe two-six, nice body on her. I asks if I could join up. She look at me like she ain't never seen a midget before, then at my dog, and runs on into the inner-sanctum and in a minute she comes out with this official-looking cat. He wearing a little Ivy-League suit with a vest and these big glasses. He tried all kinds of ways to tell me they didn't allow no niggers to join, and I play it dumb, asking questions, twisting his mind around, letting my dog lick his face. Finally I asks him how short you got to be to join. He say they didn't let no one in who taller than three feet. I look him in the eye, calm and quiet as you please, then shouts: "Three feet? Why, man, that's discrimination! I'm afraid I couldn't join no club with such an unfair policy. Some of the best midgets I know is three-foot-one!' And I jumps up on my dog's back and rides out of there. That's Charles for you!"

Only Mitchell did not laugh. Bigotry was not to him a laughing matter. The rest spun with laughter, hiding their faces on each other's shoulders.

"Say, you is out of it," Glora whispered, then kissed his ear. "Come on, I'll teach you the New York way." She embraced him.

The music had turned slow—a high tenor over a rumble. Couples stood still on the floor, their arms around each other. Mitchell wanted to pull away, but knew he had to pretend; anything to find Cooley.

"Tell me about Canada." He could just hear her above the music. Her breasts were not at all hard. He began to sweat.

"It's cold and there's a lot of snow."

"Ooooh." She squeezed him tighter. There was perfume in her hair. Suddenly, he wanted to bury his face in it, kiss her scalp, but was afraid. And now he could feel himself getting excited, was afraid of that too.

"Listen, before I forget, I want to pay." He pushed her away.

She shook her head. "Mitchell, you been with white people too damn long. You don't even know how to relax—all tied up in knots, thinking about money. This the weekend, man."

She took his hand and led him to the door, pointed: "My mama's in the kitchen. Pay her." She was angry. "And while you're there, get a couple drinks in you. That's the way white folks do, ain't it? Can't have a good time until they get drunk and start breaking things." She shook her head again. "Sometimes I think the Jesuits is right. I seen more good niggers ruined by integration!"

It was only a few steps to the kitchen. Just inside the door, a table blocked the way, a money-filled saucepan in the center. Behind the table, the kitchen was a high-ceilinged room. At one time it had been some bright color. Now it was impossible to tell what color; no one would have chosen the gray which covered the walls.

At the far end was a spattered white stove, crouching hidden behind a Black woman at least as tall and twice as wide as Mitchell. She wore a black dress decorated with large yellow sunflowers, one of which stretched across her broad back, like the picture on a team jacket.

"Is this where I pay?"

"No place else, baby." She turned now, smoke rising from an iron kettle behind her. She was the woman he had seen sitting beside the highway.

"Well?" She moved toward the table. "Ain't you got change?" She stood behind the table, large hands hanging at her sides. "It's in the pan there. Go on, I trust you."

"Didn't I see you a few hours ago on the highway?"

She wrinkled her tiny nose. "Highway?"

Perhaps he was mistaken. But . . . "You look very familiar to me."

"I ain't never been to Canada."

Mitchell was confused, decided to let the matter drop. "Is this where I pay?"

"That's what I said. Don't you light-skinned niggers never listen to anybody but white folks?"

"Why, yes." He took a five-dollar bill from his wallet. "And could I have three drinks. Do you have bourbon?"

"Course I do." She bent into a cabinet, brought out the bottle. "Three?" She squinted at him.

Perhaps three drinks were too many. "Yes." He wanted them all himself; they might relax him. "One's a double."

She poured the drinks, using a jigger glass with a thick bottom. "What's wrong now?"

"Not a thing."

"What's wrong with you, boy? You a *re*tard?" She did not wait for his answer, but returned to the stove, picked up a two-pronged fork, began to spear each piece of chicken, bringing it close to her face for inspection.

He choked down a large swallow. "It's just that I think I've seen you before."

Her back to him: "I probably look like your mama."

Mitchell smiled, almost laughed. His mother, dead now eight years, had been small and dry. "No, that's not it." He took another swallow. The alcohol could not possibly be in his arteries yet, but knowing it was on its way made him feel better. "But—"

"I get one of you at every party Glora gives." She spun around. "You light-skinned, educated boys! Young Black girls scare you, so you come out and talk to mammy."

Mitchell tried to laugh. "Really, that's not—"

"Well, mammy's a girl too and she ain't got time for scared boys." She smiled suddenly. "Unless you want to come on in the kitchen with me." She shook her head. "No, you don't want that. Go on away from here. Mammy ain't got no time no more for scared boys. Mammy wants men!"

Mitchell finished the double bourbon. "I'm not afraid."

"Then why you hanging around the kitchen?" She advanced on him, pointing the prongs of her fork at his eyes. "Go on now."

He backed away, into the darkness of the hall, and wandered, paper cup in hand, toward the dancing room. Glora was on the floor, moving inside her pink slacks. He stared at her, growing more confident all the time, certain that even across the room she would be able to feel what he was thinking about her. But she did not turn from her partner.

He stepped onto the floor, to cut in, but at that moment, saw Carlyle in a far corner talking to another man, their foreheads nearly touching. He came up behind them. "Hi, Carlyle."

"We was just talking about you." He put his arm around the other man's shoulder. "Here's a man who knows where you can find Cooley. Ain't that right, Calvin."

Calvin nodded. He was Mitchell's height and very dark, with pouches under his eyes, a thin mustache below his sharp nose. His hair was short, neatly parted. He was wearing a dark suit and white shirt. He too looked familiar, but Mitchell had to admit now that he did not know enough Black people to be able to tell them apart. He had always considered this a cliché, but realized now that it was at least partly true.

Carlyle told him that Calvin's last name was Johnson. Mitchell shook his hand, rough and cracked, but with a weak grip. "So what's happening?"

"Happening? Oh, nothing. You know Cooley?"

Calvin nodded. "I ain't seen him in about a week, but I'm pretty sure I know where he is. Carlyle says you ain't telling why you want to see him."

Mitchell realized now that, given Black people's fear and suspicion, his not telling his reasons could make it difficult to find Cooley. "You see, it's kind of private. I . . ."

"Ain't planning to kill him, are you?"

"Me?" Calvin was not joking. "No. I just want to talk to him."

"You understand my position, don't you? I wouldn't want to set up a friend of mine for a killing."

This talk of murder made Mitchell uneasy. "Sure, I know that."

"Good." He turned to Carlyle, smiled, then his tired eyes were on Mitchell again. "But I hope you won't be offended if I don't trust you for a while. I seen squarer-looking killers than you. So we'll just hang out and if you seem like you telling the truth, then maybe I'll take you to see Cooley. That sound all right to you?"

"Sure, but I really don't want to hurt him." He did not like the pleading voice, tried to harden it. "There may be some money in it for him."

"Okay. But if the deal's a good one, it'll keep, now won't it."

"I guess so." Mitchell was beginning to wonder whether it might be better just to forget finding Cooley. He could force Tam to give the baby to an adoption agency. Her mother would help him. He did not at all like the people he was meeting.

Calvin smiled at him. "I know you want to find him. And I'll help you. But Cooley and me is close, and got to stick together. The business we in, can't take no chances."

Mitchell nodded.

"Carlyle tells me you like Glora a little bit." He leaned closer. "What say you take Glora: Carlyle and me'll get us some ladies, and we can go over to a place I know of and drink up some liquor and . . . see what happens. It got lots of guest rooms."

Mitchell was about to refuse, but Calvin turned him around so that he could see Glora's pink slacks. He watched for a few moments, then agreed. It was important that he win Calvin's confidence.

Carlyle drove, Gerri-Ann (his girl?), in a light blue coat with some kind of fur collar, beside him. Calvin sat in the death seat, his arm lying on the seat, his hand, one finger ringed, just behind Carlyle's wine-colored shoulder. Glora and Rochelle (who seemed to be Calvin's girl) flanked Mitchell in the back. He could feel Glora's soft hip through slacks and outer coat. Rochelle's legs were crossed, and something—perhaps the clasp of her garter belt—was digging into him. They were leaving Harlem.

"How you doing there?" He could see Calvin's face in profile, the darkness equalizing his color, his hooked nose making him a Jew.

Glora rested her red head on his shoulder. "He doing fine. Ain't you?" Her fingers were making their way through the spaces between the buttons of his overcoat, through his suitcoat, to his shirt. Sharp nails caught in the bandagelike material of his undershirt.

"Yes." The street sign told him he was on Eighth Avenue. Then the neon signs ended and he saw the low stone wall of the park, behind it trees.

The back seat was shrinking. Rochelle seemed constantly to cross, uncross her legs. He glanced at her, found her staring at him, nodding her head. She uncrossed, recrossed her legs again, then suddenly turned away; he was looking at the back of her head, the hair in the kitchen cut into a V.

He sank down into the seat, enjoying Glora's hand massaging his stomach. So this was how Black people were by themselves. He had often seen carloads of them, had wondered where they were going, what they would do when they got there. Now he was finding out.

Then Carlyle had stopped, was parking the car. They climbed out onto the pavement, cold even through his shoes. Mitchell was still wedged between the two girls.

He dozed in the elevator, the three bourbons and two more besides, pressing his eyes shut. They woke him, made him walk—down the marble-floored hall, into Calvin's apartment, dropped him onto a large white leather sofa, put a drink into his hand.

He opened his eyes, the glass half-empty now, and watched Glora dance with Carlyle—too close, and he wondered if she was really his girl. He struggled to his feet, pushed Carlyle away, glimpsed her lavender lips before she rested her head on his chest; his hands slipped between the waistband of her pink slacks, his fingers pinched the elastic on her underpants.

The music stopped; he opened his eyes. Carlyle and Gerri-Ann were gone. So was Rochelle. Calvin sat in the middle of the sofa, rather small, looking uncomfortable. But he raised his glass to Mitchell, then pointed past him, nodding. Mitchell danced Glora in a circle until he could look down a hallway, where he knew he would find Calvin's guest rooms. He completed the circle, to signal Calvin he understood, but Calvin had disappeared.

Of course, Glora wanted to make love to him, had been flirting with him all evening, but he was not quite sure how to introduce the topic. With Tam, he had waited politely until she showed him that she would not reject him. She had been working as a reader in a publishing house then, had invited him to her apartment for dinner. They had finished a bottle of good wine, listened to some Brahms, talked, necked. Then she had guided his hand to her breast.

But this was a Black woman. He tried to remember what the Southerners he had known in the Service had told him about Black women. But even their experiences had been somewhat different. Glora was not a prostitute, and he was not planning to rape her.

The answer was simple enough—so simple in fact that he realized he must be quite drunk not to have found it immediately. Glora thought he was Black. He would simply do and say what he thought Carlyle, Calvin, or perhaps even Cooley, would do and say in the same circumstances. There was even some justice in it. Cooley had taken advantage of Tam's unhappiness. Now he, Mitchell, would take advantage of one of their women. He would convince Glora to help him find Cooley.

He began by sitting her on the sofa, his arm around her. "You never told me where you work."

"Huh?" She had been leaning, snuggling against him. She sat up slowly, blinking.

He smiled, tried to relax his face. "I asked you where you work?"

"Why you want to know that?" Before he could answer, she asked him for a cigaret. He gave her one, held a light for her, staring at her over the flame.

"I want to know as much as I can about you."

She took a drag, her lips leaving lavender on the white filter. "Why?"

He shrugged. "I think I'll be moving to New York soon and I want to see you again."

She gave him her golden smile. "Your wife won't like that a bit." Before he could ask how she knew he was married, she answered him: "Carlyle told me. He say you got a little boy." She leaned toward him, put her arms around his neck, smeared lipstick from one side of his mouth to the other. "But what I care! Maybe you'll give me a baby too, and have to come visit me."

His plan seemed to be working. He put his hand under her sweater, whispered. "Why don't"—clearing his throat—"why don't we find an empty room."

She stood up, took his hand and pulled him to his feet, smiling, and led him down the hallway, past several closed doors, where he guessed he would find Carlyle, Calvin, and their girls. They entered the last room. She closed the door, walked to a low dresser, and looked at herself in the mirror.

Then she placed her fingers to her temples, as if to hold a headache, and lifted away her red hair. Underneath, her hair was black, kinky, a round lamb hat.

For some reason, it frightened him, and he took a step backward, trying to recover himself. "I wouldn't have guessed that."

She was proud. "I know. It's a good one. I saved for six months." She crossed her arms over her breasts, grabbed the bottom of the yellow sweater. Her head popped from the neckband. Her bra, against copper skin, was light green.

Lurking near the door, he watched her go to the bed, fold back the spread. The light green straps blinked like neon. When she had finished preparing the bed, she sat down, looked at him. "Anything wrong?"

He was trying to think of what Cooley would say, but the Cooley of his imagination remained silent. "I want to tell you about my wife." He wished immediately he had not said that.

"Now?" She reached for the button on her pink slacks.

"Only that she's a bitch." He enjoyed saying it, even if it was a lie.

"I know that." She stood up, slid the slacks down over her thighs. "If she wasn't, you wouldn't be here, right?"

"Why, yes." Her underpants were lemon yellow. He closed his eyes. Opening them, he found her no more than a foot away, her arms spread to him. "I'll make up for that."

He backed up, but she kept coming. "Wait." She put her hands on his waist, began to pull his shirt out of his pants. "Do you know Cooley?"

She stopped, his shirttail between her fingers. "Cooley? Why . . . yeah, I know him." She looked confused, retreated to the bed, and sat down. Cooley certainly had a profound effect on people.

Sensing that he had thrown her off guard, he followed her. "Do you know where I can find him?"

"Look, honey, I don't want to get myself in no mess."

He sat down beside her, put his arm around her, speaking softly. "There won't be any mess. I just want to talk to him."

"About what?"

Perhaps he could tell her the truth, not that he was white, which, after the way he had completely deceived her would be too much for her, but everything else. Of course, he did not trust her. But after all she was sitting beside him almost naked, obviously had some feeling for him. He searched her face, realizing suddenly that he had seen it before, many times. The Black girl who worked in the file room at his office had the same face, and all of the girls he saw on the subway.

They were all stupid, simple girls. Each wanted only a good job, a nice home, some bright clothes. And they were willing to do almost anything to get them. He need only give her a glimpse into his world and she would tell him everything he wanted to know. "I asked you before, where do you work?"

She bit her lip. "I ain't got a job."

"How would you like a nice job in a good company?" He was stroking her plump, soft arm.

"I couldn't get no job like that." Already her dark eyes could see herself riding the subway downtown.

"Yes, you could, with my help." He kissed her ear; she tried to move away, but he held her. "I want to tell you a secret, Glora. Originally, I'm from Canada, but now I live in New York." She did not seem surprised. "And I work in a big company downtown." He remembered a movie he had seen a long time before. "I'm passing for white."

"Really?" She smiled.

"Now, I'll get you a good job in my company and all you have to do is tell me where I can find Cooley."

He saw fear in her eyes now. "Why you want to find him?"

"If I tell you, you have to promise not to tell anyone, except Cooley. You do want that good job, don't you?"

She nodded.

He sighed, hating to mouth the words, especially to someone like this. "My wife just had his baby."

"She really is a bitch, ain't she?"

He did not reply, knowing she would never understand all that had happened between him and Tam. "And I want Cooley to take the baby."

"Bye-bye job." She shook her head. "Cooley won't want no baby."

"I think he'll want this one." He decided not to tell her why. Then she would know he was not Black. Cooley might not want just any woman's baby, but this was Tam's baby—half-white. Of course he would want the baby. "It's a good job." And it would be nice to have her indebted to him, close at hand. "Well, what d'you say?"

"What do you think, honey?" She tossed herself into his arms, pushed him down onto the bed, began to kiss his face. "And I'll be good to you too." She was on top of him. He inhaled her perfume, smiling, and reaching around her back, unhooked her bra. She began to undress him.

Both naked, they slid under the covers. He could not take his hands out of her hair; it pushed against his fingers like sponge. At first he found it distasteful, but then began to enjoy it. Between kisses, she kept talking. "So you ain't from Canada. You had me fooled. I bet you really fool those white folks downtown. You so cool. And you wait until I get there. All you got to do is call me in your office. 'Glora, will you bring me them letters from so-and-so company?" I'll have my pants down before you can close the door. One time, I was working downtown, in a mail-order house, for a little white man. He looking at me all the time. So I figured maybe it'd be good for a raise and I ran into him one night, accidentally." She winked down at him. "He took me up to his place and made his play for me. You thank God you never had to make it with no pasty-faced white man." She laughed so hard she rolled off him, and almost off the bed. She crawled back to him, rested her spongy head on his chest. "Let me tell you, honey, going over, he squeal like a little fat pig: eeee eeee eeee!" She started to laugh again. "That was the last time. I bet if any white man even get close to me, I'd know it. Eeee eeee eeee! You sure you ain't passing for colored, Mitchell?"

He denied it, trying to joke, but felt as if she had thrown ice water on his stomach and thighs. For the next fifteen minutes, he tried to recover. It was hopeless. Finally, he sat up.

She looked at him from the pillow, bewildered, perhaps a little angry.

He knew that unless he gave her a reason, she would not help him, might even turn against him. "It's an old war wound," he explained. "I never know when it's going to hit me."

She sat up, her face softer, and hugged him. "Sure is terrible the sacrifices a man got to make for his country." She kissed his shoulder. "You call me when you get over it."

He dressed, took her phone number, kissed her good-bye, all the while trying to avoid her dark eyes. "I'll be all right. I'll call you tomorrow, about Cooley."

"You do that, honey." She smiled, but suddenly buried her face in the pillow. Her back began to shake, short quick little shakes as if she was giggling. He had really disappointed her.

Outside, the sky was gray, the trees in the park black. He found his car and drove home, surprised to discover that the distance between Calvin's house and his own was less than a mile.

Ernest J. Gaines

(b. 1933)

BORN ON A PLANTATION in Louisiana, Ernest Gaines spent much of his childhood there working in the fields, learning about the people and conditions he now writes about so effectively. At the age of fifteen, he moved to California, finished high school, and then entered San Francisco State College. Although his education was interrupted in 1953 by the draft, he returned to school in 1955 and received his degree in 1957.

Gaines has won several awards, including a Wallace Stegner Creative Writing Fellowship for study at Stanford. His short stories have appeared in several anthologies of black literature. His publications include his first novel, *Catherine Carmier* (1964); *Of Love and Dust* (1967); and *Bloodline*, a volume of short stories (1968).

"Just Like a Tree" is taken from *Bloodline*.

JUST LIKE A TREE

I shall not;
 I shall not be moved.
I shall not;
 I shall not be moved.
Just like a tree that's
planted 'side the water.
 Oh, I shall not be moved.

I made my home in glory;
 I shall not be moved.
Made my home in glory;
 I shall not be moved.
Just like a tree that's
planted 'side the water.
 Oh, I shall not be moved.

(from an old Negro spiritual)

Chuckkie

Pa hit him on the back and he jeck in them chains like he pulling, but ever'body in the wagon know he ain't, and Pa hit him on the back again. He jeck again like he pulling, but even Big Red know he ain't doing a thing.

"That's why I'm go'n get a horse," Pa say. "He'll kill that other mule. Get up there, Mr. Bascom."

"Oh, let him alone," Gran'mon say. "How would you like it if you was pulling a wagon in all that mud?"

Pa don't answer Gran'mon; he just hit Mr. Bascom on the back again.

"That's right, kill him," Gran'mon say. "See where you get mo' money to buy another one."

"Get up there, Mr. Bascom," Pa say.

"You hear me talking to you, Emile?" Gran'mon say. "You want me hit you with something?"

"Ma, he ain't pulling," Pa say.

"Leave him alone," Gran'mon say.

Pa shake the lines little bit, but Mr. Bascom don't even feel it, and you can see he letting Big Red do all the pulling again. Pa say something kind o' low to hisself, and I can't make out what it is.

I low' my head little bit, 'cause that wind and fine rain was hitting me in the face, and I can feel Mama pressing close to me to keep me warm. She sitting on one side o' me and Pa sitting on the other side o' me, and Gran'mon in the back o' me in her setting chair. Pa didn't want bring the setting chair, telling Gran'mon there was two boards in that wagon already and she could sit on one of 'em all by herself if she wanted to, but Gran'mon say she was taking her setting chair with her if Pa liked it or not. She say she didn't ride in no wagon on nobody board, and if Pa liked it or not, that setting chair was going.

"Let her take her setting chair," Mama say. "What's wrong with taking her setting chair."

"Ehhh, Lord," Pa say, and picked up the setting chair and took it out to the wagon. "I guess I'll have to bring it back in the house, too, when we come back from there."

Gran'mon went and clambed in the wagon and moved her setting chair back little bit and sat down and folded her arms, waiting for us to get in, too. I got in and knelt down 'side her, but Mama told me to come up there and sit on the board 'side her and Pa so I could stay warm. Soon 's I sat down, Pa hit Mr. Bascom on the back, saying what a trifling thing Mr. Bascom was, and soon 's he got some mo' money he was getting rid o' Mr. Bascom and getting him a horse.

I raise my head to look see how far we is.

"That's it, yonder," I say.

"Stop pointing," Mama say, "and keep your hand in your pocket."

"Where?" Gran'mon say, back there in her setting chair.

"'Cross the ditch, yonder," I say

"Can't see a thing for this rain," Gran'mon say.

"Can't hardly see it," I say. "But you can see the light little bit. That chinaball tree standing in the way."

"Poor soul," Gran'mon say. "Poor soul."

I know Gran'mon was go'n say "poor soul, poor soul," 'cause she had been saying "poor soul, poor soul," ever since she heard Aunt Fe was go'n leave from back there.

Emile

Darn cane crop to finish getting in and only a mule and a half to do it. If I had my way I'd take that shotgun and a load o' buckshots and—but what's the use.

"Get up, Mr. Bascom—please," I say to that little dried-up, long-eared, tobacco-color thing. "Please, come up. Do your share for God sake—if you don't mind. I know it's hard pulling in all that mud, but if you don't do your share, then Big Red'll have to do his and yours, too. So, please, if it ain't asking you too much to—"

"Oh, Emile, shut up," Leola say.

"I can't hit him," I say, "or Mama back there'll hit me. So I have to talk to him. Please, Mr. Bascom, if you don't mind it. For my sake. No, not for mine; for God sake. No, not even for His'n; for Big Red sake. A fellow mule just like yourself is. Please, come up."

"Now, you hear that boy blaspheming God right in front o' me there," Mama say. "Ehhh, Lord—just keep it up. All this bad weather there like this whole world coming apart—a clap o' thunder come there and knock the fool out you. Just keep it up."

Maybe she right, and I stop. I look at Mr. Bascom there doing nothing, and I just give up. That mule know long 's Mama's alive he go'n do just what he want to do. He know when Papa was dying he told Mama to look after him, and he know no matter what he do, no matter what he don't do, Mama ain't go'n never let me do him anything. Sometimes I even feel Mama care mo' for Mr. Bascom 'an she care for me her own son.

We come up to the gate and I pull back on the lines.

"Whoa up, Big Red," I say. "You don't have to stop, Mr. Bascom. You never started."

I can feel Mama looking at me back there in that setting chair, but she don't say nothing.

"Here," I say to Chuckkie.

He take the lines and I jump down on the ground to open the old beat-up gate. I see Etienne's horse in the yard, and I see Chris new red tractor 'side the house, shining in the rain. When Mama die, I say to myself, Mr. Bascom, you going. Ever'body getting tractors and horses and I'm still stuck with you. You going, brother.

"Can you make it through?" I ask Chuckkie. "That gate ain't too wide."

"I can do it," he say.

"Be sure to make Mr. Bascom pull," I say.

"Emile, you better get back up here and drive 'em through," Leola say. "Chuckkie might break up that wagon."

"No, let him stay down there and give orders," Mama say, back there in that setting chair.

"He can do it," I say. "Come on, Chuckkie boy."

"Come up, here, mule," Chuckkie say.

And soon 's he say that, Big Red make a lunge for the yard, and Mr. Bascom don't even move, and 'fore I can bat my eyes I hear *pow-wow; sagg-sagg; pow-wow*. But above all that noise, Leola up there screaming her head off. And Mama—not a word; just sitting in that chair, looking at me with her arms still folded.

"Pull Big Red," I say. "Pull Big Red, Chuckkie."

Poor little Chuckkie up there pulling so hard till one of his little arms straight out in back; and Big Red throwing his shoulders and ever'thing else in it, and Mr. Bascom just walking there just 's loose and free, like he's suppose to be there just for his good looks. I move out the way just in time to let the wagon go by me, pulling half o' the fence in the yard behind it. I glance up again, and there's Leola still hollering and trying to jump out, but Mama not saying a word—just sitting there in that setting chair with her arms still folded.

"Whoa," I hear little Chuckkie saying. "Whoa up, now."

Somebody open the door and a bunch o' people come out on the gallery.

"What the world—?" Etienne say. "Thought the whole place was coming to pieces there."

"Chuckkie had a little trouble coming in the yard," I say.

"Goodness," Etienne say. "Anybody hurt?"

Mama just sit there about ten seconds, then she say something to herself and start clambing out the wagon.

"Let me help you there, Aunt Lou," Etienne say, coming down the steps.

"I can make it," Mama say. When she get on the ground she look up at Chuckkie. "Hand me my chair there, boy."

Poor little Chuckkie, up there with the lines in one hand, get the chair and hold it to the side, and Etienne catch it just 'fore it hit the ground. Mama start looking at me again, and it look like for at least a' hour she stand there looking at nobody but me. Then she say, "Ehhh, Lord," like that again, and go inside with Leola and the rest o' the people.

I look back at half o' the fence laying there in the yard, and I jump back on the wagon and guide the mules to the side o' the house. After unhitching 'em and tying 'em to the wheels, I look at Chris pretty red tractor again, and me and Chuckkie go inside: I make sure he kick all that mud off his shoes 'fore he go in the house.

Leola

Sitting over there by that fireplace, trying to look joyful when ever'body there know she ain't. But she trying, you know; smiling and bowing when people say something to her. How can she be joyful, I ask you; how can she be? Poor thing, she been here all her life—or the most of it, let's say. 'Fore they moved in this house, they lived in one back in the woods 'bout a mile from here. But for the past twenty-five or thirty years, she been right in this one house. I know ever since I been big enough to know people I been seeing her right here.

Aunt Fe, Aunt Fe, Aunt Fe, Aunt Fe; the name's been 'mongst us just like us own family name. Just like the name o' God. Like the name of town—the city. Aunt Fe, Aunt Fe, Aunt Fe, Aunt Fe.

Poor old thing; how many times I done come here and washed clothes for her when she couldn't do it herself. How many times I done hoed in that garden, ironed her clothes, wrung a chicken neck for her. You count the days in the year and you'll be pretty close. And I didn't mind it a bit. No, I didn't mind it a bit. She there trying to pay me. Proud—Lord, talking 'bout pride. "Here." "No, Aunt Fe; no." "Here, here; you got a child there, you can use it." "No, Aunt Fe. No. No. What would Mama think if she knowed I took money from you? Aunt Fe, Mama would never forgive me. No. I love doing these thing for you. I just wish I could do more."

And there, now, trying to make 'tend she don't mind leaving. Ehhh, Lord.

I hear a bunch o' rattling round in the kitchen and I go back there. I see Louise stirring this big pot o' eggnog.

"Louise," I say.

"Leola," she say.

We look at each other and she stir the eggnog again. She know what I'm go'n say next, and she can't even look in my face.

"Louise, I wish there was some other way."

"There's no other way," she say.

"Louise, moving her from here's like moving a tree you been used to in your front yard all your life."

"What else can I do?"

"Oh, Louise, Louise."

"Nothing else but that."

"Louise, what people go'n do without her here?"

She stir the eggnog and don't answer.

"Louise, us'll take her in with us."

"You all no kin to Auntie. She go with me."

"And us'll never see her again."

She stir the eggnog. Her husband come back in the kitchen and kiss her on the back o' the neck and then look at me and grin. Right from the start I can see I ain't go'n like that nigger.

"Almost ready, honey?" he say.

"Almost."

He go to the safe and get one o' them bottles of whiskey he got in there and come back to the stove.

"No," Louise say. "Everybody don't like whiskey in it. Add the whiskey after you've poured it up."

"Okay, hon."

He kiss her on the back o' the neck again. Still don't like that nigger. Something 'bout him ain't right.

"You one o' the family?" he say.

"Same as one," I say. "And you?"

He don't like the way I say it, and I don't care if he like it or not. He look at me there a second, and then he kiss her on the ear.

"Un-unnn," she say, stirring the pot.

"I love your ear, baby," he say.

"Go in the front room and talk with the people," she say.

He kiss her on the other ear. A nigger do all that front o' public got something to hide. He leave the kitchen. I look at Louise.

"Ain't nothing else I can do," she say.

"You sure, Louise? You positive?"

"I'm positive," she say.

The front door open and Emile and Chuckkie come in. A minute later Washington and Adrieu come in, too. Adrieu come back in the kitchen, and I can see she been crying. Aunt Fe is her godmother, you know.

"How you feel, Adrieu?"

"That weather out there," she say.

"Y'all walked?"

"Yes."

"Us here in the wagon. Y'all can go back with us."

"Y'all the one tore the fence down?" she ask.

"Yes, I guess so. That brother-in-law o' yours in there letting Chuckkie drive that wagon."

"Well, I don't guess it'll matter too much. Nobody go'n be here, anyhow."

And she start crying again. I take her in my arms and pat her on the shoulder, and I look at Louise stirring the egg-nog.

"What I'm go'n do and my nan-nane gone? I love her so much."

"Ever'body love her."

"Since my mama died, she been like my mama."

"Shhh," I say. "Don't let her hear you. Make her grieve. You don't want her grieving, now, do you?"

She sniffs there 'gainst my dress few times.

"Oh, Lord," she say. "Lord, have mercy."

"Shhh," I say. "Shhh. That's what life's 'bout."

"That ain't what life's 'bout," she say. "It ain't fair. This been her home all her life. These the people she know. She don't know them people she going to. It ain't fair."

"Shhh, Adrieu," I say. "Now, you saying things that ain't your business."

She cry there some mo'.

"Oh, Lord, Lord," she say.

Louise turn from the stove.

"About ready now," she say, going to the middle door. "James, tell everybody to come back and get some."

James

Let me go on back here and show these country niggers how to have a good time. All they know is talk, talk, talk. Talk so much they make me buggy round here. Damn this weather—wind, rain. Must be a million cracks in this old house.

I go to that old beat-up safe in that corner and get that fifth of Mr. Harper (in the South now; got to say Mister), give the seal one swipe, the stopper one jerk, and head back to that old wood stove. (Man, like, these cats are primitive—goodness. You know what I mean? I mean like wood stoves. Don't mention TV, man, these cats here never heard of that.) I start to dump Mr. Harper in the pot and Baby catches my hand again and say not all of them like it. You ever heard of anything like that? I mean a stud's going to drink eggnog, and he's not going to put whiskey in it. I mean he's going to drink it straight. I mean, you ever heard anything like that? Well, I wasn't pressing none of them on Mr. Harper. I mean, me and Mr. Harper get along too well together for me to go around there pressing.

I hold my cup there and let Baby put a few drops of this egg stuff in it; then I jerk my cup back and let Mr. Harper run a while. Couple of these cats come over (some of them aren't so lame) and set their cups, and I let Mr. Harper run for them. Then this cat says he's got 'nough. I let Mr. Harper run for this other stud, and pretty soon he says, "Hold it. Good." Country cat, you know. "Hold it. Good." Real country cat. So I raise the cup to see what Mr. Harper's doing. He's just right. I raise the cup again. Just right, Mr. Harper; just right.

I go to the door with Mr. Harper under my arm and the cup in my hand and I look into the front room where they all are. I mean, there's about ninety-nine of them in there. Old ones, young ones, little ones, big ones, yellow ones, black ones, brown ones—you name them, brother, and they were there. And what for? Brother, I'll tell you what for. Just because me and Baby are taking this old chick out of these sticks. Well, I'll tell you where I'd be at this moment if I was one of them. With that weather out there like it is, I'd be under about five blankets with some little warm belly pressing against mine. Brother, you can bet your hat I wouldn't be here. Man, listen to that thing out there. You can hear that rain beating on that old house like grains of rice; and that wind coming through them cracks like it does in those old Charlie Chaplin movies. Man, like you know—like *whooo-ee; whooo-ee.* Man, you talking about some weird cats.

I can feel Mr. Harper starting to massage my wig and I bat my eyes twice and look at the old girl over there. She's still sitting in that funny-looking little old rocking chair, and not saying a word to anybody. Just sitting there looking into the fireplace at them two pieces of wood that aren't giving out enough heat to warm a baby, let alone ninety-nine grown people. I mean, you know, like that sleet's falling out there like all get-up-and-go, and them two pieces of wood are lying there just as dead as the rest of these way-out cats.

One of the old cats—I don't know which one he is—Mose, Sam, or something like that—leans over and pokes in the fire a minute; then a little blaze shoots up, and he raises up, too, looking as satisfied as if he'd just sent a rocket into orbit. I mean, these cats are like that. They do these little bitty things, and they feel like they've really done something. Well, back in these sticks, I guess there just isn't nothing big to do.

I feel Mr. Harper touching my skull now—and I notice this little chick passing by me with these two cups of eggnog. She goes over to the fireplace and gives one to each of these old chicks. The one sitting in that setting chair she brought with her from God knows where, and the other cup to the old chick that Baby and I are going to haul from here sometime tomorrow morning. Wait, man, I mean like, you ever heard of anybody going to somebody else's house with a chair? I mean, wouldn't you call that an insult at the basest point? I mean, now, like tell me what you think of that? I mean—dig—here I am at my pad, and in you come with your own stool. I mean, now, like man, you know. I mean that's an insult at the basest point. I mean, you know . . . you know, like way out. . . .

Mr. Harper, what you trying to do, boy?—I mean, *sir.* (Got to watch myself, I'm in the South. Got to keep watching myself.)

This stud touches me on the shoulder and raise his cup and say, "How 'bout a taste?" I know what the stud's talking about, so I let Mr. Harper run for him. But soon 's I let a drop get in, the stud say,

" 'Nough." I mean I let about two drops get in, and already the stud's got enough. Man, I mean, like you know. I mean these studs are 'way out. I mean like 'way back there.

This stud takes a swig of his eggnog and say, "Ahhh." I mean this real down-home way of saying "Ahhhh." I mean, man, like these studs —I notice this little chick passing by me again, and this time she's crying. I mean weeping, you know. And just because this old ninety-nine-year-old chick's packing up and leaving. I mean, you ever heard of anything like that? I mean, here she is pretty as the day is long and crying because Baby and I are hauling this old chick away. Well, I'd like to make her cry. And I can assure you, brother, it wouldn't be from leaving her.

I turn and look at Baby over there by the stove, pouring eggnog in all these cups. I mean, there're about twenty of these cats lined up there. And I bet you not half of them will take Mr. Harper along. Some way-out cats, man. Some way-out cats.

I go up to Baby and kiss her on the back of the neck and give her a little pat where she likes for me to pat her when we're in the bed. She say, "Uh-uh," but I know she likes it anyhow.

Ben O

I back under the bed and touch the slop jar, and I pull back my leg and back somewhere else, and then I get me a good sight on it. I spin my aggie couple times and sight again and then I shoot. I hit it right square in the middle and it go flying over the fireplace. I crawl over there to get it and I see 'em all over there drinking they eggnog and they didn't even offer me and Chuckkie none. I find my marble on the bricks, and I go back and tell Chuckkie they over there drinking eggnog.

"You want some?" I say.

"I want shoot marble," Chuckkie say. "Yo' shot. Shoot up."

"I want some eggnog," I say.

"Shoot up, Ben O," he say. "I'm getting cold staying in one place so long. You feel that draft?"

"Coming from that crack under that bed," I say.

"Where?" Chuckkie say, looking for the crack.

"Over by that bedpost over there," I say.

"This sure's a beat-up old house," Chuckkie say.

"I want me some eggnog," I say.

"Well, you ain't getting none," Gran'mon say, from the fireplace. "It ain't good for you."

"I can drink eggnog," I say. "How come it ain't good for me? It ain't nothing but eggs and milk. I eat chicken, don't I? I eat beef, don't I?"

Gran'mon don't say nothing.

"I want me some eggnog," I say.

Gran'mon still don't say no more. Nobody else don't say nothing, neither.

"I want me some eggnog," I say.

"You go'n get a eggnog," Gran'mon say. "Just keep that noise up."

"I want me some eggnog," I say; "and I 'tend to get me some eggnog tonight."

Next thing I know, Gran'mon done picked up a chip out o' that corner and done sailed it back there where me and Chuckkie is. I duck just in time, and the chip catch old Chuckkie side the head.

"Hey, who that hitting me?" Chuckkie say.

"Move, and you won't get hit," Gran'mon say.

I laugh at old Chuckkie over there holding his head, and next thing I know here's Chuckkie done haul back there and hit me in my side. I jump up from there and give him two just to show him how it feel, and he jump up and hit me again. Then we grab each other and start tussling on the floor.

"You, Ben O," I hear Gran'mon saying. "You, Ben O, cut that out. Y'all cut that out."

But we don't stop, 'cause neither one o' us want be first. Then I feel somebody pulling us apart.

"What I ought to do is whip both o' you," Mrs. Leola say. "Is that what y'all want?"

"No'm," I say.

"Then shake hand."

Me and Chuckkie shake hand.

"Kiss," Mrs. Leola say.

"No, ma'am," I say. "I ain't kissing no boy. I ain't that crazy."

"Kiss him, Chuckkie," she say.

Old Chuckkie kiss me on the jaw.

"Now, kiss him, Ben O."

"I ain't kissing no Chuckkie," I say. "No'm. Uh-uh. You kiss girls."

And the next thing I know, Mama done tipped up back o' me and done whop me on the leg with Daddy belt.

"Kiss Chuckkie," she say.

Chuckkie turn his jaw to me and I kiss him. I almost wipe my mouth. I even feel like spitting.

"Now, come back here and get you some eggnog," Mama say.

"That's right, spoil 'em," Gran'mon say. "Next thing you know, they be drinking from bottles."

"Little eggnog won't hurt 'em, Mama," Mama say.

"That's right, never listen," Gran'mon say. "It's you go'n suffer for it. I be dead and gone, me."

Aunt Clo

Be just like wrapping a chain round a tree and jecking and jecking, and then shifting the chain little bit and jecking and jecking some in that direction, and then shifting it some mo' and jecking and jecking in that direction. Jecking and jecking till you get it loose, and then pulling with all your might. Still it might not be loose enough and you have to back the tractor up some and fix the chain round the tree again and start jecking all over. Jeck, jeck, jeck. Then you hear the roots crying, and then you keep on jecking, and then it give, and you jeck some mo', and then it falls. And not till then that you see what you done done. Not till then you see the big hole in the ground and piece of the taproot still way down in it—ə piece you won't never get out no matter if you dig till doomsday. Yes, you got the tree—least got it down on the ground, but did you get the taproot? No. No, sir, you didn't get the taproot. You stand there and look down in this hole at it and you grab yo' axe and jump down in it and start chopping at the taproot, but do you get the taproot? No. You don't get the taproot, sir. You never get the taproot. But, sir, I tell you what you do get. You get a big hole in the ground, sir; and you get another big hole in the air where the lovely branches been all these years. Yes, sir, that's what you get. The holes, sir, the holes. Two holes, sir, you can't never fill no matter how hard you try.

So you wrap yo' chain round yo' tree again, sir, and you start dragging it. But the dragging ain't so easy, sir, 'cause she's a heavy old tree —been there a long time, you know—heavy. And you make yo' tractor strain, sir, and the elements work 'gainst you, too, sir, 'cause the elements, they on her side, too, 'cause she part o' the elements, and the elements, they part o' her. So the elements, they do they little share to discourage you—yes, sir, they does. But you will not let the elements stop you. No, sir, you show the elements that they just elements, and man is stronger than elements, and you jeck and jeck on the chain, and soon she start to moving with you, sir, but if you look over yo' shoulder one second you see her leaving a trail—a trail, sir, that can be seen from miles and miles away. You see her trying to hook her little fine branches in different little cracks, in between pickets, round hills o' grass, round anything they might brush 'gainst. But you is a determined man, sir, and you jeck and you jeck, and she keep on grabbing and trying to hold, but you stronger, sir—course you the strongest— and you finally get her out on the pave road. But what you don't notice, sir, is just 'fore she get on the pave road she leave couple her little branches to remind the people that it ain't her that want leave, but you, sir, that think she ought to. So you just drag her and drag her, sir, and the folks that live in the houses 'side the pave road, they come out on they gallery and look at her go by, and then they go back in they house and sit by the fire and forget her. So you just go on, sir, and you just go and you go—and for how many days? I don't know. I don't have the least idea. The North to me, sir, is like the elements. It mystify me. But never mind, you finally get there, and then you try to find a place to set her. You look in this corner and you look in that corner, but no corner is good. She kind o' stand in the way no matter where you set her. So finally, sir, you say, "I just stand her up here a little while and see, and if it don't work out, if she keep getting in the way, I guess we'll just have to take her to the dump."

Chris

Just like him, though, standing up there telling them lies when everybody else feeling sad. I don't know what you do without people like him. And, yet, you see him there, he sad just like the rest. But he just got to be funny. Crying on the inside, but still got to be funny.

He didn't steal it, though; didn't steal it a bit. His grandpa was just like him. Mat? Mat Jefferson? Just like that. Mat could make you die laughing. 'Member once at a wake. Who was dead? Yes—Robert Lewis. Robert Lewis laying up in his coffin dead as a door nail. Everybody sad and droopy. Mat look at that and start his lying. Soon, half o' the place laughing. Funniest wake I ever went to, and yet—

Just like now. Look at 'em. Look at 'em laughing. Ten minutes ago you would 'a' thought you was at a funeral. But look at 'em now. Look at her there in that little old chair. How long she had it? Fifty years— a hundred? It ain't a chair no mo', it's little bit o' her. Just like her arm, just like her leg.

You know, I couldn't believe it. I couldn't. Emile passed the house there the other day, right after the bombing, and I was in my yard digging a water drain to let the water run out in the ditch. Emile, he stopped the wagon there 'fore the door. Little Chuckkie, he in there with him with that little rain cap buckled up over his head. I go out to the gate and I say, "Emile, it's the truth?"

"The truth," he say. And just like that he say it. "The truth."

I look at him there, and he looking up the road to keep from looking back at me. You know, they been pretty close to Aunt Fe ever since they was children coming up. His own mon, Aunt Lou, and Aunt Fe, they been like sisters, there, together.

Me and him, we talk there little while 'bout the cane cutting, then he say he got to get on to the back. He shake the lines and drive on.

Inside me, my heart feel like it done swole up ten times the size it ought to be. Water come in my eyes, and I got to 'mit I cried right there. Yes sir, I cried right there by that front gate.

Louise come in the room and whisper something to Leola, and they go back in the kitchen. I can hear 'em moving things round back there, still getting things together they go'n be taking along. If they offer me anything, I'd like that big iron pot out there in the back yard. Good for boiling water when you killing hog, you know.

You can feel the sadness in the room again. Louise brought it in when she come in and whispered to Leola. Only, she didn't take it out when her and Leola left. Every pan they move, every pot they unhook keep telling you she leaving, she leaving.

Etienne turn over one o' them logs to make the fire pick up some, and I see that boy, Lionel, spreading out his hands over the fire. Watch out, I think to myself, here come another lie. People, he just getting started.

Anne-Marie Duvall

"You're not going?"

"I'm not going," he says, turning over the log with the poker. "And if you were in your right mind, you wouldn't go, either."

"You just don't understand, do you?"

"Oh, I understand. She cooked for your daddy. She nursed you when your mama died."

"And I'm trying to pay her back with a seventy-nine-cents scarf. Is that too much?"

He is silent, leaning against the mantel, looking down at the fire. The fire throws strange shadows across the big, old room. Father looks down at me from against the wall. His eyes do not say go nor stay. But I know what he would do.

"Please go with me, Edward."

"You're wasting your breath."

I look at him a long time, then I get the small package from the coffee table.

"You're still going?"

"I am going."

"Don't call for me if you get bogged down anywhere back there."

I look at him and go out to the garage. The sky is black. The clouds are moving fast and low. A fine drizzle is falling, and the wind coming from the swamps blows in my face. I cannot recall a worse night in all my life.

I hurry into the car and drive out of the yard. The house stands big and black in back of me. Am I angry with Edward? No, I'm not angry with Edward. He's right. I should not go out into this kind of weather. But what he does not understand is I must. Father definitely would have gone if he were alive. Grandfather definitely would have gone, also. And, therefore, I must. Why? I cannot answer why. Only, I must go.

As soon as I turn down that old muddy road, I begin to pray. Don't let me go into that ditch, I pray. Don't let me go into that ditch. Please, don't let me go into that ditch.

The lights play on the big old trees along the road. Here and there the lights hit a sagging picket fence. But I know I haven't even started yet. She lives far back into the fields. Why? God, why does she have to live so far back? Why couldn't she have lived closer to the front? But the answer to that is as hard for me as is the answer to everything else. It was ordained before I—before father—was born—that she should live back there. So why should I try to understand it now?

The car slides towards the ditch, and I stop it dead and turn the wheel, and then come back into the road again. Thanks, father. I know you're with me. Because it was you who said that I must look after her, didn't you? No, you did not say it directly, father. You said it only with a glance. As grandfather must have said it to you, and as his father must have said it to him.

But now that she's gone, father, now what? I know. I know. Aunt Lou, Aunt Clo, and the rest.

The lights shine on the dead, wet grass along the road. There's an old pecan tree, looking dead and all alone. I wish I was a little nigger gal so I could pick pecans and eat them under the big old dead tree.

The car hits a rut, but bounces right out of it. I am frightened for a moment, but then I feel better. The windshield wipers are working well, slapping the water away as fast as it hits the glass. If I make the next half mile all right, the rest of the way will be good. It's not much over a mile now.

That was too bad about that bombing—killing that woman and her two children. That poor woman; poor children. What is the answer? What will happen? What do they want? Do they know what they want? Do they really know what they want? Are they positively sure? Have they any idea? Money to buy a car, is that it? If that is all, I pity them. Oh, how I pity them.

Not much farther. Just around that bend and—there's a water hole. Now what?

I stop the car and just stare out at the water a minute; then I get out to see how deep it is. The cold wind shoots through my body like needles. Lightning comes from towards the swamps and lights up the place. For a split second the night is as bright as day. The next second it is blacker than it has ever been.

I look at the water, and I can see that it's too deep for the car to pass through. I must turn back or I must walk the rest of the way. I stand there a while wondering what to do. Is it worth it all? Can't I simply send the gift by someone tomorrow morning? But will there be someone tomorrow morning? Suppose she leaves without getting it, then what? What then? Father would never forgive me. Neither would grandfather or great-grandfather, either. No, they wouldn't.

The lightning flashes again and I look across the field, and I can see the tree in the yard a quarter of a mile away. I have but one choice: I must walk. I get the package out of the car and stuff it in my coat and start out.

I don't make any progress at first, but then I become a little warmer and I find I like walking. The lightning flashes just in time to show up a puddle of water, and I go around it. But there's no light to show up the second puddle, and I fall flat on my face. For a moment I'm completely blind, then I get slowly to my feet and check the package. It's dry, not harmed. I wash the mud off my raincoat, wash my hands, and I start out again.

The house appears in front of me, and as I come into the yard, I can hear the people laughing and talking. Sometimes I think niggers can laugh and joke even if they see somebody beaten to death. I go up on the porch and knock and an old one opens the door for me. I swear, when he sees me he looks as if he's seen a ghost. His mouth drops open, his eyes bulge—I swear.

I go into the old crowded and smelly room, and every one of them looks at me the same way the first one did. All the joking and laughing has ceased. You would think I was the devil in person.

"Done, Lord," I hear her saying over by the fireplace. They move to the side and I can see her sitting in that little rocking chair I bet you she's had since the beginning of time. "Done, Master," she says. "Child, what you doing in weather like this? Y'all move; let her get to that fire. Y'all move. Move, now. Let her warm herself."

They start scattering everywhere.

"I'm not cold, Aunt Fe," I say. "I just brought you something—something small—because you're leaving us. I'm going right back."

"Done, Master," she says. Fussing over me just like she's done all her life. "Done, Master. Child, you ain't got no business in a place like this. Get close to this fire. Get here. Done, Master."

I move closer, and the fire does feel warm and good.

"Done, Lord," she says.

I take out the package and pass it to her. The other niggers gather around with all kinds of smiles on their faces. Just think of it—a white lady coming through all of this for one old darky. It is all right for them to come from all over the plantation, from all over the area, in all kinds of weather: this is to be expected of them. But a white lady, a white lady. They must think we white people don't have their kind of feelings.

She unwraps the package, her bony little fingers working slowly and deliberately. When she sees the scarf—the seventy-nine-cents scarf—she brings it to her mouth and kisses it.

"Y'all look," she says. "Y'all look. Ain't it the prettiest little scarf y'all ever did see? Y'all look."

They move around her and look at the scarf. Some of them touch it.

"I go'n put it on right now," she says. "I go'n put it on right now, my lady."

She unfolds it and ties it round her head and looks up at everybody and smiles.

"Thank you, my lady," she says. "Thank you, ma'am, from the bottom of my heart."

"Oh, Aunt Fe," I say, kneeling down beside her. "Oh, Aunt Fe."

But I think about the other niggers there looking down at me, and I get up. But I look into that wrinkled old face again, and I must go back down again. And I lay my head in that bony old lap, and I cry and I cry—I don't know how long. And I feel those old fingers, like death itself, passing over my hair and my neck. I don't know how long I kneel there crying, and when I stop, I get out of there as fast as I can.

Etienne

The boy come in, and soon, right off, they get quiet, blaming the boy. If people could look little farther than the tip of they nose—No, they blame the boy. Not that they ain't behind the boy, what he doing, but they blame him for what she must do. What they don't know is that the boy didn't start it, and the people that bombed the house didn't start it, neither. It started a million years ago. It started when one man envied another man for having a penny mo' 'an he had, and then the man married a woman to help him work the field so he could get much 's the other man, but when the other man saw the man had married a woman to get much 's him, he, himself, he married a woman, too, so he could still have mo'. Then they start having children—not from love; but so the children could help 'em work so they could have mo'. But even with the children one man still had a penny mo' 'an the other, so the other man went and bought him a ox, and the other man did the same—to keep ahead of the other man. And soon the other man had bought him a slave to work the ox so he could get ahead of the other man. But the other man went out and bought him two slaves so he could stay ahead of the other man, and the other man went out and bought him three slaves. And soon they had a thousand slaves apiece, but they still wasn't satisfied. And one day the slaves all rose and kill the masters, but the masters (knowing slaves was men just like they was, and kind o' expected they might do this) organized theyself a good police force, they come out and killed the two thousand slaves.

So it's not this boy you see standing here 'fore you, 'cause it happened a million years ago. And this boy here's just doing something the slaves done a million years ago. Just that this boy here ain't doing it they way. 'Stead of raising arms 'gainst the masters, he bow his head.

No, I say; don't blame the boy 'cause she must go. 'Cause when she's dead, and that won't be long after they get her up there, this boy's work will still be going on. She's not the only one that's go'n die from this boy's work. Many mo' of 'em go'n die 'fore it's over with. The whole place—everything. A big wind is rising, and when a big wind rise, the sea stirs, and the drop o' water you see laying on top the sea this day won't be there tomorrow. 'Cause that's what wind do, and that's what life is. She ain't nothing but one little drop o' water laying on top the sea, and what this boy's doing is called the wind . . . and she must be moved. No, don't blame the boy. Go out and blame the wind. No, don't blame him, 'cause tomorrow, what he's doing today, somebody go'n say he ain't done a thing. 'Cause tomorrow will be his time to be turned over just like it's hers today. And after that, be somebody else time to turn over. And it keep going like that till it ain't nothing left to turn—and nobody left to turn it.

"Sure, they bombed the house," he say; "because they want us to stop. But if we stopped today, then what good would we have done? What good? Those who have already died for the cause would have just died in vain."

"Maybe if they had bombed your house you wouldn't be so set on keeping this up."

"If they had killed my mother and my brothers and sisters, I'd press just that much harder. I can see you all point. I can see it very well. But I can't agree with you. You blame me for their being bombed. You blame me for Aunt Fe's leaving. They died for you and for your children. And I love Aunt Fe as much as anybody in here does. Nobody in here loves her more than I do. Not one of you." He looks at her. "Don't you believe me, Aunt Fe?"

She nods—that little white scarf still tied round her head.

"How many times have I eaten in your kitchen, Aunt Fe? A thousand times? How many times have I eaten tea cakes and drank milk on the back steps, Aunt Fe? A thousand times? How many times have I sat at this same fireplace with you, just the two of us, Aunt Fe? Another thousand times—two thousand times? How many times have I chopped wood for you, chopped grass for you, ran to the store for you? Five thousand times? How many times have we walked to church together, Aunt Fe? Gone fishing at the river together—how many times? I've spent as much time in this house as I've spent in my own. I know every crack in the wall. I know every corner. With my eyes shut, I can go anywhere in here without bumping into anything. How many of you can do that? Not many of you." He looks at her. "Aunt Fe?"

She looks at him.

"Do you think I love you, Aunt Fe?"

She nods.

"I love you, Aunt Fe, much as I do my own parents. I'm going to miss you much as I'd miss my own mother if she were to leave me now. I'm going to miss you, Aunt Fe, but I'm not going to stop what I've started. You told me a story once, Aunt Fe, about my great-grandpa. Remember? Remember how he died?"

She looks in the fire and nods.

"Remember how they lynched him—chopped him into pieces?"

She nods.

"Just the two of us were sitting here beside the fire when you told me that. I was so angry I felt like killing. But it was you who told me get killing out of my mind. It was you who told me I would only bring harm to myself and sadness to the others if I killed. Do you remember that, Aunt Fe?"

She nods, still looking in the fire.

"You were right. We cannot raise our arms. Because it would mean death for ourselves, as well as for the others. But we will do something else—and that's what we will do." He looks at the people standing round him. "And if they were to bomb my own mother's house tomorrow, I would still go on."

"I'm not saying for you not to go on," Louise says. "That's up to you. I'm just taking Auntie from here before hers is the next house they bomb."

The boy look at Louise, and then at Aunt Fe. He go up to the chair where she sitting.

"Good-bye, Aunt Fe," he say, picking up her hand. The hand done shriveled up to almost nothing. Look like nothing but loose skin's covering the bones. "I'll miss you," he say.

"Good-bye, Emmanuel," she say. She look at him a long time. "God be with you."

He stand there holding the hand a while longer, then he nods his head, and leaves the house. The people stir round little bit, but nobody say anything.

Aunt Lou

They tell her good-bye, and half of 'em leave the house crying, or want cry, but she just sit there 'side the fireplace like she don't mind going at all. When Leola ask me if I'm ready to go, I tell her I'm staying right there till Fe leave that house. I tell her I ain't moving one step till she go out that door. I been knowing her for the past fifty some years now, and I ain't 'bout to leave her on her last night here.

That boy, Chuckkie, want stay with me, but I make him go. He follow his mon and paw out the house and soon I hear that wagon turning round. I hear Emile saying something to Mr. Bascom even 'fore that wagon get out the yard. I tell myself, well, Mr. Bascom, you sure go'n catch it, and me not there to take up for you—and I get up from my chair and go to the door.

"Emile?" I call.

"Whoa," he say.

"You leave that mule 'lone, you hear me?"

"I ain't done Mr. Bascom a thing, Mama," he say.

"Well, you just mind you don't," I say. "I'll sure find out."

"Yes'm," he say. "Come up here, Mr. Bascom."

"Now, you hear that boy. Emile?" I say.

"I'm sorry, Mama," he say. "I didn't mean no harm."

They go out in the road, and I go back to the fireplace and sit down again. Louise stir round in the kitchen a few minutes, then she come in the front where we at. Everybody else gone. That husband o' hers, there, got drunk long 'fore midnight, and Emile and them had to put him to bed in the other room.

She come there and stand by the fire.

"I'm dead on my feet," she say.

"Why don't you go to bed," I say. "I'm go'n be here."

"You all won't need anything?"

"They got wood in that corner?"

"Plenty."

"Then we won't need a thing."

She stand there and warm, and then she say good night and go round the other side.

"Well, Fe?" I say.

"I ain't leaving here tomorrow, Lou," she say.

"'Course you is," I say. "Up there ain't that bad."

She shake her head. "No, I ain't going nowhere."

I look at her over in her chair, but I don't say nothing. The fire pops in the fireplace, and I look at the fire again. It's a good little fire—not too big, not too little. Just 'nough there to keep the place warm.

"You want sing, Lou?" she say, after a while. "I feel like singing my 'termination song."

"Sure," I say.

She start singing in that little light voice she got there, and I join with her. We sing two choruses, and then she stop.

"My 'termination for Heaven," she say. "Now—now—"

"What's the matter, Fe?" I say.

"Nothing," she say. "I want get in my bed. My gown hanging over there."

I get the gown for her and bring it back to the firehalf. She get out of her dress slowly, like she don't even have 'nough strength to do it. I help her on with her gown, and she kneel down there 'side the bed and say her prayers. I sit in my chair and look at the fire again.

She pray there a long time—half out loud, half to herself. I look at her kneeling down there, little like a little old girl. I see her making some kind o' jecking motion there, but I feel she crying 'cause this her last night here, and 'cause she got to go and leave ever'thing behind. I look at the fire.

She pray there ever so long, and then she start to get up. But she can't make it by herself. I go to help her, and when I put my hand on her shoulder, she say, "Lou? Lou?"

I say, "What's the matter, Fe?"

"Lou?" she say. "Lou?"

I feel her shaking in my hand with all her might. Shaking, shaking, shaking—like a person with the chill. Then I hear her take a long breath, longest I ever heard anybody take before. Then she ease back on the bed—calm, calm, calm.

"Sleep on, Fe," I tell her. "When you get up there, tell 'em all I ain't far behind."

Claude Brown

(b. 1937)

CLAUDE BROWN WAS BORN in Harlem; his parents were migrants from South Carolina. He was a direct product of the undisciplined life of the ghetto, and by the time he was eight he had become involved with street gangs like the Harlem Buccaneers and the Forty Thieves and had been in trouble with the law. When he was ten, Brown's parents sent him to live with relatives in the South. Back in Harlem after a year, Claude "Sonny" Brown was committed to the Wiltwyck School for underprivileged and delinquent boys, and three years later to the Warwick Reform School. He was sent to Warwick a second and third time before he resolved that his life was not what he wanted it to be.

By 1957 Brown had completed high school, attending classes at night, and in 1961 he entered Howard University; he graduated in 1965, briefly attended Stanford University Law School, and then transferred to Rutgers University.

Although Brown's real interest is politics, he occasionally publishes articles in national magazines such as *Esquire*.

"Drugs and Harlem" comes from Chapter X of *Manchild in the Promised Land,* Claude Brown's autobiography, which has a roughness and blunt realism that lend authenticity to his portrayal of ghetto life.

DRUGS AND HARLEM

If anyone had asked me around the latter part of 1957 just what I thought had made the greatest impression on my generation in Harlem, I would have said, "Drugs." I don't think too many people would have contested this. About ten years earlier, in 1947, or just eight years earlier, in 1949, this wouldn't have been true.

In 1949, I would have answered that same question with the answer, "The knife." Perhaps all this could have been summed up in saying, "The bad mother-fucker." Throughout my childhood in Harlem, nothing was more strongly impressed upon me than the fact that you had to fight and that you should fight. Everybody would accept it if a person was scared to fight, but not if he was so scared that he didn't fight.

As I saw it in my childhood, most of the cats I swung with were more afraid of not fighting than they were of fighting. This was how it was supposed to be, because this was what we had come up under. The adults in the neighborhood practiced this. They lived by the concept that a man was supposed to fight. When two little boys got into a fight in the neighborhood, the men around would encourage them and egg them on. They'd never think about stopping the fight.

There were some little boys, like myself, who when we got into a fight—even though we weren't ten years old yet—all the young men, the street-corner cats, they would come out of the bars or the numbers joints or anyplace they were and watch. Somebody would say, "Little Sonny Boy is on the street fightin' again," and everybody had to see this.

Down on 146th Street, they'd put money on street fights. If there were two little boys on one block who were good with their hands, or one around the corner and one on Eighth Avenue, men on the corner would try and egg them into a fight.

I remember Big Bill, one of the street-corner hustlers before he went to jail for killing a bartender. When I was about seven or eight years old, I remember being on the street and Bill telling me one day, "Sonny Boy, I know you can kick this little boy's ass on 146th Street, and I'll give you a dollar to do it."

I knew I couldn't say no, couldn't be afraid. He was telling all these other men around there on the street that I could beat this boy's ass. There was another man, a numbers hustler, who said, "No. They ain't got no boy here on Eighth Avenue who could beat little Rip's ass on 146th Street."

Bill said, "Sonny Boy, can you do it?" And he'd already promised me the dollar.

I said, "Yeah." I was scared, because I'd seen Rip and heard of him.

He was a mean-looking little boy. He was real dark-skinned, had big lips and bulgy eyes, and looked like he was always mad. One time I had seen him go at somebody with a knife. A woman had taken the knife out of his hands, but she cut her hand getting it. I knew he would have messed up the cat if he could have held on to that knife.

He knew me too, and he had never messed with me. I remember one time he told me that he was going to kick my ass. I said, "Well, here it is. Start kickin'." He never did. I don't think he was too anxious to mess with me. I didn't want to mess with him either, but since Big Bill had given me this dollar and kept pushing me, I couldn't have said no. They would have said I was scared of him, and if that had gotten back to him, I know he would have messed with me.

I fought him for three days. I beat him one day, and he beat me the next day. On the third day, we fought three fights. I had a black eye, and he had a bloody lip. He had a bloody nose, and I had a bloody nose. By the end of the day, we had become good friends. Somebody took us to the candy store and bought us ice-cream cones.

Rip and I got real tight. If anybody messed with him and I heard about it, I wanted to fight them. And it was the same with him if anybody messed with me.

This was something that took place in all the poor colored neighborhoods throughout New York City. Every place I went, it was the same way, at least with the colored guys. You had to fight, and everybody respected people for fighting. I guess if you were used to it and were good at it, there was nothing else you could do. I guess that was why Turk became a fighter. He had fought so long and had been so preoccupied with fighting that he couldn't do anything else. He had to get this fighting out of his system.

With cats like Turk and many others who came up on the Harlem streets, the first day they came out of the house by themselves, at about five or six years old, the prizefight ring beckoned to them. It beckoned to them in the form of the cat around the corner who had the reputation or the cat who wanted to mess with your little brother or your little sister. If you went to school and somebody said, "I'm gon kick your ass if you don't bring me some money tomorrow to buy my lunch," it was the prizefight ring beckoning to you.

I remember they used to say on the streets, "Don't mess with a man's money, his woman, or his manhood." This was the thing when I was about twelve or thirteen. This was what the gang fights were all about. If somebody messed with your brother, you could just punch him in his mouth, and this was all right. But if anybody was to mess with your sister, you had to really fuck him up—break his leg or stab him in the eye with an ice pick, something vicious.

I suppose the main things were the women in the family and the money. This was something we learned very early. If you went to the store and lost some money or if you let somebody gorilla you out of some money that your mother or your father had given you, you got your ass beaten when you came back home. You couldn't go upstairs and say, "Well, Daddy, that big boy down there took the money that you gave me to buy some cigars." Shit, you didn't have any business letting anybody take your money. You got your ass whipped for that, and you were supposed to.

You were supposed to go to war about your money. Maybe this was why the cats on the corner were killing each other over a two-dollar crap game or a petty debt. People were always shooting, cutting, or killing somebody over three dollars.

I remember going to the store for my father on a Sunday morning. He'd given me a quarter to get him some chewing tobacco. I had to walk up to 149th Street, because no place else was open. I went up to this drugstore on 149th Street, and there were some cats standing around there. I was about eight, and they were about ten or eleven.

One of them said, "Hey, boy, come here," one of those things. I was scared to run, because I knew I wouldn't be able to outrun them all. I figured that if I acted kind of bad, they might not be so quick to mess with me. So I walked right up to them. One cat said, "You got any money?"

I said, "No, I ain't got no money."

I guess I shouldn't have said that. He kept looking at me real mean, trying to scare me. He said, "Jump up and down." I knew what this was all about, because I used to do it myself. If you jumped up and down and the cat who was shaking you down heard some change jingling, he was supposed to try to beat your ass and take the money.

I said, "No, man. I ain't jumpin' up and down."

He grabbed me by my collar. Somebody said, "He's got something in his hand." That was Dad's quarter. One cat grabbed my hand. I'd forgotten all about the guy who had my collar. I hit the boy who had my hand. Then the cat who had me by the collar started punching me in the jaw. I wasn't even thinking about him. I was still fighting the other cat to keep that quarter.

A woman came out a door and said, "You all stop beatin' that boy!"

I had a bloody nose; they'd kicked my ass good, but I didn't mind, because they hadn't taken my quarter. It wasn't the value of money. It couldn't have been. It was just that these things symbolized a man's manhood or principles. That's what Johnny Wilkes used to like to call it, a man's principles. You don't mess with a man's money; you don't mess with a man's woman; you don't mess with a man's family or his manhood—these were a man's principles, according to Johnny Wilkes.

Most girls in Harlem could fight pretty well themselves, and if other girls bothered them, they could take care of themselves. You couldn't let other cats bother your sisters. In the bebopping days in Harlem, if the girls had brothers who were scared to fight, everybody would mess with them and treat them like they wanted to. Cats would come up and say things like, "You better meet me up on the roof," or "You better meet me in the park."

It went deep. It went very deep—until drugs came. Fighting was the thing that people concentrated on. In our childhood, we all had to make our reputations in the neighborhood. Then we'd spend the rest of our lives living up to them. A man was respected on the basis of his reputation. The people in the neighborhood whom everybody looked up to were the cats who'd killed somebody. The little boys in the neighborhood whom the adults respected were the little boys who didn't let anybody mess with them.

Dad once saw me run away from a fight. He was looking out the window one day, and the Morris brothers were messing with me. I didn't think I could beat both of them, so I ran in the house. Dad was at the door when I got there. He said, "Where are you runnin' to, boy?"

I said, "Dad, these boys are out there, and they messin' with me."

He said, "Well, if you come in here, I'm gon mess with you too. You ain't got no business runnin' from nobody."

I said, "Yeah, Dad, I know that. But there's two of 'em, and they're both bigger than me. They can hit harder than I can hit."

Dad said, "You think they can hit harder than I can hit?"

I said, "No, Dad. I know they can't hit harder than you." I was wondering what was behind this remark, because I knew he wasn't going to go out there on the street and fight some boys for me. He wasn't going to fight anybody for me.

He said, "Well, damn right I can hit harder than they can. And if you come in here you got to get hit by me."

He stood on the side of the door and held on to the knob with one hand. I knew I couldn't go in there. If I went downstairs, the Morris brothers were going to kick my ass. I just stood there looking at Dad, and he stood there for a while looking at me and mumbling about me running from somebody like some little girl, all that kind of shit.

Dad had a complex about his size, I think. He was real short. Maybe that's why he played that bad mother-fucker part so strong. That's probably why he always had his knife. This was what used to scare me about him more than anything—the scar on the neck and his knife. I used to associate the two of them together.

Every night when Dad went to bed, he'd put his watch, his money, his wallet, and his knife under his pillow. When he got up, he would wind his watch, but he would take more time with his knife. He had a switchblade, and he would try it a couple of times. Sometimes he would oil it. He never went out without his knife. He never went to church, but I don't think Dad would have even gone to church without his knife. I guess it was because of that scar on his neck; he never was going to get caught without it again.

The Morris brothers were hollering, "Sonny, you ain't comin' down? Man, you better not come down here any more, 'cause I'm gon kick your ass."

They would take turns hollering up and telling me all this. Dad was standing there in the doorway, and I had a headache. I had a real bad headache, but I knew that wasn't going to help. Dad started telling me about running from somebody who was bigger than me. He said, "You'll probably be short all your life, and little too. But that don't mean you got to run from anybody. If you gon start runnin' this early, you better be good at it, 'cause you probably gon be runnin' all your life."

I just sat down there on the cold hallway tile, my head hurting.

Dad said, "Get up off that floor, boy."

Mama came to the door and said, "Boy, what's wrong with you?"

Dad said, "There ain't nothin' wrong with him. He just scared, that's all. That's what's wrong with him. The thing that's wrong is you try and pamper him too much. You stay away from that boy."

Mama said, "That boy looks like he sick. Don't be botherin' him now. What you gettin' ready to beat him for?"

Dad said, "Ain't nobody gettin' ready to beat him. I'm just gon beat him if he come in this house."

Mama came in the hallway and put her arms around me and said, "Come on in the house and lay down."

I went in and I laid down. I just got sicker until I went downstairs. They really did kick my ass. But it was all right. I didn't feel sick any more.

I remember one time I hit a boy in the face with a bottle of Pepsi-Cola. I did it because I knew the older cats on 146th Street were watching me. The boy had messed with Carole. He had taken her candy from her and thrown it on the ground.

I came up to him and said, "Man, what you mess with my sister for?"

All the older guys were saying, "That's that little boy who lives on Eighth Avenue. They call him Sonny Boy. We gon see somethin' good out here now."

There was a Pepsi-Cola truck there; they were unloading some crates. They were stacking up the crates to roll them inside. The boy who had hit Carole was kind of big and acted kind of mean. He had a stick in his hand, and said, "Yeah, I did it, so what you gon do about it?"

I looked at him for a while, and he looked big. He was holding that stick like he meant to use it, so I snatched a Pepsi-Cola bottle and hit him right in the face. He grabbed his face and started crying. He fell down, and I started to hit him again, but the man who was unloading the Pepsi-Cola bottles grabbed me. He took the bottle away from me and shook me. He asked me if I was crazy or something.

All the guys on the corner started saying, "You better leave that boy alone," and "Let go of that kid." I guess he got kind of scared. He was white, and here were all these mean-looking colored cats talking about "Let go that kid" and looking at him. They weren't asking him to let me go; they were telling him. He let me go.

Afterward, if I came by, they'd start saying, "Hey, Sonny Boy, how you doin'?" They'd ask me, "You kick anybody's ass today?" I knew that they admired me for this, and I knew that I had to keep on doing it. This was the reputation I was making, and I had to keep living up to it every day that I came out of the house. Every day, there was a greater demand on me. I couldn't beat the same little boys every day. They got bigger and bigger. I had to get more vicious as the cats got bigger. When the bigger guys started messing with you, you couldn't hit them or give them a black eye or a bloody nose. You had to get a bottle or a stick or a knife. All the other cats out there on the streets expected this of me, and they gave me encouragement.

When I was about ten years old, the Forty Thieves—part of the Buccaneers—adopted me. Danny and Butch and Kid were already in it. Johnny Wilkes was older than Butch, and Butch was older than Danny and Kid. Johnny was an old Buccaneer. He had to be. When he came out on the streets in the early forties, it must have been twice as hard as it was a few years later. Harlem became less vicious from year to year, and it was hard when I first started coming out of the house, in 1944 and 1945, and raising all kinds of hell. It was something terrible out there on the streets.

Being one of the older Buccaneers, Johnny took Butch, Danny, and Kid as his fellows. He adopted them. I guess he liked the fact that they all admired him. They adopted me because I was a thief. I don't know why or how I first started stealing. I remember it was Danny and Butch who were the first ones who took me up on the hill to the white stores and downtown. I had already started stealing in Harlem. It was before I started going to school, so it must have been about 1943. Danny used to steal money, and he used to take me to the show with him and buy me popcorn and potato chips. After a while, I stole money too. Stealing became something good. It was exciting. I don't know what made it so exciting, but I liked it. I liked stealing more than I liked fighting.

I didn't like fighting at first. But after a while, it got me a lot of praise and respect in the street. It was the fighting and the stealing that made me somebody. If I hadn't fought or stolen, I would have been just another kid in the street. I put bandages on cats, and people would ask, "Who did that?" The older cats didn't believe that a little boy had broke somebody's arm by hitting him with a pipe or had hit somebody in the face with a bottle or had hit somebody in the head with a door hinge and put that big patch on his head. They didn't believe things like this at first, but my name got around and they believed it.

I became the mascot of the Buccaneers. They adopted me, and they started teaching me things. At that time, they were just the street-corner hoodlums, the delinquents, the little teen-age gangsters of the future. They were outside of things, but they knew the people who were into things, all the older hustlers and the prostitutes, the boot-leggers, the pimps, the numbers runners. They knew the professional thieves, the people who dealt the guns, the stickup artists, the people who sold reefers. I was learning how to make homemades and how to steal things and what reefers were. I was learning all the things that you needed to know in the streets. The main thing I was learning was our code.

We looked upon ourselves as the aristocracy of the community. We felt that we were the hippest people and that the other people didn't know anything. When I was in the street with these people, we all had to live for one another. We had to live in a way that we would be respected by one another. We couldn't let our friends think anything terrible of us, and we didn't want to think anything bad about our friends.

I think everybody, even the good boys who stayed in the house, started growing into this manly thing, a man's money, a man's family, a man's manhood. I felt so much older than most of the guys my age because I had been in it for a long time before they came out of the house. They were kids, and I felt like an old man. This was what made life easier on me in Harlem in the mid-fifties than it was for other cats my age, sixteen, seventeen, and eighteen. I had been through it. I didn't have to prove anything any more, because I'd been proving myself for years and years and years.

In a way, I used to feel sorry for the cats coming out of the house at sixteen and seventeen. I knew they were afraid. I'd always been afraid too, and I wasn't afraid of what they were afraid of. I wasn't afraid of not using drugs. I sort of knew that I wouldn't have to kill anybody.

I suppose I was luckier because, when I was young, I knew all the time that I couldn't get in but so much trouble. If I had killed somebody when I was twelve or thirteen, I knew I couldn't go to the chair; I knew they couldn't send me to Sing Sing or anyplace like that.

Then the manhood thing started getting next to cats through drugs. I saw it so many times. Young cats wanted to take drugs because they used to listen to the way the junkies talked, with a drag in their voice. I used to see some of the younger cats on the corner trying to imitate the junkie drag, that harsh "Yeah, man" sort of thing.

It was changing. By 1957 the fight thing had just about gone. A man didn't have to prove himself with his hands as much as he had before. By then, when I met cats who had just come out of jail, out of Woodburn, Sing Sing, Coxsackie, and I asked about somebody, they'd say, "Oh, yeah, man, I think I know the cat," and they would start describing him by features, his height, his voice, that sort of thing. But as late as 1953, if I asked somebody, "Do you know a cat by the name K.B.?" The guy would say, "Yeah. He's left-handed, and he always fights with his left hand cocked back?"

This was something that was dying out. Now people would ask if you knew somebody by scars or the way he talked, something like that. The fighting thing didn't seem to be important any more. The only thing that seemed to matter now, to my generation in Harlem, was drugs. Everybody looked at it as if it were inevitable. If you asked about somebody, a cat would say, "Oh, man, he's still all right. He's doin' pretty good. He's not strung out yet."

I never got too involved with drugs, but it gave me a pretty painful moment. I was walking down Eighth Avenue, and I saw somebody across the street. It was a familiar shape and a familiar walk. My heart lit up.

The person looked like something was wrong with her, even though she was walking all right and still had her nice shape. It was Sugar. She was walking in the middle of the street.

I ran across the street and snatched her by the arm. I was happy. I knew she'd be happy to see me, because I hadn't seen her in a long time. I said, "Sugar, hey, baby, what you doin'? You tryin' to commit suicide or somethin'? Why don't you just go and take some sleeping pills? I think it would be less painful, and it would be easier on the street cleaners."

I expected her to grab me and hug me and be just as glad to see me, but she just looked around and said, "Oh, hi." Her face looked bad. She looked old, like somebody who'd been crying a long time because they had lost somebody, like a member of the family had died.

I said, "What's wrong, baby? What's the matter?"

She looked at me and said, "You don't know?"

"Uh-uh, uh-uh."

I looked at her, and she said, "Yeah, baby, that's the way it is. I've got a jones," and she dropped her head.

"Well, anyway, come on out of the street."

"I don't care. Claude, I just had a bad time. You know a nigger named Cary who lives on 148th Street?"

"I don't know him. Why?"

"He just beat me out of my last five dollars, and my jones is on me; it's on me something terrible. I feel so sick."

I was so hurt and stunned I just didn't know what to do. I said, "Come on, Sugar, let me take you someplace where I know you can get some help. Look, there's a man in East Harlem. His name is Reverend Eddie, and he's been doing a lot of good work with young drug addicts, and I think he could help you. He could get you into Metropolitan Hospital or Manhattan General, one of the places where they've started treating drug addicts. Come on, you got to get a cure, baby. This life is not for you."

I pulled on her, and she said, "Claude, Claude, I'm sick. There's only one thing you can do for me if you really want to help me. There's only one thing anybody can do for me right now, and that's loan me five dollars to get me some stuff, because I feel like I'm dyin'. Oh, Lord, I feel so bad."

I looked at her, and she was a part of my childhood. I just couldn't stand to see her suffer. I only had one five-dollar bill and some change. I said, "Look, baby, why don't you get off this thing? Because it's gonna be the same story tomorrow. You'll just be delaying it until another day."

"Look, Claude, I'll go anyplace with you, but I can't go now. In a little while, I'm gon be laying down in the street there holdin' my stomach and hopin' a car runs over me before the pains get any worse."

"Shit. Come on with me. I'm not gon give you another five dollars to go and give it to somebody and get bit again. Come on with me. Come on to 144th Street. I know somebody there who's got some drugs, and I understand it's pretty good. I'll get you some drugs and take care of that. Then we're gon see about doin' something for you."

"Okay. You get me high and I'll go anyplace with you after that. But first I want to go downtown. You could come with me, down around Times Square. I really appreciate this, and I'm gonna give you ten dollars."

"Shit. You gon give me ten dollars? Why don't you just go on and . . ."

"No, I ain't got the money now. I got to go down there and turn a trick. I'll give you ten dollars, or I'll give you twenty dollars if you need some money. I'll turn a few tricks for you tonight."

I wanted to hit her when she said that, because it meant she thought of me as somebody who might want her to turn a trick, somebody who would accept her turning a trick for him. But I knew that it wasn't so much me. This was what she'd been into, and she'd probably turned a whole lot of tricks. She probably thought of everybody that way now, as somebody who she could turn a trick for. I suppose that's all anybody had wanted from her for a long time.

I was hurt. I said, "Come on." I took her to Ruby's, on 144th Street. Ruby was a chick I knew who was dealing drugs. I said, "Look, you can get high right here."

I told Ruby who Sugar was. I introduced Sugar to her. I told her I wanted to get Sugar high. Ruby said, "No! I'm surprised. Damn, Sonny, you sure waited a long time to start dabblin', didn't you?"

"No, baby, it's not for me; it's for Sugar."

She said, "Oh, yeah? She looks like she's in a bad way."

Ruby told us to sit down in the living room. She had a bent-up spoon that she cooked stuff in for the poison people. She cooked some for Sugar. While Sugar was waiting for her to cook it, I asked her, "Sugar, what's been happening? The last time I heard about you, you were dancing with a popular troupe, and you were doin' good."

"Yeah, I was dancin', but I haven't done any dancin' in a long time."

"I guess not. What happened? You were doin' so good. You had finished high school. I thought you were really gonna do things; you were a damn good girl." I asked her what had happened to the young cat that she had eyes for when I wanted her to be my woman, about five years before.

"Oh, that was just one of those childish flames. It burned itself out."

"Yeah? I heard you'd gotten married. Wasn't it to him?"

"No, it wasn't to him. He wasn't mature enough for anybody to marry."

"Well, what happened with the marriage?"

"It's a long story, Claude, but I guess I owe it to you."

"No, baby, you don't owe me a thing. Save it if that's the way you feel about it."

"No, I want to tell it to you anyway. I guess you're the one I've been waiting to tell it to. . . . Do you remember a boy on 149th Street by the name of Melvin Jackson?"

"No, I don't know him."

"Anyway, he use to be in a lot of trouble, too, around the same time that you were raisin' all that hell. I think he was a year or two older than you. When you were at Warwick, he was at Coxsackie. He came out about a year after you did.

"He was a lonely sort of guy. He seemed to really need somebody. Claude, you know what I think? I think all my life, I'd been looking for somebody who needed somebody real bad, and who could need me. Who could need all of me and everything that I had to give him."

I said, "Yeah, baby, I think I know."

"We got married in '55. For about a year, we were happy. Marriage was good. I thought this was something that would last and last for a long time."

"Yeah."

"Claude, I hope you don't have anyplace to go tonight. The first thing I want to do after I get high is go down and turn a trick and get some money."

"Look girl, stop saying that. Stop saying that before I beat your ass."

She looked at me and smiled and said, "Yeah, won't you do it? I think I'd like that, just for old time's sake." And she went on with telling me about the marriage.

"For the first year, we were happy. He was working and I was working. After about a year, he started going out nights and stayin' real late. He'd get up out of bed at one o'clock in the morning, go out, and come back about four or five. At first, I thought it was another woman or something like that. I thought it was for a long time, until I found out.

"At first he just started goin' out and stayin' for a few hours. After a while, he started goin' out at night or early in the morning and not comin' back for two and three days. I got worried. After a while, I couldn't work. I had a miscarriage about a month before he started staying out all night long. I was kind of sick. I was weak, and I would get worried and couldn't go to work in the morning.

"Once, when he came home, I asked him where he'd been. He just said, 'I had to go out, baby.' I knew he knew a whole lot of shady people, because he'd been in street life for a long time, most of his life. And he knew a whole lot of characters who I didn't want him to bring around the house and who he was respectful enough not to bring around.

"I didn't ask him too much about these people. I didn't try to butt into his business, because we just had this understanding. We never talked about it. That's just the way we understood each other.

"I knew him, and I knew he loved me. I think he loved me more than anybody ever loved me in all my life before. That's what made it so bad when he started staying out at night. All that love I had finally found, the love that I'd been seekin' so strongly all my life, was being threatened. It made me sick. I'd wake up in the morning, feel that he wasn't there, and I became so scared I felt like a little kid hidin' in the closet from monsters.

"My eyes just started pushin' the water out. Heat waves would swell up and come out of my eyes in tears. That's how I felt. It wasn't a thing of body with him. It wasn't a thing of this flesh stuff. He didn't even know that I had a body when I first met him. He didn't like me; he couldn't stand having me around. One day, he said something kind, and I realized that it wasn't just me that he disliked. It was everybody. And he was lonely. He needed somebody, and I knew that the some-body could've been me.

"I'd never felt so un-alone, you know, until I met this guy. I never felt as though I had anybody or anything but him. I would've lived with him or done anything he asked. I would've went out on the street corners and tricked for him if that was what he wanted me to do, be-cause he became a part of me, and I wanted him just that badly.

"But he really loved me; he didn't expect anything out of me. That wasn't the worst part of it. I thought he was getting money from me to give to another woman, because sometimes he'd be going into my hand-bag in the middle of the night, and he'd take money out of it. Then he'd be gone. Maybe he'd come back later that night, or maybe he wouldn't come back until the next day or two days later. It scared me.

"Well, anyway, one night, he was layin' next to me, sleepin'. I should've suspected it, because I came up in Harlem, and I knew what was goin' on. I don't know, I guess I was so frightened about this other woman thing that I couldn't see the symptoms. He seemed to be almost losin' his nature. He would . . . you know how if a guy wakes up in the morning, and he's a young guy, he usually has a piss hard-on. But he'd be as soft as a rag all the time. I was wonderin' if it was just that he was gettin' tired of me. Maybe I was making him lose his nature, because he didn't want to be bothered with me any more. I just got so afraid of this . . . and I should've known. I should have known what it was.

"Anyway, he didn't eat. I became more afraid of this thing. I became afraid to ask him, 'What's wrong?' I wanted to say, 'What's wrong, Mel?' But I was scared. I was so afraid he might say, 'Look, I'm tired of you, and I got to get out of this thing.' I thought it was gonna come one day anyway. He was gonna tell me, 'Look, I got another woman, and I got to leave you.' But it was gettin' to be too much for me to keep quiet about, because when he woke up at night and started leavin', I would be awake most of these times. I'd be tellin' myself for a week, 'Look, I'm gonna ask him the next time.'

"But still I was scared; I was scared of losin' him. I'd already lost him in that love thing. He always was quiet, but now he was more quiet than he'd ever been. It seemed as though he didn't want to kiss me. If I played with him in the bed, he'd get mad, that sort of thing.

"One night, he got up, and I asked him. I said, 'Mel, turn on the light, please.' He had been nervous. I hadn't been sleepin' for over a week, because I use to lay awake just wonderin', Is he gonna go out tonight, or maybe he's gonna come back to me? Our sex life had been dwindling away to almost nothin'. I thought, Maybe tonight, maybe tonight he'll play with me. I kept hopin'.

"When he got up to dress, that night I asked him to turn on the light, he was real nervous. He just said, 'Bitch, go on to sleep, and don't bother me!'

"I was kind of hurt, because he'd never said anything like this to me. We were real sweet to each other. This was crazy. I could've never imagined him saying it to me. When he said that, I had to jump up and turn on the light. I had my scream all ready. I told you what I was gonna tell him about the other woman, and all that sort of thing.

"When I opened my mouth, I could taste the tears, and I heard myself talkin' to him in a real soft voice. I was sayin', 'Mel, please tell me where you goin'.'

"He said, 'Look, baby, go on to sleep, and don't worry about me. Try and forget me. Imagine that I never even lived, 'cause I think my life is ruined. I don't want to ruin yours. I'm goin' out tonight, and I'm not comin' back.'

"I said, 'Where're you goin'? Tell me something.'

"He got mad. He'd been gettin' irritable for a long time. He just snapped at me; he said, 'Shit, if you got to know, I'm goin' to my first love.'

"When he told me this, it stunned me. I felt as though I'd been hit in the face by a prizefighter. Everything was quiet. I was stunned, and I think he knew it. It was as though lightning had struck the house, and now all was silent.

"Then I said, 'Mel, I thought I was your first love.'

"He just said, 'No, baby, you're not my first love.' He said, 'Stuff is my first love.'

"I said, 'What do you mean "stuff"?'

"He said, 'You've heard of shit, haven't you, duji, heroin?'

"I wanted to cry. I wanted to cry. But it didn't make sense, because I was already cryin'. I didn't know what to do. I just said, 'Oh, no, no, it couldn't be.' He left."

When Sugar said that bit about "he left," she tried to smile. I felt uncomfortable. Then she said, "It seemed that I stood there in that dark room for hours with the word 'stuff' echoing in my mind. I knew but one thing in life for a whole week. All I knew was that I had to learn about stuff. I had to find out what it was that could make the man I loved love it more than he loved me. Well, Claude, baby, you can see I found out. Yeah . . . I really found out."

Ruby brought in the works; she had a makeshift syringe with a spike on the end of it. She was holding it upside down. I'd given her the five dollars when I first came in. She handed the spike to Sugar, and Sugar paid it no mind. She just rolled down her stocking and pinched her thigh. I saw the needle marks on her thigh.

She looked at me and smiled. She said, "Do you want to hold the flesh for me?"

I said, "Thanks for the offer," and smiled, but I just didn't want to help her get high. I watched as she hit herself with the spike, and I thought about the fact that just a few short years ago, to put my hand on those thighs would have given me more pleasure than anything else I was doing back in those days. I could never have imagined myself saying no to an offer to feel her thighs. Those were the same thighs that had all the needle marks on them.

I watched the syringe as the blood came up into the drugs that seemed like dirty water. It just filled up with blood, and as the blood and the drugs started its way down into the needle, I thought, This is our childhood. Our childhood had been covered with blood, as the drugs had been. Covered with blood and gone down into somewhere. I wondered where.

I wanted to say, "Sugar, I'm sorry. I'm sorry for the time I didn't kiss you at the bus. I'm sorry for not telling people that you were my girl friend. I'm sorry for never telling you that I loved you and for never asking you to be my girl friend." I wanted to say, "I'm sorry for everything. I'm sorry for ever having hesitated to kiss you because of your buckteeth."

Sugar took the spike out, and she patted herself. She started scratching her arm and went into a nod. "That's some nice stuff," she said.

I got up, went over to where Sugar was sitting, bent over, and kissed her. She smiled and went into another nod.

That was the last time I saw her, nodding and climbing up on the duji cloud.

Malcolm X

(1925–1965)

SINCE HIS DEATH IN 1965, Malcolm X has become one of the martyred heroes of the Black Movement. An aura of sanctity surrounds him. He serves as an inspiration for widely disparate groups: black revolutionaries who remember his fiery speeches and blunt denunciation of white racism, and moderates who recall his acceptance of the possibility of a worldwide, multiracial brotherhood.

The Autobiography of Malcolm X was completed with the assistance of Alex Haley soon before Malcolm's death. A revealing book, it shows above all else Alex Haley's skill in capturing the moods, ideas, and personality of Malcolm: Malcolm's initial distrust, the flowering of their friendship, the final horror of his death. In a limited way, Haley has done for Malcolm X what Boswell did for Samuel Johnson.

Malcolm X was born in Omaha, Nebraska, on May 19, 1925. His father, the Reverend Earl Little, was a Baptist minister and Garvey organizer who was perhaps motivated to enter the Garvey Movement by the violent death of three of his brothers at the hands of white men. The Little family moved often—from Omaha to Milwaukee to Lansing, Michigan. In Michigan Reverend Little met a rather suspicious end; it was widely rumored in the black community that his death resulted from his militant racial views.

After his father's death Malcolm's mother found herself unable to keep her family together. Malcolm became a ward of the state; he also became a problem child. After completing the eighth grade, he went to Roxbury, Massachusetts, to stay with an older sister. A series of small jobs followed before he became a pimp, a hustler, and a small-time thief. Sentenced to prison in 1946, he was converted to the Black Muslim religion.

Once out of prison Malcolm rose in the Muslim ranks to become second to Elijah Muhammad. In 1964 a split developed, and Malcolm X formed his own group, the Organization of Afro-American Unity. Soon afterwards, Malcolm X made a trip to Mecca which resulted in his acceptance of the orthodox Muslim religion. He then toured Africa where he stressed the need for black unity on an international basis.

Malcolm X established his center of operation, The Muslim Mosque, Inc., in New York City. On February 21, 1965, he was shot to death while addressing a meeting in the Audubon Ballroom in Harlem.

"Saved" is Chapter XI of *The Autobiography of Malcolm X.*

SAVED

I did write to Elijah Muhammad. He lived in Chicago at that time, at 6116 South Michigan Avenue. At least twenty-five times I must have written that first one-page letter to him, over and over. I was trying to make it both legible and understandable. I practically couldn't read my handwriting myself; it shames even to remember it. My spelling and my grammar were as bad, if not worse. Anyway, as well as I could express it, I said I had been told about him by my brothers and sisters, and I apologized for my poor letter.

Mr. Muhammad sent me a typed reply. It had an all but electrical effect upon me to see the signature of the "Messenger of Allah." After he welcomed me into the "true knowledge," he gave me something to think about. The black prisoner, he said, symbolized white society's crime of keeping black men oppressed and deprived and ignorant, and unable to get decent jobs, turning them into criminals.

He told me to have courage. He even enclosed some money for me, a five-dollar bill. Mr. Muhammad sends money all over the country to prison inmates who write to him, probably to this day.

Regularly my family wrote to me, "Turn to Allah . . . pray to the East."

The hardest test I ever faced in my life was praying. You understand. My comprehending, my believing the teachings of Mr. Muhammad had only required my mind's saying to me, "That's right!" or "I never thought of that."

But bending my knees to pray—that *act*—well, that took me a week.

You know what my life had been. Picking a lock to rob someone's house was the only way my knees had ever been bent before.

I had to force myself to bend my knees. And waves of shame and embarrassment would force me back up.

For evil to bend its knees, admitting its guilt, to implore the forgiveness of God, is the hardest thing in the world. It's easy for me to see and to say that now. But then, when I was the personification of evil, I was going through it. Again, again, I would force myself back down into the praying-to-Allah posture. When finally I was able to make myself stay down—I didn't know what to say to Allah.

For the next years, I was the nearest thing to a hermit in the Norfolk Prison Colony. I never have been more busy in my life. I still marvel at how swiftly my previous life's thinking pattern slid away from me, like snow off a roof. It is as though someone else I knew of had lived by hustling and crime. I would be startled to catch myself thinking in a remote way of my earlier self as another person.

The things I felt, I was pitifully unable to express in the one-page letter that went every day to Mr. Elijah Muhammad. And I wrote at least one more daily letter, replying to one of my brothers and sisters. Every letter I received from them added something to my knowledge of the teachings of Mr. Muhammad. I would sit for long periods and study his photographs.

I've never been one for inaction. Everything I've ever felt strongly about, I've done something about. I guess that's why, unable to do anything else, I soon began writing to people I had known in the hustling world, such as Sammy the Pimp, John Hughes, the gambling house owner, the thief Jumpsteady, and several dope peddlers. I wrote them all about Allah and Islam and Mr. Elijah Muhammad. I had no idea where most of them lived. I addressed their letters in care of the Harlem or Roxbury bars and clubs where I'd known them.

I never got a single reply. The average hustler and criminal was too uneducated to write a letter. I have known many slick, sharp-looking hustlers, who would have you think they had an interest in Wall Street; privately, they would get someone else to read a letter if they received one. Besides, neither would I have replied to anyone writing me something as wild as "the white man is the devil."

What certainly went on the Harlem and Roxbury wires was that Detroit Red was going crazy in stir, or else he was trying some hype to shake up the warden's office.

During the years that I stayed in the Norfolk Prison Colony, never did any official directly say anything to me about those letters, although, of course, they all passed through the prison censorship. I'm sure, however, they monitored what I wrote to add to the files which every state and federal prison keeps on the conversion of Negro inmates by the teachings of Mr. Elijah Muhammad.

But at that time, I felt that the real reason was that the white man knew that he was the devil.

Later on, I even wrote to the Mayor of Boston, to the Governor of Massachusetts, and to Harry S. Truman. They never answered; they probably never even saw my letters. I handscratched to them how the white man's society was responsible for the black man's condition in this wilderness of North America.

It was because of my letters that I happened to stumble upon starting to acquire some kind of a homemade education.

I became increasingly frustrated at not being able to express what I wanted to convey in letters that I wrote, especially those to Mr. Elijah Muhammad. In the street, I had been the most articulate hustler out there—I had commanded attention when I said something. But now, trying to write simple English, I not only wasn't articulate,

I wasn't even functional. How would I sound writing in slang, the way I would *say* it, something such as, "Look, daddy, let me pull your coat about a cat, Elijah Muhammad—"

Many who today hear me somewhere in person, or on television, or those who read something I've said, will think I went to school far beyond the eighth grade. This impression is due entirely to my prison studies.

It had really begun back in the Charlestown Prison, when Bimbi first made me feel envy of his stock of knowledge. Bimbi had always taken charge of any conversations he was in, and I had tried to emulate him. But every book I picked up had few sentences which didn't contain anywhere from one to nearly all of the words that might as well have been in Chinese. When I just skipped those words, of course, I really ended up with little idea of what the book said. So I had come to the Norfolk Prison Colony still going through only book-reading motions. Pretty soon, I would have quit even these motions, unless I had received the motivation that I did.

I saw that the best thing I could do was get hold of a dictionary— to study, to learn some words. I was lucky enough to reason also that I should try to improve my penmanship. It was sad. I couldn't even write in a straight line. It was both ideas together that moved me to request a dictionary along with some tablets and pencils from the Norfolk Prison Colony school.

I spent two days just riffling uncertainly through the dictionary's pages. I'd never realized so many words existed! I didn't know *which* words I needed to learn. Finally, just to start some kind of action, I began copying.

In my slow, painstaking, ragged handwriting, I copied into my tablet everything printed on that first page, down to the punctuation marks.

I believe it took me a day. Then, aloud, I read back, to myself, everything I'd written on the tablet. Over and over, aloud, to myself, I read my own handwriting.

I woke up the next morning, thinking about those words—immensely proud to realize that not only had I written so much at one time, but I'd written words that I never knew were in the world. Moreover, with a little effort, I also could remember what many of these words meant. I reviewed the words whose meanings I didn't remember. Funny thing, from the dictionary first page right now, that "aardvark" springs to my mind. The dictionary had a picture of it, a long-tailed, long-eared, burrowing African mammal, which lives off termites caught by sticking out its tongue as an anteater does for ants.

I was so fascinated that I went on—I copied the dictionary's next page. And the same experience came when I studied that. With every succeeding page, I also learned of people and places and events from history. Actually the dictionary is like a miniature encyclopedia. Finally the dictionary's A section had filled a whole tablet—and I went on into the B's. That was the way I started copying what eventually became the entire dictionary. It went a lot faster after so much practice helped me to pick up handwriting speed. Between what I wrote in my tablet, and writing letters, during the rest of my time in prison I would guess I wrote a million words.

I suppose it was inevitable that as my word-base broadened, I could for the first time pick up a book and read and now begin to understand what the book was saying. Anyone who has read a great deal can imagine the new world that opened. Let me tell you something: from then until I left that prison, in every free moment I had, if I was not reading in the library, I was reading on my bunk. You couldn't have gotten me out of books with a wedge. Between Mr. Muhammad's teachings, my correspondence, my visitors—usually Ella and Reginald—and my reading of books, months passed without my even thinking about being imprisoned. In fact, up to then, I never had been so truly free in my life.

The Norfolk Prison Colony's library was in the school building. A variety of classes was taught there by instructors who came from such places as Harvard and Boston universities. The weekly debates between inmate teams were also held in the school building. You would be astonished to know how worked up convict debaters and audiences would get over subjects like "Should Babies Be Fed Milk?"

Available on the prison library's shelves were books on just about every general subject. Much of the big private collection that Parkhurst had willed to the prison was still in crates and boxes in the back of the library—thousands of old books. Some of them looked ancient: covers faded, old-time parchment-looking binding. Parkhurst, I've mentioned, seemed to have been principally interested in history and religion. He had the money and the special interest to have a lot of books that you wouldn't have in general circulation. Any college library would have been lucky to get that collection.

As you can imagine, especially in a prison where there was heavy emphasis on rehabilitation, an inmate was smiled upon if he demonstrated an unusually intense interest in books. There was a sizable number of well-read inmates, especially the popular debaters. Some were said by many to be practically walking encyclopedias. They were almost celebrities. No university would ask any student to devour literature as I did when this new world opened to me, of being able to read and *understand.*

I read more in my room than in the library itself. An inmate who was known to read a lot could check out more than the permitted maximum number of books. I preferred reading in the total isolation of my own room.

When I had progressed to really serious reading, every night at about ten P.M. I would be outraged with the "lights out." It always seemed to catch me right in the middle of something engrossing.

Fortunately, right outside my door was a corridor light that cast a glow into my room. The glow was enough to read by, once my eyes adjusted to it. So when "lights out" came, I would sit on the floor where I could continue reading in that glow.

At one-hour intervals the night guards paced past every room. Each time I heard the approaching footsteps, I jumped into bed and feigned sleep. And as soon as the guard passed, I got back out of bed onto the floor area of that light-glow, where I would read for another fifty-eight minutes—until the guard approached again. That went on until three or four every morning. Three or four hours of sleep a night was enough for me. Often in the years in the streets I had slept less than that.

The teachings of Mr. Muhammad stressed how history had been "whitened"—when white men had written history books, the black man simply had been left out. Mr. Muhammad couldn't have said anything that would have struck me much harder. I had never forgotten how when my class, me and all of those whites, had studied seventh-grade United States history back in Mason, the history of the Negro had been covered in one paragraph, and the teacher had gotten a big laugh with his joke, "Negroes' feet are so big that when they walk, they leave a hole in the ground."

This is one reason why Mr. Muhammad's teachings spread so swiftly all over the United States, among *all* Negroes, whether or not they became followers of Mr. Muhammad. The teachings ring true—to every Negro. You can hardly show me a black adult in America—or a white one, for that matter—who knows from the history books anything like the truth about the black man's role. In my own case, once I heard of the "glorious history of the black man," I took special pains to hunt in the library for books that would inform me on details about black history.

I can remember accurately the very first set of books that really impressed me. I have since bought that set of books and I have it at home for my children to read as they grow up. It's called *Wonders of the World*. It's full of pictures of archeological finds, statues that depict, usually, non-European people.

I found books like Will Durant's *Story of Civilization*. I read H. G. Wells' *Outline of History*. *Souls Of Black Folk* by W. E. B. Du Bois gave me a glimpse into the black people's history before they came to this country. Carter G. Woodson's *Negro History* opened my eyes about black empires before the black slave was brought to the United States, and the early Negro struggles for freedom.

J. A. Rogers' three volumes of *Sex and Race* told about race-mixing before Christ's time; about Aesop being a black man who told fables; about Egypt's Pharaohs; about the great Coptic Christian Empires; about Ethiopia, the earth's oldest continuous black civilization, as China is the oldest continuous civilization.

Mr. Muhammad's teaching about how the white man had been created led me to *Findings In Genetics* by Gregor Mendel. (The dictionary's G section was where I had learned what "genetics" meant.) I really studied this book by the Austrian monk. Reading it over and over, especially certain sections, helped me to understand that if you started with a black man, a white man could be produced; but starting with a white man, you never could produce a black man—because the white chromosome is recessive. And since no one disputes that there was but one Original Man, the conclusion is clear.

During the last year or so, in the *New York Times*, Arnold Toynbee used the word "bleached" in describing the white man. (His words were: "White (i.e. bleached) human beings of North European origin. . . ." Toynbee also referred to the European geographic area as only a peninsula of Asia. He said there is no such thing as Europe. And if you look at the globe, you will see for yourself that America is only an extension of Asia. (But at the same time Toynbee is among those who have helped to bleach history. He has written that Africa was the only continent that produced no history. He won't write that again. Every day now, the truth is coming to light.)

I never will forget how shocked I was when I began reading about slavery's total horror. It made such an impact upon me that it later became one of my favorite subjects when I became a minister of Mr. Muhammad's. The world's most monstrous crime, the sin and the blood on the white man's hands, are almost impossible to believe. Books like the one by Frederick Olmstead opened my eyes to the horrors suffered when the slave was landed in the United States. The European woman, Fannie Kimball, who had married a Southern white slaveowner, described how human beings were degraded. Of course I read *Uncle Tom's Cabin*. In fact, I believe that's the only novel I have ever read since I started serious reading.

Parkhurst's collection also contained some bound pamphlets of the Abolitionist Anti-Slavery Society of New England. I read descriptions of atrocities, saw those illustrations of black slave women tied up and flogged with whips; of black mothers watching their babies being dragged off, never to be seen by their mothers again; of dogs after slaves, and of the fugitive slave catchers, evil white men with whips and clubs and chains and guns. I read about the slave preacher Nat Turner, who put the fear of God into the white slavemaster. Nat Turner wasn't going around preaching pie-in-the-sky and "non-violent" freedom for the black man. There in Virginia one night in 1831, Nat and seven other slaves started out at his master's home and through the night they went from one plantation "big house" to the next, killing, until by the next morning 57 white people were dead and Nat had about 70 slaves following him. White people, terrified for their lives, fled from their homes, locked themselves up in public buildings, hid in the woods, and some even left the state. A small army of soldiers took two months to catch and hang Nat Turner. Somewhere I have read where Nat Turner's example is said to have inspired John Brown to invade Virginia and attack Harper's Ferry nearly thirty years later, with thirteen white men and five Negroes.

I read Herodotus, "the father of History," or, rather, I read about him. And I read the histories of various nations, which opened my eyes gradually, then wider and wider, to how the whole world's white men had indeed acted like devils, pillaging and raping and bleeding and draining the whole world's non-white people. I remember, for instance, books such as Will Durant's *The Story of Oriental Civilization,* and Mahatma Gandhi's accounts of the struggle to drive the British out of India.

Book after book showed me how the white man had brought upon the world's black, brown, red, and yellow peoples every variety of the sufferings of exploitation. I saw how since the sixteenth century, the so-called "Christian trader" white man began to ply the seas in his lust for Asian and African empires, and plunder, and power. I read, I saw, how the white man never has gone among the non-white peoples bearing the Cross in the true manner and spirit of Christ's teachings—meek, humble, and Christ-like.

I perceived, as I read, how the collective white man had been actually nothing but a piratical opportunist who used Faustian machinations to make his own Christianity his initial wedge in criminal conquests. First, always "religiously," he branded "heathen" and "pagan" labels upon ancient non-white cultures and civilizations. The stage thus set, he then turned upon his non-white victims his weapons of war.

I read how, entering India—half a *billion* deeply religious brown people—the British white man, by 1759, through promises, trickery and manipulations, controlled much of India through Great Britain's East India Company. The parasitical British administration kept tentacling out to half of the sub-continent. In 1857, some of the desperate people of India finally mutinied—and, excepting the African slave trade, nowhere has history recorded any more unnecessary bestial and ruthless human carnage than the British suppression of the non-white Indian people.

Over 115 million African blacks—close to the 1930's population of the United States—were murdered or enslaved during the slave trade. And I read how when the slave market was glutted, the cannibalistic white powers of Europe next carved up, as their colonies, the richest areas of the black continent. And Europe's chancelleries for the next century played a chess game of naked exploitation and power from Cape Horn to Cairo.

Ten guards and the warden couldn't have torn me out of those books. Not even Elijah Muhammad could have been more eloquent than those books were in providing indisputable proof that the collective white man had acted like a devil in virtually every contact he had with the world's collective non-white man. I listen today to the radio, and watch television, and read the headlines about the collective white man's fear and tension concerning China. When the white man professes ignorance about why the Chinese hate him so, my mind can't help flashing back to what I read, there in prison, about how the blood forebears of this same white man raped China at a time when China was trusting and helpless. Those original white "Christian traders" sent into China millions of pounds of opium. By 1839, so many of the Chinese were addicts that China's desperate government destroyed twenty thousand chests of opium. The first Opium War was promptly declared by the white man. Imagine! Declaring *war* upon someone who objects to being narcotized! The Chinese were severely beaten, with Chinese-invented gunpowder.

The Treaty of Nanking made China pay the British white man for the destroyed opium: forced open China's major ports to British trade; forced China to abandon Hong Kong; fixed China's import tariffs so low that cheap British articles soon flooded in, maiming China's industrial development.

After a second Opium War, the Tientsin Treaties legalized the ravaging opium trade, legalized a British-French-American control of China's customs. China tried delaying that Treaty's ratification; Peking was looted and burned.

"Kill the foreign white devils!" was the 1901 Chinese war cry in the Boxer Rebellion. Losing again, this time the Chinese were driven from Peking's choicest areas. The vicious, arrogant white man put up the famous signs, "Chinese and dogs not allowed."

Red China after World War II closed its doors to the Western white world. Massive Chinese agricultural, scientific, and industrial efforts are described in a book that *Life* magazine recently published. Some observers inside Red China have reported that the world never has known such a hate-white campaign as is now going on in this non-white country where, present birth-rates continuing, in fifty more years Chinese will be half the earth's population. And it seems that some Chinese chickens will soon come home to roost, with China's recent successful nuclear tests.

Let us face reality. We can see in the United Nations a new world order being shaped, along color lines—an alliance among the non-white nations. America's U.N. Ambassador Adlai Stevenson complained not long ago that in the United Nations "a skin game" was being played. He was right. He was facing reality. A "skin game" *is* being played. But Ambassador Stevenson sounded like Jesse James accusing the marshal of carrying a gun. Because who in the world's history ever has played a worse "skin game" than the white man?

Mr. Muhammad, to whom I was writing daily, had no idea of what a new world had opened up to me through my efforts to document his teachings in books.

When I discovered philosophy, I tried to touch all the landmarks of philosophical development. Gradually, I read most of the old philosophers, Occidental and Oriental. The Oriental philosophers were the ones I came to prefer; finally, my impression was that most Occidental philosophy had largely been borrowed from the Oriental thinkers. Socrates, for instance, traveled in Egypt. Some sources even say that Socrates was initiated into some of the Egyptian mysteries. Obviously Socrates got some of his wisdom among the East's wise men.

I have often reflected upon the new vistas that reading opened to me. I knew right there in prison that reading had changed forever the course of my life. As I see it today, the ability to read awoke inside me some long dormant craving to be mentally alive. I certainly wasn't seeking any degree, the way a college confers a status symbol upon its students. My homemade education gave me, with every additional book that I read, a little bit more sensitivity to the deafness, dumbness, and blindness that was afflicting the black race in America. Not long ago, an English writer telephoned me from London, asking questions. One was, "What's your alma mater?" I told him, "Books." You will never catch me with a free fifteen minutes in which I'm not studying something I feel might be able to help the black man.

Yesterday I spoke in London, and both ways on the plane across the Atlantic I was studying a document about how the United Nations proposes to insure the human rights of the oppressed minorities of the world. The American black man is the world's most shameful case of minority oppression. What makes the black man think of himself as only an internal United States issue is just a catch-phrase, two words, "civil rights." How is the black man going to get "civil rights" before first he wins his *human* rights? If the American black man will start thinking about his *human* rights, and then start thinking of himself as part of one of the world's great peoples, he will see he has a case for the United Nations.

I can't think of a better case! Four hundred years of black blood and sweat invested here in America, and the white man still has the black man begging for what every immigrant fresh off the ship can take for granted the minute he walks down the gangplank.

But I'm digressing. I told the Englishman that my alma mater was books, a good library. Every time I catch a plane, I have with me a book that I want to read—and that's a lot of books these days. If I weren't out here every day battling the white man, I could spend the rest of my life reading, just satisfying my curiosity—because you can hardly mention anything I'm not curious about. I don't think anybody ever got more out of going to prison than I did. In fact, prison enabled me to study far more intensively than I would have if my life had gone differently and I had attended some college. I imagine that one of the biggest troubles with colleges is there are too many distractions, too much panty-raiding, fraternities, and boola-boola and all of that. Where else but in a prison could I have attacked my ignorance by being able to study intensely sometimes as much as fifteen hours a day?

Schopenhauer, Kant, Nietzsche, naturally, I read all of those. I don't respect them; I am just trying to remember some of those whose theories I soaked up in those years. These three, it's said, laid the groundwork on which the Fascist and Nazi philosophy was built. I don't respect them because it seems to me that most of their time was spent arguing about things that are not really important. They remind me of so many of the Negro "intellectuals," so-called, with whom I have come in contact—they are always arguing about something useless.

Spinoza impressed me for a while when I found out that he was black. A black Spanish Jew. The Jews excommunicated him because he advocated a pantheistic doctrine, something like the "allness of God," or "God in everything." The Jews read their burial services for Spinoza, meaning that he was dead as far as they were concerned; his family was run out of Spain, they ended up in Holland, I think.

I'll tell you something. The whole stream of Western philosophy has now wound up in a cul-de-sac. The white man has perpetrated upon himself, as well as upon the black man, so gigantic a fraud that he has put himself into a crack. He did it through his elaborate, neurotic necessity to hide the black man's true role in history.

And today the white man is faced head on with what is happening on the Black Continent, Africa. Look at the artifacts being discovered there, that are proving over and over again, how the black man had great, fine, sensitive civilizations before the white man was out of the caves. Below the Sahara, in the places where most of America's Negroes' foreparents were kidnapped, there is being unearthed some of the finest craftsmanship, sculpture and other objects, that has ever been seen by modern man. Some of these things now are on view in such places as New York City's Museum of Modern Art. Gold work of such fine tolerance and workmanship that it has no rival. Ancient objects produced by black hands . . . refined by those black hands with results that no human hand today can equal.

History has been so "whitened" by the white man that even the black professors have known little more than the most ignorant black man about the talents and rich civilizations and cultures of the black man of millenniums ago. I have lectured in Negro colleges and some of these brainwashed black Ph.D.'s, with their suspenders dragging the ground with degrees, have run to the white man's newspapers calling me a "black fanatic." Why, a lot of them are fifty years behind the times. If I were president of one of these black colleges, I'd hock the campus if I had to, to send a bunch of black students off digging in Africa for more, more and more proof of the black race's historical greatness. The white man now is in Africa digging and searching. An African elephant can't stumble without falling on some white man with a shovel. Practically every week, we read about some great new find from Africa's lost civilizations. All that's new is white science's attitude. The ancient civilizations of the black man have been buried on the Black Continent all the time.

Here is an example: a British anthropologist named Dr. Louis S. B. Leakey is displaying some fossil bones—a foot, part of a hand, some jaws, and skull fragments. On the basis of these, Dr. Leakey has said it's time to rewrite completely the history of man's origin.

This species of man lived 1,818,036 years before Christ. And these bones were found in Tanganyika. In the Black Continent.

It's a crime, the lie that has been told to generations of black men and white men both. Little innocent black children, born of parents who believed that their race had no history. Little black children seeing, before they could talk, that their parents considered themselves inferior. Innocent black children growing up, living out their lives, dying of old age—and all of their lives ashamed of being black. But the truth is pouring out of the bag now.

Two other areas of experience which have been extremely formative in my life since prison were first opened to me in the Norfolk Prison Colony. For one thing, I had my first experiences in opening the eyes of my brainwashed black brethren to some truths about the black race. And, the other: when I had read enough to know something, I began to enter the Prison Colony's weekly debating program—my baptism into public speaking.

I have to admit a sad, shameful fact. I had so loved being around the white man that in prison I really disliked how Negro convicts stuck together so much. But when Mr. Muhammad's teachings reversed my attitude toward my black brothers, in my guilt and shame I began to catch every chance I could to recruit for Mr. Muhammad.

You have to be careful, very careful, introducing the truth to the black man who has never previously heard the truth about himself, his own kind, and the white man. My brother Reginald had told me that all Muslims experienced this in their recruiting for Mr. Muhammad. The black brother is so brainwashed that he may even be repelled when he first hears the truth. Reginald advised that the truth had to be dropped only a little bit at a time. And you had to wait a while to let it sink in before advancing the next step.

I began first telling my black brother inmates about the glorious history of the black man—things they never had dreamed. I told them the horrible slavery-trade truths that they never knew. I would watch their faces when I told them about that, because the white man had completely erased the slaves' past, a Negro in America can never know his true family name, or even what tribe he was descended from: the Mandingos, the Wolof, the Serer, the Fula, the Fanti, the Ashanti, or others. I told them that some slaves brought from Africa spoke Arabic, and were Islamic in their religion. A lot of these black convicts still wouldn't believe it unless they could see that a white man had said it. So, often, I would read to these brothers selected passages from white men's books. I'd explain to them that the real truth was known to some white men, the scholars; but there had been a conspiracy down through the generations to keep the truth from black men.

I would keep close watch on how each one reacted. I always had to be careful. I never knew when some brainwashed black imp, some dyed-in-the-wool Uncle Tom, would nod at me and then go running to tell the white man. When one was ripe—and I could tell—then away from the rest, I'd drop it on him, what Mr. Muhammed taught: "The white man is the devil."

That would shock many of them—until they started thinking about it.

This is probably as big a single worry as the America prison system has today—the way the Muslim teachings, circulated among all Negroes in the country, are converting new Muslims among black men in prison, and black men are in prison in far greater numbers than their proportion in the population.

The reason is that among all Negroes the black convict is the most perfectly preconditioned to hear the words, "the white man is the devil."

You tell that to any Negro. Except for those relatively few "integration"-mad so-called "intellectuals," and those black men who are otherwise fat, happy, and deaf, dumb, and blinded, with their crumbs from the white man's rich table, you have struck a nerve center in the

American black man. He may take a day to react, a month, a year; he may never respond, openly; but of one thing you can be sure—when he thinks about his own life, he is going to see where, to him, personally, the white man sure has acted like a devil.

And, as I say, above all Negroes, the black prisoner. Here is a black man caged behind bars, probably for years, put there by the white man. Usually the convict comes from among those bottom-of-the-pile Negroes, the Negroes who through their entire lives have been kicked about, treated like children—Negroes who never have met one white man who didn't either take something from them or do something to them.

You let this caged-up black man start thinking, the same way I did when I first heard Elijah Muhammad's teachings: let him start thinking how, with better breaks when he was young and ambitious he might have been a lawyer, a doctor, a scientist, anything. You let this caged-up black man start realizing as I did, how from the first landing of the first slave ship, the millions of black men in America have been like sheep in a den of wolves. That's why black prisoners become Muslims so fast when Elijah Muhammad's teachings filter into their cages by way of other Muslim convicts. "The white man is the devil" is a perfect echo of that black convict's lifelong experience.

I've told how debating was a weekly event there at the Norfolk Prison Colony. My reading had my mind like steam under pressure. Some way, I had to start telling the white man about himself to his face. I decided I could do this by putting my name down to debate.

Standing up and speaking before an audience was a thing that throughout my previous life never would have crossed my mind. Out there in the streets, hustling, pushing dope, and robbing, I could have had the dreams from a pound of hashish and I'd never have dreamed anything so wild as that one day I would speak in coliseums and arenas, at the greatest American universities, and on radio and television programs, not to mention speaking all over Egypt and Africa and in England.

But I will tell you that, right there, in the prison, debating, speaking to a crowd, was as exhilarating to me as the discovery of knowledge through reading had been. Standing up there, the faces looking up at me, the things in my head coming out of my mouth, while my brain searched for the next best thing to follow what I was saying, and if I could sway them to my side by handling it right, then I had won the debate—once my feet got wet, I was gone on debating. Whichever side of the selected subject was assigned to me, I'd track down and study everything I could find on it. I'd put myself in my opponent's place and decide how I'd try to win if I had the other side; and then I'd figure a way to knock down those points. And if there was any way in the world, I'd work into my speech the devilishness of the white man.

"Compulsory Military Training—Or None?" That's one good chance I got unexpectedly, I remember. My opponent flailed the air about the Ethiopians throwing rocks and spears at Italian airplanes, "proving" that compulsory military training was needed. I said the Ethiopians' black flesh had been splattered against trees by bombs the Pope in Rome had blessed, and the Ethiopians would have thrown even their bare bodies at the airplanes because they had seen that they were fighting the devil incarnate.

They yelled "foul," that I'd made the subject a race issue. I said it wasn't race, it was a historical fact, that they ought to go and read Pierre van Paassen's *Days of Our Years,* and something not surprising to me, that book, right after the debate, disappeared from the prison library. It was right there in prison that I made up my mind to devote the rest of my life to telling the white man about himself—or die. In a debate about whether or not Homer had ever existed, I threw into those white faces the theory that Homer only symbolized how white Europeans kidnapped black Africans, then blinded them so that they could never get back to their own people. (Homer and Omar and *Moor,* you see, are related terms; it's like saying Peter, Pedro and *petra,* all three of which mean rock.) These blinded Moors the Europeans taught to sing about the Europeans' glorious accomplishments. I made it clear that was the devilish white man's idea of kicks. Aesop's *Fables* —another case in point. "Aesop" was only the Greek name for an Ethiopian.

Another hot debate I remember I was in had to do with the identity of Shakespeare. No color was involved there; I just got intrigued over the Shakespearean dilemma. The King James translation of the Bible is considered the greatest piece of literature in English. Its language supposedly represents the ultimate in using the King's English. Well, Shakespeare's language and the Bible's language are one and the same. They say that from 1604 to 1611, King James got poets to translate, to write the Bible. Well, if Shakespeare existed, he was then the top poet around. But Shakespeare is nowhere reported connected with the Bible. If he existed, why didn't King James use him? And if he did use him, why is it one of the world's best kept secrets?

I know that many say that Francis Bacon was Shakespeare. If that is true, why would Bacon have kept it secret? Bacon wasn't royalty, when royalty sometimes used the *nom de plume* because it was "improper" for royalty to be artistic or theatrical. What would Bacon have had to lose? Bacon, in fact, would have had everything to gain.

In the prison debates I argued for the theory that King James himself was the real poet who used the *nom de plume* Shakespeare. King James was brilliant. He was the greatest king who ever sat on the British throne. Who else among royalty, in his time, would have had the giant talent to write Shakespeare's works? It was he who poetically "fixed"

the Bible—which in itself and its present King James version has enslaved the world.

When my brother Reginald visited, I would talk to him about new
evidence I found to document the Muslim teachings. In either volume
43 or 44 of The Harvard Classics, I read Milton's *Paradise Lost*. The
devil, kicked out of Paradise, was trying to regain possession. He was
using the forces of Europe, personified by the Popes, Charlemagne,
Richard the Lionhearted, and other knights. I interpreted this to show
that the Europeans were motivated and led by the devil, or the personification of the devil. So Milton and Mr. Elijah Mohammad were actually saying the same thing.

I couldn't believe it when Reginald began to speak ill of Elijah Muhammad. I can't specify the exact things he said. They were more in
the nature of implications against Mr. Muhammad—the pitch of Reginald's voice, or the way that Reginald looked, rather than what he
said.

It caught me totally unprepared. It threw me into a state of confusion. My blood brother, Reginald, in whom I had so much confidence, for whom I had so much respect, the one who had introduced
me to the Nation of Islam. I couldn't believe it! And now Islam meant
more to me than anything I ever had known in my life. Islam and Mr.
Elijah Muhammad had changed my whole world.

Reginald, I learned, had been suspended from the Nation of Islam
by Elijah Muhammad. He had not practiced moral restraint. After he
had learned the truth, and had accepted the truth, and the Muslim
laws, Reginald was still carrying on improper relations with the then
secretary of the New York Temple. Some other Muslim who learned
of it had made charges against Reginald to Mr. Muhammad in Chicago, and Mr. Muhammad had suspended Reginald.

When Reginald left, I was in torment. That night, finally, I wrote to
Mr. Muhammad, trying to defend my brother, appealing for him. I told
him what Reginald was to me, what my brother meant to me.

I put the letter into the box for the prison censor. Then all the rest
of that night, I prayed to Allah. I don't think anyone ever prayed more
sincerely to Allah. I prayed for some kind of relief from my confusion.

It was the next night, as I lay on my bed, I suddenly, with a start,
became aware of a man sitting beside me in my chair. He had on a
dark suit, I remember. I could see him as plainly as I see anyone I look
at. He wasn't black, and he wasn't white. He was light-brown-skinned,
an Asiatic cast of countenance, and he had oily black hair.

I looked right into his face.

I didn't get frightened. I knew I wasn't dreaming. I couldn't move,
I didn't speak, and he didn't. I couldn't place him racially—other than
that I knew he was a non-European. I had no idea whatsoever who

he was. He just sat there. Then, suddenly as he had come, he was gone.

Soon, Mr. Muhammad sent me a reply about Reginald. He wrote, "If you once believed in the truth, and now you are beginning to doubt the truth, you didn't believe the truth in the first place. What could make you doubt the truth other than your own weak self?"

That struck me. Reginald was not leading the disciplined life of a Muslim. And I knew that Elijah Muhammad was right, and my blood brother was wrong. Because right is right, and wrong is wrong. Little did I then realize the day would come when Elijah Muhammad would be accused by his own sons as being guilty of the same acts of immorality that he judged Reginald and so many others for.

But at that time, all of the doubt and confusion in my mind was removed. All of the influence that my brother had wielded over me was broken. From that day on, as far as I am concerned, everything that my brother Reginald has done is wrong.

But Reginald kept visiting me. When he had been a Muslim, he had been immaculate in his attire. But now, he wore things like a T-shirt, shabby-looking trousers, and sneakers. I could see him on the way down. When he spoke, I heard him coldly. But I would listen. He was my blood brother.

Gradually, I saw the chastisement of Allah—what Christians would call "the curse"—come upon Reginald. Elijah Muhammad said that Allah was chastising Reginald—and that anyone who challenged Elijah Muhammad would be chastened by Allah. In Islam we were taught that as long as one didn't know the truth, he lived in darkness. But once the truth was accepted, and recognized, he lived in light, and whoever would then go against it would be punished by Allah.

Mr. Muhammad taught that the five-pointed star stands for justice, and also for the five senses of man. We were taught that Allah executes justice by working upon the five senses of those who rebel against His Messenger, or against His truth. We were taught that this was Allah's way of letting Muslims know His sufficiency to defend His Messenger against any and all opposition, as long as the Messenger himself didn't deviate from the path of truth. We were taught that Allah turned the minds of any defectors into a turmoil. I thought truly that it was Allah doing this to my brother.

One letter, I think from my brother Philbert, told me that Reginald was with them in Detroit. I heard no more about Reginald until one day, weeks later, Ella visited me; she told me that Reginald was at her home in Roxbury, sleeping. Ella said she had heard a knock, she had gone to the door, and there was Reginald, looking terrible. Ella said she had asked, "Where did you come from?" And Reginald had told her he came from Detroit. She said she asked him, "How did you get here?" And he had told her, "I walked."

I believed he *had* walked. I believed in Elijah Muhammad, and he had convinced us that Allah's chastisement upon Reginald's mind had taken away Reginald's ability to gauge distance and time. There is a dimension of time with which we are not familiar here in the West. Elijah Muhammad said that under Allah's chastisement, the five senses of a man can be so deranged by those whose mental powers are greater than his that in five minutes his hair can turn snow white. Or he will walk nine hundred miles as he might walk five blocks.

In prison, since I had become a Muslim, I had grown a beard. When Reginald visited me, he nervously moved about in his chair; he told me that each hair of my beard was a snake. Everywhere, he saw snakes.

He next began to believe that he was the "Messenger of Allah." Reginald went around in the streets of Roxbury, Ella reported to me, telling people that he had some divine power. He graduated from this to saying that he was Allah.

He finally began saying he was *greater* than Allah.

Authorities picked up Reginald, and he was put into an institution. They couldn't find what was wrong. They had no way to understand Allah's chastisement. Reginald was released. Then he was picked up again, and was put into another institution.

Reginald is in an institution now. I know where, but I won't say. I would not want to cause him any more trouble than he has already had.

I believe, today, that it was written, it was meant, for Reginald to be used for one purpose only: as a bait, as a minnow to reach into that ocean of blackness where I was, to save me.

I cannot understand it any other way.

After Elijah Muhammad himself was later accused as a very immoral man, I came to believe that it wasn't a divine chastisement upon Reginald, but the pain he felt when his own family totally rejected him for Elijah Muhammad, and this hurt made Reginald turn insanely upon Elijah Muhammad.

It's impossible to dream, or to see, or to have a vision of someone whom you never have seen before—and to see him exactly as he is. To see someone, and to see him exactly as he looks, is to have a pre-vision.

I would later come to believe that my pre-vision was of Master W. D. Fard, the Messiah, the one whom Elijah Muhammad said had appointed him—Elijah Muhammad—as His Last Messenger to the black people of North America.

My last year in prison was spent back in the Charlestown Prison. Even among the white inmates, the word had filtered around. Some of those brainwashed black convicts talked too much. And I know that the censors had reported on my mail. The Norfolk Prison Colony officials had become upset. They used as a reason for my transfer that I refused to take some kind of shots, an inoculation or something.

The only thing that worried me was that I hadn't much time left before I would be eligible for parole-board consideration. But I reasoned that they might look at my representing and spreading Islam in another way: instead of keeping me in they might want to get me out.

I had come to prison with 20/20 vision. But when I got sent back to Charlestown, I had read so much by the lights-out glow in my room at the Norfolk Prison Colony that I had astigmatism and the first pair of the eyeglasses that I have worn ever since.

I had less maneuverability back in the much stricter Charlestown Prison. But I found that a lot of Negroes attended a Bible class, and I went there.

Conducting the class was a tall, blond, blue-eyed (a perfect "devil") Harvard Seminary student. He lectured, and then he starred in a question-and-answer session. I don't know which of us had read the Bible more, he or I, but I had to give him credit; he really was heavy on his religion. I puzzled and puzzled for a way to upset him, and to give those Negroes present something to think and talk about and circulate.

Finally, I put up my hand; he nodded. He had talked about Paul.

I stood up and asked, "What color was Paul?" And I kept talking, with pauses, "He had to be black . . . because he was a Hebrew . . . and the original Hebrews were black . . . weren't they?"

He had started flushing red. You know the way white people do. He said "Yes."

I wasn't through yet. "What color was Jesus . . . he was Hebrew, too . . . wasn't he?"

Both the Negro and the white convicts had sat bolt upright. I don't care how tough the convict, be he brainwashed black Christian, or a "devil" white Christian, neither of them is ready to hear anybody saying Jesus wasn't white. The instructor walked around. He shouldn't have felt bad. In all of the years since, I never have met any intelligent white man who would try to insist that Jesus was white. How could they? He said, "Jesus was brown."

I let him get away with that compromise.

Exactly as I had known it would, almost overnight the Charlestown convicts, black and white, began buzzing with the story. Wherever I went, I could feel the nodding. And anytime I got a chance to exchange words with a black brother in stripes, I'd say, "My man! You ever heard about somebody named Mr. Elijah Muhammad?"

Faith Berry

(b. 1939)

FAITH BERRY WAS BORN in Cincinnati, Ohio, where her father, a lawyer, once served as vice-mayor. She was educated at Fisk University and in Europe before receiving her degree at Columbia University. After a stint with the *New Yorker*, Miss Berry took up residence in Paris and began writing essays on American Negro life, book reviews, and occasional "reportage" pieces for *Les Temps Modernes, Jeune Afrique,* and *Pariscope*. Returning to the States in 1967, she has published her work in *The Nation,* the *New York Times Magazine,* and the *Washingtonian,* and she has collaborated on articles and research and done translation. Miss Berry has also contributed to *Negro Digest,* most notably to its symposium on Richard Wright.

The piece reprinted here is representative of Faith Berry's involvement as a young black woman and of her strong, direct, declarative style.

BLACK TO BLACK: A LETTER TO AFRICA

July 4, 1969

Dear Brother:

I don't know if this will reach you soon. I'm writing you at the last address you gave some weeks back, and where you are in Africa I do not know. Today, which happens to be July 4, I'm going to answer your questions about what's happening with the Black Panthers as explicitly as I can.

Are the Black Panthers really real, you ask. Can they really have happened here? But consider. Could some of what you know has happened here really have happened? Slavery? The systematic extermination of the aborigines? A fraticidal war between freedom-loving Christians? These happened. And the Black Panthers are happening— a "natural" effluence of our history. Call them our Mau-Maus. Innumerable documented slave revolts notwithstanding, the Panthers represent the first organized effort on the part of black Americans to defend themselves against a system that refuses to change. They are not anarchists, though this is what they've been called; nor are they "revolutionaries," which (I read somewhere—could it have been in

Reprinted by permission of the author.

Reader's Digest!—the other day) "in the context of America's proud history" is a term of "grateful praise, like 'heroes'." George Washington, Thomas Jefferson, and Patrick Henry were revolutionaries and heroes; and so were, I suppose—if one considers them at all—Crispus Attucks, Salem Poor, and Dorie Miller. The thing about being a revolutionary and a hero in the American context, if you're black, is to fight and die for what the white man wants. And that's not what the Black Panthers aim to do. So they're "anarchists" and "militants," and both are bad words here.

I must tell you that when I first heard of the Panthers I thought they were a joke. The name itself turned me off, and I couldn't get hooked on their leader, Huey Newton, either. In every picture I saw, that cat was posing rifle in one hand, a spear in the other, and a zebra rug under his feet, looking more like an ad for a safari than like a defender of ghetto blacks. I kept thinking that revolutionaries don't pose or let themselves be posed. At the time, I couldn't take Huey Newton any more seriously than you'd take Captain Kangaroo. But then I started hearing things and reading things and witnessing things. And Huey Newton was transfigured, transformed. He became a kind of Che Guevara, and not unlike Guevara in a ravine in Bolivia—and for some of the same reasons—Newton was ambushed in a street in Oakland, California. He got four bullets in his abdomen and one in his thigh, but he lived. He was charged with murdering a policeman, but the facts were so insistently in opposition to the charge that even the anti-Negro press complained. The charge was reduced to manslaughter, and Newton is now serving two to fifteen years because he defended himself against a man who, unlawfully and without warrant, was trying to kill him.

In a recent press interview in San Francisco, a Panther said he had attended twenty funerals of Black Panthers over the past year, and that these men had been killed by police on the flimsiest pretext or on no pretext whatever.

As a political party—for that is what it is, despite its para-military trappings—the Black Panthers recently issued a ten point program and "Eight Points of Attention." Except for one of the ten points, the program sets forth what you'd expect of a political program, but point 5 is different: "We want," it says, "an education for our people that teaches us [Blacks] our true history and our role in present day society." But the "Eight Points" are worth repeating because, though they seem to contradict the general reputation the Panthers have been given, they expose them to the charge of being "Communists of the Maoist persuasion." And that charge here is deadly. The charge is based on the fact that the eight points are paraphrased from "the little red book" of Mao Tse-Tung. "Speak politely." "Pay fairly for what you buy." "Return everything you borrow." "Pay for anything you damage."

"Do not hit or swear at people." "Do not damage crops of the poor oppressed masses." "Do not take liberties with women." "If we have to take captives do not treat them ill."

I do not have to tell you that rhetoric such as this postulates power. And one of the things that the Panthers are about *is* power—black power. They have rejected the Republican-encouraged concept of black capitalism as a component of the power they seek, for they are sensitive to the probability that black capitalism would be more benevolent to black people than white capitalism has been to whites. What the Panthers say about capitalism is that in its present form it is racist and imperialistic, and that in its present form it must go. And what in effect they say about black power is that it can only be established in an alliance with the powerless of whatever skin color. Black separatism, no! The Panthers have formalized an alliance with certain white radicals, a radical organization of whites—Students for a Democratic Society. It was this move that led Stokely Carmichael, the loudest voice of Separatism (for whom I've always managed to curb my enthusiasm), to break with the BPP. You must have heard over there in Africa that Carmichael sent his African wife all the way to the States to deliver a letter of resignation, which said in part, "the alliances now being formed by the Party are alliances which I cannot politically agree with because the history of Africans living in the United States has shown that any . . . . alliance with white radicals has led to the complete subversion of the blacks by the whites through their direct control of the black organization."

It is true, of course, that whites have found it difficult to let us blacks lead ourselves and our organizations, but I think Carmichael is wrong in the instance of the BPP-SDS alliance. The Black Panthers need the SDS less than the SDS needs them, and, besides, I believe that the SDS people are John Brown-white radicals, not Abraham Lincoln-white-paternalists. However, I must declare to you that there are more people, black and white, who are against the alliance—any alliance between the races—than are for it. Black is beautiful so long as it's not politicized. Culturized (to coin a word)—okay. Wear dashikies, sandals, the Afro hair-do; set up black arts centers, take "black studies" courses, learn Swahili, talk about "soul" power, and adopt a name like Dingado. In short, cop out on the politics, the power, and dig cultural nationalism. It's not only acceptable, it's marketable.

Don't get me wrong. I'm for pride in being black, but an emphasis on "black consciousness" to the exclusion of other consciousnesses is a dangerous step in the direction Hitler and the Nazis took—and, brother, I don't want to go there. Race superiority? Crap! Black is beautiful, but so is brown and yellow and white, and as a nameless black folk poet said years and years ago, "They is altogedda in equalness."

This is not contrary to the point of view that I think Eldridge Cleaver expresses. Or maybe I'm stretching things a little. But I recall something I read in *Soul On Ice*. "There is in America today," Cleaver wrote, "a generation of white youth that is truly worthy of the black man's respect"; and I'm linking this with something I heard him say at the Peace and Freedom Party's nominating convention in Ann Arbor. He said, "I don't speak only for black people . . . but for all the dispossessed, the angry, the alienated . . . we're all going to move along together, or . . ." (and he spread his hands in a gesture of resignation); and I linked this with what I sensed about the man in the interview I had with him for the N.Y. *Times Magazine*. The man—Cleaver, that is—loves people. He hates the "system," but he loves people. Though I did not say so in the magazine piece, he made a tremendous impression on me. I'll try to analyze it when I write you next.

But I've gone on too long now. Besides, it's July 4th, remember, and there's a parade starting about now, with ranks of flags, and bands, and politicians, and soldiers, and motorized military equipment, including a flight of fighter planes and bombers. And I want to go out and jeer. As ever,

Cordially,

New Poets

EACH OF THE NEW POETS constructs a model of the world as he sees it, and each vision and each world differ from one another as much as human faces can. It may not always be possible to discuss what general qualities these writers possess, because they have not been as much influenced by the work of earlier poets as they have been shaped by the period in which they live, a period characterized at times by apparent violent change in the very way men perceive themselves and their environment. The Black Arts Movement, spearheaded by LeRoi Jones and Larry Neal, has contributed in varying degrees to their development: in moderate and extremist alike, the awareness of blackness is present.

These poets attempt to express a mode of perception perhaps made necessary by a world so complex that the resulting interdependence of all who live in it demands a more honest level of communication than was ever required before. If this interdependence causes men and women to view themselves and one another as something other than isolated individuals, then the new insight that results may at times demand expression in what is very nearly a new language: the old language, the old myths and symbols, are often inappropriate. If this new language is occasionally unfamiliar, a word or a phrase may nevertheles often suggest the tone of the poet's voice, and the tone he uses can at first convey more than the words.

A man like Lawrence Benford can call himself "a wild beast awaking," and he indicates a mood, even though the meaning of a heart "plugged with lead" may not at once be obvious. In the same way, the identity of Margaret Danner's "elevator man" is perhaps unclear, but her degree of compassion for "these others boggling in their misery" is unmistakable. The generosity of Lance Jeffers can render, through the use of the first person, the suffering of whole generations; and though Jeffers' poem is for the most part written in the accents of ordinary speech, the central ambiguity remains: does a man find refuge only in illusion, or can apparent degradation be consumed in a beauty that has an objective reality?

The new poetry is capable of great modulation in tone: it can reproduce the quiet anguish of Naomi Madgett's woman who must dread the day her child will ask, "Mommy, am I black?" It can also release an understated fury through the use of euphemisms such as Jeffers' reference to a wife's return, with her lover's "evil on her thighs."

The language may occasionally be obscene, but obscenity may be no more than an attempt to attack or destroy with words an environment that to many may appear insensible to human needs and desires. Not every poet has the patience and stamina to undermine ugliness as Jon Woodson does, by describing its effects on a little child who wonders vaguely "what to think & what to say & all that."

Lawrence Benford

Lawrence Benford, a Texan, is currently a student at Pan American College in Edinburg, Texas.

THE BEGINNING OF A LONG POEM ON WHY I BURNED THE CITY

My city slept
Through my growing up in hate
Bubbling in the back streets.
The sun shone on my city
But curved not its rays back
Into the corners where I shined shoes
With my teeth,
Where my father ate the trash of my city
With his hands,
Where my mother cared for white babies
With black breasts.
My city, yes, outstretched along
Its white freeways slept
In the warmth of its tall new building
And 100000 $ homes
Of abnormal sapiens with titles

–And I grew up!

Like a wild beast awaking
To find his mate eaten
In one second I grew up
With the fires that flamed
In my soul. Fires that burned
Holes in the soft spots of my heart.
(So as not to bleed to death)

"The Beginning of A Long Poem On Why I Burned The City." Reprinted by permission of the author from *The New Black Poetry.*

They were plugged with lead
And I went off to college
With a Gasoline can.

Margaret Danner

Margaret Danner was born in Kentucky and spent her early life in Chicago. She received her education at Roosevelt College and Loyola University. Her work has appeared in many periodicals and anthologies. She has been Poet-in-Residence at Wayne State University and is presently Poet-in-Residence at Virginia Union University.

THE ELEVATOR MAN ADHERES TO FORM

I am reminded, by the tan man who wings
the elevator, of Rococo art. His ways
are undulating waves that shepherd and swing
us cupid-like from floor to floor.

He sweethearts us
with polished pleasantries; gallantly
flourishes us up and up. No casual 'Hi's' from him.

His greetings, God-speedings, display his Ph.D.
aplomb, and I should feel like a cherub,
be fleur-de-lis and pastel-shell-like, but

instead, I vision other tan and deeper much than tan
early Baroque-like men who (seeing themselves still
strutlessly groping, winding down subterranean

grottoes of injustice, down dark spirals) feel
with such tortuous, smoked-stone greyed intensity
that they exhale a hurricane of gargoyles, then reel

into it. I see these others boggling in their misery
and wish this elevator artisan would fill his flourishing form
with warmth for them and turn his lettered zeal
toward lifting them above their crippling storm.

"The Elevator Man Adheres to Form." Reprinted by permission of the author.

Mari Evans

A native of Toledo, Ohio, Mari Evans was a John Hay Whitney Fellow, 1965-66. Her work as a poet has been used on record albums, several television specials, two off-Broadway productions, and over 30 text-books and anthologies, including Italian, German, Swedish, British, French, and Dutch works. Presently Writer-in-Residence at Indiana University–Purdue University, Indianapolis, she is also producer/direc-tor of a weekly half-hour television series, "The Black Experience."

VIVE NOIR!

i
am going to rise
en masse
from Inner City
           sick
             of newyork ghettos
           chicago tenements
         l a's slums
weary
      of exhausted lands
      sagging privies
      saying yessur yessah
      yesSIR
      in an assortment
      of geographical dialects i
have seen my last
broken down plantation
even from a
distance
         i
will load all my goods
in '50 Chevy pickups '53
Fords fly United and '66
caddys I
      have packed in
      the old man and the old lady and
      wiped the children's noses

"Vive Noir!" from *Negro Digest,* September/October, 1968. Reprinted by permis-sion of the author.

I'm tired
of hand me downs
shut me ups
pin me ins
keep me outs
messing me over have
just had it
baby
from
you . . .
i'm
gonna spread out
over America
intrude
my proud blackness
all
over the place
i have wrested wheat fields
from the forests

turned rivers
from their courses

leveled mountains
at a word
festooned the land with
bridges
gemlike
on filaments of steel
moved
glistening towers of Babel in place

sweated a whole
civilization
now
i'm
gonna breathe fire
through flaming nostrils BURN
a place for

me
in the skyscrapers and the
schoolrooms on the green
lawns and the white
beaches

                                    i'm
              gonna wear the robes and
              sit on the benches
              make the rules and make
              the arrests say
              who can and who
              can't
                        baby you don't stand
                        a
                        chance
    i'm
              gonna put black angels
              in all the books and a black
              Christchild in Mary's arms i'm
              gonna make black bunnies black
              fairies black santas black
              nursery rhymes and
                              black
              ice cream
                        i'm
    gonna make it a
         crime
              to be anything BUT   black
              pass the coppertone
    gonna make white
    a twentyfourhour
    lifetime
    J.O.B.
              an' when all the coppertone's gone . . . ?

William J. Harris

William J. Harris has spent most of his life in Yellow Springs, Ohio. His first experience in an all-Negro educational institution was at Central State College in Wilberforce, Ohio. Harris' poetry has appeared in *The Antioch Review, New Campus Writing, The Southern Poetry Review,* and others.

SAMANTHA IS MY NEGRO CAT

    Samantha is my
    Negro cat.
    Black with yellow eyes.

"Samantha Is My Negro Cat." Reprinted by permission of Moore Publishing Company from *Nine Black Poets.*

A big flat nose.
Thick features.
She came to me
from the street.
(A street nigger
with hairless ears.)
She's tough.
Been a mother too.
Has hard pink nipples.
(Yes, pink. She also has
a white spot on her neck.
She ain't pure. But
I don't care. I ain't no racist.)
She has a sad high ass.
Sway-back.
Not much to look at
but as affectionate
as any girl who's
had a hard time of it.
"Bums," said the vet
a little too objectively,
"always respond to love."

Samantha rubs against
me, sits across my
lap, purring her short-circuited purr.
(Hey, Doc, there's a wire loose
in her purr box.)

Lady, this man is
going to treat you better
than the rest.
(You say you've heard that one before.)
We'll comfort each other
in the evenings
after supper, when we stare
out on the
cold and dark street.

Lance Jeffers

Lance Jeffers, a native of Fremont, Nebraska, was born in 1919 and brought up in Nebraska and San Francisco. A graduate of Columbia (B.A. and M.A.), he has taught at Tuskegee Institute, Howard University, Indiana University, and other colleges in America and Canada.

ON LISTENING TO THE SPIRITUALS

When the master lived a king and I a starving hutted slave beneath
the lash, and

when my five-year-old son was driven at dawn to cotton-field to pick
until he could no longer see the sun, and

when master called my wife to the big house when mistress was gone,
took her against her will and gave her a dollar to be still, and
when she turned upon her pride and cleavered it, cursed her dignity
and stamped on it, came back to me with his evil on her thighs, hung
her head when I condemned her with my eyes,

what broken mettle of my soul wept steel, cracked teeth in self-
contempt
upon my flesh, crept underground to seek new roots and secret breathing place?

When all the hatred of my bones was buried in a forgotten county of
my soul,
then from beauty muscled from the degradation of my oaken bread,
I stroked on slaverysoil the mighty colors of my song, a passionate
heaven rose no God in heaven could create!

Alicia Loy Johnson

Alicia Loy Johnson was born in Chicago, Illinois, in 1944 and educated
in its public schools. She later attended Wilson Junior College and
Southern Illinois University. Her poems appear in Shuman's *Nine
Black Poets*.

ON MY BLK/NESS

my blk/ness
like
poetry
is not to be deceived

"On Listening to the Spirituals." Reprinted by permission of Moore Publishing
Company from *Nine Black Poets*.

"On My Blk/ness." Reprinted by permission of Moore Publishing Company from
Nine Black Poets.

i am the afro-asian
i am the afro-cuban
i am the afro-brazillian
i am the african
so i must not be misled.

in this town
where black men push
lawnmowers
in the center of streets/i wait my turn/for i

like him
      am pushing lawnmowers
            of truth.
i have seen my brothers
work for hrs. on
old dilapidated houses/

        i am these brothers
        working/tearing down
        old traditions and
        creating new ones.
i have seen my brothers
burn themselves
in the name of freedom &
        i too am burning
        in the name of freedom.
i have read of my brothers
laboring in the sun with
their heads up to mt. kenya/
        i am these brothers who are
        squatters/whose heads are
        raised to mt. kilimanjaro &
        mt. kenya
i am not to be deceived
my blk/ness
    like
  poetry
must not be misled.

Percy Edward Johnston

Percy Edward Johnston, born in New York City in 1930, is now Assistant Professor of English at Montclair State College. In 1961 at Howard University, his alma mater, he founded *Dasein: A Journal of Aesthetics, Literature, and Philosophy,* which he continues to edit.

TO PAUL ROBESON, OPUS NO. 3

1

A. N. Marquis[1] has erased your
Your song, your Raritain[2] relatives
Sneer. Your brothers
Fire 24 point boldface projectiles, saluting
Felons—and forget your song.

They've forgot the chorus
Of your hymn which memorialized
Oriental urban renewal;
They've forgot your song
Which stood Brooklyn on its feet
Certain technicolor leaf
Saturday afternoons.

The new song's sung
By maintanence men
Who unplug coinchaingers,
Who unscramble binary code;
By your brothers who have the
Prime trinitarian person on
Auction block,
Airconditioning machines are
More efficacious.
The new song's sung
By your billboard controlled
Sisters who nocturnally wreck
Our genetic structure.

2

She's no girl for Bootsie,
This blonde who listens to
The new song, she's more
Like an E. Simms Campbell[3]
Harem princess who's stretched out
On a padded cushion which

"to paul robeson, opus no. 3." Reprinted by permission of *Dasein* and the author.

[1] publisher of *Who's Who in America*

[2] a town in New Jersey

[3] illustrator and cartoonist who became famous for his cartoons in *Esquire* Magazine.

Conceals the tentwall covered
Taperecorder which no longer
Plays your song.
She's like one's you used to
See in Narragansett crushing
Gin-dipped olives, or pastel pink
Legs akimboed on
Room-sized carpets—
Damning the innate urge
That prods her to alight
Ellington's subway and race
Down 125th to be your
Desdemona, while you stand like
Diz or Miles in cocktail glass
Rooms, where you command even her brother
Where you face them both
In this Hilton or Sheraton ballroom,
And order greens and chitt'lins.

Naomi Long Madgett

Naomi Long Madgett (also Naomi Cornelia Long, Naomi Long Witherspoon) was born in Norfolk, Virginia, in 1923, the daughter of a Baptist minister. Educated at Virginia State College and at Wayne State University, Mrs. Madgett published her first volume of poetry when she was 17. A contributor to many periodicals, she has published work in several major poetry anthologies in recent years.

FOR A CHILD

If only the day need not come when I must tell you,
When you will stand on tiptoe looking curiously in the mirror
And ask, 'Mommy, am I black?'

If only you need not learn the cruel lesson, generations old,
And grow up with it—first a frown creeping between your eyes,
Then your careless little voice becoming more and more subdued,
And then that grim expression hovering over everything you do and say.

If only you need not understand the suffering
Inscribed on all the faces like mine
And through those tortured, early years find in your own

"For a Child." Reprinted by permission of Exposition Press Inc.

A striking resemblance to all the burdened faces
Of all oppressed people in the world.

If only the day need not come when people will stop
And tell me: 'Now that she's growing up, Bessie,
'She looks just like you.'

Oliver Pitcher

Oliver Pitcher, born in Massachusetts in 1923, was educated at Bard College and the New School of Social Research. An actor and playwright as well as a poet, he published *Dust of Silence,* his first volume of verse, in 1958.

HARLEM: SIDEWALK ICONS

Man, in some lan
I hear tell, tears wep
 in orange baloons will
bus wide open with
laughter,
Aw, cry them blues Man!

The kite
dangling from a bough-cloud is learned, knows as kin
the icon faces cracked in Harlem sidewalk squares,
the blissfully ignorant rope skipping:

'Lollypop sticks make me sick
wiggle ana wiggle, two four six'

the car brakes' sudden alarm . . . the kids' unlearned
hush. So goes the day.

Night. Black
is the air, white the kin-kite.
Labourers dream, they do, of swinging at the ball
and missing in a cosmic Yankee Stadium.
Swinging, swinging, always missing.

Dawn, Easter parader
comes wearing a cloche-cloud down to her eyes
decorated with a victim's shriek.

"Harlem: Sidewalk Icons." Reprinted by permission of Troubador Press.

Sunday
>   ah, Sunday, is here.
>   Yam skinned women with calloused dreams look
>   high, far to the kite and while wiping away
>   Saturday labour beads of sweat, webs of mourner's
>   weeping, kindred.

Monday
>   arrives on the express and waits panting
>   at the station . . .

>>   'Lollypop sticks make me sick
>>   wiggle ana wiggle, two four six.
>>   They do.'

The kite is learned.

Dudley Randall

Dudley Randall, a poet, anthologist, and short story writer, was born in 1914 in Washington, D.C. and educated at Wayne State and the University of Michigan. He has been librarian at Lincoln University in Missouri and at Morgan State College in Baltimore. A prolific contributor to periodicals, he is (in collaboration with Margaret Burroughs) editor of *For Malcolm: Poems on the Life and Death of Malcolm X.*

BOOKER T. AND W. E. B.
(BOOKER T. WASHINGTON AND W. E. B. DU BOIS)

> "It seems to me," said Booker T.,
> "It shows a mighty lot of cheek
>   To study chemistry and Greek
>   When Mr. Charlie needs a hand
>   To hoe the cotton on his land,
>   And when Miss Ann looks for a cook,
>   Why stick your nose inside a book?"

> "I don't agree," said W. E. B.
> "If I should have the drive to seek
>   Knowledge of chemistry or Greek,
>   I'll do it. Charles and Miss can look
>   Another place for hand or cook.

Some men rejoice in skill of hand,
And some in cultivating land,
But there are others who maintain
The right to cultivate the brain."

"It seems to me," said Booker T.,
"That all you folks have missed the boat
Who shout about the right to vote,
And spend vain days and sleepless nights
In uproar over civil rights.
Just keep your mouths shut, do not grouse,
But work, and save, and buy a house."

"I don't agree," said W. E. B.
"For what can property avail
If dignity and justice fail?
Unless you help to make the laws,
They'll steal your house with trumped-up clause.
A rope's as tight, a fire as hot,
No matter how much cash you've got.
Speak soft, and try your little plan,
But as for me, I'll be a man."

"It seems to me," said Booker T.—

"I don't agree,"
Said W. E. B.

Jon Woodson

Jon Woodson, born in Washington, D.C. in 1944, was educated at the University of Rhode Island. He began writing poetry in high school; in college he edited the campus literary magazine. Woodson now teaches at Lincoln University in Pennsylvania.

SATURDAY

saturday morning & i would
just be going to the pharmacy
for something inconsequential
& i would go down the street

"Saturday." Reprinted by permission of the author.

where children whirled & ran
& cut through the schoolyard
where nobody played & over to
the bridge over the creek where
the shallow creek flowed between
wavy willows for the sole purpose
of pausing & looking down
where it ran slowly over stones
& and then on down to the corner
where there would be three
ancient goldtoothed men in olive
overcoats down to their shoes
gesturing & flapping with their
sleeves shouting about bigbrimmed
hats & do she do it for nickles
& all that & after the drugstore
since it was saturday i would go
down the street to the SHABAZZ
KOSHER FISH MARKET (WE SCALE THEM
FOR YOU) to hear brother willie
talk about the white man & stare
with eyes that had never seen
the sea at the still rows of fish
that lay three deep in cracked ice
about how he was the devil but
the time will come & all that then
out again onto the bright sidewalk
down to the hardware store with
bicycles & lawnmowers in the window
where dogs pissed on the garden
display & people would be talking
about dogs always pissing on the
garden display & the hardware
store stood between the pool hall
& the liquor store & people would
be passing in cars blowing their
horns at people standing around
on the sidewalk & people would be
leaning into car windows talking
about your momma is a & your poppa
is one too or people would be
leaning out of car sipping whisky
from paper cups & old men would
be leaning out of third floor
windows smoking cigarettes watching

old women leaning out past flower
pots smoking cigarettes enjoying
the breeze & the music in the breeze
& people dancing & laughing about
last night was friday & tomorrow
is sunday because it's saturday
& it was dark in the doorway of the
pool hall & faces looked from behind
the green glass & the clock in the
COKE sign over the door showed
it wasn't morning any more & the
sun would be high & hot where
children played army on vacant lots
& everybody in the world was in
the world & probably even the dead
knew it was saturday & i would
start home going a different way
through the alleys behind houses
where some had flowers growing
& some old cars or just weeds &
the dogs barked & someone would be
hanging out clothes singing about
precious lord jesus & all that
& i would walk pondering over it all
considering it all kicking an
occasional beer can wondering what
to think & what to say & all that

Don L. Lee

Don L. Lee was born in 1942, reared in Detroit, and received his college education in Chicago. His work has appeared often in *Negro Digest* and other periodicals, and he has published three volumes of verse: *Think Black, Black Pride,* and *Don't Cry, Scream.* Mr. Lee has been Poet-in-Residence at Cornell University.

THE SELF-HATRED OF DON L. LEE

(9/22/63)

i,
at one time,
loved

my
color—
it
opened sMall
doors of
tokenism
&
acceptance.
      (doors called, "the only one" & "our negro")
after painfully
struggling
thru Du Bois,
Rogers, Locke,
Wright & others,
my blindness
was vanquished
by pitchblack
paragraphs of
"us, we, me, i"
awareness.

i
began
to love
only a
part of
me—
my inner
self which
is all
black—
&
developed a
vehement
hatred of
my light
brown
outer.

Martin Luther King, Jr.

(1929–1968)

MARTIN LUTHER KING, JR., was the most effective and distinguished leader of the civil-rights movement in recent times. As pastor of the Dexter Avenue Baptist Church in Montgomery, Alabama, he led the bus boycott in 1955 and 1956 which ended segregation and harassment of Negroes on Montgomery's buses. As president of The Southern Christian Leadership Conference, he developed techniques for non-violent protest (as had Thoreau, Tolstoi and Gandhi) based on the highest moral principles. He and his followers—though beaten brutally, set upon by police dogs and water hoses and imprisoned—brought about an end to segregation in public transportation, hotels and restaurants throughout the South. Through sit-ins, marches, boycotts, they achieved a greater degree of political and economic equality for black people everywhere and stimulated the Federal Government and the Supreme Court to take action against the indignities to which black people were subjected. A graduate of Morehouse College and Boston University, Dr. King was awarded many honorary degrees and, in 1964, the Nobel Peace Prize. His life was an inspiration to the oppressed everywhere in the world. He was assassinated on April 4, 1968, in Memphis, Tennessee, where he led protest marches in behalf of black sanitation workers.

The writings of Martin Luther King include *Stride Toward Freedom: The Montgomery Story* (1958); *Why We Can't Wait* (1963); *Where Do We Go From Here: Chaos or Community?* (1967); and numerous speeches and sermons. The passage which follows, "The World House," is from *Where Do We Go From Here: Chaos or Community?* For biographies of Martin Luther King see: Lerone Bennett, Jr., *What Manner of Man* (Johnson, 1964); William Robert Miller, *Martin Luther King, Jr.: His Life, Martyrdom and Meaning for the World* (Weybright and Tolley, 1968).

THE WORLD HOUSE ·

Some years ago a famous novelist died. Among his papers was found a list of suggested plots for future stories, the most prominently underscored being this one: "A widely separated family inherits a house in which they have to live together." This is the great new problem of mankind. We have inherited a large house, a great "world house" in which we have to live together—black and white, Easterner and Westerner, Gentile and Jew, Catholic and Protestant, Moslem and Hindu—a family unduly separated in ideas, culture and interest, who, because we can never again live apart, must learn somehow to live with each other in peace.

However deeply American Negroes are caught in the struggle to be at last at home in our homeland of the United States, we cannot ignore the larger world house in which we are also dwellers. Equality with whites will not solve the problems of either whites or Negroes if it means equality in a world society stricken by poverty and in a universe doomed to extinction by war.

All inhabitants of the globe are now neighbors. This world-wide neighborhood has been brought into being largely as a result of the modern scientific and technological revolutions. The world of today is vastly different from the world of just one hundred years ago. A century ago Thomas Edison had not yet invented the incandescent lamp to bring light to many dark places of the earth. The Wright brothers had not yet invented that fascinating mechanical bird that would spread its gigantic wings across the skies and soon dwarf distance and place time in the service of man. Einstein had not yet challenged an axiom and the theory of relativity had not yet been posited.

Human beings, searching a century ago as now for better understanding, had no television, no radios, no telephones and no motion pictures through which to communicate. Medical science had not yet discovered the wonder drugs to end many dread plagues and diseases. One hundred years ago military men had not yet developed the terrifying weapons of warfare that we know today—not the bomber, an airborne fortress raining down death; nor napalm, that burner of all things and flesh in its path. A century ago there were no skyscraping buildings to kiss the stars and no gargantuan bridges to span the waters. Science had not yet peered into the unfathomable ranges of interstellar space, nor had it penetrated oceanic depths. All these new inventions, these new ideas, these sometimes fascinating and sometimes frightening developments, came later. Most of them have come within the past sixty years, sometimes with agonizing slowness, more characteristically with bewildering speed, but always with enormous significance for our future.

The years ahead will see a continuation of the same dramatic developments. Physical science will carve new highways through the stratosphere. In a few years astronauts and cosmonauts will probably walk comfortably across the uncertain pathways of the moon. In two or three years it will be possible, because of the new supersonic jets, to fly from New York to London in two and one-half hours. In the years ahead medical science will greatly prolong the lives of men by finding a cure for cancer and deadly heart ailments. Automation and cybernation will make it possible for working people to have undreamed-of amounts of leisure time. All this is a dazzling picture of the furniture, the workshop, the spacious rooms, the new decorations and the architectural pattern of the large world house in which we are living.

Along with the scientific and technological revolution, we have also witnessed a world-wide freedom revolution over the last few decades. The present upsurge of the Negro people of the United States grows out of a deep and passionate determination to make freedom and equality a reality "here" and "now." In one sense the civil rights movement in the United States is a special American phenomenon which must be understood in the light of American history and dealt with in terms of the American situation. But on another and more important level, what is happening in the United States today is a significant part of a world development.

We live in a day, said the philosopher Alfred North Whitehead, "when civilization is shifting its basic outlook; a major turning point in history where the pre-suppositions on which society is structured are being analyzed, sharply challenged, and profoundly changed." What we are seeing now is a freedom explosion, the realization of "an idea whose time has come," to use Victor Hugo's phrase. The deep rumbling of discontent that we hear today is the thunder of disinherited masses, rising from dungeons of oppression to the bright hills of freedom. In one majestic chorus the rising masses are singing, in the words of our freedom song, "Ain't gonna let nobody turn us around." All over the world like a fever, freedom is spreading in the widest liberation movement in history. The great masses of people are determined to end the exploitation of their races and lands. They are awake and moving toward their goal like a tidal wave. You can hear them rumbling in every village street, on the docks, in the houses, among the students, in the churches and at political meetings. For several centuries the direction of history flowed from the nations and societies of Western Europe out into the rest of the world in "conquests" of various sorts. That period, the era of colonialism, is at an end. East is moving West. The earth is being redistributed. Yes, we are "shifting our basic outlooks."

These developments should not surprise any student of history. Oppressed people cannot remain oppressed forever. The yearning for freedom eventually manifests itself. The Bible tells the thrilling story of how Moses stood in Pharaoh's court centuries ago and cried, "Let my people go." This was an opening chapter in a continuing story. The present struggle in the United States is a later chapter in the same story. Something within has reminded the Negro of his birthright of freedom, and something without has reminded him that it can be gained. Consciously or unconsciously, he has been caught up by the spirit of the times, and with his black brothers of Africa and his brown and yellow brothers in Asia, South America and the Caribbean, the United States Negro is moving with a sense of great urgency toward the promised land of racial justice.

Nothing could be more tragic than for men to live in these revolutionary times and fail to achieve the new attitudes and the new mental outlooks that the new situation demands. In Washington Irving's familiar story of Rip Van Winkle, the one thing that we usually remember is that Rip slept twenty years. There is another important point, however, that is almost always overlooked. It was the sign on the inn in the little town on the Hudson from which Rip departed and scaled the mountain for his long sleep. When he went up, the sign had a picture of King George III of England. When he came down, twenty years later, the sign had a picture of George Washington. As he looked at the picture of the first President of the United States, Rip was confused, flustered and lost. He knew not who Washington was. The most striking thing about this story is not that Rip slept twenty years, but that he slept through a revolution that would alter the course of human history.

One of the great liabilities of history is that all too many people fail to remain awake through great periods of social change. Every society has its protectors of the status quo and its fraternities of the indifferent who are notorious for sleeping through revolutions. But today our very survival depends on our ability to stay awake, to adjust to new ideas, to remain vigilant and to face the challenge of change. The large house in which we live demands that we transform this world-wide neighborhood into a world-wide brotherhood. Together we must learn to live as brothers or together we will be forced to perish as fools.

We must work passionately and indefatigably to bridge the gulf between our scientific progress and our moral progress. One of the great problems of mankind is that we suffer from a poverty of the spirit which stands in glaring contrast to our scientific and technological abundance. The richer we have become materially, the poorer we have become morally and spiritually.

Every man lives in two realms, the internal and the external. The internal is that realm of spiritual ends expressed in art, literature, morals and religion. The external is that complex of devices, techniques, mechanisms and instrumentalities by means of which we live. Our problem today is that we have allowed the internal to become lost in the external. We have allowed the means by which we live to outdistance the ends for which we live. So much of modern life can be summarized in that suggestive phrase of Thoreau: "Improved means to an unimproved end." This is the serious predicament, the deep and haunting problem, confronting modern man. Enlarged material powers spell enlarged peril if there is not proportionate growth of the soul. When the external of man's nature subjugates the internal, dark storm clouds begin to form.

Western civilization is particularly vulnerable at this moment, for our material abundance has brought us neither peace of mind nor serenity of spirit. An Asian writer has portrayed our dilemma in candid terms:

> You call your thousand material devices "labor-saving machinery," yet you are forever "busy." With the multiplying of your machinery you grow increasingly fatigued, anxious, nervous, dissatisfied. Whatever you have, you want more; and wherever you are you want to go somewhere else . . . your devices are neither time-saving nor soul-saving machinery. They are so many sharp spurs which urge you on to invent more machinery and to do more business.[1]

This tells us something about our civilization that cannot be cast aside as a prejudiced charge by an Eastern thinker who is jealous of Western prosperity. We cannot escape the indictment.

This does not mean that we must turn back the clock of scientific progress. No one can overlook the wonders that science has wrought for our lives. The automobile will not abdicate in favor of the horse and buggy, or the train in favor of the stagecoach, or the tractor in favor of the hand plow, or the scientific method in favor of ignorance and superstition. But our moral and spiritual "lag" must be redeemed. When scientific power outruns moral power, we end up with guided missiles and misguided men. When we foolishly minimize the internal of our lives and maximize the external, we sign the warrant for our own day of doom.

Our hope for creative living in this world house that we have inherited lies in our ability to re-establish the moral ends of our lives in personal character and social justice. Without this spiritual and moral reawakening we shall destroy ourselves in the misuse of our own instruments.

2

Among the moral imperatives of our time, we are challenged to work all over the world with unshakable determination to wipe out the last vestiges of racism. As early as 1906 W. E. B. Du Bois prophesied that "the problem of the twentieth century will be the problem of the color line." Now as we stand two-thirds into this exciting period of history we know full well that racism is still that hound of hell which dogs the tracks of our civilization.

[1] Abraham, Mitrie Rihbany: *Wise Men from the East and from the West* (Houghton Mifflin, 1922, p. 137).

Racism is no mere American phenomenon. Its vicious grasp knows no geographical boundaries. In fact, racism and its perennial ally—economic exploitation—provide the key to understanding most of the international complications of this generation.

The classic example of organized and institutionalized racism is the Union of South Africa. Its national policy and practice are the incarnation of the doctrine of white supremacy in the midst of a population which is overwhelmingly black. But the tragedy of South Africa is not simply in its own policy; it is the fact that the racist government of South Africa is virtually made possible by the economic policies of the United States and Great Britain, two countries which profess to be the moral bastions of our Western world.

In country after country we see white men building empires on the sweat and suffering of colored people. Portugal continues its practices of slave labor and subjugation in Angola; the Ian Smith government in Rhodesia continues to enjoy the support of British-based industry and private capital, despite the stated opposition of British Government policy. Even in the case of the little country of South West Africa we find the powerful nations of the world incapable of taking a moral position against South Africa, though the smaller country is under the trusteeship of the United Nations. Its policies are controlled by South Africa and its manpower is lured into the mines under slave-labor conditions.

During the Kennedy administration there was some awareness of the problems that breed in the racist and exploitative conditions throughout the colored world, and a temporary concern emerged to free the United States from its complicity, though the effort was only a diplomatic level. Through our Ambassador to the United Nations, Adlai Stevenson, there emerged the beginnings of an intelligent approach to the colored peoples of the world. However, there remained little or no attempt to deal with the economic aspects of racist exploitation. We have been notoriously silent about the more than $700 million of American capital which props up the system of *apartheid*, not to mention the billions of dollars in trade and the military alliances which are maintained under the pretext of fighting Communism in Africa.

Nothing provides the Communists with a better climate for expansion and infiltration than the continued alliance of our nation with racism and exploitation throughout the world. And if we are not diligent in our determination to root out the last vestiges of racism in our dealings with the rest of the world, we may soon see the sins of our fathers visited upon ours and succeeding generations. For the conditions which are so classically represented in Africa are present also in Asia and in our own back yard in Latin America.

Everywhere in Latin America one finds a tremendous resentment of the United States, and that resentment is always strongest among the poorer and darker peoples of the continent. The life and destiny of Latin America are in the hands of United States corporations. The decisions affecting the lives of South Americans are ostensibly made by their governments, but there are almost no legitimate democracies alive in the whole continent. The other governments are dominated by huge and exploitative cartels that rob Latin America of her resources while turning over a small rebate to a few members of a corrupt aristocracy, which in turn invests not in its own country for its own people's welfare but in the banks of Switzerland and the playgrounds of the world.

Here we see racism in its more sophisticated form: neocolonialism. The Bible and the annals of history are replete with tragic stories of one brother robbing another of his birthright and thereby insuring generations of strife and enmity. We can hardly escape such a judgment in Latin America, any more than we have been able to escape the harvest of hate sown in Vietnam by a century of French exploitation.

There is the convenient temptation to attribute the current turmoil and bitterness throughout the world to the presence of a Communist conspiracy to undermine Europe and America, but the potential explosiveness of our world situation is much more attributable to disillusionment with the promises of Christianity and technology.

The revolutionary leaders of Africa, Asia and Latin America have virtually all received their education in the capitals of the West. Their earliest training often occurred in Christian missionary schools. Here their sense of dignity was established and they learned that all men were sons of God. In recent years their countries have been invaded by automobiles, Coca-Cola and Hollywood, so that even remote villages have become aware of the wonders and blessings available to God's white children.

Once the aspirations and appetites of the world have been whetted by the marvels of Western technology and the self-image of a people awakened by religion, one cannot hope to keep people locked out of the earthly kingdom of wealth, health and happiness. Either they share in the blessings of the world or they organize to break down and overthrow those structures or governments which stand in the way of their goals.

Former generations could not conceive of such luxury, but their children now take this vision and demand that it become a reality. And when they look around and see that the only people who do not share in the abundance of Western technology are colored people, it is an almost inescapable conclusion that their condition and their exploitation are somehow related to their color and the racism of the white Western world.

This is a treacherous foundation for a world house. Racism can well be that corrosive evil that will bring down the curtain on Western civilization. Arnold Toynbee has said that some twenty-six civilizations have risen upon the face of the earth. Almost all of them have descended into the junk heaps of destruction. The decline and fall of these civilizations, according to Toynbee, was not caused by external invasions but by internal decay. They failed to respond creatively to the challenges impinging upon them. If Western civilization does not now respond constructively to the challenge to banish racism, some future historian will have to say that a great civilization died because it lacked the soul and commitment to make justice a reality for all men.

Another grave problem that must be solved if we are to live creatively in our world house is that of poverty on an international scale. Like a monstrous octopus, it stretches its choking, prehensile tentacles into lands and villages all over the world. Two-thirds of the peoples of the world go to bed hungry at night. They are under-nourished, ill-housed and shabbily clad. Many of them have no houses or beds to sleep in. Their only beds are the sidewalks of the cities and the dusty roads of the villages. Most of these poverty-stricken children of God have never seen a physician or a dentist.

There is nothing new about poverty. What is new, however, is that we now have the resources to get rid of it. Not too many years ago, Dr. Kirtley Mather, a Harvard geologist, wrote a book entitled *Enough and to Spare.*[2] He set forth the basic theme that famine is wholly unnecessary in the modern world. Today, therefore, the question on the agenda must read: Why should there be hunger and privation in any land, in any city, at any table, when man has the resources and the scientific know-how to provide all mankind with the basic necessities of life? Even deserts can be irrigated and topsoil can be replaced. We cannot complain of a lack of land, for there are 25 million square miles of tillable land on earth, of which we are using less than seven million. We have amazing knowledge of vitamins, nutrition, the chemistry of food and the versatility of atoms. There is no deficit in human resources; the deficit is in human will.

This does not mean that we can overlook the enormous acceleration in the rate of growth of the world's population. The population explosion is very real, and it must be faced squarely if we are to avoid, in centuries ahead, a "standing room only" situation on these earthly shores. Most of the large undeveloped nations in the world today are confronted with the problem of excess population in relation to resources. But even this problem will be greatly diminished by wiping out poverty. When people see more opportunities for better education and greater economic security, they begin to consider whether a smaller

[2] Harper, 1944.

family might not be better for themselves and for their children. In other words, I doubt that there can be a stabilization of the population without a prior stabilization of economic resources.

The time has come for an all-out world war against poverty. The rich nations must use their vast resources of wealth to develop the underdeveloped, school the unschooled and feed the unfed. The well-off and the secure have too often become indifferent and oblivious to the poverty and deprivation in their midst. The poor in our countries have been shut out of our minds, and driven from the mainstream of our societies, because we have allowed them to become invisible. Ultimately a great nation is a compassionate nation. No individual or nation can be great if it does not have a concern for "the least of these."

The first step in the world-wide war against poverty is passionate commitments. All the wealthy nations—America, Britain, Russia, Canada, Australia, and those of Western Europe—must see it as a moral obligation to provide capital and technical assistance to the underdeveloped areas. These rich nations have only scratched the surface in their commitment. There is need now for a general strategy of support. Sketchy aid here and there will not suffice, nor will it sustain economic growth. There must be a sustained effort extending through many years. The wealthy nations of the world must promptly initiate a massive, sustained Marshall Plan for Asia, Africa and South America. If they would allocate just a percent of their gross national product annually for a period of ten or twenty years for the development of the underdeveloped nations, mankind would go a long way toward conquering the ancient enemy, poverty.

The aid program that I am suggesting must not be used by the wealthy nations as a surreptitious means to control the poor nations. Such an approach would lead to a new form of paternalism and a neo-colonialism which no self-respecting nation could accept. Ultimately, foreign aid programs must be motivated by a compassionate and committed effort to wipe poverty, ignorance and disease from the face of the earth. Money devoid of genuine empathy is like salt devoid of savor, good for nothing except to be trodden under foot of men.

The West must enter into the program with humility and penitence and a sober realization that everything will not always "go our way." It cannot be forgotten that the Western powers were but yesterday the colonial masters. The house of the West is far from in order, and its hands are far from clean.

We must have patience. We must be willing to understand why many of our young nations will have to pass through the same extremism, revolution and aggression that formed our own history. Every new government confronts overwhelming problems. During the days when they were struggling to remove the yoke of colonialism, there was a kind of pre-existent unity of purpose that kept things moving in one solid direction. But as soon as independence emerges, all the grim problems of life confront them with stark realism: the lack of capital, the strangulating poverty, the uncontrollable birth rates and, above all, the high aspirational level of their own people. The postcolonial period is more difficult and precarious than the colonial struggle itself.

The West must also understand that its economic growth took place under rather propitious circumstances. Most of the Western nations were relatively underpopulated when they surged forward economically, and they were greatly endowed with the iron ore and coal that were needed for launching industry. Most of the young governments of the world today have come into being without these advantages, and, above all, they confront staggering problems of over-population. There is no possible way for them to make it without aid and assistance.

A genuine program on the part of the wealthy nations to make prosperity a reality for the poor nations will in the final analysis enlarge the prosperity of all. One of the best proofs that reality hinges on moral foundations is the fact that when men and governments work devotedly for the good of others, they achieve their own enrichment in the process.

From time immemorial men have lived by the principle that "self-preservation is the first law of life." But this is a false assumption. I would say that other-preservation is the first law of life. It is the first law of life precisely because we cannot preserve self without being concerned about preserving other selves. The universe is so structured that things go awry if men are not diligent in their cultivation of the other-regarding dimension. "I" cannot reach fulfillment without "thou." The self cannot be self without other selves. Self-concern without other-concern is like a tributary that has no outward flow to the ocean. Stagnant, still and stale, it lacks both life and freshness. Nothing would be more disastrous and out of harmony with our self-interest than for the developed nations to travel a dead-end road of inordinate selfishness. We are in the fortunate position of having our deepest sense of morality coalesce with our self-interest.

But the real reason that we must use our resources to outlaw poverty goes beyond material concerns to the quality of our mind and spirit. Deeply woven into the fiber of our religious tradition is the conviction that men are made in the image of God, and that they are souls of infinite metaphysical value. If we accept this as a profound moral fact, we cannot be content to see men hungry, to see men victimized with ill-health, when we have the means to help them. In the final analysis, the rich must not ignore the poor because both rich and poor are tied together. They entered the same mysterious gateway of human birth, into the same adventure of mortal life.

All men are interdependent. Every nation is an heir of a vast treasury of ideas and labor to which both the living and the dead of all nations have contributed. Whether we realize it or not, each of us lives eternally "in the red." We are everlasting debtors to known and unknown men and women. When we arise in the morning, we go into the bathroom where we reach for a sponge which is provided for us by a Pacific islander. We reach for soap that is created for us by a European. Then at the table we drink coffee which is provided for us by a South American, or tea by a Chinese or cocoa by a West African. Before we leave for our jobs we are already beholden to more than half of the world.

In a real sense, all life is interrelated. The agony of the poor impoverishes the rich; the betterment of the poor enriches the rich. We are inevitably our brother's keeper because we are our brother's brother. Whatever affects one directly affects all indirectly.

A final problem that mankind must solve in order to survive in the world house that we have inherited is finding an alternative to war and human destruction. Recent events have vividly reminded us that nations are not reducing but rather increasing their arsenals of weapons of mass destruction. The best brains in the highly developed nations of the world are devoted to military technology. The proliferation of nuclear weapons has not been halted, in spite of the limited-test-ban treaty.

In this day of man's highest technical achievement, in this day of dazzling discovery, of novel opportunities, loftier dignities and fuller freedoms for all, there is no excuse for the kind of blind craving for power and resources that provoked the wars of previous generations. There is no need to fight for food and land. Science has provided us with means of survival and transportation, which make it possible to enjoy the fullness of this great earth. The question now is, do we have the morality and courage required to live together as brothers and not be afraid?

One of the most persistent ambiguities we face is that everybody talks about peace as a goal, but among the wielders of power peace is practically nobody's business. Many men cry "Peace! Peace!" but they refuse to do the things that make for peace.

The large power blocs talk passionately of pursuing peace while expanding defense budgets that already bulge, enlarging already awesome armies and devising ever more devastating weapons. Call the roll of those who sing the glad tidings of peace and one's ears will be surprised by the responding sounds. The heads of all the nations issue clarion calls for peace, yet they come to the peace table accompanied by bands of brigands each bearing unsheathed swords.

The stages of history are replete with the chants and choruses of the conquerors of old who came killing in pursuit of peace. Alexander,

Genghis Khan, Julius Caesar, Charlemagne and Napoleon were akin in seeking a peaceful world order, a world fashioned after their selfish conceptions of an ideal existence. Each sought a world at peace which would personify his egotistic dreams. Even within the life span of most of us, another megalomaniac strode across the world stage. He sent his blitzkrieg-bent legions blazing across Europe, bringing havoc and holocaust in his wake. There is grave irony in the fact that Hitler could come forth, following nakedly aggressive expansionist theories, and do it all in the name of peace.

So when in this day I see the leaders of nations again talking peace while preparing for war, I take fearful pause. When I see our country today intervening in what is basically a civil war, mutilating hundreds of thousands of Vietnamese children with napalm, burning villages and rice fields as random, painting the valley of that small Asian country red with human blood, leaving broken bodies in countless ditches and sending home half-men, mutilated mentally and physically; when I see the unwillingness of our government to create the atmosphere for a negotiated settlement of this awful conflict by halting bombings in the North and agreeing unequivocally to talk with the Vietcong—and all this in the name of pursuing the goal of peace—I tremble for our world. I do so not only from dire recall of the nightmares wreaked in the wars of yesterday, but also from dreadful realization of today's possible nuclear destructiveness and tomorrow's even more calamitous prospects.

Before it is too late, we must narrow the gaping chasm between our proclamations of peace and our lowly deeds which precipitate war. We are called upon to look up from the quagmire of military programs and defense commitments and read the warnings on history's signposts.

One day we must come to see that peace is not merely a distant goal that we seek but a means by which we arrive at that goal. We must pursue peaceful ends through peaceful means. How much longer must we play at deadly war games before we heed the plaintive pleas of the unnumbered dead and maimed of past wars?

President John F. Kennedy said on one occasion, "Mankind must put an end to war or war will put an end to mankind." Wisdom born of experience should tell us that war is obsolete. There may have been a time when war served as a negative good by preventing the spread and growth of an evil force, but the destructive power of modern weapons eliminates even the possibility that war may serve any good at all. If we assume that life is worth living and that man has a right to survive, then we must find an alternative to war. In a day when vehicles hurtle through outer space and guided ballistic missiles carve highways of death through the stratosphere, no nation can claim victory in war. A so-called limited war will leave little more than a calamitous legacy of human suffering, political turmoil and spiritual disillusionment. A world war will leave only smoldering ashes as mute testimony of a human race whose folly led inexorably to ultimate death. If modern man continues to flirt unhesitatingly with war, he will transform his earthly habitat into an inferno such as even the mind of Dante could not imagine.

Therefore I suggest that the philosophy and strategy of nonviolence become immediately a subject for study and for serious experimentation in every field of human conflict, by no means excluding the relations between nations. It is, after all, nation-states which make war, which have produced the weapons that threaten the survival of mankind and which are both genocidal and suicidal in character.

We have ancient habits to deal with, vast structures of power, indescribably complicated problems to solve. But unless we abdicate our humanity altogether and succumb to fear and impotence in the presence of the weapons we have ourselves created, it is as possible and as urgent to put an end to war and violence between nations as it is to put an end to poverty and racial injustice.

The United Nations is a gesture in the direction of nonviolence on a world scale. There, at least, states that oppose one another have sought to do so with words instead of with weapons. But true nonviolence is more than the absence of violence. It is the persistent and determined application of peaceable power to offenses against the community—in this case the world community. As the United Nations moves ahead with the giant tasks confronting it, I would hope that it would earnestly examine the uses of nonviolent direct action.

I do not minimize the complexity of the problems that need to be faced in achieving disarmament and peace. But I am convinced that we shall not have the will, the courage and the insight to deal with such matters unless in this field we are prepared to undergo a mental and spiritual re-evaluation, a change of focus which will enable us to see that the things that seem most real and powerful are indeed now unreal and have come under sentence of death. We need to make a supreme effort to generate the readiness, indeed the eagerness, to enter into the new world which is now possible, "the city which hath foundation, whose Building and Maker is God."

It is not enough to say, "We must not wage war." It is necessary to love peace and sacrifice for it. We must concentrate not merely on the eradication of war but on the affirmation of peace. A fascinating story about Ulysses and the Sirens is preserved for us in Greek literature. The Sirens had the ability to sing so sweetly that sailors could not resist steering toward their island. Many ships were lured upon the rocks, and men forgot home, duty and honor as they flung themselves into the sea to be embraced by arms that drew them down to death. Ulysses, determined not to succumb to the Sirens, first decided to tie himself tightly to the mast of his boat and his crew stuffed their ears with wax. But finally he and his crew learned a better way to save themselves: They took on board the beautiful singer Orpheus, whose melodies were sweeter than the music of the Sirens. When Orpheus sang, who would bother to listen to the Sirens?

So we must see that peace represents a sweeter music, a cosmic melody that is far superior to the discords of war. Somehow we must transform the dynamics of the world power struggle from the nuclear arms race, which no one can win, to a creative contest to harness man's genius for the purpose of making peace and prosperity a reality for all the nations of the world: In short, we must shift the arms race into a "peace race." If we have the will and determination to mount such a peace offensive, we will unlock hitherto tightly sealed doors of hope and bring new light into the dark chambers of pessimism.

3

The stability of the large world house which is ours will involve a revolution of values to accompany the scientific and freedom revolutions engulfing the earth. We must rapidly begin the shift from a "thing"-oriented society to a "person"-oriented society. When machines and computers, profit motives and property rights are considered more important than people, the giant triplets of racism, materialism and militarism are incapable of being conquered. A civilization can flounder as readily in the face of moral and spiritual bankruptcy as it can through financial bankruptcy.

This revolution of values must go beyond traditional capitalism and Communism. We must honestly admit that capitalism has often left a gulf between superfluous wealth and abject poverty, has created conditions permitting necessities to be taken from the many to give luxuries to the few, and has encouraged smallhearted men to become cold and conscienceless so that, like Dives before Lazarus, they are unmoved by suffering, poverty-stricken humanity. The profit motive, when it is the sole basis of an economic system, encourages a cutthroat competition and selfish ambition that inspire men to be more I-centered than thou-centered. Equally, Communism reduces men to a cog in the wheel of the state. The Communist may object, saying that in Marxian theory the state is an "interim reality" that will "wither away" when the classless scoiety emerges. True—in theory; but it is also true that, while the state lasts, it is an end in itself. Man is a means to that end. He has no inalienable rights. His only rights are derived from, and conferred by, the state. Under such a system the fountain of freedom runs dry. Restricted are man's liberties of press and assembly, his freedom to vote and his freedom to listen and to read.

Truth is found neither in traditional capitalism nor in classical Communism. Each represents a partial truth. Capitalism fails to see the truth in collectivism. Communism fails to see the truth in individualism. Capitalism fails to realize that life is social. Communism fails to realize that life is personal. The good and just society is neither the thesis of capitalism nor the antithesis of Communism, but a socially conscious democracy which reconciles the truths of individualism and collectivism.

We have seen some moves in this direction. The Soviet Union has gradually moved away from its rigid Communism and begun to concern itself with consumer products, art and a general increase in benefits to the individual citizen. At the same time, through constant social reforms, we have seen many modifications in laissez-faire capitalism. The problems we now face must take us beyond slogans for their solution. In the final analysis, the right-wing slogans on "government control" and "creeping socialism" are as meaningless and adolescent as the Chinese Red Guard slogans against "bourgeois revisionism." An intelligent approach to the problems of poverty and racism will cause us to see that the words of the Psalmist—"The earth is the Lord's and the fullness thereof—" are still a judgment upon our use and abuse of the wealth and resources with which we have been endowed.

A true revolution of value will soon cause us to question the fairness and justice of many of our past and present policies. We are called to play the Good Samaritan on life's roadside; but that will be only an initial act. One day the whole Jericho Road must be transformed so that men and women will not be beaten and robbed as they make their journey through life. True compassion is more than flinging a coin to a beggar; it understands that an edifice which produces beggars needs restructuring.

A true revolution of values will soon look uneasily on the glaring contrast of poverty and wealth. With righteous indignation, it will look at thousands of working people displaced from their jobs with reduced incomes as a result of automation while the profits of the employers remain intact, and say: "This is not just." It will look across the oceans and see individual capitalists of the West investing huge sums of money in Asia, Africa and South America, only to take the profits out with no concern for the social betterment of the countries, and say: "This is not just." It will look at our alliance with the landed gentry of Latin America and say: "This is not just." The Western arrogance of feeling that it has everything to teach others and nothing to learn from them is not just. A true revolution of values will lay hands on the world order and say of war: "This way of settling differences is not just." This business of burning human beings with napalm, of filling our nation's homes with orphans and widows, of injecting poisonous drugs of hate into the veins of peoples normally humane, of sending men home from dark and bloody battlefields physically handicapped and psychologically deranged, cannot be reconciled with wisdom, justice and love. A nation that continues year after year to spend more money on military defense than on programs of social uplift is approaching spiritual death.

America, the richest and most powerful nation in the world, can well lead the way in this revolution of values. There is nothing to prevent us from paying adequate wages to schoolteachers, social workers and other servants of the public to insure that we have the best available personnel in these positions which are charged with the responsibility of guiding our future generations. There is nothing but a lack of social vision to prevent us from paying an adequate wage to every American citizen whether he be a hospital worker, laundry worker, maid or day laborer. There is nothing except shortsightedness to prevent us from guaranteeing an annual minimum—and *livable*—income for every American family. There is nothing, except a tragic death wish, to prevent us from reordering our priorities, so that the pursuit of peace will take precedence over the pursuit of war. There is nothing to keep us from remolding a recalcitrant status quo with bruised hands until we have fashioned it into a brotherhood.

This kind of positive revolution of values is our best defense against Communism. War is not the answer. Communism will never be defeated by the use of atomic bombs or nuclear weapons. Let us not join those who shout war and who through their misguided passions urge the United States to relinquish its participation in the United Nations. These are days which demand wise restraint and calm reasonableness. We must not call everyone a Communist or an appeaser who advocates the seating of Red China in the United Nations, or who recognizes that hate and hysteria are not the final answers to the problems of these turbulent days. We must not engage in a negative anti-Communism, but rather in a positive thrust for democracy, realizing that our greatest defense against Communism is to take offensive action in behalf of justice. We must with affirmative action seek to remove those conditions of poverty, insecurity and injustice which are the fertile soil in which the seed of Communism grows and develops.

These are revolutionary times. All over the globe men are revolting against old systems of exploitation and oppression, and out of the wombs of a frail world new systems of justice and equality are being born. The shirtless and barefoot people of the earth are rising up as never before. "The people who sat in darkness have seen a great light." We in the West must support these revolutions. It is a sad fact that, because of comfort, complacency, a morbid fear of Communism and our proneness to adjust to injustice, the Western nations that initiated so much of the revolutionary spirit of the modern world have now become the arch antirevolutionaries. This has driven many to feel that only Marxism has the revolutionary spirit. Communism is a judgment on our failure to make democracy real and to follow through on the revolutions that we initiated. Our only hope today lies in our ability to recapture the revolutionary spirit and go out into a sometimes hostile world declaring eternal opposition to poverty, racism and militarism. With this powerful commitment we shall boldly challenge the status quo and unjust mores and thereby speed the day when "every valley shall be exalted, and every mountain and hill shall be made low: and the crooked shall be made straight and the rough places plain."

A genuine revolution of values means in the final analysis that our loyalties must become ecumenical rather than sectional. Every nation must now develop an overriding loyalty to mankind as a whole in order to preserve the best in their individual societies.

This call for a world-wide fellowship that lifts neighborly concern beyond one's tribe, race, class and nation is in reality a call for an all-embracing and unconditional love for all men. This often misunderstood and misinterpreted concept has now become an absolute necessity for the survival of man. When I speak of love, I am speaking of that force which all the great religions have seen as the supreme unifying principle of life. Love is the key that unlocks the door which leads to ultimate reality. This Hindu-Moslem-Christian-Jewish-Buddhist belief about ultimate reality is beautifully summed up in the First Epistle of Saint John:

> Let us love one another: for love is of God:
> and every one that loveth is born of God, and
> knoweth God. He that loveth not knoweth not
> God; for God is love. . . . If we love one another,
> God dwelleth in us, and his love is perfected in us.

Let us hope that this spirit will become the order of the day. We can no longer afford to worship the God of hate or bow before the altar of retaliation. The oceans of history are made turbulent by the ever-rising tides of hate. History is cluttered with the wreckage of nations and individuals who pursued this self-defeating path of hate. As Arnold Toynbee once said in a speech: "Love is the ultimate force that makes for the saving choice of life and good against the damning choice of death and evil. Therefore the first hope in our inventory must be the hope that love is going to have the last word."

We are now faced with the fact that tomorrow is today. We are confronted with the fierce urgency of *now*. In this unfolding conundrum of life and history there is such a thing as being too late. Procrastination is still the thief of time. Life often leaves us standing bare, naked and dejected with a lost opportunity. The "tide in the affairs of men" does not remain at the flood; it ebbs. We may cry out desperately for time to pause in her passage, but time is deaf to every plea and rushes on. Over the bleached bones and jumbled residues of numerous civilizations are written the pathetic words: "Too late." There is an invisible book of life that faithfully records our vigilance or our neglect. "The moving finger writes, and having writ moves on. . . ." We still have a choice today: nonviolent coexistence or violent coannihilation. This may well be mankind's last chance to choose between chaos and community.

Larry Neal

(b. 1937)

BORN IN ATLANTA, GEORGIA, Larry Neal was reared in Philadelphia and educated at Lincoln University in Pennsylvania and at the University of Pennsylvania. A leader in the Black Arts Movement and an apologist for the Movement, he is a poet, critic, and editor. Neal has published in *Freedomways, Negro Digest, Black Dialogue,* and *Soulbook.* He has been arts editor of *The Liberator* and is now a contributing editor of the *Journal of Black Poetry.* Larry Neal is also co-editor with LeRoi Jones of *Black Fire,* an anthology of Negro writings.

The section below is taken from "The Black Arts Movement," an article appearing in *The Drama Review* (*tdr*), Summer, 1968.

THE BLACK ARTS MOVEMENT

1

The Black Arts Movement is radically opposed to any concept of the artist that alienates him from his community. Black Art is the aesthetic and spiritual sister of the Black Power concept. As such, it envisions an art that speaks directly to the needs and aspirations of Black America. In order to perform this task, the Black Arts Movement proposes a radical reordering of the western cultural aesthetic. It proposes a separate symbolism, mythology, critique, and iconology. The Black Arts and the Black Power concept both relate broadly to the Afro-American's desire for self-determination and nationhood. Both concepts are nationalistic. One is concerned with the relationship between art and politics; the other with the art of politics.

Recently, these two movements have begun to merge: the political values inherent in the Black Power concept are now finding concrete expression in the aesthetics of Afro-American dramatists, poets, choreographers, musicians, and novelists. A main tenet of Black Power is the necessity for Black people to define the world in their own terms. The Black artist has made the same point in the context of aesthetics. The two movements postulate that there are in fact and in spirit two

Americas—one black, one white. The Black artist takes this to mean that his primary duty is to speak to the spiritual and cultural needs of Black people. Therefore, the main thrust of this new breed of contemporary writers is to confront the contradictions arising out of the Black man's experience in the racist West. Currently, these writers are re-evaluating western aesthetics, the traditional role of the writer, and the social function of art. Implicit in this re-evaluation is the need to develop a "black aesthetic." It is the opinion of many Black writers, I among them, that the Western aesthetic has run its course: it is impossible to construct anything meaningful within its decaying structure. We advocate a cultural revolution in art and ideas. The cultural values inherent in western history must either be radicalized or destroyed, and we will probably find that even radicalization is impossible. In fact, what is needed is a whole new system of ideas. Poet Don L. Lee expresses it:

> . . . We must destroy Faulkner, dick, jane, and other perpetuators of evil. It's time for DuBois, Nat Turner, and Kwame Nkrumah. As Frantz Fanon points out: destroy the culture and you destroy the people. This must not happen. Black artists are culture stabilizers; bringing back old values, and introducing new ones. Black Art will talk to the people and with the will of the people stop impending "protective custody."

The Black Arts Movement eschews "protest" literature. It speaks directly to Black people. Implicit in the concept of "protest" literature, as Brother Knight has made clear, is an appeal to white morality:

> Now any Black man who masters the technique of his particular art form, who adheres to the white aesthetic, and who directs his work toward a white audience is, in one sense, protesting. And implicit in the act of protest is the belief that a change will be forthcoming once the masters are aware of the protestor's "grievance" (the very word connotes begging, supplications to the gods). Only when that belief has faded and protestings end, will Black art begin.

Brother Knight also has some interesting statements about the development of a "Black aesthetic":

> Unless the Black artist establishes a "Black aesthetic" he will have no future at all. To accept the white aesthetic is to accept and validate a society that will not allow him to live. The Black artist must create new forms and new values, sing new songs (or purify old ones); and along with other Black authorities, he must create a new history, new symbols, myths and legends (and purify old ones by fire). And the Black artist, in creating his own aesthetic, must be accountable for it only to the Black people. Further, he must hasten his own dissolution as an individual (in the Western sense)—painful though the process may be, having been breast-fed the poison of "individual experience."

When we speak of a "Black aesthetic" several things are meant. First, we assume that there is already in existence the basis for such an aesthetic. Essentially, it consists of an African-American cultural tradition. But this aesthetic is finally, by implication, broader than that tradition. It encompasses most of the useable elements of Third World culture. The motive behind the Black aesthetic is the destruction of the white thing, the destruction of white ideas, and white ways of looking at the world. The new aesthetic is mostly predicated on an Ethics which asks the question: whose vision of the world is finally more meaningful, ours or the white oppressors'? What is truth? Or more precisely, whose truth shall we express, that of the oppressed or of the oppressors? These are basic questions. Black intellectuals of previous decades failed to ask them. Further, national and international affairs demand that we appraise the world in terms of our own interests. It is clear that the question of human survival is at the core of contemporary experience. The Black artist must address himself to this reality in the strongest terms possible. In a context of world upheaval, ethics and aesthetics must interact positively and be consistent with the demands for a more spiritual world. Consequently, the Black Arts Movement is an ethical movement. Ethical, that is, from the viewpoint of the oppressed. And much of the oppression confronting the Third World and Black America is directly traceable to the Euro-American cultural sensibility. This sensibility, anti-human in nature, has, until recently, dominated the psyches of most Black artists and intellectuals; it must be destroyed before the Black creative artist can have a meaningful role in the transformation of society.

It is this natural reaction to an alien sensibility that informs the cultural attitudes of the Black Arts and the Black Power movement. It is a profound ethical sense that makes a Black artist question a society in which art is one thing and the actions of men another. The Black Arts Movement believes that your ethics and your aesthetics are one. That the contradictions between ethics and aesthetics in western society is symptomatic of a dying culture.

The term "Black Arts" is of ancient origin, but it was first used in a positive sense by LeRoi Jones:

> We are unfair
> And unfair
> We are black magicians
> Black arts we make
> in black labs of the heart
>
> The fair are fair
> and deathly white
>
> The day will not save them
> And we own the night

There is also a section of the poem "Black Dada Nihilismus" that carries the same motif. But a fuller amplification of the nature of the new aesthetics appears in the poem "Black Art":

> Poems are bullshit unless they are
> teeth or trees or lemons piled
> on a step. Or black ladies dying
> of men leaving nickel hearts
> beating them down. Fuck poems
> and they are useful, would they shoot
> come at you, love what you are,
> breathe like wrestlers, or shudder
> strangely after peeing. We want live
> words of the hip world, live flesh &
> coursing blood. Hearts and Brains
> Souls splintering fire. We want poems
> like fists beating niggers out of Jocks
> or dagger poems in the slimy bellies
> of the owner-jews . . .

Poetry is a concrete function, an action. No more abstractions. Poems are physical entities: fists, daggers, airplane poems, and poems that shoot guns. Poems are transformed from physical objects into personal forces:

> . . . Put it on him poem. Strip him naked
> to the world. Another bad poem cracking
> steel knuckles in a jewlady's mouth
> Poem scream poison gas on breasts in green berets . . .

Then the poem affirms the integral relationship between Black Art and Black people:

> . . . Let Black people understand
> that they are the lovers and the sons
> of lovers and warriors and sons
> of warriors Are poems & poets &
> all the loveliness here in the world

It ends with the following lines, a central assertion in both the Black Arts Movement and the philosophy of Black Power:

> We want a black poem. And a
> Black World.
> Let the world be a Black Poem
> And let All Black People Speak This Poem
> Silently
> Or LOUD

The poem comes to stand for the collective conscious and unconscious of Black America—the real impulse in back of the Black Power movement, which is the will toward self-determination and nationhood, a radical reordering of the nature and function of both art and the artist.

2

In the spring of 1964, LeRoi Jones, Charles Patterson, William Patterson, Clarence Reed, Johnny Moore, and a number of other Black artists opened the Black Arts Repertoire Theatre School. They produced a number of plays including Jones' *Experimental Death Unit # One, Black Mass, Jello,* and *Dutchman.* They also initiated a series of poetry readings and concerts. These activities represented the most advanced tendencies in the movement and were of excellent artistic quality. The Black Arts School came under immediate attack by the New York power structure. The Establishment, fearing Black creativity, did exactly what it was expected to do—it attacked the theatre and all of its values. In the meantime, the school was granted funds by OEO through HARYOU-ACT. Lacking a cultural program itself, HARYOU turned to the only organization which addressed itself to the needs of the community. In keeping with its "revolutionary" cultural ideas, the Black Arts Theatre took its programs into the streets of Harlem. For three months, the theatre presented plays, concerts, and poetry readings to the people of the community. Plays that shattered the illusions of the American body poltic, and awakened Black people to the meaning of their lives.

Then the hawks from the OEO moved in and chopped off the funds. Again, this should have been expected. The Black Arts Theatre stood in radical opposition to the feeble attitudes about culture of the "War On Poverty" bureaucrats. And later, because of internal problems, the theatre was forced to close. But the Black Arts group proved that the community could be served by a valid and dynamic art. It also proved that there was a definite need for a cultural revolution in the Black community.

With the closing of the Black Arts Theatre, the implications of what Brother Jones and his colleagues were trying to do took on even more significance. Black Art groups sprang up on the West Coast and the idea spread to Detroit, Philadelphia, Jersey City, New Orleans, and Washington, D.C. Black Arts movements began on the campuses of San Francisco State College, Fisk University, Lincoln University, Hunter College in the Bronx, Columbia University, and Oberlin College. In Watts, after the rebellion, Maulana Karenga welded the Black Arts Movement into a cohesive cultural ideology which owed much to the work of LeRoi Jones. Karenga sees culture as the most important element in the struggle for self-determination:

Culture is the basis of all ideas, images and actions. To move is to move culturally, i.e. by a set of values given to you by your culture. Without a culture Negroes are only a set of reactions to white people. The seven criteria for culture are:

1. Mythology
2. History
3. Social Organization
4. Political Organization
5. Economic Organization
6. Creative Motif
7. Ethos

In drama, LeRoi Jones represents the most advanced aspects of the movement. He is its prime mover and chief designer. In a poetic essay entitled "The Revolutionary Theatre," he outlines the iconology of the movement:

> The Revolutionary Theatre should force change: it should be change. (All their faces turned into the lights and you work on them black nigger magic, and cleanse them at having seen the ugliness. And if the beautiful see themselves, they will love themselves.) We are preaching virtue again, but by that to mean NOW, toward what seems the most constructive use of the word.

The theatre that Jones proposes is inextricably linked to the Afro-American political dynamic. And such a link is perfectly consistent with Black America's contemporary demands. For theatre is potentially the most social of all of the arts. It is an integral part of the socializing process. It exists in direct relationship to the audience it claims to serve. The decadence and inanity of the contemporary American theatre is an accurate reflection of the state of American society. Albee's *Who's Afraid of Virginia Woolf?* is very American: sick white lives in a homosexual hell hole. The theatre of white America is escapist, refusing to confront concrete reality. Into this cultural emptiness come the musicals, an up-tempo version of the same stale lives. And the use of Negroes in such plays as *Hello Dolly* and *Hallelujah Baby* does not alert their nature; it compounds the problem. These plays are simply hipper versions of the minstrel show. They present Negroes acting out the hang-ups of middle-class white America. Consequently, the American theatre is a palliative prescribed to bourgeois patients who refuse to see the world as it is. Or, more crucially, as the world sees them. It is no accident, therefore, that the most "important" plays come from Europe—Brecht, Weiss, and Ghelderode. And even these have begun to run dry.

The Black Arts theatre, the theatre of LeRoi Jones, is a radical alternative to the sterility of the American theatre. It is primarily a theatre of the Spirit, confronting the Black man in his interaction with his brothers and with the white thing.

> Our theatre will show victims so that their brothers in the audience will be better able to understand that they are the brothers of victims, and that they themselves are blood brothers. And what we show must cause the blood to rush, so that pre-revolutionary temperaments will be bathed in this blood, and it will cause their deepest souls to move, and they will find themselves tensed and clenched, even ready to die, at what the soul has been taught. We will scream and cry, murder, run through the streets in agony, if it means some soul will be moved, moved to actual life understanding of what the world is, and what it ought to be. We are preaching virtue and feeling, and a natural sense of the self in the world. All men live in the world, and the world ought to be a place for them to live.

The victims in the world of Jones' early plays are Clay, murdered by the white bitch-goddess in *Dutchman,* and Walker Vessels, the revolutionary in *The Slave.* Both of these plays present Black men in transition. Clay, the middle-class Negro trying to get himself a little action from Lula, digs himself and his own truth only to get murdered after telling her like it really is:

> Just let me bleed you, you loud whore, and one poem vanished. A whole people neurotics, struggling to keep from being sane. And the only thing that would cure the neurosis would be your murder. Simple as that. I mean if I murdered you, then other white people would understand me. You understand? No. I guess not. If Bessie Smith had killed some white people she wouldn't needed that music. She could have talked very straight and plain about the world. Just straight two and two are four. Money. Power. Luxury. Like that. All of them. Crazy niggers turning their back on sanity. When all it needs is that simple act. Just murder. Would make us all sane.

But Lula understands, and she kills Clay first. In a perverse way it is Clay's nascent knowledge of himself that threatens the existence of Lula's idea of the world. Symbolically, and in fact, the relationship between Clay (Black America) and Lula (white America) is rooted in the historical castration of black manhood. And in the twisted psyche of white America, the Black man is both an object of love and hate. Analogous attitudes exist in most Black Americans, but for decidedly different reasons. Clay is doomed when he allows himself to participate in Lula's "fantasy" in the first place. It is the fantasy to which Frantz Fanon alludes in *The Wretched Of The Earth* and *Black Skins, White Mask:* the native's belief that he can acquire the oppressor's power by acquiring his symbols, one of which is the white woman. When Clay finally digs himself it is too late.

Walker Vessels, in *The Slave*, is Clay reincarnated as the revolutionary confronting problems inherited from his contact with white culture. He returns to the home of his ex-wife, a white woman, and her husband, a literary critic. The play is essentially about Walker's attempt to destroy his white past. For it is the past, with all of its painful memories, that is really the enemy of the revolutionary. It is impossible to move until history is either recreated or comprehended. Unlike Todd, in Ralph Ellison's *Invisible Man*, Walker cannot fall outside history. Instead, Walker demands a confrontation with history, a final shattering of bullshit illusions. His only salvation lies in confronting the physical and psychological forces that have made him and his people powerless. Therefore, he comes to understand that the world must be restructured along spiritual imperatives. But in the interim it is basically a question of *who* has power:

> EASLEY. You're so wrong about everything. So terribly, sickeningly wrong. What can you change? What do you hope to change? Do you think Negroes are better people than whites . . . that they can govern a society *better* than whites? That they'll be more judicious or more tolerant? Do you think they'll make fewer mistakes? I mean really, if the Western white man has proved one thing . . . it's the futility of modern society. So the have-not peoples become the haves. Even so, will that change the essential functions of the world? Will there be more love or beauty in the world . . . more knowledge . . . because of it?
>
> WALKER. Probably. Probably there will be more . . . if more people have a chance to understand what it is. But that's not even the point. It comes down to baser human endeavor than any social-political thinking. What does it matter if there's more love or beauty? Who the fuck cares? Is that what the Western ofay thought while he was ruling . . . that his rule somehow brought more love and beauty into the world? Oh, he might have thought that concomitantly, while sipping a gin rickey and scratching his ass . . . but that was not ever the point. Not even on the Crusades. The point is that you had your chance, darling, now these other folks have theirs. *Quietly.* Now they have theirs.
>
> EASLEY. God, what an ugly idea.

This confrontation between the black radical and the white liberal is symbolic of larger confrontations occurring between the Third World and Western society. It is a confrontation between the colonizer and the colonized, the slavemaster and the slave. Implicit in Easley's remarks is the belief that the white man is culturally and politically superior to the Black Man. Even though Western society has been traditionally violent in its relation with the Third World, it sanctimoniously deplores violence or self assertion on the part of the enslaved. And the Western mind, with clever rationalizations, equates the violence of the oppressed with the violence of the oppressor. So that when the native preaches self-determination, the Western white man cleverly misconstrues it to mean hate of *all* white men. When the Black political radical warns his people not to trust white politicians of the left and the right, but instead to organize separately on the basis of power, the white man cries: "racism in reverse." Or he will say, as many of them do today: "We deplore both white and black racism." As if the two could be equated.

There is a minor element in *The Slave* which assumes great importance in a later play entitled *Jello*. Here I refer to the emblem of Walker's army: a red-mouthed grinning field slave. The revolutionary army has taken one of the most hated symbols of the Afro-American past and radically altered its meaning.* This is the supreme act of freedom, available only to those who have liberated themselves psychically. Jones amplifies this inversion of emblem and symbol in *Jello* by making Rochester (Ratfester) of the old Jack Benny (Penny) program into a revolutionary nationalist. Ratfester, ordinarily the supreme embodiment of the Uncle Tom Clown, surprises Jack Penny by turning on the other side of the nature of the Black man. He skillfully, and with an evasive black humor, robs Penny of all of his money. But Ratfester's actions are "moral." That is to say, Ratfester is getting his back pay; payment of a long over-due debt to the Black man. Ratfester's sensibilities are different from Walker's. He is *blues people* smiling and shuffling while trying to figure out how to destroy the white thing. And like the blues man, he is the master of the understatement. Or in the Afro-American folk tradition, he is the Signifying Monkey, Shine, and Stagolee all rolled into one. There are no stereotypes any more. History has killed Uncle Tom. Because even Uncle Tom has a breaking point beyond which he will not be pushed. Cut deeply enough into the most docile Negro, and you will find a conscious murderer. Behind the lyrics of the blues and the shuffling porter loom visions of white throats being cut and cities burning.

Jones' particular power as a playwright does not rest solely on his revolutionary vision, but is instead derived from his deep lyricism and spiritual outlook. In many ways, he is fundamentally more a poet than

---

* In Jones' study of Afro-American music, *Blues People*, we find the following observation: ". . . Even the adjective *funky*, which once meant to many Negroes merely a stink (usually associated with sex), was used to qualify the music as meaningful (the word became fashionable and is now almost useless). The social implication, then, was that even the old stereotype of a distinctive Negro smell that white America subscribed to could be turned against white America. For this smell now, real or not, was made a valuable characteristic of 'Negro-ness.' And 'Negro-ness,' by the fifties, for many Negroes (and whites) was the only strength left to American culture."

a playwright. And it is his lyricism that gives body to his plays. Two important plays in this regard are *Black Mass* and *Slave Ship*. *Black Mass* is based on the Muslim myth of Yacub. According to this myth, Yacub, a Black scientist, developed the means of grafting different colors on the Original Black Nation until a White Devil was created. In *Black Mass*, Yacub's experiments produce a raving White Beast who is condemned to the coldest regions of the North. The other magicians implore Yacub to cease his experiments. But he insists on claiming the primacy of scientific knowledge over spiritual knowledge. The sensibility of the White Devil is alien, informed by lust and sensuality. The Beast is the consummate embodiment of evil, the beginning of the historical subjugation of the spiritual world.

Black Mass takes place in some pre-historical time. In fact, the concept of time, we learn, is the creation of an alien sensibility, that of the Beast. This is a deeply weighted play, a colloquy on the nature of man, and the relationship between legitimate spiritual knowledge and scientific knowledge. It is LeRoi Jones' most important play mainly because it is informed by a mythology that is wholly the creation of the Afro-American sensibility.

Further, Yacub's creation is not merely a scientific exercise. More fundamentally, it is the aesthetic impulse gone astray. The Beast is created merely for the sake of creation. Some artists assert a similar claim about the nature of art. They argue that art need not have a function. It is against this decadent attitude toward art—ramified throughout most of Western society—that the play militates. Yacub's real crime, therefore, is the introduction of a meaningless evil into a harmonious universe. The evil of the Beast is pervasive, corrupting everything and everyone it touches. What was beautiful is twisted into an ugly screaming thing. The play ends with destruction of the holy place of the Black Magicians. Now the Beast and his descendants roam the earth. An off-stage voice chants a call for the Jihad to begin. It is then that myth merges into legitimate history, and we, the audience, come to understand that all history is merely someone's version of mythology.

Slave Ship presents a more immediate confrontation with history. In a series of expressionistic tableaux it depicts the horrors and the madness of the Middle Passage. It then moves through the period of slavery, early attempts at revolt, tendencies toward Uncle Tom-like reconciliation and betrayal, and the final act of liberation. There is no definite plot (LeRoi calls it a pageant), just a continuous rush of sound, groans, screams, and souls wailing for freedom and relief from suffering. This work has special affinities with the New Music of Sun Ra, John Coltrane, Albert Ayler, and Ornette Coleman. Events are blurred, rising and falling in a stream of sound. Almost cinematically, the images flicker and fade against a heavy back-drop of rhythm. The language is spare, stripped to the essential. It is a play which almost totally eliminates the need for a text. It functions on the basis of movement and energy—the dramatic equivalent of the New Music.

3

LeRoi Jones is the best known and the most advanced playwright of the movement, but he is not alone. There are other excellent playwrights who express the general mood of the Black Arts ideology. Among them are Ron Milner, Ed Bullins, Ben Caldwell, Jimmy Stewart, Joe White, Charles Patterson, Charles Fuller, Aisha Hughes, Carol Freeman, and Jimmy Garrett.

Ron Milner's *Who's Got His Own* is of particular importance. It strips bare the clashing attitudes of a contemporary Afro-American family. Milner's concern is with legitimate manhood and morality. The family in *Who's Got His Own* is in search of its conscience, or more precisely its own definition of life. On the day of his father's death, Tim and his family are forced to examine the inner fabric of their lives: the lies, self-deceits, and sense of powerlessness in a white world. The basic conflict, however, is internal. It is rooted in the historical search for black manhood. Tim's mother is representative of a generation of Christian Black women who have implicitly understood the brooding violence lurking in their men. And with this understanding, they have interposed themselves between their men and the object of that violence—the white man. Thus unable to direct his violence against the oppressor, the Black man becomes more frustrated and the sense of powerlessness deepens. Lacing the strength to be a man in the white world, he turns against his family. So the oppressed, as Fanon explains, constantly dreams violence against his oppressor, while killing his brother on fast weekends.

Tim's sister represents the Negro woman's attempt to acquire what Eldridge Cleaver calls "ultrafemininity." That is, the attributes of her white upper-class counterpart. Involved here is a rejection of the body-oriented life of the working class Black man, symbolized by the mother's traditional religion. The sister has an affair with a white upper-class liberal, ending in abortion. There are hints of lesbianism, i.e. a further rejection of the body. The sister's life is a pivotal factor in the play. Much of the stripping away of falsehood initiated by Tim is directed at her life, which they have carefully kept hidden from the mother.

Tim is the product of the new Afro-American sensibility, informed by the psychological revolution now operative within Black America. He is a combination ghetto soul brother and militant intellectual, very hip and slightly flawed himself. He would change the world, but without comprehending the particular history that produced his "tyrannical" father. And he cannot be the man his father was—not until he truly understands his father. He must understand why his father allowed himself to be insulted daily by the "honky" types on the job; why he took a demeaning job in the "shit-house"; and why he spent on his family the violence that he should have directed against the white man. In short, Tim must confront the history of his family. And that is exactly what happens. Each character tells his story, exposing his falsehood to the other until a balance is reached.

Who's Got His Own is not the work of an alienated mind. Milner's main thrust is directed toward unifying the family around basic moral principles, toward bridging the "generation gap." Other Black playwrights, Jimmy Garrett for example, see the gap as unbridgeable.

Garrett's *We Own the Night* (see this issue of TDR, pp. 62–69) takes place during an armed insurrection. As the play opens we see the central characters defending a section of the city against attacks by white police. Johnny, the protagonist, is wounded. Some of his Brothers intermittently fire at attacking forces, while others look for medical help. A doctor arrives, forced at gun point. The wounded boy's mother also comes. She is a female Uncle Tom who berates the Brothers and their cause. She tries to get Johnny to leave. She is hysterical. The whole idea of Black people fighting white people is totally outside of her orientation. Johnny begins a vicious attack on his mother, accusing her of emasculating his father—a recurring theme in the sociology of the Black community. In Afro-American literature of previous decades the strong Black mother was the object of awe and respect. But in the new literature her status is ambivalent and laced with tension. Historically, Afro-American women have had to be the economic mainstays of the family. The oppressor allowed them to have jobs while at the same time limiting the economic mobility of the Black man. Very often, therefore, the woman's aspirations and values are closely tied to those of the white power structure and not to those of her man. Since he cannot provide for his family the way white men do, she despises his weakness, tearing into him at every opportunity until, very often, there is nothing left but a shell.

The only way out of this dilemma is through revolution. It either must be an actual blood revolution, or one that psychically redirects the energy of the oppressed. Milner is fundamentally concerned with the latter and Garrett with the former. Communication between Johnny and his mother breaks down. The revolutionary imperative demands that men step outside the legal framework. It is a question of erecting *another* morality. The old constructs do not hold up, because adhering to them means consigning oneself to the oppressive reality. Johnny's mother is involved in the old constructs. Manliness is equated with white morality. And even though she claims to love her family (her men), the overall design of her ideas are against black manhood. In Garrett's play the mother's morality manifests itself in a deep-seated hatred of Black men; while in Milner's work the mother understands, but holds her men back.

The mothers that Garrett and Milner see represent the Old Spirituality—the Faith of the Fathers of which Du Bois spoke. Johnny and Tim represent the New Spirituality. They appear to be a type produced by the upheavals of the colonial world of which Black America is a part. Johnny's assertion that he is a criminal is remarkably similar to the rebel's comments in Aimé Césaire's play, *Les Armes Miraculeuses* (*The Miraculous Weapons*). In that play the rebel, speaking to his mother, proclaims: "My name—an offense; my Christian name—humiliation; my status—a rebel; my age—the stone age." To which the mother replies: "My race—the human race. My religion—brotherhood." The Old Spirituality is generalized. It seeks to recognize Universal Humanity. The New Spirituality is specific. It begins by seeing the world from the concise point-of-view of the colonialized. Where the Old Spirituality would live with oppression while ascribing to the oppressors an innate goodness, the New Spirituality demands a radical shift in point-of-view. The colonialized native, the oppressed must, of necessity, subscribe to a *separate* morality. One that will liberate him and his people.

The assault against the Old Spirituality can sometimes be humorous. In Ben Caldwell's play, *The Militant Preacher,* a burglar is seen slipping into the home of a wealthy minister. The preacher comes in and the burglar ducks behind a large chair. The preacher, acting out the role of the supplicant minister begins to moan, praying to De Lawd for understanding.

In the context of today's politics, the minister is an Uncle Tom, mouthing platitudes against self-defense. The preacher drones in a self-pitying monologue about the folly of protecting oneself against brutal policeman. Then the burglar begins to speak. The preacher is startled, taking the burglar's voice for the voice of God. The burglar begins to play on the preacher's old time religion. He *becomes* the voice of God insulting and goading the preacher on until the preacher's attitudes about protective violence change. The next day the preacher emerges militant, gun in hand, sounding like Reverend Cleage in Detroit. He now preaches a new gospel—the gospel of the gun, an eye for an eye. The gospel is preached in the rhythmic cadences of the old Black church. But the content is radical. Just as Jones inverted the symbols in *Jello,* Caldwell twists the rhythms of the Uncle Tom preacher into the language of the new militancy.

These plays are directed at problems within Black America. They begin with the premise that there is a well defined Afro-American audience. An audience that must see itself and the world in terms of its own interests. These plays, along with many others, constitute the basis for a viable movement in the theatre—a movement which takes as its task a profound re-evaluation of the Black man's presence in America. The Black Arts Movement represents the flowering of a cultural nationalism that has been suppressed since the 1920's. I mean the "Harlem Renaissance"—which was essentially a failure. It did not address itself to the mythology and the life-styles of the Black community. It failed to take roots, to link itself concretely to the struggles of that community, to become its voice and spirit. Implicit in the Black Arts Movement is the idea that Black people, however dispersed, constitute a *nation* within the belly of white America. This is not a new idea. Garvey said it and the Honorable Elijah Muhammad says it now. And it is on this idea that the concept of Black Power is predicated.

Afro-American life and history is full of creative possibilities, and the movement is just beginning to perceive them. Just beginning to understand that the most meaningful statements about the nature of Western society must come from the Third World of which Black America is a part. The thematic material is broad, ranging from folk heroes like Shine and Stagolee to historical figures like Marcus Garvey and Malcolm X. And then there is the struggle for Black survival, the coming confrontation between white America and Black America. If art is the harbinger of future possibilities, what does the future of Black America portend?

Sonia Sanchez

(b. 1935)

SONIA SANCHEZ WRITES of herself:

Re Me—Sonia Sanchez—born 1935 in Birmingham, Ala—have 3 children—Anita, Morani Meusi, Mungu Meusi—have one book published—Homecoming *by broadside press 1969—have new play called* Sister Son/ji *in an anthology of blk/plays due out in Fall Edited by Ed Bullins for Bantam Books—poems in anthologies:* New Blk/poetry; L'Idea degli Antenati; Potere Negro; Black Fire
Shd be teaching in Sept at the University of Pittsburgh—

The Bronx Is Next *appeared in* The Drama Review *(tdr)*, Summer, 1968.

THE BRONX IS NEST

Characters

CHARLES
OLD SISTER
LARRY
ROLAND
JIMMY
WHITE COP
BLACK BITCH

The scene is a block in Harlem—a block of tenement houses on either side of a long, narrow, dirty street of full garbage cans. People are moving around in the distance bringing things out of the houses and standing with them in the street. There is activity—but as CHARLES, *a tall, bearded man in his early thirties, and* OLD SISTER *move toward the front, the activity lessens. It is night. The time is now.*

CHARLES. Keep 'em moving Roland. C'mon you mothafuckers. Keep moving. Git you slow asses out of here. We ain't got all night. Into the streets. Oh shit. Look sister. None of that. You can't take those things. Jest important things—things you would grab and carry out in case of a fire. You understand? You wouldn't have time to get all of those things if there was a real fire.

OLD SISTER. Yes son. I knows what you says is true. But you see them things is me. I brought them up with me from Birmingham 40 years ago. I always keeps them right here with me. I jest can't do without them. You know what I mean son? I jest can't leave them you see.

CHARLES. Yes sister. I know what you mean. Look. Someone will help you get back to your apartment. You can stay there. You don't have to come tonight. You can come some other time when we have room for your stuff. OK?

OLD SISTER. Thank you son. Here let me kiss you. Thank the lord there is young men like you who still care about the old people. What is your name son?

CHARLES. My name is Charles, sister. Now I have to get back to work. Hey Roland. Jimmy. Take this one back up to her apartment. Make her comfortable. She ain't coming tonight. She'll come another time.

ROLAND. Another time? Man you flipping out? Why don't you realize . . .

CHARLES. I said, Roland, she'll come another time. Now help her up those fucking stairs. Oh yes. Jimmy, see too that she gets some hot tea. You dig? Ten o'clock is our time. There ain't no time for anyone. There ain't no time for nothing 'cept what we came to do. Understand? Now get your ass stepping.

ROLAND *and* JIMMY *exit*.

LARRY. Hey Charles, over here fast. Look what I found coming out one of the buildings.

CHARLES. What, man? I told you I ain't got no time for nothing 'cept getting this block cleared out by 10 p.m. What the fuck is it?

LARRY. A white dude. A cop. An almighty fuzz. Look. I thought they were paid enough to stay out of Harlem tonight. *Turns to* COP. Man. Now just what you doing here spying on us, huh?

WHITE COP. Spying? What do you mean spying? You see. Well you know how it is. I have this friend—she lives on this block and when I got off at 4 p.m., I stopped by. Well. I was just leaving but this guy and another one taking someone upstairs saw me—pulled a gun on me and brought me out here.

CHARLES. What building and what apartment were you visiting my man?

WHITE COP. No. 214—Apt 10—but why are you interested?

CHARLES. Larry, bring the black bitch out fast. Want to get a good look at her so I'll see jest why we sweating tonight. Yeah. For all the black bitches like her.

WHITE COP *has turned around and seen the activity.* Hey. What are all the people doing out in the middle of the street? What's happening here? There's something going on here I don't know about and I have a right to know . . .

CHARLES. Right? Man. You ain't got no rights here. Jest shut your fucking white mouth before you git into something you wish you wasn't in. Man. I've got to call in about this dude. Is there a phone in any of these fire traps?

JIMMY. Yeah. I got one in my place during the year I lived here. It's No. 210—1st floor—1C—back apartment. I'll stay here with this socializing dude while you call.

CHARLES splits.

WHITE COP *takes out some cigarettes.* Want a cigarette?

JIMMY. Thanks man—in fact I'll take the whole pack. It's going to be a long night.

WHITE COP. What do you mean a long night?

JIMMY, *smiling.* Jest what I said man—and it might be your longest— *laughs*—maybe the longest of your life.

WHITE COP, *puffing on cigarette—leans against garbage can.* What's your name son?

JIMMY. You don't git nothing out of me 'til Charles returns. You hear me? So stop asking so many damn questions. *Moves to the right. Screams.* Goddamn it Roland. Your building is going too slow. We have only two more hours. Get that shit moving. We have to be finished by 10 p.m.

WHITE COP. Look. What are you people doing? Why are all the people moving out into the street—What's going on here? There's something funny going on here and I want to know what it is. You can't keep me from using my eyes and brains—and pretty soon I'll put two and two together—then you just wait . . . you just wait . . .

CHARLES *has appeared on stage at this time and has heard what the Cop has said. Is watchful for a moment—moves forward.*

CHARLES. Wait for what my man? Wait for you to find out what's happening? It's not hard to see. We're moving the people out—out into the cool breezes of the street—is that so difficult to understand?

WHITE COP. No. But why? I mean, yeah I know that the apartments are kinda hot and awful . . .

CHARLES. You right man. Kinda awful. Did you hear that description of these shit houses Jimmy? Kinda awful. I knew we weren't describing this scene right and it took this dude here to finally show us the way. From now on when I talk to people about their places I'll say— I know your places are kinda awful . . .

JIMMY. In fact, Charles, how 'bout—I know your places are maybe kinda awful . . .

CHARLES, *laughing*. Yeah. That's it. Perhaps. Maybe could there be a slight possibility that your place is kinda—now mind you, we ain't saying for sure—but maybe it's kinda awful—*becomes serious*. Yeah. That's the white man for you man. Always understating things. But since both you and I know that these places are shit-houses that conversation can end now.

JIMMY. What they say 'bout the dude, Charles?

CHARLES, *turns to* WHITE COP. Oh everything is cool. You can leave man when you want to, but first have a cigarette with us.

WHITE COP, *relaxing*. I would offer you some of mine but he took them all.

CHARLES. C'mon man. Give them back to the dude. And Jimmy go get Roland. Tell him to come talk a bit. What a night this has been. It's hard working with these people. They like cattle you know. Don't really understand anything. Being a cop, you probably found that too. Right?

WHITE COP, *lighting a cigarette*. Yeah. I did. A little. But the hardest thing for me to understand was that all you black people would even live in these conditions. Well. You know. Everybody has had ghettos but they built theirs up and there was respect there. Here. There is none of that.

CHARLES. How right you are my man. C'mon in Jimmy and Roland. We just talking to pass some time. Of course, getting back to your statement, I think the reason that the black man hasn't made it—you ain't Irish are you?—is a color thing—I mean even though the Irish were poor they were still white—but as long as white people hate because of a difference in color, then they ain't gonna let the black man do too much. You dig?

WHITE COP. But all this hopelessness. Poverty of the mind and spirit. Why? Things are so much better. All it takes is a little more effort by you people. But these riots. It's making good people have second thoughts about everything.

ROLAND. It's a long time going—man—this hopelessness—and it ain't no better. Shit. All those good thinking people changing their minds never believed in the first fucking place.

JIMMY, *stands up.* Man. Do you know that jest yesterday I was running down my ghetto street and these two white dudes stopped me and asked what I was doing out so early in the morning—and cuz I was high off some smoke—I said man—it's my street—I can walk on it any time. And they grabbed me and told me where everything was.

CHARLES. That gives me an idea. Let's change places before this dude splits. Let him be a black dude walking down a ghetto street and we'll be three white dudes—white cops on a Harlem street.

WHITE COP. Oh c'mon. That's ridiculous. What good would that do. Why I'd feel silly . . .

CHARLES. You mean you'd feel silly being black?

WHITE COP. Oh no—not that—I mean what would it prove? How would it help—what good would it do?

JIMMY. But what harm could it do?

WHITE COP. None that I could imagine . . . it's just that it's strange . . . it's like playing games.

ROLAND. Oh c'mon. I've always wanted to be a white dude—now's my chance. It'll be exciting—sure is getting boring handling this mob of people.

JIMMY. If you afraid, man, we don't have to.

WHITE COP. Afraid? No. OK. Let's start.

CHARLES, *jumps up—looks elated.* Then we'll jest be standing on the corner talking and you c'mon by. Oh yeah, maybe you should be running. OK?

CHARLES, ROLAND *and* JIMMY *move to one side of the stage—the* WHITE COP *moves to the other side and begins to run toward them.*

CHARLES. Hey slow down boy. What's your hurry?

WHITE COP, *stops running.* Yes. What's wrong officer?

JIMMY. Where you running to so fast?

WHITE COP. I just felt like running officer. I was feeling good so I decided to run.

ROLAND. Oh you were feeling good. So you decided to run. Now ain't that a load of shit if I ever heard one.

WHITE COP. It's true, officer. I was just thinking about the day—it was a great day for me so I felt like running—so I ran.

CHARLES. Boy! Who's chasing you? What did you steal?

WHITE COP. Steal? I haven't stolen anything. I haven't stolen anything. I haven't anything in my pockets. *Goes into his pockets.*

JIMMY *draws gun.* Get your hands out your pockets boy. Against the wall right now.

WHITE COP. But what have I done? I was just running. This is not legal you know. You have no right to do this . . .

ROLAND. You are perfectly correct. We have no right to do this. Why I even have no right to hit you but I am. *Hits* WHITE COP *with gun.*

WHITE COP, *falls down. Gets up.* Now wait a minute. That is going just a little too far and . . .

CHARLES. I said why were you running down that street boy?

WHITE COP. Look. Enough is enough. I'm ready to stop—I'm tired.

JIMMY. What's wrong nigger boy—can't you answer simple questions when you're asked them. Oh I know what's wrong. You need me to help you to remember. *Hits* WHITE COP *with gun.*

WHITE COP. Have you gone crazy? Stop this. You stop it now or there will be consequences.

ROLAND. What did you steal black boy—we can't find it on you but we know you got it hidden someplace. *Hits him again.*

WHITE COP. Oh my god. Stop it . . . This can't be happening to me. Look—I'm still me. It was only make believe.

CHARLES. Let's take him in. He won't cooperate. He won't answer the question. Maybe he needs more help than the three of us are giving him.

JIMMY. I don't know. Looks like he's trying to escape to me. Take out your guns. That nigger is trying to run. Look at him. Boy, don't run. Stop. I say if you don't stop I'll have to shoot.

WHITE COP. Are you all mad? I'm not running. I'm on my knees. Stop it. This can't continue. Why . . .

ROLAND. You ain't shit boy. You black. You a nigger we caught running down the street—running and stealing like all the niggers around him.

CHARLES. Now you trying to escape—and we warned you three times already. You only get three warnings then . . .

Noise from off stage—a woman's voice.

LARRY. Man. This bitch ain't cooperating Charles. She said she didn't have to come. Finally had to slap her around a bit.

CHARLES. Now is that anyway to act bitch? We just want to talk to you for a minute. Hear you were entertaining this white dude in your place. Is that so?

BLACK BITCH, *stands defiantly—has a reddish wig on which is slightly disheveled.* Who you? Man. I don't owe no black man no explanations 'bout what I do. The last black man I explained to cleaned me out, so whatever you doing don't concern me 'specially if it has a black man at the head.

JIMMY. Smart—assed—bitch.

BLACK BITCH, *turns to* JIMMY—*walks over to him.* That's right kid. A smart—assed—black bitch—that's me. Smart enough to stay clear of all black bastard men who jump from black pussy to black pussy like jumping jacks. Yeah, I know all about black men. The toms and revolutionary ones. I could keep you entertained all night long. But I got to get back. My kids will be coming home.

CHARLES. How many kids you got bitch?

BLACK BITCH. Two. Two boys. Two beautiful black boys. Smart boys you hear? They read. They know more than me already, but they still love me. Men. They will know what a woman is for. I'll teach them. I ain't educated, but I'll say—hold them in your arms—love them— love your black woman always. I'll say I am a black woman and I cry in the night. But when you are men you will never make a black woman cry in the night. You hear. And they'll promise.

ROLAND. Oh shit. Another black matriarch on our hands—and with her white boyfriend. How you gonna teach them all this great stuff when you whoring with some white dude who kills black men everyday? How you explain that shit to them?

BLACK BITCH *laughs—high piercing laugh—walks over to* WHITE COP. Explain this. *Points to* WHITE COP *on ground.*

BLACK BITCH. I only explain the important things. He comes once a week. He fucks me. He puts his grayish white dick in me and dreams his dreams. They ain't 'bout me. Explain him to my boys. *Laugh.* Man. I am surviving. This dude has been coming regularly for two years—he stays one evening, leaves and then drives on out to Long Island to his white wife and kids and reality. *Laughs.* Explain. I don't explain cuz there ain't nothing to explain.

CHARLES. Yeah. But you still a bitch. You know. None of this explaining to us keeps you from being a bitch.

BLACK BITCH. Yeah. I know what I am. *Looks around.* But all you revolutionists or nationalists or whatever you call yourselves—do you know where you at? I am a black woman and I've had black men who could not love me or my black boys—where you gonna find black women to love you when all this is over—when you need them? As for me I said no black man would touch me ever again.

CHARLES, *moving toward the* BLACK BITCH. Is that right? You not a bad looking bitch if you take off that fucking wig. *Throws it off.* A good ass. *Touches her face, neck, moves his hands on her body—moves against her until she tries to turn away.* No don't turn away bitch. Kiss me. I said kiss me. *Begins to kiss her face—slowly—sensuously —the* BLACK BITCH *grabs him and kisses him long and hard—moves her body against him.* Yeah. No black man could touch you again, huh? *Laughs and moves away.* I could fuck you right here if I wanted to. You know what a black man is don't you bitch? Is that what happens when you fuck faggoty white men?

BLACK BITCH *runs across the stage and with that run and cry that comes from her she grabs* CHARLES *and hits him and holds on.* CHARLES *turns and knocks her down. The white dude turns away.* JIMMY *moves toward her.*

BLACK BITCH. No. Watch this boy. You still young. Watch me. Don't touch me. Watch me get up. It hurts. But I'll get up. And when I'm up the tears will stop. I don't cry, when I'm standing up. All right. I'm up again. Who else? Here I am, a black bitch, up for grabs. Anyone here for me. Take your choice—your pick—slap me or fuck me—anyway you get the same charge.

JIMMY. Here black bitch. Let me help you. Your eye is swollen. *Doesn't look at* CHARLES. Can she go back to her place and get some things out Charles? I'll help her.

CHARLES. You have five minutes to help the black bitch then get you black ass back here. We wasted enough time. *Stoops.* Here don't forget her passport to the white world. *Throws wig at her.* And keep your mouth shut black bitch. You hear?

BLACK BITCH, *putting on her wig.* I told you I only explain important things. There ain't nothing happening here yet that's important to me. *Exits with* JIMMY.

CHARLES, *laughs.* That's a woman there. Yeah wig and all. She felt good for awhile. Hey you. Dude. You can get up now. All the unpleasantness is over. Here let me help you get cleaned up. *Begins to brush* WHITE COP *off.* We just got a little carried away with ourselves.

WHITE COP. Can I go now? I'm tired. It's been a long night. You said I could go.

CHARLES. But don't you want to go and see the bitch—see how she is —make sure she's okay?

WHITE COP. No. I don't think so. It's late. My wife will be worrying by now.

CHARLES. Isn't there anything else you want to see before you go? Can't I fill you in on anything?

WHITE COP. I've seen people moved into the street. That's all. Nothing else. I want to know nothing.

CHARLES. Would you believe that it's happening on every street in Harlem?

WHITE COP, *nervously.* I'm not interested. I just want to leave and go home. I'm tired.

CHARLES. Yeah man. You look tired. Look. Do me a favor. I want to go to the bitch's place and apologize. You know it wasn't right.

Hurting her like that. Come with me. Hey Roland. Shouldn't he come with me?

ROLAND. Yeah man. He should. After all, he knows her better than you. He can tell you what approach to use with her.

WHITE COP. No. I don't want to go. I don't want to see her again. It's all finished now. I'm tired. You tell her. Just let me go on home.

CHARLES. But man. I need you. I need you to help me talk to her. She'll listen to you. Anyway with you there, you'll keep me from getting violent again—c'mon man. Just this one thing then you can go.

LARRY'S *voice from off stage.* We ready to light, Charles—should we start now?

CHARLES. Yeah. All 'cept No. 214—we have some business there. Give us ten minutes then light it up.

WHITE COP *tries to run—* CHARLES *and* ROLAND *grab his arm and start walking.*

WHITE COP. I don't want to go. I must get home. My wife and two boys are waiting for me. I have never hurt or killed a black person in my life. Yes. I heard talk that some cops did—that they hated black people—but not me. I listened. It made me sick but I never participated in it. I didn't ever do anything to negroes. No. I don't want to go. I haven't done anything. *Begins to cry.* Holy Mother— you can't do this to me. *Screams.* But, I'm white! I'm white! No. This can't be happening—I'm white!

Tries to break away and ROLAND *knocks him out—they pull him off stage. The stage becomes light—buildings are burning—people are moving around looking at the blaze.* JIMMY, ROLAND *and* CHARLES *reappear.*

JIMMY. Well. That's that, man. What a night. Do I still have to write this up tonight Charles?

CHARLES. Were those your orders?

JIMMY. Yes. Okay. I'll do it while we wait. I'll drop it in the mail box tonight. See you soon.

CHARLES. A good job, Jimmy. Stay with them. Talk to them. They need us more than ever now.

ROLAND. We got to split Charles. We got a meeting going tonight. You know what the meeting is about man? *Take out a cigarette.* You think this is the right strategy burning out the ghettoes? Don't make much sense to me man. But orders is orders. You know what's going down next?

CHARLES, *lighting a cigarette.* Yeah. I heard tonight when I called about that white dude. The Bronx is next—Let's split.

Nathan A. Scott, Jr.

(b. 1925)

ALTHOUGH STILL A RELATIVELY young scholar, Nathan Scott, Jr. has written and/or edited eighteen published volumes and has made a prolific contribution to outstanding literary and theological journals in England and America. For his distinguished work in criticism and religion he has received five honorary doctorates.

Scott was born in Cleveland and reared in Detroit. He received a B.A. from the University of Michigan, a B.D. from Union Theological Seminary, and a Ph.D from Columbia University.

Dr. Scott has taught at Virginia Union University and at Howard University, and is now Professor of Theology and Literature and Chairman of the Theology and Literature Field in the Divinity School of the University of Chicago. He is also a priest of the Episcopal Church; Canon Theologian of the Cathedral of St. James in Chicago; Kent Fellow for the Society for Religion in Higher Education; and co-editor of *The Journal of Religion*.

Among his numerous scholarly publications are the following: *Rehearsals of Discomposure: Alienation and Reconciliation in Modern Literature* (1952); *The Tragic Vision and the Christian Faith* (1957); *Modern Literature and the Religious Frontier* (1958); *Albert Camus* (1962); *Samuel Beckett* (1965); *The Broken Center: Studies in the Theological Horizon of Modern Literature* (1966); *Ernest Hemingway* (1966); *Negative Capability: Studies in the New Literature and the Religious Situation* (1969); *The Unquiet Vision: Mirrors of Man in Existentialism* (1969).

For a study of Nathan Scott's position as a critic, see William V. Spanos, "The Critical Imperatives of Alienation: The Theological Perspective of Nathan Scott's Criticism," *The Journal of Religion*, University of Chicago, Vol. 48, No. 1 (January, 1968).

"Judgment Marked by a Cellar: The American Negro Writer and the Dialectic of Despair" appeared in Harry J. Mooney, Jr. and Thomas F. Staley (eds.), *The Shapeless God: Essays on Modern Fiction* (Pittsburgh: University of Pittsburgh Press, 1968). The version appearing here is from *The Denver Quarterly*, Vol. II, No. 2 (Summer, 1967).

JUDGMENT MARKED BY A CELLAR:

THE AMERICAN NEGRO WRITER AND THE DIALECTIC OF DESPAIR

> *The interests of a black man in a cellar*
> *Mark tardy judgment on the world's closed door.*
> Hart Crane, *"Black Tambourine."*

The Negro poet Countee Cullen began his poem of 1927, "Heritage," with the question "What is Africa to me?" And as he contemplated his own removal by three centuries "From the scenes his fathers loved,/Spicy grove, cinnamon tree," the question took on for him what was manifestly an import baffling and obscure—

> Africa? A book one thumbs
> Listlessly, till slumber comes.
> Unremembered are her bats
> Circling through the night, her cats
> Crouching in the river reeds. . . .
> > . . . The tree . . .
> Budding yearly must forget
> How its past arose or set. . . .
> One three centuries removed
> From the scenes his fathers loved,
> Spicy grove, cinnamon tree,
> What is Africa to me?[1]

"What is Africa to me?" The poet's question is clearly intended to be rhetorical. And it is precisely by such a skepticism as it implies, about the American Negro's dependence on the African past, that the interpreter of his cultural achievements would be wise to be informed. For the gulf that the anguished "Middle Passage" of long ago established between the American Negro and his African heritage could still perhaps be inchoately felt by earlier generations, as their mothers sang "Sometimes I Feel Like a Motherless Child." But today it is a gulf too depthless even to be obscurely felt. And the ancient memories that lie at the basis of Negro experience are memories not of "bats/Circling through the night" or of "cats/Crouching in the river reeds" but are rather memories of the auction block in South Carolina or Georgia, of "strange fruit hanging from the poplar trees . . . of the gallant South," and of those costly involvements of "many thousands gone" in the

---

[1] Countee Cullen, "Heritage," in *Anthology of American Negro Literature,* ed. by V. F. Calverton (New York: The Modern Library, 1929), p. 192.

Reprinted by permission of the author and the University of Pittsburgh Press.

bone and flesh of the American Adam. Nowhere else in the life of the human community have black men and white men touched one another so deeply and indelibly as in the bitter and nascently triumphant drama of the American experiment. And it now begins to be apparent that, despite superficial differences of color and ethnic style, a common cultural identity has been forged out of this drama that belongs equally to black and white alike, for each—in blood and in experience—is a part of the other; neither is "an Iland, intire of it selfe"; each is "a peece of the Continent" which both, together, have built; if either "bee washed away by the Sea," the other "is the less"; and neither can ever "send to know for whom the bell tolls," since it is in their steadfast abiding by each other that they have their "onely securitie."

So Negro literature, like all other modes of Negro expression—jazz and the spirituals and sorrow songs, painting and sculpture and dance, pulpit and secular oratory—is inseparably a part of American culture. Phyllis Wheatley, the Negro poet of the Revolutionary period, belongs as much to the time of Philip Freneau as the novelist Jean Toomer belongs to the time of Sherwood Anderson or as Ralph Ellison belongs to the period of Faulkner and Warren. And thus to take some measure of what is religiously decisive for the literary imagination among interpreters of Negro experience in this country is not to deal with forms of sensibility that are in any way tangential with respect to the central traditions of American literature. The Negro writer, to be sure, has been given a special subject by what has been special in the circumstances of his life in the United States. But the spiritual resources on which he has drawn for the shaping of his experience are in no essential way incommensurate with the environing Protestant culture that has provided the American imagination with its most basic materials; so the theological dimension of things that we confront in Negro literature is, in its fundamental terms, the same that we meet elsewhere in our literature, just as devious and duplicitous and just as riddled with ambiguity.

Indeed, it is precisely the tidiness of the late Randall Stewart's version of the religious issue in American literature that does so emphatically call it into question. What one is perhaps first struck by in his little book of 1958, *American Literature and Christian Doctrine*, is the consistency of his inclination toward a polemical treatment of his subject, and it may be that this is a polemicism made inevitable by the excessive fastidiousness of his theological orthodoxy. So strict in fact is this orthodoxy that one wonders if it may not be by way of being something less than orthodox. For Randall Stewart makes us feel that he had remembered T. E. Hulme's dictum about Original Sin being "the closest expression of . . . the religious attitude"—the notion that man is "a wretched creature" who "can only accomplish anything of value by discipline"—and Hulme's definition of "romanticism" as the view that "man . . . is an infinite reservoir of possibilities."[2] And, working with these counters, he puts forward a very rigorous (and, I suspect, a far too simple) definition of Christianity: it seemed for him to be very largely summed up in the Pauline text, "All have sinned, and come short of the glory of God." The Pauline stringency is, of course, very much a part of the Christian vision; but when adherence to it is made the single criterion of that vision, the result is a kind of rigorism that, on the one hand, cannot envisage even the possibility, say, of Emerson by any "dint of sophistry . . . [being] brought within the Christian fold"[3] and that, on the other hand, is prepared to regard as essentially Christian the kind of theatricalization of Evil into an independent world-principle that, in much of Robert Penn Warren's work, really amounts to something like a shrill and bitter Manicheism.

Professor Stewart's was, in other words, a very *literary* kind of theology. And, though the modishness which the notion of Original Sin has enjoyed in literary circles in recent years may put us in mind of a crucial aspect of the Christian testimony, this is not an idea that, taken by itself, furnishes a sufficient summation of the full Christian wisdom about human existence. Indeed, when it is made, in effect, the single criterion of the authentically Christian vision, the result, as in Randall Stewart's book, is a drastic oversimplification of the actual complexity of the relation of Christianity to modern culture. Emerson, for example, is certainly a crucial case in the American tradition; and it is true, of course, as Edward Taylor said, that, though he was "one of the sweetest creatures God ever made," there was "a screw loose somewhere in the machinery." Yet when Mr. Stewart, in effect, sides with Edward Taylor in the view that Emerson knew "no more of the religion of the New Testament than Balaam's ass did of the principles of the Hebrew grammar," he oversimplifies. For, despite all the nonsense about the "infinitude of the private man," in his stress upon the autonomy of the individual and in his protest against all external powers that thwart the individual soul, Emerson was making a kind of witness, however attenuated, to an authentically Christian conception of responsible selfhood. Or, again, in our own time, though Professor Stewart was certainly right in regarding the vision of evil in Faulkner and Warren as partaking of an authentically Christian vision (at least when these writers are considered in relation to the naturalistic positivism so pervasive in our period), he failed to take adequately into account the fact that theirs is, though, a vision of evil that is often so unremitting as to make them very much closer to the pure pessimism

[2] *Vide* T. E. Hulme, "Humanism and the Religious Attitude" and "Romanticism and Classicism" in his *Speculations,* ed. by Herbert Read (London: Kegan Paul, Trench, Trubner & Co., Ltd., 1936).

[3] Randall Stewart, *American Literature and Christian Doctrine* (Baton Rouge: Louisiana State University Press, 1958), p. 55.

of Greek tragedy than to the full wisdom of the Christian faith, whose understanding of the depth of the human predicament has always been influenced by a penitential and redemptive motif. We might say that Faulkner and Warren often seem to *believe* in Original Sin—which is never quite the stance of the integrally Christian imagination. And just as Christianly equivocal, surely, are those "Counter-Romantics" of the nineteenth century—particularly Melville—whom Stewart wanted so sharply to oppose to the heterodoxy of Emerson and Whitman.

Randall Stewart saw, to be sure, what R. W. B. Lewis was so cogently arguing in the 'fifties, that ours is a culture that may be conceived by way of the image of a debate or of an unfolding dialogue; and he also understood that one of the voices perennially opposed to the tradition of our tragic realism has been that of what Mr. Lewis calls "the party of Hope."[4] But, however inhospitably disposed one may be (for reasons of temperament or of principle) to the moral and artistic sensibility of Emerson and Thoreau and Whitman and their followers, one simply cannot go through American tradition checking off those who belong to "the party of Hope" as heterodox and checking off the tragic realists (the Hawthornes and Melvilles and Faulkners and Warrens) as orthodox. It can, of course, be done, but the procedure is not likely to make for any really useful discriminations about the actual complexities that have been operative religiously in our literature.

"The hopeful attitudes," says R. W. B. Lewis, "are pheonomena . . . about which we are today somewhat embarrassed: the culture's youthful indiscretions and extravagances. We have had to get beyond such simple-minded adolescent confidence, we suppose . . . and we sometimes congratulate ourselves austerely for having settled, like adults or Europeans, upon a course of prolonged but tolerable hopelessness. We call that state of hopelessness the human condition: something we study to realize in our literature and reflect in our behavior."[5] But, as Mr. Lewis wisely reminds us, irony remains "fertile and alive" and avoids becoming merely mordant only as long as it seeks to "feed and fatten" itself on the opposite possibilities of hope. "The new hopelessness is, paradoxically," he says, "as simple-minded as innocence," and its "chilling skepticism . . . represents one of the modes of death."[6] Nor is this cautionary word applicable only to our contemporary situation: it also has, I believe, a certain relevance to our entire tradition. Mr. Lewis is surely right in arguing, as he does in *The American*

[4] *Vide* R. W. B. Lewis, "Prologue," *The American Adam: Innocence, Tragedy, and Tradition in the Nineteenth Century* (Chicago: University of Chicago Press, "Phoenix Books," 1959).
[5] *Ibid.*, p. 195.
[6] *Ibid.*, p. 196.

Adam, that our whole literature, from Cooper to Faulkner, may be viewed under the aspect of the myth of Adam—a second Adam, who, in a new Paradise, must be painfully initiated into the difficult complexities of the moral life. He demonstrates, with great subtlety of insight, how persistently this myth has provided American literature with its constitutive themes, and he indicates how frequently the portrait that emerges is of innocence and naiveté unequipped to resist the crises and distempers of life. Indeed, it is in the discoveries born out of this disconcertion that our tragic realism has had its main source. But the trouble has been that the American Adam has sometimes been so deeply unhinged by the discovery of evil that he has, in his shock, been led to elevate evil into a principle coeval with God himself. And thus it is that this "blackness" which Melville found in Hawthorne becomes, in Melville's phrase, "ten times black" and becomes the blackness of Manicheism, a blackness, as Mr. Lewis says, that represents one of the modes of death.

In his brilliant book *The American Novel and Its Tradition,* the late Richard Chase is at one point remarking the "great practical sanity" of the English novel, the fact that it has rarely included "oddity, distortion of personality, dislocations of normal life, recklessness of behavior, malignancy of motive."[7] And this puts him in mind of the difficulty that F. R. Leavis has, in *The Great Tradition,* in fitting the author of *Wuthering Heights* into the great central line of English fiction, the line of Jane Austen, of George Eliot, of Conrad and James and Lawrence. He quotes the passage in which Dr. Leavis admits that this "astonishing work seems to me a kind of sport" and then says:

> Of course Mr. Leavis is right; in relation to the great tradition of the English novel, *Wuthering Heights* is indeed a sport. But suppose it were discovered that *Wuthering Heights* was written by an American of New England Calvinist or Southern Presbyterian background. The novel would be astonishing and unique no matter who wrote it or where. But if it were an American novel it would not be a sport; it has too close an affinity with too many American novels, and among them some of the best. Like many of the [major] fictions . . . [in the American tradition] *Wuthering Heights* proceeds from an imagination that is essentially melodramatic, that operates among radical contradictions and renders reality indirectly or poetically. . . .[8]

And, of course, Richard Chase's instinct about Emily Brontë and her assimilability into American tradition is absolutely right, for her kind

---

[7] Richard Chase, *The American Novel and Its Tradition* (Garden City: Doubleday Anchor Books, 1957), p. 2.
[8] *Ibid.,* p. 4.

of dark, narrow, sensationalistic profundity is most assuredly not at all a strange thing in our own literature; the story of Heathcliffe and Catherine Linton has far more in common with *The Marble Faun, The Scarlet Letter, Pierre, Pudd'nhead Wilson, Sanctuary, and The Sun Also Rises* than it has with any of the representative texts in English fiction. *"Wuthering Heights,"* says E. M. Forster in his little book *Aspects of the Novel,* "is filled with sound—storm and rushing wind."[9] And, at a distance, this might also be one's impression of much of American literature—eerie and frightening, mysterious and ghost-ridden, exposed to all the atmospheric tumults of the storm and the rushing wind.

So it is no wonder that not only the English Gothicism of Emily Brontë but also the German Gothicism of Franz Kafka seem to be close to us and to be a part of us: indeed, as Leslie Fiedler reminds us, Kafka's major posthumous successes have "belonged almost more to the history of our literature than his own."[10] "The terror of which I write," said Edgar Poe, "is not of Germany, but of the soul." And it is into this perilous interior that we are taken in Melville's *Pierre,* in Stephen Crane's *The Red Badge of Courage,* in Djuna Barnes' *Nightwood,* in John Hawkes's *The Cannibal,* and in James Purdy's *Malcolm.* In book after book after book, in fact, in the American tradition the glow of the scene is lurid and nocturnal: the protagonists are exhibited (in Faulkner's words [*Light in August*]) as engendering "so much more than [they] can or should have to bear"; the human adventure appears to be "an ironic and tragic affair that is beyond human rule and misrule"[11]; and the authorial intelligence that lies behind these books seems to be one which "believes in original sin, but not in divine love."[12]

Now, in the case of Hawthorne, Melville was inclined to suggest that "this great power of blackness . . . derives its force from its appeals to that Calvinistic sense of Innate Depravity and Original Sin, from whose visitations, in some shape or other, no deeply thinking mind is always and wholly free."[13] And it may well be that it is just here, in Melville's essay on "Hawthorne and His *Mosses,*" that we have the most important single insight ever to be achieved into the nature of what is theologically determinative of the slant and bias of the American imagination. It is true, of course, that, by the time of Hawthorne and

[9] E. M. Forster, *Aspects of the Novel* (London: Edward Arnold & Co., 1949), p. 134.

[10] Leslie Fiedler, *Love and Death in the American Novel* (New York: Criterion Books, 1960), p. 468.

[11] Alfred Kazin, "The Stillness of *Light in August,*" *Partisan Review,* Vol. XXIV, No. 4 (Fall, 1957), p. 533.

[12] *Ibid.,* p. 536.

[13] Herman Melville, "Hawthorne and His *Mosses,*" in *The Shock of Recognition,* ed. by Edmund Wilson (Garden City: Doubleday & Co., 1947), p. 192.

Melville, American Calvinism in the form of the Puritan movement had long since lost its original unity and power as a creative force in religious history. The process of the dissolution is sensitively traced in Richard Niebuhr's *The Kingdom of God in America*,[14] where it is shown how, following the period of the "Great Awakening," the original radicalism petered out, as a result of institutionalizing and secularizing influences. Indeed, it is not an *over*simplification of our theological history to say that, between the time of Jonathan Edwards and Reinhold Niebuhr, there is not a single theologian in the American tradition of really commanding importance, none, that is, whose achievement makes him eligible for that modern pantheon which embraces such Europeans as Schleiermacher and Kierkegaard and Ritschl and Barth. And certainly in the period of Melville and Hawthorne the Christian enterprise in this country could offer nothing more, theologically, than the equally flaccid options of Charles Grandison Finney on the one hand or Theodore Parker and Ralph Waldo Emerson on the other.

Yet, for all of the dissolution of high Calvinism that had been accomplished by the middle years of the nineteenth century, Melville's instinct about his friend was right, for the great power of blackness in Hawthorne does indeed derive "its force from its appeals to that Calvinistic sense of Innate Depravity and Original Sin," and so does it have the same derivation in Melville himself—as it does also in Faulkner or in Penn Warren in our own day. For though it is true that the "enthusiasm" of the Finneys and Moodys and Billy Grahams on the one hand and the progressivistic optimism and positive thinking of the Emersons and Mary Baker Eddys and Norman Vincent Peales on the other have, in various ways, been the sources of the main movements of popular religion in America over the past hundred years, it is also true that classic Calvinism entered deeply into the national consciousness, and it has in fact found its best expressions in our imaginative literature. Writers like Hawthorne and Melville and Faulkner and Warren have not, of course, seen *what* the great Puritans saw, but they have seen things *as* their great forebears saw them, and one feels that it is this great heritage[15]—"with its grand metaphors of election and damnation, its opposition of the Kingdom of Light and the Kingdom of Darkness, its eternal and autonomous contraries of good and evil"[16]—one feels that it is this great heritage which provides them with their fundamental terms of reference. For theirs is an

---

[14] *Vide* H. Richard Niebuhr, *The Kingdom of God in America* (New York: Harper Torchbooks, 1959).

[15] This precise distinction between *what* and *as* is, I think, borrowed from Richard Chase, though I cannot locate just where it is that it is to be found.

[16] Richard Chase, *The Democratic Vista* (Garden City: Doubleday Anchor Books, 1958), p. 34.

imagination of human existence as irremediably hazardous and problematic: it is an imagination extremist and melodramatic whose themes
are improbable and negative and horrific, the themes of the Gothic
tale of terror. And the tradition that descends from these figures is one
filled with "radical maladjustments and contradictions,"[17] a tradition
"less interested in redemption than in . . . the eternal struggle between
good and evil, less interested in incarnation and reconciliation than in
alienation and disorder."[18]

This is the sort of secularized Calvinism that constitutes a large
part of the religious inheritance whose pressure is felt by the literary
artist in American culture, and it is an inheritance felt with an especial
force by the Negro writer. He is, of course, as alienated from the
official usages of the Christian tradition as his white counterpart in the
intellectual community tends to be, perhaps even far more profoundly
so. The cliché-ridden mentality of popular journalism and sociology
supposes that nowhere in our culture does an integrally Christian
vision of things have a stronger residual life than amongst the Negro
populace, and this may still be true to a considerable extent of the
black peasantry of the rural South. But there is much which would
indicate that the Negro proletarian participates in the spiritual root-
lessness of industrial society quite as deeply as does the modern worker
generally. And the Negro intellectual has long since ceased, in any
significant degree, to approximate the astonishing picture that Professor Edward Shils offers of the religious situation of the Indian intellectual. In the brilliant account that Mr. Shils presented a few years ago
in *The Sewanee Review* of "The Culture of the Indian Intellectual,"[19]
he tells us that in contemporary India, amongst intellectuals, religious
agnosticism is an inconsequential minority position and that the historic religious traditions continue robustly to live on there in today's
intellectual community. And he maintains this to be so, even though
insisting at the same time on the profound impact of Westernizing
influence. It is a surprising line of argument which is not altogether
convincing. But should it turn out that, in this regard, Mr. Shils is more
right than wrong, the religious situation of the Indian intellectual
would then have to be acknowledged as differing most radically from
that of the American Negro intellectual whose painful experience of
the hiatus in a Christian culture between ethical profession and practice has taught him to understand religion in the terms of "ideology"
and, if pressed on the point, to say in effect, as James Baldwin does,
that "God . . . is white"[20] and that "whoever wishes to become a truly

[17] Richard Chase, *The American Novel and Its Tradition*, p. 2.
[18] Richard Chase, *The Democratic Vista*, p. 34.
[19] *Vide* Edward Shils, "The Culture of the Indian Intellectual," *The Sewanee Review*, Vol. LXVII, No. 2 (pp. 239–261) and No. 3 (pp. 401–421).
[20] James Baldwin, *The Fire Next Time* (New York: Dell, "Delta Books," 1964),
pp. 44–45.

moral human being . . . must first divorce himself from all the prohibitions, crimes, and hypocrisies of the Christian church."[21]

This is not, of course, to say that, in the case of the Negro writer, he has not found in the mythopoeic idioms and iconology of the folk religion of Negro Protestantism a rich vein of dramatic material: for the poetry of James Weldon Johnson and Langston Hughes, and the fiction of Cullen and Zora Neal Hurston and James Baldwin—to mention only a few instances—clearly have this kind of dependence. But, even in so beautifully executed and moving a book as Weldon Johnson's *God's Trombones* (1927), with its brilliant employment of the rhetoric of the old Negro pulpit, one feels the writer's position *vis-à-vis* his *mythos* to be that of a kind of archaeologist: the very shrewdness of the mimicry with which an archaic rhetoric is rendered, the almost too brilliant expertise of it, carries a suggestion of the distance at which the poet stands from the implied protagonist of the verse. And one feels much the same distance between artist and *mythos* in such a later book as James Baldwin's *Go Tell It On the Mountain* (1953), whose evocation of the world of the Harlem store-front church is, in the terms of prose fiction, as nimble a performance as Weldon Johnson's of a quarter-century earlier in the dramatic lyric. Though both writers —along with many others who might also be cited—use a religious tradition, they make us feel that what they themselves are most truly in contact with is a detritus of sentiment and rhetoric which is the last residuum of pieties effective now only in the degree to which they provide a sophisticated artist with a sort of framework for his "romance." Their distance, in short, from the position of a genuinely Christian writer (who is something else again—as in the case of a Claudel, a Mauriac, and Auden—from the writer who simply raids a religious tradition for dramatic machinery) is perhaps something like the distance between the Thornton Wilder of *Heaven's My Destination* and *Our Town* and the Eliot of *Ash Wednesday* and the *Quartets*.

So the Negro writer, for all of his occasional captivation by the charm of folk religion, represents no great exception to the general secularity of his intellectual class. Indeed, it may well be the profundity of his alienation from the Christian tradition that has left him so susceptible to the deracinative effects of the experience of exclusion which is our culture's decisive bequest to its Negro members. Yet, in a way, it is precisely this experience that prepares him to order his world in accordance with the myth of the "wounded Adam" which is a fundamental archetype figuring in that secularized Calvinism which our writers enter into the more deeply as they absorb the air and atmosphere of our literature.

In Brockden Brown's *Arthur Mervyn*, in Hawthorne's *The Scarlet Letter*, in Melville's *Billy Budd*, in James's *The Princess Casamassima*,

---

[21] *Ibid.*, p. 61.

in Dreiser's *An American Tragedy,* in Bellow's *Augie March,* in James Purdy's *Malcolm*—as in Richard Wright's *Native Son* and Ralph Ellison's *Invisible Man* and James Baldwin's *Another Country*—this is an Adam (the "wounded Adam") who is (normally) a provincial and who, with "great expectations," seeks to enter a world which, even if it is no vaster in size than Hester Prynne's village or Billy Budd's ship, is a complex and deviously ordered place. This is an Adam who comes from without the precincts of human intermingling and is "morally prior"[22] to all that, being unencumbered by familial or social attachments—and he is a stranger in the world, he is an "outsider," because he is unstained by the world's improbity. But he approaches the world not with any sort of fastidious distaste but with an enormous yearning and aspiration, for he sees it initially as a proving ground where all things may be added unto him: it is "the good earth" and a world of promises, and he applies his full energy toward winning what will be for him the great prize—namely, some definitive authentication of his really belonging to the human polity that he confronts. He wants an acknowledged "place," he wants to be accommodated. So he advances hopefully into a complex order of things the inner logic of which he does not fully grasp. But though he may succeed in doing nothing more than "leaving his mark upon the world . . . [as] a sign in which conquest may later become possible for the survivors,"[23] his own last state is likely to be greatly different from the first. For sometimes, like Antaeus, the wounded Adam—who the American imagination likes so much to contemplate—does not win access to a deeper strength through his encounter with the world, the moral weather of Experience being a climate of gale in which Innocence is bound to be undone. And even if his "initiation" is *into* society rather than *away* from it,[24] the process is likely to exact an enormous cost, so that something is lost of that first fine flush of buoyancy and good cheer with which the hero began his voyage, the maturity that he achieves being a thing of stoical sobriety and resignation, an affair of deflation and disenchantment; the wisdom of experience, in other words, proves purchasable only by the loss of something bright and lovely which is a natural *donnée* of that "simple genuine self" which Emerson regarded as "the plain old Adam . . . against the whole world."

Now it is this myth of the American as Adam, hectored and wounded by "the world," that Leslie Fiedler and Richard Lewis and numerous other recent students of American tradition have taught us to discern as having played an executive role in the shaping of our literature. And what I want now to suggest is that one of the significant

22 R. W. B. Lewis, *op. cit.,* pp. 128–129.
23 *Ibid.,* p. 128.
24 *Ibid.,* p. 115.

bodies of evidence to be adduced in this connection is that which is comprised by the work of Negro writers, of whom the chief exemplars today are doubtless the late Richard Wright, and Ralph Ellison and James Baldwin. Knowing so intimately as they do the world of the insulted and the rejected, theirs is an experience of life in the United States that has bred in them a habit of reflection whose natural fulcrum is the dialectic of innocence and experience: the "wounded Adam" is bone of their bone and flesh of their flesh. And indeed it is precisely in the extreme situation to which American history has committed these writers that we may see with an especial clarity a particular turn which the literary imagination in this country has been recurrently tempted to take, in its broodings on Adam's unlucky fate. It is the turn which, as Richard Lewis reminds us, is classically adumbrated in Melville's incident of "The Try-Works" in *Moby-Dick*.

It will be recalled that on a certain evening, towards midnight, Ishmael is taking his turn at the *Pequod*'s helm. And, from the stern, he looks down on the crew below, between the foremast and mainmast, where they are gathered around two vast boiling cauldrons into which they are pitching great masses of blubber, as "the wind howled on, and the sea leaped, and the ship groaned and dived, and yet steadfastly shot in her red hell further and further into the blackness. . . ." As Ishmael gazes down into his gloomy pit, "now and then made ghastly by flashes of redness," he falls off to sleep, just for a moment: then, just as quickly, he wakens, and, before he is even aware that he has been dozing, he becomes in a moment's flash "horribly conscious of something fatally wrong." And then it is that he realizes that, in his sleep, he has swung the tiller around, so that, now, he is able to swing it about again only just in time to keep the vessel fom flying up into the wind and possibly capsizing. "How glad and how grateful the relief from this unnatural hallucination of the night," sighs Ishmael the narrator, in retrospect. Then Melville points the moral: he says:

> Look not too long in the face of the fire, O man! . . . Turn not thy back to the compass . . . believe not the artificial fire, when its redness makes all things look ghastly. To-morrow, in the natural sun, the skies will be bright; those who glared like devils in the forking flames, the morn will show in far other, at least gentler, relief; the glorious, golden, glad sun, the only true lamp—all others but liars!

But now it is precisely this dangerous course, of looking too long in the face of fire, that the "wounded Adam" has often been tempted to take: indeed, the sign of his wound is just this fascination with the demonic, this "hypnosis by evil."[25] And, amongst the many rich exam-

25 *Ibid.*, p. 132.

ples that American literature affords, none is more deserving of attention than that body of testimony which has come from our ablest Negro writers who are, all of them, most deeply stirred by the myth of the American Adam, more especially by the myth of the "wounded Adam"—and, in the very best of them, what is perhaps of the highest interest is the degree to which "the relief from this unnatural hallucination of the night" is just barely managed, through a feat of imaginative transcendence. They all have a deep knowledge of what Mr. Auden was telling us at the end of the 'thirties, in the famous sentence of his poem "September 1, 1939," that "We must love one another or die" —and it is the general failure of love that prompts their rage, their sense of being "lost in a haunted wood."

It is surely in the inflamed and socially discarnate wraiths at the center of Richard Wright's fiction that we encounter the most drastic instances of the wounded Adam in American literature. In "Long Black Song," one of the stories in his collection of 1938, *Uncle Tom's Children,* the husband of a Negro woman who has been seduced by a white salesman says: "The white folks ain never gimme a chance! They ain never give no black man a chance! There ain nothing in yo whole life yuh kin keep from em!. . . . Ahm gonna be hard like they is! So hep me Gawd, Ahm gonna be *hard!* When they come fer me Ahm gonna *be* here!" And this is precisely the posture of the young Chicago Negro whose story is told in *Native Son* (1940), the novel that made Wright the first Negro writer to win a major reputation in American literary life. Bigger Thomas is one who intends to "be hard": indeed, as he says, "Every time I think about it I feel like somebody's poking a red-hot iron down my throat." So it is with a sullen suspiciousness that he faces the Chicago philanthropist who takes him off the relief rolls by hiring him as a chauffeur. And it is with an even greater skepticism that he views his employer's daughter and her Communist sweetheart who make gestures of fraternity toward him by inviting him to join them in a café as an equal. But this is a relation that never becomes genuinely complicated, for, at the end of their first evening together, the girl is so intoxicated that Bigger, having been entrusted with seeing her home, has to carry her bodily from the family automobile to her bedroom—into which her blind mother comes suddenly, just in the moment when he is contemplating a sexual act. And, in order to prevent the mother's knowing that he and Mary are in the room, he smothers the girl and then, in his panic, stuffs her body into the furnace. Which, in turn, leads eventually to his second crime, now against his mistress Bessie, to whom he confesses the first deed and whom he must finally remove to prevent her betraying him to the police. But he cannot ultimately avoid his nemesis and is at last captured on a South Side tenement rooftop, as a raging mob clamors for his life in the street below.

Now the engine that Wright desperately relied upon to whip this lurid fairy-tale into some semblance of probability was the courtroom defense of Bigger by his Jewish lawyer, Mr. Max—who tells us that, though there are no corpses, Bigger has committed countless murders long before the assault on Mary Dalton:

> ". . . This Negro boy's entire attitude toward life is a *crime!* The hate and fear which we have inspired in him, woven by our civilization into the very structure of his consciousness, into his blood and bones, into the hourly functioning of his personality, have become the justification of his existence.
>
> "Every time he comes in contact with us, he kills! . . . Every thought he thinks is potential murder. . . . Every hope is a plan for insurrection. Every glance of the eye is a threat. *His very existence is a crime against the state!*"

And, what is more, we are told that we have only to "multiply Bigger Thomas twelve million times, allowing for environmental and temperamental variations, and for those Negroes who are completely under the influence of the Church, and you have the psychology of the Negro people."

And thus it is that, in offering a depraved and inhuman beast as the comprehensive image of the American Negro, the novel shows itself to be overwhelmed finally by the very cancer it wants to cauterize. For, from the moment, on its first page, when Bigger is awakened by the *Brrrrriiiiiiinnnnnnnng!* of his alarm clock, until his "faint, wry, bitter smile" of farewell at Mr. Max on the final page, the novel is controlled by precisely those hopeless assumptions about Negro life which elicited its rage, and its protagonist's sense of his own identity is formed by just that image of himself which, as it lives in the larger culture, has caused his despair. So long, in other words, had Richard Wright looked into the face of fire that, when he turned away, to give dramatic substance to the hue and cry he wanted to sound, it was his tendency himself to brutalize the creatures of his imagination. Enraged as he was by the indignities that had been heaped on the Negro's head in this country, he wanted, as it were, to hold "a loaded pistol at the head of the white world while . . . [muttering] between clenched teeth: 'Either you grant us equal rights as human beings or else this is what will happen.' "[26] So, as in the wronged husband of "Long Black Song," he had to make his characters "hard"; and, in thus sweeping them into the raging abysses of violent criminality, he forged an image of *la présence noire* that is in no great way removed from the

[26] Charles I. Glicksberg, "Negro Fiction in America," *The South Atlantic Quarterly,* Vol. XLV, No. 4 (October, 1946), p. 482.

wild and lickerish nigger who inhabits the demented imagination of the racial paranoiac.

Nor was this a pathos that Wright was ever able to escape. Even in the 'fifties, after his long years of residence in Paris and tutelage under French existentialism, he was still presenting the American Negro as a wounded innocent who is an outsider, not only in a socio-logical sense but also, and more decisively, in a moral sense as well. *The Outsider* (1953), which is the most important book of this late period of his career, has as its protagonist Cross Damon, a half-educated young intellectual who bears the Negro's ancestral burden of rejection and marginality; but his concern with what is socially problematic in his situation is but one phase of a deeper concern with what is metaphysically problematic in human life. He is a man whose sense of the world has been formed by that tradition of philosophic radicalism that runs from Nietzsche to contemporary existentialists like Heidegger and Sartre, and so he is particularly alert to the reli-gious vacuum which this tradition has asserted to be at the heart of modern experience. He no longer sleeps in the old myths of the Greeks and the Jews: he has arrived at that chilling conclusion of modern nihilism, that nothing is to be preferred to anything else; and, for him, this means that the dreadful burden which man must bear today is the burden of freedom, the burden, as he says, of being "nothing in par-ticular," except what he chooses through his actions to become. This is why panic sometimes drapes the world which he looks out upon, for what he knows himself to confront is "the empty possibility of ac-tion," and he also knows that he can do what he damn well pleases on this earth. For God is dead, and everything is therefore permitted. It is this "dreadful objectivity" to which he is given access by the aliena-tion from our culture which he suffers as a Negro.

So that night when Cross walks into the room where the Fascist nigger-hater Herndon and the Communist Blount are fighting and bludgeons them both to death, he is "not taking sides . . . not prefer-ring the lesser evil." For, in the world that he knows, there are no sides to be taken; and his act is simply "a sweeping and supreme gesture of disdain and disgust with both of them!" Like Camus' Caligula, his mission as an outsider is to reveal to mankind that the human City is really a jungle and that all the disciplines and restraints of civilization are "just screens which men have used" to throw a kind of "veneer of order" over the disorder that still seethes beneath the surface. But since, as it appears, this is a mission that cannot be accomplished apart from terrorism, Wright's conclusion of 1953 entailed essentially the same mischievousness that had been implicit thirteen years earlier in *Native Son,* the notion that the natural life-movement of the Negro who bears the full burden of his situation is toward a great blasting moment of supreme destruction. Bigger Thomas is an inarticulate proletarian who enacts his role unthinkingly, whereas Cross Damon, having read his Nietzschean primers, accepts his mission with deliberateness and in the spirit of a kind of inverted messianism—but this is the only significant difference between them, for both aim, as it were, at getting outside of history altogether, through an act of consummate violence. Like Conrad's Kurtz, Cross does, to be sure, behold at last "the horror," as he gaspingly admits to Houston, the prosecuting attorney, a moment before his death; but he has, nevertheless, tested the terrible joy of his murderous orgasm: he has burst the belt and been "hard" and won through at last to the unhistorical realm of the dream—which is of revenge.

So, in the case of Richard Wright, the myth of the wounded Adam leads to a *mystique* of gratuitous violence—which there was never any large chance of his transcending, given his immoderate and melodramatic imagination of the world as "split in two, a white world and a black one, the white one being separated from the black by a million psychological miles." What begins, though, to be a little distressing is that his brilliant younger contemporary James Baldwin should have seen so clearly how unpromising was the impasse at which Wright finally arrived—as was evinced in his *Partisan Review* essay on Wright of 1949 ("Everybody's Protest Novel")—and yet should now himself, apparently, be heading towards something like the same detour.

Mr. Baldwin's essay on "Everybody's Protest Novel," at the end of the 'forties, marked his entrance into American literary life, and, in what was virtually his first major declaration, he was eager to describe and to reject that fear of the rich, complex particularity of the human individual which he had found to be a defining characteristic of "protest" fiction, from Harriet Stowe's *Uncle Tom's Cabin* to Laura Hobson's *Gentleman's Agreement;* it is, he insisted, a literature that moves wholly within the bloodless abstractions of ethical rhetoric; it asserts by implication that "it is [the human being's] categorization alone which is real and which cannot be transcended." And, for all of the simplicity of its good intentions, it is a literature which is mischief-making, in so far as the very hotness of its temperature may persuade its victims to accept the dehumanization which it would practice upon them: indeed, said Mr. Baldwin, Bigger Thomas, in admitting "the possibility of his being sub-human," is "Uncle Tom's descendant, flesh of his flesh. . . ."

Mr. Baldwin's initial purpose, then, as he said in this essay, was to insist that the task of the novelist is "revelation" of "the disquieting complexity of ourselves." And one suspects that, basically, his disaffection from Richard Wright was caused not so much by the element of "protest" in Wright's fiction—for that has perennially been an element of the greatest literature, from the *Antigone* to *The Possessed,* from *Don Quixote* to *Doctor Faustus*—as by Wright's incorrigible commitment to a violent and narrow naturalism, to an aesthetic which (in its descent from Norris and Dreiser to Dos Passos and Farrell) required the artist to view the human individual as simply an epiphenomenon of social and political process, of the pressures and counterpressures of History. Indeed, it may well be that the acute discomfort with the aesthetics of naturalistic fiction that the young Baldwin could feel, and that Wright could not, was in some measure a result of the greater internalization in the younger man of a Christian background. The religion on which Mr. Baldwin was nurtured as a youngster in Harlem was, of course, as he reports on it in various essays, a narrow and fanatical thing, breeding intensely destructive emotions and a most unwholesome asceticism: it was the very tag end of Protestant sectarian pietism, made absurdly stern and exacting in its ethic by what was neurasthenic in the experience of the black proletarian. Yet, for all of its biliousness and obscurantism, this was a religion bound to inculcate in one receiving his early formation under its auspices a sense of the multi-leveled mystery of the individual human life, and a sense of the impossibility of containing this mystery within the reductionist formulae of a Dreiser or a Dos Passos—or a Wright.

So, in his first book, *Go Tell It on the Mountain*—which proved to be one of the finest American novels of the 1950's—Mr. Baldwin, instead of hurling forth some hard-boiled and torrential blast of strident "sociology," chose as his form what German criticism has designated as the *Bildungsroman:* he undertook to produce a novel of development, and thus his theme—autobiographical undoubtedly—is the formation of a boy's character, a sensitive Negro boy who has to find his way toward some liberating sense of his own human possibilities, in the repressive atmosphere of a primitive religion of Jesus and Satan that is fanatically celebrated in the Harlem storefront church (the Temple of the Fire Baptized) and fiercely administered in the family. The young hero of the novel, John Grimes, as he faces the oppressively confining world of his family and its fanatical religion and the terrible backwater of Harlem, decides that he must revolt: "He would not be like his father, or his father's fathers. He would have another life." He is standing one day in Central Park before a slope which

> . . . stretched upward, and above it the brillant sky, and beyond it, cloudy, and far away, he saw the skyline of New York. He did not know why, but there arose in him an exultation and a sense of power, and he ran up the hill like an engine, or a madman, willing to throw himself headlong into the city that glowed before him. . . . For it was his; the inhabitants of the city had told him it was his; he had but to run down, crying, and they would take him to their hearts and show him wonders his eyes had never seen.

But this dream never comes to fulfillment, or at least not to a fulfill-ment so simple as that which the boy first imagines. For John is finally swept by his great need for reconciliation with his family and with his ancestral community, by his guilt over his awakening sexuality, by the unsubduable propensity for religious hysteria implanted in him by his nurture—he is finally hurled by all these forces onto the Threshing-Floor and swept into a high fever of spiritual convulsion in The Temple of the Fire Baptized. And though in his moment of seizure an "ironic voice insisted . . . that he rise from that filthy floor if he did not want to become like all the other niggers," and though he feels himself, as it were, in a grave, he beholds in this grave "the despised and rejected, the wretched and the spat upon, the earth's offscouring." In this moment the trouble-laden history of his father and mother, of Aunt Florence, of Praying Mother Washington and Sister McCandless and Sister Price, becomes as never before a living reality for him: "their dread testimony" and "their desolation" become his, and he knows that, only as he passes through their darkness, will he find his right course. So, at the novel's close, after the fearful night of his con-version experience is over, he walks at dawn through the filthy streets of Harlem, "among the saints, he, John . . . one of their company now." His soul is filled with gladness, for he has sworn to fight the good fight. And what is implied is that the vista he beheld that day from his "mountain" in Central Park will finally be achieved only by way of a pilgrimage involving an ascent of that Mount of Primal Pain that has been immemorially trodden by Hagar's children.

The book—which is one of the most tightly constructed and beauti-fully written novels of our period—is not, to be sure, a "protest novel," but it does become for Mr. Baldwin, finally, a passionate gesture of identification with his people. And it can now be seen in retrospect as marking the path that he was increasingly to follow in the years to come. It was succeeded, of course, by the essay in the morally fancy punctilio of Paris homosexualism which we were given in the novel of 1956, *Giovanni's Room*; and, despite Mr. Baldwin's deep engagement with the homosexual life, this is a book that strikes us as a deflection, as a kind of detour. But, throughout the 'fifties, he was busily engaged in journalism, writing about books and the theatre and his travels and various aspects of the American scene. And in all these various pieces—collected in *Notes of a Native Son* (1955) and *Nobody Knows My Name* (1961)—as he probed more deeply the meaning of Negro ex-perience in this country, his own chosen role came more and more to be that of racial ideologue and of Chief Barrister for the black multi-tudes at the bar of the American conscience. Whereas the pronoun of the first person in his earliest writings had expressed a passionately sensuous and individual intelligence, it comes increasingly in these years to take on a vast and vaguely menacing collectivist aura, so that the "I" we encounter on his pages begins no longer to stand for the intensely interesting man, James Baldwin, but for all Negroes everywhere, both the living and the dead. By some twist of his own nature and under the pressure of the rising Negro insurgency, he began himself to be "the Negro *in extremis*, a [veritable] virtuoso of ethnic suffering, defiance and aspiration."[27] This mounting militancy reaches its highest pitch in the essay of 1963, *The Fire Next Time*, and in the novel *Another Country* (1962) and the play *Blues for Mr. Charlie* (1964) which want to score many of the points already established in the polemical tracts. And, here, the loss of poise that threatens is uncountered by any such nonchalance and stability of perspective as might be afforded by a firm structure of religious belief. Mr. Baldwin's writing is, of course, both in his essays and in his fiction, abundantly embellished with religious paraphernalia—and a large part of the remarkable beauty of *Go Tell It on the Mountain* derives from its brilliant employment of Biblical idiom and imagery. But one could hardly argue that in this book the stuff of experience is being conceived Christianly, as in Graham Greene's *The Power and the Glory* or Bernanos' *The Diary of a Country Priest* or John Updike's *The Centaur*: the novel, in its conception of character and in its structure of incident, strikes us rather, at the level of systematic ideas, as being far more dependent on Freud and William James than on Pascal or Luther or Kierkegaard or Niebuhr. I did, to be sure, speak earlier of the greater internalization of Christian background in Mr. Baldwin than in Richard Wright, for, in the latter's case, what we face, in the spiritual landscape of his fiction, is a world utterly desacralized, a world in which the traditions of Christian belief and experience are as if they had never been, so uninvolved are they in the pressing existential reality of human endeavor. At least, in the case of Mr. Baldwin, it needs to be said that the memory of Christianity is still discernibly a factor in his imaginative universe, bequeathing him, if nothing more, such a sense, as Richard Wright seems never to have had, of the radical mystery incarnate in the human creature. But when Mr. Baldwin says, as he did a few years ago in an address at Kalamazoo College ("In Search of a Majority" in *Nobody Knows My Name*), that "to be with God is really to be involved with some enormous, overwhelming desire, and joy" and that he conceives "of God, in fact, as a means of liberation and not a means to control others"—when he speaks in this way, he makes us feel that he is undoubtedly a man of genuine religious sensibility, but (as is indicated by the lumpily "homemade" quality of the language) a sensibility that is quite out of touch with any of the great traditions of Christian theology and spirituality (despite his

[27] F. W. Dupee, "James Baldwin and the 'Man,'" *The New York Review of Books*, Vol. I, No. 1 (1963), p. 1.

familiarity with the Bible and his very great knowledgeableness about a particular mode of pietistic folk religion). So, in the last analysis, he has no resource for distancing himself in any way religiously from the kind of secularized Calvinism which, as a writer, is his American inheritance; and, as his work of recent years has begun to indicate, he is, finally, very nearly helpless before the power of that myth which is so much a part of this inheritance—namely, the myth of the wounded Adam. Indeed, it is just this that would seem to be so much in evidence in the tendency of his essays of the last decade—in making the pronoun "I" at once personal and collective and in thus merging a personal plight with the larger racial plight of the American Negro—to make their author (his own loneliness, his own alienation) the real beneficiary of the pity which is ostensibly sought for an entire people. "Alas, Poor Richard," says Mr. Baldwin in the title of his most recent essay on Richard Wright—and in that phrase, one feels, he distances himself too much from his first sponsor and patron, for, at last, both are to be seen as sustained by a single myth, a single mode of sensibility and belief.

Though Ralph Ellison has published thus far only one novel—*Invisible Man* of 1953—his achievement as an artist strikes us as being far less in question than either that of Richard Wright or of Mr. Baldwin, the three of them together being the most important Negro writers yet to enter American literary life. In a time when so many of our ablest novelists have chosen to seek their effects by the unsaid and the withheld, by the muted voice and the scrupulously reserved style, Mr. Ellison, like Faulkner and Penn Warren, is notable in part for being unafraid to howl and rage and bellow with laughter over the fate of man. And surely it is the uninhibited exhilaration and suppleness of his rhetoric that is a main source of that richness of texture which so distinguishes his book. But sheer verbal energy alone cannot produce a fiction that requires to be regarded as a work of art; there must also be the gift for conveying what Henry James insisted on, namely, "the direct impression" of life itself. And, in this, Mr. Ellison is superbly talented. Indeed, one of our richest satisfactions in reading his book comes from the sense of immersion in all the concrete materialities of Negro life: one hears the very buzz and hum of Harlem in the racy, pungent speech of his West Indians and native hipsters; one sees the fearful nonchalance of the zootsuiter and hears the terrible anger of the black nationalist on his streetcorner platform; and all the *grotesquerie* in the opening account of the dreary little backwater of a remote Southern Negro college has in it a certain kind of empirically absolute rightness. The book is packed full of the acutest observations of the manners and idioms and human styles that comprise the ethos of Negro life in the American metropolis, and it gives us such a sense of social fact as can be come by nowhere in the manuals of academic sociology; all this is done with the ease that comes from enormous expertness of craft, from deep intimacy of knowledge, and love.

Mr. Ellison suppresses his middle name—which is "Waldo" and which gives a certain tricky rightness to the fact that for him too, like so many other writers in the American tradition, the basic pattern of experience is something like Emerson's "simple genuine self against the whole world."[28] But, in his version of the Adamic myth, though the "simple genuine self" is "wounded" by the world, the result is neither a descent into the "cheap grace"[29] of self-pity (as in Mr. Baldwin) nor a nihilistic blast of destructive violence (as in Wright)—but, rather, it is a step forward into a further maturity, into a deepened awareness of the essential solitude that is a part of the human fate. And his hero is not undone by his discovery; indeed, by an act of transcendence, he comes to realize that, though his passage through the world has involved the special ordeals that are a part of being a Negro in the United States, he can nevertheless, as a result of what he has discovered about the basic human condition, in some measure speak "on the lower frequencies" for all men.

The protagonist of Mr. Ellison's novel is a young American Negro who has to pick his perilous way through the irrationalities of a culture which has made of him an "invisible man," and his whole effort is an effort to wrest an acknowledgment, to achieve visibility. He starts, in other words, from a point outside the world. We see him first as a timid boy about to be graduated from his high school in a southern town, valedictorian of his class, with an earnest little speech on the virtues of humility that is reminiscent of Booker Washington. Along with some of his schoolmates, he is invited to a smoker where the leading white citizens are to hear his speech and award him a scholarship. But the boys do not know in advance what the nature of the entertainment is to be that night; they are brought before a lush and naked blonde, and threatened by the crowd if they look and if they fail to look. Then, after being blindfolded, they are forced to stage a "battle royal" amongst themselves, punching and kicking one another for the obscene titillation of this degenerate mob—and then they are made to scramble for coins on an electrified rug. Finally, the valedictorian delivers his speech about humility and his gratitude to his white benefactors. And the boy later dreams that, on opening the brief-

---

[28] *Vide* R. W. B. Lewis, *op. cit.*, p. 198. Though Professor Lewis's book concentrates on the American nineteenth century, he devotes an "Epilogue" to "The Contemporary Situation," and, here, he does himself explicitly relate *Invisible Man* to the Emersonian figure.

[29] By those familiar with the literature of recent European theology, the phrase "cheap grace" will be recognized as coming from Dietrich Bonhoeffer: *Vide* his *The Cost of Discipleship*, trans. by R. H. Fuller (New York: Macmillan Co., 1949), Chapter I.

case that these gentlemen had presented to him along with his scholarship, he found an inscription: "To Whom It May Concern: Keep This Nigger-Boy Running." And so indeed he shall be running in the years to come, "skidding around corners and dashing down alleys, endlessly harried by the cops and the crooks of the world, endlessly hurrying in search of whatever it is that can sanctify human existence."[30]

The next stage in this *picaro's* journey is a Southern Negro college, where, inadvertently, on a certain day he exposes a visiting white trustee from the North to a Negro farmer's incestuous relation with his daughter and to the local Negro gin-mill—and, as a result, is ousted from the college by its unctuous and cynical president, as a punishment for his having allowed the college's donor to see what white folks are not supposed to see.

Then, the young man moves on to New York, where, after becoming involved—again, inadvertently—as a scab in labor-violence, he is taken up by the communistic "Brotherhood" after delivering an impassioned speech in the streets, before a crowd watching the eviction of an aged Negro couple from their Harlem tenement flat; his job with the "Brotherhood" is to *organize* the sullenness of Harlem Negroes. But he soon discovers that the Negro's cause is only being used to promote "the line." So, at last, in disillusionment, after a furious race riot in the Harlem streets, he dives through a manhole, down into a cellar, for a period of "hibernation." He has tried the way of "humility," of being a "good Negro"; he has tried to find room for himself in American industry, to become a good cog in the complex of the technological machine; he has attempted to attach himself to leftist politics —he has tried all these things by means of which it would seem that the Negro might achieve visibility in American life. But, since none has offered a way into the culture, he has now chosen to become an underground man. All his reversals have been due to the blackness of his skin: so now, at last, he decides to stay in his cellar, where, by way of a tapped line, he will steal the electricity for his 1,369 bulbs from Monopolated Light and Power and dine on sloe gin and vanilla ice cream and *embrace* "The Blackness of Blackness."

Now the descent into "the heart of darkness," as a movement of the spirit, as a way of coming to terms with the self, is at least as old as St. John of the Cross, and actually far older; and it is a stratagem of renewal that has its own dignity and positiveness and moral validity. So Mr. Ellison might very well have simply concluded things at this point, even though to have done so might have been to elicit from secular literati the same irritated puzzlement that T. S. Eliot's reinstate-

[30] R. W. B. Lewis, "Eccentrics' Pilgrimage" (an omnibus-review of Ralph Ellison's *Invisible Man* and several other novels), *The Hudson Review*, Vol. VI, No. 1 (Spring, 1953), p. 148.

ment of the Johannine *askésis* in the *Quartets* had provoked a decade earlier: there was already, in other words, a sufficient positivity in the negativity of that underground room—and *this* wounded Adam in *deliberately* and *lucidly* making the descent into darkness, was already no longer *merely wounded,* as the author of *The Ascent of Mount Carmel* and *The Dark Night of the Soul* might have certified. But Mr. Ellison was very eager to enlist in the "Party of Hope"; so, at the end, he has his hero speaking of his determination "to affirm the principle on which the country was built" and of his intention to play "a socially responsible role." And this is a rhetoric too stilted in tone perhaps to be altogether persuasive.

But the insecurity of vision that seems somewhat to be threatening in the last few pages in no real way invalidates the remarkable poise with which this fine artist has kept his Adam to a course that avoids at once the Scylla of rampant nihilism and the Charybdis of inordinate self-pity. And it is to be hoped that the triumph of art and of moral imagination represented by Mr. Ellison's magnificent book does but presage not only his own future but also the books that are yet to be written by the many gifted young Negro writers who are beginning to appear on the American scene.

Eldridge Cleaver

(b. 1935)

ELDRIDGE CLEAVER WAS BORN in Little Rock, Arkansas, and grew up in the Los Angeles ghetto; and, like two other well-known contemporary writers—Malcolm X and Claude Brown—he received most of his education while in prison.

Nationally known as the Minister of Education of the Black Panthers, Cleaver has lectured to academic audiences all over the nation. In his roles as lecturer, writer, and radical activist, he has served as a symbol for the entire current protest movement, particularly its violent segment. At the present writing Cleaver is being sought as a "fugitive from justice."

Eldridge Cleaver has contributed to *Ramparts, Esquire, Black Dialogue, The Liberator, Mademoiselle, New Leader,* and other periodicals. His recent speeches have been collected and published in a volume entitled *Eldridge Cleaver.*

The selection below is taken from his best-selling book *Soul on Ice.*

ON BECOMING

Folsom Prison
June 25, 1965

Nineteen fifty-four, when I was eighteen years old, is held to be a crucial turning point in the history of the Afro-American—for the U.S.A. as a whole—the year segregation was outlawed by the U.S. Supreme Court. It was also a crucial year for me because on June 18, 1954, I began serving a sentence in state prison for possession of marijuana.

The Supreme Court decision was only one month old when I entered prison, and I do not believe that I had even the vaguest idea of its importance or historical significance. But later, the acrimonious controversy ignited by the end of the separate-but-equal doctrine was to have a profound effect on me. This controversy awakened me to my position in America and I began to form a concept of what it meant to be black in white America.

Of course I'd always known that I was black, but I'd never really stopped to take stock of what I was involved in. I met life as an individual and took my chances. Prior to 1954, we lived in an atmosphere of novocain. Negroes found it necessary, in order to maintain whatever sanity they could, to remain somewhat aloof and detached from "the problem." We accepted indignities and the mechanics of the apparatus of oppression without reacting by sitting-in or holding mass demonstrations. Nurtured by the fires of the controversy over segregation, I was soon aflame with indignation over my newly discovered social status, and inwardly I turned away from America with horror, disgust and outrage.

In Soledad state prison, I fell in with a group of young blacks who, like myself, were in vociferous rebellion against what we perceived as a continuation of slavery on a higher plane. We cursed everything American—including baseball and hot dogs. All respect we may have had for politicians, preachers, lawyers, governors, Presidents, senators, congressmen was utterly destroyed as we watched them temporizing and compromising over right and wrong, over legality and illegality, over constitutionality and unconstitutionality. We knew that in the end what they were clashing over was us, what to do with the blacks, and whether or not to start treating us as human beings. I despised all of them.

The segregationists were condemned out of hand, without even listening to their lofty, finely woven arguments. The others I despised for wasting time in debates with the segregationists: why not just crush them, put them in prison—they were defying the law, weren't they? I defied the law and they put me in prison. So why not put those dirty mothers in prison too? I had gotten caught with a shopping bag full of marijuana, a shopping bag full of love—I was in love with the weed and I did not for one minute think that anything was wrong with getting high. I had been getting high for four or five years and was convinced, with the zeal of a crusader, that marijuana was superior to lush—yet the rulers of the land seemed all to be lushes. I could not see how they were more justified in drinking than I was in blowing the gage. I was a grasshopper, and it was natural that I felt myself to be unjustly imprisoned.

While all this was going on, our group was espousing atheism. Unsophisticated and not based on any philosophical rationale, our atheism was pragmatic. I had come to believe that there is no God; if there is, men do not know anything about him. Therefore, all religions were phony—which made all preachers and priests, in our eyes, fakers, including the ones scurrying around the prison who, curiously, could put in a good word for you with the Almighty Creator of the universe but could not get anything down with the warden or parole board—they could usher you through the Pearly Gates *after you were dead,* but not through the prison gate *while you were still alive and kicking.*

Besides, men of the cloth who work in prison have an ineradicable stigma attached to them in the eyes of convicts because they escort condemned men into the gas chamber. Such men of God are powerful arguments in favor of atheism. Our atheism was a source of enormous pride to me. Later on, I bolstered our arguments by reading Thomas Paine and his devastating critique of Christianity in particular and organized religion in general.

Through reading I was amazed to discover how confused people were. I had thought that, out there beyond the horizon of my own ignorance, unanimity existed, that even though I myself didn't know what was happening in the universe, other people certainly did. Yet here I was discovering that the whole U.S.A. was in a chaos of disagreement over segregation/integration. In these circumstances I decided that the only safe thing for me to do was go for myself. It became clear that it was possible for me to take the initiative: instead of simply *reacting* I could *act*. I could unilaterally—whether anyone agreed with me or not—repudiate all allegiances, morals, values—even while continuing to exist within this society. My mind would be free and no power in the universe could force me to accept something if I didn't want to. But I would take my own sweet time. That, too, was a part of my new freedom. I would accept nothing until it was proved that it was good—for me. I became an extreme iconoclast. Any affirmative assertion made by anyone around me became a target for tirades of criticism and denunciation.

This little game got good to me and I got good at it. I attacked all forms of piety, loyalty, and sentiment: marriage, love, God, patriotism, the Constitution, the founding fathers, law, concepts of right-wrong-good-evil, all forms of ritualized and conventional behavior. As I pranced about, club in hand, seeking new idols to smash, I encountered really for the first time in my life, with any seriousness, The Ogre, rising up before me in a mist. I discovered, with alarm, that The Ogre possessed a tremendous and dreadful power over me, and I didn't understand this power or why I was at its mercy. I tried to repudiate The Ogre, root it out of my heart as I had done God, Constitution, principles, morals, and values—but The Ogre had its claws buried in the core of my being and refused to let go. I fought frantically to be free, but The Ogre only mocked me and sank its claws deeper into my soul. I knew then that I had found an important key, that if I conquered The Ogre and broke its power over me I would be free. But I also knew that it was a race against time and that if I did not win I would certainly be broken and destroyed. I, a black man, confronted The Ogre—the white woman.

In prison, those things withheld from and denied to the prisoner become precisely what he wants most of all, of course. Because we were locked up in our cells before darkness fell, I used to lie awake at night racked by painful craving to take a leisurely stroll under the stars, or to go to the beach, to drive a car on a freeway, to grow a beard, or to make love to a woman.

Since I was not married conjugal visits would not have solved my problem. I therefore denounced the idea of conjugal visits as inherently unfair; single prisoners needed and deserved *action* just as married prisoners did. I advocated establishing a system under Civil Service whereby salaried women would minister to the needs of those prisoners who maintained a record of good behavior. If a married prisoner preferred his own wife, that would be his right. Since California was not about to inaugurate either conjugal visits or the Civil Service, one could advocate either with equal enthusiasm and with the same result: nothing.

This may appear ridiculous to some people. But it was very real to me and as urgent as the need to breathe, because I was in my bull stage and lack of access to females was absolutely a form of torture. I suffered. My mistress at the time of my arrest, the beautiful and lonely wife of a serviceman stationed overseas, died unexpectedly three weeks after I entered prison; and the rigid, dehumanized rules governing correspondence between prisoners and free people prevented me from corresponding with other young ladies I knew. It left me without any contact with females except those in my family.

In the process of enduring my confinement, I decided to get myself a pin-up girl to paste on the wall of my cell. I would fall in love with her and lavish my affections upon her. She, a symbolic representative of the forbidden tribe of women, would sustain me until I was free. Out of the center of *Esquire*, I married a voluptuous bride. Our marriage went along swell for a time: no quarrels, no complaints. And then, one evening when I came in from school, I was shocked and enraged to find that the guard had entered my cell, ripped my sugar from the wall, torn her into little pieces, and left the pieces floating in the commode: it was like seeing a dead body floating in a lake. Giving her a proper burial, I flushed the commode. As the saying goes, I sent her to Long Beach. But I was genuinely beside myself with anger: almost every cell, excepting those of the homosexuals, had a pin-up girl on the wall and the guards didn't bother them. Why, I asked the guard the next day, had he singled me out for special treatment?

"Don't you know we have a rule against pasting up pictures on the walls?" he asked me.

"Later for the rules," I said. "You know as well as I do that that rule is not enforced."

"Tell you what," he said, smiling at me (the smile put me on my guard), "I'll compromise with you: get yourself a colored girl for a pinup—no white women—and I'll let it stay up. Is that a deal?"

I was more embarrassed than shocked. He was laughing in my face. I called him two or three dirty names and walked away. I can still recall his big moon-face, grinning at me over yellow teeth. The disturbing part about the whole incident was that a terrible feeling of guilt came over me as I realized that I had chosen the picture of the white girl over the available pictures of black girls. I tried to rationalize it away, but I was fascinated by the truth involved. Why hadn't I thought about it in this light before? So I took hold of the question and began to inquire into my feelings. Was it true, did I really prefer white girls over black? The conclusion was clear and inescapable: I did. I decided to check out my friends on this point and it was easy to determine, from listening to their general conversation, that the white woman occupied a peculiarly prominent place in all of our frames of reference. With what I have learned since then, this all seems terribly elementary now. But at the time, it was a tremendously intriguing adventure of discovery.

One afternoon, when a large group of Negroes was on the prison yard shooting the breeze, I grabbed the floor and posed the question: which did they prefer, white women or black? Some said Japanese women were their favorite, others said Chinese, some said European women, others said Mexican women—they all stated a preference, and they generally freely admitted their dislike for black women.

"I don't want nothing black but a Cadillac," said one.

"If money was black I wouldn't want none of it," put in another.

A short little stud, who was a very good lightweight boxer with a little man's complex that made him love to box heavyweights, jumped to his feet. He had a yellowish complexion and we called him Butterfly.

"All you niggers are sick!" Butterfly spat out. "I don't like no stinking white woman. My grandma is a white woman and I don't even like her!"

But it just so happened that Butterfly's crime partner was in the crowd, and after Butterfly had his say, his crime partner said, "Aw, sit on down and quit that lying, lil o' chump. What about that gray girl in San Jose who had your nose wide open? Did you like her, or were you just running after her with your tongue hanging out of your head because you hated her?"

Partly because he was embarrassed and partly because his crime partner was a heavyweight, Butterfly flew into him. And before we could separate them and disperse, so the guard would not know who had been fighting, Butterfly bloodied his crime partner's nose. Butterfly got away but, because of the blood, his crime partner got caught. I ate dinner with Butterfly that evening and questioned him sharply about his attitude toward white women. And after an initial evasiveness he admitted that the white woman bugged him too. "It's a sickness," he said. "All our lives we've had the white woman dangled before our eyes like a carrot on a stick before a donkey: look but don't touch." (In 1958, after I had gone out on parole and was returned to San Quentin as a parole violater with a new charge, Butterfly was still there. He had become a Black Muslim and was chiefly responsible for teaching me the Black Muslim philosophy. Upon his release from San Quentin, Butterfly joined the Los Angeles Mosque, advanced rapidly through the ranks, and is now a full-fledged minister of one of Elijah Muhammad's mosques in another city. He successfully completed his parole, got married—to a very black girl—and is doing fine.)

From our discussion, which began that evening and has never yet ended, we went on to notice how thoroughly, as a matter of course, a black growing up in America is indoctrinated with the white race's standard of beauty. Not that the whites made a conscious, calculated effort to do this, we thought, but since they constituted the majority the whites brainwashed the blacks by the very processes the whites employed to indoctrinate themselves with their own group standards. It intensified my frustrations to know that I was indoctrinated to see the white woman as more beautiful and desirable than my own black woman. It drove me into books seeking light on the subject. In Richard Wright's *Native Son,* I found Bigger Thomas and a keen insight into the problem.

My interest in this area persisted undiminished and then, in 1955, an event took place in Mississippi which turned me inside out: Emmett Till, a young Negro down from Chicago on a visit, was murdered, allegedly for flirting with a white woman. He had been shot, his head crushed from repeated blows with a blunt instrument, and his badly decomposed body was recovered from the river with a heavy weight on it. I was, of course, angry over the whole bit, but one day I saw in a magazine a picture of the white woman with whom Emmett Till was said to have flirted. While looking at the picture, I felt that little tension in the center of my chest I experience when a woman appeals to me. I was disgusted and angry with myself. Here was a woman who had caused the death of a black, possibly because, when he looked at her, he also felt the same tensions of lust and desire in his chest—and probably for the same general reasons that I felt them. It was all unacceptable to me. I looked at the picture again and again, and in spite of everything and against my will and the hate I felt for the woman and all that she represented, she appealed to me. I flew into a rage at myself, at America, at white women, at the history that had placed those tensions of lust and desire in my chest.

Two days later, I had a "nervous breakdown." For several days I ranted and raved against the white race, against white women in particular, against white America in general. When I came to myself, I was locked in a padded cell with not even the vaguest memory of how I got there. All I could recall was an eternity of pacing back and forth in the cell, preaching to the unhearing walls.

I had several sessions with a psychiatrist. His conclusion was that I hated my mother. How he arrived at this conclusion I'll never know, because he knew nothing about my mother; and when he'd ask me questions I would answer him with absurd lies. What revolted me about him was that he had heard me denouncing the whites, yet each time he interviewed me he deliberately guided the conversation back to my family life, to my childhood. That in itself was all right, but he deliberately blocked all my attempts to bring out the racial question, and he made it clear that he was not interested in my attitude toward whites. This was a Pandora's box he did not care to open. After I ceased my diatribes against the whites, I was let out of the hospital, back into the general inmate population just as if nothing had happened. I continued to brood over these events and over the dynamics of race relations in America.

During this period I was concentrating my reading in the field of economics. Having previously dabbled in the theories and writings of Rousseau, Thomas Paine, and Voltaire, I had added a little polish to my iconoclastic stance, without, however, bothering too much to understand their affirmative positions. In economics, because everybody seemed to find it necessary to attack and condemn Karl Marx in their writings, I sought out his books, and although he kept me with a headache, I took him for my authority. I was not prepared to understand him, but I was able to see in him a thoroughgoing critique and condemnation of capitalism. It was like taking medicine for me to find that, indeed, American capitalism deserved all the hatred and contempt that I felt for it in my heart. This had a positive, stabilizing effect upon me—to an extent because I was not about to become stable —and it diverted me from my previous preoccupation: morbid broodings on the black man and the white woman. Pursuing my readings into the history of socialism, I read, with very little understanding, some of the passionate, exhortatory writings of Lenin; and I fell in love with Bakunin and Nechayev's *Catechism of the Revolutionist*— the principles of which, along with some of Machiavelli's advice, I sought to incorporate into my own behavior. I took the *Catechism* for my bible and, standing on a one-man platform that had nothing to do with the reconstruction of society, I began consciously incorporating these principles into my daily life, to employ tactics of ruthlessness in my dealings with everyone with whom I came into contact. And I began to look at white America through these new eyes.

Somehow I arrived at the conclusion that, as a matter of principle, it was of paramount importance for me to have an antagonistic, ruthless attitude toward white women. The term *outlaw* appealed to me and at the time my parole date was drawing near, I considered myself to be mentally free—I was an "outlaw." I had stepped outside of the white man's law, which I repudiated with scorn and self-satisfaction.

I became a law unto myself—my own legislature, my own supreme court, my own executive. At the moment I walked out of the prison gate, my feelings toward white women in general could be summed up in the following lines:

To a White Girl

> *I love you*
> *Because you're white,*
> *Not because you're charming*
> *Or bright.*
> *Your whiteness*
> *Is a silky thread*
> *Snaking through my thoughts*
> *In redhot patterns*
> *Of lust and desire.*
>
> *I hate you*
> *Because you're white.*
> *Your white meat*
> *Is nightmare food.*
> *White is*
> *The skin of Evil.*
> *You're my Moby Dick,*
> *White Witch,*
> *Symbol of the rope and hanging tree,*
> *Of the burning cross.*
>
> *Loving you thus*
> *And hating you so,*
> *My heart is torn in two.*
> *Crucified.*

I became a rapist. To refine my technique and *modus operandi*, I started out by practicing on black girls in the ghetto—in the black ghetto where dark and vicious deeds appear not as aberrations or deviations from the norm, but as part of the sufficiency of the Evil of a day—and when I considered myself smooth enough, I crossed the tracks and sought out white prey. I did this consciously, deliberately, willfully, methodically—though looking back I see that I was in a frantic, wild, and completely abandoned frame of mind.

Rape was an insurrectionary act. It delighted me that I was defying and trampling upon the white man's law, upon his system of values, and that I was defiling his women—and this point, I believe, was the most satisfying to me because I was very resentful over the historical fact of how the white man has used the black woman. I felt I was getting revenge. From the site of the act of rape, consternation spreads outwardly in concentric circles. I wanted to send waves of consternation throughout the white race. Recently, I came upon a quotation from one of LeRoi Jones' poems, taken from his book *The Dead Lecturer:*

> A cult of death need of the simple striking arm under the street lamp. The cutters from under their rented earth. Come up, black dada nihilismus. Rape the white girls. Rape their fathers. Cut the mothers' throats.

I have lived those lines and I know that if I had not been apprehended I would have slit some white throats. There are, of course, many young blacks out there right now who are slitting white throats and raping the white girl. They are not doing this because they read LeRoi Jones' poetry, as some of his critics seem to believe. Rather, LeRoi is expressing the funky facts of life.

After I returned to prison, I took a long look at myself and, for the first time in my life, admitted that I was wrong, that I had gone astray —astray not so much from the white man's law as from being human, civilized—for I could not approve the act of rape. Even though I had some insight into my own motivations, I did not feel justified. I lost my self-respect. My pride as a man dissolved and my whole fragile moral structure seemed to collapse, completely shattered.

That is why I started to write. To save myself.

I realized that no one could save me but myself. The prison authorities were both uninterested and unable to help me. I had to seek out the truth and unravel the snarled web of my motivations. I had to find out who I am and what I want to be, what type of man I should be, and what I could do to become the best of which I was capable. I understood that what had happened to me had also happened to countless other blacks and it would happen to many, many more.

I learned that I had been taking the easy way out, running away from problems. I also learned that it is easier to do evil than it is to do good. And I have been terribly impressed by the youth of America, black and white. I am proud of them because they have reaffirmed my faith in humanity. I have come to feel what must be love for the young people of America and I want to be part of the good and greatness that they want for all people. From my prison cell, I have watched America slowly coming awake. It is not fully awake yet, but there is soul in the air and everywhere I see beauty. I have watched the sit-ins, the freedom raids, the Mississippi Blood Summers, demonstrations all over the country, the FSM movement, the teach-ins, and the mounting protest over Lyndon Strangelove's foreign policy—all of this, the thousands of little details, show me it is time to straighten up and fly right. That is why I decided to concentrate on my writings and efforts in this area. We are a very sick country—I, perhaps, am sicker than most. But I accept that. I told you in the beginning that I am extremist by nature—so it is only right that I should be extremely sick.

I was very familiar with the Eldridge who came to prison, but that Eldridge no longer exists. And the one I am now is in some ways a stranger to me. You may find this difficult to understand but it is very easy for one in prison to lose his sense of self. And if he has been undergoing all kinds of extreme, involved, and unregulated changes, then he ends up not knowing who he is. Take the point of being attractive to women. You can easily see how a man can lose his arrogance or certainty on that point while in prison! When he's in the free world, he gets constant feedback on how he looks from the number of female heads he turns when he walks down the street. In prison he gets only hate-stares and sour frowns. Years and years of bitter looks. Individuality is not nourished in prison, neither by the officials nor by the convicts. It is a deep hole out of which to climb.

What must be done, I believe, is that all these problems—particularly the sickness between the white woman and the black man—must be brought out into the open, dealt with and resolved. I know that the black man's sick attitude toward the white woman is a revolutionary sickness: it keeps him perpetually out of harmony with the system that is oppressing him. Many whites flatter themselves with the idea that the Negro male's lust and desire for the white dream girl is purely an esthetic attraction, but nothing could be farther from the truth. His motivation is often of such a bloody, hateful, bitter, and malignant nature that whites would really be hard pressed to find it flattering. I have discussed these points with prisoners who were convicted of rape, and their motivations are very plain. But they are very reluctant to discuss these things with white men who, by and large, make up the prison staffs. I believe that in the experience of these men lies the knowledge and wisdom that must be utilized to help other youngsters who are heading in the same direction. I think all of us, the entire nation, will be better off if we bring it all out front. A lot of people's feelings will be hurt, but that is the price that must be paid.

It may be that I can harm myself by speaking frankly and directly, but I do not care about that at all. Of course I want to get out of prison, badly, but I shall get out some day. I am more concerned with what I am going to be after I get out. I know that by following the course which I have charted I will find my salvation. If I had followed the path laid down for me by the officials, I'd undoubtedly have long since been out of prison—but I'd be less of a man. I'd be weaker and less certain of where I want to go, what I want to do, and how to go about it.

The price of hating other human beings is loving oneself less.

Harold Cruse

Born in Petersburg, Virginia, Harold Cruse grew up in Virginia and in New York City. After finishing high school, he served in World War II.

A dramatist and critic, Cruse has edited television scripts and served as chairman of the Harlem Writers Club. His articles have appeared in *The Liberator, Negro Digest, Présence Africaine,* and other periodicals. He is the author of *The Crisis of the Negro Intellectual* (1967), from which the selection below is taken, and *Rebellion or Revolution* (1968).

POSTCRIPT ON BLACK POWER—THE DIALOGUE BETWEEN SHADOW AND SUBSTANCE

The old proverb, "Necessity is the mother of invention," was given a unique civil rights configuration when the slogan of Black Power was popularized during the summer of 1966. The necessity lay in the fact that the SNCC-CORE united front, in its direct-action-protest phase, had bogged down. Like an army that had outdistanced its supply units, it had finally been stopped by the enemy counter-attack—the backlash.

The slogan Black Power was conjured up and used in the manner of a rallying victory cry. In effect it covers up a defeat without having to explain either the basic reasons for it or the flaws in the original strategy; it suggests the dimensions of a future victory in the attainment of goals while, at the same time, dispelling the fears of more defeats in the pursuit of such goals. Yet, each and every goal was already implicit in the direct-action movements even before the slogan was projected. Black Power, then, was raised when social reality forced so-called revolutionaries to put action aside and start thinking. A movement that up to then had placed its highest premiums on practical activism now turned over a new leaf and began to get theoretical about the real *substance* of its civil rights objectives. The old slogans about "justice," "liberation," "Freedom Now," etc., were now mere shadow terms. If direct action-protest had been defeated by certain structural barriers of society, the new slogan became a commitment to deal with the real substance of those barriers that block the attainment of civil rights. Thus fears, opposition, and startled cries of alarm were immediately raised. A new threat fell across the land like an ominous shadow, even though the exact concept of Black Power has not yet been clearly defined. At this writing, as a concept it remains as vague as the former abstractions—Justice and Liberation. Although the Black Power concept is a more specific and provocative abstraction than Freedom, it is open to just as many diverse and conflicting interpretations. While it tries to give more clarity to what forms Freedom will assume in America as the end-product of a new program, the Black Power dialogue does not close the conceptual gap between shadow and substance, any more than it plots a course for the program dynamic. Whatever Black Power is supposed to mean to its adherents and its foes, its implications cannot be clearly understood unless one examines the slogan's aims and origin. Who originated the slogan? Are its aims revolutionary or reformist?

It was originated by a leading member of the radical wing of the black bourgeoisie, Adam Clayton Powell: He first mentioned it at a Chicago rally in May, 1965, and elaborated upon it in his Howard University Commencement speech of May 29, 1966. It was picked up and popularized by a leading member of the radical wing of the civil rights movement, Stokely Carmichael, from the lower-middle-class students' front. Carmichael was then joined by certain nationalist elements from integration-minded CORE, the radical wing of the civil rights movement in the North. Thus, the slogan of Black Power appeared to signal a concerted shift from SNCC-CORE radical-protest integrationism—not to nationalist separatism—but to some intermediate position between separatism and racial integration.

Since all of these diverse protest elements, separatists, nationalists, and direct actionists, had made up the sum total of what was called the Black Revolution, formal logic would conclude that this tumultuous shift to Black Power denoted a turn to a more revolutionary posture than formerly held by SNCC and CORE when their direct-action battering rams were at full strength North and South. But a closer examination of every analysis by each Black Power exponent from SNCC and CORE reveals that while the slogan cast a revolutionary *sounding* theme and a threat of more intense revolt across the land, the *substance* was, in fact, a methodological retreat to black social reforms. In pragmatic America the slogans catch the imagination while the implicit substances are glossed over and ignored. The Negro thinks and acts like the American he is; thus the leaders of the Black Revolution who seized so readily upon Black Power had never made the distinction between social revolution and social evolution, or social reform.

As this entire critique has tried to show, there can be no such thing in America as a *purely* economic, or political or civil rights revolution. There *can* be economic or political or civil rights reforms, but these are all *evolutionary* social changes that are part and parcel of the very gradualism of the NAACP. Never mind the fact that Roy Wilkins and his "class-brothers" are frightened by Black Power—that proves nothing. What a Wilkins is really saying is—"Please don't start throwing around power you don't really have, or power which you *might* have but which you obviously don't know how to use. All you are doing is scaring people (like me) and provoking other people to mobilize white power for a showdown which you are not ready for." What these gentlemen want most avidly are a number of civil rights, legal, economic, social, and educational reforms in America. But the radical direct-action civil righters (plus the nationalists) vociferously claim that this is inadequate. They say: "Those bourgeois NAACP Uncle Toms can't reform this white man's society. Man, you got to resort to revolutionary tactics if you want to shake up these white folks!" But what were these so-called revolutionary tactics? The Black Revolution included everything in the pot: sit-ins, freedom rides, demonstrations and marches of all kinds, ghetto uprisings, stall-ins, voter registration, self-defense, boycotts, black (third) party attempts, etc. These were the elements of the revolution, particularly in the South. But today when the main bulk of the direct actionists of SNCC and other have quit the South, what have they left behind? Scattered groups devoted to voter registration and economic programs for self-help. CORE has left a "cooperative marketing program for farm produce" in Louisiana. There were a few local election victories here and there, but the political reform movement of the Mississippi Freedom Democrat Party has closed its doors in LeFlore County. This is not to say that the achievements of the direct actionists are not valuable bases upon which other things can be structured, but they are still *reformist and gradualistic ideas with which not a single NAACP-er nor King passive resister could argue.* The question arises: Why was it necessary for all those idealistic and intrepid direct actionists to submit themselves to such a terrible physical and psychological battering in the South to establish a few struggling groups for local reforms in politics and economics, attempting in vain to breach the jimcrow barriers, which are, in effect, "separate" movements? It was because these young radicals did not understand, at the outset, the divergent natures of reforms and revolutionary movements for social change. They confused the methods without understanding them, thus imputing revolutionary interpretations to merely reformist methods. Hence, when direct-action methods failed against hardening barriers, they had to fall back on what few political and economic reform gains they had won. From this point on, the direct actionists advanced to the slogan of Black Power, as if to convince themselves that they were taking a revolutionary step forward, to wit: instead of radical integrationism the theme became *economic and political control by blacks in the black ghettoes and in geographical areas of black majority in the South.* But is this a step forward or backward . . . or perhaps a one-step-backward-two-steps-forward sort of gambit? Whatever it is, it is essentially another variation of the old Communist leftwing doctrine of "self-determination in the black belt areas of Negro majority"—but with certain innovations. The old Communist Party doctrine did not include the Northern ghettoes in this scheme as the Black Power exponents do. Moreover, the Communists did not envision any separatist black party movements as part of "self-detemination," nor include any separatist economic reforms for self-help (such as cooperative consumers and producers movements). For the Communists then, and forever more, trade unionism was of paramount importance. The Northern CORE found itself in the 1960's, for instance, still forced to battle for integration in certain unions such as the building and construction trades. But when the subterranean nationalists inside the organization came to the fore in 1966 in answer to Carmichael's Black Power call, they demanded that Negroes reject integration as their major aim. Negroes were called on to band themselves into a racially-oriented mass movement, using political power and economic boycotts to win complete economic and political control of Northern ghettoes and Southern counties in which they are in the majority. Except for time, place, circumstances, plus a few innovative, ideological twists, there is very little that is new in all of this.

In essence Black Power represents nothing more than a strategic retreat for a purpose. It proposes to change, not the white world outside, but the black world inside, by refoming it into something else politically and economically. In its own way and for other purposes the Nation of Islam has already achieved this in a limited way, substituting religion for politics.

Malcolm X quitted the Nation of Islam because this type of Black Power lacked a dynamic, was static and aloof to the broad struggle. He proposed to create another movement (the Organization for Afro-American Unity, OAAU) and link up with all the direct actionists and even passive resisters, believing that one must be involved in all forms of struggle wherever they are on all fronts. But after Malcolm's passing, the most dynamic of all the direct actionists gave up their dynamism and took a position almost in the lap of the Nation of Islam. They merely substituted politics for a parochial religion to go along with economics, but they added a more secular religion of Black Power invented by a Baptist minister-politician. As the fates would have it, all of this took place at a time when Powell, in whom more black political power was invested than in anyone else at the moment, was under fire from a Congressional white backlash in Washington, D.C.

On the face of it, Black Power adds up to some profound questions: Does this strategic retreat from integrationism mean that the civil righters are settling for gradual evolutionary reforms within the black communities? Can these economic and political reforms be achieved without effect on, and interaction with, the white world? Will the achievement of certain levels of Black Power enable the exponents to deal more effectively with the white world than the dynamics of direct-action integrationism? What manner of social dynamic is to be added to Black Power to make up for the dynamic that was discarded along with direct action? The real answer at this stage is that the Black Power slogan has no other dynamic than what is implied in its emotional necessity. Taken by themselevs, all purely economic and political reorganizations of any type in America can be only reformist movements, whether in black ghettoes or the white world. In order to be revolutionary in method to effect social change, such as transforming ghettoes, other dynamic elements must be added to the economic and political combination. The Black Power exponents have not understood these elements. Yet there is a unique inner dialectic at work in all this that must be examined.

For this purpose the Black Power exponents themselves have laid out their thinking for all to see. We can discount the frenetic avowals of black consciousness that made *New York Times* headlines and television panels, that frightened the bourgeois "Toms," white resisters, and lost "friends." It was but a new way of singing the same nationalist theme heard before from other quarters. But the CORE Black Power exponents came out in midwinter with a new publication called *Rights & Reviews* (Winter 1966–67), subtitled the "Black Power Issue," in which the substance of the slogan was discussed at some length. Here it was revealed that behind the brave verbalizations of Black Power, lay a muddled intellectual world of vague ideas and conceptual confusion. Sixteen articles by an interracial lineup of nationalists, Black Power integrationists, white leftwingers, Jews, Africans and others, spelled out the implicit Black Power retreat to the more leveled progression of an evolutionary black reformation. One cannot argue against this tactic since it is premature to state categorically where it will lead; but one should not, in this instance, refrain from calling reformism what it is. After all, the social realist must be aware that the New Deal heritage of the 1930's still hangs heavy over the land, and the American social dynamic has the built-in persuasion to bend all so-called revolutionary inclinations into the reformist groove. This is what Anti-Poverty is all about; it is why the Anti-Poverty program is able to buy off all the ghetto rebels with consummate ease. At a recent Anti-Poverty meeting in Harlem where an Independent Citizens' Committee* was challeng-

---

* This Independent Citizens Committee of Harlem has its roots in a rank-and-file oppositional move against the undemocratic control of HARYOU-ACT over the dispensation of Anti-Poverty funds. Active within this ICC are individuals from the Harlem Neighborhoods Association (HANA), a pioneer middleclass civic organization established in 1958. HANA grew out of the Central Harlem Coordinating Council established in 1938 for the purpose of encouraging and supporting "resident involvement and self-determination in community affairs." Harlem community politics is such that HANA was actually the creator of HARYOU and a number of other autonomous social welfare groups. The executive director of HANA, James Soler, is active in the ICC.

ing the efficiency and propriety of HARYOU-ACT's dominant role in Anti-Poverty politics, certain CORE leaders were present—and silent. It remains to be seen just how Black Power will handle Anti-Poverty issues with CORE.

But in the maiden issue of *Rights & Reviews* on Black Power, Roy Inniss opened up with "Black Power—Phase 1: Psychological Warfare," in which he said:

> There is an impelling need to emphasize the socio-psychological aspect of Black Power. We can cry "Black Power" until doomsday, but until black children stop saying, "You're blacker than me and so is your mama"; until grown black men stop using black as a curse word; until *Ebony* stops asking such asinine questions as: "Are Negro women getting prettier?" and stops carrying bleaching cream advertisements; until black people stop saying such things as: "She's dark, but pretty"; in short, until black people accept values meaningful to themselves, there can be no completely effective organizing for the development of Black Power.[1]

Mr. Inniss, a West Indian nationalist (once removed), was not merely being rhetorical about the much maligned values of "blackness." He himself is black and Africanesque. In fact, his sensitivity to this question was shown much earlier, in a *New York Times* article where he discussed his fears of "genetic destruction" through enforced "integration." Yet, if one is to discuss the color question among Negroes one cannot be as superficial as Mr. Inniss and leave it there. Granted, the Negro in America has been conditioned in many ways to a disrespect of blackness, but this is not as universal as Innis makes out. On the other hand, if Inniss truly believes that there can be no "effective organizing . . ." (even for Black Power) until Negroes stop derogating "blackness," then he will never see "Black Power," whatever he means by it. Ideas about skin-color and the social values attached thereto are like ideas about all things social. Take the notion, for example, that holds slavery as a human institution to be a good thing. Had the slaves waited for the slavemasters to *change* their views on slavery before fighting for freedom, they would never be free. For even *after* the slaves won their freedom there would still be ex-slavemasters and ex-slaves who thought that slavery was a good thing. By the same token, even after the hoped-for ascent to Black Power, there will still be Negroes who will wish they were white inasmuch as Black Power will demand more responsibility than some blacks care to assume. However, the conceptual flaws noted here in Mr. Inniss' thinking on social dynamics are typical of the social thinking of all black revolutionaries. Either they are activists without ideas or they fail to connect their ideas to the appropriate

[1] *Rights & Reviews*, Winter 1966–67, p. 5.

kind of social actions. If a person has a low opinion of himself and is unhappy because he lives in a filthy, dilapidated, rat-infested house, you cannot tell him to apply positive thinking—and "Be happy!" Happiness will begin to blossom only when he finds a way to get out of his physical trap into improved surroundings. In other words, what are the social dynamics of the program implicit in a Black Power kind of happiness?

It was noted that this Black Power magazine issue went to great lengths to play up the ideas, the imagery and the symbolism of the African Personality. All of the artwork, with exception of an amusing Jules Feiffer cartoon, relied on African tribal symbolism. One of the articles, written by a Black Nationalist-Africanist, Yosef Ben-Jochannan, asked —"What is Black Power?" He said:

> It is that power which black peoples had in Africa before the invasion and domination of Africa by the Europeans under the guise of "taking Christianity to the heathen Africans." . . . It is that power which caused Africans to build their many civilizations of high culture and institutions of science, law, medicine, philosophy, religion, etc., while Europeans were still asleep in their ignorance of the universe around and about them.[2]

Here, along with the historical romance of the African past, was an echo of Back-to-Africa Garveyism. For Ben-Jochannan, Black Power means that Negroes in America must take their "rightful place within the African community." "Why all the sudden fuss and fury against the call for Black Power?" he asks. Why the fear?—"Fear by those who allegedly lead those of us who remain on the colonial plantations throughout the Harlems of the United States of America." There is an element of truth in Ben-Jochannan's message, but also much propagandist rhetoric, and it is the rhetoric that one must watch out for. It is from a school of Harlem thought that condemns *any* effort on the part of the American Negro to seek racial equality within the American system.

Thus, within the CORE Black Power outlook reappears the old dichotomy between Du Bois-NAACPism and West Indian nationalist-Garveyism, for one must remember that CORE, the first direct-action group following World War II, merely extended the NAACP philosophy on another level. Even the present transition of the CORE philosophy to Black Power reformism is not complete, for witness the interracial lineup of the magazine content. The Black Power concept is due for a possible split between African Black Power and Afro-American Black Power, two related but different propositions in terms of emphasis. The clue to all this lies in the fact that neither in Ben-Jochan-

[2] *Ibid.*, p. 28.

nan's article, nor elsewhere in the issue, is the status of the West Indies (or the West Indian) discussed. Recall that when Black Power was first projected, the white press plus Inniss, Carmichael, and Lynch, played up the alleged Caribbean influence behind the slogan. Yet, although Ben-Jochannan discusses White Power vs. Black Power all over the world wherever it involves "the undying and unquenching energy of African peoples everywhere . . . ," he makes no reference to either the black West Indies or the British Commonwealth. The implicit, typically Garveyite, assumption here is that the black West Indies already has Black Power (poor but proud), and that the Caribbean islands, unlike the "Harlems of the United States . . ." are not what Ben-Jochannan calls "colonial plantations." For the West Indian nationalists in the United States, the Caribbean "image" must be preserved and the exact nature of the "political independence" achieved is not to be examined too closely especially since the success of Black Power (at home and abroad) is predicated on both *political and economic independence.*

However, let us see what an African representative says about Black Power in the same publication. Chief S. O. Adebo is Nigeria's Permanent Representative to the United Nations. Writing on "The Black Revolution—An African View,"[3] he discusses the "parallel movements" for freedom and independence of Africans and people of African descent in the United States:

> Where the blacks constitute the majority of the country's population, as in Africa, the movement has taken the form of a struggle to take over the exercise of the governing power; where, as in the United States, the blacks are a minority, the struggle has been one for participation on level terms with everybody else. . . .

So far even the NAACP and King would concur, but Chief Abedo added "but, fundamentally, the objective is the same, an objective which can be described as securing a square deal for the black man in this world."

On the implementation of this objective, every faction from the NAACP to the Nation of Islam—clear across the spectrum, including the Black Power exponents themselves—are divided. But, as Chief Abedo said, "The wind of change has of course caused a lot of transformation on the African continent" and in the United States. "But you will no doubt agree with me that here, as in Africa, the task still to be done is more than that which is already accomplished. For both of our communities it is a long, long way to Tipperary."

"We must coordinate and work together," Abedo advised. "In order to do this, an essential prerequisite is that we should strive to remove

[3] *Ibid.*, p. 32.

the misunderstanding created between the African and the American Negro by centuries of lack of intelligent communication between our communities." And he concluded:

> The African must recognize the American Negro as his brother, and American Negroes must acknowledge Africa as their ancestral home, and Africans as their kith and kin. This mutual understanding already exists within the top echelons both in Africa and in the United States. But this is not enough; it must go right down to the grass roots.

Again, curiously, the African said nothing, even in passing, about the West Indies, the natural home of Garveyism abroad. And, exactly who are those "top echelon" leaders in Africa and America who have this "mutual understanding" of which Adebo speaks? Such American Negro top echelon leaders would also, presumably, support Black Power. But which top leaders besides Powell support Black Power? They are not found in the NAACP, the Urban League, or in King's top echelon (the very leadership, in fact, that Ben-Jochannan sees as fearing Black Power). No, there is much confusion here both in the outlook of Africans such as Adebo and in the Afro-American Black Power exponents over the African Revolution, the alleged Black Revolution, and their parallels. There is too much romanticizing about Africa going on in certain nationalist circles; too much rhetoric and too much Garveyite Back-to-Africa lip service by certain black redemptionists in America who haven't the least intention of going to Africa unless there is the guarantee of a good job or a money-making scheme in the offing, or the possibility of a "top echelon" marriage into the African diplomatic corps.

Africans such as Chief Adebo are just as much in the dark about the inner dynamic demands of the American Black Revolution as the Black Power exponents are about the dynamic substances of their new slogan. As a result, the readiness of most Black Nationalist trends, to lean heavily on the African past and the African image, is nothing but a convenient cover-up for an inability to come to terms with the complex demands of the American reality. A Roy Inniss, for example, will have one believe that no one in the black world but the American Negro has a complex about being black. In a black African country, inasmuch as nearly everyone is black, there is no basis for any psychological conditioning of inferiority complexes. However, pick up any popular African magazine such as *Spears* from Nigeria, *Parade* from Rhodesia, *Post* from South Africa, and also *Drum* of Ghana and Nigeria, and lo and behold! There are skin-bleaching advertisements galore, also hair-straightening creams and black women in long-haired wigs—just like Harlem. Said one full-page, Madison Avenue-ish spread in *Drum:* Amazing ARTA made my skin—Lighter, Smoother, Clearer . . . Because it is Pure White." "This is how I look now that I use pure white

Arta." But, . . . "this was how I looked before. . . ." (She was *dark*, but pretty!)

Roy Inniss thinks *Ebony's* query "Are Negro Women Getting Prettier" rather asinine. But if he looks, he will observe that the African male in the United States has a female-beauty standard that parallels not only the prevailing standards of American Negro males and *Ebony* magazine, but also the standards of the vari-colored spectrum of the United Nations. On this question there is very little misunderstanding between the two ancestral progeny. The problem is deeper: The American Negro is wedded to America and does not want to return to his ancestral Africa except in fancy, perhaps. The African *has* Africa, but a severe psychic problem has cropped up among Africans sent to the United States on various assignments: Many of them have very little contact with American Negroes, feel alienated within themselves, *but do not want to return to Africa.* Alienated or no, they have become passionately attached to the ways of the cosmopolitan West, the high standard of living, the creature comforts of the affluent society. These sons of Africa do not care to share the enforced status of the American Negro (who can blame them?), but they exist from day to day, from year to year, in levels and areas of American society where for years our American Negro integrationist leadership sought to be accepted on a peer basis of merit and educational qualifications. Despite his blackness, the African is handed this status almost *gratis,* without a "civil rights" struggle. This is what he wants, and he likes it, and regrets to have to give it up. Compared to the American Negro, he is *persona grata.* Ironically, however, for the Black Nationalists and the Black Power exponents in Harlem, any American Negro from the black elite functioning in these privileged areas of metropolitan interracial life has sold out his birthright to the white power structure.

Despite the historical affinities, the African and the Afro-American dilemmas differ—each has its own qualities, peculiarities, and imperatives. And the Black Power controversy illuminates all too well the deep confusions about these imperatives. What *is* the program for Black Power? *That* is the fundamental, unanswered question. In *Rights & Reviews,* Julian Bond, formerly of SNCC, wrote: "Black Power must be seen as a natural extension of the work of the civil rights movement for the past few years. From the courtroom to the streets in favor of integrated public facilities; from the streets onto backwoods roads in quest of the right to vote; from the ballot box to the meat of politics, the organization of voters into self-interest units." This is the dialectic of reformism! But, Bond advised that "conflict and struggle are necessary for social change."[4]

4 *Ibid.,* p. 6.

However, another writer said: "Forget Black Power. There is more to it than that, and our life might perhaps become the truth of the moment we seek without the need of slogans. In times past people were content to *experience* their lives, but today one is not really living unless one has a program."[5]

Floyd McKissick, CORE's top man, wrote: "The doctrine of Black Power is this new thrust which seeks to achieve economic power and to develop political movements that would make changes that are vast and significant."[6] *But economic power for whom?* For workers? Black capitalists? Black farmers? Black middleclass? Black racketeers? Welfare clients? The crucial economic issue in the ghettoes today is Anti-Poverty, *but Anti-Poverty is not only a black issue.* How would CORE Black Power deal with this question? Or, on the question of political movements—around what particular issues would these political movements be developed? So far, the mentality of the Black Power theorists is so narrow that they see politics on merely one plane—running some black candidate for office—a hackneyed reformist tactic. No one can beat the Democrats and Republicans in the field of reform politics, especially black reform. Black radicals do not understand the art of creative politics, which is to make the superabundance of people's grievances political. But this is not all that is awry in Black Power ideology.

When one starts with the skin-color premise of a Roy Inniss on the Afro-American problem, one is, unfortunately, feeding a strong tendency within the Black Nationalist movement towards black-skin chauvinism—a policy which cannot work politically in the United States. It has never worked in the West Indies either; it can work only in Africa, it seems. But, in the United States, the American Negro group is too large and mixed with too many racial strains for the ideology of black-skin supremacy to function within the group. It can lead to the reasoning that "I'm blacker than you, and so is my mama, so I'm purer than you and your mama. Therefore, I am also more nationalistic than you, and more politically trustworthy than you and your mama, in the interests of Black Power." But inside America this is a pure fiction. The blacker skin does not always denote the deeper racial pride. In fact, some of the darkest Negroes are the most "white-minded." In America, the Negro group is more an *ethnic* than a racial group—meaning a group of mixed African, Indian, and white strains. Of course, the American-West Indian fusion of Black African-nationalists prefer their converts to be truly "black" both in pigmentation and

[5] *Ibid.*, Lorenzo Thomas, "Spontaneous History and the Ethics of a Revolution," p. 9.
[6] *Ibid.*, p. 7.

ideology, and look rather doubtfully at others. There have been several trends who have tried to exclude Negroes with non-Negroid features and straight hair, overlooking the fact that Marcus Garvey's second wife, just such a female type, wrote of Garvey: "My hair let down, thrilled him. It was long and naturally wavy, he asked me never to cut it. The first time he saw it down, curiously he felt some strands and said, 'why it is soft,' as I tossed my head, he exclaimed, 'Oh, but it is so live.'"[7] There is little doubt that Mrs. Garvey, a racial hybrid, was just as much of a Black Nationalist as the great redemptionist. And in our time, the two leading exponents of Black Power and Black Nationalism have been racial hybrids—Adam Clayton Powell and Malcolm X. The color problem among American Negroes is more complex than Roy Inniss admits.

Yet this problem among Negroes is of less signal importance today than the glaring fact that the Black Power theorists have learned very little from Afro-American history, which is of more immediate political significance than how many black Africans sat on the thrones of ancient Egypt. The trouble with the Black Nationalist Africanists is that most of their intellectual capacities are used up glorifying the most attractive aspects of Africa's pre-slavery past, while most of the African elite today have ceased being revolutionaries (if they ever were). In fact, most American Negroes who have been to Africa and back have almost as low an opinion of the African elite in Africa as some of the Africans have of the American Negroes' lack of cohesion. Hence, it would serve a very good purpose here in America for Negroes to cease romanticizing Africa and pre-feudal tribalism.

The radical wing of the Negro movement in America sorely needs a social theory based on the living ingredients of Afro-American history. Without such a theory all talk of Black Power is meaningless. One of the keys to the confusion over the meaning of the slogan, is the ambivalence in CORE's publication over the choice of historical leadership symbols and the interpretation given to the implications of these leadership trends. For example, the strong tendency of the Black Power theorists to associate only the names of Denmark Vesey, Harriet Tubman, Nat Turner, Marcus Garvey, Elijah Muhammed and Malcolm X with the social, political and ideological implications of Black Power is being absolutely false to history. Even the addition of Frederick Douglass to this historical leadership gallery is insufficient. For one thing, Douglass was no nationalist, and no pre-Civil War data is complete without the name of Martin R. Delany, the real prototype of Afro-American Nationalism.

But of more relevance to the present-day Negro movement as a whole are the twentieth-century leaders and their trends—Washington,

[7] *Garvey and Garveyism, op. cit.,* p. 186.

Du Bois, and Garvey. *These are the big three for our century.* Anyone who does not understand this cannot talk seriously about Black Power or any other slogan. But the Black Power theorists are romantics who do not understand this. Of course, spokesmen like Roy Inniss, Ben-Jochannan, etc., will find it difficult to accept this. In their conceptual scheme of things they would accept Marcus Garvey and reject Washington and Du Bois. But this is predicated not on any profound theoretical or scientific examination of historical facts but on passion, emotionalism, and prejudice. They accept Garvey without Washington because they have not examined the reasons Washington was Garvey's only American hero. Similarly, they accept Douglass without Du Bois, although it was Du Bois who upheld Douglass and carried his abolitionist-protest-civil rights trend into the twentieth century. Although in terms of economics, Elijah Muhammed carried out Booker T. Washington's philosophy of economic self-sufficiency and self-help more thoroughly than any other movement, the Black Power theorists accept the Nation of Islam, yet reject Booker T-ism. They fail to see the fallacy of such reasoning because they have no understanding of economics as a science or the different schools of economic theory and how to apply them to the Negro movement. With such an innocence about economics, politics becomes child's play once the direct-action dynamic is taken away. Unschooled in the deep politics of the Negro movement since World War One, the leaders of CORE and SNCC are unaware that even the few economic cooperatives they initiated in the South are forty years too late. How can people like this expect to cope with the economic policies of Anti-Poverty today?

In terms of economics, the Negro's heritage today is New Deal capitalism and Anti-Poverty, broadly speaking. His only "race" economics of any importance are those of Elijah Muhammed. Garvey's economic ideology which was tied to the African scene is useless today, since there is no Back-to-Africa momentum. The only leader of the big three who left behind, in writing, an economic program for the United States was W. E. B. Du Bois, yet nationalist prejudice against him prevents Negro leaders from acknowledging this. Moreover, it was Du Bois' brand of Pan-Africanism that won out in Africa, not Garvey's, *because Garvey was not a socialist but a thoroughgoing capitalist.* In terms of economics, neither Africa nor the West Indies has achieved the kind of independence and autonomy Garvey wanted. However, the unreality of Garvey's program in the 1920's meant he would have had even less chance of expunging neo-colonialism from Africa than the leaders of the African Revolution have had today. The result has been that Garveyism has failed to muster up any aid or political and economic assistance from Negroes in the Western hemisphere. The real foreign aid must come from both capitalist and socialist governments. The politics of certain African leaders are sufficiently ambivalent that they avidly seek this capitalistic and socialistic aid with one hand (for their version of Black Power), while with the other they either point the finger of criticism at the American Negro or else mouth vague platitudes about black cooperation. They simply do not understand the Afro-American's complex problem and its imperatives.

The Black Power enthusiasts practice the same dubious verbal skin-game in another way. They cannot cope with the realities of the economics of their own foreign aid, *i.e.*, Anti-Poverty, yet they talk boldly about economic independence as the basis of real power. How can such people talk seriously of cooperating with Africa when they cannot help themselves with a definitive economic program for Black Power in America? The "reluctant African" in the United States has adequate reasons for his stand-offishness. He has deep personal problems of identity to cope with, in the midst of a situation that has trapped the American Negro both physically and intellectually. The worst effect of his American conditioning is not his color-complex about blackness, but that it renders him unable to look at his own history and influence in America objectively and understand it scientifically. He is so bedazzled by the personalities of his chosen leadership symbols that he cannot peer behind the façade and examine what were the political, economic, class, and cultural trends that influenced the actions of those chosen leaders.

Another important issue the Black Power theorists evade is the class problem among Negroes. When one talks bravely about developing political and economic black power one had best start clarifying which class is going to wield this power. Better yet—which class among Negroes has the most power now? And which class will benefit from Black Power when it arrives? Here is another clue to the essential reformism inherent in the Black Power slogan: The theorists, although they snipe at the black bourgeoisie, are themselves prey to bourgeois aspirations—major or minor. This is by no means a bad thing in itself. To better one's material (if not spiritual) condition in America necessarily means adopting either the petty or the garish trappings of middle-class existence. However, the Black Power theorists are thrown into a reformist muddle involving class aspirations and economic power for the simple reason that they have no recognizable basis for economic power. To be brutally frank, some do not even know what economic theory is, while others do not want to be bothered with it. Despite their vaunted anti-Americanism, they are more American than they think. Congenitally pragmatic to the core, they are anti-theoretical. Thus, the white power structure does their economic theory and practice for them. New Deal economics, in force for thirty-four years, decides how Anti-Poverty funds are allotted to black ghettoes, but people in ghettoes have no say in how much funds or how often they are to be allotted. Is *this* economic Black Power? If not, ask any Black Power theorist what kind of politics can change this arrangement. Or better—ask any Black Power theorist whether economics determine politics, or vice versa? Ask any Black Power theorist why Anti-Poverty funds pay out so much money in middle-class salaries? Is this good or bad—for Black Power economics? You will get no clear answers.

However, from one familiar source we get some very clear convictions on the question of which class attributes and Black-Power economics go together. Discussing Black Power in the *Negro Digest* of November, 1966, our literary sojourner from the old Left, John O. Killens, had this to say:

> It seems to me there need be no strong schism at this moment between the advocates of black power and the "black bourgeoisie". . . . If one of the principle [sic] tenets of Black Consciousness is economic power, the starting place is with the black middle class. May their tribe increase. Black Power advocates are no present danger to them.[8]

When Black Power was simply Black Nationalism unqualified, Killens was by no means so certain that no middle-class Negroes were endangered. But since Black Nationalism is obviously here to stay, let us reform it nearer to the heart's desire. If John O. Killens had been told during the early 1950's that the black middle class on *Freedom* newspaper, with Robeson leading, had reformed left-wing Communism into left-wing integrationism (which is not Black Power) in the interests of the black middle class, Killens would have replied something like this —"Oh no, Robeson's *Freedom* appeals to the black working class, may their tribe increase. But this is no present danger to the black middle class." In fact, it was not. But today it should be clear to all Black Power advocates that these two "tribes"—workingclass and bourgeois —cannot both increase. Somebody has to give in, or give up, or simply "give" somewhere. Moreover, when a John O. Killens declares "all power to the black bourgeoisie" instead of the black proletariat, he admonishes: "Black Power is not an advocate of violence. It advocates non-violence, but in depth. It keeps everybody non-violent. It stays the hand of the practitioners of violence."[9] Of course, it was not long ago that Mr. Killens was upholding "violence" when "necessary."

Nothing better demonstrates the reformist ideology behind Black Power than the Killens stamp of approval. Never the originator of a single new concept, style, or exposition whether in literature or politics, Killens has been the neutralizing temporizer, the non-controversial, moderating lid-sitter par excellence. He is not averse to changing his opinions or shifting his position when necessary; but he possesses that

[8] *Negro Digest,* November, 1966, p. 34.
[9] *Ibid.*

reform politician's knack of catching on belatedly to all advanced demands and slogans, once it is certain that the establishment must bend to popular appeal. He then becomes the propagandizing expert just as if he were *always* of that opinion. Thus, it is quite proper for Killens to say of Black Power today: "It means that all the Harlems of the U.S.A. should be in the hands of Harlemites. This is the starting point for black liberation. . . ."[10]

. . . But you will find no such declaration of this tenor in a single issue of Robeson's *Freedom* newspaper in the early 1950's. *Freedomways* tried to prove that Robeson anticipated SNCC's direct action but it cannot be proven that the *Freedom* newspaper family anticipated Black Power in Harlem even when conditions existed in the Harlem radical movement of the late 1940's and early 1950's for such a slogan. Certain members of the pioneer Harlem Writers' Club, not Killens' Harlem Writers Guild, raised the idea that the black radical movement in Harlem should be run by blacks. The Harlem Writers Club, not Killens' group, forced the first conference on Negro cultural problems, the root problem of black consciousness. The leaders of the Harlem Writers Club first challenged the Committee for the Negro in the Arts' (CNA) concept of Integration in the Arts as cart-before-the-horse cultural policy in Harlem, *not* the Killens group. And, members of the Harlem Writers Club first attempted to debate these issues in their magazine *Harlem Quarterly* in 1949 and 1950, *not* the Killens Harlem Writers Guild and *Freedom* newspaper cliques. True, these issues were not debated with the thoroughness they should have been, but they *were* raised. Hence, it was the members of the Harlem Writers Club who took the brunt of the attacks, the slander, the abuse, and the ostracism from the interracial leftwing Harlem establishment. There is nothing new under the Harlem sun, but if John O. Killens had said of the black middle class—"May their tribe increase!"—in the pages of *Freedom* newspaper, everything would have been clearer for all concerned. For the black bourgeoisie *is* important as a class within the Negro movement. One cannot analyze leadership trends unless it is done within the context of the role of the black bourgeoisie. The problem is—the Black Power theorists have not done so.

The last outstanding leader was Malcolm X, but did his followers really understand the man's positive side, or his limitations, or why he acted as he did? Did they see any Afro-American historical trends repeating themselves in Malcolm X's career? Unfortunately, they did not. The editors of CORE's magazine leaned heavily on quotations from Frederick Douglass' speeches and writings. But, historically, Douglass' Abolitionism and Reconstructionism are nineteenth-century achievements that became overshadowed by American twentieth-cen-

[10] *Ibid.*

tury developments. Besides, Frederick Douglass is also the chief hero of the NAACP integrationists, hence, the Black Power fellows are in strange company, sharing "heroes." Yet Malcolm X was no hero to the NAACP worshippers at Douglass' shrine, so how then, do divergent integrationist and nationalist trends wind up honoring the same hero? Because neither integrationists nor nationalists truly understand the crucial impact of the integrationist vs. nationalist conflict within the contours of American Negro history.

The Black Power exponents who uphold Malcolm X, yet cannot come to terms with either Washington or Du Bois as historical leaders, understand neither the break between Du Bois and Washington, nor the break between Malcolm X and Elijah Muhammed. These two breaches are historically related and stem from the same root in Afro-American history, albeit under different circumstances. Malcolm X broke with the Nation of Islam because of Muhammed's refusal to participate in the broad struggle for human rights, as Malcolm X explained it. But W. E. B. Du Bois, the turn-of-the-century radical, broke with Booker T. Washington's leadership school for the same reason (as a reading of *The Souls of Black Folk* will show). Du Bois said that Washington shied away from participating in the struggle for the Negro's manhood rights. Malcolm X's break was that of a radical nationalist with the conservative nationalism of Elijah Muhammed, the latter inherited from Booker T. Washington, by way of Garvey who had "radicalized" Washington's economic philosophy.

The only way to understand this process is not to be led astray by mere slogans, but to see the fundamentals at work: the underlying conflict between integrationist and nationalist tendencies historically projected in the contrasted outlooks of Douglass and Delany. No matter how nationalistic Malcolm X remained after his break, he was forced by circumstances to swing closer to the civil rights-integrationist forces in order to participate more fully in the broad struggle.* That was why certain of Malcolm X's former followers could charge him with "selling out" by seeking an alliance with the direct-action-integrationist forces.

American Negro history is basically a history of the conflict between integrationist and nationalist forces in politics, economics, and culture, no matter what leaders are involved and what slogans are used. After Malcolm X's death, the Black Power slogan was actually a swing back to the conservative nationalism from which Malcolm X had just departed. The pendulum swings back and forth, but the men who swing

---

* Malcolm X's plan to take the Negro issue to the United Nations as a Human Rights question in 1964 had been first attempted in 1947 by W. E. B. Du Bois in collaboration with NAACP. See "Appeal to the World," A Statement on the Denial of Human Rights to Minorities in the Case of Citizens of Negro Descent in the United States and an Appeal to the United Nations for Redress (NAACP, pamphlet, 1947).

with it always fail to synthesize composite trends. W. E. B. Du Bois came the closest of all the big three to understanding this problem, when he wrote in *Dusk of Dawn:* "There faces the American Negro therefore an intricate and subtle problem of combining into one object two difficult sets of facts."[11]

The "two difficult sets of facts" Du Bois refers to are integrationism (civil rights, racial equality, freedom) versus nationalism (separatism, accommodationist self-segregation, economic nationalism, group solidarity and self-help). This was truly the first theoretical formulation of the historic conflict between tendencies, but Du Bois never developed his basic theoretical premise. He failed to go beyond this first principle into a greater synthesis of all the historical ingredients of Afro-Americana, which he knew better than all the Washingtons and the Garveys combined. Like Karl Marx, W. E. B. Du Bois was one of history's great researchers—a sifter, interpreter and recorder of historical and contemporary knowledge; but unlike Marx, he could not reinterpret his data into new conceptions of social reality. Still, he came close, albeit late in life.

It was historically unfortunate that the American Negro created no social theorists to back up his long line of activist leaders, charismatic deliverers, black redemptionists, and moral suasionists. With a few perceptive and original thinkers, the Negro movement conceivably could long ago have aided in reversing the backsliding of the United States toward the moral negation of its great promise as a new nation of nations. Instead the American Negro has, unwittingly, been forced to share in many of the corrupted values of the society—not enough, to be sure, to cancel out completely his inherent potential for social change. However, the intellectual horizons of the black intelligentsia have been so narrowed in scope and banalized by the American corrosion that Negro creativity has been diminishing since the 1920's. An examination of the pronouncements of the Black Power theorists reveal that they have not advanced one whit in their thinking, beyond the 1919 writers of A. Phillip Randolph's *Messenger* magazine. They have, in fact, retrogressed. There is not a single Negro publication in existence today that matches the depth of the old *Messenger*. CORE's new Black Power publication talks of developing "political and economic power" as if speaking for the first time. But back in the 1920's, when Randolph's writers were chastising Du Bois and boasting of how they were "correctly" giving precedence to economics and politics over culture and art, they knew what they were talking about and said it with infinitely more expertise than today's Black Power exponents. In fact, the Black Power theorists do not even know how to deal with culture and art, as the CORE publication reveals. This is shocking to contemplate.

[11] *Dusk of Dawn, op. cit.,* p. 199.

Black Power slogans reveal the depth of unpreparedness and the lack of knowledge that go along with the eagerness of the new black generation of spokesmen. The farther the Negro gets from his historical antecedents in time, the more tenuous become his conceptual ties, the emptier his social conceptions, the more superficial his visions. His one great and present hope is to know and understand his Afro-American history in the United States more profoundly. Failing that, and failing to create a new synthesis and a social theory of action, he will suffer the historical fate described by the philosopher who warned that "Those who cannot remember the past are condemned to repeat it."

SELECTIVE BIBLIOGRAPHY

I. ANTHOLOGIES AND COLLECTIONS (arranged alphabetically)
(Note: all authors in this section are editors.)

ADOFF, ARNOLD. *I Am the Darker Brother: An Anthology of Modern Poems by Negro Americans.* Macmillan, 1968.

Black on Black: Commentaries by Negro Americans. Macmillan, 1968.

ALHAMSI, AHMED AND H. K. WANGARA. *Black Arts: An Anthology of Black Creations.* Broadside Press, 1969.

BARBOUR, FLOYD B. *The Black Power Revolt.* Sargent, 1968.

BONTEMPS, ARNA. *American Negro Poetry.* Hill & Wang, 1963.

Great Slave Narratives. Beacon Press, 1969.

BRAWLEY, BENJAMIN. *Early Negro American Writers.* Univ. of North Carolina Press, 1935; Books for Libraries, 1968.

BROWN, STERLING A., ARTHUR P. DAVIS, ULYSSES LEE. *The Negro Caravan: Writings by American Negroes.* Dryden, 1941; Arno, 1969.

CALVERTON, V. F. *Anthology of American Negro Literature.* Modern Library, 1929.

CHAPMAN, ABRAHAM. *Black Voices: An Anthology of Afro-American Literature.* New American Library, 1968.

CLARKE, JOHN H. *American Negro Short Stories.* Hill & Wang, 1966.

COUCH, WILLIAM, JR. *New Black Playwrights.* Louisiana State Univ. Press, 1968.

CROMWELL, OTELIA, LORENZO TURNER, EVA B. DYKES. *Readings from Negro Authors.* Harcourt, 1931.

CULLEN, COUNTEE. *Caroling Dusk.* Harper, 1927.

CUNARD, NANCY. *Negro Anthology, 1931–1933.* Wishart, 1934.

DAVIS, CHARLES T. AND DANIEL WALDEN. *On Being Black: Writings by Afro-Americans . . .* Fawcett World, 1970.

DREER, HERMAN. *American Literature by Negro Authors.* Macmillan, 1950.

EMANUEL, JAMES A. AND THEODORE GROSS. *Dark Symphony: Negro Literature in America.* Free Press, 1968.

HILL, HERBERT. *Soon One Morning: New Writing by American Negroes, 1940–1962.* Knopf, 1963.

Anger and Beyond: The Negro Writer in the United States. Harper, 1966.

HUGHES, LANGSTON. *New Negro Poets, U.S.A.* Indiana Univ. Press, 1964.

The Book of Negro Humor. Dodd, Mead, 1966.

The Best Short Stories by Negro Writers: An Anthology from 1899 to the Present. Little, Brown, 1967.

HUGHES, LANGSTON AND ARNA BONTEMPS. *The Poetry of the Negro.* Doubleday, 1949.

The Book of Negro Folklore. Dodd, Mead, 1958.

JOHNSON, CHARLES S. *Ebony and Topaz.* National Urban League, 1927.

JOHNSON, JAMES WELDON. *The Book of American Negro Poetry.* Harcourt, 1922; rev. and enl., 1931.

JONES, LEROI AND LARRY NEAL. *Black Fire.* Morrow, 1968.

JORDAN, JUNE. *Soulscript: Afro-American Poetry.* Doubleday, 1970.

KERLIN, ROBERT T. *Negro Poets and Their Poems.* Associated Pubs., 1935.

LOCKE, ALAIN L. *The New Negro: An Interpretation.* Boni, 1925; Atheneum, 1968.

LOMAX, ALAN AND RAOUL ABDAL. *Three Thousand Years of Black Poetry.* Dodd, Mead, 1969.

LOWENFELS, WALTER. *In a Time of Revolution: Poems from Our Third World.* Vin. Random, 1969.

MAJOR, CLARENCE. *The New Black Poetry.* International Pubs., 1969.

MOON, BUCKLIN. *The Primer for White Folks.* Doubleday, 1945.

OSOFSKY, GILBERT. *Puttin' on Ole Massa: The Slave Narratives of Henry Bibb, William W. Brown, and Solomon Northrop.* Harper, 1969.

POOL, ROSEY, E. *Beyond the Blues: New Poems by American Negroes.* Dufour, 1962.

RANDALL, DUDLEY. *Black Poetry* . . . Broadside Press, 1969.

RANDALL, DUDLEY AND MARGARET BURROUGHS. *For Malcolm: Poems on the Life and the Death of Malcolm X.* Broadside Press, 1967.

ROBINSON, WILLIAM H. *Early Black American Poets.* Wm. C. Brown, 1969.

SHUMAN, R. BAIRD. *Nine Black Poets.* Moore, 1968.

SMITH, ARTHUR L. *Rhetoric of Black Revolution.* Allyn and Bacon, 1969.

TURNER, DARWIN. *Black American Literature: Poetry.* Chas. E. Merrill, 1969.

Black American Literature: Fiction. Chas. E. Merrill, 1969.

WATKINS, SYLVESTER C. *Anthology of American Negro Literature.* Random, 1944.

WHITE, NEWMAN I. AND WALTER C. JACKSON. *An Anthology of Verse by American Negroes.* Folcroft, 1924.

WILLIAMS, JOHN A. *The Angry Black.* Cooper Square, 1962.

Beyond the Angry Black (rev. of *The Angry Black*) Cooper Square, 1966.

WILLIAMS, JOHN A. AND CHARLES F. HARRIS. *Amistad I.* Vin. Random, 1970.

WOODSON, CARTER G. *Negro Orators and Their Orations.* Associated Pubs., 1925.

II. HISTORY, BIBLIOGRAPHY, CRITICISM, AND COMMENT
(arranged alphabetically)

BARTON, REBECCA C. *Witnesses for Freedom, Negro Americans in Autobiography.* Harper, 1948.

BONE, ROBERT A. *The Negro Novel in America.* Yale Univ. Press, 1958.

BRIGNANO, RUSSELL. *Richard Wright; An Introduction to the Man and His Works.* Univ. of Pittsburgh, 1970.

BRAWLEY, BENJAMIN. *The Negro in Literature and Art in the United States.* Atlanta, 1910; Duffield, 1918.

BRONZ, STEPHEN H. *Roots of Negro Racial Consciousness: The 1920's.* Libra, 1964.

BROWN, STERLING A. *The Negro in American Fiction.* Associates in Negro Folk Education, 1937.

Negro Poetry and Drama. Associates in Negro Folk Education, 1937.

(Both reissued in one volume, Atheneum, 1969).

BROWN, STERLING A., ARTHUR P. DAVIS, ULYSSES LEE, eds. *The Negro Caravan: Writings by American Negroes.* Dryden, 1941; Arno, 1969.

BUTCHER, MARGARET J. *The Negro in American Culture.* Knopf, 1956.

CHARTER, SAMUEL. *Poetry of the Blues.* Oak, 1963.

COURLANDER, HAROLD. *Negro Folk Music, U.S.A.* Columbia Univ. Press, 1963.

ECKMAN, FERN M. *Furious Passage of James Baldwin.* Popular Library, 1966.

EMANUEL, JAMES A. *Langston Hughes.* Twayne, 1967.

FARRISON, WM. E. *William Wells Brown, Author and Reformer.* Univ. of Chicago Press, 1969.

FERGUSON, BLANCHE E. *Countee Cullen and the Negro Renaissance.* Dodd, Mead, 1966.

FISHER, MILES MARK. *Negro Slave Songs in the U.S.* New Edition. Russell and Russell, 1968.

FORD, NICK AARON. *The Contemporary Negro Novel.* Meador, 1936.

GAYLE, ADDISON, JR., ed. *Black Expression.* Weybright and Talley, 1969.

GLOSTER, HUGH M. *Negro Voices in American Fiction.* Univ. of North Carolina Press, 1948.

GROSS, SEYMOUR AND JOHN E. HARDY, eds. *Images of the Negro in American Literature: Essays in Criticism.* Univ. of Chicago Press, 1966.

HOMER, DOROTHY R., ed. *Negro in the U.S.: A List of Significant Books.* 9th rev. ed., New York Public Library, 1965.

HUGHES, CARL MILTON. *The Negro Novelist: A Discussion of the Writings of American Negro Novelists, 1940–50.* Citadel, 1953.

HUGHES, LANGSTON AND MILTON MELTZER. *Black Magic: A Pictorial History of the Negro in American Entertainment.* Prentice-Hall, 1967.

HUGHES, LANGSTON, MILTON MELTZER, C. ERIC LINCOLN. *A Pictorial History of the Negro in America.* Crown, 3rd rev. ed., 1968.

JOHNSON, JAMES WELDON. *Black Manhattan.* Knopf, 1930.

LAWSON, VICTOR. *Dunbar Critically Examined.* Associated Pubs., 1941.

LITTLEJOHN, DAVID. *Black on White: A Critical Survey of Writing by American Negroes.* Grossman, 1966.

LOCKE, ALAIN L., ed. *The New Negro: An Interpretation.* Boni, 1925; Atheneum, 1968.

LOGGINS, VERNON. *The Negro Author: His Development in America to 1900.* Columbia Univ. Press, 1931; Kennikat, 1964.

McCALL, DAN. *Example of Richard Wright.* Harcourt, 1969.

MARGOLIES, EDWARD. *Native Sons: A Critical Study of Twentieth-Century Negro American Authors.* Lippincott, 1969.

The Art of Richard Wright. Southern Illinois Univ. Press, 1969.

MASON, JULIAN D., JR., ed. *The Poems of Phillis Wheatley.* Univ. of North Carolina Press, 1966.

MILLER, ELIZABETH W., ed. *The Negro in America: A Bibliography.* Harvard Univ. Press, 1966.

NELSON, JOHN H. *The Negro Character in American Literature.* Univ. of Kansas Press, 1926.

Nichols, Charles H. *Many Thousand Gone*. Brill Adler, 1963; Indiana Univ. Press, 1969.

Porter, Dorothy B. *North American Negro Poets: A Bibliographical Checklist of Their Writings (1760–1944)*. The Book Farm, 1945.

Redding, J. Saunders. *To Make a Poet Black*. Univ. of North Carolina Press, 1939.

The Lonesome Road: The Story of the Negro in America. Doubleday, 1958.

Walser, Richard. *The Black Poet; Being the Remarkable Story (partly told by himself) of George Moses Horton, a North Carolina Slave*. Philosophical Library, 1966.

Welsch, Erwin K. *The Negro in the United States: A Research Guide*. Indiana Univ. Press, 1965.

Whiteman, Maxwell. *A Century of Fiction by American Negroes (1853–1952); A Descriptive Bibliography*. Saifer, 1968.

III. POETRY PUBLICATIONS (arranged chronologically according to first publication)

Hammon, Jupiter. *An Evening Thought . . .* Broadside, 1760.

An Address to Miss Phillis Wheatley. Broadside, 1778.

Wheatley, Phillis. *An Elegiac Poem, on the Death of . . . George Whitefield . . .* Boston, 1770.

Poems on Various Subjects, Religious and Moral. London, 1773.

Horton, George Moses. *Hope of Liberty*. Raleigh, N.C., 1829.

Naked Genius. Raleigh, N.C., 1865.

Whitfield, James M. *America and Other Poems*. Buffalo, 1853.

Harper, Frances E. W. *Poems on Miscellaneous Subjects*. Boston, 1854.

Moses: A Story of the Nile. Philadelphia, 1869.

Poems. Philadelphia, 1871.

Poems. Philadelphia, 1900.

Whitman, Albery A. *Not a Man, and Yet a Man*. Springfield, Ohio, 1877.

The Rape of Florida. St. Louis, 1884.

Twasinta's Seminoles: or, The Rape of Florida. St. Louis, 1885.

An Idyl of the South. An Epic in Two Parts. New York, 1901.

Dunbar, Paul Laurence. *Oak and Ivy*. Dayton, Ohio, 1893.

Majors and Minors. Toledo, Ohio, 1895.

Lyrics of Lowly Life. New York, 1896.

Lyrics of the Hearthside. New York, 1899.

Lyrics of Love and Laughter. New York, 1903.

Lyrics of Sunshine and Shadow. New York, 1905.

The Complete Poems. Dodd, Mead, 1913.

BRAITHWAITE, WILLIAM STANLEY. *Lyrics of Life and Love.* H. B. Turner, 1904.

The House of Falling Leaves. J. W. Luce, 1908.

Selected Poems. Coward-McCann, 1948.

JOHNSON, FENTON. *A Little Dreaming.* Chicago, 1913.

Visions of the Dusk. New York, 1915.

Songs of the Soil. New York, 1916.

JOHNSON, JAMES WELDON. *Fifty Years, and Other Poems.* The Cornhill Co., 1917.

God's Trombones. Seven Negro Sermons in Verse. Viking, 1927.

St. Peter Relates an Incident . . . Viking, 1935.

MCKAY, CLAUDE. *Spring in New Hampshire.* Grant Richard (London), 1920.

Harlem Shadows. Harcourt, 1922.

Selected Poems. Bookman Associates, 1953.

CULLEN, COUNTEE. *Color.* Harper, 1925.

Copper Sun. Harper, 1927.

The Ballad of the Brown Girl. Harper, 1927.

The Black Christ and Other Poems. Harper, 1929.

The Medea and Some Poems. Harper, 1935.

The Lost Zoo. Harper, 1940.

On These I Stand. Harper, 1947.

HUGHES, LANGSTON. *The Weary Blues.* Knopf, 1926.

Fine Clothes to the Jew. Knopf, 1927.

Dear Lovely Death. Troutbeck Press, 1931.

The Dream Keeper. Knopf, 1932.

A New Song. International Workers Order, 1938.

Shakespeare in Harlem. Knopf, 1942.

In Freedom's Plow. Musette, 1943.

Fields of Wonder. Knopf, 1947.

One-Way Ticket. Knopf, 1949.

Montage of a Dream Deferred. Henry Holt, 1951.

Selected Poems. Knopf, 1959.

Ask Your Mama, Twelve Moods for Jazz. Knopf, 1961.

The Panther and the Lash. Knopf, 1967.

BROWN, STERLING A. *Southern Road*. Harcourt, 1932.

DAVIS, FRANK MARSHALL. *Black Man's Verse*. Black Cat Press, 1935.

I Am the American Negro. Black Cat Press, 1937.

47th Street. Decker Press, 1948.

HAYDEN, ROBERT E. *Heart-Shape in the Dust*. Falcon Press, 1940.

Figure of Time: Poems. Hemphill Press, 1955.

A Ballad of Remembrance. Paul Breman, 1962.

Selected Poems. October House, 1966.

Words in the Mourning Time. October House, 1970.

HAYDEN, ROBERT AND MYRON O'HIGGINS. *The Lion and the Archer*. Hemphill Press, 1948.

WALKER, MARGARET. *For My People*. Yale Univ. Press, 1942.

DISMOND, H. BINGA. *We Who Would Die*. W. Malliet and Co., 1943.

TOLSON, MELVIN B. *Rendezvous with America*. Dodd, Mead, 1944.

Libretto for the Republic of Liberia. Twayne, 1953.

Harlem Gallery; Book I, The Curator. Twayne, 1965.

BROOKS, GWENDOLYN. *A Street in Bronzeville*. Harper, 1945.

Annie Allen. Harper, 1949.

The Bean Eaters. Harper, 1960.

Selected Poems. Harper, 1963.

In the Mecca. Harper, 1968.

Riot. Broadside Press, 1969.

DODSON, OWEN. *Powerful Long Ladder*. Farrar, Straus, 1946.

HOLLOWAY, ARIEL W. *Shape Them into Dreams*. Exposition, 1955.

MORRIS, JOHN C. *Cleopatra and Other Poems*. Exposition, 1955.

JARRETTE, ALFRED Q. *Black Man Speaks*. Weinberg Book Pub., 1955.

ALLEN, SAMUEL W. (PAUL VESEY). *Elfenbein Zähne* (Ivory Tusks) Wolfgang Rothe (Heidelberg), 1956.

WRIGHT, BEATRICE. *Color Scheme*. Pageant Press, 1957.

PITCHER, OLIVER. *Dust of Silence*. Troubador Press, 1958.

MILLER, MAY. *Into the Clearing*. Charioteer Press, 1959.

JOHNSTON, PERCY E. *Concerto for Girl and Convertible*. Continental Press, 1960.

Six Cylinder Olympus. Jupiter Hammon Press, 1964.

Sean Pendragon Requiem. Dasein-Jupiter Hammon, 1964.

CUNEY, WARING. *Puzzles*. Deroos (Utrecht), 1960.

JONES, LEROI. *Preface to a Twenty-Volume Suicide Note.* Totem-Corinth, 1961.

The Dead Lecturer. Grove, 1964.

Black Magic Poetry: 1961–1967. Bobbs-Merrill, 1969.

MILLER, CLIFFORD L. *Imperishable the Temple.* Mexico City, 1962.

RIVERS, CONRAD KENT. *The Black Bodies and This Sunburnt Face.* Free Lance Press, 1962.

HORNE, FRANK. *Haverstraw.* Paul Breman, 1963.

BONTEMPS, ARNA. *Personals.* Paul Breman, 1963.

LYLE, K. L., M. RUBIN, MAY MILLER. *Lyrics of Three Women.* Linden Press, 1964.

DANNER, MARGARET AND DUDLEY RANDALL. *Poem Counterpoem.* Broadside Press, 1966.

LEE, DON L. *Think Black.* Broadside Press, 1967.

Black Pride. Broadside Press, 1968.

Don't Cry, Scream. Broadside Press, 1969.

We Walk the Way of the New World. Broadside Press, 1970.

EMANUEL, JAMES A. *The Treehouse and Other Poems.* Broadside Press, 1968.

KNIGHT, ETHERIDGE. *Poems from Prison.* Broadside Press, 1968.

RANDALL, DUDLEY. *Cities Burning.* Broadside Press, 1968.

CLIFTON, LUCILLE. *Good Times.* Random, 1969.

JOANS, TED. *Black Pow-Wow.* Hill & Wang, 1969.

JORDAN, JUNE. *Who Look at Me.* Crowell, 1969.

KEORAPETSE, KGOSITSILE. *Spirits Unchained.* Broadside Press, 1969.

MARVIN X. *Black Man Listen.* Broadside Press, 1969.

NEAL, LARRY. *Black Boogaloo.* Journal of Black Poetry Press, 1969.

REED, CLARENCE. *Not Forever Tears.* Jihad, 1969.

SANCHEZ, SONIA. *Homecoming.* Broadside Press, 1969.

GIOVANNI, NIKKI. *Black Judgement.* Broadside Press, 1970.

GROSVENOR, KALI. *Poems by Kali.* Doubleday, 1970.

SCOTT-HERON, GIL. *Small Talk at 125th Street and Lenox.* World, 1970.

THOMPSON, JULIUS E. *Hopes Tied up in Promises.* Dorrance, 1970.

IV. FICTION (arranged chronologically according to first publication)

BROWN, WILLIAM WELLS. *Clotel; or, The President's Daughter. A Narrative of Slave Life in the United States.* London, 1853. Citadel, 1969. Macmillan, 1970.

Clotelle; A Tale of the Southern States. Boston, 1864.

Clotelle; or The Colored Heroine, a Tale of the Southern States. Boston, 1867.

WEBB, FRANK J. *The Garies and Their Friends.* London, 1857; Arno, 1969.

HOWARD, JAMES H. W. *Bond and Free.* Harrisburg, Pa., 1886.

HARPER, FRANCES E. W. *Iola Leroy; or, Shadows Uplifted.* Philadelphia, 1893.

"SANDA" (WALTER H. STOWERS). *Appointed. An American Novel.* Detroit, 1894.

JONES, J. McHENRY. *Hearts of Gold.* Wheeling, 1896.

DUNBAR, PAUL LAURENCE. *The Uncalled.* Dodd, Mead, 1898.

   Folks from Dixie. Dodd, Mead, 1898.

   The Love of Landry. Dodd, Mead, 1900.

   The Strength of Gideon, and Other Stories. Dodd, Mead, 1900.

   The Fanatics. Dodd, Mead, 1901.

   The Sport of the Gods. Dodd, Mead, 1902.

   In Old Plantation Days. Dodd, Mead, 1903.

   The Heart of Happy Hollow. Dodd, Mead, 1904.

GRIGGS, SUTTON E. *Imperium in Imperio.* Orion, 1899; Arno, 1969.

   Overshadowed. Orion, 1901.

   Unfettered. Orion, 1902.

   The Hindered Hand. Orion, 1905.

   Pointing the Way. Orion, 1908.

CHESNUTT, CHARLES W. *The Conjure Woman.* Houghton Mifflin, 1899.

   The Wife of His Youth and Other Stories of the Color Line. Houghton Mifflin, 1899.

   The House Behind the Cedars. Houghton Mifflin, 1900.

   The Marrow of Tradition. Houghton Mifflin, 1901.

   The Colonel's Dream. Doubleday, Page, 1905.

HOPKINS, PAULINE. *Contending Forces.* The Colored Cooperative Pub. Co., 1900.

PRYOR, GEORGE LANGHORNE. *Neither Bond Nor Free.* J. S. Ogilvie, 1902.

GRANT, J. W. *Out of the Darkness.* National Baptist Pub., 1909.

WALKER, THOMAS H. B. *Bebbly. The Victorious Preacher.* Pepper Pub., 1910.

WARING, ROBERT L. *As We See It.* C. F. Sudwarth, 1910.

DU BOIS, W. E. B. *The Quest of the Silver Fleece.* A. C. McClurg, 1911.

   The Dark Princess. Harcourt, 1928.

The Black Flame: A Trilogy—The Ordeal of Mansart, Mansart Builds a School, Worlds of Color. Mainstream Publishers, 1957, 1959, 1961.

JOHNSON, JAMES WELDON. *The Autobiography of an Ex-Coloured Man.* Sherman, French, 1912; reprinted, Knopf, 1927; Hill & Wang, 1960.

MICHEAUX, OSCAR. *The Conquest.* Woodruff Press, 1913.

The Forged Note. Western Book Supply Co., 1915.

The Case of Mrs. Wingate. Book Supply Co., 1944.

The Story of Dorothy Stanfield. Book Supply Co., 1946.

SHACKELFORD, OTIS M. *Lillian Simmons*, R. M. Rigby Co., 1915.

DOWNING, HENRY F. *The American Calvaryman: A Liberian Romance.* Neale Pub. Co., 1917.

DREER, HERMAN. *The Immediate Jewel of His Soul.* St. Louis Argus Pub. Co., 1919.

The Tie That Binds. Meador, 1958.

SPENCER, MARY ETTA. *The Resentment.* A. M. E. Book Concern, 1921.

TOOMER, JEAN. *Cane.* Boni & Liveright, 1923; Harper, 1969.

DORSEY, JOHN T. *The Lion of Judah.* Chicago, 1924.

FAUSET, JESSIE R. *There is Confusion.* Boni & Liveright, 1924.

Plum Bun. Stokes, 1929.

The Chinaberry Tree. Stokes, 1931.

Comedy American Style. Stokes, 1933.

WHITE, WALTER. *The Fire in the Flint.* Knopf, 1924.

Flight. Knopf, 1926.

WALROND, ERIC. *Tropic Death.* Boni & Liveright, 1926.

FISHER, RUDOLPH. *The Walls of Jericho.* Knopf, 1928.

The Conjure Man Dies. Convici, Friede, 1932.

LARSEN, NELLA. *Quicksand.* Knopf, 1928.

Passing. Knopf, 1929.

McKAY, CLAUDE. *Home to Harlem.* Harper, 1928.

Banjo. Harper, 1929.

Gingertown. Harper, 1932.

Banana Bottom. Harper, 1933.

THURMAN, WALLACE. *The Blacker the Berry.* Macaulay, 1929.

Infants of the Spring. Macaulay, 1932.

HUGHES, LANGSTON. *Not Without Laughter.* Knopf, 1930.

The Ways of White Folks. Knopf, 1934.

Laughing to Keep from Crying. Henry Holt, 1952.

Simple Stakes a Claim. Rinehart, 1957.

Tambourines to Glory. John Day, 1959.

The Best of Simple. Hill & Wang, 1961.

Something in Common, and Other Stories. Hill & Wang, 1963.

Simple's Uncle Sam. Hill & Wang, 1965.

PAYNTER, JOHN H. *Fugitives of the Pearl.* Associated Pubs., 1930.

BONTEMPS, ARNA. *God Sends Sunday.* Harcourt, 1931.

Black Thunder. Macmillan, 1936; Beacon Press, 1968.

Drums at Dusk. Macmillan, 1939.

HENRY, WILLIAMS. *Out of Wedlock.* R. G. Badger, 1931.

SCHUYLER, GEORGE. *Black No More.* Macaulay, 1931.

Slaves Today. Harcourt, 1931.

CULLEN, COUNTEE. *One Way to Heaven.* Harper, 1932.

HILL, JOHN H. *Princess Malah.* Associated Pubs., 1933.

HURSTON, ZORA NEALE. *Jonah's Gourd Vine.* Lippincott, 1934.

Their Eyes Were Watching God. Lippincott, 1937.

Seraph on the Suwanee. Scribner's, 1948.

HENDERSON, GEORGE. *Ollie Miss.* Stokes, 1935.

Jule. Creative Age Press, 1946.

LEE, GEORGE W. *River George.* Macaulay, 1937.

TURPIN, WATERS E. *These Low Grounds.* Harper, 1937.

O Canaan! Doubleday, 1939.

The Rootless. Vantage, 1957.

GILBERT, MERCEDES. *Aunt Sara's Wooden God.* Christopher Pub., 1938.

WRIGHT, RICHARD. *Uncle Tom's Children.* Harper, 1938.

Native Son. Harper, 1940.

The Outsider. Harper, 1953.

Savage Holiday. Harper, 1954.

The Long Dream. Doubleday, 1958.

Eight Men. World, 1961.

Lawd Today. Walker, 1963.

ATTAWAY, WILLIAM. *Let Me Breathe Thunder.* Doubleday, 1939.

Blood on the Forge. Doubleday, 1941.

OFFORD, C. R. *The White Face.* McBride, 1943.

The Naked Fear. Ace Books, 1954.

HIMES, CHESTER B. *If He Hollers Let Him Go.* Doubleday, 1945.

Lonely Crusade. Knopf, 1947.

Cast the First Stone. Coward-McCann, 1953.

Third Generation. World, 1954.

The Primitives. New American Library, 1955.

For Love of Imabelle. Fawcett, 1957.

Pinktoes. Putnam, 1965.

(Detective stories not included here)

WOOD, O. P. *High Ground.* Exposition, 1945.

PETRY, ANN. *The Street.* Houghton Mifflin, 1946.

Country Place. Houghton Mifflin, 1947.

The Narrows. Houghton Mifflin, 1953.

Tituba of Salem Village. Crowell, 1964.

YERBY, FRANK. *The Foxes of Harrow.* Dial, 1946.

Speak Now. Dial, 1969.

(Only the last of Yerby's many novels has treated Negro themes. We give here only that novel and his first.)

BLAND, ALDEN. *Behold a Cry.* Scribner's, 1947.

THOMAS, WILL. *God Is for White Folks.* Creative Age Pubs., 1947.

MOTLEY, WILLARD. *Knock on Any Door.* Appleton, 1947.

We Fished All Night. Appleton, 1951.

Let No Man Write My Epitaph. Random, 1958.

Let Noon Be Fair. Putnam, 1966.

SMITH, WILLIAM GARDNER. *Last of the Conquerors.* Farrar, Straus, 1948.

Anger at Innocence. Farrar, Straus, 1950.

South Street. Farrar, Straus, 1954.

The Stone Face. Farrar, Straus, 1963.

WEST, DOROTHY. *The Living Is Easy.* Houghton Mifflin, 1948.

JARRETTE, A. Q. *Beneath the Sky.* Weinberg Book Supply Co., 1949.

SAVOY, WILLARD. *Alien Land.* Dutton, 1949.

DEMBY, WILLIAM. *Beetlecreek.* Rinehart, 1950.

The Catacombs. Pantheon, 1965.

KAYE, PHILIP B. *Taffy.* Crown, 1950.

REDDING, J. SAUNDERS. *Stranger and Alone.* Harcourt, 1950.

BROWN, LLOYD. *Iron City.* Masses & Mainstream, 1951.

DODSON, OWEN. *Boy at the Window.* Farrar, Straus, 1951.

When Trees Were Green (originally entitled *Boy at the Window*). Popular Library, 1967.

ELLISON, RALPH. *Invisible Man.* Random, 1952.

BALDWIN, JAMES. *Go Tell It on the Mountain.* Knopf, 1953.

Giovanni's Room. Dial, 1956.

Another Country. Dial, 1962.

Going to Meet the Man. Dial, 1965.

Tell Me How Long the Train's Been Gone. Dial, 1968.

BROOKS, GWENDOLYN. *Maud Martha.* Harper, 1953.

FISHER, WILLIAM. *The Waiters.* World, 1953.

KENNEDY, MARK. *The Pecking Order.* Appleton, 1953.

LAMMING, GEORGE. *In the Castle of My Skin.* McGraw-Hill, 1953.

KILLENS, JOHN O. *Youngblood.* Dial, 1954.

And Then We Heard the Thunder. Knopf, 1963.

'Sippi. Simon & Schuster, 1967.

MAYFIELD, JULIAN. *The Hit.* Vanguard, 1957.

The Long Night. Vanguard, 1958.

The Grand Parade. Vanguard, 1961.

SIMMONS, HERBERT. *Corner Boy.* Houghton Mifflin, 1957.

AUSTIN, EDMUND O. *The Black Challenge.* Vantage, 1958.

GIBSON, RICHARD A. *A Mirror for Magistrates.* Anthony Blond (London), 1958.

ANDERSON, ALSTON. *Lover Man.* Doubleday, 1959.

All God's Children. Bobbs-Merrill, 1965.

BROWN, FRANK LONDON. *Trumbull Park.* Henry Regnery, 1959.

HOLDER, GEOFFREY AND TOM HARSHMAN. *Black Gods, Green Islands.* Doubleday, 1959.

MARSHALL, PAULE. *Brown Girl, Brownstones.* Random, 1959.

Soul Clap Hands and Sing. Atheneum, 1961.

Chosen Place, The Timeless People. Harcourt, 1969.

WILLIAMS, JOHN A. *The Angry Ones.* Ace Books, 1960.

Night Song. Farrar, Straus, 1961.

Sissie. Farrar, Straus, 1963.

The Man Who Cried I Am. Little, Brown, 1967.

Sons of Darkness, Sons of Light. Little, Brown, 1969.

HERCULES, FRANK. *Where the Hummingbird Flies.* Harcourt, 1961.

I Want a Black Doll. Simon & Schuster, 1967.

MADDEN, WILL A. *Two and One.* Exposition, 1961.

Five More Short Stories. Exposition, 1963.

KELLY, WILLIAM MELVIN. *A Different Drummer.* Doubleday, 1962.

Dancers on the Shore. Doubleday, 1964.

A Drop of Patience. Doubleday, 1965.

dem. Doubleday, 1967.

BROADUS, ROBERT. *Spokes for the Wheel.* Kingsman Press, 1962.

COOPER, CLARENCE L. *The Dark Messenger.* Regency Books, 1962.

WRIGHT, CHARLES. *The Messenger.* Farrar, Straus, 1963.

The Wig, A Mirror Image. Farrar, Straus, 1966.

EDWARDS, JUNIUS. *If We Must Die.* Doubleday, 1963.

PARKS, GORDON. *The Learning Tree.* Harper, 1963.

GAINES, ERNEST J. *Catherine Carmier.* Atheneum, 1964.

Of Love and Dust. Dial, 1967.

Bloodline. Dial, 1968.

HUNTER, KRISTIN. *God Bless the Child.* Scribner's, 1964.

The Landlord. Scribner's, 1966.

VAN DYKE, HENRY. *Ladies of the Rachmaninoff Eyes.* Farrar, Straus, 1965.

Blood of Strawberries. Farrar, Straus, 1968.

FAIR, RONALD. *Many Thousand Gone.* Harcourt, 1965.

Hog Butcher. Harcourt, 1966.

JONES, LEROI. *The System of Dante's Hell.* Grove, 1965.

Tales. Grove, 1967.

WALKER, MARGARET. *Jubilee.* Houghton Mifflin, 1966.

PHILLIPS, JANE. *Mojo Hand.* Simon & Schuster, 1966.

ROLLINS, BRYANT. *Danger Song.* Doubleday, 1967.

REED, ISHMAEL. *The Free-Lance Pallbearers.* Doubleday, 1967.

Yellow Back Radio Broke-Down. Doubleday, 1969.

POLITE, CARLENE H. *The Flagellants* (tr. by Pierre Alien). Farrar, Straus, 1967.

HEARD, NATHAN C. *Howard Street.* Dial, 1968.

PHARR, ROBERT E. *Book of Numbers.* Doubleday, 1969.

GREENLEE, SAM. *The Spook Who Sat by the Door.* R. W. Baron, 1969.

MAHONEY, WILLIAM. *Black Jacob.* Macmillan, 1969.

McPHERSON, JAMES ALAN. *Hue and Cry.* Atlantic-Little, Brown, 1969.

WRIGHT, SARA E. *This Child's Gonna Live.* Seymour Lawrence (Dell), 1969.

BROWN, CECIL. *The Life and Loves of Mr. Jiveass Nigger.* Farrar, Straus, 1970.

WIDEMAN, JOHN. *Hurry Home.* Harcourt, 1970.

YOUNG, AL. *Snakes.* Holt, 1970.

V. AUTOBIOGRAPHY (arranged chronologically according to first publication)

HAMMON, BRITON. *A Narrative of the Uncommon Sufferings and Surprising Deliverance of Briton Hammon, a Negro Man.* Boston, 1760.

MARRANT, JOHN. *A Narrative of the Lord's Wonderful Dealings with J. Marrant, a Black* . . . London, 1785.

VASSA, GUSTAVUS. *The Interesting Narrative of the Life of Olaudah Equiano, or Gustavus Vassa, the African.* London, 1789.

ROPER, MOSES. *Narrative of the Adventures and Escapes of Moses Roper, From American Slavery.* London, 1837.

DOUGLASS, FREDERICK. *Narrative of the Life of Frederick Douglass, An American Slave.* Boston, 1845; reprinted New American Library and Harvard Univ. Press, 1960.

My Bondage and My Freedom. New York, 1855.

Life and Times of Frederick Douglass. Hartford, 1881.

Life and Times of Frederick Douglass . . . Boston, 1892; reprinted Pathway Press, 1941; Collier Books, 1962.

CLARK, LEWIS. *Narrative of the Sufferings of Lewis Clark* . . . Boston, 1845.

CLARK, LEWIS AND MILTON CLARK. *Narratives of the Sufferings of Lewis and Milton Clark* . . . Boston, 1846.

BROWN, WILLIAM WELLS. *Narrative of William W. Brown, a Fugitive Slave.* Boston, 1847.

Three Years in Europe: or, Places I Have Seen and People I Have Met. London, 1852.

HENSON, JOSIAH. *The Life of Josiah Henson* . . . Boston, 1849.

Truth Stranger than Fiction: Father Henson's Story of His Own Life. Boston and Cleveland, 1858.

An Autobiography of Josiah Henson. (*Mrs. Harriet Beecher Stowe's "Uncle Tom"*). London, 1876.

BROWN, HENRY BOX. *Narrative of Henry Box Brown* . . . Boston, 1849.

Bibb, Henry. *Narrative of the Life and Adventures of Henry Bibb* . . . New York, 1849.

(Anonymous) Truth, Sojourner. *Narrative of Sojourner Truth, Northern Slave* . . . Boston, 1850.

Narrative of Sojourner Truth, a Bondswoman of Olden Times . . . Boston, 1875.

(Anonymous) Northrup, Solomon. *Twelve Years a Slave; The Narrative of Solomon Northrup* . . . Auburn, 1853.

Ward, Samuel Ringgold. *The Autobiography of a Fugitive Negro* . . . London, 1855.

(Anonymous) Loguen, Jermain W. *The Rev. J. W. Loguen as a Slave and as a Freeman; a Narrative of Real Life.* Syracuse, 1859.

Craft, William. *Running a Thousand Miles for Freedom; or, The Escape of William and Ellen Craft from Slavery.* London, 1860.

Keckley, Elizabeth. *Behind the Scenes; or, Thirty Years a Slave, and Four Years in the White House.* New York, 1868.

Flipper, Henry Ossian. *The Colored Cadet at West Point* . . . New York, 1878.

Payne, Daniel A. *Recollections of Seventy Years.* Nashville, Tenn., 1888.

Langston, John Mercer. *From the Virginia Plantation to the National Capitol* . . . Hartford, 1894.

Washington, Booker Taliaferro. *Up From Slavery. An Autobiography.* New York, 1901.

Miller, Kelly. *Out of the House of Bondage.* Neale, 1914.

Moton, Robert Russa. *Finding a Way Out.* Doubleday, 1920.

Gordon, Taylor. *Born To Be.* Covici, 1929.

Johnson, James Weldon. *Along This Way.* Viking, 1933.

McKay, Claude. *A Long Way from Home.* Lee Furman, 1937.

Herndon, Angelo. *Let Me Live.* Random, 1937.

Du Bois, W. E. B. *Dusk of Dawn.* Harcourt, 1940.

The Autobiography of W. E. B. Du Bois. International Pubs., 1968.

Terrell, Mary Church. *A Colored Woman in a White World.* Ransdell, 1940.

Hughes, Langston. *The Big Sea.* Hill & Wang, 1940.

I Wonder as I Wander. Hill & Wang, 1956.

Handy, W. C. *Father of the Blues.* Macmillan, 1941.

Redding, J. Saunders. *No Day of Triumph.* Harper, 1942.

On Being Negro in America. Bobbs-Merrill, 1951, 1962.

HURSTON, ZORA NEALE. *Dust Tracks on a Road.* Lippincott, 1942.

WRIGHT, RICHARD. *Black Boy.* Harper, 1945.

THOMPSON, ERA BELL. *American Daughter.* Univ. of Chicago Press, 1946.

LOUIS, JOE. *My Life and Story.* Duell, 1947.

The Joe Louis Story. Grosset, 1953.

WHITE, WALTER. *A Man Called White.* Viking, 1948.

ROBINSON, JACKIE. *My Own Story as Told . . .* Greenberg, 1948.

ROBINSON, JACKIE (WITH CARL T. ROWAN). *Wait Till Next Year.* Random, 1960.

PATTERSON, HAYWOOD AND EARL CONRAD. *Scottsboro Boy.* Doubleday, 1950.

WATERS, ETHEL. *His Eye Is On the Sparrow.* Doubleday, 1951.

HORNE, LENA. *In Person: Lena Horne as Told to Helen Arstein and Carlton Moss.* Greenberg, 1951.

Lena. Doubleday, 1965.

GOODWIN, RUBY BERKELEY. *It's Good to be Black.* Doubleday, 1953.

ARMSTRONG, LOUIS. *Satchmo: My Life in New Orleans.* Prentice-Hall, 1954.

MAYS, WILLIE. *Born to Play Ball . . . As Told to Charles Einstein.* Putnam, 1955.

KITT, EARTHA. *Thursday's Child.* Duell, 1956.

ANDERSON, MARIAN, *My Lord, What a Morning!* Viking, 1956.

HOLIDAY, BILLIE (WITH WILLIAM DUFFY). *Lady Sings the Blues.* Doubleday, 1956.

MURRAY, PAULI. *Proud Shoes.* Harper, 1956.

GIBSON, ALTHEA (ed. ED FITZGERALD). *I Always Wanted To Be Somebody.* Harper, 1958.

CAMPANELLA, ROY. *It's Good to Be Alive.* Little, Brown, 1959.

DUNHAM, KATHERINE. *A Touch of Innocence.* Harcourt, 1959.

BÉCHET, SIDNEY. *Treat It Gentle.* Hill & Wang, 1960.

BATES, DAISY GASTON. *The Long Shadow of Little Rock, A Memoir.* McKay 1962.

GREGORY, DICK (WITH ROBERT LIPSYTE). *Nigger: An Autobiography.* Dutton, 1964.

BROWN, CLAUDE. *Manchild in the Promised Land.* Macmillan, 1965.

CAYTON, HORACE R. *Long Old Road.* Simon & Schuster, 1965.

DAVIS, SAMMY, JR. *Yes I Can.* Farrar, Straus, 1965.

MALCOLM X (WITH ALEX HALEY). *The Autobiography of Malcolm X.* Grove, 1965.

SCHUYLER, GEORGE S. *Black and Conservative.* Arlington House, 1966.

WORMLEY, STANTON AND LEWIS R. FENDERSON, eds. *Many Shades of Black.* Morrow, 1969.

ANGELOU, MAYA. *I Know Why the Caged Bird Sings.* Random, 1969.

BROWN, H. RAP. *Die Nigger Die!* Dial, 1969.

LACY, LESLIE A. *The Rise and Fall of a Proper Negro.* Macmillan, 1970.

VI. BIOGRAPHY (arranged chronologically according to first publication)

BROWN, WILLIAM WELLS. *The Black Man: His Antecedents, His Genius, and His Achievements.* New York and Boston, 1863.

The Rising Sun; or the Antecedents and Advancement of the Colored Race. Boston, 1874.

STILL, WILLIAM. *The Underground Rail Road. A Record of Facts, Authentic Narratives, Letters . . .* Philadelphia, 1872.

SIMMONS, WILLIAM J. *Men of Mark: Eminent, Progressive & Rising.* Cleveland, 1887; Arno, 1968.

GRIMKE, ARCHIBALD H. *William Lloyd Garrison, The Abolitionist.* New York, 1891.

The Life of Charles Sumner; the Scholar in Politics. New York, 1892.

CHESTNUTT, CHARLES W. *Frederick Douglass.* Boston, 1899.

WASHINGTON, BOOKER T. *Frederick Douglass.* Philadelphia and London, 1907.

DU BOIS, W. E. B. *John Brown.* G. W. Jacobs, 1909; International Pubs., 1962.

BRAWLEY, BENJAMIN. *Women of Achievement.* Chicago, 1919.

Paul Laurence Dunbar. Univ. of North Carolina Press, 1936.

The Negro Genius. Dodd, 1937.

Negro Builders and Heroes. Univ. of North Carolina Press, 1937.

ROBESON, ESLANDA GOODE. *Paul Robeson, Negro.* Harper, 1930.

DANEIL, SADIE. *Women Builders.* Associated Pubs., 1931.

WESLEY, CHARLES. *Richard Allen, Apostle of Freedom.* Associated Pubs., 1935.

FAUSET, ARTHUR HUFF. *Sojourner Truth, God's Faithful Pilgrim.* Univ. of North Carolina Press, 1938.

MERRITT, RALEIGH HOWARD. *From Captivity to Fame, or The Life of George Washington Carver.* Meador, 1938.

WASHINGTON, JOHN E. *They Knew Lincoln.* Dutton, 1942.

COOK, MERCER. *Five French Negro Authors.* Associated Pubs., 1943.

CUNNINGHAM, VIRGINIA. *Paul Laurence Dunbar and His Song.* Dodd, Mead, 1947.

GRAHAM, SHIRLEY. *There Was Once a Slave: The Heroic Story of Frederick Douglass.* Messner, 1947.

Booker T. Washington. Messner, 1955.

QUARLES, BENJAMIN. *Frederick Douglass.* Associated Pubs., 1948.

CHESNUTT, HELEN M. *Charles Waddell Chesnutt: Pioneer of the Color Line.* Univ. of North Carolina Press, 1952.

HUGHES, LANGSTON. *Famous American Negroes.* Dodd, Mead, 1954.

OTTLEY, ROI. *The Lonely Warrior: The Life and Times of Robert S. Abbott.* Henry Regnery, 1955.

CROMWELL, OTELIA. *Lucretia Mott.* Harvard Univ. Press, 1958.

REDDING, J. SAUNDERS. *The Lonesome Road. The Story of the Negro's Part in America.* Doubleday, 1958.

BUTCHER, PHILIP. *George W. Cable: The Northampton Years.* Columbia Univ. Press, 1959.

George W. Cable. Twayne, 1962.

REDDICK, LAWRENCE D. *Crusader Without Violence; A Biography of Martin Luther King, Jr.* Harper, 1959.

SHEPPERD, GLADYS B. *Mary Church Terrell, Respectable Person.* Human Relations Press, 1959.

BONTEMPS, ARNA. *One Hundred Years of Negro Freedom.* Dodd, Mead, 1961.

FARRISON, WILLIAM E. *William Wells Brown: Author and Reformer.* Univ. of Chicago Press, 1969.

VII. ESSAYS (book publications only; arranged chronologically according to author's first publication. For other essays see collections in I and II.)

BROWN, WILLIAM WELLS. *Three Years in Europe.* London, 1852.

The American Fugitive in Europe . . . Boston, Cleveland, and New York, 1855.

My Southern Home: or, the South & Its People. Boston, 1880.

LANGSTON, JOHN M. *Freedom and Citizenship: Selected Lectures & Addresses.* Washington, 1883.

WASHINGTON, BOOKER T., *The Future of the American Negro.* New York, 1899.

WASHINGTON, BOOKER T. (WITH W. E. B. DU BOIS). *The Negro in the South.* G. W. Jacobs, 1907.

DU BOIS, W. E. B. *The Souls of Black Folk.* A. C. McClurg, 1903.

Darkwater. Harcourt, 1920.

The Gifts of Black Folk. Associated Pubs., 1924.

MILLER, KELLY. *Race Adjustment.* Neale, 1908.

The Everlasting Stain. Associated Pubs., 1924.

BRAWLEY, BENJAMIN. *The Negro in Literature and Art.* Atlanta, 1910; Duffield, 1918.

The Negro Genius. Dodd, Mead, 1937.

JOHNSON, JAMES WELDON. *Black Manhattan.* Knopf, 1930.

REDDING, SAUNDERS. *On Being Negro in America.* Bobbs-Merrill, 1951, 1962.

SCOTT, NATHAN A., JR. *Rehearsals of Discomposure: Alienation and Reconciliation in Modern Literature.* King's Crown Press, 1952.

Modern Literature and the Religious Frontier. Harper, 1958.

The Broken Center: Studies in the Theological Horizon of Modern Literature. Yale Univ. Press, 1966.

Craters of the Spirit: Studies in the Modern Novel. Corpus, 1968.

Negative Capability: Studies in the New Literature and the Religious Situation. Yale Univ. Press, 1969.

WRIGHT, RICHARD. *Black Power.* Harper, 1954.

White Man, Listen! Doubleday, 1957.

Pagan Spain. Harper, 1957.

BALDWIN, JAMES. *Notes of a Native Son.* Beacon Press, 1955.

Nobody Knows My Name. Dial, 1961.

The Fire Next Time. Dial, 1963.

BENNETT, LERONE. *The Negro Mood.* Johnson, 1964.

ELLISON, RALPH. *Shadow and Act.* Random, 1964.

WILLIAMS, JOHN A. *This Is My Country, Too.* New American Library, 1965.

HERNTON, CALVIN C. *White Papers for White Americans.* Doubleday, 1966.

JONES, LEROI. *Home: Social Essays.* Morrow, 1966.
(ed.) *Moderns: New Fiction in America.* Corinth, 1966.

KILLENS, JOHN O. *Black Man's Burden.* Simon & Schuster, 1966.

CRUSE, HAROLD. *The Crisis of the Negro Intellectual.* Morrow, 1967.

Rebellion or Revolution. Morrow, 1968.

CLARKE, JOHN H., ed. *William Styron's Nat Turner: Ten Black Writers Respond.* Beacon Press, 1968.

CLEAVER, ELDRIDGE. *Soul on Ice.* McGraw-Hill, 1968.

Eldridge Cleaver. Random, 1969.

LESTER, JULIUS. *Look Out, Whitey!* Dial, 1968.

Search for the New Land. Dial, 1970.

COOK, MERCER AND STEPHEN R. HENDERSON. *The Militant Black Writer in Africa and the United States.* Univ. of Wisconsin Press, 1969.

GAYLE, ADDISON, ed. *Black Expression: Essays by and about Black Americans in the Creative Arts.* Weybright and Talley, 1969.

Black Situation. Horizon, 1970.

HILL, ADELAIDE C. AND MARTIN KILSON, eds. *Apropos of Africa: Sentiments of Negro American Leaders on Africa from the 1800's to the 1950's.* Humanities Press, 1969.

TURNER, DARWIN, ed. *Black American Literature: Essays.* Chas. E. Merrill, 1969.

SMITH, WILLIAM GARDNER. *Return to Black America.* Prentice-Hall, 1970.

VIII. DRAMA (book publication only)

ANTHOLOGIES, COLLECTIONS, AND CRITICAL COMMENTARY (arranged alphabetically)

ABRAMSON, DOROTHY. *Negro Playwrights in the American Theatre: 1925–59.* Columbia Univ. Press, 1969.

BOND, FREDERICK W. *The Negro and the Drama.* Associated Pubs., 1940.

BROWN, STERLING A. *Negro Poetry and Drama.* Associates in Negro Folk Education, 1937; Atheneum, 1969.

BULLINS, ED. *New Plays from the Black Theatre.* Bantam, 1969.

COUCH, WILLIAM, JR., ed. *New Black Playwrights: An Anthology.* Louisiana State Univ. Press, 1968.

DENT, THOMAS C. AND OTHERS. *The Free Southern Theatre . . .* Bobbs-Merrill, 1969.

FLETCHER, TOM. *100 Years of the Negro in Show Business.* Burdge, 1954.

HUGHES, LANGSTON AND MILTON MELTZER. *Black Magic: A Pictorial History of the Negro in American Entertainment.* Prentice-Hall, 1967.

ISAACS, EDITH. *The Negro in the American Theatre.* Theatre Arts, 1947.

JEROME, V. *The Negro in Hollywood Films.* Masses & Mainstream, 1950.

JOHNSON, JAMES WELDON. *Black Manhattan.* Knopf, 1930.

LOCKE, ALAIN LEROY AND MONTGOMERY GREGORY, eds. *Plays of Negro Life.* Harper, 1927.

MITCHELL, LOFTEN. *Black Drama: The Story of the American Negro in the Theatre.* Hawthorne Books, 1967.

NOBLE, PETER. *The Negro in Films.* Robinson Ltd. (London), 1948.

PATTERSON, LINDSAY, ed. *Anthology of the American Negro in the Theatre.* Publishers Co., 1967.

REARDON, WM. R. *Black Teacher and the Dramatic Arts.* Negro Univ. Press, 1969.

TDR (Black Theatre Issue: T-40, Summer, 1968).

WITTKE, CARL. *Tambo and Bones: A History of the American Minstrel Stage.* Duke Univ., 1930.

PLAYS IN PRINT (arranged chronologically)

BROWN, WILLIAM WELLS. *The Escape; or A Leap for Freedom. A Drama in Five Acts.* Boston, 1858.

COTTER, JOSEPH S. *Caleb the Degenerate.* Louisville, Ky., 1903; New York, 1940.

GRIMKE, ANGELINA. *Rachel.* Cornhill, 1920.

RICHARDSON, WILLIS. *Plays and Pageants from the Life of the Negro.* Associated Pubs., 1930.

EDMONDS, RANDOLPH. *Shades and Shadows.* Meador, 1930.

Six Plays for a Negro Theatre. W. H. Baker, 1934.

RICHARDSON, WILLIS AND MAY MILLER. *Negro History in Thirteen Plays.* Associated Pubs., 1935.

WRIGHT, RICHARD (WITH PAUL GREEN). *Native Son: . . . A Play in Ten Scenes.* Harper, 1941.

EDMONDS, RANDOLPH. *Land of Cotton and Other Plays.* Associated Pubs., 1942.

PETERSON, LOUIS S. *Take a Giant Step.* French, 1954.

HUGHES, LANGSTON. *Tambourines to Glory.* Day, 1958.

HANSBERRY, LORRAINE. *A Raisin in the Sun.* Random, 1959.

BRANCH, WILLIAM B. *Fifty Steps Toward Freedom. A Dramatic Presentation in Observance of the Fiftieth Anniversary of the NAACP.* New York, 1959.

DAVIS, OSSIE. *Purlie Victorious.* French, 1961.

EDMONDS, RANDOLPH. *Earth and Stars.* Florida A. & M. Univ., 1961.

HUGHES, LANGSTON. *Five Plays.* (W. Smalley, ed.). Univ. of Indiana Press, 1963.

JONES, LEROI. *Dutchman; and The Slave.* Morrow, 1964.

BALDWIN, JAMES. *Blues for Mr. Charlie.* Dial, 1964.

AMIS, LOLA JONES. *Three Plays.* Exposition, 1965.

HANSBERRY, LORRAINE. *The Sign in Sidney Brustein's Window.* Random, 1965.

BROWN, JAMES NELSON. *Tomorrow Was Yesterday.* Exposition, 1966.

WARD, DOUGLASS TURNER. *Happy Ending and Day of Absence: Two Plays.* Dramatists Play Service, 1966.

JONES, LEROI. *Baptism and the Toilet.* Evergreen, 1967.

BALDWIN, JAMES. *The Amen Corner.* Dial, 1968.

ELDER, LONNIE. *Ceremonies in Dark Old Men.* Farrar, Straus, 1969.

BULLINS, ED. *Five Plays.* Bobbs-Merrill, 1969.

GORDONE, CHARLES. *No Place to Be Somebody.* Bobbs-Merrill, 1969.

JONES, LEROI. *Four Black Revolutionary Plays.* Bobbs-Merrill, 1969.

INDEX OF AUTHORS AND TITLES

When an author is mentioned in introductory material, the citation appears in brackets [235].